THE TRUSTED ADVISOR'S SURVIVAL KIT

Peter J. Merrick, B.A., FMA, CFP, TEP, FCSI

The Trusted Advisor's Survival Kit

September 2009

Members of the LexisNexis Group worldwide

Canada	LexisNexis Canada Inc, 123 Commerce Valley Dr. E. Suite 700, MARKHAM, Ontario
Australia	Butterworths, a Division of Reed International Books Australia Pty Ltd, CHATSWOOD, New South Wales
Austria	ARD Betriebsdienst and Verlag Orac, VIENNA
Czech Republic	Orac, sro, PRAGUE
France	Éditions du Juris-Classeur SA, PARIS
Hong Kong	Butterworths Asia (Hong Kong), HONG KONG
Hungary	Hvg Orac, BUDAPEST
India	Butterworths India, NEW DELHI
Ireland	Butterworths (Ireland) Ltd, DUBLIN
Italy	Giuffré, MILAN
Malaysia	Malayan Law Journal Sdn Bhd, KUALA LUMPUR
New Zealand	Butterworths of New Zealand, WELLINGTON
Poland	Wydawnictwa Prawnicze PWN, WARSAW
Singapore	Butterworths Asia, SINGAPORE
South Africa	Butterworth Publishers (Pty) Ltd, DURBAN
Switzerland	Stämpfli Verlag AG, BERNE
United Kingdom	Butterworths Tolley, a Division of Reed Elsevier (UK), LONDON, WC2A
USA	LexisNexis, DAYTON, Ohio

Library and Archives Canada Cataloguing in Publication

Merrick, Peter J. (Peter John), 1969-
The trusted advisor's survival kit / Peter J. Merrick.

Includes contributions by various authors.
Includes bibliographical references and index.
ISBN 978-0-433-45975-0

1. Business law—Canada. 2. Business consultants—Canada.
I. Title.

KE450.C65M47 2009 346.7107 C2009-903813-7
KF390.C65M47 2009

Printed and bound in Canada.

This book is dedicated to "lifetime learners and children at heart of all ages", who regardless of their location or position in life continue to focus their values, principles and insights for the betterment of our world.

FOREWORD

During the past number of years, the image of an accounting professional has evolved from one of a traditional, conservative, green-eyeshade-clad individual to today's dynamic, tech-savvy business advisor. This evolution has not been without its struggles and some triumphs along the way. This publication by Peter Merrick stands out as a shining marker of how the world in which accountants and other trusted advisors operate has changed and merged together.

Some of the forces that have pulled the accounting and other advisory professionals (sometimes kicking and screaming) into a new world include: ever-escalating client needs and expectations; the ever-increasing complexity of the marketplace; and the survival need for these professionals to embrace new areas of business as the traditional lines of business have become increasingly commodified.

The very structure of this publication, which includes material from several different experts, reflects the complexity of today's financial world. Accolades should come Peter's way in recognition of his sensitivity to the interconnections amongst the practitioners from several different areas of the marketplace. Not only has Peter seen this network of relationships, but he has also devoted much energy to organizing and marshalling practitioners from several diverse markets, looking at the same elephant from different angles but complementary perspectives.

This publication should serve as a primer for practising accountants and other advisory consultants who are interested in knowing what this "financial services" world is all about. Trusted advisors owe it to themselves and to their clients to become knowledgeable of the broad range of products and strategies available to their clients. The material in this publication explores many creative and beneficial strategies that are generally unknown to practising accountants, lawyers and other financial professionals at this deeper level.

It is quickly apparent to the reader that although they may be aware of these products and strategies, they must find some way to forge relationships with those who possess the necessary expertise to formulate customized strategies for individual clients.

In this publication, we see a template for today's commercial marketplace in which strategic alliances, affiliations and networks are commonplace. To properly serve most clients' needs, one must bring together a host of disciplines: law; accounting; tax; insurance; employee benefits and pensions; banking; and so on.

I see it as inevitable that the trusted business and personal financial advisor is the logical central force in creating these collaborations.

Preparing this foreword has been a particularly meaningful effort for me. Many years ago, as an accounting student, I had the pleasure of working with Peter's father, Marvin S. Merrick, CA, before either of us was designated. I am sure that he would be proud of this publication and would recognize the value of this material for the practising public accountant.

Morden Shapiro, B.Com., FCA, CMC
President of Morden S. Shapiro & Associates Inc.

PREFACE

Stop!

Reading this Book will Cause you to Change!

Don't read any further if you are not prepared for change. The information contained within these pages has the power to change your career and your life FOREVER!

> "The self is not something ready made, but something in continuous formation through choice of action."
>
> John Dewey (1859-1952)

The children's story of the Tortoise and the Hare is not just for children. It is a metaphor for adults of all ages who desire more meaning out of their lives. Its moral is a simple one but equally powerful. The lesson learnt in this fable is when you commit 100% of yourself to achieving your personally defined life goals and you consistently move towards completing these goals, it does not matter how fast you move, you will eventually win your own race. What is important is that you enjoy your journey because that is where you will spend your most precious asset, your time.

You have happened upon this book for a reason. It could be that you want to change the way you practice in the realm of financial planning, or you have plateaued at a certain level in your career and you desire to achieve greater and more fulfilling success.

Carl Gustav Jung, the Swiss psychologist who is considered to be one of the 20th century's most influential thinkers, coined the term "synchronicity" in the early 1930s. Jung believed that synchronicity happened when a person experienced two or more events or coincidences at the same time and found them to be meaningfully connected. Jung believed that there was no such thing as an accident — everything had a purpose — and modern physics over the past century has validated his claim. This book has the power to be the catalyst for meaningful change in both your life and career. Now you are ready to accept this challenge.

ABOUT THIS BOOK

"There is nothing more powerful than an idea whose time has come."

Victor Hugo (1802-1885)

In the next decade, 43% of our work force will be approaching retirement and $1.3 trillion will change hands from business owners who control most of this wealth in Canada.

Canada, the economy and I have undergone change in the last two years since the publication of *The Essential Individual Pension Handbook*. Of the questions arising from that book and looming ever larger is: Why would someone want to implement the individual pension plan (IPP) option for their future?

Because they want to slow down at work or exit entirely in the most financially beneficial way they can, ensuring security and safety for their resources with a view to perhaps the most significant change in their lives: enjoying the fruits of their labour rather than the labour itself! Never before have we seen this anticipated transfer of wealth, yet very little has been researched and written on its effective preservation and distribution.

The book you hold in your hands is the result of my own personal journey of discovery; it is my attempt to add to the growing discourse in addressing the core issues of wealth preservation and its distribution. I believe that the name of this book is very fitting and timely: "The TASK" (*The Trusted Advisor's Survival Kit*). Yes, this is a survival kit whose sole purpose and promise is to provide the methodology to aid the 21st century's Trusted Advisor through this new reality. By understanding this reality, you will be better equipped to help your clients and yourself to achieve both theirs and your personalized success, which we collectively desire to manifest together.

I want to warn you that its methodology will be surprisingly simple, but don't be fooled with its simplicity. Our society loves to complicate our lives. Remember, Albert Einstein once said: "Truth by its nature is simple." All we need to do in order to create the careers and life we want is to commit to the process of change.

The Task is a call to action for Trusted Advisors of all stripes and professions to rise to the challenge and provide leadership to our clients with the very best knowledge, judgment, guidance and wisdom as humanly possible so as to assist clients to reach their desired financial and life goals, empowering us to live up to the Task of being the true professional we know lies within each of us. Weakness occurs when we look for quick fixes to fundamental problems. You would not be reading this book if you did not believe that adversity breeds the reliance to look within for what is right. This is the source that breeds heroism resulting in only a willingness to implement fundamental solutions to problems that benefit the greater good.

In our search for excellence, the only thing holding financial professionals back from capitalizing on this new reality is the lack of credible financial planning knowledge. This book is a must! When considering the income and fee potential generated from the lifetime of a truly satisfied client, the "return on investment" (ROI) that you invest in reading its pages will be astronomical and will benefit you in ways you can't imagine for yourself now. You have already decided to invest in this book, which is ultimately an investment in yourself. At the same time, I want to share with you that I am only human, with no extraordinary powers to predict your future. Only you will know if you are up for the challenge that lies ahead of you. Only you will be the final judge, knowing if the words in this book have helped you to see clearer and further. Remember, the difference between an ordinary life and an extraordinary life is the "extra" effort you make along the way.

Today, accountants, lawyers, financial planners, human resource professionals, investment advisors and insurance agents have the unique opportunity to prosper from this great challenge that our society and our economy currently face. By rising to the Task, you will not only survive it but excel through it. The question this book asks of you is: How will you stake out your claim and make your mark in this $1.3 trillion opportunity in its formative stages before this opportunity is gone forever, from all of us? As the old adage goes, "Time waits for no one."

Pierre and Nicolas

As you journey through the pages of this book, be mindful of the tale of Pierre and Nicolas. Once there were two famous lumberjacks, named Pierre and Nicolas. No one knew who the greatest lumberjack of them all was. One day, a promoter decided to host a competition between Pierre and Nicolas to see who could cut down the most trees within a six-hour period. At the end, the judges would count the cut trees and crown the winner with the title of the world's greatest lumberjack of them all.

The conditions on the day of the competition were perfect; there was not a cloud in the sky. The judge officiating the event shot his starter pistol to begin the competition. Pierre and Nicolas started cutting feverishly. Fifty minutes into the event, Pierre heard in the distance that Nicolas had stopped cutting. Pierre kept on cutting. Ten minutes later,

Pierre heard Nicolas resume. For the next five hours on the hour Pierre heard Nicolas stop cutting for ten minutes each hour.

At the end of six hours, the judge again shot off his gun to signal to both lumberjacks that the competition was over. Pierre was sure that he would be declared the victor at the end of the count because he had heard every hour on the hour that Nicolas would stop cutting for ten minutes before beginning again. He was positive that the extra hour he had been cutting would assure him of his crowning as the greatest lumberjack of them all.

The judges counted the cut-down trees and recounted several times. Then they announced the winner — Nicolas. Nicolas had been crowned the greatest lumberjack of them all. Pierre was dumbfounded. How could this be possible? Pierre approached Nicolas and said: "It's impossible that you won. It could not be done. Every hour on the hour I heard in the distance that you stopped cutting for ten minutes. I cut for an extra hour than you."

Nicolas simply replied: "I did not stop once during our competition. I was sharpening my blade!"

NOTICE TO THE READER

When writing the preface for this book, I was reminded of Plato's famous "Allegory of the Cave", which I first read two decades ago while I was a student at university. Plato wrote about prisoners living in a cave, watching shadows that they accepted as real. One prisoner frees himself of his shackles, leaves the cave, sees the sun and then returns to the darkness, temporarily blinded by the sun's brilliance, to share the truth that he had discovered. His fellow prisoners think he is crazy, yet he knows they live a life of illusion. He is bound by his innate need to free them from their mental chains. The moral of Plato's allegory as it has been interpreted throughout the millennia is that we all have the responsibility to speak our truths to ourselves and our communities, however uncomfortable the messenger feels in telling these truths. The alternative of lying in silence is even more painful.

This is reminiscent of Han Christian Anderson's story of "The Emperor's New Clothes", in which prevailing beliefs blinded people to the naked truth, and it is only through an innocent child who points out the obvious truth that the king had been swindled by his two new tailors as he paraded himself through the streets of his kingdom in nothing more than his birthday suit.

The intention of "The TASK" is to be controversial and thought-provoking. I want to state for the record that I give no apologies for this. There are, in my judgement, two main reasons why many in the financial advisory community in Canada today are reluctant to have certain convictions and a well-formed belief system to guide themselves in their personal lives and in their professional practices: (1) to do so requires coming to terms with one's own mortality in both one's career and life; and (2) it requires having clear convictions, making judgements and having an opinion of what is right and wrong and believing in something so deeply that one would be even willing to die for it.

This book is strictly intended for education and informational use only. Every attempt has been made by the author and contributors to make the content as accurate as possible. It is not intended to be an academic text; it is too practical to hold that distinction. You will notice different styles and usages of citations throughout this book. This should be expected from the number of contributors involved. What is consistent throughout is the commitment to the Task of sharing universal truths, solutions and enduring wisdom. That being said, in no way will the author, contributors and LexisNexis Canada be held liable for any actions that individuals reading this book may take or not take in the future. To be a true leader and deserving of the Trusted Advisor title, you need to take total ownership of all the choices you make in your career and life. The act of reading this book is your first step towards believing you have free will, that you have the power to set the course of your own destiny and affect others and your environment in a positive way.

HOW TO READ THIS BOOK

This book has been broken down into distinct sections. Each section or chapter can be read individually. You may read the volume chronologically as a whole depending on your own preferences. You may choose to read it in a week, a month, over the year or in the course of your career. You may want to place this book on the corner of your desk for times when a client asks you a question and you seek a quick reference to provide valuable insights, or you may turn to the TASK when you have come to a fork in your life and seek guidance. How you fit the TASK into your life and career is fully up to you.

In closing, it is important to note that financial and other solutions presented throughout this book require specialties in areas such as accounting, cross-border, legal, actuary evaluation, investment management, pension legislation, insurance, employment law and employee benefit plan construction. Many financial professionals will need to seek educational and consulting services to aid them in the set-up, maintenance and wind-up stages of these solutions. Therefore, it is well worth the time and money to hire your own Trusted Advisors to assist in the design, execution and maintenance of these solutions. It is the sign of a powerful person who admits he or she needs help and it is the act of wisdom when one seeks out this much-needed help.

All the best in your pursuits!

Peter J. Merrick
March 17, 2009

ABOUT THE AUTHOR

Peter J. Merrick, B.A., FMA, CFP, TEP, FCSI is the President of MerrickWealth.com. Since the early 1990s, Peter has had an active career in the financial planning, investment, risk management, estate, business succession planning, cross-border planning and executive benefit and pension fields. He has been retained for his expertise by some of Canada's largest financial institutions, accounting and legal firms, to provide executive benefit consulting, succession and estate planning solutions to owner-managed businesses.

Peter is a Certified Financial Planner (CFP) registered with the Financial Planners Standards Council of Canada as well as a Financial Management Advisor (FMA). In the year 2000, Peter was awarded the prestigious Fellowship of the Canadian Securities Institute (FCSI), which is recognized as Canada's highest honour in the financial services industry. In 2008 for his continued contribution in the field of trust and estate planning in Canada, Peter was invited as a full member into the Society of Trust and Estate Practitioners and awarded the TEP designation.

Peter has appeared as a regular television guest and has been seen on CBC's The National, CBC's NewsWorld, BNN, CTV and CP24 in Canada. During the past two decades, Peter has presented over 700 classes, seminars and workshops to such organizations as the Canadian Institute of Chartered Accountants (CICA), the Human Resources Professionals Association of Ontario (HRPAO) and the Financial Planners Standards Council of Canada (FPSC). He is a professional public speaker who has achieved the Distinguished Toastmaster's (DTM) designation, the highest level from Toastmasters International in the areas of public speaking and leadership. As well, Peter has taught at several post-secondary institutions in programs that lead to the Certified Financial Planning, Certified General Accountant, Certified Human Resources Professional and Certified Employee Benefits Specialist designations.

Peter is a professional financial writer, with over 306 published articles to his credit. His articles have appeared in such magazines and periodicals as *McLeans*, *CA Magazine*, *the Journal of Financial Planning*, *Ontario Dental Magazine*, *Professionalreferrals.com*, *Accounting World*, *Benefit and Pension Monitor*, *Canadian MoneySaver*, *HR World*, *CSI Infocus*, *American Funeral Director Magazine*, *Canadian Funeral Director Magazine*, *Canadian Auto Dealers*, *AdvisorWorld.com*, *Dental Practice Management*, *Oral Health*, *Lawyers*

Weekly, *The Bottom Line*, *MD Canada*, *The Bay Street Times*, *Canadian Business Franchise*, *HR Professional*, *Computer World*, *IT Ontario*, *Silicon Valley North*, *Advocis' Forum*, *The Canadian Dental Association*, *Canadian HR Reporter* and numerous publications for LexisNexis Canada Inc., Thomson Reuters and CCH Canadian Ltd.

Peter is the author of the Canadian Securities Institute's course on Individual Pension Plans and LexisNexis Canada's *The Essential Individual Pension Plan Handbook*. "The TASK" *(The Trusted Advisor's Survival Kit)* is his second published book. Currently, Peter is hard at work completing his third book, *The Trusted Advisor — Redefining Excellence in the Age of the Internet.*

TABLE OF CONTENTS

INTRODUCTION

> "We cannot solve problems with the same thinking we used when creating them."
>
> "Definition of *Insanity*: Doing the same thing over and over, but expecting different results."
>
> Albert Einstein (1879-1955)

In the early 1990s, at the beginning of my financial planning career, I was very fortunate to meet one of Canada's most successful businessmen.

He was in his late 50s and had much more life experience than me. He shared that 99.9% of the financial advisors he had met over the course of his career did not have the slightest idea of how to make money, nor did they understand what successful business people were looking for when they sought out professional advice.

He told me that when he took a risk, he got paid for it. He could buy a piece of property for a marginal amount, get it rezoned for a strip mall and then get franchises to sign letters of intent to lease for five years or more when the property was developed.

Once this was done, he would go off to the bank and borrow on the future revenue that would be generated from these highly profitable leases to develop his properties and create a residual income.

He knew that with his proven formula he could take his own money and make 100 times the amount with 1/10th the risk that any stockbroker could offer him, and he was right.

The vast majority of successful business owners are not looking for financial advisors to give them the life they want by making a killing in the stock market; these people have been able to create the life they want by themselves.

Successful business people want their Trusted Advisors to show them ways to keep their wealth. In essence, successful people want their Trusted Advisors to provide them with financial, tax, succession and estate planning holistic solutions. They don't need their advisors to sell them off-the-shelf products such as stocks, mutual funds, insurance, accounting services and legal structures to achieve their financial success. The point is that they are already successful.

Business people are looking for financial professionals who are positioned in the role of Wealth Care Specialist: someone who can see and understand the affluent and wealthy business owner's big-picture needs by constructing customized strategies to achieve their specific goals of wealth preservation, avoidance of unnecessary tax burdens, creditor protection, wealth accumulation and wealth distribution to themselves, their family, estate and charities.

Successful business owners have an understanding that a financial asset is something that puts money in their pockets, with minimum labour. They understand that a business can buy a car, but a car cannot buy a business! Liabilities are things that take money "out of one's pocket".

There are numerous advantages available to you if you own your own business, you take the risk and you have the creativity and fortitude to do something on your own. You are compensated for it. As an employee in Canada, your equation of earning an income goes like this:

- you earn;
- you're taxed;
- then you get to spend what is left over.

If you are a business owner and self-employed in Canada, our government allows you to adopt a much more favourable equation of earning an income:

- you earn;
- you spend, you income split, and you defer bonuses;
- then you are taxed on what is left over!

> "Taxes are the price we pay for civilization."
>
> Oliver Wendell Holmes, Jr.

Business owners are different from the rest of Canadians, if for no other reason than that the *Income Tax Act* favours people who work for themselves. The biggest expense business owners pay in a year is taxes. Reducing taxes legally is not only acceptable from a moral and ethical standpoint, it is also smart. In this country, there are three easy rules that keep money in your pocket and not in that of the government:

1. Find the right business structure for your business to pay less tax and protect what you have.
2. Learn to make more money by using the tax strategies of the wise, such as implementing individual pension plans and retirement compensation arrangements; incorporate active businesses; create holding companies; create family trusts; make charitable donations; create health and welfare trusts; utilize corporately owned insurances; maximize executive and employee benefit plans; and

create employee profit-sharing plans, a succession plan and an estate freeze.

3. Pay less tax legally and still sleep at night.

Highly successful people are known to make a lot of money. Too frequently, however, they fail to keep it or see it grow properly. Most entrepreneurs have everything tied up in their companies. Everyone plans for their company — their banker, their lawyer, their public accountant or other financial advisors — but who plans for them? Shrewd financial planning should separate a client's corporate needs from his or her personal interests.

When a Trusted Advisor meets with a client with an entrepreneurial background, the person and the corporation are usually indivisible. Before long, the two are extremely divisible and strategically poised for independent growth.

When the Trusted Advisor uses Wealth Care Solutions, he or she will see that the marked difference lies in the comprehensive planning system. The system combines tax planning strategies, structured life insurance strategies, disability insurance and long-term care strategies, inique investments, succession planning, cross-border planning and estate planning all into a single, integrated financial program.

Traditionally, these kinds of strategies are not implemented together. The only way to be sure you are investing in the right financial programs is to see how they work together within a single strategy.

The end result is a team of seasoned professionals who create individualized strategies to integrate the entrepreneur's entire approach to planning. The client spends a lot of time on his or her company's finances but very little on his or her investments and the tax he or she pays. Everything that a Trusted Advisor does for the client should be based on a fundamental commitment to the client's strategic plan.

Those financial professionals who will succeed in this new era will quickly identify their allies and recognize their enemies. They will build alliances with those professionals and organizations that will help them to navigate the clear blue waters towards success. To succeed in this new era, financial professionals will have to place their focus on identifying and understanding a client's total financial life and create solutions that will solve a client's most important needs and goals.

Successful financial consultants in this new era, in addition to solving their clients' current problems, must correctly anticipate their clients' future problems and develop the necessary services to solve them.

Clients will no longer pay for services and products that only meet their past needs.

Successful financial consultants whose aim is to become a Trusted Advisor must make strategic bets on the services and capabilities that they must have if they want their current clients to continue to use their services in the future while attracting new clients.

The future looks bleak for financial practitioners who lack the resources, management skills and desire to change their business model to adopt services that will best serve their clients' needs. They should be always mindful of the old adage: "If you do what you have always done, you will get what you have always gotten."

I am, however, very optimistic for the future of financial advisors who rise to the calling and invest themselves in becoming their clients' Trusted Advisor. If there is a time and need for the Trusted Advisor it is now, as the world in which clients find themselves becomes more complex. The successful Trusted Advisor is one who sees the future and embraces it while never forgetting the past and learning from it.

A TRUE STORY

The seeds of this book were first planted on Tuesday, September 11, 2001. It was a perfect day in Toronto, not a cloud in the sky. I was driving to a meeting that was going to help me surpass my sales quota for the month.

I was listening to the radio when I heard at 8:50 A.M. that a plane had just crashed into the North Tower of the World Trade Center.

As I pulled into the parking lot a few minutes later in my client's office complex, a little after 9:00 A.M., I heard the radio announcer say that another plane had just hit the South Tower of the World Trade Center.

I knew something was up, but I did not have time to think much about it because I had to get to my very important appointment.

You see, that day, I was going to implement a new investment portfolio that involved "my" client buying $600,000 of mutual funds through me.

It was an important sales day!

For the first 25 minutes of the meeting, I had my client's full attention!

Then it happened. His wife called in around 9:40 A.M. to tell him that a third plane had just crashed into the Pentagon. Our meeting at that moment ended abruptly.

There was going to be no sale that day and no big payday.

As I drove home from that meeting, I came to the personal realization that the days of just selling product for the product's sake in the financial service industry were over for me.

If I was going to be successful in the financial advisory business going forward, I would need to learn how to present and implement solutions that were going to solve clients' most important needs. It was that realization that launched me on my journey to transform my practice from that of the transactional/commission-based business model I had operated prior to September 11, 2001 to that of the client-centred/solutions-based consulting practice model that I live today.

I discovered early on during the first days of my journey that I would need to seek mentors who would assist me during this transition.

WORKING WITH THE BEST TO BECOME YOUR VERY BEST!

Over the last four decades I have discovered through the University of Hard Knocks that wisdom is best acquired by learning from those who have walked the path we desire to travel. This accumulated wisdom in the financial consulting professions makes a crucial difference in our professional development, leading us to our personal success and attracting toward us clients who appreciate the value we bring to the table as their Trusted Advisor while drawing us closer towards our own personal goals.

I believe this is best illustrated by the work of the English astronomer Sir Fred Hoyle (1915-2001). Hoyle was fascinated with the Rubik's cube and one's mastery of it. What he did so beautifully is use the example of the familiar Rubik's cube to make his point of how allowing ourselves to be guided by accumulated wisdom empowers us to achieve our end goals in a fraction of the time. This, according to Hoyle, was infinitely more powerful than doing things blindly without the proper guidance from an obliging source.

If you are not familiar with the Rubik's cube, it has six faces that are subdivided into three rows of three colour-coded sections each; there are six distinct colours being divided into an equal number of squares on each of the cube's six faces. The aim of the game of the Rubik's cube is to move the coloured squares so that all the same coloured squares are on the same face of the cube relative to the others by twisting the cube.

Hoyle proposed an interesting question, and that was: What if one asked a blind man to order the scrambled segments of the cube so they all lined up perfectly, achieving the game's objective? The blind man cannot see and, therefore, would not know if any of his twists would be moving him closer to achieving the goal of the game. Thus, the blind man would have to work by random trial and error. To be successful, the blind man would need to try every possible move. Hoyle calculated that for the blind man to be successful it would take 126 billion years to accomplish this feat, approximately ten times longer than the known age of our universe.

Then Hoyle asked another important question: What if the blind man received information about the correctness of each move/twist from an expert who had mastered the Rubik's cube before? The result: the blind man would unscramble the cube in an average of 120 moves within three minutes flat.

What this example teaches us is that the evolution towards your personal success never needs to begin from scratch, or be done alone or by a fluke of nature. I thought why invent the wheel when we can find someone who has access to a wheel factor, where we can buy it wholesale or become its distributor?

That is why in my life and professional career I have decided to seek out the experts in the areas of interest that I don't know much about but have a great desire to learn from and master, whatever the cost. I believe that to be successful in this new financial climate, one must have an inner calling to learn from the best in the hopes of becoming the very best.

If you find some of the solutions in this book revolutionary, let me quickly dispel any myths and share that these experts have spent lifetimes accumulating real-life experiences in their own financial consulting practices to arrive at these insights. Remember that formulating good opinions only comes from having access to great information from credible sources.

The common denominator shared between all these experts is that they have all advised the ultra-successful in our society and have been appointed by their clients and peers as their most Trusted Advisors. More importantly, they have had a great need to give back to their various professions and share their collective wisdom. This book is a result of their generosity.

When sitting down to write this introduction, I calculated that the accumulated experience of all the contributors combined was over 1,000 years in diverse fields. If the time spent by each contributor could be tabulated in terms of billable hours, the actual work required to create this book would cost well over $10 million.

In this book, you will be introduced to some of the most leading-edge financial planning concepts and best practices being applied to the business and personal financial planning consulting industry today and gain insight from leading innovators successfully applying these concepts to the financial planning industry on both sides of the Canadian and U.S. border.

These experts have come together to provide their intellectual property and their wisdom throughout this text. I assure you that you will find as much true value in their contributions and insights as I have gained by their individual involvement in my own personal and professional journey.

This book will have achieved its primary purpose if you, the reader, have gained the required tools necessary to enable you to transition your financial consulting practice effortlessly from that of a product-focused practice to that of a client solutions-focused financial planning practice — thus arming you, today's modern-day financial professional, to prosper in this new, challenging and very exciting environment as you emerge as the modern embodiment of the Trusted Advisor.

As I finished writing this text, a thought came to me that I would now like to share with you as you proceed with your own journey through "The TASK": true wisdom and experience are not expensive; they are absolutely priceless. The question is: Do we have the eyes to realize this fact of nature and embrace it?

Part I

The Call of the Trusted Advisor

CHAPTER 1

THE TRUSTED ADVISOR'S CHALLENGE

Peter J. Merrick

Overview

This chapter offers an overview of how the financial planning industry has changed over the past two decades. It also offers a challenge to the Trusted Advisor to break free from the shackles of old models that no longer work in order to emerge into a bright new paradigm of success.

Learning Objectives

By the end of this chapter, you should be able to:

- understand what is required of financial planning in the 21st century;
- understand how to apply the Six-Step Financial Planning Process;
- understand how to select the right clients that will make for a stratifying career;
- understand your 150 and the power of a synergy group in your professional and personal life;
- understand the three compensation models for the 21st Century Trusted Advisor for managing assets;
- understand the value of charging a retainer for the advice you provide; and
- identify what your next steps are.

> "Our greatest need is to be loved ... and to know that everything will work out ... that everything will be O.K.!"
>
> Daniel Young

WARNING: NEW LANDSCAPE AHEAD

Thomas S. Kuhn, a scientist, in his famed book originally published in 1962, *The Structure of Scientific Revolutions* (Chicago, Ill.: University of Chicago Press, 1996) first defined the term "paradigm shift". A "paradigm shift" is a revolutionary change from one way of thinking to a newer way of perceiving the world around us. It allows us to accommodate changes in the world that the old model failed to address satisfactorily. This happens when one of the basic underlying assumptions that we have been living with changes.

In 1987, the "four pillars" of the Canadian financial sector — banks, trust companies, insurance companies and investment dealers — fell down, and all these independent sectors were allowed by the Canadian government to merge. Thus, the financial sector in Canada began its own paradigm shift over the last two decades and it continues today. With this convergence of financial institutions, one-stop shopping for financial services is now possible for each Canadian consumer, and new skills are required of the 21st century financial consultant.

The financial industry is constantly evolving. For many years, people turned to stockbrokers for money matters. Then, insurance agents entered the picture. Stockbrokers are now called financial advisors, and insurance agents are sometimes financial planners. There are independent financial planners, fee-only money managers and now, even accountants who can invest client money at some accounting firms. It can be difficult to know what someone is really dealing with.

Investment advisors, insurance agents, lawyers, financial planners and accountants should be aware that their practices are no longer just competing with those of other professionals in their respective industries. Traditional brokerage firms at Canada's largest banks own brokerage houses, and banks and insurance companies are mobilizing their resources to become the semi-affluent client's financial advisor of choice in the 21st century by launching what they term the "family office".

These multi-billion dollar organizations are expanding their services to include teams of skilled professionals offering a wide variety of accounting, legal and financial services. They have created huge teams of highly qualified Chartered Accountants (CAs), Certified Management Accountants (CMAs), Certified General Accountants (CGAs), Chartered Financial Analysts (CFAs), Certified Financial Planners (CFPs), Trust and Estate Practitioners (TEPs), Fellows of the Canadian Securities Institute (FCSI), Lawyers, Chartered Life Underwriters (CLUs) and Certified Employee Benefit Specialists (CEBS), placing these experts at the disposal of clients. These new players are taking aim at the traditional accountant's, lawyer's, insurance agent's, stock broker's and financial planner's clientele by evaluating a client's tax issues, preparing individual, corporate and trust tax returns and providing tax and legal planning and other financial solutions.

In addition to offering the services mentioned above, the wealth management departments at Canada's largest financial institutions are offering expertise in areas where many lawyers, accountants, insurance agents, brokers and financial planners are weak. These services include debt consolidation, investment counselling, financial planning, succession planning, tax planning, offshore and estate and insurance services. In the process, these new players, through their holistic approach to the financial planning processes, are uncovering and identifying clients' financial issues, and providing solutions to needs that these financial advisors were unaware existed and/or had failed to address adequately and comprehensively.

MAXIMIZING YOUR PROFESSIONAL VALUE AS A 21ST CENTURY TRUSTED ADVISOR

Tom Nicolle, CA, CFA, is a very close colleague of mine and a financial professional whom I admire very much. Tom, who works from Halifax, Nova Scotia, has completed a very intensive study of the financial planning and succession marketplace in Canada. What his research shows is that in order for 21st century financial planning professionals to maximize their full intrinsic value, as with any other professional service, they would need to position themselves as dominant players in a highly specialized niche market moving in the same expanding direction as market trends while being called upon by "The TASK" to be generalists in many diverse fields. By doing this, these advisors can be compensated based on the true value they create for their clients, rather than the time they spend working on a file, and these Trusted Advisors can take advantage of a brand that recognizes them as the best in their field. When these forces come together, the true professional financial advisor has competitive advantages in the marketplace that bring both recognition and wealth.

Nicolle determined that the 21st century financial professional who takes advantage of the following three emerging trends in the financial services market will enjoy an abundance of opportunity:

1. The financial services industry predicts that in the next five to ten years, significant levels of wealth will change hands in Canada. It is estimated that much of this wealth is tied up in the equity of businesses whose owners need to plan their succession, and a large

number of these businesses are valued between $2 million and $20 million, and are family-run enterprises.

2. There are more than 150,000 advisors competing for the management of the wealth of Canadians. Most of these people are product salespeople, not solution providers. Based on statistics from various professional organizations, it is estimated that less than one-half of 1% of these advisors are true professionals capable of providing the level of sophisticated advice required for succession planning. Successful advisors will need to focus on providing business as well as financial advice to business owners.

3. Industry research suggests that there are two kinds of financial service companies that are highly valuable and profitable: those that are very large and benefit from scale, and those that are niche boutique players with specialized expertise to enable them to boost profitability. There is a need for a specialized niche model that promotes the skills of the financial consulting generalist while specializing in offering value-added succession planning services in the marketplace. However, these types of firm are rare in Canada today.

Nicolle believes that by taking advantage of these three trends, an advisor with credentials as both a business consultant and financial advisor will be positioned to fully maximize his or her true professional value in the 21st century marketplace and be deserving of the title of the Trusted Advisor with all its rewards.

21ST CENTURY CLIENT

Most people start by acknowledging that they need some help with their money. That much we know for sure. What is less certain is what sort of help they need and from what type of financial planning professional they will get that much needed help.

To make things simple, financial help falls into two categories: financial planning and money management.

Financial planning is valuable and important. The key elements of good financial planning are retirement forecasting, tax analysis, insurance analysis, business succession planning and estate planning. Note that I did not say "investing". We haven't gotten to that yet.

Under the "Six-Step Financial Planning Process" advocated by the Financial Planners Standards Council of Canada (FPSC), the 21st century Trusted Advisor continuously directs and monitors specific goals that a client has. For example, the traditional investment advisor is only going to monitor the performance of the product he or she has sold, but not make it part of the specific plan that is associated with the goal-setting process developed by the 21st century Trusted Advisor.

In a culture that is reactive by nature, people feel powerless against their circumstances, but when they use the Six-Step Financial Planning Process, clients gain control over their lives and are empowered to create and move toward living the life they want.

The six-step financial planning process allows clients to be proactive in creating a life of their choosing instead of living a life that is reactive to outside circumstances and influences.

When a client initially meets with a 21st century Trusted Advisor, the client will find that some of the questions asked are not financial in nature. For example, when a client talks about financial independence and/or retirement, the 21st century Trusted Advisor might ask things like:

- Do you want to change the way you live your life today? How?
- What result do you want to create?
- How do you spend your time?
- What would you really like to do if you were financially independent?
- How will you stay motivated if you don't do the type of work you do now?
- How will you react to not having a job?
- How would your family be affected by your retirement and health issues that may have to be considered within the plan, such as your personal life expectancy due to previous disease or family history?
- Where would you like to live?

Ordinary advisors use a structured framework to gather information about clients and overlay it with a run-of-the-mill strategy according to the client's situation. Extraordinary Trusted Advisors have learned to step back and to fully look at and appreciate the entire situation while asking, "What is really happening here to bring the client to this crossroads in his or her life, and seek the assistance of a qualified professional?" It is not that these extraordinary Trusted Advisors are any smarter than anyone else. What makes them stand out is their willingness to ask the deeper questions of:

- Why did the client do something in his or her past?
- What does the client want to accomplish in his or her lifetime?
- What legacy does the client want to leave after he or she is gone?
- What prevents the client from achieving his or her goals?
- What is the client willing to do and sacrifice to achieve his or her stated goals?

- What motivates the client to act?

Asking penetrating questions allows both the Trusted Advisor and his or her clients to achieve clarity. Having the client understand what he or she wants requires the client to make a decision; is he or she going to reach for his or her goals or ignore them? By choosing to go for his or her goals, the end result is that the client's goals just come into being naturally. A client's real vision of what he or she wants to create in his or her life is uncovered from within, not imposed or contrived by someone else, especially the advisor.

The Trusted Advisor has a fundamental understanding that none of us has control of what happens in the world around us, or, for that matter, what our governments will or won't do, but what we do have is the ability to direct what we do personally and how we choose to react to forces outside our control. The best place to start to be a proactive agent in each of ours and our clients' lives is to have in place a comprehensive financial plan. Most people do not have the time or expertise to create a financial plan for themselves, and that is the essence behind their motivation for working with a skilled Trusted Advisor.

When a client has engaged you as his or her Trusted Advisor to assist him or her in creating a comprehensive financial plan, what will be different after both of you are finished the planning process that most likely was not true before the client had engaged you?

Both you and the client will have a satisfaction of knowing that if your client dies, gets sick, becomes disabled or lives a long life, his or her family will be able to continue without compromising the client's quality of life, standard of living and goals. The financial plan will address issues such as how to protect the family business, home and cottage, pay for children's education or anything else that the client has deemed important for his or her family and himself or herself.

Within the planning process, contingency solutions will be made to protect the family business in the case of a premature death, disability or a family fight to prevent an unfortunate fireside sale and unnecessary pain for the loss. Your client will know what he or she must do in order to retire on his or her terms, at the time and place of his or her choosing. The plan addresses your client's desire of never being a financial burden to his or her loved ones, dependent on the charity of others, or at the mercy of the State. With a contingency plan in place, thus creating peace of mind for the client, a job done well, your client will live knowing that if he or she does what he or she has determined within the pages of the financial plan that he or she has identified as important, when he or she is supposed to do it, then the client will never outlive his or her money or live a life not of his or her design.

In addition, your client will be able to assist his or her children and grandchildren in establishing their own lives as contributing members of society by setting aside moneys to help them pay for post-secondary education, start businesses, purchase their first homes, help other family members, or anything else that the family deems important.

The financial plan will attend to elderly parental care issues by setting aside funds that provide the means to assist the client's parents financially and emotionally, so that the client's parents can live the rest of their days with dignity and respect. The plan will address the legacy the client wants to leave behind to his or her community, family and children in a meaningful way, with the gift of both his or her time and money.

Lastly, the financial plan will address the topic of taxes owed to the Canada Revenue Agency (CRA) by your client on his or her death, and the plan will provide the most economic way to reduce these taxes while protecting the client's family unit and its assets. This is what real clients care most about accomplishing in seeking the help of a true Trusted Adviser. This is why your role in assisting your clients through the Six-Step Financial Planning Process is so vital for everyone involved. This tested financial planning process ensures your client's and his or her family's financial health and security. It is a wonderful thing for the Trusted Advisor to be a part of ensuring the success of a family's future and a client's legacy.

THE SIX-STEP FINANCIAL PLANNING PROCESS

Every human being has an innate desire, and skill, to perceive the future. Albert Einstein said: "Imagination is everything. It is the preview of the life's coming attractions." Silvano Arieti once said:

> Creativity is one of the major means by which the human being liberates himself from the shackles not only of his conditioned responses, but also his usual choices.

By asking questions similar to those listed above, the Trusted Advisor helps his or her clients to imagine future scenarios to make better choices today. Scenarios are not predictions; they represent possible alternative futures that will help an individual navigate the present and create his or her future.

The Six-Step Financial Planning Process is not a science but an art, a disciplined way for the Trusted Advisor and the client to foresee alternative futures and make difficult decisions that will empower the client to adapt to the complex world we live in today.

This process, properly applied, empowers both the client and his or her Trusted Advisor to question the client's underlying assumptions that the client has towards his or her family, health, future work-related circumstances, retirement and estate. What is an appropriate range of alternative scenarios? What decisions does the client have to make that are affected by these scenarios? Which decisions will leave the client much better off? Asking and answering these questions will provide the greatest possible benefit from the standpoint of developing and implementing the right financial plan that will fulfill a client's goals and needs at a particular point in time.

The 21st century Trusted Advisor is really the quarterback or facilitator of the architectural plans created for a client's present and future. In essence, what separates a traditional financial advisor from a 21st century Trusted Advisor is the training in processes similar to the Six-Step Financial Planning Process that the 21st century Trusted Advisor will have received. Good financial planning is always more about process than product.

- **Step one:** The Trusted Advisor works with a client to clarify his or her present situation by collecting and assessing all relevant financial data, such as lists of assets and liabilities, tax returns, records of securities transactions, insurance policies, wills, pension plans, business ownership and share structures, *etc.*
- **Step two:** The Trusted Advisor will help the client identify both the client's financial and personal goals and objectives, as well as clarify the client's financial and personal values and attitudes. These may include providing for children's education, supporting elderly parents, selling a business or relieving immediate financial pressures that will help maintain the current lifestyle and provide for retirement. These considerations are important in determining the best financial planning strategy.

  To be effective in this process and in his or her life, the client needs to be completely and brutally honest in determining what his or her current reality is, and what he or she wants to create in his or her future. At the same time, by successfully completing Step One of this process, the client is grounded in knowing what he or she has to work with. This creates tension between what the client has now and what he or she wants to manifest in his or her life. It is this discrepancy that propels the client towards what he or she wants to create in his or her life.

Step Two of the process is also where the Trusted Advisor drills down and finds out what the client really wants and what motivates him or her by asking the most important question in a Trusted Advisor's arsenal: *What do you really want to create in your life and beyond?*

This question is powerful because it tells the Trusted Advisor if the client moves towards achieving goals or if the client chooses to move away from what he or she doesn't want. For example, a person who moves away from what he or she doesn't want might answer: "I don't want to be poor." While the person who moves towards what he or she wants would say: "I want to create a legacy to help underprivileged children have the same opportunities that I have been given in my lifetime."

The best way to appreciate these differences in underlying perceptions and motives is through the telling of the story of the traveller who comes upon two masons cutting stone during the course of his journey. The traveller asks the first mason, "What are you doing?" The mason replies: "I am cutting stone to prevent my family from starving" (moving away from what he does not want). Then the traveller asks the second mason the same question. This mason smiles and enthusiastically replies: "I am building the grandest cathedral of them all. This will stand for a thousand years and be a testament to man's ingenuity, strength of character and will" (clearly this mason moves towards his goals). Which client would you want to work with?

- **Step three:** The Trusted Advisor will help his or her client identify financial problems that create barriers to achieving financial independence. Problem areas can include too little or too much insurance coverage, or a high tax burden. The client's cash flow may be inadequate and may need to be reviewed. These possible problem areas must be identified before solutions can be found. If the client can't have it all at once, it is important for the Trusted Advisor to help the client prioritize what's important and then go like gangbusters to help the client achieve those goals before addressing other goals.

A gifted planner understands that during the process of helping the client identify potential obstacles to achieving his or her goals, the Trusted Advisor will provide tremendous value to the client by assisting the client to flush out what the client truly wants to achieve. If a client has never really gone through the Six-Step Financial Planning Process in the past, the client will most likely state as a goal something he or she does not want to bring into his or her life.

For example, when looking at what the client wants to achieve in the realm of his or her investment portfolio, the client might at first say something like, "I don't want to lose my money and be broke." This statement can be compared to someone in a row boat rowing away from the shore which he or she has come from. With this type of response, the client is always directed by what he or she does not want because that is what is at the forefront of his or her mind at all times.

The Trusted Advisor, by asking penetrating questions similar to "Through not being broke, what do you really want to bring into your life?", will help the client break free from old mental chains and establish what he or she truly wants to go forward with and build towards his or her financial planning. So let us look at how this client might answer the question:

> Trusted Advisor: "Through not being broke, what do you really want to bring into your life?"
>
> Client: "I want to reach financial independence so that my wife and family may enjoy the next stages of our lives, living in Lo Jolla, California and doing what we want on our own terms."

When a client makes this flip in his or her mental and motivational inclination from what he or she does not want to what he or she really does want to bring into his or her life, this can be compared to taking a powerful motor and placing it on the back of the row boat, where the client now moves at a blistering speed towards his or her true goals. A client's true goals are not imposed on the client by outside forces or by fear. The client now is motivated by his or her wants.

There is a world of difference between fact and speculation at this point in the process. This occurs when your client has gone through this step in the process of determining what he or she truly wants and what motivates him or her. It becomes a fact now that he or she wants to achieve these results, and that is half the battle, since most people are unclear of what they want to bring about in their lives. This can be the greatest gift that the Trusted Advisor gives the client, the gift of clarity of one's true wants.

Applying this approach during your questioning will make all the difference for the client in accepting your recommendations, implementing the plan and being fully committed for the long haul to achieving his or her most precious life goals. If your client's real goals are not identified during this step, then whatever recommendations that are made by you will not be sustainable even if the client had intentions to follow through.

- **Step four:** The Trusted Advisor will then provide written recommendations and alternative solutions. The length of the recommendations will vary according to the complexity of a client's individual situation. The Trusted Advisor knows that if the financial plan is not written down in a tangible formal document, the plan is not real in the mind of the client.
- **Step five:** A financial plan is only helpful if the recommendations are put into action. Implementing the right strategy will help the client to reach his or her desired goals and objectives. The Trusted Advisor will assist clients in the actual execution of the recommendations and in coordinating their implementation with other knowledgeable professionals, if necessary. This may include quarterbacking lawyers, accountants, investment advisors, actuaries, trustees, mortgage brokers, bankers, venture capitalists and insurance agents. By no means is this list of professionals mentioned above complete.
- **Step six:** The Trusted Advisor will provide clients with frequent reviews and revisions of their plans to assure that their goals are achieved. Clients' financial situations should be reviewed and reassessed at least once a year to account for changes in their lives and current economic conditions.

What is fascinating about this Six-Step Financial Planning Process is that once clients start achieving their goals, their goals will most likely have changed, and it is important to go through the entire process again to include these changes in the clients' financial plans. You will be amazed at what you and your clients will discover by continually utilizing this process. When both the Trusted Advisor and the client commit to the process, the universe conspires to help you both accomplish the Task and reach what was once thought to be unreachable — making the impossible, possible!

REFERRALS

Often I am asked how a Trusted Advisor can ask a satisfied client for referrals. This is much simpler than it sounds. When a client has completed the financial planning process with you, and has addressed all the core issues such that the client can now see the life he or she wants to create for his or her community, family and himself or herself, this is when it is important and appropriate to ask him or her the following question:

> *"When you achieve your goals and live the life you want, who else is in your picture?"*

The client will usually give a list of people whom he or she cares about most, such as family and friends. The client is invested in these people's success. The best follow-up question to the one listed above is:

> "*What is ________ (fill the blank with the names of the person or persons the client has identified as important to him or her) doing right now personally and financially to be in your picture of success?*"

By asking these two questions, the client in his or her mind's eye begins to see clearly that if the people he or she envisions in his or her life are not making the same preparation as the client has by planning for it, then the people the client cares deeply about will not be able to afford to live and enjoy the life that the client aims to achieve. When the client comes to his or her personal understanding of this, the client will then feel a need to get his or her loved ones and friends to go through the same financial planning process as well.

The client will feel compelled and motivated by his or her own concerns to recommend to his or her friends and family to seek the help of the Trusted Advisor who assisted the client through his or her financial planning process, so that the client's friends and family will have the personal and financial resources to enjoy their collective future together. This is all based on the sound financial planning you have helped them to achieve in the first place. When someone has a self interest to refer you, he or she will; if he or she doesn't, he or she usually won't.

LIFE'S MAIN QUESTIONS

Several years ago, I was introduced to the six questions that people ask themselves as they enter different stages of their lives. The stage at which someone begins asking each of these questions is usually tied to the individual's age and maturity. Trusted Advisors, desiring to assist clients as they ask themselves these six questions, will find that the Six-Step Financial Planning Process is their greatest ally in helping their clients reach answers to their very personal life questions at a particular moment in time. When applied properly, what is most gratifying is that both you and the client have developed an understanding of what issues the client is really grappling with and, as a result, a close partnership is forged between the both of you.

- **Life Question One:** Who am I? This is an identity question. Individuals usually begin asking this question when they are small children. When we are born we have no identity, we are given our names from our parents, we are born into a certain place and culture, and we may assume the religion of our parents. Individuals answer this question by assuming different labels that describe who they believe they are, and this is how we identify ourselves.

- **Life Question Two:** How do I fit in? Individuals begin asking this question usually when they reach their teens. It is a time when they try to figure out how they fit into their social and physical environments. When individuals begin asking this question in their development, they are highly influenced by their peers and are susceptible to peer pressure (*i.e.*, high school).
- **Life Question Three:** What will I do? Individuals begin asking themselves this question usually in their early twenties. This stage occurs when individuals try to figure out what they will do with themselves for their career, and who they may or may not partner with. This question is different from Question One because it is concerned with the actions the individuals will take in their lives; this question is not a question of identity.
- **Life Question Four:** Who have I become? The question usually arises when individuals reach their forties. Individuals wake up and realize that they are no longer planning their lives, dreaming of what they will become when they grow up, because they are grown up. Some people transition to asking this question very gracefully; others do not. This question often leads individuals into the so-called "mid-life crisis". This is also a time when individuals become serious about planning their financial affairs. For example, members of Generation X are beginning to ask this question of themselves en masse.
- **Life Question Five:** What have I accomplished? This question usually arises when individuals reach their mid to late 50s. Individuals realize that their working career is coming to an end, and a new stage of life is about to begin. At this stage, individuals are getting ready to retire from work and enter their retirement. In the area of financial planning these people are putting their financial affairs in order to make sure they have enough income to support themselves when they no longer receive income from their own labour. For business owners, this is the time when they start planning and implementing succession plans for their businesses.
- **Life Question Six:** What will my legacy be? People start asking this question of themselves after they retire. They come to the realization that they are at the end of their lives. They begin to think beyond their mortal existence and start contemplating what they will

be remembered for and what legacy they will pass on after they are gone from this life.

Individuals asking this question are quite serious about gifting their time and money to people and causes they care deeply about. It has been said that those who begin asking the question of what their legacy will be, are individuals who have the biggest impact on families, communities, society and the world long after they have departed. There is a Jewish saying that applies to many in the group asking Life Question Six:

"It is better to give with a warm hand than a cold hand."

SELECTING THE RIGHT CLIENTS THAT WILL MAKE FOR A SATISFYING CAREER, WELL DONE!

It is as true today as it was approximately 2,500 years ago when Socrates, the ancient Greek philosopher, stated probably the most profound self-actualizing statement of all time upon which all self development programs have been built ever since:

"Know Thyself!"

England's Lord Justice of Appeal John Fletcher Moulton stated over 80 years ago that the essential test of one's ethical behaviour is "obedience to the unenforceable", meaning a willingness to go beyond the law and even the spirit of the law to do what is morally right and just.

The Trusted Advisor knows that being successful means being ethical at all times, doing it right because it feels right. Knowing how to act ethically in whatever situation the Trusted Advisor finds himself or herself is not something he or she is born with; it's something he or she learns. Ethics grow stronger every time one chooses right over wrong.

Don't expect that having high ethical and professional standards are going to make you popular. Excellence is not free. You will get scarred along the way while you strive towards achieving higher standards and doing what is right. A good way to live an ethical life is to think long term as you make your way through your life and career choices. Take the approach towards the long view as you consider your actions and behaviour at all times. It is said that if you act for the moment you might be mortgaging your future. Is this what you want for yourself?

There is no one who has not made an honest mistake. But remember, there is no such thing as an honest cover-up. My father used to say to me: "Don't do anything that if you find yourself in the *Toronto Star* you are not proud of it."

Living an ethical life requires accepting high standards for yourself because nothing else will satisfy you. This means you have to make a conscious choice not to tolerate low ethical standards from yourself or those around you. You have to let everyone know that you don't allow yourself to be associated with low ethical standards and it is not acceptable to you for your ethics to be jeopardized by anyone, not your colleagues, not your employer and not your clients. You know that you are worth a lot more than that. It is said that you are what you eat, and you are seen to be that which you associate with.

You can't put anyone else in charge of your morals. Remember the words of former U.S. President Harry Truman: "The buck stops here!" You have to take total responsibility for the choices you make and not blame others for what you do or don't do. Your conscience is your greatest guide and partner to living a life based on your ethics.

> "Be not afraid of greatness: some are born great, some achieve greatness, and some have greatness thrust upon them."
>
> William Shakespeare (1564-1616)

This is why good financial planning cannot be reduced to technique; good financial planning comes from the identity and integrity of the financial professional. Technique is what you use until the authentic Trusted Advisor arrives. In essence, good financial planning comes from good people. As the author of this book, I would also like to add as an addendum to Socrates' quote above for all those who choose to provide financial advice for their careers:

"Know Thyself!
&
Know Who You Can Best Serve!"

Our most valuable asset is our time, and it is wise that we spend our time where we will get the biggest bang for each second that we have been given on this blessed earth. Before entering a client relationship, the Trusted Advisor should assess his or her added value. If you add a lot of value to the relationship, you should be paid by your clients for this value. Only you can determine what your value is. You will always receive exactly what you expect from yourself and others.

If you can't get paid for the added value you bring to a client relationship, the smartest move on your part is choosing to sit on the sidelines. Remember: you are in the professional financial advisory industry to earn a great living, while helping others and having fun. You have to value your worth and you should only work with clients who appreciate the value you bring to their table and who are willing to pay you for your value.

There is a simple law in the advisory professions: if everyone in your business can do it, you will not make money doing the same thing. In the natural world, no two species can co-exist in the same place and make their living in the same way. This basic law of nature applies for professionals who offer the same service to the same clients.

The key is to know the added value that you provide your clients so they won't go anywhere else, except to you. If you have not already done this, you should sit down and figure out what you bring to a client's life through your education, experience, code of ethics and wisdom.

A Trusted Advisor who stays true to his or her core values and mission is a very attractive professional, and the right clients will show up and appreciate him or her. How do you get people to share your core values? You can't. It is impossible. Just find people who are predisposed to share your values and purpose, attract and retain those people, and let those who do not share your values go somewhere else.

Our life span in the financial professions is relatively short, and we need to be focused on those whom we can help the most, and who can help us achieve our independent personal and financial goals in our lifetimes. Each professional relationship we have should be win/win, where we share similar values and goals and want the very best for each other. The biggest opportunities and the biggest profits don't come from playing the game differently. This comes from changing the game itself.

Robin Dunbar, author of the ground-breaking book *Grooming, Gossip, and The Evolution of Language* (Cambridge, Mass.: Harvard University Press, 1996), convincingly argues that the purpose of human communication is to bond with others. Stronger bonds are made with those we most often communicate with.

Dunbar's research shows that the average person has an invisible social network of approximately 150 people with whom the person would feel comfortable enough to have a cup of coffee if he or she bumped into a member of this group on the street. Dunbar found that the strength of social networks dilutes when these networks grow greater than 150 people. Yes, most of us know many more than 150 people, but we don't have the strong ties that we have to our 150.

With the advent of community websites such as Facebook, Twitter, Myspace and Linkedin, we have access to many more loose affiliations with tens of thousands of individuals. What is important to be mindful of here is the phrase "loose affiliations". These should not be confused with our tight personal and professional relationships.

Note: The research conducted by Robin Dunbar was used as the basis of Malcolm Gladwell's 2000 best-selling book The Tipping Point — How Little Things Can Make a Big Difference *(Boston: Little, Brown, 2000: reprinted with a new afterword by author, Boston: Back Bay Books, 2002).*

Robin Dunbar also found that within each person's network of 150 people, there is a core group of about 10-12 people who make up a smaller group of individuals whom we have vested interest in and care about dearly. If something were to happen to anyone in our core group, we would be deeply affected. We will discuss the "core group" and how we can use it to foster success in our professional careers in more detail when we explore "synergy groups" later on in this chapter.

So if there are a limited number of individuals with whom we can have quality relationships within our lives at any one time, especially during our careers, it is critical to know whom we can best serve as financial professionals and what clients to invite to our network of 150. There are spiritual vampires in our midst. By spiritual vampires I mean individuals who suck the life force out of you when you are around them or when you think about them.

These are the clients and other individuals who, when you see their names pop up on your caller ID, you don't want to talk to. To achieve longevity in any profession, we should strive to be surrounded by spiritual angels, those individuals who give us energy, who we want to be around us and to succeed just as they want us to have genuine success as well.

In a conversation I had several years ago with a colleague of mine, Derek Hill, CA, of Hill Kindly Group in Ontario, Canada, Derek shared with me that he learned to group his professional and client relationships into three distinct categories:

Group One: These are individuals who only want to win and want you to be the loser in all your dealings with them. All that matters to these individuals is that they win and you lose.

Group Two: These are individuals who want to win and don't care if you win or lose from the relationship. If you win, great; if you lose, they don't care either way.

Group Three: These are individuals whose primary goal in all their personal and professional relationships is a win/win for everyone involved. The main goal of each of these individuals in their relationships is for everyone to come out a winner and, for each party in a relationship, whether personal or professional, to always strive for that goal.

I believe that taking the time to sit down with a pad of paper and categorizing each client, professional and personal relationship into Derek's three groups is a perfect place to begin to evaluate the people we have surrounded ourselves with. Very few people ever take the time to be honest with themselves, to consciously take stock of the nature of each of their relationships with others.

INVITING THE RIGHT CLIENT INTO OUR 150

Over the last two decades, I have continually redefined the criteria of the ideal clients to join my 150, clients whom I can best help with the experience and skill sets I have acquired, and who can help me to achieve my specific goals in my life. I have come to my criteria by always asking myself the following four questions:

Question 1: What qualities do I want my perfect client to possess and demonstrate?

Question 2: What makes my perfect client tick?

Question 3: What do I want my perfect client to expect me to deliver and provide?

Question 4: What should I expect from my perfect client?

When you have found your own answers to these questions, you will know when a prospect will make a perfect client for your financial advisory practice, and is a perfect candidate to join your 150. You will be able to recognize a perfect client the moment that you meet one. An immediate spark of attraction and connection between you and this person quickly leads to mutual respect, and a profitable personal and professional relationship follows.

Below I have provided the criteria which I use to evaluate a potential and current client relationship. If my list of criteria works for you, use it; if it doesn't work for you, get rid of it. What is great about this financial profession is that you can build your own theory of business however you wish, with whomever you wish, and be very happy and successful at doing it *your way*!

Clients who best benefit from working with our company are:

(1) those who trust us and appreciate our expertise in the fields of executive financial planning, wealth management, benefit plan design, investments, succession planning and estate planning;

(2) honest with us, and are willing to fully disclose their assets, values, goals and concerns;

(3) decisive and proactive with their financial decisions that affect their businesses, their families and their lives (these individuals are motivated towards achieving their goals);

(4) extremely busy with their careers and businesses and don't have the time to manage their financial affairs and money themselves (they work in dynamic businesses and professional fields and enjoy what they do);

(5) oriented towards reaching goals such as wealth preservation, tax minimization and deferral, creditor protection, wealth accumulation, wealth distribution and being good private and corporate citizens (they understand their responsibility to invest in the future, in themselves, in others, the community as a whole and in creating a positive legacy);

(6) referred to us by a partner or client who has benefited from our professionalism, skills, solutions and performance;

(7) those who have a basic understanding of tax planning, financial planning, succession planning and corporate benefit plans (these are businesses or individuals who are highly motivated to work with our team of financial advisory professionals); and

(8) those who fully understand the value of our services, advice and relationship (it is this mutual understanding that allows us all to be successful and profitable in both our professional and personal relationships).

Typically, our services are of most value to individuals who have at least:

- $300,000 or more of combined annual income;

  or

- $5,000,000 or more of net worth.

Our services are of most value to companies with:

- $400,000 or more of combined annual income;

  or

- $5,000,000 or more of net worth.

SYNERGY GROUPS AND HOW THEY WORK TO MANIFEST YOUR SUCCESS

> "Never doubt that a small group of committed citizens can change the world. Indeed, it's the only thing that ever has."
>
> Margaret Mead

Buckminster ("Bucky") Fuller (1895–1983), referred to as the 20th century's "Gentle Genius", a visionary and inventor, when asked to describe himself, said he was a "verb" always in process. At the end of his life he had over 200 patents to his credit, coined the phrase "Spaceship Earth" and was a pioneer in the worldwide environmental movement. His most famous invention was the Geodesic Dome (the golf ball shaped building located at the Epcot Center at Walt Disney World, Florida), the most energy-efficient building ever designed in the world.

It was Bucky's fascination with the efficiency of energy that led to perhaps his greatest legacy with the coining of the word "synergy", Bucky being its biggest proponent during his lifetime, decades before it became fashionable in popular culture.

Synergy is "the phenomenon in which two or more discrete influences or agents acting together create an effect greater than that predicted by knowing only the separate effects of the individual agents": <http://en.wikipedia.org/wiki/Synergy>.

In combining the principle of synergy to our core group within our 150, we are acting on the premise that the combined energies of two or more like-minded persons is many times greater than the sum of the individual energies involved. In any great endeavour that you wish to succeed in, it is beneficial to ally yourself with others of a like mind and purpose.

In these groups, what is truly special is that we face our collective mortality by being truthful about what we fear and what we want to create, no longer avoiding but embracing our fears. This is how we make the mental shift away from what we don't want and towards creating what we do want in our lives.

By feeling comfortable in sharing our truths, we start to see ourselves as the cause of the problems we face, and this is how we invariably find our new capacity to create the results we seek. The pooling of each individual's resources in a synergy group is very valuable and cannot be understated. Through this process, invisible connections are also made among the group. These give rise to the higher principle of the group mind that acts for the benefit of all involved. Yet, you should take great care whom you allow into your synergy group because the opposite effect is also possible; that is, you might unknowingly have spiritual vampires in the midst of your core group who are sucking the life out of you, individuals who knock you down, not build you up.

It has been said that God created friends to make up for our families; thus, family will always be a part of our core group. However, our synergy group should consist of two or more persons (two to six is ideal) who meet regularly in an atmosphere of trust and harmony for the purpose of providing mutual support and encouragement and to believe for each other things that would be more difficult to conceive of or believe in alone.

Melissa Giovagnoli's and Jocelyn Carter-Miller's insightful book *Networlding: Building Relationships and Opportunities for Success* (San Francisco: Jossey-Bass, 2000) provides three useful questions that can help us populate our individual synergy groups with the right partners for our personal journeys.

Question One: Do we share the same values and goals? If an individual does not share our values and goals, then we should seriously consider moving these individuals outside of our 150, and definitely out of our core group.

Question Two: Can we work together? Someone may share our values and goals but because of differences in personality and work styles we cannot work together. If these people are members of our core group, we should move them to our 150, or even outside of that group.

Question Three: Is there opportunity for us to work together? We might answer yes to Question One and Question Two, but at this moment in time there might not be an opportunity to work together on a project. If this is the case, these individuals should be moved outside our core group and into our 150. However, if there is a genuine desire to create an opportunity amongst these individuals, they should be invited into our synergy group.

Synergy groups are not established so that individual members can solve each other's problems. Rather, such a group is established to surrender to the synergy that will be manifested in any problem areas towards resolution. When such requests are fully and properly made of the synergy group, answers and solutions occur in the most amazing way. Opportunity is manifested and real success occurs for each member of the group.

Members of a properly put together synergy group feel a compulsion to make your problems their problems, your solutions their solutions, your opportunity their opportunity and your successes their successes.

Members of your synergy group have a vested interest in each member's success when the right group is put together, and each member has a vested interest in the co-creation of business and personal opportunities for each other. A synergy group has the mindset that when one member succeeds in the group, all members do, and real miracles happen!

THREE COMPENSATION MODELS FOR MANAGING CLIENTS' ASSETS

When a client hires a Trusted Advisor, that client should know exactly how he or she will pay for that advisor's advice. This is the case whether a client is investing millions of dollars or just dabbling in the TSX.

It's also worth pointing out that until most Trusted Advisors came along, the financial advice that clients received probably cost them next to nothing. They got their information from reading *The Globe and Mail*, the *Toronto Star* or a mutual fund company's promotional material. Additional data may have come from watching television shows on The Business News Network (BNN), attending a workshop hosted by one of the five large Canadian chartered banks, or from talking to their dentist or friends and family.

This "free" information, incorrectly applied by a client, could turn out to be very costly. A client for life understands that valuable financial advice does not come cheap. He or she should be willing to pay for the right advice from a qualified financial professional.

Several years ago, I read a short piece by John Ruskin, the 19th century English social reformer, entitled: "It's Unwise to Pay Too Much". This expresses my thoughts on the subject of the true value that the Trusted Advisor provides to his or her clients:

> It's unwise to pay too much, but it's unwise to pay too little. When you pay too much you lose a little money. That is all. When you pay too little you sometimes lose everything, because the thing you bought was incapable of doing the thing you bought it to do. The common law of business balance prohibits paying a little and getting a lot. It cannot be done. If you deal with the lowest bidder, it is well to add something for the risk you run. And if you do that, you will have enough to pay for something better.

Although some advisors may feel uncomfortable talking about how they earn their keep, it is vital that clients understand how the Trusted Advisor is compensated. Whether the Trusted Advisor is starting a new client relationship or re-evaluating a current one, there are three basic models of compensation for providing the asset management solutions or any other financial advice.

Model One: The Trusted Advisor can be paid on the commissions generated when a client makes transactions. One example of this approach is the stockbroker, who earns a commission every time a client buys or sells a stock, bond or some other product purchased through the broker.

Model Two: The Trusted Advisor may be paid according to the growth or shrinkage of a client's assets. For example, some advisors' fees are set as a percentage of a client's portfolio (*e.g.*, 1% a year). If a client's portfolio grows through appreciation, then so does the advisor's fee. If assets shrink, the fee follows suit.

Model Three: The Trusted Advisor may be paid by a client per project or by the hour (*e.g.*, a flat fee for an initial evaluation of a portfolio). The client is buying the Trusted Advisor's experience, expertise and time.

Each one of these compensation models rewards the Trusted Advisor in different ways. In the first model (the "transaction or commission" base), there is a financial incentive to generate transactions in a client's account. A commission-based financial advisor might determine that the most appropriate investment for a client is 100% allocation to T-Bills. But he or she may not be able to afford to tell the client this opinion because there is almost no commission involved to reward the advisor. Even though we put the needs of the client first and act ethically, the best interests of the advisor may not always match the best interests of the client.

When an advisor is using the commission compensation model, it is important to explain all of the commissions and fees the advisor may earn from a deal. Full disclosure can help reduce any potential conflict of interest that may result from this model.

The Trusted Advisor whose pay is based on the size of the client's assets (model two) has an incentive to see those assets grow. Growth can come from appreciation of existing assets or from new assets that a client places under the advisor's management. If the client pays the Trusted Advisor a straight percentage of assets, then the client and the advisor will both want to achieve exactly the same thing — making money.

A fee-for-service-only (model three) Trusted Advisor has the incentive to take as much time as necessary to do a client's work, but has no incentive to steer the client towards any particular product. Like other professionals who bill by the hour, there is an incentive to spend more time than necessary (the "over-billing problem") to complete any project.

To some investors, this "fee-for-service-only" approach appears to be the most expensive. For this reason, very few Trusted Advisors have adopted the fee-for-service-only model. However, those who use this model have the potential benefit of obtaining increased referrals from other professionals in related financial fields. This occurs because accountants, lawyers and other professionals often feel more comfortable referring business to other professionals who are compensated in the same manner.

Investment advisors who earn their living by adopting model one (transaction or commissions) and model two (management fees on assets under management) can find it very profitable to work closely with a fee-for-service-only Trusted Advisor (model three). A fee-for-service-only Trusted Advisor, for example, may discover new investment and insurance opportunities that the referring investment advisor can implement. Think of how an investment guru who writes a newsletter can work well with a model one or model two investment advisor. The guru is compensated on a fee-only basis (via a yearly subscription to his or her newsletter, for example), while the transaction or "fees on assets under management" professional helps to implement this advice.

How do Trusted Advisors operating in model one and model two know when they have found another professional who complements their professional services working in model three? Simple. This occurs when the clients find more value in the Trusted Advisor's services when he or she is working together with that other professional to serve the clients' needs compared to when the clients have access to the Trusted Advisor's services alone. A professional is the Trusted Advisor's competitor if the clients are less attracted to what the Trusted Advisor does when the other professional is brought into the picture.

Today's clients are becoming more knowledgeable about how financial professionals are paid. An advisor who dodges this topic or gives vague answers might find his or her clients looking elsewhere for advice. As such, to be deserving of the Trusted Advisor title, you must be willing to candidly discuss your methods of compensation.

The bottom line: Stand tall and be proud of the value you bring to the table. Most importantly, be upfront with how you get paid for the valuable advice you provide. Great clients are willing to pay when they perceive that you bring value to their financial lives. Remember that as Trusted Advisors, all we truly have to sell is our time, whether we are compensated for it by earning a commission, fees on assets under-management, fee-for-service-only or a combination of these income models.

THINK ABOUT CHARGING A RETAINER FOR THE PROFESSIONAL ADVICE YOU PROVIDE

What is a retainer? A retainer fee is an advance payment paid up front for the value of the future deliverables provided by a professional advisor. The greatest value a Trusted Advisor provides to his or her clients is his or her intellectual property. Unfortunately, many who operate in the professional advisory fields choose to give away their knowledge for free in the hopes that one day soon the client will appreciate them enough to reward them by buying the advisor's services or product at some future date. This is like spilling your jelly beans in the lobby and then asking to be paid for them. As soon as a professional gives away his or her solutions for free, many clients and potential clients will unfortunately no longer see any value in using the advisor as much or at all compared to if the client first had to pay for that same advice.

Unfortunately, I learnt this lesson the hard way. Early on in my career I used to provide free employment benefit and financial planning workshops and seminars to corporations. At those meetings, very few attended, and I would be lucky if a low-level member of the company's HR team showed up. Rarely did I make enough to justify the time and money I spent to put on those events. Then when I started to charge money for those same events at companies, guess what? The events were overflowing with qualified attendees; senior VPs and Presidents would always be in the room, and this was usually followed by a lucrative consulting contract.

As the old adage goes: "Time is money." By charging a retainer to both clients and prospective clients, not only will the advisor become more profitable, the advisor will be aided in his or her time management. Retainers allow for Trusted Advisors to spend time only with clients who appreciate them for the value they provide.

By charging a retainer for an initial consultation or for a continual consulting service and making sure the retainer is always replenished for work in progress, what the Trusted Advisor has accomplished is to set himself or herself apart from the rest of the pack who don't. What the Trusted Advisor is saying to the world by charging a retainer is that he or she knows the value he or she provides to his or her clients, and that this value when shared needs to be compensated for by his or her clients.

By having a signed client engagement letter that outlines the nature of the client-advisor relationship with a fee schedule in place, this will establish the Trusted Advisor as someone who knows what he or she is doing. Clients will know who they are dealing with and what to expect. The end result is that the Trusted Advisor will feel more in control of his or her time and better appreciated for the value he or she brings to the table. In addition, once the fees the Trusted Advisor bills equal the retainer, to avoid collection problems, the Trusted Advisor should obtain an additional retainer.

When you charge a retainer, this quickly identifies clients who want to do business with you from others who don't or won't. Charging a retainer usually results in clients implementing your solutions faster because they value your advice and they have made the commitment. Thus, you will spend less time with tire kickers and share more time with clients who are deserving of your expertise and attention. Clients who appreciate you will have no issue with you being paid to provide this continuous value. Trusted Advisors who charge retainers usually end up generating more income and a steady income! Try it, see for yourself!

GOING FORWARD IN THE WORLD AS A TRUSTED ADVISOR

In this new era, financial professionals are being called upon to craft comprehensive solutions that will involve the services provided by brokerage firms, accounting and law firms, trust companies, banks, insurance agencies, mergers and acquisition firms and financial planning firms. Financial, legal and tax professionals that step up to the plate and fulfill the role of the Trusted Advisor will become the key gatekeepers to their clients, while at the same time all the other professionals and organizations desiring to serve their clientele will become little more than subcontractors.

Those financial professionals who succeed in this new era of the Trusted Advisor will quickly identify their allies. They will build alliances with clients, other professionals that complement their services and organizations that will help them navigate towards the clear blue waters of success.

To succeed in this new era, financial professionals will have to place their focus on identifying and understanding a client's total financial life and create solutions that will solve a client's most important needs.

The best plan in the world is just a plan. Entrepreneurs and business people understand this intuitively. The key to success is not the plan; it is in the execution of the steps necessary to reach the goals.

I once read an interview with Warren Buffett, founder of Berkshire Hathaway Inc., and someone I believe is the world's greatest investor. The interviewer asked Buffett if he was willing to share any of his secret personal investment strategies. Buffett laughed and said that everyone knows his strategy and his plan. It's been public knowledge since the beginning. He said that the reason he and his company are successful is that they execute the day-to-day details so that their plan becomes reality.

Today there is very little human knowledge that cannot be found in a book or on the Internet, awaiting those who have the time, interest and desire to learn. There are over 1 billion people connected to the Internet, and we have more information available at our fingertips than any other generation before us. I once heard that as information doubles, knowledge is halved and wisdom is quartered.

Keeping this in mind, no one person can understand and successfully apply the sum of this knowledge. The increase in information our world generates doesn't necessarily translate into a gain in our knowledge or a deepening of our wisdom. The person who is sick might die before finding the information that can cure the illness, while a trained doctor, through specialized knowledge and experiences, can recognize the symptoms and effect a cure within a matter of hours or days.

The skilled Trusted Advisor can provide qualified clients with sound information and effective advice to ensure their financial health. Life is too short to find the right financial way through trial and error. Most people do not notice the symptoms of their financial illness until it is too late for them. In this busy and ever complex world, people considering wealth solutions need to find knowledgeable experts who will deliver quality and value. The Trusted Advisor's clients know that information might be free but that the application of this knowledge and wisdom are not free. Cherish the clients who have the eyes to see your true value and are willing to pay for this value with which you provide them.

Remember, there are always people right now in this world accomplishing what we want to be doing, and these individuals can be our teachers to help us to achieve our desired outcomes. There are others out in the world today who are looking towards us to be their mentors. Too many advisors today think that they must have a large client base to be successful, when in fact most of us are already leaders and don't even recognize that our professions and the right clients require our leadership now. For the Trusted Advisor who recognizes this and takes a proactive role in harnessing the power of his or her core group and 150, the world of possibilities is open to him or her, for the taking.

The future is for the brave and bold who set clear and specific career and life goals, who take action towards achieving their goals, who surround themselves with the right people and, most importantly, who enjoy life!

"When the student is ready, the teacher will appear."

Lao Tzu's *Tao Te Ching*

CHAPTER 2

DEFINING THE ROLE OF THE GENERALIST

Greg Pashke

Overview

This chapter discusses the risks of increasing specialization in your practice, considers the potential benefits of generalist skills and briefly discusses how the *operational models* you use can shape and govern your performance. It then focuses on the potential role of a Generalist Profile for you as a professional financial consultant.

Learning Objectives

By the end of this chapter, you should be able to:

- understand the implications that complexity and specialization can have on the way you conduct your practice and serve your clients;
- understand how generalist skills can improve the value you provide to clients;
- understand the implications of the various "operational models" you employ and how they can shape your perceptions and behaviour; and
- Understand the implications, challenges and rewards of adopting a Generalist Profile approach in your professional and personal life.

A REALITY OF COMPLEXITY & SPECIALIZATION[1]

We do not live in a dull and mundane time. Our dynamic and vibrant society is increasingly complex and has dictated the growth, development and evolution of functionally diverse "specialists" to help society

1 Adapted from Gregory F. Pashke, "Bring Back the Generalist" in *Strategic Finance* 86:4 (October 2004) 33, a publication of the Institute of Management Accountants.

cope with and manage its affairs. The level of specialty knowledge and skills can vary from profession to profession, as an amusing tale about a mechanic and a cardiologist captures. An acclaimed motorcycle mechanic was removing a cylinder head from the motor of a vintage Harley when he noticed an eminent cardiologist in his shop. The mechanic, anxious to demonstrate his technical expertise, called the doctor over to show him his work. The mechanic stood up, wiping his soiled hands on a rag and said, "Doc, look at this engine. I open its heart, remove the valves, repair any damage and then put them back in, and when I finish, it works like new. So how is it I barely make $40,000 per year, while you make $1,700,000 when you and I are performing the same basic function?" The cardiologist smiled and whispered to the mechanic, "Try doing it with the engine running." Point made.

The financial consulting profession is but one, albeit significant, piece of an even larger complex we call *life*. It should come as no great shock that this is not your grandfather's financial consulting environment. Increasing regulatory oversight, legal formation alternatives, a growing world economy, and a plethora of new financial investment options are just a few examples. As Bob Dylan whimsically noted, "the times they are a changin'." Indeed they are.

The evidence of change and complexity is compelling. Think of how the number and scope of professional certifications has exploded over the past few decades. Think of how the breadth and depth of tested knowledge has expanded for the various designations. Think of how rare it was to know individuals with multiple designations in various fields of specialization. Today it's not an uncommon occurrence for *one* individual to possess multiple postgraduate degrees and multiple professional designations. Is all this good or does the trend carry some inherent risks?

Robert Pirsig, in his classic book *Zen and the Art of Motorcycle Maintenance*, observed:

> It's a problem of our time; the range of human knowledge today is so great that we are all specialists and the distance between specializations has become so great that anyone who seeks to wander freely among them almost has to forego closeness with the people around him.

It's interesting that this insightful comment was made over 30 years ago when arguably we lived in a simpler time and place. We should heed Pirsig's warning of the difficulty of meaningful interaction within and between professions and the public they serve. Do you remember your early days in the profession and how awkward it felt until you gradually learned the basic concepts, terms and techniques? Don't your clients and the general venue in which you practise deserve an increased awareness on your part?

What are some of the risks associated with this trend towards increasing specialization? What impact can they have on the environment in which you practise, on the other specialists with whom you interact, and on the clients whom you serve? Here's a short list to stimulate your thinking:

- **Communication Difficulties**: The technical jargon and lexicon of specialists can restrict real communication between professionals and the clients whom they serve. Each specialty tends to have its own vocabulary, terminology and imbedded assumptions. Communication with clients can be difficult even under the best of circumstances. I remember hearing a witty story about a surgeon who received a complaint from a patient about a $10,000 charge for his operating room services. The patient complained that the entire procedure only took 30 minutes and that a labour rate of $20,000 per hour seemed excessive. The surgeon mailed the patient a revised billing showing operating room services of $250 and "knowing where to cut" $9,750. *Do you tailor your communications to fit the variety and special circumstances of the clients you serve or do you stick to "technical lingo?"*
- **Breeding Ground for Charlatans:** It becomes more difficult for the public to separate the competent specialists from the charlatans who are eager to deceive. *Have you ever felt vulnerable or intimidated by experts outside your own field? How do you think your clients feel when they interact with you and competing competent and incompetent providers?*
- **Solutions in Search of a Problem:** Abraham Maslow observed that "if all you have is a hammer, every problem looks like a nail". Too often, experts with only one solution can be persuasive that theirs is the obvious choice. *Can you appreciate how important it is to tailor a solution to fit the specific needs of your clients rather than to impose one on them?*
- **A Closed Thought Process:** Ralph Waldo Emerson noted that "the field cannot well be seen from within the field". It can also be expressed as: "If you always thought what you've always thought, you'll always get what you've always got!" *Do you guard against tunnel vision and a knee-jerk response to stereotype client needs and solutions? Do you* care *enough to take adequate time to appreciate and understand the needs, aspirations and dreams of your client?*
- **Loss of Personal Confidence.** The downside here is that people feel incompetent and unable to make a decision about any aspect of their lives without consulting an expert. They become paralyzed

and do not trust in their own instincts and good judgement. They abdicate their decisions to specialists. *Do you educate, communicate in terms they can understand and help empower your clients to make the decisions that impact their lives or do you simply decide what's best for them?*

- **Limits on Career Flexibility:** Specialization carries the danger of knowing more and more about less and less. New technologies and approaches are constantly emerging but the utility of that knowledge generally has an increasingly shorter time span. *Have you assessed and will you continue to assess the career implications of the tools and techniques you employ in your professional practice? Will you have a "future focused" approach to managing your career?*

GENERALIST SKILLS CAN SHARPEN YOUR SAW

We can appreciate the need for specialists in our complex society, but we should also recognize the limitations and risks associated with that growing trend. Is there a role for a Generalist Profile and for generalist skills to help understand, integrate, communicate and make sense of all the information and knowledge being generated by the growing world of specialization?

There appears to be a growing awareness of the importance of generalist skills as well as the benefits of a broader generalist mindset. A decade ago, the American Institute of Certified Public Accountants undertook a Vision Project aimed at exploring the future role of the CPA profession in a changing environment. One of the components of that process was to predict the core competencies (skills) necessary for CPAs of the future. I submit that they have broad application to almost all professions, including the world of financial consulting. The five identified competencies are:

1. Communication and Leadership Skills
2. Strategic and Critical Thinking Skills
3. Focus on the Customer, Client and Market
4. Interpretation of Converging Information
5. Being Technologically Adept

Does anything strike you as you look at this list? If not, look at it again. The technical skills are assumed and implied. The items on that list are what I consider "generalist skills". Interestingly, these same skill sets are too often not a vital part of the normal educational curriculum. Thus there seems to be a void and disconnect between the current focus on detailed technical skills and an increasing recognition of the generalist skills necessary for the professional of the future.

What are some of the implications for professional financial consultants to consider in how they orient, educate and train themselves to provide more value to the clients they serve?

- **Professional Responsibility:** First and foremost, realize that "*specialists do not live in a vacuum*". You have a responsibility for the quality of your expertise, but you also have an inherent obligation to convey its importance in understandable terms to the public you serve. Bring clarity to your role rather than obfuscate it in technical jargon. Do you explain things in a fashion that the user of your expertise can relate to? Or do you get lots of "caught in the headlights" looks from your clients? Simplification can be challenging but very rewarding when you see *an "aha" moment* in the eyes of a valued client.
- **Seek Balanced Skill Sets:** In your pursuit of lifelong learning, seek a healthy balance between technical expertise and generalist skills. Both are important to serve your clients well. Stretch yourself by taking a Dale Carnegie course, learning project management techniques, serving as an officer in a professional organization, reading a book on strategic thinking, writing an article or joining a Toastmasters' Club to make you a more valued professional. The technical skills are important, but they have more value in a broader context.
- **Challenge and Enhance the Experts You Collaborate with:** When you deal with other professionals, challenge them to explain things in a way that both you and your client can understand. In any communication, I submit that the primary responsibility rests with the presenter. If it's not clear, ask questions and focus on the significance and implications of what these colleagues are trying to convey.
- **Think and Act in Broad Terms:** Embrace the responsibility to appreciate and communicate the bigger picture to your clients. Renowned inventor, thinker, poet and philosopher Buckminster Fuller urges us to go beyond even that to become "comprehensivists", thinking in the broadest possible terms.

Before we go further into generalist skills, a generalist mindset and levels of generalist profiles, let us first explore the implications of the business and professional models we employ in our fields of endeavour. It adds to the discussion and broadens our perspective for reflection.

IT'S A MODEL WORLD[2]

Models are everywhere. From weather maps to road maps, mathematical equations to everyday language, we rely on models (miniature representations of things) to navigate our lives and our professional world. A good model can simplify complex ideas, provide meaningful insight and communicate difficult professional concepts. We all use models, but they become so intrinsic that we sometimes forget that they are there and how they shape our perceptions and actions.

Of course, all models have their inherent limitations. It's a good idea to pause and reflect upon them occasionally. Let's review the ten traits of models:

1. **Models are not reality:** A city map can lead you to some great places to eat and visit but the map is only an approximation of what the city holds; models cannot capture all the subtleties of their subjects. We forgo something for the utility of the model. As Alfred Korzbyski, a semantic theorist of the early 20th century, explains, just as the map is not the territory, the word is not the thing. The point is particularly salient with the assumptions, mindset and tools you use in financial consulting.
2. **Models influence our perceptions:** They aid our comprehension, but that comes with a price. Robert Pirsig reminds us: "We get so used to certain patterns of interpretation, we forget the patterns are there." Members of a profession drink the same "kool-aid" and tend to view the world in the same way. There is power in a fresh perspective. Someone from outside the existing paradigm who doesn't wear the blinders that restrict those within the model can drive profound change. Are you aware of the subtle and the not so subtle influences that pervade how you think and behave?
3. **Models influence behaviour:** Pirsig captures it well: "When a new fact comes in that does not fit the pattern, we don't throw out the pattern. We throw out the fact." Keeping a healthy outlook for changing patterns and conditions is an important part of professional skepticism. Be prepared to think a bit before you throw out a fact that doesn't quite fit. It might present a valuable insight and a wonderful opportunity.
4. **Models are relative:** Some models are more advantageous than others. That's why we choose some over others. Einstein's theory of relativity explained space and time better than other available

[2] Adapted from Gregory F. Pashke, "The Use and Abuse of Models" 37:5 *The Futurist* (September/October 2003) 48, a publication of the World Future Society.

hypotheses. Recent corporate chicanery has led to major changes in corporate governance models. Keep on the lookout for alternative ways that might provide an improvement in your work.

5. **Models are culturally influenced:** There is an inherent or underlying belief structure that accompanies every discipline. People trained within the discipline begin to look at the world in the same way and have the same ingrained assumptions. This is a powerful plus, in that this can leverage the people within the discipline. The downside is the risk that some very good ideas or novel approaches get excluded because they reside outside the paradigm. Don't forget at one time all the experts thought the earth was flat or that the Atkins diet could never lower cholesterol.

6. **Models are becoming more specialized:** In almost every arena, models are becoming more complex and exotic compared to those from decades ago. And with complexity there tends to follow more esoteric terminology which begins to close off the utility of the discipline to anyone but the experts that reside within it.

7. **Models can become traps:** They can limit our worldview and prevent us from thinking in a different way. Robert Pirsig relates a good story about the old South American Indian Monkey Trap. A hollowed-out coconut which contains some rice is chained to a stake. The hole in the coconut is just big enough for a monkey's empty hand to go in, but not big enough for its fist full of rice to come out. The monkey reaches in and is suddenly trapped only by its value rigidity. It can't bring itself to let go of the rice, and so capture is the result.

8. **Models are sensitive to change:** Models may be impacted by changes in variables. Some of the changes may be obvious and direct. Others might be more susceptible to chaotic change from subtle alterations. The accounting profession in the United States is focusing on a principles-based accounting model rather than a rules-based model that carries the danger of judging something as "technically not illegal" rather than as "the most informative disclosure available". All models are sensitive to change and must evolve over time if they are to remain meaningful.

9. **Models can be nested within other models:** Morse code was a model developed to convey language via wires. Native American smoke signals were designed as a similar communications model using a different medium. Models reside within models similar to how subroutines reside within computer programs. The more complex the model, the more likely it is that smaller, less obvious mod-

els are nestled within. Keep an awareness of this as you perform your analysis and draft your recommendations.

10. **Old models die hard:** Old models can continue to influence us long after they are passé. Buckminster Fuller used to marvel at how the concepts of sunrise and sunset endure some 500 years after we discovered that the earth is round. Fuller suggested the alternate terms of *sunsight* and *sunclipse* to better describe life in a post-"flat earth" world. Are there any lingering inertia-type concepts that still influence you?

An additional observation about models is that they can be *open* or *closed.* A closed model is restrictive and limits the flexibility of those using the model. An example might be a childhood board game like Monopoly, Sorry, or Chutes and Ladders. An open model can expand, grow and evolve as things change. An example might be Linux Software that actively seeks creative collaborators to continue to build a robust and evolutionary information system.

Models play an important role in our lives as well as our professions. As model users, be aware of the ten traits of models and strive to keep your models relevant, useful and evolving by maintaining a healthy dose of professional skepticism. Remember, we live in a dynamic and complex world, and our models need to facilitate understanding rather than become roadblocks to knowledge.

THE GENERALIST MINDSET & SOME PROFILES

We've acknowledged complexity and its link to specialization. We've covered the inherent risks associated with increasing specialization. We've seen how some generalist skills can enhance specialized knowledge and we've explored the implications of the models we use to perform and function in our fields of endeavour. Now it's time to look at a generalist mindset combined with specialized knowledge. Here are some combinations or flavours to consider, with each subsequent level being broader in scope and requiring additional skills and perspective.

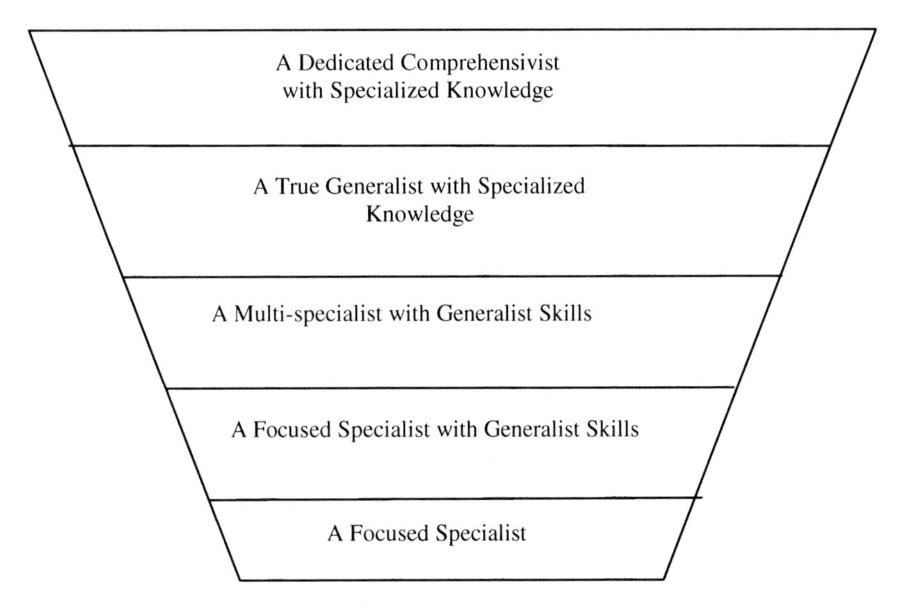

The Cone of Mindset Profiles illustrated above can be explained as follows:

- **A focused specialist** — a professional combining specialized knowledge, training and real world experience supervised by more seasoned colleagues. This is the most prevalent mindset. This will continue to be an important and valuable level within the financial consulting community.
- **A focused specialist using some generalist skills** — a growing segment of professionals with a desire to employ some generalist skills and techniques to enhance value for their clients. This level requires the acquisition and use of skills beyond the purely technical.
- **A multi-specialist using generalist skills** — a professional with expertise in two or more fields who leverages specialized knowledge through the use of generalist skills and techniques. This is similar to the prior level but harnesses the power of overlapping specialties and the potential for cross-pollination of ideas and concepts.
- **A true generalist with specialized knowledge** — a professional with broad knowledge as well as specialized knowledge in one or more disciplines who can plan, co-ordinate, manage and control teams of experts to achieve broader projects and goals and communicate the results effectively. The focus is on the broader generalist role as opposed to the mastered specialty.
- **A dedicated comprehensivist with specialized knowledge** — a broad visionary attempting to leverage many of the disciplines that

mankind and its applied technology have been able to develop. This is the high ground that few dedicated and privileged professionals will ever practise in.

We will focus our remaining discussion on the *true generalist with specialized knowledge mindset.* Here are a few examples of this mindset in action:

- **This publication:** The creative force behind this publication is Peter Merrick. Peter has assembled a virtual team of professionals from different fields of endeavour and geographic areas to design and organize a coherent reference source for those interested in and participating in the financial consulting environment. Peter was the team quarterback functioning as a field "generalist" to co-ordinate a team of specialist writers with the focused goal of a comprehensive and highly useful publication. Similar to the leader of a symphony, Peter understood the sounds that various instruments can make and how they can create a harmonious synergy together, and how to co-ordinate and time the blending of their collective efforts. Peter's role is a perfect example of the generalist with specialized knowledge in action.
- **The Iron Chef:** Are you familiar with the *Iron Chef* show on the Food Network channel? The Iron Chef must be a broad culinary generalist to take a "special ingredient" and use a creative approach to quickly pull together multiple tasty dishes. The Iron Chef must design a five-dish menu, manage a team of associates and blend appropriate spices and cooking techniques to craft flavourful dishes that demonstrate creativity, taste and presentation. The Iron Chef needs to accomplish this in a concentrated time, under extreme pressure, and then calmly yet passionately present his or her creations to a panel of expert judges. This is a pretty remarkable and impressive feat. There are many specialty cooks, such as Italian cuisine specialist, dessert creator, ingredient specialist and barbecue specialist, but the skills and scope of the Iron Chef go way beyond these quality specialists.

Why does one aspire to be a generalist and why might a professional specialist aspire to adopt a Generalist Profile?

With apologies to Jeff Foxworthy's "you might be a redneck routine", *you might be a generalist* if:

- You are perpetually curious and want to understand how things, people and processes fit together.
- You like to keep your finger on the pulse of broad trends as well as those happening in nearby professions and your own discipline.

- You enjoy asking provocative and mind-expanding questions and appreciate the power of inquiry-based learning.
- You love to ask the tough questions that no one else wants to address.
- You love lifelong learning and have a thirst to integrate knowledge.
- You like to freely jump from area to area like a bumble bee pollinating a field of flowers.
- You enjoy being the Trusted Advisor in a multi-discipline project and being the architect of integration to foster a cohesive solution that works.
- You appreciate the specialist role but envision a more comprehensive paradigm of knowledge.
- You love the world of possibilities and complexity doesn't intimidate you. It excites you. You have the ability to "cut through" the red tape and quickly grasp the bigger picture.
- You have the ability to simplify things and explain them in laymen's terms.
- You love the challenge of problem solving and get excited by the combinations and permutations of various fields of endeavour.
- You comprehend how things fit together, how they can work against each other, and you actively look for any disconnects in the facts and circumstances.
- You see the generalist role as a way to leverage specialty knowledge to improve "desired outcomes" for clients.
- You are aware of the tension between specialists and the turf encroachment that happens, but you see that as a potential creative force.
- You enjoy creating your own unique profession as a Trusted Advisor and developing a reputation as a creative problem solver and collaborator who gets things done.
- You are aware of the "unintended consequences" that can arise from focused specialists and look for ways to mitigate them.
- You love to throw yourself into learning and have a driving creative force to explore the dimensions of existing models and add to them or to build newer and more powerful paradigms.
- You appreciate the inherent danger of "routine recommendations" and the tendency for available products to supersede a comprehensive analysis focused on client needs.

- You appreciate a "strategic" as well as "tactical" approach to problem solving.

A SYNOPSIS

The goal of this chapter was to *stretch* the dimensions of your thinking. A professional aware of the risks associated with increased complexity and specialization and the limitations of the models with which he or she operates is a wiser and more valuable Trusted Advisor. A competent specialist who leverages the various levels of generalist skills and the power of the generalist mindset can even further enhance the worth of their services. Where you find your own particular comfort zone is an individual decision, for there is value in each and every level. The challenge is to use an increased awareness to guide your career of service. I hope you choose to enthusiastically embrace that challenge. *Carpe Diem*!

CHAPTER 3

GENERALISTS AND SPECIALISTS: UNRAVELLING THE MYSTERY

Fred Nickols

Overview

This chapter will explore the nature of a Generalist's practice and present a working model for understanding the differences between the characteristics and roles that separate the Generalist from the Specialist in the consulting world.

Learning Objectives

By the end of this chapter, you should be able to:

- understand what a Generalist is in the 21st century;
- understand what a Specialist is and does;
- understand how to distinguish between needing a Generalist or a Specialist, or both; and
- have a working model to understand how the Generalist and the Specialist operate in the consulting world.

INTEGRATION, NOT ADDITION

It is not the case that a consultant who is a Generalist is simply someone who has mastered more than one specialty and practises each as the occasion demands. Instead, a Generalist is a person who has not only mastered but also integrated more than one specialty. A Generalist's practice is an expanded one by virtue of synthesis or integration, not mere addition.

A consultant who has mastered more than one specialty but who has not yet integrated them is still a Specialist with a set of solutions instead of a single solution, but is still in search of corresponding problems.

Generalists can be found both within specialty fields and ranging across them. There are people, for example, who are Generalists in the field of training, that is, they are capable of developing classroom instruction or programmed instruction, of developing media, of constructing tests and of actually delivering the training. There are also people who specialize in each of these areas. And there are people who are capable in several areas of training and in other areas as well (*e.g.*, organization development, management development, performance technology and classic management consulting).

THE NATURE OF A GENERALIST'S PRACTICE

If a Generalist's practice is not simply the practice of more than one specialty, what is its nature?

The practice of a Generalist is the practice of a general problem solver. The mastery and integration of more than one specialty yield a more generalized ability to solve problems. This means a Generalist can take on problems that are ordinarily of larger scope, scale and complexity than those addressed by Specialists. This is not to say that Specialists are not problem solvers too, because they are. It is to say that the scope, scale and complexity of the problems that Specialists attempt to solve are limited by their specialties. If not, they are out of their field — and perhaps even out of their league.

To integrate areas of specialization, the Generalist must tamper with them. This is because the basic nature of a specialty is to set itself apart, literally, to be special. Tampering with specialties so as to integrate them is how a Specialist becomes a Generalist. But Generalists are also members of at least one specialty area and, as such, Generalists run the risk of castigation by their colleagues for deviating from the accepted practice. This is because Generalists continually seek to advance a practice or specialty area, not simply adhere to the current view of accepted practice. Generalists are looking for the ways in which things fit together — they have already mastered the various arts of taking them apart.

Generalists and Specialists both seek out problems. Both also seek to solve them. A major difference between the two lies in the kinds of problems sought. A Generalist will knowingly tackle problems that will or could involve specialties beyond those which the Generalist has already mastered. A Specialist who is content to remain a Specialist will not.

The goal of a Generalist is to solve the problem at hand, to engineer a fitting solution. The goal of the Specialist is to find problems that fit the solutions at hand. (This is a fine distinction being drawn here, but it is an exceedingly important one.)

TELLING THE ONE FROM THE OTHER

How, then, does a prospective client distinguish a Generalist from a Specialist? Perhaps the simplest way is to ask prospective consultants to identify themselves as one or the other. A claim to be a Specialist is easily verified. A claim to be a Generalist requires a little more effort. You might have to inquire as to the specialties they have mastered and the conceptual framework used to integrate them. If the consultant is inclined to publish, you can survey the consultant's publications. By reviewing what the consultant has written, you can get a feel for the extent to which one or more specialties have been integrated. Examine the consultant's track record. The range of projects carried out and problems tackled will tell you a great deal about the breadth of the consultant's practice.

PICKING THE RIGHT KIND

When considering a consultant for an engagement, here are a few Generalist-Specialist factors to consider.

- *Do you want help in solving a problem or in implementing a solution?*

  In the first case, you might want a Generalist, although not necessarily.

  In the second, you almost certainly want a Specialist.

- *Is your problem one that is known or thought to be solvable by the application of some particular specialty (e.g., training, reengineering or public relations)?*

  If not, then you probably require the services of a good Generalist.

  If so, then you might use either a Specialist or a Generalist who is master of that particular specialty and who is willing to confine the effort to the application of that specialty. (It is difficult, however, to keep Generalists out of related areas, so be certain they are willing to function as Specialists — unless you're also willing to live with the expansion of the project.)

- *Are your needs for control high or low?*

  If they are high, you might want a Generalist; he or she is better equipped to adapt his or her practice to your requirements.

If your needs for control are low, you might want a specialist; he or she is more inclined to ply his or her trade the way he or she sees it.

In either case, you had better check the consultant's need for control because this varies among Generalists and Specialists alike. What you want, of course, is a good match between your need for control and the consultant's tolerance for it.

WHAT IS A USEFUL MODEL?

Almost 25 years ago, I wrote and published a brief piece entitled "Generalist vs. Specialist: Whom Do I Consult?" Recently, that work led a fellow who was looking into the distinction between Generalists and Specialists to contact me. We exchanged some e-mails and telephone calls, and then he sent me a paper from two U.K. researchers who had been looking into the distinction between general managers and functional specialists in the context of developing senior managers. That paper triggered some thoughts on my part, and everything spilled forth in the form of a diagram. That diagram and some explanatory text form the content of the next section of this chapter. I hope others will find the diagram and its explanation helpful when they think about Generalists and Specialists.

Let's begin at the top.

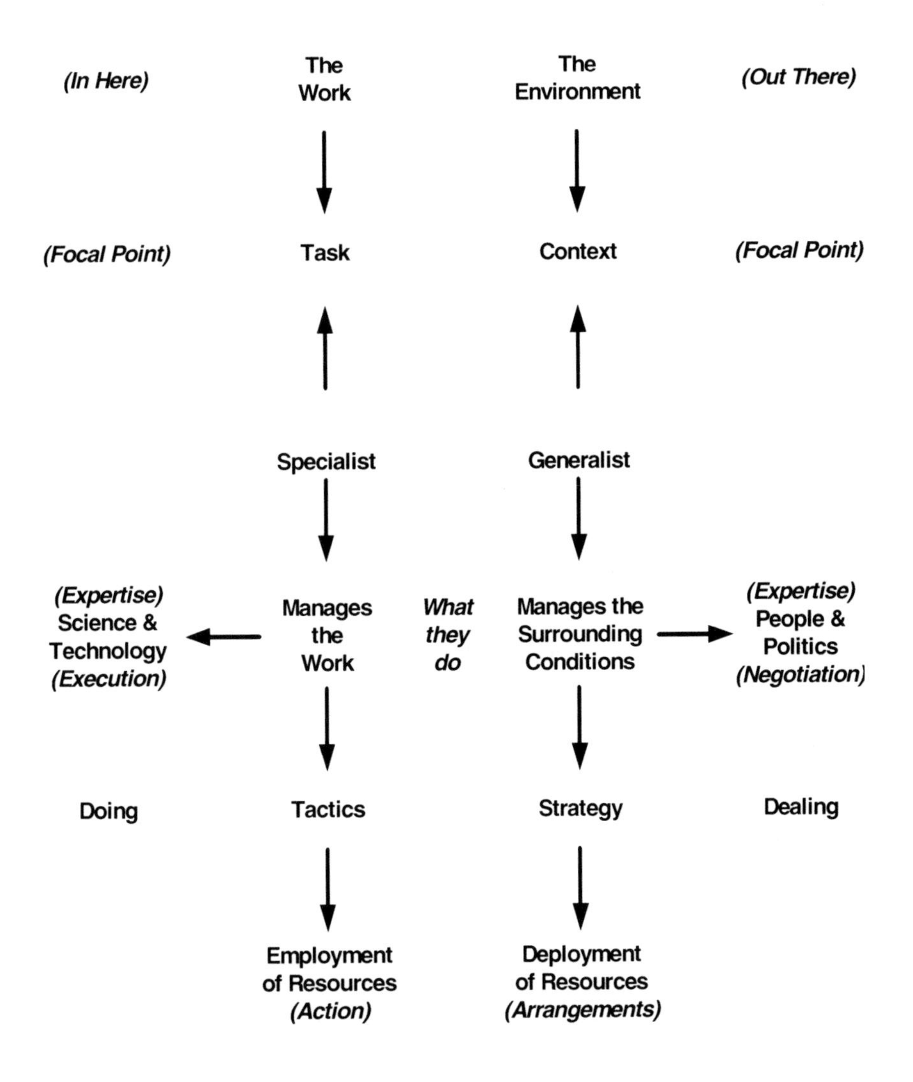

EMPLOYMENT VS. DEPLOYMENT

All organizations are concerned with their work and their larger environment, with what goes on "in here" and what goes on "out there". This same basic relationship applies inside the organization as well, where work takes the form of tasks, and the environment becomes the context for those tasks. Task and Context offer two focal points. Specialists focus on the task and Generalists focus on its context. Put another way, a

Specialist manages the work, and a Generalist manages the conditions under which that work is performed. Naturally, this calls for two different kinds of expertise. The Specialist's expertise ties to science and technology. The Generalist's expertise ties to people and politics. For the most part, the Specialist's expertise manifests itself in execution, and the Generalist's expertise manifests itself in negotiation. The domain of the Specialist involves tactics focusing on doing. The domain of the Generalist involves strategy focusing on dealing. The Specialist is concerned with the employment of resources (*i.e.*, actions) whereas the Generalist is concerned with the deployment of resources (*i.e.*, arrangements).

If all that seems an oversimplification, it might well be, but remember this: the root of the word "strategy" is the Greek *strategos*, which refers to the art of the general. That art takes the form of arranging conditions before battle so as to meet the enemy under the most favourable conditions. However, once the enemy is engaged, the focus shifts to tactics. One does not get to be a general without having first demonstrated a mastery of tactics. A Generalist, then, in the military or outside it, is someone who is skilled in execution and in negotiation, in doing and in dealing, in tactics and in strategy, in deploying and in employing resources. In terms of the diagram that popped full-blown into my mind one night, a Specialist is skilled in all that lies on the left-hand side of the diagram, and a Generalist is skilled in everything on both sides. Not all Specialists can or will become Generalists, but all Generalists have demonstrated competency as Specialists.

A SYNOPSIS

When considering the use of a consultant, it is important to know if you require the services of a Generalist or a Specialist. You might require both. Generalists are usually better at helping you define the problem. Specialists tend to frame the problem to fit their solutions. Either can be of help once the problem has been defined. Neither will be of much help if their need for control is at odds with yours. Choose your consultant with care, and give thought to the difference between a Generalist and a Specialist.

CHAPTER 4

WHAT MAKES THE 21ST CENTURY TRUSTED ADVISOR SUCCESSFUL?

Norm Trainor
Herb Koplowitz, Ph.D.

Overview

The paradigm has shifted — being a great relationship builder is not enough. To be at the top today, you need to master the art of business. This chapter will address the need for financial practitioners of old to transform their advisory practices if they are to become the Trusted Advisor that is called for in the 21st century.

Learning Objectives

By the end of this chapter, you should be able to:

- understand how the necessary skills that advisors have used have changed over the last 50 years;
- understand the complexities that have emerged within the advisory practitioner's professional world; and
- understand the new paradigm in which advisors find themselves operating and the new rules they must accept if they are to be successful as their clients' true Trusted Advisor.

Since the dawning of the Information or Knowledge Age over 60 years ago, the role of advisors has grown and evolved dramatically in advanced economies such as the United States and Canada. One manifestation of this growth is that large professional services firms employ hundreds of thousands of people worldwide. The professions of law and accounting experienced explosive growth in the last half of the 20th century. That growth will continue throughout the 21st century. In addition, consulting has become an important aspect of the service economy. The consultant of today provides advice in a myriad of sectors of our economy. The consulting arms of large companies generate multi-billion dollar revenue streams.

Given the importance of the advisory role in modern economies, it is useful to understand what makes an advisory practice successful. We address this question by exploring two issues in turn:

- What is required in the strategy of the advisory practice? In the section "The Need to Reframe the Advisory Practice", below, we will argue that the requisite strategy of advisory practices has changed over the past 30 years. In fact, the sector is now in its third set of strategic issues since the 1970s. In "Role of Complexity", we will show that what constitutes leading-edge work in an advisory practice has become increasingly complex over the past 30 years.
- What enables an advisor to implement the strategy? In "The Four Dimensions of Effectiveness in a Role", we will outline a simple four-dimensional model for understanding individual capability. An advisor can only build a practice as complex as his or her own capability can support and direct.

The section "The Three Paradigms" will show in more detail how the advisor's role has moved through paradigm changes over the past 30 years, where it might evolve to next and what will be required of one to lead a successful advisory business. We will end with a summary of our recommendations to advisors and suggest some strategic implications.

THE NEED TO REFRAME THE ADVISORY PRACTICE

The advisory role has functioned within three distinct paradigms over the last 30 years. As a new paradigm (Kuhn, 1962 — a new way of looking at the world, a new way of giving meaning) emerged, it redefined the advisory role. When a paradigm changes, the rules of the game change and the boundaries within which we operate are redefined. A new paradigm puts the previous paradigm in a new context. Continuing to apply the old rules for success to the new paradigm will usually lead to failure. Many successful individuals and companies fail when the game changes because they are unable to adapt to a new paradigm.

Let us illustrate the paradigm shifts with a personal example. When Norm started his first business over 30 years ago, he hired an accountant to help him with the financial management of the business. Back then, Norm's accountant brought skills and knowledge with regard to the accounting and tax issues in Norm's business. The accountant was a qualified CA and a partner in a small accounting firm. He provided advice on tax planning for the business and for Norm and his wife, Wendy, personally. At the time, most of Norm's financial information was paper-based. He forwarded this information to his accountant every month. The accounting firm provided bookkeeping services and prepared the financial statements and tax returns.

This was consistent with the first paradigm we will discuss, advisor as product/service deliverer. Back then, the accountant was not viewed as a resource in developing and implementing the strategies for growing the business. Often, discussions with the accountant dealt with a retrospective view of the business, *i.e.*, the preparation of the financial statements for the previous year. In summary, the common wisdom viewed skills and knowledge in accounting and taxation to be the keys to a CA's success, once he or she had mastered the basics of accounting and the *Income Tax Act*. Surprisingly, this view is still prevalent.

There are a number of problems with this approach. To begin with, technology allows financial reports and statements to be generated by people who do not have the skills and knowledge of a CA. There are software tools that provide detailed analysis of the financial health and vitality of a business. The Internet offers a wealth of financial information and knowledge. In addition, much of the basic work of accounting is now being outsourced, often to India.

With the advent of PCs and accounting software, Norm's company automated the financial management of the business, and services previously supplied by the accounting firm were taken in-house. Yet the relationship with the accountant and his firm continued to evolve and grow. As Norm's business became larger, the financial management issues became more complex. This led to increased revenue for the accounting firm. However, it also meant that other advisors became involved in financial management issues. Norm and Wendy hired a financial management firm to advise them on the management of their personal financial affairs. At various times, Norm sought out or was approached by other advisors who specialized in various aspects of the financial management of the business. To continue to add value, accountants have had to move their services up the value continuum to provide services appropriate to the consulting services paradigm. The methods accountants use to create value have evolved from preparing financial statements and tax returns to providing advice on a broad spectrum of more complex issues.

Later, Norm hired a merchant banker, who happened to be a CA, to help him with the financial aspects of his strategic planning. This particular consultant helped him build a model to develop his *pro forma* financial projections for his business over the following one and five years. The consultant also taught him the importance of Five Financial Levers: (1) Product Mix; (2) Average Revenue Per Sale; (3) Number of Sales; (4) Seasonality of his Business; and (5) Cyclicality of his Business. For Norm, the difference in the level of conversation between his accountant and the merchant banker was significant. With the merchant banker, the dialogue focused on the strategies for growing his business and realizing his vision of where he wanted to take it. With his accountant at first, the conversations focused primarily on the methods for reducing taxes and managing the financial risks facing the business. As we will illustrate later in this chapter, both levels of conversation are important. However, the higher level of discussion focuses on designing the business model, while the lower level is primarily centred on methods of running the business within the business model. A conversation about the business model is typically strategic, whereas discussions about business methods tend to be tactical. Norm's advisors had similar professional qualifications. However, they viewed the value of what they delivered through different lenses. The accounting firm's product was the provision of traditional accounting services, *e.g.*, tax returns and preparation of financial statements (specialist). The merchant banker's product was advice on the strategic direction of the business (generalist). The revenue generated by the merchant banker was higher because the work he did was more complex. The risks for Norm's accounting firm in this illustration were not immediately apparent. The accounting firm continued to provide accounting services and generate incremental revenue as a result of the growth of Norm's business. However, the higher value work that the firm could have delivered migrated to other providers. This also left the firm vulnerable to eventually losing all of Norm's business.

To survive and prosper, the advisory practice needed to move from a product paradigm in the 1970s and 1980s to a paradigm of consulting services in the 1990s, or risk being replaced by software or by other advisors perceived as bringing more value. Similarly, as we'll show in the section "The Three Paradigms", the 21st century advisor will need to move to a strategic partner paradigm. As we will explain next, these are not just changes in content of work but are also increases in the complexity of problems to be solved.

ROLE OF COMPLEXITY

It is one thing to say that providing consulting services is more complex than producing a product, but it is useful to be able to quantify the difference. Fortunately, Elliott Jaques's (1996) Requisite Organization model offers us a way to do that. Fifty years of research and consulting have shown that we can assess the complexity of work in a role by measuring the role's "time span", the length of the longest task in a role. To be clear, we are not necessarily referring to the most important task or to what takes up 95% of the person's time, just the longest task. Of course there are short, complex tasks, but they are almost always found in roles with very long tasks in them. (Note that determining the length of the longest task in a role is a profession in itself. While the time span of a role is often obvious, in many cases it takes skill and persistence to measure it at all accurately.)

The longest task in an advisory role could be any of the following:

- A bookkeeper may be given a report to prepare within a few weeks.
- A consultant may be given eight months to bring a new client's record-keeping up to standard to allow the accountant to produce reports with some confidence.
- A consultant may be asked to provide the consulting service to restructure a business within 18 months.
- After the CEO changes strategy, making the information the company has about its clients its most important strategic asset, a consultant might be given five years to change all of the systems — accounting, planning, risk management, estimating, *etc.* — and all of the interrelations among them in order to support the new strategy.

If the tasks cited above are the longest ones in each of the roles, then they provide the time span of those roles, ranging from a few weeks to five years. We can say with confidence that those roles are listed from the least to the most complex, and as we will show in the section "The Three Paradigms", what constitutes leading-edge work in advising is becoming increasingly more complex. But we can say more than that. In nature, when temperature rises, ice turns to water and water turns to steam. So too, as work becomes more complex, as the time span of a role increases, breakpoints occur that define distinct strata of role complexity. The time span of the longest task in a role identifies the stratum of the role as follows:

Stratum Time	***Span Range***
VII	20–50 years
VI	10–20 years
V	5–10 years
IV	2–5 years
III	1–2 years
II	3–12 months
I	up to 3 months

Only the very largest, most complex organizations need a CEO role at Stratum VII. The typical entrepreneurial organization will be headed up at Stratum III, IV or V.

The stratum of the work in a role becomes a critical factor for several reasons:

- You need to match the level of the capability of a person to the stratum of the role he or she is to fill. We will address this in the next session.
- You need to match the stratum of an advisor's role to the stratum of the client's role. Generally speaking, you can only be an effective thought partner with someone who is within a stratum of your own level of capability. Someone two strata above you will likely treat you as an order taker, and you are in danger of talking over the head of a client two or more strata below you.
- If you are building an organization, it is ideal to have each employee managed by a manager one stratum above. If the manager is at the same stratum, the employee will go over the manager's head to get advice and context. If the manager is two or more strata above, he or she may lose patience with the employee, and the employee may not always understand what his or her manager wants.

THE FOUR DIMENSIONS OF EFFECTIVENESS IN A ROLE

There are four dimensions of effectiveness in a role:

1. **Cognitive Capacity:** Elliott Jaques demonstrated that cognitive capacity is the key determinant of the stratum within which a professional or an employee can work. Literally, "cognitive capacity" is the potential to think, judge and solve problems. It is sometimes referred to as raw mental horsepower, the ability to exercise judgement to solve a problem or the ability to handle complexity.

   Like complexity of roles, cognitive capacity is measured in strata because one's cognitive capacity sets the upper limit of the stratum of the role in which one can succeed. The critical aspect of cognitive capacity is that, as far as we know, it matures at a predictable rate for each person. If we know your current age and current cognitive capacity, we can predict with great accuracy the level you will be able to work at 5, 10 and 20 years from now. There is no known way to accelerate the progress of your cognitive capacity.

   As we noted above, leading-edge work for advisors has been increasing in complexity. An implication is that, all else being equal, it will be the advisors with the greatest cognitive capacity who will win. Your success will be determined by your ability to leverage your cognitive capability by:

- working on those tasks that require your level of cognitive capacity;
- acquiring the skills and knowledge that can leverage your cognitive capacity;
- delegating less complex work; and
- finding support, where needed, from others with greater cognitive capacity than your own.

Cognitive capacity is the single most important factor in designing your practice and will limit the paradigm you can work from as head of an advisory practice. If you build a practice that does not require your level of capability, you will underutilize your own potential and are likely to be bored. If you attempt to build a practice beyond your level of capability, you are likely to be faced with problems you cannot solve. Your own sense of yourself is your best guide, but "The Three Paradigms" section will give you some useful pointers.

2. **Skills and Knowledge:** Cognitive capacity, the raw ability to exercise judgement, is not enough for any professional. Your success depends also on having the needed skills and knowledge, methods and facts you can use automatically to solve problems. If you are like most advisors, you have acquired the skills and knowledge to perform in your role through formal education and experience. Advisors working from the product paradigm need skills such as the ability to prepare the financial statements for a client company and knowledge of business, accounting, the *Income Tax Act*, *etc.* Typically, clients hire an advisor to provide skills and knowledge that the individual or business lacks. As we shall show in "The Three Paradigms" section, moving up from the product paradigm will require a broader range of skills and knowledge.

3. **Values:** The value you place on a task affects your performance. As a general rule, we tend to do work we value and avoid work that we do not want to perform. When we use the term "value", we are not referring to social values such as honesty or integrity. Rather, we are referring to the motivation or the desire to do a particular type of task. Like anyone else, advisors want to do work they value. Clients want advisors who value the work they are asked to perform. We all want to hire people who are intrinsically motivated to perform their assigned tasks. Moving up in the sequence of paradigms

requires not just cognitive capacity and skills and knowledge; you must also value doing the kind of work required within the paradigm.

4. **Temperament — Absence of Personal Dysfunction:** Personal issues such as alcoholism, drug addiction, uncontrollable anger and extreme anxiety can significantly impact performance in a role. The costs to businesses of personal dysfunction are enormous. These are issues that are most appropriately addressed outside the workplace in therapy or through the Employee Assistance Program in a larger organization. Self-management is an important component of effectiveness in any role. It is particularly important in an advisory capacity because of the trust people place in their advisor.

Having explained our model of personal effectiveness, we will now examine how these dimensions of effectiveness have been impacted by the changing paradigms over the last 30 years.

THE THREE PARADIGMS

We shall start with the advisor role as it existed until the late 1980s, and show how it has changed since then. For each paradigm, we will discuss the approach the advisor takes to his or her work and the capability required to work from that approach.

Up to 1990: The Product Paradigm

Advisors in the 1970s and 1980s worked primarily from the product paradigm. As we noted in the section "The Need to Reframe the Advisory Practice", the accountant then provided advice on tax planning and prepared financial statements. The skills and knowledge required centred on the profession itself, knowledge of the *Income Tax Act*, skills in preparing financial statements, *etc*.

To determine what level of cognitive capacity is required in the product paradigm, we need to understand what work is like at Strata I and II.

Stratum I, the beginning of adult capability, is characterized by two factors (see Summary Table at the end of the section):

- Someone at Stratum I can take on tasks for no longer than three months.
- Someone at Stratum I works with information *declaratively*. That is, he or she thinks of one product, method or factor at a time when making a decision.

Stratum-II work, on the other hand, is characterized by the following:

- Tasks fall into the three- to twelve-month range.*
- *Cumulative* processing of information, that is, considering several factors in order to come up with a solution itself, may require a combination of several methods.

In most cases, bookkeeping is a Stratum-I accountability. There is a limited set of procedures to use, and it is generally clear which one must be used for any situation. Accounting can be done at Stratum I, but only in the most mechanical way. To conduct a useful audit, the CA must be able to consider not just whether a particular entry or number meets requirements, but also whether any combination of factors is congruent with good accounting practices. The CA may be providing a service to the CEO of a Stratum-III organization or to someone else in a Stratum-III role accountable for administrative issues.

One can work very successfully in the product paradigm with a Stratum-II cognitive capacity.

1990 to the Present: The Consulting Service Paradigm

As noted in "The Need to Reframe the Advisory Practice" section, much of the product work of accounting is now done through software or outsourcing. To add value, the CA, as a Trusted Advisor, now needs to provide consulting services in a variety of areas such as:

- IT systems to aid financial management;
- financial implications of HR policies;
- financial implications of vendor and outsourcing contracts; and
- financial implications of selling products/services in other countries.

Note the movement from retrospective reporting in the product paradigm to forecasting and future design in the consulting service paradigm. The future-tense work can be done in a mechanical way by a cumulative-processing, Stratum-II-capable advisor, but doing the work in a value-added manner requires:

- managing projects that are intended to take one to two years to complete, *e.g.* building a client's capability to make full use of a new IT approach to financial analysis, and
- doing the *serial* processing series, of the form A→B→C, with at least three steps in them, required for complex projects, *e.g.*, surveying the

---

* At every level, there are short tasks of less than three months. What puts a role at a higher stratum is the addition of tasks longer than would exist at the lower stratum.

current financial-analysis capabilities of staff members (A) to determine the abilities required of people to be hired (B) so they can be trained (C) resulting in a staff fully competent to conduct the required financial analytical work (D).

The following two factors characterize work at Stratum III:

- work in the 12- to 24-month range; and
- the requirement for serial processing.

The Trusted Advisor may be helping function heads, working at Stratum IV in a company led by a CEO at Stratum V, to do their own jobs better.

Success in the consulting services paradigm requires:

- Stratum-III cognitive capacity;
- skills and knowledge in areas beyond accounting or law *etc.*, such as IT and HR; and
- willingness to do work outside of what is narrowly considered to be the area of professional expertise such as law or accounting.

The Future: The Strategic Partnership Paradigm

In the product paradigm, the advisor focused on work typically understood as belonging to a particular function of an organization *e.g.*, Finance, Operations, Legal Services and HR. In the consulting services paradigm, the focus expands to the impact of the consulting project on all functions of the client organization. In the strategic partnership paradigm, the Trusted Advisor's focus is on the company as a whole and on working directly with the CEO to make the company more successful. The Trusted Advisor in the strategic partnership paradigm helps the CEO to do his or her own job better. This requires knowledge of and skills in business, not just of the functions within an organization. It requires an understanding of corporate strategy and how it gets implemented. At a minimum, it requires:

- work that is intended to take two to five years to complete, *e.g.*, implementing the financial requirements of strategic change (the Trusted Advisor may be working to ensure adequate financing for the business over the next five years); and
- the ability to integrate serial developments in various departments, doing the *parallel* processing required to ensure optimal integration of the serial processes being implemented by the various departments, *e.g.*, ensuring that the growth plans of various departments

will not simultaneously create a greater need for capital than can be supported.

The following two factors characterize Stratum IV work:

- work in the two- to five-year range; and
- the need for parallel processing.

So the strategic partner must have at least Stratum-IV cognitive capacity.

But it is possible to reach a higher level of strategic partnering in which:

- projects may last beyond five years, up to ten years, *e.g.*, to convert in seven years all of the financial systems to support an evolving strategy;
- aspects of the organization need to be entirely reframed:
    - "We aren't buying output from our employees. We are renting their ability to do work, and our systems need to reflect that."
    - "Our strategy requires us to be customer-centric, not necessarily the low-cost provider. This requires revamping our entire approach to delivery."
    - "We need strategic alliances with our vendors, not just pressure to reduce their prices to us."

The reframing is, as in Stratum I, declarative processing, but at a much higher, more abstract level. The strategic partner is not immediately concerned with making an entry in a balance sheet or applying a method he or she was trained in, but with developing the abstract concept that becomes the foundation of all decisions.

The factors we described above work in the five- to ten-year range, and the need for declarative processing at an abstract level is characteristic of Stratum-V work. The accountant will either work collaboratively with the Stratum-V head of the client organization or be a strategic resource for a Stratum-VI business head.

Summary Table			
Stratum	Time Span (length of longest task)	Process	Paradigm
V	5–10 years	abstract declarative	strategic partnership
IV	2–5 years	parallel	strategic partnership
III	1–2 years	serial	consulting services
II	3–12 months	cumulative	accounting products
I	up to 3 months	declarative	bookkeeping products

IMPLICATIONS

This chapter suggests three strategic questions for the advisor:

- What is your level of capability?
- Which paradigms does that enable you to work in?
- Which paradigm do you want to work in?

Once these strategic issues are addressed, the tactical questions remain:

- If you want to work from a paradigm beyond your capability, where will you find a practice to work within which is led from a high enough level?
- What skills and knowledge do you need to acquire to be able to work in your chosen paradigm, making optimal use of your cognitive capacity?

A SYNOPSIS

The advisor's world has become much more complex than it was in the 1980s or 1990s. The recruitment, training and development of advisors must be designed to equip them to succeed and prosper in a more complex environment. Advisory firms that want their advisors to be viewed as Trusted Advisors need to broaden their focus to include both cognitive capacity, which must be recruited, and skills and knowledge beyond technical skills, which the organization can develop in its advisors. Those advisory firms that get it right will attract higher calibre individuals, develop them to much greater levels of productivity and reap the benefits of having more successful professionals.

BIBLIOGRAPHY

Jaques, Elliott, *Requisite Organization: A Total System for Effective Managerial Organization and Managerial Leadership for the 21st Century* (Arlington, VA: Cason Hall, 1996).

Kuhn, T., *The Structure of Scientific Revolutions* (Chicago: University of Chicago Press, 1962).

CHAPTER 5

DEFINING THE PROFESSION: PROFESSIONAL FINANCIAL PLANNER COMPETENCY PROFILE

Cary List

Overview

This chapter discusses the CFP Professional Competency Profile and sets out the scope of knowledge, skills, abilities and judgements that a Certified Financial Planner (CFP) professional is expected to possess in offering professional financial planning services to clients. It concludes by showing the complementary nature of the financial planning and accounting professions.

Learning Objectives

By the end of this chapter, you should be able to:

- understand the Financial Planners Standards Council (FPSC) CFP Professional Competency Profile and how the profile applies to financial planning professionals in Canada; and
- understand how the Competency Profile and financial planning services complement the profile and services offered by today's accounting professionals.

THE COMPETENCY PROFILE

When FPSC released its Competency Profile for CFP® professionals (the "Competency Profile", or "Profile") in November 2006, it represented a quantum leap forward in defining the financial planning profession in Canada. The Competency Profile lays out the entire scope of knowledge, skills, abilities and judgements that a CFP professional is expected to possess in offering professional financial planning services to clients.

While its most obvious application is to serve as the basis for the CFP certification examination, the Profile also serves as a guide to help distinguish the professional financial planner from other financial advisors, and ultimately to establish financial planning as a recognized profession in Canada and worldwide.

Since the Profile is performance-based, it clearly articulates the full set of capabilities required of a CFP professional in the performance of financial planning services, and serves as a benchmark against which to measure how financial planners are living up to what Canadians should expect from their financial planners. The Profile also helps CFP professionals to validate their own skills and abilities. It spells out the extensive breadth and depth of capabilities that a CFP professional must possess, and ultimately boosts CFP professionals' own confidence in promoting the value proposition of professional financial planning and their role in the financial services community.

FPSC's Competency Profile was developed by over 100 practising CFP professionals from across the country, under the leadership of FPSC, and with the guidance of independent certification experts. In the normal course of the competency analysis leading to the Competency Profile (often referred to as a job analysis or practice analysis by some professions), almost 1,000 CFP professionals were surveyed to validate the completed Profile.

Making a Difference Worldwide

The Profile garnered significant interest from the international CFP community as well as other unrelated professional certification bodies. FPSC donated its draft Profile to the international community of CFP certification and standards bodies through its international umbrella organization, Financial Planning Standards Board (FPSB) (of which FPSC is a member), in order that all CFP standards-setters around the world could benefit from the work in Canada. Through its work with FPSB and its affiliates around the world, the international CFP standards-setters were able to develop the first ever set of international competency standards for professional financial planners. The profile adopted worldwide reflects the extensive input of the international standards community, numerous professional certification experts and many other external stakeholders.

FPSC's approach to standards is leading certification programs away from a knowledge-based approach to a competency-based approach to certification. Such a move is necessary to ensure that the developing profession sufficiently addresses public needs. While technical knowledge is critical for competent performance, the public should be able to expect a professional to have more than just textbook knowledge, as knowledge alone does not prove competence in any profession.

When expressed in terms of specific competencies needed for CFP professionals to provide appropriate solutions to their clients, the Profile helps the public better understand the benefits of financial planning and the value of working with a CFP professional to help individuals meet their goals.

Understanding the Difference Between Licensure and Professional Certification

The Profile demonstrates the complexity and high levels of skills and knowledge intrinsic to the practice of professional financial planning. While Canadian financial services regulators play critical roles in protecting the public by imposing minimum licensure requirements that are appropriately focused on the sale of product and related advice, the competencies detailed in the Profile for CFP professionals go well beyond those which may be required in offering product advice, and thereby lie outside the scope of regulatory requirements. The Profile addresses the competencies necessary to meet the public's need for integrated professional financial planning services that span a broad range of subject matter. The interrelationships among the many facets of financial planning are becoming increasingly critical to the financial well-being of Canadians, and the public increasingly needs to be served by professionals with the appropriate integration skills who understand those interrelationships.

The Profile Is Only One Critical Element of CFP Certification

CFP certification is based on *three sets of core requirements: education, examination and experience*. Once certified, CFP professionals are then held to *three sets of professional standards: ethics*, as defined in the CFP Code of Ethics; *competency*, as assessed by the CFP Examination and ongoing continuing education requirements; and *professional practice*, as guided by FPSC's Practice Standards.

Since November 2007, the CFP Examination has been fully competency-based. The examination focuses on what candidates are expected to perform competently in practice, rather than solely on what they are expected to know. Beginning in 2010, to more fully assess some of the higher level competencies such as synthesis, integration and professional skills, FPSC will be introducing a two-level certification examination, the Professional Competence Exam 1 (PCE1) and PCE2. With this new model, the PCE2 will provide candidates with an opportunity to demonstrate their competence by providing written responses to synthesis- and integration-based questions.

Defining Financial Planning

To ensure the establishment of a consistent and clear Profile of financial planning in Canada and around the world, the financial planning community needs to rally around a singular, consistent definition for financial planning — one that resonates with financial planners and their clients alike. This internationally accepted definition is: "the process of creating strategies to help clients manage their financial affairs to meet life goals".

While financial planning practice standards are critical to CFP professionals in guiding their process so that clients can expect a consistent financial planning experience, FPSC recognizes that financial planning is about much more than the application of a process. There must be a clear and explicit explanation of exactly what a CFP professional must be capable of doing throughout the process to ensure that the clients' objectives can be achieved.

The Profile first expands the definition of financial planning in its simplest terms, at the broadest level — by defining the functions that financial planners must perform. These functions are defined by three broad categories: *collection* of information, *analysis* of information and *synthesis* of that information to achieve the desired result.

These functions are then examined with respect to each of the specific components of financial planning. "Components" refer to elements of financial planning with which people are generally familiar: *financial management, asset management, risk management, retirement planning, tax planning and estate planning*, as well as certain overarching *fundamental financial planning practices* that focus on the integration of information across multiple components — a key and distinct aspect of financial planning. Five core competencies are then identified and further defined in terms of every possible aspect of performance that may be required by a CFP professional to demonstrate each competency. These aspects of performance are defined as "elements of competency", and are categorized within each financial planning component. There are over 100 elements of competency inherent in the Profile.

FPSC recognizes that there are other skills intrinsic and fundamental to the demonstration of competent performance within all of these components that must also form part of the Profile. Specifically, a true professional cannot competently perform any of the specific functions of financial planning without applying certain generic professional skills. These skills are identified in the Profile as core "Professional Skills" and are grouped within four categories: *ethical judgement*, professional *practice*, written and oral *communication* and *cognitive* abilities. These skills are fundamental to being a professional. In demonstrating any of the core competencies of professional financial planning, CFP professionals may be required to apply any one or more of these professional skills concurrently.

The final and still critically important piece of the competency puzzle is *knowledge*. While knowledge itself does not define competency, one cannot be competent without possessing the requisite knowledge. Unlike traditional approaches to professional certification, requisite knowledge should only be determined *after* the component functions of financial planning were established. The task of defining requisite knowledge is relatively easy once the requisite competencies have been determined.

The Complete Picture

Ultimately, the complete picture of financial planning can only be found by reviewing the entire set of competencies as they are set out in the CFP Professional Competency Profile. The Profile provides a comprehensive description of the full scope of expertise required of a professional financial planner and how a CFP professional can use it to provide sound, practical and unbiased advice across the broad range of subjects that in their entirety define the financial planning profession.

THE COMPLEMENTARY NATURE OF THE FINANCIAL PLANNING AND ACCOUNTING PROFESSIONS

The Profile articulates the complete set of knowledge, skills, abilities and ethical judgement required for competent performance as a professional financial planner. Together, these define competence as a financial planning professional, as demonstrated specifically by individuals who hold the CFP® credential. There are currently over 17,000 CFP professionals in Canada and over 110,000 worldwide. What makes these professionals different from other financial advisors is the competencies articulated in the Profile. While there are a number of striking similarities between many of the competencies of a CFP professional and those of other financial advisors, a comparative review of each reveals the distinct nature of the financial planning profession, the value of financial planning and the value that financial planning professionals bring to client engagements.

All three Canadian professional accounting bodies representing Chartered Accountants, Certified Management Accountants and Certified General Accountants in recent years have released their own competency profiles. Like the Profile for CFP professionals, these documents clarify the expected knowledge, skills and abilities expected of members of the professions they define. By examining these professional profiles together with that of the CFP, we can clearly see the similarities and differences between the financial planning and accounting professions. More importantly, the examination also reveals just how complementary financial planning is to these other professions.

A Professional Is a Professional Is a Professional ...

Intrinsic to specific competencies of the CFP professional are certain fundamental professional skills — judgement, professional practice, communication and cognitive abilities — that are, in many ways, common to all professions. For example, members of all three professional accounting bodies will be entirely familiar with, and already possess, virtually all of the skills identified under these categories. As these skills are what make a true professional, they do not serve to distinguish professional financial planning from accounting; instead, they help to demonstrate, at the highest level, the core skills and abilities common to both professions.

Overlapping Competencies

There also exist several more specific areas of competence that are shared by financial planners and accountants alike. The CFP Professional Competency Profile is divided into six core components: financial management, asset management, risk management, tax planning, retirement planning and estate planning. Of these six components, one — tax planning — stands out as a clearly overlapping set of competencies with the accounting professions. Even here, however, subtle differences do exist — accountants tend to have a greater focus on corporate taxation, while financial planners focus primarily on personal taxation. Accountants also share some competencies in the areas of retirement planning and financial management. This, however, is where the competency sets diverge.

What's Different?

While professional accountants are highly competent in tax and finance, they often have little training in many other personal financial matters.

While highly competent in taxation, the non-tax issues related to asset management, risk management and estate planning fall well beyond the scope of the requisite competencies of professional accountants. Here is where the complementary nature between these professions begins to clearly emerge.

As the accounting professions grow and expand their core activities — assurance, financial accounting, finance and taxation — acquiring complementary competencies is increasingly important to the accounting professional. Responding to the needs of their existing clients, accountants are continually seeking new ways of better serving those clients, and adding more value to the engagement.

Consider the needs of the self-employed or small business owner. For these individuals, access to the breadth and depth of expertise available from a professional accountant who has earned CFP certification is invaluable. For this client segment in particular, financial planning and accounting clearly provide a tremendous complement to each other, to the benefit of the client. CFP certification helps accountants extend their expertise with these clients into the areas of asset management, risk management and estate planning. Additionally and more importantly, competence in the fundamental financial planning practices acquired through CFP certification helps accountants to understand and address the integrative nature of all of their clients' financial matters. With their already complementary skills, attainment of additional competencies that are unique to financial planning represents a logical and rewarding extension of the professional accountant's career path.

The complementary nature of the financial planning and accounting professions is one of the reasons all three professional accounting bodies support and endorse CFP certification and continue to be supporting members of FPSC.

AND WHAT OF OTHER "FINANCIAL ADVISORS"?

The term "financial advisor" is often used to describe any and all individuals acting in some advisory or sales capacity within the financial services industry. Some terms — investment advisor, for example — are reserved for individuals licensed by specific regulatory authorities to advise on, or sell, specific types of products. The CFP Professional Competency Profile distinguishes the skills and abilities of a CFP professional from those of other financial advisors, and suggests an important relationship between professional financial planners and these other advisors.

As discussed earlier, competence as a CFP professional cannot be established without the four key professional skill sets — ethical judgement, professional practice skills, communication and cognitive skills. While these competencies are fundamental to financial planning and the accounting professions — in fact all professions — they serve to differentiate the CFP professional from all other financial advisors. Financial advisors may have these skills, but they are not required by their licensing bodies to possess them all. The aggregate of these professional skills are in fact beyond the scope required for proficiency within any financial services regulatory regime.

INTEGRATION MAKES ALL THE DIFFERENCE

While some of the fundamental components of financial planning share the nomenclature of services offered by other financial advisors — many investment advisors cover asset management advice; some insurance advisors deal with risk management and estate planning; some accountants deal with tax and retirement planning; and financial counsellors deal with financial management issues — these advisors are not necessarily competent in dealing with these components together, in an integrated manner, as is required of a professional financial planner. While each of these other advisors has demonstrated, through regulatory licence requirements, his or her qualifications to sell certain products or advise on specific matters generally related to those products, it is the breadth and depth of competencies articulated in the Competency Profile that establish the unique nature of the financial planning profession and the CFP professional.

The Competency Profile reveals the important connection between regulated advisors and professional financial planners. The Canadian public clearly needs the services of both groups, and these groups clearly overlap.

The CFP professional's role is to develop strategies to help clients better manage their financial affairs, and since many of those strategies will by definition require advice regarding, and the purchase of, one or more financial products, the synergy between regulated product advice and professional financial planning is obvious. As a result, most CFP professionals are also licensed through a securities and/or insurance regulator, and most licensed securities and insurance advisors have either attained CFP certification or are working towards it.

IN SUMMARY

CFP professionals, accountants and other financial advisors with and without CFP certification must work together to assist Canadians in managing their financial affairs. The accounting profession neatly complements the financial planning profession for a distinct market segment. Likewise, financial services regulation must continue to work in concert, not in competition, with the financial planning profession and CFP certification. A clearer understanding of and respect for both the overlap and the differences in the competencies of each advisor group and of the distinctive nature of their skills and services will benefit all stakeholders of the financial services industry.

I invite you to see for yourself how the Financial Planning Competency Profile contributes to that clearer understanding. Visit <www.fpsccanada.org> to review the full Profile.

CHAPTER 6

THE "FEE-ONLY" APPROACH: THE CUTTING EDGE IN THE UNITED STATES — HOW U.S. ADVISORS PROSPER OUTSIDE OF WALL ST. BY PUTTING CLIENTS FIRST

Christopher P. Van Slyke

Overview

This chapter discusses fee-only financial planning. It outlines the main differences between the traditional commissioned financial advisor and the fee-only financial planner. It discusses the benefits of Canadian Public Accountants adopting the fee-only model to financial planning to meet their legal fiduciary duties to clients.

Learning Objectives

By the end of this chapter, you should be able to:

- have insight into the unique value that fee-only planners create for their wealthy clients and their own practices; and
- learn from the experiences of one of the leading fee-only planners in the United States.

As the founder of Capital Financial Advisors, LLC, a successful and unique wealth management firm headquartered in sunny San Diego, California, I would like to share with you a practice methodology pioneered in the United States that may be highly suitable for use by Canadian Chartered Accountants (CAs).

First, I will give a bit of the history of the financial services industry here in the United States. Traditionally, large Wall Street financial firms have been vertically integrated. That is to say, they owned the means of production (investment banks) right through to distribution and consumption (your local brokerage office). So when investors wanted financial advice, they went to the local product company and asked them which product they should buy.

I would like to illustrate the problem with this arrangement by using car dealers as an example. If you go to the Ford dealership and ask the sales representative which car to buy, the sales representative won't tell you about the Toyotas, or even tell you which Ford is right for you. In fact, the sales representative will probably try to sell you the car with the largest profit margin for the dealer. Now, everyone knows this, and would not expect anything different from a car dealer. Well, that's exactly how things are at the large bank-owned brokerage firms here in the United States, where people mistakenly think they are getting a standard of care more akin to clients of a doctor, lawyer or CA.

Stockbrokers are not looking out for investors, though the public often thinks they are. Stockbrokers are trained primarily in sales, not tax, estate planning, debt usage, risk management, investments or retirement planning.

There has to be a better way, and there is. It's called the fee-only model. In 1983 an organization called the National Association of Personal Financial Advisors, or NAPFA, was formed. The following five core principles bound its members together.

- **Competency** — requiring the highest standards of proficiency in the industry
- **Comprehensive** — practising a holistic approach to financial planning
- **Compensation** — using a fee-only model that facilitates objective advice
- **Client-centered** — committing to a fiduciary relationship that ensures the client's interest is always first
- **Complete Disclosure** — providing an explanation of fees and potential conflicts of interest

The NAPFA business model is particularly well suited for Canadian CAs. For one thing, NAPFA Registered Financial Advisors must act as fiduciaries, and CAs are already acting in this capacity. Fee-only advisors are also prohibited from linking their advice to a product sale via a commission. From what I understand, CAs are prohibited from this practice as well.

Most of the wealth management advice in the United States is given by people who have not been accredited by recognized self-regulating bodies; thus, these people are ill-trained academically, ethically and professionally. The typical broker in a bank or brokerage firm is hired through an ad placed by an employer who requires the broker to have a high school education. The broker's primary skill set would be his or her ability to sell, which is where most of the "training" that the broker gets from his or her employer is directed.

The modern fee-only firm requires the Certified Financial Planner (CFP®) designation of anyone giving advice. Contained within the CFP® requirement in the United States is now a minimum Bachelors Degree as well as specific financial planning coursework, 2,000 hours of personal financial planning-related work experience, a comprehensive two-day exam and, once the CFP® designation is earned, the successful completion of 30 hours of Continuing Education every two years. On top of that, NAPFA Registered Advisors double the 30 hours required by the CFP® Board to 60 every two years.

Though today's fee-only wealth managers may not have the golf game of a stockbroker, marketing is much easier because smart clients who are seeking true expertise will find you rather quickly by referral and reputation. You don't have to try too hard to sell people what's good for them. Plus, the firm is very easy to differentiate from the marketplace in its positioning and message.

The CFP® designation also lays the groundwork for true wealth management, which is the additional hallmark of a modern fee-only firm. Because the CFP® designation requires you to master knowledge in estate planning, tax, debt usage, risk management, investment and retirement, transition to a truly comprehensive and, therefore, superior service model is seamless. The vertically integrated product companies pay lip service to integrated comprehensive wealth management but because they don't hire qualified people to give the advice, they get what they hire — product salespeople.

Below is an illustration known as the Comprehensive Wealth Planning Wheel. It includes the services that 21st century financial planning professionals provide to each of their financial planning clients.

Another linchpin underneath the fee-only firm deals with compensation. Most of the industry links compensation to product sales in one way or another. "Do I need insurance?" the consumer asks. "Well, if I want to get paid, I better say yes", thinks the advisor. Even the so-called fee-based accounts offered by U.S. brokerages for asset management are rigged to produce excessive or expensive trading and proprietary product use. Without the fiduciary obligation and its disclosure requirements, this is, of course, not known by investors or their advisors.

We believe that advice must be separated from products for a truly client-centred experience. Therefore, we accept no compensation from anyone other than our clients directly. We receive no income from brokerages, insurance companies, lawyers or mortgage brokers. We also accept no "soft dollars", which is an industry euphemism for secret non-cash payments such as free trips or brokerage research. Thus, many of the most problematic conflicts of interest involved in wealth management are eliminated. Where conflicts of interest do exist, they are clearly disclosed in writing as a stand-alone document rather than being buried deeply in a contract, as is frequently done on Wall Street.

We generally link our fee either to the client's net worth or to the client's investment account's value. Using this method, we have two incentives that clients don't seem to mind compensating us for. First, to keep them as clients, we don't use any tricks like propriety products or long-term contracts to make people stay. Thus, we must constantly strive to exceed the expectations of our clients. Second, since our fee is linked to their net worth or investments, we have an incentive to grow wealth so we can increase our pay as a reward.

All of this makes it much easier to act as a legal fiduciary. CAs are already acting in this capacity (as are doctors and lawyers), but most of the financial service industry avoids this status like the plague. Well, of course, if you are not going to hire qualified people and you plan to hide your compensation and agenda, you had better not be a legal fiduciary, right? Fee-only planners take a fiduciary oath and practise as registered investment advisors rather than stockbrokers. Registered investment advisors are fiduciaries by definition. This provides a level of protection and confidence for consumers, as well as creating a loyal trusting client base for advisors.

Though the fee-only model is ostensibly compatible with the business practices and skill sets of CAs, the experience Certified Public Accountants (CPAs) have had in adopting it in the United States has been mixed at best. Although what fee-only planners do looks easy, it must not be, because most CPA firms have had little success in comprehensive wealth management relative to the potential of their wealthy and loyal client bases.

My view is that there are two reasons for this. First, many CPA firms became stockbroker- and insurance-licensed (after pressuring and cajoling their various professional regulatory bodies such as the American Institute of Certified Public Accountants (AICPA)), and ruined the trust they had built with their clients by giving what is essentially fee-only tax advice for years. As soon as clients saw that the CPAs were really just selling a product, they wanted nothing to do with that kind of relationship and wanted their old fee-only CPA back.

The other reason is that CPAs or Canadian CAs have a different skill set than those of us who come from the asset management and planning industry. Accountants tend be very much about today and yesterday in terms of preparing the tax return. In my experience, accountants are rather forensic as opposed to being forward-looking. Investing and planning take great courage and confidence, and advisors looking to lead clients in this way have a certain personality that is not usually found in accountants. Therefore, in most cases, either accountants in the United States have given up trying to offer comprehensive wealth management, or such financial planning business continues to languish in unfulfilled potential in its accounting practices.

While our firm has never partnered with an accounting firm, I have presented the idea of partnering to many accountants. It is my belief that rather than trying to do it themselves, the greatest potential for accountants lies in partnering with a fee-only wealth management firm that already has the infrastructure and talent to properly introduce and execute these services for existing CA clients.

In summary, CAs may want to look to the fee-only advice model promulgated by the National Association of Personal Financial Advisors in the United States as they contemplate offering wealth management services to their valued and trusting clients. The model is consistent in every way with the principles already established by CAs. Fee-only advice is fiduciary, involves no commissions and has high professional and educational standards. Furthermore, you need only to look a bit farther south to see a proven track record and lots of expertise.

CHAPTER 7

DEFINING YOUR MESSAGE IN THE NEW MEDIUM

Shay Schwartzman

Overview

The aim of this chapter is to define to the reader the important universal questions to ask before embarking on a marketing campaign. The secret to a successful marketing and advertising campaign is to stand out in a crowd by defining your product or service's benefit to the consumer and what makes it different. This chapter will outline for the reader five universal business principles that one should consider before starting a campaign. The chapter also reveals case studies of various companies that have defined their message and marketed themselves using multimedia.

Learning Objectives

Within this chapter you will learn:

- what makes a message compelling and how to cut through the clutter of the thousands of advertising messages people are bombarded with every day;
- how to effectively craft a marketing message that will be meaningful and profitable;
- how to answer questions as to why a customer would consider doing business with you; and
- multimedia and case study examples you can transpose to your business.

I love music. Music is really the universal language and many times a familiar tune gets the point across quickly and emotionally.

"*Quickly*" and "*emotionally*" are two words I would like you to remember as well.

The Four Tops sang about lost love. We as business people would sing about lost business or missed opportunities while searching for "the next big thing". Using cutting-edge systems and technologies like audio, video and multimedia as part of the lead generation, the follow-up and referral steps of the sales cycle will vault our businesses over our competition and bring us legions of new prospects and customers. Before you embark upon this journey to the future of business communication, *you must first go back to define your message.*

It's the same old song … just told (or sung) in a new way.

Now, before we continue, let's define what multimedia is. "Multimedia" is a generic term that can include: audio, in its various forms, both in CD form and electronically (*i.e.*, MP3), and video, in its various forms such as DVD and online, known today as streaming video. The word "multimedia" itself is used to describe the mixing of audio, video, animation and graphics in a single program, both online and on physical media, *i.e.*, CD, DVD, flashcards, *etc.*

For the purpose of this chapter, I will use "multimedia" in its generic sense to cover the use of audio, video and animation in its various forms and combinations. As there are many forms and uses of audio, video, animation, *etc.*, I will use the term "multimedia" to cover them all. I will give you case study examples at the end of the chapter in order to show you how you can use these marketing tools in your business. But before you decide which of these systems would be appropriate for your business, you must first define your message.

As a video and multimedia producer for over 20 years with LifeStyleMedia.ca, I have worked with CEOs of large and small corporations, public speakers, musicians, film directors, would-be artists and excons. My role, as a Trusted Advisor in my field, is to guide my clients to make the best use of their time and money when using multimedia in their marketing and sales process that would impact prospects quickly and connect with customers emotionally.

Let's understand what we are offering current and prospective customers and how our service or product is better and different than the product or service they are using right now. If they are not currently using a product or service similar to yours, then what would be the benefit to them or their business if they did?

This is your business' *unique selling proposition* (USP) or *value proposition* (VP). Once you can define that, you can then begin your marketing.

FIVE UNIVERSAL BUSINESS PRINCIPLES

The following five *universal business principles* will help you craft your message.

Principle 1: Prospects Do Not Want to Be Sold — Prospects *Will Absolutely Not* Hear What You Have to Say *Unless* You Tell Them What They Want to Hear

Let's face it, as business owners we are all salespeople. It doesn't really matter whether you are a lawyer, financial planner or accountant. Without lead generation and follow-up that is meaningful and compelling, you are out of business.

All sales begin with marketing.

Many want to believe that, like the movies, we can count on a happy ending. Think about this: one day a woman or man gets an entrepreneurial urge and decides to get into business. He or she puts out a sign, prints up some business cards, puts together a website and, presto, he or she is in business, mistakenly believing that just because he or she did all that, he or she is entitled to make a living. I wish it were only that simple.

Here is what I have discovered as a Video and Multimedia Marketer since 1998, when I got my "'Aha' moment", my epiphany, if you will, when it came to my business. *What I am about to reveal to you is the same mistake most inexperienced marketers make when it comes to marketing.*

Many professionals, once they have gone through their circle of influence and are ready to take the next step to market their business, take a look at what others in their field are doing and copy it. So if you are a lawyer, you look at what other lawyers are doing. If you are a financial planner or accountant, you look at what your colleagues are doing and you copy them. Here's the problem with this herd mentality. *Just because everyone is doing it doesn't make it right or effective.*

I urge you to look at how practitioners in your industry market themselves and you'll see what I mean. It doesn't matter what business you are in. It's pretty much all the same out there, pathetic.

It's what I call "image advertising".

Image advertising revolves around an ad, brochure or TV commercial — the advertising vehicle is irrelevant — that has a good-looking professional photo or host, the businessperson's name, a telephone number and some sort of cutesy message.

Here's the problem with "image advertising". Image ads are:

- usually big, flashy and colourful ads that feature the business owner, the owner's place of business and a "cutesy" slogan, showing off designations that no one outside the owner's industry understands.
- same old, same old vague "same-old promises" of service, quality and integrity.
- unimaginative and non-compelling. Everyone in a similar industry sees what the competition is doing and does the same thing. Consumers can't tell one professional from the other.
- trying to sell the prospect.
- look and read like ads. They give only the prospect, no benefit or reason to take action now.
- all about "me, me, me".

If you study the messages being sent to consumers in your industry, you will discover the following similarities in the message:

- We're # 1.
- We're the biggest, therefore the best.
- We sell a lot of X; therefore, you want to do business with us.
- We care about you (consumer) and/or your business.
- Do business with me — no reason, just because I put out this advertising.

As you begin to understand this and start to craft a different message, you will see how different your business can become.

Here's a statement I would like you to remember as you begin crafting your message: *Prospects do not want to be sold.*

Here's an example that we can all relate to. Think about the last time you went to a store to buy a pair of shoes or a Plasma TV. It really doesn't matter what the product is; you have a need for something. You have an event at which you want to make a good impression and want to get a new pair of shoes; it's the week before the Stanley Cup Hockey Championship and you walk into the local box store and stare up at the wall of new Plasma and LCD TVs. You are obviously in the market for whatever it is you walked into the store for. You, like most people, have better things to do with your time than walking into a store just to see what's new in the world of X.

So why is it that when the salesperson asks, "*May I help you?*", you reply, "*No, just looking*"? The reason: you do not want to be sold. This scenario is played out millions of times every day, whether it is a face-to-face interaction like the one I have described or it's a prospect's interaction with your brochure, TV or radio commercial.

You want to go as deeply as you can so you can become your prospect — to get into their mind and discover what they are thinking, and what they are talking about with friends, family or co-workers. The closer you get to this mindset, the more you can focus your marketing to become a high powered rifle finding its target, as opposed to a shotgun that just sprays pellets.

When you get it right, you will attract and convert more highly qualified prospects while using fewer resources. More importantly you will acquire higher paying, more profitable clients for life.

Principle 3: Prospects Need a Compelling Reason to Do Business with You

This is a "biggie"!

If you are not running a monopoly or a government service, the most important question you need to answer is, "Why should a prospect or a client do business with me?"

This is a fundamental question that you need to answer before attempting any marketing. If you don't know why your business exists, beyond making you money, then you don't deserve to be in business.

Here's a big "aha" for many business people. *Your clients and prospects do not care about you.*

This sounds harsh but how often do you think about the restaurant down the street? When was the last time you sat at home or in the office and said to yourself that you need to give the dry cleaner some business because you haven't been in for a while?

Unless you need something, you really don't care.

And when it's time for you to go to a restaurant or use the services of a dry cleaner, you are going to go where you get the best service, the best food, the best value, *etc.* You, like most people on this planet (though there are some altruistic folks out there but they are so few, it's hardly worth mentioning), listen to the same radio station — WIIFM, (What's In It For Me).

Ask yourself, "Why should a client do business with me, above doing business with someone else, doing what they are doing now or do nothing at all?" Unless or until you have a compelling answer to this question, you are wasting your time and money on marketing. *The answer to this question is your USP or your VP.* The clearer and simpler yours is, the more compelling it will be to prospects.

Creating a USP or VP is as easy as 1, 2 and 3:

1. Determine what your clients want.
2. Find out which of these needs you can fill.

3. Find a way to clearly state to your clients that you are the source to fill those needs.

Don't make the mistake of thinking your USP or VP is just a marketing or advertising issue. *It is the essence of your business, the strategy to lead you towards profitability* by making it the cornerstone of your conversation with prospects and customers.

So what makes *you* different?

1. What distinguishes your business from your competitors?
2. Does your business help clients make more money or save more money? Save time?
3. In your industry, are you more expensive, less expensive? Do you offer more value for the money?
4. Do you offer any guarantees?
5. Do you have a better system to benefit your clients?
6. Are you more aggressive in your programs and strategies?
7. Do you make it easier for clients to do business with you?

Here are some companies that redefined themselves in their industry and became leaders in their field. *They achieved their status by articulating a simple point of difference*:

- FED EX — *When it absolutely, positively has to be there overnight.*
- Domino's Pizza — *Fresh hot pizza in 30 minutes or less, guaranteed.*
- Craig Proctor (Top 10 RE/MAX Agent 10 years in a row, #1 for two of those years) — *Your home sold in under 120 days or I buy it.*

Now spend a moment to think about your own USP or VP.

- Your USP or VP should illicit this response from your prospect, "*How does he or she do that?*"
- You should be able to articulate this in 33 seconds or less.
- It should be clearly understood.
- Without a compelling USP or VP, you will never differentiate yourself from your competition.

Now here are what you *do not* want to base your USP or VP on:

- Quality
- Service
- Price
- Dependability

These are *empty*, *meaningless*, *unbelievable* and *completely lacking in credibility*, yet it seems everyone, in whatever field you look at, uses them and somehow thinks their message is compelling and different.

For you to define and redirect your business with a *bold and powerful* USP or VP, it *must* be benefit-driven so when a prospect reads, hears or sees it, it will be:

- Meaningful
- Relevant
- Valuable

Without these ingredients, your message will most likely fall on deaf ears.

Here's the good news: most of your competitors have *no clue* about USP or VP, but now you do. Taken seriously and implemented properly, it is a major opportunity for you to grow your business exponentially.

Your challenge right now is to develop a USP or VP that's genuinely unique.

Principle 4: If You Try to Be All Things to All People, You Dilute Your Effectiveness

When we own and manage a business, we are always looking for the next opportunity. The danger of looking for business in the wrong places is that we may well dilute our effectiveness by trying to be all things to all people. It is more important to define who you are and what you do than to try and offer a wide range of services.

When you stand for everything, you really stand for nothing.

Lawyers who specialize and are known for one thing will always have a steady stream of clients beating a path to their door. All the while, a lawyer who has a general practice will never get the big cases because he or she is known as the "Swiss army knife" of law: *good in a pinch but not when the chips are down or when it matters.*

This can be true for any profession or practice. Take the field of financial planning. Here's a personal story. I have a financial planner with whom I invest in RSPs. Nice guy, he seems to know what he is doing, but to me he is interchangeable with the financial planner in the next office to his or the financial planner who knocked on my door the other day to introduce himself. I can get an RSP just about anywhere these days; I can even do it online. So why do I use his services? He just happened to be at the right place at the right time.

Now, if I were looking to take special tax advantages in my business or wanted to set up an individual pension plan, I would seek out the services of a specialist in this field, like Peter Merrick of Merrick-

Wealth.com, who specializes in IPPs, Health and Welfare Trusts and other tax effective vehicles. Can my RSP guy guide me in these matters? I suppose he knows something about it or can get the answers, but I want to deal with someone whose specialty it is.

Here's the moral to the story. *Don't be everything to all people. Specialize and be known for one thing and be very good at it.*

McDonald's is the world's largest restaurant chain, not because its food is the best, the healthiest or the décor at its establishments is so inviting. McDonald's is known for food that is fast, moderately priced and no matter which of its restaurants you go to, the food is always the same.

McDonald's does not sell sushi, Thai or café lattes — popular foods these days. It doesn't offer fine dining, nor does it sell alcohol (in North America anyway. In some European McDonalds it does, but alcohol is not a strong selling product in these markets). The people who operate McDonald's know what business they are in and, more importantly, because they know what business they are in, they know who the prospects are that their marketing needs to speak to. They can focus their marketing efforts and be efficient with their spending.

As small- and medium-sized business owners, we often get caught up in the ego of being all things to all people or trying to capitalize on current trends and fads and wasting precious time and resources on prospects and business extensions we know nothing about. By trying to be all things to all people, we dilute who we are in the marketplace, to the point where nobody knows what we stand for.

Let's take our USP or VP examples from above. FED EX (or Federal Express) is known for delivering small parcels that are under 70 pounds. When you think of overnight express service for your documents, you think Federal Express. You would not call them if you had heavy cargo to ship.

How about Domino's Pizza? Wherever you live, does Domino's have the best pizza you can order in your hometown? Probably not. In many marketplaces, there are better tasting pizzas you can order. But when you want your pizza fast, you and the kids are hungry and you don't want to think about it too much, you call Domino's.

You may not want to grow your business to the size of a FED EX or Domino's, but if you can define who you are in your industry and become the best, you will become very popular with prospects.

That's called marketplace dominance and you can take that all the way to the bank.

Principle 5: You Must Make It Easy and Fun for Prospects to Do Business with You

If your message is hard to understand, if you are difficult to reach or if prospects have to go out of their way to get in touch with you or find it difficult to get answers to the questions they have, they won't stick around to give you a second chance. As business people, we have marketing tools available that can help us communicate with our prospects and customers 24/7. Potential customers can get the information they need, whenever they want and on their terms.

In Universal Principle #1, I wrote that prospects do not want to be sold. They do not want to speak to you until they have done their research and feel they are prepared to speak with you. Consumers are more knowledgeable and savvy today than at any point in history. Information is readily available at one's fingertips on almost any topic via the Internet. Today's clients have come to expect answers, not tomorrow, and not in a day, *but now*.

By making information inviting, easy to obtain, non-threatening, educational, inspiring and fun, you'll loft your business above your competitors.

As a business owner:

- you cannot service too much;
- you cannot educate too much;
- you cannot inform too much;
- you cannot offer too much follow-up and follow-through; and
- you cannot make calling or coming into your business too desirable.

As an audio, video and multimedia marketing expert, I work with my clients to help them communicate their points of difference and educate their prospects on the benefits of doing business with them and only them.

I now want to share with you some new media systems that will give your prospects what they want: information, in a non-threatening manner that will also set you apart as an expert in your field.

Consider the power you can wield in your field of business when you formulate an emotional, compelling and risk-free proposition to your prospects and clients. Nothing is more powerful than audio, video and multimedia when it is harnessed to the power of the Internet to get your marketing message seen and heard.

You have companies, like my company, LifeStyleMedia.ca, that understand the power of using an integrated business and marketing approach — *cutting-edge* audio-video marketing tools *bundled* with a road map to using it profitably and effectively.

The Power of Audio, Video and Multimedia

There are limitations to text. There is a magical power to the moving image that is more difficult to create in print. Think about videos you have seen, whether fiction or non-fiction, Hollywood movies or otherwise. Remember the story, the characters, the drama? *Now how does a brochure or book compare?*

Text-based materials:

- often get lost in all the clutter of other text-based materials;
- are often misunderstood (people may not get the nuance of what you are saying); and
- can have little emotional impact (people read it with their own voice, bringing with it their mood, paradigm and skepticism).

Bottom line, the effectiveness of your message may be lost.

Nothing gets your message across like video and audio. The power of moving images lets your message be seen and *heard* loud and clear. The right message, combining the right images and sound and punctuated with graphics, gets your message heard. And not *only* does the right message convey better what you say, but more importantly it conveys better what you mean. Audio and video just "say" it better!

Here are some statistics you should consider. People remember:

- 10% of what they read
- 20% of what they hear
- 30% of what they see
- 50% of what they see *and* hear together.

In addition:

- 55% of message meaning is derived from facial expression; and
- 38% of a message meaning is derived from gestures and body language.

Because of properly utilizing audio and visual messages:

- Response rates increase — up 30%
- Message retention improves
- There is uniformity of message

What it all means to you is this:

- Shorter sales cycle

- Increased prospect speed to market
- Quicker return on investment

If you *are not* using audio, video and multimedia, coupled with web 2.0 technologies, to converse with prospects and clients, you are having a one-way conversation.

In the new mediums, it's *all* about your conversation with your customer.

What does this mean to you?

- When you *generate a lead*, you want to *stand out in the crowd.*
- When you *follow up the lead*, you want to *make sure you are heard.*
- When you *build rapport* with the prospect, *you want to be trusted.*
- When you *sell a home or help a purchaser find the home of his or her dreams*, you want to *be the trusted friend so you can get referrals.*

Below are case study examples of audio, video and multimedia tools that combine the power of audio, video and web 2.0 technologies and how they offered these businesses marketing solutions.

Case Studies

Company or Group — Real Estate Agents from All Across North America

Problem

How do real estate agents generate leads and follow up those leads, efficiently using video? Once a listing or buyer agreement is signed, how does the real estate agent use technology for client retention and for customer referral?

Solution

LifeStyleMedia.ca created the Multimedia Toolkit for Real Estate Professionals.

1. For lead generation, we have developed an educational video series that is branded to the real estate agent. A link to the video is placed on the real estate agent's site. The video gives viewers information on the home selling or buying process and then invites them to order a free report for more detailed information. By asking for a report, prospects then provide their contact information so the real estate agent can follow up.

2. For lead generation and follow-up, LifeStyleMedia.ca created a series of video e-mails for both buyer and seller prospects. Once a lead is received, from whatever source (web, phone or print), the prospect is put on a series of video e-mails that give on a weekly basis good, timely and useful information on the home buying or selling process. This branded video e-mail approach keeps the real estate agent at the front of the prospect's mind, eventually to be seen as *the expert* in the field of real estate.

   As well as a video on the real estate process, the video e-mail also contains benefits for working with the agent and links back to specific landing pages on the website and a link to e-mail or a "call-me" feature. From this link, the prospect can call the real estate agent directly.

   This program is used mainly for follow-up but also for lead generation if the real estate agent had only an e-mail address.

3. Online seller presentation is a short online video/PowerPoint combination presentation that is used for follow-up and lead conversion. The Flash presentation gives the viewer a benefit-rich presentation on what makes the real estate agent different from other real estate agents in the marketplace. This is beneficial to the agent in a number of ways.

   It saves a seat for the agent at the "kitchen table" if he or she is in competition with other agents. Many times, prospects will interview a number of real estate agents before selecting one to sell their home. This presentation would be e-mailed to the prospect ahead of the agent coming over to see the house and making a complete listing presentation. This achieves the following:

   a. There are fewer cancelled appointments. Prospects are so intrigued by the offer of guarantees and benefits in the short online presentation that they want to meet the agent to hear more and get the full story.

   b. Other agents are not able to convince the prospect to sign a listing agreement with them before meeting with the real estate agent who sent them the online presentation. Prospects want to get the full presentation and meet with the agent before making their decision.

   c. The actual face-to-face presentation is much shorter and friendlier. The online seller presentation "breaks the ice" and establishes the agent as an expert in the field.

d. It helps reach out-of-town clients. In some urban areas, the sprawl can be expansive. This presentation can be used to compel prospects, particularly buyer prospects, to make the drive to visit the agent.

Result

These three tools, the streaming videos, video e-mail and online listing presentation, increased consumer response to the agent's offers and got the agents 32.7% more face time with seller and buyer prospects compared to their existing marketing mix. These results were taken over a one-year period.

Company or Group — Voice-Activated Response, Website and Lead Management Technology Company

Problem

As a technology company offering marketing tools for direct response businesses, this business has a suite of powerful tools. Educating prospects on what these tools can do for them is a challenge. Having customers understand the products and what they can do has proven to be a sure-fire way to get them to try the service. Once they try the service, over 80% of customers stay with the company on a long-term basis.

Since showing is more powerful than telling, this company commissioned LifeStyleMedia.ca to develop a system to get better message retention from the company's website and encourage viewers to take the next step and order a free special report. The importance of the special report is to capture client information in order to invite clients on a series of teleconference calls where sales are made.

Solution

1. LifeStyleMedia.ca created a presence and brand out of the company president. The first step was for the president to greet visitors on their website, generally the first point of contact that prospects made with the company. Once on the site, the president quickly caught the attention of viewers before they could "click away". He began by welcoming them to the site and gave them ample benefits for visiting. He then directed them to order free special reports. These reports are instrumental in getting the prospects' names and e-mail addresses so they can be invited to free teleconference calls where this company's sales people have more time to go over the benefits of their programs and make sales.

2. LifeStyleMedia.ca created a series of marketing tips that integrated the technology company's marketing tools and systems with tried and proven techniques. In this way, prospects and customers could see how the company's services fit into day-to-day business challenges. Six marketing tips were created in our example. Each video was approximately five minutes in length. At the end of each video there was a call to action to join the president on a series of teleconference calls where he had more time to review the benefits of their services and make sales. The videos were made available on a weekly basis for seven weeks (six marketing tips plus an introductory video).

   A DVD was also created out of the videos for direct mail use.

Result

Prospect retention of the message rose by 307%, reflecting the number of people who ended up on the teleseminar calls as a result of their first contact with the prospect on the site and the receipt of the marketing tips as video e-mails.

Company or Group — Internationally Recognized Research Pharmaceutical Company

Problem

This global pharmaceutical giant needed to create an educational video for patients participating in a drug trial for rheumatoid arthritis. The information had to be regulated by a medical body to ensure accurate and impartial claims.

Solution

The company approached LifeStyleMedia.ca with their problem, and together we and the company representatives decided that DVD video would be the best way for patients to get the information they needed so they could lead more comfortable lives. The DVD would be distributed by company sales reps to physicians who would pass it on to appropriate patients.

The production included interviews with top medical practitioners about their experience with the medical treatment, and included animations to show how the pharmaceutical interacts with the body and what effects patients should expect. The video relayed highly scientific information that was understandable, unbiased and vital to the patients involved.

Result

Patients had a greater understanding of the medication and how it affected their body. There was also better compliance with the pharmaceutical as patients felt more comfortable about taking the drug. The DVD also saved doctors time as it cut down on the number of questions and concerns being posed to them.

Company or Group — Free _Distribution Through Newspaper Chain_

Problem

A leading manufacturer and marketer of soap and toiletries was introducing a new product and wanted a sample of this new addition to their line-up to land on the cover of the morning edition of a well-known Toronto, Canada free daily newspaper. Not only did the paper have to go to press but each packet had to be affixed by hand! This was laborious but very profitable for the newspaper. How could the newspaper take this first event, use it as a learning experience and document the process so that when the newspaper took it to other advertisers, a system would be in place?

Solution

LifeStyleMedia.ca created a video documenting the logistics of the roll-out which would also serve as a promotional piece to secure more advertisers.

Result

The results were so successful that LifeStyleMedia.ca continues to create videos for media outlets, newspapers, magazines, television and radio stations across North America.

Company or Group — Film and Television Distribution Company

Problem

This company came to LifeStyleMedia.ca to create a promotional trailer for its release of *Blood and Tears* — a documentary chronicling the Arab-Israeli conflict from past to present. The problem involved taking a 90-minute film about a sensitive and complex subject and cut it to around one minute for the home entertainment market.

Solution

From script development to our use of music and rhythmic editing, we produced a trailer that captured the heart of the story.

Result

The trailer resulted in one of the best single-day cash receipts for a documentary film.

Company or Group — Internationally Franchised Coffee Company

Problem

In 2008, this firm's franchisees met in Toronto for their national conference. Head office wanted to create a series of motivational and best practices videos that would teach attendees what some of the more profitable cafés across the country were doing to achieve their success. This had to be done in an entertaining style that connected with the theme of the conference: *The Neighbourhood Oasis.*

Solution

LifeStyleMedia.ca produced and directed the opening video to support *The Neighbourhood Oasis* theme. This video delivered key messages of consumer confidence in the brand and left franchisees feeling proud of their success. Complementing this theme, we also produced a series of "Best Practices" videos that were used to help educate participants throughout the conference.

Result

The result was an informed and energized crowd eager to put new ideas to use in their business.

Company or Group — Well-Known and Loved Celebrity, Television and Radio Personality

Problem

A noted TV and radio personality wanted to take her celebrity and spin it into an online television broadcast entity. This online TV station would include original programming as well as content from other sources. The ability for uploading and broadcasting user-generated content was paramount as the theme of the project was to raise her profile using social media.

Solution

LifeStyleMedia.ca developed a WebTV portal for her. LifeStyleMedia.ca also produced the clips that are broadcast on the various channels on the WebTV portal.

This solution allowed her to use the format she is strong in, television, to reach her audience. She is not bound to any TV broadcaster, as now with the Internet she is her own television broadcaster. As well, her audience can communicate with her and the rest of her community via Webcam.

Result

The result was a wildly successful launch to 12,000 subscribers. The TV and radio personality and LifeStyleMedia.ca are partnering to sell commercial ad space, *i.e.*, *online TV commercials*, to corporate sponsors.

IN CONCLUSION

The above case studies illustrate the effectiveness of multimedia tools that are available to business people to connect with prospects and customers. There are more cutting-edge marketing tools such as these using various combinations in order to produce a successful and *profitable* marketing strategy.

But remember, before you get started, develop your USP or VP because ultimately it's your message that matters. *Whatever systems you decide to implement for lead generation, follow up, client retention and referral, you must adhere to the five universal business principles for success. They are the basic building blocks of any successful business.*

To be profitable, effective and have a business that serves your life, listen to your customers and give them ample risk-free reasons to do business with you. Marketing systems and technology change and develop over time, but the message you convey must remain consistent ... *it's the same old song.*

CHAPTER 8

MARKETING THAT WORKS FOR THE TRUSTED ADVISOR — USING THE POWER OF THE INTERNET

Galen Weston

Overview

The advent of the Internet represents the single biggest opportunity for businesses large and small in a generation, and remains a continuing challenge for all businesses in harnessing and maximizing its potential. For the entrepreneur, small business owner or self-employed advisor, an effective use of this medium can mean the difference between success and failure. The Internet can lower your costs, help close more business/deals and find customers you would never have otherwise acquired. Ignore the Internet, and you place a huge marketing advantage in the hands of your competitors.

This chapter provides some insights into developing an effective Internet marketing strategy based on the writer's own first-hand and successful experiences. It may give you some ideas about how to proceed with developing your own online marketing program.

Learning Objectives

By the end of this chapter you will:

- understand how search engines work and what search engine optimization is;
- learn how to set up your own Google ad campaign; and
- acquire the elements of a basic search engine optimization (SEO) plan and tips for maximizing the returns from your own search engine campaign.

BASEMENT TO BOARDROOM

Running a financial planning business requires the same principles as any other business. That might come as a surprise to those who believe they are entitled to make a living. Why not? You put in the time to get an Economics degree or an M.B.A. Perhaps you spent a few weeks taking the Canadian Securities Course or Insurance Licence exams. Many of you have chosen to distinguish yourselves and achieved excellence by obtaining a CFP designation. Accountants and lawyers have put many years into the process of obtaining their designations. However, the bottom line is, you all just have the minimum requirements to do the job. From a marketing perspective you have the same basic tools as every one of your competitors. On their own, those tools do not work.

The reality is you are an entrepreneur and marketing is king. So what are the options for the Trusted Advisor? Have you tried the newspaper? Doesn't work. Have you bought mailing lists? Have you tried cold calling? With the recent legislation, cold calling households is pretty much out.

Let me give you a little background on some of the things I have done and, most importantly, the mistakes I have made.

As an eager, confident yet naïve young man in my mid-twenties, I was ready to take on the world. The only problem was that I had no idea how. I had just finished four years at Humber College, studying Jazz Guitar. I had hair halfway down my back and never had a job making more then $8 an hour! Every single person I knew either was a musician or had just finished school and none of them knew what they were going to do either. But somehow I was not concerned — my requirements for living were modest. I was confident that after practically starving for the past four years, things were looking up. I was able to work through the day so there would be no more 11 p.m. – 3 a.m. shifts unloading trucks in Malton. No more begging for shifts at the local gas station in Cabbagetown. I was ready for a full-time job. I remember excitedly doing the math: $8 × 160 hours a month equals $1,280 a month. My rent was only $500, so that was going to leave $780 a month to do with how I pleased. That was exciting.

Then came the call that changed my life's direction forever. "Galen, I have been working at a penny stock broker for about a month now. They tell me I am going to be a broker soon. Maybe you should apply for a job here," proclaimed my fellow summer slave from Pikes Tent, an awning job where we spent most days hammering three-foot stakes into the asphalt used to hold down 200-foot-long event tents.

"Penny stock broker!" I said excitedly. "Wow, that sounds fantastic, but why would they hire me?" "You have an Economics degree. I don't know a thing about finance."

"Don't worry about it. They just want you to call people and ask them if they would like to receive our newsletter. They will pay you $400 a week."

I was so excited, I hung up the phone and told everyone the great news. I was going to be a penny stock-broker. Somehow my great news was not received as I had expected. Nevertheless, I was pumped.

After a quick interview I was hired.

Excited about the prospect of making $400 a week, I was determined to do a great job. I sat down at my desk and started dialing. I quickly found that I was horrible on the phone. People swore at me and told me how much money they had lost, and generally were not very pleasant. But it had no effect on my determination. Somehow it was ingrained in me to just find a way to make it happen. So I just dialed and dialed as much as I could. I was just looking for people to say yes to me. I was looking for people who might actually want to read about investing.

Within a couple of days I was called into the manager's office. I was trembling as I walked in. I was sure I was going to get fired. After all, everyone else was experienced and sounded good on the phone. I knew I had a poor telephone manner and was generating only about 15 leads when everyone else was generating 25-30. I needed this job.

Much to my surprise, I was congratulated on my efforts. My manager pulled out some printouts as he said to me, "I am not sure if you realize but we track a lot of stats here and I want to go over some of them with you."

He went on to point out that he expected us to make a minimum of 100 calls a day. "This is the average for the room", he explained. "Now, if we look at your numbers, you have called over 350 people every day you have been here. Perhaps you are not yet a great salesman, but that is exactly what we do not want. We just want you to continue to find the people who are already looking for what we are offering."

That statement really stuck with me. *You are simply looking for people who are already interested.*

Over the years I have learned that this is one of the most important concepts in marketing that you can ever learn. You need to find those who want your services. You don't need to sell people on something that they do not want. If you believe that you have a service that a large number of people do not want or already have, then find another business.

When I left my manager's office I was pumped. I was the best in the room. I understood clearly that my job was just to work hard. I didn't need to be slick or even friendly — just smile and dial. This is a numbers game and I can work the numbers.

But that was not enough. I quickly decided I wanted to be a broker. Apparently, some of them made $100,000 a year. After meeting some of them I found that hard to believe. They were not educated in finance; many of them were just like me.

So at lunch hour that day I had made my decision: I was going to be a broker. I ran off to the Canadian Securities Institute and registered for the course. Arrogantly I said to the lady at the same time that I would also like to book the exam ASAP.

"I am not sure if you are aware, but it takes six months to a year to complete this course; so I suggest you book your exam after you read through the books," she replied.

I informed her that I was in a rush to get my licence and did not wish to wait. I assured her I would study day and night.

"Fine, the next available date is in six weeks."

Back at the office I proclaimed my decision to my co-workers, who quickly explained how hard the course was and told me I was insane.

Six weeks later I was a stockbroker.

Fortunately, my nosey nature had forced me to keep my ears and eyes open. I was very disappointed to find out that the penny stock firm was really just a scam. I quickly learned that we were selling investments that did not have a real market. I learned that people never made money and everything invested went to the firm. There were lots of justifications like, "these people are gamblers and that they would gamble their money somewhere else" or "lots of real stocks go down even faster".

This did not sit well with me. I could not knowingly take someone's money. I had to believe in what I was doing.

One day, while on hold with a call to a prospect, I heard a news release instead of the usual background music. It concerned a big announcement made by the City of Toronto that carbon monoxide detectors were to become mandatory in all homes. And this was great news for a small company called North American Detectors. The stock was up 25 cents to $1 per share. I was quickly excited by the news and could imagine what would happen if this stock continually went higher. I went to the Internet and began to study. I was so excited by the story that I made my decision. I was not going to rip people off. I was going to sell people shares in North American Detectors.

I ran in to my manager's office and proclaimed the news. They said to me flatly, "You're insane! Stick to the program." I refused.

"I won't rip people off with your phony investments. I want to be a real broker." Much to everyone's surprise, they agreed to let me try.

After all, they were starting to get "heat" from the regulatory bodies, and realized it would not hurt to have someone running a legitimate business.

So I was off. Convinced I had stumbled on a gold mine, I got on the phone and started calling everyone I could to tell about this great story.

And I was successful. Within a week I had brought in over $100,000 dollars in new investments! My bosses where stunned. Never had anyone brought in so much money so quickly. The expectations were closer to $1,000 in the first few weeks.

Then there was a problem. Much to my dismay, the stock started going down. Every day it just kept going down. After another week my $100,000 had become about $50,000. I was devastated. I did not understand it; I was trying to do the right thing. My phone was ringing off the hook with angry clients. Everyone else was laughing, explaining how the company's penny stock deal went up .05 cents every eight days according to the newspaper. "The only problem is your clients are not allowed to sell it!" I retorted angrily.

To make matters worse, I was only able to make a few hundred dollars in commissions because our company was not set up to do real trading. Costs were inflated because they had to pay another firm jitney fees to do my trades.

I saw no other choice then to ask my manager to have a senior broker take over the clients for me. It was with great joy that they called my clients and told them how they could make their money back in another opportunity. They handed me a check for $8,000 and said, "Welcome to the dark side." I quit!

I was determined, however, that there was real money to be made in the financial business and that I was going to be successful. So I started to read everything I could. I realized that stories and fundamentals were not for me. I need something technical. I needed a system. So for the next few months I read everything I could on technical analysis. After "paper trading" for a few weeks I was convinced I was a master. I could make money working from home. Just master the markets.

Set up in my basement apartment with a satellite dish and some monitor screens, I was ready to go to war with the best traders on the Chicago Mercantile Exchange. Every day was a battle — in and out, up and down, winning and losing. I did okay in my self-induced ultra high stress environment. In fact I am proud to say that for over two months I broke even, in spite of the $8,000 in fees I accrued with the firm I was trading with! But I was humbled every day by the power of a market that I could not control. I was missing one key requirement for survival. Making money. I was broke.

I was confident that I was learning a great deal about the markets, and if I employed this knowledge in the regular stock markets I could make my clients a lot of money. So I decided it was time to head back to Bay Street and make another attempt at starting a real business.

A small firm offered me a salary to explore my ideas and I accepted. I was excited again! I believed that this time I had figured it out. So back on the phone I started calling up potential investors and explaining my new wonderful strategies. I predicted the financial markets on almost a daily basis to some "whales" (wealthy clients) and they bought it. I quickly convinced a small group of individuals to give me a few hundred thousand dollars to trade and I was off. And I was doing great. In a down market in the spring of 2000 I was short-selling everything in sight. I had clients who had doubled their investments to well over $150,000 after only three months. Word got out and I was able to leverage this success and build my "book" of business to almost $9 million in the first year. My end of the commissions was about $160,000 which I split with a partner.

Then the storm hit. One fateful meeting, my inexperience and perhaps immaturity came out in full force and ruined my business. Investor relations for a small public company raising funds contacted me. The business plan made sense and of course I thought it would be the next best thing. I quickly focused all my time and, even worse, a good portion of my investors' dollars on one silly story. And to my dismay the business plan was just that, a well-written document written with the intention to swindle money. I later learned that there was little or no intention to build a real business. The stock quickly fell apart and I had destroyed my "book" of business.

"It's time to go completely legitimate," I decided. No more quick schemes and no more trading, just wealth management and a long-term plan. "I have to get to a big five bank-owned firm to make that happen," I thought. So off I went. I quickly had an interview with one of the big firms. After seeing my asset accumulation of the previous year the firm was willing to overlook my stupidity and accept my reassurances that I could chalk up all the mistakes to a great learning experience.

I was thrilled! Here was the big opportunity I did not think they gave to people who did not have a degree or a rich family.

I set my goals and started to make things happen the only way I knew how. Get on the trusty old telephone with the Trade Boards' membership list. I set my lofty goals and lit up the phone lines. I remembered the numbers-game secret and made my first goal to find the money and my second goal to close it. Day in and day out I pounded the phone. It was a challenge and I will not say it did not work because it did. After three months I located $70 million on the phone by calling people and asking if they would be willing to meet with me. I would then ask how much they had invested because I learned and understood how important it was to not to be all things to all people. I decided that no matter what, I would only deal with account sizes of $250,000 plus.

After grinding it out for a few months, I was getting bored. I could not stand the day-in-and-day-out routine. I was convinced there had to be a better way. So I started to look for one.

ENTER THE INTERNET

My search quickly led to the Internet. What if I could set up a system where all the people who were already looking for a financial advisor could find me?

"I just need a website," I proclaimed to myself.

And that is how my journey to where I am today started. I went to the bookstore and got some basic web-building books and built my first rudimentary website. I focused on estate planning because I thought that was where the need was, and I was right. I started to post estate-planning articles.

To my surprise it was only a matter of weeks before I was receiving calls and e-mails asking for help. Succession planning issues, clients unhappy with their advisors and financial planning concerns were some of the many questions people were contacting me about.

I was opening accounts at a record pace. I quickly stumbled across a succession-planning opportunity that led to a record-size insurance deal.

Due to the nature of the Internet, I was getting questions and e-mails from coast to coast. I had to set up a referral network to other advisors across the country.

I began to study search engine optimization to target the kind of traffic that would bring in the client type that I was looking for.

It was not long before I realized that I enjoyed the marketing much more than I did the advising. So I knew it was time to make a decision. Do I want to be an advisor or do I want to run a referral generation company that provided advisors with prospects that were already looking for their services? I chose the latter.

With the capital I had created from my first year as an advisor, I left the brokerage firm and created my own company — ProfessionalReferrals.ca Inc.

I became a full-time marketer. In the last six years, millions of Canadians have come to ProfessionalReferrals.ca Inc. and AdvisorWorld.com to find experienced professional help in regards to estate and financial planning and all other aspects of finance.

I am going to give you many of the secrets that I have learned that help me find the people who are already looking for the services of a financial advisor, lawyer or accountant.

GENERATING PROSPECTS

First of all, before I get into marketing strategy, let me say a few things about Internet marketing as an integral and growing aspect of business in Canada. According to a recent news release from Statistics Canada, more of us than ever are turning to the Internet as a place to shop and transact business. Canadians used the Internet to purchase goods and services valuing almost $12.8 billion in orders in 2007, up 61% from 2005. Driving this increase was a larger volume of orders, up to 69.9 million from 49.4 million — an increase of roughly 40%.

The study also revealed some interesting disparities in the type of user. An overwhelming majority (91%) of people in the top 20% income group (earning more than $95,000) used the Internet. In 2007, 84% of individuals with at least some post-secondary education used the Internet, compared with 58% of those who had less education. The survey also showed that people living in urban areas continued to be more likely to have used the Internet than those from smaller towns and rural areas.

What can an entrepreneur or small business enterprise owner take from all this? Two things: first, the Internet proves to be a marketplace that deserves our attention based simply on the volume of business currently being conducted there and; second, demographics and population trends will likely fuel an ever-increasing rate in Internet transactions in the future. It is and will increasingly become a venue for higher-earning, better-educated, young urban professionals to shop for goods and services. So an online presence and an effective Internet marketing program are tools to success that the entrepreneur or small business owner simply cannot afford to ignore.

I started off this chapter by stating that advisors have many of the same tools and that does not really differentiate you. The same goes for your Internet marketing tools. Most advisors have either their own website or a presence on the web somewhere. Many of you have spent a lot of money on those sites, making them pretty. Most likely the reality is, as far as generation of new clients goes, 99% of those sites have done absolutely nothing.

What if your website was building your business for you? Imagine this: you are on the golf course on a beautiful sunny day at the same time hundreds of people are on your website, reading about great tax saving tips, creating trusts, how to file their last five years of late returns, *etc.*

They are pre-educating themselves on your products. Best of all, it could be costing you next to nothing!

While your website is building new business you could be spending more time concentrating on maximizing revenue from your current clients.

So how do you make your website generate clients quickly?

The short answer is: spend a lot of money. I'm going to preface this entire process by giving you a quick reality check on marketing. In recent years, many smart entrepreneurs and large companies have figured out that they also want to be found by all the people who are looking for financial services. That includes the big banks, insurance companies and savvy financial professionals. These people have an excellent handle on building a business and realize that it costs money to make money and are willing to spend to generate new business.

If you go into any new business without some investment capital, then the odds of success are much lower than with someone who has capital to invest in his or her business. The principals that apply to building your financial practice are the same as those that apply in any other start-up business.

You have to think of the value of a client and what you should spend to acquire a client.

What is the value of a client?

Let's look at a client that has $500,000 to invest. Let's say that your management fee is 0.75%, not including any insurance or other products. This client is worth at the very least $3,750 per year. So over the course of ten years you would earn $37,500. When you add market appreciation, that number can grow even higher. But we will leave market appreciation out because the Trusted Advisor realizes that nobody actually makes money in the market! (Sorry Peter, I just had to throw that in there!)

So over a ten-year period, you will have to decide what the cost should be. I would argue that at a minimum it should be one year's commission. If you analyze all the investment that goes into starting a new business, you will find that that is an extremely low number. Strangely enough, you will rarely find a new advisor who understands the value of a client.

SEARCH ENGINE OPTIMIZATION

The process of improving the quality and quantity of visitors to a website via "organic" or "natural" search (as opposed to pay-per-click marketing) is called search engine optimization, or simply SEO.

Many people believe that SEO can be done by simply changing around their website's content, adding more content, adding meta tags and other simple adjustments to their site. While these components are important, they are a small fraction of what needs to be done. After all, if there was some magic formula that could be incorporated on your website, then everybody could easily do it and we would all be number one in the search engines. Obviously we cannot all be number one.

So how do the search engines work?

At the risk of oversimplifying, I will ask you to think of the Internet as one giant web of websites linking to each other, hence the name World Wide Web. Google and other search engines build algorithms that try to calculate which website is more important than another. In the case of Google, a page rank is assigned to each site in its index. Google essentially uses each site that is linking to your site as a vote for your site. Some votes are worth more than others depending on the page rank of the linking site. Links from sites of the same category as your site are far more important then links from sites of different categories. So don't think that because a site has a high page rank it will automatically do wonders for your site, because unless it is also a financial site it will not likely do much at all. For example, getting a link from your friend's popular video game store to your financial planning site will probably be completely discounted by the search engines.

Here is an outline of a basic search engine optimization plan.

Keyword Selection

Keyword selection is very important. The more common the keyword, the greater the competition and the harder it is to compete for that keyword. For example, if you choose the keyword "financial advisor", as of this writing Google reports 8,870,000 results in Google.com and 1,100,000 in Google.ca. So the competition is stiff. However, it is still possible if you want it badly enough. My site <www.professionalreferrals.ca> is currently ranked #36 in Google.com and ranked #6 in Google.ca for "financial advisor". For the keyword "financial planning", I rank #1 in Google.ca. So it is possible. It just takes a lot of time and money.

It is far easier to choose keywords like "financial advisor in Markham", and (assuming that your business is in Markham) this keyword phrase is likely to generate a much better prospect for you. Your entire site needs to be focused around your core keywords, so it is very important to put time into choosing the right keywords.

Do your research. There are many paid and free tools that will help you uncover secondary search phrases that can bring substantial traffic to your site. These tools can estimate the search volume and competitiveness of a phrase.

Consider phrases that are less competitive but still have a decent search volume. Don't get too excited if your site is number one in Google for a long phrase like "financial planning expert and sushi eater". It will never bring a visitor to your site! If you add this phrase to an indexed Google page I can pretty much guarantee you that you will be number one because you will be the only site with that phrase. However, if you add the phrase "financial advisor in downtown Toronto", I would bet that you could probably do an inexpensive campaign like the one that I am outlining in this chapter and add some quality visitor traffic to your site.

A few months after you implement your optimization strategy, be sure to analyze your results. Google offers Google Analytics for free, which is likely all you will ever need for website analysis. Keep an eye on what terms people are using to come to your site. You might get one visitor reaching your site for a term like "financial advisor Toronto". If you look through Google's search results, you might find that you rank all the way down at #45 for that term and someone happened to go that far down the results to find you. Take that keyword and optimize for it. Use the tips in this chapter to focus on that term because you can likely improve on any result with a little effort and lift your pages up, bringing many more visitors.

Domain Name

Choosing a domain name is an important part of your overall search engine optimization strategy. Putting your targeted keywords in your domain name is very important although not always possible. "FinancialAdvisor.ca" is a great name but I am sure it is taken. There are other things you can do, like add your initials to the domain name. For me it might be GWFinancialAdvisor.ca. It is important to take care when choosing a domain name because if you ever have to change it you will lose all the links and history that you have acquired with Google. Try to use a short and memorable domain name. A name that is brandable and memorable can go a long way.

Content

When Google visits your site for inclusion or an update of its index it is the words that Google is looking for. So it goes without saying the content of your website is very important. You need to post high quality content on your site. You need to be the expert on the topics that you specialize in.

Long before your site will become #1 for financial planning, it will likely start to attract visitors on more niche topics such as "estate planning with a disabled child". You may not have optimized for that key phrase but it just happened to be in an article on your site. Tip: always monitor your web logs for key phrases. You might find that you already come up for a keyword phrase on the third page of the results. With a little bit of fine tuning using the tips I give you in this chapter, you may be able to improve your placement enough to get on the first page and generate yourself a few extra prospects a month from one keyword.

On-page Optimization

When writing your articles, keep these things in mind:

- **Title**: Use keywords in your title but don't overdo it. A shorter title tends to work better than a really long title.
- **H1 header tag**: Use similar keywords that you used in the page title. This helps reinforce the title.
- **H2 or H3 sub-header tags**: Use a few descriptive sub-headings above your paragraphs. This really helps readability without appearing like it was written for search engines. Be sure to add variations of the core keywords that you are targeting.
- **Bullet points:** Use bulleted lists and bold face to break up the text.
- **Write to be read:** Always write an article that people are going to want to read. Do not try to write articles that are going to fool the search engines because you are never going to fool the search engines. I will focus on this in more detail later but for now I will just say that what you do to your website is a very small part of search engine optimization.

Site-Wide Optimization

Your home page is just the start of an SEO plan. But your site is or should go much deeper than just your home page. Odds are that when a visitor comes to your site he or she will not come directly to your home page. He or she will more likely arrive at a page on your site due to a keyword combination that Google matches to the visitor's search and returns your site in the results.

Here are some tips on optimizing your site's structure:

- Use text navigation. Fancy JavaScript menus look flashy but they add little to the user's experience and objective. If visitors to your site do not find what they are looking for in seconds, they will click the back button and be gone forever! Also, Google and other search engines need to be able to "crawl" your site, and JavaScript navigations tend to make it harder for the search engine robots to do so.

- Guide your visitors around your site. Most likely, the objective of your website is to generate business. If you are going to get your visitors to perform an action, whether it be picking up the phone and calling you, filling out a contact form, providing an e-mail address to download a newsletter or downloading a white paper, you need to guide them to that action. Do not assume they are going to search for it. Adding descriptive links that are relevant within your articles is key. For example: you have an article on fee-based financial planning. Within the article you might make a reference to a research paper you have on the benefits and trends in financial planning available for download and a link to a page (*i.e.*, landing page) that requires readers to fill out their contact details and any other information you would like to know about them. Note: if you are going to make downloads available, then put links back to your website within the document. Guide the readers back to the various parts of your website that are going to lead to an action. Your pdfs might be forwarded to another reader and you'd like to get their information as well.
- Use simple "breadcrumb" navigation. Example: Home page > Level 1 > Level 2 > Current Page. This allows the user to quickly navigate your site and also allows search engines to easily understand the structure of the site.
- Use sitemaps to submit to the search engines. Sitemaps tell the search engines the location of all of your content so their "spiders" can easily index your site.
- Try to update your content as often as possible. Become an expert on your areas of expertise and post regularly, even a couple of times a week if you have the time. Content is king and the more high quality content you provide, the more likely it is that Google will pick up on your site as an authority and lift you up in the search engine results.

Link Building

The text, layout and structure of your website are important, but they are only the start. World Wide Web gets its name from the fact that it is a web of interlinking websites that are all connected in some way.

Search engine results are formulated from a very advanced and complex algorithm that analyzes the network. Sites are ranked on importance and relevance, which is determined not only by the content on your site but by the amount of links to your site from other related sites on the Internet.

It is paramount that you actively pursue links to your site. Here are some useful link-building tips:

- Make sure you produce content that other webmasters in your niche will want to link to. Be the expert.
- When possible, try to get the keywords that you have chosen to optimize for in the link text that is linking to your pages. Maybe offer the html code on your site so that other webmasters can just cut and paste it into their pages, giving you more control over the link text. Example: add a link to this article. Simply cut and paste this code on your page: <ahref=http://www.yourwebsite.com/pdflandingoage.htlml> Fee-based financial planning report</a>.
- Vary the text in your link text. It is important that links to your website look natural to the search engines. It does not look natural if every link to your site has the exact same text. Change it up every so often. Add other words to your site that might help you rank well on secondary phrases. For example: primary phrase "Fee based financial planner"; secondary phrase "Fee based financial planner in Toronto" or "Toronto Financial Planner". See the keyword research section for more information on choosing keyword phrases to optimize for.
- Submit to relevant directories. There are many directories free and paid that you can submit your site to. Dmoz and Yahoo (paid) are very important for starters. Do a Google search for <your keywords> + <add URL> to find directories in your niche.
- Exchange links with other websites. Other webmasters are more than willing to trade links with you in order to get links for their own site. Keep it relevant. It's not about getting just any link; it is about getting relative links.
- Issue press releases with links to your site. If you are paying to issue a press release, make sure that your PR person posts the press release on the Internet, and have active html links in the press release. A non-html link does nothing for your website.
- Participate in online forums. Find out what people are concerned about and help them with an informative response. Add a link to a relevant article on your site. Don't just spam forums with links to

your site. Become a valuable resource to the forum and you will reap rewards.

- Whenever possible, try to get links to your internal pages, not just your home page.
- Try to come up with valuable tools, such as unique calculators, *etc.*, that others might want to link to.

Landing Pages

A landing page is the page on your site that a visitor is taken to, or "lands on" upon clicking your ad on the search engine. The sole purpose of your site is for you to find clients, and if you are going to generate potential clients then you need quality landing pages that encourage your visitors to take an action. An action can be picking up the phone and calling you, filling out an online form to request you to contact them or providing personal information to gain access to a download or other online content.

Guide your visitors to your landing pages. Every page on your site should have a link to the appropriate landing page that will encourage your visitors to take an action.

Conversion rate optimization is the continual process of making your website and landing page generate more results from your visitor traffic. I have tested hundreds of different landing page techniques, and here is the best practices outline I have come up with through years of trial and error:

- A/B testing is extremely important. Rotate your landing pages and test various components that affect conversions. The easiest and quickest way to test your landing pages is through paid search listings. We will focus on the paid search in the next section. Following are the main components that you want to test and optimize for. Change one or two components at a time while keeping the rest of the page static so you can pinpoint what changes are improving your conversions:
    - *Headline* — This is the first line that your visitors will read on the page. This is the biggest opportunity for improvement on the page. Use headlines that clearly state the biggest benefit of your offer. Consider the entire flow of your site. If your leading link from another page captured visitors' interest, then you really want to follow through with the headline to solidify that interest. Tell them exactly what they can get on your landing page.

- *Call to action* — This is your offer encouraging a user to take an action. Example: "Call now and schedule your free wealth management consultation."
- *First paragraph* — This is your lead and it must be powerful. Outline the key benefits. Make it clear and concise and not overly wordy. Try bulleting a summary of benefits to taking the action.
- *Images* — The images you use can have a large impact on your conversion ratios. Try images that relate to your benefits. Try captions under your images that strengthen the overall objective of the landing page. Experiment with image location on the page.

BLOGS

A great way to get a website up and going and get traffic quickly is to start a blog. You can get free blog software such as that at <Wordpress.org> or you can set up a blog at <Blogspot.com>. As you update your blog, your posts are syndicated through RSS feeds around the world.

PAID SEARCH

The quickest way to start getting traffic and generating leads is through a paid search. The main paid search programs are MSN Adcenter, Google Adwords and Yahoo Search Marketing. There are smaller, tier-2 paid search programs, but they tend to drive less quality traffic to your site, so I don't recommend using them in the early stages of getting to know pay-per-click marketing.

Pay-per-click (PPC) marketing is probably the most important development in marketing in this decade. Why? First, you are only marketing to people who are looking for your service right now. Second, you are only paying when they respond by clicking through to your site. Third, pricing is determined by an ongoing real-time auction based on true market values.

As a financial advisor, there are very few marketing tactics that are truly quantifiable. PPC marketing and pay-per-lead services like AdvisorWorld.com are quantifiable. With the tools available through any of the major PPC providers, you can easily track conversions and calculate exactly how much you are paying per lead. From the conversion data you can easily extrapolate how many leads you close in order to determine your cost of acquiring each new client. You can then adjust your budgets to balance cost versus volume of new business.

The downside to PPC marketing is the competition. It is not as easy as writing a few ads and picking keywords that drive relevant traffic to your site. Many of your competitors have already found out about the value of PPC marketing and are very experienced online marketers. They have studied conversion rates and ad copy and can generate traffic less expensively then you can unless you follow the tips I am about to present.

Google, MSN and Yahoo behave in more or less the same way, but I am going to focus on Google Adwords due to the fact that they control a large share of the search traffic available.

The concept is fairly simple. You can join the Google Adwords program for free and define a budget and have your ads up and running very quickly. I recommend starting out slowly and getting comfortable with the program before raising your budgets. Mistakes in PPC marketing can be costly.

When you register your first PPC account, Google will guide you through the process of setting up a campaign. The process is relatively simple. You create a campaign that contains your geographical settings and other preferences. Then you add an adgroup, write your ads and choose your keywords. Sounds easy enough, doesn't it?

Guide to Setting up Your First Campaign

There are many resources on the Internet that will help you with the basics for setting up a campaign. I am just going to focus on some of the things that you should be aware of that might speed up the learning curve a little, particularly keeping in mind aspects that are unique to the financial industry.

- **Geo-targeting:** All of the top-tier PPC programs have extensive geo-targeting functionality. In Google, you can target your audience pretty much anyway you like. You can focus countrywide or on a province, city or even a small radius around your address. Geo-targeting is made possible by search engines looking up the IP address information of the user. If the user is within your targeted area and your bid is high enough, then your ad will display. Geo-targeting is not 100% accurate. Sometimes an IP address might be routed through an area other than that in which the person is located because he or she may be going through a proxy or a business network. The smaller an area you are targeting, the less accurate the geo-targeting will be. But on an overall basis, I find it works fairly well.

- **Budget:** You can control your daily spending on all of your campaigns in the campaign settings. Setting this amount will ensure that you never spend more than you plan to because one of your ads received a higher number of impressions than you had anticipated.
- **Advertising Networks:** Google has three main networks that it uses to display your ads. You can choose which networks you would like your ads to be displayed on:
  - Google search engines — These are the sponsored listings on Google's main search engines, *e.g.*, <google.com>, <google.ca>, *etc.*
  - Google search partners — AOL, Ask.com and Earthlink are all search engines that use Google-sponsored ads.
  - Google content network — This is comprised of sites that are part of the Google adsense program that get paid to display ads by Google. Google analyzes the pages of the websites and when the content is relevant to the key word that you are bidding on they may display your ads.

Best Practice Tip: All of the above networks are effective, and all of them will work to generate you quality traffic and, hopefully, leads that you can turn into profitable business. But I am going to share with you a tip that only PPC markets have learned from years of experience. Create one campaign for each network, each with the same keywords and ads. Why? Because this will allow you to separate your bidding and tracking and narrow down exactly what is going on with your campaigns. If Google happens to bring on a poorer performing partner search engine, you will be able to see your results decline and lower your bid on the partner sites, while leaving your bids alone where they are working.

There is less competition on the content network because many advertisers do not know how to make it work. I would recommend starting with a bid that is about 25% of your search bids. Then follow the results and impressions, and experiment with your bids. You will find that your click-through-rates are far lower than the search network rates. This is due to the fact that people who see your ad may not actually be looking for your service specifically, but while they are visiting another website your ad just happens to catch their attention. With a little experimentation, you might find that you can generate leads for a lot less than you would on the highly competitive search networks.

Adgroups

After you have created a campaign, the next step is to add an adgroup to that campaign. Adgroups are groups of ads with associated keywords. Your ad will appear when a user performs a search of one of your keywords.

The main type of ad that you will create is a text ad. Simply put, a text ad is just three lines of text with a link back to your site.

This is where it gets interesting. By writing great relevant and compelling ads, you can save yourself a lot of money and beat the competition out of a lot of clicks.

In Google and other PPC search engines, it is not just about what you spend that decides how your ad will be ranked but it is about the quality of your ads.

For example: if your ad has a click-through rate (CTR) of 0.5% and your competitor has an ad with a CTR of 5%, then his ad is being clicked on ten times more than your ad and, therefore, you are going to have to spend ten times as much for Google to make the same money off your account. So, wisely, Google has come up with a quality score, which is a combination of a number of factors. CTR is probably the most important factor in determining your quality score. You are also ranked on the relevancy of your landing page, the relevancy of the keywords in your adgroup to the ads as a whole and the historical performance of your adgroup.

See the section on optimizing your campaign structure, below, for learning more on generating the most amount of clicks and leads for the least amount of money.

Keywords

In each adgroup, you can choose any number of keywords that you wish to trigger your ads. I would advise you to keep the list short and relevant. Small groups of keywords in each adgroup will perform much better than a huge list of phrases thrown together. There are many tools available for a keyword research and I strongly advise you to take full advantage of them. One of the best tools for researching keywords is built right into your Google Adwords account. Google Keyword is an excellent research tool. You simply enter a keyword and it will return a list of related keywords and give you the monthly search volume that you can expect for each keyword.

Keyword Matching Options

There are four different keyword-matching options, each specifying a different way for a keyword to interact with search queries. With some options, you'll enjoy more ad impressions; with others, you'll get fewer impressions (but potentially more targeted clicks). By applying the appropriate matching options to your keywords, you can best meet your return on investment (ROI) goals.

Your options are as follows:

- **Broad Match:** This is the default option. If your adgroup contained the keywords "*financial advisor*", your ad would be eligible to appear when a user's search query contained "*financial*" and "*advisor*", in any order, and along with other terms such as "*financial advisor Toronto*". Your ads could also show for singular/plural forms, synonyms, and other relevant variations. For example, your ad might show on "*financial advisor*" or "*financial advisors*".
- **Phrase Match:** If you enter your keyword in quotation marks, as in "*financial advisor*", your ad would be eligible to appear when a user searches on the phrase "*financial advisor*", in this order, and possibly with other terms before or after the phrase. For example, your ad could appear for the query "*independent financial advisor*" but not for "*advisor in financial service*". Phrase match is more targeted than broad match, but more flexible than exact match.
- **Exact Match:** If you surround your keywords in brackets, such as [financial advisor], your ad would be eligible to appear when a user searches for the specific phrase "financial advisor", in this order, and without any other terms in the query. For example, your ad wouldn't show for the query "*independent financial advisor*" or "*financial advisors*". Exact match is the most targeted option. Although you won't receive as many impressions with exact match, you'll likely enjoy the most targeted clicks — users searching for your exact keyword typically want precisely what your business has to offer.
- **Negative Keyword:** If your keyword is "*financial advisor*" and you add the negative keyword "*-salaries*", your ad will not appear when a user who searches on "*financial advisor salaries*" is someone likely just researching potential jobs! Negative keywords are especially useful if your account contains lots of broad-matched keywords. It's a good idea to add any irrelevant keyword variations you see in a Search Query Performance Report or the Keyword Tool as a negative keyword.

Optimizing Your Campaign Structure

Below are two examples of the wrong way and the right way to structure a campaign.

The Wrong Way

This is an example of how *not* to structure a campaign:

Campaign Name: Financial Services Ontario

Adgroup Name: Financial Ads

Example Ad: Financial Service Company
Wealth management and life insurance
Top quality advice.
www.wealthmanagementsite.com

The destination is your website's home page.

Keywords: Life insurance
Financial advisors
Mortgage brokers
Financial planning
Investing
Stocks
Mutual funds
Financial advice
Term insurance
Estate planning
Finance
Investment advisor
Financial consultant
Tax planning

Potential Problems

- **Ad:** The ad is too vague. It does not speak directly to the keywords that the user is searching for. There is no real benefit to the user.
- **Landing Page URL**: By simply going to your homepage instead of a well-written landing page, you can count on a very low conversion rate. You need to land on a page that has a clearly laid out call to action. You might try giving something first, like a downloadable e-book.
- **Keywords**: The keyword list is far too broad. You cannot write an ad or a landing page that focuses on all of these keywords.

The Right Way

This is an example of how *to* structure a campaign:

Campaign Name: Financial Services Ontario

Adgroup Name: Financial Advisor

Example Ad: Find a financial advisor
Toronto-based financial advisor
Free consultation available
www.WealthManagementSite.com

The destination is a well-written landing page on the benefits of dealing with you and/or your organization. I recommend having a form that users can quickly fill out to provide their contact information. If you have a financial planning guide or other material, then offer it for download after they fill out the form.

Keywords: Financial advisor
Find a financial advisor
Financial planner
Financial advisor Toronto
Etc.

Successful Strategies

- **Ad:** Write an ad that is directly relevant to the keyword being searched. If your user is searching for "financial advisor", then a great way to get him or her to click on your ad is to have a headline called "find a financial advisor". If he or she is searching for life insurance, then have a headline that is about life insurance. Broad campaigns and ads are not effective. The name of the game is click-through rates, and for better CTR you need to focus on the concerns of the user.
- **Display URL Tip**: Tests have proven that an ad with Caps in the domain will receive a better CTR than a domain in all lower case. Caps make the domain stand out and easier to read than the other ads.
- **Keyword Groups:** This is a much more targeted list than the previous list. I might even just target financial advisor and make another adgroup for financial planner. If I wanted to target a fee-based financial planner, I would create a campaign just for that. The user is not looking for just a financial planner, he or she is looking for a fee-based financial planner. Target, target, target.

The difference between these two examples will equate to about 90% difference in cost. It pays to put the effort into learning PPC marketing.

Bidding Strategy

You can adjust your bids at the keyword level or you can simply set a default bid for the entire adgroup. I recommend adding keywords and constantly adjusting each keyword bid to get the best possible performance.

After your campaign is active you will see your average position in the campaign reports.

It is not necessary to always try to have your ad in the number one position. In fact, I have found that the number one position does not convert as well as lower positions, likely due to the fact that the further users look down through the results, the more motivated they are to find what they are looking for and the more likely they are to convert into a lead.

The difference between the costs per acquisition is dramatic. If it costs $2 per click to maintain the number one position, it might only cost $0.75 to maintain position number 7. If the conversion rate was 3% in the number one position then the average cost per conversion is $33. Alternatively, if the number 7 position yields a 7% conversion rate, then the average cost per conversion would be about $14. One thing you need to be aware of is that if you are further down in the list you will receive far fewer clicks and likely fewer conversions. So you have to decide the best approach for your business while keeping ROI and objectives in consideration.

Best Practices Tip:When you are first starting your campaign, you will have no history with Google so it will likely be slow in displaying your ads and require a higher bid than other more established advertisers. I recommend bidding high and fine-tuning your ads to achieve the best possible CTR. Once you have established a high CTR, you can lower your bids and likely maintain your position.

You can fine-tune your ads by adding multiple ads, and Google will rotate them automatically to find the best performing ones. Keep the ad with the highest CTR and delete the rest. Add new ads with the intention of trying to outperform the best performing ad. This will help you squeeze the best performance possible out of your campaigns.

MANAGING LEADS

When you start receiving leads from your marketing efforts, it is important that you deal with those leads effectively in order to maximize your efforts and ad spending At AdvisorWorld.com, we have generated thousands of leads from the millions of visitors that have visited our sites. Below are some of the best practices of our more successful advisors in following up Internet-generated leads.

Promptness in Contact

Speed in making the initial contact with the client is important for three reasons:

(1) It demonstrates a superior level of customer service on your part. Clients are often strongly impressed with a response that is quicker than they expected.

(2) The client may have made enquiries elsewhere; a prompt contact increases the chance that you will be the first advisor he or she hears from.

(3) The client will be more receptive to you as an advisor if his or her financial concern is still uppermost in his or her mind, as it would be with an immediate contact.

Understand the Client's Needs

Each lead carries some information about what service or product the client is looking for. Make sure you take notice and make reference to whatever information is available when you make the initial contact. Since the enquiry came through the Internet, the client is no doubt looking for a quick as well as an effective solution to his or her needs.

Sell Yourself First

People may be looking for a particular product, service or mortgage rate via the Internet, but ultimately it's a human they want to deal with — not a machine. With that in mind, be aware that whether or not you close the deal may hinge solely on one thing: the extent to which the client *likes* you and *trusts* you. Likeability and trustworthiness are factors to work on from the initial contact onwards. They should be the guiding principles with which you develop the relationship with the client. They are at least as important as all of your professional attributes taken in total.

Follow-up Communication

The most successful advisors are not reluctant to follow up with clients after the initial contact and before the deal is done. Keep in mind that other advisors may be in the picture; alacrity on your part in the initial contact and subsequent follow-ups will make it less likely the client will seek a solution elsewhere. Consider all methods of communication at your disposal. Successful advisors will utilize e-mail, phone and post when dealing with potential clients.

Since the request originally came via the Internet, the client is likely to be comfortable with e-mail communication. The advantage of an e-mail is that it provides an opportunity for a more comprehensive description of yourself and your services than is often the case with an initial voice contact via telephone. Consider an e-mail of your professional profile as part of your standard follow-up strategy.

Client Relationship Strategy

Put together a disciplined process for dealing with lead prospects, from the initial contact onwards. Use e-mails and the post to send product/services brochures after initial contacts. Don't hesitate to advertise the full range of your services, not just the specific solution the client may be seeking. As well, regard each lead as a permanent contact, regardless of whether the sale is achieved. If an amicable first impression is made, a potential client will usually not mind being regularly updated via newsletter or similar e-mails advising of product offerings, financial service opportunities, current mortgage or borrowing rates and the like. Remember, if managed properly, a lead is a lead forever.

Pitfalls to Avoid

Some common mistakes that account for failure in converting a lead to a client are discussed below.

Initial Contact Errors

Among the most common errors are the following:

- Failing to contact soon enough. Make every effort to establish initial contact as soon as the lead is received.
- Leaving poor phone answer messages. Your message should be such that the client actually looks forward to hearing from you again.

- Not calling back if failed to make contact in the first attempt. Don't rely on the client calling you.
- Calling at the wrong time. Notice that many leads will include a "best time to call" and "best number to call". They are there for a reason.
- Neglecting alternate means of contact. All leads will have an e-mail address as well as a phone number. The e-mail address provides an opportunity for a first contact when there is failure to reach the client by phone.

Moving Too Quickly

Recognize that the initial stages of the sale will be conducted remotely, via phone and in some cases by e-mail correspondence. The client may balk if you suggest a face-to-face meeting too early in the relationship. The initial contacts are the opportunity for you to sell yourself to the client.

Not Understanding Lead Generation

They're leads — not guarantees. Think about it. If a sale were a certainty, you'd have paid much more than you did for it. Some advisors seem to operate on the assumption that they can simply "show up and collect", and are perplexed when they fail. Every lead is a possibility only. Each lead requires a successful sales effort to close. Understand as well that you will not convert every lead into a sale. That's just the name of the game. Referral companies do nothing to pre-screen enquiries they send. Anyone with a computer can fill out a form, and the fact is that some leads are warmer than others. Successful advisors will have a conversion ratio they aim for that will vary depending upon the products or services they offer. Look at the big picture. Consider what your closing rate has to be in order to make the lead service pay for itself.

Unrealistic Expectations and Understanding ROI

In many businesses it can take years to break even on your investment. It is important that the purchase of leads makes sense with your budget and business plan goals. We believe that you should work with a closing average of 10%–30%. Calculate the various scenarios and track your results. Ultimately, only you can decide what ROI works for you, but here are some questions you may wish to consider.

If after one year of generating or purchasing leads you only broke even, does it still make sense to continue? Keep in mind, *a new client can provide an income stream for life and can also be a great source of referrals.*

CONCLUSION

When considering Internet marketing, I think the most important factor is that it is quantifiable. Every component can be tracked: How many visitors became leads? How many leads became clients? Your ad copy and articles can focus on the exact client you are looking for. Campaigns can be constantly fine-tuned and adjusted to become even more profitable. Get instant feedback on your ideas.

Once these Internet strategies have been adopted, the following results can be expected:

- **Save money.** Other marketing approaches can be extremely expensive. Hiring and managing a marketing staff is a huge headache.
- **Save time.** Internet marketing is largely an automated process. Once you get it up and running, the process is working for you 24 hours a day.
- **Make money.** High net worth clients use the Internet. They rarely just take someone's word for it; they go to look for an expert online. And everyone wants to deal with an expert. Be that expert.

Use an expert! If you are looking to get a campaign done quickly and want to use a proven method, visit <http://www.AdvisorWorld.com>. AdvisorWorld can find you the exact prospects that you are looking for. Through various programs, you can get your message out to millions of potential clients.

CHAPTER 9

HOW TO CATCH A WHALE!

Gordon Berger

Overview

Every professional who desires to become the Trusted Advisor to the extremely wealthy often ask themselves: where will I find these clients? What types of services are going to attract these clients? And how do I retain these clients over the long term? In this chapter, Gordon Berger, originally a public accountant, who has been in the financial services industry since 1969 and is a member of the "Quarter Century Club", a division of the Million Dollar Round Table (MDRT), and is a life member of "Top of the Table", reserved for the top 400 insurance agents worldwide, shares his insights on how to catch a whale from nearly 40 years of experience of doing just that.

Learning Objectives

By the end of this chapter you will:

- understand the value of investing in your career, social network and professional support platform to attract, sell to and service the ultra-financially successful while enjoying a satisfying career as a Trusted Advisor.

One might think that selling is a God-given gift. I used to also think so until I looked back over all the years of my career and the trials and tribulations of becoming a successful professional salesman. What I realized is that a successful path begins early on in one's life, generally in lower grade school. Shockingly, not everyone is cut out for a life in the sales arena; you have to be tough as nails.

My first manager once told me that it takes nine "no's" to get one "yes", and looking back, I realize that these numbers are totally accurate at the beginning of your career until you hone your skills and gain experience. The other rule of the road is that at the beginning of your career, you must make 20 sales approaches to get three appointments to get one sale. It sounds crazy, but it's true. Generally, these are the rules of the road and don't vary much from person to person. The other thing I noticed was that salespeople who ultimately turn into super producers start selling before they acquire much product knowledge or sales language. I remember my first $1 million sale. I secured an appointment to see a wealthy individual and before going to the appointment, I asked my manager at the time what I should try to sell him. He told me that if the prospect asked how much insurance he should have, I should tell him $1 million and not a penny less. That's exactly what I did, and he ended up buying $1 million dollars worth of insurance, which at the time was a huge sale. Nevertheless, the attrition rate is horrendous in the first two to three years. So the real question is: how does one improve the odds of success and shorten the time path to success? Another question that may be contemplated is: what does success mean to you and to the people around you?

What I've noticed over nearly 40 years in the industry is that there is no short cut to success. Overnight successes are usually finished overnight. In the next short while, I will endeavour to share with you some of the ingredients that are required to achieve long-term success.

Just before I move on, I would like to tell you a story about Joe. While walking along the street, Joe was hit by a Mack truck. The next thing he knew, he was standing in front of St. Peter at the Pearly Gates. He didn't have a clue how and why he arrived there. St. Peter then addressed him and told him that he was now dead, and explained how it happened. He went on to tell Joe that he knew that Joe had been a religious and pious man, and therefore he could get a pass directly to Heaven. Shockingly he also told Joe that he had a choice as to whether he went to Heaven or Hell.

Joe said to St. Peter, "Why would anyone want to go to Hell?", to which St. Peter replied, "Some people like to compare different options." Joe thought for a while and asked St. Peter if he decided to go to Hell, could he change his mind if he didn't like it. St. Peter told him that he could have a one-day pass, after which time he could make his decision. So off Joe went, climbing down this endless ladder towards Hell. Eventually, he came upon the cast steel doors which seemed to be the way to his ultimate end. Without wasting any time, he pounded on the doors as hard as he could, not knowing what was on the other side. Instantly, the doors started to open to reveal the most remarkable scenery Joe had ever seen in his whole life: a pristine bright blue lake with visions around the lake of every guilty and crude desire that Joe had ever had. Approaching him was a well-dressed gentleman who reached out to shake Joe's hand to welcome him to Hell. Joe immediately told the gentleman that he was expecting Hell to be something very different, that the devil would be as scary as could be. Joe stayed for a while and then decided to return to the Pearly Gates. Up the ladder he went, and ended up right in front of St. Peter. He told St. Peter that he couldn't believe how wonderful Hell was, and that he probably would live out his days there. St. Peter suggested that he take a day-pass to Heaven just to compare. He did, and shortly thereafter, returned to tell St. Peter that it was really nice, but boring in comparison. St. Peter warned Joe that this would be his final decision. Joe's decision had been made and off he went down the ladder.

There again were the vast steel doors ahead of him. He pounded on the doors, just like the day before, but this time the doors started to open, and steam and fire started emanating from the opening. All Joe could see was fire and brimstone, and bubbling pools of greenish-brown lava where once the beautiful lake was, and even more shocking was the image approaching him.

Unprepared, Joe was confronted by this scary creature with horns coming out of his head, and a tongue. Joe was shocked, and looked at the devil, and with surprise written all over his eyes said, "I don't understand; when I was here yesterday, everything was different! The pristine blue water and the visions of pleasure and satisfaction that I saw all around me are all gone! What happened from two days ago till now?"

The devil looked at him and in a very deep but hollow voice answered, "When you were here two days ago you were a prospect. Now you are a client!!!!!"

Unfortunately, many people tell the same story about their advisors. I promise you that if you follow my path as I will explain it in the following pages, you will experience a wonderful and full life, growing your business and enjoying the success that few in the world achieve. This is only my opinion, based on training hundreds of people in the art of the sale and, of course, looking back at my career to determine the formula for success. I promise to share with you my "seven habits for success" at the end of this chapter.

IN THE BEGINNING

In looking back, I wish that when I was young, I would have had a role model or mentor to help sculpt my life path. Recently, I have had the opportunity to work with about 30 different success-driven children every week for the last eight weeks at a summer camp called "Camp Millionaire". Looking into the children's hungry eyes, I was motivated to share with them what they needed to do, starting immediately, to ensure that they would achieve their goals in life. After about five minutes of questioning, I realized that even though these children were forgoing the fun of real day camp, they had never thought about long-term goals, achievement and success, so I decided to use the allotted time to assist them in learning the importance of long-term goals in their planning process. I was quick to tell them that planning can never start too early in their lives. I am sure that we have all heard someone in our lives say, "If you fail to plan, you plan to fail." Those who choose to think this is merely a trite statement will most likely experience an extreme dose of reality.

ONWARD AND UPWARD

What's interesting about my findings over all these years is that most people who turn out to be successful in life enjoy a significant amount of commonality, certain growth experiences and adventures that aid in maturing their entrepreneurial path to supreme achievement. The true entrepreneur is born with a zest to accomplish the impossible without fear of failure. Salespeople are the truest form of entrepreneur. They wake up in the morning, get in their boats and go fishing. If they happen to catch fish, they eat, and if not, they don't.

Given all this information, the conclusion to be drawn is that many people know how to find fish but don't know how to catch them. They build wonderful relationships but do not have the gift of conversion of these relationships to money-making activities, *i.e.*, "how to catch a whale".

That's where people like me come into the picture.

We are the definitive whalers who are armed with nuclear harpoons. "You find them, we will land them, filet them, pack them, sell them and make a profit." A veritable one-stop shop. However, this particular whaling ship took a lifetime to build.

I never realized that sleep-over camp would play an important role in my future life. It gave me the opportunity to meet hundreds of children who later would turn out to be doctors, dentists, lawyers, accountants and business gurus.

I spent the first of many boring years in accounting, even though I always knew I would never be an accountant. It was, however, a great stepping stone and totally required in order for me to walk the life path I chose. After graduating, I never practised accounting a single day in my life. After leaving accounting, I worked in the land development and building business for four years with some very successful tycoons, trying my hardest to find out the secrets that made them so successful. I then took all the lessons that I learned and set up my own business, which I grew for three years, and ended up selling to a very large company in the same industry.

"The Real Beginning"

So in my mid-twenties when all my friends were just starting out, I was thinking of retirement. I had sold my business and had enough capital to allow me to think that I would never have to work again.

That didn't last long ... along came my insurance agent, who happened to be an amazing broker, who successfully, after much encouragement, talked me into becoming an insurance agent. He explained to me that I had everything going for me: a network, a financial background, business experience and tenacity, all the ingredients that would ensure my success. I never looked back.

It proved to be the perfect business for me: exciting, people-oriented, creative and rewarding, with lots of hard work.

Strategically, my first major decision was to hone my business to work as a team with accountants. I realized that accountants have something that is extremely difficult to achieve in the sales world: major credibility with their clients. I figured out that instead of fighting to create this with every potential prospect, if I worked with accountants and their firms, I could achieve a long-lasting relationship with an army of professional people. My task at hand was to figure out what accountants needed in order to feel comfortable with me. The funny thing was that because I was working with my kind, most accountants felt comfortable immediately and I too was extremely relaxed and comfortable.

So for the next 30 years or so, I spent a great deal of my time educating the accounting community and lawyers in everything from "the art of the sale" to our various strategies and anything else they needed to know about estate planning and insurance products and strategies. But that was just the beginning.

I realized that in order to be referable by lawyers and accountants, I had to set myself and my company apart from my competition. How was I to do that? All I had to do was to look in the mirror and ask myself what it was that I didn't like in working with other salespeople, and then go and create a set of rules that would make it easy to refer me to any client who needed my help.

I call these rules the "Seven Habits to Success" for any business or the seven "referability" habits. Anyone who follows these rules would be hard-pressed not to achieve success way beyond their imagination. So, in order, they are:

(1) The client always comes first!

(2) If you say you are going to do something, do it!
(3) If you start something, finish it!
(4) Do it on time!
(5) Do your personal best!
(6) Do it with service excellence!
(7) Always say "please" and "thank you"!

Can you imagine working with people who know that your work ethic and commitments are at the highest level and that you aspire to live by this set of rules, understanding that no one is perfect?

Building the Whaling Ship

In 1984, I was fortunate to meet the one person who changed my life in business: Dan Sullivan. He helped me to strategize my business development to be able to grow and survive in the high net worth/high net income marketplace.

Through careful planning, I built an organization made up of unique individuals each with a depth of knowledge in their particular areas, which allowed us to build an amazing team. These people have been associated with me for 10-20 years. It is because of them that we are capable of winning in most competitive situations. A team approach is mandatory in this day and age. Sales organizations require the ability to deliver unique ideas to the marketplace. This one strategy sets our organization apart from all others in this "commoditized" world we live in.

A Few War Stories

Several years ago, I was introduced to a wealthy individual who was said to be an extremely conservative investor. After approximately two years, he decided to invest in a tax strategy using life insurance as the investment engine. For three years, everything went perfectly and the strategy performed as promised. One day I got a call from him and he said to me that he had sent in his annual cheque and when he received his statement, the interest paid to him was lower than projected. Our team went into action immediately and determined that he did something that no client had ever done: he paid the deposit before being billed, and, consequently, the insurance company parked his money in a daily interest account at 1% instead of in the program at 5.5%. We quickly calculated the interest difference and I made out a personal cheque in the amount of $34.58, and had it driven over to his office. Within moments after receiving the cheque, he called me and asked what the cheque was for and I explained what he had done and that the cheque was meant to make up his lost interest. What happened next is every salesperson's dream. He asked me to come over to the office and bring papers to double his previous investment because of our habits for success. A lesson to be learned! Support your selling proposition.

A Discussion About "On Time"

Some years ago on a Monday, a prospect met with me and the referring salesman. After one hour, the prospect asked the salesman if we could give him a presentation with real pro formas and illustrations at the end of the week because he was extremely interested in making a decision. The salesman quickly said yes, no problem; the paperwork would be ready Friday. When I heard this, I interjected that it would be at the end of two weeks Friday. The prospect was a little mixed up and I explained that we were extremely busy and would attempt to comply with his request. When the prospect left, I met with the salesman and explained what had just happened. I asked the salesman how the prospect would feel if we actually delivered the package two weeks Friday. The salesman said that he thought the prospect would be happy with that.

I then went on to ask him what the prospect would think if we delivered the package one week earlier. He thought that the prospect would be extremely happy. Then I asked him what the prospect would think if we delivered the package on the Friday he wanted it. The salesman said that he would probably be ecstatic and that he would also consider the salesman to have underpromised and overdelivered; in other words, the salesman would be referable to all the prospect's friends.

I then said, "Let's consider the situation that would normally happen." The prospect asked for the package by Friday and the salesman agreed to deliver it on Friday.

If Friday came and went, and there was no package, what would the prospect think? The salesman said that he thought the prospect would be upset and would consider that we were no better than anyone else. I then asked him what his prospect would think of us if the package wasn't delivered by the next Friday, still one week earlier than I got him to agree on. The salesman thought that the prospect would be frustrated and would probably be hard pressed to buy anything from us. By the third week, there would be no prospect.

In this particular instance, we were able to meet with the prospect on the Friday he wanted and sold him one of the largest insurance policies ever sold in Canada, times two. The premium was $4.5 million a year for five years, and as a major surprise, his brother and partner bought the same program. "Do it on time."

Let Me Count the Ways

Moving on, I determined that I needed to expand my prospecting techniques beyond these amazing referrals. Diversification is always a good thing!

Over the years as I matured in the business, I became aware that developing business could be fun, that you could do great things for the community, working in charitable causes, working on high level boards, being active in sports, travelling, and finding many other enjoyable opportunities.

What kind of organizations could I be involved in that would allow me to create value for people less able than I, and what else could I spend time on that would position me to spend time "where the whales swim"?

I want to underline the fact that the charitable endeavours were done to aid those people less fortunate than my family. The fact is that there are many benevolent business people involved in these charities.

When I look back over the years, I accumulated volunteer time in many worthwhile organizations. I was President of the Kidney Foundation of Canada, Toronto Branch, and President of ORT Toronto, a worldwide organization supporting the education of 26,000 young adults in retraining and work rehabilitation in 60 countries. I also served on the Foundation Board of the Mount Sinai Hospital for several years, was Chairman of the Cash for Life Lottery funding five major charities in Toronto and finally supported my own charity, which buses 30 underprivileged children to a computer centre twice a week, feeds them dinner, usually pizza, and teaches them computer education and study skills, and combines that with a mentoring program which teaches teens to work with these children. At graduation, we present each child with a fully loaded computer to take home with them. Given that I never worked in charitable causes to advance my business, it has been amazing to look back and note all the amazing people I have met and worked with. Over the years, these people have been instrumental in helping me grow my business.

The Importance of a Résumé

Educational background and charitable activities are of extreme interest to potential clients. They want to know that your ethics and principles are at a very high standard. That isn't enough.

Through the years I built my résumé consistently by authoring or co-authoring books and looseleaf services, giving speeches, lecturing to business grads and holding study seminars for accountants. I wrote major books on practice management for accountants and lawyers, as well as planning books for human resource people and managing partners in corporations on topics such as corporate planning, employee benefits, insurance structures, and the like.

I have also written articles on tax for the December issue of Air Canada's magazine several years in a row; this issue had their largest readership.

I was a regular participant on money programs in Toronto over many years, for radio and television.

I wanted to make sure that when a whale came into my sights, I had a résumé that would instill confidence in my ability to deliver what I promised.

The Fun Part

Hopefully my peers in the investment advisory end of the business have many interests outside work. I, too, found that if your work is fun for you, it really isn't work. So where do the whales spend their time? Well, I found out that they fly airplanes out of private airports, boat out of marinas, vacation at cottages in the North Country, travel constantly for pleasure on planes, ships and trains, spend time in Europe and spend the winters in Florida, Phoenix and places generally south.

Given that I loved and aspired to do all of the above, I designed my life around all the things I loved to do: flying my own aircraft, diving, snow-skiing at a private club, golfing, playing tennis and serious boating in the great lakes out of an amazing marina full of the "rich and famous". When travelling, I have always made it a rule to stay in wonderful hotels and travel first class or business class.

How could life be better? The funny thing is that all of these interests allowed me to surround myself with people in my target market: people or corporations with annual incomes in excess of $1 million and capital investible assets in excess of $10 million.

The Name of the Game

The name of the game is taking all of this and turning it into a profitable business, delivering value ideas and implementing them to your target market.

One of my oldest friends, Dan Sullivan of the "Strategic Coach", one of the most successful Trusted Advisor practice management organizations, once told me to

"Find the sacred cow

Kill it

Sell the meat

Make a profit"

And that's exactly what I did.

In order to exist in this incredible marketplace, many rudiments have to be put together, just like a puzzle, to allow the strategy to work.

You require a service excellence platform made up of long-standing, loyal employees who are experts in their fields.

You require product knowledge, proprietary ideas and implementation strategies which will allow you to underpromise and therefore give you the opportunity to overperform.

You require an army of centres of influence and clients who totally believe in your ability to deliver unique services and intellectual capital so they will continue to send quality referrals to your company.

You must adopt and practise the "Seven Habits to Success" all the time.

And lastly, you must continue to expand your knowledge and capabilities to grow with your clients' needs. You can never let them outgrow you.

I could go on forever and maybe I should write a book. I love this business and hope all of you can get something from this chapter that will project you into the major leagues.

"If you think you can, you will. If you think you can't, you won't."

CHAPTER 10

DELIVERING EFFECTIVE SEMINARS

Peter J. Merrick

Overview

This chapter discusses the benefits of giving seminars to build your practice and the strategies necessary to become an effective seminar presenter. Learn how to gain wealthy clients by giving excellent presentations. Understand the power you have been given with your gift of speech.

Learning Objectives

By the end of this chapter, you should be able to:

- understand the value of becoming an effective public speaker to help grow your practice;
- learn the lessons to deliver effective IPP seminars;
- learn the strategies to turn public speaking engagements into consulting opportunities; and
- understand the power of our speech.

THE VALUE OF EFFECTIVE PUBLIC SPEAKING

Becoming a good public speaker is easier said than done. It has been said that many people at a funeral would rather be in the casket than delivering the eulogy!

When I first entered my career in the financial service industry in the early 1990s, I lucked upon a book on successful marketing strategies for the financial service industry, which quickly became my Bible. One of its main tenets to achieving success as a Trusted Advisor was to commit oneself to developing the art of delivering powerful and effective presentations.

These words have always resonated in my mind and have been my catalyst for wanting to learn how to speak comfortably in front of large groups and to effectively communicate my message on whatever the topic might be at the time. During my journey over the past 18 years, I have been fortunate to have had the opportunity to deliver over 400 workshops and seminars and teach in the Certified Financial Planning (CFP™), Certified Employee Benefit Specialist (CEBS), Certified Human Resources Professional (CHRP) and Certified General Accountant (CGA) designation programs. What I would like to share in this chapter are some of the lessons I have learned about public speaking to help you on your own journey. If you choose to become an effective public speaker, you will learn how delivering presentations can help you tap into new business opportunities when delivering seminars to potential clients and centres of influences.

HOW TO DELIVER AN EFFECTIVE SEMINAR

Lesson One: You need to find your own style, and your own "voice", in a safe place, where you feel comfortable enough to practise. You can't copy someone else's style — it won't work for you. Lee Glickstein, a public-speaking guru in California, writes of "learning circles" in his book *Be Heard Now* (New York: Broadway Books, 1999). Learning circles are groups of people who meet in a supported environment to help each other find their own voice and become effective public speakers. Toastmaster's clubs also provide a good public forum and evaluation to help sharpen your skills. By just reading this chapter you will never become a great public speaker. There is no getting around practising the craft of public speaking. You have to get up and, as the Nike ad says, "Just do it!"

Lesson Two: You need to learn how to "read" your audience, and break through to the crowd. You do this by making connections with individuals, not by looking at the group as a whole. In every audience, there are people who are really supportive, and you should make eye contact with them. Speak as if you are speaking to them directly and having a personal conversation. These sympathetic listeners, these supportive people, will draw in the other members of your audience with their enthusiasm and interest. These chosen members of your audience will help you win over your entire audience. Try it the next time you get up and speak and I promise it will work miracles for you.

Lesson Three: When speaking, introduce yourself and tell a story about why you are there talking to them (how you came to be knowledgeable in your field, what you have learned and what you have to share with your audience today). That has to be communicated to your audience. At the very least, they want to be entertained, and they want you to succeed with your speech. It doesn't work when the speech is top-down, with you as the only person in the know. Remember, if people show up, it's because they want to hear your message. People want to feel connected, and as a speaker you need to learn to speak with your audiences and not at them.

Lesson Four: As a speaker, you need to be comfortable with the silences and pauses. It took me a long time to learn that when it is really quiet when I am speaking, this means that my audience is interested in what I have to say. I learned that when I heard noise from my audience while I was speaking, that meant I did not have the audience's full attention. It can get scary and unnerving when there is silence and you are the focal point of that silence. That can be the time that you begin to panic, get lost and forget what you want to say. I know it first hand. It has happened to me more than I want to recall. During those times I have trained myself to smile and look for a supportive face in the audience to encourage me to go on to my next thought.

Lesson Five: If you find yourself using "ums" and "aws", try to begin using "and" as a connector and an attention-getter instead. The word "and" allows you to transition effortlessly and smoothly from one thought to the next without missing a beat.

Lesson Six: I have learned that many of us, myself included, can't make people laugh at what we are saying, but we can allow them to find areas in our speeches to laugh at. This is done by making a statement and taking a pause. We may not have intended for something we said to be funny, but our audience might be laughing off their seats from what we have just said. Remember, the power of our pauses allows our audiences to participate and mentally catch up to us while we are making our IPP presentations.

Lesson Seven: Always keep your end in mind. You need to know what it is that you intend to communicate with your audience, and not be committed to a specific route to accomplishing your desired outcome. What if you are interrupted or the technology doesn't work for you? What then? You have to keep your presentation focused on the subject, in the room and on your message. By no means do I mean that you should not be committed to a proven process. When presenting many short seminars I have always found it most effective to follow my own universal process to present seminars.

Lesson Eight: Lastly, and most importantly, when you are speaking to your audience about your chosen topic, or about any other subject for that matter, what you are selling is not your information, but the convictions that you have about your information and about your solutions, and, finally, you are selling yourself!

HOW TO GAIN INCREDIBLE CLIENTS BY PUBLIC SPEAKING

Many times I have walked off the stage after delivering a speech for a little over an hour to a group of small business owners and their public accountants, and as soon as I have reached the bottom of the stage, a business owner has grabbed me and said, "I need to hire you now! Please let me call you later this week." The last time this happened I was asked to assist with the succession planning for a $25 million family-owned business.

From the very beginning of my career in the financial service industry, I have always believed that professional writing, teaching and speaking, apart from being lucrative in their own right, are the best methods to gain access to extraordinary clients, and lead to very stimulating work. Below I have listed five strategies I have personally adopted to establish the environment of turning speaking engagements into lucrative financial consulting contracts. I would like to share them with you now.

Strategy One: Meet the Head Honcho

Always make it a point to meet the top person or people at the event to ensure that their objectives will be met, and to begin your formal relationship with them. Do not deal exclusively with the Public Accountant, CFO, HR professional or the workshop organizer, even if those are the people making the hiring decision.

Strategy Two: Make Sure and Do Your Homework

Find out about the organization and the people you are making your presentation to. Learn as much about their history, business models, people and all the pertinent information that you can gather before you make your speech. This research will empower you to make your speech relevant to your audience and future clientele. Great places to find this key information are corporate and association websites.

The best website to find information on key individuals on the Internet today is at <www.zoominfo.com>. This website has collected comprehensive information on over 32 million business professionals and 2 million companies across the globe in every industry imaginable. Best of all, this information is free. Another great website to gather quick information about financial topics that affect Canadians is <www.AdvisorWorld.com>.

Strategy Three: Know Your Audience

Ask the organizer of the event at which you will be speaking for permission to call several of the key individuals who will be attending. This strategy allows you to learn first hand the perspective of key people who will attend your talk, and the outcome they would like to achieve by listening to you. This allows you to prepare your presentation to create the greatest impact on your audience; that, in turn, will dramatically increase your ability to turn a speaking engagement into lucrative financial consulting work.

Remember these wise words spoken 150 years ago by Abraham Lincoln:

> "When I am getting ready to reason with a man, I spend one-third of my time thinking about myself and what I am going to say, and two-thirds thinking about him and what he is going to say."

Strategy Four: Make the Call to Take Action, and Make Your Audience Know That You Are a Part of Their Solution

Describe the specific techniques, behaviour changes, new knowledge, new procedures or whatever is necessary for the group to make dramatic progress. Make it very clear that you have the specific experience, knowledge and wisdom in the area that you are talking about to assist them in accomplishing the needed transition.

Strategy Five: Always Follow Up

Bill Gates, founder of Microsoft, and author of *The New York Times*' bestseller *The Road Ahead* (New York: Penguin Books, 1996), states at the beginning of his book: "… we always overestimate the present and always underestimate the future." Not every time you make a presentation will it immediately turn into other business; have patience, and opportunities will flow your way. Our lives might not change as immediately as we hoped but when they do change, these changes are grander than we could have ever imagined.

Send either a letter or e-mail within a few days after your presentation to key people who were at the speaking venue. In these correspondences share your perspective on what was accomplished, and provide recommendations and suggestions on what can be done next to gain greater results. Let them know that you are available by offering your assistance both formally and informally.

Remember that public speaking is not for the weak at heart. Building public speaking muscles is only for those financial professionals who want to stand out above the crowd and be counted.

LAST THOUGHTS ON THE POWER OF OUR SPEECH

Each of us has been given a powerful gift. Every time we use this gift properly, we are showing an active display of our appreciation of this gift. Human beings were given three abilities that differentiate them from the rest of the animal kingdom — that of speech, a highly developed intelligence and the ability to tell a story.

Speech is not only unique to humans, but it is what makes us unique. While other animals on this planet possess some form of intelligence, only human beings have the ability to understand and analyze what is happening in the world around them and keep a distinct sense of self.

Our speech gives each of us tools to break down barriers and to connect us with others and to create and maintain relationships in a meaningful way. What differentiates us from other animals is our ability to express our thoughts, wants, emotions and insights with our language. Our language empowers us to bind time with others by sharing our experiences and insights, enabling others to learn from us without directly experiencing what we have shared with our words.

We should always be mindful that once we have said something out loud, our words bring about change in ourselves, others and the world as a whole. We should always remember these wise words attributed to Frank Outlaw, the founder of the supermarket chain BI-LO:

> Watch your thoughts; they become words.
> Watch your words; they become actions.
> Watch your actions; they become habits.
> Watch your habits; they become character.
> Watch your character; it becomes your destiny.

Why is this so? In reality nothing has changed, yet the act of speaking has the power to change how we feel, what we think and how we act in the world. Simply saying something has the power to change our world and change the realities of those who hear our words. Speech then does create reality. It affects connections between ourselves, between one person and another, and our environment.

It is very important to understand that we, as thinking and speaking human beings, use little stories called metaphors to present suggestions and ideas to the unconscious minds of others. In hypnosis, this is a practitioner's most powerful and effective tool to cause change in his or her clients. A full acknowledgement of this power requires that the user of this tool accept all of the responsibilities that come from the understanding that our words and intent do bypass our listener's conscious mind. Thus, our words have the power to affect and change another's worldview forever. With this said, then, there is very little truth behind the old saying:

> "Sticks and stones might break my bones but names will never hurt me!"

The word "metaphor" comes from the ancient Greek word "meta", which in the English translation refers to "a transfer of meaning from one thing to another". We use metaphors and symbolism to paint the picture of our communication for our listeners to derive meaning from our experiences so that they can interpret our meaning without us having to explain in literal terms, for example, that an IPP is like an RRSP on steroids.

To make your audience understand and remember who you are, give them a visual, whether by invoking a strong image or by teasing out a scenario. The more abstract your service, the more technical or foreign your business, and the more imperative it is that you *anchor* your description in visual language.

The metaphor I prefer to use to describe my company's expertise is the following:

> "At MerrickWealth.com we are Business Exit Planning Strategists helping today's successful business owner exit with success."

What this metaphor implies to the listener is that our company is skilled at putting it all together for what a successful business owner needs from a properly executed succession plan, "exiting with success". Successful business owners know either consciously or subconsciously that building and selling their business needs the assistance of both generalists and specialists to help in the design, implementation, management and winding down. This is something that every successful business owner can envision and understand — their ultimate professional goal is to leave their businesses on their terms. That is the key to this positioning metaphor, and it should be your goal as well when you create yours.

The use of our properly structured metaphors allows our families, our clients, our audiences, our professional colleagues and our communities to come to their own interpretations and make similar connections from our metaphors to their own beliefs, values and circumstances. Our metaphors allow our listeners to come to their own understanding at their own level. This is accomplished by comparing unfamiliar facts with something simple that the listener already knows. People learn more rapidly when the information relates to their own experiences.

Using metaphors and analogies in the financial planning industry allows us to distinguish ourselves in our listener's mind. A good analogy or metaphor can quickly anchor concepts, products and people into a prospect's or client's mind forever.

The power of our words should be very intimidating. One of my father's, Marvin S. Merrick's, lasting legacies to me that I would like to share with you now is the following wisdom:

> "Once something is said, it cannot be taken back; it is nearly impossible to erase its effects."

Thus, we must invest the time to train ourselves to think before we speak. We ought to speak words that are properly motivated, that are stated in the positive, and that are directed, purposeful and well thought out.

Prior to speaking, we need to have the right intentions, have evaluated whether it is an appropriate time to speak and be sure that we are being sensitive to our audience. Our words need to be sincere. People sense the truth. They know whether a speaker speaks from self-interest or for the greater good. Words spoken from the heart will enter the heart.

> "You must be the change you want to see in the world."
>
> Mahatma Gandhi

CHAPTER 11

THE "WRITE" WAY TO DEFY GRAVITY AND MOVE YOUR FINANCIAL CONSULTING PRACTICE TO THE TOP

David Leonhardt

Overview

This chapter discusses how to create credibility through writing articles and books and how to successfully court media attention to grow your financial consulting practice.

Learning Objectives

By the end of this chapter, you should be able to:

- understand the pyramid used to build credibility in prospects, clients, Trusted Advisors, colleagues and the public mind;
- understand how becoming a writer of articles and books will empower your financial consulting practice; and
- learn how to successfully court the public media to grow your financial consulting practice.

THE PUBLIC CREDIBILITY PYRAMID

There is a hierarchy of public credibility that defies logic. If you are interested in logic, the next few paragraphs will provide you with endless fodder for philosophical debates. If, on the other hand, you are interested in expanding your financial consulting practice, the next few paragraphs will provide you with endless fodder for moving up, defying not just logic but gravity.

The hierarchy begins at the bottom. The base of the pyramid is seeing your ad. If you place an ad, many people will see it, but few will call. Just above that base is receiving a cold call, which is not all that different from seeing an ad, except that there is a real human being and the opportunity to ask a question or two.

It's at the next level that gravity starts to act funny, where people hear you at a seminar. I'll go into what is funny about that in a moment. After that comes reading your article, and just above that, reading your book. We are still defying gravity, and increasingly defying logic, as we move up the pyramid.

The pinnacle of the pyramid is the media. Seeing your name quoted in a newspaper gives you superb credibility, and seeing your face on TV gives you the most. It's not for nothing that some marketers run infomercials just so they can put the "as seen on TV" moniker in their print ads.

Before giving you the information you need to make this hierarchy work for you, I suspect you want to know why this order defies logic. As with most of the sales process, and you are probably already aware of this, it is all about psychology.

Public speaking gives you more credibility than a cold call, even if the audience did not know you were going to be the speaker. Why? Because there is an assumption of credibility. Anyone can pick up the phone and call you, or place an ad, but not anyone can convince someone to let you speak. Even if it is your own seminar, the credibility of speaking over a cold call or an ad defies all logic.

One step up the pyramid, reading your article, a prospective client assumes that you had to go through a certain triage to get that article printed. So even if you typeset the article yourself and have it reprinted so that it resembles a magazine article, your credibility rises with the article. Why this defies logic is that you cannot be untruthful in an ad or in a cold call any more than you can in an article, but logic has nothing to do with it.

A book carries more weight than an article, no pun intended. Somehow being a published author is more credible than being merely a published writer. It doesn't matter if you self-publish, an author is more of an expert than a cold-caller. Period.

But the ultimate expert status is conveyed upon those who appear in the media, particularly television, which acts as the great filter of truth. Never mind that everybody says, and knows, that you can't trust everything you see on TV or read in the news; we all believe it anyway. Yes, after hundreds of media interviews on several dozen topics, from weekly local reporters to national news anchors, I can tell you that what really happens, and how much of the true story gets into the media, varies immensely from broadcast to broadcast or from article to article.

Yet, in the absence of other information, I assume that what I read or see is true. My knowledge does not interfere with my psychology, and it won't interfere with your target market's psychology, either.

Your mission to build credibility with wealthy clients is to get into the media when you can. And when you can't, hand them in person the ultimate calling card: your book. Business cards are a dime a dozen, almost literally. Hand your book to a prospective wealthy client and/or their Trusted Advisors, and offer to autograph it. Watch your sales conversion rate rise.

HOW TO WRITE A BOOK

Even if you can't write, you can be an author and a highly credible one. The first step is to come up with an idea. What special aspects of financial planning and taxation will your book be about? It needs to be more than just a run-of-the-mill how-to manual. It needs to be a little different. Put your personality into it. If you can make it visionary, you strike gold. Why? Because your wealthy clients count on you to do more than just understand the current regulations and landscape. They want you to ensure they are positioned well as the regulations and landscape change.

The next step is to organize your thoughts. Are you having problems doing this? Get a freelance editor to coach you. As the head of a freelance writer/editor agency, I can tell you that there are many brilliant people who cannot organize their thoughts for a book or an article — even if they can deliver superb reports to clients and dazzling sales pitches to prospects.

The next step, which is very important in any sector, such as in the financial service industry, where regulations prohibit hiring a ghost-writer, is to write. Never mind whether you can spell. Never mind whether English is your first language or your twenty-first. Never mind if you feel insecure about writing. Just write.

If you happen to be a brilliant writer, you might be able to write your whole book. If not, that's where a freelance editor comes in. If your book is reasonably well written to start with, any competent editor will do. If your writing is really poor, you will need an editor with writing experience.

What the editor will need is at least 25,000 words of the main ideas you want to get across. An editor can bulk it up and make it read well, but the editor cannot add any information that by regulation must be written in your own words. Make sure the editor understands the boundaries of the regulations within the financial industries.

Another great strategy if you are a poor writer is to collaborate with someone else, so that perhaps you and someone who is a great writer can leverage each other's skills, knowledge and distribution channels. You'll have to consider whom you would want to collaborate with very carefully. The ideal person is someone whose business is symbiotic, but not competitive, with yours. That is why you will often see veterinarian offices and pet food stores side by side. Likewise, optometrists and opticians. However, two competitors can easily co-write a book in a significantly large market, especially if each one has a slightly different specialty. After all, if you can move from each having 1% of the market to combined sharing 3%, isn't it worthwhile?

But there is more than just writing skills, knowledge and distribution channels that you leverage when you collaborate. You also leverage credibility. That is the premise of how this book is written. Peter Merrick is an expert in financial planning, taxation and succession planning, but he has assembled the brightest minds in various other fields to round out this book. Without those other voices, the book would have been less complete and would have had less credibility than it does. When your manuscript is complete, go to any printer who specializes in books. These printers can arrange for cover art and typesetting. Ask first to see three samples of books they have recently printed. It is absolutely important that the artwork look professional and that the print quality be impeccable. More prospective clients will judge your credibility on the quality of the printing firm you hire. Defies logic, right? Well, if you can't even choose a good printer, how can these potential clients expect you to assist them with their finances?

If a whole book is not in the cards, a quicker and less expensive route is to have a feature-length article prepared. Again, the same principles apply to the writing, although only about 800 words need to be written for a 1,600-word article. "Copies" of the article should be printed on full-colour, two-sided glossy paper, just as if they were printed for insertion in a magazine. Staple the sheets together and slip them into your information folder for each prospective client.

HOW TO GET IN THE MEDIA

Much harder than becoming a published author is to become a media spokesperson. Where do you get the credibility with the media? Where do you start? Hint: it does not involve writing a news release. The first step is to identify the media venues you want to or think you can get quoted in. Think long term. If you are thinking about getting quoted next week, you have already lost the battle.

Next, find out who controls the news. It is usually not the on-air personality, but rather a producer. At a newspaper, it might be the assignment editor or the specific reporter whose byline you see.

Follow their work religiously. Whenever they report on a topic you feel falls within your scope of expertise, write a short note. The note should not be critical. It should always be helpful. For instance, if the reporter missed some basic information, rather than criticize the piece's lack of depth, offer to share some additional information that could help with future stories.

Suggest a meeting, especially if that gives you the chance to pass along a copy of your book.

It might take several meetings, but after a while you will be seen as a good source to quote or interview on financial planning or related topics. Of course, it might lead to nothing. Getting into the news is about building relationships — friendly relationships, true, but most of all, professional relationships, based on the journalist deciding that you are a credible source of information. If a journalist doesn't like the colour of your hair, and that stands in the way of a relationship, there is very little you can do.

Similarly, if journalists already have a good source they like to call on, there is also very little you can do. But if the opportunity is there, it is up to you to forge that relationship. And here, too, there is an opportunity for collaboration, especially for a rookie journalist. If you can't answer the journalist's question at any time, find him or her someone who can. You never want to be a dead end; you always want to be a vital resource, a 100% reliable source that the journalist can always depend on that will lead to the answers and the quotes he or she needs.

In fact, when I was a spokesperson for CAA Ontario, journalists would call me up even when they were pretty sure I could not help them, because they knew I would find someone who could. Why is this important? Because I was very often also able to add an angle to their story that they had not thought of — an angle that allowed me to put in my two cents.

So you can defy gravity, along with people's logic, by moving up in the hierarchy of credibility. For obvious reasons, the higher you climb, the harder you have to work to get there. Maybe getting your face on national TV will not bring the ROI you wish. At least consider how far up the ladder you want to climb — speaking at seminars, writing articles or books, being interviewed for newspaper or TV — defying logic and gravity and increasing your business.

CHAPTER 12

HOW TO WIN THE CREDIBILITY BATTLE*

Ellen Bessner

Overview

Trusted Advisors need to be mindful that we live in a litigious society where sometimes it does not matter how much we place the needs of our clients first, some clients may be unhappy with their financial results and see redress through litigation and/or a complaint to the regulator. This chapter addresses procedures an advisor should incorporate into his or her practice to surpass the basic Know Your Client (KYC) rule and exude professionalism. Ellen Bessner, in her book *Advisor at Risk: A Roadmap to Protecting Your Business*, from which this chapter is excerpted, provides advisors with precautionary steps to enable them to establish their credibility in the eyes of regulators and judges when a client seeks to discredit an advisor's testimony and attack his or her professionalism.

Learning Objectives

By the end of this chapter, you will:

- understand the importance of asking questions at an initial client meeting, what questions should be asked and how the client's answers should be documented;
- understand the importance of creating a procedure for documenting all client communication and the results of creating a paper trail;

---

* What follows is an authorized revised reprint of Chapter 6 of Ellen Bessner's book *Advisor at Risk: A Roadmap to Protecting Your Business* (Toronto: Shore Publishing, 2008).

- understand how an advisor defending a client complaint can assist his or her lawyer to win the "credibility battle" in the eyes of regulators and judges.

SOPHISTICATION

Advisors are lulled into a false sense of security when clients arrive at their offices for the first time, asserting that they are sophisticated investors. Their expensive clothes, watches, or cars support the advisor's superficial assessment of such clients. When advisors are sued by these same clients, they are puzzled by the demand letter and subsequent claim that describes the client as unsophisticated and vulnerable. Advisors turn to me and say that the client is knowledgeable and sophisticated. The problem lies with the lack of evidence. These advisors have nothing other than mere superficial impressions. The advisor says repeatedly, "But I know he is sophisticated." While the client may very well be sophisticated, unless and until I, the lawyer, have concrete evidence, the advisor's general impression does not assist him in his defence.

Let me describe one advisor who retained me and insisted that the client suing him was indeed sophisticated, even though he had no evidence to prove it. I filed the defence on the advisor's behalf, asserting that the client was sophisticated, but I had no particulars supporting the statement. I proceeded with my examination (deposition) of the client, which the advisor's lawyer is entitled to do in most jurisdictions. As a matter of course, in the first five minutes of the examination, I asked the client about his educational background. I learned that he had taken the necessary courses to become an advisor years before but never followed through. At that point, I stopped the examination and asked the complaining client to leave the room so that I could have a discussion with the opposing counsel.[1] I explained that the client certainly understood each investment and the associated risks and that whatever the client didn't understand was his own fault, because he did not review the materials provided at the time of investing or the materials delivered thereafter. The matter was ultimately abandoned by the advisor's client. Nevertheless, the advisor and dealer had to pay me a significant sum in legal fees just to get to that stage in the proceedings.

One of the risks for advisors and dealers is that clients win judges' sympathies by saying that they were unsophisticated and relied exclusively on their advisor when purchasing investment and insurance products. In reviewing the reasons judges give for their decisions, one usually sees references to the relative sophistication of the client and the advisor. The theory is that the poor uneducated client, who knew nothing about investment and insurance products, relied upon the educated, knowledgeable, and experienced advisor, and the result was unsuitable investments and losses.

If sophistication is so important, why don't advisors take the time to collect the necessary information to defend themselves against clients who are prepared to proclaim just about anything — including their own ignorance — in order to get their money back? The short answer is, advisors haven't received enough explanation and information to appreciate the importance of sophistication and how it could determine who wins the credibility battle. Yet the issue of the client's sophistication with respect to the product he buys may be crucial to the advisor's successful defence.

In order to develop a paper trail to support an advisor's contention that the client is sophisticated, what should advisors ask clients in the first meeting? Here is a checklist:

Education

Does the client have a post-secondary education — a college or university degree, courses or certifications of any kind? What is the client's educational level, including area of focus in university or college?

Reading

Which newspapers or magazines does the client subscribe to or read regularly? In particular, does the client follow business news on TV and/or in the newspapers? Does he or she know how to follow stocks in the newspaper?

Types of Accounts

What types of accounts has the client had in the past — margin accounts, discount accounts, discretionary accounts with a portfolio manager?

Investment Decisions

How has the client made investment decisions with previous advisors? Has the client ever suggested investments, insurance products or strategies to previous advisors?

Past Vocations

As stated earlier, although most advisors ask clients about their present occupation, it also helps to know what the client's previous jobs were. As baby boomers age, many of them no longer work full time, and more of these clients take odd jobs or are retired. If the only information collected is about a client's present occupation, the advisor will not know, for example, that the client was previously a comptroller of a company. Such information would definitely support the assertion that the client was somewhat sophisticated — he or she understood numbers and presumably would have understood the statements and prospectus information delivered.

Balance Sheet and Income Statement

Does the client know how to read balance sheets and income statements? Has he or she ever done this at work?

Internet

Does the client know how to check his or her stocks on the Internet?

In gauging a client's sophistication, there are other questions and areas to explore. Perhaps advisors can think of a few such questions to add to their lists.

Armed with this information in a paper or electronic file, advisors will no longer be vulnerable to clients who say they didn't have any idea what the products were or that there was any risk that they could lose money. This information will also help advisors assess in what detail they should explain the characteristics and the risk of the products they recommend.[2]

What is the credibility battle? It is the danger of a judge or arbitrator tending to believe the client's version of events over the advisor's version. What is often a judge's greater sympathy for clients is partially based on the perception that clients know less than and are more dependent upon professionals of all kinds, including the advisor in the securities and insurance industry. In addition, professionals of all kinds, including advisors, are expected to have proof supporting their version of events. Without such proof, the advisor's most valuable assets are challenged: reputation, licence, and money.

ENHANCING CREDIBILITY

Advisors say that their clients will not regard them as professionals if they take notes during meetings. Advisors are concerned that if they take notes, it will appear to clients that the advisor is not listening to them. I believe the opposite is true. Indeed, most other professionals take notes while meeting with clients, and they are not accused of being unprofessional or not listening. When I went to meet my advisor for the first time, he sat back and just talked to me. He then attended one of my seminars and asked me why I didn't tell him to take notes during our meeting. I teased him that when I come to see him, I am paying him for his advice. If he wants to come and see me and pay me for my advice, he can book an appointment. We had a laugh.

Advisors also worry that their notes will come back to haunt them, because if they write something down, it can be misconstrued, or if the notes are incomplete, it will get them into more trouble than a blank page and a "my word against theirs" stance. I suggest that advisors are the best interpreters of their own notes, and their oral evidence will close the gaps.

Professionals take steps to protect themselves and to ensure their version of events is believed. Doctors and dentists maintain written charts for each patient, recording the date of the appointment, the subject of discussion, and the advice given. It has become a running joke that you need bad handwriting to be a doctor. I believe that doctors' notes are messy because they have to write a lot of information very quickly.

When I was last at the dentist, I saw him make a note that he had explained to me that drilling my pearly whites to fill a cavity might cause my tooth to crack, in which case I might need a root canal. (Do you think he makes such notes with all clients, or do you think it has something to do with me being a litigation lawyer?) My dentist understood the importance of managing client expectations and reducing his risk. With that note in my chart, he would win the credibility battle if I asserted that no such risk was ever explained and that I would not have had the cavity filled if I thought it was risky. Notes remind the professional that indeed they did alert clients to the risks. Without such a note, and in the face of a client who asserted otherwise, the professional, doctor, lawyer, or dentist could not be certain of having warned the client of the risks. Professional advisors tend to advise many clients each day, without taking notes. Without those notes, however, they cannot specifically recall what transpired with a particular client on a particular day. Advisors who say they do specifically recall events from months or sometimes years before the evidence is given will put their own credibility into question. An experienced lawyer could easily trip up such an advisor during a session of cross-examination.

While advisors complain that taking notes can be arduous, I ask, what side of that credibility battle do advisors want to be on?

ADVISORS HELP THEMSELVES BY HELPING THEIR LAWYERS

When examining a judge's or arbitrator's reasons for a decision, it is useful to ask the following questions:

- Why did the judge believe one party over the other — was it the credibility of the witnesses?
- What helped the winning party convince the judge that his story was more credible?

- Did the witnesses have documentation to support their own version of events?
- What could the advisor have said or done to convince the judge to believe his story?
- For those decisions that find in favour of the advisor, what evidence did the judge find compelling?

In the next section of this chapter, specific cases will be examined to determine why certain testimony was preferred. We will look at why conducting business in a manner that can render an advisor's testimony more credible may also increase client satisfaction and decrease the likelihood of complaints — the proverbial killing of two birds with one stone.

Case #1: Credibility Victory

You've likely heard many stories of advisors who failed to know their client and suffered the wrath of judges and arbitrators. Do judges and arbitrators ever believe advisors? They do. In this 2002 decision by a regulator,[3] the client, Mr. G, claimed that his advisor, Shanks, failed to learn the essential facts about him, that his recommendations were unsuitable, that accounts were churned, and that he engaged in discretionary trading.

Mr. G's net worth was about $1.25 million. Shanks opened a margin account for his client. Shanks completed his firm's new client application form, but the form did not contain specific requirements to attribute the percentage breakdown to either the risk factors or investment objectives.

Mr. G said he didn't understand how a margin account operated nor had he ever expressed any desire to speculate. He also testified that Shanks must have engaged in discretionary trading, because he had not given the advisor any instructions. Shanks testified that he recalled several discussions with his client and that Mr. G understood margin accounts. To prove this, he produced a spreadsheet Mr. G had prepared and given to him. This document served as evidence of Mr. G's sophistication and understanding. Under cross-examination, Mr. G admitted he had previously engaged in speculative investing. He also admitted that he remembered some of the conversations Shanks had described in his testimony.

Though the new client application form was lacking, the District Council concluded that Shanks had not violated his obligation to learn the essential facts about his client. The KYC form "is just the beginning of the know your client obligation.[4] and does not constitute everything embraced in this term. There is the knowledge that the broker gains as he becomes familiar with his customer and the latter's dealings in the market. Accordingly, the decision was based on what the advisor knew about the client, beyond the form.

Though the investments in the margin account were speculative, the suitability of the investments was linked to Mr. G's sophistication. Although the client said he was unsophisticated, the advisor's testimony that he was sophisticated was believed due to the documentation prepared by Mr. G that Shanks kept in his file. Shanks could recall details of conversations he had with the client, including particulars of Mr. G's experience. Furthermore, Mr. G's other speculative investments rendered his evidence less believable. The District Council decided in the advisor's favour, concluding that the investments were suitable.

On the issue of churning, which was also alleged, the District Council concluded that to prove churning, the following elements had to be present: excessive trading, the advisor exercising control over the trading, like in a discretionary account, and the advisor having an ulterior motive, for example, earning excessive commissions. Based on the client's evidence, those elements were absent.

Mr. G's inconsistencies and failure to recollect details led the District Council to favour the advisor's version of events. As a result, the advisor maintained his reputation and his licence — and he returned his checkbook to his drawer.

That is the happy ending to this credibility story.

Advisors may think that the issue of credibility in court does not affect them because they don't ever expect to be witnesses in court. But beware: with the increased number of client claims and complaints, it may not be a question of *if* but of *when* an advisor will be sued or called onto the regulator's carpet.

Good record-keeping habits can improve an advisor's credibility in court and get advisors into the habit of complying with regulatory and legal obligations.

Case #2: Credibility Problem

Let's look at another case.[5] Mr. H was an engineer in his 50s when he met Mr. B, his broker. Mr. H had previously invested heavily in stocks and options, but he did not have much money.

Mr. B was an experienced advisor with the chartered accountant designation. He specialized in option investments and developed a special strategy for index options. On Mr. B's advice, Mr. H's account consisted mostly of uncovered options — speculative and highly leveraged. Mr. H began to lose money and had to sell stock to cover a margin call. He decided to sell his entire account because he could not afford to lose any more money and instructed Mr. B accordingly. Mr. B encouraged Mr. H to hold on to the account. He did so but suffered further losses.

The dealer, through which Mr. B was licensed, sued the client for over $250,000 — the amount owing in his margin account after it was closed out. Mr. H counterclaimed against the dealer, asserting failure to supervise, and against Mr. B, asserting that he breached his duty by recommending unsuitable investments and by refusing to follow Mr. H's instructions to sell.

Both the client and advisor were witnesses. In the reasons for his decision, the judge described the advisor as follows, "He carries with him an air of knowledge, competence and assurance." The judge's description of the client was as follows, "He struck me as a sincere, soft spoken person, not aggressive or combative. While he appeared knowledgeable about the stock market he also appeared somewhat naively optimistic."[6]

The judge described the advisor-client relationship as that of teacher and student. "[The advisor] was the guru in this very specialized field and I concluded that [the client] placed his trust and reliance in him almost totally."[7]

The judge ruled in favour of the client, concluding that the "naively optimistic" client trusted his advisor.

But there is more to this matter than meets the eye. The outcome of this case may have been different if the advisor had responded properly to several red flags. There was little evidence that the advisor listened to and followed the client's instructions. Advisors need to follow their clients' instructions and document that they have done so. If the advisor had followed the client's instructions and had letters or notes to reflect the communication, he may not have received the complaint in the first place. No doubt, the advisor lost the client and suffered bad publicity, as did the dealer.

Case #3: Credibility Disaster

Insurance professionals struggle to identify potential sources of risk arising from a complicated chain of individuals intertwined in a web that even the brightest legal minds struggle to untangle. This web, referred to as "agency and principal", is well illustrated in the following recent decision.[8] Although this case is a property and casualty insurance case, its principles apply to any advisor in the securities and insurance industry.

Audio Works, an audio equipment rental business, retained a firm of insurance agents to procure coverage. The agents, in turn, approached an insurer's broker liaison and requested liability and property insurance coverage on terms that included in-transit and replacement coverage. The broker obtained coverage from the insurer for the plaintiff on substantially different terms; specifically, the policy did not provide in-transit coverage or replacement cost coverage.

What can go wrong, will go wrong — a highway accident resulted in substantial damage to transported audio equipment. The insurer denied coverage because the policy did not include in-transit coverage. The insurance agents, the insurer, the managing general agent and its employee, and the broker liaison were involved in a six-year lawsuit for the replacement cost of the damaged audio equipment.

The trial judge decided in Audio Works' favour and ordered reimbursement. The presiding judge pointed to the lack of documentation to support the broker's testimony. The broker testified that he specifically told the client that his policy excluded "in-transit" coverage; the broker didn't have any notes, letters, memos, or e-mails. Accordingly, the judge decided in favour of Audio Works, ordering reimbursement. The judge reviewed the written insurance application that specifically requested in-transit coverage and found that this documentation was evidence of what the applicant requested. Unless there was documentation specifically explaining the material differences between the application for insurance and the ultimate policy, the applicant should be permitted to rely on the application.

The lesson is that paper trails win cases. A judge is far more likely to accept the version of events supported by complete, accurate notes, correspondence and documentation. In particular, notes of all meetings and telephone conversations should be in the client file, and all agreements should be in writing and confirmed by the relevant parties. The judge is likely to accept the version of events that is supported by a systematically prepared paper trail.

Finally, judges will submit insurance agents, brokers and Managing General Agents (MGAs) to the same standards of competence expected from other professionals.

The Audio Works' litigation cost each party in the chain a hefty sum, not to mention aggravation and bad publicity. If there was evidence, other than perhaps small print on a policy that the client had been informed of the limitations to coverage, the lawsuit may have been avoided.

Different parties along the insurance industry chain work together to sell insurance products that limit a client's risk. Each of these parties is affected individually when clients sue; each must hire legal counsel to defend their respective positions; and each takes a personal or corporate hit to their reputation. Learning to manage risks can lead to better results for the insurance company, MGA, advisor, and, ultimately, the client, who should understand the limits to his or her insurance coverage.

All advisors benefit from keeping a record of events. Whether handwritten, electronic, or otherwise, notes assist advisors to remember what transpired and give them confidence that their version of events is more accurate than the client's. In court or before a regulator, evidence that supports the advisor's version of events will enable the advisor to be more convincing. The client's version, not supported by any record, will be dismissed, as will the client's claim.

WINNING THE CREDIBILITY BATTLE

The balance of this chapter explores methods to employ to win the credibility battle with clients in court and in regulatory proceedings.

The Importance of a Contemporaneous Record

Regardless of the type of record kept, it is crucial that a record be maintained that was prepared contemporaneously with the events. This simply means that the record is made at the time of the meeting or telephone conversation with the client. Some advisors prepare few or no records during the meetings and telephone calls but much later may insert a note, completed without any supporting details, into the file or forms. Such a record is not evidence of what was said during the meeting, but rather is evidence of the advisor's *best recollection* of what was discussed. Judges and arbitrators do not find notes taken after the fact to be as reliable as notes taken during the meeting.

Types of Records

Handwritten Notes

Many advisors complain that their handwriting is illegible and throw up their hands insisting that they cannot write down everything that is said. Perfection, however, is not the standard. Years later, even the most cryptic notes help advisors remember what was discussed. Poorly prepared handwritten notes are far better than no notes at all.

My handwriting is horrible. However, as messy as my notes are, they are written for each and every telephone call that I have with clients. I use a form that has a space for the date and time at the top, a space for the name of the person with whom I spoke, and a space for any action items that my assistant and I need to follow up on. For a template of my telephone form, see Appendix C of my book. Advisors can design forms to meet their own needs. I also choose coloured paper, so that these notes stand out from other written correspondence (letters or e-mails) delivered to clients. My notes and correspondence are organized on a metal spike in reverse chronological order, and placed in a yellow folder. Here are some additional suggestions for advisors preparing handwritten notes:

- Put the date and time at the beginning of the notes, and put the time again at the bottom.
- Make a horizontal line at the bottom of the page to indicate the end of the notes.
- Indicate in the notes the names of individuals at the meeting or on the telephone call.
- Put any follow-up items at the end of the notes.

Typed Notes

Because my writing is so slow and illegible, and my typing is quite good, I take my laptop to important meetings. As these notes are typed instead of handwritten, they don't need to be transcribed. After my notes are spell-checked and printed, they are filed away until they are needed.

In the financial and insurance industries, where business is conducted quickly after several telephone calls and meetings, software programs exist that simplify the recording of conversations by automatically inserting date and time. These programs permit several advisors and their assistants to insert notes and then print out a summary of conversations in chronological order. This allows each member of a team to better service clients as they can ascertain what was previously discussed with the client, without having to first track down an advisor who may or may not be in the office when the client calls. The efficiency of such a system depends on the quality and quantity of notes inserted. I have heard that assistants find the advisors' notes are often missing or too cryptic. If advisors and dealers spend money on the software, they should use it.

Some systems of storage and retrieval render the above method more efficient and less expensive. Advisors must know how to store and retrieve the notes that were taken on a computer, as the printouts of these electronic notes are invaluable if, years later, advisors and dealers are challenged by clients.

Letters or E-mails

Instead of writing time-consuming letters, some advisors send newsletters in an effort to differentiate themselves from their competitors.

While newsletters are fine, a letter or e-mail specific to the client's circumstances is often necessary. For example, if the advisor questions whether the client fully understood a conversation they had in person or over the telephone, it might be wise to clarify the exchange in writing. A letter or e-mail from the advisor clarifying the matter of concern is very powerful in court or at the regulator, particularly if it exudes professionalism and is received by the client either before he makes a decision based on the advisor's recommendations or before he suffers significant losses.

To ensure that the letter or e-mail clearly sets out the advisor's concern and reflects his or her professionalism without making damaging admissions, I recommend that advisors show their letters or e-mails to the compliance department before sending them. This kind of correspondence is a great way to avoid client complaints about advisors and/or dealers and at least supports the advisor's version of events if a complaint arises. When advisors work with clients who continually push the envelope, it is a good idea to consistently send letters and e-mails to the client, throughout the relationship.

Taping

I remember many years ago, I was speaking at a conference and someone raised his hand and asked me whether he should tape-record client meetings. I told him as long as the client was aware and agreeable, it was fine. But I couldn't envisage a client being that comfortable or agreeable. However, another gentle-looking man raised his hand and told me that he taped all client meetings, and he didn't encounter reluctance from clients because he reassured them about taping meetings. He told clients he taped because what was discussed was very important to him, and he concentrates better if he does not have to take notes. If clients are sufficiently comfortable with taping, it is an efficient way to record details of what the client has told the advisor. The gentleman at the meeting suggested that once clients get used to meetings being taped, they usually expect a tape recorder at all future meetings. However, if clients seem inhibited or uncomfortable with tape recorders, they may hold back information. For them, this method would be ineffective.

If the dealer or advisor chooses to tape meetings, a system of storing and retrieving the tapes is absolutely necessary. Advisors need to check applicable laws in their jurisdiction, which may prohibit taping or which may require obtaining client consent or taking other steps before turning on the tape recorder. Local privacy laws will likely prohibit advisors and dealers from using the tapes for purposes other than furthering the advisor-client relationship or defending themselves if sued by the client.

Advisors should keep in mind that tape recorders can, and often do, malfunction. When taping, it's a good idea to use more than one tape recorder as backup and/or to write notes simultaneously. Before a meeting, it is essential to check that batteries work. It is also smart to have extra batteries and/or an electrical outlet nearby. As for transcribing a tape, this should be done as soon as possible. The longer one waits, the harder it can be to decipher all the words on the tape.

Telephone Conversations

Many advisors have asked me whether they should tape all communication, particularly telephone conversations with clients. Setting aside my concern about the volume of tapes and the ability to store and retrieve them, my concern is that advisors will forget the tape is running. The result might be sloppy language. If tapes are maintained and if a client sues, the client's lawyer would be entitled to have a copy of the tapes. This is also the case if the regulator asks for the tapes. In most jurisdictions, regulators are entitled to have them, regardless of whether they hurt or help the advisor. I have listened to several taped conversations between advisors and their clients and, if I can generalize, these tapes may bolster the client's case and, at best, are neutral for the advisor's case. Unless advisors can install a mechanism that makes them constantly aware that the tape recorder is running, I cannot recommend this practice. I think it would be almost impossible to always remember that the tape is on and to ensure that advisors watch their "P's" and "Q's" during every conversation, with every client, every day. Some advisors use the following technique: they imagine that a regulatory compliance person listens to all conversations between advisors and clients and is always judging their professionalism. This helps them to remember the tape is running.

SUMMARY

Credibility can win the day. Appreciating the importance of credibility in court and in regulatory matters is the first step to winning the credibility battle. Advisors who use the techniques discussed in this chapter will be better equipped to win the credibility war and, ultimately, to get favourable results if a complaint is lodged. The alternative should not be an option. Using the defensive strategies outlined will mitigate losses for advisors and dealers and will boost the advisor's professionalism.

Advisors Take Action

- Question your clients and document the answers to understand and obtain evidence of their levels of sophistication.
- Maintain a record and paper trail of all communications that occur between you and the client.
- Take or record notes every time you talk to clients on the phone or in a meeting. Whether the notes are handwritten, electronic, or transcribed from a tape, they should be complete, accurate and contemporaneous.
- Write letters or e-mails, particularly to clarify a particular issue or item discussed earlier.
- When you mark trades unsolicited, ensure you have documentation to corroborate that it was indeed an unsolicited trade.

---

1 In this case, the opposing counsel was not well enough versed in this area of law or industry to comprehend the implications of his client's answer. There are, however, many other well-experienced lawyers who represent complaining clients in the industry.

2 The issue of product risk is explored in Chapter 5 of Ellen Bessner's book *Advisor at Risk: A Roadmap to Protecting Your Business* (Shore Publishing, May 2008).

3 *Gregory Pepper Shanks* (2002), IDA Bulletin 3028 (Alberta District Council).

4 *Ibid.* at 2.

5 *Nesbitt Thomson Deacon Inc. v. Haupt*, [1992] O.J. No. 552 (Ont. Gen. Div.).

6 *Ibid.* at p. 3.

7 *Ibid.* at p. 3.

8 *Audio Works Production Services Ltd. v. Canadian Northern Shield Insurance Co.*, [2005] M.J. No. 348, 2005 MBQB 209 (Man. Q.B.).

CHAPTER 13

THE MIND, METHOD AND MANNER OF LEADERSHIP

G. Scott Bowman

Overview

A thoughtful commentary about the underlying intellectual, moral and practical responsibilities of leadership, this chapter examines universal attributes necessary for any professional application. It provokes the reader to look inward and challenges his or her assumptions and attitudes about his or her own and others' leadership practices.

Learning Objectives

- Does the professional moniker of "Trusted Advisor" carry with it much more than the profession's knowledge and rules? Is there an inherent assumption of a depth and breadth of character that represents much more than mere "value added"?
- Are you interested in reliably evaluating, understanding and improving your leadership skills with clients and others?
- You will depart this chapter with more knowledge of these skills, and hopefully have more questions.

The term "Trusted Advisor" carries with it a premise of professional as well as personal competence, integrity and knowledge. It claims the presence and practice of a moral and ethical imperative that in and of itself is a barometer for leadership expectations.

As we have seen in the previous chapter by Ellen Bessner, the necessity for professional diligence and discipline is paramount in processing your relationship with your clients and in defining expectations. Do you lead your clients? Is leadership in the relationship you have with your clients critical to that relationship? Of course it is! Is a value-bound, disciplined leadership inherent in that relationship? Without question!

At the risk of flying under false colours, you should know that I am not a financial guy! My life's vocation has been the creation and development of a non-profit special boarding school for boys with great potential, who for myriad reasons require motivation, structure, discipline and great care to actualize it. For 30 years, my wife and I have laboured in the arena of educating the "whole boy", often with very distressed parents and in the face of contemporary pedagogical theory. As such, we have shouldered many defeats and rejoiced in many victories; we have known good and bad times and have, along with the raising of our own children, learned a little bit about the mind, method and manner of leadership. The only financial dictum that I have practised over these many years comes from deep Scottish roots: "You can't spend what you don't have!" It has been a most simple yet most effective financial leadership paradigm.

In its many dimensions and complexions, leadership has been scrutinized, analyzed, criticized and generally mauled by media, politicians, academics and just about everyone else in the country, it seems. And what more do we really know about it and how can we as professionals get better at it?

Many people will be happy to tell you what leadership is; just ask them! A couple of observations at most of what they consider leadership to be are all too often followed by a rapid succession of expletives clearly outlining what it isn't!

But we need to go way beyond this if we are to stand a chance of grasping the most fundamental components of the topic, particularly as it is called for in the very competitive, unforgiving world we now occupy and where we all share the responsibility of what it will look like when we hand it over to our children and grandchildren.

Allow me to make a couple of assumptions. The first is that the reader is a person whose leadership decisions have significant import for others, and that these decisions have major impact not only on clients' wealth, but more importantly, on their expectations for a quality of life based on that wealth. Further, these decisions impact your corporation, and its (and your) reputation and professional standing. With this, I assume the reader has attended professional development courses which have addressed the topic of leadership; so neither the topic nor people like me are strangers. However, I am confident some of you wish we were! Equally, I assume that at least some of what you have already read or heard did less than stimulate you to question your own mind, method and manner of leadership and move you to discover a new concept or add context to those values you hold central to your leadership ideals and duties. That is my goal in this chapter.

Please do not infer that because I have accepted the task of this topic in this text that I hold myself to be a paragon of leadership. I do not! At best, I am a lifelong pupil whose daily decisions, big and small, impact many others to whom I recognize my responsibility.

I attempt, instead, to practise a disciplined leadership in my professional life according to a moral and ethical standard as a construct for those skills I have learned from others and those I have picked up along the way.

I strive to prosecute the burden of leadership and discipline within this framework and pray that on a good day I reach the mark as often as I fall short.

Let us turn to the mind of leadership.

THE MIND OF LEADERSHIP

Leaders are obliged to think! Yes, think and think critically! They must know where they are going and why. They must also know where they are not going and why.

They are obliged to look and listen not just carefully but consistently and considerately. I always try to remember that I have two ears, two eyes and one mouth. I try to practise the math of this ratio and use it accordingly.

This does not start in a classroom, forum or group. It starts within. In order to take responsibility with others we must first come to take responsibility with and for ourselves. Why are you in this profession? Are you looking to get rich quick? Or are you in it for the long haul to assist others in their lives by bringing your knowledge and integrity to enrich their lives for their benefit and thereby enjoy the rewards of good stewardship? Do you know how your leadership style affects others? How they may perceive you and best respond to you? How does your personality in the areas of communication, problem solving, interpersonal relations and decision making impact others? Are there areas you would like to understand better and improve upon? I hope your answer is yes! This doesn't imply that you are lacking in these areas, but rather that you are a good student of leadership and therefore always anxious to learn more.

If you haven't already and are interested in learning more about yourself, how others perceive you and your leadership profile, I would suggest the Myers Briggs Type Indicator® (MBTI) and the Fundamental Interpersonal Relations Orientation-Behaviour™ (FIBRO-B) instruments. These are accessible on the web and will lead you to other reliable instruments that may be of interest to you.

A leader must be disciplined to think and take time, very often in solitude in order to make decisions and formulate action plans, always checking these against the mission at hand, the resources available, the principles and ethos of his or her profession and organization and his or her own conscience. The very delicate balance between mission and resource is of profound importance to leaders and can in many situations represent the source of its own conflict or the venue or framework to understand and resolve larger conflict.

Those readers who may be senior executives or CEOs know very well that the essence of command lies not in the tabulation of accurate numbers, data and forecasts. These are undoubtedly important and ought never to be misunderstood or ignored. They are, however, so often not the arena of decision-making. The essence of command is nuance! In this context, all of the information a leader can muster and bring to bear on a decision is analyzed, weighed and balanced with principle, mission and resource. This is the arena of nuance and by definition is characterized by solitude, requiring knowledge, reflection, determination and courage to proceed. Here, the leader must marshal the very best of communication and motivation skills conveying the plan to others and in so doing capture their commitment, always keeping the objectives in mind.

It is true of all leaders and all relationships that expectations are the crucible of evaluation. It has been my experience that a relationship most often breaks down when expectations for that relationship are not declared and agreed upon at the onset, or change in the course of the relationship and remain undeclared and unacknowledged. This applies to both professional and personal relationships. For the Trusted Advisor, knowing what your clients' real expectations are of you could not be more important. Knowing and acknowledging your clients' expectations and clarifying yours is a critical constituent of your relationship at the onset, and once done and reviewed throughout, your relationship can go a long way to ensuring you are not left in the situation of having to defend yourself later on.

I meet with all parents when they enroll their son in our school. The most important exchange we have involves my asking them to write down their expectations of the school for their son and addressing these directly. Most of their expectations are within the bounds of our contractual agreement, already signed by them, but some are not. These are the most critical. I let them know very clearly that if their expectations are beyond our purview, our principles, ethics or simply our capability, that we cannot fulfill these. I inform the parents that if they are truly committed to an expectation that we cannot meet, they should look for another school. Following this, I let them know exactly what the school's expectations of them are and ensure that they understand and agree with them.

In order to do this, I have to accurately know our capabilities, our values, our various resources and our faculty's commitment very well. I also have to be able to evaluate our clients' capabilities, values, various resources and commitment to their son doing well at our school over a number of years. In other words, we have a professional relationship that is defined in a number of ways, the most important being acknowledging what each of us expects from the other regarding the most pressing, emotionally taxing and potentially rewarding issue in their life right now — their son!

Making difficult decisions, formulating the plan and following it in practice in both its letter and spirit, the leader must finally keep in mind the obligation of responsibility. Even in the vortex of the storm the leader must personify the values of his or her profession with integrity.

Of this process, Sir Winston Churchill said, "I am certainly not one of those who need to be prodded. In fact, if anything, I am the prod!"

Dr. Albert Schweitzer said, "Example is not the main thing in influencing others. It is the only thing!"

And Henry Kissinger stated, "If you don't know where you are going, all roads lead to nowhere!"

When considering the quality of leadership, we see that it is an ongoing process of thought and consideration. Its efficacy is largely dependent upon our values, our motives and our willingness to dedicate ourselves to the professional standard of always learning and how we critically think through these lessons. It is our obligation, as our decisions affect others directly and carry great import, to ensure we nurture the right lessons and strive always to make the right choices. How can we as professionals train ourselves to develop the good habits of right choice, particularly in matters that can only be prosecuted in the arena of nuance?

I have learned that stories can convey moral and intellectual truth in a way that contemporary prose often cannot, particularly with young people! Over 30 years in my vocation, I have collected two large ringed binders of such stories and I often convey them to our boys following the breakfast meal at school. I hope the following is found to be worthy of your thought or, more particularly, the young person that I sincerely hope still lingers within you. It is by the greatest of all authors: unknown.

An old Cherokee warrior sat with his grandson, who was a high-spirited adolescent, and observed the tension of his youth. The boy spoke of this tension to his grandfather, plaintively describing the angst he felt between what he was told was the right thing to do by his parents and the tribe, but wanting so badly to do otherwise, to have fun and be free of the shackles of his elders' expectations. His grandfather reflected that he was very familiar with this. He told his grandson that he, as well as all human beings, has a battle that rages within him!

"It is a battle between two wolves," the old warrior cited. "One wolf is good and brings us joy, peace, love, respect, humility, truth, generosity, compassion, faith and wisdom. The other wolf is evil and brings us anger, envy, greed, jealousy, hatred, arrogance, selfishness, false pride, self possession, superiority, detachment from others and lies."

The boy thought of this, became very still and asked his grandfather, "Which wolf wins the battle?"

His grandfather answered, "The one you feed."

THE METHOD OF LEADERSHIP

There are many styles or types of leadership. Which is best? I don't know! In truth, I think good and effective leaders use many of these in hybrid form to the benefit of the outcome. Rather than examining and debating these, let's look to a couple of practical suggestions that no leader, regardless of style, can be without. Two of the three we'll look at have already been mentioned.

Communicate. This doesn't mean talk! It means listen attentively and carefully, watch closely and carefully and ask questions intelligently and carefully. Learn something new about your business every day and teach something old about your business every day. In order to do this you have to get out of your chair, away from your computer and out of your office, and move around. Please understand that everything you do, even those things you do unknowingly, have meaning for those around you. It often isn't what you say that causes people to remember what you have said, but rather how you say it. An assumption wrongly made and stubbornly or even unwittingly pursued can have disastrous effects.

Another story may demonstrate the point. This is an alleged transcript of the actual radio conversation of a United States naval ship with Canadian authorities off the coast of Newfoundland a few years ago.

Canadians: Please divert your course 15 degrees to the south to avoid collision.

Americans: Recommend you divert your course 15 degrees to the north.

Canadians: Negative. You will have to divert your course 15 degrees to the south to avoid collision.

Americans: This is the Captain of a United States Navy ship. I say again, divert your course.

Canadians: No. I say again, divert your course 15 degrees south to avoid collision.

Americans: This is the aircraft carrier USS Lincoln, the second largest ship in the United States Atlantic fleet. Three destroyers, three cruisers and numerous support vessels accompany us. I demand that you change your course 15 degrees to the north. I say again, that is one five degrees north, or countermeasures will be undertaken to ensure the security of this ship and its task force.

Canadians: We are a lighthouse. Your call!

Ask questions. Give your undivided attention to the person giving the answer. For that moment nothing is more important. Always remember the person's name. The next time you want to say something to him or her, he or she is much more likely to receive your message properly and act upon it.

Speak of the values, principles and mission of the organization to someone every day. This is not preaching. It's reaching! It's reaching your people at the level of your vision and commitment and inviting them to join you. Be present and be patient. Listen a lot and talk a little. Remember the ratio of two eyes, two ears and one mouth and employ the math. Communication is more watching and listening than speaking. Be consistent. Predictability in integrity and action is the hallmark of a professional. This in no way smothers creativity or critical thought. I have a very good friend who is in the financial business and is a millionaire many times over. He is consistently creative and predictably brilliant!

Motivate. Evaluate and overcome! A good leader is obliged to accurately evaluate a situation, make decisions and provide structure for resolution. It's not a leader's job to make everyone happy. It's the leader's job to provide the challenges and trail markers that will stimulate people to do well and accomplish the mission.

A leader demonstrates his or her caring for his or her people and the mission by ensuring both are properly orchestrated to do the very best.

Train, train and then train some more. A great leader once told me, "If you fail to plan, you plan to fail!"

Unless you plan on being a self-serving leader (one who controls people and contains information for his own gratification) rather than a serving leader (one who serves the people and the mission), it is impossible to do it all yourself. You have to train people. Many organizations, regardless of size, render only lip service to training and pay substantially when it is needed the most. Good leaders encourage their people to continue their education, take on new challenges and expand their horizons and then apply it all to enrich others around them.

Always disseminate principles. In their book *The Secret: What Great Leaders Know and Do*, Blanchard and Miller point out that, "Profit is simply the applause. People are more motivated when a leader disseminates his own commitment, vision and spirit." Loyalty is indeed a two-way street. Integrity begets integrity! Strength of character is the venue by which good leaders find the best solutions, not necessarily their solutions.

General Norman Schwarzkopf declared, "If you have to choose between professional knowledge and strength of character, give me strength of character every time!"

How do we determine true strength of character? How do we see through the shiny veneer to a duplicity that lies beneath the surface and is surely feeding the evil wolf? We are all subject to the fast and easy talker, the slick salesman, the one who indeed can read others well and determine their needs, but rather than offering good stewardship, he manipulates and cons people for his own selfish ends. Indeed, it's very difficult at times and we regret our misplaced faith. Perhaps the only true way to be able to accurately detect true strength of character is to consciously work on our own and thereby recognize similar substance in others.

If we are to be truly "stand alone" professionals in our respective vocations, perhaps there is a common method of leadership that in its principles may be generalized to all. Perhaps it is a conviction to work every day to reach a balance in life that demands an internalized discipline whose purpose is the communion with good, and to value this so strongly that, having fed the evil wolf and suffered its betrayal, we lead with a sense of responsibility for that good in those we lead and those we influence.

THE MANNER OF LEADERSHIP

When speaking of the manner of leadership, character and confidence become our focus.

Casual observation often leads people to conclude that the successful person at the helm is a "born leader". Strength of character goes a long way to support this observation.

My experience has been that whether or not a leader is born or taught, or in the best case a combination of both, he or she embodies a certain "manner". This has little to do with barking orders, coming up with slick slogans or simply just getting others to do the things they should. That's called supervision.

Rather, it is a unique and very often hard-earned confidence born of a combination of a very strategic mind and a disciplined and scarred will that has learned to do those things it would rather not do! For example, we would all rather do a hobby or watch a favourite movie or television program than confront a serious issue with our children or a colleague. There is always a choice and so very often in life the right choice is always the harder one. It is for those who have learned or wish to learn to put what they "want" aside in service of what they "ought" that leadership truly beckons. My grandfather, who was a new immigrant to this country, always used to say, "Many are called, but few are chosen." Are you called and are you choosing to be chosen? Is your character and its strengths and weaknesses worthy of being a "Trusted Adviser"?

What are the presiding characteristics of this manner? Integrity. Doing the right thing! Feeding the good wolf and communicating its truth to your profession and your clients. The personality traits of this manner are a strong personal ethic and a strong work ethic over a long term; loyalty to principles, not profit; courage to say no in the practice of those principles; commitment to service and stewardship; and common sense and decency in dealing with others.

I'm old enough to have grown up with the term "common sense" as a very active part of my lexicon or rather my parents' lexicon. I can't tell you the number of misdemeanours I committed as a boy that flew in the face of "common sense". I was a "common sense" delinquent in adolescence and either I have improved just a little with years, or the term has become less familiar. It is a critical constituent of the manner of good leaders.

Some years ago, I went searching for it again and found that "common sense" is not all that common anymore! In my search I stumbled upon this wonderful story, again by my favourite author, unknown, and have shared it many times at breakfast with our boys at the Academy.

A Remarkable Obituary

Today we mourn the passing of a beloved old friend, Mr. Common Sense.

Mr. Sense had been with us for many years. No one knows for sure how old he was, since his birth records were long ago lost in bureaucratic red tape.

He will be remembered as having cultivated such value lessons as: when to come in out of the rain, why the early bird gets the worm and that life isn't always fair. Common Sense lived by simple, sound financial policies (don't spend more than you earn) and reliable parenting strategies (adults not kids are in charge).

His health began to rapidly deteriorate when well-intentioned but overbearing regulations were set in place. Reports of a six-year-old boy charged for sexual harassment for kissing a classmate, teens suspended from school for using mouthwash after lunch and a teacher fired for reprimanding an unruly student only worsened his condition.

Mr. Sense declined even further when schools were required to get parental consent to administer aspirin to a student, but could not inform the parents when a student became pregnant and wanted an abortion.

Finally, Common Sense lost the will to live as the Ten Commandments became contraband, churches became businesses and criminals received better treatment than their victims.

Common Sense gave up the ghost when a woman failed to realize that a steaming cup of coffee was hot. She spilled it in her lap and was awarded a huge financial settlement.

Common Sense was preceded in death by his parents, Truth and Trust, his wife, Discretion, his daughter, Responsibility, and his son, Reason. He is survived by two estranged stepbrothers: My Rights and Ima Whiner.

Not many attended his funeral because so few realized he was gone.

I have often found that one of the practical ways to identify the manner of leadership is by a leader's manners! Good manners are engrained as they have disciplined themselves to make bad manners unnecessary.

In Dr. Lewis Sorleys' Pulitzer nominated book *Vietnam Chronicles*, which documents the actual transcripts of classified tapes of General Creighton Abrams during his command of American troops in Vietnam from 1968 through 1972, we see a pristine example of this.

The book is a working manual on the best kind of leadership. One of the many striking attributes of General Abrams' manner of leadership was his unwavering capacity to listen and to coach those around him and, even in very dark and dangerous times or when he had to become confrontational, he did so with the kind of good manners that leaves both the subordinate and the situation enhanced by his integrity.

Don't get me wrong. Abrams was no pushover or "shiny" soldier. He was a very tough man. When he gave it to you, you got it straight. But that's all you got. One never got rancour or vindictiveness or acrimony. He gave praise in the same dignified manner.

Good manners, combined with common sense, strong personal and professional ethics, and communicating the right message with the true confidence, is a pretty impressive leadership manner!

The task of leadership is to achieve difficult tasks, often in a delicate balance of vision, mission, logistics, tactics, resource, manpower and principles.

In contrast, many pundits purport that leadership is solely situational and that the old question of whether or not the times make the man or the man makes the times is an antiquated intellectual exercise. Rather, in our modern "tuned in and turned on" hectic world, leadership must necessarily be a compilation of demands and opportunities, an amalgam of influences and pressures, real or contrived, that no man can truly lead as the task is too vast and the partisan interests too great. Political correctness demands compromise as a premise to thought or action, and the weakest link in the chain by merit of that weakness wields the defining spirit of that compromise. It has even been hypothesized that we are witnessing fewer and fewer leaders because our modern world does not reward them in a material sense as it may once have. I don't think any of this is true.

I think it may well be that our society of late has become so focused on immediate self-gratification, the supremacy of the ethos of comfort, quick-fix solutions, personal power and money making that we have forgone the integrity of service, stewardship and true mastery in our vocations.

I encourage each of you in your journey as leaders. It is a hefty burden that exacts a hefty tariff. If it's the genuine article, it will bring scorn more often than glory, solitude more often than the company of friends and questioning more often than concurrence.

I have one last thought of a most personal nature to offer, if I may.

The defining moments of leadership are not those public or even intimate vignettes, regardless of how good or bad they may turn out.

Rather, the defining moments of leadership reside in those times of solitude when you are all alone with the weight of a decision and the only company you have is your conscience.

My very best wish for you is that you find yourself in good company.

PART II

INDIVIDUAL PENSION PLAN (IPP) ESSENTIALS

CHAPTER 14

UNDERSTANDING THE INDIVIDUAL PENSION PLAN (IPP) HISTORY AND MARKET FORCES

Peter J. Merrick

Overview

This chapter presents the concept of the Individual Pension Plan (IPP). The chapter then describes the history of pensions and IPPs in Canada. It concludes by describing the market forces driving the growth of the IPP industry.

Learning Objectives

By the end of this chapter, you should be able to:

- explain what an Individual Pension Plan is;
- provide the historical background behind the Individual Pension Plan in Canada; and
- understand the market forces driving the Individual Pension Plan solution.

WHY READ THIS?

To be successful in the Individual Pension Plan (IPP) arena today you need a lot of luck. "Luck" in this book has not been defined in the traditional sense of the word. "Luck" means when your preparation meets with opportunity. You need to be prepared to be able to identify and act upon every opportunity that presents itself to you so that you will create your own luck.

Incorporated businesses looking to add a benefit for their owners and top executives are beginning to learn about this little-known tax deferral and tax minimization structure called the IPP. The IPP is what many in the financial industry are calling an "RRSP on Steroids", a "Super-Sized RRSP" or an "RRSP Upgrade". An IPP is a defined benefit pension plan for usually one person, a husband and wife, a small group of employees or a family. All members of an IPP need to be *bona fide* employees of companies that sponsor the plan.

An advisor who gains one IPP client aged 49 today will create over $350,000 of commissionable and fee income over the next 15 years. Research indicates that the IPP market will experience unparalleled growth, from 11,500 registered plans in 2008 to over 300,000 within 15 years for Canada's richest Canadian households. Three hundred billion dollars of new investable assets are now up for grabs.

The only thing holding financial professionals back from capitalizing on this new IPP market is the lack of credible IPP and proper financial planning knowledge. This section of this book is a must! When considering the income and fee potential generated from each IPP client, the "return on investment" (ROI) could be astronomical.

IPPs are a successful person's answer to registered retirement savings plans. IPPs are sanctioned by the Canada Revenue Agency (CRA) and offer one of the best tax and retirement savings solutions for individuals 40 years old and older who have a T4 income of more than $122,222 for 2009, who work for an incorporated business and who historically have maximized their RRSPs and pension contributions.

IPPs offer significant amounts of additional tax-deferred income to be set aside for a business owner's and top executive's retirement. The IPP tax solution allows for hundreds of thousands of additional tax-deferred income dollars (from an incorporated business) to be invested into an IPP structure above and beyond the average RRSP funding allotments. Thus, owners/executives are allowed non-taxable interest that compounds until retirement and the money is withdrawn from the plan.

In 2004, at the annual consultation held by the CRA on Registered Pensions, a discussion ensued on "how Individual Pension Plans (IPPs) were a 'new' and uncommon type of pension plan some years ago, but now represent more than 1/3 (6,500 of 19,000) of the inventory (defined benefit pension plans). This type of plan design presents more compliance risk and the growth of this segment continues to increase. Although an IPP usually covers only one member, they require a disproportionate amount of attention when compared with plans covering hundreds of members. Consequently, a lot of audit activity has been focused on the IPP segment." As a result, the CRA Registered Plans Directorate intends to enhance its focus to monitor IPPs.

Advisors planning to enter the IPP market will need to acquire a basic understanding of tax laws, accounting, actuary evaluations, investment management, pension legislation, employment law and employee benefit plan construction as they begin to offer this specialized pension solution to their clients. Many employers and their financial advisors will need to seek educational services to aid them in the IPP set-up, maintenance and wind-up stages.

IPP vs. RRSP

How good are IPPs vs. RRSPs? Imagine a 45-year-old owner/executive who has worked for the same company since 1991 and has averaged a T4 income of more than $125,000 a year. If she and her employer decide to "max-out" her IPP contribution room and RRSP going forward (using a yearly rate of return of 7.5%), she will accumulate $7,042,649 in registered retirement assets by the time she turns 71. Opting for this tax solution, this individual would have a registered retirement yearly benefit at age 71 of $561,252 fully indexed to the consumer price index.

In comparison, if this same owner/executive only utilizes her RRSP option from 45 years of age to 71, she would only accumulate $5,083,364 in registered retirement tax-sheltered assets. This amount of RRSP assets on an annual basis would generate $405,110 of retirement income from age 71 and beyond.

The decision is clear. The owner/executive who implements both the IPP and RRSP tax solutions as part of her retirement plan would have an additional $1,959,285 of tax-sheltered assets in her registered retirement plans and have an additional $156,152 in annual retirement income.

On the next page is a table that shows the accumulated dollar value for the business owner/executive with both an IPP and an RRSP. On the page following that is a table that shows the accumulated dollar value for the owner/executive with only an RRSP.

With IPP

		IPP				RRSP					
Year	Age	Beginning Balance	Contri-bution	Interest Income	Ending Balance	Beginning Balance	Contri-bution	Interest Income	Ending Balance	Total With IPP	Retirement Pension per Year
2008	45	313,400	91,202	26,863	431,465	0	8,500	313	8,813	440,278	N/A
2009	46	431,465	25,002	33,281	489,748	8,813	600	683	10,096	499,844	N/A
2010	47	489,748	26,877	37,721	554,346	10,096	600	779	11,475	565,821	N/A
2011	48	554,346	28,893	42,640	625,879	11,475	600	883	12,958	638,837	N/A
2012	49	625,879	31,060	48,085	705,024	12,958	600	994	14,552	719,576	N/A
2013	50	705,024	33,390	54,106	792,520	14,552	600	1,113	16,265	808,785	44,027
2014	51	792,520	35,894	60,761	889,175	16,265	600	1,242	18,107	907,282	49,933
2015	52	889,175	38,586	68,109	995,870	18,107	600	1,380	20,087	1,015,957	56,568
2016	53	995,870	41,480	76,218	1,113,568	20,087	600	1,529	22,216	1,135,784	64,024
2017	54	1,113,568	44,591	85,160	1,243,319	22,216	600	1,688	24,504	1,267,823	72,364
2018	55	1,243,319	47,935	95,014	1,386,268	24,504	600	1,860	26,964	1,413,232	81,784
2019	56	1,386,268	51,530	105,868	1,543,666	26,964	600	2,044	29,608	1,573,274	92,274
2020	57	1,543,666	55,395	117,815	1,716,876	29,608	600	2,243	32,451	1,749,327	104,127
2021	58	1,716,876	59,550	130,958	1,907,384	32,451	600	2,456	35,507	1,942,891	117,466
2022	59	1,907,384	64,016	145,411	2,116,811	35,507	600	2,685	38,792	2,155,603	132,408
2023	60	2,116,811	68,817	161,295	2,346,923	38,792	600	2,931	42,323	2,389,246	149,235
2024	61	2,346,923	73,978	178,743	2,599,644	42,323	600	3,196	46,119	2,645,763	168,306
2025	62	2,599,644	79,526	197,902	2,877,072	46,119	600	3,481	50,200	2,927,272	189,590
2026	63	2,877,072	85,490	218,928	3,181,490	50,200	600	3,787	54,587	3,236,077	213,744
2027	64	3,181,490	91,902	241,996	3,515,388	54,587	600	4,116	59,303	3,574,691	240,882
2028	65	3,515,388	98,795	267,292	3,881,475	59,303	600	4,470	64,373	3,945,848	271,635
2029	66	3,881,475	106,205	295,021	4,282,701	64,373	600	4,850	69,823	4,352,524	306,313
2030	67	4,282,701	114,170	325,407	4,722,278	69,823	600	5,259	75,682	4,797,960	345,510
2031	68	4,722,278	122,733	358,690	5,203,701	75,682	600	5,698	81,980	5,285,681	389,840
2032	69	5,203,701	131,938	395,136	5,730,775	81,980	600	6,171	88,751	5,819,526	440,013
2033	70	5,730,775	141,833	435,031	6,307,639	88,751	600	6,678	96,029	6,403,668	496,840
2034	71	6,307,639	152,470	478,687	6,938,796	96,029	600	7,224	103,853	7,042,649	561,252

Note: Chart provided by Westcoast Actuaries Inc. of British Columbia.

Without IPP

		IPP				RRSP					
Year	Age	Beginning Balance	Contri-bution	Interest Income	Ending Balance	Beginning Balance	Contri-bution	Interest Income	Ending Balance	Total Without IPP	Retirement Pension per Year
2008	45	0	0	0	0	313,400	20,000	24,241	357,641	357,641	N/A
2009	46	0	0	0	0	357,641	21,000	27,596	406,237	406,237	N/A
2010	47	0	0	0	0	406,237	22,000	31,278	459,515	459,515	N/A
2011	48	0	0	0	0	459,515	23,210	35,318	518,043	518,043	N/A
2012	49	0	0	0	0	518,043	24,487	39,755	582,285	582,285	N/A
2013	50	0	0	0	0	582,285	25,833	44,623	652,741	652,741	35,533
2014	51	0	0	0	0	652,741	27,254	49,959	729,954	729,954	40,174
2015	52	0	0	0	0	729,954	28,753	55,805	814,512	814,512	45,351
2016	53	0	0	0	0	814,512	30,335	62,205	907,052	907,052	51,130
2017	54	0	0	0	0	907,052	32,003	69,207	1,008,262	1,008,262	57,549
2018	55	0	0	0	0	1,008,262	33,763	76,863	1,118,888	1,118,888	64,750
2019	56	0	0	0	0	1,118,888	35,620	85,228	1,239,736	1,239,736	72,712
2020	57	0	0	0	0	1,239,736	37,579	94,364	1,371,679	1,371,679	81,648
2021	58	0	0	0	0	1,371,679	39,646	104,336	1,515,661	1,515,661	91,636
2022	59	0	0	0	0	1,515,661	41,827	115,215	1,672,703	1,672,703	102,746
2023	60	0	0	0	0	1,672,703	44,127	127,078	1,843,908	1,843,908	115,172
2024	61	0	0	0	0	1,843,908	46,554	140,007	2,030,469	2,030,469	129,165
2025	62	0	0	0	0	2,030,469	49,114	154,094	2,233,677	2,233,677	144,668
2026	63	0	0	0	0	2,233,677	51,816	169,434	2,454,927	2,454,927	162,148
2027	64	0	0	0	0	2,454,927	54,666	186,132	2,695,725	2,695,725	181,653
2028	65	0	0	0	0	2,695,725	57,672	204,303	2,957,700	2,957,700	203,610
2029	66	0	0	0	0	2,957,700	60,844	224,068	3,242,612	3,242,612	228,202
2030	67	0	0	0	0	3,242,612	64,191	245,560	3,552,363	3,552,363	255,812
2031	68	0	0	0	0	3,552,363	67,721	268,921	3,889,005	3,889,005	286,829
2032	69	0	0	0	0	3,889,005	71,446	294,306	4,254,757	4,254,757	321,701
2033	70	0	0	0	0	4,254,757	75,375	321,882	4,652,014	4,652,014	360,935
2034	71	0	0	0	0	4,652,014	79,521	351,829	5,083,364	5,083,364	405,110

Note: Chart provided by Westcoast Actuaries Inc. of British Columbia.

A LITTLE PENSION HISTORY — FROM YESTERDAY TO TODAY!

The legendary documentary filmmaker, Ken Burns, creator of the acclaimed mini-series: *The Civil War* (1990), *Baseball* (1994) and *JAZZ* (2001), once remarked during an interview "that if we want to know where we are and where we are going, we first need to know where we have been". So let us begin by looking at an 89-year history of Canada's ever-changing tax, retirement and pension environment.

1919: The federal government, two years after the introduction of personal income tax, introduced legislation that allowed employees to make tax deductions for their contributions into pension plans.

1938: The federal government passed legislation that allowed employers to deduct their contributions to employee pension plans with no caps on the amount that could be deducted.

1941: The Canadian government during the Second World War placed strict wage freezes on the entire economy to control inflation during the war. Employers across Canada en masse started providing their people with pensions and other deferred income benefit plans that legally allowed them to work around the wage freeze and offer additional compensation to their employees without actually raising wages. In 1951, the Canadian government removed these wage freezes.

1947: The federal government placed limits on the amount of contributions that both employees and employers could make into pension plans.

1957: The federal government introduced Registered Retirement Savings Plans.

1971: The federal government placed limits on the amount of foreign property that pension funds and other registered tax-deferred retirement plans could hold within them to a maximum of 10%. The foreign content rules were introduced to ensure that a substantial proportion of tax-deferred retirement savings were invested in Canadian companies and to support the development of Canada's capital markets.

1972: The *Act to amend the Income Tax Act*, S.C. 1970-71-72, c. 63, was passed into legislation. The modern day *Income Tax Act* (ITA) was born. Before 1972 capital gains were not taxable in Canada.

1976: The federal government set defined benefit pension plan (DBPP) limits at $1,715 per year of service to a maximum of $60,025 promised annual defined pension retirement benefit. This remained the maximum until 1990. In 1976 the maximum defined benefit earnings was set at nine times the national wage at the time.

1978: Up until 1978 the only form of retirement income that someone could purchase from an RRSP was an annuity for life based on the surviving spouse or what is referred to as a last survival annuity. The federal government that year introduced two more additional options. One was the option to purchase a term certain annuity until the owner of the plan turned 90 years old. The other new option was the creation of the Registered Retirement Income Fund (RRIF).

1984: The federal government's Marc Lalonde, then the Liberal federal Finance Minister, proposed increasing RRSP contribution limits. In 1989, RRSP yearly contribution limits were to be increased to $15,500, which would put them in sync with the maximum benefit enjoyed by members of defined benefit pension plans. This proposed legislation to increase maximum RRSP contributions to $15,500 did not become a reality until 2004.

1987: The federal government knocked down the barriers separating the "four pillars" of the Canadian financial sector — banks, trust companies, insurance companies and investment dealers — and all these independent sectors were permitted to merge their services. With this convergence of financial institutions, one-stop shopping for financial services would be possible for each Canadian consumer.

1990: The federal government passed legislation amending the *Income Tax Act* which overhauled how the government grants taxed assistance for all pensions, RRSPs and other registered deferred income plans in Canada.

1990: The federal government set defined benefit pension plan limits at $1,722.22 per year of service to a maximum of $60,278 pension benefit per year for 35 years of employment service. This was considered to be enough to provide for a 70% pension for an individual earning a T4 income of $86,111. This limit remained until the 2002 federal budget.

1990: The federal government amended the *Income Tax Act* to include in section 147.1 designated plans to be created as of 1991 (S.C. 1990, c. 35, s. 16). A designated plan is a pension plan where more than 50% of the pension credits are for a specific person. This individual is an active member of a pension plan who may be a connected person to the employer of the plan and/or who earns two and one-half times the year's maximum pensionable earnings (YMPE).

A connected person is a person who owns directly or indirectly 10% or more of capital stock in a company or a related corporation. It also includes a person who does not deal at arm's length with a company. This includes a spouse or a common law partner. It should also be noted that if someone were a connected person at any time in the history of the employer who sponsors an IPP, the CRA would always consider him or her a connected person. This amendment to the ITA gave birth to the Individual Pension Plan.

For example, if a business owner had sold 91% of his or her interest in his or her company in 1995 and only owns 9% of the IPP sponsoring company in 2006 at the time the IPP is set up for him or her, then according to the CRA rules this member will be considered for IPP purposes a connected person. Simply put: "Once a connected person, always a connected person!"

1990: Pension adjustments (PA) were first reported in that year to offset RRSP contribution limits for the first time in 1991. The PA is based on what is referred to as the Factor of 9. This is a pension credit formula used to determine the pension credit in a defined benefit pension plan. The federal government created the Factor of 9 to equalize the tax-assisted savings between all defined contribution plans and defined benefit plans. The Factor of 9 states that for every $1 of defined benefit pension benefit promised to a member, the government considers that $9 of funding will be required to deliver that same benefit. However, this relationship is an average over a plan member's entire working career (later on in this book we will see how the Factor of 9 benefits older employees and puts younger employees at a disadvantage). It should be noted that the PA reported for defined contribution pension plans (DCPP) and deferred profit-sharing plans (DPSP) are equal to the actual dollar amounts invested in those plans.

1990: RRSP maximum contribution limits for 1991 were set at $11,500 and were to increase to $15,500 by 1995 to put them at par with the maximum defined pensionable benefit.

1990: The foreign content limit for Registered Pension Plans and RRSPs were doubled in 1990 from 10% to 20%.

1990: The federal government instituted a policy that allowed for unused room in an RRSP to accumulate starting in 1991. Before this was introduced by the federal government, if an individual did not use his or her RRSP room in the year that it was granted, he or she would lose the opportunity to contribute that amount in future years.

1991: The first modern Individual Pension Plans were registered with the CRA and given pension registration numbers for reporting to the CRA.

1992: RRSP maximum contribution limits of $15,500 for 1995 were pushed back to 1996.

1995: The maximum RRSP contributions for 1996 were frozen at $13,500. This maximum limit lasted for seven years.

1997: The federal government implemented Pension Adjustment Reversal (PAR) into the *Income Tax Act*. PAR restores the RRSP contribution room for an employee who was terminated from a registered pension plan (RPP), or increases the room by the difference between the total employee's PAs that were reported while he or she was a member of these plans and the actual pension transfer value to an RRSP. A PAR is calculated based on when membership in the plan is terminated. The RRSP room generated by PAR can be used by the individual to make RRSP contributions in the year of termination or it can be carried forward for use in future years. Before the federal government enacted PAR, when a member of a defined benefit pension plan left a plan, if he or she had lost RRSP room due to large pension adjustments that did not represent the actual amount vested within his or her DBPP, the former plan member would not have been able to recover the lost RRSP room.

2000: The federal government increased foreign content limits for RPPs and RPPs from 20% to 25% for 2000, and to 30% for 2001.

2003: The federal government increased yearly funding limits for RRSP contributions, and pension benefit limits for all RPPs. The new limits for RRSPs were set at $14,500 for 2003, $15,500 for 2004, $16,500 for 2005 and $18,000 for 2006. Money purchase registered pension plans limits were set at $15,500 for 2003, $16,500 for 2004 and $18,000 for 2005. Defined benefit plan maximum pension benefit limits for accredited years of service were increased from $1,722.22 to $1,833 for 2004, and to $2,000 for 2005 for each year of employable service. When these plans reach their new maximum funding amounts as stated above, these amounts will increase with the average wage.

2004: The first of a series of Individual Pension Plan articles were published in *CA Magazine*, starting in the January 2004 issue. *CA Magazine* is a publication owned by the Canadian Institute of Chartered Accountants. These articles are accredited with launching the current boom in IPPs.

2005: RRSP and RPP limits were increased. Set limits for RRSP contributions were increased to $19,000 for 2007, $20,000 for 2008, $21,000 for 2009, and $22,000 for 2010. Set limits for defined contribution pension plans contributions were increased from $18,000 to $19,000 for 2006, $20,000 for 2007, $21,000 for 2008 and $22,000 for 2009. Set limits for defined benefit plan limits were increased to $2,111 for 2006, $2,222 for 2007, $2,333 for 2008 and $2,444 for 2009. All these limits are to be indexed to the average wage growth, starting in 2010 for defined contribution pension plans and defined benefit plans, and in 2011 for RRSPs.

2005: The foreign content limits for RPPs and RRSPs were removed. This marked a fundamental change in the federal government's policy to direct moneys from RPPs and RRSPs to support the Canadian capital markets.

2005: The CRA's Registered Plans Directorate decided that it would shift its focus from an all-encompassing review of IPP documents when IPPs are first registered to a selective review of plan documents based on risk, and to more audits of IPPs on an ongoing basis.

For the first 14 years of the modern IPP history, the CRA placed its focus on pre-registration review. Going forward, the CRA's resources will be going towards audits of plans that are already registered. This means that the registration process of IPPs will be relaxed and made more quickly, but if an IPP is found not to be compliant with regulations, these pensions will be deregistered.

2005: The CRA increased the amount of funds that needed to be transferred from RRSPs, DPSPs, DCPPs and other DBPPs, in a qualifying transfer to purchase IPP past service pension credits.

2006: In Ontario, a Risk-Based Pension Investment Monitoring Program and Investment Information Summary Form (IIS Form) was mandated to be submitted every year by sponsors of IPPs to the Financial Services Commission of Ontario (FSCO). It is believed that other provincial pension regulators will follow FSCO's lead and implement a similar risk-based pension investment monitoring process.

This form allows FSCO to reduce the risk that members of individual pension plans will not receive the benefits promised to them by their IPP sponsors due to poor investment performance and management within these plans:

- The IIS Form requests asset information, queries the status of the Statement of Investment Policies and Procedures (SIPP) and assesses compliance with the federal investment regulations and the SIPP.
- The plan administrator must certify as to the accuracy of the information on the IIS Form.
- Only the defined benefit component of a hybrid plan should be reported on the IIS.

Plans flagged by the automated assessment process will be subject to a further review. FSCO will follow up with the plan administrator if there is any non-compliance with the investment regulations or standards related to IPPs.

2007: This marks the 50th anniversary of the RRSP.

2007: The first formalized course provided on IPPs in Canada was offered by the Canadian Securities Institute for financial consultants nationwide.

2007: The first book on IPPs in Canada is published by LexisNexis Canada Inc.

2007: The Canadian federal budget for that year set the maximum retirement age for an IPP member to begin withdrawing his or her pension until December 31st after the IPP member's 71st birthday from age 69. Also in the same budget, senior couples were now all permitted to pool their retirement pension income. But there are some specific eligibility rules. IPP lifetime pension payments can be split between spouses regardless of the age of the pensioner to provide up to 50% of the promised yearly benefit to the non-participating spouse.

2007: Canadian judges have cleared the way for the CRA to confiscate from two taxpayers, Susanne Greenhalgh and Charles Ross, their pension savings, that is, their entire IPP savings, hers from more than 30 years as a St. Catharines teacher and his from serving as a Sault Ste. Marie police officer. The CRA now has court backing to revoke registration of individual pension plans. Financial advisors, IPP sponsors and IPP members have been placed on notice that the CRA is monitoring all IPPs going forward to make sure that these plans are compliant.

2007: Canada's Minister of Finance and the U.S. Treasury Secretary signed a new protocol to the Canada-U.S. tax treaty. They agreed that both countries will give mutual tax recognition of pension contributions. Before this amendment to the Canada-U.S. tax treaty, all contributions made into an IPP were considered a taxable benefit for U.S. residents living in Canada or Canadians residing in the United States.

2008: The federal government and Ontario pension regulators (*Pension Benefits Act*), which both govern the majority of IPPs in Canada, amended their requirements for Locked-in Retirement Accounts (LIRA) and Locked-in Income Funds (LIFs). These amendments will impact the deregistration of IPPs, giving members of these plans more options when winding down their IPPs as follows:

- Money invested in an IPP can be transferred into a LIRA until the individual reaches the age of 71.
- No longer are individuals who own LIRAs or LIFs obligated to purchase an annuity by the end of the year in which they reach 80 years of age. Consequently, owners of LIRAs and LIFs will be able to keep their LIF after age 80.

- Upon the death of the LIRA or LIF owner, the spouse or joint partner will be authorized to make a direct transfer of the survivor benefit into his or her own RRSP or RRIF where permitted by the federal *Income Tax Act.*
- Owners of LIRAs who are age 55 or over with total assets in all their locked-in accounts that make up less than 40% of the Year's Maximum Pensionable Earnings will have the option of directly transferring the money to an RRSP or RRIF.
- Non-residents of Canada as determined by the CRA for the purposes of the federal *Income Tax Act* may apply to withdraw the money in their LIRA or LIF account two years after their official departure date from Canada.

With these new rules governing LIRAs and LIFs, members of IPPs have greater flexibility to collapse their IPPs into these types of registered plans and are permitted to access these moneys as a result of these new LIRA and LIF rules. Canadians moving savings from a locked-in to an unlocked registered savings vehicle would not be subject to taxes. But funds withdrawn from the savings vehicle would be subject to federal income tax.

2008: The Canadian federal government introduced the tax-free savings account (TFSA) in its February 2008 budget. In many ways, the TFSA mirrors the RRSP and registered education savings plan (RESP). As with RRSPs, there is an annual contribution limit, but the contributions are not deductible. Unlike RRSPs, the contributions and income that accumulate in a TFSA are not taxable on withdrawal. A TFSA therefore lets investments grow tax-free.

Starting in 2009, individuals 18 years of age and older who are resident in Canada may contribute a maximum of $5,000 to a TFSA each year. This amount will be indexed as of 2010 and rounded to the nearest $500. Unused contribution room can be carried forward to future years. Accumulated amounts may be withdrawn from the TFSA as needed at any time. The tax benefit will not be lost if you withdraw an amount from a TFSA because you will gain contribution room equal to the withdrawal, making a TFSA much more flexible than an RRSP, where the contribution room is lost. The contributions and income that accumulate in a TFSA are not taxable on withdrawal.

2008: The federal government made amendments to the federal *Bankruptcy and Insolvency Act*, protecting RRSPs, RRIFs and deferred profit-sharing plans from seizure by creditors in case of bankruptcy. The federal Act now protects RRSPs/RRIFs only in the case of a bankruptcy. On the other hand, the Act provides creditor protection of locked-in plans even before bankruptcy. As a result, the federal changes are limited in their application, since a person could only benefit from the protection if he or she declares bankruptcy and is subsequently sued. Under these new rules, if a creditor files a claim before a person has declared bankruptcy, then the RSP/RIF is not protected. The pension legislation provides a greater level of protection, since the assets in a locked-in plan are protected from creditors in all cases, not just bankruptcy.

2008: The CRA released an actuarial bulletin on how postponed retirement actuarial increases on pensions are to be determined for members over the age of 65. The increases for benefits accrued after age 65 would be affected — instead of having the increase determined from age 65 to the actual retirement or valuation date, it would now be from the age when benefits are being accrued (*e.g.*, 66, 67 and 68) to the actual retirement or valuation date.

2009: The Accounting Standards Board (AcSB) of the Canadian Institute of Chartered Accountants (CICA) has been working on new financial reporting standards for private businesses. It is expected that the number of specific financial disclosure requirements for reporting IPPs for privately owned businesses and corporate financials will be adopted in early 2010. These reporting standards are expected to be less stringent for business owners who own more than 50% of a company and have IPPs set up for themselves or their family members.

MARKET FORCES DRIVING THE INDIVIDUAL PENSION PLAN SOLUTION

Similar to the adoption rate of RRSPs, which were first introduced in 1957 and did not become popularized in Canadian culture until the late 1970s when banks were allowed to sell RRSPs, IPPs are predicted by industry experts to become as commonplace for Canada's top earners in the next 15 years as RRSPs are today, as Canada's highest income earners trade in their RRSPs for the much more tax- and retirement-efficient IPP structure.

Let us look at some of the forces driving the growth of the IPP solution.

According to the Canadian Taxpayers Federation, in 2000, 22 million Canadians filed tax returns. Of those, 598,700 (2.7% of tax filers) earned more than $100,000 in T4 income. Potentially, an additional 600,000 business owners and executives have the ability to pay themselves T4 incomes of more than $100,000 if there is a tax incentive, such as the IPP, for them to do so.

The richest 10% of Canadian families have an average net worth of $980,903, accounting for 53% of national wealth in 1999. At that time, 72% of the $420 billion held in RRSPs were owned by the top 20% of affluent families. This 20% also owned 94% of the $92 billion invested in stocks outside RRSPs and 81% of the $80 billion invested in mutual and investment funds outside RRSPs.

According to the Canadian Federation of Independent Businesses, in the 1990s, there was an explosion of self-employment in this country. Currently there are 2.3 million self-employed Canadians and 1.1 million active incorporated businesses in Canada. With 75% of Canada's over one million businesses that employ fewer than five people, it can be assumed that most of the IPPs in this country will be created by owners of Canadian Controlled Private Corporations (CCPCs) looking for a strategy to take money out of their corporations in a tax-effective way to help them prepare for retirement.

According to Statistics Canada, in the 2001 census, the median age of the average Canadian worker was 41.3 years old. Today 43% of working Canadians are within ten years of retirement. The creation of an IPP only makes sense for individuals aged 40 or older. The IPP maximum contribution for a 40-year-old is approximately $22,762 and will increase at a compound rate of 7.5% annually compared to the maximum RRSP 2009 contribution limit set at $21,000.

It is hypothesized that the IPP market will experience a growth similar to that of the mutual fund industry in Canada. The Investment Fund Institute of Canada reports that in 1990, the mutual fund industry was $24 billion. At the end of 2000, it had grown to $430 billion. The IPP market is on the verge of the same kind of explosive growth as more Canadians earn $100,000 and prepare to enter retirement en masse beginning in 2010.

In 2005, 230,000 Canadians were classified as millionaires, a growth of 7.2% from 2004, according to Merrill Lynch. High-net-worth Canadians were defined by Merrill Lynch as individuals who had financial assets over U.S. $1 million; this excluded their cars and homes. The majority of Canada's millionaires (70%) were older than 50 years of age.

According to the tenth annual World Wealth Report, the largest group (32%) of the wealthy in Canada earned their money through their employment. The next largest group was business owners (26%), followed by those who had inherited their wealth (16%).

Boomers are looking for both tax and investment solutions that will provide them with wealth preservation, CRA-sanctioned tax minimization and deferral capabilities, creditor protection, wealth accumulation and wealth distribution solutions, and the IPP delivers on all five of these criteria.

IPP specialists predict that over the next 15 years, if half of the people who currently earn $100,000-plus choose to upgrade their RRSPs to an IPP, there will be more than 300,000 of these DBPPs in place across Canada. Currently, there are approximately 11,500 registered IPPs across Canada representing approximately $3 billion of total assets invested.

It is inevitable that the 20% of affluent Canadians who own 72% of the over $500 billion in RRSPs in 2009 will opt to migrate much of their RRSP assets into IPPs. If the average IPP accumulates $500,000, there will be more than $150 billion sitting in IPP assets or much, much more when additional voluntary contributions (which will be explained in the last chapter of Part II) are added into the IPP asset mix. Given an average asset management fee of 2% per year, the assets held within IPPs will generate between $3 to $5 billion or more in recurring investment fees paid annually.

In addition, each IPP (to remain registered) will require actuarial and trustee administration, billing approximately $1,500 a year, generating approximately $450 million annually or more.

In real terms, an IPP will need to be accounted for on a company's corporate financial statement. The average cost for the total IPP new accounting services will roughly generate 2.4 million billable hours (IPP set-up) and also create 1.2 million in (ongoing) annual billable hours.

Lastly, the emerging IPP industry will create about $3 to $6 billion in new annual revenue for Canada's 68,000 Chartered Accountants, 35,000 Certified Management Accountants, 60,000 Certified General Accountants, 100,000-plus financial advisors and 2,600 actuaries which is not calculated into Canada's current gross domestic product formula, yet.

CHAPTER 15

IPP FEATURES, BENEFITS AND LIMITATIONS

Peter J. Merrick

Overview

This chapter begins by explaining the basic features and benefits of the Individual Pension Plan (IPP). It then goes on to detail the liabilities created by adopting the IPP solution. The chapter concludes by outlining the key differences between the IPP and the Registered Retirement Savings Plan (RRSP).

Learning Objectives

By the end of this chapter, you should be able to:

- list the features and benefits of the IPP;
- list the liabilities of the IPP; and
- list the differences between an IPP and an RRSP.

IPP FEATURES, BENEFITS AND LIMITATIONS

In a nutshell, the IPP is essentially an RRSP upgrade, with two main differences: IPPs have significantly higher limits for contributions and they have restricted collapsibility options. In most provinces, IPPs cannot be fully collapsed unless the plan holder is critically ill, is severely disabled or has fallen on financial hardships. In essence, if the IPP is set up and maintained properly, the IPP effectively guarantees its member an income for retirement.

Let us explore the features, benefits and limitations of an IPP in more detail.

Features and Benefits

Contribution for Current Service

Contributions to the IPP are far greater than what can be contributed into an RRSP for individuals over the age of 40. In essence, the older a person is the greater the divide between what can be contributed into an IPP and what can be contributed into an RRSP on his or her behalf. In 2008, the maximum current service contributions that can be made into an IPP for an individual aged 71 could be as much as $54,236 compared to the maximum RRSP contribution of $20,000, a $34,236 difference in favour of the IPP.

Contributions for Past Service

For owners/executives, the IPP funding formula is more generous than the RRSP contribution limits. The plan normally allows companies to contribute for the pension plan member for years of service prior to the set-up of the plan going back to 1991 for connected persons. For non-connected persons, IPP funding contributions can go back further than 1991 to when the IPP member became an employee of the IPP sponsoring company.

If the first year of the set-up of an IPP is 2008 for a connected person, the past service and current service funding contribution/corporate deduction for a connected person could be as much as $630,106 for an individual who is 71 years old.

The table below shows the maximum corporate deduction a corporation may be permitted by Canada Revenue Agency (CRA) for a connected person based on the age of the plan member for 2008.

Table of Allowable IPP Contributions

(2008 Tax Deductibility for Corporations)		
Age in 2008	**Past Service from January 1, 1991**	**Current Service**
40	$44,399	$21,822
45	$79,623	$23,970
50	$118,315	$26,330
55	$160,815	$28,922
60	$207,497	$31,769
65	$262,815	$35,143
71	$575,870	$54,236

Note: All assumptions in the table above are based on a 2008, $116,667 maximum annual pensionable income and an RRSP Qualifying Transfer of $313,400. Contributions are determined by the actuary.

Catch-up Contributions

Contributions that are not made into the IPP for a particular year can be made up in following years. If the IPP employer/plan sponsor makes a catch-up IPP contribution, this contribution will include an additional amount to compensate for the loss of income that would have been generated within the IPP based on a 7.5% rate of annual return. This additional contribution is a deduction for the employer and a non-taxable benefit for the IPP member.

Employees Earning Less Than $122,222 for 2009 per Year and at Least 40 Years of Age

The age of a potential IPP member is the most crucial factor in determining if the IPP is a person's best retirement solution. IPP contributions for a member of at least 40 years of age and earning less than $122,222 for 2009 per year will still produce a proportional advantage over RRSP contributions. Later in this book, you will learn why contributions into an IPP for older plan members will always be greater than contributions into an RRSP for the same individual.

Luring Key People to Your Organization

By using an IPP as part of a total executive benefit package, a company can attract people who are currently employed and are members of a defined benefit pension plan. Traditionally, such candidates may not have wanted to leave an employer or defined benefit plan before retirement because tax rules prevented them from transferring the full value of their pension credits to a locked-in RRSP. Now a company can avoid such an obstacle by creating an IPP for these employees by transferring existing pension plan assets to the new IPP without tax implications. Opting to utilize this IPP benefit, the full commuted value from a previous employer's defined benefit pension plan can be transferred to the IPP at the new place of employment without a maximum transfer age value limit and triggering taxes to the IPP member.

Creditor Proofing

Creditors of the plan member or the incorporated business cannot seize assets held within the IPP in most situations provided that the IPP was created in good faith. However, all annual payments made to the retired employee are taxable earnings and could be seizable.

To summarize the changes, the *Bankruptcy and Insolvency Act* (Canada) now protects RRSPs/RRIFs only in the case of a bankruptcy. On the other hand, the pension legislation provides creditor protection of locked-in plans even before bankruptcy. As a result, the federal changes are limited in their application, since a person could only benefit from the protection if he or she declares bankruptcy and is subsequently sued. Under these new rules, if a creditor files a claim before a person has declared bankruptcy, then the RSP/RIF is not protected. The pension legislation provides a greater level of protection, since the assets in a locked-in plan are protected from creditors in all cases, not just bankruptcy.

Extended Contribution Period

A company has 120 days after its year-end to make an IPP contribution which will be considered an expense for the company in the previous business fiscal year. Contributions into an RRSP that can be applied back to the previous calendar year need to be made within the first 60 days after the start of the New Year.

Ownership of Plan Assets

At retirement, the IPP member owns any actuarial surplus. It may be used to upgrade pension benefits, or the plan holder may pass it on to his or her spouse, heirs or estate.

Greater Compounding on Interest on a Tax-Deferred Basis

Albert Einstein once remarked that one of the greatest human inventions was the creation of compound interest. The value of earning compound interest within the IPP in a tax-deferred way should never be understated. Let us look and see why it makes sense in the long run to save for retirement within a tax-deferred vehicle such as the IPP, where interest compounds tax-free until it is withdrawn.

Imagine you have a 55-year-old client, John Doe, who has owned an incorporated business since 1991, with a T4 income of more than $200,000 and a marginal tax rate in Ontario of 46.41%. This client is serious about saving for retirement and in the next ten years, when he reaches 65, he plans to retire. By creating an IPP for himself this year, your client will be able to defer $189,737 immediately from taxes from his company's and his personal income. This money will then compound tax-free until he withdraws from the plan. The next year John Doe will be able to contribute an additional $31,091 tax free into his IPP, and the contribution into the IPP will increase by 7.5% annually until he retires (the investment chosen for this example earns 7.5% annually). When John Doe reaches 65, he will have accumulated $927,536 in his IPP.

If this client decides not to create an IPP for himself and instead chooses to take this same amount of money out of his business, after having paid the personal marginal tax rate of 46.41% for the purpose of saving for retirement, and where all his investment returns are also taxed at his marginal rate, then his financial situation becomes much different. The first year after taxes, John Doe will be left with $101,680 to invest. The following year, after taxes, the $31,091 he takes out of his business, as personal income, will leave him with $16,662 to contribute to his non-IPP investment, and this annual contribution will grow at 7.5% (the investment chosen for this example earns 7.5% annually as well; this is the prescribed actuary growth rate set by the federal government for defined pension plans). At age 65, he will have an accumulated value in his non-IPP of $395,437.

Based on the stated assumptions, this particular client's IPP option will yield an additional $532,099 more than his non-IPP alternative with a ten-year period from ages 55 to 65. That is the power of tax-free deposits and compounding.

Guaranteed Lifetime Income to IPP Members, Their Spouses and Heirs

This pension plan offers a predictable retirement income. An actuary determines the current annual cost of the future retirement income. Spousal pension benefits may be upgraded to 100% at the time the member retires or at the plan member's death. Adult children with disabilities may also receive pension benefits after the IPP member's death.

Terminal Funding

One of the most attractive features of the IPP is the possibility of terminal funding. The IPP member may elect to receive his or her pension benefit as early as age 50 without reducing the promised pension benefit.

While the CRA restricts the benefits that can be pre-funded, the plan can be amended at retirement to provide the most generous terms possible. Some of these include full consumer price indexing and early retirement pension with no reduction as well as bridge benefits to compensate for CPP/QPP and Old Age Security (OAS) that IPP members will not receive until age 65.

Imagine an IPP has been created for a 49-year-old owner/manager. As of January 1, 2005, this owner/manager has T4 earnings of $100,000 and has maintained this level of income since 1991. It is safe to project that the owner/manager's income will remain at $100,000 annually adjusted to inflation until retirement. Assume that this IPP member will retire at age 60 on January 1, 2016, with 25 years of pensionable service (1991 to 2015). Before the retirement benefit begins to be paid out of the IPP, there is a window of opportunity for the company to make a one-time $251,000 terminal funding contribution to the IPP, in addition to regular IPP government-prescribed funding contributions and annual growth calculations when this IPP member retires.

Estate Planning

IPPs are the perfect vehicle to transfer assets from one family member to another in a tax-effective way. With an RRSP on the death of a second spouse, all assets within the RRSP become taxable. If an able adult child joins a business in which an IPP has been set up for the parent(s), the child can be added as a member of the IPP. Upon the death of the parent(s), any assets that have not been used to pay benefits to the retired parent(s) from the IPP can be transferred to the child who is a member of the IPP for the purpose of funding the promised pension benefit to the child without causing taxes to be triggered.

An alternative is that upon the death of the IPP member, the assets are available to be transferred to the spouse, to another beneficiary or to the member's estate.

Flexible Funding Options

Moneys can be used to fund the IPP that have accumulated in retained earnings of a company. Funding can come from outstanding bonuses owed to owners/executives by the employer making the employee's contributions into the IPP. Another option would be for the employer to obtain financing/loans from a financial institution. The business can access funds tax-effectively from a corporately owned Universal Life Policy by collateralizing the policy through loans from a bank using the cash value as the collateral, or shareholder loans. All interest on loans to fund an IPP in addition to all other IPP expenses are tax-deductible for the sponsor/employer and are a non-taxable benefit for the IPP member.

Limitations

Under the Age of 40 IPPs Are Ineffective and Detrimental for Tax-Efficient Retirement Savings

The value of defined benefit pension credits (the amount, determined actuarially, that is needed to be invested in a defined benefit pension plan to deliver the promised pension benefit) greatly varies depending on an IPP member's age. For individuals under the age of 40, his or her pension adjustment is over-valued, meaning that less money will actually be put aside tax-effectively within an IPP rather than if the individual utilized an RRSP or defined contribution pension plan. For individuals over the age of 40 the reverse happens. Their pension adjustment is under-valued, meaning that more money can be put away tax-effectively within an IPP than could be invested in either an RRSP or a defined contribution pension plan.

For example, if a 25-year-old earned $100,000 and is credited a $2,000 IPP benefit for this year's earning, his pension adjustment would be $18,000, giving him RRSP room of $600 due to the pension adjustment offset (multiply plan benefit by 9, then subtract the pension adjustment offset (9 × benefit − $600)). However, the true amount invested in his IPP to generate the promised benefit of $2,000 would only be approximately $3,940 ($1.97 × benefit), not the $18,000 attributed to his pension adjustment for our 25-year-old. His pension adjustment represents $14,060 more than he had actually invested for his year of pensionable service.

On the other hand if a 71-year-old earned $100,000 and is credited the same $2,000 IPP benefit this year, his pension adjustment would be $18,000, giving him RRSP room of $600 once the pension adjustment offset is factored in as for our 25-year-old. But the actual amount invested in our 71-year-old IPP to generate the promised $2,000 pension benefit would be much greater, <u>$54,236</u> ($27.12 × $2,000 pension benefit). The 71-year-old is able to have an additional $36,236 more tax deferred than his pension adjustment states was invested in his IPP. What is really unfair to the 25-year-old is that he receives the same promised pension income when he retires as the 71-year-old as they both receive pension adjustments of $18,000, but the 71-year-old gets to have $50,296 more put away tax deferred for his pension than our 25-year-old friend.

Pension adjustment offset is the minimum level of RRSP room that someone is given when they are participating in a defined benefit pension plan. Up until 1996, it was $1,000, and then from 1997 to the present, it is $600 per year for members of a defined benefit pension plan. The pension adjustment offset gives members of a defined benefit pension plan a minimum RRSP contribution room for any given year that they are members of defined benefit pension plans.

IPPs Are Expensive to Set up and Maintain

The set-up fees for an IPP can range from $1,500 to $5,000 depending on the complexity of the plan. Annual administration fees range from $500 to $2,000. It should be remembered that the plan sponsor could write off these IPP fees. In comparison, the cost for having a self-directed RRSP can range annually from $0 to $250, which cannot be written off at all by either the employer or the RRSP owner.

Before implementing the IPP solution, a cost-benefit analysis should always be completed for each situation. For example, in the case of an employer/business owner who is considering an IPP for himself or herself for 2008 with a set-up fee of $3,500, who is 40 years of age, who earns $200,000 annually with a marginal tax rate of 46.41% and who is not permitted to make any past service contributions into the plan, his or her corporation will be permitted to make a current service contribution of $21,822 this year into an IPP on the business owner's behalf. The business owner will also be given an RRSP contribution of $20,000 based on his or her previous year's income for a combined corporate and personal tax deduction of $45,322 ($21,822 IPP contribution + $3,500 set-up costs + $20,000 RRSP contribution).

By creating an IPP, the business owner and corporation will have personal tax savings of $21,034 compared to only making his or her $20,000 RRSP 2008 contribution, which would provide a tax savings of $9,282. By completing a cost-benefit analysis for this business owner, it will be clearly illustrated that the IPP/RRSP option will deliver an additional $11,752 tax savings over and above the RRSP contribution-only option.

IPPs Are Too Complex

IPPs are, first and foremost, defined benefit pension plans. Each IPP has to be approved by the CRA, and in most instances IPPs need the approval of provincial pension regulators.

There is a need for annual filings and triennial actuarial reports filed with the CRA to validate contributions by the plan sponsor into these plans. In addition, there are special accounting procedures that must be applied to the corporate financial statements by IPP-sponsoring companies, as well as investment restrictions for assets held within the IPP that are not required of ordinary RRSPs.

IPPs Are Contractual Employment Arrangements

The employer/IPP plan sponsor is required to make annual contributions into the plan. These mandatory contributions are not dependent on the sponsoring company showing a profit or loss on its books.

IPPs Have Withdrawal Restrictions

An RRSP can be collapsed at any time and the RRSP holder will then pay taxes on the proceeds withdrawn from his or her plan based on his or her marginal tax rate. IPP assets are usually locked in and cannot be accessed by the plan member prematurely.

An IPP member can opt for several choices with the pension plan when his or her employment is terminated or when the plan member retires. At termination or retirement, pension plan funds may be used to pay out the plan benefit as promised. The IPP can also be transferred to or invested in the following financial instruments: Annuity (single or joint and last survivor); Locked-in Investment Retirement Account (LIRA); Life Income Fund (LIF); and Locked-in RRIF (LRIF) (where applicable, as some provinces do not require IPPs to be transferred to a locked-in plan at all). The pension plan can be transferred to a new employer pension if the new employer is willing to offer an IPP. If the IPP was registered in Quebec and the IPP member is a connected person, he or she has the option to transfer the assets from the plan to an RRSP and then take a lump-sum withdrawal, after applicable taxes have been withheld.

In 2008, the federal government allowed owners of LIRAs age 55 or over with total assets in all their locked-in accounts less than 40% of the Year's Maximum Pensionable Earnings to have the option of directly transferring the money to an RRSP or RRIF.

IPPs Restrict the Use of Spousal RRSPs

Contributions into an IPP can be made only into an employee's plan. Hence, income-splitting through contributing into a Spousal RRSP is extremely restricted to what is left over after the IPP member's pension adjustment has been subtracted from his or her RRSP contribution limit. Usually the RRSP amount left to invest into a Spousal RRSP is only the pension adjustment offset, which is $600 per annum. However, since 2007, the federal government allows IPP lifetime pension payments to be split between spouses, regardless of the age of the pensioner, to provide up to 50% of the promised yearly benefit to the non-participating spouse.

IPP Surpluses

If the investments within an IPP do very well, delivering better than the actuarial investment return assumptions of 7.5%, a surplus will result in an IPP. A company/sponsor in this situation will not be permitted to make additional contributions into an IPP on behalf of the plan member until the surpluses have vanished. In the years that the plan runs surpluses, a company/sponsor will not receive a deduction until contributions into the plan are permitted to resume.

In years that an IPP is running surpluses, where the IPP member is accruing pensionable credits, a pension adjustment will be generated, even though no funds are being contributed into the plan on the IPP member's behalf. The result: the IPP member's ability to contribute into an RRSP or any other registered plan will be deeply restricted to only the pension adjustment offset of $600 per annum.

IPP Underfunding

Depending on the province that an IPP is registered in, if a plan is underfunded based on actuarial assumptions and valuations, an employer/sponsor of an IPP may be mandated to make contributions into a plan, to make up for deficits in the plan. In some cases, making up for deficiencies in funding into an IPP is desirable if a company has positive cash flow.

On the other hand, mandatory IPP contributions may place a heavy burden on a business/IPP sponsor who might not have the ability to fully fund a promised IPP benefit at the time that contributions have been mandated to occur.

IPP Revocation of Plan Registration (Worst-Case Scenario)

If it is determined that an IPP is not in compliance with governing Pension Acts and the CRA's Registered Plans Directorate's regulations, the registration of an IPP may be revoked at any time. To remain registered by the CRA, IPPs must at all times satisfy four criteria:

1. The IPP must comply with all laws and regulation governing Registered Pension Plans; all filings must be up to date.
2. The company/sponsor must be established for a reason other than to establish a pension plan prior to the plan being set up and/or the transferring of pension benefit assets from another defined benefit pension plan from another employer to the IPP.
3. The employee/employer must have a *bona fide* employment relationship between the plan member and his or her company.

4. If assets from another defined benefit pension plan have been transferred to an IPP, the member of the IPP needs to expect to have earnings at a similar level from the new employer as the member earned from the prior employer. The rule of thumb is that these earnings from the new employer should be similar to that of the old employer for three years.

The best-case scenario resulting from this worst-case scenario is that, when an IPP's status is revoked, the IPP immediately turns into a retirement compensation arrangement (RCA). The former registered IPP will have to then immediately forward 50% of all plan assets to the CRA on behalf of the plan member. These funds will be refunded to the RCA plan member at a later date when money is withdrawn from the RCA.

In the very, very worst-case scenario, the CRA may not permit the assets from the IPP to be rolled over into an RCA. Thus, taxes will be charged on all assets held in the former IPP. Heavy interest charges may be levied by the CRA for overdue taxes owed by both the IPP sponsor and the member of the plan.

An RCA is a plan defined in subsection 248(1) of the *Income Tax Act*, R.S.C. 1985, c. 1 (5th Supp.), providing supplemental pension benefits to owners/managers and key employees of incorporated businesses. Contributions to an RCA are 100% tax deductible by the employer and are not taxable for the employee until the money is withdrawn from the RCA.

Money that is invested into an RCA through a trustee is divided equally between two accounts. The first account is called the RCA investment account. The second account is referred to as the refundable tax account, and this account is administered by the CRA. Fifty per cent of the deposits into the RCA are forwarded to the refundable tax account, and 50% of the earnings earned within the RCA investment account are also forwarded to the refundable tax account every year. All funds in the refundable tax account are refundable to the recipient of the RCA when the recipient begins to withdraw his or her money. When money is withdrawn from an RCA, tax will be paid by the beneficiary of the RCA at his or her marginal tax rate. (RCAs will be covered further in Chapter 49.)

Note: Over the past several years, the CRA has been cracking down on registered IPPs, especially a Tailored Individual Pension Plan (TIPP). A TIPP is an IPP in which the pension adjustment is inappropriately low in relation to the benefit promised by the pension. The CRA frowns upon TIPPs and on plan sponsors and members of plans that have been deemed TIPPs. Sponsors, plan members and advisors run the risk of having these pension plans deregistered and paying high interest and tax penalties to the CRA.

Possible Heavy Fines and Penalties (Worst-Case Scenario)

It is important to understand that an IPP is a registered pension plan and because of this simple fact, extra care must go into the set-up, maintenance and wind-up of these plans.

If for any reason an IPP is in violation of the federal government's *Pension Benefits Standards Act, 1985*, R.S.C. 1985, c. 32 (2nd Supp.), *Income Tax Act*, *Income Tax Regulations*, C.R.C., c. 945, or provincial Acts, an individual who contravenes any provision, or who avoids compliance, is guilty of an offence under these Acts. Individuals found liable for violating these Acts on their first conviction can be fined up to $100,000 or be imprisoned for a term not exceeding 12 months, or both. In addition, a corporation/sponsor of an IPP that is convicted of violating these Acts and regulations may be fined up to $500,000.

IPP VS. RRSP

The following is a brief comparison between an IPP and an RRSP:

Quick Overview	**RRSP**	**IPP**
Contribution limits	18% of individual's previous year overall T4 income.	Established by actuary according to the CRA rules and both federal and provincial pension Acts. Contributions are based on the IPP member's current age and current income received from the IPP sponsor.
Contributions	Deducted by the individual.	Contributions and costs are deducted by the company and are not subjected to payroll taxes.
Creditor protection	Yes: Since 2008. The federal Act now protects RRSPs/ RRIFs only in the case of a bankruptcy. On the other hand, the pension legislation provides creditor protection of locked-in plans even	Yes.

Quick Overview	**RRSP**	**IPP**
	before bankruptcy. As a result, the federal changes are limited in their application, since a person could only benefit from the protection if he or she declares bankruptcy and is subsequently sued. Under these new rules, if a creditor files a claim before a person has declared bankruptcy, then the RSP/RIF is not protected. The pension legislation provides a greater level of protection, since the assets in a locked-in plan are protected from creditors in all cases, not just bankruptcy.	
Investment risk	Lies with the individual.	Lies with the employer because if the performance is not up to the formula amount, the employer must make additional contributions.
Additional contributions	If poor investment performance, no additional funds can be added to these plans.	If the investment performance is poor (less than 7.5% per annum), the company/sponsor in most jurisdictions has to make additional contributions to fund the plan.
Past service	Taxpayer may have unused room that can be used to make further contributions.	Past service recognition, receive credit for previous years' income for funding retirement savings. IPPs can be funded back to 1991 for connected persons.
Current funding	Contributions can be made within 60 days after the end of the calendar year.	Contributions allowed 120 days after corporate year-end.
Transfer of assets to other family member	No: On the death of an RRSP holder, assets held within the RRSP can be	Yes: If other family members are placed on IPP as members of the existing

Quick Overview	**RRSP**	**IPP**
upon death other than that of the spouse	transferred tax-free to a surviving spouse or a dependent child. Upon the death of the spouse or the time a child is no longer deemed dependent, all RRSP holdings are subjected to taxes of the deceased spouse's estate or former dependent child's marginal tax rate.	plan, upon death of one of the members of the plan. Assets within the IPP can be transferred successfully without triggering taxes. IPP benefits can be transferred to a dependent child without triggering the assets within the IPP to be deregistered.

CHAPTER 16

ROLES AND RESPONSIBILITIES

Peter J. Merrick

Overview

This chapter introduces the roles and responsibilities of each party who is involved in the implementation, maintenance and wind-up processes of an Individual Pension Plan.

Learning Objectives

By the end of this chapter, you should be able to:

- list the roles and responsibilities of different parties involved in the IPP.

THE KEY PLAYERS

Who is involved in the set-up, maintenance and wind-up of an IPP? The key players that can be easily identified are the employer/sponsor of the plan, the administrator, the custodian, the trustee(s), actuary, investment manager/financial advisor and the IPP member. Each of these players must work within defined roles and follow sound IPP governance.

IPP Sponsor

The IPP sponsor is the company that creates an IPP for a *bona fide* employee. IPPs are usually only sponsored by incorporated businesses or incorporated professional corporations. The sponsor is responsible for providing continuous T4 income records to allow the actuary to properly determine the beneficiary IPP funding levels. Since an IPP is usually a pension for just one person, it is usually more cost-effective that the sponsor of a plan also be the administrator of an IPP. From this point on in this chapter, the terms "sponsor" and "administrator" will be interchangeable.

IPP Administrator

The IPP administrator, as mentioned earlier, is usually the employer/sponsor of an IPP. For an IPP to become a registered pension plan, it is required that an administrator be appointed. The administrator is either a person or a group of people, or sponsoring company with the responsibility for the set-up, maintenance and winding-up of an IPP. It is a must that the IPP administrator resides within Canada.

The IPP administrator/sponsor is placed in a key position where it must decide that it will create an IPP compensation package for an owner, executive or a *bona fide* employee of the sponsoring company. After it has been decided that an IPP will be created, the administrator will appoint an investment manager/financial advisor to manage an IPP's assets. Even though an investment manager has been appointed, the administrator still has fiduciary duties to make sure the IPP assets are properly managed according to the investment policy statement (IPS), and that the plan is fully funded. The administrator/sponsor is responsible for appointing the actuarial firm that will complete the needed actuarial calculations that are required by the Canada Revenue Agency (CRA) and the various provincial pension regulators for an IPP on an ongoing basis.

In the world of IPPs, it is usually the investment manager/financial advisor who works with the sponsor/administrator to select the actuarial firm. The administrator/sponsor is responsible for providing the needed financial data to the actuarial firm, so that an IPP quote can be produced by the actuary to show the financial benefits, liabilities and responsibilities of providing an IPP.

The administrator/sponsor will appoint a custodian who will actually hold the IPP assets. If the custodian is an insurance company, there may be no need to appoint a trustee, if certain conditions are met, which will be discussed later on in the trustee(s) section of this chapter. However, if the custodian of the assets of an IPP is a financial institution or financial firm, the administrator/sponsor will need to appoint a trustee(s) to manage/direct the investment manager on how to manage the funds in the IPP.

During the IPP set-up stage, the administrator/sponsor must decide what the amortization period to fund the past service contribution to the plan (1-15 years) will be. The administrator/sponsor then applies to the CRA to register the IPP by completing Form T510, "Application to Register a Pension Plan", *and* Form T244, "Registered Pension Plan Annual Information Return". These forms will indicate whether or not a plan is a designated plan and if the plan member is a connected person.

Once a plan has achieved designated plan status (IPP), it continues with this status unless the CRA changes its status.

Other duties and responsibilities of an IPP administrator/sponsor include filing actuarial reports with the CRA. Administrators must provide the CRA and pension authorities with annual information returns and triennial actuarial evaluations. It is the IPP administrator/sponsor that applies to the CRA for past service pension adjustment (PSPA) for IPP members. IPP administrators must make sure that pension adjustments (PAs) and PSPAs are produced and reported to the CRA and the various provincial pension regulating bodies. IPP administrators are responsible to pay all registration fees for the IPP to both federal and provincial regulating bodies if these fees are applicable. IPP administrators will be responsible to pay out pension benefits to IPP members when these members are eligible to receive a pension benefit.

Lastly, IPP administrators are responsible for providing members with information about their plans in a timely manner. This information includes:

- **Pension Plan Booklet**: The administrator/sponsor of the IPP must provide this within 60 days after an individual has joined an IPP.
- **Annual Statement**: The administrator/sponsor of the IPP must provide an annual statement of the plan to an IPP member within six months after the year-end of the plan.
- **Termination Statement**: The administrator/sponsor of the IPP must provide this to an IPP member within 30 days after the member has retired from the sponsoring company. The administrator/sponsor of the IPP is responsible for advising the member within 60 days before retirement what his or her retirement options are.
- **Pension Adjustment Reversal (PAR)**: If the IPP plan member decides to transfer/cease being a member of the IPP and transfer his or her IPP funds to an RRSP or a defined contribution pension plan (DCPP), the plan administrator has to report a PAR that is greater than nil to both the CRA and the employee by submitting a Form T10, "Pension Adjustment Reversal", to the CRA on behalf of the former plan member. PAR restores RRSP contribution room for an employee that was terminated from a registered pension plan (RPP) or a deferred profit-sharing plan (DPSP). PAR increases a former RPP and DPSP member's RRSP contribution room by the difference between the total employee's PAs that were reported, while a member of these plans and the actual pension dollar transfer value to an RRSP.

- **Survivor Benefit Statement**: The administrator must provide a survivor benefit statement within the first 30 days after the estate of an IPP member has provided a certified death notice of the plan member.

Custodian

The custodian is the entity that actually holds the assets inside the IPP. Either an insurance company or a financial institution or financial firm usually holds assets in an IPP. In the case where there has not been a contract of insurance to invest IPP assets in a "group insurance product", the administrator of an IPP will have to draw up a trust agreement and appoint as the custodian a corporate trustee or a three-party trustee to hold the assets within the IPP.

Trustee(s)

If an IPP invests its assets in anything other than in a group insurance product/insurance pension fund held by an insurance company, then the administrator/sponsor of the IPP must appoint a trustee(s) to administer the IPP assets while these funds remain registered in the IPP. A group insurance investment product should not be confused with individual segregated funds offered by insurance companies. IPPs that hold individual segregated funds need to have a trustee(s) appointed to administrate the assets.

The reason why IPPs that hold group insurance investment products do not require a trustee(s) appointed to them is that these types of products have a built-in maturity date after the IPP member's 71st birthday. Pension law requires that a trustee(s) be appointed for RPPs with assets that do not have a maturity date after the pension plan member's 71st birthday. Regular investments and segregated funds do not have built-in maturity dates, so a trustee must be appointed on these types of IPPs to ensure that these plans do mature after the 71st birthday of the plan member.

A trustee(s) can be a trust company or at least three individuals who live in Canada, and who are charged to promote the financial security of a pension fund through sound investment policies and practices. If the trust for the IPP is set up using three trustees/individuals, at least one of these individuals needs to be completely independent from the corporation sponsoring the IPP and the IPP member.

What is expected of a trustee is something that has been considered by the courts over the years, and can now be found in the provincial

Trustee Acts. The rule has been expressed that the trustee must show ordinary care, skill and prudence, and that he or she must act as a prudent person of discretion and intelligence would act in his or her own affairs.

The most popular method to date of setting up an IPP is by using the three-person trusteeship structure. Unfortunately, many individuals accepting a trustee role in this type of IPP structure do not have a full comprehension of their responsibilities and duties. Trustees risk serious liabilities if they are in violation of the *Income Tax Act*, the *Income Tax Regulations*, the various Trustee Acts and Pension Acts and the common laws surrounding fiduciary responsibilities of trustees.

Before someone accepts the position as a trustee to an IPP, that person should have a firm understanding of the IPP itself and the information contained in all documents concerning the administration of the trust.

These duties include hiring and overseeing professional advisors and service providers in carrying out the responsibilities of the trust. IPP trust administration includes maintaining all trustee documentation and receiving and depositing all contributions into the IPP trust fund. The trustee(s) should know all the IPP's professional advisors and service providers and understand their roles. The trustee(s) should review the reports of each advisor. The trustee(s) should become familiar with the legal duties and responsibilities for a trustee and should be familiar with the assets held in the IPP and how these assets have been invested within the plan.

The trustee(s) is responsible for helping put together the information to file a T3P form to the CRA. The T3P form is entitled "Employees Pension Plan Income Tax Return". The T3P form must be filed within 90 days after the year-end of the trust. If this form is late, the CRA can impose penalties for filing late.

Prudent Trustee Investment Guidelines

Unless it has been specified in the trust documents, trustees must act unanimously on any decisions that are made concerning IPP trust assets. Some IPP trusts allow for the majority of the trustees to make decisions or for one of the trustees to act on behalf of all the trustees. If the trustees allow one of their members to manage and control IPP assets, all trustees are still responsible for what decisions are made and how IPP assets are cared for.

Beneficiaries of trusts should be able to expect an objective test of what is careful, skillful and prudent, and the trustee must document his or her conduct. Section 27 of the Ontario *Trustee Act*, R.S.O. 1990, c. T.23, is set out below as a representative example of the provincial Trustee Acts' investment guidelines that an appointed trustee to an IPP must follow.

Note: The investments guidelines within the Trustee Acts are complementary to the investment guidelines outlined in the various Pension Acts across Canada that are discussed in depth in Part III of this book.

Section 27 of the *Trustee Act* provides:

> 27. (1) *Standard of care* — In investing trust property, a trustee must exercise the care, skill, diligence and judgment that a prudent investor would exercise in making investments.
>
> (2) *Authorized investments* — A trustee may invest trust property in any form of property in which a prudent investor might invest.
>
> (3) *Mutual, pooled and segregated funds* — Any rule of law that prohibits a trustee from delegating powers or duties does not prevent the trustee from investing in mutual funds, pooled funds or segregated funds under variable insurance contracts, and sections 27.1 and 27.2 do not apply to the purchase of such funds.
>
> (4) *Common trust funds* — If trust property is held by co-trustees and one of the co-trustees is a trust corporation as defined in the *Loan and Trust Corporations Act*, any rule of law that prohibits a trustee from delegating powers or duties does not prevent the co-trustee from investing in a common trust fund, as defined in that Act, that is maintained by the trust corporation and sections 27.1 and 27.2 do not apply.
>
> (5) *Criteria* — A trustee must consider the following criteria in planning the investment of trust property, in addition to any others that are relevant to the circumstances:
>
> 1. General economic conditions.
> 2. The possible effect of inflation or deflation.
> 3. The expected tax consequences of investment decisions or strategies.
> 4. The role that each investment or course of action plays within the overall trust portfolio.
> 5. The expected total return from income and the appreciation of capital.
> 6. Needs for liquidity, regularity of income and preservation or appreciation of capital.
> 7. An asset's special relationship or special value, if any, to the purposes of the trust or to one or more of the beneficiaries.
>
> (6) *Diversification* — A trustee must diversify the investment of trust property to an extent that is appropriate to,
>
> (a) the requirements of the trust; and
>
> (b) general economic and investment market conditions.

(7) *Investment advice* — A trustee may obtain advice in relation to the investment of trust property.

(8) *Reliance on advice* — It is not a breach of trust for a trustee to rely on advice obtained under subsection (7) if a prudent investor would rely on the advice under comparable circumstances.

(9) *Terms of trust* — This section and section 27.1 do not authorize or require a trustee to act in a manner that is inconsistent with the terms of the trust.

(10) *Same* — For the purposes of subsection (9), the constating documents of a corporation that is deemed to be a trustee under subsection 1 (2) of the *Charities Accounting Act* form part of the terms of the trust.

Actuary

When an IPP is to be created, an administrator is required to appoint an actuary. An actuary is a person who is a Fellow of the Canadian Institute of Actuaries. Actuaries are business professionals who apply their knowledge of mathematics, probability, statistics, and risk theory, to real-life financial problems involving future uncertainty.

With the setting up, ongoing maintenance and wind-up of an IPP, actuaries are needed to complete the IPP's required valuation reports and to certify in these reports that an IPP is properly funded to deliver the promised benefit for an IPP member. The other main responsibilities that are delegated to the actuary of an IPP are to draft the IPP plan documents, create board resolutions for the sponsoring company to sign, review insurance contracts or trust agreements where the IPP assets will reside and file with the CRA and/or provincial regulators. Actuaries complete triennial valuations that must be submitted every three years to both the CRA and, in some provinces, provincial pension regulators.

IPP Investment Manager/Financial Advisor

The IPP investment managers/financial advisors are appointed by plan sponsor/administrators and trustee(s) (if a trustee(s) has been appointed). They are charged with working with the IPP administrator and trustee(s) to develop a written investment policy statement (IPS). The IPS aim is to provide the IPP with guidelines for the long-term financial and investment decisions that will be made for assets within the plan. It generally includes investment objectives (return requirements and risk tolerance), constraints (cash requirements and timing issues) and guidelines for achieving the IPP's funding objectives.

IPP investment managers/financial advisors are charged with the responsibility of selecting and managing the investments that are invested in the IPP fund. Investment managers are responsible for making sure that the activities within the pension fund comply with the IPS and federal and provincial pension guidelines. Lastly, investment managers/ financial advisors are charged with the responsibility of reporting the activities within the IPP fund back to the administrator and trustee(s) (if a trustee(s) has been appointed) and actuary of the IPP.

IPP Member/Participant

The IPP member/participant is a designated employee of a company who is deemed or has been deemed to have contributions made to an IPP on his or her behalf. In most cases, IPPs are set up for connected members of organizations.

In most situations, because IPPs are created for a connected member, these individuals are usually involved in making the decision to create IPPs for themselves. They may help in the selection of the IPP's administrator, investment manager, custodian, trustee and actuary. The member will provide past earning data and provide a complete list of current RRSP, DCPP, DPSP, Locked-in RRSP holdings and accumulated unused RRSP room amounts to assist in the first actuary evaluation. When an IPP is approved, the member will receive from the CRA an approval notice that the member will have to provide to the custodian of the IPP. The member will also assist in transferring assets from his or her RRSP, unused RRSP room and/or other registered pension plans for the qualifying transfer that is required before the IPP can receive past service funding for prior years of service before the IPP was created.

The IPP member is also responsible for providing names of spouse, common law spouse or heirs to be beneficiaries in the event the member dies.

CHAPTER 17

INDIVIDUAL PENSION PLAN PROCESS

Peter J. Merrick

Overview

This chapter lays out the processes involved in the life cycle of an Individual Pension Plan, from the set-up through to the ongoing maintenance and deregistration stages.

Learning Objectives

By the end of this chapter, you should be able to:

- list the steps involved in the process of the implementation stage of the Individual Pension Plan solution;
- list the steps involved in the process of the maintenance stage of the Individual Pension Plan solution; and
- list the steps involved in the process of the winding-up stage of the Individual Pension Plan solution.

IPP PROCESS FOR NEW PLANS

The table below shows the life cycle of an Individual Pension Plan (IPP) through its set-up phase.

Step 1	A company/future administrator requests a quote to determine how much can be put into an IPP to fund a benefit for a potential IPP member. Information data such as date of birth and T4 earnings dating back to 1991 if earned by a connected person is gathered. If the individual is not a connected person, T4 earnings used to calculate pensionable benefits can be collected dating back to the time the employee began working for the sponsoring company.

	Determine IPP suitability by getting a quote from an actuary or a firm that specializes in setting up IPPs.
Step 2	The company/sponsor will need to review the quote to determine if the IPP is the best solution for the potential IPP member.
Step 3	The Plan sponsor decides to establish an Individual Pension Plan.
Step 4	The Plan sponsor appoints an administrator, a custodian, trustee(s) if needed, an actuary and an investment manager/financial advisor to design, register and manage the IPP.
Step 5	IPP documents such as the following are prepared: • Trust Agreement (if applicable) • Board of Directors Resolutions • Actuarial Valuation Report • Actuarial Information Summary/Cost Certificate (if applicable) • Application for PSPA (if applicable) • Application for Registration of Pension Plan CRA Form (T510) • Investment Objectives Guidelines • Locking-in Agreement (if applicable) • Letters to the CRA and Provincial Authority (if applicable) • Past Service Pension Adjustment Certification Form T1004 (if applicable) • CRA Connected Person Information Return Form T1007 (if applicable) • Beneficiary Designations • Pension Plan Text A folder of all documents for the IPP sponsor's and IPP member's records are prepared.
Step 6	IPP documents are filed with the CRA and provincial regulating authorities. The administrator pays fees for filing and registering IPP.
Step 7	The CRA provides a temporary registration letter with a temporary seven-digit IPP registration number. Permanent IPP status has not been granted yet.
Step 8	Once the CRA has provided a temporary IPP number, the sponsoring company can now make contributions for past service and current service. However, the qualifying transfer will not occur yet at this stage. The IPP must first receive final approval from the CRA.

Step 9	If all filings are completed properly, the CRA will give formal approval of the IPP by sending a registration letter to the sponsoring company and its appointed advisors.
Step 10	At this point, the IPP member must start the qualifying transfer process. These funds will originate from the IPP member's RRSP, RRSP's unused room, locked-in plans, DPSPs or pension plans or a combination thereof, and will be transferred to the IPP. The CRA requires that the qualifying transfer process be completed within 90 days of the date that the IPP was formally registered by the CRA.
Step 11	The CRA's formal letter is sent to the sponsoring company of the IPP. This letter permits contributions to the IPP to be deducted as expenses off the sponsoring company's corporate tax return.

Note: Depending on the jurisdiction in which an IPP is registered, a cheque by the plan administrator for the IPP's registration will have to be paid directly to the regulatory pension authorities (see table below for these dollar amounts by jurisdiction).

PROVINCE	REGISTRATION FEE
Alberta	$70
British Columbia	$200
Federal	$10 per member
Manitoba	$100
New Brunswick	$100
Newfoundland	$500
Nova Scotia	$100
Ontario	$250
Prince Edward Island	N/A
Quebec (if non-connected person)	$500 + $7.15 per member
Saskatchewan	$100

ONGOING IPP ADMINISTRATION REQUIREMENTS AND PROCESS

The table below shows the life cycle of an IPP through its maintenance phase.

Step 1	The administrator/sponsor will need to provide the actuarial firm all T4 earnings of the IPP member for the current year of service. The member's pension adjustment (PA) is calculated based on the previous year's earnings, and this will be shown on the IPP member's T4. The sponsoring company is required to include a PA and the plan's registration number for each IPP member on its T4 slip.
Step 2	A statement showing the IPP's assets for the previous year is required to be produced and forwarded to the IPP's actuary. In this statement, the following must be provided: • Opening market and book value • Contributions • Transfers • Distributions • Closing market and book value *Note: The financial or insurance institution that holds the IPP assets will provide this information.* This information is required so the actuary, plan administrator and trustee can complete a T3P Employees' Pension Plan Income Tax Return if the IPP has been set up with a trust agreement with either a formal trustee or a three-person trustee arrangement. Also, what needs to be prepared for submission to keep the IPP registered are: • Financial Statements • Pension Statements • CRA Annual Information Return (Depending on the province of registration, a Joint Annual Information Return may need to be filed with both the CRA and the provincial regulators.) • Census of Trust Pension Fund (Statistics Canada may select the IPP at random to provide information regarding the assets in the IPP fund.)
Step 3	The Registered Pension Plan Annual Information Return is submitted to the CRA on CRA Form T244 and, if needed, to the provincial regulators with the applicable fees for approval to keep the IPP registered.

Step 4	Sponsors of IPPs in Ontario are mandated to submit the Risk-Based Pension Investment Monitoring Program and Investment Information Summary Form (IIS Form) every year to the Financial Services Commission of Ontario (FSCO) to ensure that the assets held in the IPP are being properly managed and that the IPP will generate enough returns on investments to provide the promised benefit for the IPP member.
Step 5	Every three years, a triennial valuation must be completed on behalf of the IPP. A triennial valuation is an actuarial valuation that reports on the strength of a registered IPP and that must be filed with the CRA every three years. The valuation is used to set current service contributions for the next three years. It also determines if the IPP has a surplus or deficit in meeting its benefit obligations.

TERMINATION OF IPP MEMBER AND IPP WIND-UP

The table below shows the life cycle of an IPP through its winding-up phase.

Step 1	If an IPP member stops being a member of the IPP, or the plan winds up, he or she has transferring rights. The options available to a former member of an IPP include the following: 1. He or she can transfer the commuted value of the accumulated IPP to another registered pension plan. 2. He or she can transfer the commuted value of the accumulated IPP to an LIRA, LIF, or LRIF, or to an RRSP only in the Province of Quebec if the IPP member is a connected person. 3. He or she can transfer the commuted value of the accumulated IPP to purchase an annuity.
Step 2	A wind-up for purposes of an IPP is deemed to be in effect on the date determined by the sponsor of the plan. This date is referred to as the effective date. On the effective date, accrual IPP benefits for the member of the plan will end even though the member may continue working for the sponsoring company. In addition, on the effective date the member of the IPP is fully vested in

	the plan and all assets are the member's according to government formulas. IPP sponsors on wind-up of the plan must provide written notice to the IPP member of the proposed termination of the plan.
Step 3	An IPP will be considered to be wound up after the proper documentation has been filed with the CRA and provincial regulators, and funding requirements have been met by the sponsoring company.
Step 4	If the IPP assets are not yet vested with the member of the IPP, Form T10 is filed with the CRA. The T10 is a form that reports the pension adjustment reversal (PAR) to the CRA on behalf of the former RPP member. The T10 restores the RRSP room that was reduced as a result of membership in a pension plan or DPSP, a portion of which the member is no longer entitled to as a result of termination from the plan. PAR increases a former RPP and DPSP member's RRSP room by the difference between the total employee's PAs that were reported while he or she was a member of these plans and the actual pension value transferred to an RRSP.

CHAPTER 18

APPLICABLE PENSION LAWS AND REGULATIONS

Peter J. Merrick

Overview

This chapter provides the foundation for understanding the applicable pension laws, regulations and industry standards that apply to the implementation, maintenance and wind-up of an IPP. The aim of this chapter is to unleash the key components of the Canadian pension sector that up until now have been known to only a few government officials, actuaries and employee benefit consultants.

Learning Objectives

By the end of this chapter, you should be able to:

- understand pension laws governing Individual Pension Plans;
- understand the tax laws and tax regulations governing Individual Pension Plans; and
- understand the actuary formulas that are used to determine an Individual Pension Plan's funding requirements.

A thorough understanding of the basic legislative intent behind tax rules, Pension Acts and pension standards can assist in understanding the complexities behind the adopting of the IPP solution. Understanding the intent behind the various rules impacting IPPs should be the aim of every financial professional involved in recommending, implementing, maintaining and winding up IPPs. IPPs are built on several key foundations, and within this chapter we will address the cornerstones that make the IPP solution possible today.

FRAMEWORK FOR DEFINED BENEFIT PENSION PLANS REGISTERED UNDER THE DIFFERENT PENSION BENEFITS ACTS

Across Canada, there are 11 legislative bodies that have authority to govern registered pension plans. The 11 jurisdictions and the names of the Acts regulating pensions are:

Federal: *Pension Benefits Standards Act, 1985*, R.S.C. 1985, c. 32 (2nd Supp.)

Alberta: *Employment Pension Plans Act*, R.S.A. 2000, c. E-8

British Columbia: *Pension Benefits Standards Act*, R.S.B.C. 1996, c. 352

Manitoba: *Pension Benefits Act*, C.C.S.M., c. P32

New Brunswick: *Pension Benefits Act*, S.N.B. 1987, c. P-5.1

Newfoundland and Labrador: *Pension Benefits Act, 1997*, S.N.L. 1996, c. P-4.01

Nova Scotia: *Pension Benefits Act*, R.S.N.S. 1989, c. 340

Ontario: *Pension Benefits Act*, R.S.O. 1990, c. P.8

Quebec: *Supplemental Pension Plans Act*, R.S.Q., c. R-15.1

Prince Edward Island: *Pension Benefits Act*, S.P.E.I. 1990, c. 41 (unproclaimed)

Saskatchewan: *Pension Benefits Act, 1992*, S.S. 1992, c. P-6.001

One of the main purposes of the federal and provincial Pension Benefits Acts is to set out minimum standards for registered pension plans to ensure that the rights and interests of pension plan members, retirees and their beneficiaries are protected. Pension standard legislation governs such matters as who is eligible for membership in a defined benefit plan, vesting and portability of the pension, death benefits and disclosure. The two basic tenets that are found in all the pension legislation across Canada are:

1. Each Pension Benefits Act has far-reaching rules and guidelines regarding how pensions within their jurisdictions behave and function.
2. Each Pension Benefits Act places the responsibility upon pension regulators to make sure all pensions within their jurisdictions comply with the rules and regulations and empowers these regulators with the authority to enforce rules, regulations and laws sanctioning them to fine violators and to take criminal action against such violators.

While setting up an IPP is voluntary in nature for an employer, once an IPP is registered, a pension sponsor has a legal obligation to follow all the pension rules that govern it, with no exception. IPPs must be registered federally with Canada Revenue Agency (CRA) and with every provincial pension regulatory body, with the exception of British Columbia, Manitoba and P.E.I. In Quebec, an IPP does not have to be registered with the provincial pension authorities if the IPP was created for a connected person. However, for all other members who are not connected persons to the IPP sponsor, these plans have to be registered with the Quebec provincial regulator.

As it applies to IPPs, federal and provincial Acts require registered pension plans' promised benefits to be in accordance with standards set out in these Acts. Defined benefit pension plans must file actuarial valuations every three years, or more frequently, as required by these Acts. If these valuations show a pension plan's assets to be less than its liabilities, payments must be made into the plan to eliminate the deficiency over a prescribed period of time, provided that this has been legislated by the Pension Benefits Act and pension authority that the IPP is registered with. In addition, these Acts require that the administrators of these plans file an Annual Information Return (AIR).

Actuarial valuations for the purpose of defined benefit pension plans are conducted using two different sets of actuarial assumptions: "solvency valuations" use assumptions consistent with a plan being terminated, while "going-concern valuations" are based on the plan continuing in operation.

If a solvency valuation reveals a shortfall of plan assets to plan liabilities, the IPP usually requires its plan sponsor to make special payments into the IPP, sufficient to eliminate the deficiencies over a five-year period.

For example, if an IPP has been set up for both a husband and wife with an unfunded liability of $160,543, this IPP has a solvency deficiency of $121,121, which requires the company/sponsor to make special payments of $2,301 per month over a five-year period to eliminate this deficiency.

Where a deficiency exists on the basis of a going-concern valuation, these Pension Benefits Acts require special payments to eliminate the going-concern deficiency over 15 years. Using our example of an IPP being set up for both a husband and wife with an unfunded liability of $160,543, it will require the sponsoring company to make a minimum special payment of $1,461 per month over the next 15-year period to fund the liability of the going-concern deficiency.

In general, the payments that a plan sponsor must remit to a plan in a given year include the amount necessary to cover the ongoing current service costs associated with the plan, plus any "special payments" required in that year to pay down a funding deficiency over the relevant time period.

Again, using our example, the company/IPP sponsor for this husband and wife IPP will have to make a minimum IPP contribution equal to $2,301 per month to fund the solvency deficiency, and $1,461 per month for the underfunded liability.

Note: In the example above we are using an IPP set up in Ontario and are following rules that apply specifically to Ontario. If the company/sponsor makes the full $160,543 contribution into the IPP this year, all solvency and underfunded liabilities requirements will have been met and this plan will be fully funded for the years of service credited to this husband and wife.

INCOME TAX ACT

It was not long ago when the federal government passed Bill C-52 into law in 1990 to amend the *Income Tax Act*, R.S.C. 1985, c. 1 (5th Supp.) (ITA) to include registered pension plans (RPPs) formally as part of the Act. An RPP is a pension plan that has been set up by an employer, and registered by the CRA, to provide a specified employee(s) with a pension when he or she retires. An RPP exists when there is a formal arrangement made by an employer (sponsor) to contribute on behalf of an employee (member) to a registered pension plan. RPPs and the definition of who can be a member of a plan are defined in section 147.1 of the ITA.

As of 1991, the CRA allowed designated pension plans (DPPs) to be registered. These types of plans are referred to as Individual Pension Plans. A designated pension plan is a pension plan where more than 50% of the pension credits are for a specific person. These individuals are active members of a pension plan who may be connected persons to the employer of the plan or who earn approximately two and one-half times the year's maximum pensionable earnings (YMPE). The 2008 YMPE has been set at $44,900, so a designate plan applies to IPPs that have been set up for individuals who earn over $116,667 annually and are to receive a pension benefit at 65 for the 2008 year equal to 2% of his or her earnings for a maximum credited benefit of $2,333.33.

Other important areas that both the ITA and its supporting *Income Tax Regulations*, C.R.C., c. 945 (REG), cover are how an IPP sponsor needs to be engaged in an active business and the IPP member needs to be a *bona fide* employee who receives either a T4, T4A or T4PS for active income from the sponsoring business. Both the IPP sponsor and IPP member need to be separate legal entities from one another for an

IPP to be allowed to be set up and maintained by a business/sponsor for a plan member.

For example, an unincorporated doctor cannot create an IPP for himself or herself because he or she would be both the IPP sponsor and IPP member. The unincorporated doctor could create an IPP for one of his or her employees because in this situation there would be two separate legal entities, the doctor (IPP sponsor) and the doctor's employee (IPP member). However, an IPP can be set up for a doctor who has an incorporated professional corporation because in this instance, there would be two separate legal entities: the incorporated practice (IPP sponsor) and the doctor (IPP member).

Also defined in both the ITA and REG are the guidelines for the types of investments that can be held within an IPP. The types of investments that can be held within an IPP will be covered in more detail in Chapter 25 of this book. Both the ITA and REG state that an actuary must show how contributions and asset amounts held in an IPP have been determined. Actuaries must certify all amounts that are invested into an IPP, using an approved IPP funding formula. The ITA and REG outline the guidelines on how IPP benefits are to be paid out to a member of an IPP and what the available options are for an IPP member whose plan is winding up or if the member decides to transfer assets out of an IPP to another type of registered deferred income plan.

INCOME TAX REGULATIONS

The *Income Tax Regulations* are complements to the ITA. The REG specify the terms and conditions of applying the ITA. Since the IPP is classified as a designated plan, the amount of possible pensionable benefit earned per year of credited service for an IPP member is set within subsection 8500(1) of the REG. It states:

> "defined benefit limit" for a calendar year means ...
>
> ...
>
> (b) 1/9 of the money purchase limit for the year ...

A money purchase plan is also referred to as a defined contribution pension plan. This is a registered pension plan with the CRA in which the contribution amounts are defined but the benefit of the pension received at retirement is not defined. Contributions limits for DCPPs are set for 2006 ($19,000); 2007 ($20,000); 2008 ($21,000); 2009 ($22,000); and 2010 (indexed to the average wage).

Based on the 1/9th formula, defined benefit maximum pension limits (per year of service) have been set as follows: 2006 ($2,111); 2007

($2,222); 2008 ($2,333); 2009 ($2,444); and 2010 (indexed to the average wage).

Example

$22,000 DCPP contribution ÷ $9 = $2,444 DBPP pensionable service limit per each year of service up to 2009

Outlined in subsection 8515(7) of the REG are the assumptions and methodology that are to be used as guidelines by all actuaries across Canada in determining the maximum funding contributions permitted into an IPP based on the IPP member's age. The assumptions and methodology presented in this section include:

(a) the projected accrued benefit method used to determine actuarial liabilities and current costs;

(b) a valuation interest rate of 7.5% per year;

(c) a salary increase rate of 5.5% per year;

(d) a rate of increase in the Consumer Price Index of 4.0% per year;

(e) retirement at age 65;

(f) assumed continuous employment until retirement;

(g) at retirement, member assumed to be married to a person who is the same age;

(h) no pre-retirement mortality;

(i) post-retirement mortality based upon the 1983 Group Annuity Mortality Table using 80% of the average of male and female rates; and

(j) plan assets valued at their fair market value.

These actuarial assumptions and methodology are used to determine the contribution needed to produce a 2% IPP benefit for a person earning a T4 of $116,667 in 2008. This defined benefit pension formula produces a larger contribution amount made by an IPP sponsor for plan members older than 40 years of age than if this same IPP member/person made a maximum $20,000 RRSP 2008 contribution for the same year.

The table below compares the allowable maximum IPP contributions based on the member's age and the maximum RRSP contribution for 2008.

Age at January 1, 2008	**IPP Contribution Rate of Income**	**IPP Contribution $**	**RRSP Contribution Rate of Income**	**RRSP Contribu-tion $**
40	18.7%	$21,822	18%	$20,000
45	20.5%	$23,970	18%	$20,000
50	22.5%	$26,330	18%	$20,000
55	24.6%	$28,922	18%	$20,000
60	27.0%	$31,769	18%	$20,000
65	30.1%	$35,143	18%	$20,000

Note: The above calculations may vary depending on the actuarial firm performing the IPP Quote and Valuation because how the actuary chooses to interpret subsection 8515(7) may be very different. To avoid problems with IPP registration, it is recommended that you contract an actuarial firm that has a pre-approved Specimen Plan Text with the CRA.

CHAPTER 19

APPLICABLE PENSION INDUSTRY STANDARDS

Peter J. Merrick

Overview

This chapter addresses issues that are as diverse as accounting, actuary evaluation, pension legislation, employment law and marital and common law relationship breakdown.

Learning Objectives

By the end of this chapter, you should be able to:

- determine what jurisdiction an IPP should be registered in;
- understand pension adjustment and the Factor of 9 as they relate to an Individual Pension Plan;
- understand the role qualifying transfers play as it relates to funding a pension for past service;
- understand how the creation and maintenance of an IPP impacts on RRSP contributions in the first year of the plan and the years that follow the initial registration;
- understand how deficits, surpluses and excess surpluses are determined in the IPP funding formula;
- understand the differences between the career average formula and the final average as they apply to IPP calculations;
- understand how terminal funding works;
- understand how transferring IPP assets out of an IPP to a locked-in plan and Age Transfer Factor work;
- understand the significance of Accounting section 3461, Employee Future Benefits, in the Canadian Institute of Chartered Accountants (CICA) Handbook; and
- understand how IPPs are dealt with during a divorce or the ending of a common law partnership.

REGISTRATION WITH THE PROPER PENSION AUTHORITIES

Each IPP must be registered with the CRA Pension Directorate. However, where the IPP member shows up for work physically in Canada determines the provincial jurisdiction in which an IPP is registered and the pension authority under which an IPP will be governed. Currently, IPPs are not required to be registered in the Provinces of British Columbia and Quebec if the participant is a significant shareholder of the corporation (connected person). If the IPP has been set up for a group of individuals, the registration of the plan will depend on where the majority of the plan members show up for work.

Suppose an IPP is set up for only one executive who lives in Ottawa, Ontario, but who works in an office in Hull, Quebec. This plan would fall under the jurisdiction of Quebec, not Ontario. If an IPP is set up for a husband, wife and their oldest son, who are all *bona fide* employees of a company where the husband and wife work in Ontario and the son works in Alberta, the IPP will be registered in Ontario and governed by the pension authority within Ontario.

FACTOR OF 9 (DETERMINING PENSION ADJUSTMENT)

Our entire Canadian private and corporate tax-assisted retirement saving system is based on what is referred to as the Factor of 9. The Factor of 9 is a pension credit formula used to determine the pension credit in a defined benefit pension plan for any given year. The federal government created the Factor of 9 to equalize the tax-assisted savings and benefits between all defined contribution pension plans (DCPP), deferred profit-sharing plans (DPSP) and RRSPs to defined benefit pension plans (DBPP).

The Factor of 9 states that for every $1 of defined benefit pension benefit promised to a member, the government considers that the equivalent of $9 of funding would have to be invested in a defined contribution pension plan or RRSP to deliver the same end benefit. However, this relationship is an average over a plan member's entire working career.

The main assumptions that the Factor of 9 are based on are as follows:

- It assumes that the DBPP member will receive the maximum benefit that can accumulate in any year, which is 2% of the plan member's pre-retirement employment income per year according to the maximum pension benefit limits set by the federal government each year.

- It assumes that the DBPP member will not retire until he or she has accumulated 35 years of accredited pension service in the plan. It also assumes that RRSP and DCPP contributions would have been maximized during that 35-year period.
- The internal compound rate that the funds within a DBPP, DCPP, RRSP and DPSP are assumed to be growing at is a real rate of return of 3% per year.
- Upon retirement the member with the amount invested in a DBPP, DCPP and RRSP would have enough funds to be withdrawn for a 21.4-year period after retirement.

The Factor of 9 is used to come up with an IPP member's pension adjustment (PA). To calculate the PA, the yearly promised benefit that is earned by the member of a defined benefit plan is multiplied by 9. Whatever the amount calculated by the Factor of 9 is, even if all of the RRSP room is wiped out using this formula, the government will always give members of defined benefit pension plans a pension adjustment offset (PA offset). Up until 1996, the PA offset was $1,000, and then from 1997 to the present it was reduced to $600 per year for members of a DBPP.

Example

For 2009, a maximum IPP annual PA equals 2% for a maximum pension credit of $2,444 for a maximum income of $122,222 (where $2,444 × 9 = $22,000). This IPP member will be given RRSP room of $600 for this year.

In this case, the PA would be $22,000, which is equal to the money purchase plan (DCPP) maximum contribution limit for 2009. However, due to the PA offset in this example, the CRA will give this IPP member an RRSP contribution room of $600 for 2009. The CRA automatically gives the PA offset to every plan member to make it simpler and fair because the PA/Factor of 9 formula is based on 2% of the income of a plan member based on a public sector government-defined benefit pension plan. While the majority of private sector-defined benefit pension plans are based on providing 1% of the member's income for pension per year for the plan member, these lower pension benefit plans require a lot less funding to provide promised benefits. The PA offset amount can be used to contribute into either an individual's RRSP or, if the plan member has a spouse, into a spousal RRSP.

All in all, for members of defined benefit pension plans who are younger than age 40, the actual amount needed to be invested into an IPP to produce the promised $1 of pension benefit at age 65 is less than the assumed $9 that the Factor of 9 uses; the actual amount needed to fund a defined benefit pension benefit in the future could be as low as a $1 to $3 contribution today for younger employees. For older IPP members (aged 40 to 71) the factor to deliver $1 of pension benefit tomorrow may be as high as $10 to $27.

The reason for the variance of the actual dollars needed to fund the same benefit is due to older members of a DBPP having less time value for the investments in their IPPs to compound in order to deliver the promised defined benefit; therefore, more money has to be invested into an older member's IPP to deliver the same benefit as a younger plan member's.

PAST SERVICE PENSION ADJUSTMENT (PSPA)

One of the main reasons the IPP funding formula is more generous than the RRSP limits is due to the fact that a company/sponsor can contribute into an IPP for the pension plan member for his or her years of service prior to the set-up of the plan going back to 1991 for a connected person, or, for a non-connected member, a company/sponsor can contribute into a DBPP/IPP going as far back as the date that the member was hired by the sponsoring company.

It is important to understand that when an employer contributes into an IPP for past service, this new contribution reduces an individual's RRSP deduction limit for any pension benefits earned in a year after 1990 for the following years through the reporting of a PA. Thus, when past service credits are bought for an IPP member going back to 1990, a retroactive adjustment is required of the IPP member to give up some of the RRSP room he or she had in past years. This is referred to as past service pension adjustment (PSPA).

What does that mean, and are there any possible exceptions to the rule for funding an IPP for a connected person for employment years prior to 1991?

Imagine that we have a business owner (connected person) who has been working for his incorporated company for 28 years since 1980, and who decides that he wants his company to sponsor an IPP for himself. In this situation, his company would be restricted to funding his pension for only his years of service going back to 1991.

This restriction would not apply to non-connected persons. If this same business decided to create an IPP for a key executive who was a non-connected person who started working for this company at the same time in 1980, the company would be permitted to fully fund this key executive's pension benefit for the full 28 years of service since 1980.

The possible exception to the rule for a connected person to have an IPP funded by his or her company for prior years of service before 1991 would be for the company to also create an IPP for a non-connected member for the same years of credited service. So it is possible for the owner/connected person (this should be investigated with an actuary) to have his or her company fund his or her IPP for the full 28 years that he or she had received a T4 income since 1980, provided that the company also funded an IPP benefit for the same 28 years of service for its key executive (non-connected person).

It should be noted that funding of an IPP for pensionable service after 1990 is permitted by the CRA in the form of one lump-sum contribution, and this is a fully deductible expense for the IPP sponsor in the year that the contribution is made. On the other hand, funding of the IPP for pre-1990 service, if permitted by the CRA, cannot be fully deducted by the sponsor in the year that it is made. An IPP-sponsoring company is only permitted to spread out a pre-1990 contribution for the purposes of deductions over a number of years going forward after the IPP was registered with the CRA.

2/3 Pensionable

It should be noted that for pre-1990 pensionable service recognized after June 7, 1990, the maximum pensionable benefit limit for pre-1990 pensionable service funding is $1,150.00 (2/3 of $1,722.22) for years up to and including 2003, and 2/3 (two-thirds) of the maximum pension limit for years after 2003. In the pension industry, this is referred to as 2/3 pensionable.

QUALIFYING TRANSFER

The CRA's PSPA funding requirements for an IPP consist of two parts:

Part One: Direct deposits made by the employer only or by both the employer and employee for the purpose of buying past service pension credits.

Part Two: A qualifying transfer from the IPP member's RRSP, Deferred Profit-Sharing Plan (DPSP), Locked-in RRSP, money purchase plan (DCPP) or the member's unused RRSP room.

Below is a chart that shows the maximum qualifying transfer amount needed by a connected person to receive a maximum pension benefit for each year of pensionable service, starting back from 1991 to December 31, 2007, that would be required by the CRA to be transferred into his or her IPP.

YEAR	(1) MAXIMUM T4 EARNINGS ($)	(2) DOLLAR OFFSET ($)	(3) MAXIMUM PSPA ($)
1991	69,444	1,000	11,500
1992	69,444	1,000	11,500
1993	75,000	1,000	12,500
1994	80,556	1,000	13,500
1995	116,667	1,000	20,000
1996	116,667	1,000	20,000
1997	116,667	600	20,400
1998	116,667	600	20,400
1999	116,667	600	20,400
2000	116,667	600	20,400
2001	116,667	600	20,400
2002	116,667	600	20,400
2003	116,667	600	20,400
2004	116,667	600	20,400
2005	116,667	600	20,400
2006	116,667	600	20,400
2007	116,667	600	20,400
	(3) = (1) × 2.0% × 9 – (2)		313,400

The maximum PSPA amounts above are for 2008 only. As it has been mentioned before, depending on the actuary completing the initial IPP valuation, the qualifying transfer amount may vary.

HOW PSPA AND QUALIFYING TRANSFERS WORK TOGETHER

Imagine we have a 50-year-old male owner/executive who has worked for the same company since 1991 to the present (2008), and he has averaged a T4 income of more than $116,667 a year during that same period. An IPP is set up for this individual this year, and a past service calculation has been performed by an actuary. It has been determined that the total liability for the IPP for past service (1991 to 2007) totals $431,715. Of this IPP's past service liability, the actuary has determined that $313,400 must be funded by a qualifying transfer. The IPP sponsor will make up the remaining $118,315 of unfunded liability for past service for the IPP.

Note: In our example, if the IPP member does not have enough funds in RRSPs, Deferred Profit-Sharing Plans (DPSP), Locked-in RRSPs, money purchase plans (DCPP) or unused RRSP room equal to $313,400 to make a qualifying transfer, the member will not be able to buy back past service credits going back to 1991 when the member received T4 income from the company.

IPP IMPACT ON RRSP CONTRIBUTIONS FOR THE FIRST YEAR OF THE PLAN

In the first year after an IPP has been registered with the CRA, a connected person's RRSP contribution limit will be reduced by the CRA by 18% according to a formula based on the member's T4 income in the 1990 tax year. The IPP member's RRSP contribution limit will be reduced by a maximum of $11,500, which was the maximum RRSP contribution limit for 1990.

This decrease in the IPP member's RRSP contribution limit for a connected person for the first year the IPP has been registered with the CRA only pertains if the PA for 1990 was $0. If the IPP member who is a connected person had a PA reported for the year 1990, this reduction in RRSP deduction limits does not apply. In the second year after the IPP has been established with the CRA, the plan member will only receive a PA offset of $600, which can be contributed to his or her RRSP, or to a spousal RRSP.

Example

Imagine that an IPP is registered in 2008 for a connected person who earns $100,000 for the same year, who has also received a T4 income from his or her company starting back in 1990, where the connected person did not get a PA for that year. Lastly, this connected person was eligible for the maximum RRSP contribution for 1990. This connected person's allowable RRSP contribution for 2008 would be $6,500 ($18,000 possible 2008 RRSP contribution without IPP – $11,500 maximum RRSP contribution for 1990 = $6,500 allowable 2008 RRSP contribution).

If the connected IPP member in this example did not work for the sponsoring company in 1990, he or she would receive the full $18,000 RRSP contribution limit for the first year of the plan.

The 1990 rule does not apply to IPP members who are not connected persons. Thus, in the first year of an IPP's registration, the member's RRSP room for a non-connected member will not be reduced. Using our example from above, if a person was not a connected person and earned $100,000 and did not report a PA for 1990, this IPP member's maximum RRSP contribution limit for the first year of the plan would be the full 18% of his or her income or $18,000 for the first year of the plan.

In all of our scenarios listed above for both connected and non-connected members, every year following the first year of the plan, the member's contribution limit would be reduced to $600 per year thereafter until the plan is wound up or the member reached age 71.

The IPP Registration Effective Date

The effective date is the date that an IPP is considered to have been registered with the CRA. This date is outlined in the IPP documents. This date cannot be before January 1st of the year that the application for registration of the IPP is made to the CRA. When setting up an IPP, registration must be sent to the CRA within 120 days of the corporate year-end. Additionally, it must occur within the same calendar year. Contributions must be made within 120 days of the corporate year-end, regardless of calendar year.

Thus, a company with a corporate year-end of March 31st has until July 31st to send the documents to the CRA and make the contributions. A November 30th year-end will require documents to be submitted by December 31st (calendar year-end), but contributions do not have to be made until March 31st of the following year.

IPP DEFICITS, SURPLUSES AND EXCESS SURPLUSES

Deficits: The plan could be in a deficit position because the IPP fund returns were lower than anticipated due to the average industrial wage (AIW) rising faster than expected, or for any other reason such as a lower return of assets within the IPP. As a result, the actuary will require additional contributions to be injected into the plan in order to finance the deficit. Note that this deficit may be amortized over a maximum period of 15 years.

Surplus: The actuary will not require a contribution holiday or a decrease in contributions if the IPP surplus does not result in an excess surplus.

Excess Surplus: The actuary will require a contribution holiday or a decrease in contributions if the plan is in an excess surplus position. The excess surplus represents the lesser of 20% of the actuarial liabilities or the greater of 10% of the actuarial liabilities and two times the contributions for current service.

IPP RETIREMENT DATE AGE

All IPP members must begin taking pension benefits from the plan by December 31st in the year that the member turns 71 years old. This is similar to RRSP rules, which require that RRSPs be collapsed by the same date.

CAREER AVERAGE IPP VS. FINAL AVERAGE IPP

IPP final benefits that are promised to the member of the plan can vary depending on the status of the plan member (connected or non-connected person status) and the structure of the plan. The two main structures for determining the final IPP pension benefit are as follows:

Career Average Earnings IPPs

These IPPs are used to calculate the total annual pension benefit that a connected person can receive from his or her IPP. Career average earning IPP benefits are structured to pay out a pension benefit to a plan member based on the member's entire career during which he or she was eligible to acquire pension credits from the plan. Each year is treated equally in the weighting of the career average and capped at the CRA-prescribed pensionable amounts.

Career Average Formula

Annual Pension Benefit = Career Average of Pensionable Earnings × Years of Pensionable Service

Career Average IPP Example		
Year	**Earnings**	**Pension 2% of Earnings**
1998	$50,000	$1,000
1999	$50,000	$1,000
2000	$50,000	$1,000
2001	$50,000	$1,000
2002	$50,000	$1,000
2003	$75,000	$1,500
2004	$75,000	$1,500

Career Average IPP Example		
Year	**Earnings**	**Pension 2% of Earnings**
2005	$100,000	$2,000
2006	$100,000	$2,000
2007	$100,000	$2,000
Annual Pension due at age 65		$14,000

Final/Best Average Earning Defined IPPs

These IPPs provide for the payout of pension benefits to the IPP member that are based on the member's pensionable length of service and the average earnings of the IPP member for a stated period of time. This formula can only be used for a non-connected person. Usually the best IPPs for non-connected members are based on an average of the top three earning years that are capped at the CRA-prescribed pensionable amounts.

Final/Best Average Formula

Annual Pension Benefit = Average of Final/Best Average Pensionable Earnings × Years of Pensionable Service

Final/Best Three-Year Average IPP Example		
Year	**Earnings**	**Pension 2% of Earnings**
1998	$50,000	$1,000
1999	$50,000	$1,000
2000	$50,000	$1,000
2001	$50,000	$1,000
2002	$50,000	$1,000
2003	$75,000	$1,500
2004	$75,000	$1,500
2005	$100,000	$2,000
2006	$100,000	$2,000
2007	$100,000	$2,000
Annual Pension due at age 65		$20,000

TERMINAL FUNDING

IPPs allow for additional funding at retirement that in the IPP world is referred to as "Terminal Funding". Additional voluntary funding is allowed at retirement for the purpose of providing early retirement benefits/bridge benefits to supplement IPP members' incomes until they are eligible for full CPP and OAS benefits at age 65, full post-retirement CPI indexing and an unreduced pension benefit for a surviving spouse.

This amount is calculated by an actuary and includes unreduced early retirement benefits back to age 60, and 3% per annum prior to age 60 bridging benefits. Terminal funding creates another opportunity for additional tax-deductible contributions for employers and tax deferral for former employees that could be in the hundreds of thousands of dollars.

Example

Imagine that an IPP has been created for a 50-year-old owner/manager. As of January 1, 2007, this owner/manager has T4 earnings of $111,111 or more from 1991 onward. Assume that the member will retire at age 60 on January 1, 2017 with 26 years of pensionable service (1991 through 2016). His restricted funding liability at age 60 would be $1,240,000, while his terminal funding liability would be $1,501,000. Thus, the potential terminal funding opportunity for this member would be $261,000 ($1,501,000 less $1,240,000).

TRANSFERRING IPP ASSETS OUT TO A LOCKED-IN PLAN

For IPP members who want or need to wind up their IPPs, they have several options. They can purchase an annuity, a Life Income Fund (LIF), a Locked-in Retirement Account (LIRA) or a Locked-in Retirement Income Fund (LRIF).

In section 8517 of the *Income Tax Regulations*, C.R.C., c. 945, there is a prescribed formula of how much money within an IPP can be transferred to another registered plan without triggering taxes on the amounts that are not allowed to be tax-sheltered. The dollar limits that are allowed to be tax-sheltered within an IPP in most cases are much greater than permitted when transferred to a LIRA, LIF or LRIF.

AGE TRANSFER FACTOR

In the pension industry there is a formula that is used to determine how much money can be transferred out of an IPP to another type of registered plan to avoid being taxed. This formula is based on the IPP member's age and is referred to as the "Age Transfer Factor".

The Age Transfer Factor formula is written out as follows:

Permitted Transfer Tax Deferral Assets = Promised Annual Pension × Age Transferred Factor

Example

Imagine that you have a client who is 50 years of age, and who had an IPP created for him or her. This client has 15 years of credited pension service to date. At age 60 this client decides to wind up his or her IPP and transfers as much as is permitted of the 25 years of pension credits to a LIRA. At the end of 2016, there will be $1,307,104 sitting in the IPP to fund a promised retirement pension benefit of $83,060 per year. This individual will only be permitted to transfer $955,190 into the LIRA ($83,060 × 11.5 Age Transfer Factor = $955,190). The remaining $351,914 ($1,307,104 – $955,190 = $351,914) cannot be transferred into a LIRA. This surplus money will become deregistered and become fully taxable at the client's top marginal tax rate. If the client lives in Ontario and has the top marginal tax bracket of 46%, the client will have to pay the CRA $161,880 in taxes on this deregistered money.

The chart below shows the different Age Transfer Factors for the different ages used to determine the amount of money that is permitted to be moved from an IPP to a LIRA on a tax-deferral basis.

Age	Transfer Factor
Under 50	9.0
50	9.4
51	9.6
52	9.8
53	10.0
54	10.2
55	10.4
56	10.6
57	10.8
58	11.0
59	11.3
60	11.5
61	11.7

Age	Transfer Factor
62	12.0
63	12.2
64	12.4
65	12.4
66	12.0
67	11.7
68	11.3
69	11.0
70	10.6
71	10.3

Retiring Allowance

Using the example above, if your client were to be terminated from employment at the time that he or she transferred moneys from his or her IPP to a LIRA, none of the $351,914 taxable funds that could not be transferred to the LIRA on the IPP termination would be eligible to be considered part of a retiring allowance, eligible to be put into an RRSP.

A retiring allowance is an amount of money that an employer pays to an employee in recognition of long service with a company or an amount paid for loss of employment or position. The CRA may allow the taxpayer who receives a retiring allowance to defer part or all taxes on the amount by making payment into an RPP or LIRA if certain criteria are met. A retiring allowance must be paid directly from a former employer to a former employee. A retiring allowance cannot originate from the surplus taxable amounts that could not be transferred from an IPP to a LIRA.

Some rules that apply to retiring allowances include the following:

- An individual who is eligible for a retiring allowance can transfer the eligible part of that allowance into his or her RRSP or RPP within 60 days of December 31st.
- He or she can transfer $2,000 for each year or part year of service before 1996 in which he or she was employed.
- He or she can also transfer an extra $1,500 for each year or part year of service before 1989, as long as he or she was not entitled to receive any benefits earned under a pension plan or DPSP from contributions an employer made for each such year.
- These transfers do not reduce IPP or RRSP contribution room.

ACCOUNTING SECTION 3461, EMPLOYEE FUTURE BENEFITS, IN THE CICA HANDBOOK

The IPP for many is, first, a tax solution and then, second, a retirement strategy. What many experienced financial advisors who have successfully implemented the IPP solution know to be true is if a client's public accountant is not behind the IPP solution for his or her client, the IPP will not be implemented. It does not matter how much the investment advisor or actuary tries to convince the client to adopt the IPP solution, the IPP will not happen without the public accountant's support for the creation of an IPP.

Traditionally, the big four accounting firms (Pricewaterhouse Coopers, Ernst & Young, Deloitte & Touche and KPMG) prepared financial statements for corporations offering large defined-benefit pension plans for hundreds of employees. Now with the emergence of the IPP, hundreds and even thousands of smaller public accounting firms and public accountant sole practitioners will be producing financial statements for incorporated businesses offering the IPP solutions to their key people. This is why it is important for financial advisors entering the IPP market to become familiar with the accounting standards that the Canadian Institute of Chartered Accountants (CICA) has adopted when showing IPPs on business clients' financial statements.

In the mid-1980s, the CICA began to develop the accounting standards that would be applied to all retirement plans that employers promised to provide to their employees. These accounting procedures would pertain to both registered and non-registered plans, showing all current and future pension costs and obligations of sponsoring employers. The aim of these standards was to harmonize the accounting procedures for pension plans and their expenses, thus allowing for the comparability of pension expenses and liabilities between one sponsoring company and another.

In 1999, the CICA introduced into the CICA Handbook Section 3461, which required sponsors of DBPPs and IPPs to provide minimum disclosure on their financial statements that included the following components: the current service cost of the IPP, plus interest cost on the accrued benefit obligation, minus the expected return on plan assets, plus the amortization of any past service costs arising from a plan initiation or amendment, minus the amortization of any net actuarial gain or loss, plus any amount immediately recognized as a result of a temporary deviation from the plan, plus any increase or decrease in a valuation allowance, plus a gain or loss on a plan settlement or curtailment.

Note: Audited financial statements that meet Accounting Section 3461, "Employee Future Benefits", in the CICA Handbook and show an IPP's strength may need to be filed annually with pension regulators as well.

However, under certain circumstances, filing certified statements of IPP strength by an actuary may suffice. Even though financial statements may not be required to be filed with IPP regulatory bodies, companies sponsoring IPPs will still have to account for these IPPs in their corporate books.

The Accounting Standards Board (AcSB) of the CICA has been working on new financial reporting standards for private businesses since 2006. It is expected that the number of specific financial disclosure requirements for reporting IPPs for privately owned businesses on corporate financials will be adopted by 2010. These new standards will significantly reduce reporting requirements for IPPs in comparison to the existing Section 3461 of the CICA Handbook. The AcSB in principle has agreed to simplify the approach to accounting for defined benefit plans for business owners who own more than a 50% interest in the enterprise sponsoring an IPP for themselves or for their family members.

All other IPPs that are set up for members who own less than 50% of a sponsoring company or for their family members will continually need to follow existing accounting principles laid down in Section 3461. The proposed accounting reporting method used for plans that qualify as a controlling shareholder's IPP will use the actuarial funding valuation as a basis for the measurement, and recognize all actuarial gains and losses and past service costs in income when they occur.

MARRIAGE AND COMMON LAW RELATIONSHIP BREAKDOWN AND THE IPP

According to Statistics Canada there are approximately 146,000 marriages each year. Of those, 38% of first marriages and 60% of second marriages will end in divorce. The story these numbers don't tell us is the one where a growing number of adults choose to live together.

Larry Lipiec, a lawyer and author of the book *I Had Dreams of a Happy House Now I'm a Former Spouse*, published by Continental Atlantic Publications, challenges societal taboos by addressing the legal and financial realities of relationships in the 21st century.

He points out that marriage and common law cohabitation are not just personal relationships; under Canadian law, they are treated as business relationships/partnerships. One should be mindful that the rules that apply to the division of family assets also apply to the division of IPP assets and IPP pension benefits as well.

In regard to the division of IPP assets, assets will be divided according to provincial legislation and/or court orders if they exist. The recipient spouse of an IPP asset division is allowed to transfer the awarded IPP assets to his or her RRSP, avoiding paying taxes on the transfer.

IPP asset divisions after the end of a common law relationship or a marriage breakdown are valued using two methods:

The Value Added Method Formula: This formula for the division of IPP assets subtracts the value of the pension earned before the legal union of the couple from the value of the pension at the time of the official separation. Once that amount is determined, the split of the IPP assets occurs at the prescribed provincial and federal matrimonial asset division rates.

The Pro-Rata Method Formula: This formula for the division of IPP assets divides the value of the IPP assets on the date of legal separation based on how long the couple was married and the pension credits that were earned in the IPP. Once this amount is determined, assets are split between the divorcing spouses according to the prescribed provincial and federal matrimonial asset division rates.

How do these formulas work?

Imagine that a couple legally separates after 10 years of marriage. The husband has been a member of an IPP for 15 years, 10 of which he was married. On the day of the couple's marriage, the IPP was valued at $150,000, and on the date of the legal separation, the IPP assets were valued at $500,000. This couple lives in a progressive family law province where all assets accumulated during a marriage are split evenly, 50/50, upon divorce.

Using the value added method to determine how much of the IPP assets would be legally the wife's, you will find that she would be entitled to $175,000 of the assets of the plan.

Formula

$175,000 transfer to spouse = $500,000 value of pension on date of separation − $150,000 value of pension on the date of marriage ÷ 50% division of matrimonial assets

Using the pro-rata method in our example above, you will find that the husband would be required to give his ex-spouse $166,500 of his IPP assets upon the date of their official separation.

Formula

$166,500 Transfer to spouse = $500,000 value of pension on date of separation × 10/15 or 66.6% of the time that the IPP was accumulating pension credits during the marriage ÷ 50% division of matrimonial assets

IPP members in Newfoundland & Labrador, Saskatchewan, Quebec, Ontario, Prince Edward Island and Alberta cannot transfer more than 50% of their IPP benefits that were accrued during the marriage to the other spouse upon divorce.

In British Columbia, there are no provisions in the provincial pension legislation for the splitting of pension plan assets or pension benefits. Divorcing spouses in British Columbia have to trade off other matrimonial assets, permitting the IPP member spouse to keep the full IPP.

IPP members who live in Manitoba are given a choice under their provincial legislation where they can agree with their former spouse either to split 50/50 the IPP assets or benefits that had accumulated while they were married or to exchange assets, allowing the IPP member to keep the entire pension.

PREDECESSOR EMPLOYER AND SPONSORSHIP OF AN IPP

A predecessor employer can sponsor an IPP provided that it meets the following definition in section 8500 of the *Income Tax Regulations*:

> "predecessor employer" means, in relation to a particular employer, an employer (in this definition referred to as the "vendor") who has sold, assigned or otherwise disposed of all or part of the vendor's business or undertaking or all or part of the assets of the vendor's business or undertaking to the particular employer or to another employer who, at any time after the sale, assignment or other disposition, becomes a predecessor employer in relation to the particular employer, where one or more employees of the vendor have, in conjunction with the sale, assignment or disposition, become employees of the employer acquiring the business, undertaking or assets;

In essence, where it is important to know this rule is when a client is selling his or her company and is planning to retire. The company that the client is selling can first establish an IPP and then during or after the transaction can transfer the IPP to a new corporate entity such as the client's holding company without causing any adverse tax implications. The CRA allows these types of IPP transfers of sponsorship because the CRA does not view that the new company sponsoring the IPP was established for the purpose of transferring benefits from a prior pension plan, but that the new company was established for other legitimate reasons.

CHAPTER 20

IPP MISCELLANEOUS

Trevor R. Parry

Overview

This chapter begins by describing the options for companies making a final contribution to an IPP for its member. It continues by looking at the retirement options that an IPP member has available to receive a payout from the plan. It concludes by discussing the merits of having family IPPs and who best to name as beneficiaries of the IPP after the member has died.

Learning Objectives

By the end of this chapter, you should be able to:

- understand the value of an IPP sponsor making a final contribution into an IPP prior to an IPP member retiring;
- understand the options available for IPP members at retirement;
- understand the pros and cons of designating classes of beneficiaries for IPP assets after a plan member's death; and
- understand the recent IPP developments that could impact implementing the IPP solutions.

INTRODUCTION

We are all aware of the tax benefits that are afforded by the additional deductible contributions to IPPs over RRSPs. However, there are several other additional benefits to IPPs which often go overlooked. Most significant among these are: additional funding on retirement; investment expense deductibility; Employer Health Tax (EHT) savings; and creditor protection. It is critical to raise these issues with the companies that are considering establishing an IPP. While tax is a critical determinant, these other benefits are so significant that they must be weighed in the decision-making process.

The additional funding on retirement allows the company to make one large, final payment into the IPP. This amount varies by retirement age and length of service, but is frequently six figures, ranging to over $1 million. This funding provides two significant benefit enhancements to the plan. The first is additional indexing. Many plans have a built-in indexing provision. Additional funding enhances this indexing level. Over the length of a plan member's retirement, this can have a significant impact on the total amount of pension received. The second benefit applies only to those plan members who retire prior to age 65. The additional funding provides a benefit-bridging provision for those who retire early. Enhancing both the reduced pension and Canada Pension Plan (CPP) benefits is a distinct advantage for the early retiree.

In order to take advantage of the additional funding, either the IPP must be maintained on retirement or the assets must be used to purchase an annuity. Rolling the assets into a Locked-in Retirement Account (LIRA)/Locked-in Retirement Income Fund (LRIF) will result in a surplus which will cause the assets to be taxable in the participant's hands in the retirement year.

The deductibility of investment expenses can provide a significant benefit to a business owner setting up an IPP for himself or herself. At age 71, an IPP participant could find himself or herself with $500,000 or more in the plan. A 3% management fee would result in a tax deduction of $15,000, meaning a savings of approximately $5,000 for that year alone, simply by having these assets held in an IPP.

In Ontario, an employer is required to pay a 1.95% EHT on all payrolls over $400,000. Contributions made to an IPP are not defined as income subject to this tax. This means that a company making $450,000 worth of contributions will save $8,775 over the life of the plan versus simply paying the money out as salary or bonus. The same holds true with the other provinces that maintain a payroll-based health tax. These provinces — Quebec, Manitoba and Newfoundland — all maintain health taxes on payroll in excess of 2%. In the case of Quebec, the tax escalates, and as such the savings realized by implementing the IPP for owners/managers has profound effects.

CREDITOR-PROOFING ASSETS

Creditor-proofing is something that anyone in business, or professional practice, should seek to implement. However, creditor-proofing may be difficult for some. For instance, the lack of a uniform approach to professional corporation rules across Canada means that in some provinces the assets of the professional corporation can be creditor-proofed through the use of a holding corporation, while in others that is impossible. Some business owners have utilized segregated funds to creditor-proof invested assets. While this strategy has merit, it also has severe limitations and costs. Segregated funds carry higher management expense ratios (MERs) than other mutual funds and will erode capital over the accumulating years.

As a pension is a trust, with the plan member enjoying beneficial ownership, the assets of the pension are creditor-proof. An IPP properly designed may also provide creditor protection for any plan surpluses that may arise. Therefore, traditional business owners and incorporated professionals alike may creditor-proof substantial assets from personal and corporate creditors.

The IPP, however, will not provide protection from the results of marriage breakdown. The net family property (NFP) calculation, which will give rise to equalization payments, will include pension assets in that calculation. Including the employed spouse in the IPP from plan inception may mitigate the effects of an NFP calculation in the future.

It should be noted that recent changes to the *Bankruptcy and Insolvency Act* have now afforded protection for RRSPs in bankruptcy matters. While not full creditor protection, and protection inferior to that available in an IPP, it is an important step in the right direction for policy makers.

RETIREMENT OPTIONS

On retirement, an IPP participant has three options on how to handle the assets in his or her plan: rolling the funds into a LIF, purchasing an annuity or drawing a pension directly from the IPP.

Rolling the funds into a LIRA discharges any further obligations to the plan. A wind-up is performed, and any surplus or deficit is calculated. Once any deficit is funded, the company no longer has any responsibilities to the pension. The subsequent pension will be based on the performance of the assets inside the plan and standard maximum/minimum withdrawal calculations for LIRAs. The additional funding on retirement is not available under this option.

While many individuals might consider the plan wind-up to be the most likely scenario for the eventual disposition of their IPP, the facts might be quite different. The parameters of a wind-up calculation are established by the CRA, and the result is that too often a sizable surplus exists. A surplus of this nature must be paid out as income. This will result in considerable taxation in a single year. While the IPP may have provided considerable tax relief throughout its existence, no one likes to stomach a tax bill that can be in the hundreds of thousands of dollars. Additional funding at retirement is also not permitted in the case of plan wind-up, which will further deprive the plan sponsor of considerable tax relief. While business owners may require plan wind-up for their non-connected employees, where possible, wind-up should be avoided for their own plans.

The purchase of an annuity will, like the plan wind-up, relieve the sponsoring company of any further obligations, but it will not result in the creation of a large taxable liability through a wind-up calculation. The pension will be based on the annuity rates at the time the annuity is purchased, and the entire asset may be used to purchase the annuity. This option will allow for an additional funding payment to be made on retirement. The annuity may be purchased at any time. If the plan was maintained beyond retirement as a formal pension plan, and in later years the plan sponsor wishes to dispense with the plan, the annuity is the only option. If, for instance, the company is sold after the IPP member reaches age 71, and no corporation exists to sponsor the plan, or age or infirmity makes continuance and maintenance of the plan too difficult, then the purchase of the annuity can make tremendous sense.

The final retirement option is to leave the plan intact and begin withdrawing a pension from it. This option still requires triennial valuations, and the sponsoring company is still responsible for funding any deficits. This plan allows for the additional funding on retirement, as well as an indexed pension with known annual payments. If the company is willing to maintain sponsorship, this is usually the preferred option for pension payouts. It should be noted that terminal funding of an IPP is a simple procedure. A waiver must be filed with the CRA, which retains the right to refuse the funding. The plan could also be held to continue as a designated plan, which would greatly curtail flexibility in retirement for the plan sponsor. While terminal funding does provide a significant tax deduction, a careful review of options involving the actuary and financial planner is strongly recommended.

IPPs provide several mechanisms to transfer assets from the plan participant to the beneficiary after the participant's death. By law, the spouse is always the primary beneficiary of an IPP. If the spouse has predeceased the participant, the assets will flow to the estate or surviving children based on the beneficiary designation.

DISPOSITION OF PENSION WITH A SINGLE PLAN MEMBER

On the death of the sole plan participant, the disposition of plan assets will depend on whether or not the plan participant has begun taking a pension. If the participant has not retired before death, the assets in the IPP will roll to the spouse in a tax-free transfer into either a LIRA or an RRSP, depending on the applicable provincial regulations. If the participant has retired, the disposition will depend on the election made at retirement. The most common practice is to have the pension pay a reduced pension benefit from the IPP (with 66 2/3% of the original amount) to the surviving spouse for the remainder of his or her life. When the spouse dies, any remaining assets will be paid to his or her designated beneficiary.

If there is no surviving spouse at the time of death, the plan assets will be paid in a lump sum to the designated beneficiaries: either the named children in equal installments or the deceased's estate.

DISPOSITION OF A PLAN WITH MULTIPLE MEMBERS

It is strongly advised that only spouses or parents and adult children be placed together in the same IPP plan. All members of the plan must be employees of the sponsoring company. If a deceased participant has a surviving spouse, and has not retired, the assets representing the commuted value of his or her pension will be dealt with as if he or she was the sole plan member, as described in the section above.

If there is no surviving spouse, but the participant has adult children who are part of the plan, and the participant has begun taking a pension, the situation changes. In this case, the assets in the IPP other than any of the remaining guaranteed benefit payout to pay the heirs of the deceased plan member or to the plan member's estate will remain in the plan and create a surplus for the remaining plan members. The company would then be required to take a contribution holiday until this has been utilized.

One recent change that affects this multi-generational IPP is the issue of additional funding available upon retirement. The CRA now requires that where said funding is to be made for a plan member, his or her portion of the pension plan must be separated from the larger plan and moved into the plan member's own individual plan. This reduces the efficacy of the plan somewhat as it forces the plan sponsor to make a choice. Either additional funding is made, or the larger plan is maintained. In most cases, the plan sponsor would choose not to make additional funding payments as the estate planning elements associated with the multi-member plan outweigh the one-time deduction associated with additional funding at retirement.

ASSIGNING MINOR CHILDREN AS BENEFICIARIES

When electing beneficiaries on an IPP, the participant and spouse should always select their estate if there are minor children. Depending on the applicable provincial regulations, there will be negative consequences for minor children if they inherit funds from a pension plan.

In Ontario, naming a minor child directly as a beneficiary will result in the intervention of the Children's Lawyer (Public Guardian), who will administer the pension assets until the child reaches the age of majority. By designating the estate as the primary or contingent beneficiary, the intervention of this government agency will be precluded. While applicable probate and provincial taxes may attach to the pension asset, the individual will have far more control over those assets if the will is properly drafted. The executor or estate trustee will be able to invest and direct the pension assets according to the deceased's wishes.

This is particularly important in the case of incapacity of any minor beneficiaries. If a child is developmentally handicapped, the parent may wish to provide detailed and specialized terms regarding the distribution of assets and income from those assets. The use of testamentary trusts, which can be quite detailed, is possible only through the use of a will, and the designation of the estate as the beneficiary of pension assets.

PAST SERVICE: WHEN TO SET UP THE PLAN

Since the IPP does, in most cases, generate significant tax relief to the sponsoring company because of the ability of that company to fund past service contribution, there has been some discussion as to when to put the pension plan in place. One position that has been advanced is that the sponsoring company should wait to establish the plan in order to maximize the past service contribution, and therefore enhance the tax relief. While technically correct in that waiting will generate larger contributions and deductions in the future, for many people, waiting may be impractical.

For instance, if a 45-year-old individual were to wait until age 65, he or she would be entitled to a past service contribution of $713,000. The question that this raises is simple: how many corporations have $713,000 on hand to fund past service? Waiting to maximize a past service contribution focuses purely on the tax relief represented by these initial contributions, and may in most cases make the IPP impossible to implement for the vast majority of corporations. Also, if a company were able to make this large, one-time contribution, how much of that contribution would offset corporate tax at the higher levels? It is quite likely that some of the $713,000 would be deductible at the small business tax rate, and, as such, the deduction would not be maximized.

In discussing IPPs with accountants, advisors and entrepreneurs alike, it is my experience that tax relief, while usually the primary reason for plan implementation, is not the only reason that leads to the IPP option. Financial planning concerns must be presented to the client. For instance, the ability to creditor-proof assets is a significant benefit for many, particularly those whose businesses are in economic sectors with a higher risk of litigation, or professionals who are constantly concerned about defending claims of malpractice or professional negligence. By waiting to fund a larger past service contribution, in the future, the sponsoring company may be forced to retain significant assets for considerable periods of time, the result being that these assets could be at risk to creditors.

Both plan sponsors and members must also consider what the individual does in the interim period while he or she builds up the larger past service contribution. Invariably the individual will utilize his or her RRSP as the primary retirement funding vehicle. This in essence means that the individual, by waiting to create a larger corporate deduction in the future, is forgoing considerable benefits for a considerable period of time. For instance, the ability to deduct investment management fees, which is a facet of the IPP and not available in the RRSP, must be considered. How many dollars could have been deducted by the sponsoring company in the 20-year wait?

As with all financial planning strategies, a balance must be struck. Tax considerations are key, but must be tempered by the nature of the underlying enterprise. For instance, professional corporations, most notably medical corporations, must look at the end benefit the IPP provides as being at least as important a consideration as the tax deduction provided by past service funding. For medical corporations, where sale of the professional corporation is effectively an impossibility, a concentration on accumulation of wealth in a disciplined and foreseeable fashion should trump tax concerns. For this reason, professional corporations should consider an IPP, and the tax tail should not wag the financial planning dog.

CHANGE IN DIVIDEND TAX TREATMENT: REGISTERED PLANS IN JEOPARDY

In response to the wholesale conversion of corporations into income trusts, the federal government has moved forward in implementing changes introduced by the previous federal government, by changing the way in which dividends will be taxed. This has led some people to postulate that compensation strategies for owners/managers will change and that we will see a reduction in traditional T4 income in favour of dividend-based income. This argument is specious, as we are not aware of how these tax changes will manifest themselves.

Both plan sponsors and members must look at what "eligible dividends" will be subject to the new tax regime, especially since such dividends are those paid by Canadian public companies and not private corporations. While it may reduce the large shareholder bonuses paid in the past, the dividend tax changes will not reduce the need to create *bona fide* deductions for companies, and this is very much what IPPs do.

There is a strategy espoused by some individuals for dividend payments to completely eclipse T4 income, but this is dangerous. Such a strategy would eliminate a business owner's involvement in many retirement savings programs. Participation in the Canada Pension Plan would cease, which might have negative effects on an individual's future retirement plans, and as dividend income is not earned income, the use of an RRSP would be eliminated. It would also not be illogical for the CRA to seek redress through future tax changes if a wholesale conversion to dividend-based remuneration takes place. Participation in company-funded disability and critical illness insurance programs, along with company accident and sickness plans, would be eliminated through a switch to an all-dividend stream of income. The tried and true saying that "pigs get fat and hogs get slaughtered" is something everyone should consider when examining "radical" strategies.

CONCLUSION

The tax relief provided by IPPs remains the primary reason for establishing a plan. Canadians are an overtaxed lot, and business owners are acutely aware of this fact. The advisor team owes a duty to the client to explore thoroughly all means of safe tax deferral and reduction, but it also owes a duty to explore other aspects of all strategies. The IPP presents the sponsoring company and plan member with significant benefits above and beyond pure tax relief. The ability to know with certainty the future income that will be provided by the IPP is of tremendous benefit in properly building a comprehensive retirement plan. Additional tax relief provided by deductibility of investment fees, actuarial fees and additional contributions to fund plan deficits must be considered. Creditor-proofing is a must in our growingly litigious society. Estate planning benefits are also clear.

Demographics and economic and taxation realities will give rise to a significant increase in the use of IPPs, and, as professionals and advisors, we must always understand that thorough due diligence is the hallmark of service.

CHAPTER 21

ACTUARIAL CALCULATIONS FOR INDIVIDUAL PENSION PLANS

Stephen W.I. Cheng

Overview

This chapter goes into the workings of the formulas that are used by actuaries to perform the various actuarial calculations involved with the set-up, maintenance and wind-up of an IPP.

Learning Objectives

By the end of this chapter, you should be able to:

- understand what actuaries must calculate and certify for an IPP to be registered;
- understand pension limits and know the percentage of increases to these limits; and
- understand IPP pension plan governance.

INTRODUCTION

A defined benefit plan, such as an Individual Pension Plan (IPP), defines the pension a member is to receive upon retirement via a formula. For a *connected person*,[1] the IPP formula is typically 2.0% of the member's *career average* indexed T4 earnings. The IPP formula for a *non-connected person* is usually 2.0% of the member's *highest three-year average* indexed T4 earnings.

An *actuary*[2] is required by the *Income Tax Act*, R.S.C. 1985, c. 1 (5th Supp.), and by pension regulators[3] to calculate and certify the contributions

---

[1] A person who owns directly or indirectly 10% or more of any class of shares of a company or who is not dealing at arm's length with such a person.

[2] A Fellow of the Canadian Institute of Actuaries.

[3] Pension regulators include the applicable provincial pension regulatory authorities or the Office of the Superintendent of Financial Institutions (OSFI), the federal pension regulator for pension plans sponsored by employers in the federally regulated industries such as banking, telecommunication, interprovincial trucking and agriculture.

needed to properly fund this formulaic pension promise. The actuary is required to update the calculations every three years by the applicable pension legislation. Any contributions certified in an actuarial valuation report are deductible for tax purposes if made within four years of the effective date of the valuation. For administration simplicity and convenience, most plans follow the triennial actuarial valuation cycle (once every three years) for both pension legislation and tax legislation purposes.

PENSION LIMITS

The maximum annual pension payable to a member of a defined benefit plan is restricted by the maximum pension limit (MPL). The MPL amounts, expressed in annual pension per year of pensionable service, are summarized as follows:

TABLE 1

Year of Retirement	Defined Benefit MPL $	Increase %
2003 and prior	1,722.22	
2004	1,833.33	6.45
2005	2,000.00	9.09
2006	2,111.11	5.56
2007	2,222.22	5.26
2008	2,333.33	5.00
2009	2,444.44	4.76
2010 and after	Indexed to AIW*[4]	

* Average Industrial Wage index

---

[4] The AIW Index has increased since 1990, as per the table below:

Year	Aggregate AIW Index 12 months ending each June 30th	Increase %
1990	6,206.66	
1991	6,507.68	4.85
1992	6,751.07	3.74
1993	6,954.92	3.02
1994	7,051.57	1.39
1995	7,155.60	1.48

PENSION PLAN GOVERNANCE

Pension plans are governed by the *Income Tax Act* and the *Income Tax Regulations*, C.R.C., c. 945, as well as the applicable federal or provincial pension legislation.

The Registered Plans Directorate of Canada Revenue Agency (CRA) regulates pension plans registered according to the *Income Tax Act* and Regulations for income tax purposes. The CRA determines:

(a) whether the plan submitted for registration satisfies the primary purpose test of a pension plan (the moneys contributed are to be used for pension purposes), whether the employer (plan sponsor) and the employee (member) have a *bona fide* employment relationship, whether the employer is an active company, whether the employee receives pension-eligible compensation (*i.e.*, T4 income), *etc.*;

(b) the deductibility of employer contributions; and

(c) whether the plan maintains its formal registration status.

The federal and provincial pension regulators administer their respective Pension Benefits Acts. These Acts govern *minimum* pension standards such as vesting, locking-in, spousal benefits and minimum pension plan funding requirements. Provincial Pension Benefits Acts protect the member's rights to a properly funded pension.

IPPs are usually established for owner-managers and highly compensated executives and feature many *maximum* plan provisions (such as the formula pension and the post-retirement indexing of pension payments) to take full advantage of company pension deductions under the *Income Tax Act*. Given these circumstances, some pension regulators have decided to exclude IPPs from almost all provincial pension regulation, as shown in the following table:

1996	7,239.76	1.18
1997	7,439.67	2.76
1998	7,541.09	1.36
1999	7,627.22	1.14
2000	7,775.85	1.95
2001	7,925.59	1.93
2002	8,071.92	1.85
2003	8,205.75	1.66
2004	8,351.58	1.78
2005	8,531.25	2.15
2006	8,857.60	3.83
2007	9,101.39	2.75

PROVINCE	EXCLUSION FOR CONNECTED PERSONS	EXCLUSION FOR HIGHLY COMPENSATED EMPLOYEES
British Columbia	Yes	Yes
Alberta[5]	Yes	No
Manitoba	Yes	Yes
Quebec	Yes	No
Prince Edward Island[6]	Yes	Yes

The actuary in performing and reporting of actuarial calculations is subject to the professional standards promulgated by the Canadian Institute of Actuaries. These standards include:

(a) Consolidated Standards of Practice — General Standards (May 2002);

(b) Standard of Practice for Determining Pension Commuted Values (February 2005); and

(c) Statement of Principles on Revised Actuarial Standards of Practice for Reporting on Pension Plan Funding (March 2005).

ACTUARIAL VALUATIONS

Actuarial valuation reports for IPPs commonly show three actuarial valuations — maximum funding, going concern and solvency. Maximum funding and going-concern valuations assume that the IPP will continue in active status. Most IPPs use the maximum funding valuation results for the purpose of the going-concern valuation as well. Solvency valuations assume that the IPP will be terminated as at the valuation date.

An actuarial valuation shows:

(a) the financial position of the plan; and

(b) employer's current service contributions for the member.

As at the valuation date, the financial position of the plan compares the actuarial value of assets to the actuarial liability. If assets exceed the

[5] From August 2006, the Alberta pension regulator does not require the filing of documents, actuarial valuation reports and annual filings for IPPs for connected persons.

[6] As at this writing, Prince Edward Island has not promulgated any pension legislation. Therefore, all pension plans, including IPPs, are not subject to provincial pension legislation.

liability, then the plan has an actuarial surplus. If the liability exceeds assets, then the plan has an unfunded liability.

The actuarial liability measures the present value of pension benefits accrued by the member prior to the valuation date, *i.e.*, past service benefits. The current service contribution measures the present value of pension benefits expected to be accrued by the member in the current year.

ELIGIBILITY FOR PAST SERVICE BENEFITS

For calendar years 1990 and after, any pension benefit provided by the employer in a given year would reduce the pension plan member's RRSP deduction limit for the following year through the reporting of a pension adjustment (PA) on the member's T4.

Before an employer can provide past service pension benefits to, or make a past service pension contribution on behalf of, an IPP member, the *Income Tax Regulations* require that the IPP member satisfy the condition on "RRSP deduction limit lost". This condition must be satisfied through one or a combination of the following methods:

(a) a reduction in the member's unused RRSP contribution room carried forward;

(b) a withdrawal from the member's RRSP on a taxable basis so as to free up the necessary RRSP contribution room (this method is rarely used as the member makes a taxable withdrawal from an RRSP — defeating the purpose of setting up a new IPP, which is to achieve more tax sheltering); and/or

(c) transfer the amount on a tax-free basis from the member's existing RRSP account to the IPP (this most common method is referred to as a "qualifying transfer from RRSP to IPP"). *Note that only the member's own personal RRSP* (*i.e.*, the IPP member must be the annuitant of the RRSP) can be used. *Spousal RRSP* (*i.e.*, a plan under which the IPP member is the contributor but not the annuitant) funds *cannot be used* for this purpose.

If the "RRSP deduction limit lost" condition cannot be satisfied, the employer must either:

(a) reduce the number of years of past service benefits being recognized; or

(b) postpone the recognition of past service to a future date until the RRSP funds have accumulated to the required transfer amount.

Some individuals may wish to have a selected number of years recognized immediately and have other past years recognized only when remaining RRSP funds can accumulate to the required transfer amount.

Recognition of past years of pensionable service at IPP implementation is voluntary and at the discretion of the employer. Bear in mind that for a plan that is subject to an applicable pension legislation, the employer must contribute a minimum amount based on the amount of current service contribution and the amortization of a deficit amount.

Recognition of additional years of past service for the IPP member would also result in an additional minimum funding obligation for the employer. The employer should take the mandatory minimum employer contribution into consideration to ensure that he or she is comfortable with the resulting mandatory minimum pension funding requirements.

For a new IPP effective on January 1, 2008, the maximum "RRSP deduction limit lost" for past service benefits from January 1, 1991 to December 31, 2007 is $313,400 calculated as follows:

Year	(1) T4 Income	(2) Benefit Entitlement	(3) RRSP Deduction Limit Lost
2007	≥ $116,667	$2,333.33	$20,400
2006	≥ $116,667	$2,333.33	$20,400
2005	≥ $116,667	$2,333.33	$20,400
2004	≥ $116,667	$2,333.33	$20,400
2003	≥ $116,667	$2,333.33	$20,400
2002	≥ $116,667	$2,333.33	$20,400
2001	≥ $116,667	$2,333.33	$20,400
2000	≥ $116,667	$2,333.33	$20,400
1999	≥ $116,667	$2,333.33	$20,400
1998	≥ $116,667	$2,333.33	$20,400
1997	≥ $116,667	$2,333.33	$20,400
1996	≥ $116,667	$2,333.33	$20,000
1995	≥ $116,667	$2,333.33	$20,000
1994	≥ $116,667	$1,611.12	$13,500
1993	≥ $116,667	$1,500.00	$12,500
1992	≥ $116,667	$1,388.88	$11,500
1991	≥ $$116,667	$1,388.88	$11,500
Total			**$313,400**

(2) = (1) × 2.0%

(3) = (2) × 9.0 − $600 for years after 1996

(3) = (2) × 9.0 − $1,000 for years 1995 and 1996

(3) = years 1991 to 1994 had lower maximum benefit entitlements

MAXIMUM FUNDING ACTUARIAL VALUATION

A maximum funding valuation, as its name implies, calculates the maximum deductible contributions allowed under the *Income Tax Act* and its Regulations to a Designated Plan, which is defined as a pension plan primarily for the benefit of specified individuals. "Specified individuals" as defined in the tax legislation include connected persons and employees whose remuneration exceeds 2.5 times the YMPE (Year's Maximum Pensionable Earnings as defined in the Canada Pension Plan).

Section 8515 of the *Income Tax Regulations* specifies the following assumptions that must be used for the purpose of a maximum funding valuation:

(a) actuarial liabilities and current service contributions are to be determined using the projected accrued benefit method;

(b) valuation interest rate is 7.5% per annum;

(c) wage increase is 5.5% per annum;

(d) Consumer Price Index increases by 4.0% per annum;

(e) the member will survive to age 65;

(f) the member will retire at age 65 (if the member is over age 65 as at the actuarial valuation date then the member is assumed to retire immediately);

(g) the member's employment with the plan sponsor will continue until retirement;

(h) at retirement, the member is married to a person who is the same age as the member;

(i) post-retirement mortality rates are based upon 80% of the average of the male and female rates set forth in the 1983 Group Annuity Mortality Table;

(j) the actuarial value of assets equals the fair market value of assets as at the valuation date;

(k) pension payments are payable monthly in advance;

(l) pension payments are increased each year by 1.0% less than the percentage increase in the Consumer Price Index; and

(m) pension payments are guaranteed for five years, with 2/3 of the pension continuing to the member's surviving pension partner.[7]

Consider the January 1, 2008 actuarial valuation for a maximum-provision IPP for a connected person with the following characteristics:

(a) date of birth: October 31, 1949;

(b) 1995 T4 earnings: $50,000 and had 12 months of service; and

(c) 2008 expected T4 earnings: $120,000.

To determine the actuarial liability in respect of 1995:

(a) calculate the member's retirement date (first day of month coincident or following attainment of age 65): November 1, 2014;

(b) calculate the duration from valuation date to assumed date of retirement: six years and ten months;

(c) determine the indexed T4 earnings as at the valuation date by multiplying 1995 T4 earnings by the AIW[8] in 2007 ($9,101.39) and dividing by the AIW in 1994 ($7,051.57), yielding $64,534.49;

(d) determine the indexed T4 earnings as at the retirement date as $88,982.92 ($64,534.49 × 1.055 raised to the 6th power);

(e) calculate the MPL in the year of retirement as $3,194.79 ($2,444.44 × 1.055 raised to the 5th power);

(f) calculate the projected annual pension in the year of retirement as $1,779.66 ($88,982.92 × 2.0%);

(g) choose the lesser of the result in (f) and the result in step (e) to arrive at the projected annual pension with respect to 1995 ($1,779.66);

(h) determine the interest discount from the valuation date to the member's retirement date as 0.610064 (1.075 raised to the negative 6.833333th power);

(i) calculate the annuity factor for a $1.00 per year pension payable monthly commencing at age 65 as $14.5263; and

(j) multiply the result of (g) by the result of (h), and multiply that by the result of (i) to derive the actuarial liability in respect of 1995 to be $15,771 ($1,779.66 × 0.610064 × $14.5263).

To determine the current service contributions for 2008, 2009 and 2010:

---

[7] Pension partner includes spouse, common law partner or same-sex partner as per applicable pension legislation.

[8] See note 4, above, for details.

(a) calculate the member's retirement date (first day of the month coincident or following attainment of age 65): November 1, 2014;

(b) calculate the duration from valuation date to assumed date of retirement: six years and ten months;

(c) determine the indexed T4 earnings as at the retirement date as \$165,461.14 (\$120,000 × 1.055 raised to the 6th power);

(d) calculate the MPL in the year of retirement as \$3,194.79 (\$2,444.44 × 1.055 raised to the 5th power);

(e) calculate the projected annual pension in the year of retirement as \$3,309.22 (\$165,461.14 × 2.0%);

(f) choose the lesser of the result in (f) and the result in step (e) to arrive at the projected annual pension with respect to 1995 (\$3,194.79);

(g) determine the interest discount from the valuation date to the member's retirement date as 0.610064 (1.075 raised to the negative 6.833333th power);

(h) calculate the annuity factor for a \$1.00 per year pension payable monthly commencing at age 65 as \$14.5263;[9] and

(i) multiply the result of (g) by the result of (h) and multiply that by the result of (i), and multiply that by 1.075 raised to the 0.5th power[10] to derive the current service contributions for 2008 to be \$29,355[11] (\$3,194.79 × 0.610064 × \$14.5263 × 1.036822). The

---

[9] A joint and survivor annuity (with the member aged 65 and the survivor aged 65), which pays the survivor \$0.667 per year after the member's death, which is guaranteed for a period of five years and which is increased each year by 3.0% (1.0% less than the percentage increase in the Consumer Price Index).

[10] Our company's practice (Westcoast Actuaries Inc.) is to assume that IPP current service contributions are to occur during the middle of a calendar year. Other actuarial firms may, for example, assume that current service contributions are made at the beginning of a year.

[11] The CRA requires that actuarial valuation reports express current service contributions for connected persons as a percentage of their T4 earnings up to a dollar maximum. In this example, the report would state that the 2008 current service contributions are 25.2% of T4 earnings up to \$29,355. The percentage is derived by dividing \$29,355 by the member's expected 2008 T4 earnings up to a maximum earnings level of \$116,667 (the 2008 MPL of \$2,333.33 divided by 2.0%).

The CRA's reasoning is that because a connected person can control his or her own T4 earnings, it does want the employer contribution made after the member has received T4 earnings. In this case, if the member had \$10,000 of T4 earnings in January 2008 and February 2008, *etc.*, then the employer should contribute \$2,520 in February 2008 and \$2,520 in March 2008, *etc.*, until the dollar maximum of \$29,355 is attained. In other words, the CRA does not want the employer to contribute \$29,355 until the member has received at least \$116,667 in T4 income for 2008. Of course, if, for example, the member received a bonus of \$120,000 of T4 earnings in January

2009 current service cost would be $31,557 ($29,355 × 1.075). The 2010 current service cost would be $33,924 ($31,557 × 1.075).

GOING-CONCERN ACTUARIAL VALUATION

The purpose of a going-concern valuation is to provide appropriate funding for the benefits being accrued, assuming that the plan continues indefinitely.

The actuary sets the assumptions for the going-concern valuation. The main assumption would be the interest assumption. In the current economic environment, an appropriate interest rate would likely be in the range of 5.0% to 7.0% per annum. The lower the interest rate, the higher the actuarial liability and current service contributions.

The actuary could choose to employ an actuarial value of assets which smooth the past market value of assets rather than employing simply the market value of assets. As such, the actuarial value of assets would show less variance.

Other assumptions would be consistent with the provisions in the plan text and consistent with each other. For example, if the interest rate was 5.5% per annum, then the wage increase rate would be 3.5% per annum, and the increase in the Consumer Price Index would be 2.5% per annum, *etc.*

The key point is that, most likely, the employer contributions calculated under the going-concern valuation would be higher than the employer contributions calculated under the maximum funding valuation.

SOLVENCY VALUATION

The purpose of a solvency valuation is to provide appropriate funding for the benefits being accrued, assuming the plan terminates as at the valuation date.

The method of calculating the solvency deficiency and special payments to amortize that deficiency is specified by the various provincial Pension Benefits Acts. Fortunately, the method of calculation is the same across all provinces.

If the solvency valuation reveals a solvency deficiency, additional funding by the employer is required to ensure such deficiency is eliminated in five years. Certain adjustments to be made to the solvency assets to determine the solvency excess or solvency deficiency are as follows:

2008, then the employer could immediately thereafter contribute $29,355 in respect of the member's 2008 current service contributions.

(a) Solvency assets equal the sum of:

  (i) market value of investments; and

  (ii) any cash balances and accrued receivable income items less amounts payable (and wind-up expense allowance — assumed payable from the plan).

(b) Solvency asset adjustment equals the sum of:

  (i) the impact of using an asset adjustment method which smooths out market gains/losses over a period of up to five years; and

  (ii) the present value of the special payments that are scheduled for payment within five years after the valuation date.

The hypothetical wind-up method is not technically an actuarial cost method (which deals with the allocation of the costs of the plan to various periods) but rather a method of estimating the liabilities of the plan should the plan be terminated. The primary requirement of this method is to comply with provincial Pension Benefits Acts. The solvency liabilities have been calculated as the present value of accrued benefits (all of which would be vested upon plan termination) for all members, whether active, retired or entitled to a deferred pension.

Assets are valued at market value adjusted for any receivables or payables as at the date of valuation, reduced by expected plan wind-up expenses.

The accrued benefit cost method was used to determine the solvency liabilities. Under this method, for each member, the accrued actuarial liabilities are determined as the present value of all benefits earned to the valuation date.

Members who are eligible to retire as at the valuation date are assumed to retire immediately. All other members are assumed to retire at age 65.

The benefits reflected in the valuation were those in effect at the valuation date. No allowance was made for subsequent benefit increases.

Pensions in payment were valued for retired members. Deferred pensions commencing at age 65 were valued for deferred vested members.

Actuarial assumptions[12] as at January 1, 2008 include:

(a) During the deferral period prior to pension commencement, interest rates are 4.50% per annum for the first ten (10) years followed by

---

[12] These assumptions are in accordance with the Canadian Institute of Actuaries Standard of Practice for Determining Pension Commuted Values, effective February 1, 2005.

5.00% per annum thereafter. After pension commencement, interest rates used are 3.52% per annum for the first ten (10) years followed by 3.77% per annum thereafter.

(b) During the deferral period prior to pension commencement, the salary scale is 2.95% per annum for the first ten (10) years, followed by 3.19% per annum thereafter.

(c) After pension commencement, pensions in payment are indexed at 0.95% per annum for the first ten (10) years, followed by 1.19% per annum thereafter.

(d) A member eligible to retire at the valuation date is assumed to do so. Otherwise the member is assumed to be eligible for a deferred vested pension at age 65 based on accrued benefits as at the valuation date.

(e) The member is assumed to terminate as at the valuation date, with full vesting of accrued benefits.

(f) Gender-distinct mortality rates are taken from the UP-94 Table projected forward to the year 2015, using mortality projection Scale AA.

(g) Ninety per cent of members are assumed to have a pension partner. Female pension partners are assumed to be three years younger than male members. Male pension partners are assumed to be three years older than female members.

A sample calculation is shown below:

ITEM	$
Actuarial Value of Assets (a)	142,708
Solvency Expenses (b)	2,000
Solvency Assets (c) = (a) – (b)	140,708
Solvency Asset Adjustment (d)	35,440
Total Solvency Assets (e) = (c) + (d)	176,148
Solvency Liabilities (f)	273,103
New Solvency Excess (Deficiency) (g) = (e) – (f)	(96,955)
Solvency Ratio (h) = (c) / (f)	51.5%

EMPLOYER CONTRIBUTIONS

The employer should make contributions in the range of the minimum required contribution and the maximum deductible contribution specified in the actuarial valuation report.

In determining the employer contributions to be made for any year, consideration should be given to various items, including:

(a) the estimated value of benefits being accrued in a year;

(b) the funded ratio of the plan (actuarial value of assets divided by actuarial liability);

(c) the anticipated cash flow required to provide plan benefits; and

(d) external factors affecting the employer's cash management.

The maximum contribution limit for 2009 will depend on the level of employer contributions made in 2008 and a reasonable amount of interest. Similarly, the maximum employer contribution limit for 2010 will depend on the level of contributions made in 2008 and 2009, plus a reasonable amount of interest.

The above contribution levels do not anticipate changes to any of the following in the future:

(a) changes to provision of the plan;

(b) changes in actuarial basis or assumptions;

(c) experience gains (or losses); or

(d) a significant change in membership of the plan.

Should any of the above occur, a re-examination of the employer's contribution may be necessary.

Under subsection 147.2(1) of the *Income Tax Act*, an employer contribution to a registered defined benefit pension plan is deductible in computing the employer's income for a taxation year if:

(a) it is paid in the fiscal year or within 120 days from the end of the fiscal year;

(b) it was not deducted in the previous year; and

(c) it is an eligible contribution under subsection 147.2(2) of the *Income Tax Act*.

Subsection 147.2(2) of the *Income Tax Act* defines an eligible contribution as one which:

(a) is made on the recommendation of an actuary;

(b) is approved in writing by the Minister;

(c) is based on an actuarial valuation prepared as of a date that is not more than four years before the day on which the contribution is made; and

(d) is not in excess of prescribed limits if the plan is a designated plan.

A designated plan is one in which the total pension credit for members who either are connected with the employer or earn more than two and one-half times the year's maximum pensionable earnings exceeds 50% of the total pension credit for all the members under the defined benefit provisions of the plan. The prescribed limits are determined by using actuarial assumptions set forth in subsection 8515(7) of the *Income Tax Regulations*.

CONCLUSION

Actuarial calculations for IPPs are complicated. The key is for the employer to make contributions between the minimum required under the various Pension Benefits Acts and the maximum deductible contribution allowed under the *Income Tax Act*.

Note that the maximum deductible contribution allowed under tax legislation overrides the minimum contributions required by applicable pension legislation. For example, consider an IPP with a surplus of $2,500 on the maximum funding valuation basis prescribed in section 8515 of the *Income Tax Regulations* and a $5,200 annual payment required to amortize a solvency deficiency pursuant to pension legislation. The minimum required contribution is $5,200 plus the member's current service contributions. The maximum deductible contribution is the member's current service contributions. The employer should make contributions equal to the member's current service contributions.

CHAPTER 22

MAXIMIZING IPPS WITH IMFS AND AVCS — A POWER-CHARGED OPTION

Kurt Dreger

Overview

This chapter introduces the concept of utilizing investment management fees (IMFs) and additional voluntary contributions (AVCs) in conjunction with an IPP to maximize retirement savings for both IPP sponsors and IPP members.

Learning Objectives

By the end of this chapter, you should be able to:

- describe what IMFs and AVCs are; and
- understand the long-term benefits of utilizing IMFs and AVCs in conjunction with an IPP to maximize retirement savings for both IPP sponsors and IPP members.

IMFS AND AVCS

So far within the pages of this book, we have covered many concepts related to getting the most out of an IPP. In this chapter you will discover the power behind applying two new concepts — the investment management fees (IMFs) and additional voluntary contributions (AVCs) in conjunction with an IPP to create maximum tax relief and retirement savings for the IPP member.

An IMF is the fee that someone pays a financial institution to manage his or her investment/retirement assets. An AVC is the additional funds that can be invested within an RPP in addition to the prescribed amounts set out in the Registered Pension Plan (RPP) plan text. The unique value proposition of an AVC is that it is not subject to the locking-in provisions found in RPPs.

What is important to understand is that funds held within an IPP are usually held at a financial institution of some kind, and these institutions charge some kind of IMF to manage these IPP funds.

As stated in Chapter 15 of this book, IMFs as they relate to IPPs are a deductible expense to the IPP-sponsoring company. As an example, consider that ABC Company (client) sets up a 2009 IPP for the 50-year-old owner named Mr. Owner (plan member). To fund the past service, Mr. Owner was required to transfer $250,000 from his personal RRSPs into the IPP, and ABC Company contributed $100,000 for remaining past service contribution. As well, ABC Company makes a $24,000 contribution for 2009 service.

If we assume an IMF of 2% and a net rate of return of 5.5%, the IMF for 2009 would be $7,878. An invoice would be produced in early 2010 and sent to ABC Company. This would continue each year until the IPP is wound up. Each year, the IMF invoice amount would be fully tax deductible to ABC Company. There is no taxable benefit to Mr. Owner. As you can see from Figure 1, below, the IMF invoice grows each year and represents one third of the IPP payments up to age 65. These are significant dollars not to be ignored.

Figure 1: Impact of Invoicing the IMFs

Assumptions

IMF	2.00%
Net Rate of Return	5.50%
Gross Rate of Return	7.50%
RRSP Transfer	250,000
Past Service Contribution	100,000

Age	IPP Current Service Contribution	IPP IMF Invoice	Total IPP Payment	IPP Fund End of Year
50	24,000	0	24,000	393,910
51	25,800	7,878	33,678	450,179
52	27,735	9,004	36,739	512,688
53	29,815	10,254	40,069	582,057
54	32,051	11,641	43,692	658,964
55	34,455	13,179	47,634	744,151
56	37,039	14,883	51,922	838,430
57	39,817	16,769	56,586	942,685
58	42,803	18,854	61,657	1,057,886
59	46,014	21,158	67,171	1,185,088
60	49,465	23,702	73,167	1,325,446

Age	IPP Current Service Contribution	IPP IMF Invoice	Total IPP Payment	IPP Fund End of Year
61	53,175	26,509	79,684	1,480,221
62	57,163	29,604	86,767	1,650,786
63	61,450	33,016	94,466	1,838,643
64	66,059	36,773	102,832	2,045,428
65	0	40,909	40,909	2,196,721
Total	**626,841**	**314,133**	**940,973**	

One note of consideration when invoicing the IMF is the effect on the funded position of the IPP at the time of the actuarial valuation. By paying the IMF, the IPP has basically provided itself with a gross rate of return which will provide a better funded position than a net rate of return.

Had the IPP been in a deficit position with a net rate of return, there would have been additional contributions to fund the deficit. This would have a similar effect of paying for the IMF.

As well, should the IPP investments perform exceedingly well, the IPP may be in an excess surplus position, thus eliminating some future employer contributions. Paying for the IMF can contribute to IPPs getting to an excess surplus position earlier.

As you can see, invoicing the IMF in an IPP is a feature that should be considered for an IPP sponsor and IPP member.

NEXT STEP

Consider the same IPP client from above and also consider that Mr. Owner has an additional $500,000 in his RRSPs. He is paying either management expense ratios (MERs) or IMFs or some sort of management fee for his RRSP assets, and these fees cannot be tax deductible to ABC Company.

However, Mr. Owner can transfer this $500,000 of RRSPs into the IPP. Since he has already transferred $250,000 of his RRSP assets into the IPP to fund the past service, the remaining $500,000 of transfer will be deemed as AVCs.

The IPP now has essentially two sub-accounts: regular contributions and AVCs. The regular contributions are the sums of the current service costs and total past service funding going into the IPP. The AVC is the RRSP transfer not associated with the past service funding. Now the IMF on IPP and AVC assets is a deductible expense to ABC Company.

If we assume an IMF of 2% and the net rate of return of 5.5%, the IMF for 2009 would be $18,428 when you include Mr. Owner's AVCs.

An invoice would be produced in early 2010 and sent to ABC Company. This invoice is almost equal to Mr. Owner's 2010 IPP current service contribution and is almost greater than the 2010 RRSP limit. As you can see from Figure 2, below, the IMF invoice grows each year and represents almost one-half of the IPP payments up to age 65 when we consider the AVCs. This is a significant tax-sheltering opportunity not to be ignored.

Figure 2: Impact of Invoicing the IMFs with AVCs

	Assumptions	
	IMF	2.00%
	Net Rate of Return	5.50%
	Gross Rate of Return	7.50%
	RRSP Transfer	250,000
	Past Service Contribution	100,000
AVC =	Additional RRSP Transfer	500,000

Age	IPP Current Service Contribution	IPP IMF Invoice	Total IPP Payment	IPP Fund End of Year
50	24,000	0	24,000	921,410
51	25,800	18,428	44,228	1,017,532
52	27,735	20,351	48,086	1,122,904
53	29,815	22,458	52,273	1,238,375
54	32,051	24,767	56,819	1,364,867
55	34,455	27,297	61,752	1,503,385
56	37,039	30,068	67,107	1,655,023
57	39,817	33,100	72,918	1,820,973
58	42,803	36,419	79,223	2,002,528
59	46,014	40,051	86,064	2,201,098
60	49,465	44,022	93,487	2,418,216
61	53,175	48,364	101,539	2,655,549
62	57,163	53,111	110,274	2,914,910
63	61,450	58,298	119,748	3,198,271
64	66,059	63,965	130,024	3,507,776
65	0	70,156	70,156	3,768,187
Total	**626,841**	**590,855**	**1,217,698**	

Although not locked in under pension legislation, once made, AVCs must remain in the pension plan during the entire period of a person's employment. They cannot be accessed by the employee while still employed. There is one exception to this rule, and it occurs if the pension plan is subsequently amended so that it no longer has the provision allowing AVCs. In that case, the AVCs accumulated in the plan to that date may be rolled over into an RRSP on a once-and-for-all basis.

On termination of a person's employment due to retirement, AVCs are an exception, allowed under the *Income Tax Act*, R.S.C. 1985, c. 1 (5th Supp.), to the rule regarding pension contributions. Although AVCs cannot be withdrawn until the termination of employment, they can be paid on termination as a lump-sum payment should the employee choose to receive it in that fashion, rather than as an annuity for life.

You should note that assets that are held as AVCs are not commingled with the IPP assets at the time of an actuarial valuation. This means that the AVC funds do not impact the surplus/deficit position of the IPP.

The IPP is no longer an isolated product where you only compare the difference of the actuarial funding amounts vs. the RRSP limits to weight the IPP benefits. You should also consider the positive impact of invoicing the IMFs to the IPP sponsor.

CHAPTER 23

INDIVIDUAL PENSION PLANS: DANGER STRAIGHT AHEAD

Peter J. Merrick

Overview

This chapter addresses the issues of transferring a non-connected person defined benefit pension plan into a connected person's Individual Pension Plan.

Learning Objectives

By the end of this chapter, you should be able to:

- understand what the three options that members of corporate DBPPs usually have available to them when they leave employment and membership of their pension plan;
- know what protection members in DBPPs have if the sponsor of their plans cannot meet pension funding obligations;
- qualify to be a self-employed incorporated consultant for tax purposes by meeting the CRA's four tests to individuals to determine if their relationship is that of an employee or an independent consultant; and
- determine if it is wise for a non-connected member of a traditional DBPP to consider transferring DBPP assets into an IPP.

This chapter is a direct result of the publication of the book *The Essential Individual Pension Handbook* (LexisNexis Canada, 2007). Immediately after its release, I began to receive a flurry of calls and e-mails from members of Defined Benefit Pension Plans (DBPPs) with over 25 years of service in their company-sponsored plans. These calls were coming from people who worked at Bell Canada, Inco, Falconbridge, Hydro One, Ontario Power Generation, Bruce Power, General Motors and Ford, in addition to members of the Ontario Teachers' Pension Plan and Ontario Municipal Employees Retirement System (OMERS). These members were all asking the same question: could I review their retirement choices regarding their DBPPs?

When someone is leaving employment, his or her DBPP usually provides the following options:

- **Option One:** keeps the member's money in the company DBPP;
- **Option Two:** transfers the member's pension to a new employer's plan (in this case the viability of transferring all of the member's DBPP assets into a newly created Individual Pension Plan (IPP); or
- **Option Three:** transfers the member's entire vested portion of his or her pension out, where an allotted amount would be transferred into a locked-in RRSP and the remaining amount would be deregistered and taxed in the taxpayer's hands.

The question you might be asking is: why are so many members of DBPPs seriously considering transferring their money out, especially now?

I would like to share with you my own experiences to provide some insight into this question. Several years ago I presented at an outplacement workshop where the majority of attendees were former Nortel employees. One man had brought with him an article from the *Ottawa Citizen*. It reported that Nortel's DBPP was underfunded by $2 billion.

Up until that moment, I had never considered that employer-sponsored DBPPs may not be able to meet their pension obligations. Once I started thinking about it, I couldn't stop. This is actually what initiated my journey to learn more about IPPs in the first place.

Consider this: as the baby boomers start to retire en masse, beginning in 2010, Canada could see combined pension and health-care costs exceeding 30% of our total gross domestic product. In recent years, Canadian companies and their employees have seen their pension assets plummet at the end of 2000 when, according to Statistics Canada, two-thirds of pension plans in Canada were in the red.

In the old economy, the average employee would work for the same company for 35 years. In their pension calculations, actuaries of DBPPs would make the assumptions that male and female workers would retire at 65, and the majority would die by 68 and 72, respectively. Now actuaries of these same plans need to factor in that today, a minimum of 10% of all DBPP male pensioners will live beyond 91, and female pensioners beyond 94.

All those telephone calls and e-mails I received from members of DBPPs asked the following:

> "What if there is not enough pension money to go around when I retire?"

The answer for most DBPP members is not a very appealing one. When a company that sponsors a DBPP goes bankrupt and there are any funds left over, employees would be paid two weeks' salary, then secure and unsecured creditors are paid, followed by preferred share owners and then common share owners. If there is anything left over this will go towards paying pension obligations. When a DBPP cannot meet its obligations, retirees will get first claim on the assets of the plan. Next will be employees who are eligible for pensions. The remaining money is then divided among the rest.

For DBPPs that are registered in Ontario, many are supposedly covered by that province's Pension Benefits Guarantee Fund (PBGF), which offers limited protection for the over one million DBPP members within its borders. If a DBPP in Ontario has insufficient funds, the PBGF will guarantee only the first $1,000 per month of pension benefits. The problem with the PBGF is that it does not have enough money in its reserve (approximately $200 million) to cover payments if even one of the large pensions in that province were to hit the financial skids. Plus, the government does not provide any guarantees to defined benefit pensions as it does for money held in savings, checking accounts and GICs protected under the Canadian Deposit Insurance Corporation (CDIC). This reality does not give much comfort for a DBPP member who has over $1.6 million sitting in his or her plan which many of the pension members calling me had in their retirement plans.

As a result, many DBPP members who are reviewing their pension options are seriously considering transferring their pensions to a new employer's plan, which means creating their own IPP to gain additional protection and deferred taxes.

REVOCATION OF PLAN REGISTRATION

Guess what? The financial wolves are out promoting this option to these pension members and so are their firms. Why not? The investment advisor at first glance seems to be a big winner if someone transfers his or her entire DBPP to an IPP. Imagine that you have an individual who has $1.6 million sitting in his or her pension and he or she transfers all of it to a newly created IPP. If the investment firm charges 2% in management fees every year on assets under management within 15 years, the fees paid will be well over $500,000. Not a bad trade-off when this individual saves over $480,000 in taxes today by transferring the entire pension into an IPP that can compound tax-free until withdrawn, don't you think?

Well, let's look again at some people who took that advice to transfer lump sums out of their DBPPs to their own IPPs. During the summer of 2007, Canadian judges cleared the way for the Canada Revenue Agency (CRA) to confiscate from two taxpayers, Susanne Greenhalgh and Charles Ross, their pension savings, that is, their entire IPP savings, hers from more than 30 years as a St. Catharines teacher, and his from serving as a Sault Ste. Marie police officer. The CRA now has court backing to revoke registration of IPPs. Financial advisors, IPP sponsors and IPP members have been placed on notice that the CRA is monitoring all IPPs going forward to make sure that these plans are compliant.

This is what the CRA has to weigh in on transferring DBPPs to IPPs to new companies for the purpose of avoiding taxes:

> We have noticed a trend in which individuals near normal retirement age leave large employers and establish their own corporation. The individual is hired by the corporation, and the corporation sponsors an IPP for the individual that recognizes the prior service under the public sector pension plan. Once the IPP is established, the full commuted value of the individual's prior pension is transferred to the IPP, as the transfer rules of the *Income Tax Act* do not limit transfers from one defined benefit plan to another. We are concerned that while some of these IPPs may be acceptable, many will not meet the requirements for registration under the Act.
>
> The primary purpose of every registered pension plan must be to provide retirement benefits to individuals in respect of their service as employees. This requirement is reflected in the Act as a condition of registration. If it is determined that a plan is established for a reason other than this primary purpose, it will not qualify for registration under the Act.
>
> The first issue we have with these arrangements is the legitimacy of the employee/employer relationship. Our concern is that the reason the corporation and the pension plan are being established is to avoid the transfer rules of the Act. If there is not a bona-fide relationship that has the employee rendering legitimate services to the employer, the plan will fail the primary purpose test.
>
> Even if this relationship is established and nominal earnings are received, there may still be an issue with the primary purpose test. The Act only permits a pension plan to base retirement benefits on the earnings received from an employer who participates in the plan. In most cases, the earnings with the new corporation are much lower than what was received with the prior employer, and therefore the benefits under the IPP are significantly lower than the benefits that the individual would have received from the prior plan. This creates a large surplus in the IPP.
>
> When an individual foregoes a substantial retirement benefit by transferring the associated funds to a recently established IPP that provides a much smaller retirement benefit, it can be argued that the primary purpose test is not met. In these cases, we may conclude that the primary purpose of establishing the IPP was to facilitate a transfer of funds from a prior plan that would have been limited by the Act had it been transferred to an RRSP. The

> conclusion that the primary purpose condition is not met is further supported by the fact that following the transfer, the IPP holds significant surplus assets rather than providing retirement benefits of a level comparable to those that would have been paid from the prior plan. As mentioned earlier, if the primary purpose of a plan is for any reason other than providing retirement benefits with respect to the individual's service as an employee, the plan will fail to qualify for registered status.
>
> If it is apparent at the time of registration that the IPP will not meet the primary purpose test, the CRA will refuse to register the pension plan. Unfortunately, in many cases, it will not be apparent until a year or two later that the primary purpose test was not met. This situation can be more problematic for individuals as they may have already transferred funds into the IPP.
>
> If it is determined that a registered plan does not, and never did, meet the primary purpose test, the plan's registered status can be revoked as of the original effective date. The consequences to the member could be financially devastating if the CRA was to revoke the registration of the plan upon discovering that the purpose for incorporating a company was simply to establish a pension plan to hold the transferred pension for a specific member. The impact of this action is that all the assets of the plan would become taxable.

If the CRA determines that an IPP does not comply with governing Pension Acts or the CRA's Registered Plans Directorate regulations, the CRA may revoke the IPP's registration. To remain registered, IPPs must at all times satisfy four criteria:

1. The IPP must comply with all laws and regulations governing registered pension plans; all filings must be up to date.
2. The sponsor must have been established for a reason other than to create a pension plan, prior to the plan being set up and prior to the transfer to the IPP of pension benefit assets from another defined benefit plan from another employer.
3. There is a *bona fide* employment relationship between the plan member (employee) and the sponsoring company (employer).
4. If assets from another defined benefit pension plan have been transferred to an IPP, the member of the IPP must expect to have employment earnings from the new employer similar to earnings from the prior employer for three years.

CONNECTED PERSONS' INDIVIDUAL PENSION PLANS

Even if an IPP is established at a new company that meets all four criteria mentioned above with funding of the new IPP originating from the transferring of assets from another DBPP, if the IPP member is now a connected person to the new company sponsoring the plan, that is, a person who owns more than 10% or is related to someone who owns more than 10% of the sponsoring company, this individual will only be permitted to transfer money from the older pension plan to fund pension maximum credits of the new IPP dating back to 1991. It is very plausible that hundreds of thousands of dollars within the older pension plan will not be eligible to be transferred into the newer IPP.

In the worst-case scenario, if a connected person's IPP is created with the transfer of moneys from a non-connected defined benefit plan, the surplus funding into the IPP will be taxable in the hands of the new plan member. In addition, interest will be charged on the taxes that were determined to be owing on the surplus funding into the IPP. Perhaps fines will be charged and/or the entire connected-person IPP may be fully deregistered resulting in the entire IPP becoming taxable in the hands of the member. In addition, there could be fines that range from $100,000 to $500,000 with the potential for a prison term for pension offences.

In many situations after the connected-person rules are factored in with the cost of setting up and maintaining an IPP for a non-connected member who is currently a member of a DBPP, who would meet the four criteria for IPP plan registration, when terminating employment from a former employer, he or she is better off leaving his or her pension with his or her former employer if permitted to do so. This individual would also be better off transferring the allowable moneys from his or her former pension plan into a Locked-in Investment Retirement Account (LIRA) and being taxed on the surplus rather than creating a connected person's IPP for himself or herself.

PROPER REGISTRATION OF AN IPP

There are many members of the existing DBPPs who are highly skilled professionals who know their value and that there is a high demand for their skills in the various industries within Canada and around the world. These individuals are willing to give up company benefits and job security for career flexibility and for the favourable tax treatment they receive from the CRA for being self-employed.

To qualify to be a self-employed incorporated consultant for tax purposes, the CRA applies four tests to individuals to determine if their relationship is that of an employee or an independent consultant. These tests ask the following tests:

(1) *To what extent does the employer control how the work is done?*

This test looks at who has the ability to determine how, when and where the services are performed. The more flexibility the independent consultant has in these matters, the more likely he or she will be considered an independent consultant.

(2) *Who owns the tools?*

The basic tools of an independent consultant are generally the phone, computer hardware and the consultant's technical ability, experience and education. Part of the CRA's test is whether the consultant has his or her own office outside the premises of the company he or she is consulting for.

(3) *Does the independent consultant pass the integration test?*

This test is designed to determine if the consultant's services are ancillary to the other company's primary business activities. The greater the extent to which the independent consultant's services are considered integral to or integrated into the company he or she consults with, the more likely the CRA will deem that there is an employer/employee relationship.

(4) *What are the chances of profit and loss?*

The last criteria the CRA uses to determine whether a consultant's status is that of an independent consultant or employee is the potential for profit and loss. An example would be liability concerns for a system failure. In an employee relationship, an employer shoulders this type of liability.

If a member of a company pension plan decides to go this route and become an independent consultant, he or she must meet all four of these criteria provided that he or she does not take a consulting contract from his or her former employer for at least two years after he or she leaves his or her employment. Even though the independent consultant might have his or her own company that now bills his or her former employer directly, the CRA will for tax purposes consider this person an employee and will tax the consultant and his or her former employer accordingly. And if the independent consultant has established an IPP, the CRA will deregister the plan.

THE IPP NUMBERS FOR THE TRANSFER OF A NON-CONNECTED DBPP TO AN IPP

For example, let's just say a 55-year-old individual has 35 years of pensionable service in a defined benefit pension plan with $1,689,212 of assets accumulated within it that can be commuted out of this plan. This individual has an option to take retirement as of January 1, 2009 and receive a pension benefit income or take the money out of the plan entirely and be fully taxed on the surplus cash. In most cases, he will be better off opting to take his pension from his former employer or to transfer money into a LIRA than he would be legitimately permitted to tax defer in a connected person's IPP.

Below is an analysis of what this individual would be allowed under the CRA IPP rules to justifiably transfer for legitimate reasons amounts from a non-connected person DBPP to a connected person IPP, if they transferred the money to an IPP sponsored by a newly created consulting company which the individual owns. The following two assumptions were used to calculate how much of the assets of the $1,689,212 within his DBPP would be eligible to transfer from a former employer plan to a newly created IPP:

- Allowed Past Service Credits for the new IPP would only be 18 years, not the 35 years accumulated in his former pension plan. The IPP yearly pension credits are only available for the new IPP starting from January 1, 1991 to December 31, 2008 inclusive.
- Calculations used to determine the IPP funding formula are based on career average pension plan for T4 earnings, not the best of three years average salary that the former pension was based on:

Tax Year	T4 Earnings
2008	$125,000
2007	$125,000
2006	$111,000
2005	$100,000
2004	$95,000
2003	$95,000
2002	$80,000
2001	$80,000
2000	$80,000
1999	$80,000
1998	$66,000
1997	$66,000
1996	$66,000
1995	$55,000
1994	$55,000

Tax Year	T4 Earnings
1993	$50,000
1992	$50,000
1991	$50,000
18-Year Career Average	$79,389

Note: The above table provides a listing of the individual's salary for each year from 1991 to 2008 and a career average of his salary during that period.

Based on these assumptions the eligible moneys legitimately allowed to be transferred from his previous employer's DBPP to an IPP is $397,791. This is much less than the option his current DBPP provides him with to transfer $755,958 of pension assets into a locked-in RRSP. By opting to transfer money into a locked-in RRSP, this individual has the opportunity to legitimately tax shelter/defer an additional $358,167 into a locked-in RRSP than by transferring pension money into a connected person IPP.

Based on these calculations above, a Trusted Advisor should strongly recommend that this individual not consider the IPP option to take money out of his current employer's pension plan to fund it, but rather first consider keeping his current plan in place or the option to transfer the allotted amount into a locked-in RRSP and pay the tax on the moneys that could not be tax-sheltered in an RRSP.

CHAPTER 24

DISABILITY AND INDIVIDUAL PENSION PLANS

Ian Quigley

Overview

This chapter looks at the issues that impact the Individual Pension Plan (IPP) when a plan member becomes disabled. It explores strategies that allow both an IPP sponsor and IPP member during a member's disability to maximize the IPP and other retirement benefits while minimizing costs to the employer through the use of salary continuation plans.

Learning Objectives

By the end of this chapter, you should be able to:

- understand the risks of an IPP member becoming disabled during his or her working career;
- list the options for both an IPP sponsor and IPP member to fund the IPP in the event of the member becoming disabled, depending on whether the IPP member is either a connected or a non-connected member; and
- understand how the implementation of a salary continuation plan can be an effective strategy that complements the IPP solution.

A REAL RISK REQUIRING REAL ATTENTION

Individual Pension Plans (IPPs) are back in vogue as a retirement planning tool in the small business environment. The target seems to be senior executives and owner-managers looking to generate a tax-sheltered pool of retirement savings in excess of what RSP programs will allow. While retirement remains a stiff challenge for many, other risks inherent in the financial planning process should also be reviewed, including the risk of disability.

Disability risk is called "morbidity" risk. Morbidity risk is a real and serious threat to the net worth of many Canadians including those contemplating IPPs. While death only causes 3% of mortgage foreclosures in Canada, disability is reported to cause 48%. This comes as an alarming statistic to many advisors and planners. Various options exist to offset the financial risk of being disabled, including a number of approaches from a tax perspective. Here lies a strong area for solid financial planning and advice giving.

In 2001, a research organization (LIMRA) did a survey called "Tracking the Opinions of the Public in Canada". This survey measured the public's attitude toward insurance and other financial products in Canada. Some of the interesting facts to note from this survey were that only 39% of households reported to be using an insurance agent or broker, and of those households, only 47% had discussed disability insurance. This is somewhat surprising in light of the risk of disability and the need for attention in planning against this risk. The survey went on to illustrate that while few had addressed the issue, many Canadians are concerned about their ability to replace their income in the event of a disability. As a matter of fact, it ranked third on the list of concerns, with 70% of Canadians commenting that they share this concern.

Looking at a Statistics Canada "Health and Activity Limitations" survey from 1991, we see that the disability rate in Canada is 17.7%, meaning one in five Canadians are struggling with a disability issue. A 1985 Statistics Canada Commissioners Disability Report further illustrates the risk of a disability occurrence with the chance of a disability lasting 90 days or more exceeding 30% for males and females all the way up to age 50.

Statistics such as these may lead a person to question the threat a disability would have on the planning available within an IPP. Certainly, the effect of a disability needs to be addressed by all planners reviewing such pension plans for their clients.

DISABILITY CREDITS

The effect of a disability event on an IPP depends on whether the plan has been registered for a connected person. Many IPPs are arranged for senior staff including owner-managers. As a result, many IPPs are considered what are termed "connected person" plans and, therefore, subject to connected person plan rules.[1] A connected person is one who:

---

[1] Subsection 8500(3) of the *Income Tax Regulations*, C.R.C., c. 945.

- owns, directly or indirectly, at least 10% of the issued shares of any class of the capital stock of the employer, or of any other corporation that is related to the employer;
- does not deal at arm's length with the employer; or
- is a specified shareholder of the employer under paragraph (*d*) of the definition of "specified shareholder" in subsection 248(1) of the *Income Tax Act*, R.S.C. 1985, c. 1 (5th Supp.) (ITA).

In a connected persons plan, disability periods are exempt from creditable service. This means that even if the employee receives taxable employment income during a period of total disability, the pension plan would not be able to generate pensionable service.

This fact will then lead a planner to recommend a potentially different set of options to a disabled connected person versus a disabled non-connected person.

DISABLED CONNECTED PERSONS

A disabled connected person is the most likely candidate requiring such advice, as most Individual Pension Plans are set up for this market. You may note that the plan text required of these pension plans defines disability as "total and continuous disability". As a result, if you give advice to a disabled connected plan member, you may want to establish the details and conditions of the disability. For example, a person may qualify for disability benefits under an insurance contract but not be disabled severely enough to lose pensionable credits from the pension plan. If this is the case, more options present themselves as discussed for non-connected persons later in this chapter.

In the event of a total disability, most connected plan members will probably look at terminating their IPP. At plan termination comes the potential to negotiate a terminal contribution from the plan sponsor that may pair well with the disability planning outlined in the unanimous shareholders' agreement (USA).

Terminal Funding: A Retirement Enhancement

Retirement enhancements become available to plan members when the plan is terminating,[2] and result in a negotiation between the plan member and the plan sponsor (often the same party with a connected person

[2] Unless they are a federal member of Parliament, their terminal funding has been prenegotiated.

plan). Some people view this as offering a "retirement package", and it is paid into the pension trust by the sponsoring company on a tax-deductible basis. Plan members can secure packages as follows:

- an early unreduced retirement benefit prior to age 65;
- improving the pension payout to full indexation from (CPI) — 1%; or
- "bridging" the equivalent CPP payout until age 65 paid from the pension plan.

A retirement with plan enhancements will cause the obligations of the plan to increase. This will increase the funding requirements of the plan and, therefore, the tax-deductible contributions of the plan sponsor. This funding comes from the company (tax-deductible contribution) and goes into the tax-sheltered pension trust on behalf of the member(s).

Estimates made on terminal deposits[3] are dependent on the age of the plan member and how long the plan member was in the pension plan (including backdating from past service benefits).

Below is a chart that illustrates how much money can be terminally funded at specific ages for plan members who earn the maximum pensionable income.

	Age of Retirement:		
Age entering the plan:	60	62	64
45	$ 500,000	$ 400,000	$ 300,000
50	$ 300,000	$ 250,000	$ 200,000
55	$ 180,000	$ 170,000	$ 120,000
60	$ 125,000	$ 90,000	$ 70,000

Note that if the trust is dispersed, there are *Income Tax Act* prescribed maximums that can be transferred into a LIRA or LIF account.

Terminal Funding: Disability Buy-Out Programs and Disability Lump-Sum Insurance

Coincident to the terminal funding opportunity may rest a disability buy-out clause in the USA. Some USAs will offer to repurchase shares of a disabled person after a set period of disability.[4] Some, or all, of this can be insured on a lump-sum basis with an insurance company. Basically,

---

[3] Ian Quigley, *Tax and Compensation Strategies* (Toronto: Thomson Carswell, 2005).
[4] Often 12 months.

the insurance company pays the policy amount to the company tax-free, and the company then has funding available for the share repurchase. A challenge is that the share repurchase[5] will often lead to taxable gains to the disabled person and then be invested in a taxable environment going forward.

If the share repurchase, outlined in the USA, were to be worded in a flexible manner, it might be able to coincide with the terminal funding available in the pension plan. The issue here is that the USA contractually binds the company to the disabled member, when the terminal funding in the pension plan cannot be predetermined. Nonetheless, the two events can work well together.

For example, a partner becomes disabled. One year later, the insurance proceeds are received by the sponsor company tax-free. The sponsor company then decides to pay out the pension plan on a tax-deductible basis. The disabled member of the pension plan now has a boosted IPP with tax-sheltered investing. Hopefully, the tax boost will better prepare the member to deal with the financial consequences of being disabled.

DISABLED NON-CONNECTED PERSONS

Non-connected persons can continue to receive pensionable service on employment income received even if they are disabled. This may sound contradictory to many people, as how would a disabled employee receive taxable employment income while being disabled? The answer depends on the structure of the disability insurance.

One traditional approach to obtaining disability insurance is through an employer-sponsored plan. Here, the employer simply sponsors the plan and the plan is considered by Canada Revenue Agency (CRA) as an "employee-pay-all plan". Employee-pay-all plans are programs where the employee pays out of his or her after-tax income the cost for the disability insurance. The employer simply acts as a facilitator of the disability coverage. As the premiums are paid with after-tax dollars, and the contracts are in essence owned outside of the corporation, the potential payout is paid as tax-free dollars to the disabled employee.

The other traditional approach of obtaining disability insurance on an individual basis is through an individual disability contract. Here as well, the premiums are paid with after-tax dollars, and the contract is in essence held individually or outside of the corporation. The contract as it

[5] Either corporate or personal repurchase.

is paid with after-tax dollars will have a payout that is characterized with tax-free dollars.

WAGE LOSS REPLACEMENT PLANS

A "wage loss replacement plan" or "salary continuation plan" (SCP) is a formal arrangement between the employer and its employees. Here, the arrangement offers provisions for indemnification of lost income in the event of sickness, maternity or accident. Simply put, lost wages are covered.

Most income and benefits earned by an employee are taxable in the year earned. This includes the value of board, lodging and other benefits with only a few limited exclusions. One of these exclusions is the cost of a "group sickness or accident insurance plan". An employer may therefore outsource the risk of covering wages in the event of a disability by purchasing a disability insurance contract. The cost(s) of this contract is borne by the employer on a non-taxable basis to the employee.[6]

In the event of a disability, the benefits received by the employee will be taxable due to a loss of income and pursuant to a sickness or accident insurance plan, disability insurance plan or income maintenance plan.[7]

Items to note[8] with regards to a wage loss replacement plan include the following:

- benefits are paid on a periodic basis;
- the arrangement may be formal or informal;
- if a contract of insurance is used, it is part of the plan but not the plan in itself;
- the CRA will assume that the program is a wage loss replacement plan unless the contrary can be established; and
- the plan must be an "insurance plan" but does not require an insurance company.

A Technical Interpretation letter written in 1997[9] contained a review of a proposed wage loss replacement plan where an individual was both an employee and a shareholder. The CRA stated it was a question of fact whether a benefit had been conferred on the individual in the capacity of a shareholder or in the capacity of an employee. Where a

---

6 Subparagraph 6(1)(*a*)(i) (ITA).
7 Subparagraph 6(1)(*f*)(ii) (ITA).
8 IT – 428 "Wage Loss Replacement Plans".
9 TI9640485.

benefit is granted to an individual, the benefit will be presumed to have been conferred upon him or her by reason of being a shareholder, unless the benefit is available to all employees of that corporation or the benefit is comparable in nature and quantum to the benefits generally offered to employees who perform similar services for and have similar responsibilities to other employers of a similar size.

This is an important comment because it removes the issue of shareholder versus employee and reminds us that programs such as a wage loss replacement plan are specifically designed for employees. The issue of shareholder status is not one of concern unless a bias has been taken to offer benefits specifically to those with shareholdings. This TI letter moves on to discuss a situation of multiple wage loss replacement plans and comments that it is possible for an employer to offer multiple wage loss replacement plans to employees under different terms and conditions. The TI letter concludes with comments in regards to individually purchased disability contracts being grouped together and used as part of a wage loss replacement plan, and favourably comments that this is a reasonable strategy to be undertaken.

Each province carries its own Insurance Act, which may affect the ability of an employer to offer a wage loss replacement plan. Specifically, the Province of Alberta has made it illegal to self-fund a wage loss replacement plan, but an insured arrangement through an insurance provider is considered onside. This is a trend that we should see in Canadian provinces as a response to events like the Eaton's bankruptcy, where employees lost disability benefits due to the bankruptcy of their employer.

Tax Savings Used to Purchase More Insurance

A properly structured wage loss replacement program would take the tax savings from the deductible premium and apply it towards a larger insurance policy. With the larger taxable insurance policy, you then have to look at the post-disability tax rate to determine where the higher net payout would be achieved.

Assuming tax rates do not change, the wage loss replacement program should offer an employee the same net income as the employee-pay-all approach. It has to be this way, as insurance companies cannot offer preferential underwriting to one method versus the other, or arbitrage would enter the system.

For example, an employee wanting to purchase a $48,000 disability policy outside the corporation will have a policy cost of $200/month ($2,400/year). The policy pays $48,000/year tax-free in the event of disability. To pay the $2,400/year policy cost, the employee will have to draw $4,000/year of salary at a 40% tax rate. The premiums are paid with after-tax dollars and the payout is tax-free.

The same employee could be offered participation in a wage loss replacement plan. Here, the disability premiums would be a non-taxable benefit, but any payout would be taxable. As a result, the employer for the employee should be able to purchase a larger taxable policy. At a tax rate of 40%, the employee would have to have obtained a $6,667 per month benefit so that after 40% tax ($2,667), the same net income is achieved. There is no extra risk for the insurance company as the same net income is found in both approaches. Using similar logic, the cost of the policy should also be the same. The $2,400 per year after-tax cost would now become a $4,000 pre-tax cost.

Here is the point of indifference:

Personal Policy

- Premium cost $4,000 in taxable salary, leaving $2,400 after-tax.
- Policy offering $4,000 per month in tax-free disability benefits.

Wage Loss Replacement Program (Taxable Policy)

- Premium cost $4,000 as a direct business expense.
- Policy offering $6,667/month in taxable disability benefits. After 40% tax, this would leave the executive $4,000 of net income.

In reality, most taxpayers will find that their tax rate decreases during a disability period. A salary continuation program can be arranged for those starting at a high tax rate (executives) as simply an arbitrage on underwriting assumptions. If the underwriter assumes that there is to be no tax rate change pre- and post-disability for the insured, but the executive insured feels that a spread could be achieved in the system, this is a worthwhile strategy to investigate.

More Than a Simple Tax Arbitrage

Although there is clearly a tax arbitrage available for those starting at a high tax rate, there is more opportunity for planning in a salary continuation program than in tax arbitrage. An SCP offers an employee a non-taxable employee benefit that the employee could not achieve independently from the company. The company would in essence own the disability policy and could use it as a negotiating tool for executive compensation purposes. In addition, some corporate taxpayers simply find it easier to cut a corporate cheque for things such as insurance coverage, rather than a personal cheque.

It is possible that the disabled employee would qualify for a disability tax credit, thereby reducing his or her post-disability tax rate.

Should the disabled employee require medical needs not offered by the health care system, he or she could use the medical expense tax credit again, reducing his or her disability tax rate.

As the disability income is paid in a taxable format, it is possible for the employee to do other tax planning in the disability period, working to achieve a disability rate lower than assumed by the program. Enter the Individual Pension Plan.

Wage Loss Plans and an IPP

Because the income from an SCP program is considered employment income, it would create pensionable contribution opportunities for non-connected plan members. Income is paid to the employee from the insurance contract, but is considered taxable employment income. The sponsor company could continue making IPP deposits on behalf of the employee, allowing the employee to maintain retirement savings plans while dealing with the disability disruption.

A second option is to leave the pension plan. A connected member who would not continue to gain pensionable credits from the IPP could return to an RSP program. Deposits made into the RSP account would reduce taxable income and boost the results of the wage loss program. This could offset the lost tax benefits from the pension plan for connected persons owing to a disability event.

CHAPTER 25

IPP REGULATOR INVESTMENT CONSTRAINTS

Peter J. Merrick

Overview

This chapter provides a general outline of the constraints that are placed on investment managers/financial advisors managing Individual Pension Plan assets by regulating bodies.

Learning Objectives

By the end of this chapter, you should be able to:

- list the regulatory constraints placed on the management of assets held within an Individual Pension Plan; and
- list and describe the main types of investments held within an Individual Pension Plan.

REGULATORY ENVIRONMENT

Individual Pension Plans (IPPs) are highly regulated, and they must always comply with the investment rules that are found within the *Income Tax Act*, R.S.C. 1985, c. 1 (5th Supp.), *Income Tax Regulations*, C.R.C., c. 945, Canada Revenue Agency's (CRA) Registered Plans Directorate and federal and provincial Pension Benefits Acts under which IPPs are governed. The trustee(s), custodian, administrator, investment manager and other appointed advisors to the IPP have a fiduciary duty to the beneficiary of the IPP to ensure that these plans' assets are invested properly to deliver the promised benefits to their beneficiaries.

When investing IPP assets, all parties involved must follow the prudent person rule, which means restricting the discretion in the IPP account to investments that a prudent person seeking reasonable income and preservation of capital might buy for his or her own portfolio. Lastly, investment risk for the overall asset mix within an IPP should be well diversified.

All IPPs in Canada are required by law to have a formalized Investment Policy Statement (IPS) that states the procedures and goals for the assets held within the IPP and its position on loans.

When an investment manager/financial advisor is developing the IPS for an IPP and investing IPP assets, the investment manager/financial advisor must always take the restraints placed on defined benefit pension plans into account.

If the investments within an IPP do very well, delivering better than the actuarial investment return assumptions of 7.5%, a surplus will result in an IPP. A company/sponsor in this situation will not be permitted to make additional contributions into an IPP on behalf of the plan member until the surpluses have vanished and a new actuarial evaluation stating that there are no surpluses left in the IPP has been filed with the proper regulators.

In the years that the plan runs surpluses, a company/sponsor will not receive a deduction until contributions into the plan are permitted to resume. In years that an IPP is running surpluses, where the IPP member is accruing pensionable credits, a pension adjustment will be generated, even though no funds are being contributed into the plan on his or her behalf. This results in the IPP member not having the ability to contribute into an RRSP or any other registered plan except his or her allowable pension adjustment offset amount of $600 per year.

Depending on the province in which an IPP is registered, if a plan is underfunded based on actuarial assumptions and valuations, an employer/sponsor of an IPP may be mandated to make contributions into a plan in order to make up for deficits in the plan. In some cases, making up for deficiencies in funding in an IPP is a positive if a company has a positive cash flow. On the other hand, mandatory IPP contributions may place a heavy burden on a business/IPP sponsor's cash flow, and the business/IPP sponsor might not have the ability to fully fund a promised IPP benefit at the time that contributions have been mandated.

INVESTMENT

In paragraph 8502(*h*) of the *Income Tax Regulations* are the directives of investments permitted into registered pension plans and their restrictions.

Note: In addition, it is important to investigate the investment restrictions that are mandated by the federal and provincial Pension Benefits Acts.

Permitted Investments Within IPPs and Other Defined Benefit Pension Plans

The following is a list of investments that are permitted within IPPs and other plans:

(a) bonds, debentures, notes, coupons, term deposits, guaranteed investment certificates, insurance contracts and mortgages;

(b) shares listed on a recognized stock exchange by Canadian regulators;

(c) derivatives, which could be used for hedging a portfolio risk;

(d) real estate holdings;

(e) mutual funds and other managed money products.

As of the end of 2005, there are no longer any foreign content restrictions placed on RPPs or RRSPs.

Prohibited Investments Within IPPs and Other Defined Benefit Pensions

The following is a list of IPP limitations:

(a) An IPP is limited to holding up to 10% of its entire book value in any one entity, affiliates and associates. The only exception to this rule is holdings in government guaranteed issues.

(b) An IPP is limited to holding up to 5% of book value of any parcel of real estate up to 25% total book value of assets in real estate holdings.

(c) An IPP is limited to holding up to 15% of book value of any resource property up to 25% total book value of assets. Resource property types of assets are grouped in with real estate holdings.

(d) An IPP may not hold property that is a share of the capital stock of, or a debt of, an employer who is sponsoring the IPP.

(e) An IPP may not hold property that is a share of the capital stock of, or a debt of, a person who is connected with the employer who is sponsoring the IPP.

(f) An IPP may not hold property that is a share of the capital stock of, or a debt of, a person or partnership that controls indirectly or directly the employer who is sponsoring the IPP.

(g) An IPP may not hold property that is a share of the capital stock of, or a debt of, a member of the IPP.

(h) An IPP may not hold property that is a share of the capital stock of, or a debt of, a person or partnership that is not at arm's length from the employer, a person who is connected to the employer, a plan member or a partnership to the IPP.

It is important that all investments held within an IPP first go through an in-depth screening process to ensure that they meet the guidelines placed on pension assets by the CRA and provincial pension regulators.

Currently, most assets held in IPPs today have not gone through a proper screening process to determine their appropriateness for these plans. The CRA and pension regulators across Canada have initiated an aggressive audit process of assets held in IPPs over the last few years. If IPP portfolios are found to be offside of the pension investment guidelines, pension plan sponsors, administrators, trustees and investment managers risk fines and penalties, and offside IPPs risk being deregistered.

CHAPTER 26

DEALING WITH POSSIBLE OBJECTIONS AND HOW TO PRESENT THE IPP SOLUTION!

Peter J. Merrick

Overview

This chapter serves as a primer for the financial professional to apply the concepts and principles behind value selling the IPP solution to prospective clients.

Learning Objectives

By the end of this chapter, you should be able to:

- find your market;
- deal with a prospective IPP client's objections to adopting this solution;
- handle and neutralize a prospective IPP client's attempt to negotiate on fees; and
- present the IPP solution to a prospect in a way that he or she will see value and take action to receive the value of an IPP now.

FINDING YOUR NEW MARKET

The quote which I have read and heard, even borrowed, hundreds of times during the past two decades while being in the financial industry (and I am sure that if you have ever been to a financial advising training session or conference, or read a book on practice management or investing, you would have heard it, and even used it, yourself), with many variations, goes like this:

> When Willie Sutton the bank robber was asked why he robbed banks, he replied: "Because that's where the money is."

A financial professional who aims to provide financial services to the wealthy must know the fine distinction between someone who is affluent and someone who is wealthy. An affluent individual is a person who has a very good cash-flow statement. A wealthy individual is a person who has a solid net worth statement. Many people in our society confuse affluence and wealth. Great clients have both.

If you decide to be a serious Individual Pension Plan (IPP) consultant, then there are plenty of hard decisions and tough calls to make, but it is definitely worth the time and effort to chart this course of action. For many financial advisors entering the IPP market, it is a pleasure for them to abandon low-end clients and to, instead, deal with serious clients with serious money to invest for the long haul.

In W. Chan Kim and Renée Mauborgne's book *Blue Ocean Strategy: How to Create Uncontested Market Space and Make the Competition Irrelevant* (Boston: Harvard Business School Press, 2005), these two authors/consultants use the "blue ocean" metaphor to illustrate to their readers how companies can easily grow their businesses in practically competitor-free environments.

They define "red oceans" as market niches that have been well developed and are overcrowded by predators and competitors. When entering red oceans, you should be mindful that they are bloody and financially dangerous (*i.e.*, launching a new mutual fund company in 2009 in an already overcrowded industry with several thousand funds offered in the Canadian marketplace would be swimming in a red ocean). "Blue oceans" are untapped market spaces with the "opportunity for highly profitable ground-breaking growth for those who have the courage to step forward and take the plunge". Be mindful of the old adage:

> If you do what you have always done, you will always get what you have always gotten.

An advisor who chooses to offer the IPP solution to qualified prospects is one step closer to operating a financial planning practice in the blue ocean. Those advisors already providing IPP services know that they free up more time to develop deeper relationships with top-notch clients, which in turn earn a greater income for the advisor with far less effort.

To succeed in finding one's blue ocean within the IPP marketplace, a financial advisor will have to learn how to qualify the right clients, present the IPP solution and deal with a prospect's objections to implementing the IPP solution.

UNIQUE VALUE PROPOSITION (UVP)

Successful Trusted Advisors the world over are aware of the unique value they bring to their clients. Each one of us has a unique value proposition to offer to those who have the ability to recognize and appreciate this value. Some people can immediately recognize a unique value proposition and act upon it, while others may not recognize it at first, but, through time and experience, will eventually come to recognize a unique value proposition and then act upon it. Yet others will never see the value in another, no matter how much time passes or how much may be done to prove that value. In our professional lives, many may be called, but a chosen few will be selected to work with the new 21st century Trust Advisor.

This is why it is so imperative to keep in mind that when the new 21st century Trust Advisor markets, what he or she is accomplishing is building a brand in the mind of his or her prospects and clients. In this competitive marketplace, only by building a brand can you differentiate your *unique value proposition* from your competitors. The simplest method to accomplish this is by contracting and narrowing the focus of services that your practice specializes in so that clients and prospects are not confused by what you do, and they know exactly what you do, how your services will benefit them and how to find you.

The difference between a flower and a weed is a judgement. Surround yourself with people who see you as a rose and not a dandelion.

PEOPLE PAY FOR VALUE, KNOW YOUR VALUE

Several years ago a CEO of a very successful multi-million dollar business wanted to redesign his company's logo in order to show the values his company stood behind. He visited over a dozen design studios and none of their design departments could come up with a logo that could express the message he was looking for.

After several months of looking for a design company that could help him, he was directed to a little boutique studio that had a reputation for coming up with design miracles. When the CEO arrived at this studio, he was met by the marketing team. They asked him what he was looking for, and the VP of Marketing said to the CEO, "This sounds like a job for George."

At that moment, the VP of Marketing of the studio picked up the phone and called George into the room. George had been the head of the design department at the company for over 20 years. George proceeded to listen for two minutes as the CEO described what he desired the new logo to portray. George thanked the CEO and then proceeded to pull out his sketchpad and draw. At the end of two minutes, George picked up his sketchpad, showed the CEO his design and asked: "Is this what you have been looking for?"

The CEO immediately jumped up and said that it was exactly what he had been looking for all these months. The CEO then asked how much it would cost. George replied $100,000. The CEO gasped and then replied: "That is crazy! I saw with my own two eyes that you only spent two minutes drawing the logo." George turned to the CEO and calmly said: "It took me 20 years to be able to draw the logo in two minutes."

QUALIFY, QUALIFY, QUALIFY

When you provide a service, your main aim should always be to satisfy your client's need. This is why it is so important that the IPP be presented only to prospects and clients that have an inherent need for this solution. Why waste the time of both the prospect and advisor if the prospect has not been properly qualified?

My good friend Stephen Cheng, principal of Westcoast Actuaries Inc., has created an IPP Feasibility Study. This study will help the advisor determine whether the IPP prospect should be immediately eliminated or if the IPP prospect merits any further attention. The study asks the following 11 qualifying questions:

1. Does the employee want a pension from a "supersized RRSP"?
2. Does the employer want larger deductions than an RRSP can provide?
3. Do the employer and employee want the IPP for the long term?
4. Is the employee at least age 40?
5. Does a *bona fide* employer-employee relationship exist?
6. Does the employee receive T4 income?
7. Is the employee willing to follow investment guidelines?
8. Is the employee willing to have IPP moneys locked in?
9. If the IPP is subject to provincial pension regulation, is the employer willing to make regular contributions?
10. Is the employer willing to make additional contributions if a triennial actuarial valuation reveals that investment earnings were less than 7.5% per year?
11. Is the employer willing to forgo making contributions if a triennial actuarial valuation reveals that investment earnings were more than 7.5% per year?

If the prospect answers "no" to *any* question, then the advisor should simply state that the prospect is not a good candidate for an IPP at this time, and the advisor should move on to the next prospect. If the prospect answers "yes" to *every* question, then the next step is to show the prospect an IPP quotation. Thus, the advisor and prospect's time will be spent most efficiently.

Qualified IPP Prospective Clients and Where to Find Them

In the best selling book *The Millionaire Next Door*, written by Dr. Thomas J. Stanley and Dr. William D. Danko (New York: Pocket Books, 1998), the authors point out the difference between someone of affluence and someone who is wealthy. As mentioned earlier in this chapter, an affluent individual makes a great income and has a solid cash flow; however, individuals may spend more than they make and, therefore, their net worth is often very low. A wealthy individual has assets and saves more than he or she earns. Often advisors confuse affluent and wealthy individuals, but there is a difference, which must be understood by the 21st century financial consultant. Dr. Stanley and Dr. Danko describe the typical millionaire who lives next door as follows:

- Male, age 57, is married to his first spouse, with an average of three children.
- Two-thirds are self-employed business owners or professionals.
- Total average realized household income is $131,000 per year.
- Average household net worth including all personal and business assets is $3.7 million.
- On average, typical millionaires realize less than 7% of their wealth as their income. Hence, they live well below their means.
- They live in neighbourhoods where they are outnumbered three to one by families that are not millionaires.
- They are extremely busy, spending between 45 and 55 hours per week working.
- They save and invest 20% or more of their household's income per year.
- They only hold about 20% of their family's wealth in publicly traded securities.
- Their most trusted advisors are their accountants, lawyers and financial planners. They overwhelmingly recommend that their children go into these professions to serve the wealthy like themselves.

SOME TIPS ON PRESENTING THE IPP SOLUTION TO QUALIFIED PROSPECTS

It is very important to understand that when communicating with a qualified prospect, our focus is not just on what we are saying; we should also be focused on how we are saying what we are saying. Our intended response from our prospects and clients is the sole purpose of our sales presentations. The quality of an IPP presentation is an inverse function of its length.

No one in the financial planning business ever became a great communicator of anything until he or she learned to transcend the facts of what is being sold and speak to the real needs of a prospect or client. Never state the attributes of the IPP in terms of what it is not.

The act of practising to perfect an IPP sales presentation is more important than all the sales training in the world, or, for that matter, the material contained within the pages of this book. An IPP sale is only made after the Q&A is done and you have gained conceptual agreement with the client that the IPP solution is best for him or her. Without this, the IPP for any client will not be maintainable and sustainable. Remember, there is no such thing as failure in the game of life; there is only feedback. Practice, practice and more practice equals success!

DEALING WITH POSSIBLE OBJECTIONS

Many prospects may believe that the cost of setting up an IPP is too expensive. Fees are often considered to be too high because the financial advisor presenting the IPP solution has not established an adequate matrix showing prospective IPP clients the cost they will incur if they do not set up an IPP. By that I mean a client has not been properly "educated" about the true savings being derived/generated. So the true worth of the IPP is not accurately understood. Consequently, the prospective client cannot possibly make a reasonable return-on-investment calculation, because the client does not truly understand the total return on his or her IPP investment.

I learned this firsthand when I first began presenting the IPP solution many years ago. The cost of setting up an IPP was approximately $5,000, compared to having a self-directed RRSP with trust fees that ranged from $0 to $250 yearly. I quickly learned that I had to show the clients with their own numbers what the true short- and long-term costs would be if they did not implement the IPP solution, and use those same numbers to illustrate what the true benefit was going to be.

If prospective IPP clients say that implementing the IPP solution is too costly, it is best to immediately turn their resistance into a question about their perceptions of what constitutes value. Most financial advisors presenting the IPP solution today fall into the trap of focusing on the clients' reluctance to spend, rather than on their inability to see long-term value. Qualified clients may initially say no to the IPP solution for the following three reasons:

One: The perception of value by the prospect is too small, and the financial advisor has to re-educate the prospect about the true benefits. The prospect may be thinking in terms of one year, although the savings will be gained indefinitely.

Two: The urgency for the prospect is not sufficient enough to take action now. The prospect may believe that living with his or her current retirement vehicles is satisfactory. The financial advisor must be able to demonstrate that the prospect's retirement options are deteriorating and that every passing day causes more lost opportunity to save on taxes and compound more dollars in a tax-effective way for retirement.

Three: The client is looking for a discount on fees for the IPP. The prospect appreciates the value of the IPP solution but wants to see if the financial advisor can be moved on fees because other people have been, or the prospect is simply a natural bargainer. If the financial advisor allows his or her fees to be moved, they will be.

Remember, successful business people know that the key component of cost-effectiveness is value. And if the prospective IPP client does not perceive value in your product or service, the lowest price for setting up and maintaining the IPP solution will mean nothing to him or her.

HOW TO PRESENT THE TRUE INTRINSIC VALUE OF THE IPP SOLUTION

When you present the IPP concept, the opening statement about this solution should define the client's core financial need. Articulating the IPP concept is the one critical and indispensable way to begin any IPP presentation. The IPP concept must be presented and seen as the solution to the client's problems. Always come to an agreement with the client that the need you are addressing is indeed his or her actual need. For example, the client is looking for a solution to reduce corporate taxable income and defer moneys for retirement in a tax-effective way.

Always stress to prospective clients what the IPP solution will do for them. By letting clients know what the IPP will do for them in achieving their financial goals, you are presuming that the client accepts the IPP solution. If the prospect is properly qualified, the IPP sales process is almost complete.

If the clients desire to know, share with them how the IPP works. In more cases than not, the only people who want to know how the IPP works are the clients' public accountants. When you take your car to get it fixed, you want to know that you can trust your mechanic and that your car will start and go from point A to B without any trouble. Very few people actually want to know the inner workings of their automobiles, and 99% of the time this is true for their IPPs. What IPP prospects and clients want to know is that the IPP is sanctioned by the Canada Revenue Agency and that if they use you and your firm to implement and maintain the plan, everything will run smoothly without a hitch.

Always go on the offensive in raising the issue of risk and limitations of the IPP solution. Don't be scared of telling your prospects and clients the risks and limitations of the IPP solution as you are closing your presentation. The limitations that are associated with the IPP solution were presented in detail earlier, in Chapter 15. If you are honest with prospects and clients, and share with them what the risks and limitations of the IPP are, prospects and clients will begin to see you as not just another sales person painting only the best-case scenarios. You will be seen as someone they can trust and want to do business with for a long, long time.

The key to becoming successful in the IPP marketplace is to always focus on the long-term value that the IPP solution will bring to the client. Focusing on output rather than input sounds simple, but you must have the confidence to approach selling the IPP solution in this way.

Lead clients to think in terms of the end by emphasizing, for example, how much more money the clients will have in their pockets at the end of 10, 15, 20 and even 40 years after they have implemented the IPP solution. By learning how to show clients how much greater their tax savings and tax deferred income will be if they opt for the IPP solution, you give the clients reason to act now rather than later.

The best way to get potential IPP prospects' attention is to speak in terms of the economic language they understand best, that of the bottom line and the impact of implementing or not implementing the IPP solution will have on their corporate bottom line and their retirement income.

In essence, this converts buying reasons (emotion) into dollar-sized justifications, allowing the client to see in terms of return on investment (ROI). Successful advisors in the IPP market know how to move an IPP prospective client's attention to the outcomes of the IPP engagement and the impact the results will have on a company's long-term business plan and the IPP member's retirement plan. This avoids the task and commodity concerns and instead puts the focus on the results, which are near and dear to the IPP prospective plan sponsors' and plan members' hearts.

If a prospective IPP client is only certain of the cost of implementing the IPP solution but has a vague idea about the end results, the prospect may inevitably tip toward a lesser type of retirement plan such as the traditional RRSP, which would clearly be an outdated option for the properly qualified prospect to take. Consequently, it is incumbent upon the financial advisor to provide the client with the proper matrix with which to measure the IPP solution's results and convert those results into a calculable ROI specific to the prospect's situation.

There are two types of metrics a financial advisor must prepare before attempting to achieve conceptual agreement with a prospect. These will empower the prospect to agree to implement the IPP solution:

1. *Short-term measures*. This includes the immediate savings that are generated when the IPP solution is created.
2. *Long-term measures*. This includes showing how much the prospective IPP client would be better off over the long term had he or she adopted the IPP solution.

Here is how to put these concepts to use.

Imagine you are presenting the IPP solution to a 55-year-old client named John Doe, who has owned an incorporated business since 1991 and has a T4 income of more than $100,000 and a marginal tax rate in Ontario of 46%. This client is serious about saving for his retirement during the next ten years. When he reaches 65 years of age, he plans to retire, and he is properly qualified for the IPP solution.

Step 1: When presenting the IPP solution to this client, you should show him the immediate short-term benefits created by implementing the IPP, which include a $161,851 deduction for his company and a non-taxable benefit for himself. Explain how this money will then compound tax-free within the IPP until it is withdrawn.

Step 2: Show how in the following year John Doe's company will be able to contribute on his behalf into his IPP $27,934, and these contributions will increase by 7.5% annually until he retires (the investment mix in his IPP earns 7.5%).

Step 3: Conclude this portion of your presentation by showing John Doe that when he reaches 65, he will have accumulated $815,583 in his IPP to provide him with pension benefits.

Step 4: Next, show John Doe how his situation would look different if he had chosen not to follow your recommendation to create an IPP for himself. This is called "lost opportunities!" Prepare an example of what his financials would look like if he had taken the same amount of money out of his company, after having paid his personal marginal tax rate of

46%. Then place what was left over into a non-registered investment earmarked for his retirement savings.

The first year after taxes, John Doe would be left with $87,400 to invest for his retirement. The following year, after taxes, he would make a $15,084 contribution to his non-registered retirement investment. His contributions into this plan would grow at 7.5% (the investment mix in his non-registered portfolio earns 7.5% and all growth of these investments are taxed at 46%).

Step 5: Show the client that had he opted for the non-IPP strategy at age 65, he would have only accumulated $351,113.

Step 6: Show the client that had he taken your recommendation to set up an IPP today, at retirement, based on the stated assumptions, he would have earned $464,470 more in retirement savings than he would have by investing in the non-registered investment.

Below is a table that shows the accumulated savings that the business owner in the example would have by opting to implement the IPP solution over not implementing the IPP solution.

Registered IPP Investments vs. Non-registered Investments Table

Years	IPP Annual Deposit (annually increase by 7.5%)	IPP Balance at the end of year (growth rate of 7.5%)	Non-Registered Investment Annual Deposit (annually increase by 7.5%)	Non-Registered Balance at end of year (growth rate of 7.5%)	Accumulated difference at the end of IPP year period
1	$161,851	$173,990	$87,400	$90,910	$74,451
2	$27,934	$217,068	$15,084	$110,250	$106,818
3	$30,029	$265,629	$16,216	$131,544	$134,085
4	$32,281	$320,254	$17,432	$154,958	$165,296
5	$34,702	$381,577	$18,739	$180,672	$200,905
6	$37,305	$450,298	$20,145	$208,881	$241,417
7	$40,103	$527,181	$21,656	$239,794	$287,387
8	$43,110	$613,063	$23,280	$273,637	$339,426

9	$46,344	$708,863	$25,026	$310,656	$398,207
10	$49,819	$815,583	$26,903	$351,113	$464,470

After you have presented these two scenarios to a qualified prospective client, and he or she still doesn't take action to implement the IPP solution, all I can recommend to you at this point is to quote Oscar Wilde when he said:

> The definition of a cynic: "*A man who knows the price of everything and the value of nothing.*"

And if that doesn't work, begin saying the "Serenity Prayer" by Reinhold Niebuhr (1892-1971):

> God grant me the serenity to accept the things I cannot change; courage to change the things I can; and wisdom to know the difference.

CHAPTER 27

PENSION SPEAK

Peter J. Merrick

Learning a language is akin to acquiring a new code cipher. "Pension Speak" refers to a language that is spoken by individuals who have developed a mastery in Canadian pension, tax, accounting and actuarial terminology. You will encounter many terms as you delve into the world of Individual Pension Plans and other advanced planning solutions, and the aim of this appendix is to provide you with a working lexicon of the most commonly used terms and concepts.

Glossary

2/3 Pensionable refers to pre-1990 pensionable service recognized after June 7, 1990. The maximum pensionable benefit limit for pre-1990 pensionable service funding is $1,150 (two-thirds of $1,722.22) for years up to and including 2003, and two-thirds of the maximum pension limit for years after 2003.

Accountant is a tax professional, who keeps, audits, and inspects the financial records of individuals or businesses and prepares financial and tax reports. In Canada, there are three recognized accounting professional designations, which are: Chartered Accountant (CA), Certified General Accountant (CGA) and Certified Management Accountant (CGA).

Accrual Accounting is a form of accounting that matches revenues to expenses at the time in which the transaction occurs rather than when payment is received.

Accrual Rate is the rate, usually specified in the benefit formula of a defined benefit pension plan as a percentage of earnings, at which pension benefits are earned. Example: 2% of pensionable earnings for each year of service restricted by the defined benefit maximum pension limit.

Accrued Benefit Obligation is the actuarial present value of benefits attributed to an IPP member's service performed as of a specific date.

Active Member is a member of an IPP to whom a pension benefit has accrued under the provisions of the plan during the year that contributions to the plan have been made.

Actuarial Assumptions are the estimates of future events that will impact upon the cost and obligations of the employer to provide a retirement benefit. These events may include administration costs, rate of return on IPP assets, mortality tables, *Income Tax Regulations*, Average Indexed Wage and retirement age.

Actuarial Gains and Losses are the changes that occur in the accrued benefit obligation of the IPP assets as a result of experiences that differ from the actuarial assumptions.

Actuarial Valuation is the report by an actuary of the financial strength of an IPP.

Actuarial Valuation Report (AVR) is a report that determines the funding level of a pension plan as of a specific date and the appropriate contributions to be deposited into the pension fund for the periods between the next actuarial valuation.

Actuary is a person who is a Fellow of the Canadian Institute of Actuaries. Actuaries are business professionals who apply their knowledge of mathematics, probability, statistics and risk theory to real-life financial problems involving future uncertainty.

Additional Voluntary Contributions (AVCs) are typically described as additional funds set up in a Registered Pension Plan (RPP) that are in addition to the prescribed amounts set out in the RPP plan text. AVCs are not subject to the locking-in provisions found in Registered Pension Plans.

Administrator is either a person or a body of persons with the ultimate responsibility for administrating an IPP. In most cases, the administrator for an IPP will be the trustee or the employer.

Annual Information Return (AIR) is also referred to as a Form T244. An annual Information Return is a form that must be filed with the CRA every year for each Registered Pension Plan in Canada within 180 days of the plan year-end. The AIR reports activity that occurred within an

IPP during the past year and the health of the plan. If an AIR is filed late, penalties may be charged to the IPP by the CRA.

Annuity is a contract between an individual and an insurance company for a guaranteed interest-bearing policy with guaranteed income options.

Applicable Pension Laws refer to the requirements based on the *Income Tax Act*, *Income Tax Regulations* and all statutes of Canada and provinces of Canada that apply to IPP.

Asset is approved property held with the Individual Pension Plan.

Asset Allocation refers to diversifying investments in different categories such as cash, fixed income and equities.

Assets Under Management (AUM) refer to the total investment funds that are managed by another.

Average Indexed Wage (AIW) is the measure of the average weekly wage published by Statistics Canada.

Beneficiary means the person or persons legally designated by the plan to receive any benefits payable under the plan as a result of the IPP member's death.

Beta refers to a stock's exposure to the overall market and its sensitivity/volatility in relation to the overall market.

Blue Ocean is a metaphor that illustrates how companies can easily grow their businesses in practically competitor-free environments.

Bridge Benefit is also referred to as a CPP Offset. A temporary supplement to a pension, usually paid from the early retirement date until the normal retirement date of age 65 or death, whichever comes first.

Canada Revenue Agency (CRA) administers tax laws for the Government of Canada and for most provinces and territories and various social and economic benefits and incentive programs delivered through the tax system.

Canadian-Controlled Private Corporation (CCPC) is defined under the *Income Tax Act* (subsection 125(7)) as a corporation that has been incorporated in Canada and where the majority of outstanding shares are held by Canadian residents.

Career Average Earning Defined Benefit Pension Plan is a pension benefit that the IPP will pay out to a plan member based on his or her entire career average earnings during which he or she was eligible to acquire pension credits from the plan. Each year is treated equally in the weighting of the career average and capped at the CRA prescribed pensionable amount. Career Average Earnings are used to calculate the total annual pension benefit that a connected person will get from his or her IPP.

Cash is money invested in T-bills, and in chequing and savings accounts.

CICA Handbook, Section 3461, Employee Future Benefits are the accounting standards set by the Canadian Institute of Chartered Accountants that oblige companies to make changes in several key areas in their financial reporting in relation to IPPs and other defined benefit pension plans. Accrual accounting is required for retirement and post-employment benefits. Organizations operating in the private sector are required to accrue the cost of all employee future benefits including Individual Pension Plans.

Common Law Partner is a person of the opposite sex or the same sex who is the natural or adopted parent of the IPP member's child. The common law partner has been in an intimate relationship with the member of the IPP and has been cohabiting with the member for 12 consecutive months or lived with the member previously for 12 consecutive months.

Commuted Value refers to the amount of money that needs to be set aside today, at current market interest rates, to provide sufficient funds to pay for a pension when a plan member retires. It shows how much a benefit is worth today. Commuted values express the lump-sum value of a promised benefit, usually from a defined benefit pension plan. The commuted value takes into account the benefits, interest and mortality rates.

Company refers to an employer who sponsors an IPP for an owner, executive or employee.

Connected Person is a person who owns directly or indirectly 10% or more of capital stock in a company or a related corporation. It also includes a person who does not deal at arm's length with a company. This includes a spouse or a common law partner.

Consumer Price Index (CPI) measures monthly and yearly changes in the cost of 300 goods and services commonly bought by Canadians.

Contract for Insurance refers to IPP funds that are held under a contract with an insurance company. If the administrator of an IPP elects to have IPP money held with an insurance company, the administrator of the IPP will not have to appoint trustees to administer plan assets.

Cost-of-Living Adjustments refer to the adjusted salaries and pensions based on changes in the CPI. Typically, salaries and pensions are adjusted annually.

Credited Service is the continuous service that a member of a plan has accumulated from the effective date and during which the company made contributions or was deemed to make contributions on behalf of the member of the IPP.

Creditor is either a person or legal entity to whom money is due.

Current Service Cost refers to the expenses connected with the funding and the administration of a defined benefit plan on an annual basis.

Custodian is the entity that actually holds the assets inside the IPP. The custodian can be either an insurance company or a formal trustee or a three-party trustee.

Deemed Registration of an IPP is deemed registered with the CRA January 1st of the calendar year that an application to register an IPP has been made.

Deferred Income Plans are retirement savings plans recognized and registered with the CRA that allow immediate deductions for employed individuals or their companies where taxes paid on the money in these plans are not taxed until withdrawal. These plans include RPPs, RRSPs, RRIFs, LIFs, LIRAs, LRIFs and Locked-in RRSPs.

Deferred Pension refers to when a member's employment or pension plan terminates and the pension benefit is not payable until the pensionable age.

Deficit may occur in an IPP because the fund returns in the plan were lower than anticipated due to AIW rising faster than expected, or for any other reason. As a result, the actuary will require additional contributions to be injected into the plan in order to finance the deficit. Note that this deficit may be amortized over a maximum period of 15 years.

Defined Benefit Maximum Pension Limits (per Year of Service) are the following: 2006 ($2,111), 2007 ($2,222), 2008 ($2,333), 2009 ($2,444), 2010 (indexed to the average wage).

Defined Benefit Pension Plan (DBPP) is a traditional pension plan registered with the CRA that pays workers a specific monthly benefit at retirement. These plans either state the promised benefit as an exact dollar amount or specify a formula for calculating the benefit. Within these plans, the contributions are not defined, but the benefits are defined.

Defined Contribution Pension Plan (DCPP) is a registered pension plan with the CRA and is governed under the federal and provincial Pension Acts depending on the province a DCPP is registered in. A DCPP is also referred to as a money purchase plan. In these plans, the contributions are defined but the amounts that will be withdrawn are not defined.

Designated Plan is a pension plan where more than 50% of the pension creditors are for a specific person. These individuals are active members of a pension plan who are connected persons to the employer of the plan or who earn two and one-half times the year's maximum pensionable earnings (YMPE).

Disability is the inability to work due to illness or injury.

Early Retirement is the date prior to a member's Normal Retirement Date, when the member actually retires. This date can be the first day of any month within 15 years of the member's Normal Retirement Date and no earlier.

Earnings mean the amount of pensionable earnings as defined in the IPP text that is used to calculate pensionable benefits earned.

Effective Date is the date that an RPP is considered to be registered with the CRA. This date is outlined in IPP documents. This date cannot be before January 1st of the year that the application for registration of the IPP is made to the CRA. The Effective Date also refers to the date that the membership into an IPP is terminated.

Employer Health Tax (EHT), previously known as OHIP in Ontario, is paid by employers who exceed a certain payroll amount to the Ministry of Health. The amount paid by each employer goes towards covering health care for Ontario residents who hold a valid Ontario Health Card. Once a business's payroll reaches $400,000 (whether it takes five months or five years to reach), it must pay EHT.

Equities are ownerships in companies.

Excess Surplus represents the lesser of 20% of the actuarial liabilities or the greater of 10% of the actuarial liabilities and two times the contributions for current service. The actuary will require a contribution holiday or a decrease in contributions if the IPP is in an excess surplus position.

Factor of 9 is a pension credit formula used to determine the pension credit in a defined benefit pension plan. The federal government created the Factor of 9 to equalize the tax assisted savings between all Defined Contribution Pension Plans and RRSPs to Defined Benefit Pension

Plans. The Factor of 9 states that for every $1 of defined benefit pension benefit promised to a member, the government considers that $9 of funding will be required. However, this relationship is an average over a plan member's entire working career. To calculate the Factor of 9, the benefit earned by the member of a defined benefit plan to determine an IPP member's PA is to multiply the defined benefit promised to the member of the IPP in a year by 9, then subtract the PA offset (9 × benefit – $600).

Fiduciary is any person or entity that has any power or authority over the control, management or disposition of the funds of any employee benefit plan, including anyone who provides investment advice for a fee or has discretion with respect to the administration of a plan.

Fiduciary Duty represents a very high level of standard of care in dealing with assets on behalf of a beneficiary. If the duty and standards are not met, the offending fiduciary could be legally liable for the consequences.

Final Average Earning Defined Benefit Pension Plan is the pension benefit that is paid out to the IPP member based on length of service that is pensionable and the average earnings of the IPP member for a stated period of time. This formula can only be used for a non-connected person. Usually the best IPPs for non-connected members are based on an average of the top three earning years that are capped at the CRA-prescribed pensionable amount.

Fixed Income is money invested in GICs, bonds and mortgages.

Hybrid Plan refers to a Registered Pension Plan that has features of both defined benefit pension plans and defined compensation pension plans.

IIS Form is a Risk-Based Pension Investment Monitoring Program and Investment Information Summary Form that has been mandated in Ontario to be submitted every year by sponsors of IPPs to the Financial Services Commission of Ontario (FSCO).

Income Tax Act is the primary source of all income tax legislation in Canada. The *Income Tax Act* lays down the rules of taxation in Canada.

Income Tax Regulations are complements to the ITA. The Regulations specify the terms and conditions of applying the ITA.

Indexing refers to the pension increases for a pension plan member or the member's survivors. It is calculated each year by using Consumer Price Index (CPI) data published by Statistics Canada. The increases are based on a comparison of the 12-month average of the monthly CPI for the year just ended, to the 12-month average of the monthly CPI for the previous year.

Individual Pension Plan (IPP) is a defined benefit pension plan for just one employee as defined in section 147.1 of the Canadian *Income Tax Act*. IPPs provide senior executives and business owners with the opportunity to achieve maximum tax relief combined with a maximum Registered Pension Plan (RPP).

Initial Value Message is a statement of value an advisor could bring to a prospective IPP client based on prior experience and success in a particular market segment with similar companies and individuals. It is used early in the sales process to generate interest in a discussion.

Investment Management Fees (IMF) are the fees that clients pay a financial institution to manage their investment assets.

Investment Manager is an individual or organization appointed by the trustee or administrator of an Individual Pension Plan to manage the assets of the plan pursuant to federal and provincial laws and regulations pertaining to the investment of pension assets.

Investment Policy Statement (IPS) refers to the written guidelines that are used for the IPP's long-term financial and investment decisions. It generally includes investment objectives (return requirements and risk tolerance), constraints (cash requirements and timing issues) and guidelines for achieving an IPP's objectives.

Lifetime Retirement Benefits are benefits promised to be paid to members of defined benefit plans from the time the benefit starts paying to the time of the member's death and the death of the member's spouse.

Locked-in Plan is a registered plan where money has been transferred from a pension plan to a personal registered retirement account where there are restrictions to accessing the money to ensure that there will be an income stream during retirement for life. Lock-in Plans include Life Income Funds (LIF), Lock-in Retirement Accounts (LIRA), Locked-in Retirement Income Funds (LRIF) and Locked-in RRSPs (LRRSP).

Luck is when preparation meets opportunity.

Matching Service is the contributions to fund an IPP for non-connected persons for years of service prior to 1991.

Member/Participant is a designated employee of a company who is deemed or has been deemed to have contributions made to an RPP.

Money Purchase Plan is also referred to as a defined contribution pension plan. This is a registered pension plan with the CRA in which the contribution amounts are defined but the benefits of the pension received at retirement are not defined. Contribution limits are set for 2006 ($19,000), 2007 ($20,000), 2008 ($21,000), 2009 ($22,000), 2010 (indexed to the average wage).

Morbidity refers to the incidences of disability in a given population.

Mortality refers to the incidences of death in a given population.

Normal Retirement is the first day of the month following a member's 65th birthday.

Office of the Superintendent of Financial Institutions (OSFI) is the Ontario entity making sure pension plans governed by the Ontario *Pension Benefits Act*, R.S.O. 1990, c. P.8, comply with this Act.

Participating Employer is an employer that has made or is required to make contributions to an IPP for an employee or former employee.

Past Service Pension Adjustment (PSPA) reduces an individual's RRSP deduction limit for any pension benefits earned in a year after 1989 for the following year through the reporting of a Pension Adjustment.

Payback is the time it takes to recover the amount invested, commonly expressed in months or years.

Pension Adjustment (PA) is a plan member's total pension credits earned for the prior year. A PA reduces the amount that a member can contribute into his or her RRSP. For IPPs, the PA is nine times the approximate amount of the annual pension accrued in the year for defined benefit pension plans, minus the pension adjustment offset. It should be noted that the PA reported for Defined Contribution Pension Plans and Deferred Profit-Sharing Plans is equal to the actual dollar amounts invested in those plans.

Pension Adjustment Offset is the minimum level of RRSP room that someone is given. Up until 1996, it was $1,000, and then from 1997 to the present, it has been $600 per year for a member of a Defined Benefit Pension Plan. The pension adjustment offset gives a member of a Defined Benefit Pension Plan a minimum RRSP contribution room for any given year.

Pension Adjustment Reversal (PAR) restores RRSP contribution room for an employee that was terminated from a registered pension plan (RPP) or a deferred profit-sharing plan (DPSP). PAR increases a former

RPP and DPSP member's RRSP room by the difference between the total employee's PAs that were reported while the employee was a member of these plans and the actual pension transfer value to an RRSP. PAR is calculated based on when membership in the plan is terminated. The RRSP room generated by PAR can be used by the individual to make RRSP contributions in the year of termination or it can be carried forward for use in future years.

Pension Benefits Guarantee Fund (PBGF), which is available only in Ontario, was created to offer limited protection for the over one million DBPP members within Ontario's borders. If a DBPP in Ontario has insufficient funds, the PBGF will guarantee only the first $1,000 per month of pension benefits. This fund does not protect designated plans such as the IPP.

Pension Credit is the value of a pension benefit that a member of a plan earns under an IPP in a calendar year. Pension credits are totalled to determine an IPP member's PA with his or her employer.

Pensionable Age refers to when a member of a pension is entitled to an unreduced pension.

Pensionable Service refers to the number of years that a member of a defined benefit pension plan has accredited to his or her retirement since becoming a member of a plan.

Portability refers to the right to transfer locked-in or vested benefits to another registered plan when a member leaves the service of an employer.

Postponed Retirement is the earliest of the first day of the month on which the member actually retires after his or her Normal Retirement Date and December 31st of the calendar year in which the member reaches the age of 71.

Projected Unit Credit Funding is a funding method that takes into account all the benefits that may be paid under a fund for a member of an IPP. A level of contributions is set so it covers both the benefits that have already accrued and benefits associated with membership in the future. Projected benefit funding methods include individual funding, aggregate funding, attained normal age funding and entry age normal funding.

Pro-Rata Method is a formula used for the division of IPP assets during the divorce of a married couple. The formula divides the value of the IPP assets on the date of legal separation based on how long the couple was married and pension credits for the IPP were earned. Once this amount is determined, assets are split between the divorcing spouses according to the prescribed provincial and federal matrimonial asset division rates.

Provincial Pension Regulators (PPRs) administer their respective provincial Pension Benefits Acts.

Prudent Person Rule as it applies in this book refers to the restrictions and the discretion that a prudent person would have in seeking to achieve a good investment return while achieving the preservation of capital.

Qualifying Transfer is a direct transfer of a lump-sum amount from an unmatured RRSP, a money purchase plan, locked-in plan or a DPSP. A qualifying transfer is made to pay for all or part of the cost of the past service benefits related to the PSPA.

Qualifying Withdrawal is an amount a member of a Registered Pension Plan is allowed to withdraw.

Reciprocal Transfer Agreement is an agreement between two or more plans to transfer an appropriate sum of money from the pension fund of one employer directly to the pension fund of another, to fund benefits of an employee who leaves the first employer to enter employment with the second employer.

Registered Pension Plan (RPP) is a pension plan that has been set up by an employer and registered by the CRA to provide specified employees with a pension when they retire. An RPP exists when there is a formal arrangement between an employer to contribute on behalf of an employee to a trust.

Registered Plans Directorate is a special division in the CRA responsible for all program activities related to the provisions of the *Income Tax Act* for the registering and monitoring of employee pension plans, retirement savings plans, retirement income funds, deferred profit-sharing plans, supplementary unemployment benefit plans, education savings plans and registered investments.

Registered Retirement Savings Plans (RRSPs) are savings plans for individuals, including the self-employed, who have been registered for the purposes of the federal *Income Tax Act*. RRSP contribution limits are based on *earned income*. RRSPs provide retirement income at retirement based on accumulated contributions and return on investment in the plan. Contributions to an RRSP are tax-deductible, the *investment income* in it is tax-deferred and payments from it are taxable. Annual contributions are limited to 18% of earnings up to a maximum of $21,000 in 2009.

Remuneration refers to all salaries, wages, bonuses, vacation pay, honoraria, commission, taxable allowances, the value of taxable benefits and any other payment that a member of an IPP receives as an employee of a sponsoring company.

Retirement Benefit is the benefit paid out to a member of a pension plan on a periodic basis.

Retirement Compensation Arrangement (RCA) is a plan defined in subsection 248(1) of the *Income Tax Act*, providing supplemental pension benefits to owners/managers and key employees of incorporated businesses. Contributions to an RCA are 100% tax deductible by the employer and are not taxable for the employee until the money is withdrawn from the RCA.

Retiring Allowance is the amount of money that an employer pays to an employee in recognition of long service with the company or an amount paid for loss of employment or position. The CRA may allow the taxpayer who receives a retiring allowance to defer part of or all taxes on the amount by making payment into an RPP or RRSP if he or she meets certain criteria.

Return on Investment (ROI) is defined as net income divided by investment. ROI is often used in a general sense, referring to the overall return on investment of the IPP initiative for both the sponsor and the member of the plan.

Risk-Based Pension Investment Monitoring Program and Investment Information Summary Form (IIS Form) is a form that sponsors of IPPs must submit every year to the Financial Services Commission of Ontario (FSCO). This form allows FSCO to reduce the risk of members of individual pension plans not receiving the benefits promised.

Salary is the active income an employee receives for providing service to an employer.

Solvency Requirements is a calculation to determine the funding requirement to properly fund a defined benefit pension plan if it is to be terminated and wound up.

Specimen Plan is an IPP text that has been pre-approved by the CRA. Specimen Plans are frequently used by administrators or consultants who market IPPs. When sponsors of IPPs registering IPPs use the same consultant or administrator, the approved Specimen Plan document contains the same terminology and identical wording. When an IPP uses an approved Specimen Plan, the CRA will quickly register the IPP as soon as it has been determined that the IPP plan matches the Specimen

Plan. Specimen Plans for IPPs have within them approved IPP text, funding formulas and other documents.

Sponsor is a company that sponsors an IPP for an employee. IPPs can only be sponsored by incorporated businesses or incorporated professional corporations.

Spouse is a person who is married to an active IPP member, inactive IPP member or retired IPP member.

Statement of Investment Policies and Procedures (SIPP) must be provided each year by sponsors of pension plans registered with the Province of Ontario to the Financial Services Commission of Ontario (FSCO). Sponsors must submit a written Statement of Investment Policies and Procedures that meets the guidelines of the Office of the Superintendent of Financial Institutions (OSFI). This documentation is used to help ensure that individual pension plans are operating in the best interests of plan members.

Surplus in an IPP will not require a contribution holiday or a decrease in contributions if the IPP surplus does not result in an *excess* surplus.

T10 is the form that reports the Pension Adjustment Reversal to the CRA on behalf of the former RPP member. The T10 restores the RRSP room that was reduced as a result of membership in a pension plan or terminated DPSP, and the member is no longer entitled to a portion of his or her pension benefits.

T1004 is a Past Service Pension Adjustment Certification Form.

T1007 is a CRA Connected Person Information Return Form.

T244 is a CRA form in which the IPP Annual Information Return is reported to the CRA.

T3P is an IPP Trust income tax return. The T3P must be filed within 90 days after the year-end of the Trust. T3Ps must be filed by the IPP trustee(s). If this form is late, the CRA can impose penalties for filing late. T3Ps only have to be filed by IPPs that have formal trust agreements. If investments of an IPP have been invested in a contract of insurance such as in a segregated fund, there is no T3P filed.

T4 is a slip that reports an individual's earned income from his or her labour.

T4PS (profit-sharing) is a slip issued to employees of a company who participate in a company's employee profit-sharing plan.

T510 is a form that the sponsor/administrator submits to the CRA when applying to register an IPP. This form is an application for registration of a pension plan. This form indicates that an IPP is a designated plan. Once an IPP has been given plan status, it continues to hold this status unless the CRA changes its status.

Tailored Individual Pension Plan (TIPP) is a defined benefit plan created for an individual where the PA is inappropriately low in relation to the benefit promised by the pension. The CRA frowns upon TIPPs and upon plan sponsors and members of plans that have been deemed TIPPs. An IPP designated as a TIPP runs the risk of being deregistered.

Tangible Benefit is a benefit that can be monetarily quantified.

Terminal Funding may occur if the member of the IPP retires prior to age 65. Then the plan could be amended to provide an unreduced pension plus a bridge payment from early retirement to normal retirement. Terminal Funding creates an underfunded liability and an opportunity for a company to make further contributions to an IPP.

Third Party Administrator is an organization that processes health plan claims but does not carry any insurance risk.

Transfer refers to the act of conveying the title of property.

Transfer Factor is a formula that is used to determine how much money the CRA will permit to be transferred on a tax-deferral basis from an IPP to an LIRA, RRSP, LIF or LRRSP without triggering taxes. This formula is based on the age of the IPP member.

Triennial Valuation is an actuarial valuation that reports the strength of a registered IPP and that must be filed with the CRA every three years. The valuation is used to set current service contributions for the next three years. It also determines if the plan has a surplus or deficit. Based on the Triennial Valuation, it is determined whether the IPP will meet its benefit obligations or not.

Trust is a legal arrangement in which one person or entity (settlor) transfers legal title to a trustee (fiduciary) to manage the property for the benefit of a person or institution (beneficiary).

Trustee(s) can be a trust company or at least three individuals who live in Canada and who are charged to promote the financial security of a pension fund through sound investment policy and practices. If an IPP has been set up with a Trust Agreement instead of a contract of insurance, a T3P tax return must be filed with the CRA within 90 days of the year-end of the Trust.

Unfunded Liability occurs when there are fewer assets in the IPP fund to meet the IPP's pension benefit obligations.

Unique Value Proposition (UVP) refers to the unique value an advisor offers to his or her clients. However, not everyone has the ability to appreciate this value. Advisors are called up to work with those clients who perceive this unique value.

Valuation is an actuarial examination of a pension plan to determine whether contributions are being accumulated at a rate sufficient to provide the funds out of which the promised pension can be paid when due. The valuation shows the actuarial liabilities of the plan and the applicable assets.

Value-Added Method is a formula for the division of IPP assets during a marriage breakdown. The formula subtracts the value of the pension earned before the legal union of the couple from the value of the pension at the time of the official separation. Once that amount is determined, the split of the IPP assets occurs at the prescribed provincial and federal matrimonial asset division rates.

Value Assessment is the consultative process of identifying the business impact of an investment, according to the client's decision-making criteria, and assembling the business case that explains it.

Value Assessment Methodology is a methodology for selling that focuses on how you produce value for clients.

Value-Based Pricing is based on the value of the product or service to the client, not the cost of production.

Values are the principles and standards we set for ourselves either consciously or unconsciously.

Vesting means that a member of a pension is entitled to get the pension benefits that he or she has built up according to the pension plan formula.

Wind-up is the process whereby an employer discontinues a defined benefit pension plan.

Year's Maximum Pensionable Earnings (YMPE) is the average Canadian national wage determined and adjusted yearly by Statistics Canada and reported by the CRA. The YMPE is the maximum amount of annual earnings, not including reductions for the year's basic exemption, upon which benefits and contributions for purposes of the Canada Pension Plan and Quebec Pension Plan are based.

PART III

INVESTING 101

CHAPTER 28

INVESTMENT PHILOSOPHY

Christopher P. Van Slyke
Peter J. Merrick

Overview

This chapter discusses arguably the most advanced investment strategies and management for IPP portfolios around today. It combines several methodologies that include Modern Portfolio Theory, the three-factor model and fixed-income strategies.

Learning Objectives

By the end of this chapter, you should be able to:

- understand the basics of Modern Portfolio Theory;
- understand the basics of the three-factor model; and
- understand the basics of fixed-income strategies.

MODERN PORTFOLIO THEORY

In 1990, Harry Markowitz, William Sharpe and Merton Miller, three noted financial economists, won the Nobel Memorial Prize for Economics for their work in developing Modern Portfolio Theory as a portfolio management technique. Modern Portfolio Theory has been used to develop and manage investment portfolios for large institutions, as well as for individual investors. There are four components to Modern Portfolio Theory.

Investors Inherently Avoid Risk

Investors are often more concerned with risk than they are with reward. Rational investors are not willing to accept risk unless the level of return compensates them for it.

Securities Markets Are Efficient

The "efficient market hypothesis" states that while the returns of different securities may vary as new information becomes available, these variations are inherently random and unpredictable. Assets are repriced every minute of the day according to what news comes out. As new information enters the market, it is quickly absorbed into the prices of securities, and thus hard to capitalize on. In fact, advancing information technology and increased sophistication on the part of investors are causing the markets to become even more efficient.

The implications of the efficient market hypothesis are far-reaching for investors. It implies that one should be deeply skeptical of anyone who claims to know how to "beat the market". One cannot expect to consistently beat the market by picking individual securities or by "timing the market".

Focus on the Portfolio as a Whole and Not on Individual Securities

The risk and reward characteristics of all of the portfolio's holdings should be analyzed as one, not separately. An efficient allocation of capital to specific asset classes is far more important than selecting the individual investments.

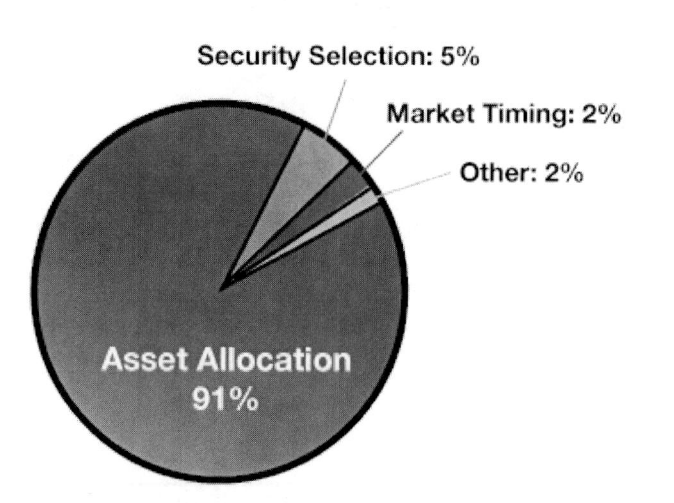

Source: "Determinants of Portfolio Performance" published in the Financial Analysts Journal (August 1986) by Gary P. Brinson, L. Randolph Hood and Gilbert Beebower.

As the pie chart shows, your asset allocation can determine over 91% of the performance variation of an investment portfolio. How the investment dollars are allocated far outweighs the potential effects of individual security selection and market timing. This will be further explored in Chapter 29.

Every Risk Level Has a Corresponding Optimal Combination of Asset Classes That Maximizes Returns

This is called the "efficient frontier". Portfolio diversification is not so much a function of how many individual stocks or bonds are involved, but the relationship of one asset to another. This relationship is referred to in the investment world as "correlation". The higher a correlation between two investments, the more likely they are to move in the same direction.

The efficient frontier represents the range of hypothetical portfolios that offer the maximum return for any given level of risk. Portfolios positioned above the range are unachievable on a consistent basis. Portfolios below the efficient frontier are inefficient portfolios (too much risk, not enough reward). The ideal portfolio exists somewhere along the efficient frontier.

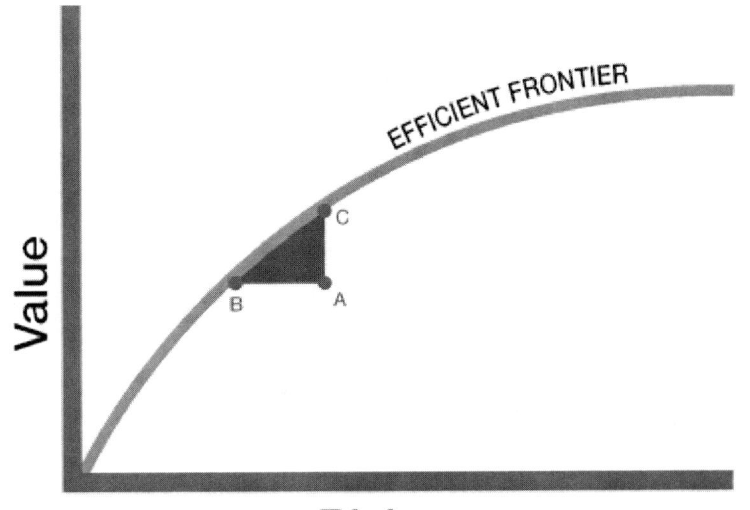

The portfolio represented by point A is inefficient because there are portfolios with the same value but less risk (Portfolio B); there are portfolios with the same risk but more value (Portfolio C); and there are portfolios with a combination of these two conditions. The efficient frontier, as originally defined in Modern Portfolio Theory, is a line that represents the continuum of all efficient portfolios.

THE THREE-FACTOR MODEL

Most finance academics and investment professionals acknowledge that there are three primary factors influencing equity portfolio returns:

(1) **Exposure to the overall market (beta)** — The term beta refers to a measure of an investment's volatility, relative to an appropriate asset class or the overall market.

(2) **The percentage invested in large company stocks versus small company stocks** — Over time, small company stocks have higher expected returns than large company stocks. This is because stocks of small companies are riskier than those of large companies, and investors demand a premium for this risk.

(3) **The percentage invested in growth stocks versus value stocks** — Over time, value stocks have higher expected returns than growth stocks. Value stocks are those that sell at lower prices relative to their earnings and book values. They are perceived by investors to be riskier than growth stocks, and investors demand a premium for this risk as well.

FIXED INCOME

The role of fixed income in a portfolio is not only to produce income, but also to reduce volatility. The best way to accomplish this is to employ the following strategies:

- use shorter maturities (maturities under five years);
- use high quality issues;
- use a variable maturity approach; and
- use a diversified global approach while hedging all currencies.

Together, Modern Portfolio Theory, the three-factor model and fixed-income strategies, along with the institutional approach that will be discussed in Chapter 29, can help form an overall investment philosophy for the management of a clients portfolios.

CHAPTER 29

INVESTMENT POLICY STATEMENTS, ASSET ALLOCATION AND REGULAR REBALANCING OF PORTFOLIOS

Peter J. Merrick
Christopher P. Van Slyke
Charles Stanley

Overview

This chapter discusses the benefits of creating an Investment Policy Statement (IPS) and adopting an allocation approach towards the management of investment assets. Then it evaluates the different types of asset management vehicles that are most commonly used today. The chapter concludes by making the case for using money management products to manage money.

Learning Objectives

By the end of this chapter, you should be able to:

- understand the importance of an IPS;
- describe what asset allocation is and the value of applying its principles to managing investment assets;
- describe regular rebalancing of investment portfolios;
- list the five-step process of proper portfolio management;
- understand the basics of the institutional approach;
- list the main types of money-managed products that are held today; and
- understand the argument for using money managers to manage products to hold client assets in.

INVESTMENT POLICY STATEMENT (IPS)

One way clients can take control over how they react to their investment portfolios going up and down is to create an investment policy statement (IPS). An IPS is a written document that articulates the client's overall investment goals and how those goals will be accomplished. It's designed to take the emotion out of investing and keep our clients on track, regardless of how the markets or the economy behave.

The main tenet behind an IPS is its focus on detail. The IPS should not be a general statement. The areas that must be contained within an IPS are the client's specific investment objectives, desired annual return, asset allocation, any tax management strategies, benchmarks, rebalancing methods and monitoring procedures.

The client's Trusted Advisor should work with his or her client to identify the client's investment goals, such as university, travel, retirement date and length, gifts to pass at death, charitable donations and a whole host of other things that the client identifies as being important to him or her.

Some questions that should be asked while drawing up the IPS are:

- How much should the client set aside in cash reserves?
- Will the client be making regular withdrawals for living expenses?
- Will the client need to make large lump-sum withdrawals from his or her investment portfolio in the future, and how will that be accommodated within the IPS?
- What role will taxes play in your client's investing strategy?
- Does your client want to crystallize tax losses in order to minimize taxable gains?
- Will your client be invested primarily in deferred income tax plans, such as Registered Retirement Savings Plans, Individual Pension Plans, Registered Education Savings Plans and Retirement Compensation Plans?
- What is your client's investment time horizon for each of his or her very specific goals?

All these factors need to be addressed and incorporated into the client's IPS. Once these questions and many more are answered by the client, only then can the Trusted Advisor and his or her client determine the necessary investment rate of return that will accomplish the client's goals.

Remember, a portfolio is not designed to simply make as much money as possible. It is designed to accomplish specific goals. That is where the IPS is able to restrain both clients and their advisors from overreaching or panicking. For example, if the IPS determines that earning 6% annually is sufficient enough to accomplish a client's goals, both the client and his or her Trusted Advisor will be less tempted to jump on the band wagon of a particular mutual fund or stock just because it might earn 500% (or, possibly, lose 100%).

As the client's primary advisor, you should be asking if the investment risk your client is willing to take matches his or her goals? For example, perhaps your client wants or needs a 7.5% real rate of return to accomplish his or her goals, but the client isn't willing to invest in anything other than Government of Canada Bonds. Historically, from January 1, 1926 through December 31, 2006, the compounded annual rates of return have been 12.4% for Small-cap Stocks, 11.2%, for Large-cap Stocks, 5.8% for Corporate Bonds and 5.3% for Government Bonds.

During that same period, inflation measured by the CPI was 3.1%. Thus, the compound annual rate of return net of inflation from January 1, 1926 through December 31, 2006 shows a truer story. A client's portfolio would have compounded annually after inflation 9.3% for Small-cap Stocks, 8.1% for Large-cap Stocks, 2.7% for Corporate Bonds and 2.2% for Government Bonds. This is not even taking into consideration how these returns would have been reduced by marginal tax rates. After inflation and a 38% marginal tax rate, a client's real rate of return on Government Bonds over this period would have yielded 0.18% compounded annually. That's it!

Faced with these realities, if this had been your client, he or she would have had to either adjust his or her goals or be willing to take greater risk in his or her investment portfolio to have achieved his or her goals.

The IPS Specifics

The client's IPS will identify what asset classes and investment vehicles are the most appropriate for his or her goals. What are the limits placed on the different asset classes of investments in the IPS? For example, the client's IPS might permit for maximums of 60% in stocks, maximums of 60% in fixed income and maximums of 100% cash in his or her portfolio. The client might want the IPS to specifically state that the portfolio will not invest in certain types of investments, such as tobacco or military companies.

Just the act of writing down these issues, factors and details forces your client to clearly think out his or her investment strategies and stay on course, versus going this way and that way, resulting in the client never really going anywhere because the client did not have any set plan. This is what happens with most clients and their money.

Just remember that the major problem with investing money in the year 2009 for most people is that they spend too much time looking at the day-to-day prices of their holdings and not enough time in allowing for true long-term growth. Having an investment policy statement helps the client stay the course and achieve his or her very important life and financial goals. Assisting a client create his or her very own IPS is one of the true values that the Trusted Advisor can provide for the client.

ASSET ALLOCATION

Here's a shocking story: a banker with Bear Stearns had 100% of his investment assets in Bear Stearns stock (a prestigious bank stock, no less). Bear Stearns stock was selling for $171 per share in the first week of January 2008. When a deal for JP Morgan to buy Bear Stearns was initially struck, it was for $2 per share. That is a loss of 98.8%, which is about as close as you can come to losing it all without actually doing so. Fortunately for Bear Stearns investors, it has come up a little since then, but still represents a tragic loss of capital to those who invested in the Bear.

It has only been eight years since Enron went bust and many of the 22,000 employees who "drank the cool-aid" and had all their retirement money in Enron stock lost it all. Everyone knows about the Enron debacle, even people who have never bought a stock in their lives. But did anyone learn the lesson of Enron? We don't mean the one about not cheating in the board room, but the one about safety in diversification or, to put it another popular way, "not putting all your eggs in one basket". Apparently, this investment banker didn't learn.

Why would someone do what is now obviously such a stupid thing? Well, if you had an investment that since 1985 had outperformed the S&P 500 Index and even beat Warren Buffet's Berkshire Hathaway Inc., would you be tempted to depart from prudence, give in to greed and overload into that investment? That was the story with Bear Stearns. It was a great ride up followed by a horrific crash, one of historic proportions.

There are less sinister reasons than the typical greed and fear cycle to explain why someone might concentrate his or her holdings in one company or one sector. In Canada, public accountants and other Trusted Advisors have been known to frequently make the unwittingly imprudent recommendation to clients. "Just buy the banks. They always do well and pay a good dividend." That has been largely true, but is it prudent advice? Could you be taking on an unrealized liability by making that kind of narrow off-the-cuff recommendation? Is it prudent? Investment prudence begins with an understanding of how the capital markets work.

Markets Work: Academic research makes it clear that financial markets around the world are essentially efficient, that is, all public information that can be known about a stock is known by market participants, and stocks are priced accordingly, that is, the price is essentially always correct. The implication of the Efficient Markets Theory is that it is a futile effort to try to pick stocks or time the markets in order to "beat the market". It can't be argued about whether or not the markets are perfectly efficient; they probably aren't. However, the question for an investor is: "Is there enough inefficiency in the market so I can profit from it?" All academically sound studies have answered this question with a resounding "No!"

Risk and Reward Are Related: Most people understand this at its most fundamental level; in order to have more reward, you must take more risk. In other words, risk is rewarded — but not all risk. Bear Stearns is but the latest example.

Asset allocation means that as an investor, an individual allocates proportions of his or her liquid assets within his or her portfolio into different asset classes. In asset allocation, an individual or, in our case, an investment portfolio can be in one or a combination of three main categories:

(1) equities — ownership in companies;

(2) fixed income — money invested in GICs, bonds and mortgages; or

(3) cash — that is money invested in T-bills and in chequing and savings accounts.

Studies have shown that asset allocation is the single greatest determinant of investment performance. It has been shown that approximately 91% of the total long-term return of an investment portfolio is due to the asset allocation.

Unaware of this, many people blindly sink money into this or that investment without ever formulating an asset allocation model that is in sync with their financial goals and investment personality.

Once a client's investment objective for his or her portfolio has been determined, a Trusted Advisor helps the client formulate an investment policy statement for his or her portfolio. As current markets have proven, it is wise to allocate current and future investment assets in a well-balanced portfolio that includes equities, fixed income and cash. Designing this type of portfolio is like keeping your money in separate pockets and in a separate pair of pants.

All asset classes move in cycles, and each asset class has its own cycle. Typically, when one or two asset classes are performing well, the other asset classes may not be performing as well. By having a well-defined asset allocation strategy in place, the financial ride is much smoother to achieve the capital requirements to deliver a clients financial objective.

Let's go through an example of asset allocation diversification and how this can work for the typical investor. Let's imagine a set of twins, Gwen and Joan. Both are 40 years of age.

Gwen invests $1 million in a 7% bond, which matures in 20 years. Joan also invests $1 million for 20 years but separates the money into five $200,000 investments. The first investment loses everything, the second earns nothing, the third earns 4%, the fourth earns 7%, and the fifth earns 15%. At age 60, Gwen's investment has grown to $3,869,700, while Joan, who has practised asset allocation, has grown her initial investment to $4,685,300. Joan's practice of asset allocation has yielded her an additional $815,600 over Gwen's strategy of placing all her money in one asset class. This is the true power of asset allocation.

Let's imagine that a client decided to put all of his or her assets into a technology portfolio at the end of the bull market of the 1990s. Then in the middle of 2000, the very foundations of the technology sector in the stock market began to crumble, free falling into negative territory. This client could now be hurting, even though nine years have passed; in addition, he or she might not be a client anymore. With asset allocation, it does not need to be this way.

History shows that equities (stocks) are more risky than fixed income (bonds). The value of a dollar in 1927 invested in large U.S. stocks was worth $3,286 by the end of 2007. That same dollar invested in U.S. Bonds was worth $76 by the end of 2007. During that 80-year period, there was much more volatility (risk) with stocks than with bonds. Also, if a person invested his or her $1 in small U.S. stocks instead of large U.S. stocks, that dollar would have become $16,643 instead of $3,286. Additionally, if one had only invested in large U.S. value stocks, that $1 would have become $14,517 instead of $3,286. Small stocks and value stocks were more volatile (risky) than the large U.S. stocks — and, they paid off with greater return.

Diversification

Portfolios that are structured to provide comprehensive asset class allocation both domestically and internationally have the advantage of only taking the risk of the market, not the individual business risk of a Bear Stearns or an Enron. Consequently, the diversified portfolio is "safer" and will outperform over time. Buying "the banks" is a limited strategy that leaves a tremendous amount of non-systematic risk in the portfolio. When there is a difficult time for financial stocks, banks get hit, even if they aren't the bad guys. They are part of the financial sector and will be affected by the sector as a whole.

Sector investing leaves the investor with inadequate diversification. Proper diversification requires the purchasing of multiple entire asset classes — small cap stocks (all of them), large cap stocks (all of them), international developed markets stocks (all of them) and emerging markets stocks (all of them). This will provide true diversification, eliminate non-systematic risk (the business risk of individual companies or sectors) and guarantee the investor the return of the capital markets. Now, that is prudent. Of course, depending on the circumstances and purposes of the investment portfolio, some short-term fixed income assets will be appropriate to reduce the systematic risk of the stock market further.

For example, consider the comparison between the Dow Jones U.S. Banks Index and the S&P 500 Index from February 7, 2003 to May 23, 2008, a little over five years. The S&P outperformed all along and was really a better place to be from early 2007 onwards.

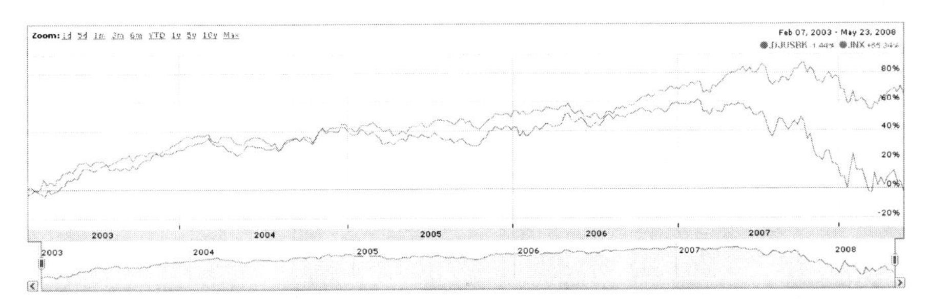

Chart from Google Finance May 23, 2008

Structure Determines Performance

Asset allocation explains most of the variation in portfolio returns. What is meant by asset allocation? This means how much of those large-cap stocks, small-cap stocks or bonds I will place in a portfolio. Actually, there are more well-defined dimensions of the market like large value stocks, small-value stocks, international value stocks, emerging market stocks, emerging market value stocks and emerging market small stocks, as well as various kinds of bond investments.

A fully diversified portfolio will have some amount of all of these "asset classes" in a proper recipe that maximizes return for a given level of risk. This is the essence of what is known as Modern Portfolio Theory. A good cook will have a good recipe that won't leave the cooking to *ad hoc* mixing of ingredients; likewise, a good investor will have an excellent investment plan that doesn't leave the choosing of investment vehicles to the vagaries of stock picking and market timing investment managers.

So, what are the lessons to be learned here?

1. Capital markets do work, but a limited number of holdings (as opposed to the complete asset class) are not required to (and frequently won't) reward you with capital market returns. You might just own a few Enrons and Bear Stearns (a bank, by the way), and for a while take a magic ride on the flying carpet, but you may eventually fall off the carpet from significant heights and find out that it hurts to fall from so high — *so diversify*!
2. Take only as much risk as you can afford to take, both emotionally and financially. Some people are emotionally risk takers, but their financial condition says they can't afford to take as much risk as their intestinal fortitude will allow. Even a diversified portfolio has risk and it should be appropriate for you.
3. If you don't know how to structure an investment portfolio in a scientific way, then hire a fee-for-service CFP® Practitioner or other qualified professional who can. What you spend in fees will probably be far less than what you would lose by trying to be a non-professional investment do-it-yourselfer. In all likelihood, you will come out far ahead over time by associating yourself with a truly qualified professional who acts in a fiduciary capacity on your behalf.

IPP: REGULAR REBALANCING OF PORTFOLIO

Along with asset allocation, regular rebalancing of an investment portfolio is an essential element of long-term investment success. Rebalancing is a fundamental part of the process of reaching a client's financial goals in the most effective way while lessening the overall instability of the total investment portfolio.

An example of how effective rebalancing can be is illustrated in a study conducted by T. Rowe Price of Baltimore, Maryland, a top investment manager. What T. Rowe Price did was construct two $10,000 model portfolios made up of 60% equity, 30% fixed income and 10% cash.

Using historical data spanning a 25-year period from the end of 1969 to September 1995, T. Rowe Price invested one portfolio using the original mix and never rebalanced at all.

The identical portfolio invested at the same time was rebalanced every three months to the original target allocation of 60% equity, 30% fixed income and 10% cash.

At the end of the 25-year and nine-month period, the rebalanced portfolio grew from $10,000 to about $145,000; the untouched portfolio grew to $141,000. By following a disciplined rebalancing asset allocation approach to investing, clients are joining the ranks of the world's greatest investors by buying low and selling high. You do this by constantly trimming the asset classes that have done well and replenishing the asset classes that have decreased in value.

From time to time, as clients' lives change, as do laws and economic conditions that regulate and govern our economy, it is very important to re-evaluate the asset allocation mix within our clients' portfolios and modify and help them modify their investment policy statements to reflect these changes.

What makes the asset allocation approach the approach for long-term investing is that it eases the turbulence that happens while investing, and empowers both the client and his or her Trusted Advisor to stay the course to achieve the desired outcome, that is, larger amounts of money to enable them to live the life of their choosing.

THE FIVE-STEP PROCESS TO PROPER PORTFOLIO MANAGEMENT

Step One

Determine the amount of equity and fixed income exposure that will be in the investment portfolio. This primarily depends on the client's goals, resources, time horizon and risk capacity and tolerance. Just as an example, many pension managers recommend a blend of 60% equities and 40% fixed income. This is referred to as a "60-40" balanced portfolio.

Step Two

Add asset classes to increase expected return and decrease volatility. Securities are grouped together according to similar risk and return characteristics called "asset classes". After establishing the equity-to-fixed income ratio, begin adding other asset classes for two reasons. Either they increase the expected return, or they help lower volatility. As mentioned in the previous chapter, there is a vast amount of research available today that demonstrates that portfolio returns over time are influenced by three primary factors:

- the amount invested in equities versus fixed income;
- the amount invested in large company stocks versus small company stocks; and
- the amount invested in growth companies versus value companies.

When it comes to diversification, the number of investments owned in a portfolio is not what is important. How effective these assets are diversified in the portfolio is what really matters. If most of the funds in a portfolio are invested in the large cap growth asset class, then the portfolio does not have proper diversification. These investments will probably move up and down together, not independent of each other.

Step Three

Adjust the portfolio for constraints. Once the "model" portfolio has been developed and agreed upon by the client, it is time to turn the attention to implementing the investment strategy. This step requires the reviewing of the portfolio for portfolio constraints to adjust asset weighing accordingly. A constraint may be a limitation of the percentage of one holding within the portfolio, a stock that the client just cannot part with, illiquid positions or regulatory restrictions. The model portfolio is then tweaked to accommodate these particular constraints.

Step Four

Choose the correct investment vehicle for each asset class. The final step of implementation is selecting the best investment(s) for each asset class. For diversification and better risk/reward ratios, experts generally prefer institution-managed money products.

Step Five

Review, monitor and adjust. Investment portfolio management is not something that is set once and forgotten about. Markets change everyday, and so do our clients' needs and goals. A portfolio needs to be frequently reviewed, monitored and, if needed, adjusted to restore the portfolio to its desired asset allocation. This could be the most important step of all.

INSTITUTIONAL APPROACH

Institutions managing investment assets have long out-performed the average investor for a variety of reasons as shown below.

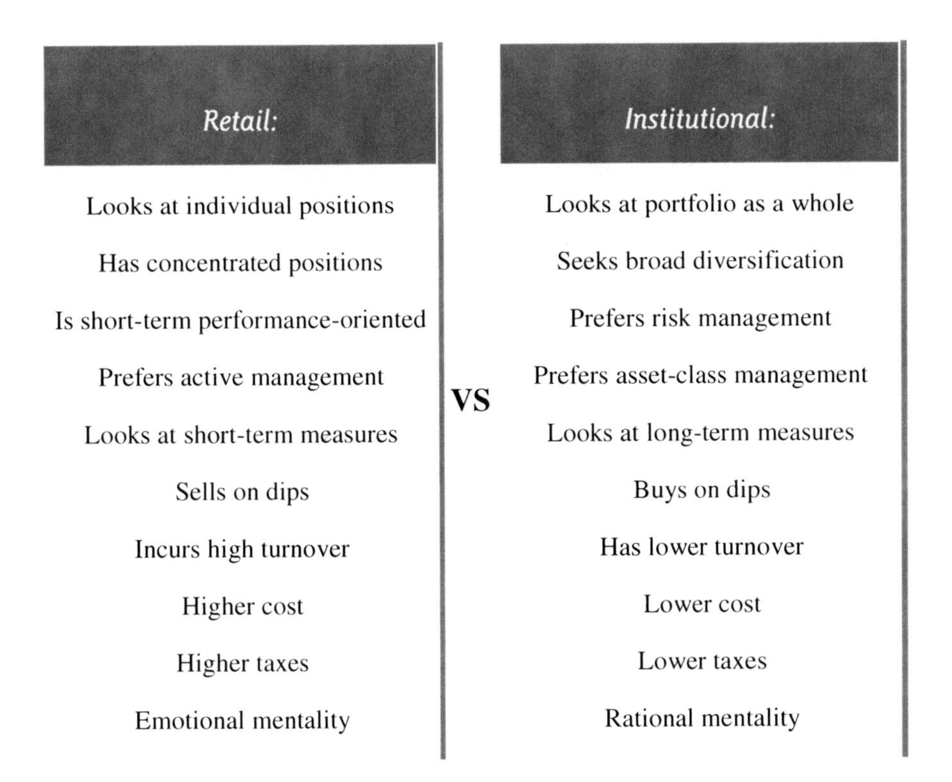

Retail:		Institutional:
Looks at individual positions		Looks at portfolio as a whole
Has concentrated positions		Seeks broad diversification
Is short-term performance-oriented		Prefers risk management
Prefers active management	VS	Prefers asset-class management
Looks at short-term measures		Looks at long-term measures
Sells on dips		Buys on dips
Incurs high turnover		Has lower turnover
Higher cost		Lower cost
Higher taxes		Lower taxes
Emotional mentality		Rational mentality

Chart above provided by Capital Financial Advisors, LLC of La Jolla, California.

There are several sound types of investment management vehicles that an investment manager operating under the direction of a client can use. These are as follows:

- Investment assets could be invested in pooled funds. The fees are much lower than mutual funds and they can all be written off.
- Assets can be invested in pension funds; with these types of investments either for government registered or non registered assets.
- Assets can be invested in either mutual funds or insurance segregated funds.
- Lastly, assets can be invested in a discretionary investment account where the investment manager will choose the types of holdings placed in the IPP fund portfolio.

Overall, the best strategy for managing assets is to have designed a well-balanced portfolio that meets the client's present and future income benefit needs. The Trusted Advisor will help clients monitor and review this strategy regularly.

THE CASE FOR MONEY MANAGEMENT

Many people in the media have objected to managed money products because they say it adds another layer of people who charge fees.

Successful investors like Warren Buffett believe markets are not always efficient. According to pundits of the efficient market theory, the price of a stock reflects a company's true underlining value. Those that believe in the efficient market theory believe that no single entity can affect the prices of stocks or bonds.

In reality, the managers of Canada's largest money management firms, mutual fund companies and pension management firms can buy a significant percentage of a Canadian company's stock, causing the price of that stock to go up, as other buyers follow in the wake of these mutual fund companies' and pension management firms' purchases.

Those who buy Canadian shares from full service or discount brokerages usually have no idea when the buying began.

So what are mutual funds, money managed accounts and pool funds anyway? They are a collective of sorts, where people have pooled their financial resources together, under one roof, and hired the same professional management.

These managers claim that an individual investor may be able to buy the same stocks cheaper on his or her own, but he or she would not have bought the same stocks at the same time with the same knowledge.

If markets were perfectly efficient, and research did not make a difference, then relative fund performance would be based on chance.

If it were that easy to make money from investing in stocks, individual investors would only need to watch business news programs. But information in an efficient market is disseminated randomly.

From experience, it can be argued that although information may be random at its outset, its development is sequential. Stories have a beginning, middle and end. Sometimes hearing the news and acting on it first provides an advantage.

Sometimes having the wisdom not to react will prove more successful. Sometimes it helps to know the people releasing the information in the first place.

Wisdom comes from making mistakes and then learning from those mistakes. These lessons can be expensive, especially for someone using his or her own money, such as a hobbyist.

Money managers are people, like you and me. Maybe they are no smarter than anyone else, but they have the time and money to find that garage in Richmond Hill, Ontario's Silicon Valley North, where two recent grads from Waterloo University are working on the next Internet breakthrough.

Pension and money management managers are more likely to find out which companies in India or China will grow and which national government is about to fall. Efficient markets require that access to information be, if not free, at least equal.

Fund managers claim that their information is not random, but the result of well-developed methodologies and access to information, which, although public enough to avoid security violations, is too fresh to be widely disseminated.

In the Canadian Securities Course text (note that every registered Investment Dealer Association stockbroker is required to take the Canadian Securities Course before he or she can become licensed), it states that for a portfolio to be well diversified, it would need to hold between 15 to 30 stocks to avoid a single company's risk, that is, the risk that a company's management team might do something stupid.

Some people can afford the time and the money to design their own portfolios. Owning this many companies in a portfolio requires multiple costs for transactions and time for tracking, following and measuring performance. This all leads us back to the initial question.

If someone believes in perfectly efficient markets, that there is no truth to the herd mentality, that research does not matter and that there is no value in delegating his or her investing, then there is no reason for these individuals to buy money management products.

The financial industry has gone through a fundamental change from being transaction based — buying and selling — to one focused on fees and the gathering of assets. By placing clients into money-managed products, Trusted Advisors will be able to focus on providing solutions to solve clients' very real needs instead of getting caught up in the day-to-day administration of choosing what stock or bond to buy or sell.

Over the years, the best criteria for picking an excellent money manager to run a client's portfolio are as follows:

- Make sure that the money manager has done better than the average of the money manager's peers for a meaningful period of time, say ten years.
- Make sure that the money manager has been running money for a while and has some combat experience, meaning managing money in both the boom years of the late 1990s and the bust years of the early part of the 21st century.

- Make sure that the money manager is a long-term investor. The money manager should be an owner of stocks and bonds. The money manager should not rent them.

You and your clients can have a pleasant investment experience over time if you follow academically sound principles of investments whether you do it yourself or hire a professional with a good cook book.

CHAPTER 30

THE "SAFE HARBOUR" FOR PRUDENT FIDUCIARY INVESTING — HOW YOU CAN PROTECT THE TRUSTEES YOU ADVISE FROM UNNECESSARY RISKS, COSTS AND TAXES WHILE EARNING CAPITAL MARKET RETURNS

Charles Stanley

Overview

After a careful reading of the pertinent legal documents and their commentaries,[1] one concludes that a strategy of investing in pure passive low cost asset class funds, including Index Funds and Exchange Traded Funds (ETFs), is the safe harbour or default standard for fiduciary trust investing. Active investment strategies increase costs, risks and taxes over the comparable passive asset class strategies. While active strategies are permitted, a trustee who decides to incorporate active strategies should be able to objectively justify why he or she is accepting greater risk, greater costs and greater taxes for the trust by employing these active investment strategies.

Learning Objectives

By the end of this chapter, you should be able to:

---

[1] The pertinent documents in California include the California *Uniform Prudent Investor Act* (UPIA) and the American Law Institute's Restatement [Third] of Trusts. The Ontario documents include the Ontario *Trustee Act*.

- know the similarities and differences in the legal framework for prudent investing strategies for trustees in Canada and the United States (specifically Ontario and California);
- know that there is a "safe harbour" investment strategy for trustees that incorporates two key provisions:
  a. required diversification and its purposes:
     i. to eliminate non-systematic risk,
     ii. to create efficient portfolios, and
  b. pay only costs that are reasonable and appropriate to the trust and the strategies implemented; and
- inform the trustees you advise about these key concepts to help them avoid liability in their oversight of their investment portfolios.

PURPOSE

Fiduciary liability is a growing concern. Our purpose is to demonstrate that in both Canada and the United States, low cost passive asset class or "index" investing is the safe harbour or default standard for fiduciary trust investing, and any departure to active investment strategies that increase risk and costs, while allowable, should be demonstrably justified. We will compare and contrast the legal framework for fiduciary trust investing between California and Ontario, since these are the two communities most affected by cross-border concerns between Canada and the United States. (Most Canadians immigrating to the United States move to California, Arizona or Florida. Both California and Arizona are community property states, and trusts are drafted under state law. None of these distinctions between community property and common law change the principles of prudent investing addressed in this chapter. All three states have their form of the *Uniform Prudent Investor Act*.)

SIGNIFICANCE

Every California trustee and co-trustee is accountable to the *Uniform Prudent Investor* Act (UPIA). Every Ontario trustee is accountable to the Ontario *Trustee Act*. The importance of the UPIA is emphasized by the fact that it is placed under "Duties of Trustee" in the California Probate Code, and failure to follow the UPIA constitutes a breach of trust for which a trustee is liable to be removed and liable for damages. This is especially significant for attorneys, accountants, trust officers and private fiduciaries who act as trustees, since they are held to the standard of professional trustees rather than non-professional trustees. Since the trustee is liable for failure to follow the Act, it is assumed to be malpractice for an attorney or CA to fail to advise the trustee of his or her responsibility under the Act. The principles of prudent investing incorporated in the UPIA are applicable to all fiduciary investing, whether under the typical family trust arrangement, charitable funds or any other trust format.

DEFAULT LAW

Default law means that the provisions of the law will apply if the provisions of the trust don't spell out a different provision. It appears that the Ontario *Trustee Act* puts more emphasis on the sufficiency of the trust language[2] than is the case in California or the United States in general. While both jurisdictions have similar language in law, the courts in the United States have tended to give more weight to the requirements of the UPIA in the absence of very strong language in the trust overriding the language of the statute. In particular, this has applied to the requirement to diversify assets. There are a few cases in which trustors authorized the trustees to retain either Kodak or IBM stock and not diversify the position. Without going into the detail of these cases, the end result is that if a trustor truly wants to have a future trustee retain an asset, then that trustee would be well advised to use very specific and demanding language that essentially forbids the trustee to diversify from that position. Otherwise, if it would be deemed prudent to diversify from that single position, the courts will most likely side with diversification. It would appear to me that this would be more likely in the United States than in Canada, but any Canadian would do well to take this under advisement.

ACTIVE VERSUS PASSIVE INVESTING — DEFINING ACTIVE AND PASSIVE INVESTMENT MANAGEMENT

Active management is the traditional way of building a stock portfolio, and always incorporates some form of stock picking and/or market timing. Regardless of their individual approach, all active managers share a common thread: they buy and sell securities selectively, based on some forecast of future events. This is the form of investment strategy you hear or read about almost exclusively in the financial press/media

---

[2] Ontario *Trustee Act*, R.S.O. 1990, c. T.23, s. 68; California UPIA §16046(b).

and is practised by the vast majority of professional investors (stock brokers and investment advisors whether retail or institutional).

Passive or index managers or equilibrium-based investors (similar but distinct approaches to passive investing) make no forecasts of the stock market or the economy, and no effort to distinguish "attractive" from "unattractive" securities. Their goal is to hold virtually all of an asset class or dimension of the market. For example, they will often construct their portfolios to closely approximate the performance of well-recognized market benchmarks such as the Standard & Poor's 500 index (large U.S. companies) — Canada's version would be the TSX — Russell 2000 index (small U.S. companies) or Morgan Stanley EAFE index (large international companies).

There is an ongoing debate that argues whether it is "better" (meaning who will outperform) to invest with passive or active investment strategies. This chapter is not one of those. While we will comment on that question, the premise is not whether one is "better" than the other, but, rather, how a trustee establishes an investment policy which most nearly fits with the criteria of prudence delineated by the UPIA and the Restatement [Third] of Trusts, including the commentary in California and the *Trustee Act* in Ontario.

THE TRUSTEE'S DUTY TO DIVERSIFY

California UPIA § 16048: Duty to Diversify Investments

> 16048. In making and implementing investment decisions, the trustee has a duty to diversify the investments of the trust unless, under the circumstances, it is prudent not to do so.[3]

The Prefatory Note to the (Uniform Prudent Investor) Act (as promulgated by the National Conference of Commissioners on Uniform State laws) states that the Act "draws upon" the Restatement [(Third) of Trusts] ("Restatement"), while the Reporter for the Act notes that the Act "codif[ies]" the Restatement. A commentator observes: "[The Act's] tie to the Restatement is significant, because it is the Restatement that provides numerous examples of prudent and imprudent investing, as well

---

[3] California Probate Code, Part 4, Article 2.5. Section 27(6) of the Ontario *Trustee Act* provides:

> (6) A trustee *must* diversify the investment of trust property to an extent that is appropriate to,
>
> (a) the requirements of the trust; and
>
> (b) general economic and investment market conditions.

as providing the underlying rationale of the rules that are now part of the [Act]."[4]

In California, a great deal of investing by trustees of personal trusts, even when done in conjunction with professional investment advisors and stock brokers, is done without being informed by the law and the commentary around it.

The purpose of diversification is twofold: first, it is to eliminate, or at least substantially reduce, uncompensated or non-systematic risk. This is a basic tenet of Modern Portfolio Theory. The commentary to the Restatement says:

> In understanding a trustee's duties with respect to the management of risk, it is useful to distinguish between diversifiable (or "uncompensated") risk and market (or non-diversifiable) risk that is, in effect, compensated through pricing in the marketplace. *The distinction is useful in considering fiduciary responsibilities both in setting risk-level objectives and in diversification of the trust portfolio.*
>
> In the absence of contrary statute or trust provision, the requirement of caution ordinarily imposes a duty to use reasonable care and skill in an effort to minimize or at least reduce diversifiable risks. ... these are risks that can be reduced through proper diversification of a portfolio. *Because market pricing cannot be expected to recognize and reward a particular investor's failure to diversify, a trustee's acceptance of this type of risk cannot, without more* [*i.e.*, a rational examination of the portfolio's risk], *be justified on grounds of enhancing expected return.* What has come to be called "modern portfolio theory" offers an instructive conceptual framework for understanding and attempting to cope with non-market risk. The trustee's normal duty to diversify in a reasonable manner, however, is not derived from or legally defined by the principles of any particular theory. See Reporter's General Note on Comments e through h for discussions of asset pricing, types of risk, and the advantages of diversification.
>
> Another aspect of risk management deals with market risk, often called "systemic" or "systematic" risk, or more descriptively for present purposes, simply non-diversifiable or compensated risk. The trustee's duties and objectives with respect to this second category of risk are not as distinct as those with respect to diversifiable risk. They involve quite subjective judgments that are essentially unavoidable in the process of asset management, addressing the appropriate degree of risk to be undertaken in pursuit of a higher or lower level of expected return from the trust portfolio. In this respect the trustee must take account of the element of conservatism that is ordinarily implicit in the prudent investor rule's duty of caution. *Opportunities for gain, however, normally bear a direct relationship to the degree of compensated risk.* Thus, although an inferred, general duty to invest conservatively is a traditional and accepted feature of

---

[4] W. Scott Simon, *The Uniform Prudent Investor Act: A Guide to Understanding* (Camarillo, CA: Namborn Publishing 2002) at 3.

> trust law, that duty is necessarily imprecise in its requirements and is applied with considerable flexibility.[5] [author's emphasis]

The first purpose of diversification then is to eliminate uncompensated or non-systematic risk to the extent possible. Compensated or systematic risk is the risk of the market, a risk that one cannot reduce or eliminate by diversification. It is clear in modern investing that there is no investment that is free of risk. The UPIA and the *Trustee Act* call for an investment portfolio that is risk-efficient, that is, the portfolio only takes risk for which it will be compensated and where the risk is appropriate for the trust.

PASSIVE INVESTING AND COMPENSATED RISK

Passive investment strategies involve purchasing virtually all the securities in the relevant segment or dimension of the market. For example, if the relevant segment of the market is the S&P 500 Index, a passive investor will hold all 500 stocks in the same approximate weight as the market and will only change them when the index is changed. In the case of international stocks in the mature markets, one would buy virtually all of the stocks in the MSCI EAFE Index (Europe, Australasia and the Far East). These relevant indices represent "the market" we are investing in. If I hold the entire universe of securities in "the market", by definition I am taking only the market risk — no more and no less. As soon as I decide that I will employ an active strategy and only pick what I believe to be securities with the greatest short-term promise (short term meaning until I decide that they no longer hold superior promise), I reduce diversification and take on a greater risk that I will not perform as the market performs, both in terms of volatility and returns. I now have what is termed in the Restatement Comments in Section 227 "uncompensated" risk. My choice of securities that is less than "the market" will either outperform or underperform and will have either more or less volatility as defined by standard deviation. *All Active strategies, by definition, take on uncompensated risk.* Failure to diversify on a reasonable basis in order to reduce uncompensated risk is ordinarily a violation of both the duty of caution and the duties of care and skill.[6]

The second purpose of diversification is to create "efficient" portfolios. Modern Portfolio Theory was developed from the Nobel Prize winning work of Harry Markowitz. Among other things, it has taught us

---

[5] Section 227 of Restatement of Law [Third] Trust, Comment e.

[6] *Ibid.*

about the significance of asset allocation.[7] Proper asset allocation allows us to create investment portfolios that are deemed "efficient", that is, they are designed to provide the greatest return for a given amount of risk. The creation of portfolio models under this theory assumes asset classes (as represented by indices like the S&P 500, the MSCI EAFE, *etc.*) made up of compensated risk only. The introduction of uncompensated risk dilutes the reliability of an asset allocation model. The degree to which risk is being controlled is called into question.

PASSIVE STRATEGIES AND INVESTMENT COSTS

California UPIA § 16050: Costs and Expenses

> 16050. In investing and managing trust assets, a trustee may only incur costs that are appropriate and reasonable in relation to the assets, overall investment strategy, purposes and other circumstances of the trust.[8]

With all investment strategies there are costs. These costs include commissions, advisor fees, transaction fees, mutual fund internal expense ratios, research costs, bid/ask spreads and market impact costs. Passive investment strategies cost less than active strategies.

Internal Expense Ratios (IER) in the United States and Management Expense Ratio (MER) in Canada

All mutual funds have an internal expense ratio that represents the cost of the fund doing business and making a profit. Most actively managed funds in the United States include in the IER a fee known as a 12b1 fee that was authorized by the SEC to fund marketing efforts of no load

---

[7] Gary P. Brinson, L. Randolf Hood, and Gilbert L. Beebower, "Determinants of Portfolio Performance" (1986) 42 *Financial Analysts Journal* 39 and again Gary P. Brinson, Brian D. Singer and Gilbert L. Beebower, "Determinants of Portfolio Performance II: An Update" (1991) 47 *Financial Analyst Journal* 44 and again William E. O'Rielly and James L Chandler, Jr., "Asset Allocation Revisited" (2003) 13 *Journal of Financial Planning* 94 all indicate that in excess of 90% of an investment portfolio's variability of returns is determined by the Asset Allocation.

[8] California Probate Code Article 2.5. Section 27 of the Ontario *Trustee Act* provides:

> 23.1 (1) A trustee who is of the opinion that an expense would be properly incurred in carrying out the trust may,
>
> (a) pay the expense directly from the trust property; or
>
> (b) pay the expense personally and recover a corresponding amount from the trust property.
>
> (2) The Superior Court of Justice may afterwards disallow the payment or recovery if it is of the opinion that the expense was not properly incurred in carrying out the trust.

mutual funds. The typical IER fee is around .25%; it can be more, and with "C" shares it is typically 1.00%. Most passively managed funds in the United States do not include a 12b1 fee, especially those that are designed for use in institutional settings. The IER of the average stock mutual fund according to leading investment research firm Morningstar is 1.51% compared to the MER of 2.51% in Canada.[9] The passively managed index funds at Vanguard, a client-owned investment management company, for example, average .22%. This gives the passively managed Vanguard portfolio a 1.29% advantage against U.S. funds and a 2.29% advantage against Canadian funds.

> The more rigorous academic studies [of internal expenses] find that expense ratios generally detract from fund performance. On average, fund managers are unable to recoup the expenses that funds pay via better performance. These findings suggest that basing fund investment decisions at least partially on fees is wise. Lower cost funds have a smaller drag on performance that active managers must overcome. Taken to their logical conclusion, these results may suggest that index funds, accompanied by the lowest expense ratios in the mutual fund industry, are a more logical long-run investment choice than more expensive actively-managed funds.[10]

This issue of cost is a greater problem for Canadian investors than for U.S. investors. The average Canadian MER is about 1% greater than the average U.S. IER. A small part of that cannot be avoided by more efficient management because it is attributable to the Goods and Services Tax (GST) at a 5% rate. Beyond that, there is a difference in the distribution systems between Canada and the United States. It seems to me that the use of low cost asset class funds is even more important in Canada than the United States due to the significant delta between the cost of actively and passively managed funds.

The following chart illustrates the long-term impact of fees on investment returns. For many trust-owned investments, this kind of long-term perspective is required.

---

[9] Larry MacDonald, "Keeping up with the Deep Thinkers", *Canadian Business Online* (May 29, 2003), online: <www.canadianbusiness.com>. See also Janet McFarland and Rob Carrick (with files from Keith Damsell), "The fee crunch: Not all investors get value for money", GlobeAdvisor.com (June 24, 2004), online: <www.globeadvisor.com>.

[10] Jason Karceski, Miles Livingston and Edward S. O'Neal, *Mutual Fund Brokerage Commissions*, a report commissioned by Zero Alpha Group (January 2004) at 2.

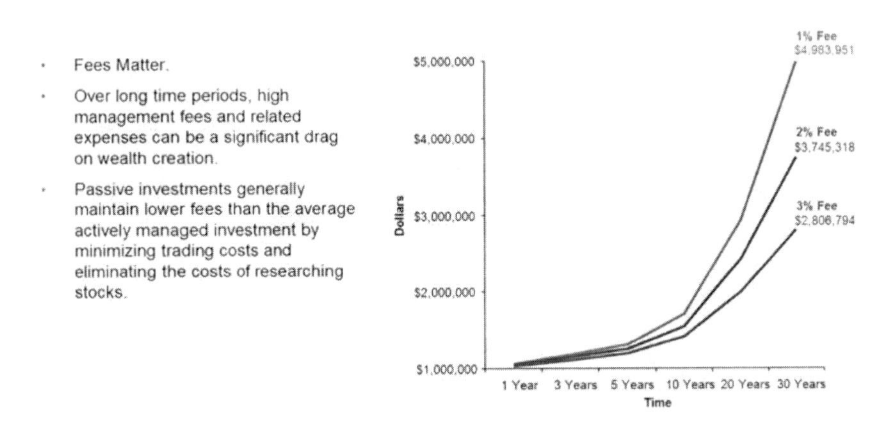
Fees Matter.
Over long time periods, high management fees and related expenses can be a significant drag on wealth creation.
Passive investments generally maintain lower fees than the average actively managed investment by minimizing trading costs and eliminating the costs of researching stocks.
Assumed 6.5% Annualized Return over 30 Years
1% Fee
$4,983,951
2% Fee
$3,745,318
3% Fee
$2,806,794
$5,000,000
$4,000,000
$3,000,000
$2,000,000
$1,000,000
Dollars
1 Year
3 Years
5 Years
10 Years
20 Years
30 Years
Time

Chart provided by Dimensional Fund Advisors (2000).

Turnover Ratio and Brokerage Costs

By definition, passively managed funds have a low turnover rate. It is the policy of passive funds to buy their universe of stocks and hold them until they no longer fit the specific universe the fund is to emulate. Actively managed funds, however, generally have significant turnover. Turnover creates brokerage commissions that are not reported in fund prospectuses. To find these costs, one must order a copy of the Statement of Additional Information (SAI) and then decipher it from what is often pooled reporting for the entire family of funds — a task that takes some amount of speculation.

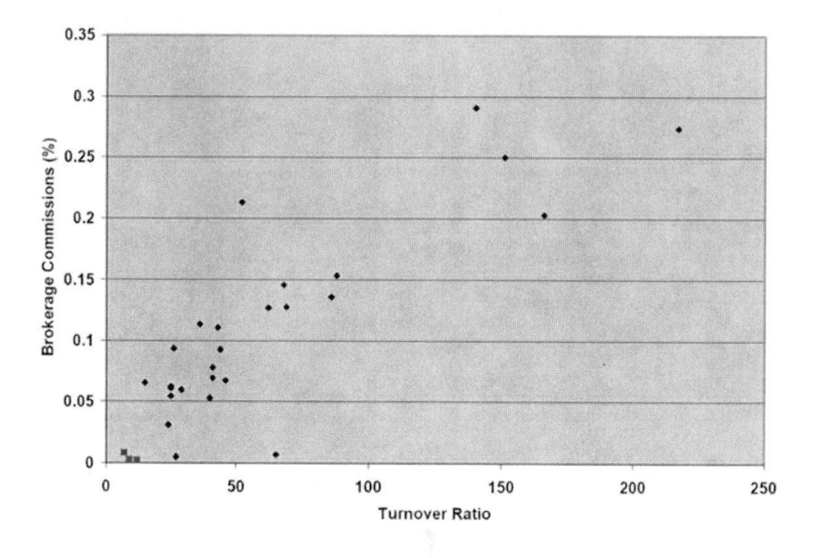

Exhibit 1: The relationship between brokerage commissions and turnover for the 30 largest retail domestic equity funds in 2001.

Source: Jason Karceski, Miles Livingston and Edward S. O'Neal, Mutual Fund Brokerage Commissions *(Zero Alpha Group, 2004).*

For 2001, Morningstar data shows that turnover for the average U.S. domestic equity fund was 106%. The average turnover for these largest 30 funds (in Exhibit 1) is 57% — half that of the average fund. There are 3 index funds in this sample of 30. If we separate these out, the average commission rate for the actively managed funds is 11.3 basis points [.113%]. This contrasts to an average of .45 basis points [.0045%] for the index funds (the three dots in the bottom left of the chart).

Bid/Ask Spread Cost

In addition to brokerage commissions, there is another implicit cost to investors created by the spread between the bid (sell price) and ask (buy price) for a stock. After explaining their methodology for deriving the "average" cost of the bid/ask spread, Karceski, Livingston and O'Neal concluded, "A fund with a turnover ratio of 100% would thus incur 36 basis points [.36%] per year in implicit trading costs."[11] Carrying the logic a step further, we can estimate that a comparable large passive portfolio such as the Vanguard Index 500 fund with a turnover ratio of

---

[11] *Ibid.* at 7.

5%[12] would incur implicit trading costs of 1.8 basis points [.018%] per year, a reduction of 2000%.

Market Impact Cost

An additional implicit cost is incurred when a mutual fund, as a large investor, actually moves the prices of the stocks in which it transacts. If a fund wishes to sell a very large amount of a stock, this significant selling pressure may actually reduce the price at which the fund is able to sell the stock (which is obviously bad for the fund). This change in the stock price driven by large trades is called market impact.[13]

Academic researchers have suggested that commissions represent less than half of the total cost of trading for institutional investors. Therefore, while commissions represent a quarter of a point per year for the average fund, total trading costs likely surpass a half of a percentage point for the average fund.[14] These are costs that are not disclosed in the prospectus or in any commercially available investment database. Karceski, Livingston and O'Neal have called for the disclosure of at least the brokerage costs of mutual funds to be disclosed in their prospectuses.

Exhibit 2, below, portrays the more complete picture of costs in four of the largest mutual funds in the Morningstar U.S. database. Exhibit 3, below, portrays four high turnover funds and the undisclosed costs which significantly outstrip the disclosed IER. As you can see, the disclosed PBHG large-cap IER understates the true costs by approximately 740%.

---

[12] Morningstar Premier online service (March 19, 2007) <http://quicktake.morningstar.com/fundnet/Snapshot.aspx?Country=USA&Symbol=VFINX>.

[13] Jason Karceski, Miles Livingston and Edward S. O'Neil, *Mutual Fund Brokerage Commissions*, a report commissioned by Zero Alpha Group (January 2004) at 3.

[14] *Ibid.* at 6-7.

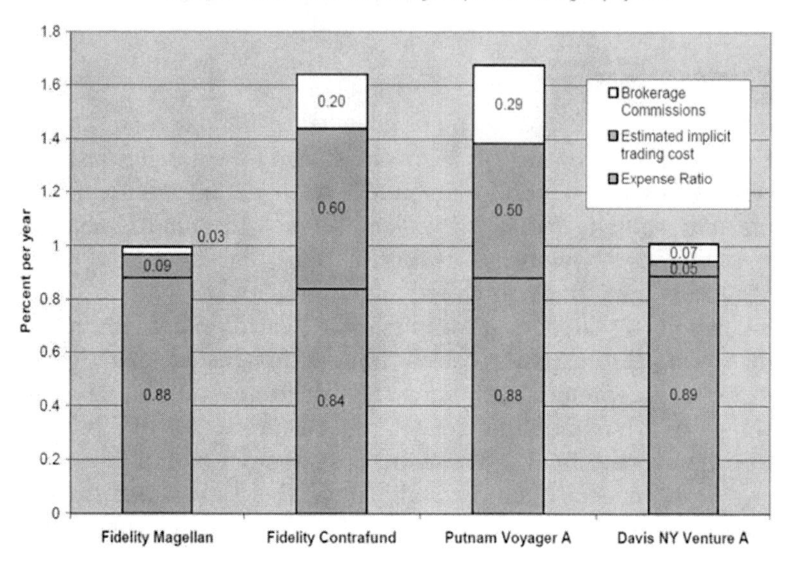

Source: Jason Karceski, Miles Livingston and Edward S. O'Neal, Mutual Fund Brokerage Commissions *(Zero Alpha Group, 2004).*

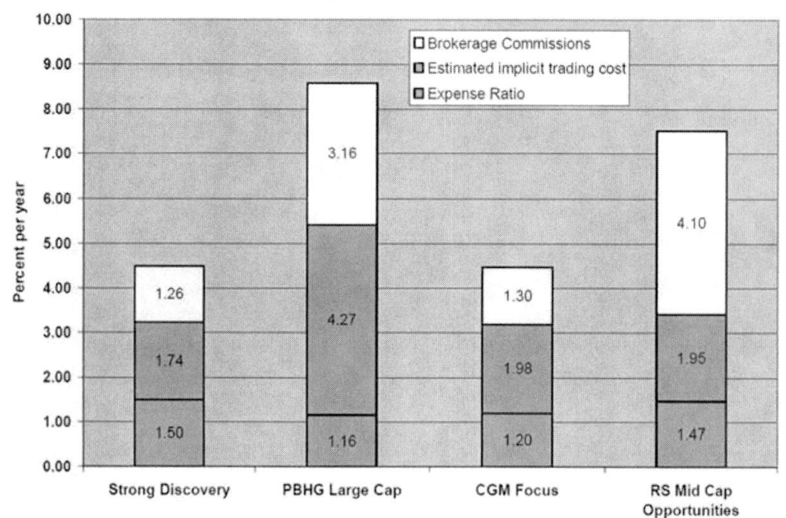

Source: Jason Karceski, Miles Livingston and Edward S. O'Neal, Mutual Fund Brokerage Commissions *(Zero Alpha Group, 2004).*

If we apply the same methodology to the Vanguard 500 Index Fund as was applied in the above actively managed scenarios, we find that the IER is .18%, brokerage commissions are .0045% and the implicit trading costs from the bid/ask spread are .018%, for a total of .2025% compared to 8.59% for the PBHG large-cap fund.

In all fairness and in the interest of full disclosure, Karceski, Livingston and O'Neal state:

> We have some reservations about the use of this data to draw over-arching conclusions. First, it appears as though the data is subject to errors. Although we delete outliers, there may still be errors in this data. It is also possible that some of the observations we delete are, in fact, valid. Second, we are forced to allocate commissions across the funds in a registrant [Fund Family]. The ad hoc measures we construct are the best we can do with the data we have.[15]

This study is one of the few attempts by academics to determine the impact of these investing costs and was handled with the best of efforts to arrive at reliable analysis, so, while acknowledging the possibility of error, at the same time I believe the conclusions are reasonable and valuable in the measurement of the relative cost impacts between active and passive investing strategies. When a trustee makes good fiduciary decisions regarding investment strategy, this allows the trustee to observe the relative value in the use of low cost passively managed asset class funds as compared to the various actively managed alternatives.

PASSIVE MANAGEMENT OUTPERFORMS ACTIVE MANAGEMENT OVER TIME

> If "active" and "passive" management styles are defined in sensible ways, it *must* be the case that:
>
> (1) before costs, the return on the average actively managed dollar will equal the return on the average passively managed dollar and
>
> (2) after costs, the return on the average actively managed dollar will be less than the return on the average passively managed dollar.
>
> These assertions will hold for *any* time period. Moreover, they depend *only* on the laws of addition, subtraction, multiplication and division. Nothing else is required.
>
> . . .
>
> To repeat: Properly measured, the average actively managed dollar must underperform the average passively managed dollar, net of costs. Empirical analyses that appear to refute this principle are guilty of improper measurement.[16]

---

[15] *Ibid.* at 7.

[16] William F. Sharpe, "The Arithmetic of Active Management" (1991) 47 *The Financial Analyst's Journal* 7.

Many people would think this is an outrageous statement except for the fact that it comes from one of the leading financial academics in the United States, William F. Sharpe, winner of the Nobel Prize in Economics in 1990 and the Stanco 25 Professor of Finance, Emeritus at Stanford University.

Of course, averages are made up of all data points. In this case, it includes some actively managed funds that potentially outperformed the passive fund along with those that underperformed. Random statistical expectations tell us that some fund managers will outperform the market in any given year. They also tell us that it will probably not be the same active manager consistently outperforming year after year. Studies of manager performance have supported this position.[17]

JUSTIFYING ACTIVE STRATEGIES VERSUS PASSIVE STRATEGIES

The Restatement Commentary, below, warns trustees about the perils often associated with active investing. These include the greater risks, and higher costs and taxes of stock picking and market timing.

> Active strategies, however, entail investigation and analysis expenses and tend to increase general transaction costs, including capital gains taxation. Additional risks also may result from the difficult judgments that may be involved and from the possible acceptance of a relatively high degree of diversifiable risk. These considerations are relevant to the trustee initially in deciding whether, to what extent, and in what manner to undertake an active investment strategy and then in the process of implementing any such decisions.
>
> If the extra costs and risks of an investment program are substantial, these added costs and risks must be justified by realistically evaluated return expectations. Accordingly, a decision to proceed with such a program involves judgments by the trustee that:
>
> a) gains from the course of action in question can reasonably be expected to compensate for its additional costs and risks;
>
> b) the course of action to be undertaken is reasonable in terms of its economic rationale and its role within the trust portfolio; and
>
> c) there is a credible basis for concluding that the trustee — or the manager of a particular activity — possesses or has access to the competence necessary to carry out the program and, when delegation is involved, that its terms and supervision are appropriate.[18]

---

[17] Mark Carhart, "On Persistence in Mutual Fund Performance" (1997) 52 *Journal of Finance* 57.

[18] Restatement §227, Paragraph h.

This Commentary suggests that the trustee meet a two-part test to determine the prudence of implementing an active investment strategy. This two-part test asks:

(1) Are the extra costs, taxes and risks of the proposed strategy "substantial"?

(2) If they are, can they be "justified by realistically evaluated return expectations?"

Consequently, the trustee who conducts this test should consider whether:

1. the proposed investment strategy's gains can reasonably be expected to overcome its additional costs and risks;
2. the strategy is suitable to the risk/return profile of the trust portfolio and the facts and circumstances of the trust or its beneficiaries; and
3. the trustee (or its agent) has the requisite competence to carry out and monitor the strategy.

The Commentator suggests that it is very difficult to "beat the market" through any means of active investment management. The objective of using an active rather than a passive investment strategy is to beat the returns a passive (market) investment strategy would provide.

> Economic evidence shows that, from a typical investment perspective, the major capital markets of this country are highly efficient, in the sense that available information is rapidly digested and reflected in the market prices of securities. As a result, fiduciaries and other investors are confronted with potent evidence that the application of expertise, investigation, and diligence in efforts to "beat the market" in these publicly traded securities ordinarily promises little or no payoff, or even a negative payoff after taking account of research and transaction costs. Empirical research supporting the theory of efficient markets reveals that in such markets skilled professionals have rarely been able to identify under-priced securities (that is, to outguess the market with respect to future return) with any regularity. In fact, evidence shows that there is little correlation between fund managers' earlier successes and their ability to produce above-market returns in subsequent periods.[19]

The test for deciding whether to use an active strategy initially requires an estimate of expected returns. How does one reasonably determine that the active strategy will exceed the future return of the market benchmark and therefore outperform the passive strategy?

---

[19] Restatement §227, General Note on Comments e through h: Introduction to Portfolio Theory and Other Investment Concepts.

Track Record Selection

The most common method, although warned against constantly, is what I will call the "track record" method. What has the track record of this manager/strategy been in the past? The first and glaring problem with this approach is the warning found on every mutual fund prospectus in the country: "Past performance is no guarantee of future results." Second, evaluating past performance is always a matter of "how you slice the pie", or how you determine the time frame for the sample of past performance. A track record can be tremendously different if the time frame is changed by as little as one quarter.

Outstanding track records always represent greater risk than the market because, by definition, the stock picking that selected less than all the market stocks in question is underdiversified relative to that market.

Lastly, track records don't account for taxes or commission loads.

> For example, Fidelity Magellan generated an average annual pre-tax return of 18.3% over the ten year period from mid-1985 to mid-1995. But once the reality of taxes (and commission loads) is taken into account, the after-tax return drops to 12.7%. This turns a track record that seemingly widely outperformed the market into one that came close to underperforming it.[20]

Skillful Manager Selection

The other method of manager selection is to attempt to find "skillful" money managers separate from their track record. There are now many independent consultants and institutions dedicated to identifying these most skillful or "Best of Class" money managers. These include companies like Frank Russell Company, Callan Associates, Wilshire Associates and SEI Investments. The criteria will include things like:

1. the money manager's investment philosophy and style;
2. their discipline in making buy/sell decisions;
3. the consistency of the application of their process and the stability of their personnel; and
4. while it is not specifically listed as a component, the manager's performance track record, as it is inevitably a significant part of this analysis.

While this is all admirable and undoubtedly an honest effort,

> A [Frank] Russell [Company] analyst notes, "If I have to base future expectations, I want to base it on skill as opposed to identification of good per-

---

[20] W. Scott Simon, *The Uniform Prudent Investor Act: A Guide to Understanding* (Camarillo, CA: Namborn Publishing, 2002) at 113.

formance." But this reasoning, like that used to justify track record investing, may have some flaws. Russell's own studies indicate that it takes a long time to identify skill statistically. In fact, a money manager must have a track record of at least 15 years — and sometimes as much as 80 years or even longer — before it's even possible to eliminate sheer luck as the source of the manager's superior performance. Even when a manager is found to be skillful statistically (based on the track record of past performance), that's no indication that it will be skillful in the future.[21]

It is, therefore, difficult to establish reasonably that an active strategy is a superior choice to a low cost passive strategy. W. Scott Simon identified five specific reasons to consider low cost passive investing as the safe harbour or default standard for prudent fiduciary investing:

1. First, the zero sum nature of financial markets means that all passively managed money invested in a particular market will earn the market return.
2. Second, the costs and taxes associated with passive investing are relatively lower.
3. Third, passive funds are broadly diversified so they are relatively lower risk.
4. Fourth, passive funds don't experience style drift.
5. Fifth, passive funds aren't subject to "manager risk" like active investment products.[22]

THE ROLE OF THE FINANCIAL ADVISOR

One might conclude from the foregoing that the cost of an Investment Advisor is an unnecessary burden on the trust. That is a naïve and costly conclusion. So, what is the role of the Investment Advisor under this regime and why are the advisor's fees appropriate?

First, The California UPIA and the Ontario *Trustee Act* are predicated on the dominance of the Noble prize winning Modern Portfolio Theory. These Acts and others like them around the world have codified Modern Portfolio Theory as appropriate for fiduciary investing. To meet the requirements of the applicable statutes, one must be able to implement Modern Portfolio Theory. Most non-professional investors do not have the capacity to do so. As one who advises trustees, you should be recommending that they hire a professional capable of implementing Modern Portfolio Theory and the other criteria of the applicable statutes.

---

[21] *Ibid.* at 114.
[22] *Ibid.* at 122-23.

Second, there are several choices for implementing passive asset class investments. Some of those are not available in some jurisdictions. Some are structured differently and have unique advantages over others — a subject that goes beyond the scope of this chapter. For example, while the popular American Vanguard Index Funds would certainly meet the criteria in this chapter, there are some drawbacks to Index investing that can be overcome by the use of passively managed asset class funds like those offered by Dimensional Fund Advisors and available only through approved Investment Advisors. Properly structured ETFs are also a viable option.

The professional advisor will be able to assist the trustee: (1) in the creation of a proper asset allocation that is science based, not emotionally driven; (2) in the selection of appropriate investment strategies for filling in the various asset class selections; (3) in monitoring their performance; (4) in facilitating appropriate rebalancing of the portfolio over time; and (5) in documenting all of this in a professionally drafted Investment Policy Statement.

All of the above is done in the context of the particular trust and its requirements. The discipline brought to the process by a truly qualified professional Investment Advisor is well worth the annual fees charged by professional advisors. However, this is one of those fees that must be reviewed by the trustee to be sure it is reasonable and appropriate to the trust and the investment strategies used by the trust. Unexamined fees can become excessive and may not be justified.

CONCLUSION

Both the California UPIA and the Ontario *Trustee Act* contain two sections that significantly speak to investment strategy: the duty to diversify in order to reduce or eliminate uncompensated risk and develop efficient portfolios; and the duty to only incur costs that are appropriate and reasonable in relation to the assets, overall investment strategy, purposes and other circumstances of the trust. Included in costs to be considered are tax costs.

(1) By definition, a low cost passive asset class mutual fund or ETF reduces uncompensated risk as much as possible. Any active strategy, because it holds something less than the full market dimension it is chosen to represent, by definition, contains uncompensated risk.

(2) Due to its essential buy and hold strategy, a low cost passive asset class fund, ETF or Index Fund is lower in all costs: lower IER or MER, lower brokerage costs, lower bid/ask spread costs and a

lower potential for market impact negatively affecting investment performance than a comparable active strategy.

(3) A low cost passive asset class fund will generally not underperform the market dimension it is chosen to represent by more than the costs of investing. Most actively managed funds underperform the "market" most of the time — few outperform, and those that do generally do not persist in that outperformance over the investment time period required by most trusts.

(4) Since it is apparent from the *Trustee Act*, the UPIA, the Restatement and the Commentary and Notes on the Restatement that a trustee should take only compensated risk unless he or she can justify active uncompensated risk, and since the UPIA requires trustees to pay only reasonable costs, it is apparent that the use of low cost passive asset class funds is the default strategy or safe habour for prudent fiduciary investing for trustees.

It is then my conclusion that those professionals who advise trustees must look carefully at the basic investment strategies that are being implemented. There should be a rational justification of any active strategies being proposed or implemented against a comparable passive strategy in regard to risks, costs and taxes. Can the fiduciary justify the active strategy as being more prudent for the trust than the passive strategy? If not, then a passive strategy should be used to implement the investment portfolio.

CHAPTER 31

SOCIALLY RESPONSIBLE INVESTING: NOT A NEW INVESTMENT TREND

Peter J. Merrick
Eugene Ellmen

Overview

This chapter lays out the case for socially responsible investing (SRI) for today's modern investor.

Learning Objectives

By the end of this chapter, you should be able to:

- understand what socially responsible investing is;
- understand the emerging influence of the "cultural creatives" subculture in the developed world;
- learn about the new trend of socially responsible investing occurring in the Canadian institutional marketplace; and
- understand how you can make a difference when you invest in SRI.

> "We do not inherit this land from our ancestors; we borrow it from our children."
>
> Haida Indian Proverb

WHAT IS SOCIALLY RESPONSIBLE INVESTING?

Over the past decade, we have worked with hundreds of corporations, non-government organizations, families and individuals to help them to invest their money so they can create a better future. Collectively, we have learned through experience that in reality, money is something we have chosen to trade our life energy for. In the last 60 years, money has dematerialized from paper into electrical pulses of 0s and 1s, with trillions of dollars swirling around the world every minute. The truth is that when we invest our money, we are really casting a vote on the type of future we want to create. When North Americans poured billions of dollars into the Asian markets in the early 1990s, world attention focused on the potential of the Asian tiger.

In the late 1990s, technology was the focus. Perhaps the reason for the collapse of both these investing fads was that they were based on greed and fear, not long-term sustainable financial growth.

We are living in the most exciting, challenging and critical time in human history. Never before has so much been possible, and never before has so much been at stake. Around us are environmental, social and economic crises, along with extreme geopolitical tensions. It is evident that the roots of these crises lie within us: our materialism, our yearning for power, our love of money and our fear of each other.

The world's population in 1900 was 1.5 billion people. Forecasters predict that by 2050 the population will reach 9.1 billion; this will all have happened within 150 years. Humanity has consumed more of the world's resources since the end of World War II than all previous human generations. In society, many buy into the myth that more stuff breeds more happiness.

The truth is that Gross Domestic Product (GDP) includes warfare, pollution, consumerism, divorce and crime as economic gains in the economy. But there is no value given for caring for dependents, housework and volunteering. However, without these worthwhile human endeavours, our social fabric will break down.

Our actions are turning humanity into an endangered species. We are threatening our future and the future of our planet.

> "The future is not to be forecasted, but created. What we do today will decide the shape of things tomorrow."
>
> Sir Arthur C. Clarke

In the 21st century, many investors have come to believe that we can do good for society with our investments and do well financially at the same time. Most of us would prefer to invest in companies that share the same values we do; if only we could outpace the S&P 500 or TSX at the same time. Now that goal has become more than an ephemeral New Year's resolution.

Yet the fact is, investing that reflects investors' values is both possible and profitable. Socially responsible investing, once largely dismissed as a novelty for the politically correct, is now considered to be a smart and lucrative way to make money in the long run.

If you feel this way, you are not alone. Toronto-born Paul Ray, a sociologist, and his wife, Sherry Anderson, a psychologist, now living in

California, drew upon 13 years of survey research studies on 100,000 adults to find that as of the year 2000, there were 50 million people in the United States and 90 million in the European Union who would identify themselves as cultural creatives (*The Cultural Creatives: How 50 Million People Are Changing the World* (New York: Three Rivers Press, 2001)). According to Ray and Anderson, what makes someone so is being an "individual who cares deeply about ecology and saving the planet, about relationships, peace, social justice, and self-actualization, spirituality and self-expression". Such individuals have a burning desire to have their values reflected in their careers, investments and community.

The ranks of cultural creatives have been growing by leaps and bounds over the last 50 years. They want their money manager and financial advisor investment processes to be rigorous and demanding. But they want one more element put into the mix. They want to invest in responsible companies.

Socially responsible investing is about striking an appropriate balance: finding that golden meaning between a life that neither bows down to money nor neglects financial responsibilities, getting a good return for yourself without forgetting about others.

The overall amount of money (or assets under management (AUM)) invested in one or more of the three main SRI strategies (screening, shareholder advocacy and community investing) grew to $2.29 trillion in 2005. Nearly one in ten dollars is now invested in SRI (9.4% of the $24.4 trillion) in total assets under professional management in the United States, according to the U.S. Social Investment Forum. According to this report, SRI assets have grown by 258% within one decade, outpacing the growth of the overall market.

A PERSPECTIVE ON CANADIAN AND INTERNATIONAL PENSION PLANS

This growth in socially responsible investment is being reflected in new approaches to pension management in Canada and Europe.

Across the Atlantic, large and very influential pension fund managers in the United Kingdom and Europe are banding together to conduct research into the impact of social and environmental analysis on pension returns. These fund managers believe that investment in socially responsible and sustainable companies with good governance structures will pay off in long-term value and lower long-term risk.

A group of European pension fund managers and asset firms managing hundreds of billions of euros has established the Enhanced Analytics Initiative, a process to establish incentives for investment brokers to begin analyzing non-financial factors. In addition, institutions such as the giant ABP pension fund and asset manager in the Netherlands (the second largest pension fund manager in the world), the Norwegian Government Pension Fund and the Fonds de Reserve (the state pension managers in France) are all using social and environmental analysis as part of their investment selection and management.

In Canada, several large pension managers have signed the United Nations' Principles on Responsible Investment (UNPRI). The Canada Pension Plan Investment Board, the British Columbia Investment Management Corp. and the Caisse de depot et placement du Québec are among the largest pension fund managers in Canada. They have also signed the UNPRI treaty, pledging to look into socially responsible investment strategies and analysis.

Not only is pension management an issue, but so too is the topic of shareholder voting. As fiduciaries responsible for the investment of billions of dollars worth of assets, Canadian pension managers are in a position of owning shares in every major company in Canada, as well as the largest international corporations. With this ownership comes responsibility for the voting of shares in these companies. Every year, shareholders raise important issues of social responsibility, environmental well-being and corporate governance with major Canadian and international companies. Pension plan managers have a responsibility to cast their votes on these issues with care, and with the pension plan members' interests in mind.

Pension regulation is one of the drivers of these new approaches. The United Kingdom, Germany, France and other countries now require pension fund managers to disclose the extent to which they take social and environmental factors into account in their investment decision-making. By providing regular information on these issues to plan members, European pension fund managers are providing their members with an additional level of knowledge about their investment policies. These disclosures answer important questions from plan members about the social responsibility of their pension asset managers. Such a proactive approach heads off costly and divisive stakeholder debates over questions like tobacco or military investments.

In Canada, mutual fund managers are now required by Canadian securities commissions to reveal how they vote on such issues, disclosing their voting policies and showing exactly how they vote on shareholder resolutions. The requirement follows similar rules in the United States, driven by the belief that mutual fund managers were asleep at the switch when executives were raiding corporate coffers at Enron, WorldCom and other companies. More vigorous attention to voting would have placed management under greater scrutiny, reducing losses to investors. It is only a matter of time until pension fund managers are brought under similar shareholder voting disclosure rules.

The debate about pension funds during the last few years has centred on the issue of pension deficits. Rich benefit packages and accounting rules encouraging fund managers to overestimate future returns combined with lower stock values and bond yields have led to a crisis in the funding of many of Canada's largest defined benefit pension plans. There is no doubt that significant reform is needed to put the funding of these pensions back in order.

But pension fund managers are also going to have to answer the questions of how social responsibility, sustainability, corporate governance and proxy voting fit into their long-term investment vision. The short-term funding issues are only a part of the puzzle of the pension problem. Equally important is the need to reform investment policies to take account of the long-term issues of responsible and sustainable business. As major investors in Canadian business, pension fund managers will need to look carefully into these issues. Not every pension plan manager will answer these questions in the same way. But now that these questions have been asked, they will need to be answered, and disclosure to plan members is the best way to ensure that plan members get the information they need.

WHERE TO FIND GOOD INFORMATION TO INVEST

Established in 1989, the Social Investment Organization (SIO) is the national non-profit association for the socially responsible investment (SRI) industry in Canada. The SIO has more than 400 members across Canada, representing SRI mutual fund managers, financial institutions, investment advisors, asset managers, institutional investors, individual investors and non-profit organizations with an interest in responsible investment. Its members serve more than half a million depositors and investors in Canada.

The mandate of the SIO is to take on a leadership role in furthering the use of social and environmental criteria within the investment community, to raise public awareness of socially responsible investment, to establish the case for environmental/social analysis with other investment organizations and to provide a forum and information source on socially responsible investment for its members and the public.

The SIO defines SRI as the process of selecting or managing investments according to social or environmental criteria. The SIO estimates that there is approximately $65.5 billion in socially responsible investment assets under management in Canada.

MAKE A DIFFERENCE

In November 1992, 1,700 of the world's leading scientists, including the majority of Nobel laureates in the Sciences, issued the greatest appeal to the human residents of this planet by publishing a warning to humanity that stated:

> "Human beings and the natural world are on a collision course."

Further in 2007, 600 climatologists came to a consensus under the auspices of the United Nations Intergovernmental Panel on Climate Change (IPCC). They published a dire report that predicted dramatic and dangerous short- and medium-term global changes in temperature and sea levels. They stated that the Earth's biosphere will most likely survive these changes but humanity might not be so lucky.

It is not too late to make a difference. On May 2, 2005, Bob Hunter, one of the founders of Greenpeace and one of our mentors, died of cancer at the age of 63. You might remember Bob as the quirky guy who used to read the newspaper in his bathrobe every weekday on Toronto's City TV *Breakfast Television*. Bob's indomitable spirit fired the direct action mode of the environment protection movement and created Greenpeace. In Bob's last book, *Thermageddon: Countdown to 2030* (New York: Arcade Publishing, 2003), Bob persuasively argued that around the year 2030, the climate change for our planet would be irreversible, what he called "Thermageddon", and he reviewed the scientific evidence to support this theory. Included in his discussion was the role each North American citizen plays in contributing towards global warming patterns in the world. Throughout his book, he expressed grave concern for the kind of world that his generation was leaving his grandchildren and the grandchildren of the world. His lasting challenge was for each of us to do his and her part to make this a better world after we depart it than how we found it.

One of Bob's most admirable traits was that he was not just a man of the spoken and written word, he was a man of action. On a very cold day in March 1976, Bob and Paul Watson, co-founder of Greenpeace, stood on an ice floe off the coast of Labrador, Canada as a large sealing ship approached them. The ice cracked and split beneath their feet as Watson said to Bob, "When it splits, I'll jump to the left and you to the right." Bob looked straight ahead and calmly said, "I'm not going anywhere." Because Bob stayed, Watson stayed, and the two of them brought that seal killing ship to a dead stop.

Bob Hunter's life proves that each and every one of us can make a difference. It is a moving call for action backed by deeds and facts. One way we can do our part is by acting on the belief that there is absolutely no conflict in doing what is right by investing our portfolios in companies that respect the environment, treat their employees well and conduct their businesses ethically while earning a good solid return. Plus, this type of investing just feels good because it is good!

> "Our Future evolution will not be decided by the strongest but by the survival of the wisest."
>
> Jonas Salk

TAKING THE NEXT STEP

In 1992, the Center for Ethical Business Cultures in Minnesota put forth a fairly representational statement of five ethical principles known as the Minnesota Principles. These principles are intended to act as a compass for both clients and their Trusted Advisors to create an investment and business community that supports both society and the environment as a whole. As you navigate these new waters towards a sustainable and a more ethical world, these principles can assist both you and your clients in making better, well informed ethical decisions that benefit all:

- **Principle One — Stimulating economic growth is the particular contribution of business to the larger society.**
  We understand that profits are fundamental to the fulfillment of this function.
- **Principle Two — Business activities must be characterized by fairness.**
  We understand fairness to include equitable treatment and equality of opportunity for all participants in the marketplace.
- **Principle Three — Business activities must be characterized by honesty.**
  We understand honesty to include candour, truthfulness and promise-keeping.
- **Principle Four — Business activities must be characterized by respect for human dignity.**
  We understand this to mean that business activities should show a special concern for the less powerful and the disadvantaged.
- **Principle Five — Business activities must be characterized by respect for the environment.**
  We understand this to mean that business activities should promote sustainable development and prevent environmental degradation and waste of resources.

Remember: Act locally today by investing your money in SRI, and think globally about how we will all be doing our part in making this a better world for our grandchildren's tomorrows!

CHAPTER 32

THE IMMIGRANT INVESTOR PROGRAM — A GREAT OPPORTUNITY

Peter J. Merrick

Overview

This chapter addresses the Canadian Immigrant Investor Program and the opportunities it offers both new immigrants and advisors who assist clients who come to Canada under this program.

Learning Objectives

By the end of this chapter, you should be able to:

- understand the criteria for the qualification of immigrants who are eligible to immigrate under this classification.

According to Citizenship and Immigration Canada's 2001 statistics, of the 250,643 people who immigrated to Canada, 4,087 qualified under the investor, entrepreneur and self-employed immigration categories. Mendel Green, of the law firm Green & Spiegel in Toronto, believes that business and investor immigrants are one of the main economic drivers helping Canada to remain competitive and prosperous in the 21st century.

"Every one in this country benefits from these people choosing Canada to become their home. They start businesses, employ Canadians, pay taxes, buy homes and send their children to university. They make this a better country for all of us," says Green, who has been practising immigration law since 1962 and is listed in *The Canadian Legal LEXPERT Directory* as a "leading immigration practitioner — most frequently recommended".

The Immigrant Investor Program was created in 1986 by Citizenship and Immigration Canada. Quebec administers its own program. Since the Canadian and Quebec governments initiated their programs, over 21,000 immigrants have qualified under this category. They have invested over $6.5 billion into these programs, with the bulk of this money going to Quebec (57.4%).

Citizenship and Immigration Canada defines an investor immigrant as someone who has successfully operated or controlled or directed a business or commercial undertaking and has accumulated through his or her own efforts a net worth of at least $800,000 CDN. Immigrant investors must also make a minimum investment of $400,000 CDN in an approved investment fund. This class of immigrant has no conditions imposed upon admission to Canada. These immigrants can pursue whatever business opportunity in Canada they wish and live where they like, once their initial investment is made.

Immigrants who meet these requirements must use one of 11 approved Citizenship and Immigration Canada financial institutions to facilitate the financing of their Immigrant Class investments. All are members of the Canada Deposit Insurance Corporation (CDIC). Each $400,000 investment is collected by these institutions and forwarded to either Citizenship and Immigration Canada or the Quebec Immigration Office. The interest earned from this money is to be used for government grants to Canadian and Quebec companies to help foster economic growth.

Quebec has done a much better job of promoting Canada to prospective wealthy immigrants and having these immigrants choose to invest in Quebec for two simple reasons. First, Quebec has paid a commission to financial institutions from the start of its program; this has facilitated the promotion and recruitment of immigrant investors in the Quebec program.

This money incentive has helped support an infrastructure of offices and agents around the world to promote Quebec and Canada. In addition, a financial institution that has successfully processed an applicant in Quebec usually receives its commission in 6 to 12 months. This commission ranges from $30,000 to $50,000.

Citizenship and Immigration Canada redesigned its immigrant investor program, effective April 1, 1999. A $28,000 commission is now paid to an approved financial institution for aiding in the facilitation of the application process. However, payment of this commission takes a minimum of three years according to agents participating in this program.

Many immigrants who do qualify for the investor immigrant program choose not to put up the full $400,000, but only place a down payment of $120,000 at one of the approved institutions. They are able to arrange financing to borrow the other $280,000. Their $120,000 is non-refundable.

Many immigrants prefer this option to giving the government the full $400,000. These immigrants are business people first, and they prefer this option because they believe that they can make better use of their own money than having the entire amount sit with the government for five years earning nothing (no interest).

Some immigration consultants earn up to $100,000 for the successful processing of these immigrants — between the popular Quebec program and a finder fee they receive from the financial institution administering these funds. Immigration consultants are driving the Investor Class immigrants to Canada. For every lawyer who brings a financial institution a client, three clients come from an immigration consultant.

There is an ethical issue about immigration consultants receiving a commission. Unlike lawyers and financial advisors in Canada, they are not regulated. Many of these consultants do not operate in Canada, most likely because they would not be qualified to do so. For a number of years, Citizenship and Immigration Canada has been working on regulations to govern the ethics and activities of immigration consultants. The question many are asking themselves is, will this policy be enforced and, if it is, will it have teeth?

Lawyers and Trusted Advisors who receive commission for acting as agents, directing funds to financial institutions and participating in either the Canadian or Quebec programs have both an ethical and moral responsibility for full disclosure to their clients that they will be receiving a commission. Many ethical financial professionals and lawyers do disclose to every client who qualifies under the investor program all the fees and commissions their firms will be receiving. They also direct these clients to seek a second opinion from another non-connected firm to avoid any perception of a conflict of interest.

This program is a noble venture, but the federal government has not made it a priority to process these applications. While visiting Green & Spiegel, I had the pleasure of meeting an applicant who had first applied under the Investor Program in April 2001. His net worth is well over $10 million U.S., he operates a very successful bottle recycling plant in the Middle East that employs over 400 people and he wants to immigrate to Canada to open a similar plant, where he plans to employ 45 people.

As of my visit in late 2003, the federal government had yet to review his file. In September 2003, he finally received his receipt from Citizenship and Immigration Canada for his immigration-processing fee, which he had paid over two years earlier. Even though this successful businessman's application has not been processed, he still wanted to immigrate to Canada. Green said that his client could very easily obtain a visa to the European Community within months of his application without the bureaucratic hassles.

This country is losing thousands of qualified business people to Australia, New Zealand and the European Community every year. Business people want to be treated in a proper businesslike manner by government officials, which should be efficient, timely and professional.

Green showed me a list of files that have yet to be processed by the government dating as far back as 1996. These are files of very qualified business and investor class immigration applicants who have a collective net worth of well over $200 million.

We don't know how good we have it in this country — incredible people from around the globe want to make this their home. It's because our multicultural society works, and we are an example for the world. Qualified immigrants come to this country to enjoy the freedoms that many of us take for granted, to make a better life for their children and themselves, and most of all they want to contribute to both our society and economy.

The federal government acknowledges that the proper attention has not been given to business and investor immigrant applicants over the past few years. Hoping to address this problem, Citizenship and Immigration Canada is placing a minimum quota on the number of business and investor immigrant files that must be processed each year. This will be the first time the federal government has identified how many cases must be approved. In the past, the government had not distinguished business and investor immigrants from the rest of the immigration classes.

Business and investor immigrants respect professionals, have a need for their advice and are willing to pay for their services. They have a clear understanding that to succeed in Canada they will need to hire a host of professionals to establish themselves. In addition to their immigration lawyer, many will need chartered accountants, certified financial planners, real estate agents, corporate lawyers, real estate lawyers, investment professionals, international tax lawyers and corporate benefit consultants. Business and investor immigrants are the clients everybody wants and those from whom Canada will benefit most, by inviting them to join our country's rich mosaic.

PART IV

EMPLOYEE BENEFITS AND COMPLEMENTARY RETIREMENT SOLUTIONS

CHAPTER 33

THE TRUSTED ADVISOR'S PRACTICE GROUP EMPLOYEE BENEFITS TOOL KIT

Gordon Berger
Jeffrey Berger

Overview

In recent years, non-cash and deferred compensation programs have become extremely complex because of new legislation and changes in the business environment. Their planning and management require a broad spectrum of specialized knowledge and a thorough analysis of options. This chapter covers individual and group insurances, retirement plans and other non-cash benefits for you and your employees. It presents options and examples that can help you plan this vital aspect of your practice. It will also outline how you can protect your firm, your employees, yourself and your family financially by knowing how to select the right employee benefits.

Learning Objectives

By the time you complete this chapter you will:

- understand the purpose of non-cash compensation;
- understand the different types of advisory practices and the unique benefit considerations for each; and
- understand how to go about selecting employee benefits, and setting up, maintaining, and reviewing employee benefit programs.

NON-CASH AND DEFERRED COMPENSATION

Non-cash compensation refers to forms of remuneration other than salary, such as employee benefits and vacation. A non-cash and deferred compensation program may be established for yourself, your partners or your staff in the form of employee benefits.

Critical Importance

Individual and group insurances, retirement plans and employee benefits are critically important because they can:

(1) protect your income, your practice and your family;

(2) save you and your employees out-of-pocket medical and/or dental expenses; and

(3) give you a competitive edge in motivating and retaining partners, staff and support staff.

Co-ordinated Management

An advisory firm is a business first and foremost. One of its primary reasons for existence is to generate income. As with any other business, a successful advisory practice requires knowledgeable, thorough and co-ordinated management of all its operations. You must carefully consider the effect that one decision may have on another. This means that you should not approach non-cash compensation in piecemeal, one element at a time. Your personal interest, along with those of your firm and your employees, must be seen as a unit, as a dynamic, changing organism. In other words, your financial planning must be holistic.

Options

Certain aspects of non-cash and deferred compensation, such as pensions, whether they are provided privately or by government, are regulated by statutes and regulator guidelines. You may have many choices regarding insurance and other compensation arrangements. There are a large number of policies and plans to choose from for both yourself and your employees. If you are well informed, you can select those which give all the protection you and your employees need and those that will provide you with the most financial clout. For example, some components of insurance can be used as collateral for borrowing money to build your practice or for some other purpose.

Tax Implications

You may already realize that retirement plans and other benefits constitute an increasingly important and larger part of employee compensation. However, you may not be aware of how these plans and benefits can be a valuable resource for you personally, even if you are a partner and not an employee of your firm.

There are also implications to consider. Contributions to certain insurance and retirement plans are deductible for you or your firm; others are not. Insurance premiums paid by your firm and offered to your employees as benefits may or may not be taxable for your employees. Sound planning on your part and careful management of the plans you put into place can substantially reduce your own taxes and the taxes paid by other members of your firm. The key is holistic planning. This will ensure that all your non-cash and deferred compensation plans are tax effective.

DIFFERENCES AMONGST FIRMS

The way you set up your non-cash compensation program is determined to a large extent by the size and nature of your firm. For the purposes of this chapter, we will classify advisory firms into the following categories:

(1) sole practitioners;

(2) small firms with 2 to 5 partners;

(3) medium-sized firms with 5 to 25 partners; and

(4) large firms, often national organizations, with 25 or more partners/executives/lawyers/accountants/planners.

Sole Practitioners

As you know, in a sole practitioner's practice, the Trusted Advisor is, for all intents and purposes, the firm. In many instances, the only support staff is a secretary and/or receptionist. The sole practitioner may also hire other advisors as support staff or use the support of other firms.

Sole practitioners are considered to be self employed. Consequently, they do not qualify for employment insurance (EI) and may not participate in certain group benefits. On the other hand, a sole practitioner can establish a Registered Retirement Savings Plan, and if they are incorporated they may have registered pension plans. If he or she has staff, they can all participate in a group medical and dental plan. Self-employed advisors must contribute to the Canadian Pension Plan (CPP). They are required to pay both the employer's and employee's share of the contribution. If you have a support staff, you must abide by the employment regulations in your province of practice. If there are at least three people in your firm, including the owner, you may be able to set up a group insurance plan, although the benefit structure may be limited. You could also set up a pension plan for your employees but that could be costly. Many small firms will help their employees save for retirement by utilizing a Group RRSP. Sole practitioners who have incorporated and receive T4 income are eligible to set up an IPP for themselves.

While it may be perceived at first as expensive, not having insurance coverage could place you in the precarious position, since you and your staff may not have any protection in the event of illness, accident or death. Insured benefit plans are usually administered on behalf of small firms by themselves or their other Trusted Advisors, which may include brokerage firms and insurance agencies. Administration often includes providing written and other materials to help explain benefits to the firm's employees.

If you are a sole practitioner, you would be advised to take out disability insurance to cover any business-related loan and office overhead expense to ensure that your fixed overhead costs may be paid in the event of your disability owing to illness or injury. You should also purchase personal life insurance and personal disability insurance as protection for your family. These forms of insurance will financially protect your practice, your family, yourself and your estate in case of death or disability.

Small Partnerships

Many of the considerations that apply to sole practitioner also apply to small partnerships. In some situations, the small partnership has an advantage over the sole practitioner. Partners may not take advantage of EI benefits, but if they have their own individual corporations, they may create a registered pension plan for themselves. They may participate in group insurance plans that included disability, health, dental or other such coverage. It is usually advisable for partners in a small firm to purchase insurance to fund a buy/sell agreement, personal life insurance, office overhead expense coverage and personal disability and critical care insurance. Their business income can thus be protected in case one of the partners becomes disabled, critically ill, dies or wants to sell out. The staffs of a small firm are subject to the appropriate provincial employment standards and are covered by EI and CPP.

Medium-Sized Practices

There is more flexibility in establishing benefits packages for medium-sized practices. Although the same legal restrictions apply to partners with regard to EI and pension plans, as in smaller firms, the medium-sized firm has more options in how to insure various benefits. It has, for example, the option of self-insuring short-term disability or being insured by an insurance company. The choice is weighed according to the degree of risk the partners are prepared to take. It is usually wisest to ensure coverage with potential catastrophic claims, such as life and disability coverage. There may also be greater expectations on the part of staff and partners for a comprehensive benefit plan, including such benefits as health insurance, retirement plans and maternity leaves.

To accommodate these needs and demands, a medium-sized practice can more easily introduce the "cafeteria" approach to a benefit plan. It may also decide to implement a "top-hat" or "Cadillac" approach to the benefit plan for partners and senior staff. Although there is still a need for protection, should one of the partners die or become disabled, this is not as vital for the medium-sized practice as it is for the sole practitioner or small partnership. Unless the success of the firm depends on one or more partners, the knowledge, skill, reputation and income-earning ability of the firm is not as dependent on any single individual.

Note: Most advisory firms take the approach that an advisor who is a partner is not entitled to any compensation if he or she leaves the firm — except for work in progress and any undrawn income. The approach may be stated as, "You come into the firm with nothing, and you leave with nothing." This approach, however, does not take into account the real needs of retiring partners. When they leave the firm, the only retirement income they might possess is from an IPP, RCA, RRSP, CPP and old age security. A comprehensive, well-planned retirement program, including deferred compensation and deferred profit-sharing plans, would largely answer these needs. Retirement options and tools have been discussed in other chapters of the book. In addition, or as an alternative, it is possible to structure a highly effective partnership retirement plan that meets the real needs of retiring partners and has a zero cost feature.

Large Firms

A large advisory firm should approach its non-cash compensation programs on a well-structured basis. Once it has identified the objectives of its benefit plan and determined its employees' needs, the firm can proceed to develop a comprehensive and attractive non-cash and deferred compensation program. The large firm must contribute to CPP and EI for all its employees.

The large firm has the option of insuring them or establishing a trust for those contingencies. It is unwise to assume that there will be enough money in the firm's general operating budget to meet demands as they arise, unless there is a deliberate provision for these contingencies. The large firm may package its benefit program in whatever style it prefers. The "top-hat", new style "cafeteria", "standard cafeteria" or traditional approaches may all work because the firm has the necessary volume and cash flow to meet the insurer's underwriting guidelines. When determining the type of plan to offer, the large firm may need to hire a seasoned executive/employee benefit consultant to determine the demographic of its partners and staff. This will have an effect on the kind and amount of insurance needed. Of course, market and industry practice and employee demands are also a strong influence.

The volume of the benefits and consequent premium cash is a determining factor in assessing whether it is financially beneficial for the firm to assume some of the administrative tasks of the insurance company. The insurance companies provide premium reductions for those firms prepared to maintain the monthly billing statements. A firm of sufficient size may even consider using the insurance company merely as a means of carrier administration. Risk exposure may be limited by insuring individual or total claims over predetermined levels. The larger firms may also have the financial flexibility to access customized benefit communication programs and also customized in-house administration software systems at extremely affordable costs.

REQUIREMENTS AND OPTIONS IN SETTING UP EMPLOYMENT BENEFITS

The Choices

In deciding which benefits are most suitable for your firm, you are faced with a multitude of choices. Insurance is available on an individual basis for personal protection and, more economically, on a group basis for the security of the members of the group. It may also be purchased for the protection of your practice. Further, some coverage may be obtained from the professional associations your firm belongs to.

Statutory benefits include the Canadian Pension Plan (CPP)/Quebec Pension Plan (QPP), Employment Insurance (EI) and provincial health plans. The various provincial Employment Standards Acts provide required minimum standards for such benefits as vacations and maternity leave. Employer-sponsored programs encompass a full spectrum of benefits, including life, disability and critical illness insurance, retirement and health plans. Savings and investment programs and a sundry of other plans, such as group home and auto insurance, may also be included in your benefits package.

FACTORS TO CONSIDER

Your Personal Plans

Before you set up any plan or look at the specifics of any single program, you should define the reasons for establishing a plan and what it is you want to accomplish. A good plan will assist you in attracting and retaining valuable employees and encouraging skilled professionals to become partners of your firm. For these reasons, it is important to take into account the real needs of your employees and partners in selecting a plan design. The needs of your partners, professional staff and yourself may vary considerably from those of your support group.

Not only do today's partners and employees evaluate salaries when comparing employment opportunities in other advisory firms or general companies in the same geographic area, but they also look at the total compensation package, including group insurance, retirement plans and other benefits.

Employee Policy

Benefit plans are costly and generally reflect 25-40% of your payroll costs. Therefore, it is important that you maximize the return on every dollar invested by ensuring that the plan is geared to the employees' needs and its value properly communicated. Your compensation objectives should accurately reflect your overall policy towards employees and partners, which, in turn, is governed by your business targets.

Your benefits package is one of the most effective ways in which you can communicate your employee-relations philosophy. The philosophy need not be contained in a formal document, but it must be clearly understood by all. Some firms, for example, provide benefits only because they have to, and they provide them at a minimum level. Others are very aware of the tax advantages, for both the firm and their employees, that may be acquired through employee-benefits programs, and they operate accordingly. Yet, other approaches are more paternalistic; the employer takes responsibility for a major part of the employees' financial well being.

Demographics

One potential pitfall of which you should be aware is that it is easy to be swayed by benefit plans that fulfill only your immediate and personal needs. For example, vision-care programs may be most attractive to owners who wear glasses, older employees may be more concerned with pension plans and life insurance, or staff with young families may be attracted to comprehensive health and dental programs.

The demographics of your employee group, such as age, sex, marital status and income levels, should be among the deciding factors in the plan design you select. In this way, you can maximize the value of your benefit dollars and also provide benefits useful to you, your partners and your staff. For example, a predominately young, single, female staff member may not be interested in a plan that includes life insurance equal to two times annual earnings and excludes provisions for dental care. The plan would be even less attractive were the staff required to share in the cost. The lower-income earners may be reluctant to contribute to the cost of a benefit plan, but this reluctance may not be apparent in the higher-income groups, whose income protection needs are greater.

Demographics also determine the cost of your benefits. In the case of individual and group life insurance, premium rates are based on demographic factors. For example, in life insurance, a high average age attracts higher premium rates, while a high female participation in the group, because of the lower mortality factor of women, helps to reduce the premium rate.

Budget

Once you have determined your firm's objective and your employees' needs, your next step is to calculate the levels of benefits you can afford. A limited budget will restrict the extent of the benefits that you can offer. One way to resolve this restriction is to persuade your staff to share in the cost. Employee cost-sharing enables you to offer more extensive benefits.

Just as you budget for payroll, you can budget for your benefit plan. One quarter of every dollar in your payroll may be internally budgeted for benefit coverage. The future cost of the benefit plan will be reflected by the make-up of the group, the benefit level, inflation and the previous year's experience. Your benefits consultant may assist you in matching objectives to plan design and your budget. Once you have agreed to the plan's specifications, the consultant will request proposals from the insurers, which will be analyzed and presented to you. This will give you the opportunity to select a plan in light of your established budget. Some consultants may be capable through computerization, to generate fairly accurate cost models before going to market.

If you have never had a benefits plan, it is best to start with a basic plan, since it can always be upgraded in the future. However, once you have a plan, it may be extremely hard on employee morale to reduce the coverage or introduce cost-sharing later on. The plan should be upgraded from time to time to maintain adequate protection and to keep it competitive.

Approaches

After you have determined your budget and have investigated the needs of your employees to determine the plan design, you then have to decide on the approach you will take in offering the package to your employees. There are various ways of doing this. Once again, the ultimate choice must be one that is compatible with the way your firm is organized and its managerial style.

Traditional Approach

Traditionally, a firm decided which benefits it was going to provide to all of its employees, regardless of age, status or other personal characteristics. It also decided whether benefits premiums were to be paid in full by the firm or whether costs would be shared with employees. With this approach, all staff members were required to participate in the various plans. There was no room for choice or for employees to buy additional coverage. It did not matter if the plan met the needs of any particular individual, nor did it matter if the individual could obtain better coverage or lower premiums elsewhere.

Although this approach is inflexible and is now viewed negatively by many employees, it is the simplest one to administer. If a firm's employees all fit into a similar demographic pattern, this approach may work effectively.

"Standard Cafeteria" Approach

An alternative in benefits planning is the "cafeteria" approach. This approach blends core and optional programs. The employer still selects all the benefits that will be offered in the plan. All employees have to be covered under the core programs, for example, group life insurance, but the employees are able to choose those they want from the optional group. In addition to their own contribution, the staff members may also be assigned a given dollar amount for optional benefits coverage, which they may allocate to the optional benefits selected. They may also, in some instances, increase the value of coverage they receive under the compulsory part of the plan.

The "standard cafeteria" approach is usually more popular among employees than the traditional method. It gives them some freedom in selecting the benefits and level of coverage that best meets their immediate and long-term needs.

"New Cafeteria" Approach

The "standard cafeteria" approach has evolved even further. Under the "new cafeteria" style of benefits coverage, statutory insured benefits such as CPP and EI are included. Other benefits — for example, retirement plans, pensions and vacations — may also be part of the mandatory package. Employees may be covered under any of the offered plans, up to a predetermined dollar amount. The amount is usually a percentage of earnings or a minimum dollar amount, whichever is greater. Employees can thus determine the level of protection they require within the parameters provided by the plans. This approach is particularly attractive to employees who have benefits protection from other sources, such as a spouse's plan.

"Top-Hat" Approach

Participation in "top-hat" or "Cadillac" benefits plans is usually restricted to senior executives, partners or owners of a firm. This type of approach provides these individuals with additional or increased levels of protection in recognition of their value to the organization. The "top-hat" plan can allow for such benefits as *carte blanche* health and dental coverage, and group insurance and financial programs such as deferred compensation, profit sharing, IPPs or RCAs. In order to hire, motivate and retain good senior-level employees, a "top-hat" plan has become almost a necessity today.

INSURED VS. SELF-INSURED VS. NON-INSURED

An advisory firm has three choices in determining how to finance its benefits program; each involves varying degrees of risk:

(1) A firm may opt for total security by having an insurance company underwrite all its benefits.

(2) A firm may take on the risk itself by self-insuring some or all benefits.

(3) A firm may not insure any benefits, therefore assuming the role of insurer.

Underwriting a Plan

When an insurance company agrees to insure or underwrite a benefits plan in its simplest form, it assumes the liability or risk for claims on that plan in exchange for payment of monthly premiums. The premiums are determined by the type and level of insurance, the demographics of the insured group and the geographical area of the firm.

When benefits are covered by an insurance company, the risk is spread over a large group. Because large numbers of firms and individuals participate in these plans, the insurance company is able to build up enough of a fund to meet any reasonable compensation claim. Most firms prefer to have benefits that may have a long-term liability, such as long-term disability, underwritten by an insurance company. The reason for this is the substantial ongoing liability that may be incurred in the event a claim is made.

Self-insuring a Plan

Some firms treat certain benefits, such as short-term sick leave, as self-insured plans, which are met from current cash or through established reserves. They feel that the claims against such plans will ultimately cost less than paying monthly premiums to an insurance company. The firm is protected against open-ended liability because of the limited duration of the claim, for example, six months. If a cash reserve is established and there are no claimants, a further cash outlay may not be required. The capital and interest will continue to accrue over time until the plan may become self-funding.

Non-insured Benefits

The greatest risk for a firm is to have non-insured benefits. It assumes that it will have sufficient funds to provide benefits whenever there is a claim. The firm does not insure its benefits with an insurance company, nor does it establish a self-insured program. Depending on the nature of the benefits being offered and the firm's financial resources, the advantages and disadvantages of this option should be carefully considered before it is taken.

THE PURPOSE OF INSURANCE

Protection

The purpose of insurance is to provide firms and their employees and dependents with cash in the event of death, disability or some other event.

Employee Morale

If an advisory firm provides enough insured benefits to meet the expected needs of its partners and employees, it has a head start in achieving or maintaining high employee morale; employees have always expected adequate cash compensation for their output. Today, they also expect to be protected financially against unforeseen events that would prevent them from providing for their own needs and those of their dependents.

PERSONAL VS. GROUP INSURANCE

The ultimate deciding factor for insurance is short- and long-term cost. The more comprehensive and substantial the insurance coverage, the higher the premiums and the greater the cost to your firm. Depending on the organizational and legal structure of your firm, you, as individuals, might also be eligible for protection under group rates. Even if this is the case, you probably would want and need additional coverage beyond that offered in the group benefits package. Although initially more costly, individual insurance is tailor-made to a person's particular situation.

HOW TO SET UP OR REVIEW A BENEFITS PLAN

So far, we have discussed options to consider in planning your non-cash and deferred compensation program. These sections outline the steps to take once you have considered the options and are ready to actually set up or review your plan.

The multi-disciplined and complex nature of insurance, retirement and other benefits may require you to deal with several companies or persons when establishing or reviewing your benefits plan. For this reason, it is vital that you deal with someone who can co-ordinate these activities for you on a timely basis. A benefits consultant can help you design a plan that is competitive with the costs and benefits provisions of other advisory firms or other organizations with which you compete for employees and talent. Generally, an insurance company will then underwrite the benefits offered under your plan. Finally, a plan administrator may help you take care of day-to-day administration. Your employee benefits consultant should be a professional who, in addition to helping you design your plan, can keep you up to date on changing legislation as it applies to you. All Canadian provinces have provincial regulations that monitor benefits plans and employee rights. Federal legislation sets out the CRA regulations that govern the benefits and contributory levels for certain employee benefits plans. Ideally, you should deal with a company that is familiar with all aspects of individual and group insurance, retirement planning and other non-cash and deferred compensation.

How to Set up a Plan

Survey

The first step is to survey your profession to determine trends among familiar firms. You need to find out the types and levels of benefits that are being offered by firms of a similar size, in the same sort of practice and so on. You conduct an informal survey yourself or hire an employee benefit consultant to do it for you. A well-chosen consultant will already have information concerning the benefits plans offered by other firms of your size and type that operate in a similar style. If you have not had previous experience in this field, you will likely save time and money by engaging the services of a professional benefit consultant.

Employee Needs

Your next step is to understand your own, your partners' and your employees' needs. This includes an analysis of their age groups, marital status, length of service and other demographic factors mentioned earlier. Now you may begin to design your benefits program. Again, a consultant could help you. Together, you would design a program that both meets the specific needs of your firm and is competitive with other firms.

Quotes

After you have set up your plan design, either you or your consultant should request a number of insurance companies, fund managers, plan administrators and other professionals to provide you with a proposal outlining the services they would offer, contractual provisions and costs. Usually, you will be able to narrow down to two or three companies that could meet your criteria regarding plan design, provisions and cost. In many instances, premium or service costs quoted by the selected companies are similar, so your final selection may be based on other criteria such as which supplier can best assist you in administering and servicing your program and communicating it to your staff.

Implementation

Once you have chosen your supplier or suppliers, you can begin to implement your plan. First, sign a master agreement with the supplier and deposit funds to get the plan going. Second, prepare memos, booklets and/or other communication materials to announce the plan to potential participants and to stipulate the requirements they must meet to join the plan or receive benefits. Third, enroll people in the plan by asking them to fill out the appropriate forms.

Administration

When the plan is in place and participants are enrolled, the plan should be administered on a day-to-day basis. This involves such things as keeping track of information on participants, collecting premiums, handling claims, answering questions and preparing reports on plan activity. As previously discussed, a small- to medium-sized firm would usually find it most cost-effective to have its plan administered by an insurance company or a third party administrator. A larger firm would consider going to a company that specializes in benefits plan administration or doing the administration in-house.

How to Review and Upgrade a Plan

If you already have a benefits plan, you should review your plan every two or three years. This will ensure that your plan remains competitive in terms of both the benefits it offers and its cost. If your firm expands rapidly, plan reviews are especially important. As the number of employees grows, you have more flexibility in both the type and level of benefits you can offer. For instance, you might be able to introduce optional benefits for one or more groups of employees such as senior staff. In addition, you might be able to save money, since the cost per dollar of benefits may drop as the number of plan participants increases. The steps you go through in reviewing and possibly upgrading your benefits plan are similar to the steps you took when you set up the plan:

(1) Analyze market trends among similar firms.

(2) Re-examine the needs of your employees.

(3) Adjust your plan design as necessary.

(4) Do a feasibility study, as discussed below.

(5) Go to market with the changes.

(6) Communicate the changes to potential participants.

(7) Enroll new participants or alter the plan for current participants.

(8) Re-evaluate your method of administration and make whatever changes are necessary.

The key step is conducting a feasibility study. Rather than going to the market for quotations, the study provides a detailed analysis of your plan and takes into account the benefits your plan currently provides, the premiums being paid and the plan's claims experience. This is done to determine whether or not you need to go to the market in the first place. If the study indicates that your rates are in line, then you might still wish to go to the market to obtain better service than you are getting to improve contract provisions.

If you do not audit your non-cash compensation program regularly, it may soon be out of date. The benefits industry has been changing dramatically in the types of products offered, so if you have not seriously examined your non-cash compensation, you may have the wrong contracts for your firm or be paying too much in premiums.

PLACES TO GO FOR HELP

If you are starting up an advisory firm, you may need to get advice on the specific choices available to you and guidance on selecting appropriate options and implementing your new program. If your firm is already established, you may benefit from dealing with a consultant who knows everything your firm is doing in this field. An outside specialist can help you monitor your program, keep abreast of new options as they become available and recommend improvements that may save you money or improve benefits.

ADMINISTRATION

Determining who is to administer your non-cash compensation program is largely dependent on the size of your program. A small program is probably best run by an insurance company. But the larger the program becomes, the more complicated its reporting requirements. So with a larger program, it may save you money to administer it in-house or have an outside administrator look after it for you.

Outside administration is a highly specialized field practised by only a few companies. Large benefits consulting firms sometimes provide benefits administration services for their clients. However, these are rarely more efficient than in-house administration and almost always cost more. There are two common approaches to benefits administration:

(1) Accounting approach — typically taken by large consulting firms and insurance companies, whose purpose is to meet basic reporting needs such as who is covered under the program, the level of benefits for each person and which cheques are to be issued each month; and

(2) All-inclusive approach — full reporting to meet the needs of the client, insurer, employee, accounting department and human resources department, using information maintained in a centralized system.

The all-inclusive approach may appear to be more expensive at first glance. But the money it saves and the advantages it offers make it far more cost efficient in the long run.

COMMUNICATIONS

Very few aspects of non-cash compensation are neglected more than communications. Typically, a firm will go to a lot of trouble and expense to identify its financial objectives, analyze its employees' needs, draw up a first-rate benefits program, implement it with precise efficiency — and stop at that. Such a firm will, more often than not, forget that one of the principal reasons for setting up a benefits program is to attract, retain and motivate employees. It will neglect to tell each individual member or staff what his or her benefits are and how they relate to total compensation.

Sound communication is essential to group retirement and group insurance plans. In addition to the reasons already stated, there are also disclosure laws, particularly with regard to pensions and retirement programs, governing the information that must be revealed to employees regularly. These laws vary from province to province. In most cases, an employee joining a firm receives a benefits booklet and a five-minute briefing about the booklet's contents. The employee places the booklet into the bottom drawer of a desk and never looks at it again. The only time the booklet comes out of the drawer is when the employee may need to make a claim. But at all other times, the only thing the employee notices are the deductions coming off his or her pay-cheque. Employees therefore question whether this amount is really worth it — that is, unless they make very large claims against their plan, which most people do not.

Ideal Situation

Ideally, every person working for the firm receives the following:

(1) a well-prepared benefits booklet and perhaps an audio-visual presentation;

(2) a detailed oral explanation of all benefits and options;

(3) a periodic and thorough review whenever the benefits or the employee's circumstances change; and

(4) regular reinforcement of the idea that benefits are a major part of the employees' compensation.

The purpose of this process is to ensure that every staff member clearly understands what he or she is getting and what it is costing him or her, and, more importantly, what it costs your firm as part of your entire compensation package. In your communications, you should also clearly define what your firm is doing for its employees in addition to the benefits provided by various government plans.

With regard to group insurance, the booklet is drafted by the insurance company, and in many cases this is merely a verbatim transcription of the contract. The insurance company takes credit, as though it were giving benefits away to employees and not collecting premiums from the firm. In other words, the booklet is geared to protecting the insurance company instead of communicating to employees. True communication provides the information the employees want and states your corporate philosophy.

Caution

Employers who do not communicate are missing the point — they may not want to spend that little extra, perhaps $10 per employee per year, to multiply substantially the value of their benefits program. With the advent of computers, the Internet and e-mail, it is now much easier to integrate and communicate benefits information, even in the form of a personalized annual benefits statement. Until now, calculating benefits entitlement and values and retirement and death benefits was onerous and costly. Today, it is as easy as pushing some buttons.

What to Do

Unless you have in-house communications specialists to take on the task, do not try to do it yourself. Instead, spend the money on a benefits communications specialist to do it properly.

COMPREHENSIVE HELP

Because there is the danger of isolating one specific area of non-cash compensation from another, the individual needs from that of the group, a comprehensive consultant may identify cost savings by switching policies from an individual to a group basis in areas such as disability insurance. If several partners wanted this coverage, they would be able to obtain a discount of up to 15% by purchasing as a group. But discounts are one thing; having the right benefits package and making sure all of its elements work together is another. Not only do type, quantity and cost of benefits have to be addressed, but so does the quality.

Traditionally, the benefits consulting field has been segregated into two areas: individual and group. This segregation does not make much sense any more because the *Income Tax Act* and various regulations regarding pensions and other retirement plans, insurances and other benefits integrate individual and group needs. So in your financial plan, the individual side should mesh with the group side to achieve economies of scale on both sides.

One of the problems you are likely to encounter is that most benefits plans are designed for mass consumption. Typically, when one or more individuals want specific provisions, they are denied. The broad-based comprehensive financial consultant who becomes the Trusted Advisor will have proven relationships with different insurance carriers and other financial providers and carry a certain amount of clout with them to customize plans for specific needs.

CONCLUSION

Your objective in benefits planning is to provide real motivation to people, augment compensation and cover on a group basis the insurance and other retirement and compensation needs of your staff, your partners and yourself. Your advisory firm is faced with an infinite number of options in designing its benefits package. The careful and cost-efficient selection of the right options to achieve your objectives is critical. With a careful analysis of the options, and a clear understanding of the implications of those choices, you are more likely to produce an effective and meaningful result.

CHAPTER 34

CAPITAL ACCUMULATION PLANS — MAKING INDIVIDUAL FINANCIAL PLANS A CORE EMPLOYEE BENEFIT

Peter J. Merrick

Overview

This chapter outlines the rule and intent surrounding the Joint Forum of Financial Market Regulators' Capital Accumulation Plan Guidelines, which hold Canadian employers to a higher standard for the sponsoring of defined contribution plans, stock option plans, group RRSP, employee profit-sharing plans, stock purchase plans and deferred profit-sharing plans. This chapter concludes by arguing the value of employers offering individual financial planning as an employee benefit to its work force as a core benefit program.

Learning Objectives

By the end of this chapter, you will:

- understand the Joint Forum of Financial Market Regulators' intent behind its Capital Accumulation Plan Guidelines; and
- understand why companies that provide individual financial planning as a core employee benefit will meet its guideline obligations while providing the best return on investment for their corporate employee benefit dollars.

CAPITAL ACCUMULATION PLANS (CAPs)

Employers offer company-sponsored savings plans because they want to reward loyal employees and encourage their people to save for retirement.

During the last few years, the media has had a field day reporting the financial woes of older Canadian workers who are now having to delay their retirement. At a recent financial education workshop that my firm was hired to present, a 62-year-old executive vice-president shared his story with me. He was placing his retirement on hold because the value of his corporate-sponsored retirement savings plan (in which most of his retirement savings were invested) had drastically dropped in value as a result of the meltdown in stock market.

The Canadian Council of Insurance Regulators, the Canadian Association of Pension Supervisory Authorities and the Canadian Securities Administrators created what is known as the Joint Forum of Financial Market Regulators in 1999. It is a national organization that addresses issues concerning the growing integration of the financial services sector and the harmonization of financial services regulation across the country.

One of the issues that the Joint Forum has addressed is the regulation of capital accumulation plans (CAPs). In addressing this issue, the Joint Forum's main aim is to strengthen consumer protection and outline corporate responsibility for their employment benefit plans. In 2006, the Canadian Association of Pension Supervisory Authorities (CAPSA) mandated that all CAPs comply with guidelines developed by the Joint Forum of Financial Market Regulators.

There are over $80 billion in CAPs. Over three million Canadians are members of them. CAPs include all group RRSPs, defined contribution pension plans (DCPPs), deferred profit-sharing plans (DPSPs), employee profit-sharing plans (EPSPs) and all other types of employee non-registered savings plans in which employees make investment decisions.

POTENTIAL RISK FOR EMPLOYERS

As employees learn their legal rights, a company's fiduciary obligations could perhaps be the most worrying of all for employers. In Canada, employers have been found liable for failure to bring the terms of benefit policies to the attention of employees.

Several years ago, Bell Canada was caught off guard, as many other Canadian companies in the coming years will be as the baby boomers begin to retire en masse. Many of its retirees received a large cash settlement from Bell Canada as a result of allegations that this company had not communicated to its employees the inherent risk of the group RRSP that it had set up and was promoting to its employees. Even though Bell Canada was not making contributions on behalf of its employees, it still chose to settle the dispute rather than fight it out in court.

Canadians have a newfound interest in class action litigation. Justice William O. Douglas, the longest-serving justice in the history of the U.S. Supreme Court, once wrote, "The class action is one of the few legal remedies the small claimant has against those that command the status quo." Class action lawsuits have seen more success in the last decade than they had in all the previous decades of the previous century, and it appears that our Canadian courts are now prepared to certify class action suits for breach of employment-related obligations.[1]

"It is not proposed that plan administrators and employers would be held harmless for investment losses of members," says the Joint Forum's first report, released in April 2001. Ultimately, if employees do not get what they expect from their company's sponsored retirement plans, there may be lawsuits relating to the product itself.[2]

In essence, employers offering CAPs have reason to be very concerned. The types of lawsuits we might expect are probably only limited by the imagination of the lawyers pursuing them. Websites have popped up all over the Internet, offering free services to the public, motivated to help the Davids of this world receive protection and justice from the corporate Goliaths.

Companies must be aware that if a lawsuit is pending against a sponsor of a CAP, there most likely would be disclosure in the notes of the company's financial statement in accordance with the generally accepted accounting principles which will impact investor and consumer confidence alike.

The most recently updated Joint Forum CAP Guideline outlines the roles and responsibilities of plan sponsors/employers for providing access to investment decision-making tools and cautioning employees that they ought to obtain independent investment advice. It is suggested that members of CAPs work with a professional advisor, who follows a strict code of conduct.

THE NEW FRONTIER

Employees in today's employment environment need to take responsibility for their careers and finances. It is important that employees don't perceive their company pension plan, benefit plan or group RRSP to be

---

1 Peter Merrick, "Individual Financial Plan Should Be the Core Benefit" *The Lawyers Weekly*, vol. 23, no. 23 (October 17, 2003).

2 *Ibid.*

their retirement plan, as it once used to be. Now employers are finding a need to help employees distinguish between the company's retirement plan and their employees' financial plans, and to help their employees to build contingency plans in case they lose their jobs through downsizing, getting sick, dying too soon or living too long.

In this new era, there is confusion over the distinctions between the meanings of "information", "education" and "employee personal financial knowledge" among both employers and employees. The Joint Forum is trying to clarify these differences. A company that just provides information about its pension, RRSP and other benefit plans has most likely not met its fiduciary responsibilities or moral duties. Just providing benefit information only adds to their employees' confusion (information overload).

THE SOLUTION

The Joint Forum of Financial Market Regulators has initiated raising the fiduciary responsibility bar on all employer-sponsored savings plans. A wise solution to mitigating potential future liability/risk for all employer-sponsored CAPs would be for companies to set aside between 1 and 5% of the total compensation for their people and to hire an independent financial planning solutions provider. Thus, their employees would then individually create and maintain a comprehensive financial plan custom-tailored for them alone.

"When Sears Roebuck proved that they earned 200 million dollars extra in 1997 as a result of improving employee satisfaction by four per cent, they paved the way for us to capture the true cost of poor well-being. Sears not only found a correlation between employee satisfaction, customer loyalty, and the bottom line, they found a causal link!" says Danielle Pratt, author of *The Healthy Scorecard — Delivering Breakthrough Results that Employees and Investors Will Love!* (Victoria, BC: Trafford Publishing, 2001).

How effective could financial planning be in increasing a company's bottom line?

Imagine we are dealing with a technology company that has a specialized department of 20 highly skilled software engineers who earn an average of $100,000 per year, with a total payroll of $2 million. The company's gross annual revenue attributed to the vital work of each of these employees is $1 million for a total of $20 million from this one department. Each year, the company has a personal turnover of 20% (four employees) from this department's workforce. To replace each engineer who leaves the department with another qualified engineer, it costs this company $30,000 in finder fees to pay a head hunting firm for assistance to find one replacement. It takes an average of 18 months for the replacement computer engineer to learn his or her job effectively and to generate a profit for the company.

This year, the company has decided as a retention strategy for this department to implement a financial planning benefit for each of its 20 employees. It has earmarked the equivalent of 5% of its total payroll ($100,000) for this department towards the creation of a personal financial planning benefit. The aim of this benefit is to give each employee the wherewithal to take responsibility and be empowered to integrate the company's entire benefit plan with what they are doing outside the company with their entire financials, thus creating a community and a strong feeling among the employees toward the company that they belong to. The goal of this new benefit is to create an environment that gives each of these engineers peace of mind, with a new ability to see how his or her personal success relates to the company's success in a tangible way, through the creation of the personal financial planning benefit. The desired goal is to create a greater commitment towards the company, reduce turnover and increase productivity.

At the first year anniversary of the financial planning benefit, the company witnesses its turnover drop by 50% (two employees leaving compared to the four the year earlier) and the productivity for each employee increase by 10% ($2 million). For a $100,000 investment in the first year of implementing this financial planning benefit program, this company has made a quantifiable return on its investment of $4,260,000 in productivity gains and a reduction in employee turnover in its first year. After ten years of implementing this benefit plan, the company could see a return on its investment of $42,600,000 in productivity gains and a reduction in employee turnover for as little as its $1 million investment into this benefit and its people.

RETHINKING CORPORATE BENEFIT PLANS

Canadian employers need to rethink corporate benefit plans. In the 21st century, the individual financial plan should be the modern company's core employee benefit. The financial plan makes the distinction between the financial planning process and the old world's focus on financial products. A financial planning benefit solution is the one tool that will help employers surpass regulatory benchmarks in the most cost-effective way.

A financial plan helps employees understand how their employee benefit programs form a part of their financial foundation while understanding that their employee benefit programs are not the total foundation for them to get the life they want as they plan their future and retirement.

CHAPTER 35

COMPARING 401(K)S WITH GROUP RRSPS

Peter J. Merrick
Robert Keats

Overview

This chapter details the similarities and differences between the U.S. 401(k) and the Canadian Group RRSP.

Learning Objectives

By the end of this chapter, you will:

- have a basic understanding of the rules that govern the U.S. 401(k); and
- have a full appreciation of how the Group RRSP can mirror the American 401(k) for U.S. employers who are operating in Canada.

Some time ago, a U.S. company sent an e-mail that read as follows: "Peter, I am the chief financial officer with a mid-sized software company in New York state. My company has just purchased a Canadian firm with more than 200 employees. We are seeking your assistance to help us with the set-up of an equivalent to the 401(k) plan for our new Canadian workforce. Can you refer us to a competent resource?"

The Canadian equivalent to the 401(k) is known as the Group RRSP. Unfortunately, very little has been written to act as a primer comparing 401(k) plans to similar employee registered retirement plans for American companies that are in the process of locating in Canada or that have acquired a Canadian company.

This should be very surprising to the reader since Canada is the United States' largest trading partner of goods and services, with more than $518 billion of cross-border trade in 2007, according to the U.S. Census Bureau. This partnership has been accelerating since 1984, when then-Prime Minister Brian Mulroney declared Canada "open for business" with the dismantling of the Foreign Investment Review Agency, a Canadian protectionist agency, coupled with the passing of the *Investment Canada Act*.

A December 2005 report by the Canadian Centre for Policy Alternatives showed that Canadian-owned companies valued at more than $620.7 billion had been taken over by non-resident-controlled corporations since Investment Canada started keeping records of these transactions in 1985. Just in the last two years, $156 billion worth of domestic companies have been sold into foreign hands. Of those, the majority of these takeovers were by U.S. interests. This has all occurred within a country which Statistics Canada says has a population of 33 million people, a 2007 GDP of $1.274 trillion and a national debt of only $467.3 billion. In the latter part of this decade, Canada has successfully avoided an economic recession while maintaining the healthiest financial statements of all the Group of Eight Nations (G8).

All things being equal, if we were to remove the Canadian publicly funded health care system from the equation, the difference between the Canadian and U.S. economies are marginal at best. The Fraser Institute's Economic Freedom of the World 2007 Annual Report says that the United States and Canada ranked together with Britain in fifth spot as the most economically free, open and competitive economies in the world today.

It is this continuous trend towards integration of the economies of the United States and its partner to the north that has prompted us to create this primer to decipher the secret code between the U.S. 401(k) and the Canadian Group RRSP to help demystify these two great retirement plans for employers on both sides of the 49th Parallel.

401(K) VERSUS GROUP RRSP

The story of the 401(k) begins in 1978, when the U.S. Congress amended the Internal Revenue Code to add section 401(k). The birth of the RRSP occurred more than 20 years prior, in 1957, when the Canadian federal government passed legislation amending the Canadian *Income Tax Act* to include these retirement plans. Both retirement plans are similar in that they allow workers to save for retirement while deferring income tax on the saved money and earnings until withdrawal.

Found within the plan text of both the 401(k) and the Group RRSP is the voluntary nature of membership for all employees. For an employee to be eligible to participate in a 401(k), he or she has the choice to become a member of this plan on the first day of each calendar quarter, following his or her date of employment. Eligibility and membership in a Group RRSP is similar to that in the 401(k). However, in a Group RRSP, there is no legislative requirement to limit or grant eligibility. Employers may set eligibility rules for their Group RRSPs to suit their needs.

The normal retirement age for a 401(k) participant is after his or her 65th birthday or an alternative retirement date if the employer decides to set its own retirement date. The earliest that a 401(k) participant can withdraw income is at age 59½ without a 10% early withdrawal penalty, and the latest is at age 70½, when the required minimum distribution rules apply.

The normal retirement date for a Group RRSP member is very flexible and may be set by the employer at age 65 or earlier. Group RRSP participants can enjoy the benefits of a registered plan until December 31 of the year after they turn age 71. At that time, members must convert all their RRSPs into a Registered Retirement Income Fund (RRIF) or an annuity, and begin withdrawing money from their retirement plan.

Other main differences between the 401(k) and the Group RRSP revolve around the maximum allowable employer matching contributions rules and eligibility rules.

401(k) employer contributions can be up to 100% of an employee's pre-tax compensation. 401(k) employee maximum contribution limits for 2008 for individuals under age 50 are $15,500 and for 401(k) participants age 50 and older limits are $20,500 annually. The maximum employee and employer contributions to a 401(k) plan for plan year 2008 is the lesser of $45,000, or 100% of compensation. As of 2009, 401(k) maximum contribution limits will be indexed to inflation.

In 2007, the IRS allowed a new and exciting option that most employers have adopted for the 401(k) programs. This new option is called the Roth 401(k), in which the employee may choose to put a portion of his or her contributions into the Roth 401(k) versus the regular 401(k). Employees contribute to the Roth 401(k) program, although no current deduction against income is provided, and all the proceeds in the Roth 401(k) grow and may be withdrawn under the normal Roth 401(k) rules without ever being taxed over the lifetime of the employee and employee's beneficiaries. The Canadian Tax-Free Savings Accounts (TFSAs) were created by the Canada Revenue Agency (CRA) to provide Canadians similar benefits to the U.S. Roth 401(k) or Roth Individual Retirement Accounts (IRAs). Eventually, it is expected that the TFSA may be incorporated into Group RRSP type programs in Canada in the future once employees start to demand this option.

The maximum contribution into a Group RRSP (both employer and employee) allowed by the CRA is the lesser of 18% of last year's earned income of the employee — up to a maximum of $20,000 in 2008, $21,000 in 2009, $22,000 in 2010, and indexed thereafter. If the 401(k) maximum contribution amounts are not used in the year that they are awarded, the member of the plan is not allowed to carry that unused room forward to future years to make contributions into these plans. Unused RRSP room can be carried forward indefinitely. In addition, an individual can accumulate unused RRSP room going back to 1991.

The rules for vesting the employer's contributions into the 401(k) for the member differ greatly from those of the Group RRSP. The vesting rule of an employer's contributions for the 401(k) by law is via a graduated formula so that 100% is vested within six years. However, employers have the option to adjust the vesting schedule to any earlier date that they may choose. The Group RRSP vests an employer's contributions in the employee's hands as soon as the employer contributions are remitted to the employee's RRSP account.

SALARY DEFERRALS

However, employee salary deferrals into a 401(k) are immediately 100% vested — that is, the money that an employee has put aside through salary deferrals cannot be forfeited. When an employee leaves employment, he or she is entitled to those deferrals, plus any investment gains (or minus losses) on his or her deferrals.

Many American companies can remain at ease knowing that an RRSP can accommodate the 401(k) contributions formula. Employee and employer contributions are remitted monthly for both the Group RRSP and 401(k). If the employer matches the employee contribution, these matching contributions are also remitted monthly.

Within both the 401(k) and the Group RRSP, transfers from other similar registered plans are allowed into these plans. In addition, moneys within these plans may be transferred out to similar registered plans as well. Transfers into both the 401(k) and the Group RRSP and transfers out to other registered retirement plans will not trigger taxes by either the Internal Revenue Service (IRS) or the CRA for their members choosing to do so.

Participants in a 401(k) may be permitted to access funds free of the 10% early withdrawal penalty from these plans subject to the rules set within the individual 401(k) plan text for reasons other than retirement. These allowable 401(k) withdraws may occur for the purchase of a primary residence or to avoid foreclosure on a primary residence. 401(k) funds can also be used to pay for post-secondary schooling within a 12 month period, medical expenses and funeral expenses. Most 401(k) plans also have a loan provision where participants can borrow from their plans for any purpose. For example, a participant can have a line of credit without any penalties or income taxes on the withdrawal unless they fail to repay the loan.

In regards to the Group RRSP, registered assets are not assignable and cannot be used as collateral for a loan, except for an interest-free, tax-free withdrawal for Home Buyers' Plans or other eligible Canadian government programs such as the Lifelong Learning Program.

Under the RRSP Home Buyers' Plan, the maximum that can be withdrawn is $20,000, and the withdrawal amount must be repaid into any RRSP within 15 years in no more than 15 equal yearly installments. Although $20,000 can be withdrawn from an RRSP over four years to pay for a post-secondary education using the Lifelong Learning Program, the most that can be taken out of an RRSP in one calendar year is $10,000. The participant has ten years to repay the money borrowed from his or her RRSP. Required moneys not repaid back into the Group RRSP — for either the Home Buyers' Plan or the Lifelong Learning Program — are counted as income by the RRSP member for that year and are taxed.

U.S. employees with 401(k) plans have optional withholding on withdrawals for retirement, and the Group RRSP has taxes withheld on funds withdrawn from these plans. With a Group RRSP, the plan must allow for withdrawals at the employee's discretion. However, deterrents from withdrawing funds can be imposed, such as eliminating the right to future employer contributions for a period of time.

U.S. CITIZENS LIVING AND WORKING IN CANADA

Prior to the fifth protocol of the Canada-U.S. Tax Treaty, as effective in 2009, citizens living in Canada could not contribute to Canadian group RRSPs, defined contribution plans or any similar Canadian registered plans and deduct the contributions from their U.S. taxable income. Consequently, U.S. citizens living in Canada who wanted to participate in Canadian registered retirement plans were effectively double-taxed in that they were taxed on the contributions by the IRS and were taxed by Canada again on any withdrawals. This new fifth protocol to the Canada-U.S. Tax Treaty now allows U.S. citizens transferred to Canada for employment, for the first five years of residency in Canada, to deduct contributions in both Canada and the United States for all Canadian registered plans, providing the contributions do not exceed what would normally be allowed by the IRS had the contributions be made to similar

U.S. plans with a U.S. employer against U.S.-sourced employment income.

BREAKING THE LOCK ON LOCKED-IN RRSPS

Canadians or U.S. citizens who have worked for employers within Canada find, much to their disappointment, that a good portion of their defined contribution pension benefit is "locked in" when they leave the company before retirement age. This lock-in is a result of employment pension plan regulation at the provincial level. All ten provinces and the four territories have such legislation, designed to prevent employees from spending their accrued pension benefits before retirement age. In effect, the provinces feel that the employees aren't responsible enough to roll their pension benefits into an RRSP and leave it there only for their eventual retirement, so they force the employees to roll the vested company contributions of their pensions into a Locked-in Retirement Account (LIRA).

Funds cannot be withdrawn from a LIRA, except in special emergency situations as defined by the applicable provincial legislation. At the normal retirement age set by the original company plan in which the employee was a member, the LIRA owners, if they wish to make withdrawals, can convert their LIRAs to Life Income Funds (LIFs) or Locked-in Retirement Income Funds (LRIFs). These both operate like Registered Retirement Income Funds (RRIFs) except that the start date at which withdrawals can be made for most provinces is age 55, and there is a maximum withdrawal rate each year, as well as the usual RRIF minimum. One additional option for LIRA holders is to use the LIRA funds to purchase a life annuity.

Until the year 2000, LIRA holders who became non-residents of Canada had no options other than the two mentioned above. This subjected U.S.-resident LIRA holders to numerous reporting requirements annually to the IRS and state tax authorities, potential double income and/or estate taxes, estate-planning issues and investment planning issues, not to mention currency risks. Review the previous section of this chapter for more details of the concerns of U.S.-resident RRSP/LIRA holders. In other words, being locked in with your RRSPs (in the form of a LIRA, LIF or LRIF) as a U.S. resident is somewhat punitive!

After much lobbying of provincial governments to provide relief for non-resident owners of LIRAs, Alberta, British Columbia, Saskatchewan, Ontario, Quebec and New Brunswick finally came through with legislation, effective on various dates from July 1999 to February

2007, respectively. As of these dates, LIRA owners from these six provinces can break the locks on their LIRAs if they can get written confirmation from the CRA that they are indeed non-residents. If the LIRA owner is married, a spousal waiver of any benefits from the LIRA is also required. The LIRA owner can obtain the CRA written confirmation by filing an appropriately completed Form NR73, Determination of Residency Status. The LIRA owner should receive an answer approximately eight weeks after submitting the NR73 to the CRA. In 2005, Manitoba introduced provisions into its *Pension Act* that allow those over the age of 55 to unlock up to 50% of a LIRA.

Employees of federally regulated industries, such as airlines, railroads and communications companies, regardless of their provinces of residence, can also qualify to break the lock-in on their LIRAs obtained from these companies. To qualify, they must currently be and have been non-residents of Canada for at least two years. By providing proof of non-residency (using form NR73 as noted above) to the LIRA trustee, he or she can break the lock-in and forward the funds to you, less the 25% non-resident withholding tax.

Dealing with RRSPs and LIRAs as a non-resident of Canada can be a tricky business. We recommend, at all times, that you seek the advice of an experienced and qualified cross-border financial planner.

INFORMED DECISIONS

In both Canada and the United States, there are rules revolving around what employers and plan sponsors are required to communicate to their plan participants about their plans to help their members make informed decisions. All 401(k) plans must follow the *Employee Retirement Income Security Act* (ERISA). ERISA is a federal law that sets minimum standards for most voluntarily established pension and health plans in private industry to provide protection for individuals in these plans.

ERISA requires plans to provide participants with plan information including important information about plan features and funding, sets out the fiduciary duties for those who manage and control plan assets, requires plans to establish a grievance and appeals process for participants to get benefits from their plans, and gives participants the right to sue for benefits and breaches of fiduciary duty.

Most providers offering Group RRSPs have procedures that are consistent with ERISA and that comply with the Canadian Capital Accumulation Plan (CAP) Guidelines. CAPs include all Group RRSPs, defined contribution pension plans, deferred profit-sharing plans, employee profit-sharing plans and all other types of employee non-registered savings plans in which employees make their own investment decisions. One of the guidelines is that employers are responsible for providing access to investment decision-making tools and for cautioning employees that they ought to obtain independent investment advice.

Obviously, setting up Canadian retirement benefits such as Group RRSPs, defined contribution pension plans, retirement compensation arrangements, employee profit-sharing plans, defined benefit pension plans or group medical and dental plans for American companies located in Canada requires specialties in areas as diverse as the Canada-U.S. Tax Treaty, the *Employee Retirement Income Security Act* (U.S.) and Canadian Capital Accumulation Plan Guidelines, as well as accounting, actuary evaluation, investment management, pension legislation, employment law and employee benefit plan construction.

Many employers and their Trusted Advisors will need to seek educational services to aid them in the set-up, maintenance and wind-up stages of these employee group benefits. Therefore, it is well worth the time and money to hire skilled certified consultants, financial planners and lawyers who possesses this expertise to assist in the design, implementation, maintenance and wind-up of these solutions.

CHAPTER 36

UTILIZING ALTERNATIVE TAX SAVINGS PLANS — EMPLOYEE PROFIT-SHARING PLANS, DEFERRED PROFIT-SHARING PLANS AND TAX-FREE SAVINGS ACCOUNTS

Peter J. Merrick

Overview

This chapter introduces the concept of the employee profit-sharing plans (EPSP). It then describes the long-term opportunity that an EPSP in conjunction with an Individual Pension Plan (IPP) creates. Also explored are the benefits of corporate clients creating deferred profit-sharing plans (DPSP). Lastly, the tax-free savings account (TFSA) is introduced.

Learning Objectives

By the end of this chapter, you should be able to:

- describe what an EPSP is;
- list the benefits that an EPSP provides for both a sponsoring company and for the member of the plan;
- understand how the creation of an EPSP creates funding opportunities for the IPP and what the long-term benefits are;
- understand the benefits of offering employees DPSP; and
- understand the rules and benefits of the new federal government's TFSA.

EPSP: HOW IT WORKS

Established under subsection 144(1) of the *Income Tax Act*, R.S.C. 1985, c. 1 (5th Supp.), the EPSP is a special purpose trust that allows the beneficiaries of the plan to share in the profits of a company. EPSP employer contributions are taxable as income to the employee and tax deductible as a compensation expense to the company. One of the great benefits of EPSPs is that they are treated as IPP eligible earnings for members of pension plans.

EPSPs are non-registered savings plans in which the employer contribution is computed by reference to an incorporated company's profits. The minimum employer contribution is 1% of current year profits or $100 per employee per year. Under an EPSP, investment earnings are taxable, any vesting rules or withdrawal restrictions may be established and no maximum contribution limits or investment restrictions apply. Both employer and employee contributions are permitted.

The flow chart below shows a simplified step-by-step process of how a company sets up an EPSP and deposits profits into the plan for members.

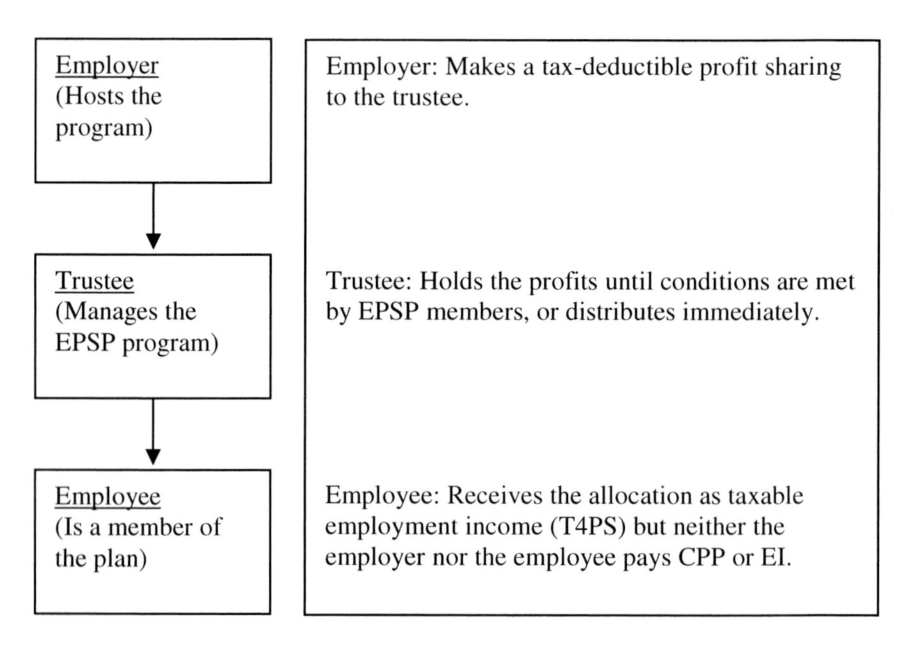

EMPLOYEE BENEFITS

- **Maintain RRSP Contribution Room:** Contributions made to the EPSP by the employee and employer will not reduce the employee's registered retirement savings plan (RRSP) contribution room. Allocated profits qualify as "earned income" for RRSP and IPP purposes and the RRSP carry-forward rules.

- **No Impact On IPP/RPP Contributions:** Members of an EPSP can still accumulate pension credits for their IPPs, allowing their employers to still be able to contribute into their plans on their behalf.
- **Employer Matching:** Many employers will match an employee's contribution to an EPSP as additional compensation.
- **Tax:** Yearly income tax is calculated on an EPSP; however, Canada Pension Plan (CPP) and Employment Insurance (EI) contributions are exempt.
- **"Kiddie Tax":** The "kiddie tax" rules should not apply to income received by minor children from an allocation from an EPSP, if they are *bona fide* employees of the business.

EMPLOYER BENEFITS

- The company accrues a payment to the trust that is fully deductible by the company if it is paid within a certain time period (up to a maximum of 120 days after the sponsoring company's year-end).
- No source deductions (CPP, EI and Income Tax) are required with respect to the amount allocated to the employee.
- An EPSP can be used for income-splitting purposes.
- All amounts paid from an EPSP to an employee are not subject to a reasonableness test, unlike salaries.
- There is no requirement that all employees be included or that those employees be treated equally under the EPSP trust. The decision to share profits and the selection of the employees with whom they are shared is totally discretionary.

How the EPSP works: A trust called the Employee Profit-Sharing Plan for XYZ Company is set up usually using a three-person trust agreement. The EPSP sponsoring company makes the contribution to the trust. All funds in the trust account must be allocated to the participants of the plan at the end of the fiscal year. The company issues a T4PS (profit-sharing) slip.

What you need to know: The table below shows what working Canadians and their employers have been contributing to CPP and EI.

EPSP's — Maximum Combined Employer and Employee Contributions

Year	CPP	EI	Total	Percentage Increase
1966	$158.40	-	$158.40	-
1975	$241.70	$323.44	$564.14	257%
1985	$759.60	$1,348.88	$2,108.48	273%
1995	$1,701.00	$3,051.38	$4,752.38	125%
2000	$2,659.80	$2,245.20	$4,905.00	3%
2002	$3,365.20	$2,059.00	$5,424.20	11%
2004	$3,663.00	$1,853.28	$5,516.28	2%
2005	$3,722.40	$1,825.98	$5,548.38	1%
2006	$3,821.40	$1,750.00	$5,571.40	1%
2007	$3,979.80	$1,728.00	$5,707.80	1%

KEY STRATEGIES OF AN EPSP

The following are examples of how an EPSP trust works and what its benefits in financial planning are.

"Golden Handcuffs" (Employee Loyalty)

An EPSP is an excellent incentive for senior employees. It can drive employee loyalty to an employer by delivering on a payout through continuous years of service. An employer can set up an EPSP with certain stipulations. See the following example:

- Each year, should profit be available, the trustee will receive a payment equal to 15% of an employee's base salary.
- Upon 25 years of service or age 60, the accrued balance plus growth will be released to the EPSP member/employee.

In this situation, the employee is presented with an opportunity so good, so "golden", that the employee becomes literally handcuffed to the employer so as to receive the funds from the EPSP, thus creating "golden handcuffs".

Tax Deferral

EPSPs can also be used as an alternative to salary bonuses to maintain the small business tax rate. EPSP payments must be made within 120 days of the fiscal year-end. If that date happens to fall in the next calendar year, the trustee would have until the end of the calendar year to allocate the payment to beneficiaries. Those beneficiaries would need to remit tax by April 30th of the following year. The end result is the potential for up to 12.5 months of tax deferral. With a traditional approach of paying salary bonuses, source deductions would be due within the same tax year as opposed to the additional 12.5 months of tax deferral gained by the EPSP.

A Practical Application for Investing CPP Contributions Saved in an IPP

Loss or reduction of EI and CPP benefits can be offset by properly investing the savings. In most cases, flexibility to invest these contributions should more than make up for the lost benefits. Let's see how!

Imagine that the owner of a Canadian-controlled private corporation (CCPC) establishes an EPSP for the year 2006. In the first year, both this business owner and his spouse are the only beneficiaries of the plan, and each earns more than $41,000 of profit-sharing income (through the EPSP trust).

The business owner, his spouse and his CCPC will not need to make any further CPP contributions. After the EPSP has been established, the savings will include employer/employee CPP contributions equalling $3,722.40 each, or $7,444.80 combined.

If the business owner decides to invest the $7,444.80 CPP savings to fund his IPP into a balanced portfolio that earned 7.5% annually, within ten years the business owner will have accumulated $15,344.

Now let's take this a step further. If our owner invests both the employer and employee CPP contribution into an IPP each year in the same balanced portfolio that compounds annually at 7.5%, assuming his contributions based on savings on CPP contributions will rise with the average industrial wage rate of 2.5% per year for the next 25 years until he turns 69 years old and has to withdraw funds from an IPP, our owner will have contributed $254,305 that would have been ear-marked for CPP contributions into his IPP. The value accumulated within his IPP before it would be needed to be withdrawn as pension at age 69 would be $679,390.

Below is a graph showing how much the savings of not having to make CPP contributions will grow within an IPP over a 25-year period.

IPP Contributions and Growth

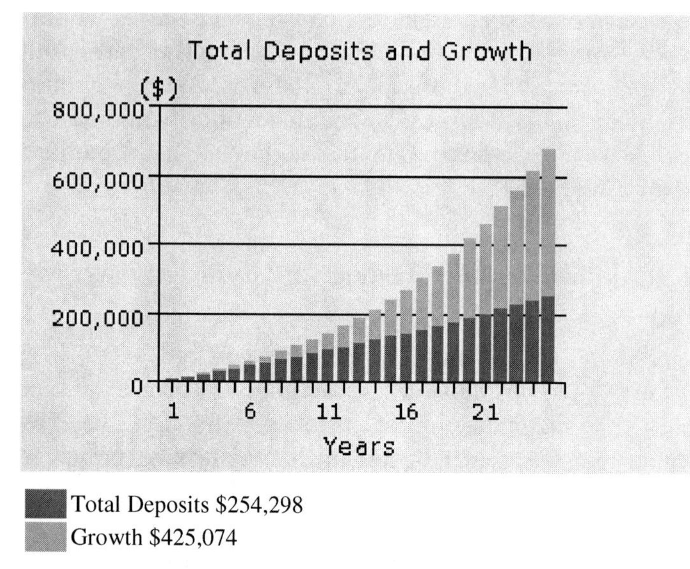

Income-Splitting Opportunity

This strategy is a practical example of how the EPSP can be effectively used to split income between spouses, generating both tax and CPP savings that can be used to make contributions into an IPP. This example illustrates the benefit of using this money to fund an IPP over a 25-year period.

Business Owner's Gross Income: $175,000
Income Tax Payable on Income: $64,400 (36.8% Average Tax Rate)
After Tax Income to Owner: $110,600

An EPSP is established for the owner and his spouse, who is an employee of the CCPC.

Business Owner's Gross Income: $100,000
Spouse's Gross Income: $75,000

Income Tax Payable to Owner: $30,000 (30% Average Tax Rate)
Income Tax Payable to Spouse: $19,125 (25.5% Average Tax Rate)
Total Tax Payable: $49,125

Net Income to Owner: $70,000
Net Income to Spouse: $55,875

Total Net Family Income: $125,875

Note: Difference in net tax payable and net family income with EPSP: $15,275 in 2006 dollars. This tax savings could even be greater if the business owner employed his children, and they were members of the EPSP as well.

LONG-TERM BENEFIT ANALYSIS OF ESTABLISHING AN EPSP

If the business owner and his spouse invested their combined savings of taxes and CPP contributions of $22,719.80 ($15,275 tax savings + $7,444.80 CPP contribution savings), which increased with CPI of 3% to subsidize a joint family IPP for the next 25 years, our owners will have contributed $828,354 into an IPP from these moneys. If these contributions within the IPP portfolio compounded annually at 7.5% for the next 25 years until they retire at age 69, when they will have to start withdrawing theses funds from their IPP, the value accumulated within the family IPP would have grown to $2,173,498.

The graph below illustrates the power for our example of taking the savings from both tax and CPP contributions and investing them into an IPP and letting them grow tax sheltered for 25 years. At the end of this period, because of the implementation of this strategy, the accumulated amount in the IPP will be $2,173,498.

IPP Deposits and Growth

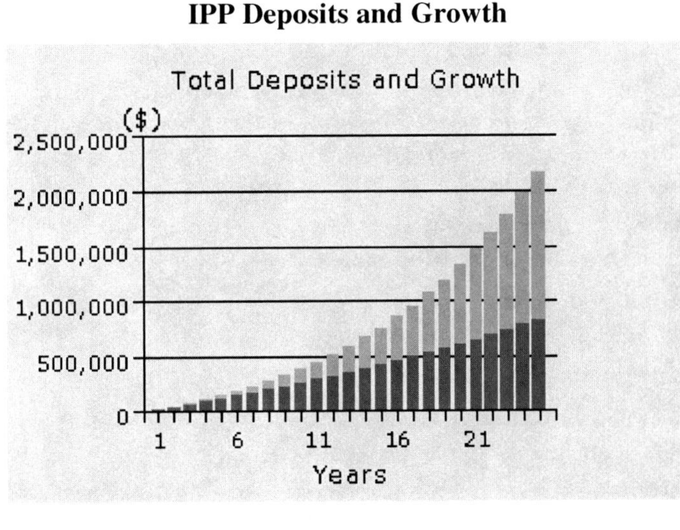

Values after 25 yrs

Growth $1,345,144

Total Deposit $828,354

Under certain circumstances, an EPSP can be used as an alternative to traditional remuneration strategies to effectively defer tax and facilitate income-splitting.

REQUIREMENTS

There are some guidelines that a company must follow before setting up an EPSP:

- It is essential that the payments from the business to the trust be calculated using the profits of the business. This means that the payments must be a percentage or share or part or all of the profits derived from the business.
- There must be an obligation on the business to make the payments in accordance with a formula in which profits are the principle variable. These payments must be made in any year where the business enjoys profits.
- A trustee is required, and a bank account in the name of the trust must be established.

EMPLOYER NEGATIVES

There are always benefits and negatives to any opportunity in life. The following is a short list of negatives which you might want to consider before implementing an EPSP trust:

- Like any plan, there are initial costs and maintenance fees to consider. There are legal and accounting fees associated with the analysis and drafting of EPSP trust documents. Average start-up costs for an EPSP trust vary depending on the size of the company. Generally, companies are able to recoup these costs within the first year of this trust being established.
- Like the introduction of the "kiddie tax", the CRA always has the ability to cut short the use of legitimate tax strategy.

Remember that an EPSP is a worthwhile consideration when:

- a corporation routinely follows a policy of "bonusing-down" to the small business limit (currently $400,000 federally);
- a corporation is expecting a large one-time increase in income;
- a corporation's current business structure prevents the business owner from effectively income-splitting with members of his or her family; and

- a business wants to reward key employees for contributing to the success of the business in a tax and financially effective way.

The creation of an EPSP creates the opportunity for an incorporated business to use money saved that would have been ear-marked for taxes and CPP to be redirected to partially fund an IPP. This is a strategy worth investigating.

IS A DPSP RIGHT FOR YOUR CLIENT'S BUSINESS?

Recently, I met with a client who owned a small business. For the last ten years he had been paying bonuses to his employees based on his profits. The problem he felt was that after he took off all the required taxes that he had remitted to the CRA on his employees' behalf, the result was that most of his people were left with little more than half of what he had indented to share with them. He asked me if there was an employee benefits plan that:

(1) could enable him to reduce contributions in the years he was not profitable; and

(2) allowed his employees to receive their entire bonus in a tax-effective way.

The answer that immediately popped into my head was the deferred profit-sharing plan (DPSP)!

These plans are not widely used in Canada today. However, DPSPs are one of the most powerful employee benefit tools available today that an employer can include in its arsenal to attract and retain top notch personnel. In a nutshell, employers and employees appreciate the DPSP because it rewards employees for helping a company earn profits. A DPSP is a simple and flexible arrangement; a company/plan sponsor distributes a portion of the company's pre-tax profits. DPSPs are arrangements where an employer may share with either all or a designated group of employees the profits from the employer's business.

Contributions and administration fees are tax deductible for the employer and accumulate, tax-sheltered, in the plan for the benefit of the employee(s) or former employee(s), until paid out of the DPSP as stated in subsection 147(1) of the *Income Tax Act*. In years that a DPSP sponsor is not profitable, the employer only needs to contribute 1% of an employee's income.

Usually the amounts payable by the employer under a DPSP are calculated as a portion of profits (*e.g.*, 10% of profits as defined in the plan), but can be a fixed dollar amount per plan member or fixed percentage of payroll.

DPSP MISCELLANEOUS

- A connected person (an individual who owns directly or indirectly more than 10% of a company) is not eligible to participate in a DPSP.
- Employer contributions into a DPSP are limited to the lesser of 18% of the employee's compensation for the year or a dollar limit equal to one half of the defined contribution pension plan limit as follows: 2006 — $9,500, 2007 — $10,000, 2008 — $10,500, 2009 — $11,000 and 2010 — indexed.
- Contributions are not added to members' earnings and are not subject to payroll taxes such as EI and CPP.
- Unlike a Group RRSP or pension plan, only employer contributions are allowed under a DPSP. Most employers use a DPSP as a complement to a non-contributory Group RRSP (*i.e.*, an RRSP with no employer contributions).
- DPSP contribution reduces the employee's RRSP room for the following year (allows full RRSP contribution for the current year). The reduction shows up as a pension adjustment amount on the employee's T4.
- Contributions vest in members after two years and are not locked in. Usually a DPSP member has the right to withdraw vested benefits from the plan at any time. Contributions can be cashed out or used to purchase an annuity.
- Depending on the plan, DPSP members may withdraw their holdings while they are still employed. Terminated employees can withdraw the full vested amount subject to taxation.
- The DPSP requires trustees, with at least one trustee being fully independent of the employer and plan member(s), and all trustees must be residents of Canada.
- All DPSPs must comply with the rules laid out in the CRA's Informational Circular 77-1R4.

INVESTIGATE THE NEW TAX-FREE SAVINGS ACCOUNT (TFSA)

The federal government introduced the new tax-free savings account (TFSA) in its February 26, 2008 budget. The first plans were registered in January 2009. Some experts expect that during the next decade, over $100 billion will accumulate in these plans.

Many consider the TFSA to mirror the RRSP and registered education savings plan (RESP) in many ways. Both the TFSA and the RRSP have annual contribution limits. But where the TFSA differs is that its contributions are not tax deductible for the contributor, similar to the RESP. In addition, unlike in the RRSP, contributions and income that accumulate within a TFSA are not taxed upon withdrawal. A TFSA permits clients to grow their investments tax-free (*i.e.*, interest, dividends and capital gains) on money that is in the plan because it has already been taxed as income.

Any individual (other than a trust) who is a resident of Canada and 18 or older is eligible to establish a TFSA. There is no age maximum for an owner of a TFSA to stop contributing to or withdrawing from the plan. A TFSA is administered in the same way as an RRSP: an account has to be opened with an authorized issuer; your client must provide his or her social insurance number; and loan expenses and interest are non-deductible for these plans.

How Does a TFSA Work?

As of 2009, individuals may contribute a maximum of $5,000 into a TFSA each year. Contribution amounts will be indexed beginning in 2010, with the Average Industrial Wage (AIW) and rounded to the nearest $500. Unused contribution room can be carried forward into the future indefinitely as long as the owner is alive. Accumulated amounts may be withdrawn from the TFSA as needed and at any time. The tax benefit will not be lost if your client withdraws an amount from a TFSA. Every time money is taken out of a TFSA, your clients will regain contribution room equal to their withdrawal, making a TFSA much more flexible than an RRSP, whereas in an RRSP the contribution room on funds withdrawn is lost forever.

So, for example, if a client contributes $4,000 to a TFSA in 2009, his or her contribution room for 2010 will rise to $6,000 ($5,000 current service contribution limit in 2010 and $5,000 limit minus the $4,000 actually made for 2009). Now imagine it is 2018, your client decides to take out $50,000 from his or her TFSA to purchase a cottage. Your client now has the ability to recontribute $50,000 into his or her TFSA after tax with the ability to grow again in the TFSA tax free because the government allows your client to regain that contribution room equal to the withdrawal. This does not affect his or her current year TFSA's contribution room.

A TFSA would generally be permitted to hold the same investments as an RRSP. This would include mutual funds, publicly traded securities, GICs, bonds and certain shares of small business corporations. TFSAs are not allowed to hold investments in any company where the owner of the plan is a connected person (owns 10% of a company or is related to someone who owns more than 10% of a company).

RRSPs Versus TFSAs

Since the federal government introduced the creation of the TFSA, many analyses have been completed to determine which is better for a client to take advantage of: the RRSP or the TFSA? Overall, the consensus is that TFSAs are best if the client expects his or her taxable income to be higher on withdrawal than when he or she made his or her contributions to the plan. RRSPs make more sense for a client when his or her tax rate is expected to be lower than when he or she starts to withdraw funds from the plan than when he or she made his or her contributions and took the tax deduction.

In March 2008, Jamie Golombek, CA, CPA, CFP, CLU, TEP, formerly at AIM Trimark Investments and now at Tax and Estate Planning, CIBC Private Wealth Management, made the following analysis, comparing the TFSA to the RRSP benefit:

TFSA vs. RRSP Example

	RRSP	**TFSA**
Pre-tax income	$5,000	$5,000
Tax (40%)	N/A	($2,000)
Net Contribution	$5,000	$3,000
Growth at 6% over 20 Years	$16,035.68	$9,621.41
Tax upon Withdrawal	$6,414.27	$0
Net Cash	$9,621.41	$9,621.41

The two plans shown above in the table are meant to be tax-neutral. The chart above compares the after-tax accumulation over 20 years of $5,000 in employment or business income earned by an individual, subsequently invested through a TFSA or an RRSP.

In the TFSA scenario, the $5,000 is taxed upfront, when earned, at the individual's marginal tax rate (assumed to be 40%) and the after-tax amount of $3,000 is invested in the TFSA. Since this tax is literally "pre-paid" and since the earnings and growth inside the TFSA are not taxed during the accumulation phase, nor are they taxed upon withdrawal, the after-tax value after 20 years, assuming a 6% growth rate, is $9,621.

In comparison, take the example of $5,000 of income that you don't pay tax on because it is put into your RRSP and a deduction is claimed for it. The $5,000 invested grows to $16,036 and is ultimately taxed upon withdrawal in 20 years at 40%. You net exactly the same amount after-tax, or $9,621, as the TFSA.

TFSA vs. Non-registered Investment Taxable Account

Imagine we have two clients, Client A and Client B, who each earns over $150,000 per year, both intending to invest $5,000 annually over the next 35 years, aiming to earn 7.5% compounded. Their individual investment holdings are placed in diversified portfolios, with their annual returns from 40% interest, 30% dividends and 30% capital gains. Client A invests into a TFSA, and Client B invests into a Non-registered Investment Taxable Account. Client A in his TFSA at the end of this period accumulates $799,657, and Client B within his Non-registered Investment Taxable Account only accumulates $480,281. Client A's TFSA will generate $319,376 more than Client B's Non-registered Investment Taxable Account.

TFSA Planning Opportunities

No Attribution Rules: Spouses can contribute into their spouses' TFSA with no fear that the earnings within these plans will be attributed back to their income.

No Old Age Securities (OAS) Clawbacks: Money withdrawn from a TFSA is tax-free so income taken out of these plans will not trigger an OAS clawback.

Ownership of Private Business Shares: If an individual or non-arm's length person owns less than 10% of a private business' shares, he or she can hold those shares in his or her TFSA.

Other Rules and Restrictions

Another bonus is that neither income earned in a tax-free account nor withdrawals will affect Canadians' eligibility for income-tested benefits and tax credits, meaning everything from Guaranteed Income Supplement (GIS) and OAS pension payment to payments under programs such as the National Child Benefit and Employment Insurance benefits.

Individuals may contribute to their own TFSA with funds provided by their spouse without the spouse's annual contribution room being affected. Moreover, the attribution rules will not apply to income earned on those contributions.

Generally, earnings that accrue in the account after the account holder's death will be taxable, while those that accrued before death would remain exempt. However, it would be possible to maintain the tax-free status of the earnings if the account holder names his or her spouse or common-law partner as the beneficiary of the plan.

TFSA vs. RRSP Review

Below is a chart that compares the new TFSA to the RRSP.

Benefits	**TFSA**	**RRSP**
Minimum age	18 years	No minimum
Age limit for contributions	No Limit	Year of 71st birthday
Contribution limit	2009: $5000 (indexed in subsequent years)	2009: Up to $21,000 2010: Up to $22,000 (indexed in subsequent years)
Limit as a percentage of earned income	No limit	18%
Carrying forward of unused contribution room	Every year	Every year

Benefits	TFSA	RRSP
Ability to replace withdrawn dollar amounts into the plan	Yes	No
Tax deductibility of contributions	No	Yes
Tax on growth within the plan	No	No
Taxation on withdrawals	No	Yes
Impact on OAS and GIS	No	Yes
Ability to use assets within the plan as security for loans	Yes	No

Remember: EPSPs, DPSPs and TFSAs offer incredible benefits, and it is well worth the time to investigate if these savings plans suit your clients' needs.

CHAPTER 37

STRATEGIES OF BALANCING EMPLOYEE HEALTH CARE COSTS WITH AN OWNER'S RETIREMENT GOALS

Peter J. Merrick
Andrew Duckman
Scott Maclagan
Stan Risen
Trevor Parry

Overview

This chapter will explore in depth some of the key issues currently challenging the traditional insurance model and will show how an alternative insurance solution known as an ASO (administrative services only) model offers an attractive cost-effective option that can impact the owner's retirement strategy in a positive way by finding money to fund the business owner's retirement solutions. It concludes in providing tax-effective methods to turn health care costs that are not covered by traditional medical and dental plans into legitimate deductions for employers and non-taxable benefits for employees while controlling costs.

Learning Objectives

By the end of this chapter, you should be able to:

- understand the new developments in health care;
- develop a basic understanding of the ASO model to manage rising health care costs for employees;
- understand how adopting the ASO model for health care can help fund a business owner's Individual Pension Plan (IPP);

- understand the benefit of creating health spending accounts for both executives and business owners; and
- understand the essence of health and dental plan cost containment.

FINDING THE MONEY

One of the reasons the IPP solution remains relatively underutilized by owners of small- to medium-sized companies in Canada today is the lack of available corporate funds to make the large initial and ongoing investments that are required into the Individual Pension Plan (IPP) to ensure maximum results.

One fruitful area to look for potential funds is at the business' employee group insurance. Most owners of small and medium-sized businesses offer their employees group benefit plans from traditional insurance carriers. Perhaps the greatest difficulty with this model is the constant rise in annual premiums, often as high as 15% per annum. In many cases, a simple re-evaluation and subsequent remodelling of the group benefit insurance model can deliver significant cost reductions and contain the year-over-year escalation. By adopting an alternative insurance solution, businesses owners will not only realize these cost savings, but can also use these new found savings to fund their IPP or other retirement solutions.

In the face of Canada's public health care crisis, providing employees with adequate and competitive health and dental coverage has never been more important. In 2005, more than $142 billion was spent for health care in Canada with 70% of the costs paid for by the federal and provincial governments' publicly funded system. Corporate Canada paid for most of the remaining 30% of non-essential medical and dental expenses, according to the Canadian Institute for Health Information and Statistics Canada.

While employer medical and dental plans were originally designed to be supplementary to the publicly funded government plan, as a result of the federal and provincial cutbacks in health care services, employers and private insurers across this country have had to alter and redesign their medical and dental plans to keep up with emerging trends of higher claims and new cost realities. In an age where publicly covered services continue to be reduced, we are likely to see Corporate Canada's share continue to increase in the coming years.

In the midst of these economic pressures on the current health care system, employees are demanding an enriched company medical and dental benefit plan. While the traditional corporate employee medical and dental benefit plan in Canada provides coverage for semi-private hospital rooms, prescription drugs, dental, chiropractors, physiotherapists, vision care, extended health coverage and travel medical insurance, employees are asking for more options then ever before. Opinions on what to add are largely influenced by age and experience — items like teeth-whitening can compete with orthotics. Older employees want expanded drug coverage, while younger workers are concerned about their deductibles. The end result is that employees want choice and employers want/need to contain their costs.

The vast majority of Canadian small- and medium-sized businesses offer medical and dental benefits to their workforces by utilizing insurance carriers. With the consolidation frenzy of the last decade, the number of insurance carriers has dwindled in an effort to make the Canadian players more globally competitive. This new, streamlined landscape has been good for the carriers, but not for the small- and medium-sized Canadian businesses, which have been underserved by the carriers because the carriers are focused on delivering shareholder value with big premium clients that pay $500,000 or more in annual premiums.

The increasing pressures on the current health care system, the consolidation of the insurance industry and the growing employee demand for more flexible and expanded coverage is having the greatest impact on the small- and medium-sized Canadian business. With health and dental care coverage escalating by approximately 15% for health and 7% for dental, small- and medium-sized employers are facing uncontrollable and unpredictable costs to their businesses to provide these benefits. Employers have tried to curtail these costs by introducing annual limits, co-insurance, deductibles and exclusions to their medical and dental plans.

Upon closer review of the average group medical and dental policy for small- to medium-sized businesses, usually only 60% to 75% of the overall premium dollars are earmarked for payment for eligible claims. The remaining portions of these premiums are used to pay administration costs, create reserves, pay commissions and earn insurance carriers profits for shareholders.

As an alternative to the traditional medical and dental insurance solution, some employers are choosing to move towards the administrative services only (ASO) model offered by traditional insurance companies and third party administrators. There are generally three components to this model:

(a) *Self-Insurance* — The employer self-insures, assuming the cost of all claims.

(b) *Stop-Loss Insurance* — To reduce the risk of a large employee claim, stop-loss insurance provided by a traditional carrier or specialty provider is combined with the self-insurance to pay out claims beyond a certain level. The premium for this reduced level of insurance is reasonably affordable.

(c) *Third Party Administrator* (TPA) — In order for Canada Revenue Agency (CRA) to allow the cost for medical and dental plans to be tax deductible for the employer and the benefits to be non-taxable in the hands of employees, the administration of these plans operated through the ASO model must be handled by a third party. In addition, having employees submit claims directly to the employer would contravene the *Privacy Act*.

By avoiding a great deal of the administrative costs and reserves incurred by traditional insurance companies, this model allows the employer to pay more claims with every dollar spent, and offers greater flexibility when designing a plan. Under the ASO model, the company assumes the cost of predictable claims and purchases stop-loss insurance for the catastrophic risk for unpredictable large claims.

But what if an employee has a large drug claim or hospital claim? Can the plan sponsor afford the risk of self-insurance?

To reduce the likelihood of incurring a significant claim from an employee, insurance is still a wise purchase. Statistically, most employees spend less than $1,000 per year on eligible health claims. The premium for insurance coverage over a specific amount such as $5,000 per individual is reasonably affordable. In this case, the extra insurance is truly insurance. The company is assuming the cost of predictable claims, and purchases insurance for the catastrophic risk of unpredictable large claims. This type of insurance is referred to as stop-loss insurance.

For companies with fewer than 150 employees, the key factor is selecting the appropriate stop-loss level. As the deductible or stop-loss level increases the corresponding premium is reduced. However, the level of risk increases should the company incur a major claim. Regardless of the cost of the stop-loss insurance, the company will only tolerate a certain level of risk. The key is understanding claims activity and choosing a level of stop-loss insurance at which the risk tolerance and savings are in harmony.

To illustrate the savings from the ASO model with stop-loss insurance, we will use a ten-employee company. The total health claims for the previous 12 months were $9,000, and the total dental claims were $7,000.

	Traditional Insurance
Health premiums	$13,000
Dental premiums	$11,000
Total cost	$24,000

	ASO with stop-loss ($5,000 level)
Health claims	$15,200*
Dental claims	$7,000**
Stop-loss premium	$2,000
Administrative cost	$1,680
Total cost	$22,680
Saving	$1,320 (5.5%)

* As a rule of thumb, 80% of all claims come from 20% of all employees — in this scenario, two employees incurred $6,600 worth of health claims each, costing the stop-loss carrier $1,600 per employee based on a $5,000 stop-loss deducible. Other employees incurred health claims of $2,000. The $2,000 and first $5,000 of claims for the two employees is borne by the company. A total of $3,200 is paid by the stop-loss insurer.

** The dental claims are fully self-insured by the company and will cost the company the full $7,000. There is no stop-loss for dental. Unlike health, which could have a catastrophic event, dental has built-in limits of coverage and therefore there is no need for dental stop-loss insurance.

In the example, the company would save $1,320 or 5.5% by converting to a self-insurance model with a stop-loss policy. In the worst-case scenario, where all employees have high average health claims one year, the company's exposure is still capped at $5,000 per employee. However, while the likelihood of such an event occurring is extremely minimal, the impact on the following year with ASO would still be less than with traditional insurance that reimburses from the first dollar and includes "inflation and trend" factors in their renewal rates ranging from 15% to over 20%.

Employers contemplating utilization of the ASO approach must recognize that they are fully responsible for the cost of the actual paid claims plus administration expenses and premium taxes, less any recovery from the stop-loss insurer. The presence of stop-loss insurance does not guarantee that it will protect the company for a high average level of claims just below the stop-loss deductible amount.

ASO AND INSURED PLANS IN ACTION ENABLING A BUSINESS OWNER TO FUND HIS OR HER IPP

Imagine a 55-year-old man who owns a small transportation company in Ontario with approximately 90 employees, who has drawn a T4 income since 1991 of $100,000 annually and who has struggled with the rising costs of his company's group benefit premiums, which have been increasing at an annual rate of 10% per year over the last three years. In a competitive industry with only 5% profit margins, the company had to take immediate action. The company outlined that it wanted to achieve three objectives when reviewing its group insurance plan with its employee benefit specialist:

(1) Provide an enhanced medical and dental plan that would be attractive to new and existing personnel.

(2) Maintain and, if possible, reduce expenditures on its balance sheet.

(3) Fund an IPP for the business owner's retirement.

After a thorough consultation, the corporate benefits program was re-engineered to meet the company's main objectives. This was accomplished by modifying the existing fully insured group plan to an ASO model with stop-loss insurance. After the new solution was implemented, annual premiums went from $403,562 to $239,706, a 40% savings in year one alone. In year two, the premiums for the ASO and stop-loss insurance increased by only 5.5%, down from the 10% premium increases seen under the traditional group insured plan.

Based on the above assumptions, this company will realize an accumulative savings by transitioning from the traditional group-insured plan to the new ASO and stop-loss insurance plan, totalling $3,345,439 over the next ten years (see the table, below). Had the employer paid for the entire plan, these savings would have been equivalent to the company generating $67 million of gross revenue during the same ten-year period.

Projected Ten-Year Savings

Year	Traditional Insured Annual Premium Based on an Annual 10% Renewal Increase	Cumulative Premiums Paid	Annual Premiums for ASO and Insured Model Based on an Annual 5.5% Renewal increase	Cumulative Premium Paid for ASO plus insured Model	Cumulative Savings for Transitioning to the ASO and Insured Model	Gross Revenue Equivalent to Cumulative Savings
1	$403, 562	$403, 562	$239, 706	$239, 706	$163,856	$3,280,397
2	$443,918	$847,480	$252,890	$492,596	$354,884	$7,104,777
3	$488,310	$1,335,790	$266,799	$759,395	$576,395	$11,539,427
4	$537,141	$1,872,931	$281,473	$1,040,867	$832,064	$16,657,921
5	$590,855	$2,463,786	$296,954	$1,337,821	$1,125,965	$22,541,819
6	$649,941	$3,113,727	$313,286	$1,651,107	$1,462,620	$29,281,652
7	$714,935	$3,828,662	$330,517	$1,981,624	$1,847,038	$36,977,700
8	$786,428	$4,615,090	$348,695	$2,330,319	$2,284,771	$45,741,115
9	$865,071	$5,480,161	$367,874	$2,698,193	$2,781,968	$55,694,999
10	$951,578	$6,431,739	$388,107	$3,086,300	$3,345,439	$66,975,688

COST-SAVINGS OF THE ASO MODEL USED TO FUND AN IPP

In the example provided above, the business owner saved his company $163,856 in the first year by having his company adapt the ASO model, which goes directly to the company's bottom line. The savings created could easily be redirected to fund the business owner's IPP, helping him meet his last objective of funding his retirement in a cost-effective way.

This business owner, at 55 years of age, with a T4 income of $100,000 from his company since 1991, has now found existing money within his company to make the $161,851 contribution to fund the IPP. The $161,851 IPP contribution will be a full deduction for the business and a non-taxable benefit for the business owner in the first year of the IPP. All future contributions into the IPP will also come from the savings from switching to the ASO model.

HEALTH AND WELFARE TRUSTS

Adopting the ASO model allows employers the additional benefit of providing either health and welfare trusts (HWT) or enhanced benefits for key executives within an organization. An ASO can be structured to provide varying reimbursement limits to a different classification of employees (*e.g.*, executive, part-time staff, *etc.*). Each employee classification can be assigned an annual reimbursement limit, with different classes of employees having differing reimbursement limits.

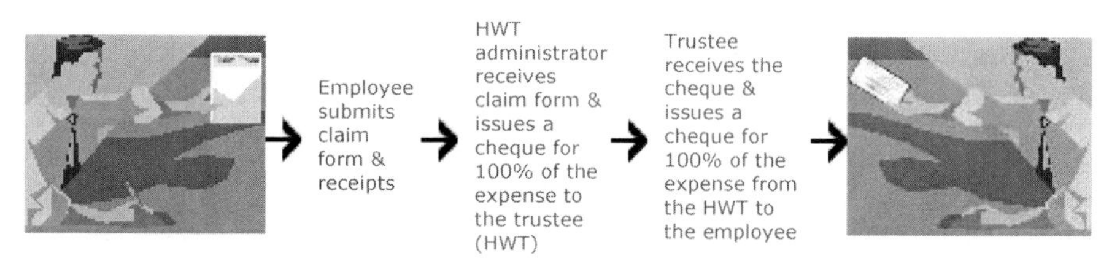

Illustration was provided with the permission of Gordon B. Lang & Associates Inc.

In this competitive employment environment, employers looking to attract and keep key people are finding that offering enhanced executive medical and dental plans gives these employers an edge over their competitors aiming to achieve the same results. Enhanced executive medical coverage using the ASO model for key people within an organization, in addition to traditional health care coverage, can include the rest of an individual's costs, such as the following:

- insurance premiums paid by the executive/employee or the individual's spouse for private health and dental plans;
- cosmetic dental and medical treatment;
- over-the-counter drugs, provided they are prescribed by a physician;
- drugs for conditions sometimes excluded under conventional plans;
- laser eye surgery;
- professional services of a dietician, acupuncturist, psychologist or nutritionist;
- dental care (preventive/restorative/orthodontic);
- medical equipment and devices;
- allowing of critical illness (CI) and long-term care (LTC) insurance premiums to be deductible to the company;
- facilities and services — special school, alcohol/drug addiction counselling, nursing home care, institution for mental or physical handicap, licensed private hospital, semi-private or private charges in a hospital, care of a person who has been certified as mentally incompetent, care of a blind person, full-time attendants in a nursing home and fertility clinics; and
- specialized private schools, camps and other educational institutions — an owner of an incorporated business (and/or his or her dependants) who has been diagnosed as having a learning disability has the ability to make business tax deductions for expenses that are related to the learning disability through the use of the health and welfare trust solution.

The cost of specialized private schools, camps and other educational institutions can be put through a health and welfare trust in accordance with the rules set down in subsection 118.2(2) of the *Income Tax Act*, R.S.C. 1985, c. 1 (5th Supp.), provided that the following three criteria have been met:

Criteria One: A qualified person has certified that the individual has a learning disability.

Criteria Two: A qualified person certifies that the individual with the learning disability requires the equipment, facilities and personnel specialties provided by a named private school, camp or other educational institution.

Criteria Three: The specialized private school, camp or other educational institution has the required equipment, facilities and personnel to assist the individual with his or her learning disability needs.

"The Numbers Speak for Themselves ..."

Imagine that you have a client who has an incorporated business in Ontario, earns a T4 income of $200,000, and has a marginal tax rate of 46.4%. This client has a son who has been diagnosed with a learning disability by a certified child psychologist (Criteria One met).

The psychologist recommends in writing that the best educational facility in Canada to meet this boy's learning and developmental needs as a person with a learning disability is the Robert Land Academy (RLA), a boarding school in Wellandport, Ontario. RLA has been widely recognized by qualified persons during the past 31 years in meeting the special needs of boys with learning disabilities (Criteria Two met).

RLA currently has in place the facilities and personnel to meet the educational needs of boys who have been diagnosed with learning disabilities (Criteria Three met).

The school fee for attending RLA for the entire 2009-2010 academic year is $35,500.

Now let us compare this client's two options and find out what the final financial outcomes for each are. In Option 1, the client plans to pay for the entire school fee with his after-tax dollars. In Option 2, the client has set up a health and welfare trust with his company and plans to pay for the entire school fee through the trust.

In Option 1, the client will have to earn approximately $66,231 of personal income before taxes to pay with after-tax dollars the school fees of $35,500. The school fees will have to be paid before the client can be eligible to apply for a personal medical expense tax credit (METC).

In Option 2, the client's company, through the health and welfare trust solution, will pay $39,000 ($35,500 school fees plus $3,500 administration fee of 10%) into the trust. The total savings this client and his company receive for opting for Option 2 and setting up the health and welfare trust and then claiming the RLA school fees through the trust is $27,231 over staying with Option 1. This savings equals approximately 75% of RLA's entire school fees.

Critical Illness and Long-Term Care Through a Health and Welfare Trust

For many businesses, the use of a health and welfare trust can be instrumental in providing health benefits and planning for contingencies. The use of an HWT to make the pure insurance portions of CI premiums and long-term care premiums deductible allows a company to provide these benefits on a more cost- and tax-effective basis.

The CRA has issued various rulings concerning CI and LTC policies purchased by a health and welfare trust over the last few years.

1. CRA Interpretation Bulletin IT-85R2, July 31, 1986, set out key requirements needed to constitute an HWT and requires that benefits would be restricted to one or more of the following: group sickness and accident insurance plans and private health service plans.
2. CRA Technical Interpretation TI-2003-0026385, December 10, 2003, held that CI policies, which provide only CI coverage, would constitute an accident and sickness plan.
3. A CI insurance policy held by a health and welfare trust is not considered a "life insurance policy" and, therefore, is not a taxable benefit to an employee. A return of premium benefit payable on death, or at the expiry of the term of the coverage or after a certain claim-free coverage period, may result in the disallowance of tax deductions of all contributions to the HWT.
4. Under CRA Interpretation Letter 2002-0160155 dated April 3, 2003, and subsequent CRA letters, a group CI policy may be purchased by the plan, and where such a policy contained no provision for life insurance coverage or for a refund of all, or a portion, of the premiums paid on termination of the policy or on death of the insured employee, it was viewed as a legitimate investment by the plan resulting in no taxable benefits to the employees.
5. A similar situation applies with an LTC policy, where such a policy would be a legitimate investment by the plan, providing it did not contain any return of premium benefits providing a premium refund similar to that for CI policies.

There are two types of CI and LTC policies — individual and group plans. These are generally issued by distinct departments of life insurance companies. Either type of policy may be purchased through a health and welfare trust.

Individual Policy and Split-Dollar Agreements

Individual policies generally provide additional benefits or riders in the form of return of premium benefits. Although the company may find such riders highly attractive, should the premium for such riders be paid through the HWT, it invalidates the HWT, *i.e.*, it disqualifies the eligibility of all contributions made to the HWT. The approach is to prepare a "split-dollar" or "shared ownership" agreement. The cost of pure insurance is funded through the HWT, and the company will pay the premiums for all of the various return of premium benefits and riders. Care must also be taken to ensure that shareholder employees are eligible for such benefits as a result of their employment with the company as opposed to their company ownership and that a policy would be issued on each life.

Flow Chart of an HWT with Critical Illness Insurance or Long-Term Care

(Individual Policy Situation)

1. Health and welfare trust is established
2. Sponsoring company purchases CI insurance or LTC insurance

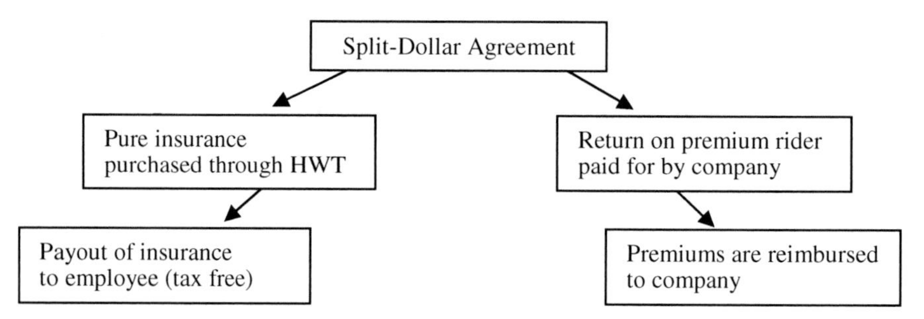

Group Policy

Group CI policies tend to be simpler than individual policies and can usually be issued without any return of premium benefits or riders.

Requirements

Whether individual or group policies are used to fund critical illness insurance through a health and welfare trust, the company should ensure the following:

1. The HWT has been properly set up and that no taxable employment benefits or shareholder benefits have been created.
2. The critical illness and/or long-term care benefits constitute a "group sickness and accident plan" by purchasing either a group plan or series of individual plans which will be deemed part of the company plan.
3. No form of return of premium benefits or riders are funded through the HWT. If the company wishes to purchase these riders, they should have their employee benefit consultant prepare a split-dollar/shared ownership agreement. If the company does not require these riders, the insurance company should be instructed to

issue the policy as pure insurance without any such benefits riders, in particular, any embedded return of premium benefits on death.

THE ULTIMATE SOLUTION TO HEALTH AND DENTAL PLAN COST CONTAINMENT

If employers are to be able to afford health and dental benefits in the future, we believe there has to be a fundamental change in the approach taken to the provision of these benefits in Canada. No longer can the "traditional group insurance plan" incorporating annual compound rate increases be afforded by most employers, and in particular small employers of fewer than 25 employees, which make up over 95% of all Canadian employers.

Employees have to become part of the solution, rather than the cause of increasing claim costs. Few employees have any sense of the true cost of the benefits provided and only look at benefits as an entitlement, rather than a part of their overall compensation.

Canadian employers today are seeking alternatives to the cost spiral being experienced with the traditional group health and dental plan offered by insurers. Many benefit plan administrators (third party administrators), insurance brokers and others are offering versions of what is termed a "cost plus" program, under which an employer pays a set-up fee and then the actual cost of eligible medical or dental expenses plus a handling fee of 10% of the claim, plus applicable taxes.

These plans are claimed to be "private health services plans", as defined in the *Income Tax Act*, Regulations and associated Interpretation Bulletins. However, in the eyes of the CRA, based on our discussions with the CRA, most of these plans are "offside" and not an eligible business expense.

The Federal *Income Tax Act* is supplemented by a number of Interpretation Bulletins that are intended to clarify various aspects of the Act. Interpretation Bulletin IT-339R2 (August 8, 1989) defines the meaning of a "private health services plan (PHSP)". Under point 3 on page 2 it states:

> A private health services plan qualifying under paragraph (a) or (b) of the definition in subsection 248 (1) is a plan in the nature of insurance.

In this respect, the Bulletin states that the plan must contain the following elements:

(a) an undertaking by one person,

(b) to indemnify another person,

(c) for an agreed consideration,

(d) from a loss or liability in respect of an event,

(e) the happening of which is uncertain.

[emphasis added]

It is the element of "risk", as required by item (e) above, that many "cost plus" plans do not contain and therefore would not qualify as a PHSP. Proponents of these plans have added "stop loss" or "out-of-country" insurance, but this is not what the CRA intended or requires. As all claims are paid in full, there is no element of risk as required under IT-339R2.

A corporate employer, in order to provide coverage for items not covered by its group medical and or dental program, often utilizes "cost plus" to cover such expenses for senior management staff. This is considered acceptable by the CRA.

The CRA and the Department of Finance have had ongoing discussions for many years regarding the future of "cost plus" plans, as they are aware that there are many thousands of such plans that do not meet the requirements of IT-339R2. The primary area of concern is the fact that under many plans there is no "element of insurance".

There was a tax case in which a significant shareholder in Whistler, B.C., set up a cost plus plan to cover a $35,000 knee operation he had in the United States in 2004. Not only was the medical expense claim disallowed, but he was penalized and fined because his plan was not eligible in the eyes of the CRA as it covered only one person — a shareholder — not an employee.

The Need for Cost-Controlled Health and Dental Benefits

Employers of all sizes, but particularly small- to medium-sized employers, have faced compounding premium rate increases under traditional insured group health and dental plans for the past decade, regardless of the actual claims experience of their own group. In recent years, insurers have utilized arbitrary "inflation" and "trend factors" ranging from 15% to 20+% when calculating the renewal rates. When asked to justify the level of these increases, insurers have been unable to do so.

Large corporate employers have been able to "self-insure" their benefit costs under what is termed an "administrative services only" (ASO) arrangement with an insurer. While this may enable them to have some degree of control over the inflation factors utilized, they have to recognize that *they will ultimately bear the full cost of their own group's claims experience, plus administrative costs and applicable taxes.*

Many large employers have added a "stop-loss" insurance policy in an attempt to "cap" their potential liability. However, if the stop-loss protection purchased is based on an individual employee's claims in excess of say $5,000 or $10,000 per policy year, it may not have any impact whatsoever. A new "aggregate stop-loss" policy covering all claims in excess of a predetermined amount per certificate is now available and may assist in controlling an employer's ASO costs, but that is yet to be determined.

Smaller employers have not been able to afford this ASO approach because of the wide swings in cost that can occur from year to year. They have been forced to resort to the traditional insured plan with its compounding rate increase. A new approach to the provision of benefits, and in particular health and dental benefits, is therefore required.

Traditional solutions to the cost spiral have included restrictive drug formularies, increased deductibles and co-insurance factors, drug utilization reviews and restrictions on certain drug categories, as well as revised cost sharing arrangements placing a greater burden on employees. These measures have had limited success as employees have not been required to effectively manage the limited employer dollars available for health-care.

Over the years, employees have developed an attitude that the employer's program is there to be taken advantage of and have no comprehension of the true costs being borne by the average employer. Insurers for their part have simply increased the premium rates at renewal to cover their losses and have included the aforementioned inflation factors to ensure that they have adequate funds to pay the escalating claim costs and to meet their bottom line pre-tax profit objective of at least 15%.

Many employers have contributed to the problem by continuing to provide open-ended plan designs, which invite abuse and cost increases. There has been little or no communication with employees to make them part of the cost solution, rather than the problem.

Controlling Immediate and Long-Term Costs

Benefit costs can represent a significant percentage of an employer's overall compensation costs, particularly where benefits are part of a collective agreement. Most employers cannot afford to follow down the compounding cost increase road and must act more prudently in the provision of benefits, because of not only the immediate, but the long-term costs.

With the introduction of the Canadian Institute of Chartered Accountants (CICA) Accounting Standards in Canada in 2000, employers who have been providing post-retirement benefits are now reviewing the future cost of these benefits and eliminating them wherever possible as they must be reported on their financial statements each year as a future liability.

The end of mandatory retirement is also impacting on benefit plans as the cost of providing health benefits to those 65 years of age and older rises dramatically. Many employers are taking the position that while they will allow and in some cases encourage employees to work beyond age 65, they are not obligated to continue benefit protection. Post-age 65 workers on the other hand want continued health and dental coverage as a minimum.

Flex Benefit Plans

Over the past 25 years or so, major Canadian employers introduced "Flex Benefit Plans" in an effort to control costs. Under a true full-flex plan, literally every benefit component is subject to review and scrutiny, and employees are given the responsibility of selecting benefits to match their personal needs. Often a mandatory core program of life and disability benefits is required to be selected by each participant. Employees may also be allowed to trade the cost value of certain benefits and even vacation time in the design of their own program.

The implications of a full-Flex program for the employer usually include increased benefit administration responsibilities and related costs, and most certainly more effective ongoing employee communications. This is required to ensure that employees really understand the choices and implications of these choices on their own financial security and that of their families. For the small- to medium-sized employer, a full-Flex plan is not a realistic or an affordable option.

The Defined Contribution Solution

Several years ago, many employers in the United States, faced with even higher health care costs than Canadian employers, moved to a "defined contribution" approach. Under this arrangement, *a specific dollar amount is provided to all employees* regardless of marital status (this is because an employer does not typically pay someone more based on the fact that he or she has dependants). Employees with dependants are required to pay the full additional cost of covering their dependants.

The trend to defined contribution plans is now well entrenched in the United States, but more significantly, a new trend has emerged whereby employers are utilizing "individual health plans" rather than "group plans" to provide employees with health and dental protection in order to avoid the compounding cost increases. These are often referred to as "consumer driven health plans" in U.S. media publications.

American employers many years ago were sold on "managed care programs" through health maintenance organizations (HMO) and preferred provider organizations (PPO) and their purported ability to control costs. Unfortunately, these solutions did not work as promised, hence the resulting trend to defined contribution and individual plans under which employees must take ownership for their own health care utilization and costs.

The solution for Canadian employers to achieve cost control is to adopt a "defined contribution" approach to the provision of health and dental benefits. This enables an employer to establish a defined amount per employee that will be contributed towards the cost of benefits in the form of a Health Spending Account (HSA), which will not be subject to "inflationary" cost factors normally imposed by a traditional group insurer.

Employers are then able to effectively budget their future benefit costs under this approach. Employees know the amount they will have to spend on health and or dental benefits for themselves and any dependants, and can purchase optional individual health or health and dental coverage to supplement the amount available under their HSA (the HSA is a sub-plan under HWT).

Flexible Benefits, But Defined Contribution Approach

Utilizing an HSA as the primary vehicle for health and dental benefits enables an employer to define the annual employer contribution to the program and therefore control the employer's cost. The employer can vary the annual contribution by class of employee or on any basis desired. Employees cannot contribute directly to the plan. However, the employee and employer at the expiry of a contract can renegotiate the "compensation arrangement" under which the employee requests that the employer direct pre-tax earnings to the employee's HSA.

The medical expenses that may be claimed are outlined in Subsection 118.2(2) of the *Income Tax Act* and in IT-519R2, and are much broader than permitted under any group benefits program. Benefits received from the HSA (a "private health services plan") are not considered taxable income in the hands of employees (except in Quebec).

Often HSAs are included as part of an overall "Flex Benefit Program", but can also be offered independently of any other health benefit. As the employer's contribution is fixed on an annual basis, there is the "risk" that some claims incurred by employees will not be paid due to the claims exceeding the amount available in the HSA. This is the element of insurance the CRA requires under IT-339R2.

An employer could self-administer the HSA according to the CRA, or contract with a third party administrator, or an insurance company, to administer the plan. There is no indication in any CRA materials that a "trustee" is required. We would not recommend self-administration by an employer as this would require that all claims be submitted to the employer for approval and this would contravene the *Privacy Act* regarding the confidentiality of health information.

The employer can deduct contribution to an HSA as a business expense as it is a contribution to a "private health services plan". Sole employees of their own corporation may have to prove that the deduction is being claimed as the result of being an employee and not because he or she is the significant shareholder.

The CRA T4002, "Business and Professional Income Guide", outlines the basis under which a sole proprietor may deduct premiums payable to a PHSP. The sole proprietor who has no employees may deduct up to $1,500 for himself or herself, plus $1,500 for a spouse and $750 for each child from his or her business income. If there are employees, additional rules come into play.

True Cost Control for Canadian Employers

A "defined contribution" approach which includes an HSA as the basic health and dental coverage, plus "catastrophic" insurance protection of $25,000 per person per policy year ($1 million lifetime) for drugs, hospital and private duty nursing out of hospital, enables an incorporated self-employed entrepreneur as well as an employer of any size to essentially "freeze" their cost for health and dental protection. It provides internal equity amongst employees, as all employees, whether single, couple or family, receive the same employer contribution amount. Employers can vary the contribution amount based on position, length of service or earnings if desired.

Under this approach, there is no annual increase for "inflation or trend" as under a traditional group program — the employer cost is increased only when and if the employer decides that he or she can afford to do so. There is no increase because of actual paid claims as employees can only claim up to the net amount after administration fees in their personal HSA account. It is the only approach that provides an employer with total cost control while providing employees with maximum flexibility as to what health or dental expenses they use their fund to cover.

In a "benefits by choice" variation of this program, the employer's contribution is made to a "flexible account", and the employee is then responsible for allocating the available funds to:

1. the HSA alone;
2. the HSA and a Retirement Savings Plan (RSP) in any percentage desired; or
3. the RSP only — the employee has full spousal health and dental coverage or has minor medical and dental expenses. The amount allocated to the RSP is considered taxable income, but the employee receives a receipt for having made an RSP contribution.

This variation provides employees with maximum flexibility, yet the employer's cost is still controlled.

FINAL ANALYSIS

Regardless of whether employers continue with traditional group insurance plans or adopt the ASO model or the HSA, employers need to review their plan designs and understand where employee spending is occurring. It is strongly recommended that the employer include stop-loss insurance coverage with a reputable provider, along with a group pooled out of province, out-of-country travel insurance program. Under the ASO model, the cost of benefits is directly claim-driven versus premium-driven under the old traditional insurance carrier plan model. This also applies to utilizing the HSA to control employer costs.

Third party administrators and insurers will report all claims made by the employee by category (drug, dental, paramedical, hospital, vision) to the employer. In accordance with the *Personal Information Protection and Electronic Documents Act*, S.C. 2000, c. 5, the employees' names are not disclosed owing to federal privacy laws. With this information, employers together with their administrators are equipped to act to control skyrocketing medical and dental costs. If an employee or employee's family has large drug claims, a drug cost management program can be initiated.

While it is strongly recommended, if the employer chooses not to include stop-loss insurance coverage in its ASO or HSA program, there are additional provincially funded drug programs that employees can access that have high drug utilization. This falls outside the scope of employer-provided coverage, but represents an additional option that individuals can access when drugs are not covered by their employer. In the case of Trillium, Ontario's provincial drug program, residents must pay an out-of-pocket deductible based on their family net income and the number of their dependent children. The provincial drug formula is reviewed regularly, and not all drugs are covered by these provincially funded drug plans.

A FINANCIAL WORD

ASO, HWTs and HSAs require specialties in employment compensation, adjudication of eligible claims and benefit plan construction. Therefore, if you are evaluating the suitability of these medical and dental plan alternatives for your clients or for yourself, it is well worth the time and the money to hire the right professionals to assist in the design, implementation, maintenance and adjudication of claims within these alternative medical and dental plan solutions.

There are clearly several unique benefits in forgoing the traditional insurance model and, instead, adopting these alternative medical and dental models. In addition to increased flexibility and greater control over the plan, the alternative models offer considerable cost savings. By playing a more active role and taking on the increased risk associated with the ASO model, the business owner is able to reduce administration fees, eliminate reserves and cut out unnecessary benefits.

For the individual business owner looking for the most effective way to save for retirement, these alternative models also have the added "benefit" of providing the means to fund an individual IPP or other retirement solutions along with a whole host of other cost and tax-saving benefits.

CHAPTER 38

SEVERANCE — EMPLOYER OBLIGATIONS AND BENEFIT ANALYSIS

Peter J. Merrick
Andrew Duckman
Stephen Cheng

Overview

This chapter provides a basic overview of severance packages and the surrounding issues that a Trust Advisor needs to be familiar with. The aim of this chapter is to empower the Trusted Advisor to assist clients who find themselves going through this financial and career transition to maximize their results.

Learning Objectives

By the time you finish this chapter you will:

- understand the basic legal aspects surrounding severance in Canada today;
- understand the financial side of employees who have lost their jobs;
- understand the issues in valuing the loss to an employee of losing his or her employee benefits; and
- know the basic ways of calculating the lost employee benefits.

We can choose to use whatever language we like: downsizing, rightsizing or firing. In the end, the result of losing one's job can be devastating. Companies provide severance packages for a range of reasons, and most firms are good corporate Canadian citizens, wanting to help their former employees. Their reasons vary from wishing to be known as fair so they can, perhaps in the future, recruit top talent when the economy improves, or they may want laid-off workers to have some reason to sign legal agreements designed to protect the company.

LEGAL ASPECTS

The last thing a company would want to do would be to put in place a downsizing program and then be sued for it. Right off the bat, they'd pay more money for legal fees — and their HR staff would be trapped in legal proceedings. Unfortunately, many employers and employees negotiate severance packages at the time the employee is fired.

Many companies have found that the best way to avoid any confusion or misunderstanding between themselves and their employee at the time of termination is to have a written company policy in force on termination and a severance package which is agreed upon when every employee signs his or her employment contract.

Each province has a piece of legislation similar to the Ontario *Employment Standards Act, 2000*, S.O. 2000, c. 41 (ESA). The ESA establishes minimum standards for termination and severance pay. Further, the common law requires employers to provide employees who are terminated without cause with notice or pay in lieu of the notice or a combination of the two. In reality, what a separation package is doing is providing employees with money in lieu of reasonable notice.

One of the most significant requirements under employment standards legislation is the minimum standard for notice of termination and severance pay. In Ontario, the ESA obliges employers to provide notice of termination to employees who are terminated in most instances who have been employed for three months or more at the time of their termination.

This notice of termination requirement increases with each year of employment to a maximum of eight weeks' notice owing to an employee who has been employed for eight years or more.

An employer is also required to provide an employee with severance pay if, at the time of termination, the employee has been employed for five or more years and the employer has a payroll of $2.5 million or more or is terminating 50 employees or more at one time. Severance pay is also tied to the employee's length of employment and increases for every year of employment to a maximum entitlement of 26 weeks of severance pay. For example, an employee who had 10 years of employment at the time of termination with an employer who had a payroll of $3 million would be entitled to 18 weeks (10 weeks of severance pay and 8 weeks' notice of termination), assuming that the employer did not give the employee notice of his or her termination.

Common law employee entitlements are almost always greater than entitlements under ESA legislation, which are just minimums and which employees and employers are not permitted to contract out of in an employment contract. Under the common law, there are generally three factors which courts consider in determining the reasonable period of notice to which an employee terminated without cause is entitled: the employee's age, length of service and the character of the employment (*i.e.* labour or management). Senior executives with longer service may be entitled to as much as 24 months' notice, with some recent cases seeing courts award greater periods where there are unique circumstances.

When the economy was very hot, not so long ago, many highly qualified individuals were lured away from secure positions to join new companies, only to find that within a year they were unemployed. This type of situation is referred to as "inducement or luring".

In these cases, the new employer under the common law could find itself responsible for paying damages to these employees, with the courts giving consideration to not only the length of employment with the employer, but also the period of employment with the previous employer.

During the past decade, an emerging trend in Canada has been the move northward of American employment principles. For example, class action lawsuits are seeing more success in the last few years than they have in the previous decade. It appears that our Canadian courts are now prepared to certify class action suits for breach of employment-related obligations.

This exposes an employer to a group of employees who may be more apt to withstand the financial pressures of litigation than the individual employee might otherwise have been equipped to.

When one considers the employment issues which arise when an organization has to make the difficult decision to restructure and reduce headcount, prudence warrants engaging a qualified employment and labour lawyer and employee benefit specialist.

THE FINANCIAL SIDE OF SEVERANCE PACKAGES

Typically severance packages include some or all of the following:

- some form of lump-sum severance payment and/or a severance payment paid out over a set period of time;
- an extension of group benefits, such as medical and dental plans, for a predetermined period, or a sum compensating for past benefits;
- an option for the employee to convert group life insurance to a private policy;
- a provision for the employee to obtain financial planning and outplacement services for a specified period of time; and

- if the company has a pension plan, there are usually three options given to terminated employees:
  (1) an option to keep their money in the company pension plan,
  (2) an option to transfer their pension to a new employer's plan, or
  (3) an option to transfer their entire vested portion of their pension into a locked-in RRSP.

(The law requires that the plan administrator of a pension plan give former employees a Termination Statement within 30 days of being let go, if these employees are entitled to a deferred pension.)

An organization may need to make the following arrangement for laid off employees:

(1) Employees may need to look at their Notice of Assessment from Canada Customs and the CRA to see what RRSP contribution limits are, to know how much severance they can invest in their RRSP in order to reduce taxable income for the year. A company may arrange to direct a portion of the severance payment directly into the employee's RRSP before the payroll department calculates taxes that will be withheld.

(2) If a company has a defined benefit pension and the employee decides to transfer the vested amount into a locked-in RRSP, by leaving the defined benefit pension plan the individual is eligible for the Pension Adjustment Reversal (PAR). PAR was created by the federal government to address lost RRSP room for employees who participated in a company's defined benefit pension plan as a result of termination from their pension plans. As a rule of thumb, a person's PAR will be equal to the amount by both his or her company's and his or her contributions to his or her pension plan exceed the lump-sum amount he or she will receive when he or she is terminated from the pension plan. (Pension plan administrators are required to report an employee's PAR by December 31 of the year of termination from the defined benefit pension plan.)

(3) If the former employee was involved in the company's Registered Pension Plan and started working for the firm in 1995 or earlier, he or she should be able to transfer at least $2,000 of his or her severance payment to his or her RRSP for each year of service before 1996. And if the employee's employment goes back to 1988, he or she may be able to top this up by another $1,500 for each year before 1989 in which the company's pension plan contributions did not vest in his or her name.

THE COST OF LOST EMPLOYMENT

Background

Whether in the face of a global recession, such as the one we are currently experiencing, or in better times when companies restructure and let employees go, there is always an emphasis on the compensation to be paid to departing employees. The law is awash with cases that deal with the number of weeks or months of severance to be paid for years of service. Severance packages also include compensation payable on account of lost employee benefits. The traditional way of determining this compensation, however, is outdated and results in unimaginable sums of money owed to employees remaining in the hands of employers.

In many situations, employees who are not covered by a collective agreement are, with greater frequency, signing written employment contracts which reduce or eliminate any entitlement beyond what is provided by provincial employment legislation. The starting point for determining the entitlement of an employee terminated without cause is whether there is a written employment contract that sets out the rights of the employee and employer upon his or her termination.

Terms like "termination pay" and "severance pay" have defined meanings in the ESA. Frequently, employers use phrases such as "severance package", "termination package" and "lump sum payment" which do not in themselves have definitions, and consequently the actual document must be reviewed by a qualified expert.

An indispensable factor of any payment by an employer beyond the minimum entitlement mandated by provincial employment legislation is a release by the terminated employee. There are important provincial distinctions in compensating terminated employees, *i.e.*, in Ontario, the employee need not show that he or she incurred an expenses in obtaining compensation for employee benefits during the notice period; however the law in B.C. is that the employee must incur the expense to purchase the employee benefit formerly provided by the employer, and only then can the terminated employee collect the expense incurred.

Employee Benefit Analysis

The current methodology for calculating compensation for lost employee benefits is, in reality, not very good. However, very few in the legal, financial or accounting professions acknowledge that the old matrix for calculating benefits for severance packages is obsolete. Very few lawyers, financial advisors and accountants completely understand how to properly arrive at the true value of lost employee benefits when they are assessing client severance packages. This has resulted in thousands and even hundreds of thousands of dollars of benefits being unaccounted for in individual employee severance packages. These dollars remain with the company. The result of inadequate analysis may very well be subject to future liability claims against advising legal counsel and other Trusted Advisors who have failed to investigate the true cost of their client's loss of employee benefits.

What Is at Risk?

As an example of the cost of inaccurate assessment of the cost to employees of losing their employee benefits, consider the instance of one of Canada's largest telephone companies which initiated a company-wide early retirement package for its senior older workforce. In the aftermath of this initiative, employee benefit consultants estimated that between $50 million and over $100 million of severance compensation was lost because the former employees and their Trusted Advisors did not seek the proper advice to determine and get what was legitimately owed to them.

The Traditional Approach

The typical methodology that employment lawyers have used, and continue to use in many cases, to value the loss to employees of losing their employee benefits is to find out what the employer had paid for those employee benefits per month or week, and then multiply that dollar amount by the number of months or weeks of severance the employee was entitled by law to receive. This amount would then be added to the salary portion of the severance package. For example, if an employer had paid a total of $2,000 per month for a former executive's benefit package and the former executive was awarded 20 months of severance, then he or she would be offered $40,000 to compensate for the loss of those benefits, in addition to his or her salary severance. This compensation would usually be taxed at the former executive's marginal rate.

What Is an Employee Benefit Really Worth?

In early 2007, Ian Wright, a lawyer and partner at Scott, Petrie, Brander, Walters & Wright LLP, in London, Ontario, approached our firm on the issue of valuing the loss of employee benefits to a terminated employee. Ian believed that the typical methodology to calculate the loss to employees of losing their employee benefits did and does not accurately calculate the value of this loss to the terminated employee using general principles of contract law.

As a general principle, an innocent party (the terminated employee) is entitled to recover his or losses so that the terminated employee is in the same position as he or she would have been in had the breaching party (the employer) performed its obligations.

The issue that Ian had with the typical methodology of valuing lost employee benefits during the notice period (*i.e.*, the cost by the employer of the terminated employee's premium over the notice period) is that this methodology does not represent what it would cost the terminated employee, *as an individual*, to purchase comparable benefits privately and place him or her in the same position benefit-wise for the notice period.

The theory put forward by Ian is that the value of the lost employee benefits to the terminated employee is the cost to which the terminated employee would be put to replace the employee benefits by purchasing identical employee benefits individually in the marketplace for the reasonable notice period, in after-tax dollars. This results in a significantly greater dollar amount for the loss of employee benefits than simply asking what amount the employer would have paid to provide employee benefits, typically under a group insurance plan.

Issues that the traditional approach neglected to address include the following:

- Employers are able to deduct their employee benefit contributions as a business expense while their employees receive these same benefits either tax-free or tax-deferred. If the same or similar benefits were purchased by a former employee privately, this individual would have to pay with his or her after-tax dollars, leaving fewer dollars in the pocket of the affected former employee.
- Employers are able to buy employee benefits at a reduced cost from insurance companies or other benefit providers because the cost of administration and risk of loss/cost of paid out benefit for these providers is spread out over a number of employees who form the group. A former employee would not enjoy such an economy of scale or dilution of risk. Instead, a former employee would be insured only on an individual basis. For such individual coverage, there is no dilution of the risk of loss to an insurance company or other benefit provider and any such provided would have proportionately higher costs of administration. As a result, a former employee would pay a substantially greater amount per benefit than those same benefits cost the employer, and there is a question as to

whether some of those benefits would even be available to an individual.

- Lastly and of critical importance, the vast majority of employee group benefit plans do not discriminate between whether someone is healthy or not and/or whether someone is a smoker or not. However, this does not apply when an individual applies privately for individual medical and dental, critical illness, short- and long-term disability, long-term care or life insurance coverage. For example, smokers will pay substantially more for individual insurance coverage than they would if they were a part of group coverage. And for former employees who have health issues, there is the very real prospect that they will not qualify individually and will be denied coverage altogether.

The following is a summary of several Ontario court decisions in which the issue of the value of employee benefits was considered by the court and a brief summary of the court's conclusions:

- The Ontario Court of Appeal in *Davidson v. Allelix Inc.*, [1991] O.J. No. 2230 (Ont. C.A.), confirmed the law in Ontario that a wrongfully dismissed employee may claim, in addition to lost salary, the pecuniary value of lost benefits flowing from such dismissal.
- Soon after the *Davidson* decision, the case of *Alpert v. Les Carreaux Ramca Ltée*, [1992] O.J. No. 769 (Ont. Gen. Div.), concluded that the dismissed employee, Mr. Alpert, was entitled to compensation for the loss of coverage under the employee medical plan "... calculated by reference to the cost to the defendant [employer] of maintaining the plan in favour of Mr. Alpert". *Note: This method of calculating the compensation for the loss of coverage was suggested by Alpert's counsel.*
- The *Alpert* decision was followed in the *Connolly v. General Motors of Canada Ltd.*, [1993] O.J. No. 2811 (Ont. Gen. Div.), where the judge, although dismissing the claim of the dismissed employee because the employer had cause to terminate Connolly, nevertheless went on to conclude that on the issue of compensation (had Connolly been wrongfully dismissed), "... the measure of the 'pecuniary value' was the amount the employer would have had to pay to maintain the benefits for the benefit of the employee during the notice period".
- However, in the case of *Habraken v. MacMillian Bathurst Inc.*, [1995] O.J. No. 1951 (Ont. Gen. Div.), affd [1998] O.J. No. 282 (Ont. C.A.), the court was again faced with the issue of valuing the

dismissed employee's benefits for the reasonable notice period. The court noted that "[n]o specific evidence was offered as to the value of these benefits to the employee or the cost to the employer". *Note: In* Habraken, *both employer and employee requested the court "to calculate these damages according to a percentage of the plaintiff's annual salary of $46,500".*

Since the *Davidson* decision, Ontario courts have frequently resorted to the typical methodology of valuing the loss of employee benefits to the terminated employee over the reasonable notice period. Some cases, such as *Habraken*, have utilized a percentage of the terminated employee's salary for purposes of valuing the lost employee benefits over the reasonable notice period. The theory and method of valuing lost employee benefits for the reasonable notice period as advanced by Ian Wright has not been considered or adopted by an Ontario court.

EMPLOYEE BENEFIT ANALYSIS — THE TRUE COST OF LOST EMPLOYMENT

How to Evaluate a Lost Employer Contribution into a Group Medical and Dental, Short-Term and Long-Term Disability, Critical Illness, Long-Term Care and Life Insurance

Case Study

In this scenario, we have a 52-year-old executive (Michael) who has worked for the same company for over 24 years. The company he worked for is a large national retailer that was recently purchased by an American firm. Michael started his career in the field, working at one of the stores, and over 20 years worked his way up to a vice president position. After his company was acquired he was told that his services were no longer needed in the same capacity and his role would change drastically. He was very disappointed with his new duties. Michael looked at it as a demotion and was offered a severance package.

Key Facts

Michael: Age 52, smoker, with some known health issues

Marla (wife): Age 50, smoker

Two Sons: Age 18 in school dependant, age 25 not dependant

Michael and his family relied heavily on his benefits. Over the last three years, Michael had some health issues that included high blood pressure and insomnia, and he did not do well on his stress test with his physician. Both Michael and his wife smoke and they are worried about their ability to get private insurance and wanted to make sure that they received the best severance package possible. Michael's lawyer contacted us at SeveranceOptions.com to review the benefits offered by his previous employer and estimate what the cost would be to replace his benefits with similar individual insurance coverage.

SeveranceOptions.com assessed Michael's existing benefits and the health of both Michael and Marla. We surveyed the market and assumed that Michael and Marla were insurable at standard rates even though Michael had been under the care of his doctor regarding his health issues, which could have resulted in a decline or higher insurance rates charged by insurance carriers.

If Michael were to purchase similar employee benefits, the cost would be entirely an after-tax expense for him. In this analysis, it was assumed that Michael had a marginal personal tax rate of 46% in Ontario based on a salary of $150,000, which is a reasonable assumption for his income.

We conducted a market survey in September 2008 to find individual benefits for Michael similar to the ones offered to him when he was employed by the national retailer. During our market survey, we found that only a couple insurance companies offered private coverage similar to the coverage provided through his previous employer (life insurance, dependent life insurance, accidental death and dismemberment, long-term disability insurance with a 119-day wait period, payment to age 65, critical illness coverage and health and dental coverage).

If the old matrix for calculating benefits were used and Michael were compensated for 24 months of lost insurance benefits based on what his former company would have paid for his insurance benefits, he would only have been eligible for $13,925.28 to mitigate his loss. After we had performed an extensive market analysis, we determined that the true cost for Michael to buy similar insurance benefits on his own for a 24-month period for himself and his family would cost him $57,424.32 in before-tax dollars. By having this analysis completed it was identified that there was a $43,499.04 difference between what the company paid for these benefits and what the truer reality would be if Michael were to purchase these same benefits on his own.

The end result would be that Michael's legal council would be able to negotiate a much more favourable severance package for Michael based on the truer loss of his insurance benefits.

Benefit Analysis and Comparison Chart

Below is a table that shows the cost of insurance benefits that Michael's company would have paid and what Michael would pay for those same benefits.

Age of Executive: 52

Age of Executive's wife: 50

Age of Executive's Dependant male child: 18

Medical and Dental Benefit Plans	Estimated Life, Group Medical and Dental Plan	Individual Insurance Program with After-Tax Dollars	Individual Insurance Program Pre-tax Using a 46% Average Tax Rate
Life Insurance @ $400,000	$96.00	$286.58	$435.31
Dependent Life ($10,000/$5,000)Spouse/Chil d	$2.00	$2.75	$4.17
Accidental Death and Dismemberment ($400,000)	$12.00	Included	
Long-Term Disability (119 days, year regular occupation to age 65 @$6,300/mth	$113.00	$423.84	$643.81
Critical Illness @ $100,000	$90.00	$290.00	$440.51
Health & Dental	$267.22	$554.00	$836.54
Travel Insurance	Included	$18.00	$27.34
Monthly Premiums	**$580.22**	**$1575.17**	**$2,392.68**
Annual Premiums	$6,962.64	$18,908.40	$28,712.16
18 Months of Premiums	$10,443.96	$28,353.06	$43,068.24
24 Months of Premiums	$13,925.28	$37804.08	$57,424.32

Note: This table is based on the following.
Life and Accidental Death and Dismemberment, $4,000
Long-Term Disability based on monthly benefit, $6,300
Health, 100% coverage on Drugs
Dental, 80% Coverage, maximum $2,500 Basic and Major combined Coverage
Travel Insurance, $1,000,000

How to Evaluate a Lost Employer Contribution into a Group Registered Retirement Savings Plan, Defined Contribution Pension Plan, Deferred Profit-Sharing Plan, Employee Profit-Sharing Plan, Employee Stock Option Plan and Employee Stock Purchase Plan

These plans are referred to as Capital Accumulation Plans (CAPs) because the contributions on the employee's behalf are defined but the future benefits are not. CAPs give the employee investment choices of what he or she can invest the money in, while on the other hand Defined Benefit Pension Plans do not give the employee this choice. Usually, employers will contribute a set percentage into these types of plans based on an employee's salary. It is important to note that contributions in these plans are usually based on pre-tax amounts and may or may not be taxable immediately in the employee's hands. This is dependent on whether or not the CAP is registered with the CRA as a retirement plan.

For example, if an employer had set up a Defined Contribution Pension Plan (DCPP), where the employer promises to contribute on behalf of its employee 9% of the employee's salary and this employee had earned $150,000 salary per year, the employer would have contributed into the DCPP for this employee $1,125 per month or $13,500 per year.

If this employee had worked for this company for 20 years and had been fired, this employee would be eligible to receive the employer's contribution into this plan for 10 months of severance to mitigate his or her loss. This employee for the 20 months of severance would need $27,000 for the loss of the employer's contribution into his or her DCPP.

How to Evaluate a Lost Employer Contribution into a Deferred Benefit Pension Plan

Most labour lawyers tend to adopt a "unit value" approach to estimate the present value of pension loss on severance or wrongful dismissal cases that involve defined benefit pension plan members. This may potentially lead to a significant understatement of the present value of pension loss if the terminating pension plan member would qualify for unreduced early retirement benefits in the near future absent the termination of employment.

Legal counsel often rely on the commuted value of pension figures quoted by the pension plan administrator to estimate the present value of pension loss. For example, if the commuted value of pension is $400,000 for the member's 20 years of participation in the plan, most lawyers would simply divide the $400,000 by 20 years to arrive at a "unit value" of $20,000 per year of pensionable service. If they consider a notice or severance period of two years to be appropriate, the compensation that they may be seeking for pension loss is only $40,000, *i.e.*, two years at $20,000 per year.

Under certain circumstances, the use of the "unit value" approach would significantly understate the present value of pension loss, particularly situations where the member is very close to being eligible for unreduced immediate retirement benefits. The example below would shed some light on how much an employee who has been let go may be shortchanged if the legal counsel is not attentive to details. This may even lead to the legal counsel being sued for giving bad advice.

Sample Pension Loss Calculations

This example provides an illustration of a situation where the actual present value of pension loss is much more significant than the amount suggested by the "unit value" approach.

Pension Plan Information

Pension Benefit Formula:	Annual pension equals 2.0% of best three-year average salary per year of service.
Indexing:	Fully indexed to increases in the Consumer Price Index (CPI).
Normal Retirement Age:	Age 65.
Normal Form of Pension:	Life annuity guaranteed five years.
Early Retirement Date:	Anytime after age 55.
Early Retirement Reduction:	None if retiring from active employment with *age plus service equalling 85 years or more (the 85-point rule)*. Otherwise reduction factor is 1/3% per month that the early retirement date precedes age 65.

Plan Member Data

Gender:	Male
Age at Termination:	55.0
Years of Credited Service:	27.0
Best Three-Year Average Salary:	$80,000
Date of Termination:	November 1, 2008

The member's accrued annual pension payable at age 65 is:

$80,000 × 2% × 27 years = $43,200

Alternatively, the member can commence an immediate pension at age 55 with a reduction of 40% (1/3% per month is equivalent to 4% per year and hence 40% reduction for 10 years if pension were to commence at age 55).

Alternatively, the member's immediate pension payable at age 55 is:

$43,200 × (1 – 40%) = $25,920

The commuted value of pension determined as at the date of termination (November 1, 2008) in accordance with the Canadian Institute of Actuaries Standard of Practice for Determining Pension Commuted Values (the CIA CV Standards) is about $442,000 for a deferred pension of $43,200 at age 65 or about $540,000 for an immediate annual pension of $25,920 at age 55. Taking the greater of these two amounts, the conclusion may be that the pension is worth $20,000 for each year of pensionable service (*i.e.*, pension is worth $540,000 for 27 years of service, which means $20,000 per year).

If the labour lawyer feels that the appropriate notice or severance period is two years, he may only seek damages of $40,000 ($20,000 per year times two years) with respect to the loss of pension. However, that is not the proper way to determine pension loss.

The lawyer should take into account the fact that had the employee remained an active employee and pension plan member for another two years (the notice or severance period), he would have qualified for full unreduced pension at age 57 under the 85-point rule (*i.e.*, age 57 plus 29 years of service = 86 years > 85 years required for unreduced pension).

Assuming that the member's best three-year average salary would remain at $80,000, his annual pension payable at age 57 without reduction would be:

$80,000 × 2% × 29 years = $46,400

The commuted value as at November 1, 2008 for a pension plan member age 55 with a deferred pension of $46,400 per annum commencing at age 57 is about $846,000. As compared to the current commuted value of $540,000, the present value of pension loss would be about $306,000, which is significantly higher than the $40,000 loss estimated using a "unit value" approach.

How to Mitigate Your Professional Risk

The true value of a lost employee benefit is not a rote calculation. It is vitally important to determine with some accuracy the higher cost to a former employee of replacing those lost benefits with similar benefits paid for with after-tax dollars based on the former employee's marginal tax rate. It is also important to determine whether certain of the lost benefits may not be available to an individual privately for any reason. As a result, the actual financial compensation for the lost benefits, which mitigates a former employee's loss, becomes much greater than has been traditionally provided.

It is well worth the time and the investment to hire an expert in group employee benefits with credentials and experience to complete a proper evaluation of true cost of lost benefits to a former employee. Under the circumstances, the sizeable benefit is definitely worth the marginal cost.

BEYOND THE FINANCIALS

Several years ago, Peter was very fortunate to meet a gentleman who would become one of his greatest mentors, who had a profound influence on the way Peter viewed layoffs and severance packages. This gentleman had developed a system called "Beyond The Financials". It arose out of his experience in the early 1980s; he had a specialty practice in early retirement, severance and pension plan wind-ups. Remember those days? During that period he had more than 1,000 one-on-one discovery interviews with ordinary people who were going through transitions, transitions they could not understand, and when he would sit down and present the financial severance package, he would quickly realize that there was never enough money in the world because these people were emotionally hurt.

As employees learn their legal rights, a company's fiduciary obligations could perhaps be the most worrying of all for creating potential employer liabilities. In Canada, employers have been found liable for failure to bring the terms of benefit policies to the attention of employees. From Peter's mentor's experience with severance packages, the pattern he noticed emerging as a solution to help people deal with being let go was to have them visualize the life that they wanted to create, to see a new life beyond the one they had just left.

Employees in today's employment environment need to take responsibility for their careers and finances. It is important that employees not perceive the employer's pension plan, benefit plan or the company group RRSP as their "retirement plan". Many employers are confused about a company's fiduciary obligations to employees in regards to company benefit plans.

This confusion arises over the distinct differences between the meanings of "information", "education" and "employee financial knowledge". When a company just provides information about its pension, group RRSP and other benefit plans, 99.9% of these employers are not meeting their fiduciary responsibilities because the information just adds to the confusion of their employees. And having an education program for employees about benefit packages only goes so far to explain what they need to know.

Education is not enough without employees having the knowledge and the wherewithal to take responsibility and be empowered to integrate the company's benefit plan with what they are doing outside the company with their entire financials.

In addition to helping with financial planning, employers should offer tangible assistance with job search, retirement and life transition. These so-called "career transition services" might be offered in-house or handled by a company specializing in providing such assistance. It is also important to understand that the employees left behind after a downsizing are also hurt. Employers don't want their employees to believe that they will receive vastly different severance payouts from one round of layoffs to the next and their remaining staffers to believe that they have no assurance that they will get anything.

Individually, employers have no say over the direction of the Canadian economy, but what employers do have control over is how they choose to navigate with their employees through their careers and life transitions. It is how corporations act during these transitions that will result in creating or losing goodwill in the labour force and marketplace.

PART V

ACCOUNTING AND FINANCIAL PLANNING

CHAPTER 39

BEYOND TRADITIONAL TAX SOLUTIONS FOR BUSINESS OWNERS

Peter J. Merrick
Mort Shapiro

Overview

At the end of 2004, Peter Merrick began a very engaging dialogue with Mort Shapiro, President of Morden S. Shapiro & Associates Inc. Management Consultants, and a fellow columnist at *The Bottom Line*. Their talks focused on how the roles of the public accountant and financial planning professional were in the process of being redefined as they converged upon one another. What follows is a revised reprint of their two articles that appeared in the October 2006 issue of *The Bottom Line* newspaper, a LexisNexis publication. Shared within this chapter are some of the insights that were gained from their lengthy discussions, which continue today.

Learning Objectives

By the end of this chapter you will:

- understand the responsibility that Trusted Advisors must take in defining the roles they play with their clients;
- understand what the profit distribution trap is and what questions the Trusted Advisor might ask to avoid it; and
- understand some of the strategies that may be employed other than the traditional salary/dividend/bonus to business profits.

"Thin Ice" (Article One)

Mort Shapiro

In recent years, clients' needs have become increasingly varied and sophisticated, particularly so in the areas of wealth accumulation, management and preservation. Satisfying these needs has become increasingly complex in today's taxation and regulatory infrastructure. At the same time, clients have become more knowledgeable and aware and increasingly tend to focus on maximizing their economic well-being by managing their financial affairs as effectively as possible.

It's important for public accountants to understand that if clients have needs, they'll find ways to satisfy those needs. The areas of wealth accumulation, management and preservation are no exception to this rule. Although it may seem logical to many clients that their accountants would address these needs, such is not always the case. And unfortunately, when accountants do address these needs, they often do so with a deficiency of knowledge and expertise, which feeds the following "thin ice" factor.

THE "THIN ICE" FACTOR

It's well recognized that today's public accountants practise in a litigious environment. Risk management is a mantra in the business world. To render advice without sufficient expertise or knowledge is akin to skating on "thin ice". Not only does it create a real vulnerability from a litigation viewpoint, but it also exposes the practitioners to a possible breach of their professional rules by not sustaining their competence in those areas on which a client relies due to their professional status. The reality is that whether or not they realize it, most public accountants are constantly practising in the areas of wealth accumulation, management and preservation, and are often on "thin ice" when they do so.

It's because of these concerns, that in this issue I join with my fellow columnist Peter Merrick to address a common "thin ice" scenario which I encounter in the course of my work in the world of public practice.

THE PROFIT DISTRIBUTION TRAP

In the all too common annual "how shall we distribute/allocate this year's corporate net income?" meeting, practitioners tend to focus on traditional salary/bonus/dividend mixes which are based on the integration of personal and corporate tax rates and are designed to minimize current tax burdens and maximize (to some extent) the availability of disposable after-tax income in the present. However, this traditional practice now often requires new levels of knowledge and expertise in order to keep the practitioner from giving inappropriate advice.

For many clients, traditional strategies are often recommended without an appropriate workup of a client's goals, needs and wishes (for the short-, medium- and long-term periods). Even if this has been done at some previous date, circumstances may have altered a client's strategic goals.

Every profit distribution strategy has within it an implicit strategic plan. The "thin ice" develops when the implicit plan is not known to or appreciated by the client, who, with the choices available to him or her may have chosen to achieve some alternative goal, need or wish which might not necessarily have minimized current tax burdens and maximized (to some extent) the availability of disposable after-tax income in the present.

The accountant's dilemma may be rooted in any or all of the following factors:

- The client's current goals, needs and wishes (for the short-, medium- and long-term periods) may not be known to the accountant, who then uses conventional planning strategies (*i.e.*, maximizing tax-paid disposable income when much of it ends up being redundant cash, but outside the client's corporation) which may not be well aligned with the client's goals.
- The accountant may not be aware of strategies and techniques that are available to achieve alternative goals (*i.e.*, the broad range of insurance products, deferred compensation plans and other such vehicles).
- The accountant may not have the skills needed to guide the client through an intensive inward-looking process to develop a personal strategic financial plan (*i.e.*, to identify and evaluate quality of life and life cycle events which must be addressed and reduced to very practical financial terms and then explored at an emotional and psychological level).
- The client may not be prepared to pay the accountant to explore his or her personal financial goals, needs and wishes (*i.e.*, "just tell me how to do it").

The accountant's vulnerability is rooted in the eventuality that clients may discover, after the fact, that they had choices as to how they could have managed their wealth differently, which choices you as their accountant did not present to them. It's possible that had alternatives been presented to the clients, they would have chosen the path recommended by you as their accountant. But they or their heirs or legal representatives will be tempted to attack you for, at the very least, not having informed them of their alternatives (*i.e.*, you took away their opportunity to make a choice).

I've asked Peter Merrick to address this example of the annual profit distribution strategy, and comment on the traps into which accountants all too easily fall. After familiarizing yourself with Peter's cautionary words, I invite you to consider using the following self-assessing checklist (this can be applied to an individual accountant or to a firm as a whole):

- Do I realize what goals and objectives are implicit in the financial recommendations that I make to my clients (*i.e.*, what is being primarily achieved by my recommended strategy)?
- Do I lead my clients through the process of developing goals and objectives for a financial strategic plan?
    - If yes:
        - Do I have the appropriate skills to do so (*i.e.*, interview skills/counselling/mediation if dealing with a family unit, *etc.*)?
        - Do I have appropriate expertise and knowledge to appreciate what alternative strategies are available to achieve a broad range of goals and objectives (*i.e.*, the latest developments in legal and tax regulations/new and emerging financial products)?
    - If no:
        - Do I communicate in writing to my client the range of goals that my recommendations do and do not achieve?
        - Do I have the client confirm in writing that I have recommended that he or she undertake the process of developing goals and objectives for a financial strategic plan *or* that I have made such a recommendation and he or she has rejected it?
- Whatever my responses were to the foregoing self-assessing questions, do I do these things on a regular, periodic basis so as to be satisfied that the information with which I am working is current

(*i.e.*, the birth of a child/the illness of an aging parent/the development of a medical crisis/disability, *etc.*)?

The opportunities for delivering real value to clients are there for the taking as are the traps for delivering poor, incomplete or (as your client might argue) incompetent service. These opportunities flow from real needs which real clients have. To ignore them is to ignore the reality of the world in which you practise.

Be mindful of the fact that any attacks on your performance in this arena will generally come from persons of wealth. And they usually have the financial wherewithal to be serious attackers.

Readers should consider whether any of the strategies outlined by Peter Merrick would have been appropriate for one or more clients, either to adopt or at the very least to consider. If there are such scenarios and if they were not adequately considered, then you may have (unknowingly) been practising on "thin ice".

How to Skate Around Thin Ice (Article Two)

Peter J. Merrick

In this month's column Mort Shapiro has posed several thought-provoking questions. He's asked me to address his scenario from the perspective of a Certified Financial Planner (CFP), in order to provide public accountants with some fresh insight.

I personally find it useful to keep in mind that in this developing era of convergence, most client financial problems are multi-dimensional. Efficient solutions tend to reach beyond the scope of the traditional public accountant's skill set.

Most clients' issues, be they strategic business planning, estate planning, succession planning, charitable giving, investments or insurance issues, are as significant to the client as their tax issues. In order to successfully service their clients' needs, public accountants must ensure that they are capable of considering this broad range of concerns.

Mort has asked me to examine the common profit distribution trap from the perspective of this broader landscape. This trap usually arises during the annual review meeting between the public accountant and his or her client. The traditional question inevitably arises: "How shall we distribute/allocate this year's net corporate income?" Many public accountants fall into the trap of recommending a stand-alone salary/bonus/dividend mix without considering the alternatives. This single dimension strategy is built on two underlying assumptions:

(1) No obvious tax-planning opportunities exist for corporate-held investments funded from undrawn net income and so there tends to be a reluctance to leave funds in the corporation.

(2) The client is often presumed to wish to maximize the quantum of after-tax dollars in his or her hands today.

The problem with the latter assumption is that the accountant will likely have assumed this to be the client's goal without having explored its validity. In fact, the clients' goals may not be tax-driven at all. The accountant's exposure, which flows from the traditional assumption, is rooted in today's common client expectation that their accountant is capable of providing overall advice on the client's long-term financial welfare and is a knowledgeable and capable strategic thinker.

Mort Shapiro has identified the annual net profit distribution meeting as a "thin ice" scenario. He speculates that a problem could/will arise if clients subsequently learn that they had other options (other than the salary/bonus/dividend mix recommendation made by the accountant) that would have better suited their needs by yielding greater overall benefits for them and better supporting the clients' goals in both the short and long term.

Opportunities often exist whereby corporate funds created from undrawn net income can compound tax-free within the company and/or tailored executive benefit plans. These opportunities are often viable and complementary to the traditional salary/bonus/dividend mix strategy. These alternatives are available through financial solutions which may take the form of: corporate class money-managed products, corporate interest rate swaps, retirement compensation arrangements, individual pension plans, employee profit-sharing plans, corporately owned universal life insurance, and health and welfare trusts. (This is not an exhaustive list of the alternatives.)

CORPORATE CLASS MONEY-MANAGEMENT PRODUCTS

This is a strategy whereby a third party money-management company invests the client's corporate funds. This investment structure allows a business to invest its funds in tax effective investment type accounts that allow for the switching between fund classes of shares within the same fund corporation without triggering capital gains for the client corporation. As with many vehicles, there are limitations: assets will attract tax if they are withdrawn from the third party money-management company.

CORPORATE INTEREST SWAP

An *interest* rate *swap* contract consists of exchanging two types of investment instruments without actually exchanging these investments. This is a strategy whereby the client purchases units in a fund held by a third party money-management firm. The money market returns will be taxed as capital gains only on sale. Funds invested in such corporate interest rate swaps allow the business to have access to this money in a secure way while at the same time delaying the taxation of the returns on such moneys and leveraging the deferred tax dollars.

INDIVIDUAL PENSION PLANS (IPPs) AND RETIREMENT COMPENSATION ARRANGEMENTS (RCAs)

Owners who are employed by an incorporated business should consider creating a "Supersized RRSP" in the form of an Individual Pension Plan (IPP) or a Retirement Compensation Arrangement (RCA). Contributions to these two vehicles for older clients will exceed the maximum allowable RRSP limits, are fully deductible by the sponsoring company and are a non-taxable benefit for the individual. Increases in the total value of the assets held in the vehicle are tax-deferred until withdrawn. IPPs and RCAs offer the potential for significant amounts of additional tax-deferred income to be set aside for retirement.

CORPORATELY OWNED UNIVERSAL LIFE INSURANCE (UL)

Universal life insurance allows tax-sheltered growth within the policy. A corporate-owned life insurance contract can tax shelter much of your client's retained earnings in the cash-value portion of the policy, provided the premiums are not deducted. Your clients can access these funds for their businesses or personal use throughout their life by collateralizing the policy through loans from the policy or from a bank. For example, your client might borrow funds annually in order to increase his or her retirement cash flow.

Make sure your client has the appropriate documentation and guarantee fees in place to avoid a personal benefit (which forces your client to pay a lot of unnecessary personal tax). Any related bank or policy loans would be repaid automatically upon your client's death from a portion of the policy proceeds. At the same time, a credit to the corporate capital dividend account would be created equal to the full policy proceeds. Another added benefit is if your client has put this type of policy in place, then if he or she becomes critically ill or disabled, he or she will be entitled to have the entire cash value paid out to him or her, without any requirement to repay the policy tax-free.

HEALTH SPENDING ACCOUNTS (HSAs)

An HSA is a bank account created by the corporation to be used and whose deposits are available exclusively for health care expenses. By having an HSA, business owners are able to convert health care expenses into 100% business deductions equal to the deposits into the HSA in the year. Payments of these health care expenses are treated as a non-taxable benefit to the business owner. The business owner determines the contribution amount each year and also determines how to spend the benefit dollars. Unlike traditional medical and dental plans, if the deposits are not spent in the current year, then the funds remain in the account, available for future use. In essence, "if you don't use it, you don't lose it".

EMPLOYEE PROFIT-SHARING PLAN

An employee profit-sharing plan (EPSP) is a special purpose trust that allows the beneficiaries of the plan to share in the profits of a company. The allocation to an EPSP is taxable in the hands of an employee and a deductible expense for an employer. An EPSP is a non-registered savings plan in which the employer contributions are computed by reference to a company's profit. The advantages of an EPSP are that they attract neither Employer/Employee Canada Pension Plan nor EI contributions. EPSPs allow for more control over retirement assets. They are treated as pension or RRSP eligible earnings. Source deductions and withholdings are not required by the EPSP trustee or employer.

EPSPs also allow for income-splitting opportunities. All amounts paid from an EPSP to an employee are not subject to a reasonableness test, unlike salaries. The "kiddie tax" rules should not apply to income received by minor children through an allocation from an EPSP, if they are *bona fide* employees of the business. Contributions to the EPSP can be made up to 120 days after corporate year-end salaries.

PAYING CAPTIAL GAINS INSTEAD OF SALARY

Clients who own incorporated businesses can structure their cash withdrawals as capital gains rather than salary or dividends. Capital gains are taxed only on one-half the income earned. So an individual who has used up his or her lifetime capital gains exemption, who pays himself or herself $300,000 in capital gains and who has an Ontario personal marginal tax rate of 46% will pay $69,000 of tax as compared to taking the same amount out as regular income, which would require paying the Canada Revenue Agency $138,000 in personal taxes.

THE BOTTOM LINE

As Mort Shapiro has suggested, if clients' needs are not being satisfied by their accountant, then there is a very real possibility that the clients will have those needs satisfied by someone else and may attack their accountant if a strategic opportunity has been lost. Today's public accountant should at least be aware of options such as those noted above and should be prepared to bring these alternatives to their clients' attention in the event that they would address client needs beyond the traditional salary/bonus/dividend mix recommendation. Such service is the best strategy for avoiding "thin ice".

In order to ensure that you are satisfying your clients' needs, consider asking them the following question:

"What do you want to achieve this year with your money?"

Make sure that your clients understand your question. This question should elicit whether the clients' goals for their money in the current year are for consumption, retirement or estate purposes. Each type of goal requires a different set of tailored solutions, which may or may not include the traditional salary/bonus/dividend mix recommendation.

This question also implies that the practitioner should ask the same question each year because as every public accountant knows, life changes and so do clients' needs and goals from year to year. If a public accountant fails to identify and address these new changes in the goals and direction of a client's life, then that practitioner risks skating on "thin ice".

CHAPTER 40

DIVIDENDS VS. SALARY AND BONUS

John Nicola

Overview

Taxes play a large part of every business owner's life and financial planning. This chapter's purpose is to help the Trusted Advisor question traditional tax strategies and to think in new ways to help clients best minimize and defer their taxes.

Learning Objectives

In this chapter, the objective is to make a case for the following:

- Incorporated business owner/professionals earning less than $400,000 per year should not take any salary. That also means no more RRSP or IPP contributions. The same would be true for paying salaries to low-income spouses.
- Ideally, all income would be paid (in the above example) as dividends and structured to make total taxable incomes for a husband and wife equal.
- Continuing to pay dividends to a family trust for children over 18 still makes sense under the right circumstances.
- Future retirement savings would occur at the corporate level (perhaps in a holding company). If the asset mix is combined with the right compensation approach, then the tax on corporate investments can be reduced from its initial rate of 47.8% to as little as 5% (we realize this is a huge difference, so please see example below).
- For practitioners earning more than $400,000 per year, the latest tax law presents a number of outcomes. However, in general, income would be taken in a combination of ways:
  - no "bonus down" to $400,000;

- salary — only to the extent that RRSP/IPP contributions can be maximized (approximately $112,000); and
- dividends — for the balance of income required, ideally through a trust or to other shareholders with lower tax rates.

INTRODUCTION

George Harrison wrote the song "Taxman" during a period of time when the highest marginal rate of tax in England was 95%. Perhaps if he had John Maynard Keynes as a financial advisor, he would have fared better and complained less. It was, after all, Keynes who wrote: "The avoidance of taxes is the only intellectual pursuit that still carries any reward."

For over 20 years, self-employed business owners and professionals have been able to incorporate their businesses and practices in parts of Canada. Certain "rules" about how one takes his or her compensation and splits income with other family members have become ingrained in our thinking. For example:

- take a large enough salary to maximize your RRSP contribution ($105,555 in 2007 for the 2007 contribution maximum of $19,000, roughly increasing to $111,111 and $20,000 respectively in 2008);
- split income with low-income spouse if possible and pay him or her a "reasonable" salary;
- distribute after-tax corporate earnings by way of a dividend to a family trust (now restricted to children over the age of 18);
- if you earn more than $400,000 after expenses, you should "bonus down" and pay personal taxes on that income rather than the high-rate corporate income (which is currently 31.5% for 2008, but scheduled to drop to 27% by 2012 in British Columbia);
- taxes on investments held inside a company are higher than when those investments are held personally.

What if some of these "rules" are outdated or, while correct, only reveal half the story? What if these rules are costing you more in taxes and lost retirement savings than other approaches to compensation that are both safer and simpler?

Let's first look at the following case study.

CASE STUDY: A TALE OF TWO DENTISTS

Assume John Wilson is a dentist who makes $400,000 after expenses, but before tax, in his incorporated practice. He is married to Mary, who earns income only from the practice. They need about $120,000 per year to live on and they want to maximize their RRSP contributions as well. In this case, we'll further assume that Mary receives an income of $40,000 per year as a salary and he receives $160,000 (before taxes, RRSP deductions, and CPP premiums). The table below shows the net result for 2008.*

	John	Mary
Gross Income	$160,000	$40,000
Personal Tax	$42,737	$4,082
CPP Premiums	$4,098	$3,614
RRSP Contribution	$20,000	$7,200
Spendable Income	$92,865	$25,104
Total Taxes and CPP ($ and %)	$54,531	27.27%
Total Savings	$27,200	13.6%
Spendable Income	$118,269	59.1%

**We have used 2008 tax rates and CPP premiums. Income based on $200,000 paid in salaries and the balance of $200,000 earned is assumed to be retained in the company and tax paid at the small business rate of 15.5% in 2008 for British Columbia.*

So how might this have worked if they had received their $200,000 cash compensation in the form of dividends? As in the chart above, we assumed that corporate income above $200,000 (the amount necessary to pay dividends) was retained in the company and tax was paid at the small business tax rate of 15.5%.

	Dr. John Wilson Inc.	John	Mary
Gross Income	$200,000		
Corporate Tax	$31,000		
Dividend		$63,000	$63,000
Personal Tax		$4,000	$4,000
Spendable Income		$59,000	$59,000

Corporate Savings	$43,000		
Total Taxes Corporate and Personal	$39,000	19.5%	
Total Savings	$43,000	21.5%	
Spendable Income	$118,000	59%	

So how do these two approaches compare?

- With dividends, total taxes for John and Mary are about $15,500 per year less as a result of three major factors: CPP does not have to be paid; there is a reduced corporate tax rate; and the total income is being split more evenly than when John and Mary take a salary.
- Savings are now in the company, and amount to about $15,800 more than RRSP savings.
- When they retire, John and Mary will pay about 30% less tax on dividends taken from their company than withdrawals from their RRSPs.
- There is less risk of a tax reassessment for Mary with dividends vs. salary.
- While they do lose future CPP benefits (but not benefits accrued so far), in most cases the amount they will lose is considerably less than the premiums they will have to pay.

For the majority of incorporation businesses earning less than $400,000 per year, dividends are a more effective and safer way to take compensation.

So that leaves two big questions:

(1) *What do business owners and professionals who earn more than $400,000 per year do?*

(2) *How can one reduce the taxes one has to pay on investment earnings inside a company?*

The first question was made slightly more complicated by the new dividend rules that came out in early 2007. It is best for individuals in this category to review with their accountants, as early in the year as possible, what approach is best for them. Below are some guidelines:

- Salary should not be more than the amount required to maximize your RRSP/IPP contributions. For 2008, that will be approximately $112,000.
- If you have investment income in your company and have accrued Refundable Dividend Tax on Hand (RDTOH), you should take sufficient dividends to get it back. This can lower your tax on investment income by more than 50%.
- Income-split as much as possible and if you have a family trust (with beneficiaries who turn 18 years of age or older in 2008), then review with your accountant how best to use it.
- These new rules have rendered the option of taking dividends as one's income as good as, if not better than, salary at every income level for many individuals. We have developed an analysis tool to assist our clients and their accountants in determining the right mix of salaries and dividends for different situations.

To answer the second question, a quick primer on corporate tax rates on investment income is necessary. If you are going to take the dividend approach, you will be investing corporately. Companies have to pay a high tax on investment income that is subject to tax credits. Space does not permit us to go into this in great detail, but the table below will help.

Corporate Investment Tax Rates	Initial Tax Rate	After RDTOH
Interest	46.7%	20.1%
Dividends (from Canadian Companies)	33%	0%
Capital Gains	23.35%	10.1%

We can make two key observations from this table:

1. It is much better to pay taxes after we have received back the refundable taxes available (RDTOH). This will happen automatically if we take our compensation in the form of dividends.
2. The lowest tax rates for a company are on capital gains and dividends from Canadian companies. That means we should focus on holding long-term appreciating assets and dividend-paying stocks in our company portfolio, and move interest-bearing assets and income trusts to our registered plans (RRSPs and IPPs). If we do this well, we can reduce our long-term corporate tax rate on investment income to 5% (the average of the dividend and capital gains rate

after RDTOH). The table below shows how the tax rate can get to such a low level.

	Initial Corporate Tax	RDTOH (paid back)	Net Corporate Tax
Dividends (from Canadian Companies)	33%	33%	0%
Capital Gains Income	23.35%	13.3%	10.1%
Average	28.2 %	23.2%	5%

So for small business owners such as incorporated dentists, it seems that it is indeed "the best of times".

There is one caveat: in order to get back RDTOH, you need to ensure that the dividends you receive come from a company that has RDTOH. If you have both a holding company and an operating company, you may find that all of your RDTOH is in the holding company. If that is the case, then taking dividends from your operating company will not trigger any refunds of taxes and will be far less effective. Review with your accountant how best to integrate compensation structure into your tax planning.

We do not all need to have the intellect of John Maynard Keynes to reduce our taxes. We simply need a better understanding of how the rules work and when they change.

CHAPTER 41

ACCOUNTING 101 — USING FINANCIAL STATEMENTS & ACCOUNTING TECHNIQUES TO ASSIST YOUR CLIENTS GET THE GREATEST RETURN ON THEIR COMPANIES AND INVESTMENTS

John Parkinson

Overview

This chapter sets out to explain accounting in straightforward terms to those who are not accounting specialists. It describes the four main financial statements and the process that is used to develop them. The chapter shows how accounting information is used for planning, for control and for making both short-term and long-term decisions in relation to buying securities and in evaluating and maximizing a client's company's value.

Learning Objectives

By the end of this chapter you will have learned:

- a brief history of accounting;
- financial and management accounting;
- what the balance sheet tells you;
- what the income statement tells you;
- what the statement of changes in financial position tells you;
- how to use accounting ratios; and
- management accounting techniques.

INTRODUCTION

Why would you want to study the accounting reports of organizations?

One assumption is that you have some cash to invest.

Traditionally, you would want to understand the financial statements of a company if your client was totally averse to any risk so that your client could invest his or her money in government securities. Your client would not earn much interest (as of this writing, early 2008, your client could get about 3¼% interest by lending to the Canadian government). If your client is only prepared to expose himself or herself to a very low risk, you can invest his or her money in guaranteed investment certificates (GICs) issued by the major banks. The interest rate, as of early 2008, would be 3¾% for any of the large Schedule One bank GICs that mature in one year.

If your client is prepared to expose himself or herself to higher levels of risk, he or she would have to invest in company shares. In return for the higher risk, your client will expect to get a higher return. This is where the financial reports come in.

You as your client's Trusted Advisor will want to measure the riskiness of a company's financial reports; this will give you some strong clues. A company's financial reports will show whether the company had liquidity problems, and they will show whether or not the company has borrowed so much that it may have difficulty paying back the loans. There ought to be a higher level of return to the investor from a higher risk company.

The financial return you and your client are hoping for is, of course, in the future. Unlike lending to the government or lending to a bank, when your client buys shares in a company, there are no guarantees about the future. What you and your client hope and expect is that the company will make a profit, and that this profit will be passed on to the client either in the form of a dividend, or in the form of a higher market price for the shares. The financial reports can tell you how well the company did in the past, and this is valuable input into estimating how well it will do in the future.

So the financial reports are one of the sources of information that investors use to assess the expected risk and return of investment in a company. To use the financial reports intelligently requires that you understand the way those reports are created and understand the way the information in the reports feeds into analyzing their risk and return through accounting ratios.

A second assumption, which is in line with this book, might be that your client has a company and is considering selling it. This is the reverse of the situation described above, and some slightly different analytical tools would be required on your part as your client's Trusted Advisor.

You have to be clear in your own mind what it is you are selling, as that is the value proposition your client will be offering to any potential purchaser. Traditionally, the investment advisors neglect to include a client's company in the client's overall balance sheet, which should include both the client's business and personal interests.

It may be that the client's company has physical assets which are the main attraction to any purchaser. For example, the company may own a valuable plot of land, but not much else. In that situation, the financial statements are really not much help, as they tend to value assets on the basis of their acquisition cost. Rather than rely on the balance sheet (which is a list of the cost of assets), it would be better to have the assets professionally valued and use that to determine the value of the company.

It may be that the company assets are overshadowed by the potential to earn income. The income statement will demonstrate past achievements in earning income. By examining the trend over time, reasonable estimates of the growth that has occurred and hence the growth that can be expected in the future can be made. The value of the company is the future earnings potential, discounted back to the present.

There are several numbers that appear on the income statement that present themselves as the income of the company. Probably the most relevant one is the operating income, or, as it is often called, the earnings before interest and taxation (EBIT). This represents the results of the business activities that the company has engaged in, without adding the confusion of interest payments (which are a function of the type of investment used to finance the company) or taxes (which are largely beyond anyone's control).

A third assumption would be that your client owns a company, and you both want to make sure it is operating at its optimum level of profitability. Management accounting can help here.

For example, management accounting through budgetary control can tell the manager whether he or she is on track to meet his or her plans and expectations.

Management accounting can also distinguish between the effect of reducing recurring costs by one dollar (it adds one dollar to EBIT) and the effect of increasing sales by one dollar (which will usually add something less than one dollar to EBIT, depending on the contribution margin ratio). Importantly, management accounting will inform the manager whether it is worthwhile adding $1,000 to fixed costs, if the result is the addition of $10,000 to revenue. This is done by using the cost-volume-profit model. This, in turn, depends on being able to classify the costs reported in the income statement as those that are variable and those that are fixed.

So, whatever the business situation, and whatever decisions face the owner or manager, a sound understanding of financial statements is necessary for all stripes of Trusted Advisors that clients will lean on going forward into the 21st Century.

A BRIEF HISTORY OF ACCOUNTING

The history of accounting is a close parallel to the history of civilization.

Not long after mankind abandoned the nomadic lifestyle, settlements started to use crude accounting records to show how much corn and other goods the king had in the royal storerooms, and where it had come from. From these humble beginnings, writing was developed.

During the middle ages, when mercantilism took over from subsistence farming, double entry bookkeeping was developed to keep accurate records of merchants' transactions. But it was still only a record-keeping system; accounting had not then developed its reporting function. Individual merchants did not need accounting reports because they could "eyeball" their assets and liabilities.

The industrial revolution gave rise to the corporation, in which multiple shareholders owned the business, but professional managers ran it on a day-to-day basis. The accounting response was to create regular reports for the shareholders so that they could be assured that the managers had looked after their affairs properly. Initially, only an annual balance sheet was prepared. Later, an annual income statement was added to show how successive balance sheets were connected. The statement of changes in financial position (the cash flow statement) was added much more recently (in the latter part of the 20th century. Management accounting techniques were also developed to improve the efficiency of the manufacturing process.

When, in the middle of the 20th century, marketing overtook manufacturing as the dominant theme of the successful business, the scope of management accounting was extended to include more precise profitability reports and techniques such as break-even analysis.

We now live in the information age, where virtually all accounting record-keeping is done on computers. This enabled the instant and virtually costless creation of large amounts of sophisticated accounting reports. In larger businesses, this is done through Enterprise Reporting Systems (ERPs), such as SAP, Peoplesoft and Great Plains. In smaller concerns, even Quickbooks, Accpac and Bedford are capable of delivering complex reports and analyses quickly and easily.

So, as the nature of commercial activities has increased in sophistication, accounting has matched its activities to the needs of the day. It is important for the businessperson or the investor to know what accounting can do to help him or her, and what limitations it has.

FINANCIAL AND MANAGEMENT ACCOUNTING

Financial accounting refers to the underlying record-keeping system (bookkeeping), and the production of regular general purpose reports intended primarily for shareholders and users outside the organization. These reports include the balance sheet, the income statement and the cash flow statement. Each of these is described in more detail below.

The Financial Statements

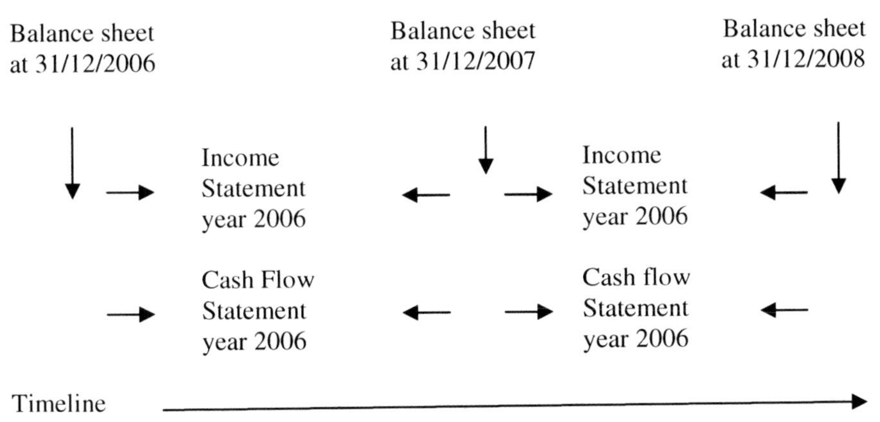

The shareholders need to have these reports to know that the managers who run large companies on a day-to-day basis have exercised good stewardship over the resources that the shareholders have put at their disposal.

In addition to shareholders, other users would include the tax authorities, stock exchange regulators and individuals who are considering investing in, or lending to, the company.

These records and reports are now compulsory for companies where ownership is split among many shareholders. It is also sensible for an organization that is owned by a single individual to prepare the same reports so that the owner can make the same sort of judgements about his or her own company and his or her behaviour as its manager.

Because of the intended use of these accounting reports, it is a primary expectation that they be accurate. One way of assuring accuracy is for independent auditors to carry out detailed checks on the records and the reports, though as was observed in the recent cases such as Enron and Worldcom, even an audit does not guarantee that the reports are accurate and meaningful.

Management Accounting

Management accounting is not for public consumption. Instead it is a set of techniques used internally to guide and inform the managers about how best to make business decisions, and to control ongoing activities. Management accounting includes budget preparation, budgetary control, ratio analysis, cost allocation, cost behaviour and break-even analysis, to mention the most important ideas. Clearly, a short chapter such as this does not allow for a description of these complex tasks in detail but brief summary will be provided later. The reader who is interested can follow this up in any management accounting textbook.

In most cases, management accounting uses the same underlying records as financial accounting. Occasionally it will organize the data differently. For example, when the hydro bill is paid in a manufacturing company, the financial accountant wants to know how much has been paid in total for hydro, as it is his or her intention to report hydro expense in the income statement. The management accountant would be more interested in distinguishing the monthly fixed cost of hydro from the cost based on usage, as distinguishing between fixed costs and variable costs is key to both budgetary control and break-even analysis. So, the same underlying transaction could be recorded in different ways to support different accounting activities.

Because it is essentially an internal activity carried out by or on behalf of the management, management accounting is a voluntary activity, rather than a compulsory one, and is prepared as needed, rather than according to financial accounting's regular annual cycle: for management accounting, timeliness is more important than precision.

The key consideration for management accounting is that it is intended to help management achieve the organization's strategic objectives, whatever they might be.

What the Balance Sheet Tells You

Sears Canada Ltd.: Balance Sheet as at December 2006: $ million

Assets:		Liabilities:		
Current assets:		Current liabilities:	1,575	
Cash:	747			
Receivables:	145	Long-term liabilities:	733	
Inventories & other:		Total liabilities:		2,308
	1,056			
Total:	1,948			
		Equity:		
Long-term assets:	1,145	Shares:		
			16	
		Retained earnings:	769	
				785
Total assets:	3,093	Liabilities & equity;		3,093

The balance sheet is a list of the assets of the organization, the liabilities of the organization and the difference between the two — the owners' equity.

The assets and liabilities in the balance sheet are not complete: they are restricted to monetary items that have arisen as a result of recordable transactions. So internally generated goodwill may be a real asset in every sense of the word, but it is typically excluded from the balance sheet, however valuable it might be. Even where an asset appears in the balance sheet, it is possible that its stated value may be less than its economic value. A plant asset, for example, may have been amortized to zero, but it may still be in regular use. A parcel of land may be valued at its cost, yet its market value may be much higher. There is a consistent theme of economic conservatism in valuing the assets that appear in the balance sheet. Great pains are taken to avoid reporting assets at excessive values, but reporting assets at less than their values is considered acceptable. Originally this was done to protect creditors, but the effect now is to make the balance sheet less useful than it might be.

The assets are listed in order of their liquidity. At the top of the list the most highly liquid items (such as cash and bank accounts) appear. These are followed by assets that will soon turn into cash (such as receivables). Then come assets that will take longer to turn into cash (such as inventory). All the assets mentioned so far are called current assets, as it is intended that they will be available for paying liabilities within a year. The subtotal of all current assets is shown on the balance sheet. Current assets feed into the calculation of liquidity ratios, as will be shown later. Current assets are valued either at their cost or, where it is less, at their realizable market value.

Valuing Current Assets at the Lower of Cost or Market Value

Inventory of fuel:	
Quantity (obtained by measurement at tank):	100,000 litres
Cost:	$0.50 per litre
Replacement cost:	$0.75 per litre
Selling price:	$1.00 per litre

Balance sheet will show:	
Inventory of fuel at lower of cost or market value:	
100,000 litres @ $0.50 per litre:	$50,000

Other assets, such as land and plant and equipment are not intended to be liquidated; instead they are acquired with the intention of being used to create wealth. They are listed by type of asset on the balance sheet. These long-term assets do not last forever, and eventually their use and the passage of time will exhaust all their value. To reflect this, their value on the balance sheet is their original cost, less amortization, amortization being an annual expense that recognizes their gradually losing value over time. The subtotal of all long-term assets is shown on the balance sheet.

Amortization

Cost of moulding machine: 1st January 2005:	$50,000
Expected life:	4 years
Expected residual value in 4 years:	nil
Annual amortization expense: 2005 to 2008:	$12,500 per year

Taken together, the current assets and the long-term assets represent the total assets of the business. That is a good measure of the size of the business. (Other measures of size include total sales and number of employees). The different measurement bases for the assets and the omission of some important assets make total assets a slightly problematical measure of size, but its usefulness generally exceeds its shortcomings.

Listing the liabilities has fewer valuation problems than listing the assets. The amount that is expected to be paid to settle the liability is typically a single, unambiguous figure. As with the assets though, on the balance sheet a distinction is drawn between current liabilities (which have to be paid within a year) and long-term liabilities (which are due to be paid more than a year from the balance sheet date. This, too, helps in liquidity evaluation.

If all the assets of the business were sold for precisely their balance sheet values, and all the liabilities were paid off, what would be left over would be its net worth. That is shown on the balance sheet as the owners' equity.

Owners' equity will show some details of where it came from, including the amount of share capital (money paid to the company by investors to buy shares) and the retained earnings (profits made by the company, but not paid out to investors as dividends). However, these categories are less important than the total, and the total is this "plug" figure of the assets minus the liabilities of the business. Owners' equity is a residual of the recording and valuation of the company's assets and liabilities.

If you are going to use the balance sheet to value a company, the first stage would be to consider the assets reported: that would be the total assets less the total liabilities. This net asset figure is always identical to the shareholders' equity. Dividing the shareholders' equity by the number of shares in existence gives a figure for the asset backing of each share, which is a crude expression of how much each share is worth. If the market price of a share is higher than the reported net assets per share, then the buyer is being asked to pay for something not reflected on the balance sheet. That may or may not be logical.

Net Assets per Share

Sears Canada: 2006:

Total assets:		$3,093.00
Less total liabilities:		2,308.00
Net assets:	$ 785.00	
# Shares (million):	107	
Net assets per share:		$ 7.34
Market price: close 2006:	$ 26.76	

One reason for a discrepancy between the asset backing and the market share price would be that the assets are reported at less than their true values, and this is a likely consequence of the use of cost as a valuation approach for long-term assets, and conservatism being applied to uncertain situations.

Another reason would be that the company has the ability to make more than expected levels of profit from the assets it has. This could result from owning unique patents, or the possession of unique skills by its employees.

An extreme example would be the Coca-Cola Company. Experts agree that the brand Coca-Cola is worth billions of dollars, but its value is not included in the company's balance sheet. As a result, the asset backing for this company bears no relation to the market price of the shares.

If the buyer of a share believes that he or she is buying a stake in the assets of the company, the calculation of net assets per share would be vital. However, unless the buyer is going to acquire all the shares and sell off the assets, it is probably less important to think about asset values, and more important to think about how much earnings they can create. That is reported through the income statement and the earnings per share.

What the Income Statement Tells You

Sears Canada Ltd.: Income Statement for the Year 2006: $ million

Revenues:			5,933	
Cost of merchandise sold, operating administrative and selling expenses:	5,468			
Amortization expense:	152	5,620		
Operating income:			313	
Interest expense:	48			
Unusual items:	25			
Income taxes:	87	160		
Net income:				153

The income statement shows how much better off the organization has become through its business activities over a period of time. To show how much better it has done, it reports all the income generated and then deducts the related business expenses that were incurred over the same period. The net of these two is the operating profit.

Calculating the revenues is generally fairly straightforward, but a couple of points are worth noting.

Firstly, revenue is the wealth created, not the cash received. So goods or services delivered are included, whether or not the invoices have been paid. Unpaid invoices are treated as assets in the balance sheet and are called accounts receivable. If the balance of accounts receivable changes then there will be a significant discrepancy between the revenue reported and the cash flow. This is called accrual accounting and is a principle that also extends to calculating expenses.

Secondly, there are occasions when the amount of revenue reported is not totally clear. A recent case involved the Xerox Corporation. Xerox was in the habit of signing multi-year contracts for its photocopiers. In order to maximize the reported profit, the entire revenue steam for the contract was reported as revenue in the year the contract was signed, even though the services had not been delivered. When this emerged, Xerox was forced to restate its profits, and a lot of investor confidence evaporated. The company had not properly matched the revenue against related expense, and it had anticipated the profit on the contract.

The essential point is that revenues should be well matched to the reporting period covered by the income statement.

When an organization prepares the income statement, it will find that the expenses are generally more troublesome than revenues because there are more categories of expense than there are categories of revenue, and their behaviours are more complex. The overriding principle is that the expense reported should be matched against the revenues reported and the time period involved.

Direct costs are almost always the largest expense. These refer to the immediate costs that are necessarily incurred when revenue is earned. In a retail shoe store, for example, the sale of a pair of shoes for $100 means that a pair of shoes that was previously an asset (inventory) is no longer owned by the company. The shoes will have to be replaced to put the company back to the same position. So the cost of the shoes sold (perhaps $60) becomes an expense.

The effect of making the sale (+$100) and incurring the direct cost (–$60) is shown in the income statement as a subtotal of gross profit.

In retailing, the cost of the inventory sold is the direct cost of making the sale. In manufacturing situations the direct cost is more complex, involving not only materials used, but also manufacturing wages and manufacturing overhead, but the principle is the same.

In addition to direct costs, there are indirect or overhead costs. These are expenses incurred to support the business activities such as advertising, employees' salaries, rent, property taxes, utilities and the like.

These indirect costs also have to be correctly matched to the time period covered by the income statement. If the company has used hydro to heat its premises, the correct expense to report is the cost of the hydro used, as revealed by the hydro bills received. Whether or not they have been paid (or even paid in advance) is irrelevant.

Deducting the expenses from the gross profit leaves a subtotal called the operating income. This is intended to report the net effect of the business activities over the time period reported on, which is typically one year.

There are a number of further deductions from the operating profit before we get to the bottom line, including interest expense and taxes.

Interest expense is treated as a special case as it arises not from the business activities of buying or selling, but as a result of the choices made about how the company is financed. Two identical businesses (for example, two Tim Hortons® franchises) might have been established, one financed entirely by the owner having invested his personal wealth, the other being mostly financed from borrowed money. If the interest expense were to have been deducted with all the other expenses, then it would be impossible to tell which of the two was more efficient. By deducting interest expense after operating income has been calculated, the operating income is left as an unambiguous measurement of how well each business was run.

Tax expense is also treated as a special case and is deducted from operating income in the same way as interest expense. Taxes, too, are regarded as something different from other expenses, not controlled by the managers and potentially distracting from the meaning of the operating income.

After the deduction of interest and taxes from operating income, the balance is called net income or net earnings. This is important as it measures the net increase in wealth that applies to the shareholders.

As with the balance sheet, this net income can be related to the equity through the calculation of the earnings per share (EPS). To do this the net income is divided by the number of shares in existence.

Earnings per Share

Sears Canada: 2006:

Net income ($ million)		153
# Shares (million):	107	
Earnings per share:		$ 1.43

The EPS of different companies can be compared. In a perfect world, the EPS of similar companies would be the same and would reflect a fair return on the market price of the share, but we often find that they differ.

The trick here is that a figure for past earnings is used in calculating the EPS, but the buyer is actually buying an expectation of future earnings, and opinions about the future are highly likely to differ. EPS differences exist because buyers have different perceptions of how well individual companies are going to do in the future.

As an additional wrinkle, the EPS as calculated may not be representative of the future EPS because of uncertainty about the number of shares that might exist in the future.

For example, many companies find it a good motivational tool to award their managers the right or option to buy shares in their company at advantageous prices. By doing this they give managers a stake in the success of the company and they don't have to pay any cash out immediately. However, this results in the situation that the number of shares in issue can change dramatically and, as a result, the EPS can fall to a significantly lower figure. Companies report not only the current EPS but also a fully diluted EPS that assumes that all of the possible shares get issued. This ought to mean that the buyer is not surprised if it happens.

The final piece of information that you are likely to see at the end of the income statement concerns dividends.

When the company makes a profit (*i.e.*, there is a net income reported by the income statement), it has a choice.

On the one hand it can keep the profit inside the company and reinvest it in whatever business opportunities it sees as valuable. This is referred to as ploughing back the profits. If this done, the shareholder will not see any direct benefit from owning shares, but he or she ought to see an indirect benefit. Because additional assets have been created (net income is a recognition that net assets have increased), the company should have more assets per share and make more earnings per share; however, shares are being valued by prospective purchasers, and the share price should increase. The shareholder who needs cash to pay for groceries should be able to sell some of his or her shareholding and still be no worse off than when he or she started.

On the other hand, the company can declare a dividend. This is a payment made to shareholders out of profits. It reduces the cash assets within the company and (in the absence of taxes) makes an equal increase in the cash assets of the shareholder.

An extreme example of dividend payments is the income trust, which is constructed so as to pay all profits back to shareholders (and is also designed to minimize taxes). Most companies, however, tend to pay a dividend of part of the profits and retain the balance for reinvestment.

Any income not paid out as dividends is added to the balance sheet as part of the equity under the title retained earnings. In mature companies, the retained earnings account can be significantly larger than the share capital account.

What the Statement of Changes in Financial Position Tells You

The double-entry bookkeeping system goes back to the 12th century. Balance sheets, to measure the wealth of the business, became common in the 18th century. The income statement, to measure the change in wealth over a year, became popular in the 19th century. In the 20th century, a combination of rampant inflation and rapid change in the business environment led to companies going bankrupt despite the fact that they reported profitable operations and had plenty of assets on the balance sheet. The problem was that these companies were running out of cash.

A good example is the Rolls Royce Co. Although most people will recognize the name as the maker of excellent automobiles, its business is actually more concentrated in areas such as aero-engineering. In the 1970s, Rolls Royce put so much money into developing the new RB 211 aero-engine that the company ran out of cash!

The accounting response was to require all companies to produce yet another report: the statement of changes in financial position (SCFP). This shows the sources of all cash flowing into the business and the destinations of all cash flowing out of the business. This forces organizations to think about cash flow more carefully and enables investors and lenders to make better informed investing and lending decisions.

Sears Canada Ltd.: Statement of Cash Flows for Year 2006: $ million

Cash flow from operations:				
Net income:				153
Add: non-cash expenses:			270	
Deduct: increase in working capital & other items:		(173)		250
Cash used in investing activities:				
Purchase of capital assets:	50			
Sale of capital assets:		(5)		
Other items:		7		(52)
Cash used in financing activities:				
Repayment of long-term debt & other:	(510)			
Issuance of long-term debt:		300		
Dividends paid:		(13)		(223)
Net decrease in cash:				(25)

The SCFP identifies three specific areas of cash flow, and links them to the change in cash for a period (normally one year, just like the income statement).

The first reporting heading is the cash flow from normal business operations. The starting point is the net income. In some businesses, the net income will be equal to the cash flow, but the application of the accrual approach to accounting makes it untrue in most businesses. The two biggest adjustments are for amortization and for working capital.

Amortization is where the original cost of a long-term asset is treated as an expense in the years when its value is used. As such, it is an expense that does not represent any cash flow; the cash flow took place when the asset was bought, and that is reported as cash used in investing activities. So amortization expense (and any other non-cash expense) is added to net income.

Increases or decreases in non-cash working capital (inventory, accounts receivable, accounts payable, *etc.*) are part of normal business operations. They are not shown as expense or revenue (because they are treated as assets or liabilities on the balance sheet), but they do require cash flow; you cannot increase your inventory, for example, without spending money to do so, but until the inventory is sold it is an asset, not an expense. So the increase in net non-cash working capital is deducted from net income.

Net income, plus amortization expense, less any increase in non-cash working capital is reported as the cash inflow from operations.

An organization reporting a positive cash inflow from operations is seen to be self-sustaining, all other things being equal, while the organization reporting a cash outflow from operations is hemorrhaging cash and is probably doomed.

The second reporting heading is cash flow that arises from investing activities. Investing means the purchase of long-term assets (less, of course, any sales). A company that makes no investments is static, while growing companies constantly invest in new assets and new technology. To make these investments, however, either they have to have cash from operations (see above) or they have to raise new cash through financing (see above).

The third reporting heading is the cash flow from financing activities. This summarizes the cash inflow from issuing new shares or from borrowing, less the cash used in repaying shares or repaying loans.

In the short-term, an organization can maintain its liquidity by financing activities, but only in the short-term.

The net effect of cash flows from (1) operations, (2) investing and (3) financing will equal the increase or decrease in actual cash balances over the year.

How to Use Accounting Ratios

The financial reports (balance sheet, income statement and statement of cash flows) provide valuable information about the activities and wealth of an organization. That information is enhanced by the calculation of a number of key ratios which show the relationship between accounting numbers. This enables comparison of organizations of different size, and it enables comparison against norms or expectations. In this way, qualitative judgements may be made to better inform investing or lending decisions. Accounting ratios may be calculated in respect of liquidity, profitability, leverage, efficiency and stock market prices.

Liquidity ratios are the most important accounting ratios. A liquidity ratio compares the short-term obligations to the cash and other resources that are available to pay them. Inadequate liquidity can lead to creditors foreclosing on the organization and forcing it into bankruptcy. It is therefore essential to monitor liquidity as the wise investor will avoid companies with liquidity problems.

The current ratio compares current assets (cash, receivables and inventory) against current liabilities. You will recall from the description of the balance sheet that current assets and current liabilities are those expected to be settled within one year, so the timing of both is similar.

Current ratio:
Current assets/current liabilities:
$1,948/$1,575 = 1.2:1

The norm, or expected value, for the current ratio is 2:1. In a liquid firm, there should be $2 of current assets for every $1 of current liability. Sears is showing a low level of liquidity in 2006.

The quick ratio compares available current assets (cash and receivables, but not inventory) against current liabilities.

Quick ratio:
Cash and receivables/current liabilities:
$892/$1,575 = 0.6:1

The norm, or expected value, for the quick ratio is 1:1. In a liquid firm, there should be $1 of current assets for every $1 of current liability. As with the current ratio, this shows a low level of liquidity.

The second most important ratio type measures profitability. In a profitability ratio, the earnings are compared with the resources used to create them.

The return on assets ratio compares operating income against total assets. It is a measure of the efficiency with which assets have been used. It is expressed as a percentage.

Return on Assets

Sears Canada: 2006:

Operating income/Total assets:
$313/$3,093 × 100 = 10.1%

For the shareholder, the most important ratio is the return on shareholders' equity, which is similar to the return on assets, but income is measured on an "after-tax and interest" basis (*i.e.*, net income), and the comparison is with the shareholders' equity (*i.e.*, excluding all debt).

Return on Equity

Sears Canada: 2006:

Net income/Shareholders' equity:
$153/$785 × 100 = 19.5%

This ratio is, of course, based on the balance sheet numbers, and does not represent the return that an investor would actually get. For that, it would be necessary to compare the earnings per share with the market price of a share.

Market-Based Return on Investment

Sears Canada: 2006:

Earnings per share/Market price of a share:
$1.43/$26.76 × 100 = 5.3%

Because the market price ($26.76) is substantially higher than the net assets per share reported in the balance sheet, if you were to buy a share of Sears Canada, you would only get a return of 5.3%, based on 2006 results.

From the perspective of the manager running a company, a key question is how the return on assets (and hence, the return on equity) can be increased. Part of the answer to that question lies in the return on sales ratio (another profitability ratio) and part is through efficiency ratios, which we deal with next.

Return on Sales Ratio

Sears Canada: 2006:

Operating income/Sales:
$313/$5,933 × 100 = 5.3%

The managers can work with this ratio to improve results. If the gross margin (*i.e.*, the sales markup) can be increased without reducing total sales value, then this ratio will increase. That could be done by reducing input costs, which is a strategy followed very assiduously by Walmart. Or the markup could be increased, as is done by sellers of luxury goods. As another approach, if the expenses are reduced, then every dollar saved goes straight to the bottom line as an increase in operating income; so every expense should be rigorously examined to see if it is truly necessary (in that it supports the business model) and, where it is necessary, that its amount is minimized.

Efficiency ratios also lead to possibilities for improving the management of the organization. Efficiency, in this context, means maximizing the sales per unit of assets. The total asset turnover ratio compares sales with assets.

Total Asset Turnover Ratio

Sears Canada: 2006:

Sales/Total assets:

$5,933/$3,093 = 1.92 times.

For every dollar of assets, Sears made sales revenue of $1.92 in 2006. Improvement can be directed at making higher sales revenue with the same assets; making the same revenue with fewer assets or using a combination of the two.

Additional efficiency ratios can be calculated by comparing any individual asset grouping (receivables, inventory, long-term assets, *etc.*) to sales. The message is always the same: the greater the sales for a given level of assets, or the lower the asset base for a given level of sales, the more efficiently the firm is operating. As an extreme example, moving to a just-in-time inventory management system increases the inventory turnover ratio to infinite levels or, if you want to express is differently, reduces the inventory holding period to zero.

These efficiency ratios are linked by the return on sales ratios to the return on assets ratio.

Return on assets: operating income/total assets 100
Sears 2006: $313/$3,093 × 100 = 10.1%

Relate both elements in the equation to sales:

Return on assets: (operating income/sales × 100) × sales/total assets
Sears 2006: ($313/5,933 × 100) × ($5,933/$3,093)
5.3% × 1.92 times = 10.1%

Management Accounting Techniques

There are many management accounting techniques that can be used to aid decision-making. We will restrict ourselves to describing two of them: budgetary control and the break-even model.

The budget is the financial effect of the business plan, and all organizations prepare budgets for their future operations. After the actual results are available, it is usual to compare them with the budget to see how closely they match.

This is an example of management by exception. Once the budget has been accepted by all the people involved, it defines an acceptable level of performance. If the actual results are substantially the same as the budget, then the actual performance level may be treated as acceptable too. At this point, no managerial action is required.

If, however, there is a significant shortfall between the actual results and the budget, then it becomes necessary for management to take action. The dollar value of the difference is called a variance. Management will want to know not only the amount of the variance but also what happened and why, and what action has been taken to correct the situation. So variances trigger investigation and action.

Variances pinpoint the area where the problem occurred and they put a precise dollar value on the effect. Variances do not, however, explain the causes, nor do they identify appropriate corrective action.

Variances can be broken down into as fine a level of detail as management wants. For example, the overall sales quantity variance could be a single number or it could be broken down into the effect of selling too few units (the sales volume variance) and selling products at prices different from budgeted prices (sales price variance). In turn, the sales volume variance could be broken down into the volume variance that happened in each of the main markets (geographical variances). The finer the variances are broken down, the more precise the remedial action can be.

Variances are typically reported to cover the following areas of activity:

- sales (price and volume);
- direct materials (price and efficiency);
- direct labour (price and efficiency);

- manufacturing overhead (spending and efficiency);
- selling overhead (spending and efficiency); and
- administrative overhead (spending and efficiency).

Taken together, all the variances reported should explain the deviation between the actual results and the budgeted results, and should enable management control.

The other technique we shall describe is the cost-volume-profit (CVP) model, which is a very useful tool for planning and understanding the effect of some business decisions.

The underlying theory of CVP is that all financial activities can be accurately categorized as behaving in two ways with respect to sales activities: either they are variable or they are fixed in relation to sales.

Sales dollars are assumed to go up or go down exactly in proportion to sales quantities.

Certain costs are also expected to rise or fall in direct proportion to the increase or decrease in sales quantities, and these are called variable costs. These would include: raw material usage, manufacturing labour, some manufacturing overhead and sales commissions.

If a sale is made, two things happen: firstly, the dollar value of the sale comes in and, secondly, the dollar value of the variable cost is incurred. The net (sales revenue less variable cost) is called the contribution margin, and represents the marginal benefit to the organization of making that sale. Conversely, if an expected sale is not made, then the contribution margin represents the marginal loss.

The other type of behaviour is that of the fixed costs. Fixed costs are those that do not change as a result of increases or decreases in sales levels. Fixed costs would include some manufacturing overhead and a lot of administrative and selling overhead. Examples would include: rent, property taxes, supervisory salaries, travel expenses, advertising, amortization and so on.

To break even, the organization needs to create enough sales activity so that the contribution margin completely covers the fixed costs. To make a profit, the organization needs to make additional contribution margin beyond the break-even point.

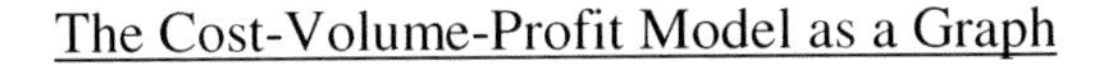

The Cost-Volume-Profit Model as a Graph

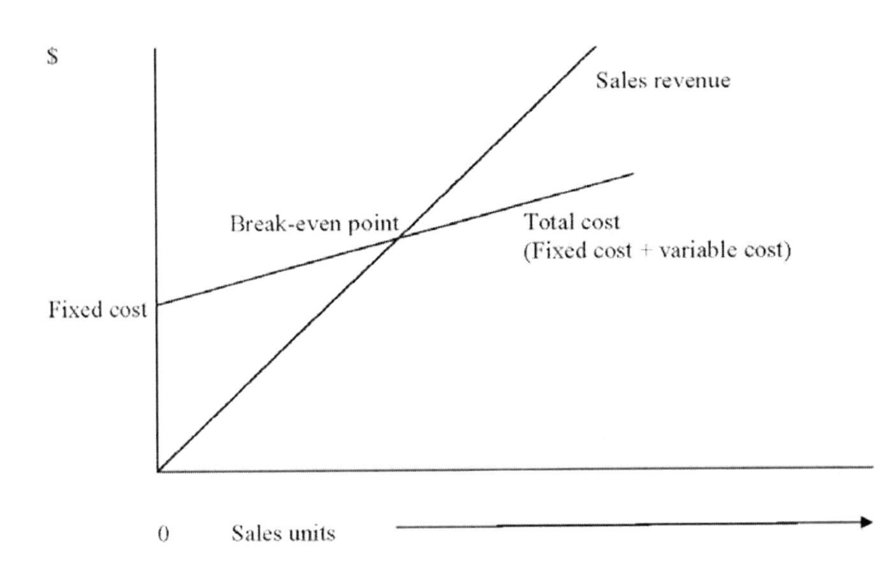

The CVP model can be used to estimate whether a business is capable of making a profit (does the company expect to sell enough to go beyond the break-even point and, if so, by how much?). It can also be used to focus on the marginal effect of a business decision, such as increasing expected sales through additional spending on advertising.

Below are examples of break-even calculations for the following scenario.

The Vegetarian Delight Restaurant sells delicious tofu sandwiches for $3.50 each. Every sandwich costs $2 for raw material, wrapping, *etc.* Fixed costs (rent, wages, *etc.*) total $600 per week. How many sandwiches must the restaurant sell each week:

(1) to break even?

(2) to make a profit of $300?

(3) to justify an advertisement in the local newspaper costing $240?

The contribution margin per sandwich is $1.50 (selling price of $3.50 less variable costs of $2 = $1.50).

Solution (1) — Breaking even:

Breaking even is achieved where contribution margin is enough to cover the fixed costs:

$600 fixed costs/$1.50 = 400.

If the restaurant sells 400 sandwiches per week, it will break even. (And conversely, if it does not think it can sell 400 sandwiches per week, it should not go into this business.)

Solution (2) — Sales needed to make a profit of $300:

The contribution margin (still $1.50 per sandwich) now has to pay for the fixed costs of $600 and also create the profit of $300 (total $900):

$900/$1.50 = 600.

By selling 600 sandwiches per week, the restaurant can generate a profit of $300.

Solution (3) — Sales needed to justify $240 of advertising:

The contribution margin is still $1.50; the restaurant will need additional sales that generate enough contribution margin to cover the $240:

$240/$1.50 = 160.

By selling an additional 160 sandwiches, the restaurant will justify (but only just) the advertisement. If the ad brings in more than 160 additional sandwich sales, the restaurant will increase its profit.

The CVP model is very useful in simple circumstances. For example, it is a very good representation of most retail situations, where all costs can be described as either fixed or variable. However, the more complex the underlying business model, the less representative the CVP model is of the economic reality. For the most complex organization (manufacturing of multiple products for example), a more complex model such as Activity Based Costing becomes necessary.

SUMMARY

Accounting information is critical to maintaining an edge in managing both personal and business affairs. While it is possible to run anything on a "seat of the pants" basis, only where accounting information is brought into the picture is excellence possible.

In organizational terms, accounting plays a key role in planning (through budgeting), executing (through resource allocation) and controlling (through comparison of actual results with their planned outcomes).

PART VI

WEALTH PRESERVATION AND SUCCESSION PLANNING

CHAPTER 42

THE MOST ELUSIVE PRIZE OF ALL — $10 TRILLION

Thomas Deans

Overview

This chapter offers advisors a contrarian approach to family business succession planning. It's an approach that helps business owners to pursue the "longevity" of their wealth by abandoning the longevity of their operating businesses as a fundamental business objective.

Learning Objectives

By the end of this chapter, advisors will be able to:

- gain confidence to wade into the most complex and confounding issues confronting high net worth business owner clients by helping answer the question: "Who will own and lead my business in the future?";
- acquire a rare generational view that acknowledges the role of business as an instrument of wealth creation and its great limitations as a substitute for family;
- understand that advisors who can assist their clients with their business succession planning will not only manage that client's wealth but likely the next generation's wealth as well;
- learn that every advisor brings his or her own bias to the subject of succession planning and that the key to successful planning means bringing the right questions to the advisor's clients to unlock the plan that is appropriate for them; and
- believe that every business has a beginning, middle and end and that the key to succession planning means helping business owners find their "end" before the end finds them.

One of the best publicized pieces of data in the family business literature notes that only 30% of all closely held businesses successfully pass to the second generation and that only 3% will survive to the third generation.

On the heels of this data is the cultural belief that the progeny of second and third generation family business owners are lazy, incapable spendthrifts with no discernable work habits. The famed expression "shirtsleeve to shirtsleeve in three generations" further supports this popularized notion that somehow families who try to pursue the "longevity" of their business will fail — the implication being that the "drive" or work ethic of the succeeding generation is absent. Having met hundreds of second and third generation business leaders my firm belief is that often — but not exclusively — the opposite is true.

So what accounts for the high attrition rate of businesses that attempt to retain control of businesses over multiple generations? My experience is that businesses that gift the controlling interest to family are more apt to define themselves and their wealth by their operating business. They are committed to "longevity" as the principle driver of their succession plans. In these families, the company has been so successful at branding itself in the marketplace that the family has itself been inculcated with the notion of itself as "the business".

When businesses are gifted, the succeeding generation often, but not always, removes the sale option from the table — intuitively we all know it's hard to sell a gift. In this scenario, businesses lose a valuable wealth protection maneuver, specifically the discipline to probe the market for their value, assessing in whose hands the businesses' assets can deliver a higher return on invested capital. Trusted Advisors who develop a world view, an historical view and appreciation for the rhythm of business will shape family fortunes in profound ways. Trusted Advisors who read David S. Landes, *Dynasties: Fortunes and Misfortunes of the World's Great Family Businesses* (New York: Viking, 2006) will be left with a chilling reminder of how quickly great family businesses can evaporate their wealth.

When families pursue "longevity" as opposed to "wealth protection" as a fundamental objective, the seeds of generational wealth destruction are clearly sown. This view has less to do with family dynamics and more to do with the general life cycle of business in general. The great Forbes statistic that of the 100 largest U.S. firms in 1900, only 16 remained in business in the year 2000, offers a stark reminder of just how temporary businesses are. Let's remember that these were the best branded, best capitalized, arguably the best managed firms, and that four generations — 100 years later — we see a failure rate of 84%. As we ponder the universe of the typical advisor who interacts with the owners of something other than the 100 largest firms, we know the chances of the businesses they touch lasting 100 years are even more improbable.

But what accounts for our obsession with the multi-generational firm — why do we bestow upon these enterprises an elevated status and admiration? Why do the media, investors and the business community at large fete the family business dynasty? Why is it that consumer products companies especially imply in their branding that their fourth generation family business is more successful than a third generation business, a second better than a first, *etc.*? What is it about the longevity of a business that fascinates and lures business owners to buy into this approach to wealth management despite the data to suggest that it is the ultimate crap-shoot?

The answer, in part, relates to the advice business owners receive from their advisors, who are often themselves in awe of the wealth creation machine and persona of the great business founders. Advisors after all know better than most just how many businesses fail to make it past the five-year mark. When it comes to advising an owner of a 35-year-old family business on succession planning, it can feel like showing up uninvited to the owner's thanksgiving dinner without a bottle of wine. But the great business owners — especially founders — are the most blind to preserving their wealth — most blind to the seeds of wealth destruction that they plant by failing to plan and execute their last deal — *the sale of their business*. The high net worth clients who intimidate their advisors with their extraordinary track record of wealth creation are the most in need of strong independent counsel. It is the ageing high-net-worth business owner who needs reminding that wealth creation is a fundamentally different exercise than wealth preservation and that long-term planning and sound succession principles should drive their thinking.

WHY WEALTH MANAGEMENT ADVISORS ARE DIFFERENT FROM ACCOUNTANTS AND LAWYERS

Everyone who approaches the subject of succession planning brings their own bias. My family's business history is punctuated by three generations of founders and sellers; never once have we gifted an operating business to the next generation. My bias is that families ought to pass wealth, that families ought to pass entrepreneurial values to their children and that the only sustainable legacy is the family itself, and that wealth, like the businesses that create wealth, is temporary and fleeting.

The traditional bias of most accountants and lawyers is business "continuity", that is to say, perpetuating the business forward in family hands. For it is family that these two professions view as the best chance of maintaining the business — it is these two professions that historically have had the most to gain by supporting the traditional approach to succession planning that encourages the act of "gifting" controlling interest of shares to family members. The sale of a family business at the end of a founder's long run of success to a competitor or private equity firm usually spells the end of the file. The tragic implications of this singular approach or bias will increase in numbers as the demographic bulge of business owners moves in unprecedented numbers closer to their end without either a plan or a wish and a prayer for their succession. That is of course unless *financial advisors* gain the courage, knowledge, savvy and experience to offer a competing vision of succession planning, one that focuses not on perpetuating operating businesses, but rather a vision driven by wealth preservation. This will not be easy.

Trusted Advisors who master the art of offering a contrarian view of succession planning, one that drives the execution of a liquidity event, will not only manage their client's wealth but the succeeding generation's wealth as well. These advisors will create their own versions of Multi-Family Offices as a consequence of their "generational wealth preservation world view". This is not a zero sum game between accountants and lawyers on the one hand and wealth management advisors on the other. Rather, the former two will see how the shifting of wealth from operating businesses to family holding companies will generate significant accounting and legal work as the next generation puts capital to work in the next great enterprise — ideally enterprise uniquely fitted to its own skills and aspirations. The Multi-Family Office concept will really take flight when all three professions understand that gifting shares of closely held family businesses will continue to destroy families and their wealth with blinding speed. The corollary is that when succession planning goes well, the rewards will always flow to the advisors who saved the family from itself. What do I mean by this?

Some Context

Ninety per cent of all North American businesses — 24 million in total — are family owned and collectively worth more than $10 trillion. More than half of these ageing, tired business owners intend to retire over the next ten years. More than half of business owners have failed to formally articulate their succession plans. Most have given little thought about who will own and operate their business when they die. Most believe that in the event of their death the rolling of shares to a surviving spouse or children via provision in their will is their plan — full stop. That the children and spouse have never met senior management or chaired a board meeting is often of little consequence or pause for thought — the succession plan is complete. Little thought is given to how quickly their life's work, in their absence, will be reduced to a full contact sport.

Sadly, what the most extraordinary generation of talented, hard-working, prudent and frugal entrepreneurs fail to appreciate is the speed at which their *gift* will destroy wealth, relationships and their intended legacy. Why? Rare is the family that produces generation after generation of offspring that shares the passion to propel a founder's business and legacy forward. Even rarer, as noted earlier, is the business whose products and services stay in demand for more than one generation. Furthermore, those smaller families that started in the 1960s offer business owners fewer *succession* options today. The children of business owners who were encouraged by their parents to pursue their education and dreams went on in unprecedented numbers to heed that advice. Consequently, the traditional family business succession plan began to die in the 1960s in the quietest, most loving, self-inflicted and naïve way. The last chapter is about to unfold for millions of ageing family business owners as they ponder their dwindling options. Tragically, business owners who elect to ignore business succession planning will dishonour the intelligence of a generation that has created extraordinary cities, culture, philanthropy and commerce, which created the very wealth of our nation. The time has never been more ripe for advisors to play a magnificent role to reshape our society and our culture and redefine our relationship to wealth itself. The Trusted Advisor can and must do this by teaching business owners that gifting businesses to family is an act of hubris — a tried and disastrous approach that will not only wither wealth on the vine but destroy families from the inside out. Now, when I offer this perspective in my public lectures, I am always quick to clarify that while I'm suggesting operating businesses not be gifted, I am suggesting that wealth be gifted. And it is the deft hand of the wealth advisor who can manage wealth, spread risk and preserve wealth.

HOPE FOR A NEW SUCCESSION PLANNING APPROACH

Trusted Advisors need to understand that every family is different, every family business is different and they are not required to come with a set of succession planning answers but rather a new set of questions. Succession planning has always failed in the past when advisors came with their biases, came quickly to the rescue with their estate freezes and came with their tax-efficient plans without first understanding some basic information about the family and its individual and collective aspirations.

If the questions to guide families from destroying their wealth weren't so simple, the destruction of wealth wouldn't be so sad. Oddly enough, the questions advisors can put to business owners and their family centre around simple themes, the most important being clarifying whom and when the business will be sold to. If not sold to family, then to whom? The response to these questions offers advisors great insights into what kind of client they are dealing with. Business families should address questions such as the following:

- To whom do I want to sell my business?
- Are my children prepared to risk their capital to buy the business?
- Will I put in place special compensation for my children if they help sell the business?
- Does everyone acknowledge that we will always entertain outside offers to sell?

Businesses that offer up answers to these and other questions are prime candidates to work well with advisors. Business owners who never get around to answering the questions, offering vague excuses, will waste an advisor's time in the same way that they will waste their own family's time and wealth in pursuing something that can't be had — a business that seeks immortality.

This being said, I am a great believer that Trusted Advisors will be the purveyors of a new business succession planning paradigm and that some business owners will pay attention. Business owners, who can be convinced of the wisdom to ask their children poignant, direct questions now, will create a lasting and sustainable legacy long after they have gone. The questions zero in on the succeeding generation's appetite to risk their own capital today to purchase the stock of their parent's business. Most children will pass on the offer and give parents a glimpse into the future of how their business will be treated after they have died. When a business is simply gifted, children are denied the very opportunity that made their parents great — the opportunity to live and learn the lessons of risk and reward. Planted are the seeds of generational wealth destruction. When children are gifted shares in an operating company, they often stay for all the wrong reasons — because it is easy. Instead of driving the sale of a business to maximize shareholder value, a second or third generation family member often runs the business as he or she found it. If selling a gift is difficult, changing it fundamentally is equally difficult and consequently seldom done. When one contemplates the 3% success rate of businesses that make it to the third generation, one need look no further than the stifled innovation caused by gifting. Trusted Advisors who can remind their business owner clients about the perils of gifting will bring a contrarian view that will resonate profoundly with founders. The pandering advisors who advocate perpetuating a business into the reluctant or ill-suited hands of family has never served anyone particularly well — including the advisors themselves.

But this approach begs the question, how do the children afford to purchase the controlling interests of a significant family business? The answer lies in gifting *wealth*. When children are told that they will receive a living gift and at the same time told that shares in the family business are available to buy, the outcome will reveal volumes. Children that forgo consumption and purchase shares will be authenticating their ownership and gain the intellectual freedom to drive change in the business they have invested in. But more profoundly, children won't make the investment unless they understand the business, understand where that business is in its life cycle and understand what the likely return on invested capital will be. The earlier this process can start the better. When parents and their children ask themselves the same questions — what are the strengths, weaknesses, opportunities and threats to this business, and what does this business look like in five years — when both generations collaborate in answering these questions, they will be answering a fundamental question — is there a buyer in the house? If it is decided that the business won't be sold to family, it behooves advisors to help their business owner clients work on alternative plans. Private equity, competitors, key managers, Employee Share Ownership Plans, individual investors — the list is long.

Indeed, the really smart business families pursue all of their selling options concurrently, dispassionately probing the market for value. It takes great introspection and self-awareness for business owners to see their "end" to drive their business to its conclusion. Nothing that feels so utterly wrong is so utterly right when it comes to protecting generational wealth. Typically lacking is a methodology for a family business to find the end before the end finds the business. Family businesses are always relatively easy to start, yet it is their conclusion, a method for planning their finality that confounds most. Even when family businesses are sold to the next generation, I find it interesting that this event is "celebrated" as "continuation", as "succession" or most erroneously as "passing" the business. Why not celebrate this event as the conclusion of its ownership by the preceding generation? To do otherwise is to diminish the risk-taking assumed by the succeeding generation and to imbue it with what can be one of the greatest wealth destroying ideas to haunt family businesses — the burden of legacy, the burden of pursuing longevity as an end unto itself.

Non-family business leaders are seldom compensated for maintaining continuity of ownership; rather, their overriding objective is to increase shareholder value. The most successful family businesses understand this; seldom do they confuse their passion for *a* business with their passion for business — a subtle but crucial distinction required in family businesses for the protection of relationships and wealth.

But members of a family in business together know that the very notion of selling their business can be a lightning rod for emotional turmoil — selling can feel like failure. And yet nothing should be further from the truth. Indeed, for families that manage their succession well, selling a family business is the only legitimate succession goal worth pursuing, be it a sale to a family member, to a competitor or to a financial investor. This simple idea of forcing an "end" to ownership is the secret to preserving wealth and family relationships.

This perspective is based on my own personal involvement in a family business. In 2007, we sold our family business — gone was our ownership of the plastics manufacturing business founded by my father in 1973. After all the years of risk-taking, hard work and passion, the business — with plants in Canada and the United States — was no longer in our family's control. Our family brand, our legacy, was dead — or perhaps not.

On a sunny July morning in 2007, six months after working for the new owners, I drove out of the parking lot one last time from the business that I had run for almost ten years. The journey home that morning felt oddly exhilarating. There was no lamenting the business as *lost*, but instead a gut feeling that something new and extraordinary was about to begin — the first hint that our family business was still very much alive. With our family relationships intact and our capital preserved, our business could reinvent itself like it had done a previous generation ago when my grandfather sold his publicly traded chemical company — the business he had started in 1957. In the preceding months to my grandfather's business being sold, I watched his company stock rocket from $3 to $21. This left an indelible mark on my own understanding of the nature of business. I saw succession as driving a business to be sold.

I had no idea that evidence of my father's business legacy would emerge only two weeks later when I sat down and typed the first word of a 43,000-word manuscript that would become the best-selling book *Every Family's Business: A Blueprint for Protecting Family Business Wealth* (Orangeville, ON: Détente Financial Press, 2008). Only through the process of writing did I realize that as founders and sellers, our approach to succession planning was different than the experience of so many other family businesses. Our approach differed from those more inclined to preserve their legacy by passing their business to the next generation, either through its discounted sale or through its gifting.

The succession planning principles that have guided three generations of our family are distilled in 12 questions — questions that fundamentally put wealth preservation ahead of all other considerations — especially *family employment*. The cornerstone of our succession planning method involves an assessment of the risks to the business and defusing the *emotional* pull of legacy. Never was the notion of *longevity* of the business a compelling succession goal for any member of our family. My father and grandfather's inherited knowledge and experience told them that every product and service has a beginning, middle and end, that the key to business is knowing where you are in that life cycle.

One of our 12 questions was whether my father, the controlling shareholder, wanted to sell shares and whether I wanted to buy. This simple, routine question led us to a collaborative decision to sell to a third party. Markets can devour family businesses blinded by the pursuit of generational longevity. Market threats to my father's wealth were the same threats to mine. But what compels the succeeding generation to drive the sale of a business and put himself or herself out of work? The answer is straightforward — and it's precisely what the leadership of non-family businesses put in place to preserve their own shareholder value and management continuity.

A key component of any family business succession plan is agreeing to a compensation formula for the succeeding generation in the event that the controlling shareholder elects to sell to a third party. When this important step is taken, the succeeding generation should have an incentive to explore acquiring controlling interest of the family business at market value, as well as an economic incentive to probe the market for its sale. So simple, yet in practice so seldom done. Transparency, mutual trust and respect are essential to successful succession planning. It is through the honest declaration of future ownership intentions that the generations in a family business can work collaboratively on their plan to protect their wealth.

In our family business it was easy to pursue these two different succession tracks concurrently. With my economic interest aligned with that of my father, finding the end of our business became our goal, my goal. Its sale, if not to me, to someone, was the desired outcome. Controlling an outcome feels good. The legacy for us was never a company *name* but rather the capital we preserved together — capital that is now available to be reinvested in a business or many businesses that offer better returns for the risk. In my book I describe selling a family business as "creative destruction trumping the benign, wealth destroying idea of family legacy". Advisors who can help families embrace a broader definition of legacy and work collaboratively on a plan by adopting a method that puts wealth preservation first will succeed in the boardroom, and around the dining room table.

With my lineage punctuated with family business founders and sellers, my grandfather and father's business legacies feel very much alive in my business today. My business feels oddly like a third generation family business with that familiar drive to create and preserve wealth. I look forward to passing my family's legacy of entrepreneurship and capital into the trusting and respectful hands of my children one day, making it four generations in a row. But this transfer will only take place after we answer the 12 questions together and everyone agrees that my business, our family business, is always for sale. The experience and knowledge offered to the next generation to create and preserve wealth is the only *sustainable* legacy that can be gifted. Ask a Rothschild, a Desmerais or a Munk and he will tell you that knowing when to exit a business is as important as knowing when to invest in one. The pursuit of legacy — narrowly defined as the longevity of *an operating business* — is fool's gold.

Advisors who can offer their business owner clients a contrarian view of succession planning will emerge as most Trusted Advisors — trusted because they understand that the only plan worth pursuing is one that is built collaboratively by the family itself.

CHAPTER 43

SUCCEEDING AT SUCCESSION: THE EXIT PLANNING SPECIALIST

Peter J. Merrick
James Sbrolla
Charles Stanley
Lynn Mason

Overview

During the coming decade, Canada will experience the transition of wealth through the exchange of ownership of over $1.3 trillion worth of businesses from our ageing entrepreneur population, which has driven our economy to be one of the most admired in the world. This chapter outlines the basic issues related to succession planning for a business and gives an overview of some strategies that will result in assisting entrepreneurs to exit their businesses on their own terms, achieving their wealth preservation and wealth distribution goals.

Learning Objectives

By the time you complete this chapter you will:

- understand the value of creating a Sales Side Offering Memorandum;
- understand how to identify clients who might be candidates to sell their business;
- have a handle on when is the right time to sell;
- know who the three types of business buyers are;
- understand what an equity partner is and what he or she can bring to the table;
- understand what an Employee Share Ownership Plan is and how it works;
- understand how a business raises money without giving up ownership; and

- understand the capital pool concept and how it can be used to achieve a business owner's succession planning goals.

INTRODUCTION

According to a recent Canadian Institute of Chartered Accountants (CICA) survey, succession planning is still a very small part of total billings for most Chartered Accountant firms across Canada and is likely to grow in importance. The survey found that 60% of firms expect succession planning to account for at least 5% of total billings in the future, and 17% expect it to account for more than 10%.

Canadians are ageing. Canadian entrepreneurs are ageing even faster. Over the next ten years, more than half of the country's small- and medium-sized family business owners are expected to retire. According to studies by the Canadian Federation of Independent Business (CFIB), Canadian family business owners are generally not adequately prepared for the business succession matters they will have to address. The numbers reflect this. Only 10% have a formal written plan; 38% have an informal unwritten plan; while 52% have no plan at all.

The majority of business owners have not even started to discuss their exit plans with their family members, business partners, or Trusted Advisors, *i.e.*, the exit planning specialists. An estimated $1.3 trillion in business assets is expected to change hands over the next decade, representing the largest turnover of economic control in Canadian history. And yet the CFIB studies indicate that 60% of respondents feel it is too early to plan for business succession. Many family business owners are underestimating the challenging issues they will have to address, the time it will take to do them and the emotional decisions they may have to make.

These statistics are unfortunate, and the apparent lack of preparation could backfire on some business owners. Succession planning should be a deliberate process and not a one-time event. Business owners should realize that the best time to plan is when there is time to both properly evaluate alternatives and seek input from professional advisors to assist them in their exit planning. A client may not want to be forced to accelerate succession planning because of illness, divorce or death, yet prudence and foresight are still important.

Business succession planning is an investment in the future of your practice, your clients' companies, their employees, and customers. Planning is the key to future success for everyone whose efforts have helped the business to grow. The existence of a succession plan emphasizes both your client's commitment and your commitment to their company's long-term growth, and creates confidence among shareholders, lenders, employees and suppliers.

CREATING A SALES SIDE OFFERING MEMORANDUM

One of the best investments that a business owner can make in his or her company is to create and maintain what is referred to as a Sales Side Offering Memorandum (SSOM) or a Prospectus. The SSOM and the company financials provide an objective overview of a client's company and that company's valuation in the marketplace. The value of this document is that when a client decides to sell his or her business, the client will be prepared to do it on his or her own terms with realistic expectations. A SSOM can provide meaningful information for the client, his or her Trusted Advisors, *i.e.*, lawyers, wealth managers and accountants, along with the potential buyers.

In this way, when it is time for the business owner to sell his or her business, he or she will get the maximum sales price for his or her goodwill. The SSOM will add value to the business simply through the organization of documents and information which create an overall picture of his or her financial position in the marketplace. This allows the owner to anticipate the kinds of information that prospective buyers will ask and request. Thus, your clients can frame the sales dialogue.

A company effectively creates a SSOM for it by first completing a market valuation analysis for the company. The Market Valuation Analysis will provide the company with the following scenarios to evaluate:

- growth fuelled by a capital infusion;
- growth by acquisition and a capital infusion;
- growth by merging with a complementary firm;
- sale of some or all of the shares of the company; and
- sale of a division or component of the company.

A client will need the assistance of his or her Trusted Advisors in the process of creating, maintaining and reviewing the SSOM to provide the following services and deliverables:

- review current financial statements and projections;
- review the current business plan and financial model;
- meet and assess key senior management;
- develop detailed financial projections using researched and documented market metrics;

- develop a detailed pro forma revenue and expense model, cash flow statement and balance sheet statement;
- develop the firm's valuation range using standard and accepted valuation methodologies;
- document the internal capital structure; and
- document the scenarios that express future plans for the company.

HOW TO IDENTIFY CLIENTS WHO MIGHT BE CANDIDATES TO SELL THEIR BUSINESS

The most important reason cited by business owners for wanting to sell their business is the prospect of creating financial independence for themselves and for their families. By doing so, they afford themselves the time to enjoy their lives, doing what they truly love without the financial constraints they have experienced up to this time while having the vast majority of their net worth tied up in their companies. There are five key factors that indicate when a business owner is a candidate for selling the family business.

According to Rudolph Dorner, president of M&A Inc. in Cambridge, Ontario, which has brokered the sale of 74 corporations valued at between $2 million and $100 million over the last 20 years, there are five key indicators that a business owner is a candidate for selling his or her business:

(1) **Age:** The business owner is age 50-55 or he or she has been in the business over 20 years. At this stage, the business owner is ready to do something else or wants to enjoy the fruits of his or her labour.

(2) **Fatigue:** The owner demonstrates a lack of daily enthusiasm for the business. The owner has travelled across North America, building his or her business too many times and has dealt with too many employee problems.

(3) **Money:** The owner wants to take some or all of his or her equity (most of which is in the company) off the table. He or she wants to secure his or her family's future.

(4) **Future:** The future of the business is not as bright as it once was for reasons of competition, currency exchange, technology or whatever.

(5) **Partners:** The long-term arrangement has finally hit a major snag. Think of the McCain and the Steinberg Families in Canada.

Note: The McCain family owns one of the largest food processing companies in the world, and in the 1990s there was a power struggle as to who would control the company. The Steinberg family owned one of Canada's largest grocery store chains. After Sam Steinberg's death, a power struggle developed between his two daughters.

WHEN IS THE RIGHT TIME TO SELL?

The number one question that many successful business owners ask themselves and their Trusted Advisors is: "When is the right time to sell?" Before considering selling his or her business, your client needs to discover what his or her individual financial independence number is. This "magic number" is the amount of capital that will be needed for the client to live on for the rest of his or her lifetime. The number is "magic" because it can turn a business owner into a business seller. This number can only be understood when you work with the client to help in the development of a complete financial plan detailing everything the client desires to accomplish in this lifetime and beyond. If it is determined that by selling the company today your client can meet the magic number, then your client is a prime candidate to sell the business. If your client cannot reach the magic number by selling the business today, the client will need to develop new strategies to grow the business until such time when the sale of the business will generate that personal magic number.

The second question that business owners ask of their Trusted Advisors when contemplating selling their business is: "To whom should I sell my business?" Generally speaking, there are three primary categories of potential purchasers to consider in any exit/succession planning exercise:

- family members (whether active or passive in the business);
- key managers/senior employees of the business;
- third party purchaser (which may be a strategic buyer such as a competitor or key customer/supplier of the business, or a purely financial buyer such as a private equity fund, merchant bank or investor).

The Family Business and the Family

Often Trusted Advisors have corporate clients whose businesses are owned by multiple family members. Inevitably, the time will come when the older generation of shareholders will want to "pass the baton" to the younger generation. Of course, these older shareholders have put in many years of hard work and don't want to risk their future financial security on the younger generation's ability to profitably manage the business. When they remove themselves from active involvement in the business, they generally want to be "cashed out" or something very close to it.

In these circumstances, there is a very real need for clarity among the various shareholders regarding the vision for the business and their role in it, since each will have a "horse in the race" when it comes time to make decisions on strategies and tactics. Therefore, a discussion of specific planning strategies or tools is futile, unless it is done in the greater context of exactly what the shareholders desire to accomplish. Many of the tools, techniques, strategies and tactics used in estate and exit strategy planning involve irrevocable decisions that clients might not fully appreciate. Consequently, as a Trusted Advisor to your client, the importance of this clarity cannot be overstated.

Ike Did It Right: Successful Family Succession Planning

Peter, a taxation specialist, had known a car dealership owner, Ike, for several years, ever since his public accountant, Ronald, whom they both trusted, introduced them. Ronald wanted Peter to implement some tax minimization and tax deferral solutions for Ike, focusing on executive compensation, pension and succession exiting strategies. Although Ike owned several car dealerships in Southern Ontario and had plenty of business sense, he still felt that he could benefit from some outside advice.

In 2004, Peter learned that Ike had benefited from the tax strategies he had implemented, and achieved the goal of transferring one of his dealerships to his son Pat. Peter was fascinated with Ike's story. He had read many studies about the desire of entrepreneurs to transfer their business to another family member, typically their children, when it was time to retire. However, most of those businesses ended up being sold to third parties. This is usually because younger family members lack the money to buy their older relatives out or simply have no interest in running the business.

Ike, by seeking professional advice from his Trusted Advisors at every stage of the process, avoided the usual pitfalls and made possible another generation of car dealership owner success. This story goes back to 1992.

The Long View

When asked to reflect on Pat's achievements since 2004, Ike will tell you that he and his son owe much to sound financial preparation. Equally vital was the professional help they sought, especially from his public accountant, lawyer and financial planner.

Ike had always believed in a flexible business strategy that looks ahead five, even ten years. Pat first expressed an interest in joining the family business as early as 1992. Ike's planning prepared him for the day when Pat was finally ready to join the family business and make this his career.

Part of being a mature business owner is considering your succession and exit strategy with every business decision you make, in other words, taking the "long view". In 1992, Ike told his public accountant of his desire to eventually sell his business to his children. As their family accountant and most Trusted Advisor, Ronald's role was to provide guidance and help him develop a business model and tax plan to facilitate this still far-off goal.

Setting up a Trust

Ronald recommended that Ike reorganize his corporate structure to allow for an estate freeze on the future value of his business. An estate freeze limits the growth of capital property you hold during your lifetime; any future growth in the capital property is transferred to your heirs. Ike shared ownership of the operating company with his children through a "family trust". The children would be the trust's beneficiaries.

A trust is not a separate legal entity from the group or individuals who set it up. It is a device for holding property or assets for the benefit of a specific person, group or organization, known as the beneficiary (in this case, Pat and his sister Ellen). The person creating a trust (Ike) is called the grantor, donor or settler. When a trust is established, an individual or corporate entity is designated to oversee or manage the assets in the trust. This individual or entity is called a trustee (again, Ike).

With Ike's new business structure in place, it allowed for his business' future profits and assets to accumulate in the family trust, with dividends to be paid through it to the children. This helped Pat and Ellen to accumulate funds in the most tax advantageous way: (a) because they were in a lower tax bracket than Ike, and (b) because he could maintain control of the assets and split the income with his children. The future trust also allowed Pat to accumulate his own funds in his own name to provide him the equity with which to buy this location from his father.

The Individual Pension Plan

Ike's trusted accountant also made two other recommendations that helped guarantee Ike's own financial well-being once retirement approached. First, he recommended that Ike create an individual pension plan (IPP).

Universal Life Insurance

Ronald's second suggestion was for Ike to purchase (through his new corporate structure) a corporate-owned universal life (UL) insurance policy. UL insurance allows for tax-sheltered growth within the policy. A corporate-owned life insurance contract can tax shelter much of your retained earnings in the cash-value portion of the policy. You can access these funds for personal business use throughout your life by collateralizing the policy through loans from the policy. For example, as a retired business owner, you might borrow funds annually to increase your retirement cash flow.

Any related bank or policy loans will be repaid automatically upon death from a portion of the policy proceeds. A credit to the corporate capital dividend account (CDA) would be simultaneously created, equal to the full policy proceeds. Should Ike ever become disabled or critically ill, the corporate-owned UL insurance policy entitles him to the entire cash value without any requirement to repay the policy. Thus, a corporate-owned UL policy can provide the following benefits for a business owner who chooses to adopt it:

- corporate deposits can be deductable;
- all personal deposits can be deductable over time;
- large annual deductions are provided each year against income for the rest of your life;
- the owner receives tax-free retirement (even tax-free death), with savings protected from creditors; and
- the corporation or personal deduction creates an annual cash-on-cash return of approximately 60%, in a plan on which taxes will never be paid.

The Next Generation

With Ike's financial future secured, he turned his attention to the succession challenge itself. The challenge for the car industry, like all businesses today, is finding candidates who will bring value to the brand. Auto dealership owners must be competent in business management, marketing, relationship management and resource management.

To protect its brand, the auto company holds the final say over who will be granted franchise rights. The auto company must simply ensure a proper fit between the next generation and its dealership system. Most well-established car dealership network systems have created a set of step-by-step guidelines for current owners and their successors:

1. All parties (in this case, Ike, as parent, Pat, as would-be next-generation owner and the auto company) must be involved in all steps of the succession planning and transfer-of-ownership process.
2. The new family member must show an interest in and commitment to owning the business and have already worked in the business in a senior management position. He or she must demonstrate a capability to work successfully in the business. The auto company will also help by establishing a training program for the next generation dealership owner candidate.
3. The auto company will still hold final approval for any transfer of ownership. The next-generation candidate must complete an application (like any other applicant). He or she must also have the financing in place to purchase the dealership. Once the applicant's training program is complete, the auto company invites the next-generation applicant to an interview. The panel then determines the family member's suitability to take over the reins.

In 2004, Pat met and far exceeded the panel's requirements. With the foresight of his father, the help of the auto company's next-generation training program and Ike's Trusted Advisors, Pat became an owner of his own dealership, just like his father before him. As one senior executive at the car company's head office recalls, "Ike must have had some incredible advisors because he did everything right in preparing his business and his son to take over his dealership."

The value of this long-term planning is not limited to car dealerships. Business owners of all stripes must consider the future and prepare for the day when their life's work must be passed along. A good place to start is to ask your clients if they see their children taking over their family-owned business in 5, 10 or even 20 years. If they do, the time to start planning for it is now, and clients should begin by seeking planning advice from trusted and competent professionals.

Private Equity Partners

We are currently in a very tight credit environment. Family-owned businesses usually don't carry enough retained earnings in the company to be able to "cash out" the older generation. So, in a tight credit market with insufficient retained earnings, other options need to be considered. One option is the use of a private equity partner.

Private equity is another method of raising capital for both growing and mature businesses. Different from "angel investors" or true "venture capitalists", private equity investors are looking for mature and well-managed companies that are leaders in their defined markets and have significant upside in their growth potential.

In addition to investing for growth, private equity firms will provide capital to support complete ownership "transitions". This can include founders who are reaching retirement, and/or families who have inherited businesses that they do not intend to operate. Private equity is also suited for owners who wish to lower their risk (*i.e.*, "take some chips off the table"), or who recognize their need for assistance in taking their business to the next level.

Industry Interests

Most private equity funds will look at deals in a wide range of industry sectors. However, once they have completed a transaction in a specific sector, it often makes sense to build in the same sector, particularly when there is an opportunity for consolidation. Leveraging existing investments is a strong premise of private equity.

Regardless of industry focus, most private equity funds avoid early stage companies, real estate and operating turnaround situations. Making "good companies" better, through their involvement, is a core private equity principle.

There are many advantages to accessing private equity rather than some of the other sources of capital available in the market place. First, private equity funds generally have some level of involvement in the businesses that they invest in and this can bring knowledge and experience that these businesses may not have previously had. Second, private equity funds bring relationships that can offer business opportunities that would never have been realized without them.

The attitude in private equity is that it brings more than capital to the table. In reality, private equity becomes partners with the ownership/management group. Private equity works closely with management teams on issues related to acquisitions, financial structure and strategic planning. The relationship also goes well beyond these things. Private equity partners can help with enhancing many intangibles. Partnering with the largest private equity funds throughout North America can bring relationships and credibility that are unique and helpful to many independent businesses.

Example of Partnering

What follows is an example of how this technique of partnering with a private equity firm was recently employed to resolve a major conflict between competing family interests.

Maintaining control of the family business and maintaining harmony among multiple generations of shareholders with divergent interests are the major challenges confronting the owners of many family-owned businesses. Other issues, including the desire for asset diversification by all shareholders and ongoing capital demands of the business, can create additional obstacles to peaceful coexistence. Frequently, indebtedness incurred to buy out inactive shareholders severely restricts a company's ability to expand and, in times like now when credit is tight, can lead to its demise.

The presence of a restless bloc of shareholders precipitated the agreement to sell a substantial interest in Freedom Communications, Inc. At the time, it was one of North America's few remaining family-owned media companies. Founder R. C. Hoiles started the company in 1935 with the purchase of the Santa Ana Register (now the Orange County Register in Orange County, California) and expanded it into a media conglomerate. Freedom's assets included 8 television stations, 27 daily newspapers and 37 weeklies. Daily circulation approximated 1.2 million subscribers.

Citing the company's underperformance in recent years, older family members demanded a buyout of their shares or an outright sale of the entire company. Another group of Hoiles' descendants, representing approximately 40% of the company's voting stock, argued that the value of keeping the business in the family and protecting its unique philosophical heritage outweighed the financial rewards of selling out to a competing media concern. This was clearly a case where clarity between the shareholders and their Trusted Advisors about their true goals was imperative to arrive at an acceptable solution.

To address the conflicting objectives, the company's board of directors elected to partner with Blackstone Communications Partners and Providence Equity Partners to purchase the stock of the older family members under an agreement that enabled remaining shareholders to retain operating control of the family business. Funds provided by the equity firms and a JP Morgan Chase Bank debt facility were used to make the purchase. Competing bids had been submitted by Lee Enterprises, Inc., E.W. Scripps and Gannett Co., Inc., publisher of *USA Today*, which would have resulted in the sale of the company upon approval by a majority of the shareholders. However, this alternative was rejected as being inconsistent with the goals of the younger generation of shareholders. Again, significant clarity of the goals and values of all shareholders was critical to achieving the successful exit strategy that was achieved.

Private Equity Sources

Blackstone, Provident, and other prominent private equity groups continue to provide a flexible and dependable source of capital for established, family-owned companies. Investors in these funds include public and private entity pension plans, major universities, insurance companies, investment banks and high net-worth individuals. Private equity transactions can take the form of leveraged acquisitions, buyouts or recapitalizations. There is substantial latitude in the structuring of each deal to accommodate the unique requirements and objectives of the various shareholders in the family business. In the Freedom Communications transaction, for example, Provident and Blackstone purchased a substantial position in the company while leaving key family members in control.

After making an investment in a family business, private equity partners will seek to continue or accelerate its growth. Through a base of professional relationships, equity partners can create business development opportunities for the company. The group can offer financial expertise and access to strategic industry relationships and resources, and serve as a primary source for additional growth capital. The investment in a family-owned company by a prominent private equity firm provides additional credibility to the business and a solid foundation for its future expansion or sale.

Capital Availability

Private equity firms are under increasing pressure from their limited partners and other capital sources to invest idle funds. John L. Chapman, Ph.D. and NRI Fellow (Economics) at the American Enterprise Institute, estimates that the worldwide volume of private equity capital exceeds $1.4 trillion, and that $800 billion of that total is held by American PE firms. This abundance of capital, combined with a relatively limited number of attractive target companies, has generated intense competition among private equity groups, hedge funds and corporate acquirers to consummate transactions. As a result, valuations, as reflected by multiples of EBITDA (earnings before interest, taxes, depreciation and amortization), are steadily increasing for family-owned businesses that are performing well. Moreover, the private equity firms have become much more flexible in negotiating the terms and structures of their equity investments.

Ideal Candidates for Investments

Although private equity firms are as diverse as the operating companies in which they seek to invest, there are many common characteristics that private equity investors find attractive in potential candidates. In general, these investors look for well-managed companies which generate annual operating income in excess of $1 million. Many funds have significantly higher earnings thresholds. On the other hand, companies pursued as "add-ons" for an existing company within an equity fund's portfolio of businesses may be somewhat smaller. Targeted businesses may compete in a broad spectrum of industries and supply a wide range of products and services through diverse distribution channels. Accordingly, successful manufacturing, wholesale, retail and service businesses are of interest to these seasoned investors.

The criteria private equity firms consider when evaluating potential investment opportunities include:

- consistent and growing businesses;
- stable revenue streams;
- expansion opportunities;
- predictable cash flows;
- the current market position of a business within its industry; and
- the presence of meaningful barriers to entering the company's market segment or geographic region.

Finally, a private equity partner will seek assurances that remaining family members and operating managers will continue with the enterprise and endeavour to increase sales and profits to achieve maximum value for all shareholders. And most importantly, you, as your clients' Trusted Advisor, will remain a key member of the team to help your clients transition as $1.3 trillion worth of Canadian-owned businesses are sold in the coming decades.

Canadian Private Equity Venture Capital Perspective

Bay Street, Canada's equivalent to Wall Street in the United States, has a wide cast of characters. As companies look to raise capital and build their businesses, it is often difficult to know who's who and where these different players fit in. Fortunately, there is an association that brings some structure to this otherwise complicated world of business and finance. This association, Canada's Venture Capital and Private Equity Association (CVCA), was established in 1974 to represent the interests of the private risk capital industry. Currently, it has approximately 120 full member companies comprised of venture capital, mezzanine and buyout funds, and over 1,200 individual members. The CVCA also has a large number of associate members that are drawn from the ranks of the leading accounting, legal, insurance and human resources service providers in Canada. There are also a growing number of international members comprised of foreign-headquartered entities with Canadian operations. Member funds have more than $65 billion in capital under management.

Members actively collaborate to increase the flow of capital into the industry and to expand the range of profitable investment opportunities. This is accomplished by the CVCA undertaking a wide variety of initiatives, ranging from developing comprehensive performance and valuation statistics to promoting the industry's interests with governments and regulatory agencies.

The CVCA has members across the country that are active in financing a wide range of companies in many industries and at all stages of development, from start-up firms that are just beginning to mature companies whose shares are traded on public stock exchanges. The venture fund members have most of their investments in high technology sectors, including information technology, telecommunications, clean-tech, life sciences and biotech. The mezzanine and buyout members operate across a broad range of industries, including manufacturing.

To help educate those interested, the CVCA offers a Professional Development program to its members as well as an extensive series of networking events that culminates in the Annual Conference. the Professional Development program, which is comprised of four half-day seminars on topics that are of interest to members and to non-members alike, and are held concurrently in over half a dozen cities.

The Canadian Private Risk Capital Industry has a number of defining features:

(1) It is characterized by an active, hands-on investment style. The industry works closely with portfolio company executives to position firms for growth and development. The industry pays considerable attention to ensure a proper alignment of interests between investors and portfolio companies' management in order to maximize the opportunities for accelerated growth.

(2) It is "patient" capital that is concerned with building long-term value in portfolio companies. In this regard, for instance, venture fund investments' hold periods can range from five to eight years.

(3) The contribution of the private equity investor often goes beyond providing capital and extends to identifying new markets, customers and technologies, and to assisting in recruiting top-level executive talent.

The private risk capital industry is a vital component of the financing ecosystem in Canada. CVCA members work together with other groups in this ecosystem, from angel investors to financial institutions and stock exchanges, in Canada and abroad, in order to provide Canadian industry with the edge that it needs to succeed in today's ultra-competitive global economy.

To be able to continue to provide that edge and to build on it, Canada's venture capital and private equity industry must attract more capital. Presently, Canada's venture capital industry is, on a proportionate basis, half the size of its U.S. counterpart. Thus, the CVCA, as the industry's only national trade association, is actively involved in various initiatives that are specifically designed to attract more capital into the industry from both domestic and international sources.

The CVCA website, <www.cvca.ca>, contains a listing of all its members with links to funds' own websites where information about their broad investment criteria, including industry and geographic preferences, and the usual size of investments, can be found. Through the growth and development of the CVCA, capital markets are maturing and providing a great service to Canadian companies and to the economy in general.

Employee Share Ownership Plan

As your client's Trusted Advisor, you can help him or her create his or her own buyers who will buy at the best price. This is done via the vehicle known as an ESOP (Employee Stock Ownership Plan) or in Canada (Employee Share Ownership Plan).

When you structure the ESOP, any of the first three choices to sell a business to, *i.e.*, to family, employees or a third party, may end up being the effective owner of the business, that is, he or she may end up having control of the business and being the trustee of the ESOP, the one who votes the shares in any company voting decisions. Technically, employees are the owners, but they do not have the right to vote shares in the ESOP.

One interesting feature here is that your client doesn't have to go out and find a buyer and risk the loss of confidentiality about his or her exit plans to leave the business. Your client creates their own buyer. This is known as a 100% ESOP Buy-Out. So how does this work?

In oversimplified terms, your client creates a Qualified Retirement Plan (QRP) for his or her corporate employees known as an Employee Stock Ownership Plan. Right now, your client owns the stock in the company. The company borrows the money from a financing institution to purchase the stock. The company loans money to the ESOP, which in turn purchases your client's stock from him or her at a value established by an independent outside valuation firm (probably a higher value than a negotiated price with an outside buyer). Now, your client does not own the stock, but he or she controls it by being in charge of the ESOP (as trustee), which controls the shares.

The company loan and the ESOP loan must be paid back. Over the next three to five years, the company funds the ESOP with tax deductible cash contributions on behalf of your client's employees, which contributions are used to repay the loans, and shares are attributed to employees. Your client continues to run the company profitably during the debt elimination time, so the risk of someone else running the company and failing is eliminated. This structure could happen with a third party buyer through a buyout plan.

Your client has now extracted the maximum value from the company and rewarded loyal employees with an ownership stake in the company. If your client has family in the business, he or she may arrange for the family to have control of the business going forward as trustee of the plan that owns all the shares. This is a regulated plan, so you can't just do anything you want. There are regulations that must be followed and you will want to have true ESOP experts as part of your wealth management team to make sure it is done properly.

Raising Money Without Giving up Ownership

There are many reasons why business owners can often find themselves in a situation where they need to raise new funds but don't want to give up a share in their business. It may be a strategic move to acquire a competitor or there may be a need for additional cash to support operations. It is not uncommon for businesses to find themselves in a situation where a new piece of equipment is needed to facilitate growth but funds are limited as the customer base has not as yet begun paying for the added production.

If the owner of a business decides not to raise "equity financing", there are two traditional forms of "debt" that can be utilized — senior and subordinated. Senior debt comes in three forms: an operating revolver (also referred to as a line of credit), a term loan and a capital lease. Senior debt means that the lender will have preference on the asset he or she has security on over any other lender, including the business owner.

An operating line of credit is set up on the basis of the amount of accounts receivable the business owns which is reassessed monthly. Most commercial lenders will lend between 60 and 80% of the value of the accounts receivable. This form of debt is usually the cheapest as interest rates are set at prime to prime plus 2%. Another attractive feature to this debt instrument is that there is no defined repayment schedule.

A term loan is similar to an operating line of credit but it takes into account the tangible assets of the business such as buildings, property, inventory, *etc.*, excluding the business' accounts receivable. Most commercial lenders will lend between 40 and 60% of the value of the tangible assets depending on the condition of the asset. This form of debt usually charges interest at a rate of prime to prime plus 4%. Different from the operating line of credit, the term loan will have defined repayment terms.

Most people are familiar with the purchase of a car or a new piece of equipment and taking a lease out with the manufacturer or a third party leasing company to buy the asset. But what most business owners often neglect is the hidden value of the tangible asset once the lease is paid off and often fully depreciated on the balance sheet. There are companies that lend money as capital leases against assets that have been fully written off but where the market value is greater than zero. The interest cost of this debt instrument is similar to a term loan and will usually have a three- to five-year repayment schedule.

Subordinated debt is a different type of debt instrument. Much like an equity investor, this type of lender often looks at the business as a whole. The lender will consider the value of the assets that are secured and those that are unsecured. He or she will consider the cash flow the business has generated and should generate in the future. If you have a lender with an operating revolver in place, a subordinated debt lender may be the best option. This lender will charge more for the loan than the senior lender, in most cases prime plus 8% to prime plus 10%, but he or she will postpone his or her security to other lenders. This type of debt instrument has a fixed repayment plan.

In any case, it is important to recognize that the lender will want to be very comfortable with the business' ability to service the debt. The lender will want to see the company's historical performance, understand the business strategy going forward, assess the business plan and, depending on the term of the loan, may want to see a three- to five-year plan. Careful consideration of your client's business' needs and matching it up with the right form of financing can lead to a very productive outcome. Happy debt hunting!

Capital Pool Concept Is Gaining Market Traction

Raising capital has long been a challenge for growing businesses, but this has been particularly true in recent years. The tough market has been compounded by currency and interest rate fluctuations that have made lenders reluctant to take big new positions in this turbulent environment.

In addition to many traditional ways to access capital for growth, there is a comparatively new method that is gaining popularity, and it is called the capital pool company (CPC) program. New regulations have paved the way for this vehicle to be attractive for Canadian industry.

The concept originated in Western Canada, where junior capital pools were used to finance oil and gas exploration. These vehicles were designed to offer an alternative to businesses that didn't want the drama and large costs of a traditional initial public offering (IPO).

A CPC is a blind pool listed on public exchange that has capital and seasoned management but no operating business. Its primary objective is to identify and acquire an early stage business moving to public company status. Revisions to the pool have been approved to increase the amount of capital that can be invested to $2 million and to streamline the shareholder approval process.

The CPC program is available to emerging companies at a time when a traditional IPO would not be suitable. The IPO route can cost upwards of $1 million in fees and administrative costs alone. Unless a company is raising $5 million to $10 million, the fixed cost burden can be prohibitive. The CPC route has capped commissions and legal and accounting fees so that they are not overwhelming. There are many companies that could make great use of $500,000 to $2 million in growth capital. Each must meet the minimum listing requirements for the exchange.

These requirements vary depending on the industry and seniority of listing. The requirements for the most senior industrial issuer include adequate working capital for 12 months, $50,000 of pre-tax earnings in the last year or in two of the last three years and $500,000 of net tangible assets.

The CPC program is a multistep process. The mechanics work like this:

1. founders set up a new company and invest a minimum of $100,000 to establish a pool;
2. an investment firm is engaged to find at least 300 investors who subscribe to the pool;
3. the pool is now between $250,000 and $2 million and ready to acquire an operating business; and
4. the founders identify a target company that is acquired by the pool, resulting in public status.

The operating business now has the capital to grow and to meet reporting requirements for a public listing. There are numerous benefits to being a public company. The status offers entrepreneurs capital, visibility, an exit strategy and a means of employee and management participation.

It also means public shares can be used as currency for acquisitions, and it gives the outside world (including people in the sector) the opportunity to share in the firm's growth. There are also drawbacks to being a public company. There are costs for maintaining the public listing; and it can be a distraction watching the share price fluctuate.

Public status opens financial information of the company to the outside world. Given these benefits and drawbacks, the CPC option is just one that growing companies should consider as part of their long-term strategic planning.

Getting Out — Third Party Buyers

Based on our professional experience working with business owners before, during and after the sale of their company, we have found that selling to a third party is the best option for a business owner to get out of his or her business completely. The advantages of selling to a third party over selling to family or key managers are that your client has a better probability of selling the business for cash and the odds are greater that your client will get a premium for it and surpass the ever-important magic number. If the negotiations fall apart, your client will not have to worry about continuing a relationship with the third party again. This cannot be said when dealing with family or key managers.

There are a number of key steps in selling a business. First, it is essential to choose a reputable business broker. Forget the ads or solicitations in the mail. Ask around for a personal reference from someone who has sold his or her business. Expect to pay about 5% on the first $10 million and 1% thereafter for the broker. Legal and accounting fees will cost 1.5% of the selling price. The broker will value your client's business. Over the last 20 years in Ontario, good businesses have sold for an average of 3.54 times normalized EBITDA (earnings before interest, tax, depreciation and amortization — normalized for the owner's wages and non-recurring costs).

The valuation of a business should not cost more than $5,000. The broker should also provide a statement showing the net funds available to the vendor from the sale after transaction costs and taxes.

Once your client has decided to sell his or her business and has selected a business broker to represent him or her, the broker writes the SSOM describing your client's company in full detail as discussed earlier in this chapter. It is wise for the client to prepare the SSOM as a part of the ongoing management of his or her company well before he or she contemplates selling the company. It usually takes two and a half days of the seller's time to supply the raw information, and this should be assisted by all the client's Trusted Advisors.

What is helpful during this process is for the seller to provide a list of every potential buyer that he or she can remember, think of or imagine to the broker. The broker will also solicit buyers, sign them to a non-disclosure agreement, screen non-serious buyers and present the company in its best light. The seller will meet with the potential buyers to discuss company history, current and future operations and any role the seller is willing to play in the business transition. The seller should expect to meet a maximum of five potential buyers. If more buyers are introduced, the broker is not screening carefully enough.

When an offer is presented, the broker will provide a signed offer in the form of a letter of intent. He or she will review it with the seller and point out any advantages or deficiencies. He or she should not advise your client to accept or reject it. The broker should only advise if the deal is at, above or below market, and that is all.

If the deal is acceptable, the broker will procure a deposit, $100,000 being a standard deposit on deals in this segment. A standard good deal has the following earmarks: 75% cash up front, maximum 25% vendor take back (VTB). The VTB is to be guaranteed by a pledge of shares, guarantee of the purchaser and the purchaser's principals. The deal should have specific terms to allow excess cash to be stripped out of the company prior to close.

The seller should have already sat down with his or her Certified Financial Planner, public accountant and other Trusted Advisors to put in place solutions to generate and strip out excess cash. Working with tax and financial planning specialists will go a long way to minimize the tax liability triggered by the sale. One of the best ways for your clients to successfully meet their needs is for their Trusted Advisors to think beyond traditional tax-based solutions. Most business owners' issues, be they related to strategic business planning, estate planning, succession planning, charitable giving, investments or insurance, are as significant as anything tax-related, and these must be addressed as well.

Opportunities often exist whereby corporate-held moneys created from undrawn net income and/or proceeds from the sale of a business can compound tax free within holding companies and/or be invested in tax-favourable, tailored executive benefit plans.

These opportunities can be achieved through several means, including individual pension plans, retirement compensation arrangements, corporate-owned UL insurance, employee profit-sharing plans, family trusts, holding companies and health and welfare trusts. By implementing any of these strategies the business owner can benefit by tax savings of hundreds of thousands and even millions of dollars.

The buyer will then do a 90-day due diligence investigation to determine if the facts presented about the business are true. It is important to note that this process will be intrusive and tedious in the extreme. The broker's job is to minimize the disruption by organizing the information in the manner most useful to the buyers and their lawyers, accountants and certified financial planners.

Next is the share purchase agreement prepared by the buyer's lawyers. The terms will be strongly tilted to the buyer's advantage. The broker working with the seller's lawyer and/or his or her own specialist will make sure balance is restored. Expect there to be anywhere from three to ten turns at the merry-go-round before there is full agreement. The seller stays out of this process, letting the lawyers and his or her broker apply their craft. The vendor will formally review the final version.

The Last Steps Towards Peace of Mind

Just prior to closing, the broker will provide a projected balance sheet to the new owners, as well as a payout statement to the vendor showing all costs, projected taxes and net funds receivable from the sale. The day after closing the broker will usually hand-deliver the cheques and ensure the funds are deposited into the correct entity as per the tax plan. The broker's job is not done until the funds due on the VTB are collected and in the vendor's account.

CONCLUSION

You now possess a basic primer to map out whether a client is ripe to consider selling his or her business or not. There are Trusted Advisors who can bring value to your clientele throughout the preparation, the sales process and long afterwards. The best advice we can give is this — find out your client's "magic" number. The longer they have it firmly in their heads the better. If the client is considering selling, as your client's exit planning specialist, you need to begin the process today.

For those clients who don't know their magic number yet, seek out their Trusted Advisors and communicate with them what you need to move forward. Let the Trusted Advisors help create a pathway towards the next stage in the process and for your client's next step in their life's journey.

For business owners who have been putting off succession planning, there is no time like the present to explore their options. This process involves answering tough questions and exploring scenarios that may not please all family members, shareholders, managers or employees; but it is important that you assist your business-owner clients to address them.

Below are seven tough questions:

1. Do you want to sell the entire company in due course?

2. Do you want to sell some now and achieve the rest of your liquidity later?
3. Is it important to you that ownership remain with family members or managers?
4. Do you want them to maintain control or just have minority equity participation alongside a new owner?
5. Is the incumbent group of family members or managers even capable of taking over and managing the business?
6. How will they finance the purchase of your shares?
7. Can they gain the confidence of lenders and investors, or are you prepared to finance their acquisition?

The first step should be to have a professional business valuation firm prepare an assessment of the value of the company, and it should reflect normalization adjustments to account for unusual, non-recurring or one-time items, such as excessive remuneration and family perks. It is important for the business owner to be realistic with respect to valuation expectations, or considerable time will be wasted. Accountants and lawyers should be involved in estate planning, and, any share reorganization or tax structuring matters.

Answering these questions can be time-consuming and should not be rushed. Most owners, and in fact most businesses, are not ready for the sale process to begin immediately. The valuation conclusion and business review process often indicate that some management depth, capital structure and profitability issues should be addressed before proceeding, not only to support valuation expectations, but to have a more saleable business.

This is why many owners find a gradual exit less alarming than an immediate one. If you can prudently diversify the family net worth by taking some chips off the table now, you will have helped your clients to better plan for the sale of the rest of the company, and probably at an improved valuation. This also generally leads to a smoother transition, and gives the owner a better chance to evaluate next-generation managers, transfer business relationships and responsibilities, and identify and manage risks that a strategic buyer will consider down the road.

When buying a property, one always considers resale value. The same consideration should be entertained when building a business. This involves drafting and regularly updating a written strategic plan (SSOM) for the future priorities and direction of the business, creating an organization chart that allows for the evaluation of those senior managers best qualified to meet the company's challenges (whether family members or not), and that strives to make the founder replaceable so that the business can continue to grow and prosper.

Following these steps and starting succession planning early should ensure an effective process. With due consideration given to the range of issues and emotions that family business owners face, you, as one of your client's Trusted Advisors, *i.e.*, their exit planning specialist, can help make this transition smooth and rewarding.

CHAPTER 44

HELP YOUR CLIENTS UNLOCK UP TO 74% OF THEIR BUSINESS VALUE OR WATCH THEM LOSE IT

UNLOCKING THE HIDDEN VALUE AND WEALTH INSIDE BUSINESSES PROVIDES AN UNPRECEDENTED AND TIMELY OPPORTUNITY FOR TRUSTED ADVISORS AND THEIR CLIENTS

Harish Chauhan

Overview

What is the biggest and best reason for your clients to *keep* or *make* you their Trusted Advisor? This chapter aims to provide you with that reason.

Business owners, with the help of their Trusted Advisors, are always looking for ways to make more money, have more success and protect their wealth.

Intangibles, including goodwill, account for up to 74% of the purchase price of a company. Consequently, business owners are at significant personal risk and financial loss if they are not well advised on how to harness the full value locked up in their intangible assets.

Advisors can either help their clients build wealth by maximizing, structuring and better managing these assets or ignore these assets and, by default, bear witness and responsibility for their client's loss.

This chapter introduces a solution — the Unifying Philosophy (UPh). Outperforming slogans, missions and vision statements, the UPh is an "operational asset" that helps build more "extractable" value in a business while reducing company-specific risk. This chapter focuses on:

- how Trusted Advisors can more effectively grow their practices, gain more clients and generate more revenues by helping their clients unlock 74% of their business value;
- how their clients are losing money right now without having a UPh and can achieve greater success with a UPh; and

- how much more their clients' companies could be worth if they properly implemented a UPh.

With the solutions presented in this chapter, Trusted Advisors now have an essential blueprint to help their business owner clients grow their businesses successfully — reducing risk and enhancing profitable value for both the short and the long term.

Learning Objectives

1. Intangibles represent enormous potential for value maximization, wealth creation and future risk minimization when managed effectively.
2. The UPh is a solution to unlock and compound value across intangible assets and drivers effectively. When implemented and managed successfully by Trusted Advisors, the UPh helps business owners grow their companies more easily and successfully — maximizing profitability, value and wealth with less risk, complexity and day-to-day stress of growing a business.
3. Using a client case example, Navigant Consulting's Sean Cavanagh, CA, CBV, illustrates how a Toronto-based bakery succeeds at:
   (a) growing revenue, profitably despite intense competition and price sensitivity;
   (b) increasing gross margin by 9%;
   (c) increasing profit margin by almost 10%;
   (d) reducing company risk by about 10%;
   (e) improving the day-to-day management of the business;
   (f) enhancing the quality of work life, staff management and customer loyalty (especially with premium pricing); and
   (g) improving company EBITDA (earnings before interest, tax, depreciation and amortization) by 250% in five years.
4. Trusted Advisors have a solution, via the UPh Authorized Advisor and Strategy program, to:
   (a) provide added value to existing clients (thereby generating higher margin revenues quickly);
   (b) gain a competitive advantage delivering a distinguished and differentiated service offering (complete with customized advisory tools, processes and deliverables);
   (c) attract more of the "right" clients (those who want a better, integrated advisory solution from your firm);

(d) grow their practice area, profile and market reach (the expertise to unlock intangibles is a growing market niche ideal for industry leading firms ready to grow); and

(e) increase revenue by increasing their services, adding value and increasing their involvement with their clients.

INTRODUCTION

> "This chapter provides excellent information regarding the steps needed to prep a company for sale in order to maximize sale proceeds. All business owners and their advisers should study this chapter's blueprint and implement its directives, especially as companies approach the desired time to explore a sale."
>
> Lynn Mason, Principal
> Global Capital Markets Incorporated

Imagine that you are 60 years old, wanting to retire after 30 years of building a business from scratch to $20 million in annual revenues. And despite showing strong profitability year after year, you find out that you will only be able to sell the business for a fraction of what you believe it's worth.

How does that make you feel? What cash will you retire with? What legacy will you have left for your life's work? How will this impact your current lifestyle and the future of your family, children or grandchildren?

Sadly, this could be the case for many owners — to lose most of their potential wealth upon exit. Who's to blame, the owner or the owner's advisors? Was it the owner's fault because, although he or she is well advised, he or she chose not to act early enough to build value effectively; or is it the advisors' fault — because although they know how to build value, they for whatever reason failed to convince their client to do just that, build value in his or her business and effectively structure it for maximum exit value and wealth creation?

Whose responsibility is it to ensure that the owner understands what it means to truly build a valuable business — one that is valuable every day until it is sold and that this value can be extracted tax-efficiently at any point?

We know all to well that "a business is only worth what someone is willing to pay for it". That's the truth. But when the majority of the selling price of a company includes its intangible assets and goodwill, up to 74% (PriceWaterhouseCoopers, 2003), it represents too much money for the owner and his or her advisors to dismiss any action on maximizing these assets effectively.

> "According to recent PricewaterhouseCoopers' analysis of the US market, intangible assets and goodwill constituted 74 per cent of the average purchase price of acquired companies in 2003 (with, respectively, intangible assets representing 22 per cent and residual goodwill 52 per cent). These findings are certainly in tune with the increasing attention now being paid to the management of intangible assets by companies in the US and worldwide."
>
> Reporting the value of acquired intangible assets (article) by Tony Hadjiloucas and Richard Winter, PricewaterhouseCoopers, London

Putting yourself in your clients' shoes may be the best way for you, as their Trusted Advisor, to genuinely see and think about the choices and consequences your clients have about how they grow their business so that it improves their quality of life.

Some Things You May Already Know

- Most business owners have only one chance to successfully transition out of their business (this poses tremendous risk for owners to do any planning, selling or exiting their business by themselves).
- A business is the largest asset business owners own (this also means that most of their wealth is locked up in their business).
- Most owners believe their business is worth more than someone is willing to pay for it (this means they may have an unrealistic expectation of their exit value or proceeds for retirement/succession).
- Business owners are too busy managing their business to think about planning for their inevitable exit (the opportunity cost of ignoring their exit value may result in the greatest loss of wealth on retirement — yet this is when they need it the most as ageing retirees are wanting a higher quality of life).
- Most business owners find out a "more realistic" value of their business when it's too late — when they are at the deal table; there's not much that anyone can do to substantially enhance value because efforts to enhance measurable value takes time.
- Retirement is not what it used to be. Now referred to as "activement" it is becoming the best time to enjoy one's life and do all of the things that one did not do before (this means that one needs more money to live a full and active lifestyle, not to mention having the ability to pay for increased costs of health care and health risk due to ageing).
- Pressures of supply and demand may force "baby boomer" owners to sell or exit at a lower than desirable price — unless of course

they have an exceptionally valuable business for which they can command a premium.

- Business owners may deny the need for doing any substantial value enhancement (especially regarding intangibles and the commercialization of goodwill), exit or succession planning, but that just may mean that Trusted Advisors need to be more proactive and do a better job in communicating the tangible benefits of doing so early enough and translating the significant, inevitable risks in *not* doing so early enough. This responsibility in educating owners lies in the hands of advisors, not business owners, for is that not the professional obligation of the retained Trusted Advisor?

THE $10 TRILLION BABY BOOM TRANSITION OPPORTUNITY HAS STARTED (2006 TO 2024) — HOW ARE YOU SEIZING IT?

The following statistics are reason enough to investigate new ways of serving your clients and deciding how you will seize this window of opportunity:

- Over the next 20 years, more than 90 million people will be retiring in the United States and Canada. These are the "baby boomers", the generation born between 1946 and 1964. (Richard E. Jackim and Peter G. Christman, *The $10 Trillion Dollar Opportunity* (Palatine, IL: The Exit Planning Institute, Inc., Dog Ear Publishing, 2005))
- More than 9 million baby boomer businesses will begin to exit their businesses over the next 15 years. (Richard E. Jackim and Peter G. Christman, *The $10 Trillion Dollar Opportunity* (Palatine, IL: The Exit Planning Institute, Inc., Dog Ear Publishing, 2005))
- Over the next 10-15 years, more than 70% of these businesses are expected to change hands. (Richard E. Jackim and Peter G. Christman, *The $10 Trillion Dollar Opportunity* (Palatine, IL: The Exit Planning Institute, Inc., Dog Ear Publishing, 2005))
- The vast majority of the wealth is held as stock in more than 12 million privately owned businesses. (Richard E. Jackim and Peter G. Christman, *The $10 Trillion Dollar Opportunity* (Palatine, IL: The Exit Planning Institute, Inc., Dog Ear Publishing, 2005))
- Owners who are 45 years or older tend to be more receptive to the importance and the need for a comprehensive exit plan. (Richard E. Jackim and Peter G. Christman, *The $10 Trillion Dollar Opportunity* (Palatine, IL: The Exit Planning Institute, Inc., Dog Ear Publishing, 2005))

- 66% of them have no retirement or succession plan. (Canadian Federation of Independent Business, *CFIB Research: SME Succession: Update*, October 2006)
- 74.3% of family firms are striving for growth and expansion. (Planning for Success: The Canadian supplement to the 2007/2008 PwC Global Family Business Survey (PriceWaterhouseCoopers, 2007))
- More than 65% of private business owners surveyed believe their companies could be worth significantly more. (Canadian private companies navigating their way to success: A survey of 350 owners/CEOS (Deloitte, June 2006))

Clients Confirm Unprecedented Opportunity

It's one thing to read the numbers vs. seeing it for yourself. Having worked with successful business owners from some of Canada's best firms (Profit 100, Innovators Alliance, and Canada's 50 Best Managed) I was amazed to find that most of the companies that were surveyed answered "no" to the following four questions:

(a) Would your company prosper without the current owner or leader?

(b) If you were to sell your logo as a brand, do you think you would get a good price for it?

(c) Does your shareholders agreement consider the impact of brand value and other intangible assets?

(d) Are your advisors aware of how the company brand and related intangible assets are best managed throughout your wealth management strategy and succession plan?

This showed me clearly that both current and future cash and exit value proceeds were at risk. The award-winning profitability and success of these companies didn't mean that their wealth and business value were protected from being at risk. It also revealed that their greatest wealth potential (locked up inside their business, brand, goodwill and related intangibles) was not being well managed — at least neither they nor their advisors were aware of it. And lastly, there was a big gap in what their current advisors are doing and could be doing in this area to serve their clients' needs better.

These client findings alone represent a significant opportunity for Trusted Advisors in providing a range of services (services that unlock and manage newfound value) to the very large, and underserved, private and family business owner market.

Intangible asset value and brand wealth management is clearly an unprecedented and timely opportunity especially suitable to Trusted Advisors and existing fully integrated accounting, financial, estate and wealth management firms who are seeking a competitive advantage and revenue growth.

Additionally, Trusted Advisors and their firms can protect themselves from potential professional liability by helping their clients become more proactive about creating better, measurable value in their intangibles so that owners can grow and exit successfully.

Bottom Lines

1. The best "ticket" successful business owners have to prosper from their business, *while growing the business and upon exit*, is to effectively maximize and monetize most of the value in their business — thereby providing optimal liquidity of proceeds for them to enjoy throughout their remaining living years.
2. Trusted Advisors who position themselves to successfully help their clients maximize, manage and monetize intangibles — the largest portion of potential value within their clients' business — will not only become champions of industry, they will benefit from market leadership and distinctive competitive advantage with more value — added service and product revenues for years to come.
3. Despite what you may believe or what your personal experience has been to date with your current clients and prospects, the numbers above tell the real story. Your future success as the Trusted Advisor rests in how you can serve the "new and current" needs of this growing, underserved market.

WHY INTANGIBLES CAN BE LUCRATIVE

Even though many will argue that intangibles are just that, things that you can't see and therefore cannot be truly measured or therefore do not have much value, this cannot be further from the truth. The facts and statistics will prove many such skeptics and experts wrong, especially given that we are in the age of information, technology and knowledge — an age where markets and industry survive and compete on brands and intangibles. In their comprehensive study of more than 10,000 companies across 32 countries over a six-year period, Brand Finance U.K., an established brand valuation firm, notes that intangibles continue to be on the rise. The total enterprise value of intangibles is in excess of $31.5 trillion (66% of enterprise value), exceeding the value of tangibles

(34% of enterprise value) (Global Intangible Tracker, December 2006 report and December 2007 report (Brand Finance)).

Intangibles can deliver the best return on investment because they can grow *exponentially* in value over time. When well managed, these assets can accrue value like a compounded interest savings account. For example, BMW's brand value shot up \$6.7 billion in a span of six years, as determined by Interbrand and *BusinessWeek Magazine* (vs. Mercedes during the same time period growing marginally at \$0.7 billion in brand value), shown in Figure 1 and Figure 3.

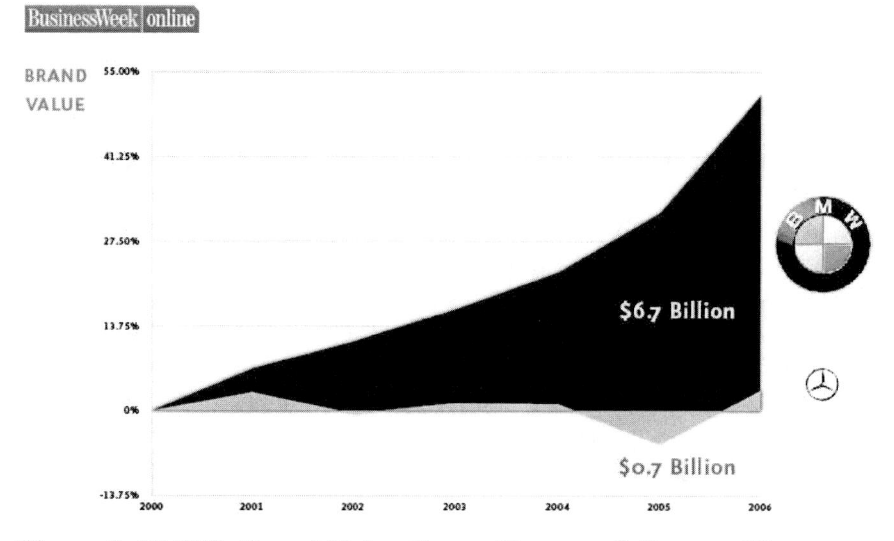

Figure 1: BMW's Brand Value Grows Exponentially over Time

On the other hand, tangible assets, although more easy to manage and quantify, only grow linearly in value — at a fixed rate every year. Real estate, equipment and inventory appreciate or depreciate consistently year after year. Due to their nature, they do not have exponential returns. This is illustrated in Figure 2.

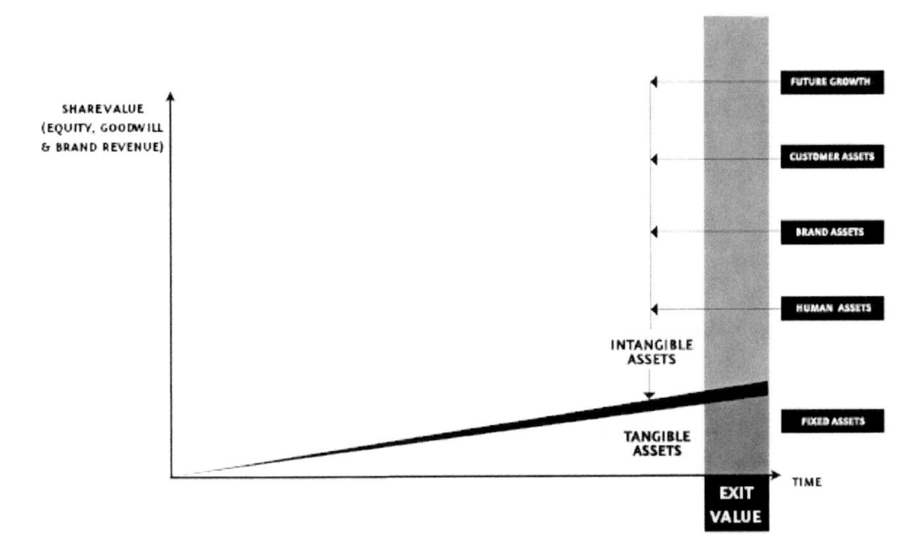

Figure 2: Tangible Assets Produce "Straight Line" Growth in Value

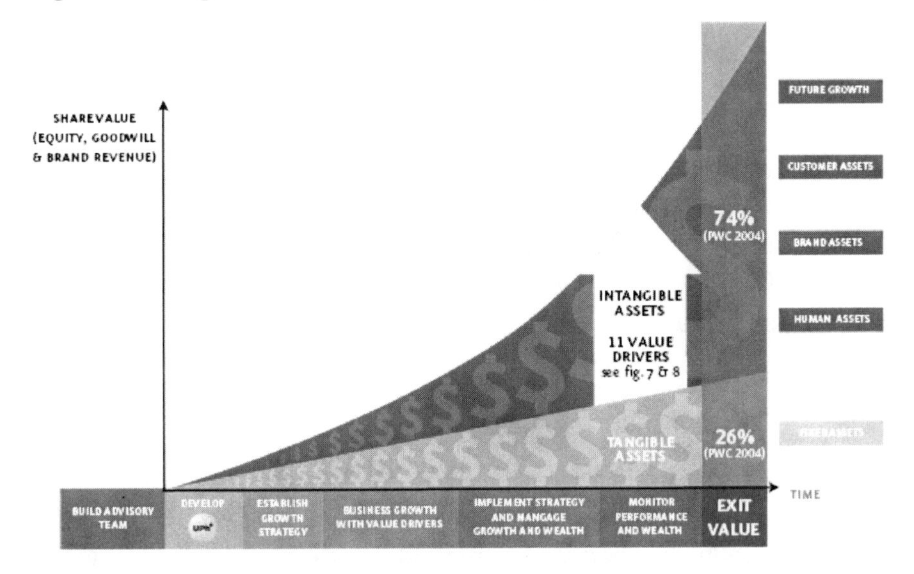

Figure 3: Intangible Assets Can Produce "Exponential" Growth in Value

As potentially lucrative as they may be, intangible assets require great know-how to maximize, manage and measure — hence more advisor involvement. There are 11 basic drivers that make up the group of intangibles. Most of these 11 drivers, if not all, must be harnessed successfully to maximize measurable value. The question is how? This is discussed later in this chapter, in the section "Why Unlocking Value Is Difficult *Without* a UPh", and illustrated in Figures 7 and 8.

Bottom Lines

Do you want to grow value linearly or exponentially over time? Do you want to *risk* or *gain* premiums on your brand and goodwill?

I have yet to find a business owner who would not want to create exponential value (and returns on his or her time and money) in his or her business and not get paid a premium on his or her brand, goodwill and related intangibles he or she has developed in his or her business.

True value creation results from how well you manage intangibles to drive company revenue growth and day-to-day performance.

THE TALE OF TWO OWNERS: A COMPARISON OF WEALTH CREATION AND SUCCESSION RISK

Helen is a homeowner and Bob is a business owner. Both have owned their assets for 20 years and are ready to sell and move on.

What can Helen expect when selling her home?

- The value in her home has increased with the natural increase in the real estate market over the past two decades.
- Due to a renovation, she has multiplied the dollars she invested in the kitchen and bathroom since it has enhanced the resale value.
- The likelihood of finding a buyer to pay the price she wants is relatively high.
- She will get paid in one lump sum on closing.

What can Bob expect when selling his business?

- The value in his business may not have increased with the natural increase in his industry over the past two decades.
- He may not be able to pinpoint how he has increased the resale value in his business or precisely identify if and how he has multiplied his original investment or whether he will get paid what he wants for his goodwill.
- The likelihood of finding a buyer to pay the price he wants depends on many factors that he may not be fully aware of at the time of sale unless he is well advised in advance.
- He may not get paid in one lump sum on closing of the deal — he may be subject to an earn-out, payment terms or even a final settlement based on continued profitability with the new owners.

How do Helen's and Bob's situations compare?

	MARKET VALUE Ability To Create Wealth During Ownership
HELEN'S HOME	Increases proportionately with the growth of the market (e.g. street, neighbourhood, city and regional value)
BOB'S BUSINESS	Increases or decreases with industry, regulatory or overall economic conditions
COMMENTS	Helen's initial investment may have multiplied simply because the market value has multiplied over the 30 years. Can Bob expect the same for his initial investment in his business?
AS BOB'S TRUSTED ADVISOR(S) YOU COULD...	a) Earn Bob's trust by getting Market Value information straight from industry experts – especially if this means reaching outside your expertise – If you were Bob wouldn't you want your advisor to do the same for you? b) Show Bob that market value for a business is more volatile than that for homes and that Bob would be wise to get time on his side by building value as early as possible c) Help Bob protect his personal stake in the business by ensuring he understands that building a valuable business (one that one would want to buy and pay decent money for) requires sufficient investment of time and advisor involvement upfront to do it right d) Show Bob that you are the "go-to" advisor because you know which expert to bring in when needed – with every advisor you bring to Bob you prove that his interest comes before yours – (i.e. you will find him the best person to help him, especially when its outside your expertise or if it is doesn't involve or benefit you – be the primary advisor not the sole advisor

Table 1: Market Value Comparison

	KNOWLEDGE OF VALUE DRIVERS
HELEN'S HOME	High: Kitchen and bathrooms are commonly known to increase the resale value of property higher than any other room/area in a home
BOB'S BUSINESS	Minimal: Unless Bob speaks to the right experts (i.e. Business Valuator, M&A or Investment Banking Advisor) he will not have the foresight to know where he can focus on building business value that can easily increase his personal wealth on exit. For a general list of business value drivers See figures 7 and 8 What value drivers will make the most impact on the sale price of the business is highly specific to Bob's business, industry, market condition and competition–the need for experts to get involved early to inform Bob is essential
COMMENTS	Helen benefits from foresight – she knows that she will get more than her money back for every dollar she invests in her kitchen and bath. Bob, Bob, however, doesn't know where he can invest in his business to increase its value effectively.
AS BOB'S TRUSTED ADVISOR(S) YOU COULD...	**f)** Introduce him to experts who would arm Bob with the foresight of how he could grow his business in a way that will maximize his personal stake (i.e. enhance the value in a way that it can successfully extracted); specifically this means identifying the key value drivers (considering both tangible and intangible assets) that would specifically enhance Bob's business **g)** Work with Bob - 5, 10, 15 or even 20 years in advance of his exit helping him to increase his value, protect his equity and ensures 'cashes out' richer than ever (No matter how informed Bob is about exit value and wealth creation options when he is 60 and selling his company he will not have the time to do anything **h)** Know how Bob could be paid more for his business because he commercialized his Goodwill effectively, increased his Brand and related intangible assets, and employed best exit planning practices as early in Bob's business life as possible

Table 2: Comparing Knowledge of Value Drivers

	VALUE ENHANCERS
HELEN'S HOME	Additional money can be made on the sale of the home by: - cachet of the home being popularized by the magazine - preparing the home for sale with a staging firm - set up an auction sale - promote the quality of professional construction (labour and materials) - maximize neighbourhood and regional developments that make living there ideal
BOB'S BUSINESS	Value enhancers for a business, first and foremost, requires time – time to work with the expert, time to research what is the optimal for the business and time to implement in the business
COMMENTS	A last minute can of paint can measurabley increase the sale value of a home – there are little if any last minute options available to the owner to increase value for the business
AS BOB'S TRUSTED ADVISOR(S) YOU COULD...	a) Earn Bob's trust by getting Market Value information straight from industry experts – especially if this means reaching outside your expertise – If you were Bob wouldn't you want your advisor to do the same for you? i) Inform Bob that there are no "last minute specials" for dressing up a business for sale (versus a home) – it requires: - 3-5 years for the preparation of sale - 5 yrs or more for most value enhancement programs (like the UPh) to take substantial and measurable effect to enhance value and commercialize goodwill j) Help Bob prepare his business for sale since day one – knowing that that inevitable day will come when Bob will come to back to the trusted advisor for help – why not be proactive and don't get caught k) Remind Bob or better show him others who have sold their business for less, that's "too late to turn back" to find out that you will not get what you want when sitting at the deal table to sell the business

Table 3: Comparing Value Enhancers

	ABILITY TO EXTRACT WEALTH UPON EXIT
HELEN'S HOME	Homeowners have complete liquidity of their asset on sale – after all costs and existing mortgages are paid. With effective tax planning most of the cash proceeds can be pocketed and enjoyed.
BOBS BUSINESS	Unless the business is automated and can be instantly transferred to new management, there is most often an earn out period of typically 3-5 years. Sometimes this earnout may be subject to maintaining or improving earnings. Payment terms are very sensitive to how valuable your business is and how low the risk inherent in the transition – lower risk, higher value equals better terms.
COMMENTS	A profitable business is not necessarily a valuable business. Some investments in the business will make more money now and provide a higher selling price later - the trick is which ones? (i.e. which value drivers provide a higher return on investment) Creating value requires time (a minimum of 1 year), the earlier one starts the better. Growing a valuable business whose value you can 'cash in on' requires a team of experts working together (this team is best coordinated by the Lead Trusted Advisor (Generalist).
	ABILITY TO EXTRACT EQUITY
HELEN'S HOME	Upon sale or even refinancing, should you qualify, equity in a home can be extracted relatively easily and at any time there is sufficient equity built in to do so.
BOBS BUSINESS	How much an owner like Bob will get paid for his goodwill and any equity he has built up in his company over 30 years is directly proportional to how well he has commercialized his goodwill: - How well can his company run when he is not there? - How many customers will be lost or gained when new owners take over

Table 4: Comparison of Wealth and Equity on Exit

	MARKET CONDITIONS ON SALE
HELENS HOME	In most cases market conditions will have improved (increased real estate value) since the time a property was originally purchased.
BOBS BUSINESS	Risks are very high when determining the market condition on sale of a business. One law, an act of mother nature, a large merger or simply a change in buying patterns can positively or negatively change the value of a business overnight. The variables are many and ever changing – timing, relationships and negotiation clout is critical to a successful sale.
	BUYER PROBABILITY
HELENS HOME	Finding a buyer for a home is rather straightforward – list, promote, show, negotiate offers, close. Price, Location and the home's 'personality' are major factors in attracting the right buyer.
BOBS BUSINESS	It's not everyday that an owner sells his business and sits down with buyers. Hence finding buyers and dealing with them can be risky – especially when its your own business. A professional M&A or Investment banking advisor is crucial to increasing the odds for sourcing the right buyer or transaction for exit (for example - the business becomes a 'platform company for a roll up instead of being sold'.

Table 5: Comparing Market Conditions and Buyer Probability

Bottom Lines

Creating and extracting value in a business is not as straightforward as it is in residential real estate. Growing business value successfully therefore requires more advisor assistance due to the complexity and risks involved — but the rewards can be substantial for doing it right.

Business owners have too much to lose if they dismiss or minimize the value locked up inside their intangibles and business. The incentive to involve their Trusted Advisors more proactively couldn't be clearer.

Being the busy business owner, Bob's chances for success are low unless he gets the right help to show him the way to growing his business right. The right way for Bob to grow his business is to:

- grow profitably while growing measurable value, thereby protecting Bob's livelihood, lifestyle and future wealth;
- continually prepare for that one, inevitable day when he can exit richer and happier — hence reaping all the rewards for the life he invested in his business.

How does Bob, with the help of his advisor(s) increase his chances for success, unlock his hidden value and overcome the complexity and risk involved in growing his business in the best way possible?

THE UNIFYING PHILOSOPHY (UPh) — A SOLUTION TO UNLOCKING VALUE AND CREATING PROSPERITY

> "Harish has developed and honed an intriguing process to identify and assess intangible assets and the drivers that build value. The Unifying Philosophy (UPh) provides the 'glue' to focus and align organizational effort. The result is a superior wealth creating environment and an enhanced exit strategy."
>
> Greg Pashke CMC®, CBA, CMA, CFM, MBA, CPA
> Pashke Consulting

Necessity Is the Mother of Invention

In 1996, at the age of 29, I was asked by a successful family business owner to rebrand his 25-plus-year-old company because he was facing stiff competition from Toyota. Understandably, he was concerned, even frightened, about the future of his business. In my first meeting with him he asked me, "How will the brand you design make me money?" I replied, "It can't make you a lot of money unless you spend more money building it and promoting it — like Toyota." Regardless of how great his brand could ever be, he could never beat Toyota. I struggled to find a solution to help my client grow his business and compete. Could a mission or vision statement, marketing slogan or strategic plan be used to compete against Toyota and the other competitors he has? I was not convinced.

Having built over 150 corporate logos, brand identity systems and corresponding strategies for private entrepreneurial firms, I realized then and there, that logos and brand investments (on their own) are hard to justify (cost vs. benefit). If that is the case, then why do them? And I realized that traditional tools (like mission/vision statements, strategic plans and slogans) have limited benefits. What could I do to help my client survive, compete and thrive?

I asked him to give me a chance to solve his problem. I said to him, "You are obviously doing something right in your business because you have been in business for so long. To continue your success we must identify 'this distinct or unique competitive advantage', ensure it reflects your history (goodwill or 'what you are known for') and the way you do business (business and revenue model), package it up (brand identity promise) and promote it (marketing)." The process by which I selected key stakeholders, interviewed them, compiled and presented the findings, and established a statement for my client, described the first making of the Unifying Philosophy (UPh) for my client — Quality to Lift Your Profits®.

The UPh — A Process and a Product

As it is not the purpose of this chapter to present the UPh at length, the information provided has been abbreviated to provide a preliminary understanding of what it is, how it is developed and the way it works.

The UPh is a facilitated, strategic process consisting of five major steps. It involves the company's stakeholders to engage in specific strategic discussions (20 to 50 two-hour sessions) that result in the development of the company's "DNA" in six words or less. The UPh is built with four to seven management drivers that readily implement this "DNA" into all areas of the company (across all departments and throughout all ranks). This makes it operational throughout the company and is therefore not just a statement of words.

As a product, the UPh is an explicit customer benefit statement of six words or less that is formally trademarked and structured as an intellectual property asset in a holding company. As the UPh is continually implemented, promoted and recognized over time, throughout the market, with customers and by staff, it aggregates value across associated intangible and tangible assets.

Examples of a UPh

Service Companies

Quality to Lift Your Profits® (forklift dealership)
Making Vacancy Profitable® (hospitality financier)
Building Reliability® (freight management and logistics)

Manufacturing/Distribution Companies

Freshness on Time® (baked goods manufacturer and distributor)
Better Airflow by Design® (industrial fan manufacturer and distributor)
Ultimate Indian Food Pleasures. Serving Life.® (food manufacturer and distributor)

The UPh is similar to the "Hedgehog Concept" presented by Jim Collins in his indispensable book *Good to Great: Why Some Companies Make the Leap ... and Others Don't* (New York: HarperBusiness, 2001). In comparing hedgehogs vs. foxes, he explains, "Hedgehogs, on the other hand, simplify a complex world into a single organizing idea, a basic principle or concept that unifies and guides everything."

The Hedgehog concept goes beyond mere strategy:

> Good-to-great companies attained a very simple concept that they used as a frame of reference for all their decisions, and this understanding coincided with breakthrough results.... A Hedgehog Concept is a simple, crystalline concept that flows from deep understanding about the intersection of the following three circles:

1. What you can be the best in the world at
2. What drives your economic engine
3. What you are deeply passionate about … .

By this explanation, the UPh is a formal process to develop a company's DNA or Hedgehog concept. The distinctive process by which a UPh is built (from stakeholders inside the company) and how it is structured (holding company as a trademark), expressed (specifically six words or less) and used by everyone throughout a company (on a daily basis) is what separates the UPh from its counterparts (taglines, positioning statements and slogans).

What Is *Not* a UPh

Mission statements, vision statements, slogans or taglines are the counterparts to a UPh. They may look the same but they work very differently and are not necessarily made for the same reasons. In my 18 plus years of practice, I have yet to see management or staff proudly living their mission statement or marketing slogan.

But do not to take my word for it. The best way to realize the effectiveness of a mission statement or similar is to find out for yourself. As a Trusted Advisor, you may be a principal, partner, owner or key staff in a firm, so it may be safe to assume that you ought to have a mission, vision of some sort to keep your firm focused on success. If so, how would you answer the following:

- What is your mission and vision statement (can you recall it from memory)?
- How do you apply it to enhance what you do for your firm every day (does it help you make better decisions that are for the common good of the company)?
- Do your customers know your mission/vision or slogan and does it help them buy your services?
- How does your mission/vision statement or company slogan maximize you or your firm's shareholder value? If so, how does it do that?

How you answered the above may show you how well your current mission, vision or company tagline performs.

From your own experience in the above exercise, you may better understand why companies who have implemented their UPh successfully have demonstrated outstanding performance and replaced the need to have mission/vision statements and company slogans/taglines.

Client companies with a UPh have shown that they grow faster, sell better, hire effectively, manage efficiently and are more profitable than when they were without one. A more comprehensive cross-examination of the UPh can be found in my book *Unconventional Business* <www.unconventionalbusiness.com> or in success stories available at <www.businessbyphilosophy.com>.

Famous Honourable UPh Examples

The Ultimate Driving Experience® (BMW)
Better Sound Through Research® (BOSE)
The World On Time® (FedEx)

What Does the UPh Do?

The UPh helps address the biggest and most burning questions that management, staff, suppliers and customers wonder about a company every day. This is presented in Figure 4. Addressing these questions and defining how a company works and why it works that way is crucial for the business to compete and grow effectively and successfully. Many a business faces growth challenges because its problems grow as its business does.

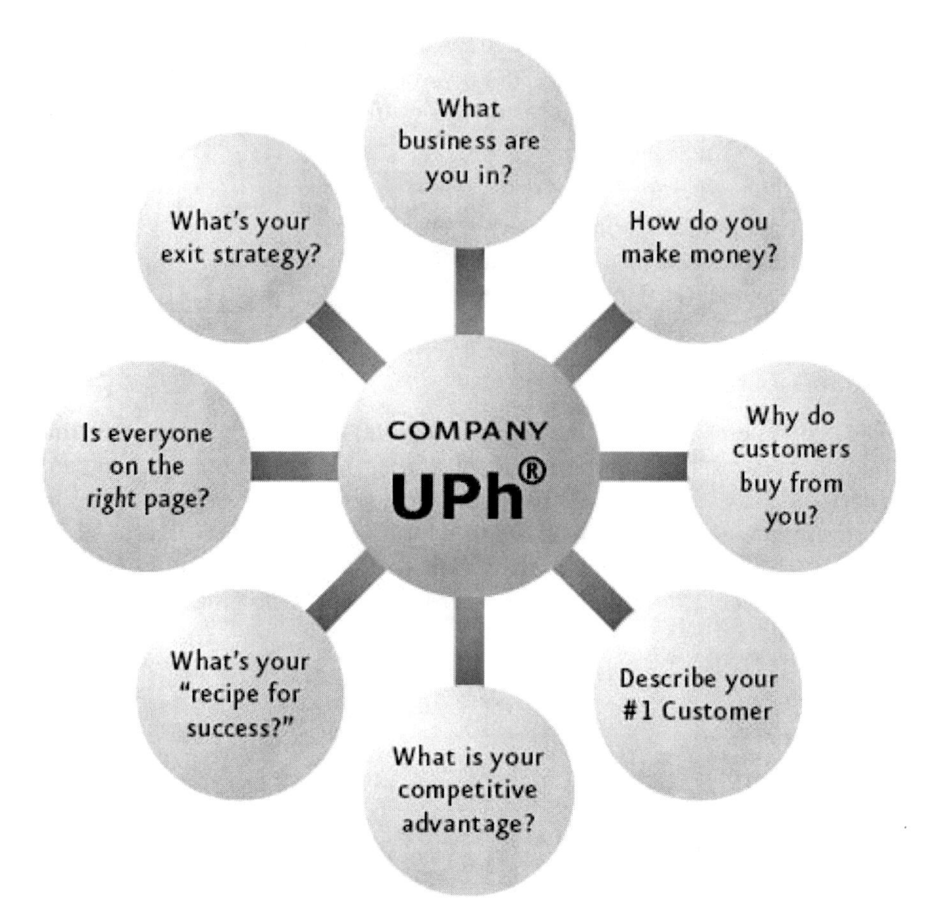

Figure 4: Questions Addressed by the UPh

Figures 5 and 6 show the impact of a UPh and a non-UPh based company. The UPh helps a business to synchronize all of its various components to maximize *value*, *harmony*, *innovation* and *performance* throughout an organization. Without a UPh, a business often struggles to establish order throughout the organization especially as the company grows. These struggles only increase over time, and as the company expands in size, reach and geography. Organizations without a clear focus of its "DNA" increases its *intangibility* of assets, *conflict* amongst its people and departments, *chaos* throughout its systems or processes and *deficiency* of its resources.

Figure 5: Company Impact When Growing and Managing *Without* a Uph

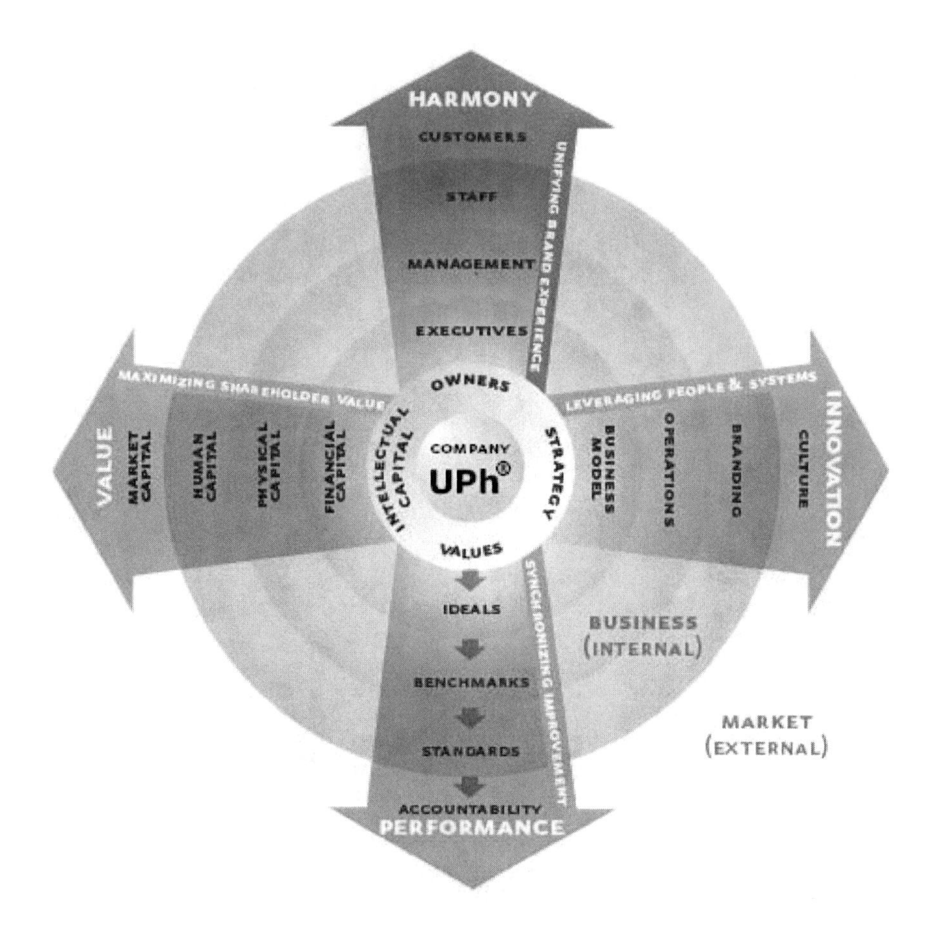

Figure 6: Company Impact When Growing and Managing With a Uph

Why Unlocking Value Is Difficult *Without* a UPh

Growing a business is one of the toughest challenges owners and leaders face. Aside from daily operations, challenges, victories and crises that unexpectedly pop up, a business owner still must build a valuable company to truly succeed. When does an owner have time to learn how to build value and do it successfully?

Steven Hacker, CA, CBV and Senior Manager, Financial Advisory at Deloitte in Toronto, helped to provide a simplified list of 11 generic business value drivers for intangibles as shown in Figure 7.

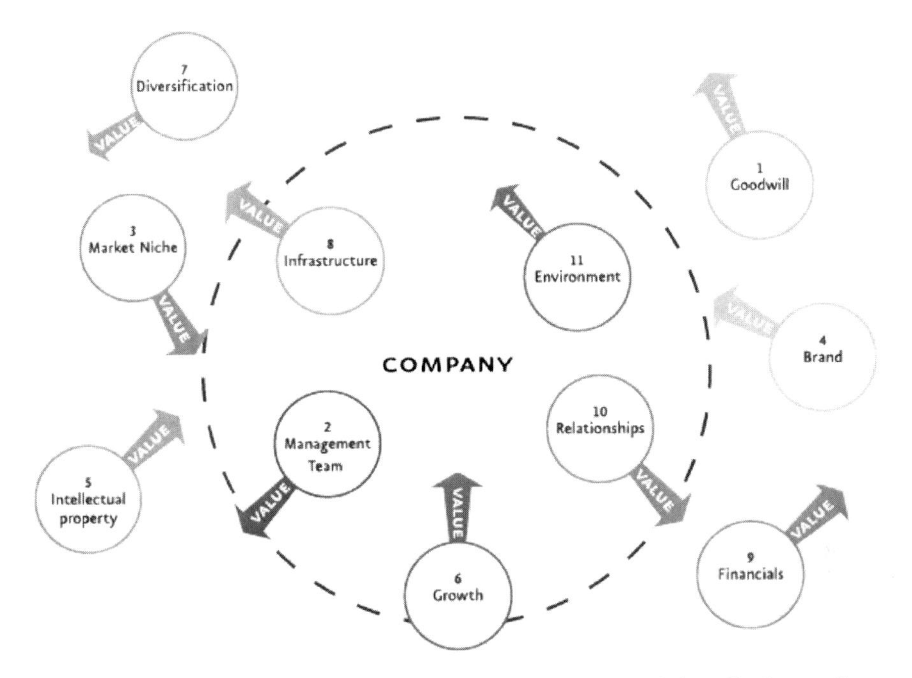

Figure 7: Value Drivers Are Disconnected, Requiring Independent Value Creation

When you look at it, you can't help but wonder: "Is the business owner supposed to enhance these 11 value drivers every day or run the company? And how do they enhance one driver without detracting value from another (for example: diversification and market niche can be contradicting value drivers — how do you have a focused market niche yet be diversified at the same time)?

The challenge becomes obvious — business owners overlook *enhancing their value drivers* when they have daily pressures growing their company. To their detriment, they end up growing a business that doesn't create or maximize its business value.

A particular solution, used by successful businesses, is to focus on *one thing* that drives their business on a daily basis, grows profitability and maximizes value *simultaneously*. The UPh is that *one thing*. By implementing it day in, day out, the UPh helps owners and leaders save time, save money, prevent risk and compound value across all drivers. This is illustrated in Figure 8.

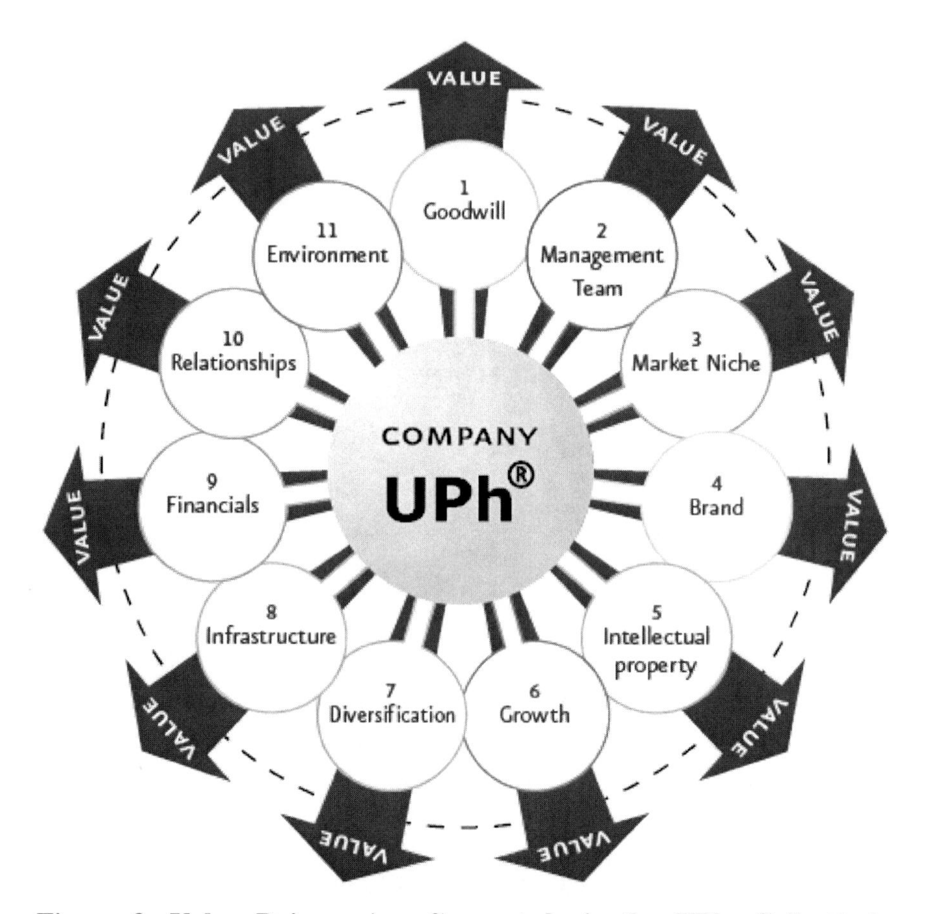

Figure 8: Value Drivers Are Connected via the UPh, Collectively Compounding Value

A good reason for your clients to make or keep you as their most Trusted Advisor is for you to show them how you can help them unlock value that already exists in their business. By developing and "operationalizing" their UPh, they can now realize value that they have not been able to harness before. The best part is that the more successful your clients are the more opportunity there is to realize more value. And just because they have been successful or have very profitable businesses, this doesn't necessarily mean that they have realized the full value, potential and wealth locked up inside their business. A large portion of business value and their personal wealth still could go unrealized.

So what does it take to build and implement a UPh into a company?

Four Steps to Building and Implementing a UPh Successfully

Leading advisors and their business owner clients can utilize the following steps to better understand the UPh and how it helps to grow their businesses successfully.

STEP 1 ASSESSMENT	STEP 2 STRATEGY
"How can I grow my business for long-term value and personal prosperity?"	*"How can I get everyone on the right page and going in the same direction?"*
a) UPh Financial Analysis* Before investing in a UPh project, owners will find out, in financial terms: • How much money they could lose if they don't have a UPh? • How much money they can expect to make with a UPh? • How much their business could be worth if they develop a UPh? • How much personal financial risk they are taking if they don't have a UPh?	**c) Unifying Philosophy (UPh)** Building a unifying philosophy is a once in a lifetime investment for a business. It consists of a 4-part program that engages stakeholders (from owner to staff) through a series of twenty to fifty strategic sessions (3-hour sessions). The end result is a company UPh, your business DNA, in 6 words or less. This 'DNA' or UPh is then trademarked, structured as a business asset and implemented throughout the company at all levels.
b) UPh Business Assessment* Understanding the financial payoff, owners can learn how the UPh will specifically help their company by using these 3 tools: **Brand Assets Checklist** – Helps owners uncover areas in which they could make more money from their Brand investments and protect this 'new' wealth **Brand Diagnostic** – If your Brand is not built or functioning properly, you will not make money with it or from it. This diagnostic determines the 10 Strengths, Weaknesses, Alignments, and Conflicts with your Brand and what to do about it. **ROI Calculator** – Analyzes 7 areas in your business and identifies how the UPh process specifically improves your: Strategy, Operations, Revenue Model, Sales & Marketing, Shareholder Value & Wealth, Branding, and Corporate Culture	**Benefits:** ✓ Helps clarify and execute vision ✓ Unifies leadership, staff, suppliers to customers ✓ Streamlines the organization to identify and service its #1 Customers ✓ Synchronizes and maximizes key value drivers throughout the business ✓ Engages management staff to work from one, right page and go in the right direction ✓ Reduce inefficiencies, dysfunction and conflict between management, departments, staff and customers ✓ Accelerates revenue growth, maximizes profitability, and shareholder value
*Qualified Advisors are eligible to receive training to perform these assessments with their clients. Approved advisors can benefit from these turnkey, high margin, and high client value product offerings.	

Table 6: Steps to Building a UPh: Assessment and Strategy

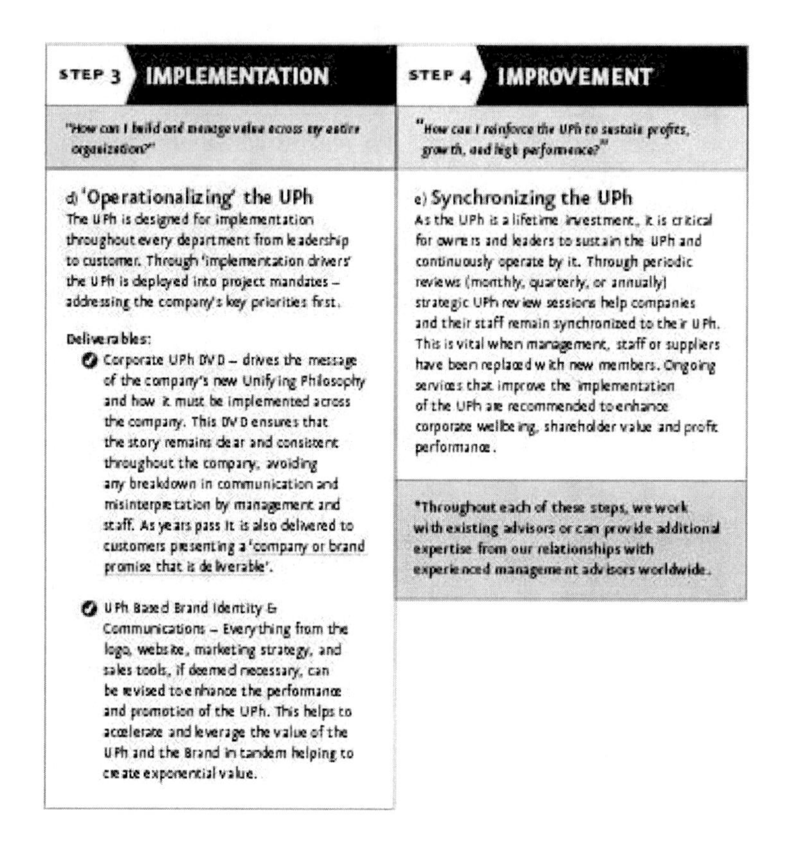

STEP 3 IMPLEMENTATION	STEP 4 IMPROVEMENT
"How can I build and manage value across my entire organization?"	*"How can I reinforce the UPh to sustain profits, growth, and high performance?"*
d) 'Operationalizing' the UPh The UPh is designed for implementation throughout every department from leadership to customer. Through 'implementation drivers' the UPh is deployed into project mandates – addressing the company's key priorities first. Deliverables: • Corporate UPh DVD – drives the message of the company's new Unifying Philosophy and how it must be implemented across the company. This DVD ensures that the story remains clear and consistent throughout the company, avoiding any breakdown in communication and misinterpretation by management and staff. As years pass it is also delivered to customers presenting a 'company or brand promise that is deliverable'. • UPh Based Brand Identity & Communications – Everything from the logo, website, marketing strategy, and sales tools, if deemed necessary, can be revised to enhance the performance and promotion of the UPh. This helps to accelerate and leverage the value of the UPh and the Brand in tandem helping to create exponential value.	**e) Synchronizing the UPh** As the UPh is a lifetime investment, it is critical for owners and leaders to sustain the UPh and continuously operate by it. Through periodic reviews (monthly, quarterly, or annually) strategic UPh review sessions help companies and their staff remain synchronized to their UPh. This is vital when management, staff or suppliers have been replaced with new members. Ongoing services that improve the implementation of the UPh are recommended to enhance corporate wellbeing, shareholder value and profit performance. *Throughout each of these steps, we work with existing advisors or can provide additional expertise from our relationships with experienced management advisors worldwide.

Table 7: Steps to Building a UPh: Implementation and Improvement

The UPh — Showing You the Money

What are the real financial and non-financial benefits for a business owner to develop a UPh for his or her business? How much return and how soon?

To illustrate the financial, value and risk impact of the UPh on a business, Sean Cavanagh, CA and CBV of Navigant Consulting, has been generous enough to provide the following explanation:

> *Harish presented me with a past client to analyze the impact of the UPh on the value of the business at a very general and high level. The valuation was to be contrasted between the time before and after the implementation of the UPh, relying on only a cursory review and limited financial information; a professional determination of valuation was not available. However, I was able to discuss how the UPh affected various*

aspects of the corporate risk in the company and the impact on profitability as determined by the information he presented.

B&A Bakery had been a prime distributor of bread products throughout southern Ontario since the mid '80s. The company was acquired by the Sunderji family in 1991, when it was producing $2 million in revenue. In six years, the family worked long and hard, doubling annual revenues to $4 million. The younger of the two sons had a desire to double revenues again to $8-10 million within five years by producing "parbaked" bread, that is, dough partially baked then frozen to be cooked in minutes after purchase. The company went into full expansion mode by purchasing a new 50,000 square foot building for $2 million and a $500,000 freezer that would produce the bread with an equity injection and a $1 million secured loan in 1997.

However, the "build it they will come" philosophy did not work and there was need for a more robust plan to fulfill the vision. Customers were not grasping the rationale for the parbaked product or why or what B&A Bakery was doing or trying to do. The staff also did not understand how to work in the new business operations; the whole work environment was in chaos with owner frustration at their inability to implement a great product opportunity.

Management, rather than addressing the operational issues that existed, chose to focus solely on increasing revenue. It was their belief that higher revenues meant higher business value. Their goal of doubling revenues was predominantly on their minds. They had no clear financial information reporting structure that could provide relevant cost data or cash flow analysis to assist in problem identification. The cursory review demonstrated that there were no human capital, sales, purchasing, competition or any other operating policies. All employees acted independently of one another. Morale was low, productivity suffered.

Along with increasing revenues as a corporate goal, one of the company's value initiatives was branding. The concept of branding was not fully understood but they knew all successful companies had a brand and they wanted to create one. Management's intention was to change the old and tired B&A Bakery name/brand and create a new one. In the spring of 1997, it became clear to the Sunderji sons that branding is not just about a nice logo and a tag line; a successful brand requires building a corporate philosophy and value system in-

corporated into every aspect of their business operation. This corporate philosophy then resonates throughout the organization and into the production of a product that customers will be loyal to and pay more for.

Within three months, the Sunderji sons had established their strategy for competitive advantage and positioning strategy, their unifying philosophy or UPh: Freshness On Time®. The rollout of the UPh exercise resulted in a new company structure consisting of a parent corporate brand, Breadsource, facilitating their longstanding goodwill to be successfully transitioned into a new entity. In addition, a retail brand, "B&A Bakery", was retained and a secondary retail UPh was developed for it: Big Value and Appetizing Taste®. This redefined the historic B&A, adding new life to a name that had a good reputation in the industry.

The UPh solution helped reposition and revitalize the bakery brand asset because customers and suppliers knew the B&A name and associated it with good value and quality. The full cost of the UPh program was $75,000. The two UPh brands were codified across the companies into their information systems, operation policies and corporate philosophy. All corporate decisions were filtered for how it impacted on either UPh: "Freshness On Time" or "Big Value and Appetizing Taste".

Within the first year of implementing the UPh programs, the youngest son spearheaded tremendous change in operations to implement Freshness On Time into every aspect of how they baked and shipped bread. Implementing the UPh included new staff training, new policies and procedures on distribution, and mixing/baking/packing to consistently deliver Freshness On Time every time, every day. Full implementation cost was $250,000 over the first year.

The conversion to deliver their main UPh, Freshness On Time, succeeded; customers, existing and new, appreciated the brand as they disassociated Breadsource from the day-old bread the competition was delivering. By 2003, revenues were reaching $8 million; double revenues were achieved. But doubling revenues does not necessarily translate into increased profitability and corporate value. The results of the UPh being successfully implemented on the company were found to be broader and more significant than initially thought:

1. *Advanced information systems had been implemented to monitor cost and production in a real time basis. They were instantly able to get information that would provide accurate relevant information on cost and production.*
2. *New production and process controls removed all one-day-olds from their deliveries. This allowed the bakery to charge more per unit for 100% fresh bread. Wastage rates of 6% reduced to less than 1%, thus contributing to the gross margin increase of 6% by 2003.*
3. *Product pricing to customer pricing was once "the best deal you can make". This was changed to a uniform, higher margin pricing schedule, which contributed to increasing gross margins by an additional 3% after three years. There were a few customers that were let go and revenue did dip in the first year. However, margins increased and net income was the same.*
4. *Distribution radius doubled from 200 km to 400 km. The larger footprint enabled the increase in high value, high margin customers who needed fresh bread daily. Cost of goods sold increased by only .05% with most costs passed on to the customer.*
5. *Staff morale was improved due to easier working standards to follow, better training, improved work culture and ethic and continued investment into the company's growth, all emanating out of the UPh. This stability and vision gave employees confidence that the company's future was bright and their jobs were secure. $25,000 in cost savings was achieved in the first year from lower recruitment, retraining, fewer sick days taken and less requested overtime pay. Productivity also increased.*

The impact of UPh on the business operations was significant. B&A had previously been achieving only the industry average profit margin of 37%. Subsequent to the UPh implementation, B&A increased its profit margin to over 46% by 2003. The after tax profit margin also increased by almost 10% denoting a bottom line impact of the UPh.

A company with higher margins has the ability to be competitive in times of recession, increased competition, supply shocks, etc., because they can be more price-competitive when needed. With a well-established brand, customer loyalty and efficient operations, they are less affected by price chal-

lenges from competitors. This market position clearly decreases risk within the company.

The full cost of implementing the UPh throughout the business was $325,000. These costs were recovered over several years. The recovery period was impacted by the need to streamline operations in sync with the UPh. This resulted in a period of decreased sales as the company eliminated over 5% of is customer sales to conform with the new "freshness" policy. The same level of net income, however, was achieved. The cost of the UPh and its implementation was paid back in two years, which is a good return on investment; however, there is also a corresponding overall increase in corporate value.

In corporate valuation, there is a cost/benefit concept. One expects the benefit to increase as the cost increases; in the same way, if an investment has higher risk, we desire a higher rate of return. A company is valued not only on the basis of the cashflow it achieves, but also the risk of that cash flow; a risk/return profile has to be determined.

In B&A, not only did revenues increase, but they were from higher priced products than the competition and they produced higher margins as well. Therefore, compared to a competitor with the same $8 million revenue level, B&A's revenues were better quality because they were less risky. This in turn drove up the corporate value.

The analysis of corporate value does not end here. The corporate value of two companies can be compared using the same key operational criteria:

1. *employee morale;*
2. *information systems;*
3. *human resources policies;*
4. *defined business vision and focus;*
5. *superior credit relationships.*

If each of the two companies have the same revenue levels, a company that has these established higher operational attributes for these criteria will demand a higher value than a company that does not have them regardless of what the financial position states.

Operational risk was reduced at B&A through the adaptation of their UPh. Many small businesses have a 2-3x cash flow multiplier representing a 33% to 50% required rate of return reflecting the risk associated with the company. If we *assume that through the UPh implementation, in 1997 there could be an estimated 6% decrease in corporate risk or less required rate of return, this would translate into an additional $675,000 in corporate value. By 2002, this risk or required rate of return decrease was estimated to be 9% lower than in 1997. With the increase in cash flow from higher sales, the corporate value in 2003 increased by an estimated $7.8 million; bringing the multiplier to between 3x and 4x cash flow.*

The UPh investment of $325,000 translates into a two-year cash payback and over a 2,200% return on investment in just over five years. The UPh provided increased profitability and lower risk in the business requiring a lower rate of return. The UPh created a brand that was identifiable.

Using hindsight in the analysis, management now understands that without the UPh, they would not have:

1. *doubled revenues;*
2. *considered a plan to increase margins;*
3. *avoided the longer-term potential of bankruptcy if revenues and margins had continued to decline.*

With UPh, their business succeeded in:

1. *growing revenue and profitability despite intense competition and price sensitivity;*
2. *increasing gross margin 9%;*
3. *increasing profit margins almost 10%;*
4. *reducing company risk by about 10%;*
5. *improving the day-to-day management effectiveness of the business;*
6. *enhancing the quality of work life, staff management and customer loyalty (especially with premium pricing);*
7. *improving company EBITDA 250% over five years.*

Because the UPh has resulted in improving the quality of revenue and business value, this business family has achieved a strategy for prosperity regarding the growth and succession of their business.

Sean Cavanagh is available to provide Trusted Advisors with additional insight on the value and risk impact of the UPh at <sean.cavanagh@navigantconsulting.com>.

Bottom Lines

Business owners and their advisors may struggle to grow value across their intangibles without a UPh.

With a UPh, business owners have a *unifying* strategy to grow value, profitability and performance throughout their company. This ultimately helps them build the business the way they want.

The UPh has been proven to help "everyone get on the same page and move in the same direction". This quickly empowers all staff to apply the UPh in everything they do and know when their actions are not true to their company UPh. This helps improve company culture and everyday performance leading to long-term success and prosperity.

Sean has outlined seven key financial and non-financial benefits, in the case of Breadsource, to provide business owners with an example of how outstanding success can be achieved by midmarket companies using a UPh. Everyday owner operator, family firms can capitalize on their long-standing efforts and create greatness with financial prosperity and protect everything they have invested in their business.

Companies, like Breadsource who capitalize on their UPh, have increased their options for a truly rewarding exit or succession: transitioning to the next generation more seamlessly, selling the business at substantially justified premiums or engaging in more mergers and acquisitions (M&A) activity (*i.e.*, rollup) wherein the family can take money out of the business (reducing risk) while increasing the value of their equity as they acquire more companies, implementing their UPh throughout each acquisition. Such an exercise would be the difference between selling a $15 million (single UPh company) company vs. selling a $50-100 million company (group of branded companies operated by one governing UPh).

By recommending and helping manage the UPh, advisors can play a more vital and proactive role in helping their clients realize new value, wealth and success.

How Trusted Advisors Can Seize Opportunity

Unlocking current and newly found value represents immense opportunity for advisors because it delivers significant value and benefit to their clients.

The UPh program is designed to be modular. Qualified Trusted Advisors can be trained to perform the UPh Assessment (Step 1) of the 4-Step program. The Assessment Step includes turnkey questionnaires and tools that help to uncover issues and successes that business owners can improve upon. This in turn provides more opportunity for additional advisory work that Trusted Advisors or their firms are already set up to do. In essence, it is an added enhancement to what they already do. The

Assessment Step is aimed to quickly show the business owner the financial and non-financial benefits of developing the UPh and the risks in *not* doing so.

Because the UPh is an asset that realizes more value and reduces business risk (ultimately protecting the owner's interests), it uncovers enormous opportunity for qualified Trusted Advisors to *justifiably* play a more active role in serving their clients. Business owners have a better incentive to include their advisors in helping them build value that can ultimately be extracted to provide them with more wealth, profits and improved quality of work life.

The following illustration, Figure 9, demonstrates how the UPh helps a Trusted Advisor take the lead and quarterback client profitability, value and wealth issues with the appropriate specialists. The Trusted Advisor who takes this initiative and wins the client's confidence to consider the UPh is the ideal one to lead that client when working with other specialists.

As every advisor is vying for their client to elect them, the race is only won by that special advisor who can clearly show the client a better way to prosperity.

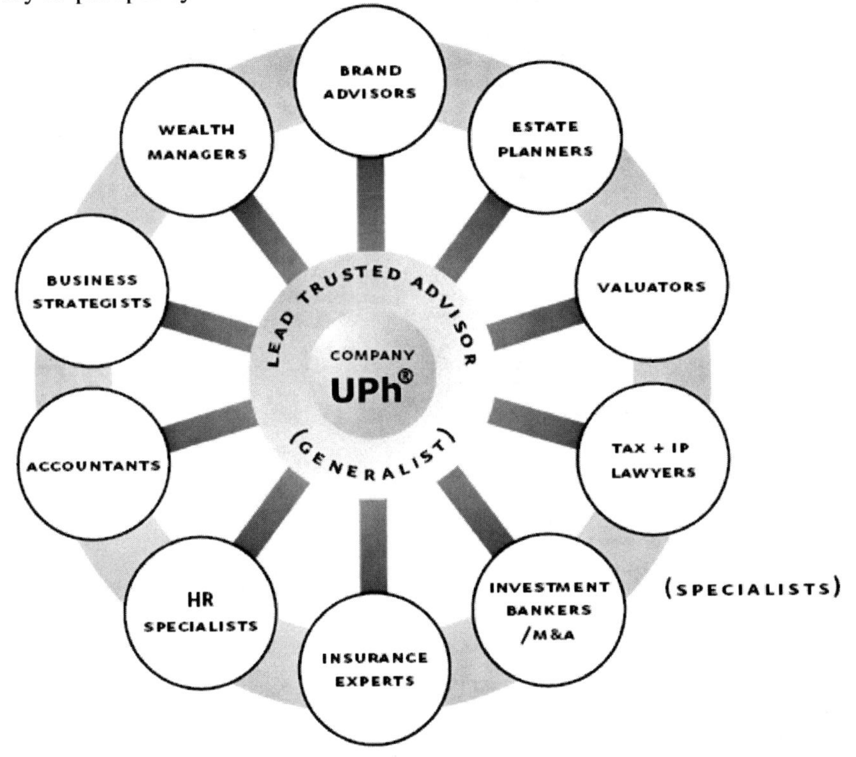

Figure 9: Trusted Advisors Spearheading the UPh Lead Other Specialty Advisors

How Do Trusted Advisors and Business Owners Benefit from a UPh?

Trusted Advisors are always looking for ways to grow their practice while providing more client value add. This, however, is easier said then done, since advisors, like their business owner clients, face daily challenges that often distract them from performing the right tasks that could grow their business the way they want.

What is for certain is that there are four fundamental ways to grow a business:

1. Increase the number of customers (of the type you want).
2. Increase the transaction frequency.
3. Increase the transaction value or "average sale".
4. Increase the effectiveness of each process in your business.

But how do you execute these steps and become successful? While discussing those solutions is not the purpose of this chapter, it can be mentioned that the UPh does help companies grow in each of these four ways. The following Tables 8-14 help to describe both Trusted Advisor and business owner benefits.

	FINANCIAL ADVISORS Tax, Estate, Exit, Succession, Accounting, Valuations
HOW ADVISORS AND THEIR FIRMS CAN GROW, COMPETE, AND PROFIT BECAUSE THEIR CLIENTS HAVE A UPh	For those accounting firms looking for - improved market differentiation - stronger competitive advantage - increased client revenue and growth - higher margin services with lower risk The UPh can be a distinct strategic add-on service offering. The UPh process clarifies the ultimate exit or end goal of a business owner, with a viable means of getting there and in doing so the financial advisors have a clearer roadmap by which to advise their clients. And as a result of their UPh, business owner clients become more receptive to the vital role their financial advisors play in protecting their increased wealth. Without a UPh, an owner may not be as convinced that their Goodwill can be effectively commercialized and 'cashed in.' With a UPh this may be a new possibility. Implementing the UPh creates the need for more proactive planning because more value created means more tax, estate, valuation insurance liability and considerations.
A PARTIAL LIST OF ADVISORY SERVICES REQUIRED BY CLIENTS WHO HAVE DEVELOPED A UPh FOR THEIR BUSINESS (BASED ON ACTUAL CLIENT CASES OR RECOMMENDATIONS)	Creation of new holding companies in favourable tax jurisdictions Business valuations Increased tax advisory Succession planning Increased growth financing Pricing, Revenue Model and Costing analysis

Table 8: Benefits to Financial Advisors

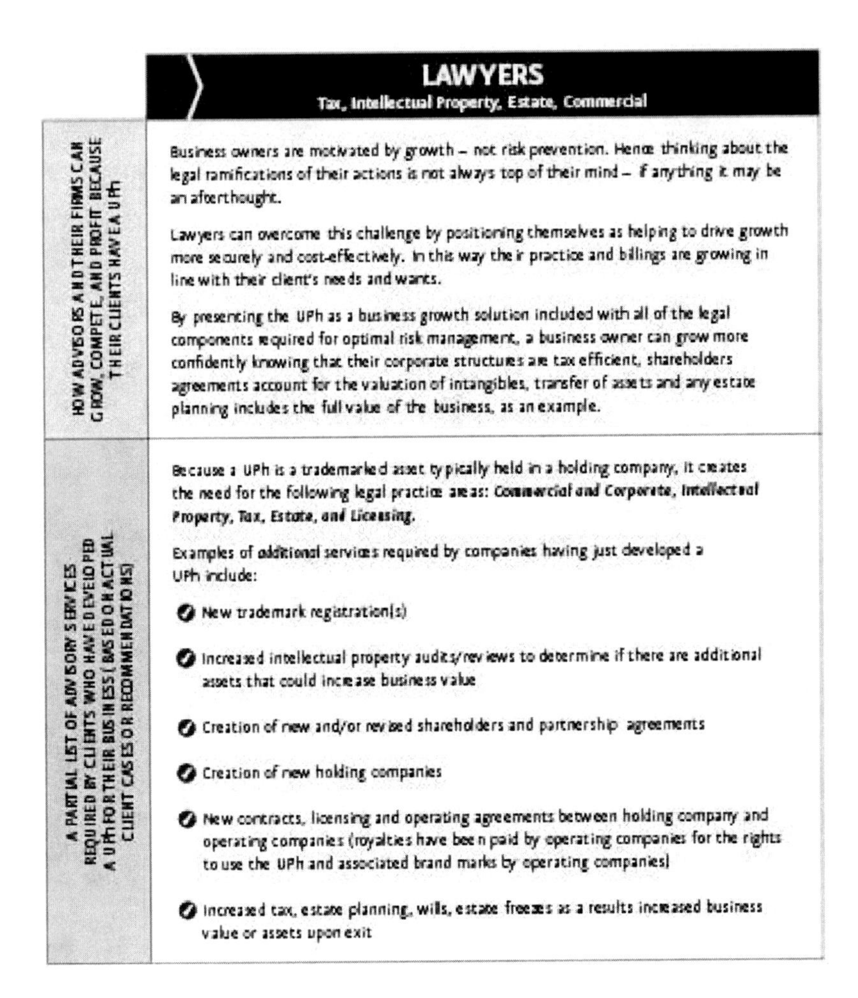

	LAWYERS **Tax, Intellectual Property, Estate, Commercial**
HOW ADVISORS AND THEIR FIRMS CAN GROW, COMPETE, AND PROFIT BECAUSE THEIR CLIENTS HAVE A UPh	Business owners are motivated by growth – not risk prevention. Hence thinking about the legal ramifications of their actions is not always top of their mind – if anything it may be an afterthought. Lawyers can overcome this challenge by positioning themselves as helping to drive growth more securely and cost-effectively. In this way their practice and billings are growing in line with their client's needs and wants. By presenting the UPh as a business growth solution included with all of the legal components required for optimal risk management, a business owner can grow more confidently knowing that their corporate structures are tax efficient, shareholders agreements account for the valuation of intangibles, transfer of assets and any estate planning includes the full value of the business, as an example.
A PARTIAL LIST OF ADVISORY SERVICES REQUIRED BY CLIENTS WHO HAVE DEVELOPED A UPh FOR THEIR BUSINESS (BASED ON ACTUAL CLIENT CASES OR RECOMMENDATIONS)	Because a UPh is a trademarked asset typically held in a holding company, it creates the need for the following legal practice areas: ***Commercial and Corporate, Intellectual Property, Tax, Estate, and Licensing.*** Examples of additional services required by companies having just developed a UPh include: • New trademark registration(s) • Increased intellectual property audits/reviews to determine if there are additional assets that could increase business value • Creation of new and/or revised shareholders and partnership agreements • Creation of new holding companies • New contracts, licensing and operating agreements between holding company and operating companies (royalties have been paid by operating companies for the rights to use the UPh and associated brand marks by operating companies) • Increased tax, estate planning, wills, estate freezes as a results increased business value or assets upon exit

Table 9: Benefits to Lawyers

	INSURANCE ADVISORS Life, Key Person, Disability, Critical Illness, IPP, RCA
HOW ADVISORS AND THEIR FIRMS CAN GROW, COMPETE, AND PROFIT BECAUSE THEIR CLIENTS HAVE A UPh	Full service insurance and advisory firms ideally want clients to have their policies current and accurately reflect adequate coverage. Clients, however, are reluctant to pay high premiums unless there is very good reason to do so. A UPh for a company is the catalyst for a client to obtain the right insurance vehicle for the highest insurable amount required. Clients also overlook the fact that most of the risk of a successful business is locked up in one/few person(s) – the KEY person(s). As a solution, the UPh helps to reduce this risk from the KEY person(s) as the UPh becomes more institutionalized throughout the company. Advisors can better justify their recommendations because the new found value released and created by the UPh (new profitability, cashflow, goodwill and intangibles) means that more liability and risk needs to be insured. The greater the value released, the greater the insurance required. It becomes a win-win for the client and advisor.
A PARTIAL LIST OF ADVISORY SERVICES REQUIRED BY CLIENTS WHO HAVE DEVELOPED A UPh FOR THEIR BUSINESS (BASED ON ACTUAL CLIENT CASES OR RECOMMENDATIONS)	Clients seldom like to pay more premiums than they need to; however as business value increases and more wealth can be created in their business then their willingness to protect and maximize this wealth becomes very different. Intangible assets, unlike tangible assets, can grow exponentially in value over time. This increased wealth potential and consequent tax liability requires additional insurance advisory. This may include: • Helping the purchase the right kind and adequate amount of insurance as early in the business as possible to secure the best possible price for premiums • Consistent reviews and updating of insurance, estate, wealth transfer and investment planning option (typically policies are updated to reflect an increase in the death benefit as a result of an increase in business value) • Pension planning and renewed succession planning discussions may also result in improved client value add

Table 10: Benefits to Insurance Advisors

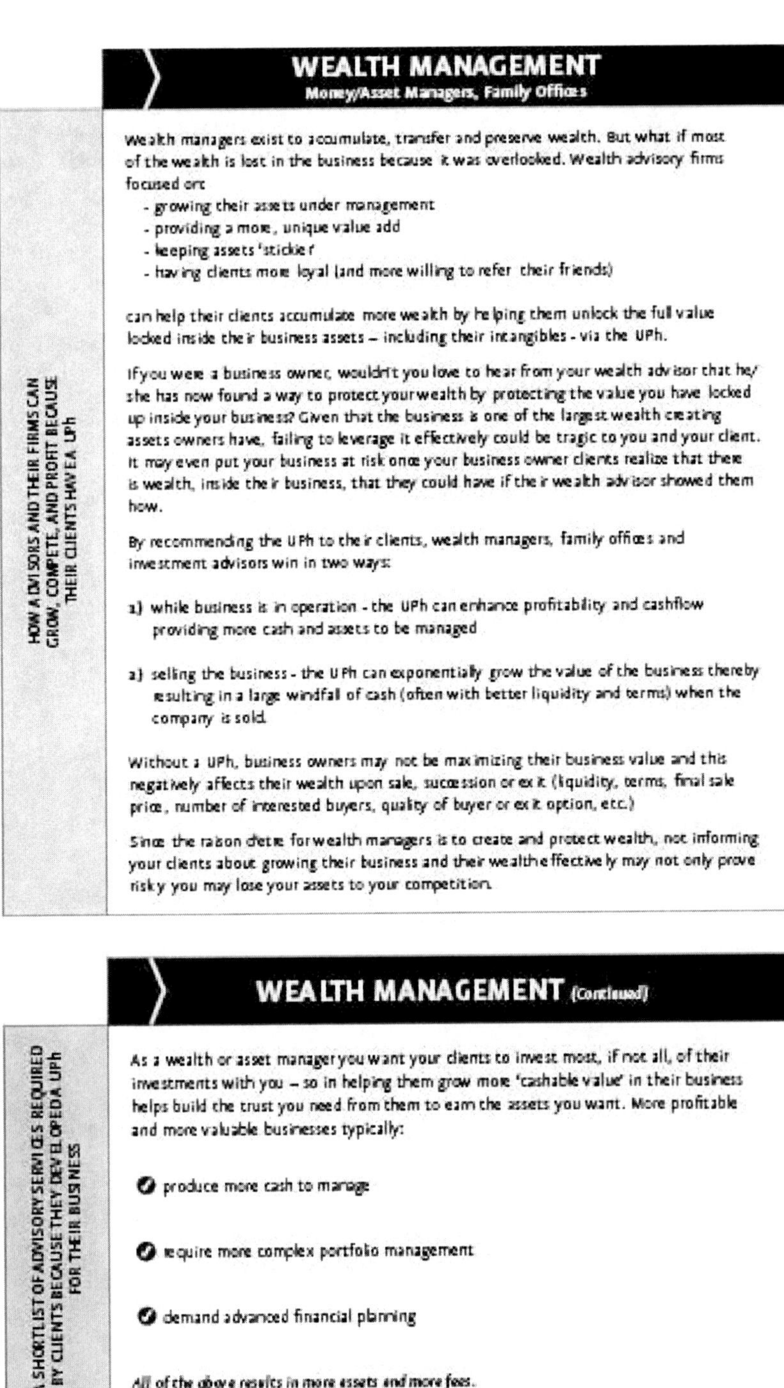

WEALTH MANAGEMENT

Money/Asset Managers, Family Offices

HOW ADVISORS AND THEIR FIRMS CAN GROW, COMPETE, AND PROFIT BECAUSE THEIR CLIENTS HAVE A UPh

Wealth managers exist to accumulate, transfer and preserve wealth. But what if most of the wealth is lost in the business because it was overlooked. Wealth advisory firms focused on:

- growing their assets under management
- providing a more, unique value add
- keeping assets 'stickier'
- having clients more loyal (and more willing to refer their friends)

can help their clients accumulate more wealth by helping them unlock the full value locked inside their business assets – including their intangibles - via the UPh.

If you were a business owner, wouldn't you love to hear from your wealth advisor that he/she has now found a way to protect your wealth by protecting the value you have locked up inside your business? Given that the business is one of the largest wealth creating assets owners have, failing to leverage it effectively could be tragic to you and your client. It may even put your business at risk once your business owner clients realize that there is wealth, inside their business, that they could have if their wealth advisor showed them how.

By recommending the UPh to their clients, wealth managers, family offices and investment advisors win in two ways:

1) while business is in operation - the UPh can enhance profitability and cashflow providing more cash and assets to be managed

2) selling the business - the UPh can exponentially grow the value of the business thereby resulting in a large windfall of cash (often with better liquidity and terms) when the company is sold.

Without a UPh, business owners may not be maximizing their business value and this negatively affects their wealth upon sale, succession or exit (liquidity, terms, final sale price, number of interested buyers, quality of buyer or exit option, etc.)

Since the raison d'etre for wealth managers is to create and protect wealth, not informing your clients about growing their business and their wealth effectively may not only prove risky you may lose your assets to your competition.

WEALTH MANAGEMENT (Continued)

A SHORTLIST OF ADVISORY SERVICES REQUIRED BY CLIENTS BECAUSE THEY DEVELOPED A UPh FOR THEIR BUSINESS

As a wealth or asset manager you want your clients to invest most, if not all, of their investments with you – so in helping them grow more 'cashable value' in their business helps build the trust you need from them to earn the assets you want. More profitable and more valuable businesses typically:

- produce more cash to manage
- require more complex portfolio management
- demand advanced financial planning

All of the above results in more assets and more fees.

Table 11: Benefits to Wealth Management Advisors

<table>
<tr><th></th><th>COMMERCIAL BANKING
Lending Institutions (Debt or Equity)</th></tr>
<tr><td>HOW ADVISORS AND THEIR FIRMS CAN GROW, COMPETE, AND PROFIT BECAUSE THEIR CLIENTS HAVE A UPh</td><td>Lenders require that their investments are paid back (debt) and provide desirable returns on time or earlier (equity). "Get your money out" or "get more for your money" is the goal.

Lenders can minimize their risk and maximize their returns by having their clients (current and prospective) manage and operate their business with a UPh in place first.

Since the UPh helps the management team 'get on the same page' and 'grow in the right direction' their ability to perform, use funds, and deliver results improves. With their UPh, management and staff are clearer, more focused and efficient to do what they need to do on a daily basis.

When overall business performance is improved, through better management and follow through by staff, investors and lenders can become highly esteemed and rewarded trusted advisors. Clients will be better funded and thereby more loyal because they have become more successful.</td></tr>
<tr><td>A SHORTLIST OF ADVISORY SERVICES REQUIRED BY CLIENTS BECAUSE THEY DEVELOPED A UPh FOR THEIR BUSINESS</td><td>The UPh process and statement helps company leaders and staff become clearer on where they are going and how they are getting there. In most cases, UPh clients require additional financing to make operational, staff, strategic, and marketing enhancements. Examples of past enhancements made by clients have been:

• $1Million+ customized Enterprise Resource Planning (ERP) Software system
• Purchase of a new baking business to expand its UPh Branded food product line
• Revised packaging design across 30+ food products, consisting of two staple brands
• Revised warehouse planning, new health & safety, quality control certifications
• New hires with improved employee performance management systems and training programs
• New branding, marketing, advertising and sales initiatives
• Real Estate holdings were divested to expand distribution into new countries complete with warehouse, new staff, and logistics
• Revitalized R&D to establish new product lines, new brand lines and new strategic partnerships</td></tr>
</table>

Table 12: Benefits to Commercial Banking Advisors

TRANSACTION ADVISORY

Investment Banking, M&A, Private Equity, Turnaround

HOW ADVISORS AND THEIR FIRMS CAN GROW, COMPETE, AND PROFIT BECAUSE THEIR CLIENTS HAVE A UPh

How do you ensure more transactions succeed especially when deals are so prone to failure. Regardless of the reasons for deal failures, owners and their advisors can improve their readiness and their positioning in the deal by having a UPh performed in advance. Results of a UPh pre- merger, rollup, acquisition, management buyout, sale, restructuring, or financing, or investment from new ownership range from improved offers, better terms, aligned objectives among stakeholders, less conflict and anxiety, and more favourable valuations. Because transactions are complex in nature, each case must be reviewed uniquely to verify the benefits of the UPh.

Private Equity or Investment Banking firms with an active management and shareholder interest can realize improved earnings, increased return on equity, and perhaps earlier exit timeframes on invested capital - with the successful implementation of a UPh.

Improved Stakeholder alignment, explicit clarity on strategy, operational enhancement and control, staff engagement, customer qualification and service and value creation are a some factors on how companies with a UPh become more profitable and valuable.

Valuable companies enjoy more quality transactions (desirable partners, investors, terms, structures, exit and growth options, negotiations and liquidity).

A SHORTLIST OF UPh CLIENT ACHIEVEMENTS

Transactions that have proceeded successfully as a result of the stakeholders participating in a UPh process include:

Forming Strategic Alliances & Joint ventures

After investing 3 years wooing a potential equity partner for a new corporation, this senior executive who underwent a UPh program to develop the underlying philosophy, business strategy and platform for the new firm, realized within weeks that they were the wrong partners simply because they refused to participate in the UPh program. Such non-action and lack of interest clearly revealed that they weren't interested in creating a common future. Instead of pursuing the equity arrangement, this executive created contract agreements to distribute the product instead. This new awareness saved both parties from wasting more time and money in what would have been a failed partnership.

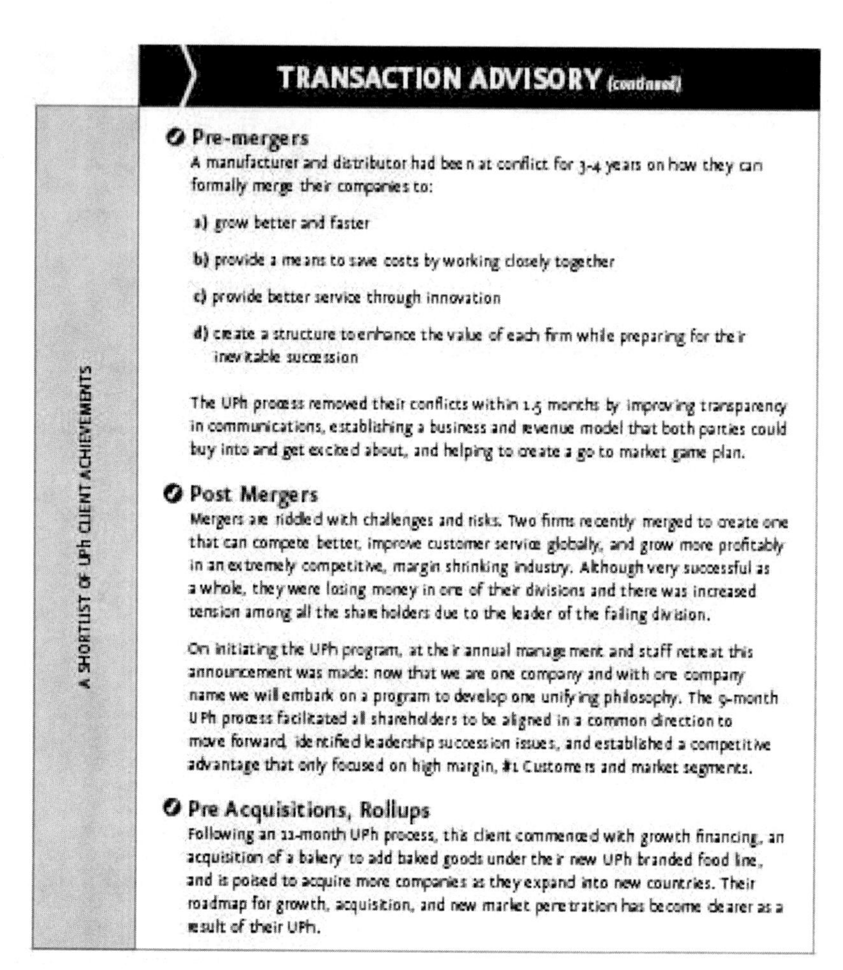

TRANSACTION ADVISORY (continued)

A SHORTLIST OF UPh CLIENT ACHIEVEMENTS

Pre-mergers

A manufacturer and distributor had been at conflict for 3-4 years on how they can formally merge their companies to:

a) grow better and faster

b) provide a means to save costs by working closely together

c) provide better service through innovation

d) create a structure to enhance the value of each firm while preparing for their inevitable succession

The UPh process removed their conflicts within 1.5 months by improving transparency in communications, establishing a business and revenue model that both parties could buy into and get excited about, and helping to create a go to market game plan.

Post Mergers

Mergers are riddled with challenges and risks. Two firms recently merged to create one that can compete better, improve customer service globally, and grow more profitably in an extremely competitive, margin shrinking industry. Although very successful as a whole, they were losing money in one of their divisions and there was increased tension among all the shareholders due to the leader of the failing division.

On initiating the UPh program, at their annual management and staff retreat this announcement was made: now that we are one company and with one company name we will embark on a program to develop one unifying philosophy. The 9-month UPh process facilitated all shareholders to be aligned in a common direction to move forward, identified leadership succession issues, and established a competitive advantage that only focused on high margin, #1 Customers and market segments.

Pre Acquisitions, Rollups

Following an 11-month UPh process, this client commenced with growth financing, an acquisition of a bakery to add baked goods under their new UPh branded food line, and is poised to acquire more companies as they expand into new countries. Their roadmap for growth, acquisition, and new market penetration has become clearer as a result of their UPh.

Table 13: Benefits to Transaction Advisors

BUSINESS & MANAGEMENT CONSULTING

Strategic Planning, Operations, Sales and Marketing, Human Resources, Human Capital, Organizational Development, Process Improvement, Technology and Systems, Branding, Public Relations, Advertising, and Customer Service

HOW ADVISORS AND THEIR FIRMS CAN GROW, COMPETE, AND PROFIT BECAUSE THEIR CLIENTS HAVE A UPh

Specialists providing these services can enhance client success while creating more consulting work for themselves by integrating the UPh into their current offerings. By doing so the solutions they provide will in most cases:

- Become better integrated into other areas of the business
- Deliver results beyond their scope of work
- Have more longevity and probability of even more success

Companies without a UPh, don't have an explicit focus that they are truly aware of – they struggle to unanimously agree on:

- what makes us a great company
- what do we stand for
- why are we unique or distinctive
- why should customers buy from us

Without a clear focus and strong motivation, companies are reluctant to spend money, commit resources, and hire the right people to do the right thing. Instead when a company has invested in a UPh, they are clear about doing one thing and only one thing – implement their UPh across the company so every staff follows it and every customer buys because of it. Therefore consultants who mobilize the UPh are hired more readily, kept on projects longer and paid more to deliver results.

Clients can better justify such spending because their deliverables help to 'operationalize' their UPh ultimately increasing business performance, profitability, and value.

Example: President or Owner wants to increase sales revenues and profitability. What do they do first: build a UPh or hire a sales specialist? Doing the UPh is like 'curing the disease' versus 'treating the symptom'. When doing the UPh first some results that can be achieved simultaneously (sample list) include:

- Uncovering internal issues as to why sales revenues are low
- Identifying the key value proposition for the company
- Refining the revenue model or sales strategy if needed
- Engaging the sales, customer service, operations, marketing staff to further uncover company wide issues issues that may hinder sales and profitability
- Improving the target customer profile focusing the company to serve more profitable customers
- Defining the organizations' ideal competitive advantage or strategic DNA (the UPh statement) to help it sell more, better, faster

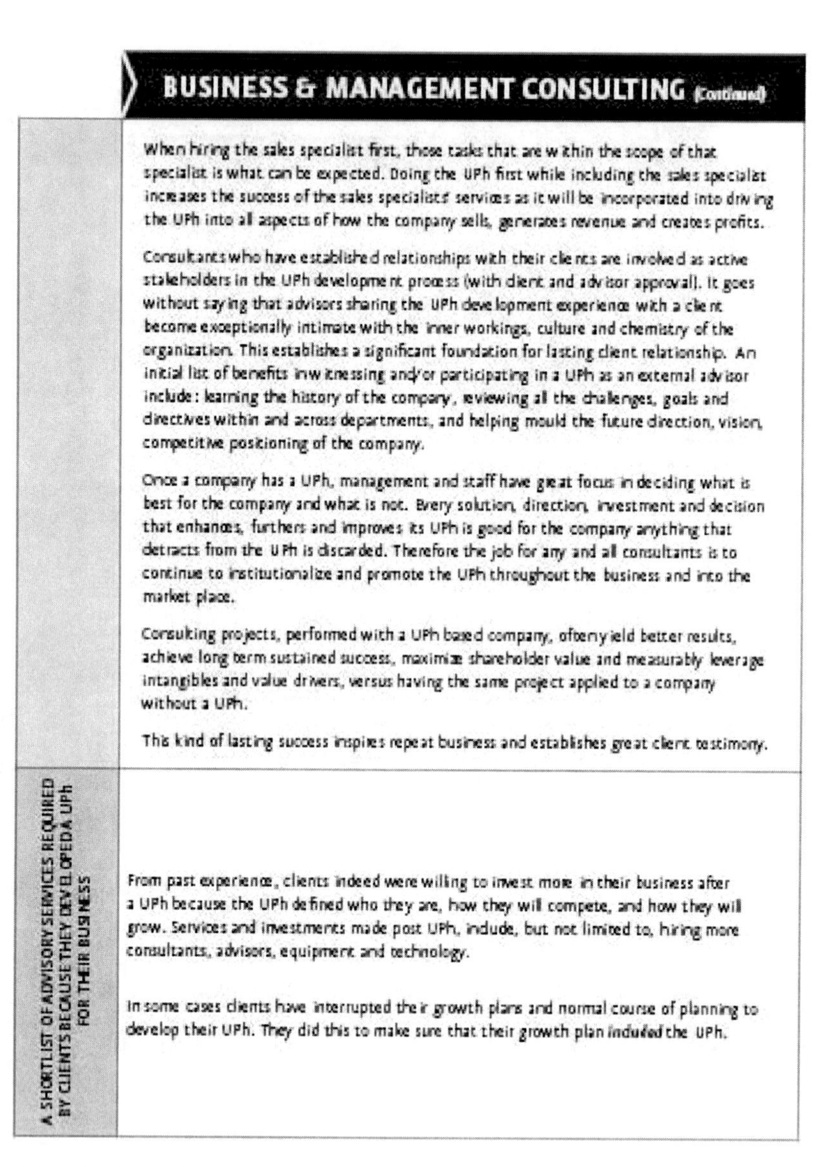

BUSINESS & MANAGEMENT CONSULTING (Continued)	
	When hiring the sales specialist first, those tasks that are within the scope of that specialist is what can be expected. Doing the UPh first while including the sales specialist increases the success of the sales specialists' services as it will be incorporated into driving the UPh into all aspects of how the company sells, generates revenue and creates profits. Consultants who have established relationships with their clients are involved as active stakeholders in the UPh development process (with client and advisor approval). It goes without saying that advisors sharing the UPh development experience with a client become exceptionally intimate with the inner workings, culture and chemistry of the organization. This establishes a significant foundation for lasting client relationship. An initial list of benefits in witnessing and/or participating in a UPh as an external advisor include: learning the history of the company, reviewing all the challenges, goals and directives within and across departments, and helping mould the future direction, vision, competitive positioning of the company. Once a company has a UPh, management and staff have great focus in deciding what is best for the company and what is not. Every solution, direction, investment and decision that enhances, furthers and improves its UPh is good for the company anything that detracts from the UPh is discarded. Therefore the job for any and all consultants is to continue to institutionalize and promote the UPh throughout the business and into the market place. Consulting projects, performed with a UPh based company, often yield better results, achieve long term sustained success, maximize shareholder value and measurably leverage intangibles and value drivers, versus having the same project applied to a company without a UPh. This kind of lasting success inspires repeat business and establishes great client testimony.
A SHORTLIST OF ADVISORY SERVICES REQUIRED BY CLIENTS BECAUSE THEY DEVELOPED A UPh FOR THEIR BUSINESS	From past experience, clients indeed were willing to invest more in their business after a UPh because the UPh defined who they are, how they will compete, and how they will grow. Services and investments made post UPh, include, but not limited to, hiring more consultants, advisors, equipment and technology. In some cases clients have interrupted their growth plans and normal course of planning to develop their UPh. They did this to make sure that their growth plan included the UPh.

Table 14: Benefits to Business & Management Consulting Advisors

Key Things to Remember About Using or Recommending the UPh

- The UPh is beneficial regardless of exit option (sell, keep, transition, grow, M&A). How the UPh and its performance and value are managed in each exit scenario is what matters.
- A company builds a UPh only once in its lifetime. This is the way in which the UPh, as an asset and business driver, compounds value

over time. Advisors benefit by having their client develop a UPh because the client requires ongoing advisory and management of their UPh.

- More money is found when intangible assets and value drivers are well managed, monitored and monetized. Due to the increased sophistication and complexity of intangibles and their potentially lucrative payoff, advisors and their clients are *both* given incentive to work more closely and frequently together throughout the UPh process.
- Value, like equity, requires time to grow. Therefore the sooner a UPh is developed and implemented, the sooner value enhancement and success can be achieved.
- Because the UPh program is a vital undertaking (in that it typically "re-organizes" a business to help the owner(s) in becoming clearer about his or her personal and business goals and mission), it is recommended to develop a UPh in advance of most financial planning, legal structuring, consulting or transaction work; any post-UPh advisory work will help cement the UPh and its benefits for the client's personal and business well-being. *Additionally, advisors may want to incorporate the UPh's payoffs (improved revenues, goodwill and business value) in their financial, legal and wealth planning, rather than not include it and fall short of the results that the owner or you expected.*
- No company runs perfectly, so improvements can always be made. My experience working with Profit 100 and 50 Best Managed firms (including a Platinum member firm) uncovered financial, legal and wealth management advisory work that could be referred to the right specialists (since their current advisors, as indicated by my clients, were not addressing these issues). The more successful the firm, the more it can benefit from developing its UPh because it has more success to protect and resources to gain.

The Ideal Trusted Advisor and the Business Owner Client

Business owners, like any tough customer, seldom want to pay more advisory fees or take time away from growing their business to meet with their advisors. But when they put more money in everyone's pocket to do so, the incentive becomes obvious. The ideal Trusted Advisors to recommend the UPh are those who already know that they and their clients are "leaving a lot of money behind" and want to do everything they can to help their clients extract it, effectively.

The ideal Trusted Advisor or advisory firm (based on past successes), who can benefit the most from having their clients develop a company UPh, is retained to (and earned the trust and right to):

- advise their clients about strategic and long-term issues, not just tactical ones;
- deliver solutions, not products;
- solve complex issues; and
- remain proactive, not reactive, to the needs of the clients' family, business and their respective futures.

Business owners and leaders who are ideal for developing a UPh for their company are:

- open and forward-thinking with a desire to build the best business possible by helping their clients in the most effective way (vs. someone who says, "we have been successful doing it this way for years so why change now");
- have invested money in strategy, change management or transformation programs before and are looking for a secure return on their investment strategy;
- aware that their business value and personal wealth is at risk and are ready to maximize business value (throughout all their assets) and protect their shareholder interests (especially in preparation of an exit or transition);
- challenged in growing their business successfully (they are often time-strapped and looking for new ideas to do things differently);
- asking the right questions of their advisors (often striving to improve and do things better);
- facing multiple issues throughout the business simultaneously (staff, growth, revenue, sales and operations) that have been difficult to overcome in the past;
- afraid to leave a lot of money on the table when selling or transitioning their business and realize they could be.

CHAPTER TAKE-AWAYS

1. Intangibles represent enormous potential for value maximization, wealth creation and future risk minimization when managed effectively.
2. The UPh is a solution to unlock and compound value across intangible assets and drivers effectively. When implemented and

managed successfully by Trusted Advisors, the UPh helps business owners grow their companies more easily and successfully, maximizing profitability, value and wealth with less risk, complexity and day-to-day stress of growing a business.

3. Sean Cavanagh, Navigant, describes the positive financial impact and business risk reduction merits of the UPh based on how second generation leaders of a family business used their UPh to more than double revenues in five years.

4. Many professional firms and Trusted Advisors have hourly fees, and may not participate or enjoy a form of leveraged or passive income on their time. Nor do they enjoy the fact that they often lose a valuable account when the client sells his or her business. In the midst of a transition boom, many accounts will be lost, and professional service firms must find new ways to rightfully keep clients and win new ones.

   This chapter provides Trusted Advisors and select firms with a solution to:

   - provide added value to existing clients (thereby generating higher margin revenues quickly);
   - gain a competitive advantage in delivering a distinguished and differentiated service offering (complete with customized advisory tools, processes and deliverables);
   - attract more of the "right" clients (those who want a better, integrated advisory solution from your firm);
   - grow their practice area, profile and market reach (the expertise to unlock intangibles is a growing market niche ideal for industry-leading firms ready to grow); and
   - increase revenue by increasing their services, adding value and increasing their involvement with their clients

5. Even though most companies need a UPh, not every company is ready for it. Trusted Advisors and their business owner clients must be steadfast to invest the necessary time and resources to engage in a business transformation process to build lasting value. Even though it provides near immediate results in the business, the UPh is hardly a quick fix.

   The UPh program remains for those who are driven to build the most valuable business possible, achieve the most desirable exit and transition options available to them and are prepared to do what it takes to reap those rewards.

It's not a process that is recommended for "lifestyle" business owners who have no desire or need to build a professionally managed enterprise.

CONCLUSIONS — DOING WHAT'S RIGHT

The choice remains yours: either help your clients unlock up to 74% of the value or watch them lose it.

Sooner or later your clients will come to know why they *lost value* in their business or *lost wealth*. They would *lose value* because they didn't build a valuable, saleable company — one that is better or safer to buy. And they would *lose wealth* either by not making enough money while growing the company or by leaving some money on the deal table when negotiating a sale, buy, rollup, merger, acquisition *etc*.

Sooner or later your clients will come to know that there are solutions available to build extractable value effectively — if only someone would have told them. Will that be you?

So:

- Who do you think they would blame first for any loss — themselves or their advisors?
- Who was supposed to (because they are retained to) help, advise and prevent them from missing out on growing their business better (and unlocking the full value of their business — including intangibles that affect 74% of their potential sale price)?
- Who could have helped them make the right choices when *it was time* to do so (and does not wait until the end when their client is at the deal table defending the value of his or her business)?

Save yourself and your client from the risks in ignoring the value locked inside their most lucrative and precious assets — intangibles.

I therefore invite you to do what's right for your client and safe for your practice by informing yourself and advising your client on the full benefit of unlocking business value, using all intangible and tangible assets, effectively.

Imagine what your clients will say when you show them how to build more extractable value and protect their wealth — especially when few other advisors have.

You will not only become (or remain) their Trusted Advisor, you will, aside from making more money, provide distinctive client value. This distinguishable market advantage earns you and your firm every right to keep the clients you have (and possibly their successors as clients) while gaining new ones that you have always wanted to have.

CHAPTER 45

THE TRUSTED ADVISOR'S SURVIVAL GUIDE — A GUIDE TO PRIVATE EQUITY

WHAT EVERY TRUSTED ADVISOR SHOULD BE ABLE TO TELL OWNERS ABOUT ACCESSING OTHER PEOPLE'S MONEY AND THE POWERFUL DIFFERENCE IT MAKES IN GROWING PERSONAL AND FAMILY WEALTH

J. B. Loewen

Overview

The person who can impact the most on the future wealth of a business owner is the Trusted Advisor. With this responsibility, every Trusted Advisor needs to understand that private equity is no longer for the big companies but is available at all levels. It is in the Trusted Advisor's own best interest to understand why private equity has taken the place of the public market, how it works and what the outcomes are for your client, the business owner.

Gathering together skills and talent of the private equity investor is the competitive advantage. Bringing in private equity at least five years before a transition will ensure the business transitions to the legacy.

This chapter is a guide to private equity — what every Trusted Advisor should be able to tell owners about accessing other people's money and the powerful difference it makes in growing personal and family wealth.

Learning Objectives

By the end of this chapter you will be able to:

- identify clients who would benefit from accessing private equity;
- advise your client to plan for the business and its long-term survival;
- understand how traditional finance is changing;

- know the difference between public and private capital — why private money is taking over from the initial public offering (IPO);
- know the value that the private equity fund team offers and when to use it;
- use the checklist to assess if your client's business would fit private equity;
- help your client understand how ownership and control differ;
- advise on how different levels of investment result in different outcomes;
- analyze how much risk your client, the owner, can bear; and
- guide your client in decision-making — does he or she want to be in control or to be rich?

Did you know that private equity buyers of owner-managed companies increase the value by a third of the sale price (on average) within just three to five years?[1] What does that mean for Trusted Advisors? Do you really want to let your clients leave 30% of their company's worth on the table for the new owners?

Absolutely not.

You probably already know that new owners of the company would find many levers with which to grow the business within the first five years of taking control. You may also get frustrated by how often your client's ideas on how to develop the revenue streams seem to remain out on the golf course, not in the boardroom. You have most definitely asked the difficult questions and yet are frustrated that the owners do not take enough action.

TRUSTED ADVISORS ADD WEALTH

As a Trusted Advisor, you want to bring the best solutions to your clients. By being ahead of the crowd on how to help the business succeed by tapping into this interesting type of capital, your clients will recognize that you are helping show opportunities to explore.

Private equity people will be contacting your clients, and if you have already helped to go through the key questions to answer, both your clients and the private equity partners will appreciate your knowledge. If your clients decided on using private equity, if you were the one to initiate the process, you are more likely to be retained.

---

[1] Ernst & Young, *Private Equity Report*, 2008.

As a Trusted Advisor to many business owners, you know the shocking truth that some businesses grow simply because they know where to get money — not because they have a better strategy, more motivated staff or leaner business processes. It's comes down to knowing how and where to get the smart cash.

The other fact you will probably not know is that by bringing in private equity partners at least five years *before* a succession date, the business will grow at a far more profitable rate than if the owners are left to their own devices. As a Trusted Advisor, your role can be to help owners get over their fear of giving up partial equity and to reframe the question from one of ownership to one of wealth creation. It is as simple as asking the question, "Do you want to be in control, or do you want to be rich?"

Then, if you want to make money from your company, why would you leave wealth on the table for the next owners? Why not work side-by-side with private equity partners to grow the business and increase its worth? Those companies that remain too small are going to have a difficult time surviving over the next decade as the global marketplace gathers strength.

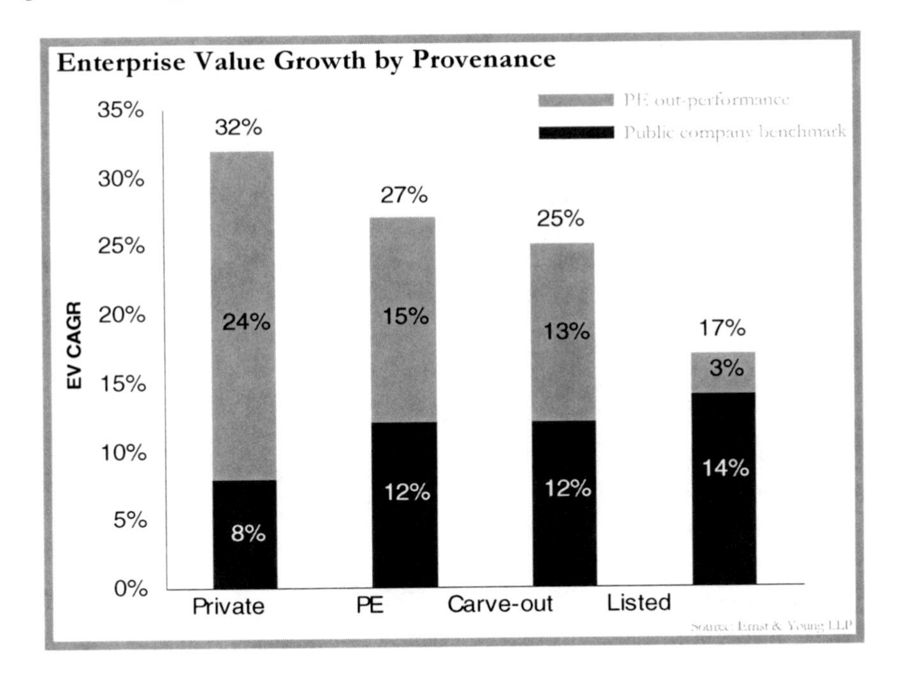

Trusted Advisors are the number one influencer to help a business owner think five years down the road. Since private equity has only recently become the best alternative to bank money, advisors may not be familiar with how private equity funds work. Think of it like smoking; business owners who use banks as a sole source of funds will seriously stunt their growth. This chapter is a guide to private equity — what every Trusted Advisor should be able to tell owners about accessing other people's money and the powerful difference it makes in growing their personal and family wealth.

IS THE COMPANY MAKING ENOUGH CASH?

Most business owners believe that their company does not make enough cash — even when revenues soar as high as the Rockies. There is also a belief that money is not something to discuss with others. Add to this the embarrassing discomfort owners have of inviting someone to take a look under the hood of their company and provide a diagnostic of their finances. Yet these same owners are scared out of their minds of being beaten to the customer by brash new competitors (bolstered up by newly available investor money).

If these owners produce technology, how can they make sure that their product gets to the market fast enough? If they sell a service, how can they come up with fresh ways to bring back fickle clients? If they are rooted in manufacturing, how can they set up a plant outside North America — as every consultant seems to be urging with all the Wisdom of Solomon? Let's face it, this new competition from other countries is challenging for many Canadian companies because they think they do not have the cash. This is simply not true anymore.

Will the business benefit from private equity?

1. Can it grow fast (*e.g.*, software, oil, biotechnology, telecommunications, mobile technology, infrastructure, day care, baby-boomer products)?
2. Would it be tough to do it in India, or China? Can it have high patent, or be knowledge-based (*e.g.*, health care, medical devices, technology)?
3. Is it family-owned, a mature business with steady clients?
4. Can the business model be expanded to other locations?
5. Could the business be done in other countries?

Now, your clients, like cars, come in all sizes and styles: there are young founders hammering away at their keyboards on weekends, and others with their prototype bits and pieces scattered across the garage where their spouse's car ought to be parked. Then there are those owners who have been at it a while with good revenues but costs hoovering up the cash flow. And let's not forget those 40-year-olds in family businesses who are chomping at the bit to take over from Pops but wondering how on earth to buy him out. Money is required to take businesses to the next level.

On the home stretch of business ownership, there are those 50-ish and 60-something CEOs out there, increasingly aware that even the Rolling Stones are getting closer to converting their tax-sheltered savings into annuities. They are growing vaguely uneasy with all the talk of thousands of companies coming up to the sell point as the baby-boomer owners prepare to retire. Much of this transfer of assets will involve deals of $25 million or less.

Your advantage as a Trusted Advisor is that you already know the intricate details of the business. The owner trusts you and can talk to you openly, or more openly than most. If the business has revenues of $10 million, not profits, there will be a private equity fund interested in partnering with the owners with the goal of selling in five years. That sale could be to the business owner's employees, his or her children, another private equity fund or a strategic buyer, usually a larger competitor. Your job is to make sure that your client gets to take some chips off the table now and then again in five years.

WHAT IS PRIVATE EQUITY?

Private equity partners with owners of companies bring capital but also *energy* to the business. Private equity partners typically buy shares in a company (as little as 10% or up to 90% — it depends what the owner wants). The term "private equity" embraces various types of private equity investments (as illustrated below), with each type determined by the stage of maturity of the company.

Type of Private Equity Investment

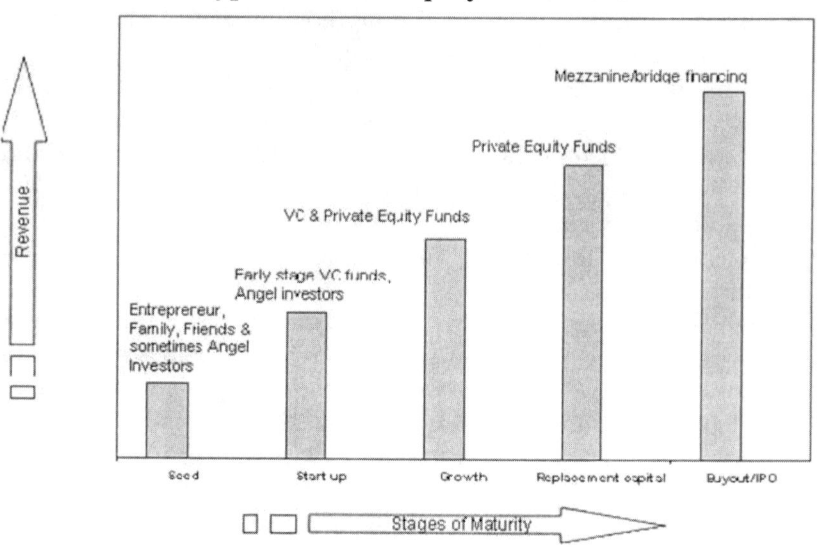

Being a new industry, it is difficult to come to agreement about a definition shared by all stakeholders, as some think it is for companies making $50 million and more, while others believe it begins with seed stage financing. The label of private equity can cover the full gamut — from the top end private equity buyouts through to institutional funds, venture capital, angels and the start-up seed funds. It's all privately held money.

For simplicity, we will place angel capital, venture capital and private equity all under the same umbrella of "private equity". However, each of the stakeholders will be dealt with separately because despite the search for investment process being similar enough for this book, there is a world of difference between venture capital and private equity investors' *raison d'être*.

Winning Companies Partner with Private Equity

Have you eaten Domino's Pizza, driven a Hertz car, worked out at Good Life Fitness, watched an Imax movie, driven a skidoo, used PayPal, eaten a Harvey's hamburger, Swiss Chalet chicken or Ace Bakeries French bread, tasted Sweets from Heaven or Purdy's chocolates, bought Pethealth insurance for your dog or enjoyed a glamorous flight with Porter Airlines? All these companies took on private equity partners.

None of these achievements was racked up by entrepreneurs working all by themselves, but through partnerships with private equity investors bringing a sharp insistence on strategy, hard-earned business skills and their much-needed injection of "patient capital".

Chances are you have heard of Blackberry by Research in Motion (RIM), Open Text, or Sleeman and Upper Canada beer. All of these start-ups grew with the added power of private equity partners. Then there are the hidden companies in the economy which supply equipment to manufacturers, like Bermingham Construction, or develop technology for mobile phones, create medical devices, supply nursing homes and so on.

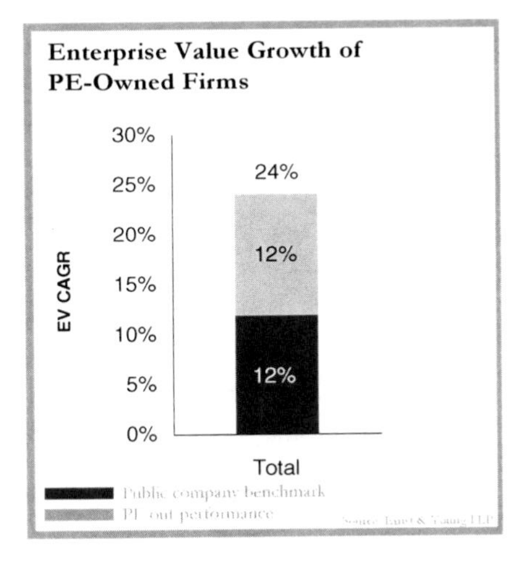

What all of these companies will tell you is that private equity helped their company. By working together, the market-savvy entrepreneur and the experienced venture investor can create something bigger that neither could do on his or her own — a growth business developing far beyond the familiar backyard.

HOW IS PRIVATE EQUITY DIFFERENT?

Business financing is getting better. It is how money lending should be. Indeed, many business owners can get more optimistic about their future, as *never in the history of commerce has so much financial opportunity been made available to previously neglected stages of business.*

At first blush, private equity is assumed to be the big buyouts by the large firms such as KKR's historic takeover of RJR Nabisco, or the BCE failed deal — a $1.8 billion deal — by Teacher's Pension Fund, Torstar and Woodbridge. Headlines are full of private equity deals such as Ford, Dunkin Donuts, Hertz, Toys-R-Us and other Fortune 500-sized businesses which are out of your league. It is true that the private equity source of capital has experienced unprecedented growth since 2001, but it is not only headline-grabbing deals that account for it.

These billion dollar deals are about 1% of all the private equity deals in terms of number of deals done, not by the dollar amount. In reality, according to research by McKinsey & Company's Private Equity Canada 2006 survey, the best prospects for private equity in North America are with thousands of small, privately owned companies that are currently experiencing competitive and succession transitions. Though the majority of deals are in the small- to mid-sized market, they do not make the front pages. After all, where's the glamour in a $10 million revenue trucking company where the CEO makes a fair wage and the highest extravagance is buying warehouses to develop supply chain expertise?[2] But when you research what falls into the bucket of private equity, large deals make up a very small part of most of the money available for companies like the ones you advise.

TRADITIONAL FINANCE IS MORPHING

Conventional financing — the corner banks with their strict lending ratios and tables, the public stock markets with their regulation and pressure for quarterly results — have created the pressure for capital that can deal with higher risk.

The music industry ignored its early warnings, and the blinkered finance industry is doing likewise. Sources of money for smaller, riskier companies are growing rapidly. Investors are creating fresh ways of rewarding those who take the risk of building companies — people like your clients, business owners.

To give you an idea of the changes happening, try to imagine a billion years ago, when the world's land mass was all one lump. We call it Pangaea, surrounded by the salty waves of the Panthalassen Sea. Then something happened, a trigger event, perhaps a volcano, and the land began to split into awkwardly shaped lumps. How unthinkable that what seems so permanent can change into something entirely different, previously unimaginable.

Something similar has happened to the finance industry model. Its trigger event was the arrival of computers and the Internet. Just as technology knocked typewriters out of the ballpark as a way to get ideas into print, so it has knocked the old-style business of finance. Exactly like Pangaea's slow breakup and its transformation into a whole new world, investment money is breaking away from the mass of public

---

[2] McKinsey & Co. 2007 study of private equity.

capital pools, and collecting into odd-sized chunks of private cash, otherwise known as private equity. With technology, more people can set up their own fund and invest in other businesses. They can manage to do this successfully as there is now technology to watch daily performance, with access to spreadsheets and detailed drill-down into financial spreadsheets which was just not available even ten years ago. The Internet opens up the ability to research industries very, very fast and in fact-crunching detail. As a result, the money available to invest in companies such as your clients' firms is going to be tracked, all issues are attacked quickly, performance is managed better and more financial rewards will be given to those working directly on the company.

Ignoring all of this, the public market — represented by stock markets, brokerages, big bank investment bankers — is gamely trying to hold the pieces together, ignoring the fact that they no longer have a monopoly on information about companies any more. They are not the only ones who can do a cost analysis or a sensitivity spreadsheet. Very much like the Industrial Revolution's destruction of specialized guilds for making shoes or spinning cotton, the Internet takes specialized knowledge that used to belong exclusively to the banks and now makes it accessible to all.

As laptops replaced typewriters, the private equity model became the alternative to the traditional public stock markets and the corner banks. Today, anyone can afford computers to design and print their own contracts and documents. And today, all types of businesses (and business ideas) can access a variety of previously unimaginable financial sources and manage their investments with sophisticated Excel spreadsheets that would have been impossible 15 years ago. The Internet makes it possible for small groups of investors to manage a portfolio of company investments. In addition, the Internet websites enable the flow of cash by sharing knowledge of companies in much the same way the public markets did when they first evolved.

All too often, the public money allows companies to list and then they are ignored, orphaned with values dragging. Private equity gets involved with the business in a way the public market has lost by taking the long-term risk to invest in non-tangibles of R&D and innovation. Frankly, it is the aloof "give me the money" and treating the company as an ATM machine approach to investing that is tearing apart public money.

For similar reasons, you may have noticed that the music industry is crumbling, despite the frantic efforts of the big boys desperately propping up the crumbling walls. They try anything they can think of to legislate the old business model into permanence, even to such ridiculous extremes as suing teenagers (their primary clients!) for downloading tunes illegally.

While the traditional recording industry is one of the highest-profile casualties of the new information era, the public capital markets, the Dow Jones, *etc.* are also finding technology altering their game forever. Technology allows music lovers to access their favourite tunes in a hundred different ways, such as downloading music from the rock groups themselves, purchasing albums directly from small labels or buying just one hit song from Apple's iTunes. No longer do you have to buy an album full of lousy B-siders to get your one hit. In the same way, no longer is the IPO the be-all and end-all for ambitious business owners. Today, entrepreneurs can access capital for their companies in a hundred different ways.

Business owners' old ways of thinking now need to catch up to the new geography of money. No longer do companies have to get listed on the stock market to gain access to money. As a Trusted Advisor, you need to be able to understand this change and how to help your clients take advantage of this.

CHALLENGES FACING CEOS AND OWNERS

Before we look at this private money — private equity — it is worthwhile knowing the reasons why the stock market is no longer the primary place to access money. It will help you understand how private equity works and why CEOs enjoy it.

First of all, public companies are being legislated to the eyeballs as regulators request more forms to be filled out. As we've seen, today's public markets are feeling the turmoil of the bad apples (Enron, Madoff) who spoil the whole of the stock market. Companies pick up the tab and grapple with the soaring costs of complying with ever-tightening rules and regulations thought up by bureaucrats. The Sarbanes Oxley regulations are the death rattle of the Wall Street stock market model. Market forces are begging for a better way of doing things because public companies are drowning in that sea of paperwork and sucking out time and energy in filing reports that prove they are not embezzling funds through the compensation committee or money laundering for terrorists. Managers' time is taken away from the competitive battle. London has so far not subjected its venture capital exchange (AIM) to such a level of bureaucracy, which results in North American companies opting to list there first.

Another knock against the current industry model is the short-term outlook of the public stock markets. CEOs are hounded to raise revenues every quarter, which is rarely good for any business' long-term value. And no one can make excuses and say, "How could we have known that this quarterly braying for rising revenues would cause the markets to damage their own companies?"

The alarm bells were sounding more than a decade ago when MBA finance professors' favourite exam question was, "For 30% of your marks, show how a CEO can boost the stock in their publicly traded company." It was a clever exercise and it aptly demonstrated how a quarterly earnings focus wears a company thin. After all, there are only so many times you can water the wine. The problem is, this common question — designed to teach students how to recognize a company being asset-stripped — has now become the actual demand of shareholders playing the stock market. They have influence as shareholders are owners of the public businesses.

Who can blame the CEO's either? Show beleaguered CEOs a public shareholder who is willing to wait for a long-term R&D strategy to take effect while the balance sheet flatlines, and they will gasp in disbelief. Shareholders have proven to have the attention span of a kindergarten class with the ice-cream van driving past: they run to the next attractive deal as fast as their little legs can carry them. At Berkshire Hathaway Inc., Warren Buffett's strategy was the opposite of that of the rest of Wall Street — he actually invests and holds. For years. What a radical strategy. Who would have thought?

Inevitably, the costs of this alarming popularity of such short-term investment strategies, with their rigid quarterly focus, are caught up with the public markets — which once enjoyed a monopoly on efficient capital.

ADDING VALUE IN NEW WAYS

Wall Street and Bay Street's purpose is raising money to throw at innovation. It does achieve this and has done a wonderful job for decades. But a rock has been thrown into the pond: technology. Banks are no long the guild controlling the lending business. The ripple effect is that the market has found a new way to be more efficient. Goodbye to those uninvolved shareholders whose prime question is, "Is this company being run to feed me profits?" Now you have private equity teams with their skills and global rolodex, whose prime question is, "How can we collaborate with the management team and current owners?" The KPMG report on building private equity value says, "The private equity's firm's core objective is to add value to a deal above and beyond historical returns."[3] Who can blame companies for dumping the old for this new model.

How, you ask, will this private equity money work for the companies I advise? What is so new, does it cost more and how much control do they want?

THE BIG DIFFERENCE PRIVATE EQUITY BRINGS

The common attribute of good private equity investors around the world is that many are strategically brilliant. The best people in private equity have been entrepreneurs who cashed out. They can walk through the soil of an unknown field and instantly know the blood and sweat involved in getting that level of sweet, moist richness. They have planted their own business seeds in the topsoil of loans and bank financing. They have lived through the seasons it takes to germinate and grow a good crop, to get past the heartbreak of hailstorms and reap the rich harvest. They know seeds cannot be expected to produce green fields the very next quarter. They appreciate the life flow of business. They know what it takes to bring seeds and plants to maturity. They respect what has gone into making your business.

Use private equity to ...

- Inject capital for growth (minority investment)
- Give liquidity to owner (buyout control)
- Make transition from your business supporting your lifestyle to the discipline of a professionally managed business
- Change or step up strategy
- Add to communication competence
- Re-energize the business, refresh the team
- Manage risks

John Seminerio, an engineering graduate from Waterloo, started up the high-tech business Abatis in Vancouver, and partnered with the private equity firm Celtic House to get seed money. Abatis sold for over $2 billion and Seminerio went on to repeat his success. Now Seminerio has a hand in the venture capital funds Yaletown and Magellan Angel Partners, where he puts his remarkable leadership talent into the growth of the high-tech sector of the economy[4]. Imagine having the privilege of receiving personal attention from such a successful serial entrepreneur.

---

[3] KPMG in Canada, Building Private Equity Value (2007), <www.kpmg.ca/en/issues/durabilityPrivateEquity.html>.

[4] Gosia Brestovacki, Alumni Communication Officer, University of Waterloo Engineering, 2005 December Achievements, online at: <www.engineering.uwaterloo.ca>.

So you see how private equity can do far more than lend you money: private equity can help you grow revenues more than you could on your own or with a bank loan. The impact to your business is that private equity wants to see your business do well because it gets its money back and more. It also reaps the uplift of bonus performance. Private equity is in it for the same end game of profits as seriously as the owner.

LENDER *AND* OWNER

Your client may ask why he or she would want private equity investors if the bank will lend money for less and his or her business is ticking along well enough. Why invite trouble? *I would have to give up bits of my business in the form of shares, right? Is it really worth giving up precious equity for this unknown partner?*

The simple answer is yes.

In much the same way as banks or public markets, private equity money is held by professional funds and former entrepreneurs. The difference is that these investors are looking to become directly involved in your business. Some owners find this hugely alarming. They imagine an invading army rushing into their business, boots and clattering armour echoing around their offices and plants, while employees hide behind their desks trembling and praying that these newcomers will be nice and not shoot anyone.

This is the understandable instinct of a business owner. Yet the ownership is not forever. You have the option of buying back your company, earning shares as the five years proceed. Many top entrepreneurs use private equity for many years, changing funds every five years. They know the value.

THE BENEFITS OF PRIVATE EQUITY

When the announcer yelled out, "The winner of the media category, Ernst & Young Entrepreneur of the Year — *Somerset Entertainment*!" Andy Burgess grinned and bounded up to the stage to collect the award. It all looked so easy to be standing there in a tuxedo, waving the trophy, but this moment of appreciation came from painful years of slogging late into the night.

Andy Burgess is one of the owners of Somerset Entertainment, which produces and distributes specialty music initially to gift stores and other non-traditional retailers throughout North America, using those interactive displays where you can push a button and listen to the CDs.

The company has 28,000 displays in over 18,500 locations, which now include mass merchants and specialty stores.

With business and music awards filling their shelves, Somerset Entertainment made various acquisitions and moved from $5 million in revenues to $11 million, until eventually it was achieving $21 million in revenues. It bought a distributor and in 1998, levered up with four flavours of debt: term debt, mezzanine debt at 17% interest rate, revolving credit and a vendor take back loan. Then the cracks began to show.

The Buffalo distribution fulfillment centre had been shipping comfortably to over 100 different retail points when Andy asked, "Can you do higher volume?" Naturally, the distributor answered, "Yes!" when in fact that was far from the truth. Somerset had been a company with $8 million revenues and $2 million in EBITDA (earnings before interest, tax, depreciation and amortization) but had grown its supply chain with a distributor who turned out to be slow, with the uncanny ability to mess up orders. The distributor would say that it had shipped goods — the display case with CDs — and Somerset would then invoice the retailer, who turns out had not received anything except a bill. It was October — prime pre-holiday selling time with the Christmas season around the corner. Not good!

American retailers are the toughest sons of guns and were furious at being bamboozled. They told Andy they did not get the goods, but then told him not to bother coming around any more — they were through. Yikes! In one fell swoop, Somerset had gone from being swift deliverers of orders to slow, unreliable duds.

"We hit $36 million in sales with $8.5 million in EBITDA but our debt was at $15 million and for the first time, we stressed about breaking covenants. We got a valuation of $15 million and, with reluctance, we decided to go with a private equity investment of $21 million."

In hindsight, Andy says getting private equity was great for the company's motivation. It took the edge off the worry about money and retirement. "With private equity buying part ownership, we were allowed to take a large chunk out for ourselves straight away but still retain control. I had been working very hard and it was good to get $6 million out for the founder and owners."

The money meant Somerset could pay off its debt straight away and still have $4 million to make acquisitions. Andy says, "With that extra cash, we set up an office in Chicago which has turned out to be the vital springboard into the American market, taking Somerset to the next level. We have had a bad year in there, but we did not have to worry about the business blowing up. The peace of mind meant we could focus on battoning down the hatches to the storm and finding a new way forward."

The private equity partners proved to be great sounding boards when Somerset was making acquisitions. They were more aggressive in wanting the growth but respected Somerset's decision to step away from some identified targets.

"Also, when we nearly lost a key person," Andy adds, "they did bring him around and get him to stay."

Andy says, "When you are an entrepreneur working your butt off, it is great to get that cash pay out as well as have cash to grow the business. With private equity you get the best of both worlds — the cash liquidity without the rigorous scrutiny of the public market."

Not every company can go public, as this is an intense process and you may not get the necessary check marks next to your client's chart:

Is Your Client Ready for Public Market Money?

- they are making enough money,
- they are profitable,
- they have a strong growth curve for their revenues,
- they have a decent management team, and
- they are a good size.

Andy says, "At the time of the private equity deal, we were too small. With private equity investors, we got to retain control *and* we got liquidity. Private equity took us back from the brink with risky debt and looming covenants. They were the stepping stone to getting big enough until in 2005, Somerset did our initial public offering (IPO). Selling those secondary shares was sweet, too."

As Andy Burgess stood on the stage and let the applause of the audience sweep over him, it struck him how far Somerset Entertainment had come and what a ride it had been so far.

LEGACY BUSINESS OR LIFESTYLE?

Make no mistake: fund managers and venture capitalists seek out companies that appear to promise a good investment. They do want to fund a business where you are deeply committed and passionate. They want to grow your business into a legacy that goes beyond you.

Is your client at that stage where he or she may wish to let his or her business grow beyond him or her? Perhaps your client is ambitious enough to want his or her business to grow beyond his or her lifetime. You know that time creeps up awfully fast: help him or her to get on it while he or she is still energetic. Now consider an alternative — private equity. It can transform a business from an asset that merely supports a

Am I ready for investors — A quick self-test

- Do you want a business that suits your lifestyle or to grow?
- Can you take criticism?
- Can you share decision-making?
- Can you take advice and act on it?
- Do you have a succession plan?
- Do you have a written description of how partnership would look to you?
- Have you got legal information, financials organized?

lifestyle to a professional business that can afford the rigour required to make it up to the public stock market. With entrepreneur experts assisting companies, the odds of making it are increased.

Many businesses that make the transition from 100% owner controlled, with a nice lifestyle, to a legacy, from making a living to building a long-term, sustainable business, take on investment partners.

IMPORTANT DECISIONS

Okay — so the Stage 3 Legacy owner says, "I want to see this business expand aggressively. This is not an owner-controlled business. I want to see how far this business can go. Maybe even to being a Fortune 500 company." This is a fundamental and deeply personal decision, to go for the Stage 3 Legacy and seek private equity partners, as each owner has a widely differing set of decision criteria and risk parameters.

It is impossible to reach Level 3, and take on private equity, without answering two questions honestly:

Decision 1: Do I need to be in personal control of the business? Do I have personal comfort with a partnership with strong, talented people? Will I be able to let go of control? Do I have the skills to be a team player?

Decision 2: What level of risk can I bear? How much of this company do I want to personally carry? Could I do more for the business with OPM — other people's money? How much money does the business realistically need — $500,000, $1 million, $2 million, $5 million, $10 million, $21 million like Somerset Entertainment, or more? How much do I want my partners to help me? Would I like to reduce my risk by selling off an equity stake by 25% or maybe 75%?

Decision 1: Personal Control

A mushroom business in the United States (let's leave out the company name) had aspirations to grow and build a new plant and was getting close to signing up private equity partners, giving 51% control over to private equity partners, when the CEO called a fund manager in for a meeting. He said, "You know guys, I've run this business by myself for 20 years and I don't think I'm able to answer to anyone else. I don't think I can do this partnership. At first I was excited about it, but then I realized I'm too set in my ways. I think I'm going to stick with bank debt, which requires nothing of me."[5]

This feisty entrepreneur knew that he was a Stage 2 business and was content to remain as captain of his own ship. A Stage 3 owner would be ambitious enough to put aside his ego and move over to make room for other experts giving strategic opinions. This mushroom expert knew he had taken the business as far as he could on his own. *For his business to move to the next stage of investment, he knew it would require partners,* but he preferred to stay with what he knew and could control. He worried that if he opened the gate to private equity, the horse would bolt — with equity as the surprise jockey wielding the whip and charging off toward the horizon.

"We respect that owner's honesty," says the fund manager. "Absolutely. When dealing with private equity, it is important to understand what being a partner means." When you speak to your clients, business owners, the most important advice for you to emphasize is:

1. You must be prepared emotionally — probably the most critical but overlooked issue.
2. Your books must be straight.
3. Understand that the private equity partner brings far more to the table as its value-add.
4. Be honest about who you can work with (*i.e.*, personal dynamic is important).
5. Ensure that your ideas and goals are similar to those of the private equity partners.

Paradox of Success: Changing Leadership Style

The irony of owner-run companies is that their current success has often grown as a result of their autocratic leadership style. The challenge in

---

[5] Ed Reicklemen, keynote speaker, Canadian Innovator's Forum, CEO Roundtable, Toronto, May 2007.

moving to Stage 3 is adapting to a team of peers — partners — and learning together. It is not an easy evolution. The business founder will need to rein in and even put aside that very same dominating ego and personality that pushed, prodded and pulled the business to its current level. Only then is he or she ready to invite in partners.

Decision 2: Level of Investment and Risk

The second question entrepreneurs or CEOs need to ask is, how much risk are they willing to carry on their own? Being the sole decision-maker, with the bulk of ownership, raises the risk profile of the mushroom farmer's business. What would happen if he got hit by the proverbial bus? With strategic private equity partners, his business would not need to die too. His family and employees might appreciate that spread of the risk!

Also, there is the stretch of growing a business. A food-processing company CEO was happily engrossed by his business, and making a great deal of money. Inspired by a speech by Apple founder Steve Jobs, however, his true dream became to grow the company more. This CEO knew that he had the drive but worried about putting so much of his personal money at stake. He could not afford to take the risk, nor could he go to the public markets at that stage. To help his company evolve, the CEO sold 75% of the company's shares to private equity partners. They helped build up the staff, create systems and identify acquisitions. Ironically, *his 25% share ownership ended up giving him more financial return than if he had kept 100% to himself.* How incredibly satisfying when the more difficult course turns out also to be the best! Of course, if you're following Steve Jobs' advice, you must know the risks to growing. One additional point — Jobs may have lost his spot at Apple for a decade, but he says the company made it through that period due to the private equity financial partners in place.

Risk is relative. A medical device company wanted to launch a new product. As the owner knew it would cost $3 million to bring it to market, he weighed the risks: "Right now, I'm profitable. If all goes well, the product will grow my $50-million company to $60 million, with a cash flow of $1 million. If it does not go well, I'm in the hole for $3 million and it will take me five years to break even and get back to where I am now."

Pass!

But private equity partners will be lured to the possibility of growth. They catch a glimpse of the big fish in the dark water and appreciate the gleam of its scales; they will pick up the harpoon and take on the struggle, bleeding from holding the line, facing unbelievable adversity to bring home the fish others can only admire from the shoreline. That medical device company's CEO settled on admitting to the conservative nature of his personal and financial goals. "I built this business in my garage and now it has to fly without just me. Let's get in partners and share the risk." He got enough cash off the table to cover his retirement and compensate for all the hungry years, but he was still able to stay around to enjoy the new growth with the partners who brought valuable new skills — vision, contacts and patient capital through the storm. Heaven forbid you hit a rainy patch when financed by a bank.

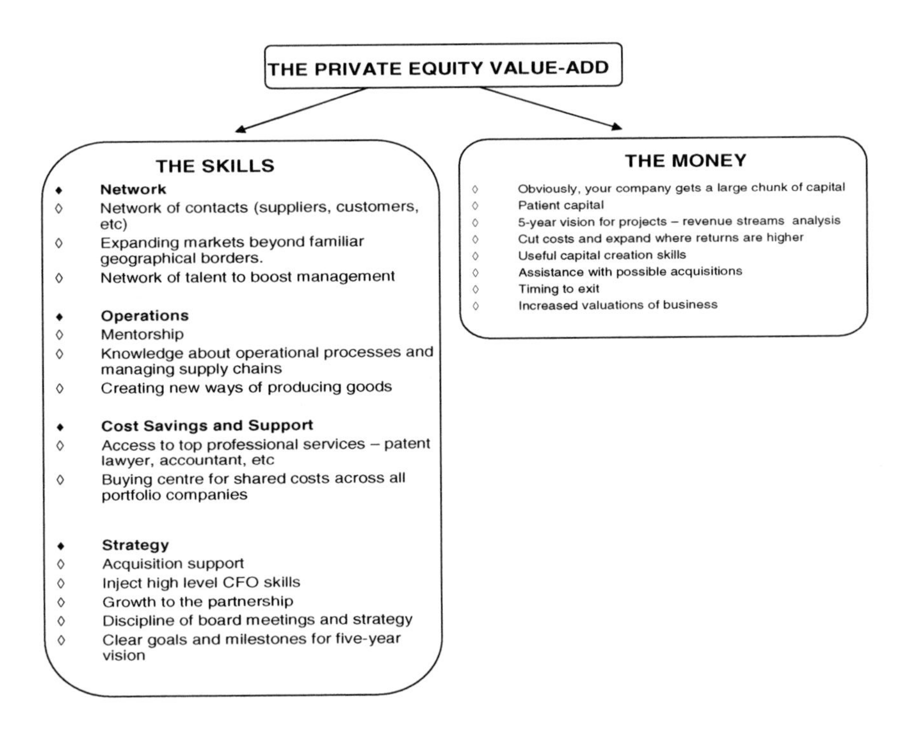

DECREASE OWNERSHIP BUT GAIN GROWTH

As a business owner, you set your risk by the amount of shares you sell to a private equity firm. It is vital to realize that you control the level of effort the fund will bring to your revenue growth.

You can sell:

- 100% or 90%, and walk away from the company. By selling 90%, you can keep shares and get some upside to the new ownership.
- 75%, and keep some control but benefit from the skills and Herculean effort put in by your new partners.

- 30%, and take on a minority shareholder — you cannot expect these partners to be hugely hands-on for that amount.

The level of ownership by financial partners will determine how much motivation and skills you can expect from them. Private equity partners will not be motivated to do a great deal of heavy lifting for just 30% of the rewards. Stage 3 owners appreciate that the more ownership is shared by the investor, the more effort the investor will make to help build revenues.

Valuation and Future Value

	Controlled	Shared	Majority	Sell
Ownership	30%	50%	75%	100%
Partnership role	Likely more silent	Board skills and strategy	"Heavy lifting" and active participation	Take over and you walk away

MORE VALUE FOR YOU

Private equity is a way "to get more juice out of a lemon", says Kenneth Langone, co-founder of Home Depot, and he does not have a problem with that, "It ain't complicated. We tend to mystify simple math."[6] If you understand the math, you will get how the private equity model will help you boost the value of your business.

MATH FORMULA FOR PRIVATE EQUITY

How does private equity come up with a value for a business? Likewise, if you understand the math for private equity investors, you will understand how they assign value to your business. Here's a simple way to understand it and to explain it to your clients.

How much will private equity help you in developing your business? Much like when someone buys a house, the bids vary depending on who is making an offer and what or whom he or she judges to be of value. Investors have reasons too. Imagine you have a house, and now you are going to share that investment with a private equity investor. Do you and your partner want it to suit your owner-controlled goals or is it for investment and resale, and, then, what return do you want?

---

6 Ben Levisohn, "The Joy of Private Equity" *Business Week* (8 August 2007), online <www.businessweek.com>.

The three variables for private equity in deciding valuation or how much to pay for a business can be explained using the house example:

- *Growth* — You rely on holding the house and getting a return because the neighbourhood went up in value. This is the "Buy, fix and sell" method.
- *Leverage* — You fix up the house and the neighbourhood rises in value. This is the "Buy, add value while paying down the debt and sell" method.
- *Multiple arbitrage* — You buy by borrowing other people's money. You develop the house as well as wait for the value of the neighbourhood to rise. This is the "Buy, arbitrage and sell" method.

Growth is when the fund pays five times the earnings and, a few years down the road, sells at seven times the earnings and the private equity is happy with that as it has made some money. The fund may pay seven times the earnings, knowing that there is the ability to grow the company at 10% over the next four years. Would you be satisfied if you buy a house, live in it for five years, pay the bills and the value of the neighbourhood goes up by 10%? It gives you a solid profit. One CEO, irritated by the use of EBITDA, declared his company to be worth a multiple of 13 times, thus assuming that he could grow his company at 23% a year. That is how valuation works — future earnings potential of the company. If you bring in partners and are confident that you can grow your business at 23% per year over the next five years, by all means expect such a steep multiple. Otherwise, now that you understand how debt is used as one of the key value levers, much like buying a house, you can see how funds would be challenged to see future profits.

DO YOU WANT TO BE IN CONTROL OR DO YOU WANT TO BE RICH?

There you have it — a rapid trip around the world of private equity. The big question to pose to your clients is whether they would like to be in the driver's seat or shift over and share. They can go it alone or they can widen the circle and include experts.

You can run far when alone. Have you ever noticed though, if you do fundraiser runs, that you run farther and more energetically when you are surrounded by a group of similar minded, focused people?

As a Trusted Advisor, you are the person most likely to introduce your clients to this interesting money. I can tell you one thing: if you are not telling your clients, your competitors will be.

CHAPTER 46

THE NUTS AND BOLTS OF AN ESTATE FREEZE — KEY CONSIDERATIONS

Corina Weigl*

Overview

For most business owners, succession planning can be a complicated affair. This chapter is meant to clarify this process by providing an overview of one of the most common tools in succession planning for a business owner — the estate freeze. While this tool is applicable to any business owner, this chapter will focus on the family business owner.

Learning Objectives

By the end of this chapter, you should:

- understand what an estate freeze is, its purpose and the issues to address when considering implementing an estate freeze;
- appreciate the decisions to be made when planning to implement an estate freeze; and
- know what the steps are to implement an estate freeze.

Not surprisingly, each family has its own set of considerations, and each family plan will require customization. Nevertheless, there are many similar issues to address when considering, planning or implementing an estate freeze for families.

* I would like to thank Joanna D. Gorman, Student-at-Law at Fasken Martineau DuMoulin LLP, for her assistance with this chapter.

CONSIDERING AN ESTATE FREEZE

What Is an Estate Freeze?

An estate freeze essentially involves reorganization of the future growth in value of a business in favour of the hands of the next generation.[1] The current business owner "freezes" his or her interest in the business at a particular point in time by exchanging this interest in the business for fixed value "freeze shares".[2] New shares reflecting the future growth in value of the business would then be issued to the next generation, either directly or *via* a discretionary family trust,[3] so that this next generation would participate in any future increase in value of the business.

This can be accomplished while allowing the owner to maintain control of the business before it (and its future value) is transferred to the next generation. To ensure this continued control, a discretionary family trust, coupled with voting shares, are commonly used. The future value of the business is then transferred to the next generation without triggering any immediate income tax liabilities, while allowing the owner to maintain control of the business.

While there are other means to achieve the concept of a "freeze" (*e.g.*, a direct gift of the business to the next generation), these other means will result in immediate tax liabilities and/or not being able to maintain control. In my experience, the corporate structure coupled with a discretionary family trust, is the most common type of estate freeze. It allows for control to be maintained by the owner, while also deferring the realization of any tax liabilities.

---

1 The focus of this chapter is on providing the future growth to the next generation of the owner. A freeze can, however, also be a reorganization of value in favour of management, employees or a third party.

2 An estate freeze can also involve the reorganization of the ownership interests of other appreciating assets. This chapter will, however, not address an estate freeze of this nature. Rather, it will focus on an estate freeze in the context of an incorporated family business. "Freeze shares" are shares the value of which is fixed at an amount equal to the value of the business at the time of the transaction.

3 A discretionary family trust is a vehicle for the ongoing ownership of the new "growth shares". More detailed information regarding this vehicle is provided in the section "Acquisition of New Equity Shares by a Discretionary Family Trust", later in this chapter. The beneficiaries of a family trust would often include the current and future children and the issue of the current and future children of the owner. To the extent the owner intends on benefiting other family members, the class of beneficiaries could include other family members.

What's the Purpose of an Estate Freeze?

I often recommend implementing an estate freeze because of the deferral of income tax liabilities that are otherwise imposed upon death. To understand why, certain aspects of capital gains[4] taxation need to be reviewed. For instance, under the federal *Income Tax Act*,[5] capital gains taxation is not limited to sale transactions. There are actually several circumstances where a capital gain is triggered, even though a sale transaction has not occurred. One such circumstance is with respect to death.

Generally speaking, each individual is deemed to have disposed of his or her property immediately before his or her death. If that deemed disposition gives rise to the realization of a capital gain, then income taxation will follow in the year of death as if the property were actually sold. There is an ability to defer the imposition of this tax liability, in particular, if the transfer of assets on the property owner's death is to the property owner's surviving spouse, or to a trust for the surviving spouse's exclusive benefit during his or her lifetime.[6]

The main drawback regarding the deemed disposition created by death is that there are no proceeds of sale available to satisfy the exigible taxes. This often creates difficulty with respect to a significant illiquid asset, such as a family business. Very significant amounts may have to be borrowed or premature sales made in order to generate sufficient funds to satisfy the tax liability. When this is the case, I often suggest that owners acquire life insurance to ensure the liquidity exists to satisfy the tax liability.

It is in this context that an estate freeze serves its main purpose. An estate freeze fixes the burden of capital gains taxation on death. In effect, the owner's current equity in a family business is translated into a non-growth asset. For example, equity[7] shares which today may be worth

---

4 A "capital gain" is defined as "the profit realized on a disposition of certain properties by a taxpayer where the property is not property described in inventory. There is a capital gain where the proceeds of disposition exceed disposition costs plus the cost (or the "adjusted cost base") of the property", pursuant to sections 39 and 40 of the *Income Tax Act* (Canada), R.S.C. 1985, c. 1 (5th Supp.). Joanne E. Magee, ed., *Insight into Canadian Income Tax 2007-2008* (Toronto: Thomson Canada Limited, 2007) at 350.

5 All references to the "Act" are to the *Income Tax Act* (Canada), R.S.C. 1985, c. 1 (5th Supp.), as amended.

6 Under the Act, the definition of "spouse" includes common law spouses of a one-year duration and same-sex relationships.

7 References to "equity", "common" and "participating" shares are intended to refer to those shares of a corporation that reflect the value of the corporation after its liabilities (including all issued and outstanding preference shares) are accounted for.

millions of dollars, but are subject to growth with the increasing value of the business, are exchanged for non-participating preference shares with a fixed value equal to the current fair market value[8] of the owner's equity shares. New equity shares are then issued to the next generation or to a trust for the benefit of the next generation. Thus, any future growth in the value of the business is translated to the new equity shares. The capital gains tax on the capital growth which occurs after the date of the freeze is deferred until the holders of the new common shares pass away or the business is sold.

In my experience, the resulting deferral may be extremely valuable. However, income tax consequences are not the only relevant factor.

Another purpose an estate freeze serves is to implement a structure that allows for some income splitting with family members. In the context of a family unit, income-splitting refers to the shifting of assets from a high tax rate taxpayer to a lower tax rate taxpayer, thereby allowing a family unit to benefit from more after-tax dollars. Needless to say, the tax rules do not support this type of planning. To discourage it, various rules, referred to as the "income attribution rules", exist. These rules must be considered whenever income-producing assets are transferred from a taxpayer to a related taxpayer, in a situation where taxes may be reduced.

A third purpose of an estate freeze might be to use or multiply access to the $750,000 lifetime capital gains exemption associated with the disposition of "qualified small business corporation shares"[9] ("QSBC shares" and the "Capital Gains Exemption"). This will be discussed in greater detail below.

Lastly, an estate freeze serves as a form of creditor protection for the owner by converting the owner's equity interest in the business into fixed value preference shares that may have priority on a liquidation of the business.

---

[8] "Fair market value" means the price that the property would have brought at the time, considering its highest and most profitable use, if then offered for sale in the open market.

[9] The $750,000 lifetime capital gains exemption allows a taxpayer who disposes of shares that qualify as "qualified small business corporation shares" to shelter up to $750,000 in capital gains thereby not having to pay taxes on up to $375,000 of taxable capital gains. To qualify as QSBC shares, the shares must satisfy asset use and minimum share ownership tests, outlined in subsection 110.6(1) of the Act.

Should an Estate Freeze Be Implemented? Is It the Right Time?

What Are the Non-tax Considerations?

While the income tax savings can be substantial, the income tax consequences are not the only relevant factor. Before engaging in an estate freeze, a prudent advisor must address several considerations that are not income-tax related.

First, the owner must be comfortable that his or her assets are more than sufficient to meet his or her needs for his or her lifetime, as well as those of his or her spouse, if the spouse does not have independent means. One must also consider the owner and spouse's desired standard of living, making sure it will always be maintained. Do not forget to take into account the future impact of inflation and potential emergencies or special unforeseen circumstances that may arise during the lifetimes of the owner and spouse.[10] If they are not comfortable with the current state of their financial affairs such that they may require some of the future value of their business, remember that an estate freeze need not be a 100% freeze. A lesser percentage of an owner's interest in the business could be subject to a freeze.

Second, make sure to consider the stage in life of the next generation at the time of implementing the freeze or when shares of the corporation may ultimately be distributed to the next generation. Any reorganization that proposes to transfer the future growth in value of a business to the next generation must consider the family law implications that may arise in respect of their direct receipt of equity shares of the business, or their being a beneficiary of a discretionary family trust, and thereby potentially receiving equity shares of the business from the trust at some point in the future.

Third, do not forget to undertake a thorough assessment of the ability and desire of the next generation to continue the family business. If a client were to tell me that it is unlikely that the business will be continued, then I would suggest that from an economic and family harmony perspective, the business should be sold while the owner is alive and active in the business. In this context, an estate freeze may not be a fruitful exercise.

Another important consideration is the "softer" issue related to prematurely putting significant wealth in the hands of the next generation, and

---

[10] Perhaps the biggest unknowns of a financial nature are: how long will the owner and his or her spouse live; what kind of care will the owner and his or her spouse require in their *golden years*; and what will the costs of that care be?

the impact on the owner's psyche if he or she no longer has total control of his or her "other child" — the business itself.

What Are the Tax Considerations?

Capital Gains Exemption

There is a silver lining for business owners in certain situations. The shares issued to the next generation, either directly or through a discretionary family trust, may qualify for the $750,000 lifetime capital gains exemption for QSBC shares defined earlier as the "Capital Gains Exemption". As noted earlier, the Capital Gains Exemption will shelter up to $750,000 of capital gains if the shares are actually transferred to the next generation before the shares are sold or deemed to be sold. In this regard, make sure to consider:

(i) whether the company satisfies the test for being a "Small Business Corporation" ("SBC"); and

(ii) whether the shares satisfy the test for being QSBC shares.

The definitions of a SBC and a QSBC share are very complex. An otherwise qualifying share can easily fall offside. The definition of a QSBC share has three components which must be met. They are outlined below. However, to ensure the shares qualify as QSBC shares, one should obtain advice from the company's accountant. Further, given the "holding" periods described below, planning to use the Capital Gains Exemption may need to begin well prior to a potential sale or estate freeze.

- **Small Business Corporation Test:** At the time of their disposition, the shares of the company must be shares of a SBC. A SBC is a Canadian-controlled private corporation ("CCPC") where all or substantially all[11] of the fair market value of the CCPC's assets are used principally[12] in carrying on an active business primarily[13] in Canada, or are shares of the capital stock of another SBC connected to the company.
- **Holding Period Shareholder Test:** The individual shareholder (including a trust), or a person or partnership related to the individual shareholder, must own the shares during the two-year period before the sale of shares.

---

[11] "All" or "substantially all" is defined to mean 90% or more.

[12] Greater than 50%.

[13] Greater than 50%.

- **Holding Period Asset Test:** Throughout the two-year period before a sale, the company's shares must have been shares of a CCPC of which more than 50% of the fair market value of its assets were mainly used in an active business carried on primarily in Canada by the corporation or a related corporation and/or shares of other qualifying connected corporations. For the shares of a corporation to qualify as QSBC shares, this test must be met at each point in time during the two-year period.

Double Tax Potential

Another tax consideration is the potential for double tax that arises on the owner's death. Remember that a company is a separate taxpayer from the shareholder/owner. Therefore, a deemed disposition on death by a shareholder/owner of the shares of the company he or she owns will result in the realization of accrued capital gains, without a corresponding realization by the company of the accrued capital gains on the underlying assets of the company. However, certain strategies can ease this outcome, particularly as it arises on death. These strategies must be implemented within the first year of the shareholder/owner's death. Therefore, one must consider any post-mortem planning that will need to be in place, even when the initial freeze is considered.

Equally important are factors related to the size of the company's refundable tax or capital dividend account[14] balances, as well as the impact of the eligible dividend tax regime introduced in 2007.

GAAR

Lastly are considerations relating to the General Anti-Avoidance Rule ("GAAR"). However, it is beyond the scope of this chapter to discuss those considerations.

---

[14] The "capital dividend account" is essentially the untaxed fraction of capital gains. It includes any amounts received as capital dividends from other corporations, so that the 'tax-free characteristic' of any particular amount is preserved even if paid through a chain of holding corporations.

PLANNING AN ESTATE FREEZE

When Can You Use an Estate Freeze?

The estate freeze structure is a great way to transfer the future growth in value of assets to the next generation. However, it only applies to the following types of assets:

- incorporated businesses;
- real estate holdings;
- unincorporated investment assets; and
- partnership assets.

As noted, this chapter will only discuss considerations related to an estate freeze in the context of an incorporated business, with emphasis on the family business.

What Are the Options for an Estate Freeze Structure?[15]

Section 85 — Holding Company Freeze

Overview

Subsection 85(1) of the Act allows certain properties to be transferred by a taxpayer to a taxable Canadian corporation (the "transferee corporation") for proceeds equal to an amount elected by the taxpayer and the transferee corporation. While the amount is subject to certain restrictions, to avoid triggering taxes, it would typically equal the tax cost of the properties transferred. Members of the next generation would acquire newly issued common or equity shares of the transferee corporation either directly or *via* a discretionary family trust of which they could be beneficiaries.

Subsection 85(1) can be used in many contexts, such as:

- to transfer an unincorporated business to a corporation without income tax consequences (I often recommend this to clients, since it provides some protection to the owner from claims of creditors, or it allows for the small business deduction to be claimed in respect of the income of the business);

[15] There are several options for structuring an estate freeze. This chapter will focus on the two more common options: a section 85 "holding company" freeze and a section 86 "internal" freeze.

- to transfer a business from one corporation to another as part of an estate freeze;
- to transfer shares of one corporation to another as part of an estate freeze;
- to trigger a capital gain, crystallizing all or part of the owner's Capital Gains Exemption; or
- any combination of the above.

What Are the Rules?

Subsection 85(1) applies if a taxpayer disposes of any property that is "eligible property" to a "taxable Canadian corporation" for consideration[16] and that includes shares of the transferee corporation. The taxpayer and the corporation must file a joint election. These requirements will be discussed below. Subject to certain limitations, the elected amount is deemed to be the taxpayer's proceeds of disposition of the property and the corporation's cost of the property. The basic structure of an estate freeze using a holding company structure appears in Diagram 1, below.

Diagram 1

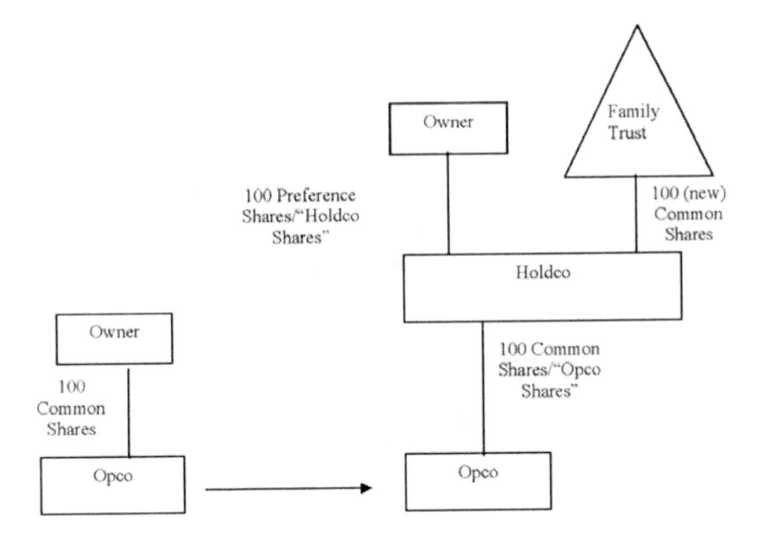

[16] "Consideration" within a legal context is generally defined as the "cause, motive, price, or impelling influence which induces a contracting party to enter into a contract. ... Some right, interest, profit or benefit accruing to one party, or some forbearance, detriment, loss, or responsibility, given, suffered, or undertaken by the other. ... It is a basic, necessary element for the existence of a valid contract that is legally binding on the parties": *Deluxe Black's Law Dictionary*, 6th ed., *s.v.* "consideration".

In this case, the owner will be disposing of his or her shares in his or her operating company (referred to throughout as "Opco Shares") to a holding company (referred to throughout as "Holdco"). To effect this disposition, the Opco Shares must qualify as capital property.

In this context, Holdco must be a "taxable Canadian corporation".[17]

The owner must receive shares of Holdco (referred to throughout as "Holdco Shares") as full or partial consideration for the transfer of Opco Shares to Holdco.

A joint election must be filed by the owner and Holdco on a prescribed form[18] and by a certain date. This form is to be filed at the owner's taxation centre separate from any tax returns. While the Act allows for such forms to be filed late or amended, the client will likely be exposed to penalties as a result. For this reason, responsibility for filing the election should be documented in writing.

Provincial corporate tax legislation may also require that an election be filed. In some provinces, a valid election filed under section 85(1) is deemed to also be a valid election for purposes of the provincial counterpart.

What Are the Limitations on the Elected Amount?

A prudent advisor must understand the limitations on the amount that may be elected in respect of the Opco Shares which the owner transfers to Holdco. If the elected amount falls offside one of the limitations, the amount will be deemed to have met the limitation. However, tax consequences may arise if the deeming provisions apply.

The elected amount impacts both the owner and Holdco. First, the cost of the Opco Shares to Holdco will generally be equal to the elected amount. Second, the proceeds of disposition of the Opco Shares to the owner will generally be equal to the elected amount. Accordingly, it is important to understand the limitations that are imposed on what the elected amount can be.

The limitations are as follows:

- The elected amount cannot exceed the fair market value of the Opco Shares. If it does, then the owner will be deemed to have received a shareholder benefit equal to the difference between the elected amount and the fair market value of the Opco Shares.

---

[17] The Act defines this to be a corporation that was not exempt from tax under Part I of the Act. A corporation is a "Canadian corporation" at any time if it is resident in Canada at that time and if it was either incorporated in Canada or resident in Canada from June 18, 1971 to the particular time. See subsection 89(1) of the Act.

[18] Form T2057.

- The elected amount cannot be less than any non-share consideration received by the owner on the transfer.[19] Therefore, if I want the transfer to have no tax consequences to the owner, then the owner cannot receive non-share consideration, such as debt, that is greater than the adjusted cost base[20] of the Opco Shares. If the elected amount is less than any non-share consideration, it will be deemed to equal the non-share consideration. If the non-share consideration is greater than the adjusted cost base, it will trigger the realization of a capital gain to the owner and a resulting tax liability.
- The elected amount cannot be less than the lesser of the fair market value of the Opco Shares and their "cost amount". In other words, the owner cannot create an artificial loss.
- If the fair market value of the Opco Shares transferred to Holdco exceeds the greater of (i) the fair market value of the consideration received by the owner (*i.e.*, the Holdco Shares and any non-share consideration) and (ii) the elected amount otherwise determined under the Act, and any part of the excess value is a benefit that the owner wanted to confer on a person related to him or her, then the elected amount will be increased by that part of the excess associated with the benefit. To ensure an appropriate elected amount is chosen, the owner should obtain advice from Opco's accountant concerning the cost base of the Opco Shares. Further, the owner should obtain an appropriate valuation of the Opco Shares. Lastly, I always include a "price adjustment clause" in the share conditions of the Holdco Shares received by the owner. This concept will be discussed in greater detail later in this chapter.

What Are Some of the Pitfalls?

Experience has taught me that whenever a section of the Act provides benefits to taxpayers, there is the potential for unintended results. Some

---

[19] The owner may wish to receive non-share consideration in the form of a promissory note. For example, where the Opco Shares have an adjusted cost base that is other than nominal, the receipt of a promissory note equal to the adjusted cost base of the Opco Shares will allow the owner to extract the adjusted cost base on a more efficient basis (*i.e.*, without having to call for the redemption of any preference shares of Holdco with the ensuing need for Opco to ensure it can, from a corporate solvency point of view, pay dividends to Holdco thereby allowing Holdco to redeem preference shares).

[20] Pursuant to section 54 of the Act, the term "adjusted cost base" means: for property other than depreciable property, the cost of the property to the taxpayer adjusted as a result of certain transactions. See the section for a more detailed description of the term.

of the more common pitfalls in connection with a section 85 holding company estate freeze are discussed below.

- **V-Day Shares:** If the Opco Shares which the owner intends to transfer to Holdco include shares of the same class, some of which were acquired prior to December 31, 1971 (commonly referred to as "V-Day") and some after that date, the adjusted cost base of the pre-V-day and post-V-day shares must be determined separately. Separate elections are also made in respect of each group. If this is not carried out, adverse tax consequences may arise to the owner. If this is an issue, the company's accountant ought to be consulted.
- **"Boot"[21] Received:** A prudent advisor will ensure that the amount of any non-share consideration received by the owner does not give rise to a deemed dividend.[22]
- **Paid-Up Capital of Holdco Shares:** The amount which can be added to the paid-up capital[23] of the Holdco Shares received by the owner will be limited by subsection 85(2.1) of the Act. For corporate purposes, the stated capital of the Holdco Shares must be restricted to the amount of the paid-up capital.
- **Double Taxation:** I mentioned above that a transfer of Opco Shares to Holdco may result in double taxation, particularly on the death of the owner. This arises because the accrued gain on the Opco Shares is also built into the Holdco Shares received by the owner. As a result, the same gain can be taxed once on the disposition of the Opco Shares by Holdco, and again on the disposition of the Holdco Shares by the owner. This is particularly the case if Opco Shares must be sold by Holdco on the death of the owner. Post-mortem strategies are available to alleviate this burden. They must, however, be implemented within the first anniversary of the owner's death.
- **Stop-Loss Rules:** Occasionally, I am presented with a situation where the owner, his or her spouse or a person or group of persons with whom the transferor is related directly or indirectly controls Holdco. In this context, any capital loss realized on the transfer of the Opco Shares to Holdco will be denied.

---

[21] Non-share consideration is often referred to as "boot".

[22] It is beyond the scope of this chapter to discuss the implications of subsections 84.1(1) and 212.1(1) of the Act.

[23] "Paid up capital" generally represents a return to shareholders of the capital originally invested in the corporation.

- **Corporate Attribution Rule:** The rule in subsection 74.4(2) applies to both holding company freezes implemented under section 85 and internal freezes implemented under section 86 will be discussed in greater detail in the section "Implementing an Estate Freeze", below.

Section 86 — Internal Company Freeze

Overview

Where a holding company freeze is inappropriate, given the client's situation, a section 86 internal company freeze is often a useful tool to consider. It allows an owner of equity or common shares in a company to convert those shares into preference or "freeze" shares, on a tax-deferred basis. New common or equity shares are acquired by the next generation either directly or *via* a discretionary family trust of which they are a potential beneficiary.

What Are the Rules?

Section 86 applies where, in the course of a reorganization of the capital of a corporation, the owner disposes of shares of the capital stock of the corporation, usually common or equity shares (referred to throughout as the "Old Shares"), in exchange for property received from the corporation that includes other shares of the corporation. These other shares are the preference or "freeze" shares (referred to throughout as the "New Shares").

To use this tool properly, an advisor must ensure that the Old Shares are "capital property" to the owner. The Old Shares must also represent all of the shares of the particular class owned by the owner at the time of the disposition. If the Old Shares are shares of a wholly owned operating company that have been held by the owner since incorporation, it is likely that the Old Shares qualify as capital property.

There are a couple of other things that the owner must do in order for this section to have effect. First, he or she must dispose of all shares of a particular class that are owned by him or her at the time of the disposition.

Second, as consideration for the disposition of the Old Shares to the corporation, the owner must receive shares of capital stock of the corporation. Like a section 85 freeze, the owner can also receive non-share consideration.

Both of these conditions can be implemented by the filing of articles of amendment to the company's articles of incorporation. In particular, a reorganization of capital of a corporation may include: (i) a transaction which adds, changes or removes any rights, privileges, restrictions or conditions attaching to the shares of a corporation; or (ii) a transaction, pursuant to which the shares of any class of a corporation are changed into a different number of shares of the same class or into the same or a different number of shares of another class.

When these conditions are met, the section applies automatically. There is no need for an election to be filed. If, however, an election under section 85 is filed, then section 86 will not apply. In my experience, there may be circumstances where this is preferable.

Diagram 2, below, shows a section 86 internal company freeze.

Diagram 2

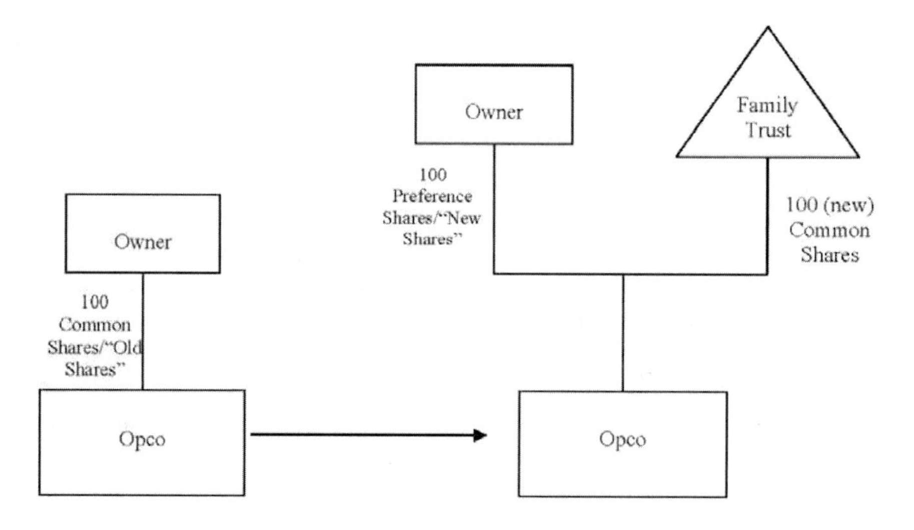

What Are the Tax Consequences?

If the owner receives non-share consideration, then the cost of the non-share consideration is deemed to be its fair market value at the time of the disposition of the Old Shares. This will affect the cost to be allocated to the New Shares received by the owner.[24] In particular, the cost of the New Shares is equal to the adjusted cost base of the Old Shares less the fair market value of the non-share consideration.

---

[24] There are special rules that apply when there are different classes of New Shares issued to the owner.

The proceeds of disposition of the Old Shares is equal to the cost of the New Shares plus the fair market value of any non-share consideration received.

Therefore, to avoid triggering a tax liability to the owner on the exchange of his or her Old Shares, I would ensure that the fair market value of any non-share consideration received does not exceed the adjusted cost base of the Old Shares.

Where the Old Shares were held by the owner on December 31, 1971 (being V-Day) and thereafter without interruption until the time of the reorganization, special rules may apply to determine the adjusted cost base of the New Shares. If there is potential for the New Shares to drop below the V-day value of the Old Shares, one may want to avoid the application of these special rules. Otherwise they may prevent the owner from realizing the capital loss.

If the rules of section 86 are complied with, the result is that the realization of the capital gain accrued on the Old Shares at the time of the reorganization will be deferred until a subsequent disposition of the New Shares by the owner.

What Are Some of the Pitfalls?

As expected, where provisions of the Act potentially give a benefit to taxpayers, there are unintended results which may occur. I will outline some of the more common pitfalls to be avoided below.

- **Shareholder Benefit:** Make sure that the fair market value of the New Shares and other consideration received by the owner is equal to the fair market value of the Old Shares disposed of by the owner. If this is not the case, the owner will incur increased tax liabilities in the form of a shareholder benefit.
- **Deemed Gift:** Alternatively, if the value of the New Shares and other consideration received by the owner is less than the value of the Old Shares, subsection 86(2) may deem the owner to have realized a capital gain in the course of the reorganization. It will apply if any portion of the excess value of the Old Shares (referred to as the "gift portion") is a benefit that the owner intended to confer on a person related to the owner. If these conditions are satisfied, the following rules will apply:
  (i) The owner is deemed to have disposed of the Old Shares for proceeds of disposition equal to the sum of the gift portion plus the value of any non-share consideration received. This may trigger a capital gain.

(ii) Any capital loss which would otherwise result from the disposition of the Old Shares is deemed to be nil.

(iii) The cost to the owner of the New Shares received is deemed to be the amount by which the adjusted cost base to the owner of the Old Shares exceeds the sum of the fair market value of the non-share consideration and the gift portion. This may be less than the adjusted cost base otherwise determined, thereby increasing future taxes owing.

- **Deemed Dividends:** If the value of any non-share consideration received for the Old Shares is greater than the paid-up capital of the Old Shares, the corporation will be deemed to have paid a dividend equal to the amount by which the value of the non-share consideration exceeds such paid-up capital. The amount of dividends deemed received will reduce the taxpayer's proceeds of disposition of the Old Shares. The taxpayer may also realize a capital loss on the exchange if the adjusted cost base of the Old Shares to the taxpayer is greater than their paid-up capital. It is often the case that the owner or his or her spouse controls the corporation immediately after the exchange. In that situation, the capital loss is deemed to be nil and the amount of the loss otherwise determined is added to the adjusted cost base of the New Shares.
- **Corporate Attribution:** The rule in subsection 74.4(2) applies to both holding company freezes implemented under section 85 and internal freezes implemented under section 86. This will be discussed in greater detail in the section "Implementing an Estate Freeze", below.

IMPLEMENTING AN ESTATE FREEZE

What Are the Steps to Implement an Estate Freeze?

Section 85 — Holding Company Freeze

To implement a section 85 holding company freeze, there are 12 general steps to be followed. They are listed below.

1. Determine the fair market value of the Opco Shares.
2. Prepare a director's resolution of the value of the Opco Shares.
3. Create a corporation with the following authorized share capital: (i) a fixed number of preference or "freeze" shares (*i.e.*, the Holdco Shares) with the share attributes described elsewhere in this chap-

ter; (ii) an unlimited number of "thin voting" shares with the share attributes described elsewhere in this chapter; and (iii) an unlimited number of common or equity shares. These must include the right to participate in the future growth in value of Holdco (and thus indirectly Opco) beyond the value of the Holdco Shares issued to the owner, and may include discretionary dividend and voting rights.

4. Produce a Share Purchase Agreement stating that the owner agrees to sell the Opco Shares to Holdco in exchange for the Holdco Shares and any non-share consideration to be received as part of the transaction. This Agreement will also document responsibility for the filing of the joint election Form T2057. It may also include the fair market value of the Opco Shares and the attributes of the Holdco Shares. Lastly, it will usually include a price adjustment clause, described in greater detail below.

5. Determine the fair market value of the consideration received by Holdco in exchange for the issuance by Holdco of the Holdco Shares to the owner.

6. Surrender for cancellation the owner's share certificate for the Opco Shares.

7. Issue the share certificate to the owner for the Holdco Shares.

8. If a discretionary family trust is to own the new common shares of Holdco, create a discretionary family trust by (i) executing a trust agreement among the settlor and the trustees, and (ii) settling the discretionary family trust by having the settlor transfer property to the trustees.

9. Acquire new common shares of Holdco for nominal consideration by the trustees of the discretionary family trust with either debt financing from a bank or other third party, or (potentially) a gift to the trustees of the subscription proceeds. If the latter option is chosen, you must ensure that the donor of the subscription proceeds is not a beneficiary of the trust. If the donor is a trustee, he or she must be one of three trustees acting by majority decision. Otherwise, the future distribution of any shares from the trust to any one of its beneficiaries will have potentially serious tax consequences.

   If the owner is not freezing his or her entire interest in Opco, *i.e.*, only a partial freeze is being implemented, then the owner may also need to acquire some of the new common shares of Holdco.

   Also be mindful of family law issues applicable to members of the next generation. If there are such issues, the owner may want to acquire the new common shares of Holdco and then gift those common shares to the trustees of the trust. This could provide some family law protection to the next generation.

The next generation can also acquire the new common shares of Holdco directly. Make sure that the children are qualified to become shareholders, and that control mechanisms are put in place for the owner. Again, if family law issues are relevant, the owner may wish to acquire the new common shares and then gift them to the next generation. This can only be considered where the children are over the age of majority.

10. Have those persons (*e.g.*, the trustees of the discretionary family trust) who are acquiring the new common shares of Holdco execute subscription documents for those shares.
11. Issue share certificates for the new common shares of Holdco to those persons (*e.g.*, the trustees of the discretionary family trust) who are acquiring the new common shares of Holdco.
12. If the owner is to maintain control of Opco *via* "thin voting" shares of Holdco, execute subscription documents for the "thin voting" shares of Holdco by the owner and issue the same to the owner. See discussion below.

Section 86 — Internal Company Freeze

To implement a section 86 internal company freeze, there are 11 general steps to be followed. They are listed below.

1. Determine the fair market value of the Old Shares.
2. Prepare a director's resolution of the value of the Old Shares.
3. Direct a shareholders' resolution authorizing an amendment to the articles of the corporation to create the New (or freeze) Shares, and to change the existing Old Shares into the New Shares.
4. Prepare and file articles of amendment to create the New (or freeze) Shares, and to change the existing Old Shares into the New Shares.
5. Surrender for cancellation the share certificate for the Old Shares.
6. Issue a share certificate for the New Shares.
7. If a discretionary family trust is to own the new common shares, create a discretionary family trust by (i) executing a trust agreement among the settlor and the trustees, and (ii) settling the discretionary family trust by having the settlor transfer property to the trustees.
8. Direct the trustees of the discretionary family trust to acquire the new common shares of Opco for nominal consideration with either debt financing from a bank or other third party, or (potentially) a

gift to the trustees of the subscription proceeds. If the latter option is chosen, ensure that the donor of the subscription proceeds is not a beneficiary of the trust. If the donor is a trustee, he or she must be one of three trustees acting by majority decision. Otherwise, the future distribution of any shares from the trust to a beneficiary thereof will have potentially serious tax consequences.

9. If the owner is not freezing his or her entire interest in Opco, *i.e.*, only a partial freeze is being implemented, then the owner may also need to subscribe for some of the new common shares of Opco. To execute this properly, ensure that the owner has disposed of all of his of her Old Shares. This may require the conditions of the new common shares to be slightly different from the conditions attached to the Old Shares.

   Alternatively, if there are family law issues applicable to members of the next generation, the owner may want to acquire the new common shares of Opco, and then gift those common shares to the trustees of the trust. This may provide some family law protection to the next generation.

   It is also possible for the next generation to acquire the new common shares directly. In that case, the children must be qualified to become shareholders, and control mechanisms must be put in place for the owner. Again, if family law issues are relevant, the owner may wish to acquire the new common shares and then gift the new common shares he or she has acquired to the next generation. Again, this can only be considered where the children are over the age of majority.

10. Have those persons (*i.e.*, the trustees of the discretionary family trust) who are acquiring the new common shares of Opco execute subscription documents for those shares.

11. Issue share certificates for the new common shares of Opco to those persons (*i.e.*, the trustees of the discretionary family trust) who are acquiring the new common shares of Opco.

Does the Owner Have the Capital Gains Exemption to Utilize?

As a Trusted Advisor, you need to determine whether the owner has part or all of the Capital Gains Exemption in respect of the disposition of "qualifying small business corporation" shares (defined earlier as "QSBC shares"). The Capital Gains Exemption will allow an owner to extract up to $750,000 of capital growth from the corporation without paying the associated capital gains tax. To do this, consider whether the corporation is a "small business corporation" and whether the shares qualify as QSBC shares. See earlier discussion.

If you determine that the owner has part of the Capital Gains Exemption available and the shares to be "frozen" qualify as QSBC shares, then consider whether the estate freeze transaction should be structured to crystallize the balance of the Capital Gains Exemption available to the owner. This will reduce the ultimate tax liability the owner will realize on a future redemption or disposition of the Holdco Shares or New Shares the owner received on the freeze transaction. Given that it is never certain that a tax benefit which allows a taxpayer to extract capital growth from a business without paying taxes will continue to exist, if the owner has not fully used the Capital Gains Exemption it is highly recommended that he or she "use it or (potentially) lose it".

There are two basic options available to crystallize the Capital Gains Exemption. First, in the context of a section 85 transaction, the elected amount can be greater than the adjusted cost base of the Opco Shares by the amount of the Capital Gains Exemption remaining. This can also be accomplished on a section 86 transaction by filing a form T2057 election. Second, the owner could receive non-share consideration equal to the adjusted cost of the Opco Shares or the Old Shares plus the amount of the Capital Gains Exemption remaining to the owner.

What Rights or Attributes Should the "Freeze Shares" Have?

To avoid the adverse tax consequences referred to earlier, the fair market value of the Holdco Shares, or the New Shares as the case may be (and any non-share consideration), received by the owner must equal the fair market value of the Opco Shares (in the case of a section 85 freeze) or the Old Shares (in the case of a section 86 freeze). This will require an assessment of the fair market value of the Opco Shares or the Old Shares.

With respect to the value of the Holdco or New Shares (also referred to as the "freeze" shares received by the owner), the Canada Revenue Agency ("CRA") generally accepts that the fair market value of shares that are redeemable at the option of the holder is equal to the redemption amount. Accordingly, the redemption amount of the Holdco Shares or the New Shares should be fixed at the fair market value of the Opco Shares or the Old Shares, less any non-share consideration received by the owner. To ensure that the value of the Holdco or New Shares received by the owner as consideration is maintained, the following rights and conditions should be attached to those shares:

1. the shares are redeemable by the corporation at an amount equal to the fair market value of the Opco Shares or Old Shares;

2. the shares are retractable at the option of the owner at the same amount;
3. in the event of a liquidation, dissolution or winding-up of the corporation, the shares have a preference on the distribution of the corporation's assets to receive an amount equal to the redemption or retraction amount;
4. the shares must not be subject to a restriction on transfer other than that required to qualify the corporation as a private company under corporate law;
5. the shares may or may not have voting rights but, if the relevant corporate law statute does not so provide, they should at least have voting rights on any matter involving a change to the rights, conditions or limitations attaching to them;
6. the shares cannot permit the corporation to pay dividends on, or redeem, other classes of shares if the payment of such dividend or the redemption of such shares would result in the corporation having insufficient net assets to redeem the shares;
7. while a dividend right is not vital, the CRA prefers that the freeze shares pay a reasonable dividend rate (any dividend rate cannot, however, exceed a reasonable rate; the dividend rate is typically non-cumulative but it can be cumulative);[25] and
8. there is a price adjustment mechanism, which will be described in greater detail below.

Is It Important to Ensure the Fair Market Value Is Accurate?

Equally important to the rights and conditions discussed above is ensuring that the redemption/retraction amount of the Holdco Shares or New Shares received by the owner is equal to the fair market value of the Opco Shares (in the case of a section 85 freeze) or the Old Shares (in the case of a section 86 freeze). This requires two things.

First, make sure to include a price adjustment clause. It allows the parties to a transaction to adjust the price if the CRA subsequently challenges the value assigned to the subject matter of the transaction.

A price adjustment clause takes one of two forms. It may be a clause forming part of the rights and conditions attaching to the Holdco Shares or the New Shares received by the owner. This condition will

---

[25] A non-cumulative dividend right means that if a dividend is not declared for a particular period, the shareholder will not be entitled to a dividend for that period when dividends are ultimately declared.

provide for an adjustment of the redemption/retraction amount to reflect the fair market value of the Opco Shares or the Old Shares exchanged. Alternatively, a price adjustment clause may be included in the purchase and sale agreement or share exchange agreement to provide for the issuance of additional shares or cancellation of issued shares without payment, such that the net number of Holdco Shares or New Shares will reflect the fair market value of the Opco Shares or Old Shares exchanged.

Be careful. A common mistake is not ensuring that the price adjustment clause contained in the share conditions of the Holdco Shares or New Shares is effective. To guard against this, the owner and the corporation should be able to show that they have reasonably attempted to determine the value of the Opco Shares or Old Shares to be disposed of. The parties should also demonstrate that all consequential adjustments will be made if the redemption amount is adjusted pursuant to such conditions.

In IT Bulletin IT-169R, the CRA will recognize any adjustment clause, provided the following conditions are met:

> (i) The agreement reflects a bona fide intention of the parties to transfer the property at fair market value and arrives at that value for the purposes of the agreement by a fair and reasonable method.
>
> (ii) Each of the parties to the agreement notifies the Department by a letter attached to his return for the year in which the property was transferred
>
> (A) that he is prepared to have the price in the agreement reviewed by the Department pursuant to the price adjustment clause,
>
> (B) that he will take the necessary steps to settle any resulting excess or short-fall in the price, and
>
> (C) that a copy of the agreement will be filed with the Department if and when demanded.
>
> (iii) The excess or shortfall in price is actually refunded or paid, or a legal liability therefor is adjusted.

How Can the Owner Maintain Control?

In most cases, the owner will want to maintain control over the business even after he or she has frozen his or her current equity position and allowed the next generation to benefit from the future appreciation in value of the business. There are three major ways to ensure that the owner maintains control, which may be used independently of one another or concurrently. Each will be discussed below.

Attach Voting Rights to Freeze Shares (i.e., Holdco Shares or New Shares)

The simplest way to ensure the owner has control is to include voting rights in the share conditions attached to the shares issued as consideration to the owner, and as part of the section 85 holding company freeze (*i.e.*, the Holdco Shares) or as part of the section 86 internal company freeze (*i.e.*, the New Shares). Unfortunately, this has some drawbacks.

First, members of the next generation may include children who are active and inactive in the business. If voting control is attached to the only class of shares the owner receives as consideration (*i.e.*, the Holdco Shares or the New Shares), the owner may be creating a situation where a future transfer of such shares to the next generation results in the inactive children having some control of the business. This may lead to a situation prone to disputes.

Second, the owner may wish to rely upon the future redemption amount of the shares issued to him or her (*i.e.*, the Holdco Shares or New Shares) as his or her source of income in retirement. If this is the case, the level of control the owner has will decline with each share redemption made. This means that at some point, control may prematurely shift to the next generation.

Create a Separate Class of "Scrip" or "Thin" Voting Shares

Another way to ensure that the owner has control is to create an additional class of shares in Holdco or on the reorganization of the share capital of Opco where the only right attached to shares of that class is the right to vote. The subscription price would be nominal. The owner would then subscribe for a sufficient number of shares of this class to ensure that he or she can control the company for all purposes. The benefits of this approach are the corollary of the drawbacks referred to above.

First, the owner can decide which member(s) of the next generation will obtain control of the company, separately from determining which member(s) should benefit from the value of his or her freeze shares or the future value of the company.[26]

Second, the owner could redeem his or her Holdco Shares or New Shares without causing a dilution in his or her control of the company.

---

[26] This may be particularly important where the freeze shares are to be held in a spousal trust for the benefit of the owner's spouse, but one or more children will be instrumental in managing the ongoing operation of the business such that control should devolve to those children separate from the value attributed to the freeze shares which will be needed to benefit the spouse.

Acquisition of New Equity Shares by a Discretionary Family Trust

Owners often want the flexibility to determine which members of the next generation ought to benefit from the future value of the business, in what proportions and at what moment in time they are to benefit. Providing for the acquisition of the new common shares of Holdco (on a section 85 freeze) or of Opco (on a section 86 freeze) by a discretionary family trust will give them such flexibility. Otherwise, the owner would be allowing the next generation to become direct owners of the new common shares. This will be discussed in greater detail below, under the heading "What Are the Benefits of Using a Discretionary Family Trust?"

What Are the Options for the New Equity/Common Share Acquisition?

Outright Acquisition

As part of either a section 85 holding company freeze or a section 86 internal company freeze, those members of the next generation who are intended to benefit from part or all of the future growth in value of the business after the freeze transaction can subscribe for the new common shares of Holdco or Opco directly. It goes without saying that this ought to be considered only in the context of competent adult members of the next generation. Serious consideration will also need to be given to the permanent nature of this decision — once an individual is a direct shareholder, he or she has legal rights that cannot be ignored. Lastly, consideration needs to be given to the family law implications applicable to members of the next generation.

Gift After Marriage

An alternative is for the owner to first acquire the new common/equity shares of Holdco or Opco personally. The owner would then gift the new common/equity shares of Holdco or Opco to those members of the next generation who are intended to benefit from part or all of the future growth in value of the business after the freeze transaction. Clients often choose this scheme because it may offer some protection against the family law implications if members of the next generation are already married at the time of the freeze transaction.

Acquisition by a Discretionary Family Trust

What Is a Discretionary Family Trust?

A trust is not a legal entity like a corporation. Rather, it is a relationship based upon the separation of legal ownership of property from beneficial enjoyment. This relationship arises when a person (called the "settlor") transfers property, whether real or personal, to another person (called the "trustee")[27] to hold for the benefit of other persons (called "beneficiaries"). The trustee has legal authority over the property while the benefit of the property ultimately accrues to the beneficiaries and not the trustee.

The trust deed contains terms describing how the trustee must manage the property for the benefit of the beneficiaries.

In the context of the discretionary family trusts, the settlor would establish the trust by transferring nominal non-income-producing property to the trustees. The settlor is often a person who is related to the beneficiaries. The trustees will often be the owner and two other persons.

The beneficiaries of a family trust would generally include the current and future children, and the descendants of the current and future children of the owner. They may also include the owner and his or her spouse, but pay attention to the "income attribution values" referred to earlier and the corporate attribution rule discussed below. Depending on the owner's wishes, the class of beneficiaries can also include other family members. However, I strongly discourage expanding the class of beneficiaries beyond the children and their descendants, unless it is likely that other family members are intended to benefit from the future value of the corporation.

The trustees of a particular family trust should acquire the new common shares in Holdco or Opco by borrowing a nominal amount from a bank, and using the borrowed funds to subscribe for such shares for nominal consideration. I often recommend this third party borrowing to avoid the implications of certain income tax attribution rules of the Act. However, if family law issues are a concern for a beneficiary, it may be possible for the owner to acquire the common shares and then to gift them to the family trust after the marriage of such beneficiary. However, this ought to be done alongside the freeze transaction.

---

[27] This is often referred to as the settlor "settling" or "establishing" the trust.

What Are the Benefits of Using a Discretionary Family Trust?

There are many benefits of using a discretionary family trust to provide for the transfer of future value of a family business to the next generation. They are listed below.

- **Flexibility:** The use of a discretionary trust will allow the owner to postpone the following decisions: (i) which members of the next generation he or she wishes to benefit, and (ii) when to transfer the future value of the business.[28]
- **Control:** Pending distributions of the capital of the trust (*i.e.*, the new common shares of Holdco or Opco or the proceeds of sale therefrom), the trustees control the trusts' assets. As noted, the owner would be one of three trustees.
- **Multiplying the Capital Gains Exemption:** The Capital Gains Exemption provides a significant exemption from capital gains tax on the disposition of QSBC shares. Using a discretionary trust to hold QSBC shares can dramatically increase the amount of capital gains that can be exempted from tax on the future sale of the corporation or the new common shares of the corporation. This is carried out by enabling the beneficiaries of the family trust to utilize their own capital gains exemption in respect of the shares owned by the trust. Further, as capital gains realized by minors are not subject to the income attribution rules under the Act, there is the added benefit of income-splitting.
- **Creditor-Proofing Assets:** If potential creditor claims of members of the next generation is an issue, holding the new common shares of Holdco or Opco in a discretionary trust may offer some protection.
- **Privacy:** Subject to the obligations under the Act, a discretionary trust is a private arrangement that does not have to be registered with any government agency. Nonetheless, a trust is a taxable entity for income tax purposes. As such, the trustees must file tax returns in respect of the income earned by a trust on its assets. The trustees must also enclose a copy of the trust deed when filing the first tax return for the trust.

---

[28] Due to subsection 104(4) of the Act, it is generally advisable to transfer the assets of a trust to the beneficiaries prior to its 21st anniversary.

What Are the Issues That Need to Be Considered?

To establish a discretionary trust, there are three main issues to be considered, each of which is noted below. The resolution of each of these issues is dependent upon the goals to be achieved and ensuring that the income attribution rules and the corporate attribution rule (discussed below) of the Act do not apply.[29]

- *Who will be the settlor?* — The person establishing the trust (*i.e.*, the settlor) should be a person who is neither the owner nor a potential beneficiary. Generally a family member (*i.e.*, parent or sibling) or a close friend of the owner is chosen. A family member is the preferred person. This person will transfer a nominal asset to the trustees to settle the trust. Note that the settlor *cannot* be a potential beneficiary of the trust. However, the settlor could be a trustee provided that there are three trustees, acting by majority.
- *Who will be the trustees?* — One of the trustees should be the owner. How many more trustees are named depends on a number of other considerations which will not be discussed here. When choosing trustees, it is important to bear in mind that if a majority of the trustees are or become non-residents of Canada, the trust would also cease to be resident in Canada for income tax purposes. The trust would become resident of another jurisdiction instead. There is a departure tax imposed on a trust that ceases to be resident in Canada.
- *Who will be the beneficiaries?* — The settlor should not be a beneficiary. There are no other restrictions on choosing the persons who could be included in the class of potential beneficiaries. Nevertheless, it is important to note that even though the trust will be a discretionary trust, the exercise of discretion in favour of certain beneficiaries and not others exposes the trustees to potential complaints from non-recipient beneficiaries. As a result, the bigger the class of potential beneficiaries, the bigger the potential risk to the trustees. While this risk may not be overly significant, it is important that the list of potential beneficiaries not simply be expanded for expediency. Rather, you should establish who the owner may potentially want to distribute future value of the company to, taking into account any future family needs or dependency relationships.

  If any of the beneficiaries are or might become resident of the United States for U.S. income and/or estate tax purposes, explore

[29] If the income attribution rules apply, then the income earned on the relevant assets is attributed to one taxpayer while another taxpayer enjoys the benefits of that income. However, it is beyond the scope of this chapter to discuss these rules.

the implications of the U.S. income and estate tax rules when preparing the terms of the trust deed. Since these rules are extremely complicated, it is advisable to engage U.S. counsel to provide advice with respect to the terms of the trust at the time of its initial drafting.

How to Avoid the Corporate Attribution Rule

As noted above, any time a taxpayer transfers or loans property to a corporation, consider the potential application of the attribution rule in subsection 74.4(2) of the Act.[30] If that rule applies, the taxpayer will have to include in income as interest an amount equal to an annual percentage of the value of the property loaned or transferred.

The subsection will apply if one of the main purposes of the loan or transfer of property by the taxpayer to the corporation is to reduce the income of the individual and to benefit a "designated person"[31] in respect of the taxpayer. Since this is a purpose-based test, it is not necessary that a designated person actually receive income in order to satisfy it.

An exception to the rule exists if the corporation is a small business corporation. The exception must, however, be satisfied annually.

If the corporation does not qualify as a small business corporation annually, a further exception exists. In particular, if the only interest that the designated person has in the corporation is a beneficial interest in shares of the corporation held by a trust, and, by the terms of the trust, the person may not benefit from any of the income or capital of the trust while being a designated person, *i.e.*, under age 18 in the case of a child, then the purpose test of the rule will not be met. If this exception is to be relied upon, the trust must be drafted to fit within the exception.

---

[30] An exchange of shares pursuant to section 86 is considered to be a transfer of property to a corporation which may lead to the application of subsection 74.4(2).

[31] "Designated person" is defined as a spouse, a non-arm's length minor, or a niece or nephew. The captured individual must also be a "specified shareholder" of the corporation. In general, a beneficiary of a discretionary family trust who owns shares in the corporation will meet the test for being a "specified shareholder".

CHAPTER 47

FAMILY BUSINESS SUCCESSION PLANNING — HOW TO BE MORE THAN A TACTICAL PRACTITIONER

Grant C. Robinson

Overview

We are all trained to deliver tactical solutions to our clients. We feel it is our responsibility to give our clients the *right* answer. Unfortunately, many business owners are confused by different messages from different advisors. This chapter is about helping your clients get to *their* right answer, not *your* right answer. It is designed to provide you with a more holistic and more client-directed approach to succession planning.

Recently, I moderated a panel of three business owners who had played a key role in three very different business transitions. Each of them admitted that the technical aspect of their transition accounted for a mere 20% of the plan. The other 80% was what they called the "softer issues" — or what I call "communication and relationships".

These entrepreneurs faced many challenges in dealing with the three different *circles* of their business: the ownership, the day-to-day management of the business and the personal or family area (where the business directly or indirectly impacts the shareholder's family). As they discovered, the issues that arise don't always fall cleanly into one of these three major areas but often overlap two or more *circles*.

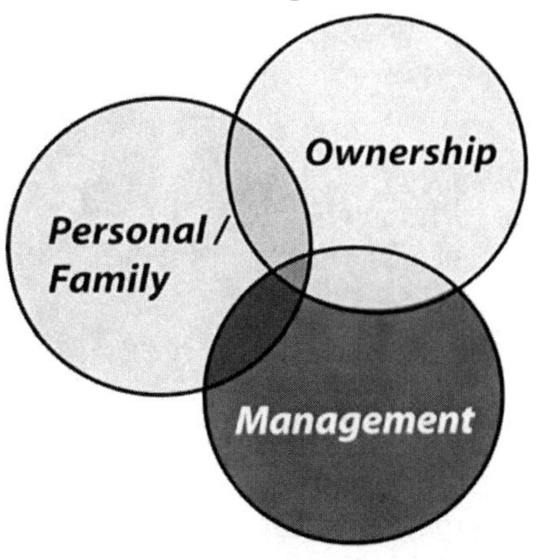

Adapted from the 3-circle Model by Tagiuri & Davis

So when a succession plan focuses solely on the tactical

solutions for a share transfer, it could address as little as one-third of the complexities facing a typical business family. Advisors need a process and tools to guide their clients through the whole family business journey, including the complexities which can't be resolved with an estate freeze, an insurance policy or an investment program.

This holistic succession planning process applies to all family businesses and business families. Business families are those who are impacted by the business even if only one member of a family works or owns shares in the company. Business families include the local car dealer, the large manufacturing plant that is a family-controlled public company, and all accounting or legal partnerships. In other words, it applies to most of you! If you run your own book of business, your practice has all the features of a family business. You can use this same approach to deal with your own transition.

A picture is worth a thousand words, so this chapter will provide you with messages and tools that are visual in nature. The tools were designed not only to facilitate a dialogue with your clients, but also to enhance the communication process in your clients' own lives.

Learning Objectives:

From this chapter, you will learn the following:

- Tactical consulting only goes so far. It is the process consulting that can better position you as a Trusted Advisor and at the same time provide ways to meet the next generation so you can maintain the client relationship into the future.
- To some business owners, succession means death or castration, and no one wants to come to a meeting to talk about these two topics. Succession planning is actually a transition process. Transition planning is something entrepreneurs understand as they have transitioned through different stages to get to where they are today. Your role is to help them see that their inevitable exit is just another transition.
- Entrepreneurs need to treat this final transition just like any other project in their business, as something that needs planning, resources and execution.
- There are structured, fun and enlightening ways to have initial or difficult conversations with your clients and their families, and ultimately move them forward. You will discover a process that instead helps business families collectively clarify a *bigger future* and the steps to get there.

- There is a process that is flexible enough to be adapted to different client situations. As you explore this process, consider how you might use it in your professional and private life. I have always felt that I have been a better practitioner when I have been able to first apply concepts to myself. It gives me a chance to walk a mile in my clients' shoes before I offer comments on whether or not it is appropriate for them.

THE TRANSITION PLANNING PROCESS

It is important to be very conscious of the fact that, as professional advisors, we are trained to plan and deliver the tactical solutions related to our profession of origin. We feel we add value to our clients by providing them with this advice on how to solve their problems. However, when it comes to family and people issues, the technical issues often get in the way.

When you are coaching an entrepreneur or business family, it is critical that you view their business and family life as a journey as opposed to a discrete event. For this journey to be successful, their greatest need is to learn how to communicate effectively, how to problem-solve together, and how to make informed decisions. I call this process consulting. The advisor's role is not to provide the answer but to guide clients so that they can come to their own conclusions.

In my experience, about 75% of advisors work solely within their profession of origin delivering tactical solutions, and have little or no interest in getting involved in helping entrepreneurs enhance their communications and decision-making processes.

As you reflect back on the work you have done with your clients, think about the times when you designed great plans for which there was a lot of initial enthusiasm, but no follow-through or implementation. These great plans ended up sitting on the shelf. The reason is typically a lack of confidence on the part of the entrepreneur or the business family in where they were going.

I encourage you to consider how you might integrate a process consulting approach into your services. If it is not a role with which you are very comfortable, learn about the process and then partner with a process consultant to take your clients through the stages of self-discovery. When they have enough confidence in how their problems can be resolved, you can then design the technical and tactical solutions.

The approach and the tools you will see in this chapter are very visual, and simplified to better allow entrepreneurs to understand the concepts. The tools are for creating conversations and are designed to identify problems or opportunities and define the obstacles and strategies that need to be implemented. This is a process consulting approach.

THE LINE OF CONFIDENCE™

It is important to understand why succession planning strikes fear in the hearts of the majority of business owners.

Business owners associate *succession* with *retirement*. The dictionary definition of retirement is to "take something out of use" — not a picture that excites many entrepreneurs whose DNA says to keep building. For many, retirement means death.

The idea of a *transition* — moving on to the next stage — is much more palatable and something business owners can endorse. They understand that just as their business transitioned many times from its beginning until now, it will continue to transition. Transition planning is the journey to a bigger future. Inevitably, that bigger future requires engaging others, which prepares the way for the inevitable leadership transition.

There is a natural process for transitioning from one stage to another. We all unconsciously follow this process. The Line of Confidence™ depicts it well.

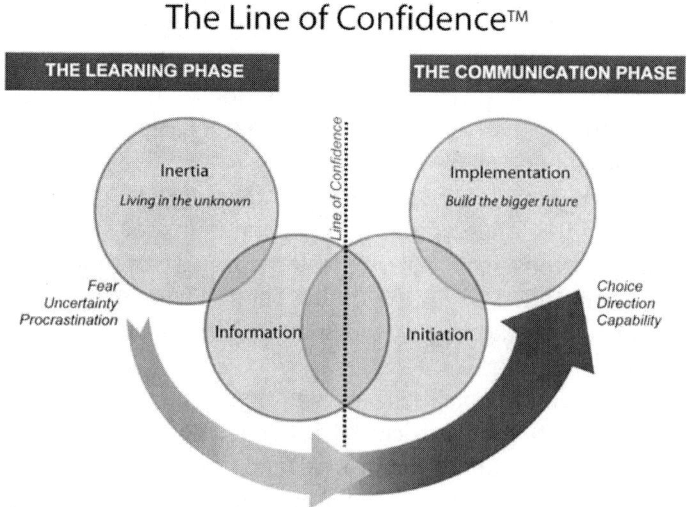

There are four overlapping circles, and the Line of Confidence is the dividing line between the learning and communication phases.

In every new project, we begin in the Inertia Stage where we are unclear or unsure about how to move forward or what the outcome might be. Before we can take action, we have to understand enough about the process and feel fairly confident about the likelihood of success. This is the Information Stage. Once we get that confidence, we move into the Initiation Stage, where we can break the tasks into manageable pieces and take the first steps forward. As our confidence grows we eventually reach the Implementation Stage, where we can achieve our bigger future and celebrate our accomplishments. It is unreasonable to expect anyone to move directly from Inertia to Implementation.

When it comes to transitioning a business, all owners start out in the Inertia Stage. At this point, they are not actively pursuing the transition process. Quite often that's because they are less than 50 years of age and oblivious to the inevitabilities in life, including death and taxes! On the other hand, they may be paralyzed by fear and uncertainty — or plain old procrastination. The fact is, none of them are immune to the need to create a sustainable organization and family system and protect their wealth and personal legacy.

When the decision-maker in a business family is in this stage, there won't be any movement on a transition plan. They don't know what they don't know. The uncertainty or fear of the unknown is one of the greatest challenges in transitioning a business. There is a need for all family members — whether they are first, second, third or fourth generation — to understand the process and get clarity on where they are going and what their individual roles might be. So the first step is to move the business owner, together with his or her family, from the Inertia Stage into the Information Stage.

The Information Stage is the area where entrepreneurs and their families can explore and learn, and gradually gather confidence. Here they identify possible roadblocks. They learn about tactical issues and governance issues. They get to ask questions.

People will stay in the Information Stage until they not only understand where they are going and what they are committing to, but also how they will get out of it if it doesn't work. Eventually they will reach the Line of Confidence™. The Line of Confidence™ is not something anyone can define. It is more of a gut feeling that there is a clear path forward and a likelihood of success. All family members need to cross the Line of Confidence™, and a key aspect of your role is to help them get there.

Once across the Line of Confidence™, they enter the Initiation Stage. This Initiation Stage is what most professionals refer to as a succession plan. This is the tactical area where the insurance products are purchased, the investments outside the business are made, the estate freeze is put in place, the business plan is prepared and the roles and responsibilities within the business are identified. These tactics are essential to enabling the choice to transition to either a family or non-family member, and on a timetable that fits the entrepreneur.

The final step is to move into the Implementation Stage. This is where the transition to clients' bigger future ultimately takes place. Success is measured on whether the decision-making has moved from one person, group of people or generation to another person, group of people or generation. The transition of the decision-making is what enables continuity and is the real goal of a succession plan.

The Line of Confidence™ is a napkin tool. It can be explained anywhere, any time, even on the back of a napkin! It is a template for the transition planning process and illustrates to clients how the system works and where they are in the process.

The rest of the chapter explores a tried-and-true approach to take clients through the Learning Phase and across the Line of Confidence™ towards their bigger future.

Moving out of Inertia

Finding a way to get to their reality is the key to moving your clients beyond the Inertia Stage.

The reality for the majority of entrepreneurs is that exiting their business means risking their equity, giving up control or causing conflict in their key relationships. I use the following visual to open the discussion about the fears and uncertainty that entrepreneurs typically experience.

Changing Lanes Without a Major Collision

The sedan in the fast lane represents the current leader of the business with no plans to slow down or allow another vehicle into that lane. These are the entrepreneurs who feel they still have a lot to offer and are not ready to retire. They may feel there isn't another driver with enough experience to drive at this speed. Handing the vehicle to a junior driver might result in a serious accident or, worse still, a complete write-off of their pride and joy. On the other hand, they may find it difficult to choose from a group of other drivers already on the highway, each of which is pushing to be the driver of the lead car. One such driver is in the pickup that has just entered the highway. In its hurry to speed up and take its place in the fast lane, it has already had one near collision.

Likely the drivers in the fast lane are somewhat aware of the possible road conditions up ahead but feel confident in their ability to deal with whatever comes. After all, they have years of driving experience with wet and stormy weather and icy roads, so it should be easy to still maneuver the vehicle when the fuel warning light comes on! The reality is, most of them are entering an area of unfamiliar territory and do not have the experience to deal with the potential hazards ahead — hazards such as crossing three lanes of a busy highway to reach the exit ramp.

Changing lanes suddenly, without any prior signal, will surely result in a major collision.

Eventually, every entrepreneur will exit his or her business, either from a conscious decision arising from an opportunity to travel a different highway, or something beyond their control. Planning ahead to deal with all possibilities will ensure that entrepreneurs signal their intentions far enough in advance to avoid any serious collisions. It gives them more control over the outcome. Entrepreneurs like to be in control!

Some of the simplest concepts have the greatest impact on people. "One Day You Will Sell" is one such concept. It illustrates how business owners can address the inevitable, yet protect their wealth, keep the control that is so important to them and still preserve important relationships. It validates their fears and uncertainty and gives them confidence that there is a solution.

The "One Day You Will Sell" concept brings the reality to two choices. Business owners will either sell *involuntarily* as a result of death, disability, bankruptcy, a franchisor pulling the franchise or some other factor beyond their control, or sell *voluntarily* under their terms and conditions — *i.e.*, to follow a different lifestyle. Many entrepreneurs don't think of their death as a sale. It is important to get people to understand that if they hold onto the business until they die, the business is still sold.

Whether selling *voluntarily* or *involuntarily*, there are only two categories of buyers. There is either a sale to a family member or someone inside the business, or a sale to someone outside the business. If the business owner chooses to pass the baton to someone else in the family, it is an internal sale. Regardless of whether or not moneys change hands, transition to new ownership is a sale.

Rarely do I find a business owner who doesn't want a voluntary sale. To ensure a successful voluntary sale, entrepreneurs need to have a healthy business, a healthy family or personal situation, and a healthy ownership focus. In other words, all three circles need to be healthy. To achieve this end, entrepreneurs need to prepare the family area through communication and supporting people on a personal level. To address the ownership circle, they need to ensure there is liquidity on death, a good rule book (shareholders' agreement) and investments outside the business to fund their lifestyle. In the third circle, they must protect the wealth engine by preparing a solid track for the business with evidence that the management team can adapt to changing circumstances and run the business with formalized roles and responsibilities.

Enabling the choice to sell internally requires the entrepreneur to consider the possibility that the next generation does not want to be in partnership after mom and dad are gone. Tactics must allow for enough liquidity should one or more of the next generation wish to "sell" their ownership.

Planning for a possible external sale requires tactics to manage the resulting wealth. I have heard entrepreneurs comment that they will just sell the business to someone outside the family so they do not have to address the impact an internal sale will have on family relationships. While selling the business undoubtedly takes away the issues of who will run the business and what roles, responsibilities and authority people will have, it doesn't address the fact that the wealth stays in the family and needs to be managed. I have seen destructive family situations arise after a family business has been converted to cash. My observation is that when the wealth is invested in the business, there is a family identity, a responsibility to the community and a pride in the ownership that binds the family. When a business is sold externally, that identity and purpose can disappear. When the wealth has no clear purpose, it can have a very negative impact on the family. We have all heard such stories in the media. On the other hand, some of the more successful external sales are where wealthy families have redefined that purpose in a philanthropic pursuit. They have adopted a responsibility to a community and clearly articulated their commitment within the family group. Our role as advisors is to ensure business families are aware that an external sale doesn't necessarily get rid of the issues. Indeed, they can become more pronounced.

The pursuit of a bigger future and the ability to ensure a voluntary sale leads families further into the Information Stage, where they will learn more and get clarity around the ultimate purpose for their wealth. Preparing each circle for sale will trigger many difficult but important conversations. The result of these conversations will be the need for many of the tactics that comprise a traditional succession plan, including managing the tax bill and ensuring there is enough liquidity in the business to offset any uncertainty that customers, lenders, suppliers and employees might have as a result of the owner's exit.

"One Day You Will Sell" is also a napkin tool. The message is successful because it focuses on the client's bigger future. It is the pursuit of this bigger future that drives the tactics — not the solutions that are typically imposed by professional advisors. From this visual, entrepreneurs are now able to see that there is a process for addressing the inevitable while still protecting their wealth, keeping the control that is so important to them and preserving important relationships.

Moving Through the Information Stage

Once beyond the Inertia Stage, your business owner clients are anxious to identify what the bigger future might be and what needs to be done to achieve it.

I recommend an experiential process incorporating a variety of discovery exercises which require the family to talk to each other. For example, don't ask family members what their vision is; find a way for them to talk to each other about what interests and excites them. This approach is vital to ensuring a common interest or a "we focus" going forward.

Identifying the bigger future involves putting into context what has been created and the opportunity that exists going forward.

Setting the Stage

Stephen Covey's "*Begin with the End in Mind*", the second habit in *The 7 Habits of Highly Effective People: Powerful Lessons in Personal Change* (New York: Simon & Schuster, 2004), is a proven approach. The House on the Hill is a visual with which entrepreneurs and business families can easily identify. It is not as easy to draw on a napkin, although I certainly have done so.

In this visual, the smaller but comfortable cottage on the left represents what the entrepreneur has today. The objective is to transition to the next stage — depicted as the house on the hill. This house on the hill is bigger and more substantial, and has some significant features. First of all, it is on a hill so it should be a loftier goal. Called the Stewardship House, it represents an opportunity for families to build a legacy — a legacy that comes about as a result of multiple generations adopting a responsibility to take the family wealth, using it during their lifetime and passing it along to the next generation, much bigger and more significant than what they themselves received. Successful transitions evolve from an identified "we focus", so it is vital to get input from all stakeholders by engaging them in the process of building the house on the hill.

This visual goes on to depict the key steps in building their house on the hill. As with all structures, the foundation needs to be solid. The foundation of the house on the hill is one of trust and leadership, without which any entity will crumble. Transitioning a business requires this same solid foundation.

The pillars of the house speak to the four components that are essential for a strong, stable structure: the direction, the roles, the ground rules and the measures.

- Direction is fundamental. You need to know which way to point the ship when you leave the harbour. It's not likely that all individuals in a business family will choose the same path, but they can arrive at the same destination, provided they start out in the right direction and have a chart to guide them.

- Building the bigger future will require clarity around roles, and, even more importantly, the responsibilities and authority that should accompany each role. Clearly defined roles provide leadership, are the basis for establishing compensation and contribute to successful management of conflict situations.
- Roles and leadership should be allocated based on required skill sets so that not only does the organization function at optimum levels, but individuals also have the opportunity to personally succeed and excel. Why put an individual in the role of CEO when in fact he or she is much more comfortable and competent playing a completely different role in the organization? When people consistently operate outside their core strengths, you'll see individual burnout and dysfunctional families. On the other hand, there is a greater sense of personal fulfillment and a willingness to contribute to something meaningful when people are in the right roles.
- Ground rules are absolutely necessary for working cohesively in building the bigger future, particularly in the process of professionalizing the business and creating structures for people to have safe conversations and open communication.
- Finally, the measures are required because most entrepreneurs have a perfection standard which tells them that no matter how successful they have been in the past, they could have done better. It is important to take time to recognize what has been accomplished and celebrate those accomplishments while at the same time trying to set the bar higher and move to the next level. There needs to be a true appreciation of success which can only come through taking stock of what has been accomplished.

Once the foundation and the pillars have been erected, it's time to put the roof on. The roof symbolizes success on two levels. First, there is the fun that represents the sense of accomplishment and having made a difference. The other is the financial security that generally accompanies the building of a bigger future.

The final aspect of this picture is the gap between the two entities. This gap represents the roadblocks that the entrepreneur must navigate on the journey towards the bigger future. There are two components to this gap. The first is a bridge containing numerous hurdles, and the second a pond filled with alligators. The bridge represents the way forward but the hurdles can trip up the travellers. The alligators represent the external threats that can destroy anyone who loses his or her footing on the bridge and falls into the pond. There are risks in transitioning businesses just as there are risks in life and anything we do. The more business families can understand about the obstacles, the better they can overcome them. The more they learn and practise, the easier the journey will be. They definitely need a map and a guide for the journey so they will be less likely to trip over the hurdles and fall into the alligator-filled waters.

Using a visual like this to explain the many components for building their house on the hill has had a much greater impact on the entrepreneurs and business families I have worked with than a 50-page report or an Excel spreadsheet. It is a concept that gets conversations flowing. It is a great motivator for identifying their specific house on the hill and what they personally need to do to build it.

Becoming Future-Focused

Transitioning their business will surely present entrepreneurs with some challenges. They will be faced with situations involving debate and disagreement and will need to find a way to a keep the bigger future in focus while they strive for a positive outcome.

First they need to understand that conflict is a fundamental component of success. The secret is to ensure that they enable *positive conflict*, which can lead to something better, rather than *negative conflict*, which has the power to destroy.

The Change Equation is another napkin tool, and one I use to explain the role of conflict in the transition planning process.

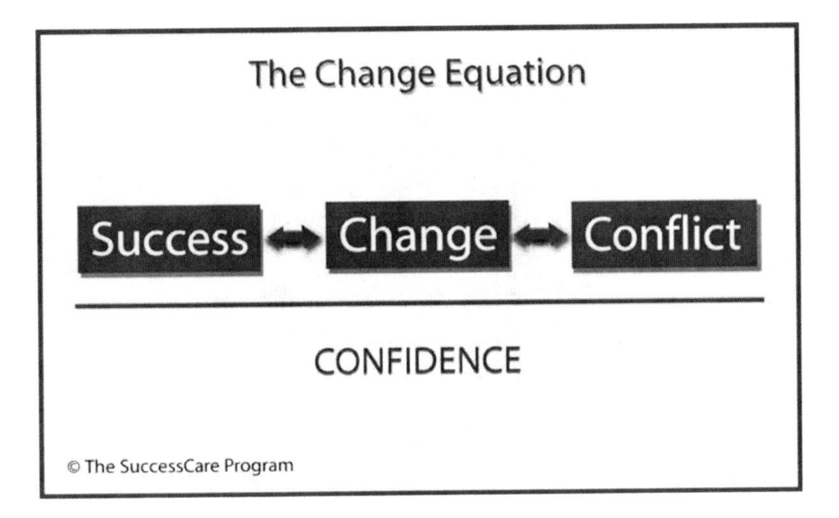

The top line of the Change Equation can be true whether read from left to right or right to left. Going from left to right, achieving *success* will undoubtedly mean embracing *change*. *Conflict* is a natural by-product of change. If this conflict is managed appropriately, the equation also works in reverse. Effective working teams know that multiple ideas and perspectives can lead to a greater outcome. The conflict that results from these multiple ideas fuels the change which ultimately leads to greater success. This process can work just as well for business families, provided they have enough confidence and believe in their ability to create the positive conflict that leads to this greater success. To manage the differing perspectives, there needs to be a formal process for communication, problem-solving and decision-making.

So how do you create positive conflict? The answer of course lies in another napkin tool!

The Positive Outcome Model (which originated from a concept established by CDR Associates and profiled in the book *The Conflict Resolution Toolbox* by Gary Furlong (Mississauga, Ont.: J. Wiley & Sons Canada, 2005)) illustrates the process for helping business families focus on their common interest and reach a positive outcome.

The left side of this model represents the past and provides important information for building the bigger future — the house on the hill. These are the facts that exist today and are particularly valuable in determining what worked in the past and should be re-created, and what hasn't worked and should be avoided.

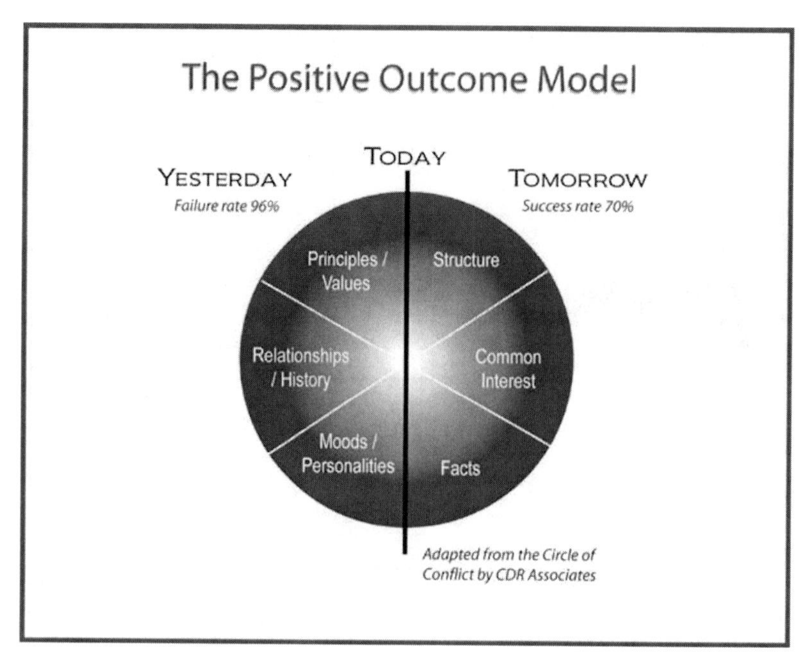

As I work with families and entrepreneurs, I emphasize that the objective is to understand the past, not from a perspective of changing it or coming to peace with it, but simply to get the facts required to promote the *common interest*. Indeed, our informal statistics indicate that trying to build a *common interest* by forcing people to adopt a different perspective fails 96% of the time. Do not try to change the facts. Accept the realities and take what works to the right side of the model, where you can focus on the future.

Remember to use discovery exercises that fit the experiential model referred to earlier in the chapter — an approach that requires the family members to talk to each other. I use a variety of tools to clarify *principles*, *values*, *history*, *relationships*, *moods* and *personalities* so that all members of the group have an opportunity to contribute. At the end of the day, they are better able to understand each other and can be more collaborative moving forward.

When you get people to focus on the right side of the model, where they can clarify and articulate a *common interest*, you can create a *structure* where it is safe not only to have conversations and ask questions, but ultimately to make decisions with all the *facts* on the table. The success rate in finding a go-forward track is now considerably higher.

I want to be clear: this doesn't mean that everything is perfect and everyone will all commit to working together. Sometimes the common interest is *not* to be in business together. If this is what the family wants, and it can be accomplished without destroying the family unity, you can still have a very positive outcome.

I use this approach with entrepreneurs, partnerships, management teams, advisory boards and even not-for-profit groups. It is an overreaching visual from which I facilitate the process of defining and promoting the common interest.

Read on for an example of how I dig into the history to enable positive conflict, and use this positive conflict to define the common interest in building a bigger future.

Clarifying the Bigger Future

The first step in beginning with the end in mind is to determine what the entrepreneur's house on the hill looks like.

In helping business owners visualize their house on the hill, it is important to have an understanding of the *history* and *relationships* of both the business and family, be able to take an inventory of where they are now and then discuss what the future could be.

I use a very simple but effective tool called The SuccessChart™ to guide the discussion around what the future might be. This napkin tool is based on a chart consisting of an X and Y axis, but its power lies in the ability to create a visual representation of what has occurred since the business was founded (or the time the current generation took over).

The SuccessChart™ has two components.

First, it is a forensic tool that inventories what worked and what didn't work during the various stages of the business. Seeing how people have impacted the business and getting their perspective on the events that contributed to building the organization they have today is an important step in engaging all stakeholders. It uncovers information that doesn't come to light in typical conversations. It allows the advisor to extract the intangibles such as core principles, successful strategies for overcoming obstacles, and cornerstones for success. It reinforces lessons learned and helps the family understand the relevance of celebrating successes and victories while learning from prior challenges. Finally, it brings ignored issues to the forefront and makes it much easier to identify the fears, uncertainty and procrastination that are stopping business owners from planning for the inevitable transition.

When using this tool a second time with one long-time client, we collectively discovered that the client had a pattern of buying $2 million businesses and growing them. This nugget turned out to be an important business model which, had we not reviewed the past and reflected on the client's story, would have been completely missed. From identification of this pattern, the client's confidence in building a bigger future took a huge step forward.

Second, the SuccessChart™ is a powerful discovery tool in determining the future direction of the family and the business. It is important to extrapolate what the future could be according to what they have achieved in the past. The key in this part of the exercise is to identify a future that truly resonates with entrepreneurs — one that excites them. The tool is then used to establish if there is a common interest within the family. Do the family members all have the same vision of the future?

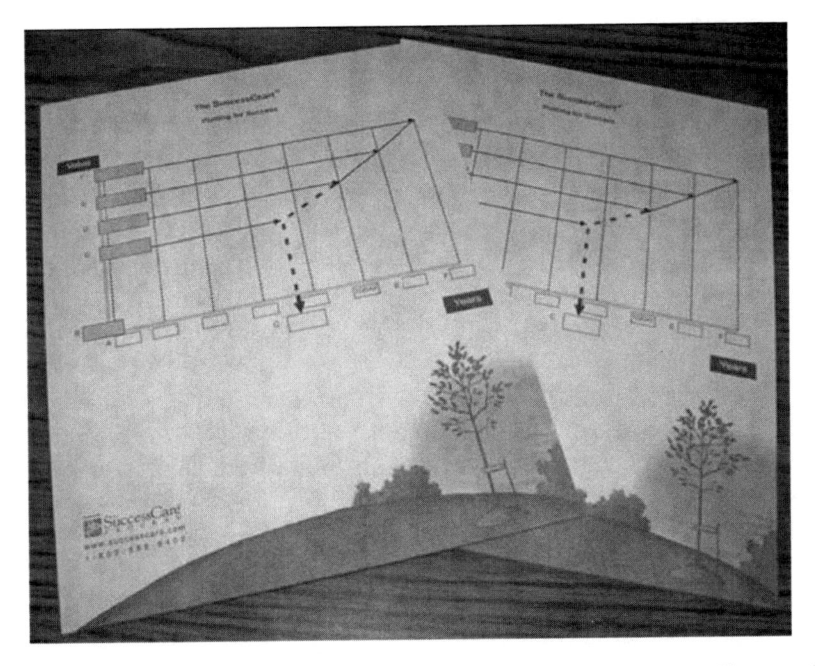

Often, especially in economic downturns, you will have clients who are unsure if their business even has a future. The reality is, if they have a critical mass today and follow best practices, they can continue to grow, even if it is at a slower rate for a while. There are questions you can ask to draw out that reality. One of these questions is: "What might the business be like today if you had started, however many years ago, with what you have today, knowing what you know today and had that same number of years to build it?"

Two things happen when you ask this question. The first is a realization for entrepreneurs that if they had started with what they have today and had been able to grow from that base, their business or equity would be significantly greater and the choices and opportunities available to them would have increased exponentially. Second, the entrepreneur realizes that it is unlikely that he or she will be able to re-create his or her career now — he or she personally doesn't have enough years left. However, the entrepreneur can see that there is a way to obtain that same result through the next generation. This leads to discussions about why the family should work as a team and what the members can accomplish together. It leads to the definition of their common interest and is very much the foundation for a legacy.

Uncover the Obstacles

As the visual of the House on the Hill depicts, there will undoubtedly be obstacles to overcome in building the bigger future. I encourage you to coach your clients to identify as many of these obstacles as possible before any work is done on building the house. It is likely very clear to you what the roadblocks are and equally clear how to manage those roadblocks. However, your solutions are not their solutions. In a client-focused consulting approach, it is vital that all solutions clearly address the client's reality. Let me share some of the ways I help business families focus on their reality.

The Three-Circle Model helps explain many of the conflicting issues facing families in business together. I use it as a tool not only to help families understand the complexities, but also to gain greater insight into the issues for myself. But first, I will review the base message the model delivers.

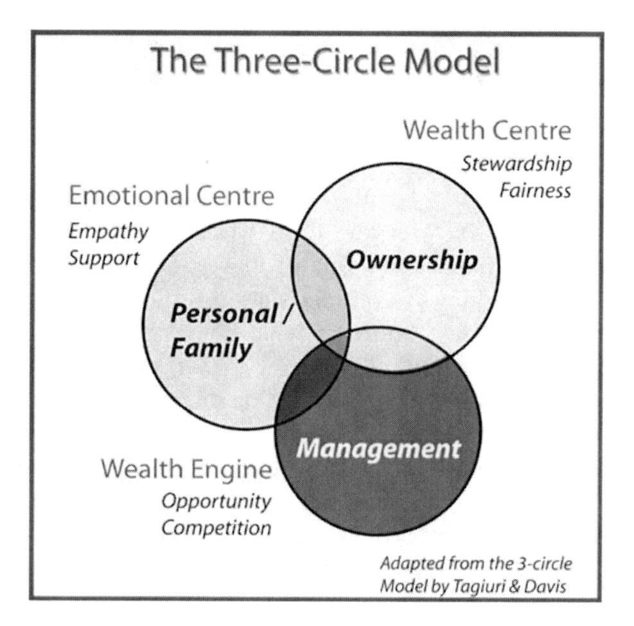

The Personal/Family circle is for developing relationships and promoting individual successes. I call it the Emotional Centre, as its objectives are to provide support and empathy for individuals and the family unit as a whole. Issues can arise when these personal/family objectives overlap or clash with business objectives, so it is important for families to have a clear philosophy around who they are and what they stand for.

The Ownership circle focuses on the protection and preservation of the ownership of the business and other assets over the long term. I refer to it as the Wealth Centre, as its objectives are to ensure that the wealth has purpose and can enable legacies. It is important to have a clear ownership philosophy for the ongoing management of assets. Ownership of the family assets is based on the principles of being fair and equitable. Note that equitable does not necessarily mean equal. Issues can arise from differing views on the purpose of the wealth and what constitutes fairness.

The Management circle is the Wealth Engine for the business. It focuses on processes and products and the ability to reinvent the business and adapt to changing times. The objectives are to ensure that the business is always competitive and looking for opportunities for growth. To survive, all businesses need to be efficient and effective. Failure to uphold these objectives or confusing them with the objectives of the family or ownership circles will ultimately have a significant impact on both the family and the preservation of its wealth.

When issues arise in entrepreneurially led or family businesses, it is not always clear into which area or circle they fit. It is quite possible they will reside in one of the overlapping areas. One of the keys to managing the obstacles to building a bigger future is to identify the circle in which the issue belongs and then resolve it based on the corresponding principles or objectives.

The Three-Circle Model is very powerful when used as a discovery and diagnostic tool. When it is used to open up discussions about "where they are today" and "where they want to go", it also highlights some of the current and potential obstacles in achieving a common interest.

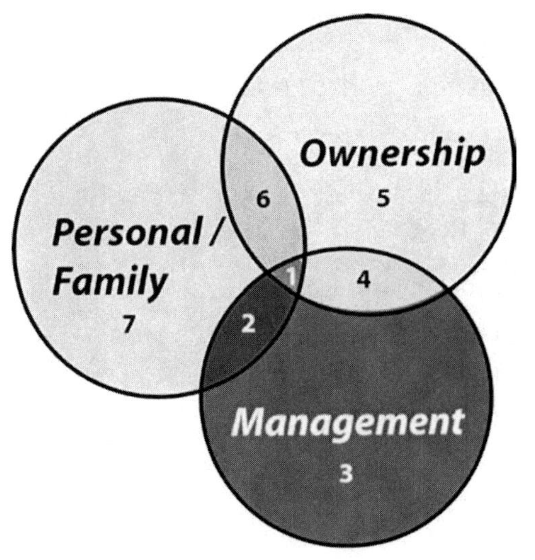

In the "where are they today" version, each person independently determines where in the three circles each family member and stakeholder plays a role. For example, those family members who neither own shares nor work in the business are placed in category 7. Someone who is not a family member but does have ownership and works in the business would belong in category 4. While this may seem pretty straightforward, a follow-up comparison of all the individual charts usually reveals some differences, some of which can be quite significant. Sometimes, the group will have different ideas on who has ownership. Other times, estranged relatives, in-laws or step-children show up on some charts and not in others.

We all tend to make our perceptions become our reality. The discussion that ensues is a great opportunity to highlight the dangers of perceptions and the need for facts. It shows the need for greater clarity and perhaps even further definition of what constitutes a family member, an owner or an employee.

It is also interesting to see how family members suddenly understand the source of a particular conflict. In one situation, when a son-in-law who was renowned for his continuous objections to business policies was shown to belong only in the Family circle, it became clearer to all that his comments were unqualified. He had no firsthand knowledge of that particular business system, as any business perspective he had came through his wife. His opinions were perceptions and not necessarily a match for the facts. When using this exercise, I encourage people to first fill in the circles independently and then compare results.

The next step is the "where do they want to go" chart, where players are placed in the roles they may play ten years into the future. A ten-year timeframe will move teenagers up into career choices and may see some parents or senior managers move to retirement. I like to characterize timeframes in terms of five-year car leases. A timeframe of two car leases brings more of a reality to the discussion.

Again, it is always interesting to note the discussions that arise from the different responses within a connected group. More importantly, the chart indicates potential gaps in leadership and highlights the urgency of planning to fill these gaps.

The Three-Circle Model is a napkin tool that can be used anywhere at anytime, and the second tool I use to uncover the obstacles.

So what is the first tool? It's not only one of the most powerful ways of collecting confidential information from all the key players in the business, but it is a great way for the entire advisory team to collaborate. Read on to learn how to use the "Where Are You Now" Discovery Questionnaire.

The "Where Are You Now" Discovery Questionnaire provides the advisor, the business owner and the individual family members with a benchmark for where they are now in terms of the day-to-day operation, succession and contingency planning. It is also designed to identify building blocks for the future and to highlight areas for concern.

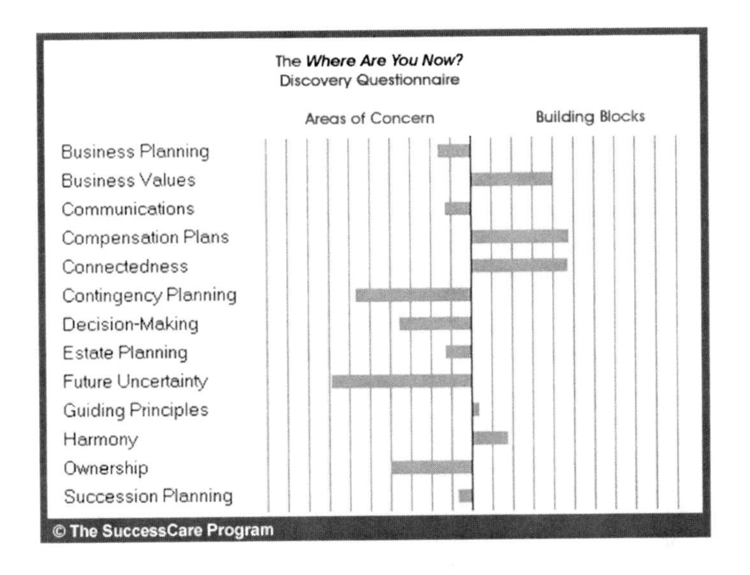

Each member of the business or family independently answers questions about 13 components that are critical to a successful transition. The individual results are then compiled to produce a consolidated report that identifies both the areas where the family or group is consistent in its perceptions, and the areas where differing perceptions indicate obstacles to a successful transition. Each respondent is assured of confidentiality as his or her viewpoints are anonymously blended with the others in the group.

Not only is this a valuable tool in identifying the common interest and the hurdles that need to be overcome to ensure a voluntary internal or external sale, it is a great way to engage the entire group in the process of building the house on the hill. Each person has the opportunity for input without fear of criticism.

This questionnaire also enables better collaboration among the members of the entrepreneur's advisory team. When this information, which has come directly from the client, is circulated among the advisors, it can be the basis of a more integrated, multi-disciplinary approach.

The greatest benefit to using both these tools and others like them is the fact that your clients uncover the obstacles themselves. They own them. They are now more open to finding the solutions to these obstacles. They are moving closer to the Line of Confidence™.

Crossing the Line of Confidence

You have helped your clients determine their bigger future, and conducted some diagnostic tests to identify existing or potential hurdles and alligators. The information both you and your clients have gathered about where they are now and where they want to go is hugely valuable. The next objective is to build their confidence that the obstacles can be resolved and ensure that they have clarity around the process for constructing their house on the hill.

In keeping with the experiential nature of the process, the approach is to have the entire team engage in a problem-solving exercise.

I use a tool called the SuccessStrategies Worksheet™, which is structured to get all the obstacles on the table before any solutions are designed. This tool also allows the members of the business family to come up with the solutions themselves. There is greater motivation on their part to move forward with a plan than when the advisor provides the answers. Advisors often find ways to navigate the technical roadblocks, only to find the process grinds to a halt because some less obvious obstacles have been overlooked.

In the first step of the SuccessStrategies Worksheet™, the participants craft a goal that projects their bigger future. I use a large group facilitation technique that captures everyone's viewpoints so they can collectively articulate a goal that the entire group can support and be excited about.

The next step is to inventory all the obstacles. Many of these obstacles were identified going through the Information Stage, but the group will find others as it goes through this experiential process. Typically, these obstacles stem from external threats or internal weakness, communication issues, individual limitations and business issues such as finances or systems. I have conducted this facilitation countless times and will predict that members of any business family or group will arrive at a list of between 10 to 15 obstacles that could stop them from getting to their stated goal. The really important part is that they are identifying the problems themselves.

Once the group is satisfied that all the obstacles are on the table, the group goes to the beginning of the list and collaborates on finding a strategy that addresses the first obstacle. The key here is to define an overreaching strategy, not a specific tactic. (The tactics are developed during the Initiation Stage of the Line of Confidence™.) The group then reviews the rest of the obstacles to determine if that same strategy will have some level of positive impact. It is amazing to see just how many obstacles one strategy can influence. The process is repeated for the next and subsequent obstacles until every one of them has been addressed.

Generally speaking, at the end of the exercise all the obstacles are addressed by a total of four to six strategies. The group's confidence rises to a new level. There are only four to six things to do (albeit considerable in size) and, more importantly, it knows exactly why it is doing them. Both the family and the entrepreneur are empowered. Now there is a focus on the common interest.

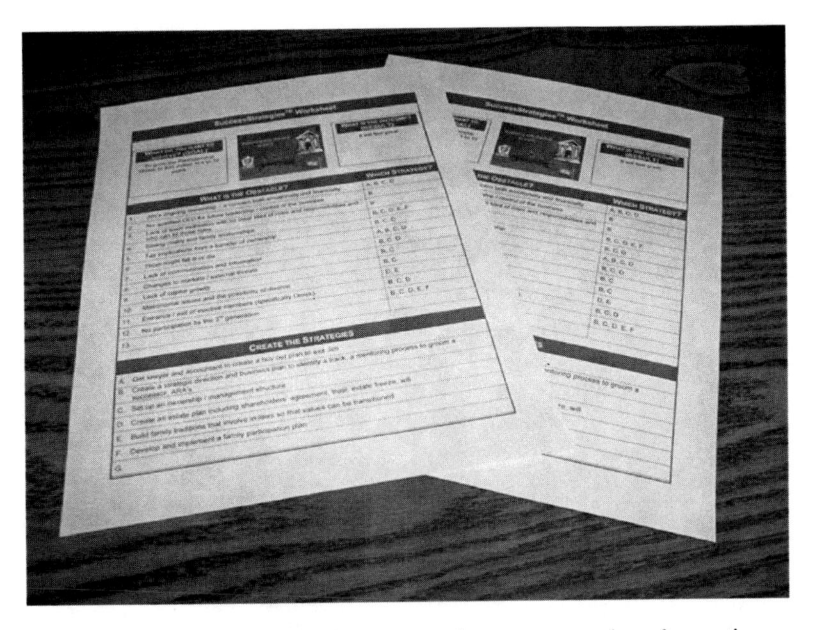

Remember, the key in this process is to ensure that the entire group participates in the problem-solving process and there is collaboration in developing the strategies. As members of the group arrive at the solutions themselves, they take ownership of them. They now have the confidence to move forward and initiate these strategies.

Getting across the confidence line is the core of the overall process consulting approach and is the driver for the entire Communication Phase, or the right side of the Line of Confidence™ model. Don't be tempted to move straight into the Initiation Stage, where the majority of advisory services fit. You will make a bigger and better sale if your approach is more family-directed.

The ultimate goal of the right side of the model is to get to the Implementation Stage, where the decision-making can move from one group to another. This obviously takes time and a lot of communication. As shown in the Positive Outcome Model, it requires structure and a lot of facts, and its success relies heavily on the process consulting approach. Business families need advisors who can guide them through the development of concepts such as a Family Business Senate that enables communication, problem-solving and decision-making in all three circles of the business. But that's a topic for another book!

CHAPTER 48

BUSINESS EXIT PLANNING AND PREPARATIONS — CRITICAL LEGAL CONSIDERATIONS

Jordan Dolgin

Overview

This chapter addresses critical legal issues applicable to the process of "exit planning" for business owners.

With a greater awareness in these areas, the professional is better equipped to assist his or her client and the client's legal advisors to: (1) assess areas of vulnerability which a potential buyer might use to negotiate lower exit transaction values; and (2) develop a plan for eliminating or mitigating the impact of such areas of vulnerability and thereby yield higher exit transaction values.

Learning Objectives

By the end of this chapter, you should be able to:

- understand the importance of legal aspects of exit planning preparations;
- identify some of the basic legal investigations necessary to getting organized in order to engage in proper exit planning;
- identify some of the more common business "skeletons" or "value threats" which can impact the exit planning process; and
- better assess the impact of "value threats" to a potential buyer and learn ways to eliminate, manage and/or mitigate their impact on the exit planning process.

INTRODUCTION

To the seasoned professional, any client who is undergoing the exercise of implementing an individual pension plan, retirement compensation arrangement and/or universal life insurance policy is already embarking upon the process of examining ways to extract value from his or her business on a "tax-preferential" basis and "better prepare" for his or her eventual retirement.

In my experience, clients who match this profile are often ready to consider a more holistic approach to a full exit from their business. Exit (or succession) planning will need to be tailored to the individual owner and to the nature of his or her expected or anticipated exit. The nature of the exit will ultimately depend upon the identity of the purchaser of the business.

Generally, there are three primary categories of purchasers to consider in any exit/succession planning exercise:

- family members (whether active or passive in the business);
- key managers/senior employees of the business; or
- a third party purchaser (which may be a strategic buyer such as a competitor or key customer/supplier of the business, or a purely financial buyer such as a private equity fund, merchant bank or angel investor).

GETTING ORGANIZED — WHAT'S IN YOUR CLOSET?

This part will quickly examine certain "places" where lawyers can and should look to assess whether a particular business may have problems or deficiencies which may give a potential buyer a reason to withdraw from negotiations, or ammunition to negotiate lower exit transaction values.

Public Searches

There are a number of publicly available searches which you can undertake against corporations and individuals when it comes to exit planning preparations. The more typical searches fall into the following categories:

- corporate existence/profile
- bankruptcy
- *Personal Property Security Act* (PPSA)
- *Bank Act*

- real property
- executions/court judgments
- litigation

Corporate searches will report on whether a given Canadian federal or provincial corporation has an "active status" and will also identify the subject corporation's current directors, officers, registered office address and a listing of publicly filed documents (such as articles of incorporation, articles of amendment, annual reports, *etc.*). It will be important to review these searches and to confirm that the applicable corporate information is accurate or to rectify any deficiencies. In some cases, this search will indicate that a given corporation's status is in "default" and permit the lawyers to rectify any governmental deficiencies prior to the applicable governmental authority taking any steps to prematurely terminate the corporation's existence or status.

Although hopefully not applicable, it is always desirable to obtain searches against key individuals and corporations to confirm that no filings have been made and that no proceedings either by a party seeking creditor protection or by creditors seeking enforcements of their rights against a given debtor are under way.

PPSA searches (and the equivalent searches in other relevant Canadian provinces or foreign jurisdictions where key business assets are located) will identify secured creditors of relevant corporations and individuals. Hopefully, the results of these searches will only show known current secured creditors, but surprises do sometimes appear. For example, sometimes a creditor who has been paid in full some time ago will continue to appear on this search if the parties forgot to process the necessary discharge before the expiry of the original registration period. Other times, a person may have filed a PPSA registration without the knowledge of your client (this person may be either a disgruntled unsecured creditor who did not get paid or a potential creditor whose deal was not concluded with your client). A potential buyer will obtain PPSA search results against the target business and its individual owners, so you might as well check these databases first and correct any inaccuracies well before your exit negotiations commence.

In Canada, security interests may sometimes be filed/registered by banks under federal banking legislation in addition to filings under the PPSA, and it is important to obtain these results as well to ensure they are accurate.

To the extent that real property (*i.e.*, land and buildings) is proposed to be sold to a potential exit buyer, it would be prudent to obtain full title searches and identify any issues which a buyer may object to or use as a basis to negotiate better exit pricing.

Any buyer will be concerned about existing litigation involving the target business (or its owners) and/or formal judgments obtained against the target business (or its owners). Litigation and execution searches will reveal any pending lawsuits or actual judgments which you and your clients will want to identify long before negotiations with a potential exit buyer commence.

Material Agreements

Every business enters into contracts (of varying degrees of importance) in order to govern its relationship with various key stakeholders, such as shareholders/founders, employees/contractors, customers, suppliers, landlords, equipment lessors and bankers, to name just a few. In the context of exit planning, these various agreements need to be identified, catalogued and reviewed to ascertain their impact, if any, on the exit planning process. For example, do these material contracts contain provisions which give a key stakeholder a right to terminate the contract if its approval is not first obtained prior to any "change of control" or "assignment" to a new party? In other cases, material contracts may not obtain consent or approval requirements, but may merely give a third party some favourable rights to increase prices, extend terms or obtain some benefit (*e.g.*, golden parachute) should a buyer terminate the agreement following the exit, *etc.* In any event, material contracts are clearly an area of critical examination for any client seeking to prepare for an exit transaction.

Note: Special consideration should be made in the case of company obligations under pension or other benefit arrangements. Corporate pension and benefit documentation should be carefully reviewed to ascertain how they may impact exit planning. For example, to what extent might unfunded obligations need to be "topped-up" prior to closing, or what hidden charges or benefits might create a future cost to a buyer not otherwise known to it at the time of the exit closing?

Material agreements may also exist at the individual level in the form of personal guarantees which the owners have given to lenders and other key suppliers relating to the business. In such case, it will be important for these personal guarantees to be addressed as part of the exit transaction. Other types of material agreements which involve the individual owners include shareholder loans and corporate-owned insurance policies. A proper exit planning exercise will consider how these agreements need to be addressed with a potential buyer as well.

Apart from restrictions on ownership changes, material agreements should be reviewed from the perspective of "risk allocation". In cases where contractual terms involving customers of the business include limited warranties, liability exclusions and liability limitations, your client may be able to demonstrate fewer "customer skeletons" to a prospective buyer of the business.

Industry-Specific and Other Regulatory Considerations

Certain businesses will need to obtain and maintain key governmental licences, permits and registrations under industry-specific municipal, provincial and/or federal government legislation. Proper exit planning will involve the identification and listing of these key licences, permits and registrations, and an understanding of any special conditions which a buyer may or may not be able to satisfy and/or whether or not these key licences, permits and registrations may be transferred to a potential buyer. Where a buyer is a competitor of the business, it will likely have its own industry-specific registrations, licences and permits.

Even in cases where there may be no unique industry-specific regulation which imposes any special licensing or permit requirements over the target business, it may be prudent for your client and your client's counsel to consider the impact of other Canadian federal and/or provincial legislation as part of your exit planning preparations. For example, notices and/or approvals from the federal Competition Bureau or Industry Canada under the *Competition Act* (Canada) or *Investment Canada Act* (Canada), respectively, may be required as part of the exit transaction depending upon the size of the deal and the size/residency of the buyer and seller. In the context of an exit structured as an "asset sale", the provisions of Ontario's *Bulk Sales Act* and *Retail Sales Tax Act* (among others) may also need to be considered.

Review of Corporate Records/Minute Books

Although every corporation is required by law to maintain its corporate records on an annual basis, many corporations do not have current and up-to-date minute books and corporate records. As part of any exit planning (and any tax audit planning), corporate minute books should be reviewed by counsel to ensure that the following matters are properly provided for:

- changes in registered office
- changes in board size
- changes in director and officer appointments and resignations
- issuances, redemptions and transfers of shares

- declaration of dividends and bonuses
- shareholder loans and loan security
- approval of material transactions/contracts
- authorization of articles of amendment and name changes
- approval of financial statements
- fixing/changing of fiscal year-end
- appointment of accountants/auditors
- shareholder agreement approvals

While most minute book "deficiencies" can be rectified, it is important to identify these well in advance of any exit negotiation, particularly where the exit transaction is likely to take the form of a sale of shares, since the buyer will likely want certain legal opinions relating to share capital which your client's legal counsel may be unable to give unless the minute books are in proper condition and in good standing prior to the closing of the deal.

Review of Existing Corporate Structure

Proper exit planning preparations would not be complete without a thorough examination of the existing corporate structure of the target business and consideration of the various assets which are (or are not) intended to be sold to a potential buyer.

For example, if holding corporations constitute part of the corporate organizational structure, do the shares of the holding corporation need to be sold to the buyer in order to take advantage of any available capital gains exemption to individual sellers? If so, will a buyer likely be prepared to purchase the business at the "holding company" level? The answer is typically "yes", but the seller will need to be responsible for any "skeletons" at both the operating company *and* the holding company levels.

Will non-core assets inside the holding company (or the operating company) need to be "cleared out" prior to the sale because they are to be excluded from the sale? If so, what are the tax implications of these purifying transactions?

If the sellers intend to retain key real property (held in a separate company) used by the business, and lease that same property to the buyer as part of the deal, has a suitable lease been put in place before closing? If not, this will need to be addressed as part of the exit transaction.

IDENTIFYING SKELETONS — WHAT ARE YOUR "VALUE THREATS"?

This part will review the types of "skeletons" which, in my experience, are somewhat common and which the client's legal and other advisors should pay careful attention to as part of the exit planning process. In practical terms, you should really think of these "skeletons" not merely as unseemly warts or blemishes on the otherwise shiny complexion of the stellar business your client wants to present to a potential buyer, but as "value threats". By "value threats", these skeletons may either cause a buyer to completely abandon the sale process or (more likely) be used by a buyer opportunistically to extract better pricing or other deal terms from your client.

Minute Book Deficiencies

As mentioned above, a review of most corporate minute books will reveal minor (and often major) issues. Some of these problems are simply matters that have not been noted in the corporate records. In any event, they are most often able to be corrected if identified early enough. The area of greatest concern often relates to whether corporate shares have been validly issued, since many exit transactions are structured as share sales. Most buyers' counsel will (time permitting) insist on receive closing legal opinions from the seller's counsel pertaining to corporate existence and other typical minute book matters, so it is important to identify and address minute book deficiencies early in the process.

Asset Ownership and Encumbrances

Where the core value of a business rests with ownership of a key asset or group of assets, any problems with "title" to such asset will cause major issues with your client's buyer. The most obvious example of this is in the area of intellectual property and, in particular, ownership of the copyright subsisting in source code comprising software.

Under Canadian law and absent an express "assignment of title", ownership of the copyright subsisting in computer software remains with the author of the copyright. In the case of employees, the copyright created in the works they author belongs to the employer, but this is not the case with independent contractors. As a matter of practice, where a non-employee individual contractor and/or software development company built all or part of any key proprietary software used in and/or exploited by your client's business, you should ensure that some form of development agreement was signed and/or that intellectual property rights (*i.e.*, copyrights) were assigned from the developer to the owner of the selling company. Otherwise, title issues will likely arise and create significant problems for your client in executing an exit strategy.

Similar "chain of title" issues might exist with other key assets such as real property.

Additionally, as noted above, a review of the public search results might indicate certain "stale" PPSA encumbrances which will need to be discharged given that your client has long since paid off the debts owed to the applicable secured party. In other cases, registrations which were intended to only encumber specific assets (*e.g.*, motor vehicles or leased equipment) may have been filed to broadly cover all of your client's assets. In these cases, a buyer will want to see a letter from such secured parties confirming that their security does not extend to the assets being acquired by the buyer and that they release the buyer from any claims against such assets. Obviously, from a buyer's perspective, any unacceptable asset encumbrances will need to be addressed before closing, and your client will want to avoid any last minute surprises in his or her deal.

Share Capital Ownership Issues

Simply put, who owns your client's company? You are likely tempted to respond by saying "the client". However, consider the following questions:

- Were the legal formalities relating to any historical share redemptions or share purchases followed properly?
- Were any options or similar rights granted to any former employees, contractors or others early on in the evolution of the business?
- Were any creditors granted any rights to convert their debt into shares?

If the answer to any of these questions is "yes", your client may not be the 100% owner of his or her business, and there may be "phantom" owners who may surface during the exit process if you and your client are not careful in your exit planning.

Opportunistic Litigation

There are often a number of historical (or current) third parties who have unresolved disputes with your client and are just looking for some additional leverage to coerce a settlement. The exit process may be the leverage they are looking for. Once word gets out to the trade that your client is engaged in the sale process, all sorts of opportunistic plaintiffs may emerge from the shadows and commence real (or frivolous) litigation or complain to some governmental or regulatory agency.

Examples include:

- former employees or consultants who were granted stock options;
- former employees who were terminated under less than ideal circumstances;
- resentful competitors who have lost significant market share;
- former shareholders who sold out under less than ideal circumstances;
- large customers who may allege "product liability" issues; and
- large suppliers who may threaten to terminate favourable supply contracts.

Tax Audit/Reassessment Issues

One very typical and significant area of exit planning preparations involves assessing audit risk relating to historical income, commodity taxes and source deductions. This can be particularly problematic for businesses that have made extensive use of independent contractors or for businesses that have failed to collect and remit GST or PST. As part of any exit preparations, it would be prudent for the client's tax advisors to review the operations of the business for the past three to four years, as well as tax returns covering the same period, and comment on areas of possible audit risk which a buyer's tax advisors may identify and which may give rise to potential price negotiations.

Product Warranty/Liability Issues

Part of any exit preparations should include an assessment of any isolated and/or widespread issues of product liability and the warranty/insurance-related costs associated with those issues. As noted above, the extent to which customer agreements contain limited warranties, liability exclusions and liability limitations may assist in mitigating the costs of any product liability issues and thereby reduce the impact of these issues in any exit negotiations.

Environmental Issues

Whether your client is a landlord or tenant, environmental risks are becoming more prevalent; therefore, your client should review its operations and the history of the former tenants of the premises it occupies to ascertain whether any environmental contaminants may have been created, generated, used and/or disposed of within or in proximity to such premises during the past ten years. Depending on the facts, a buyer might be expected to ask for copies of any historical environmental audits and/or requisition its own environmental audit. Any negative results of such audit will be used by a buyer to seek price and other concessions from your client; thus, it would be best to discover any environmental issues long before a buyer is at the table.

Contractual Restrictions on Assignments/Changes of Control

As mentioned above, it is critical to identify any material contracts which may be adversely impacted by the completion of a sale of the business. If a buyer's interest is dependent upon, for example, the continuity of long-term customer contracts and/or a key supplier relationship, the cessation of such relationships may be fatal to your exit negotiations.

Regulatory Restrictions on Assignments/Changes of Control

As mentioned above, it is critical to identify any legislative restrictions and/or special conditions attaching to any existing permits, licences and/or registrations held by the business which are not transferable to the buyer. Unless the buyer has its own licences and/or can independently obtain them, the inability to transfer key permits to it may be fatal to any exit transaction.

Domestic/Foreign Law Risk

Depending upon the industry in which your client operates, and the nature of its products, services and/or customers, your client's business will be subject to a large number of domestic Canadian federal, provincial and municipal laws of either general or specific application. It will not come as a surprise to you that many businesses are non-compliant with some of these laws (although often it is to a degree which, on balance, will not have a material adverse impact on the business). However, a proper exit planning process should identify any areas or potential areas of non-compliance with general and industry-specific laws. More often than not, your client will be quite familiar with the laws affecting its own industry but less familiar with laws of general application (*e.g.*, provincial consumer protection legislation).

Moreover, many Canadian businesses have some level of foreign business activity. This may be limited to customers that are resident in other provinces or countries or may extend to the existence of employees or agents resident in such jurisdictions and/or some physical or permanent establishment in such jurisdictions. In these cases, the business may have extensive (and often valuable) business activities in such jurisdictions and be unknowingly offside various foreign business and tax laws. In such cases, the possibility of foreign legal risk may provide a buyer of the business with leverage to negotiate favourable price concessions and/or cause it to abort negotiations.

ASSESSING "VALUE THREATS" — SEE WHAT A BUYER SEES

Not every buyer will care about every "skeleton" to the same degree. While it is incumbent upon your client and your client's advisors to undergo the process of identifying potential "value threats" as I have identified above, it may not be practical (or possible) to incur the cost and time necessary to address all of these considerations, especially when the expected exit date is well into the future.

However, if for any given "value threat" your client is able to answer "yes" to any of the following six questions, then chances are that the particular threat should be addressed sooner rather than later:

- **Impact on Title:** Does it affect or impair the very ownership to the assets or shares which a buyer wants to acquire?
- **Nature of the Problem:** Is it a recurring circumstance (as opposed to an isolated or one-time event)?
- **Impact on Key Relationships:** Does it materially impair or threaten the existence of any valuable relationships which the business has with any key customers, suppliers or other stakeholders?
- **Cost to Fix:** Is the cost (in money's worth and time) to rectify the "skeleton" substantial?
- **Business Continuity:** Does it materially impair the ability of a buyer to continue to operate the business following the exit in the same manner in which your client operated the business prior to the exit?
- **Who Should Bear the Risk:** Is it a risk which no buyer is likely to want to assume, and which most buyers will expect a seller to fix or accept responsibility for?

STRATEGIC CONSIDERATIONS AND MANAGING "VALUE THREATS"

In light of the six questions posed above, the following are six basic strategic considerations aimed to assist you in discussing with your clients how to handle some of the "value threats" identified by the exit planning process:

- **Assess Your Negotiating Strength:** If you believe your client has (or will have) superior bargaining strength in the exit negotiations, you may (aggressively) take the position that your client need not address any "skeletons" at this stage, and address them only if necessary after the exit negotiations have commenced.
- **Don't Wait/Start Early:** In the case of any opportunistic litigation which this process identifies, it is often prudent (and less costly) to take steps to negotiate a settlement with the other party long before exit negotiations commence. As you can appreciate, the cost of settling will likely go up once the other party learns that your client is trying to sell the business.
- **Communications and Confidentiality:** Your client needs to take steps to carefully control the exit planning process and avoid leaks wherever possible.
- **Contractual Renewals, Etc.:** To the extent that the planning process has identified any negative contractual provisions which arise in connection with any exit or "change of control", your client should try to negotiate changes (or deletions) to these provisions as part of any contract renewal talks. Obviously, the new agreements which are being negotiated with new stakeholders from time to time should be reviewed carefully by your client's counsel to ensure that unfavourable exit provisions are not included in the final signed copies.
- **Be Proactive:** To the extent that your client is offside any important laws, consider the costs of compliance and implement corrective measures without delay and before these issues lead to litigation or regulatory action. Additionally, if there are any areas of inadvertent non-compliance with tax legislation, your client and your client's tax advisors should consider to what extent applicable tax fairness legislation or voluntary disclosure procedures might be used to reach a lower-cost resolution well before any exit negotiations commence.
- **Fix the Easy Ones First:** Your client may find that, for example, fixing minute book deficiencies and contacting old creditors to dis-

charge stale PPSA registrations may be "low hanging fruit" in the process of implementing exit preparations.

PULLING IT ALL TOGETHER

You and your clients should consider exit planning as part of the other planning exercises undertaken in other parts of this book. Proper exit planning requires the client and the client's key advisors (including legal, tax, accounting, insurance, pension/benefits and financial) to identify key "value threats" to a successful exit, and to develop/execute a strategy to eliminate, manage and/or mitigate those threats for the sole purpose of helping the client to ultimately unlock upon exit the maximum after-tax liquid value from the client's business.

EXIT PLANNING PREPARATIONS — LEGAL CHECKLIST

The following is a non-comprehensive listing of pertinent legal matters to consider in the context of exit planning preparations:

A. Getting Organized — What's in the Closet?

Obtain public search results

Review material agreements

Consider legislative/regulatory licensing requirements

Review corporate minute books

Review corporate structure

B. Identifying Skeletons/Value Threats

Minute book deficiencies

Issues affecting asset ownership/encumbrances

Share capital ownership issues

Opportunistic litigants

Tax audit/reassessment risk

Product warranty/liability issues

Environmental issues

Contractual restrictions on assignments/changes of control

Regulatory restrictions on assignments/changes of control

C. Assessing Skeletons/Value Threats

Consider impact on title to shares/assets

What is the nature of the problem — recurring vs. isolated?

Is there any negative impact on key relationships?

What is the cost to fix — material vs. *de minimus*?

Can the business continue "as is"?

Who should bear the risk?

D. Managing Skeletons/Value Threats — Strategic Considerations

Assess your negotiating strength — will buyer let it slide?

Neutralize potential litigants via early settlement

Loose lips sink ships — preserve exit confidentiality

Negotiate away third party approvals upon contract renewals

Be proactive — address legal compliance issues early on

Fix the easy ones first — begin at the beginning

CHAPTER 49

RETIREMENT COMPENSATION ARRANGEMENTS

Trevor R. Parry

Overview

This chapter introduces the concept of the retirement compensation arrangement (RCA). It then describes how an RCA can be used in conjunction with an IPP to maximize retirement savings for high-income earners employed by incorporated businesses.

Learning Objectives

By the end of this chapter, you should be able to:

- describe what a retirement compensation arrangement is;
- list the benefits that an RCA provides for both a sponsoring company and for the member of the plan; and
- understand how the creation of an RCA will provide additional retirement funding and other opportunity above that of an IPP for top earners within a corporation.

INTRODUCTION

For many companies and government agencies, providing adequate retirement income for their senior and most valued employees presents a problem. Frequently, the pension limits allow for providing only a fraction of required income. It requires innovative planning to address this "pension gap". Historically, annuities were purchased and claimed as deductible expenses by firms, with the future stream of income providing the extra income required to address the shortfall. The RCA rules brought uniformity to the situation, setting out how employers might fund pension gaps going forward. The RCA rules have also been, and are still, used in a punitive fashion as an anti-avoidance mechanism. The general rule is that a firm may wish to establish an RCA, but should avoid having one imposed upon it.

In 1986, the federal government introduced new measures called the retirement compensation arrangement rules. As described in subsection 248(1) of the *Income Tax Act*, R.S.C. 1985, c. 1 (5th Supp.), RCA "means a plan or arrangement under which contributions ... are made by an employer or former employer of a taxpayer ... to a custodian in connection with benefits that are to be or may be received or enjoyed by any person on, after or in contemplation of any substantial change in the services rendered by the taxpayer, the retirement of the taxpayer or the loss of an office or employment of the taxpayer ...".

RCA STRUCTURE

The RCA is a trusteed pension structure that allows for higher contribution limits than traditional pension plans. All contributions are tax deductible to the sponsoring corporation and taxed in the hands of the plan member when they are withdrawn. As it is based on a defined contribution structure, there are no inherent required rates of return on the investments held inside the trust, and contributions and withdrawals are at the discretion of the sponsoring company and plan member, respectively. A company may sponsor several different RCAs or a single RCA with multiple members, depending on the situation.

Corporate Employment

One prerequisite for establishing an RCA is having a corporate sponsor in place to settle the RCA trust and to make contributions to the RCA. Partnerships and sole proprietorships are prohibited from establishing RCAs. In addition to a corporate sponsor, the beneficiary of the RCA plan must have a current or prior employment relationship with the sponsoring company or predecessor company. Frequently, a situation develops where an RCA makes good business sense but cannot be put in place because the intended plan member, usually the owner-manager, has not been paid with employment income. Instead, payments of director fees, management fees and dividends replaced traditional earned income. While this may give rise to a short-term tax advantage, it can severely limit tax-planning flexibility. Long-term solutions, including the use of not only RCAs, but RRSPs and IPPs, cannot be implemented.

Trust

RCA trusts vary in how they are drafted. There is no requirement for a corporate trustee to be retained to manage the trust, although in certain situations, the sponsoring company may prefer such a provision. Where the plan member is a U.S. citizen and therefore is required to file with both the Canada Revenue Agency (CRA) and the Internal Revenue Service, corporate trustees may be preferred as they are more likely able to deal with this dual filing responsibility. Corporate trustees may also be preferable in situations involving public companies where rigorous shareholder reporting and potential conflict of interest can be avoided.

In most cases, a corporate trustee is not required. A tripartite board of trustees, or, in certain cases, a single individual, will suffice. In the case of the single trustee, the individual should be at arm's length from the company. A lawyer or accountant would traditionally fill this role. The tripartite trust allows for greater flexibility and may suit the owner-manager's situation better than a corporate or single trustee. In this situation, two individuals who are employees of the sponsoring company may act as trustees together with one arm's length individual. The trust itself will vary in the drafting, but it must clearly set out the powers, rights and protections afforded the trustees. This is particularly important in cases where the RCA may be pledged as security pursuant to a leveraging transaction.

Plan Text

The RCA will also include an RCA agreement or plan text. This is a critical document as it outlines the RCA plan. It sets out definitions of parties and the component elements in the RCA. It details plan member eligibility, vesting provisions (if required), nature and timing of contributions, contingencies for change of control of the sponsoring company, benefit descriptions and options, options upon disability of a plan member, options upon death of a member, funding and administration and any and all other issues that the plan sponsor feels the need to dictate. This plan text should also closely resemble a pension document as this is *prima facie* evidence that the structure is in fact an RCA and not a salary deferral arrangement (SDA).

Beneficiaries

Upon the death of the last living plan member, the trust assets are not subject to a deemed disposition as with RRSP/RIF and IPP assets. Instead, the named beneficiaries will commence a schedule of withdrawals, which will exhaust the assets of the trust within the next 20 years. This can be of significant benefit where the RCA assets are large, and a one-time lump-sum withdrawal would result in substantial taxation.

The plan member's spouse will automatically become the primary beneficiary upon the death of that plan member unless otherwise set out in the plan documents. In the event that the spouse has predeceased the plan member, the named beneficiaries, or contingent beneficiaries, will receive the plan assets without probate fees. Where a plan member has minor children, the member should name his or her estate as the contingent beneficiary to avoid the unwanted presence of the Public Trustee, who would otherwise take control of the assets until the individual children reach the age of majority.

Actuarial Certificate

Contributions that are made by a sponsoring company to the plan for the benefit of the employee(s) must be reasonable in the eyes of the CRA. Until recently, there was only conjecture as to what reasonableness would entail; it was not unusual to see some RCA contributions have no reasonable basis.

The CRA dealt with this issue in its September 16, 2005 letter:

> As the Act is silent with respect to the determination of whether or not a contribution to an RCA is reasonable, it is always a question of fact and depends on the circumstances surrounding each plan. Contribution amounts that are clearly supported by either an actuarial valuation or the use of some other formula based calculation may be more justifiable; however reasonability must be weighted taking into account all relevant factors.[1]

While the CRA says that it will accept formula-based calculations, there is the possibility for misuse and undercutting of the very concept of reasonableness. For instance, inclusion of dividend income, prohibited by the actuarial valuation method, would produce an RCA contribution that does not truly reflect pensionable or earned income.

Concerning the CRA letter, Gordon Lang writes:

> I would assert that the use of a best 3 year earnings formula for the purposes of calculating the earnings base for an RCA, when combined with other reasonable Actuarial Assumptions and Methods is reasonable. In the case of Company Owners, they often have life cycle earnings quite unlike those of regular employees. They will start as Company Founder then as the business increases may take on the titles of Chairman, President & CEO. As they wind down their involvement with the business they may ultimately be only a Director of the Company. Their final 5 years earnings as depicted on their Company T4's

[1] CRA letter: 2005-13240117 (16 September 2005).

> may well thus relate only to their period of Company service as a Director. Thus, basing their earnings, for the purpose of reasonableness, on the average of the final 5 years earnings is patently unreasonable. Earnings for RCA purposes should be based on actual T4 earnings and not on future earnings which may either be unreasonable or indeed based on fiction.[2]

The actuarial certificate is a document prepared and signed by an accredited actuary setting out the rationale for, and limitations to, any RCA contributions. Earned income, namely T4, T4A and T4PS (profit-sharing) income, may be used to calculate the RCA benefit. The average of the best three years will allow for a comprehensive approach in ascertaining contribution limits. If the plan member has income from a variety of related companies, then each of those companies may contribute to a single RCA, and the actuarial certificate will reflect this. The certificate accounts for how much of the contribution will arise as a result of past service and how much will be able to be contributed each year.

The company may contribute up to the limit set out in the certificate. The contributions are not mandatory, and if the maximum allowable contribution or past service is not used up in a given year, that amount will accumulate for contributions in future years. The chart below sets out a typical contribution ceiling schedule.

RCA inception date:	March 1, 2006	
Age:	49 years old	
Income:	$200,000 (three-year average)	
Retirement date:	65	
Example of current year service and past service amounts		
Maximum Actuarial Unfunded Liabilities (past service)		$1,404,800.00
Calendar	**Current Service**	
2006	73,800.00	(10 months)
2007	91,900.00	
2008	95,300.00	
2009	98,900.00	
2010	102,600.00	
2011	106,400.00	
2012	110,400.00	
2013	114,500.00	

---

[2] May 2005 article available online through Gordon B. Lang & Associates Inc.'s portal <www.gblinc.ca>.

Calendar	Current Service	
2014	118,800.00	
2015	123,300.00	
2016	127,900.00	
2017	132,700.00	
2018	137,700.00	
2019	142,900.00	
2020	148,300.00	
2021	153,900.00	
2022	159,700.00	

The member's first year contribution is $73,800. When coupled with the past service amount of $1,404,800, his *total first year maximum contribution room is $1,478,600.*

The RCA may also be used in combination with other retirement plans such as the IPP. While participating in an IPP or traditional group pension (RPP) will affect contribution limits to the RCA, the use of a personally funded RRSP will not have the same effect. As the RRSP is a personally funded and held asset, it has no bearing on RCA calculations.

Refundable Tax Account

Once the RCA trust is established and registered with the CRA, contributions may be made. To make a valid RCA contribution, the sponsoring company will issue two cheques, each for exactly 50% of the total contribution. One cheque will be made out to the plan custodian, usually an insurance or trust company, bank or investment company. The second cheque, for the remaining 50%, will be forwarded to the CRA. This remittance is a payment of refundable tax, and upon registration of the RCA trust, the CRA will assign a refundable tax account (RTA) to the RCA for this and any future contributions.

The RCA, unlike an RRSP or IPP, is not a tax-sheltered vehicle *per se*. While final taxation does not occur until the plan member receives a payment of benefit from the RCA, the plan itself is subject to ongoing refundable tax requirements. Fifty per cent of all realized interest, dividends and capital gains, net of fees and losses, is remitted to the RTA annually. For many people, the retarding of asset growth due to refundable tax is something to be avoided and has led to a variety of investment strategies implemented within the RCA.

Filings

Because the RCA is a trust, it has specific reporting requirements that are set out in legislation. The trustees will gather the relevant information regarding investment returns from the plan custodian in order to prepare this annual return. In the case where the RCA invests in a life insurance policy, the insurance company will be deemed to be the plan custodian.

Once the prerequisites have been established, the RCA plan itself can be put in place. The RCA is a trust that is registered with the RCA unit of the CRA. Completion and filing of a T733 is required to obtain an RCA account number. It is critical to remember that RCAs must be established and funded before the conclusion of the fiscal year. While the CRA will grant a grace period of 14 days following the fiscal year-end to receive the refundable tax remittance, those individuals establishing these plans, and their advisors, should be conscious of deadlines. The penalties for late remittance are onerous; 10% of the refundable tax is assessed for first-time tardiness, and this increases with each subsequent transgression.

In addition to the initial application for an RCA account number (Form 733), the trustees are also required to file a series of documents by March 31st of each year. Those documents include a Part X1.3 Tax Return, a T737-RCA Return for reporting employer contributions, a T4A-RCA Summary and a T4A-RCA Form for refunds of contributions to the employer and payments to beneficiaries. If payments are to be made to non-resident beneficiaries, an NR4 Summary and an NR4 Form for payments must be filed as well. The annual RCA Guide prepared by the CRA is an excellent and user-friendly resource for all those individuals responsible for the administration and reporting of RCAs.

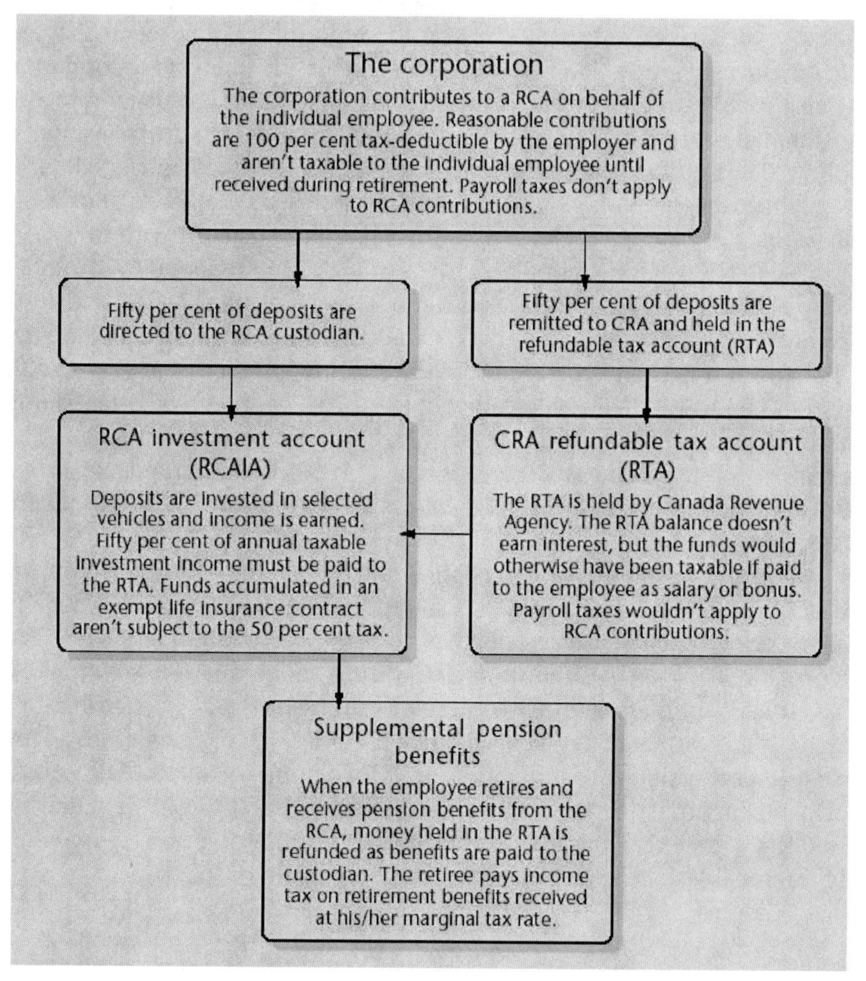

Flow chart above provided by AdvisorWorld.com Inc.

RCA APPLICATIONS

To understand why an RCA is used, and to identify scenarios where its introduction might be of aid, we must first determine the benefits or effects of the RCA. Generally, the RCA is a retirement planning tool that allows the plan member to defer income to a time and place of his or her choosing.

Advantages

By understanding the key benefits of the RCA — postponement of significant tax payments, flexibility of contributions and withdrawals, creditor proofing and estate planning — we can determine the scenarios where the RCA may be a timely and beneficial strategy.

RCAs offer a great deal of flexibility both in contributions and withdrawals. Once the limits are set, companies can fund any amount not exceeding those limits. The creation of an RCA does not automatically confer a liability on the employer. Also, remaining funding room can be carried forward, allowing almost complete company discretion as to when and how much a company will contribute to the RCA. Likewise, once the plan member has undergone a material change in employment, he or she has complete flexibility as to when he or she withdraws the funds. There is no set schedule and no age at which he or she must begin drawing.

The principal advantage of this flexibility is tax deferment. Contributions made into an RCA are not taxable until they are withdrawn from the plan. This allows the plan participant to take money that would normally be taxed at a high rate and instead have it placed in an RCA, intending to withdraw it in years when he or she is in a lower tax bracket. Additionally, some foreign tax jurisdictions may allow for the funds to be withdrawn at significantly lower rates than if the participant remained a Canadian resident.

Being that it is a trust, the RCA is protected from creditors of both the sponsoring company and the participant, unless otherwise bound by an agreement pledging the RCA assets as security. This may be of significant interest to those companies and professional corporations that find themselves in markets in which the risk of litigation is a practical concern.

The RCA documents may be prepared to remove any company role after initial contribution, or a letter of understanding may be prepared by all relevant parties setting out that the RCA is to be funded with a single contribution, and the sponsoring company will have no legal tie or future responsibility to the RCA or plan member after funding.

Where a business has multiple family generations employed, a single RCA can be created for the whole family unit, allowing contributions that were driven by the parents' income to be passed down to the children, taxed only on withdrawal by the children, not on the death of the parents. Even with only a single participant in the plan, on death the beneficiary has a full 20 years to collapse the RCA, spreading out the tax burden.

Drawbacks

There is no firm case law or legislative direction that subjects RCA assets to inclusion in net family property (NFP) calculations in divorce proceedings. While there is reason to argue that these assets might be exempt from such proceedings, it is more probable that the RCA will be included and therefore not survive divorce. The RCA is likely to be seen as a pension plan, and a review of the key documents would in most cases indicate intention to create something very much akin to a pension plan. All of this forces the conclusion that the RCA is more likely to be incorporated into NFP calculations.

An employer must avoid creating a salary deferral arrangement when establishing an RCA. If an employee is otherwise entitled to an amount of remuneration pursuant to his or her employment contract, and that remuneration becomes an RCA contribution, the CRA is likely to find an SDA and levy tax, interest and penalties. If, however, an employment contract clearly stipulates that the amount and nature of remuneration are to be determined solely at the discretion of the employer, then it is likely that no SDA will be found to exist. Finding an SDA in the situation where an owner-manager contributes to an RCA is highly unlikely as these individuals' overall compensation varies each year with the profitability of the firm.

If an employee were to leave the company, and the vesting provisions had not been satisfied, that employee may have a cause of action where it can be proven that the employee was otherwise entitled to the plan contributions as a performance bonus pursuant to the employment agreements. While not insurmountable, this presents a challenge to counsel in drafting such agreements to allow for the RCA to be established and funded, without the threat of future litigation.

Employee Contributions

In certain circumstances, an employee may be required to contribute to his or her RCA. This was addressed by the CRA in the aforementioned letter:

> The Act does not specifically dictate what level of benefits may be provided under an RCA. However, an employee may only deduct amounts paid in the year as contributions under an RCA to the extent that the conditions in paragraph 8(1) (m.2) was intended to be a relieving position which would in part permit, within limits, the deduction of employee contributions where they are required under the terms of an unregistered pension plan that also meets the RCA definition. Consequently, before any amount will be deductible under paragraph 8(1) (m.2), the plan or arrangement has to be a pension plan. Where it is established that the plan or arrangement constitutes a pen-

sion plan, an employee contribution will be deductible under paragraph 8(1)(m.2) of the Act where all of the following conditions are satisfied:

(a) the amount is paid to a custodian of the arrangement who is resident in Canada;

(b) the taxpayer was required, by the employer's conditions of employment, to contribute the amount; and

(c) the amount contributed to the RCA in the year does not exceed the amounts contributed to the RCA in the year by any other.[3]

Where the above requirement has been satisfied, the employee contribution can be accepted by the custodian and be deducted by the employee. This situation is rarely encountered, but may exist where a company wishes to put an RCA in place but missed the filing deadline. As a result, contributions are made by the employees and matched by the sponsoring company, with the resulting deduction facilitating the intended tax result.

RCA INVESTMENTS

There are effectively no rules as to what an RCA can invest in. The CRA has recently opined that direct or indirect investment of the assets of the RCA trust in the sponsoring company is something that should be avoided as it may result in a questioning of the intent behind creating the RCA in the first place. If we therefore assume that RCAs will invest in arm's length investments, there is a wide array of choices open to the RCA trustees. In certain cases, the RCA trustees will direct the investments of the trust, and in other instances the company may appoint an investment manager to direct these affairs.

While an RCA may invest in any securities, it might be advantageous to look at investments that have certain tax-efficient characteristics. Tax-sheltered or tax-efficient investments that minimize the annual remittances to the refundable tax account are, *ceteris paribus*, preferable to other types of investments. There are a host of investment options that will wholly or partially achieve this goal, including life insurance and certain tax-efficient types of pooled investments.

Insurance

For many people, the use of permanent life insurance contracts, either whole life or universal life, inside the RCA is the preferred investment option. Offering a wide choice of underlying investments, the cash value

---

[3] Canada Revenue Agency, Document 2005 — 13240117 at 3.

(CV) of the contract will grow tax-sheltered, eliminating the need to remit annually to the RTA.

When the plan member commences withdrawals from the RCA, he or she may do so by either "leveraging" the insurance policy or taking cash withdrawals from the policy. The former strategy would see the policy pledged as collateral to a financial institution which, in return, would forward a loan or loans to the plan member. The death of the plan member results in the death benefit being paid to the RCA trust, which in turn repays the lending institution. The latter strategy does not require a lending institution but gives rise to ongoing refundable tax remittances. These withdrawals are deemed taxable dispositions requiring 50% of that disposition to be remitted.[4]

One drawback of the "insured RCA" approach is that on the death of the insured, the normally tax-free death benefit is received by the RCA trust and is paid out to the named beneficiary(s) as taxable RCA income. This is unfortunate as these death benefits are usually a considerable amount. The sponsoring company should give consideration to a "split dollar" insured RCA strategy. In that instance, the RCA and the company would share the ownership of the insurance contract, with the CV being owned by the RCA trust and the death benefit being owned by the sponsoring company. With the growth of the CV sheltered, the value of the RCA asset is maximized due to the lack of annual remittance. Upon retirement, that CV may be drawn down or leveraged to provide for the income needs of the plan member. Upon the death of the plan member, the death benefit will be paid to the corporation, creating a credit to the capital dividend account. This in turn will be paid out to the shareholders tax-free.

The split dollar strategy, while initially more expensive since it requires a specially tailored contract and actuarial report on the validity of the split, allows for more comprehensive financial planning.

The buy-sell provisions, common in most shareholder agreements, and frequently unfunded by the company, may now be funded, making corporate succession planning a reality. The company also bears the cost of insurance as a non-deductible expense above and beyond the RCA contribution (which of course remains deductible).

While the insured RCA route may be preferable in many cases, it is not unusual to see a combination of insurance- and investment-based product solutions. Often lack of insurability due to medical issues, or lack of time needed for accumulation in the CV, mitigate against the use

---

[4] J.T. Cuperfain and F. Marino, *Canadian Taxation of Life Insurance*, 2nd ed. (Toronto: Thomson Carswell, 2002) at 203.

of insurance in an RCA. It is also possible that as a result of the underwriting process, the contribution to the RCA cannot all be sheltered in an insurance contract, and provision should be made to find a suitable tax-efficient investment vehicle.

Tax-Efficient Investments

Certain types of mutual funds, known as corporate class funds, may operate tax-sheltered, providing a significant benefit inside an RCA. Exchange-traded funds and certain hedge funds have been used to satisfy a need for tax efficiency. The trustees, investment manager and investment advisor will have to thoroughly examine the tax efficiency and risk of each proposed investment.

LEVERAGED RCAs

The ability to use the RCA for corporate financing is an opportunity in financial planning that is attractive for many candidates, both lenders and borrowers. For that reason, most of Canada's chartered banks have established lending programs to allow for the front-end leveraged RCA. Banks and other lenders find the secured nature of the transaction attractive, and, as the RTA is a receivable of the trust, banks will often lend up to 90% of the total value of the RCA.

In essence, the ability to leverage an RCA lies in the laws of trusts. It is a standard provision of most trusts that the trustees may pledge the assets of that trust as collateral or security to facilitate lending. While the trust indenture will have some substantial modifications and characteristics germane to RCAs, the provision for the trustees to pledge the RCA assets will be found in most RCA trust indentures. That said, the RCA is a retirement plan and must always maintain its *bona fide* status as such. There is generally believed to be a stipulation that the plan members must have unimpeded access to the trust assets, as benefit payments, upon the stated retirement date of the individual.

This rule has been translated into a practice enforced by lenders that the loans which are made, and secured by the RCA, must be repaid in full by the retirement date of the plan member. To do otherwise would create an "evergreen" scenario in which the loans are not repaid during the lifetime of the plan member. A loan on trust assets of a retirement plan that is not repaid until the condition that follows retirement, that is, death, is at its core not a retirement plan, and consequently such a plan is not an RCA, and will, and should, attract the scrutiny of the CRA.

Proceeding carefully and with the right team of professionals advising all parties is the only way to undertake leveraged RCA transactions. The sponsoring company will retain legal counsel to advise it on the terms of the loan. The bank or client will be required to obtain a tax opinion from an approved accounting or law firm, setting out to the lender that the RCA is an RCA and not a salary deferral arrangement or other non-RCA structure, and, as such, the bank can realize on its security interest in the event of default or in enforcing the terms of the lending agreements.

Each lender will have a somewhat different approach to the transaction. Some will insist on acting as trustee, while others will insist on a separate corporation (investment corporation) to be created to service the loan between RCA trust and the sponsoring company.

The lender will insist on low risk investments in the RCA trust. Often, the assignment of a death benefit of a life insurance policy will be part of the transaction. Some lenders will insist on a personal guarantee provided by the principals of the sponsoring company. Each lender will have different requirements, and costs will reflect this.

In addition, to the due diligence that the lender will perform on the prospective borrower, the purpose of the loan must be considered. A direct payment of the loan proceeds or diversion of those proceeds to an individual shareholder or shareholders will likely not meet with approval.

Care should be given not to lend the invested portion of the RCA back, directly or indirectly, to the sponsoring company. While not strictly prohibited, the CRA has opined that this type of transaction might question the intent of the RCA.

WITHDRAWING FROM RCAs

Withdrawals from the RCA may commence upon a substantial change in the nature of employment of a plan member. The plan member will request payment from the trustees who, provided that they are satisfied the member may make such a withdrawal, will pay out the requested amount. The trustees will make all necessary withholdings and remit to the proper authorities. The individual will then claim this income on the annual T1 General return.

Before any distribution is made, the trustees will need to inform the CRA of the intention to commence withdrawals. This is done by obtaining a Remittance Number for Tax Withheld from a Retirement Compensation Arrangement. The trustees will complete a T735 form to initiate this process. The particular regime for withdrawals is set out in a very detailed fashion in *Retirement Compensation Arrangements Guide* available from the CRA.

For every dollar withdrawn from the RCA trust, the RTA will refund 50 cents to the investment account.

If the plan member is not a Canadian resident, the trustees will be responsible for remitting the required withholding tax to the CRA.

APPLIED RCAs

In practice, the RCA is an effective solution in many different cases. As the CRA is also now looking toward intent in assessing RCAs, retirement must always be the primary planning goal in RCA practice.

There are two primary focuses of RCAs: employee compensation and owner-manager solutions. Employee compensation includes executive compensation planning, severance, non-resident issues and employee retention. Owner-manager solutions include profit management, leverage strategies, business exit strategies and non-residency planning.

Employee Use

Executive Compensation

Supplemental Executive Retirement Plans (SERPs) have existed in Canadian business for years. They are promises, usually put in place through a resolution of the board of directors, that establish a retirement plan for a key employee that goes beyond the pension limitations set out by the CRA. Often, the retirement package offered to a key executive is a make-or-break element of the employment relationship. For many large Canadian companies, these SERPs appear as unfunded liabilities; they are paid out of cash flow as needed.

This unfunded, non-segregated structure creates significant problems for both the employer and employee. A change in control or bankruptcy of the sponsoring company could result in the SERP promise being unenforceable, leaving the employee in a rather precarious situation. The company may also not like to have large unfunded liabilities on its balance sheets. These concerns make funding the SERP critical. Some firms have used letters of credit to fund SERPs, but this must be seen as a stop-gap measure.

Corporations are beginning to address this funding challenge by embracing the RCA. The RCA may be established for either a single employee or an entire class of employees. The employees' retirement needs are being addressed through a creditor-proof vehicle. The employer has cleaned up its balance sheet. Employee loyalty is enhanced.

In this situation, the RCA acts very much like a large RRSP where assets can grow and pay out enhanced but not specific income upon retirement of the plan member.

Care must be taken to assure that a SERP does not constitute a salary deferral arrangement.

Severance

One of the unfortunate facts for today's employee is that lifetime employment with one company is an exception to the rule. Severance is therefore something that companies should incorporate in their planning. The RCA is of particular use in this area.

A large severance package in one year will give rise to significant taxation. If the departing employee can mitigate the tax liability by dividing the large lump sum into smaller amounts occurring over several tax years, the result is usually a significant reduction in overall tax paid. The RCA is the vehicle that will accomplish this.

The RCA is funded as the plan member is terminated. Because termination constitutes a substantial and material change in the nature of employment, the former employee is legally entitled to commence withdrawals at leisure.

If an individual finds employment soon after his or her termination from the previous firm, he or she may not need to access the RCA for many years. The RCA can then provide a new source of retirement income for the future. If the plan member needs income, the member may withdraw it in amounts of his or her choosing. Using Ontario tax rates, a $400,000 severance payment (excluding other income) would result in taxation of $168,055, while redirecting that lump-sum payment into four $100,000 RCA payments, each occurring in a separate year, would result in tax of $29,374 annually, or $117,496 in total. That is a considerable savings in tax.[5]

Non-resident

International firms with subsidiary operations in Canada may find the RCA quite useful because it provides a means of equalizing benefits that executives in other countries are able to receive. For instance, both the United States and United Kingdom have far more expansive pension

---

[5] Ernst & Young 2009 Personal Tax Calculator, online: <http://www.ey.com/CA/en/Services/Tax/Tax-Calculators-2009-Personal-Tax>.

limits. The RCA allows the Canadian executive to receive a pension comparable to his or her foreign colleagues.

Retention

The use of vesting is critical in understanding the efficacy of a group RCA. In traditional pension plans, the plan member is said to be vested (entitled to the beneficial ownership of his or her pension asset) after two years of membership in the plan.

The RCA has no such rules concerning vesting. The plan sponsor may include in the RCA agreement/plan text a deferred vesting provision. While we encourage firms to avoid being Draconian with regards to vesting, the use of this provision will go a long way to retaining a key employee. Traditionally, the plan member would see the benefit vest after five or ten years of service. There would likely be an acceleration clause that would result in immediate vesting upon change of control of the sponsoring company.

As the majority of the employee group that would be party to this type of RCA will not be fully vested for many years, the employer should give consideration to creating a single group RCA. The plan custodian, or retained actuary, can demonstrably assist the trustees in preparing the annual filing requirements, such as accounting for each plan member's share of the RTA.

Owner Use

Profit Management

Where a company's overall tax strategy is to limit profit to $300,000 (soon to be $400,000) to take advantage of the small business tax rates for qualified business corporations, the usual means of achieving this is to pay bonuses to the shareholders. The company is then able to pay a low rate of tax. This strategy, while advantageous to the corporation, gives rise to considerable tax payments for the individual owner-manager. The company, if operating in provinces that impose payroll or employer health taxes, will also have to pay these as a result of the "bonus down" strategy.

In many cases, the creation of an RCA may be a preferable strategy. RCA contributions would likely be equal to what otherwise would have been paid out as a shareholder bonus. The company receives tax relief for the contribution, and escapes having to pay the provincial tax, finding itself in the same or preferable situation as having paid out bonuses.

The individual may find this strategy preferable. Typically, the person receiving the bonus will already be in the top tax bracket; the bonus is thus taxed at the top rate. If tax rates at withdrawal are lower than when the initial contribution was made to the RCA, then the taxpayer has reduced his or her overall taxation.

Leveraging

The most common uses for a leveraged RCA are:

- providing additional working capital to the sponsoring company;
- expanding of business operations;
- acquiring competitors;
- buying out other shareholders; and
- flushing the shareholder loan account.

The primary determination for leveraging the RCA is: Will the strong internal rate of growth outweigh the cost of borrowing? While loans are usually quite favourable in terms of interest, the associated legal, actuarial, banking and accounting costs must be considered.

Businesses that enjoy strong cyclical growth, such as builders and real estate developers, are just two categories of businesses that have utilized this strategy. The strategy is now being used to facilitate orderly transfer of ownership amongst shareholders or between generations in family business scenarios.

Exit Strategy

It is an unfortunate fact that entrepreneurs, while they may do some planning for their own retirement, do little planning for the retirement of their business. Too often, owners assume that their real retirement income will come from the sale of their business. They plan on the $500,000 life capital gains exemption for sale of shares of a qualified small business corporation. The unfortunate fact is that the sale that the owner intends to undertake is rarely the sale that the owner ends up getting.

The vast majority of Canadian business owners do not sell the shares of the corporation, but rather enter into asset sale transactions. Typically, the purchaser does not in most cases wish to purchase the liabilities of the business that would attach in an equity sale. Most franchises require a franchisee to sell the franchise back to the parent company through an asset sale.

The effect of this is profound. Entrepreneurs who expect to pay very little tax on the sale of their company because of preferential tax treatment on capital gains will find that they face a rather daunting tax bill in the year of sale. This is because selling assets generates income to the company. When the final accounting is completed on the sale, an entrepreneur might find a tax debt equivalent to almost half of the value of the business.

The use of a tax postponement strategy, made possible by instituting an RCA, may be the critical and timely piece of financial planning that the business owner needs. The strategy is straightforward. Once the contribution limits have been established, the sponsoring company will fund the RCA. In many cases, the long period of employment that the owner-manager(s) has(ve) accumulated allows for considerable contribution room. The contribution will often offset all of the tax liability associated with the sale of assets.

The result is secure income, enjoyment of retirement and substantial reduction of tax. Of course, the efficacy of the RCA strategy is reduced with substantial income from other sources such as rents, royalties or associated fees from other business interests. However, for the vast majority of Canadian business owners, the primary retirement income will be from the RCA and other registered plans.

A company that sells its assets, creating a taxable income of $3,000,000, would normally attract considerable tax, even with two owners to split the bill. In Ontario, they would each owe $666,801 in taxes, and the company would have $50,700 of Employer Health tax to pay. Even in Alberta, which enjoys much more reasonable levels of tax, the shareholders would owe $573,247 each on their 50% ownership of the company.

The advantages of tax postponement as allowed through the use of the RCA are clear. It is unlikely that the business owner will need to take a single payment of $1,500,000. He or she is more likely to need income of $150,000 per year. That would mean that the tax on that income (excluding other income) would be $52,030 in Ontario and $46,747 in Alberta. Projecting forward, that would result in tax savings of about $150,000 per person over a ten-year period.

An RCA may have a role in an anticipated share sale. In order to safeguard the ability to claim the lifetime capital gains exemption, the RCA could be put in place in earlier years to create an ongoing corporate purification strategy. Passive asset problems, which may jeopardize the exemption, can be avoided by managing the creation of retained earnings through RCA contributions.

As the vast majority of Canadian entrepreneurs will attempt some form of change of control of their business (most through asset sale) in the next 15 years, it is essential that they learn about the benefits of tax postponement through the use of a properly established RCA.

Non-resident

An RCA participant who changes his or her legal residency may be able to withdraw his or her RCA pension assets at considerably lower tax rates (15% to 25%) than he or she could by remaining in Canada. Care should be taken to consult with an international tax expert to make sure that the participant meets the residency requirements and to determine the actual tax treatment.

CONCLUSION

The RCA is a vehicle that has enjoyed expanded use in recent years. For employers wishing to fashion superior compensation, retirement and retention strategies, the RCA can be a straightforward approach to achieve these key goals and to remove unfunded liabilities from the balance sheet. For the business owner looking to defer or reduce tax, find alternative financing strategies and reduce tax upon the sale of his or her enterprise, the RCA is a vehicle that he or she must consider.

With taxation burdens staring employers and entrepreneurs in the face, the time to consider the RCA, in the light of its flexibility and positive consequences, is now.

PART VII

FAMILY AND ESTATE WEALTH DISTRIBUTION PLANNING CONSIDERATIONS

CHAPTER 50

GO DEEPER FOR MORE HIGHLY SATISFIED CLIENTS

Charles L. Stanley

Overview

This chapter offers an overview of the tremendous value to both the Trusted Advisor and the client of a discovery process that is holistic rather than limited to the traditional financial or estate data questionnaires.

Learning Objectives

By the end of this chapter, you will be able to:

- understand the value of "values" questions and relationship building with clients;
- understand the difference between a salesperson and a consultative advisor — the new paradigm of advice vs. sales;
- understand that a proper in-depth discovery process brings leadership to the planning process;
- understand that "highly satisfied" clients are those who believe your work product meets their personal values, goals and concerns;
- understand that "highly satisfied" clients help you grow your business, while merely "satisfied" clients may actually cost you money and future business; and
- learn about different practice models for holistic discovery.

There are well over 100 different tools, techniques, strategies, tactics and combinations thereof to enable high net-worth individuals and successful business owners to manage their wealth in accordance with their values and goals in life. Discovering the appropriate combination must begin with clarity about the wealth holder's values, goals, people and causes they hold in highest esteem. Discussing or proposing specific strategies or tools is futile unless it is done in the context of exactly what the wealth holder desires to accomplish in terms of both their goals and the values that control how they accomplish those goals. The importance of this clarity cannot be overstated, since many of the tools, techniques, strategies and tactics involve irrevocable decisions. One would not want to make an irrevocable decision only to find out later that it will prohibit one from accomplishing what one really wants us to accomplish.

THE NEW PARADIGM

The historic paradigm of the financial services world is that of salesman. While there have been attempts in the past several years in the United States and Canada to change the paradigm, it has been difficult to do so. The major institutions, insurance companies and major wirehouse securities brokerages have been the bastion of high level salespersons since their inception. The compensation structures of both of these industry segments also mitigate against the desired change of paradigm. Today, we all want to be seen as "Trusted Advisors" or as "consultants" rather than as salespersons. Of course, the question is, are we really Trusted Advisors and consultants or merely more sophisticated salespersons? And, yes, I know, we are all salespersons of our services and, "nothing happens until someone sells something". But, we can either be a product salesperson or sell clients on the advisory relationship and provide valuable service rather than product. What we really are will betray us sooner or later whether we are a salesperson or an advisor. (As a side note, will the financial system realignment that took place in the fall of 2008 with the demise of Lehman Brothers and the loss of the independence of Merrill Lynch, and who knows what else by the time it is done, result in a more consultative and fiduciary industry? Personally, I hope so.)

Case Study — Family Financial Philosophy[1]

Rick Harmon (age 56) is a third generation independent Funeral Director who owns three funeral locations and a crematorium in the greater San Diego area of Southern California. Rick is married to Francine (Frannie), his first and only wife of 35 years, and has three children, Ricky (33), George (31) and Marianne (28). All three of the children are happily married. Ricky and George are both involved in the family funeral business. Marianne's husband is an attorney who practises corporate

[1] During the course of this chapter, the text within boxes provides an example of how a family financial philosophy statement is developed and used.

transactional law with a major national firm, and she is a stay-at-home mom to their two small children.

The Harmons are a dedicated, Christian, family-centred extended family. Rick Harmon has thought deeply about the implications of his Christianity on how he runs his business, and has worked hard to pass on these values to his children, especially the boys, who are involved with him in the family business.

Typically, when engaging in Estate Planning and Wealth Management, the majority of time during the planning is spent in plan design — as much as 80% to 90% — with minimal time devoted to step one, discovering what the client's values, goals and objectives are. One of the world's oldest adages may be the reason: *follow the money*.

Most Estate Planning advisors are paid only when a plan is implemented. For example, an attorney is paid to create documents, an insurance professional is paid when he or she sells your client a policy, an accountant is paid to do the tax analysis and a stock broker is paid to handle the securities transactions. They are all paid for plan implementation; nobody gets paid to delve into, clarify and document your client's values and objectives.

But how can you, as a Trusted Advisor, design an effective plan if you don't understand your client's values, goals and objectives? That is like firing your gun and then running out in front of the bullet and holding up the target in front of the bullet. You must first get clearly sited on the target before you pull the trigger.

In addition to "following the money", there is also an "advisor bias" created by differing levels and types of training and expertise. As Stephen Covey put it, "People see the world *not* as it is, but as they are."

Consider four "advisors":

- insurance professional;
- investment professional;
- attorney; and
- accountant.

Pose a problem to each of them separately and ask for a solution. I'm willing to bet you will get four different solutions, each from their own different perspective.

Because different advisors have different opinions, it's difficult for a client to know who's right. When this occurs, more often than not, the end result is … *nothing*! Your client does nothing, because they aren't sure who or what is correct.

This "advisor bias" creates confusion for you as a Trusted Advisor who's trying to take responsibility for the estate plan. When people become confused by the process, all they want to do is get out of the process ... end the conversation ... eliminate the anxiety. So, they do nothing, and nobody is served.

These issues of "follow the money" and "advisor bias" are part of the old paradigm and don't fit in with the new paradigm of a truly consultative Trusted Advisor.

The Harmons' four locations represent substantial hard asset wealth estimated at approximately $4.5 million. Rick and Francine's home is estimated at $1.5 million. Other assets bring their personal holdings to $9 million.

Rick and Francine want their boys to be able to take over the businesses in about ten years or so. They want to position the company for growth, since it will need to support two owner-families after Rick and Francine retire from the business. Rick and Francine definitely do not want to have to sell their business to one of the corporate funeral companies that are buying up all of the well-run funeral businesses (like Rick and Francine's) that they can. Rick and Francine believe there is a significant cultural difference between the family-run business and the corporate funeral providers. Family-run businesses have greater flexibility to do what they want to meet the needs of their grieving families, whereas the corporate entities have their company policies and shareholder value to consider at all times.

I believe there really is a desire on the part of a significant percentage of the industry to move from the sales paradigm to the "advice" or "consulting" paradigm. In order for this to happen, there will have to be a shift not only in compensation methods, but also in practice methodology because "sales" and "advice" are really different businesses with different goals. In the sales world, the goal is to sell the product and make profit for the salesperson and the manufacturer of the product (the insurance company or brokerage firm). The person who buys the product is a customer. In the advice world, there are no customers, only clients. The "product" is the impartation of wisdom about financial matters in the context of the client's life. The advisory relationship is a long-term relationship. In the sales business, the only value to the ongoing relationship is to be there when another sales opportunity comes up. Insight into the client's life is only material to help with a better sales presentation.

CLIENT LEADERSHIP

How many times have you heard of high net-worth families approaching their estate planning and never actually implementing a plan? Anecdotally, I have heard responses in the realm of four out of five being non-implementers. I don't know if there have been any true academic studies of the question. However, if we take the anecdote as reasonably accurate, we must ask the question, "Why?" Why do four out of five families that embark on the estate planning process not reach the other shore? I believe I can answer the question at least in part. Research done by Russ Alan Prince sheds some interesting light on this question. In his book *The Private Client Lawyer Now and In the Future*, Prince surveys 154 families with a net worth of $7.5 million or more along with 619 lawyers who devoted more than 51% of their practices to the private client and found that "among the wealthy who understood their estate plans, nearly nine out of ten of them thought that the recommended legal solutions did not deal with their personal goals, wants, needs and objectives".[2] Notice that this is among the one of five that did follow through and implement an estate plan. But, what was their satisfaction level? Not good. Their perception was that their needs weren't being met.

Estate taxes are a concern for Rick and Frannie, especially since Congress has failed to clarify the future of the estate tax regime they will have to deal with. The Harmons have considered establishing some kind of charitable fund that will support their Christian charitable commitment and particularly their commitment to the geographic areas where their businesses are located, but aren't clear on just what to do or how to do it.

They have concern about treating their children equitably. Since the boys will be involved in the business, how should the ownership be divided? Should Marianne have ownership, since she won't be involved in running or working in the business?

This takes me back to my opening paragraph, "There are well over 100 different tools, techniques, strategies, tactics and combinations thereof to enable high net-worth individuals and successful business owners to manage their wealth in accordance with their values and goals in life. Discovering the appropriate combination must begin with clarity about the wealth holder's values, goals, people and causes they hold in

[2] Russ Alan Prince, *The Private Client Lawyer Now and in the Future* (Overland Park, Kansas: Wealth Management Press, 2003) at 90.

highest esteem. Discussing or proposing specific strategies or tools is futile unless it is done in the context of exactly what the wealth holder desires to accomplish as the end game." In Prince's survey, over 90% of those who actually understood their plan felt their plan missed the target. I believe it is because the drafting attorney didn't really know what made his clients tick. It seems that Prince agrees: "... by fully understanding the wants, needs and expectations of their clients, private client lawyers will avoid the major reason why affluent clients decide not to implement completed estate plans."[3]

I know I jumped from financial services to the practice of law, but the principle is the same. In both cases, there is a tremendous need to know your client fully so that when a solution is offered, it is based on the clients clearly stated and documented needs, wants and desires and not based on the "advisor's" limited offerings. A truly professional Trusted Advisor will not only get to know his or her client, but in the process help his or her client to know himself or herself better as well. Many times in my career I have had clients respond to a query with something like, "Gee, I don't know how I feel about that subject. Help me think through it." Of course, they didn't use those words, but if you really listen, you will hear them say that more often that you might think. If you have never heard that kind of statement, then you aren't probing deeply enough. If you haven't helped them gain clarity on important issues, how can you provide a solution that fits them?

Rick and Frannie met with an estate attorney to create an estate plan. They had one "discovery meeting" where the attorney reviewed their "intake sheet" to get the facts — citizenship, marriage status, heirs (and possible disinherited people), approximate value of assets, business form, etc.

They returned two weeks later to see what the attorney would propose. He recommended a trust as the vehicle to avoid probate and assure the use of both estate tax exemptions. He also recommended an Irrevocable Life Insurance Trust (ILIT) to purchase a $4 million last-to-die life insurance policy to pay estate taxes.

They rejected the plan because, while it was fine as far as it went, it didn't address their philanthropic interest or their concern about how to deal equitably with two sons who are involved in the business and a daughter who is not.

---

3 *Ibid.* at 81.

When a client is presented with a plan for wealth management that is built around the best perceptions of you and the other wealth management team members as to what the client wants, there is a much greater probability that it will be implemented and the client will be happy with the outcome.

So, how does one go about developing this kind of understanding of a new client without spending years getting acquainted? Well, there are a few different models being practised that I am aware of and they don't all fit all clients. The methodology you use should be appropriate to the clientele you serve and to your business model and targeted market.

John Bowen of CEG Worldwide teaches an approach that is relatively quick and repeatable, using mind mapping software that can be very effective. Another approach was developed by the late Scott Fithian[4] and creates a several page document referred to as the Family Financial Philosophy. There are some "wealth coaches" who arrange for weekend or weeklong family retreats to delve into this kind of understanding together. Prince has developed what he refers to as The Whole Client Model™,[5] in which he identifies six categories of questions: goals, relationships, assets, advisors, process and interests. As would be expected, the Prince model is very similar to the Bowen model, since both are associated with CEG Worldwide. I have worked with a couple of these models with varying success, depending on both my own skill, or lack thereof, and the level of interest and commitment of the client.

I believe that this kind of "discovery" process, if done well, has great value not only to the Trusted Advisor but also to the client. In-depth questions can take a client to places he or she has never gone before — maybe I should label this the Star Wars method. Clients should find new clarity for their lives during this process, just as the client's Trusted Advisor will have gained understanding. If a Trusted Advisor does a good job in leading the discovery process, he or she will have added significant value to the client before he or she ever makes a single financial recommendation. This is where the Trusted Advisor really begins to provide leadership to his or her client.

One of the most potent qualities you can bring to your clients is your leadership in their lives. To some, that will sound scary, but everyone needs to experience leadership when entering new areas of life if they are to avoid wasted time and effort. Boiling down personal values,

---

4 Scott C. Fithian, *Values-Based Estate Planning: A Step-by-Step Approach to Wealth Transfer for Professional Advisors* (New York: John Wiley & Sons, Inc., 2000). Fithian's book goes into great detail in explaining his system.

5 Russ Alan Prince, *The Private Client Lawyer Now and in the Future* (Overland Park, Kansas: Wealth Management Press, 2003) at 78.

goals and objectives to concrete personal planning strategies isn't something most clients have dealt with before. They may be great business strategists, but the dynamic changes when it becomes personal planning instead of business planning. Leadership here is of phenomenal value to your client.

Bowen adds to the Prince model. Prince includes questions in the areas of goals, relationships, assets, advisors, process and interests. Bowen adds "values" to the list, using Bill Bachrach's questioning process, asking, "What, about money, is important to you?"[6]

Scott Fithian's model incorporates two parallel processes: one is the traditional gathering of "hard data"; the other is the development of the Family Financial Philosophy that will eventually incorporate the hard data as well. Fithian's model is more extensive and takes a much greater commitment from both the Trusted Advisor and the client. Not all clients are willing to invest that much in what they thought was going to be the creation of their estate planning documents. Fithian used to encourage members of his coaching program to take the following position: "This is how we do it and if you don't want to do it this way then you may need to find another advisor." This does have an advantage. All of your clients will be of a temperament to do in-depth thinking and evaluation, and you will have a deeper relationship with all of your clients if you require this depth. It also means you will have fewer clients and it will be a practical necessity that they all be high net-worth or ultra high net-worth families. You can't afford to spend this much time and resource, without a substantial fee for this service. Less than "high net-worth" clients will generally not be willing to make the financial commitment even if they are prepared for the commitment of time and emotion. If you aren't prepared to go upmarket exclusively, then you may not be able to be insistent on every client going through as in-depth a process as Fithian has created.

The advantage of the Bowen model is that, it takes less time and still allows for a greater discovery process than most advisors are typically trained to do. The initial interview, the discovery time, should take approximately two hours.

There is a quiz in Fithian's book that is intended to uncover whether or not a prospective client would be a good candidate for his in-depth system. I think it is a good tool for all Trusted Advisors to complete

---

[6] Bill Bachrach, *Values-Based Selling: The Art of Building High-Trust Client Relationships for Financial Advisors, Insurance Agents and Investment Reps* (San Diego, CA.: Aim High Publishing, 1996).

themselves from the perspective of what they think they are doing for their clients. Here is the questionnaire:[7]

Yes	No	I feel that I (my clients) understand the estate planning process.
Yes	No	My (clients') estate plan accurately reflects my (their) personal values.
Yes	No	My (clients') estate plan is based on clear, written objectives.
Yes	No	I (my clients) have defined how much I (and my spouse, if applicable) (they) will need in order to be assured of financial independence for the rest of my (our) (their) life.
Yes	No	I (my clients) have identified a specific and appropriate inheritance for my (their) heirs.
Yes	No	I (my clients) know how much estate tax will be due upon my (their) death, both if my (their) estate were settled today and if it were settled by my (their) normal life expectancy.
Yes	No	I (my clients) have used the estate planning process as a way to share my (their) values with my heirs.
Yes	No	I (my clients) understand the concept of social capital.
Yes	No	I (my clients) have taken the necessary steps to capture and direct my (their) social capital legacy in a way that is consistent with my (their) personal values.
Yes	No	My (clients') professional advisors work as a team in developing appropriate strategies for me (them) to consider.
Yes	No	I (my clients') am confident that my (their) heirs are prepared to manage their inheritance effectively.
Yes	No	I (my clients) am (are) satisfied with past experiences in making charitable gifts of time and money.

It may be appropriate for you to change the words "estate plan" to "wealth plan" or some similar terminology. The key is to personalize it to how you work. Now, ask yourself these questions with the perspective of, "Can my clients answer most of these in the affirmative?" If you believe they can, then you are doing an excellent job of knowing your clients and advising them accordingly. On the other hand, if you are not so sure that most of your clients could answer in the affirmative, maybe it is time you considered adding some additional efforts in knowing your clients in precise ways. Now, take a real risk and ask your clients to answer this questionnaire. You will find out if you have done as good a job as you think. You may discover some significant areas where you can improve your worth as a Trusted Advisor.

---

7 Scott C. Fithian, *Values-Based Estate Planning: A Step-by-Step Approach to Wealth Transfer for Professional Advisors* (New York: John Wiley & Sons, Inc., 2000) at 199.

Rick and Frannie were referred by a Funeral Director friend to an advisor at Total Client Wealth Management, LLC (TCWM) to develop a personalized wealth plan. Charlie, the advisor from TCWM, spent several hours probing and questioning the Harmons about their values, goals, relationships and interests. Charlie compiled a report of his findings and asked Rick and Frannie to review it to see if he had misunderstood or overlooked any important issues. Together they finalized this document, which became the guide for Charlie and the other experts on the planning team to create a plan. The team members included Charlie, an estate attorney, the Harmon's CPA and a Philanthropic Advisor from one of their esteemed charities. With the document as their guide, the team of experts developed a plan to accomplish the following:

1. *Position the business for growth so it will support two owner families, not just one.*
2. *The business would also be positioned to provide Rich and Frannie with a comfortable retirement.*
3. *Their daughter, Marianne, would receive cash and a small non-voting equity position in the business, while the boys will own most of the stock and manage the business. The small position for Marianne will provide some cash flow but, just as important, a true connection to the family business.*
4. *The estate plan includes a family foundation. The Board of Directors will be headed up by Marianne and include the boys as Directors also.*
5. *An Irrevocable Life Insurance Trust will provide liquidity to purchase the business assets from the Foundation later, and allow the Foundation to diversify its investment portfolio without jeopardizing the family business.*

PUTTING THE CLIENT FIRST AND "IN CHARGE"

There is another very powerful result if you help your client reduce the results of this discovery to a good written document. It puts the client in charge. If that statement sent chills down your spine, then you aren't ready for this new paradigm. Salespeople are taught to be in control and close the sale. A real Trusted Advisor or consultant is client-centric. The *client* is supposed to be in charge of the process so he or she knows that what he or she is getting is what he or she wants and needs. You have the ability to serve your clients in a way that is still quite unique: you help them get control of their planning process by *leading* them through an excellent job of discovery, reducing it to writing and then presenting strategies that will support your clients' expressed values, needs and goals, not one that sort of sounds like an attempt but doesn't really fit, but pays a good commission or creates good billable time and fees quickly.

What are the common elements to all of these methods? First, they all go way beyond the factual data of traditional financial data gathering. They are centred on the client as a whole family (or person in the case of single clients) and recognize that good decisions for the client are decisions that are in concert with his or her deeply held values and beliefs. Sometimes the client isn't even aware of his or her beliefs, since he or she has never carefully thought about ultimate questions that much.

There is a certain danger in doing this kind of counselling. You may, and probably will at some point, uncover issues that a couple has either buried or never addressed. They may find it difficult to deal with some issues about which they discover they have real conflicts. My advice in those instances is to let them know that you are not a marriage counsellor and so will not attempt to referee a resolution to the issue for them, and for your purposes will not address that issue in your documentation. They can choose to get further help with an appropriate professional (which you can help them with from your list of vetted professionals that you have developed over the years of your practice, right?).

The second common element is that all of these discovery methods are built as "client first". The inquiry process begins with the client and his or her values, not his or her assets and income; that comes way later. There is a television advertisement that I haven't seen for a while now, but you will surely recognize it. It betrays the misunderstanding of the major institutions. The branding line is simply "Total Merrill". The implication is supposed to be that Merrill Lynch has all the answers in-house, so don't involve any of those lesser institutions, just let Merrill take care of it all. But what it really says is, "This is all about Merrill Lynch, not about the client." What your branding line should be is "Total Client".

The third common element is the fact that solutions are simply strategies that take the client to the place you have discovered that he or she wants to go. The Trusted Advisor is never trying to make the client fit the advisor's solution. The solutions are never about how cool they make you look as a professional or about how big a commission you can earn or how much in fees you can generate, but about how well you have served your clients. If you take these values into your practice, you will be a better Trusted Advisor and will serve your clients better.

Highly satisfied clients are clients who perceive their advisors as advisors who "know what is really important" and "help to crystallize my needs and wants".[8] Highly satisfied clients do more business with their advisor and will enthusiastically refer other clients to their advisor.[9]

Incorporating an in-depth discovery methodology into your practice is one of the single most productive steps you can take. You will be able to make better recommendations to your clients, and your clients will be more satisfied with you as a Trusted Advisor because you will "know what is really important" to your client, and you will have "helped them to crystallize their needs and wants".

THE PAYOFF

So what is the payoff for you, the Trusted Advisor, if you add a more in-depth discovery process to your practice model?

1. You will gain a greater level of trust from your clients and find greater success in their enthusiastic implementation of the plans that are developed in concert with the team of experts.
2. You will increase your own personal sense of satisfaction with your work and with your client relationships.
3. You will have more "highly satisfied" clients who will not only continue to be active clients, but will make positive introductions to their friends and associates. That, of course, means more clients and more profits.
4. You will find that you will be changed personally by this intimate exchange with some wonderful human beings who just happen to be your clients. Your profit will be much more than mere dollars, as important as they are.

Happy discovery![10]

---

[8] Russ Alan Prince, *The Private Client Lawyer Now and in the Future* (Overland Park, Kansas: Wealth Management Press, 2003) at 71.

[9] *Ibid.* at 61.

[10] The characters Rick and Frannie and their family are a fictitious family based on the reality of many client experiences over my career. If it resembles reality, then I have done a good job of making up a story.

CHAPTER 51

POWERS OF ATTORNEY

Garry M. Cass

Overview

Powers of attorney are very important and powerful documents. Until recently they have often been underappreciated and misunderstood. This chapter will explain the concept of the attorney as substitute decision-maker, the uses and limitations of continuing powers of attorney, the due diligence that a professional advisor must carry out before relying on a power of attorney and the challenges of working with an attorney.

Learning Objectives

By the end of this chapter, you should be able to:

- satisfy yourself as to the validity of a continuing power of attorney and whether it is suitable for its intended use;
- determine how best to work with a client's attorney should it become necessary to do so to best look after your client's interests; and
- define the limits of the actions that the attorney should take without court sanction.

POWER OF ATTORNEY

Powers of attorney have recently hit the mainstream spotlight: unfortunately, not for a good reason. Due to a rash of fraudulent transactions and the resultant loss of substantial amounts of money by one party or another, the public is learning firsthand about the misuse of these valuable documents, but little about their benefits.

For the professional advisor, powers of attorney are both good and bad news. If used correctly, they promote key beneficial results:

1. there is a decision-maker in place should a client be absent for a period of time and is unable to give immediate instructions should he or she be called for;
2. there is a decision-maker in place should a client become mentally incapable of managing his or her own financial affairs; and
3. there is consistency if the forward-looking advisor and client have arranged for the advisor to meet the attorney(s) before the attorney(s) are actually required to become decision-makers.

The purpose of this chapter is to:

1. familiarize the non-lawyer reader with the concept of power of attorney;
2. summarize what to look for before accepting a power of attorney;
3. outline the limitations on the use of powers of attorney;
4. set out basic parameters for working with the attorney(s) in the management of a client's account; and
5. briefly discuss alternatives to a continuing power of attorney.

WHAT IS AN ATTORNEY?

An attorney is a substitute decision-maker.

WHAT IS A POWER OF ATTORNEY?

A power of attorney is the document by which an attorney is appointed. Powers of attorney are governed by statute and there are legal requirements that must be met before they will be considered valid.

It is extremely important that any professional advisor who is going to be relying on a power of attorney:

1. be familiar with the legal requirements for making one in the jurisdiction where he or she lives;
2. if relying on a power of attorney drawn in a different jurisdiction, he or she must satisfy himself or herself that the document was properly drawn on its face to meet the local requirements of that jurisdiction;
3. satisfy himself or herself that his or her jurisdiction has reciprocity with the jurisdiction where the document was prepared (reciprocity means that each jurisdiction recognizes documents prepared in the other); and

4. in all cases make sure that the power of attorney can be used for the intended purpose.

TYPES OF POWER OF ATTORNEY

For individuals there are two types of power of attorney: a continuing or enduring power of attorney for the management of property; and a personal care power of attorney. This chapter will deal primarily with the former.

CONTINUING OR ENDURING POWER OF ATTORNEY (FOR MANAGING PROPERTY) (CPA)

This is the power of attorney document that most professional advisors will be asked to rely on.

At common law, a power of attorney automatically ended at the death, bankruptcy or mental incapacity of the donor. To address this shortcoming, legislation allows for powers of attorney to continue in effect (or endure) where the donor has become mentally incapacitated.

A continuing power of attorney (CPA) may be very broad and all-encompassing in nature or it may be for a limited purpose. Examples of the latter include such things as authorizing the sale or refinancing of real or personal property or authorizing someone to enter into a contract on your behalf. A power of attorney in such limited scope as this generally terminates after the action contemplated has been undertaken and performed.

Generally, the document you will be faced with is an all-encompassing continuing power of attorney. This type of document will permit the attorney to make virtually any type of decision relating to the donor's property. The most benign use of a CPA is when it is used to pay the donor's ongoing expenses such as mortgage (or rent), property taxes, insurance, utilities, *etc*.

Unless there is a limitation in the document, however, it can also be used for more aggressive purposes such as:

1. reorganizing an investment portfolio;
2. refinancing or selling or buying real property;
3. making new investments on behalf of the donor that are in keeping with the attorney's investment philosophy, which may or may not be the same as that of the donor; and
4. making business decisions.

Unless there is a restriction in an all-encompassing CPA, the only real limitations on its use are those set out below.

WHAT TO CONSIDER BEFORE ACCEPTING A CPA

In the perfect world, a professional would know the name of each client's lawyer and that the client had prepared a CPA with his or her lawyer. He or she would also know if a client switched lawyers or made a new CPA. In the perfect world, the professional advisor would also know who was designated as the attorney from time to time.

In the real world, however, this information can be elusive. In far too many cases, clients have concentrated on their businesses and accumulating wealth but have taken no precautionary steps to deal with eventualities such as disability. In other cases, clients have relied on kit forms of CPA available online, from stationers or in some cases from lawyers who sell generic documents but do not supervise completion of the forms or offer legal advice on how to complete them, or a government which also does not supervise completion of the forms or offer legal advice on how to complete them. The result is a potential minefield for the professional advisor especially when he or she cannot go back to the client for answers to any concerns he or she may have because the client has become incompetent.

Adding to the difficulty faced by professional advisors is the vastly uneven expertise and sophistication of the attorneys themselves and their ability to transact business on behalf of the donor. In some instances, a donor is very sophisticated, listens to the suggestions of the professional advisor but ultimately makes his or her own decision. In some instances, a less sophisticated donor relies more heavily on the advice of his or her professional advisor. When an attorney is introduced into the equation, the attorney may be more or less knowledgeable than the donor. In addition, there are two other key issues that a professional advisor must come to grips with:

1. The attorney may not agree with the way the donor has transacted his or her business and may seek to change it. In the case of a financial advisor, for instance, this may be significant if the attorney seeks to dismantle an investment plan that a donor has put in place because the attorney does not understand or is more or less risk averse than the donor.

2. The trust level that exists between a client and a professional advisor will not exist between the advisor and an attorney when they have never met each other and never worked with each other before.

It is very important for a professional advisor to realize that his or her role changes when dealing with an attorney. When a professional advisor deals directly with a client, the client is ultimately responsible for his or her own decisions, and the advisor and client develop their own methodology for working together. When a professional advisor works with an attorney, however, there is a paradigm shift for the following reasons:

1. Both the advisor and the attorney are supposed to have the best interests of the client/donor[1] at heart but each may have different views on how to achieve this goal.
2. The needs of the client/donor may have changed, and if this is the case the advisor and the attorney must agree on what the new direction is to be.
3. Often attorneys initially know little about the client/donor's business and finances, and there is a learning curve that must be anticipated. This is especially important when immediate actions are called for.
4. An attorney is taking on responsibility for someone else's business and finances in addition to his or her own. Time is often an issue. An attorney may not be as available as the actual client/donor was.
5. Personalities.
6. You may have to deal with multiple attorneys who do not always agree with each other, let alone you.

In short, when a professional advisor starts to work with a client's attorney, it is like starting a new relationship with a new client. One cannot assume that the "old rules" apply and that the same assumptions can be made as when the advisor was dealing directly with the client/donor. To do so without laying a proper foundation potentially puts the client/donor at risk and/or may result in the loss of the account if the attorney is not comfortable with and does not trust the advisor.

AUTHENTICATING A CPA

In this day and age fraudulent CPAs have been used to commit all manner of unscrupulous acts and to rob innocent people of their assets. Therefore, before accepting a CPA, it is very important for a professional advisor to authenticate it. I suggest the following procedure be followed:

1. Insist on receiving either an original signed power of attorney document or a copy that has been notarized by a lawyer.

---

[1] Client/donor means your client who is also the maker of the CPA (the donor).

2. If the document was prepared and signed at a lawyer's office, ask for an affidavit of execution and verification of identity of the donor signed by both of the witnesses.
3. If you have a sample of the donor's signature on file, compare the file signature with the signature on the power of attorney document.
4. If you are concerned that your client, the donor, was not mentally capable at the time he or she made the power of attorney, ask for a written opinion from the lawyer who prepared the document or for the results of a capacity assessment if one has been carried out. In the absence of either, you must use your best judgement.
5. If your client, the donor, has indicated to you previously that someone other than the attorney named in the document you have received is his or her attorney, make inquiries. You should make sure that you have received the latest CPA and that it has revoked all previous CPAs. Alternatively, the CPA you receive may be for a limited purpose, and the person named in the limited CPA has been selected to carry out the particular task.
6. If the CPA has been prepared on a kit form and not by a lawyer, you also have to be concerned that the formal requirements of signing the CPA have been met. Of particular importance is that the document has been properly witnessed. People who cannot be witnesses include: the attorney, the attorney's spouse/partner, the spouse/partner or child of the donor or someone that the donor treats as his or her child and someone under 18 years of age. Please check your local legislation for a complete list of ineligible witnesses.
7. In some cases you may want to talk to the witnesses to satisfy yourself that they actually knew the person who signed the CPA as donor. (This is a case where having a signature on file really helps.)

JOINT ATTORNEYS AND JOINT AND SEVERAL ATTORNEYS

In some cases, you will be presented with a CPA that names more than one person as attorney. Such a CPA will refer to the attorneyship as being "joint" or "joint and several". If the CPA does not say "joint and several" on its face, it is "joint".

When a CPA is "joint", all of the named attorneys must agree to a course of action, and all of the attorneys must sign whatever documents are required to give effect to that action. This presents two major challenges to a professional advisor:

1. scheduling meetings at times that are mutually convenient; and

2. dealing with different personalities. If the choice of attorney was made carefully, your client would have considered the ability of people to work together and reach decisions and would only have people he or she knew were compatible. Often though, attorneys may be strangers to each other, or, worse still, have polar opposite outlooks. These people have been chosen for reasons known only to your client. On some occasions a person does not even know he or she has been named as an attorney and is skeptical about what lies ahead. The job of professional advisors in this case is to forge a working unit for the benefit of the client.

When a CPA names multiple attorneys who are "joint and several" it basically means that they are interchangeable, that anyone can conduct business and make decisions on behalf of your client. This arrangement is much more flexible than a joint CPA, *but* where attorneys are not compatible, care must be taken to insist on unanimity on major decisions. No major decision should be made on a "who gets there first basis".

SUBSTITUTE ATTORNEYS

When you first receive a CPA, you should also look to see if a substitute attorney has been named in the document.

If there is only one attorney named, the substitute attorney will assume responsibility if the named attorney dies, becomes incapable or is or becomes unable or unwilling to continue being the attorney.

If there is more than one attorney named, there are a few different possibilities to consider:

1. The substitute attorney will only assume responsibility if all of the named attorneys die, become incapable or all become unable or unwilling to continue being the attorneys.
2. The substitute attorney steps into the shoes of an attorney who dies, becomes incapable or is or becomes unable or unwilling to continue being the attorney so that the number of attorneys originally named is preserved.

The wording of the CPA will give you the answer to which of the foregoing possibilities applies. It will also let you know how many successive alternates there are before the number of attorneys starts to drop. Most people who appoint multiple attorneys wish to preserve the number for as long as possible; so you will usually be faced with the second possibility.

This is important information. CPAs for individual clients are typically used in three different situations:

1. the client is going to be absent for a period of time and leaves the attorney in charge in his or her absence;
2. the client becomes incapable of managing his or her business and finances as a result of accident or illness; or
3. the client reaches an age or state of health where he or she could continue to manage his or her own business and finances but prefers not to.

In the first situation, the professional advisor knows that his or her client will be returning after a defined period of time and can usually delay major decision-making until his or her return. Also, if a really important decision is required, the advisor often has a way to contact his or her client directly.

The second and third situations are different. In each of these situations, no one knows if the attorney will be acting for a short time or for many years. The longer an attorney acts, the more likely that an attorney himself or herself may die or become incapable of acting or may grow too old to want to continue. In these situations, responsibility would fall to the substitute attorney.

The very real question that professional advisors and attorneys are faced with, therefore, is: "To what degree do you keep substitute attorneys in the loop?" There is no single real answer to this question. On the one hand, as long as there is a named attorney acting, the substitute has no authority and may regard this type of communication a waste of time. If the client/donor's situation is relatively straightforward, a substitute attorney can usually step into the role fairly easily should he or she be required to do so. On the other hand, if the client/donor's situation is complicated, there may be a tremendous challenge for a substitute attorney not up to speed with the assets and situation he or she is now taking control of to get up to speed. Depending on the circumstances, it may be prudent to insist that the substitute attorney agree to stay informed and be like an understudy to the lead actor — ready to step in at a moment's notice.

EFFECTIVE DATE OF CPAs

In addition to authenticating a CPA, it is important for a professional advisor to ensure that the CPA is effective for immediate use.

CPAs may become effective documents:

1. immediately once they are signed;
2. if there is postponed effectiveness, on a specified date or when a specific contingency happens; or

3. on a specifically stipulated day.

Typically, a postponed effectiveness provision would provide that the CPA only became effective upon the donor becoming mentally incapable of managing his or her own finances and the document would provide a means to make this determination (*e.g.*, a letter from one or more qualified medical practitioners). If you, as a professional advisor, are presented with a CPA containing a postponed effectiveness clause, you must make sure that you also have the documentation determining the incapacity before you attempt to implement any action with the CPA. The proof documentation must be appended to the CPA as this is what makes it effective.

LIMITATIONS ON CPAs

Subject to any restrictions contained in a CPA, an attorney can do almost anything with the property of the donor that the donor could do if capable. Restrictions set out in a CPA can present challenges to both an attorney and an advisor. Unless restrictions are very well spelled out, a difficulty may arise in determining whether an attorney has the authority to perform a particular act; in other words, it depends on interpretation, which in some circumstances may require a court application for directions. Even where there are no written restrictions, statutes that govern the creation of CPAs present some significant limitations. For example, an attorney may not do any of the following things on behalf of a donor:

1. make a gift or otherwise dispose of the donor's property for the benefit of anyone other than the donor — unless the CPA provides otherwise;
2. make a will;
3. delegate his or her authority — unless the CPA provides otherwise; and
4. perform acts which are personal to the donor (*e.g.*, swear an affidavit on the donor's behalf).

Also, as an attorney is not able to make a will on behalf of the donor, it is entirely likely that he or she cannot perform other acts which have testamentary implications (*e.g.*, changing beneficiary designations on life insurance policies/RRSPs/RRIFs).

The most important thing for an advisor to keep in mind, however, is that an attorney cannot stop a client/donor from dealing with his or her own assets. Just because a client/donor puts a CPA into effect does not preclude the client/donor from making his or her own decisions. The use of the CPA is for the convenience of the client/donor and to provide flexibility (if the client/donor is a snow bird for instance), not to transfer decision-making capability. To achieve this goal would require a court to find that a client/donor of a CPA had become mentally incompetent and incapable of managing his or her own finances. This is very important to remember in cases where the client/donor is deteriorating and starts making questionable decisions. The client/donor does not have to voluntarily submit to capacity testing and may in fact refuse to co-operate. A court application to determine competence can often be expensive and bitter and leave lasting emotional wounds that never heal. The professional advisor must always be aware of this if a client has voluntarily put a CPA into effect before becoming mentally incapable. It is not unusual to feel caught between a rock and a hard place.

MULTIPLE CPAs

It has been my experience that in most cases where the client/donor is married, his or her spouse will be named as attorney.

However, if a client has complex business dealings, he or she may decide to have more than one CPA. For example, a businessperson may choose to have a different attorney manage his or her business interests than his or her personal accounts and investments.

If this is the case, it is important for the professional advisor to have copies of all relevant CPAs and to make sure that none of them inadvertently revokes any of the others. It is also important to remember that the decisions made by an attorney running a business may have tremendous impact on the well-being of the client/donor. Issues include whether to continue to operate the business or to sell it and all of the individual decisions that have to be made to come to an overall conclusion. Some of the individual decisions include the following:

1. Can the business be continued profitably in the absence of the client/donor?
2. What, if any, is the cost of hiring employees to replace expertise lost by the absence of the client/donor? How will profitability be affected?
3. Can the attorney oversee the business "*in absentia*" or does the attorney have to become a hands-on manager and give up his or her regular job/career in order to do so? Is he or she willing to do so?
4. Who are the potential buyers for the business?
5. Should all or only a portion of the business be sold?
6. If the business is very dependent on the goodwill generated by the client/donor himself or herself (*e.g.*, a professional practice), how

long does the attorney have to sell the practice before the clients/patients start to go elsewhere?

ESTATE PLANNING BY AN ATTORNEY

Estate planning in the traditional sense means ordering one's assets to minimize taxes and transfer costs upon one's demise. Estate planning usually requires input from several professional advisors — a lawyer, accountant, investment advisor and insurance professional. While a client is of sound mind, he or she takes advice from his or her professionals and creates a plan accordingly. The client decides who his or her beneficiaries are going to be, whether they are going to be absolute beneficiaries, beneficiaries of trusts, how much they are to receive and when they are to receive it. Since no two clients are exactly the same, no two plans are exactly the same. As long as an individual is mentally capable, he or she is free to change all or any individual aspect of his or her estate plan, subject to any limitations that he or she may have agreed to in writing.

As previously mentioned, one limitation on an attorney is that an attorney cannot make a will on behalf of the donor of the power of attorney.

In recent years, the extent to which an attorney can estate plan on behalf of an individual who had become incompetent has been tested several times in the courts. In one case, the attorney sought to reorganize the assets of the incompetent by using an estate freeze to moderate taxes when the incompetent person died. In a second case, the attorneys of the incompetent were his children, who moved his assets into a trust in an attempt to escape the clutches of an opportunistic caregiver who married their father when his mind was already frail. A third case dealt with a situation where a scheme of annual donations was proposed to the family of a woman who had had a brain hemorrhage and stroke at age 63, in order to lessen U.S. tax upon her death. In a fourth case, beneficiaries of an incompetent's will went to court after her attorneys tried to effect some estate planning that the beneficiaries believed adversely affected their interests.

The courts in each of these cases examined the effect of the proposed estate planning:

- In the first case, the court decided that the proposed estate freeze was permissible in part because the new shares were to be issued to a trust, the incompetent was the exclusive beneficiary of the trust during his lifetime, the trustee was to have unlimited authority to encroach on the capital of the trust (if necessary) for the incompetent's care and maintenance and, if the incompetent were to recover, he could require the corpus of the trust to be transferred back to him. If the incompetent died, the assets in the trust would be distributed in accordance with his will.

- In the second case, the court recognized the authority of attorneys to create the trust, but the trust failed because the attorneys went too far and gave interests to people other than the incompetent. Therefore, the trust denied the incompetent the right to revoke his will by marrying, and denied his spouse any rights she may have had under Ontario's *Family Law Act* (for equalization) and *Succession Law Reform Act*.
- In the third case, the court rejected the planned gift because it was concerned that a depletion of the incompetent's estate might not leave enough to look after her needs, given that her life expectancy was unknown.
- In the fourth case, the court acknowledged that the maker of a will is free to change his beneficiaries while he or she is mentally capable. However, when he or she becomes mentally incapable and therefore can no longer change a will, this has the effect of giving the beneficiaries an entitlement.

The conclusions to be drawn by professional advisors are as follows:

- Complex estate planning should be approved by a court of competent jurisdiction before being undertaken by an attorney.
- No provisions that have the effect of being testamentary in nature will be permitted.
- If the value of the estate might be significantly decreased as a result of the plan, it will not likely be approved by a court.
- A court will not allow a plan if the effect is to deny the incompetent person or another party his or her rights.
- If a client and his or her advisors anticipate the need for complex and sophisticated planning, the client should do the planning himself or herself.

ALTER EGO TRUSTS AND JOINT SURVIVOR TRUSTS

An unmodified CPA is really a very straightforward document to read and comprehend. However, as has been mentioned above, there are limitations on a CPA that must be addressed specifically by the donor if an attorney is to be able to do certain things.

The CPA is a general use document. Most specific modifications to the document are relevant only for some of the uses. Presenting a highly modified CPA to some third parties presents a problem: it may make them question the document as a whole and delay their acceptance of it or, worse, have them reject it. It is hard to create one document that can be all things to all people.

One solution is for a client/donor to have multiple CPAs, as discussed above.

Another solution is to suggest that clients who qualify consider utilizing an alter ego trust or a joint survivor trust.

An alter ego trust is for use by an individual, and a joint survivor trust, by a couple. To be eligible, the client(s) must be at least 65 years of age and residents of Canada. In most cases the client is the one who settles the trust and is the trustee until his or her death or incapacity. During the client's lifetime, or the lifetimes of the couple in the case of a joint survivor trust, he or she (or they) is (are) the only one(s) entitled to the capital and the income of the trust.

Either of these trusts provides a number of very valuable advantages:

1. Assets inside the trust are not subject to probate. As a result, there is no time delay in dealing with them, and there are no probate type fees or taxes. In some provinces this can represent significant savings.
2. Privacy. Once an application to court for Letter Probate/Certificate of Estate Trustee is made, the contents of the documents become public, and anyone who is interested can see the contents of the court file. Since the assets in an alter ego trust or joint survivor trust are not subject to probate, the public has no way to find out the assets of these trusts unless they are leaked.
3. The trust document is a better place to more fully deal with estate planning issues.
4. The trust is a CPA substitute for the assets inside it. If the original trustee becomes mentally incapable, the substitute trustee(s) assume(s) control, and the trust continues.

It is important to note, however, that the trustee does not assume control of assets outside the trust and has no way of doing so. Therefore, the client still needs to have a CPA to cover these. If the assets which require specific planning are inside the trust, however, the CPA can be left largely or totally unmodified as the individual instance requires and likely will not come under undue scrutiny.

Despite their advantages, alter ego trusts and joint survivor trusts are not suitable for all purposes. These trusts are living trusts as opposed to testamentary trusts. They are created by individuals during their lifetime. Income taxed in living trusts is taxed at the highest marginal rate from the first dollar earned. Income tax in a testamentary trust receives the benefit of the same graduated income tax rates as individuals receive. Therefore, if an alter ego trust or joint survivor trust provides that on the death of the original beneficiary(ies) there is to be a further trust rather than an outright distribution of its assets, the income earned and taxed in that subsequent trust will be taxed at a higher rate than if a similar trust was created through a will. Deciding the proper mix and allocation of assets is an exercise for the individual and his or her Trusted Advisors.

PERSONAL CARE POWER OF ATTORNEY

In addition to the CPA, most clients will have a personal care power of attorney or some form of health care directive.

The duties of the personal care attorney are many and varied. They deal with the non-financial aspects when a client becomes mentally incompetent. At one end of the spectrum are the important matters such as shelter, food and clothing. Is the client going to live at home? What type of caregiver service is required? What type of special equipment is required? Or, is the client unmanageable at home and must be placed in a care facility? Does the client still need a caregiver and special equipment?

At the other end of the spectrum are the emotionally charged issues that surround giving or withholding medical treatment and the right to die with dignity.

Often the personal care attorney is not the same person as the property attorney named in the CPA. This is not unusual because most people have people that they trust to carry out one role better than the other.

What is most important when there are different attorneys for personal care and for property, however, is that they are able to communicate with each other. The personal care attorney needs to know what funds are available in order to be able to make decisions about all of the shelter, caregiver and equipment matters. On the other hand, if funds are limited, the property attorney has to make sure that the reasonable requirements of the client are funded.

Professional advisors should be aware of the issues that the attorneys are facing together in order to be able to offer proper advice. This is particularly important in the case of investment advisors who have to give advice on how to set up an account to balance preservation of capital, growth and liquidity.

IN SUMMARY

CPAs are incredibly important, useful and powerful documents. Once they are put into use, they take on a life of their own. A CPA gives an attorney almost complete control over another person's assets.

Until recently, CPAs were also the "Rodney Dangerfield" of legal documents — they did not get enough respect. That, however, is now quickly changing.

For professional advisors, CPAs provide the means to continue to provide meaningful advice to benefit clients who have become mentally incapacitated. Prior to relying on the CPA presented to you, however, it is extremely important that you:

1. be familiar with the legal requirements for a CPA in the jurisdiction where you live;
2. if relying on a power of attorney drawn in a different jurisdiction, satisfy yourself that the document was properly drawn on its face to meet the local requirements of that jurisdiction;
3. satisfy yourself that your jurisdiction has reciprocity with the jurisdiction where the document was prepared (reciprocity means that each jurisdiction recognizes documents prepared in the other);
4. in all cases make sure that the power of attorney can be used for the intended purpose;
5. authenticate the CPA;
6. develop a working relationship with the attorney(s) that preserve(s) as much as possible the intentions of your client;
7. advise the attorney(s) not to make decisions which are out of the ordinary before he or she (they) consults (consult) with the client's lawyer and any other professional advisors whose advice may impact the decision; and
8. keep comprehensive notes of your meetings with the attorney(s).

And above all, encourage your clients to do their planning well in advance and do so proactively, rather than as a reactive response to a crisis that has occurred in the life of a relative or friend.

CHAPTER 52

TRUSTS — "CAIN AND ABEL", "THE EVIL STEPMOTHER" AND "THE TRUSTEE YOU CAN'T TRUST"

Peter J. Merrick
Charles L. Stanley

Overview

This chapter discusses the most common reasons for a trust to be attacked after the settlor of the trust has died. This chapter shares steps that can mitigate the risk of a trust being attacked.

Learning Objectives

By the end of this chapter, you should be able to:

- understand the three main reasons trusts get attacked in court; and
- know what you and your client can do to resolve the issues that might cause a trust to be attacked in the future.

There are three kinds of trial cases concerning the deceased and his or her estate plan or lack thereof that make it to the courts:

- The Cain and Abel
- The Evil Stepmother
- The Trustee You Can't Trust

The "Cain and Abel" refers to the sibling rivalry that has lasted since childhood and is now being carried out with high stakes in court. "The Evil Stepmother" refers to the sad family dynamic that takes place when a parent remarries after either the death of the other parent or a divorce. The new spouse is viewed by the spouse's children as an interloper stealing the inheritance of the deceased spouse's children.

"The Trustee You Can't Trust" is untrustworthy for various reasons. The trustee may be simply naïve, may be negligent and may be malicious. In any case, he or she can't be trusted.

Most of the readers of this chapter already understand the benefits of creating a trust for their families and encouraging their clients to follow suit, so we are not intending to encourage people to create trusts with this chapter.

We know that legal trusts are supposed to help avoid probate and other taxes. Well, they do if there is no contest or trustee challenge. Then they often wind up in court. Could it happen to your family or your clients because of the way the estate plan is drafted, or because of the way the trustee performs his or her duties?

If you have two children (or more) who fit the "Cain and Abel" scenario, it is difficult to eliminate the problem with a mere drafting of the trust. This is really a sibling rivalry issue. If your children have this kind of problem, don't be like an ostrich and stick your head in the sand and hope it won't resurface after you are gone. Deal with it now. But how?

- *First possibility* — Discuss it with your estate planning attorney to see if he or she has any wisdom to share after his or her years of estate planning work and observation of other families who have faced similar issues.
- *Second possibility* — Get the rivals in the same room and explain to them clearly what you are intending in your estate plan and why. We know this can have its own set of difficulties because you will have to make it known what you may not want to disclose now.

  Let them express their displeasure with your plan, if they have any. It is possible that clearing the air now will stave off an eruption later.
- *Third possibility* — Have a meeting with the rivals and your estate attorney. Have the plan reviewed in front of them and give them an opportunity to air any disappointments. If you don't want to make any adjustments to your plan, there is now a third party witness to this discussion who may be able to help stop litigation later on.

"The evil stepmother" is also not so easy to solve. A remarriage (particularly if it takes place later in life after the children are older and have spent most of their lives with their nuclear family intact) may result in a step-parent who is difficult for the adult children to adjust to. If the new spouse is younger than the biological parent, it becomes more difficult because the life expectancy of the survivor is often quite a bit longer and, under many estate plans, the children have to wait until the step-parent is deceased before they will enjoy their inheritance. The children may also have to sit by and watch a step-parent live large on what they consider their inheritance. Their solution is to sue the step-parent and trustee and hopefully regain control of their inheritance.

The truth about both the "Cain and Abel" scenario and "The Evil Stepmother" scenario is that most of the time it isn't really about the money. It is about some emotional and relationship issues that are being manifest through trust litigation. A case in point: a beneficiary to a trust, from which he was to receive $1 million, sued the trustee and the other beneficiaries. He was very belligerent and when he didn't win the first time around, he sued the attorneys, claiming they had not done their jobs correctly. Along the way it became apparent to the judge that the claimant was not going to deal reasonably and so he ruled that 100% of the costs of litigation were to come out of the claimant's share of the trust, the $1 million he was to inherit. When the claimant had used up all of his $1 million from the trust, he continued to pursue the litigation. There was nothing left for him to inherit. This case was obviously not about the money.

"The Trustee You Can't Trust" is untrustworthy for various reasons. The trustee may be simply naïve, may be negligent and may be malicious. In any case, he or she can't be trusted. The naïve trustee simply doesn't know what his or her responsibilities are. Ignorance is no excuse. If you are a trustee, you need to know what your responsibilities are.

So if you are a naïve trustee, what can you do? You can either educate yourself and fulfill the responsibilities or resign. You shouldn't consider an alternative. Unfortunately, there is little available for a non-professional to read in order to learn how to be a trustee.

There are three key documents to read and understand. The first document is the trust itself. Be sure you know the trust provisions; you are obligated to manage trust assets according to the trust. The second document is the legislation that governs trusts in Canada, and the third is the *Income Tax Act*. It is a lot to grasp, especially if you aren't used to reading legal language.

If you consider these three things and take notes about things you need to clarify, you can make an appointment with your estate attorney to go over these items. It will cost you for a couple of hours of attorney time, but it just may save you and/or the heirs many thousands of dollars and possibly a lifetime of human relations that could be destroyed through an unnecessary trust fight.

Another aid can be your investment advisor. If you hire a Certified Financial Planner® (CFP) or Trust and Estate Practitioner (TEP) who has a good grasp on trust administration, he or she may be able to help you understand your duties and alert you to when you really need to consult an attorney. He or she should also work with you to create an Investment Policy Statement that is written to support the trust's purposes and goals.

A knowledgeable CFP or TEP will require a complete copy of the trust because he or she is accepting a role as a co-fiduciary along with you, and has to know the trust provisions as well in order to manage the trust assets in accordance with the trust's purposes and goals.

A trust is a wonderful tool to avoid probate, keep your affairs private and save administration costs in most cases, that is, as long as no one challenges the trust or its administration in court. So what is our point here? Actually, there are three:

1. Make sure your trust is drafted the way you want it and that you and your spouse/co-trustee understand it and your responsibilities under the trust and the law. If you don't, educate yourselves. You won't get that education at a marketing seminar, so you will have to do your own homework.
2. Trust contests are more often about relationships between the parties to the trust than they are about the actual inheritance. Look hard at your family and its relationships, and don't be naïve about potential harmful relationships that could cause a great deal of grief when money and inheritance are introduced into the relationships. Do what you can now to deal with these difficulties.
3. Consult with your Trusted Advisors and don't be afraid to spend a little consulting money now when it might do some good.

It may save that amount in future litigation costs. We know this reads like a negative chapter, but it is actually the hard and real stuff of planning. Estate planning is as much about these relationships as it is about taxes and transfers, maybe even more. In our opinion, what is the "stuff" ultimately worth if there aren't loved ones to share it with?

CHAPTER 53

MODERN ESTATE PLANNING — THE HIGH PRICE OF NOT TALKING

THE FAMILY MEETING — A PRE-EMPTIVE STRIKE AGAINST ESTATE LITIGATION

Ian Hull

Overview

This chapter is focused on the estate plan and on tools which can be utilized to ensure that the goals of a testator are achieved while, at the same time, maintaining the family dynamic.

Learning Objectives

By the end of this chapter you should be able to:

- understand the basic tools used in planning an estate;
- understand how family dynamics play a role in estate planning;
- understand the benefits of a family conference on the estate planning process;
- recognize components of an estate plan which lead to litigation;
- identify ways to reduce the likelihood of estate litigation;
- recognize alternatives to litigation and when they are beneficial to an estate;
- understand the underlying trust concepts and the ownership structure created by a trust; and
- recognize the different types of trusts used in estate planning and their intended purpose.

INTRODUCTION

As the transfer of wealth from one generation to the next proceeds in Canada, the inevitable growth in estate litigation will no doubt continue. In fact, statistically, the transfer of wealth in Canada is moving along at an extraordinary rate.

Trusted Advisors continue to be faced with clients who come to see them, hoping to create an estate plan that is geared in part to either resolving future conflicts or facing those conflicts in the estate planning process itself.

There currently exists an excellent regime whereby lawyers, estate planners, accountants, insurance agents and other allied professionals work together with the client to create a plan that makes sense both from a tax standpoint and from the family dynamics perspective.

Many of these existing estate plans work as the percentage of estate matters that are litigated continue to be proportionately relatively small. However, while the amount of litigation, on a percentage basis, may be small, two difficulties arise in the litigation context. First, even that small percentage of estate litigation that does get created on the death of the client is usually extremely painful for the family, both financially and emotionally. Second, even when you think you have all the "t"s crossed and the "i"s dotted, the advent of estate litigation usually occurs on a fairly random basis. In other words, no matter how hard you try, if the underlying family dynamics have not been considered, then even the best laid plans may well fall into the "black hole" of estate litigation.

Presumably, more than just good documentary planning on the part of your client is now needed.

Historically, the whole estate plan was structured without the input of those who are most affected by the result, namely, the family members. It is the additional component of the family dynamics that is a significant instigator of estate litigation.

Within the confines of the estate litigation arena, the process and the fight can be incredibly harmful to family relationships. These proceedings are often emotionally devastating and financially problematic.

Before examining some of the common causes of and possible alternatives to estate litigation, it is helpful to consider the main estate planning techniques.

WHAT IS A WILL?

A will is a written statement that sets out how the testator wants his or her assets to be disposed of on death. A will creates an almost unchangeable estate plan, which after death can only be varied if everyone with a financial interest in the estate agrees. As a result, it is important that it accurately describes the testator's wishes. After death, a will provides a framework for the appointment of an executor who is responsible for the administration of the estate. A will gives the executor the power to deal with assets belonging to the deceased and to distribute them to the beneficiaries selected.[1]

POWERS OF ATTORNEY

A power of attorney is a document which allows the grantor to plan for situations where he or she may become incapable and unable to make decisions about his or her property or health. With a power of attorney, another person is appointed (known as the "attorney"), although that person does not have to be a lawyer, to make those decisions on behalf of the grantor. A power of attorney is only effective during the lifetime and terminates upon the death of the grantor.[2]

There are two different types of powers of attorney: one is a power of attorney for property, which allows the attorney to manage property for the grantor; and the other is a power of attorney for personal care, which allows the attorney to make health care decisions for the grantor if he or she becomes incapable of making those decisions himself or herself. The same person does not have to be appointed to both positions.

TRUSTS

Trusts offer a number of benefits as an estate planning tool, from lowering or deferring taxes to providing a more flexible method of distributing assets. In examining the benefits, it is important to understand the basics of how trusts work.

A trust is created when the settlor transfers ownership of certain assets to a trustee, who holds and manages the assets for the benefit of the beneficiaries. The beneficiaries are able to enjoy the benefits of the assets but do not legally own them. For example, if you transfer your cottage to your brother in trust for your children, your brother legally owns the cottage, but your children, and not your brother, are entitled to use the cottage.

Trusts can be either *inter vivos* trusts, which are created during the lifetime of the settlor, or testamentary trusts, which are created in a will

---

1 I.M. Hull, *Advising Families on Succession Planning: The High Price of Not Talking* (Markham, Ont.: LexisNexis, 2005) at 9.

2 *Ibid.* at 47.

and take effect on death. Different tax rules apply to the two types of trusts: *inter vivos* trusts are taxed at the highest marginal tax rate and testamentary trusts are subject to the graduated tax rates that apply to individuals.

There are many different types of trusts that may be useful as part of an estate plan. These include:

- **Income Trusts:** An income trust gives the beneficiaries the income earned by the trust's capital assets (like an investment account, for instance). For greater flexibility, the trustee may also be given the right to decide how much income should be paid to the beneficiaries. The trustee may even be given the right to pay part of the capital to the beneficiaries over a period of time as well.
- **Spendthrift Trusts:** If a family member does not handle money well or has a history of financial problems, the settlor may be concerned about giving him or her access to a large sum of money. A spendthrift trust ensures that a beneficiary will have the income needed, while preventing depletion of the capital.
- **Trusts for Special Needs Beneficiaries:** Children with special needs often require considerable ongoing financial support. A trust can secure their long-term future. A special form of trust is created to ensure that the child isn't disqualified from receiving provincial disability support benefits.
- **Spousal Trusts:** Transferring property to a trust for the benefit of a spouse allows a deferral of the capital gains taxes that will arise on death until the trust disposes of the property or the surviving spouse dies.
- **Family Trusts:** These are useful for income-splitting amongst family members, particularly if the family owns a business.
- **Incentive Trusts:** An incentive trust is used to motivate beneficiaries who expect to inherit a large amount of money to lead a productive life.

Advantages of a Trust

Trusts offer many advantages, both to the settlor and the beneficiaries:

- **Tax Reduction:** Since testamentary trusts are taxed at the same graduated rates as individuals, they can be used to income-split amongst the beneficiaries. In addition, money can be distributed from the trust so as to minimize the tax consequences to the beneficiaries. For example, capital gains, which are taxed more favourably than other types of income, can be paid by the trust to the beneficiaries and taxed in their hands.

- **Protection from Creditors:** Assets that are held in a trust are usually protected from the beneficiaries' creditors.
- **Money Management:** If a child inherits a large sum of money at a young age, he or she may not be able to properly manage that money. If the money is held in a trust, the trustee can ensure that the child's living costs and other appropriate expenses are covered, but can delay distributing the bulk of the funds until the child is older and more financially responsible.
- **Gifts to Minor Children:** In Ontario, children can't legally own property until they are 18. If you want to leave assets to minor children, you must create a trust or the Office of the Official Guardian will administer the money until the child turns 18.
- **Dispute Resolution Between Children:** Transferring a contentious asset, like a cottage, to a trust for the benefit of your children allows the trustee to make decisions about that asset and can reduce the conflict between the children.
- **Protection for a Second Spouse:** A trust can balance the needs of children from a first marriage with the needs of a second spouse. It is possible to transfer property to a trust that will provide income to a spouse during his or her lifetime. On that spouse's death, the children will receive the remaining capital from the trust.[3]

BRINGING IN THE FAMILY — PROTECTING THE FAMILY FROM LEGAL CHALLENGES

Trying to convince your client to open up the full family dynamics during his or her lifetime is a difficult sales pitch. Typically, your client does not even want to deal with the issue of death one-on-one with you, as the Trusted Advisor, let alone face the prospect of bringing in various family members, including those who are non-blood-related.

Having said that, it only takes one dissatisfied beneficiary to start estate litigation. That's what the pre-estate family conference is designed to prevent.

When preparing an estate plan, the client inevitably wants to leave his or her family with a legacy that is accepted, rather than a costly dispute that will erode the value of the estate and may permanently destroy family relationships.

---

[3] *Ibid.*

Traditional estate planning focuses on developing a comprehensive estate plan, including a will disposing of assets. While this is important, it does nothing to prevent unhappy family members from bringing a legal action to challenge a will — and it really does take only one disappointed beneficiary to start litigation and deplete the value of an estate.

In my experience, having litigated over estate matters ranging from those that were planned almost to perfection right through to those that were a mess (often created by either the planning process itself or the client, *i.e.*, homemade wills or handwritten wills), the ability of a Trusted Advisor to accurately predict that an existing estate plan will run smoothly after death is, in our view, very much in doubt.

Currently, disputes come from all angles within the client's world and they are usually very surprising to the family members. For example, your client might be quietly sending $500 per month to relatives overseas, an amount that would not attract much attention to him or her when he or she prepares an estate plan but may, nonetheless, result in a claim by the relatives against the assets of the estate as dependants upon your client's death.

More to the point of the family dynamic itself, many family members do not know and understand the nature and effect of the will itself. As an illustration, many matters are litigated over the question of executor's compensation. In particular, if one family member is chosen over another as executor, the fact that that individual was chosen may bring with it an emotional consequence after your client's death. One brother may be upset by the fact that he is not "running the show", so to speak, and an easy way to get at his sister/executor is to make trouble in the context of the compensation that she might claim.

Another example of a problem that may arise in a well-planned, carefully constructed estate plan is the transfer of wealth through a family-run company. For instance, if one of the siblings is currently running the company and is given the shares of the parent, it may be an entirely justified, fair and/or equal distribution in the context of the other siblings; however, the event itself may either come as a surprise to the other siblings or, more importantly, be seen as an unequal distribution which is challenged in the context of an estate litigation proceeding.

What Is the Solution?

Of course, there is no definitive solution to this problem as the frailties of human nature prevail, and it is impossible to predict with certainty that any steps taken before death on behalf of your client will result in the perfect, unchallenged and undisrupted administration of his or her estate.

However, there are two aspects which should be considered:

The Existing Approach

There is simply no substitute for good, effective and comprehensive estate planning. By using well-qualified counsel, with the assistance of the necessary allied professionals and Trusted Advisors, one takes a giant step forward in the preventative strike regime.

From a documentary standpoint, consideration should be given to the drafting techniques employed through the estate planning process. For example, the use of *inter vivos* trusts, trusts within the will, *in terrorem* clauses (*i.e.,* levying a cost on those who choose to litigate) included in the will and other drafting tools can go a long way toward creating a "bulletproof" estate plan.

The Family Meeting Approach — Enter the Professionally Mediated Family Conference

Notwithstanding all of the efforts on the part of your client to create an estate plan that is protected from attack, the one important consideration missing in the existing approach is the role of the beneficiaries themselves.

In fact, arguably, the whole estate planning process should also be looked at from the bottom up, and this view from the bottom should, in my opinion, be conducted live, as opposed to being projected by the client's estate planning professionals.

A family conference provides a client with the opportunity to explain his or her wishes to family members and to describe the intended disposition of the estate. It provides a forum for discussion that ensures both the testator and the intended beneficiaries are comfortable with the proposed dispositions.

It also allows the parties to address the emotional issues that may arise around the will and, if necessary, make changes to the estate plan so that everyone is satisfied.

I hope to provide an overview of the steps which can be taken to protect an estate plan, and explain how the pre-estate family conference can play an integral role in the estate planning process.

To the extent that it is possible, full, direct family participation in the estate plan can add another important and effective pre-emptive strike against problems after death.

As to the "sales pitch", this will presumably be a five-minute discussion with your client, advising him or her that if the estate plan comes under attack for any reason, which can ultimately never be entirely foreseen or predicted, then tens of thousands of dollars will be spent on lawyers, accountants and other professionals cleaning up the mess. This prospect alone will, no doubt, send shivers down your client's back. However, you will also likely be faced with the sensible reaction on the part of your client that if his or her beneficiaries can't get along, then so be it. Further, then, your client's impression may be that it will be the beneficiaries' loss if they want to fight amongst themselves.

Having said that, the one thing that will likely resonate in your client's mind, in any event, is the fact that his or her whole estate plan can be fought over and substantially restructured, ignoring many of his or her wishes in the context of a fight later in the day.

Finally, your client needs to understand that the impact of the estate plan may result in emotional strife that could ruin relationships or make it worse within the family for the rest of their lives, and bitter feelings may be harboured in respect of your memory.

In my experience, the three-part combination of an incredible waste of money, completely ignoring the testator's wishes and the lifelong emotional impact on the family will leave its mark on your client's mind.

PROTECTING YOUR ESTATE FROM CHALLENGES

A will is the cornerstone of any estate plan. One of the best ways of protecting an estate from challenges is to ensure that a will is professionally drafted and distributes all included assets to the intended beneficiaries. Here are several steps that can be taken during a testator's lifetime to reduce the likelihood of a successful will challenge:

- **Proof of Mental Capacity:** A will is invalid if the testator didn't have the mental capacity to sign it when the will was made. The testator should ask his or her lawyer or doctor to take detailed notes on his or her mental capacity and ability to provide and understand instructions at the time of the will signing.
- **Guarding Against Claims of Undue Influence:** A will can be challenged on the basis that someone has forced the signing of a document that does not reflect the real intentions of the testator. Those who are elderly, unhealthy, frail or highly dependent on one person when making a will should consider having their lawyer and doctor prepare detailed notes on their mental condition at the time.
- **Ensuring the Will Is Properly Executed:** A will can be challenged if it is not properly executed. The drafting lawyer will ensure that the will is properly witnessed and that the witnesses sign the necessary affidavits. Any changes later made to the will must also be properly signed and witnessed.
- **Documenting Any Gift Made During Lifetime:** If large gifts are made during the testator's lifetime, make sure that the appropriate

legal documents are prepared and that a lawyer makes notes as to the mental capacity of the client. This is particularly important if the client is making unequal gifts — for example, if monetary gifts are made to only one child.

- **Drafting Wills to Protect Against Challenges:** Careful will drafting can help reduce estate challenges. For instance, a will can contain a clause providing that if a beneficiary challenges the will, he or she loses his or her right to receive anything from the estate. Another possibility is to have all beneficiaries sign a contract stating that they will not challenge the will. A lawyer can help with the decision as to what might work best in this particular situation.

THE HIGH COSTS OF ESTATE LITIGATION

Protecting an estate from challenges becomes even more important when consideration is given to the financial and emotional costs involved in defending an estate during the litigation process. Individuals generally focus on the fees and disbursements paid to their lawyer, but the emotional costs of litigation can leave family members permanently estranged.

Traditionally, the estate was ordered to pay the costs of all of the parties involved in litigation, regardless of who was successful. However, in recent years, courts have moved away from this approach and are focusing on the success the parties achieve in the litigation. This can mean that parties may have to bear their own costs, or that someone who unsuccessfully challenges a will may be ordered to pay the estate's costs.

There are several stages in estate litigation, and costs climb as you move through each stage. These stages and their approximate costs are as follows:

Stage	Approximate cost
Obtaining an order organizing the litigation	$5,000 to $10,000
Collecting and disclosing evidence to establish the case	$2,000 to $20,000
Attending discoveries to give sworn evidence	$10,000 and up, plus the costs of preparing the transcripts ($2.00 to $3.50 a page, with an approximate length of 200 pages)
Preparing for and attending a pre-trial conference	$3,000 to $7,500
Preparing for and attending at trial	$15,000 to $30,000 a day for trial, plus fees for preparation time
Appeal of court's decision	$40,000 and up

MEDIATION

Mediation is a non-binding process in which interested parties attempt to reach an agreement on the issues between them with the help of a trained mediator. Mediation is far less costly than the court process (overall mediation costs generally range from $7,500 to $25,000) and allows people to reach an agreement themselves, rather than have a decision imposed on them by a judge. The downside, of course, is that if mediation is unsuccessful, you'll have to pay both the mediation costs and the subsequent litigation costs, which will add to your financial burden.

MOST FREQUENT CAUSES OF ESTATE LITIGATION

Even if a comprehensive estate plan is in place and all the necessary steps to bulletproof the will have been taken, the estate may still wind up the subject of litigation. Here are some of the most frequent causes of estate challenges:

- **Lack of a Comprehensive Estate Plan:** It's important that the estate plan cover all assets and that it's kept up to date, so that it reflects any changes in personal circumstances or intentions.
- **Inadequate Estate Planning Advice:** Make sure to obtain advice from estate planning professionals (lawyers, accountants, financial planners or insurance professionals) about a specialized estate plan. Obtaining professional advice also reduces the likelihood of poorly drafted documents that may create confusion about the testator's true intentions.
- **Acrimonious Family Members:** If family members are acrimonious and believed likely to challenge the wishes of the testator, make sure the estate plan is as enforceable as possible. Keep in mind that if an estate dispute starts, family members may adopt positions that are completely unreasonable and be resistant to all rational advice.
- **Actions of Your Personal Representatives:** The executors and trustees appointed must behave in a scrupulously fair manner towards all family members. Make sure the individuals selected will be able to set aside any pre-existing feelings they may have about any stated intentions with respect to the estate plan or the beneficiaries, and will be able to establish a good relationship with family members.

THE FAMILY CONFERENCE SOLUTION

Protecting families from the high costs of estate challenges by using a family conference to solve disputes before they become litigious is a reasonable alternative. With the assistance of a mediator, the conference can be used to tell family members about any intended estate plans and, hopefully, obtain their approval of that plan.

Before the Family Conference

There are a number of steps which need to taken before a family conference takes place to ensure that it runs smoothly, including determining whom to invite. In general, invites should be given to all of the adult members in the family who may be affected by the estate plan. At a minimum, the spouse and children should attend.

Deciding where to hold the conference is also important. A neutral location, such as the mediator's office, is usually the best choice.

Finally, an agenda should be prepared before the meeting to ensure that all of the relevant issues are addressed. The mediator will work with the client and his or her lawyer to prepare the agenda and become familiar with the estate plan and any issues that are likely to be contentious.

At the Conference

The meeting will generally start with the mediator explaining his or her role to the family members and outlining the rules governing the meeting. Typically, the mediator asks family members to sign two agreements at the beginning of the meeting:

- the family conference agreement, which emphasizes the neutral role of the mediator and the confidential nature of the meeting (it also provides that the mediator cannot be subpoenaed or required to give evidence about the Family Conference); and
- the rules for the family conference, which are designed to promote an atmosphere of mutual respect and courtesy.

The meeting often continues with the mediator outlining the family conference process and providing a brief outline of the proposed estate plan. The client, and possibly his or her spouse, will also provide brief opening statements, which reiterate any goals for the family conference. The lawyer will then provide a detailed explanation of the estate plan and answer questions that any family members may have.

Once all family members have been fully informed of the details of the estate plan, they can be split into smaller groups or caucuses where they can openly discuss their concerns. The mediator will move between the caucuses and the parents to determine what issues are dividing the family. The mediator will promote negotiation on these issues and suggest possible ways of resolving them.

The ultimate goal of the family conference is to have all family members sign a family constitution, approving the estate plan and agreeing not to contest the will. If the meeting goes well, this can happen in a single session. In some cases, subsequent meetings will need to be held.

Need for Full Disclosure

Essential to the success of the family conference is full disclosure of the details of the estate plan to all family members. Without this forthrightness, an atmosphere of mistrust could poison the process. In addition, if after the client's death family members discover that the deceased did not fully disclose the details of his or her estate plan, they are more likely to challenge your will.

There are a number of sensitive topics that may be difficult to discuss with family members, including unequal treatment of children, spendthrift beneficiaries and succession issues with respect to the family business. The mediator can help plan the best way to address these topics with the family.

What if Some Family Members Won't Attend?

Some family members may refuse to attend the family conference. If that occurs, the rest of the family should still meet so that their agreement to the proposed estate plan can be obtained. Once the family constitution is signed, the mediator can then send it to the non-participating family members and invite them to sign it as well.

In some cases, all family members may attend the family conference, but some family members may refuse to approve the proposed estate plan. If that happens, the Trusted Advisor, be it the lawyer, accountant or estate planner, may want to suggest amending the estate plan to satisfy as many of their concerns as possible without sacrificing personal goals. It is critical that all family members receive a copy of the family constitution, even if they have chosen not to sign it.

Even if some family members won't sign the family constitution, it is likely that a court will nevertheless consider the process favourably upon a will challenge. It will also be difficult for these family members to argue that the testator lacked testamentary capacity or was unduly influenced, because the lawyer will have comprehensive notes about the family conference. In addition, circulating the family constitution to all family members demonstrates a clear intention as to the desired asset distribution.

In the end, whether or not all family members participate in the process or agree with the result, holding a family conference and developing a family constitution are key steps in protecting an estate from litigation.

After the Conference

Once the family constitution is signed, the lawyer and other professional advisors will prepare the necessary documents, including wills, trusts, powers of attorney and deeds of gift, to implement the estate plan. Once this is complete, a diligent regular review of the estate plan is necessary to make sure it continues to reflect the client's wishes. Under normal conditions, the estate plan should be reviewed every few years. If substantial changes are made to the estate plan, another family conference will need to be held.

INCENTIVE/PURPOSE/PRODUCTIVITY TRUSTS

Introduction

One of the important consequences of the considerable transfer of wealth from the baby boom generation to its children and grandchildren is the individual impact it will have on those beneficiaries. Having said that, in my experience, the "problems of wealth" resonate at all levels, even when relatively modest inheritances are passed on to the next generation(s). The extent of this phenomenon is illustrated by the fact that new terminology has surfaced in the United States to describe the baby boomer children as "trust babies", and the enjoyment of the new wealth as the epidemic of "affluenza".

As a result, it may be worthwhile to explore the concept of how one can deal with the potentially unmotivated child who has received the financial protection of being named as a beneficiary in a substantial trust. The key, of course, is to incentivize that beneficiary.

Essentially, it has been suggested that one use the traditional trust mechanism to revise that existing structure to help encourage or discourage certain types of behaviour on the part of the particular beneficiary. Of course, no matter what legal arrangements are created, the fundamental questions are the same: What does it take to motivate people and what is the best way to facilitate the development of a productive individual?

The Current System

To date, Trusted Advisors have generally focused their attention on creating an estate plan that is fundamentally based on avoiding tax and, typically, if there is a need to protect either the surviving spouse during his or her lifetime or the children of that relationship, creating a life interest arrangement. In this situation, an individual (*i.e.,* executor/trustee) is charged with the management of the capital and, at all times, the balancing of the interests of the life tenant and the capital beneficiary.

A recent trend coming out of the United States is to add a twist to the traditional estate planning process by trying to draft into trust documents language that will control the behaviour of the beneficiaries.[4] Essentially, the suggestion of those who propound the incentive trust approach is that estate planners need to move away from the traditional approach of drafting an estate plan with the goal of tax savings, creditor protection and estranged spouse protection, and begin to draft trust documents that will assist to modify the behaviour of the beneficiaries.

Trusts for Children

In considering adding a new layer to the whole trust drafting process, one must give some thought to the fundamentals behind the creation of a trust and why trusts themselves are used for the protection of children.

The obvious goals of a settlor/testator are to protect the financial interests of minor beneficiaries, and while many clients do not like to admit it, an obvious result of any trust arrangement is the fact that the settlor and/or testator is given the privilege of, in some measure, "ruling from the grave".

In her article "Incentive Trusts: Considerations, Uses and Alternatives",[5] Marjorie Stephens considers those the traditional reasons for creating a trust for children. She notes that there are obvious problems that come from this traditional estate planning technique, including the fact that the money received by the children/beneficiaries may act as a disincentive to future education. Furthermore, those children may begin

---

[4] For a comprehensive review of the incentive trust concept, see Marjorie J. Stephens, "Incentive Trusts: Considerations, Uses and Alternatives" (2003) 29 ACTEC Journal 5.

[5] *Ibid.*

to depend on the trust money and not rely solely on their own personal resources. She goes on to say that the most important consideration in respect of distributing the wealth, in the context of a trust environment, is a determination as to when the particular child becomes mature enough to handle both the income and the capital of the trust.

Obviously, it is up to the estate planners and lawyers to create a protection system that typically results in the income and capital being given to the beneficiaries, with a view to eventually having them receive the money without any "strings attached". In fact, ideally, most settlors and/or testators would prefer that the income, and capital if necessary, of the trust be used for support of the children up to the age of 20, and then focus the spending, when the children are in their 20s, solely on education. The prospect that the child will enjoy the income for any other purpose, during his or her 20s, is not as desirable for many clients. However, it is difficult to control the use of the income, and capital, even in the best of circumstances.

Drafting Challenges

Historically, motivating the child beneficiary was not something that was typically addressed in the structure of the trust document. The concept underlying an incentive trust is that the trustee will reward certain behaviour. For example, the trust could be drafted in such a way that the more productive the child is financially, the more money he or she will receive from the trust. The purpose is obvious, namely, encouraging the child to live a productive life.

The concept of the incentive trust was, in part, first developed in a *Wall Street Journal* article dated November 17, 1999, entitled "Trust Me, Baby". Some suggestions made in that article included the idea of matching earned income and creating a specific fund to set up a business or professional practice. Another suggestion was that the monthly income could be paid to a stay-at-home mother or father, or specific language could be included to deny distributions if the child did not enter into a premarital agreement when he or she married. More dramatic suggestions included drafting trust clauses which provided that the child would be denied any money from the trust if he or she failed a drug test, and in an effort to incentivize the child, the trust could include a clause that provided for more money to the child if he or she was receiving therapy.

Obviously, these types of clauses create their own problems, and one has to give consideration to whether or not they are capable of being administered. This is presumably the lawyer's challenge. As with any trust document, broad language usually needs to be incorporated so that unknown future events can fall within the confines of the drafting language. Therefore, it is difficult to draft in all of the desirable behaviour in the context of an incentive trust.

From an administration standpoint, if the specific benefit is tied to specific behaviour, then it is not that difficult for the trustee to attend to the administration of the assets. However, given the necessity for broad and vague language in the drafting, encouraging a productive child can be much more difficult to administer.

At the outset, it is suggested that the following steps be considered:

(1) the objects and purposes of the trust need to be defined;

(2) consideration must be given to broad and specific behaviours that need to be encouraged; and

(3) consideration must also be given as to whether or not the provisions of the trust, as drafted, can indeed be administered.

Psychological Considerations

In her article, Marjorie Stephens sets out some of the psychological considerations that are relevant to the structure of a trust designed to incentivize behaviour. The starting point for any incentive trust is the idea that the settlor/testator is trying to motivate an individual. The two presumptions are that: (a) money can motivate that particular individual; and (b) the settlor/testator will use his or her power wisely and that the individual appointed to administer those powers will do so judiciously.[6]

Marjorie Stephens notes that, in her view, one should not try to use the reward method to control an individual as that does not motivate a beneficiary. In fact, the key to success is that the child takes control over his or her own life and that the use of the exercise of control enables or encourages the child to do so.[7]

The foundation to any incentivizing behaviour is the confidence that the child believes he or she can get things done. In the process of motivating the child and creating a confident child/beneficiary, there must be economic independence for that individual.

In Marjorie Stephens' view, one should not draft "bail out" provisions in the trust. Rather, every effort should be made to foster a feeling that the child must take responsibility for his or her own conduct. Encouraging independent decision-making, accepting responsibility for the consequences of one's actions and establishing and fostering strong

---

[6] *Ibid.* at 14.

[7] *Ibid.* at 12-13.

relationships are the foundations to creating economically independent and competent beneficiaries.[8]

Practical Considerations

In an effort to reach the goal of a financially independent and confident child/beneficiary, one needs to address practical considerations when drafting the trust provisions.

Obviously, the greatest need for economic assistance for the child is usually between the ages of 20 to 40, and, therefore, a careful distribution scheme needs to be set out during this period of the child's life.

Marjorie Stephens notes that:

> Money is not the "problem". Individuals are not "de-incentivized" by money, but rather by the dynamics around the money. Money means control over the individual, not by the individual. ... The solution to this problem, as is suggested, is proper, comprehensive communication.[9]

As a consequence, it is recommended that one start to discuss the financial arrangements and the emotional issues surrounding financial support at an early stage. Sometimes it is useful to involve the child directly in the decision-making process, including investments and distribution.

Knowledge is a form of control, and releasing that information is an important part of the shift in control. Essentially, as the beneficiary matures, so does trust in that beneficiary, and therefore a proactive approach to involving the beneficiary in the process is important.

CONCLUSION

In summary, while the concept of incentivizing beneficiaries and influencing behaviour through the trust mechanism is novel, it seems to me that small steps can be taken to develop an estate plan that moves toward creating confident and financially independent children. This process involves both creative drafting and important psychological considerations in the confines of the family unit — and requires the unified assistance of one's Trusted Advisors.

---

[8] *Ibid.* at 13.

[9] *Ibid.* at 14.

BIBLIOGRAPHY

Bandura, Albert, *Self-efficacy: The Exercise of Control* (New York: W.H. Freeman and Company, 1997).

Covey, Stephen R., *The 7 Habits of Highly Effective People: Powerful Lessons in Personal Change* (New York: Simon & Schuster, 1989).

Czikszentmihalyi, Mihaly, *Flow: The Psychology of Optimal Experience* (New York: Harper Collins, 1990).

Donohue, P. Daniel, "Drafting for Flexibility in Light of Possible Tax Reform" (Big Sky Regional Meeting, American College of Trust and Estate Counsel, Keystone, Colorado, May 18-20, 2001).

Frimmer, Paul, "The Use of Special Trustees" (Big Sky Regional Meeting, American College of Trust and Estate Counsel, Keystone, Colorado, May 18-20, 2001).

Gibson, Rowan, ed., *Rethinking the Future: Rethinking Business, Principles, Competition, Control & Complexity, Leadership, Markets and the World* (London: Nicholas Brealey, 1999).

Hopkins, Kate, *et al.*, "Drafting Strategies for Advanced Planning" (Conference on Advanced Estate Planning Strategies, State Bar of Texas Continuing Legal Education, Santa Fe, New Mexico, April 18-19, 2002).

McCue, III, Howard, "Guiding (Controlling?) the Children and Grandchildren: Planning and Drafting to Influence Behaviour" (34th Annual Philip E. Heckerling Institute on Estate Planning, Miami Beach, Florida, January 10-14, 2000).

Santrock, John W., *Life-Span Development*, 6th ed. (Dubuque, Iowa: Brown & Benchmark, 1997).

Stephens, Marjorie J., "Intrinsic Motivation" (School of Human Development Masters Program, University of Texas at Dallas, April, 1984).

Wernz, Ann Hart, "The Challenges of Drafting and Administering Discretionary Provisions in Trusts" (Notre Dame Tax and Estate Planning Institute, South Bend, Indiana, September 1997).

CHAPTER 54

PLANNING FOR CLIENTS AND FAMILIES WITH SPECIAL NEEDS

Kenneth C. Pope
Marie L. Cassis
Peter Sokoloski

Overview

This chapter will show you how to advise and assist families with family members with disabilities and special needs. It explores the issues that accountants and financial advisors will need to discuss with your families or with friends of special needs individuals with disabilities. In order to maximize available benefits and to plan for lifelong care, especially after the parents have passed on, specific planning tools such as Henson Trusts are needed. Insurance funding for trusts is a standard part of the estate plan. Disability-related tax credits must be put in place, the recently rolled out Registered Disability Savings Plans (RDSPs) must be considered and Lifetime Benefit Trusts to receive RRSPs and RRIFs on a tax-free basis must be anticipated.

This chapter will show you how to make sure that your clients have peace of mind about their estate arrangements to provide for children with disabilities, how to recapture between $5,000 and $20,000 of their tax dollars and how to reduce or remove taxation on RRSPs and RRIFs on death.

At a very conservative minimum, one Canadian family household in eight is either the parent or the sibling household of a person with severe disabilities who receives provincial disability benefits. In Ontario alone there are more than 500,000 households who fall into this statistic.

This does not include all of the people with disabilities who do not receive provincial supports, such as those receiving financial and other supports from workplace disability pensions, personal injury structured settlements and Canada Pension Plan disability benefits.

Any professional advisor who has not identified this core concern for those families has failed the "know your client" test; they have also lost the opportunity to assist these families in the course of their practice, which is a lost business opportunity.

Learning Objectives

By the end of this chapter, you will be able to:

- familiarize yourself with estate planning options for clients whether they have their own special needs or, more commonly, are the family, friend or guardian of someone with special needs;
- understand how the focus of estate planning shifts when planning for disability-related needs;
- maintain focus on how disability-related needs are protected by specialized trust, tax and succession planning tools and techniques; and
- know what to say and start the planning process when your client says, "I just want to live 60 seconds longer than my daughter who has disabilities."

KNOW YOUR CLIENT'S SPECIAL NEEDS

While the "know your client" issue is very important for all your clients, those who need to include special needs planning require even more careful financial planning given the inherently high costs associated with disabilities. Do you think that this will not affect many of your clients? Well, think again. While degrees of disability may vary substantially from client to client, keep in mind that many disabilities are not visible to the naked eye; if you do not ask the questions, you may not truly get to know your client. In addition to this, note that disability rates rapidly increase with age,[1] and with a large segment of the population at or approaching retirement, most advisors and accountants will represent either people with disabilities or someone who cares for a person with disabilities, whether or not they are aware of the fact.

Clearly understanding client core concerns will necessarily shift your focus from simple investment and retirement matters to facing the complex interaction between disability financial assistance programs, benefits and a range of tax and trust implications.

If the person with the disability is your client, then depending on the disability, your ability to communicate with your client may require

---

[1] 2006 Participation and Activity Limitation Survey: Disability in Canada, online: Statistics Canada <http://www.statcan.gc.ca/bsolc/olc-cel/olc-cel?catno=89-628-XIE &lang=eng#formatdisp>.

means such as electronic devices or alternatives to speech where applicable. We become so used to communicating with words that we forget that many persons with severe speech or language impairments may rely on, for example, facial expressions, gesticulations, symbols, flashcards, sign language, finger-spelling or button-pushing to get their message across.

If your client has limited mobility, consider arranging home visits rather than having the client come to your office. Some financial advisors regularly visit clients at home or in a nursing home because it affords them, firsthand, the opportunity to see how they live and to familiarize themselves with their clients' daily challenges. You may notice that it is often easier to get to know someone when they feel comfortable in their own surroundings. Because we live in a world that is not geared for people with special needs, do your best to make yourself and/or your business accessible.

Always remember that with disabilities come higher anticipated living costs, so there will often be a need for more prudent investment planning. You will need to safeguard capital to a large extent and to assist with paying for disability-related items and the often high costs of care/assistance, sometimes both future and ongoing.

How much personal health information should I ask? Keep in mind that some clients will be more than happy to give you plenty of disability-related information, while others will be very short in their answers. Help your client to understand that the more informed you are, the better able you will be, as a financial professional, to build a realistic investment plan, taking into consideration the pragmatic planning of disability-related costs — some obvious and many unapparent.

Some clients may not be willing to offer much detail, while others will be impressed to see that you, as their financial advisor or accountant, are taking a truly personalized approach to their financial planning. Doing so can build trust between you and your client, and can in turn make matters like thorough disclosure that much more likely, hence affording you a clearer picture of available assets.

Do not hesitate to take the "know your client" exercise to a much more detailed level when dealing with clients with special needs, or those who care for a special needs person. The extra time you take at this stage will help you gain insight into your client's financial expectations. You may even wish to draft a new "know your client" form specifically drafted to capture all of the relevant disability-related information and costs.

Across Canada, the huge number of families who have children with disabilities is astounding, and constitutes a segment of the population that is both large and identifiable — as professionals, you need to be aware that not asking your client the appropriate questions may be akin to professional negligence. Since "know your client" is often the preliminary step when meeting new clients, make a stellar first impression by taking into serious consideration "know your special needs client" where appropriate.

If the parents of children with special needs are your clients, be clear on the clients' comfort level *vis-à-vis* investment risk. This is a very appropriate point to consider in the use of life insurance as an estate back stop, to ensure that even if nothing else is left there will be at least a certain sum available to fund a testamentary trust for the child. In my experience, the parents are very prepared to live modest lives themselves to protect capital for this purpose, not realizing that they can usually fund the trust more economically with life insurance than with savings. The "return on investment" is almost invariably higher from this vehicle than from uncertain or very conservative investments.

I recall a 71-year-old client mother I assisted about eight years ago. Her husband was deceased, and she was subsisting in the family home supported only by her own OAS and GAINS income plus her son's provincial benefits. She also had $200,000 in a bank account for "security of capital" earning very little interest, and $300,000 in a RRIF which she intended to encroach upon at the required minimum amounts so there would be more left for her son.

She had no idea that when she died the RRIF income would be taxed at the maximum rate applicable, depending mostly on whether she died in January or December of the year of her eventual demise.

The money in the bank was shifted to a conservative segregated mutual fund, and a designation was made to the Henson trust we had created in her will, which would then be received promptly and without incurring estate administration tax.

She then had a policy of Term to 100 insurance put in place on her life, to be designated to the trust as well. This was funded by the untaxed withdrawals she made from the RRIF, after making use of her own personal exemptions together with the "disability" and "caregiver" tax credits that were available due to her son's marked disability and his living with her.

Even given her age and the fact that she smoked, it was still a much better plan than to simply wait to die and have a large RRIF taxed in her hands in the year of death.

Don't hesitate to collaborate with knowledgeable estate lawyers and other professionals who have experience in this area. In my experience, I have found a collegial approach both personally rewarding and very effective for the client.

PROVINCIAL DISABILITY BENEFITS

Once a qualifying child with disabilities reaches the age of 18 years, there are provincial disability benefits available that include financial, medical and other support benefits. While the disability benefits vary from province to province, it is important that you understand how you can provide financial planning to help special needs families and recipients of provincial disability assistance benefit from additional moneys. Special care must be taken so as not to jeopardize their benefits as this could translate into lost income, including lost dental and drug prescription coverage (a costly item to replace on a dollar-for-dollar value).

Many provincial disability programs fall under the umbrella of social services, with little difference between basic social assistance and disability benefits. Depending on your client's jurisdiction, or the jurisdiction of his or her loved one with special needs, consult the appropriate provincial ministry for specific qualification requirements. At minimum, certification of the disability by a medical doctor and asset-testing will be required for acceptance into the program.

Do not expect the staff operating the benefit programs to be of more than minimal assistance, or to inform you of benefits or services that could be made available if you know what to ask for. To be charitable at best, it is more often the case that provincial disability benefit programs are fraught with staff who provide misinformation about program eligibility to persons with disabilities, often forcing the applicant into inappropriately spending down their assets, inheritance, *etc.* Recently, I heard the term "bureaucratic disentitlement" used to described the denial of benefits and supports which should actually have been provided by the disability benefits program, and it sounds apt to me.

Because the amounts received annually from provincial disability programs leave the recipient living under the poverty line, any assistance you can provide in terms of financial planning is crucial to that family and will also provide peace of mind to your clients, providing for additional needs and costs often associated with disabilities. Get to know what other financial options are available within the relevant jurisdiction, as it varies from province to province.

Take the time to either familiarize yourself with the relevant provincial disability rules and directives or find a local organization and/or lawyer who deals regularly with this subject matter.

In Ontario, recipients of the Ontario Disability Support Program (ODSP) are allowed to inherit money without affecting their benefits, but there are some key limitations. For instance, if an ODSP recipient receives a straight inheritance (not a Henson trust within a will) he or she can inherit $100,000. Currently, any amount can be withdrawn specifically for disability-related items and services, but no more than $6,000 can be withdrawn annually for any use. This is not the case with the Henson trust, as explained in further detail below.

There are different levels of support available from the provinces. For instance, someone living in a "room and board" situation may receive a lower amount to cover shelter, while someone in a rental situation may receive a higher amount to cover rent, utilities, water, *etc.* For the information specific to your client's jurisdiction, see the relevant provincial ministry. In Ontario, it is the Ministry of Community and Social Services that delivers the ODSP.

Referring back to "bureaucratic disentitlement", I recall having a 50-year-old woman referred to me by a legal aid clinic in a small town. Five years before, she had inherited a sum of money from her mother and she had reported this to the local ODSP office. Instead of telling her what could be done to allow her to have this inheritance and continue receiving benefits, the ODSP office cut her off. She proceeded to live on her inheritance, reducing it to $15,000. Five years later, she heard about what she could have done, did those things with the help of a lawyer who assisted her, *pro bono*, and took the new information to the local office. The response was not to reinstate benefits but to tell her, "You didn't do it then, and now it's too late." This is obviously incorrect, and I had everything put back in place in about ten days, using an alternate technique which completely side-stepped the question of whether this was an appropriate response. Unfortunately, the new arrangement restored benefits but not the money she had spent over the years.

HENSON TRUST

The optimal estate planning arrangement for clients to provide for persons with special needs is called a "Henson" trust (a form of absolute discretionary trust). Named after a landmark case in Ontario in 1989, assets left by way of a will or other designation to a Henson trust does not disqualify the recipient from provincial benefits even if assets exceed allowed limits. Sadly, by the time the fight between the trustees and the Ontario government was resolved at the Court of Appeal level, Audrey Henson, the special needs person for whom her father had made provisions in his will, died. The silver lining in this tragedy is the fact that Audrey's painful fight cleared the way for families of persons with disabilities to find a vehicle that could make the all-too-real difference between living in stark poverty and having supplementary personal and special needs paid for by the trust, without jeopardizing provincial benefits.

You can create a Henson trust in a will by leaving an inheritance to a Henson trust (*testamentary* Henson trust), or you can create a Henson trust while the person is still living (*inter-vivos* Henson trust) so that the beneficiary does not have to wait for the benefactor to pass before receiving from the Henson trust. In conjunction with the very modest financial benefits provided by the provinces (maximum just over $1,000 per month in Ontario), the Henson trust can help to provide for supplementary special needs. This can mean the difference between living in poverty and living in modest comfort.

The key to creating a true Henson trust is in the wording, which must make it clear that, at the absolute discretion of the trustees named to manage the Henson trust, income and capital is to be paid out for the benefit of the named beneficiary of the trust. Poor drafting of a trust can result in it failing to meet the testator's true intention, and without the proper wording, the Henson trust can fail. For example, the language must indicate that the trustees have full and absolute discretion to pay out of the trust and that they are not required to pay out to the beneficiary upon demand. The beneficiary does not ever "own" the trust; unlike normal discretionary trusts, it does not "vest" in the beneficiary, who simply receives whatever payments or distributions are made directly from the trust to pay third parties for goods and services for the beneficiary, as directed by the trustees.

One of the keys to making a Henson trust work well over the lifetime of its special needs beneficiary is in the choice of trustees and planning for replacement trustees. Because the beneficiary cannot direct the trustees to pay out, it is crucial that trustees be chosen very carefully in terms of their ability to understand the trials and tribulations faced by the beneficiary as well as prudently investing the trust. Your role here is very important. Trustees will often look to their trusted financial professionals for prudent trust/capital investment advice. Once again, a careful review of all foreseeable disability-related costs will be important as you balance the need for payments and distributions over the beneficiary's lifetime.

Trustees are most typically family members or friends rather than corporate trust companies, although these can also be appropriate. Depending on the age of the beneficiary and the trustees, your client may wish to spell out in detail who will be replacement trustees and, where applicable, how multiple trustees will make decisions, replace themselves and when to wind down the trust. It is always helpful to name trustees of different age groups as part of common sense estate planning; you do not want to see a trust set up with all three trustees, for example, being over the age of 80, with the beneficiary being in his or her teens. Many families do not have more family trustee alternatives than one or two siblings or cousins at the most, so the net may have to be cast over a larger group before appropriate trustees are named.

My trust arrangements almost invariably provide the initial trustees with the power to replace themselves as time goes by, either while alive or by appointment in their own wills. The wording for this is not complicated, and it avoids future court and legal costs, as well as minimizing potential future litigation associated with trustee replacements.

Given the absolute power of the trustees, and the common provision that the ultimate distribution of the trust assets remaining when the beneficiary dies go to the surviving siblings or their children, there is a potential for a conflict of interest on the part of the sibling trustees. This issue and the family dynamics must always be discussed with the client testators and dealt with accordingly.

Because drafting of the trust is key to how it will be interpreted by provincial authorities, contact a lawyer who specializes in trusts, and is familiar with Henson trusts, to set up the necessary vehicles to assist with your client's estate planning goals. Ask him or her how many of these arrangements he or she has drafted for clients, and whether any have come into place after the testator has passed on. The larger part of my estate practice is not settling the estates of my special needs families, but rather being brought on the file when incorrect arrangements or no arrangements have been put in place, and the executors and trustees come to my office to have me help them sort out the mess. It is worth noting that not all provinces have either formally accepted the Henson trust as an allowable asset or had the concept tested in their courts.

RRSP ROLLOVERS TO AN ADULT DEPENDENT CHILD AND LIFETIME BENEFIT TRUSTS (LBTs)

Consider a common scenario. A mother (spouse predeceased) dies holding a sizeable RRSP or RRIF. The income falls into her income in the year of death and is taxed accordingly, often at a high marginal rate. Although it has been possible since 2003 to have this registered asset roll over to an adult dependent child or grandchild, as it would to a spouse, there are various *Income Tax Act* (ITA) requirements to allow this to take place. The new registered asset could and often would result in provincial benefits being cut off, and in many cases a court application to have someone appointed guardian of the child's property and person would be necessary to provide a legally authorized party to handle the rollover and manage the asset if the child lacks competence. Still, there are now, and will be in future, many family situations where this must be addressed rather than paying excessive income taxes. This variable also has an impact on the overall estate plan and the distribution of the estate in many cases. If the estate consists of a house and the RRIF of a similar value being divided between two heirs, it requires more planning than simply providing for the estate to go equally between the two if one receives the RRIF directly on a deferred taxation basis.

In an effort to protect registered retirement savings and/or registered retirement income funds from being eaten up by taxes at the time of your client's death, the Lifetime Benefit Trust (LBT) is a new option whose most recent incarnation was last sighted in Bill C-10 during the last Parliamentary Session, but unfortunately died on the Order Paper when Parliament was prorogued in December 2008. Hopefully, we will still see this new type of trust re-emerge on the Order Paper and eventually see the light of law.

The LBT will be a valuable tool when your client wants to leave a personal trust in his or her will for a special needs, financially dependent, child, grandchild or spouse, with the additional comfort of knowing that the RRSP or RRIF assets he or she dedicates to the LBT could be protected from creditors with an election to deem the RRSP or RRIF assets to have been received by them, with the possibility of a tax-deferred rollover of said assets to that special needs family member.[2]

Since the goal of the LBT is to leave a certain portion of your estate to your special needs, financially dependent family member, attention must be paid to properly defining relevant terms such as "financially dependent". If the dependant's income for the year preceding death was less than the basic personal amount ($9,600 for 2008), the financial dependence definition is met. If the dependant is mentally or physically infirm, add to the "basic personal amount" the disability tax credit amount[3] ($7,020 for 2008) for a 2008 total of $16,620[4] to meet the definition of "financially dependent" for the purpose of setting up an LBT.[5] Because this income threshold is most likely higher than the amounts received in the hands of the special needs beneficiary, from provincial disability benefits, government program benefits should

---

[2] Tim Cestnick, "Help an infirm dependant with lifetime benefit trust" *The Globe and Mail* (11 September 2008), online: <https://secure.globeadvisor.com/servlet/ArticleNews/story/gam/20080911/RCESTNICK11>.

[3] For a complete definition of "mental and physical impairment", see the section in this chapter on Disability Tax Credits and see also the *Income Tax Act*, R.S.C. 1985, c. 1 (5th Supp.).

[4] Tim Cestnick, "Help an infirm dependant with lifetime benefit trust" *The Globe and Mail* (11 September 2008) at 1, online: <https://secure.globeadvisor.com/servlet/ArticleNews/story/gam/20080911/RCESTNICK11>.

[5] The term "financially dependent" is formally defined in the *Income Tax Act* in subsection 146(1.1) and provides the formula for calculating financial dependence.

remain intact and unchanged. Where provincial disability programs require trust reporting to satisfy income reporting requirements, one need report only the amounts disbursed directly to the disabled beneficiary.

The LBT is a true trust, and it is structured and worded to meet the terms required by the ITA. It has terms different from those in a Henson trust, so it will almost certainly be created to run parallel with the Henson trust, which is intended to hold inheritances and proceeds of designated assets.

The LBT trustee(s) may have absolute discretion on the amounts paid out to the disabled beneficiary. The trustee discretion can provide much-needed assistance, especially when the beneficiary suffers from a mental disability that affects his or her ability to manage money. All too often, we have seen the best laid plans go astray when large sums of money are received by someone who does not possess the same abilities as those of the prudent trustee and, before you know it, funds are spent and scattered in the wind, leaving little, if anything, to show of the inheritance. Look to your clients' choices of trustees and take the time to discuss the importance of choosing trustees and their replacements, and clarifying their obligations to the beneficiary. The more in-depth discussions that take place (and are noted) while your client is alive will help to keep everyone directly involved on the same page in terms of duties and expectations. Trustees are required to consider the needs of the beneficiary, including his or her comfort, care and maintenance.[6]

Like a testamentary Henson trust, LBTs will also be incorporated into your client's will. Your client will not have to decide whether a Henson trust or an LBT is most beneficial because it is not an *either/or* situation. For example, your client could potentially set up a Henson trust for the estate and set up an LBT for the RRSPs. If desirable, several beneficiaries can be named to the Henson trust, while the LBT is limited to only one beneficiary; the addition of other beneficiaries may disqualify the LBT, which is supposed to be used only by the beneficiary during his or her lifetime.[7]

As long as the special needs child is the ultimate recipient of the retirement savings (RRSPs, RRIFs), tax can be deferred and possibly eliminated completely if the special needs child has no other taxable

---

6 Murray Sklar, "Estate Planning: The New Lifetime Benefit Trust", *The Estate Planner*, iss. 162 (July 2008) at 2, online: <http://www.cch.ca/newsletters/Financial Planning/september_2008> (paid smdsubscription required).

7 Alison MacAlpine, "Vehicle helps parents care for disabled children", online: <http://www.investmentexecutive.com/client/en/News/ImprimerDetail.asp?Id=46896&cat>.

income.[8] The potential for tax savings is considerable when one uses the personal amount and the disability amount.

Another important provision of the LBT is the need for the RRSP or RRIF funds passing, in the will, to the disabled beneficiary, to be put into a special form of annuity.[9] Proposed amendments to the ITA include allowing the annuity to be acquired by the trust or the estate of the deceased individual, rather than by or on behalf of the child.[10] Our current understanding is that the qualifying beneficiary will be allowed to deduct the purchase price of a *qualifying trust annuity*[11] where a trust is the annuitant and the financially dependent disabled child is the sole beneficiary under the trust.[12] This is helpful where the disability affecting the beneficiary is mental in nature *and* affects the beneficiary's ability to establish or administer the account.

Once the qualifying life annuity (for the life of the disabled beneficiary or for a fixed term equal to 90 years minus the age of the disabled beneficiary) is purchased with the RRSP or RRIF proceeds, the LBT begins receiving the annuity payments. It will be very interesting to see how the expected lifetime of the beneficiary is calculated, and what efforts will be made to determine if the annuity should be specially rated and shortened based on the nature of the disability.

Any amounts paid out of the LBT to the beneficiary (whether income or capital) will be taxable to the beneficiary and the fair market value of the annuity at the time of the beneficiary's death will be taxable to the beneficiary upon his or her death.[13] If there is a guaranteed period or fixed term associated with the qualifying trust annuity, there is a

---

8 Guy Desmarais of Collins Barrow, "Estate Planning — the Finer Points: Special Issues for Those with Special Needs", online: <http://www.collinsbarrow.com/news_showArticle.asp?articleID=240>.

9 Annuity purchased for the Lifetime Benefit Trust must be a qualified lifetime annuity.

10 "Planning for Registered Retirement Savings Plan" by M. Hoffstein, H. Carr, C. Weigl and L. West of Fasken Martineau DuMoulin LLP, *Estate Planning Bulletin* (March 2006) at 5, online: <www.fasken.com>.

11 Note that complete definitions of the types of qualifying trust annuities are located in the proposed legislated changes. See LEGISinfo on the 40th Parliament — 1st Session for the exact proposed wording, online: <http://www.parl.gc.ca/legisinfo/index.asp>, and click on Bill C-10. If you click on Bill C-10 for the current, 2nd Session, you will be brought to the current budget tabled in Parliament and this is not the same legislation.

12 "Planning for Registered Retirement Savings Plan" by M. Hoffstein, H. Carr, C. Weigl, and L. West of Fasken Martineau DuMoulin LLP, *Estate Planning Bulletin* (March 2006) at 5, online: <www.fasken.com>.

13 Tim Cestnick, "Help an infirm dependant with lifetime benefit trust" *The Globe and Mail* (11 September 2008) at 3, online: <https://secure.globeadvisor.com/servlet/ArticleNews/story/gam/20080911/RCESTNICK11>.

requirement that if death occurs during the guaranteed period or fixed term, any amounts that would otherwise be payable after the death of the taxpayer must be commuted into a single payment.[14]

It remains to be seen when the LBT will become law. Worth watching will be the Canada Revenue Agency's (CRA's) interpretation of any LBT-type vehicle that applies the proposed legislation to otherwise valid wills containing LBT provisions governing the RRSP/RRIF proceeds after death to the qualifying beneficiary.

I'm aware of an existing estate in which an RRSP was designated to an LBT prepared according to the terms of the proposed amendments to the ITA. The testator died and the estate was settled, but the final decision of what to do with the RRSP proceeds was delayed for a year or more. Since the legislation was intended to be retroactive to 2003 once passed, I have been advised that the elections and arrangements intended to roll over the RRSP have been made, and that the parties are now waiting for the legislation to be put in place. This was a brave tactical decision, but even if it is unsuccessful the result will be no worse than not making every effort.

TAX CREDITS

In my experience, when I have asked parents of children with cognitive and developmental disabilities (which clearly qualified them for the disability tax credit) if they had applied for the credits, 45% answered "no" or "unsure" to this question! The realm of tax credits is one huge area that is often overlooked in terms of helping clients lower their payable income tax, as discussed below in greater detail. In addition to lowering taxes, qualifying for tax credits can also be a requirement for applying for other money-saving vehicles such as the Registered Disability Savings Plan.

To qualify, a person must have a *severe and prolonged impairment* (expected to last at least 12 months).

The filing process can be onerous, because it requires the involvement of a medical professional and there is sometimes disconnect between how physicians complete forms and how the CRA civil servants process applications at the various centres across the country.

---

[14] Murray Sklar, "Estate Planning: The New Lifetime Benefit Trust", *The Estate Planner*, iss. 162 (July 2008) at 2, online: <http://www.cch.ca/newsletters/Financial Planning/september_2008> (paid subscription required).

Because many applications are not accepted on first submission, specialized assistance is often required in dealing with Disability and Caregiver Tax Credit filings, as discussed below.

The Disability Tax Credit (DTC)

The disability amount can be found on line 316 (for self) and line 318 (transferred to a supporting relative) of your client's tax return. The disability tax credit is a non-refundable tax credit for individuals who have a severe and prolonged impairment in physical or mental functions. In order for an impairment to be considered prolonged, it must be expected to last, or have lasted for a continuous period of at least 12 months.[15]

Asking clients whether or not they currently apply for or receive the disability tax credit (DTC) for themselves or for a family member does not often translate into a clear answer. Very often, clients are unsure as to whether or not they are or have already qualified for the disability tax credit.

The individual must be "markedly restricted"[16] in at least one of the following categories: speaking, hearing, walking, elimination (bowel or bladder functions), feeding, dressing, performing the mental functions of everyday life, life-sustaining therapy to support vital function and the recently introduced cumulative effects of significant restrictions.

To qualify as having a severe and prolonged impairment, one must have the "T2201 Disability Tax Credit Certificate"[17] (hereafter referred to as T2201) form certified by a qualified professional related to the impairment: for example, a medical doctor, physiotherapist, optometrist, psychologist, audiologist, speech-language pathologist or occupational therapist. The qualified practitioner must certify on the T2201 that the impairment meets specific conditions within the set category, which varies depending on the impairment.

If the medical practitioner charges your client to complete the T2201, the client can claim this as a medical expense on line 330 of his or her tax return. We will discuss medical expenses briefly, later in this

---

15 Canada Revenue Agency, T2201 Disability Tax Credit certificate form, 2008.

16 "Markedly restricted" has been defined by CRA as "all or substantially all the time, and even with therapy (other than life-sustaining therapy) and the use of devices and medication, either: [1] Your patient is unable to perform at least one of the basic activities of daily living ...; or [2] It takes your patient an inordinate amount of time to perform at least one of the basic activities of daily living".

17 The T2201 form can be found on CRA's website, online: <http://www.cra-arc.gc.ca/E/pbg/tf/t2201/>.

chapter. Doctors and other professionals are usually helpful and co-operative in this process, with some exceptions. They are busy with their practice and this may appear to be just one more piece of paper to complete. I recommend that the applicant make sure that it is understood that a reasonable fee for the service is quite appropriate, as this may assist the doctor to find the time to focus on the task at hand.

Your clients should be able to retroactively file for the disability amount, back ten years, due to the Tax Payer Relief Provisions in the ITA.[18] The DTC can be a very lucrative tax savings measure for your clients. To give you a brief overview — in 2008, the DTC amounts to over $1,600 in tax savings. When one files for the full ten-year period, the possible tax savings amounts to over $13,000[19] for adults and approximately $20,000 for children 18 or under who qualify.[20]

If your client with the impairment does not have a taxable income, he or she can transfer his or her credit to a supporting relative, such as a parent, grandparent, child, grandchild, aunt, uncle, niece and nephew. You may also transfer the disability amount to a brother and sister but since this was only introduced in 2001 you may only retroactively transfer the amount to that date. The disability amount can be transferred in either its entirety or as the remainder of what the dependant was unable to claim himself or herself.

A majority of the categories of impairment are relatively straight-forward to assess, with one important exception. The "mental functions necessary for everyday life" is often times difficult to assess for eligibility due to the large amount of grey area contained within this intangible category. As a result, it's not unusual to have a medical professional hesitant to certify that a patient is markedly restricted in this category. Fortunately, there have been a few resources released by medical associations to assist medical professionals with assessing their clients.

One document released by the Canadian Psychological Association (CPA) in response to suggestions they made to the House of Commons Sub-Committee on the Status of Persons with Disabilities attempts to assist medical professionals with deciphering what qualifies as a being markedly restricted in the "mental functions necessary for everyday life".

In the document "Eligibility of Persons with Impairments in Mental Functions for the Disability Tax Credit: What Qualified Persons Need to

---

[18] Canada Revenue Agency, "IC07-1 Tax Payer Relief Provisions" (31 May 2007), online: <http://www.cra-arc.gc.ca/E/pub/tp/ic07-1/ic07-1-e.pdf>.

[19] This is approximate because it depends on a number of variables.

[20] The disability tax credit (DTC) is in combination with the supplement for children for the DTC and the Canada child tax benefit.

Know about Attesting to Eligibility",[21] the CPA goes on to further define and clarify the category by stating that "... an individual can be markedly restricted if their only impairment is memory or adaptive functions (which includes abilities related to self-care, health and safety, social skills and common simple transactions) but not if their only impairment is problem solving, goal setting or judgment. An individual must be impaired in problem solving, goal setting *and* judgment in order to qualify".[22]

In 2005, the CRA introduced a new category of eligibility, "Cumulative effect of significant restrictions". This category is useful for individuals who are disabled but not restricted enough to qualify as being markedly restricted. It should be noted that because this category was introduced in 2005, you may only file retroactively back to that point. Significantly "restricted" has been defined by the CRA to mean that "although your patient does not quite meet the criteria for markedly restricted, his or her ability to perform the basic activity of daily living or vision is still substantially restricted".[23] In other words, if an individual takes an inordinate amount of time to dress, feed himself or herself and walk a few city blocks, taking all restrictions into consideration may be enough to qualify as being markedly restricted. This is a welcome addition but unfortunately another ambiguous threshold that will require further redefining at a later date.

As a side note, it is recommended that you only complete the cumulative effect category if you must. In one instance, the CRA failed to notice that a client had not only been certified by the doctor as qualifying for the cumulative effect category, but had also been certified as being restricted in mobility back to 1998. This resulted in the client only being found eligible back to 2005, even though the doctor clearly stated his patient has been markedly restricted prior to 1998. As a result, all the information had to be resubmitted, with emphasis on the mobility restriction rather than the cumulative effect category, and the usual process time on the CRA's end doubled from three to six months. Unfortunately, this was likely due to the oversight of one or two CRA employees.

Many people are unaware that you can make a disability amount claim against an estate. With elderly individuals, often times the last few years of their life can be a trying time; more often than not an individual

---

[21] Canadian Psychological Association, "Eligibility of Persons with Impairments in Mental Functions for the Disability Tax Credit: What Qualified Persons Need to Know about Attesting to Eligibility" (February 2008), online: <http://www.cpa.ca/cpasite/userfiles/Documents/advocacy/tax%20credit.pdf>.

[22] *Ibid.*

[23] Canada Revenue Agency, T2201 Disability Tax Credit certificate form, 2008.

can be affected by a number of age-related disabilities such as arthritis, dementia, *etc.* The 2001 Participation and Activity Limitation Survey indicated that seniors represent the highest rate of disabilities in Canada, with 41% being restricted within their group.[24] Keeping this in mind, it is easy to see that many elderly clients who have children with disabilities also likely qualify for the disability tax credit for themselves. We try to shift our focus to the larger family, looking *up the tree*, as it were, rather than solely focusing on the child with disabilities.

If the client did not manage to file the disability amount while he or she was alive, then fortunately it is not too late to do so *post mortem.* When applying for probate and settling estates, we frequently also back-file for the disability and caregiver credits, which usually total about $18,000. This certainly is enough to pay legal and estate fees in most cases.

In order to make a disability amount claim against an estate, your client will require: the deceased person's death certificate or funeral director's statement; the deceased person's social insurance number and a complete copy of the will or other legal document such as a Certificate of Appointment of Estate Trustee with a Will or a Certificate of Appointment of Estate Trustee without a Will.[25] It should also be noted that you can transfer a dependant disability amount to an estate as well if it is beneficial to do so, if the credit applies but was not used. This typically recaptures $13,000 for the estate.

When assessing your client's tax return, you should also be aware that any attendant care costs in excess of $10,000 will disqualify your client from claiming the disability amount as well. If you are able to keep the attendant care costs below $10,000, then you can claim both under what is known as the *part-time attendant care rule*. This would only be beneficial to your client if it produced a higher claim than the full-time attendant care costs.[26]

The "preferred beneficiary election" is available to trustees of trusts when the beneficiary qualifies for the disability tax credit due to his or her being "markedly restricted in the activities of daily living". This provides an alternative way to attribute income to the low-income child,

---

[24] Department of Finance Canada, "Tax Expenditures and Evaluations — 2004", online: <http://www.fin.gc.ca/taxexp-depfisc/2004/TaxExp04_e.pdf>.

[25] Canada Revenue Agency, "Preparing Returns for Deceased Persons — 2008", online: <http://www.cra-arc.gc.ca/E/pub/tg/t4011/t4011-08e.pdf>.

[26] Gena Katz, CA, CFP, "Taking Care — Clients Helping Their Parents with the Bill Can Claim Certain Tax Credits", online: <http://www.advisor.ca/images/other/ae/ae_0806_takingcare.pdf>.

rather than following the "paid or payable" rule to have income declared in the beneficiary's hands.

Income can be deemed to be "phantom" income of the child without actually giving it to the child, in turn spending it as after-tax capital in ways that benefit the child without affecting provincial disability benefits.

Additional Supplements for DTC-Qualifying Minors

There are additional tax credits and child disability benefits which substantially increase the recapture outcomes for children. In a recent case involving a divorced mother of two boys, aged 14 and 12 with disabilities, we successfully recaptured $52,000, a substantial amount for a teacher (in this case), almost equivalent to her net take-home pay for an entire year.

In another example, two retired parents in their 60s handle daily needs for their two adult daughters, both with disabilities, and three grandchildren, one of whom is also developmentally disabled. We grouped the disability, caregiver and child disability amounts, transferred them to the taxpaying parents and grandparents, and recaptured $42,000 in total for one family. As you can imagine, this is a very gratifying part of the practice.

If your client's child is 28 or under and qualifies for the disability tax credit, your client may also claim the *supplement for children with severe and prolonged impairments* for the years when the child was under 18. There are no extra eligibility requirements once the child can claim the disability amount. This supplement was introduced in 2000 and as such can be retroactively filed back to that date, and allows for an approximate additional $640[27] in tax savings for each year. This amount is, however, reduced dollar-for-dollar by any child care, medical expense claims or attendant care expenses in excess of $2,399.[28]

The Child Tax Benefit (CTB) and the Canada Child Disability Benefit (CDB)

The Child Tax Benefit (CTB) is a federal, refundable tax credit made up of the National Child Benefit (NCB) and two supplements, the National

---

[27] This is approximate because the federal amount is $4,019, multiplied by the lowest marginal tax rate of 16% equals $643.04.

[28] Christine Van Cauwenberghe, *Wealth Planning Strategies for Canadians 2009* (Toronto: Thomson Carswell, 2008) at 263.

Child Tax Benefit Supplement for lower-income households and the Child Disability Benefit (CDB).

The CDB is a tax-free benefit for families who care for children with disabilities under the age of 18. It is a supplement to the monthly CTB for children who already qualify for the DTC. The individual claiming the tax credit must be the child's primary caregiver, the child must qualify for the CTB, and both parents must have filed tax returns for all years being retroactively filed. The CDB may be retroactively filed back to its introduction in July 2003.

The CDB amount is calculated using a base amount, which is associated with the number of children in the household that receive the CTB. You are eligible to receive the full CDB amount if your client's adjusted family net income is less than the base amount for the family size. For instance, a family with one child claiming the CDB would have to be making less than $37,885 in 2008 to claim the full amount. The CDB would not be fully eroded until the family net income exceeds $150,000. The CDB provides up to $2,395 per year, at $199.58 a month (for the period July 2008 to June 2009).[29]

The Caregiver Tax Credit (CTC)

The caregiver tax credit found on line 315 of the federal tax return is available to individuals who provide in-home support for a relative who is a dependant, is over 18 and resides with the supporting relative in his or her residence at some time in the year. The dependant must be your client's child, grandchild, brother, sister, niece, nephew, aunt, uncle, parent or grandparent in order to qualify. If it is difficult to determine an individual's primary residence, a general rule of thumb is that it is usually the address from where the individual files his or her income tax, subject of course to the CRA's rules governing residence. The CTC is currently worth approximately $600 in annual tax savings. Similar to the disability tax credit, it can be retroactively filed for ten years, which can result in an overall tax savings of approximately $5,000. The CTC erodes dollar-for-dollar if the dependant's income exceeds $13,986[30] and becomes completely eroded if it tops the $17,745 threshold.

You cannot claim both the caregiver tax credit and the amount for an infirm dependant 18 or over.

---

[29] Canada Revenue Agency, "What is the Canada Child Disability Benefit?" (8 February 2009), online: <http://www.cra-arc.gc.ca/bnfts/fq_cdb-eng.html#q1>.

[30] Paul B. Hickey and Sandra Bussey, *Tax Planning 2009: For You and Your Family* (Toronto: Thomson Carswell, 2008).

Amount for Infirm Dependants over 18

The amount for infirm dependants over the age of 18 can be of limited use to some but not all. Unfortunately, this amount is income-tested and the individual cannot have an income greater than $9,906 to take full advantage of this credit.[31] If the individual is receiving disability-related support from the Ontario Disability Support Program (or your client's provincial equivalent), by the time the support is calculated against the individual's net income, he or she receives little if any of the credit at all. If your client receives disability support, which most clients do, then it is best to use the caregiver tax credit found on line 315 instead. Clients who are currently using line 306 and not receiving any benefit from it should send in T1 adjustments to reverse these amounts before putting the correct caregiver amount in place. Unfortunately, it is not uncommon to see respected accountants and financial advisors alike suggesting their clients use line 306 instead of line 315 on their tax return when they receive disability support or their net income exceeds the above threshold.

Medical Expense Claims

Medical expense claims are one of the most commonly used tax provisions in the ITA. Individuals are able to claim the portion of the expenses that exceeds the lesser of the two following amounts: 3% of the individual's net income for the year or a fixed amount, which was $1,614 in 1997 (the amount is indexed to inflation). For a full list of what is accepted and not accepted as a medical expense, please refer to the CRA's website.[32]

One interesting bit of information that many people are unaware of is that you can claim your child's tuition as a medical expense if it has been prescribed for the child by a psychologist or other medical practitioner. Often, a child with special needs will greatly benefit from having a smaller teacher-to-student ratio. In order to qualify, you must meet the following conditions: the school must specialize in teaching students with learning disabilities; the school must certify that your client's child is enrolled in this school because of a learning disability, and due to the lack of appropriate resources and services in the public school system,

---

[31] Canada Revenue Agency, "Are you eligible for the amount for infirm dependents over 18?" (8 February 2009), online: <http://www.cra-arc.gc.ca/tx/ndvdls/tpcs/ncm-tx/rtrn/cmpltng/ddctns/lns300-350/306/lgbl-eng.html>.

[32] Canada Revenue Agency, list of accepted medical expenses, online: <http://www.cra-arc.gc.ca/tx/ndvdls/tpcs/ncm-tx/rtrn/cmpltng/ddctns/lns300-350/330/llwbl-eng.html>.

the child needs to access the specialized services of the prescribed school.[33]

As you can see, disability-related tax provisions can be very valuable to clients with special needs. The government realizes that there are certain costs associated with supporting a special needs person, and has adopted many different tax credits, deductions and provisions to ensure that he or she is compensated for some of his or her support. Unfortunately, the onus lies with the tax filer to complete his or her taxes in the most beneficial way, and many people with disabilities and/or their caregivers do not know how, or do not have the time to properly do this. By improving the special needs component of professional financial education, advisors, accountants and others will be better equipped to ensure that they are maximizing their client's options and saving all the money he or she rightfully ought to have.

REGISTERED DISABILITY SAVINGS PLAN (RDSP)

The recent addition of the Registered Disability Savings Plan (RDSP) requires that any new plan beneficiary already qualify for the DTC, so the DTC application being accepted is critical to the set-up of the RDSP for special needs clients. Only one RDSP account may be set up per qualifying individual, and only that beneficiary is entitled to any payments, unlike other registered plans such as the Registered Education Savings Plan (RESP), where you can have multiple plans per person and where effectively tax-free returns of contributions are allowed. You can potentially transfer an RDSP from one financial institution to another once the rest of the financial institutions come on board (the rollout by all the major banks, except one, has been less than stellar, to say the least).

This new type of registered savings plan will help friends and families build financial security for the special needs person in their lives. This is not an alternative to setting up a trust for a person with disabilities, but should be used in conjunction with other vehicles, such as Henson trusts, insurance products, segregated funds and LBTs to build a solid financial plan.

Similar to the RESP, contributions are not tax-deductible, and earnings and growth accrue on a tax-deferred basis.

---

[33] Canada Revenue Agency, Income Tax Interpretation Bulletin No.: IT-519R2 (consolidated), "Medical Expense and Disability Tax Credits and Attendant Care Deduction", section 29, at 8, online: <http://www.cra-arc.gc.ca/E/pub/tp/it519r2-consolid/it519r2-consolid-e.pdf>.

Anyone can contribute to an RDSP; you do not need to be related in any way. The contributions grow tax-free until withdrawn, at which time a proportion of the plan (earnings and growth received) is taxable and will need to be declared as income in the hands of the beneficiary at that time. Persons receiving provincial disability benefits can set up an RDSP, without going through an asset-test and without it affecting provincial disability benefits, where applicable.[34] Unlike RRSPs, there are no maximum annual contribution restrictions. There is a maximum of $200,000 that may be contributed to any one RDSP over the course of its lifetime, and all contributions must be made before the beneficiary's 60th birthday.

People with disabilities receive approximately $12,000 in untaxed social benefits each year in most provinces, or less. If they also work, employment income will offset provincial benefits to varying degrees. In my experience, it is unusual to find a disability benefit recipient who nets more than $21,287 per annum from both sources. Children under 18 do not receive disability benefits.

If the beneficiary's income level is less than $21,287 (if under 18, use family's net income level, and if over 18, use the beneficiary's net income only), the beneficiary should receive annual Government of Canada Disability Savings Bonds, to a lifetime maximum of $20,000 per RDSP. Add to this the Canada Disability Savings Grant, if the beneficiary's income is $75,769 or less, for an additional $3,500 per year, to a lifetime maximum of $70,000.[35]

Simply put, if the beneficiary over the age of 18 meets the appropriate income levels, an initial contribution of $1,500 can result in $4,500 in matching government funds. However, with every plan there are pitfalls to note. Be aware that there are complex rules governing the withdrawal of funds from RDSPs that could potentially see the beneficiary having to repay government grant and bond moneys if withdrawals are made before the funds have vested for a period of ten years.[36]

---

[34] As of February 14, 2009, the following provinces and territories officially exempted RDSP income from affecting provincial benefits: British Columbia, Alberta, Saskatchewan, Manitoba, Ontario, Quebec (partially), New Brunswick, Nova Scotia, Prince Edward Island, Newfoundland, Northwest Territories and Yukon.

[35] The amount to be received under the Canada Disability Savings Grant and Bond are graduated depending on income levels. See online: <www.hrsdc.gc.ca> for income specific amounts.

[36] Current discussions with the federal government regarding the complexity of the current ten-year-hold-back rules are under way. The federal government is being asked to loosen the restrictions to make it easier for financial institutions to administer the RDSP.

Beneficiaries will only receive grant and bond moneys up until the year in which they turn 49 years old.

If maximum matching contributions have been made since the child turned 18, then when he or she turns 38, there will be no further federal contributions available. The total of $90,000 grants and bonds available will already have been maximized. If the plan is set up for a child at a young age, the end of contributions will be earlier, but the growth on the total contributed will presumably be larger than if the plan is set up at a later age.

Maximize the sources of contributions to an RDSP. Ask your client for a list of potential contributors and send them a letter informing them that an RDSP has been set up for the special needs person in their life and show them how to contribute and what it could mean for the intended beneficiary's quality of life. Some clients may only be able to provide a limited amount of contributions and you want to try to maximize contributions so that matching government contributions are received annually, for the potential maximum of 20 years, allowing room before the $200,000 lifetime limit is reached.

The governing legislation and regulations outline the two forms of payments allowed under the RDSP: Lifetime Disability Assistance Payments (LDAPs); and Disability Assistance Payments (DAPs). LDAPs are mandatory payments in the year the beneficiary turns 60 years of age, calculated by a legislated formula as follows:

FMV of the RDSP / 3 + (life expectancy – age)

DAPs, however, must be specified at the time the plan is set up. Whoever is responsible for setting up the plan will need to mention this and check the bank account agreement regarding lump-sum withdrawals. RDSP payments are "blended" on a *pro-rata* basis, since the contributions were made with after-tax dollars, while the grants and bonds, as well as interest/earnings on the whole plan, are taxable.

For assistance with running RDSP scenarios and calculating the potential returns, there is a great tool available at <http://rdspadvisor.org>, where you will find a valuable RDSP Calculator to crunch those numbers. This is a great website, full of recent news, developed by parents of special needs children who have spent a great deal of time and effort lobbying the government and providing a great support network for families affected by special needs.

As beneficiaries of RDSPs near their retirement years, they can find comfort in knowing that RDSP income will not affect their entitlement to: Old Age Security (OAS) payments, GST credits and the CTB.

In the event of the RDSP beneficiary's death, the plan's value is paid out to the beneficiary's estate, subject to the ten-year-assistance holdback rule (note: all RDSP beneficiaries should have a current will reflecting the inclusion of the RDSP otherwise the RDSP will likely have to be disbursed according to the relevant provincial rules of intestacy, in other words, as if they had died without a will).

Currently, we have encountered a hiccup in the administration of the RDSP, specifically regarding the difficulties of parents of special needs children who are over the age of 18 and lack the requisite competency to sign Continuing Powers of Attorney for Property. In early 2009, organizations such as PLAN went back to the government, asking for a loosening of the rules governing the opening of RDSPs. Parents of special needs children who are over the age of 18 and lack the necessary competency to sign powers of attorney have been turned away from financial institutions until they provide proof of formal guardianship standing. While some provinces such as British Columbia and Manitoba already have alternative arrangements such as Representation Agreements in place, others like Ontario do not, and are currently requiring parents to seek formal guardianship status, which is a lengthy (could take a year if not more) as well as costly (minimum of $5,000) process to embark upon.

Since discussions with the relevant government authorities are still under way, it remains to be seen how flexible the provinces will make the currently complex and rigid rules. Unfortunately, there is a real disconnect between the goals of the program and the rules and regulations governing its administration. This is often the result of policymakers drafting in isolation of their intended audience. Further consultations with leading organizations such as PLAN Canada should help policy writers understand how to tweak what is working and discard what is unnecessarily complicated and arguably overly onerous for families already coping with life's own complications.

For a list of financial institutions currently administering RDSPs, please see the federal government's Human Resources and Development website at: <http://hrsdc.gc.ca> for details.

PENSION PLANS

Pension plans are a valuable part of estate planning. They are often the fruit of many years of diligent work on the part of the client (employee), and the prudent investments and expenditures of the pension managers (employer), always with the same intention: to provide financially for the later periods of our lives.

Pensions typically have a survivor pension, as part of the overall succession plan for spouses and children when the main income earner has passed on.

We realize that a spousal pension may well result in the loss and clawback of other benefits, such as federal and provincial income supplements (GAINS) and OAS benefits. The efforts we make to split income and reduce the usurious rates of taxation in Canada are generally defeated when one spouse dies and passes on pensions, investments earning income and other family assets to the surviving spouse.

A family with a child or children with disabilities in which both parents have committed themselves to caring for all their children as their needs require would benefit from specialized advice when planning for retirement with private corporate Individual Pension Plans (IPPs) as well as public sector pensions across Canada.

It is entirely feasible for an IPP to designate a survivor pension for a spouse, obviously, and from there, a pension for an "adult dependent survivor", such as a child with disabilities, is a small step.

Various statutory pensions provide "adult dependent survivor" pensions for children with disabilities. Ontario examples of these include: Teachers pensions, OMERS pensions, OPG Ontario Power Generators pensions, OPSEU and others.

The difficulty is that pension income will be offset dollar-for-dollar from provincial disability benefits! A 100% offset is not a good use of well-earned pension income. This is not why parents work hard all their lives, to remove and replace the provincial share of support for their children. The legislative intent of provincial disability benefits is to continue a sharing of support from the province, the community, the family and the person with disabilities.

The better plan is to have the pension income paid to a testamentary Henson trust, created by the will of the parent, rather than paid to the child. It is also feasible to have the pension paid to the trust upon the death of the pensioner rather than on the death of the spouse if this is preferable for tax efficiency, depending on the tax bracket of the surviving spouse. There is no sense in giving income to a surviving spouse to be taxed at high marginal rates, thereafter used to provide for the child, when it may be taxed at reduced rates at the start.

Another alternative, which will be appropriate when considering the future plan of care for a child with disabilities, is to commute the pension into a lump sum and have this directed to the trust. This could then be used to purchase shelter for the child, or to be reinvested according to "prudent trustee investment guidelines". In Ontario and other provinces, such guidelines have replaced the approved list of investments defined by statute (to which professionals found workarounds anyway).

For example, it may be appropriate to invest in dividend-earning stocks rather than interest-earning assets, to make use of the dividend tax credit and further reduce taxation.

Pensions are a major source of income later in life for both wealthy families and lower income families. Both will also often have a Registered Retirement Savings Plan (RRSP/RRIF). For higher income earners, this is a component of their overall investment and retirement strategy, designed to allow asset growth without annual taxation of the income earned. Unfortunately, upon retirement, this RRIF income is subsequently taxed at high rates in the hands of the contributor or the spouse.

In addition to IPP beneficiaries, there are going to be hundreds of thousands of unwitting "adult dependent survivor" pensions coming into play as the "baby boom" generation retires. Relatively few of these employees even know that such pensions for their children exist. These pensions often become known to the family only after the pensioner has passed on and the family seeks estate settlement assistance from knowledgeable accountants, financial planners and lawyers.

The same is true of the OMERS pension, another Ontario provincially legislated pension, which provides a pension for adult children with disabilities. The general rule for Canadian pensions is that the disability must be a result of early onset or young adult disabilities.

The disabilities may be any combination of physical, mental health and cognitive developmental disabilities. Establishing the facts of the disability and pension applicability takes place after the death of the parent(s), but documentation can be put in place beforehand.

From an accounting standpoint, if these families are properly advised, they will create testamentary and *inter vivos* Henson trusts to provide for their children. These trusts will be created both while the parents are alive and upon each of their deaths. This will generate trust accounting and tax filing work equivalent to probably over 200,000 new client files in Ontario alone.

Due to the common use of the "preferred beneficiary election" for the trusts, depending upon circumstances, the tax returns for the beneficiary may also require attention.

For a thorough discussion of pension plan options, see Part II: Individual Pension Plan (IPP) Essentials, in this book.

INSURANCE PRODUCTS

We see the television advertisements daily; it seems everywhere we turn these days, we are inundated with offers to purchase insurance. While every insurance policy needs to be reviewed on its own merits, insurance policies are one way to help minimize the chance of debt after death and are an additional vehicle to planning for your client's special needs, or those of the special needs person in your client's life. For a comprehensive look at insurance and annuity options, see Part IX: Personal Risk Management and Maximizing Estate Benefits (Chapters 62–67) for specifics.

Clients are often preoccupied with two matters: concerns about the child with disabilities and financial stability to care for their loved ones after they are gone. Add to this the fact that personal debt levels are rising while real estate values and investment portfolios are dropping and it is not difficult to envision an estate falling short of its financial goals. Insurance products can often play a key role in bridging a financial gap, and can even be used to fund Henson trusts.

You will need to consider what type of insurance will provide the best protection for the dollars spent. While individual term insurance may be suitable for a "clean living" (healthy, non-smoking) person, it may not be cost-effective for someone already dealing with health issues. You need to find a balance between cost and coverage, tailored to your client's financial goals and expectations. For instance, does your client plan to pay for large items such as the education and care of a special needs person? These are not only expensive items but require payout over a number of years, so keep this in mind when planning.

Discuss if any children will need to be covered under the policy, if a family term policy may be appropriate or if a universal life insurance product may be more suitable. Because some disabilities are genetically passed, and may not manifest until later in life, you need to know what could reasonably happen to the health, and consequent needs of your client and his or her loved ones, and try to plan for many possible outcomes by choosing the appropriate insurance products and addressing critical illness clauses. Permanent illness needs to be matched with the right insurance product, preferably one that is permanent rather than term based, but I defer to the insurance experts on these options.

As previously mentioned in this chapter, any potential cash that can be left to a person receiving provincial disability benefits must be structured so as not to affect their eligibility for income assistance.

Financial planning, insurance and investment needs are often weighted by concerns about providing for a child with disabilities over the course of the child's lifetime. Insurance products often play a key role in the financial planning to fund, for example, Henson trusts, as well as other options.

From a marketing perspective, almost one in ten people is directly affected by disability issues. This is a very identifiable niche market that is unknown to or ignored by many financial professionals.

Until raised by amendments to the applicable regulations to the ITA, the test was the amount of the personal exemption, which is $10,320 in 2009. If the adult child had income greater than this amount, which virtually all adult children with disabilities do (resulting from provincial disability benefits), he or she was disqualified from a tax-deferred rollover of registered retirement assets.

This test amount was raised in 2003 and indexed, making it greater than disability benefits in all of the provinces; thus, the rollover is achievable subject to other factors which may make such a designation complicated or self-defeating.

Accountants preparing tax returns for special needs clients who do not ask the right questions are particularly at risk. You may know there has been an annual contribution, but this does not mean your job is done when you are preparing the tax return for filing. Knowing but not advising about the implications of beneficiary designations will come back to haunt such professionals in the very near future. The fees they may have earned in preparing the tax return will not warrant claims made for negligent advice. This sort of claim is already coming back to bite the tails of lawyers who did not prepare Henson trusts for clients when they "knew or should have known" that there was a child with disabilities. Most of my estate practice involves sorting out "no trust" estates or advising executors when flawed trusts have been drafted.

One possible result will be that errors and omissions insurance premiums will rise. The courts will hold lawyers and other professionals to the test of perfection and likely find against them without mercy or qualification.

Another possible result will be the liability of the partners of retired professional accountants and advisors and those who find themselves liable as partners of those retired professionals. In the majority of cases that I've dealt with, I have been able to find a "fix" to this problem, by mitigating the damages and putting the estate and beneficiary onside with the provincial authorities. I am now starting to see situations where my best efforts are not enough, and disability benefits and other life supports are being cut off. This is tragic and unnecessary for all concerned.

I have a client situation in which we were able to have a sympathetic judge in a small town actually amend by court order the terms of a will designating insurance to a person with disabilities, but with no Henson trust, thus creating one! This is cutting edge, but it will not be available across the board.

Much to the advantage of the partners of the senior retired solicitor who drafted the will in this case, their liability has ended, and a quantified settlement will be reached with LawPro, the lawyers' indemnity company.

REGISTERED RETIREMENT SAVINGS PLAN (RRSP)

This brings us to the question of designating the RRSP to a Henson trust. This is not presently workable except for IPP owners. Proposed amendments to the ITA which would allow for this have not yet been brought into effect.

An IPP owner, however, is free to have the RRSP transferred over to the IPP by way of an additional voluntary contribution, and then direct the benefits to a Henson trust. This is the ideal solution to the problem.

If a parent designates an RRSP to a child with disabilities, which is very common when a spouse is out of the picture due to death or divorce, there are factors which a professional advisor must consider and discuss with the parent. A Trusted Advisor who places the annual contributions might well know of this designation, while an accountant or lawyer often would not, unless he or she were already aware of the parent's actions, so do not forget to ask the right questions so that no asset is overlooked for planning purposes.

For lower-income families, RRSPs are often a cruel trick played on them by well-meaning financial advisors and institutions. At retirement, drawing on RRSPs may often result in substantial clawbacks of GAINS and OAS income. Every dollar of other income starts to come into the clawback equation for both GAINS (at 50% of each GAINS dollar) and a graduated clawback of OAS at higher levels of income. Trusted Advisors in particular should consider these factors from the client's perspective when also considering their commissions and fees.

What both tax bracket families would like to do is shelter this RRSP asset and have it available at lower rates of taxation or clawback for the benefit of their children with disabilities when they have passed on.

To do so would require that it be "rolled over" to the child or to his or her Henson trust to protect provincial disability benefits. It is common knowledge that such a rollover can be made to a dependent child under age 18, subject to annuitizing the fund and paying it out in equal shares in the years remaining until age 18. For a child over age 18, the rules are less well known.

This adult dependant rollover is now feasible. As a result of federal regulatory changes in 2003 after the budget in February of that year, the financial dependency test (income of the child in the year prior to the death of the parent being less than the personal tax exemption level) that a child with disabilities must meet to allow this rollover has been adjusted upward, and, in the majority of cases, the test can be met.

Foremost is the fact that the rollover of an RRSP in excess of certain limits directly to a child receiving ODSP will disqualify him or her from benefits, and the receipt of funds from the RRSP will again affect benefits. Currently, this appears to be the case in all provinces. Specialized advice is needed to decide on the parent's best course of action.

REGISTERED EDUCATION SAVINGS PLAN (RESP)

Gone are the days when special needs children were simply expected to stay at home with their parents. Nowadays, many special needs children will go on to attend university or college, but those are not their only options, and attendance at alternative educational institutions will need to be appropriately costed out and planned for. RESPs facilitate the saving of funds for such opportunities by allowing your clients to earn investment income in a tax-deferred environment.

Individual plans can be set up for the benefit of an individual beneficiary while family plans accept contributions for more than one beneficiary. While there is no longer a maximum annual contribution to an RESP, the maximum lifetime contribution per beneficiary cannot exceed $50,000. These contributions are not tax-deductible. The federal government provides a grant of 20 cents for each dollar contributed, up to a maximum of $500 each year and a lifetime limit of $7,200. These Canada Education Savings Grants (CESGs) are only paid on the first $2,500 contributed each year and only if an annual contribution is made. A large lump-sum contribution might compromise these grants, but the interest accumulating tax free on a lump sum of $50,000 (presuming, for example, that grandparents decided to endow this amount as an "early" inheritance) would generate much more tax-free growth than the grants provide. This option may be suitable for some of your clients.

Additional grants for families with income below $74,000 are now available. The grant on the first $500 contributed will be 40% for families with incomes below $37,000, and 30% for families with incomes between $37,000 and $74,000. Contributions can be made for a period of 21 years.

RESPs must be terminated by the end of the year that includes the 25th anniversary of the plan.

If your client has chosen to set up an RESP for a special needs child that will attend an alternative to university or college, remember that in order for the funds to be disbursed from an RESP, a facility must be deemed a "designated educational institution" with a "qualifying educational program" under the Canada Student Loans plan. Alternatively, it can be certified by the Minister of Human Resources as an educational institution that provides courses related to the development or improvement of skills in a given occupation or vocation.

A "qualifying educational program" cannot span less than three consecutive weeks. Full-time students must spend at least 10 hours weekly on program-related courses or work, while part-time students must devote at least 12 hours monthly of their time. The in-class portion of a recognized apprenticeship can also count as time spent. Part-time students can access up to $2,500 of RESP funds per 13-week semester, or greater amounts, subject to approval by the plan's administrators.

Curricula can be specifically created to meet the special needs of adult children. For example, a couple of years ago, a group of "exceptional families" in Ottawa arranged a series of approved continuing education classes designed for their 25 children at Algonquin College in Ontario, all of whom had graduated from high school at the age of 21.

Your clients may not be aware of the options available to special needs children; let them know that RESPs can be useful tools for all children, regardless of disabilities. It is just a matter of thinking outside the box and customizing educational needs specific to the person. Even if a special needs child cannot physically attend a classroom setup, he or she may be able to access distance education via correspondence classes, participate via online or study via a variety of apprenticeship programs.

Once the money from the RESP has been distributed to the beneficiary, the income earned in the plan plus the amount of federal contributions is taxed as income of the beneficiary. As a student, the child will not likely have much other taxable income and will be eligible for tuition and education tax credits; therefore, he or she will have little to pay in taxes.

RESP funds should only be used to pay for education-related expenses such as tuition, books and tutors. If a residential or meal plan comprises part of the child's program, it is very important that the plan not be paid with RESP funds. Similarly, RESP money should not be used to pay for things that are covered by provincial disability benefits such as shelter, clothes and food. Inform your client that separate paperwork should be kept so as to clarify the flow of funds in the event of a deemed overpayment, surprise clawback or audit of some kind.

Parents can now have up to $50,000 of the income that accumulates in the RESP transferred into their RRSPs, to the extent that they have unused contribution room available. Alternatively, they can withdraw RESP income and pay tax at their marginal rate plus an additional 20% to offset the interest earned on the grant portion.

It is now possible to roll over or transfer educational assistance payments without tax implications to another family member, so long as the beneficiary is under 21 years of age and is related by blood or adoption. In the case of an RESP in the family plan format, educational assistance payments can be paid out to another family member as long as the same qualifying criteria are followed.

THE BIGGER PICTURE

The advice you provide your clients will often be the trigger that encourages the client to seek further professional assistance, be it for will drafting, trust creation, completion of medical forms, tax filing, insurance designations, powers of attorney, guardianship matters, setting up RDSPs or pension planning. Some clients may have already considered a few of the options you will present to them, but I hazard a guess that very few will ever present an already thorough estate plan; they all need to be constantly tweaked as new laws are enacted, as tax rules change and as their financial holdings vary in value. Periodically, it is worth your while to revisit clients after having completed a comprehensive financial plan, to discuss any new goals and to confirm those already in existence.

Do yourself a favour and build periodic reviews with clients into your work calendar. The more up to date the estate plan and the clearer you and your notes are regarding the planning priorities and current and foreseeable disability-related needs, then the better equipped you are to assist your client and his or her family when life events come to pass, and people you have perhaps never seen before in your life look to you for direction and help during, what can often be, the most trying times of their lives.

CHAPTER 55

GIFT GIVING CONSIDERATIONS — PLANNED GIFTS AND FOUNDATIONS

Gwen Benjamin

Overview

Over the coming decades Canada will experience the largest shift in our demographics as its population ages. As more Canadians approach their greying years, many will begin to consider their legacy and this will have a far-reaching impact for charities. There will likely be an impact on the nature of donations, with financial assets and gifts in kind becoming more important. Charitable giving and the creation of foundations are likely to become more popular vehicles for the distribution of charitable funding. This chapter outlines the considerations that Trusted Advisors must consider when guiding their clients with their estate planning and gifting to be a proactive force in their clients' lives.

Learning Objectives

By the end of this chapter you should be able to:

- understand the importance of incorporating philanthropy into the conversation with clients;
- understand the choices that a client has when he or she has decided to gift money to a charity or foundation and the legal and tax consequences of each choice; and
- understand the positive impact both a client and his or her Trusted Advisor can achieve through planned gift giving as a part of a client's overall financial and estate plan.

TALKING ABOUT PHILANTHROPY

When we meet with a new client, we have to be mindful of obtaining as much information about the client and his or her family as we need so as to prepare a suitable estate plan for the client. A good checklist is critical to ensure that you don't miss information about the client's circumstances — age, citizenship, dependants, previous marriages, *etc.* How many of us have the client's philanthropic goals on that checklist?

I have come to believe that if I fail to ask the client about his or her views on charitable giving — current practices and future dreams — I may have missed opportunities for him or her; mostly a missed opportunity to realize his or her wishes, but also missed opportunities from a tax and family legacy perspective.

Sometimes a client simply wishes to leave a small legacy to a charity that he or she has supported for many years — it might be a church that he or she attended, or a hospital that helped him or her with a loved one. But often a client with no close family ties or, in the event of a failure to vest of his or her estate because of there being no beneficiaries to take, wishes to leave the residue of his or her estate to one or more charities.

The thorough trusted advisor will explore the client's wishes in this regard.

WHAT SHOULD YOU KNOW ABOUT PLANNED GIVING?

Planned giving simply refers to making charitable gifts in a structured manner. Planned gifts can be made at death — by will or by designation — or during a lifetime. Like an estate plan, there is no "one size fits all"; rather a planned gift should be tailored to fit a client's needs, both from a philanthropic and from a financial perspective.

Our tax system encourages philanthropy. Under the *Income Tax Act* (ITA) a tax credit is available for individuals making a gift to registered charities and certain other entities. This chapter focuses on gifts made to Canadian registered charities.

The combined tax credit in Ontario for donations over $200 is 46.41%[1] in 2008. The threshold for the amount of income that can be sheltered by a tax credit for a charitable gift given by an individual is 75% generally. If the gift exceeds this limit (or even if it does not but it isn't claimed in the year), the excess amount of the gift may be carried forward and must be claimed ahead of gifts in each of the current years

[1] This is calculated on taxable income that exceeds $123,185. The federal credit is currently 15% of the first $200 and 29% of the amount over $200.

over the next five years. This annual limit of 75% is also increased by 25% of taxable capital gains arising on the donation of a capital property. Thus, if a piece of land is donated and a taxable capital gain of $100,000 arises on that donation, the annual limit, in that instance, would be increased by 25% of that amount, or $25,000.

In the year of death and the immediately preceding year, this general threshold of 75% is increased to 100%. This is an important rule to know, as the client can make a very meaningful gift in the year of death, and, because of this rule, eliminate income which arises in the year of death and potentially the year preceding death.

When a gift is made, the donation receipt will indicate the amount of the gift that is eligible for the tax credit — the "eligible amount". The eligible amount of the gift is generally the value of the gift less any benefit or advantage which the donor receives for giving the gift. So, for example, if your client makes a donation to a registered charity and receives a ticket to a ballet performance, the amount of the donation receipt will be the amount, if any, by which the donation made exceeds the price of the ticket. If the value of the advantage or benefit exceeds 80% of the value of the donation, no gift is deemed to have been made under proposed amendments to the ITA. In that case, the donor would have to satisfy the Canada Revenue Agency (CRA) that there was an intention to make a gift. Naming rights (such as having a hospital wing bear the family name) are not generally considered to be a benefit or advantage that will reduce the eligible amount of the gift.

There are many other technical rules in the ITA which deal with charitable donations and the tax credit that is available for individuals. It is not necessary to know these rules in great depth, provided that you have an advisor to whom you can send the client to plan a gift.

In the last few years, the gifting of publicly traded securities has become extremely popular. This is largely a result of the fact that these assets can be gifted with no capital gains arising. As a result of this tax exemption, the gift to the charity can be more meaningful than an after-tax gift of cash, for example. Until recently, this exemption only applied when the securities were gifted to public foundations or charitable organizations. Now, under proposed new rules, the gift of publicly traded securities may be given, exempt from capital gains tax, to any registered charity, and there are certain other rules which will govern the amount of interest that any charity can have in a given corporation. These new proposed rules are aimed at preventing self-dealing, and they are referred to as the "excess business holding" rules. While these excess business holding rules are fairly complex, they seek, in essence, to limit the amount of interest in a certain corporation that the charity can hold.

GIFTS MADE IN THE YEAR OF DEATH

When a deceased taxpayer has made charitable gifts (bequests) in a will, the ITA deems the donation to have been made immediately before the taxpayer died. As noted above, to the extent that the gift cannot be used in the year of death to offset income, it can be carried back to the immediately preceding year.

When gifts are made in a will, it is very important to ensure that the chosen charity or charities have been properly identified. The Charities Directorate of the CRA has a very helpful website to be found at <www.cra-arc.gc.ca> which contains an online search vehicle for registered charities. These registered charities can be searched by name, by registration number or by designation. When your client advises you that he or she wishes to make a gift to a certain charity, double check the identity of that charity on the website to be sure that the charity is correctly identified in the will. Consider also discussing with the charity any gift in respect of which your client wishes to attach a specific purpose. The purpose of the gift must be within the objects of the charity.

While larger gifts are often made in the will, gifts can also be structured as direct designations, such as direct designations of life insurance, RRSPs and RRIFs. If these gifts meet certain conditions, they may also be deemed to have been made in the year of death.

In the case of life insurance, one can name the charity as the beneficiary of the life insurance proceeds in the policy itself. This avoids estate administration tax on the proceeds and also provides a gift which qualifies for the charitable tax credit. There are also other ways to make charitable gifts with life insurance — for example, one could assign the life insurance policy itself to the charity. If the gift is made by making the charity the owner of the policy, the individual who pays the premiums qualifies to receive a tax receipt for those premiums. However, that individual would not receive a charitable tax credit for the insurance proceeds in the year of death or in the year preceding death.

There are many papers written on the different types of gifts which will qualify for the tax credit. Another valuable source of information is the charity itself. Often charities will have helpful information available to potential donors on the various types of gifting. One should always seek independent advice, however, and not rely solely on the charity, as it may not represent your client's interests.

ENDOWMENTS

If your client wishes to make a significant gift, you will want to consider how the gift will be structured. Many clients wish to establish gifts that will go on in perpetuity — commonly called "endowments". The benefit of this type of gift is that the capital will be exempted from the general disbursement quota of the charity (although subject to a 3.5% disbursement quota), which, in theory, will allow the capital of the gift to grow. Generally, an endowment is structured as a donor-advised fund, with the donor having the ability (sometimes with his or her family) to advise the charity as to where the donations should be made but with the board of the charity making the final decisions on granting. Generally, these endowments are held by public foundations, such as a foundation that is affiliated with a hospital, a community foundation or an institutional foundation.

Sometimes clients wish to put stringent conditions on gifts. While there may be issues as to whether there is actually a "gift" (see commentary above regarding the advantage or benefit under taxation rules), which must be a voluntary transfer of property, the gift will possibly fail if the charity can't accept the gift. Each charity has its own objects and by-laws. If the charity's by-laws and objects do not contemplate the type of activity that the donor is requesting, then the charity will not, from a constitutional perspective, be able to accept the gift.

PRIVATE FOUNDATIONS

For some, the donor-advised fund or conditional gift with a public foundation is not enough. Take, for example, your client, John Smith.

John Smith is retiring. He has been active in the business community for 40 years and although he enjoys golf and sailing, he is dreading the separation from a community that he feels comfortable in and thrives in. He is actively looking for something to get his teeth into. A friend mentions to him that he has set up a private foundation for his family. John, being inquisitive, asks what his friend is referring to. The idea of having his own family's charity is very appealing. He likes the idea that he can be a director of the foundation and manage its investments, making gifts to various operating charities over time. Not only would this fill some of the empty time to come, but it would be a legacy for his family, putting the family name on various philanthropic activities for years to come.

What is a private foundation? In short, it is a name of a type of registered charity, designated by the CRA's Charities Directorate to be a foundation and to be private.

There are three types of charities that are registered by the CRA, but firstly, they all must be charities. When John attends your offices to ask about the private foundation, you explain that the foundation he is thinking of must devote all of its resources to its charitable purposes, a concept developed in the 17th century by the courts in England. There are four categories: relief of poverty, advancement of education, advancement of religion and purposes beneficial to the community. All charities must also meet a public benefit test — that is, to be charitable, the entity is not just benefiting a group of individuals, but the broader community.

The Charities Directorate will examine the entity's plans and, assuming that it finds the entity will meet the charitable purposes test, determine whether to designate the registered charity as a charitable organization, public foundation or private foundation. Charitable organizations are typically active organizations, such as hospitals, food banks or educational facilities. These organizations carry out their own charitable activities and devote all of their resources to carrying out those activities. Public foundations are either funded or governed by the general public. They usually do not undertake charitable activities themselves; instead, their role is to provide funding for charitable purposes. For example, a foundation may be created to raise funds for a hospital.

Private foundations are similar to public foundations, except they are funded and/or governed privately rather than by the general public. You explain to John, that if he is thinking of setting up a foundation that will only be run by his family, he is thinking of a private foundation.

John is a bright, accomplished business person with experience in the asset management and investment areas. He has a finance background and would be competent to run such a foundation and would know to get the help he needs in areas where he lacks experience. The rest of his family might be a different story.

Private foundations are attractive to people who want to maintain control over the assets and how they are used, while receiving a tax receipt. Often, people feel they are better at investing the assets than an unknown person sitting on a charity board would be.

However, managing a private foundation is hard work. All registered charities have a disbursement quota that must be met. The disbursement quota has been referred to above. You explain to John that the purpose of the disbursement quota is to ensure that charities spend their funds on activities that carry out their charitable purposes and discourage charities from saving funds rather than spending them on charitable activities, and keep a reasonable limit on expenses related to management, administration and fundraising. A charity's disbursement quota is the amount the charity must spend on activities, including, in the case of private and public foundations, making gifts to other registered charities, to carry out its charitable purposes. These funds include salaries paid to people who carry out those charitable activities. Meeting the disbursement quota can be challenging, and the penalties for failing to do so can be severe. A charity's disbursement quota is set each year and is based on the amount of receipted donations and gifts received by the charity in the previous year. You explain to John that there are also other rules to comply with. An information return must be filed annually with the Charities Directorate. There are other government departments interested in the charity. As John lives in Ontario, you tell him about the Public Guardian and Trustee, who monitors charities in this province. Some of these issues, and others, make one wonder whether or not the private foundation is the best alternative. There are other possibilities. In some cases, it might be better to plan a gift to the charity of choice directly. You may be able to negotiate a permanent endowment with the charity, and there may be naming rights that go with the endowment. Alternatively, a community foundation or other public foundation might be an answer. While these charities are not able to provide total control, and the board must exercise its own discretion, your client could establish a donor-advised fund which would provide the tax incentives of a public foundation and more of a feeling of a private foundation in terms of consultation and direction. If your client is committed to the private foundation plan, notwithstanding the drawbacks that have been mentioned above, the next step is to consider the vehicle through which the foundation will be run. Private foundations may be trusts or non-share capital corporations.

Typically, the non-share capital corporation is used, particularly if the foundation will hold any real property. If the private foundation will only operate in Ontario, then one could incorporate under the Ontario *Corporations Act*, but if there will be a cross-Canada element to the foundation, one might be more inclined to register under the federal Act. There is a new federal Act proposed. In June 2009, Bill C-4, the *Canada Not-for-profit Corporations Act*, received Royal Assent. This Act will modernize the current federal Act which has been in existence since 1917. One of the modernizing features will be a move to articles of incorporation from the current application for letters patent, which is required under both the federal Act and the Ontario *Corporations Act*. Until the Bill is proclaimed in force, the current federal Act prevails.

If after considering the options, your client decides to incorporate under the Ontario Act, your next step is to assist him or her with the two-step process that such an incorporation may entail. The objects of the charity must be drafted, keeping in mind the parameters relating to charitable objects referred to above. If the charity will simply be a conduit, making gifts to charitable organizations such as hospitals and universities, the objects will be simple. The government of Ontario has also provided "pre-approved" objects which can be used even in circumstances where the charity will be conducting a charitable activity, such as the relieving of poverty. However, if the "pre-approved" objects are not used, then an application must be made first to the Public Guardian and Trustee. The Public Guardian and Trustee will review the objects of the charity to ensure that the objects are charitable from Ontario's perspective. It is possible that the CRA and Ontario would disagree — except in the case of pre-approved objects which have already passed the scrutiny of the CRA. The CRA has recently released its updated list of pre-approved objects. Once the approval of the Public Guardian and Trustee has been obtained, the application for letters patent can then be granted. The next step involves the application to the Charities Directorate of the CRA itself. An application form is filed with the Letters Patent and Bylaws. In my view, the most important part of the application is the Statement of Activities. Here, the CRA is ensuring that not only will the charity be governed by charitable objects, but its actual activities will be charitable. Again, this is easy if John is considering a foundation that will be a mere conduit — but not so easy if John wishes to start a foundation that will be carrying on its own charitable activities.

The process of incorporation and registration can take months. It can be very frustrating for a client from the corporate world who is used to establishing a private corporation in days, not months. It is important to ensure that your client has a complete understanding of this issue — again, it may lead to a decision to use a public foundation in cases where there is a timing issue and a gift must be made by year-end, for example.

Even if John decides to proceed with the private foundation, it is possible that he won't have the family legacy that he was hoping for. Many individuals picture their children and grandchildren carrying on the family philanthropy through the foundation, but forget that they may be the only family member willing to put the time and effort into the running of the foundation — are they being realistic about what their children and grandchildren are willing and able to do?

CONCLUSION

For every client who knows that he or she wishes to set up a foundation, or establish an endowment, there is a client who knows that, to the extent possible, he or she would like to participate in philanthropy. It is your job, as the Trusted Advisor, to help these clients bridge the gap between a desire and an outcome. Much of this is through education which can be achieved over time as your relationship with your client deepens. But unless you ask that initial question, you may never know what doors you leave shut for the client.

CHAPTER 56

FAMILY LAW

Steven Benmor

Overview

This chapter explains how family law impacts the redistribution of income and assets, and the rights of spouses to spousal and child support, following a breakdown of a marriage.

Learning Objectives

By the end of this chapter, you should be able to:

- explain the financial impact of marriage and separation;
- determine the redistribution of assets and debts following separation;
- appreciate the liability for child support and spousal support;
- identify the process necessary to provide advance protection of assets and income; and
- understand the sequence of events leading to a final settlement.

INTRODUCTION

More than any other area of law, family law has the greatest influence on Canadians' financial and retirement plans. With one-half of all marriages ending in separation, every person — whether single or married — must be conscious of the effects of marriage, cohabitation and separation on his or her income and assets. Moreover, every professional dispensing financial advice must be aware of the implications of marriage and divorce upon wealth management.

Family law creates rights and obligations. Those rights and obligations are between individuals, including spouses, children and sometimes other family members. Therefore, it is necessary to first determine if such a relationship exists and what legal obligations stem from the formation of that relationship.

Clearly, a marriage between a man and a woman creates legal obligations, which include the right to property and support. But Canada has become a beacon of progress in recent years and has included cohabiting spouses and same-sex partners in this same category, thereby entitling all types of spouses to the same rights historically afforded to only married heterosexual couples.

PROPERTY

Only marriage, whether heterosexual or same-sex, creates a financial partnership in property. Ontario's *Family Law Act*[1] states in its preamble that:

> Whereas it is desirable to encourage and strengthen the role of the family; and whereas for that purpose it is necessary to recognize the equal position of spouses as individuals within marriage and to recognize marriage as a form of partnership; and whereas in support of such recognition it is necessary to provide in law for the orderly and equitable settlement of the affairs of the spouses upon the breakdown of the partnership, and to provide for other mutual obligations in family relationships, including the equitable sharing by parents of responsibility for their children;

Canadian law places special emphasis on the sanctity of marriage and, in doing so, automatically grants each spouse the right and expectation to share in the asset growth (and loss) of the other spouse when the marriage ends.

Ontario's *Family Law Act* provides a formula for dividing the value of assets and debts that were acquired during the marriage. This method is called "equalization of net family property". Upon separation, each spouse fills out and swears a financial statement in a prescribed form. The financial statement lists all assets that each spouse owned on two dates — the date of marriage and the valuation date. The financial statement must include full and frank disclosure of all assets and debts that each spouse owned on the date of marriage and the valuation date, as well as any property that is excluded from equalization. The financial statement is used to calculate each spouse's "net family property". In the end, the spouses' net family properties are equalized, so that each spouse is left with one-half of the assets accumulated during marriage.

Valuation Date

There are two dates that determine the exact financial rights that accrue to each married spouse — the date of marriage and the "valuation date".

---

[1] R.S.O. 1990, c. F.3.

Ontario law specifically provides that the increase in the value of each spouse's net worth from the date of the marriage to the valuation date is to be equalized, or equally shared. Although the most commonly used date is the date that the spouses separate from one another, it is not always separation that ends a marriage.

The valuation date is defined in subsection 4(1) of Ontario's *Family Law Act* as the earliest of the following dates:

1. The date the spouses separate and there is no reasonable prospect that they will resume cohabitation.
2. The date a divorce is granted.
3. The date the marriage is declared a nullity.
4. The date one of the spouses commences an application based on subsection 5(3) (improvident depletion) that is subsequently granted.
5. The date before the date on which one of the spouses dies leaving the other spouse surviving.

In attempting to ascertain the correct date of separation for the purposes of valuing the spouses' assets and debts, there are cases where a difference of a few days or months can result in a very different calculation of the net family property and the equalization payment. For example, one spouse may claim that they had separated on an earlier date when the family assets were greater, resulting in a greater financial settlement, while the other spouse may be relying on a later date, after financial losses were experienced. In such cases, the spouses may elect to proceed to court to seek a judge's ruling on the date of separation so as to then ascertain the values of the family's assets for equalization. The spouses will then be required to gather evidence and proceed to a trial in an effort to convince the court of the date when the parties began living separate and apart. In some cases, this date may be known only to the parties who continued to reside in the same home long after they decided to separate.

One example of the challenges of this legislation is the case of *Anderson v. Anderson*,[2] decided by Mr. Justice Bolan. The main dispute in that proceeding was the determination of the "valuation date" of the assets accumulated during the marriage. The husband claimed that the separation took place in 1971, while the wife claimed that it took place in 1987 — a spread of 16 years. The effect of either side of this debate would have a critical effect on the final financial settlement between the spouses. After a lengthy trial, including the testimony of the spouses, their daughter, the husband's girlfriend and others, Mr. Justice Bolan stated:

---

[2] [1994] O.J. No. 1915 (Ont. Gen. Div.).

> The Court will look at the sum total of the acts and attitudes of the husband and wife to determine whether or not the parties, even although under the same roof have terminated the partnership and repudiated the marriage in such a way that they have become sole proprietors with separate and not interlocking lifestyles with no physical or emotional commitments one to the other.[3]

By way of comparison, the law in British Columbia fixes the date for the quantification of the spouses' assets and debts. British Columbia law provides "triggering events". A triggering event is not the same as the date of separation. In British Columbia, each spouse is entitled to an undivided one-half interest in each family asset upon the occurrence of a triggering event such as the signing of a separation agreement or a court order terminating the marriage — thus providing a more precise date that is transparent and controlled by one or both of the spouses.

Excluded Property

Irrespective of the valuation date, Ontario's *Family Law Act* excludes certain assets from being equalized with the other spouse. In fact, the definition of "net family property" is the value of all the property, except "excluded property", that a spouse owns on the valuation date, after deducting the spouse's debts and other liabilities and the value of property, other than a matrimonial home, that the spouse owned on the date of the marriage, and after deducting the spouse's debts and other liabilities that the spouse owned on the date of the marriage.

Excluded property refers to property that is not equalized with the other spouse. That is, excluded property is kept by one spouse and not shared with the other.

This includes the following:

1. property (other than a matrimonial home) that was acquired by gift or inheritance from a third person after the date of the marriage;
2. income from such property (if the donor or testator has expressly stated that it is to be excluded from the spouse's net family property);
3. damages, or a right to damages, for personal injuries, nervous shock, mental distress or loss of guidance, care and companionship, or the part of a settlement that represents those damages;
4. proceeds, or a right to proceeds, of a policy of life insurance that are payable on the death of the life insured;

---

[3] *Ibid.* at para. 43, quoting from *Buller v. Buller*, [1979] O.J. No. 4370, 26 O.R. (2d) 92 at 98 (Ont. Co. Ct.).

5. property (other than a matrimonial home) into which property referred to in paragraphs 1 to 4 can be traced; or
6. property that the spouses have agreed by a domestic contract is not to be included in the spouse's net family property.

Calculating Values

After the preliminary determination of the date of marriage and the date of separation is made, then the spouses must ascertain the values of all assets and debts on these two dates. Thereafter, the legislation provides the formula to be applied to determine the final equalization payment that must be paid by one spouse to the other.

Subsection 5(1) of Ontario's *Family Law Act* provides that "the spouse whose net family property is the lesser of the two net family properties is entitled to one-half the difference between them." This is called the "equalization payment". That is, the assets and debts are not actually divided. It is the *value* of the assets and debts that are shared and that generate a figure that may be satisfied with the transfer of money, assets or both.

Pensions

A spouse's pension is treated the same as any other asset the spouse accumulated during the marriage. That means that the spouse with the pension receives a credit for the value of the pension on the date of marriage, but will share with the other spouse the rise in the value of the pension during the marriage and ending on the date of separation. The pension is typically valued by a professional actuary to determine its value on the date of separation.

Net Family Property Statement

An example of the calculation of a spouse's net family property and equalization payment is demonstrated in the chart below, which is called a Net Family Property Statement.

Net Family Property Statement

ITEM	Wife	Husband
1. Assets Owned at Separation		
Matrimonial Home	$150,000.00	$150,000.00
Jewellery	$1,000.00	$0.00
Car	$13,000.00	$2,000.00
Bank Accounts	$700.00	$10,000.00
RRSP	$15,000.00	$1,000.00
Pension	$9,000.00	$1,000.00
Investments	$7,000.00	$500.00
TOTAL 1.	$195,700.00	$164,500.00
2. Debts and Liabilities at Separation		
Mortgage	$75,000.00	$75,000.00
Loan	$5,000.00	$0.00
Real Estate Commission on Matrimonial Home	$7,500.00	$7,500.00
Disposition Costs of RRSP	$2,000.00	$150.00
TOTAL 2.	$89,500.00	$82,650.00
3. Property Owned at Marriage		
Jewellery	$1,500.00	$0.00
TOTAL 3.	$1,500.00	$0.00
4. Excluded Property		
Inheritance of Car from Father	$13,000.00	$0.00
Life Insurance Proceeds from Death of Aunt	$0.00	$10,000.00
TOTAL 4.	$13,000.00	$10,000.00
5. Net Family Property	$91,700.00	$71,850.00
6. Equalization Payment	**Wife pays to husband:**	**$9,925.00**

Box 1 lists the assets that each spouse owned, either solely or jointly, on the date of separation.

Box 2 lists the debts that each spouse owed, either solely or jointly, on the date of separation.

Box 3 lists the assets and debts that each spouse owned or owed, either solely or jointly, on the date of marriage.

Box 4 lists the assets that are excluded.

Box 5 illustrates the calculation of each spouse's net family property.

Box 6 illustrates the calculation of the equalization payment.

In this example, the wife owes the husband an equalization payment of $9,925.00. This is in addition to the husband's share of the matrimonial home that is jointly owned, after deducting the jointly owed mortgage. Thus, the spouses may agree to sell the home and divide the sale proceeds or allow for one spouse to purchase the other spouse's interest in the home, after adjusting for the equalization payment.

Debts and Liabilities

It is not unusual for marriages to suffer because of a family's financial difficulties, growing debt loads, a spouse's loss of employment, the reduction or loss of the wife's employment income when children are born and many other events that may occur within a family that place undue financial stress on the marriage.

In some cases, the financial stress may cause marital breakdown and separation. It is in these situations where a spouse who turns to a lawyer for legal advice discovers that Ontario property law does not require spouses to share their family debt.

Subsection 4(5) of Ontario's *Family Law Act* provides that:

> If a spouse's net family property as calculated under subsections (1), (2) and (4) is less than zero, it shall be deemed to be equal to zero.

In effect, spouses who are separating and who have an unequal distribution of debts amongst them, or a couple where the bulk of the family assets are held by one spouse while the other spouse holds the family debt, are likely to suffer even greater hardship than they experienced prior to separation.

To illustrate this dilemma, the next two examples demonstrate cases of financial hardship.

Example A — Both Spouses End Marriage with a Significant Debt Load

ITEM	HUSBAND	WIFE
1. Assets Owned at Separation		
Car	$5,000.00	$0.00
RRSP	$3,000.00	$1,000.00
Wedding Rings	$500.00	$500.00
Household Contents	$2,500.00	$2,500.00
TOTAL 1.	$11,000.00	$4,000.00

ITEM	HUSBAND	WIFE
2. Debts & Liabilities at Separation Student Loans Credit Cards Joint Line of Credit	 $8,000.00 $6,000.00 $5,000.00	 $15,000.00 $4,000.00 $5,000.00
TOTAL 2.	$19,000.00	$24,000.00
3. Net Family Property (Total 1 minus Total 2) Husband's NFP = –$8,000.00* Wife's NFP = –$20,000.00* * *Calculated value was negative and becomes nil as the legislation does not permit a negative net family property figure.*	* $0.00	* $0.00
4. Equalization Payment	Husband pays to wife:	$0.00

In this example, the husband has a negative net family property of –$8,000 and the wife has a negative net family property of –$20,000. Applying subsection 4(5) of the *Family Law Act* will result in each person being individually liable for the debts held in his or her name alone and be jointly responsible for the joint line of credit. In effect, this family's debt is not equalized and will result in tremendous hardship on the wife.

Example B — One Spouse Holds Assets and Other Spouse Holds Debt

ITEM	HUSBAND	WIFE
1. Assets Owned at Separation Matrimonial Home Household Contents Car	 $0.00 $10,000.00 $0.00	 $200,000.00 $10,000.00 $20,000.00
TOTAL 1.	$10,000.00	$230,000.00
2. Debts & Liabilities at Separation Line of Credit Credit Cards	 $150,000.00 $30,000.00	 $0.00 $0.00
TOTAL 2.	$180,000.00	$0.00
3. Net Family Property (Total 1 minus Total 2) Husband's NFP = –$170,000.00* * *Calculated value was negative and becomes nil as the legislation does not permit a negative net family property figure.*	* $0.00	$230,000.00

ITEM	HUSBAND	WIFE
4. Equalization Payment	Wife pays to husband:	$230,000.00

In this example, the husband has a negative net family property of –$170,000, but due to the application of subsection 4(5) of the *Family Law Act*, he is deemed to have a nil value for his net family property. This would result in the wife paying him $115,000 as an equalization payment — one-half of her net family property of $230,000. After accounting for the husband's negative net family property of –$170,000, he would leave the marriage with $55,000 in debt, while the wife would have assets of $115,000.

MATRIMONIAL HOME

Despite the general principles that apply to property owned on the date of separation, Ontario law places the spouses' rights to a matrimonial home in a separate category.

Section 18 of Ontario's *Family Law Act* states:

> Every property in which a person has an interest and that is or, if the spouses have separated, was at the time of separation ordinarily occupied by the person and his or her spouse as their family residence is their matrimonial home.

Therefore, by definition, the date that is used to determine whether a property is a matrimonial home is the date on which the spouses separate. On that date, if they were "ordinarily occupying" a property and treating it as their "family residence", then that property (or properties such as a cottage or chalet) is a matrimonial home, as defined in the legislation, and therefore each spouse is afforded two rights to the property — whether or not they are registered on title.

The spouses are entitled to the right of possession and the right to an equalization of that asset.

As regards the right of possession, Ontario law is very strict. A married spouse who resides in a matrimonial home is permitted to remain in possession after separation, even though he or she is not registered on title. The registered owner of the property, which may be the other spouse but in some cases is the other spouse's family, would need to obtain a court to order vacant possession of the home.

As regards the right to an equalization of the matrimonial home, the general rule is that Ontario law does not permit a spouse who entered the marriage with the matrimonial home, or received it as a gift or inheritance, to exclude it from the equalization process. This equally applies to moneys with which one spouse entered the marriage, or to inherited or gifted moneys — if such moneys were used to purchase or renovate the matrimonial home. In all these cases, the total value of the matrimonial home must be equalized with the other spouse. No deduction for its value on the date of marriage, or exclusion based on an inheritance or gift, is permitted. There are a few exceptions to this general rule; however, the spouse who is the registered owner bears the onus of seeking such a departure from this rule.

COMMON LAW SPOUSES

Ontario's *Family Law Act* makes a distinction between spouses who are married and spouses who are not married but cohabit. To the outside world, these two sets of families appear exactly the same. They both consist of two spouses living in the same home. They have children together. They own property together. They share all aspects of their lives together. The children refer to them as "mom" and "dad". They lead their lives together in the exact same way.

But, according to Ontario's *Family Law Act*, once these two different families separate, the married spouse has rights that the unmarried spouse cannot enjoy. Specifically, the unmarried spouse is not entitled to an equalization of net family property.

Ontario's *Family Law Act* consists of different Parts including Part I, which grants property rights, Part II, which grants rights to a matrimonial home, and Part III, which grants support rights.

The definition of a "spouse" in Parts I and II is limited to married spouses. The definition of a "spouse" in Part III expands this definition to include "persons who are not married to each other and have cohabited, (a) continuously for a period of not less than *three* years, or (b) in a relationship of some permanence, if they are the natural or adoptive parents of a child".

Therefore, married spouses have rights to share in the growth of their assets during marriage and rights to matrimonial homes, but unmarried spouses do not.

The fairness of this legislation has been the subject of debate. This debate was ultimately elevated to the Supreme Court of Canada in 2002. In the landmark decision of *Nova Scotia (Attorney General) v. Walsh*,[4] the Supreme Court of Canada was asked to conclude that excluding unmarried spouses from provincial matrimonial property laws is discriminatory. That case involved Susan Walsh and Wayne Bona, who

---

[4] [2002] S.C.J. No. 84, [2002] 4 S.C.R. 325 (S.C.C.).

cohabited for ten years. They had two children together. After they separated, Ms. Walsh applied for spousal support and child support. She also sought a declaration that the definition of a "spouse" in Nova Scotia's *Matrimonial Property Act* was unconstitutional because it failed to provide her with the right to an equal division of matrimonial property — a right that is available to married spouses.

In an 8-1 decision, the Supreme Court of Canada ruled that excluding unmarried spouses from provincial matrimonial property laws is not discriminatory because the distinction reflects the differences between married and unmarried relationships and respects the fundamental personal autonomy and dignity of the individual. The highest court stated that the decision to marry, or not to marry, is personal and that many common law couples have chosen to avoid marriage and its legal consequences. They are free to marry each other or take other steps if they want to enjoy the benefits available to married couples.

Even though an unmarried spouse does not enjoy the right to an equalization of net family property, he or she naturally has the rights to property that is registered in his or her name or that is owned jointly with the other spouse.

Furthermore, in respect of spousal support, Ontario's *Family Law Act* makes no distinction between spouses who are married and spouses who are not married but cohabit, provided that the expanded definition of "spouse" is met.

MARRIAGE CONTRACTS

Whether married or not married, it is possible for cohabiting spouses to avoid the automatic operation of the law upon separation. For those spouses who wish to plan ahead and avoid the usual process of the law regarding equalization of net family property and spousal support when they separate, they may decide to enter into a marriage contract, also known as a prenuptial agreement, or cohabitation agreement.

So as to avoid the unpredictable financial consequences of separation, many people who marry, remarry or reside with a spouse enter into a contract so as to decide, in advance, on the financial consequences of the relationship ending.

A marriage contract is a written agreement that permits a couple that intends to marry to agree in advance on issues such as property division and support in the event that the marriage ends. More often, people are getting married later in life or for a second time. If they own property that they wish to protect, or want to confirm that they will not be expected to support their spouse after they separate, then they may agree to terms that are incorporated into a marriage contract.

The best time to enter into a marriage contract is many months before the marriage. Once married, each spouse immediately obtains family law rights, which can only be waived or limited by a marriage contract that is signed by both spouses. If the marriage contract is prepared after marriage and one of the spouses refuses to sign it, these rights will not be limited or waived.

The question of whether a marriage contract would truly provide the protection desired caused a stir in the family law community after a judge in British Columbia decided to set aside the contract because it was unfair to the wife. This very topic was so contentious that it was appealed to the provincial court of appeal, and then to the Supreme Court of Canada.

In the case of *Hartshorne v. Hartshorne*,[5] the Court ruled that Kathleen Hartshorne was bound by the terms of a marriage contract that she had signed on her wedding day in 1989.

The Hartshornes were both previously married and divorced. They began to cohabit in 1985 and had their first child in 1987. After they married in 1989, their second child was born. They were both lawyers (the wife articled for the husband's law firm). The husband brought assets worth $1.6 million into the marriage, including a home, two recreational properties, RRSPs, savings and his law practice, while the wife entered the relationship with no assets and heavily in debt. On the day of the wedding, the husband insisted that the wife sign a marriage contract that allowed both spouses to protect their pre-marriage assets, except for their matrimonial home. In this regard, the wife was to be entitled to a 3% interest in the matrimonial home for each year of marriage up to a maximum of 49%. Both spouses consulted with separate lawyers and obtained independent legal advice. The wife's lawyer advised her that the contract was grossly unfair. She nevertheless agreed to sign the contract with a few amendments, including a clause confirming her right to spousal support. According to the contract, the wife was entitled to property worth $280,000 on separation, while the husband was entitled to property worth $1.2 million.

After they separated in January 1998, the wife commenced divorce proceedings against her husband for custody of the children, child support, spousal support and a division of property. The wife argued that the marriage contract should not be upheld because it was unfair and

---

5 [2004] S.C.J. No. 20, [2004] 1 S.C.R. 550 (S.C.C.).

because she had given up her own law career to take care of their two children.

The husband relied upon the contract to avoid the usual legal procedure for equalizing family property upon separation. The husband further argued that, in keeping with the spirit of the contract, they managed their finances separately: there was no commingling of funds, there were no joint accounts of significant value and the assets that the husband brought into the marriage remained in his name. The husband argued that his wife knew what she was signing and agreed to be bound by its terms.

If the wife had been successful in setting aside the contract and receiving an equalization of the family property, she would have received $654,000, as opposed to $280,000.

In the end, the Court ruled that when a couple's circumstances at the time of separation were within their contemplation at the time that they signed the marriage contract, then they both should be bound by the terms of the contract. In this case, the Court ruled that the Hartshornes' financial and domestic arrangements unfolded exactly as they had expected. Regarding the wife's argument that she had given up her own law practice to take care of the children, the Court concluded that it was a decision that she had made prior to the marriage and it was not realistic to assume that she had not understood the consequences of this choice.

For spouses who do not intend to marry but do intend to cohabit, yet still wish to avoid the unpredictable financial consequences of a separation, they may enter into a cohabitation agreement. Such an agreement is very similar to a marriage contract. Subsection 53(2) of Ontario's *Family Law Act* provides that the cohabitation agreement is deemed to be a marriage contract upon marriage.

SEPARATION AGREEMENTS

Despite the many laws that set out a spouse's rights following separation, Part IV of Ontario's *Family Law Act* does grant separating spouses the right to settle their affairs in their own unique and personal manner — which may be very different from the automatic process of the law regarding equalization of net family property and support.

Section 54 of Ontario's *Family Law Act* provides that the spouses may agree on their respective rights and obligations, including:

(a) ownership in or division of property;

(b) support obligations;

(c) the right to direct the education and moral training of their children;

(d) the right to custody of and access to their children; and

(e) any other matter in the settlement of their affairs.

Normally, when spouses separate and a marriage contract was not previously executed, the spouses retain counsel to negotiate and execute a separation agreement — which finalizes their affairs.

It is worth noting that the spouses may lose the protection of their separation agreement if they reconcile and cohabit for a period greater than 90 days. Indeed, there have been cases where one spouse has argued that the separation agreement did not survive their reconciliation, and sought a court order that all property that the other spouse owned at the time of their final separation be equalized once again.

CHILD SUPPORT

Usually, a spouse who does not have day-to-day care and control of the children will be responsible for paying child support. The parent with day-to-day care and control of the children is called the custodial parent. The other parent is called the access parent or non-custodial parent, and is the payor of child support. The amount of child support is based on the access parent's income and on the extraordinary expenses of the children.

Since Canada and each province enacted the *Child Support Guidelines* in 1997, the monthly amount of child support is primarily based on the income of the non-custodial parent, the number of children in the family and which province the children reside in. There are published Tables that set out the amount that the access parent must pay to the custodial parent. The Table amounts are for the children's ordinary expenses such as food, clothing and shelter. For example, an access parent of two children in Ontario who earns $40,000 per year will pay to the custodial parent a Table amount of $601 per month (non-taxable). The custodial parent's income becomes relevant where the children have special or extraordinary expenses such as daycare, extracurricular activities and private school tuition. In most cases, the parents share these costs in proportion to their incomes.

The *Child Support Guidelines* state that there is a presumption that the access parent pays the custodial parent child support according to the payor's annual income and the Table amount. But the court is given the discretion to deviate from the Table amount and reduce the amount of child support payable if the payor has the children in his or her care for 40% or more of the time during the course of a year. This discretion is based on section 9 of the *Child Support Guidelines* and the 2005 decision of *Contino v. Leonelli-Contino.*[6] In that case, the Supreme Court of Canada set out guidelines for considering a deviation from the Table amount. The Court stated that there still is a presumption in favour of the Table amount. However, the parent seeking a deviation may establish that a reduction in child support is in the children's best interest.

Step-parents may be liable for child support. The term "parent" has been used in various ways, at different times and in diverse settings. This stems from Canadian society applying its changing social norms, its rich cultural diversity, its advances in biotechnology and its modernization movement to the meaning of "parent". As a result, presently a "parent" can be anyone who resides with the child, a child's relative who assumed the task of being the child's primary caregiver, a surrogate mother, a sperm donor, an egg donor, *etc.*

Subsection 2(2) of Canada's *Divorce Act* and section 5 of the *Child Support Guidelines* specifically provides that a step-parent, after separation, may be liable to pay child support even where the child's biological parent is supporting the child.

The test that is customarily used to determine whether such a liability exists is derived from the legislation that places the liability for child support upon a spouse who "stands in the place of a parent" and the decision of the Supreme Court of Canada in *Chartier v. Chartier.*[7]

Whether one is an access parent, biological parent or step-parent, the sum payable for child support is not fixed, but varies from year to year based on factors such as the age of the children and whether they are still dependants, the income of the non-custodial parent and the division of parenting time. For this reason, it is common for spouses to annually review and vary separation agreements and court orders regarding child support.

Child support is paid as long as the child is a dependant. Usually, a dependent child is one who is under the age of 18 years. In some instances, child support may continue past the age of 18 years if the child is not financially self-sufficient because of an illness or disability or because the child continues to attend full-time studies.

SPOUSAL SUPPORT

Spousal support, previously called alimony, is one of the most challenging subjects that is broached after a family separates. In determining the rights of a spouse to collect spousal support, or the obligation of a spouse

---

6 [2005] S.C.J. No. 65, [2005] 3 S.C.R. 217 (S.C.C.).

7 [1999] S.C.J. No. 79, [1999] 1 S.C.R. 242 (S.C.C.).

to pay spousal support, there are three questions that need to be considered.

1. Is a spouse entitled to support?
2. What is the amount of support that should be paid?
3. What is the duration for which support should be paid?

When asked to determine the answers to these questions, family law lawyers and judges are forced to make extensive inquiries into the lives of the spouses from the beginning — including even before the spouses met. This analysis examines an exhaustive list of factors such as: the length of the spouses' cohabitation and marriage; their standard of living during their cohabitation; the spouses' ages, incomes, income potential, needs and budget, education, and health and employment capacity; any barriers to economic self-sufficiency; any retirement or loss of employment, remarriage, assets, debts and income tax considerations (since unlike child support, spousal support is usually taxable income to the recipient and is tax-deductible by the payor); ongoing child-care responsibilities; educational, career or business concessions; and opportunities experienced due to the marriage.

Moreover, each spouse swears to a financial statement which contains a monthly budget. This way, the spouses' total monthly income and expenses are ascertained and considered to determine the resolution of spousal support, including entitlement, quantum and duration.

The federal government commissioned the *Spousal Support Advisory Guidelines*. These guidelines provide a mathematical calculation of a proposed range of spousal support sums based on certain inputs such as the spouses' ages and incomes. These guidelines have been used in negotiations, mediations and trials. They have been routinely used as a system of checks and balances for lawyers and judges regarding the quantification of spousal support. Like many other benchmarks and tools, they provide general guidance and do not address the particular circumstances of any one family, as described above.

TAX CONSEQUENCES

For many spouses experiencing separation, the financial implications are confusing, as well as devastating. Assets are divided, and support is paid. In many cases, the tax implications of these transactions may be even more challenging for the ex-spouses. However, certain general provisions regarding the tax consequences of separation are set out in the *Income Tax Act*.

The Table amount that is paid for child support is paid with after-tax dollars and is received free of taxation. Most of the additional expenses paid for the children attract no differential tax treatment. However, child-care expenses such as daycare or private caregiving do result in specific tax treatment. Generally, following a separation, the spouses will proportionately share the children's child-care expenses. During marriage, the spouse with the lower income will claim a deduction for such expenses, which often results in a reduction of the tax liability to that spouse. Following separation, this favourable tax treatment is often shared during the year through the reduction of the monthly share of the child-care costs paid by the access parent.

Spousal support payments that are received in a particular calendar year are generally taxable as income to the recipient and deductible by the payor if the spouses are separated and the payments are made in accordance with a court order or separation agreement. Such tax treatment applies to payments made in the same year or in the immediately preceding full calendar year. These payments must be periodic, such as monthly, and not be a lump-sum payment. There are specific tax provisions for third party payments for spousal support.

Generally, an equalization payment is not taxable as income to the recipient and deductible by the payor. However, there are provisions in the *Income Tax Act* that permit the spouses to transfer the tax cost on the transfer of capital assets to the spouse who ultimately disposes of the property to a third party.

In all cases of separation, the financial and tax implications of such matters must be calculated and resolved with professional tax advice.

CONCLUSION

The purpose of this chapter was to provide a general overview of the family law issues that arise upon the separation of spouses. This information is not meant to be considered as legal advice or even legal information that can be relied upon by a spouse experiencing a separation. It should not be relied upon by any advisor providing assistance to such a spouse. For legal advice, a legal opinion or legal representation relating to a person's individual circumstances, a spouse is urged to consult with his or her own lawyer.

Separation and divorce is an emotional, financial and legal process. It requires extensive planning to address the needs of children, family finances and immediate actions that need to be taken to protect each spouse's individual interests.

Despite this chapter's general overview of family law, each spouse has particular rights, including the rights to custody of, and access to, children, child support, spousal support, possession and ownership of matrimonial homes, property division and divorce. In this situation, every spouse must learn what immediate actions must be taken for his or her own protection. This can only be done through a direct professional relationship between the spouse and a family law lawyer who will advise, guide and facilitate a safe, speedy and just conclusion.

CHAPTER 57

THE THREE RETIREMENTS

Gilles R. Marceau

Overview

In this chapter, you will learn about the three stages of retirement.

Learning Objectives

By the end of this chapter, you should be able to:

- understand the three stages of retirement and learn how to integrate the Individual Pension Plan, retirement compensation arrangement and Health and Welfare Trust to optimize an individual's golden years.

Most self-employed professionals and business owners in their mid to late 50s concern themselves with providing retirement income during their lifetime. And with a third of their lives still left to live, many are beginning to realize their needs are different as they think about the various stages of life they will transition to, be it semi-retirement, full retirement, or retirement at the end of their lives.

We call these stages "the three retirements".

FIRST RETIREMENT — SEMI-RETIREMENT

The *First Retirement* encompasses trading "at work time" to "do the other things I want to accomplish in my life". At this point, the driving force is not money but internalized feelings of accomplishing other goals in one's life.

For the most part, our culture defines its members by what they do, not by who they are. Our identities are often dependent upon our occupations and/or what we own. "Being" rather than "doing" must become the primary focus of our lives in order to enjoy this stage of retirement. The First Retirement is all about the transition to "being". This means that true wealth is time!

This may mean you need to find tax-effective ways in which to bridge the income gap without using those assets required to support a longer-term income stream when full retirement arrives. More on this later!

The Retirement Compensation Arrangement — The Unknown Tax Strategy

The retirement compensation arrangement (RCA) gives the business the opportunity to achieve maximum tax relief while maximizing the owner's retirement income. Just as importantly, the income stream can be matched on a year-by-year basis to the owner's personal requirements.

RCAs were introduced by the Department of Finance as an unregistered supplemental retirement plan established by a company to provide additional retirement benefits beyond that provided through a Registered Retirement Savings Plan/Deferred Profit-Sharing Plan and/or through a Registered Pension Plan.

Statistics Canada in its January 1, 2003 research paper entitled "Pension Plans in Canada" identified that from a modest start in 1991 (249 trusts and $200 million in assets) the value of RCAs as of the end of 2001 grew to 2,051 trusts with $5.3 billion in assets.

Contributions were nearly $1.1 billion in 2001, with the total number of potential beneficiaries at about 12,000 persons in 2001.

RCAs are very flexible in that:

- The funding of the RCA can be tied into the company's accomplishment of corporate profitability, thereby enabling the company to make RCA contributions when the funds have been earned. Such funding is tax-deductible for the company in the year the contribution is made.
- A business owner or self-employed professional who started the company/practice 30 years ago and incorporated only in 2006 can obtain service for every year he or she has been in the business/practice.
- There are no requirements for when the pension must start. While registered plans (*e.g.*, RRSPs) must start income by end of the year in which the self-employed individual turns 69, RCAs have no requirement. Thus, they are excellent in meeting the variable income needs of the business owner if "stop and go income" is required to support the First Retirement Stage.
- Participation in the RCA does not generate a pension adjustment, nor does it affect or reduce RRSP room. It is a supplemental retirement program.

- There are no restrictions on investments.

This *First Retirement Stage* involves a transition to a new way of living and requires a period of adjustment. If an individual wishes to maximize his or her options, it is necessary to take control of the future, to the extent that this is possible. What can be controlled should be controlled. Life choices can then become a real possibility with the individual determining the direction of his or her life, rather than wandering aimlessly into the future.

This trade-off between "at work time" and "doing the other things I want to accomplish in my life" can be referred to as "the semi-retirement period".

It is a period that most self-employed individuals will enjoy until they arrive at that period in time in which their energy levels do not permit them to "keep such a pace". The natural ageing process begins to affect a person's ability to continuously do.

SECOND RETIREMENT — FULL RETIREMENT

The *Second Retirement* relates to "slowing down" due to the ageing process. The topic of ageing is one that many prefer to avoid. Yet, it is a process all of us must go through. We can prepare for ageing only if we talk about it. While it may be difficult for some people to picture a situation 20 years in the future, it is an essential discussion to ensure that personal plans also address potential needs.

For example, during the *First Retirement Period*, decisions about where to live may be based on work-related factors. At the *Second Retirement Stage*, the housing decision becomes part of the individuals' personal planning choices. Whether individuals remain in their current homes or communities ultimately depends on what they want out of life.

To be old and dependent is an ugly existence in a culture that values youth, productivity and functionality. Western culture does not appear to like its elderly, and this may be another reason why many people do not actively plan for this part of the life cycle. Planning for it means we must face its inevitability.

The Second Retirement should allow a smooth transition that takes into consideration the ageing process. The Second Retirement should include the ability to cope with life, to maintain emotional well-being, to continue to make valued contributions to all facets of life and to *feel worry-free financially*.

The objective in the *Second Retirement Phase* — full retirement — remains unchanged. It is to create wealth for retirement sufficient to maintain a person's lifestyle *for the last 25-30 years of life without having to worry about outliving one's money and to accept life as it is and make the best of it.* This stage is defined through the following question:

"What else, other than work, defines you?"

The Individual Pension Plan — Another Relatively Unknown Tax Strategy — Creating a Guaranteed Income Stream You Cannot Outlive!

Historically, many business owners have maximized their RRSP contributions, hoping that investment growth and the sale of their business would provide the retirement income required to maintain their current lifestyle.

Unfortunately, RRSPs have not performed well, and business owners are realizing (as they approach full retirement) that their businesses are not easy to sell.

The solution could be an Individual Pension Plan (IPP).

Legislation governing IPPs provides twice the savings room (contributions) for suitable business owners/professionals by providing 50% to 75% more retirement income than RRSPs.

The IPP legislation may be an appropriate way to maximize retirement income for the owner while giving the business the opportunity to achieve maximum tax relief.

The structure of the IPP is that of a defined benefit pension plan for one or more people. There is a promise of a specific income stream based upon years of service and earnings. Thus, there is downside protection. In the event that the plan suffers lower than expected returns, the company has the ability to make additional tax-deductible contributions to adequately fund the plan. By their structure, defined benefit pension plans usually provide 40% more income than a normal RRSP.

THIRD RETIREMENT — RETIREMENT AT THE END OF LIFE

The *Third Retirement* represents that stage in which our health may affect our finances.

For example, the effects of possible long-term health care needs on an investment portfolio that is designed to provide income to the surviving spouse or the provision of alternative living accommodations to the spouse who can no longer care for himself or herself on a day-to-day basis are significant lifestyle-related issues that will have significant effects on the capital/income requirements. While this stage may be an uncomfortable subject, you need to get through the reluctance barrier to ensure that you have plans that anticipate real potential situations.

A 2005 RBC Insurance/Ipsos-Reid survey found that 34% of respondents were worried about the cost of care in their old age.

How a Health and Welfare Trust and/or Retirement Compensation Arrangement Can Be Used to Fund Future Health Care Expenses

RCAs are essentially not regulated by the Canada Revenue Agency as long as they are "reasonable" and not camouflaged salary deferral arrangements. Any pension promise of under 100% of pre-retirement earnings is reasonable. Thus, a $200,000 per annum business owner can create a $200,000 per year pension.

This limit may allow you to take into consideration any future health care costs that may be a significant part of the retirement plan. On the other hand, you may prefer to establish a Health and Welfare Trust (HWT), which is specifically set up to pay current and future medical expenses.

Both the RCA and HWT contributions are tax-deductible to your company in the year they are made. The difference is that benefits payable from the HWT are tax-free, whereas income from the RCA is taxable. The health spending account converts health care expenses into 100% business deductions.

The HWT Is a Benefit That Can Also Be Enjoyed Today

All traditional health care costs, like dental, prescription drugs and vision care, are eligible, but the HWT extends to cover the rest of your costs: family orthodontic, cosmetic and restorative dental, laser eye surgery, cosmetic surgery and even long-term care costs for elderly dependants. This may allow you to put more aside for the future.

ONLY YOU CAN BE YOUR LIFE'S ARCHITECT

When you know what you want to accomplish, then you can make the appropriate decisions relating to the financial support of your retirement needs.

LIFE IS NOT A DRESS REHEARSAL

Life is about taking charge and control to accomplish those things that are important to you. It is only when individuals take responsibility by making a major effort to solve their problems, adapt to changing circumstances and look forward to the future that they can say they have done a total job of retirement planning.

This can best be achieved if your planning incorporates the same process for personal retirement planning as that which we use for business planning: you want to become a successfully retired person.

CHAPTER 58

DO YOU AS A TRUSTED ADVISOR GO THE EXTRA MILE? SIX STEPS TO HELPING SURVIVORS HANDLE FINANCIAL DECISIONS ALONE!

Peter J. Merrick
Charles L. Stanley

Overview

This chapter teaches Trusted Advisors how to provide the needed assistance to clients after the death of their significant other to avoid rash financial decisions that might disrupt the rest of their lives.

Learning Objectives

By the end of this chapter, you should be able to:

- apply the six-step process to helping clients with the financial and life transition after their significant other has died.

It's not every day a Trusted Advisor can go beyond the call of duty for a family in need, but for some professionals, this is the norm rather than the exception. All Trusted Advisors have the innate understanding that their primary role is to provide a professional and sympathetic service to grieving loved ones.

Most people perceive the role of a funeral director as someone who will make their funeral arrangements on their behalf. They do so partly for reasons of convenience, at a stressful time, and the funeral director ensures that the arrangements are carried out with dignity, to ensure the funeral arrangements are carried out in accordance with the deceased's and the family's wishes.

The funeral director is sometimes called upon to make the necessary payments on behalf of the family and the deceased that include cemetery or crematorium fees, doctor's fees and minister's fees, and to organize the collections for charities. Funeral directors are asked to arrange for copies of the death certificate of the deceased so that life insurance benefits can be paid and financial accounts accessed.

What could be neglected, but should never be ignored, is the potential for a grieving spouse to make rash financial decisions at the time of the death of his or her partner. Yes, Trusted Advisors, as counsellors, are positioned to help. Acting as the circuit breaker and being the gentle voice of reason, your kind and genuine words and insight may be what it takes to prevent a grieving spouse from making the wrong financial decisions that will affect his or her well being for the rest of his or her life.

"Sudden Money" sounds like a good idea. But when you have always made financial decisions together with your spouse, whom you have just buried, it can be almost paralyzing. Even if one is fairly sophisticated about financial matters, the context for decision-making has now changed; it is done alone, without the consideration of a spouse.

Stereotypically, one would think of a widow whose husband had always handled the financial matters for the home, but experience says it is true of widowers as well. We have had many attorneys tell the stories of professional men, widowers, sitting in their offices shortly after the funeral, quietly sobbing and asking, "What do I do next?"

Previous financial planning decisions were based on goals to be accomplished together, things to do and enjoy together. Now, those goals may go away because they can no longer be shared with the spouse they were intended to be shared with. A little gentle direction can have potentially powerful positive effects in the life of a grieving survivor, be it widow or widower. Here are some thoughts you can consider the next time you have the need for some kind of positive reinforcement for one of your survivor clients.

Step One: Of course, there are some things that won't wait for a survivor to get refocused on his or her life ahead, but other than those truly urgent items, we recommend strongly that your client make no significant (and definitely no irrevocable) financial decisions for at least six months, other than investing any new money (like life insurance proceeds) in a short-term investment like a T-Bill Fund, Money Market Fund or short-term GICs.

Step Two: Encourage your client to ask himself or herself, "What needs to happen over the next one to three years to make you happy about your personal progress?" This can include big things like that MBA she never pursued because she stopped to raise the kids, or that trip to Europe that was never taken because "we were too busy". These are deep considerations that can be quite motivating and cause one to become forward looking again. Financial decisions can then be made in the context of new life goals.

Step Three: If your client doesn't already have a relationship with a competent financial planner, recommend he or she hire a fee-only Certified Financial Planner™ practitioner to help him or her through the process of estate administration. During the administration time, your client can begin to think out loud with his or her financial planner about his or her future.

Step Four: As your client completes the estate administration process, it will be time to consider his or her own "new" estate plan. Estate considerations along with investment and cash flow considerations should result in a new "single life" financial plan to support his or her new life.

Step Five: Encourage your client to plan and invest for a long and fulfilling life.

Step Six: Have a list of Certified Financial Planners™, attorneys, and public accountants who are both technically and emotionally equipped to help survivors. This is tremendous value added for you and will not only be of great help to your clientele, but will move clients toward being "highly satisfied" with your service and recommend your services to friends and family when their time comes. There is a huge economic difference between merely "satisfied" clients and "highly satisfied" clients as demonstrated in the study by Russ Alan Prince and put forward in his book *The Private Client Lawyer* (Oakland Park, KS: Wealth Management Press, 2003), which was discussed in Chapter 50.

Do you really think in terms of the needs of your clients or in terms of performing the service? If you are focused on the service rather than on the people who are your clients, you run a good chance of having merely satisfied clients. Focus on the people and you will have a much greater chance of producing highly satisfied clients.

Whether your client is someone who has always handled the finances, the spouse who never handled the finances or a survivor who suddenly has to make decisions about major amounts of "new" money from life insurance or retirement plan benefits, he or she may think of his or her financial "wind-fall" as too small to command serious attention. Consider this: $150,000 invested in a solid well-managed investment earning an 8% average annual compounding rate of return will grow over 30 years to more than $1,509,399 (nothing to laugh at).

As Certified Financial Planner™ practitioners who were in the business in the 1990s during the run up to the tech bubble, we observed many people's fortunes grow almost overnight as a result of being paid in employee stock options only to see those same individuals lose it all through poor financial and tax planning or ill-conceived life choices in the early 2000s.

Each survivor has the opportunity to be either a wise or a foolish steward of the financial assets and income in his or her life. Wise counsel from competent mature professional advisors can go a long way toward helping that survivor be a wise steward and be able to enjoy the fruits of his or her stewardship for the rest of his or her life and, if the assets are substantial, possibly affect several future generations of his or her family. Speaking a few well-placed words of caution at the right moment to a grieving spouse that will cause him or her to stop and count to ten before making any financial decisions could be what ultimately makes all the difference in this person's life. When a truly empathic Trusted Advisor has acquired the wisdom to know when to step in and be the voice of reason at a time of family crisis, this is when the true authentic professional has arrived.

By encouraging your clients to clearly identify what matters most to them, you will be deepening your skill as an authentic communicator. Your clients will have a powerfully positive experience with you and your service, and you will experience greater fulfillment in your vocation. Your client's positive experience may produce a "highly satisfied" client and result in more referrals to you and your services. As a widow's or widower's first counsellor, if you are not comfortable or don't feel qualified to start the conversation about these financial decisions, perhaps you should direct your survivors to work with a fee-only Certified Financial Planner™ who specializes in this area. Remember, an ounce of prevention is worth more than a pound of cure.

Part VIII

Offshore Investing

CHAPTER 59

CHOOSING YOUR OFFSHORE TAX HAVEN

Andrew Rogerson

Overview

In this chapter, you will learn what characteristics to look at when selecting an offshore tax haven.

Learning Objectives

By the end of this chapter, you should be able to:

- understand what characteristics to look for when evaluating an offshore jurisdiction;
- understand the types of asset protections that the most popular offshore tax havens offer; and
- understand the privacy that offshore jurisdictions provide.

Turquoise seas, pristine coral, endless and near-deserted white sandy beaches with iconic palm trees; a holiday is but a dream for most bankruptcy lawyers and their clients. This became reality for me many years ago, when I was briefed to appear in the Court of Appeal in a, then, little-known but quite exotic tax haven. I stayed. I went on to help clients establish and defend structures that put their hard-earned wealth out of harm's way, away from vexatious litigants and hostile spouses. What follows is an overview of asset protection using some of the more popular tax havens.

As a preliminary point, though, I should say that prior to considering any form of offshore structure, one should always look first at structuring within Canada. Domestic structures may be appropriate in terms of ease of establishment and cost. Since asset protection and tax structuring may be available onshore, one should always look, initially, at the means of achieving one's ambitions within the domestic context.

JURISDICTIONS

There are many offshore jurisdictions in which a trust may be established. Some are extremely successful. For example, Cayman is the world's fifth largest banking centre with $1.3 trillion in deposits, of which $935 million are interbank bookings, not personal or corporate accounts. The British Virgin Islands (BVI) are home to 700,000 offshore companies. Bermuda enjoys the third highest per capita income in the world, that being US$70,000 compared to US$43,500 for the United States. The Turks and Caicos Islands, whilst smaller, is a niche jurisdiction, offering a friendly and efficient boutique service against a backdrop of wonderful beaches and fine hotels. Many offshore finance centres (the new name for "tax havens") are current or former British Colonies and/or associated states located in the Caribbean, North Atlantic and the Channel Islands. They are characterized by the following:

- zero or minimal income tax;
- legislated bank secrecy;
- similar legal system to Canada (based on English common law with a generally independent and non-corrupt judiciary); and
- strict regime of supervision by financial services authorities, generally headed by experienced non-local people (which require trust companies and banks to maintain heavy insurance coverage).

Most of the offshore jurisdictions provide similarly attractive regimes, so the decision as to which one to use will, to a degree, depend on personal preference. Skilled and efficient trustee and corporate services are available in most of them. One important factor to consider in selecting a jurisdiction is the ease with which one can travel there. In the modern telecommunications era, it is not essential to ever step foot in the jurisdiction. However, there is much to be gained by making at least an initial visit to familiarize oneself with the jurisdiction in general and the trustees in particular. This consideration may make the North American investor select the Turks and Caicos Islands or the Bahamas over, say, Lichtenstein or even the Cook Islands. Ease of communication having regard to time zones is also a very important factor to consider.

ASSET PROTECTION

Historically, trusts evolved as a means of protecting assets. This was achieved by having another trusted person hold legal title of assets on behalf of (or in trust for) another. Tax considerations aside, which I will deal with below, asset protection is still by far and away the most important reason for establishing an offshore trust. Persons of substantial means who are, or may be, at risk in the future from unwelcome litigation should give consideration to establishing a trust. Once assets are transferred into the name of the trustees, after a prescribed period, creditors are no longer able to execute against such assets. This is because the settlor has divested himself or herself of legal ownership. One may obtain asset protection by establishing trusts both in Canada and offshore. The advantage of establishing a trust in one of the offshore finance centres is their prevalent debtor-friendly regimes. These shorten the period of time in which a creditor may bring proceedings to attack the establishment of the trust/settlement of specific assets into trust. The jurisdictions range geographically from the Bahamas to the Cook Islands. Trusts established in the debtor-friendly jurisdictions are typically referred to as Asset Protection Trusts.

The Cook Islands regime provides considerable hurdles for a creditor to overcome. Firstly, he or she must seek the leave of the court in Rarotonga to even bring the action. Secondly, if leave is granted, he or she must prove beyond reasonable doubt (the criminal standard) that the transfer into the trust was made with the intention of defrauding a creditor. No action may be brought in respect of any transfer that took place before, or more than two years after the cause of action arose. If the settlement takes place within the two-year window, then the creditor must bring an action in the settlor's home jurisdiction within 12 months of the transfer of assets to the Cook Islands trust, alleging some sort of debt or damages. He or she must then commence a further action in the Cook Islands' courts within two years of the transfer of assets into the trust. If the creditor does not comply with both of these limitation periods, then the claim will be statute-barred.

The Cook Islands regime marks the high watermark of debtor friendliness. Caribbean jurisdictions such as the Turks and Caicos Islands have similar regimes but are slightly more neutral. In the Bahamas, *The Fraudulent Dispositions Act*, 1991 establishes a two-year limitation period for creditors' attacks on asset protection trusts; the attacker has to prove fraud against the settlor. Even if fraud is proved, beneficiaries who have *bona fide* received benefit from the trust are permitted to retain what has been distributed to them. In Barbados, creditors have three years to apply to set aside the terms of a trust. An intention to defraud, on the part of the debtor, must be established. A successful creditor can only set aside such parts of the trust as have caused him or her prejudice, not the balance.

Once established, as indicated above, legal title rests with the trustees, and the settlor and/or his or her family may become beneficiaries and entitled to receive discretionary distributions. It is well settled that with a properly established trust, there is no right on the part of the beneficiaries to require payments to satisfy their creditors. Accordingly, execution against such a beneficiary could prove fruitless.

Some of the advantages of utilizing offshore trusts for asset protection purposes include the following:

- The geographic distance between Canada and the offshore centre makes an action against the trust more difficult to pursue than in Canada. To use an extreme example, the distance, as the crow flies, between Calgary and Rarotonga, Cook Islands is 11,670 kilometres. To fly there from Calgary takes a minimum of 24 hours in the air and requires one to change planes in Los Angeles and Papeete, French Polynesia.
- Foreign judgments normally are not recognized in offshore jurisdictions. A plaintiff will therefore have to litigate the entire action afresh in the offshore court, always assuming that the offshore court agrees to accept jurisdiction, which it may not.
- Should the action be permitted, then substantial costs will be incurred in prosecuting the action offshore.
- Time zone differences make it difficult to speak to lawyers by telephone. Distances preclude satisfactory conferences and briefing of witnesses ahead of travel to the offshore jurisdiction. Lawyers' hourly rates may be substantially higher than in Canada, owing to the difficulty of attracting lawyers willing to practise in such locations.

It will be logistically difficult and expensive to transport witnesses to give evidence.

The laws governing the trust will be those of the offshore jurisdiction — not those of Canada. The laws of the offshore jurisdiction are likely to be much more favourable to the debtor than to the creditor. Generally, the self-interest of an offshore finance centre is best served by a legal regime that upholds the sanctity of a trust under attack from a disgruntled creditor of the settlor. In most offshore finance centres, a high proportion of the population is employed in the trust and banking sector. Allowing trusts to easily collapse ultimately leads to the destruction of an important industry. Overseas investors will be unwilling to have their trust administered in a jurisdiction that allows the interests of overseas creditors to prevail.

The net result of the above is to discourage frivolous lawsuits and to encourage reasonable settlement offers from more legitimate complainants.

FREEDOM FROM PROBATE (IMPOST AND CONFIDENTIALITY)

Upon death, details of assets that have to be probated become a matter of public record. There is no requirement to make public details of assets that one settles into trust prior to one's death. Probate fees (however described) are charged in most provinces on the value of assets probated on death. These charges cannot be levied if the assets are already settled into an *inter vivos* trust, as the assets no longer form part of one's deceased estate. This is another excellent reason to establish an offshore trust.

EASE OF ADMINISTRATION OF ASSETS AND CONTINUITY

One problem that manifests itself, particularly in the context of family businesses, is that of ownership of shareholding in the holding corporation by siblings, irrespective of their knowledge of the business and involvement in its day-to-day activities. For example, one child may have dutifully entered the family business upon completion of his or her education. Another may have pursued a career as a musician. It is unlikely that the latter sibling will be able to make the same contribution to business discussions as the former. Also, health or psychiatric problems may hinder family members, who have the best intentions, from properly exercising their rights as shareholders. Family disputes and the lack of capacity can frequently bring down a family business. An offshore discretionary family trust can be utilized to overcome these problems. Ownership of shareholding is vested in the trust. The trustees decide who will sit on the board of directors. The trust receives dividends paid by the company. The trustees then distribute income received by the trust from the company according to the needs of the beneficiaries, having regard to their duties as trustees, which require them to act in an even-handed manner. Further, upon the death of any family member, there is no issue pertaining to transfer of ownership of shares. The interest of the deceased in the trust is transferred on, according the provisions of the trust deed.

PERPETUITY PERIOD

Most offshore jurisdictions have codified their trust law to provide for a fixed term for trusts to, typically, 80 years. In 2004, the Bahamas extended their perpetuity period from 80 years to 150 years. In April

2006, the Bailiwick of Jersey amended its trust law to provide for trusts of unlimited duration.

POLITICAL STABILITY

Strange as it may seem, many Canadians have fears as to the complexion of future Canadian governments, in a state that may or may not include Quebec. Some prefer the prospect of having assets held in a trust based in, say, the Isle of Man, which is politically stable and conservative. The legislature of that country, the Tynewald, is 1,000 years old, making it the oldest parliament in the world. The "offshore" world now also includes Switzerland, whose political confederation dates back to August 1, 1201. It has enjoyed legislated neutrality in international conflicts since 1815. The trust industry is prominent in both countries exemplified here.

CANADIAN TAX SAVING

In a nutshell, offshore trusts are now unlikely to be of assistance in making any substantial saving of Canadian income tax. An explanation of the legislative framework is described below. However, there are other structures that will achieve this end in appropriate circumstances. As indicated above, the primary reason for client consideration should be asset protection.

IBCs AND DOUBLE TAX TREATY WITH BARBADOS

Barbados, like most offshore finance centres, provides a favourable tax regime for International Business Corporations (IBCs). IBC status is given to companies that are carrying on the business of international manufacturing or international trade or commerce. Broadly speaking, these activities have to be carried out in Barbados, with exports or the provision of services being to countries outside the Caricom area. Currently, Barbados' taxation of IBCs is at the rate of 2.5% for the first US$10 million of their profits and gains, reducing to 1% on such over $30 million. Pursuant to section 13.1 of the *International Business Companies Act* (1991), dividends paid by an IBC to a non-resident are free from withholding tax.

Barbados has a double tax treaty with Canada, which was signed on January 22, 1980.

Pursuant to paragraph 113(1)(a) of the *Income Tax Act*, R.S.C. 1985, c. 1 (5th Supp.), dividends from active business income earned by foreign affiliates based in treaty partner countries (such as Barbados) are effectively exempt from Canadian tax when distributed to Canadian resident shareholders (individual or corporate).

OFFSHORE BANKING LICENCES

Having one's own bank is a very valuable asset. It opens the door to all manner of financial transactions using funds originating from Canada. The appropriate category of banking licence is widely known in the offshore world as a "Class B" licence. This permits overseas investors to establish a bank that may conduct business with clients located anywhere but the country of the bank's incorporation.

In Barbados, this type of licence is known as an Offshore Banking Licence. Minimum capitalization is BDS$2 million authorized and BDS$1 million issued. These figures are due to be increased, and the Central Bank is already applying higher limits. A licensed bank pays an initial and continuing annual fee of BDS$25,000. The Central Bank requires quarterly balance sheet reporting and filing of full annual accounts, along with a list of the licensee's directors (one of whom must be a Barbadian). There are 53 licensed offshore banks in Barbados. Offshore banks pay corporation tax on the same basis as IBCs. They are exempt from withholding tax on payments to non-residents or other offshore entities, from customs duties on goods and materials imported for their offshore business, from estate duties on any of their shares, securities or assets owned by a non-resident, and from property transfer tax on the transfer of shares, securities or other assets. Their offshore transactions are exempt from exchange control, and they are exempt from *ad valorem* stamp duty. Obtaining a banking licence is a matter of meeting fairly standard (but strict) criteria as to a good character of owners and the ability to provide skilled personnel to run the operation.

Another alternative is Panama, where the licence is known as a "restricted licence". Required capitalization is a minimum of 3 million Balboas (equivalent to US$3 million). Panama is a sophisticated and stable world-banking centre. It has approximately 80 banks, of which 30 are operated under a restricted (overseas) licence.

WHICH JURISDICTION?

Shortlist jurisdictions that have the asset protection regime and professional services that you and your advisor feel comfortable with. Go and have a look. Find out which jurisdiction leaves you with a good feeling. Sample the beaches and the fine hotels and restaurants in the context of an easy plane ride from Canada. Find a place that you enjoy going to so that meetings with trustees and bankers are a pleasurable experience.

CHAPTER 60

THE CANADIAN'S BEST TAX HAVEN? CONSIDERABLE TAX RELIEF MAY BE CLOSER THAN YOU THINK!

Robert Keats

Overview

This chapter discusses how to assist Canadians to obtain substantial tax relief, using the tax havens that create the best tax and other financial benefits with the least disruption of the clients' family and lifestyle.

Learning Objectives

By the end of this chapter, you should be able to:

- understand the critical advantages that the United States offers to Canadians seeking tax relief over the traditional tax havens;
- understand how to recognize the hidden costs of tax havens and how these costs can actually be higher than paying tax at the Canada/U.S. Tax Treaty rates; and
- learn how to successfully assist clients to maintain their desired lifestyle while utilizing tax haven-type tax reduction strategies through U.S. residency.

INTRODUCTION

Many wealthy Canadians will move lock, stock and barrel to one of the tax haven islands in the middle of nowhere, but few, including their advisors, will consider one of the best tax havens available to Canadians — the United States. Besides the obvious that most Canadians can drive to the United States in about an hour, this chapter will discuss the main reasons why the United States may be one of the best retirement and/or tax planning alternatives for many business owners, executives and other high net-worth/high-income Canadians.

I was asked to speak to a group of largely retired Canadians who were holding a conference in Dublin, Ireland a few years ago, and who were looking at going offshore for their retirement. After a long and successful career paying more than half of their earned income to the various Canadian governments in the form of income taxes, sales taxes, goods and services taxes, land transfer taxes, *etc.,* these Canadians were asking whether there was relief available in their retirement by moving to a tax haven now that they were no longer tied down to businesses or jobs in Canada. There were speakers at this conference from virtually all the major tax havens in the world pontificating on the many possible tax and other benefits of their particular country. The United States as a tax haven never came up in any of the conversations until I had my turn to speak, and, initially, many thought I was crazy even to mention the United States and tax haven in the same sentence, an oxymoron of sorts. The purpose of this chapter is to explain to the Canadian advisor why the United States can be the best tax haven for almost any Canadian in the majority of situations and their advisor should be the one guiding them in their best interests. After a career of over 30 years involving assisting Canadians doing business and/or retiring outside Canada, I have definitive proof that the United States should always be at or near the top of the list for any Canadian looking for tax relief and year-round warmth and sunshine.

Here are the key discussion points that an advisor should review with clients who are seeking tax relief by living most or all of the year in a warmer climate. I will explain the logic and the understanding of each of these points over the next several sections of this chapter, as well as give specific examples of the many positive results from Canadians who have used the United States as their tax haven:

- Media Perceptions — The Venerable IRS
- The United States — Only Tax Haven You Can Drive to
- Reduce Income Tax to Levels of Traditional Tax Havens
- Canada/U.S. Tax Treaty
- Small Business Owners Can Reap Huge Rewards
- Medical Access — Double Dip
- Familiar Lifestyle
- Numerous Immigration Options
- Tax-Free Rollovers on Investment Real Estate

THE VENERABLE IRS

One of the main reasons why most Canadians and any of their Canadian advisors never consider the United States as a country in which they can get substantial tax benefits is the United States' venerable Internal Revenue Service (IRS). I wish I had a dollar every time I heard a Canadian advisor tell clients, "You don't want to move to the U.S.; you will have to deal with the IRS." The IRS over the years has done one of the best negative marketing campaigns ever to get taxpayers to comply with its many and complicated rules. By throwing somebody in jail and fining renegade taxpayers great amounts of money and then getting it splashed all over the newspapers, the IRS strikes fear into the hearts of many. After all, it was the IRS that got Al Capone back in the 1930s, not the police or the FBI. This fear of the IRS ensures a much higher level of compliance by taxpayers to the rules.

However, the truth be known, for those who have a desire to follow the rules and understand how to use them to their advantage, the IRS rules are much clearer in most cases, and the IRS is as easy or easier the majority of the time to deal with than the Canada Revenue Agency (CRA). Taxpayers in the United States have many more basic rights than taxpayers in Canada. For example, the burden of proof standards by the IRS require a much higher barrier for the IRS to attempt to attack a taxpayer without good solid proof that he or she is in violation. In addition, the IRS can actually be sued for costs and recovery of legal fees through the appeals and court proceedings if the IRS has been proven wrong, particularly when it gets overly aggressive. The IRS has a Dispute Resolution Section that works very well to resolve those unjustified tax assessments that you cannot get answers to through the standard channel of calls, letters and e-mails that go unanswered by the usual IRS staffers or that are answered in a non-responsive way. The dispute resolution option allows the taxpayer to bypass all the normal channels after a certain time period of non-resolution to get the problem resolved in a matter of weeks. Under CRA rules, some problems seem to go unresolved, with a great deal of time and expense wasted unnecessarily by both the taxpayer and the CRA. However, do not get me wrong; even though there are more taxpayer rights in the United States, the IRS, like the CRA, is no picnic to deal with under the best of circumstances. My main point is that taxpayer odds are just better in the United States, dealing with the IRS, than they are in Canada, dealing with the CRA, for those who generally follow the rules and don't push them past prudent limitations. Taxpayers should not fear the IRS any more or less than the CRA unless they are intentionally planning on breaking the rules.

THE UNITED STATES — THE ONLY TAX HAVEN CANADIANS CAN DRIVE TO

It is a well-known fact that 90% of the Canadian population lives within 150 kilometres of the U.S. border. This means that most Canadians are a one- to two-hour drive from their best potential tax haven. For those who choose not to drive, there are numerous other travel options to allow Canadians very easy access to most any desired major U.S. location, generally much easier than even travelling between major Canadian cities. This ease of physical travel options to and from the United States should not be underestimated. One of the biggest complaints Canadians have going to one of the traditional tax haven islands is that in most cases your only options are to fly with sometimes more than one connecting flight on the island puddle-jumper-type aircraft. These limited travel options are exacerbated when there is a medical emergency, particularly if the patient is not able to travel by air back to the United States or Canada to get the required potentially life saving medical assistance. An important complaint I have heard from Canadians who have gone offshore is that if they have left their kids and grandkids back in Canada the difficult travel means they don't get to see the family as much and as often as they would like for weddings, graduations, birthdays, bar mitzvahs, *etc.* A real dilemma often arises if a family member left in Canada is terminally ill and the offshore family members want to spend time with that person in his or her last days but they may jeopardize their entire tax plan because they are spending too much time in Canada with the sick relative. These are lifestyle issues that, if they are important to the family, are much easier to deal with where the family travels back and forth across the U.S. border rather than to an island in the middle of the ocean, and where the Canada/U.S. Tax Treaty protects their tax plan.

One Canadian from Alberta who had a net worth measured in 11 digits and whose advisors had sent him to one of the offshore Caribbean tax havens could last only six months on the island before he was bored stiff talking to the locals at the corner bar about fishing or other things that mattered little to him. He came charging back to Canada, saying, "I don't care what tax I have to pay; I'm not going to be imprisoned on an island." Had this individual's advisors spent time understanding the life planning issues important to this taxpayer, they would have found that a move to the United States would likely have been more appropriate to maintain his desired lifestyle while at the same time receiving most or even all of the tax benefits of the island tax haven.

Since the traditional tax havens have no tax treaty with Canada, and therefore no treaty protection, as noted in the next section of this chapter, Canadian taxpayers who exit Canada must clearly sever all ties and leave nothing they own back in Canada. They should not even visit Canada for the first two years, and then only on a very short-term basis to ensure the CRA doesn't try to attack them and deem them to be residents of Canada, obliterating all of their critical tax planning. Without treaty protection, it is quite easy for the CRA to use the most minor of issues to deem an ex-Canadian resident still a taxpayer in Canada and attempt to tax him or her as if he or she has never left Canada. One thing as minor as leaving furniture in storage in Canada, holding a Canadian driver's licence or leaving an automobile in Canada can send the CRA on a rampage to tax the expatriate as a full Canadian deemed resident.

Moving to an offshore tax haven is a major and disruptive change in lifestyle for these Canadians, and it often raises the question in their minds, "Why have we worked so hard all our lives to obtain financial independence and then not be able to choose the lifestyle that we want?" However, when these Canadians choose the United States as their tax residence and follow the tiebreaker rules of the Canada/U.S. Tax Treaty, Canadian travel and personal ties with Canada are not nearly as much a concern based on the great deal of protection the taxpayer has from the treaty if the CRA were to attack their residency status in the United States. Consequently, their lifestyle needs to change very little, particularly if they already had a primary residence in the United States that they have been wintering in for many years already. In summary, lifestyle and life planning needs for clients are important, and advisors who ignore these issues in favour of tax savings from some far-off island will inevitably result in a very unhappy client.

REDUCE INCOME TAX TO LEVELS OF TRADITIONAL TAX HAVENS

To most advisors, including me, the proof that the United States is an equal or better tax haven than the traditional tax haven countries or islands comes from actual tax results and comparisons. We, at my firm, Keats, Connelly and Associates, Inc. (KCA), have CAs, CPAs, JDs and other tax professionals who over the years have prepared thousands of U.S. and Canadian tax returns for the Canadians and Americans living outside their respective native countries. Over years of reviewing all of these complex returns, I have found a definite pattern of substantial tax savings for Canadians completing a cross-border move to the United States emerge. In short, the results were so spectacular that we started comparing the taxes paid by these Canadians to the taxes paid by other Canadians who have gone offshore to one of the traditional tax havens. The surprising bottom line was that in many cases, Canadians actually paid a lower rate of income tax in the United States than in other tax havens. In addition, when a broader comparison was done to include the "hidden tax" of the tax haven, which I discuss later in this chapter, the United States for these Canadians was consistently the hands-down winner. The main purpose for this entire chapter is to make Canadian and U.S. advisors more aware of the tax planning opportunities available for Canadians in the United States without having to send their clients "offshore".

There are numerous examples I could use to illustrate my "proof is in the numbers", but I have tried to choose what I would consider to be more typical clients. These clients have enough income and assets that had they gone to Canadian advisors, seeking relief from high Canadian taxes, the advisors would have possibly recommended them to go offshore, with the United States likely never even being mentioned as an option. In order to protect client confidentiality, I have eliminated names and some of the more obvious details or changed them enough so as to maintain confidentiality while using the facts to illustrate the income tax comparisons adequately.

The first example involves an individual who was a retiring key executive at one of Canada's largest corporations at the time his cross-border plan was developed. His key advisors at the time, in 1994, were one of the big four accounting firms provided for and paid for by the company. He came to KCA, seeking better tax-reducing retirement options than what his advisors were providing, which consisted primarily of "pay the tax or go offshore", neither of which was acceptable to him. This executive had a superior pension and supplementary executive retirement plan provided by the company as well as real estate in Canada and the United States. He and his wife had a combined net worth of over $10 million, including the present value of all pension benefits. Their combined income, which consisted primarily of portfolio income and pension, in the tax year 2007 was $747,000. They paid a combined husband and wife U.S. tax of $6,700 and used foreign tax credits of $59,800 for a total U.S. federal and state tax due of $66,500. The estimated Ontario tax for that year was $336,000 if they had remained Canadian residents with the identical income. The estimated tax haven tax for that year, had they gone offshore, would have been in excess of $150,000, consisting primarily of the 25% non-resident withholding tax that the CRA would have taken on his pensions. This tax differential amongst Canada, a tax haven and the United States has been consistent throughout the 14 years this couple has been resident in the United States. So it doesn't take much of a math major to calculate that the executive and his wife have saved several millions of dollars more in taxes as U.S. residents in retirement rather than as offshore residents, not to mention even larger tax savings when compared with a retirement in Canada. This couple also has had a much better lifestyle in the U.S. Sunbelt compared to offshore, where the executive and his wife never would have been able to be close to their family and receive the kind of medical treatment they need over the years had they been resident on one of the tax haven islands. This is an interesting tax anecdote for this couple, because the Canada/U.S. Tax Treaty eliminates the 100% Old Age Security (OAS) clawback tax (a benefit the husband and wife would not get if they lived in a traditional tax haven or in Canada), amounting to savings of over $150,000 for the period of residence in the United States to date, just for this one simple gift from the CRA through the treaty. Since they invested their OAS clawback savings in their U.S. portfolio, over the 14 years of U.S. residency so far, with an average after-tax portfolio return in excess of 7%, their portfolio has grown by an additional several hundreds of thousands of dollars solely due to the OAS benefits they received as U.S. residents. These benefits would be clawed back if the husband and wife were either Canadian residents or residents of the traditional tax haven.

The second example illustrating the United States as an equal or better tax haven for Canadians involves a very different set of circumstances consisting of a successful businessman involved in creating, developing and selling his own companies in the public market. He decided that he wanted to retire in the late 1990s, and because his adult children/grandchildren were spread throughout the United States and Canada, his wife would not even remotely agree to go offshore. His advisors at the time he came to KCA for cross-border planning were one of the big four accounting firms and various attorneys located in more than one Canadian province. The combined net worth of this couple was in excess of $10 million. In 2007, the couple's combined income was $521,000, consisting primarily of investment portfolio income. The husband and wife paid U.S. federal and state tax of $33,800 and used foreign tax credits of approximately $60,000 for a total U.S. tax of $93,800. Their estimated Ontario tax for that year was $234,000, and the approximate tax haven comparative tax was $78,000, plus an additional $12,000 for the OAS clawback, for a total of $90,000. The husband and wife still keep a large Canadian residence in which they spend four to five months a year with their family and then the remaining seven to eight months they spend at their beautiful U.S. Sunbelt residence close to their children and grandchildren. Because of their residual business connections, they were able to develop qualifications necessary for free U.S. Medicare, giving them complete access, for the rest of their lives, to the U.S. medical system with excellent Medicare supplemental insurance coverage, something they never would have been able to achieve had they lived in the traditional tax haven.

For the third and final example, I show yet quite a different set of circumstances in the form of a Canadian broker from a large Canadian brokerage firm who wanted to change careers and move to the United States in 2006. The broker and his wife still had two children living at home and one already married and living in the United States. Because this was a change in career and there were still dependent children who needed to be educated, an offshore island would have severely stifled this family's opportunities, another very real limitation to individual lifestyles in offshore jurisdictions. The broker's planning advisors when he and his wife came to KCA for their cross-border planning were a large U.S. firm. In 2007, the broker and his wife had income of $1,001,000. They paid U.S. tax of $26,600 and used foreign tax credits of $283,300 for a total U.S. federal and state income tax of $309,900. Their estimated Canadian federal and provincial tax on the same income would have been $380,000, while the tax haven tax would have been around $350,000. The exact tax haven tax in this instance is difficult to determine because we assisted this broker in negotiating his buyout package from the brokerage firm such that the majority of the buyout was considered a retirement benefit under the Canada/U.S. Tax Treaty. Absent the treaty, the CRA may have taxed this benefit as full employment income at maximum Canadian rates rather than as a retirement benefit that would be subject to a lower rate of non-resident withholding tax.

In summary, of all three of these examples which were created using actual numbers from real tax returns, the message should be very clear that the generally accepted oxymoron of the "United States — an excellent tax haven for Canadians" is not an oxymoron at all. In general, the higher Canadians' income — providing that income is a typical mix of portfolio income, pension income or registered retirement plan-type income — the better the United States is suited for advisors to use as a tax haven for their clients. The primary driver for this equivalent to tax haven benefits in the United States is the Canada/U.S. Tax Treaty in conjunction with the knowledge of what to do on a tax-free basis in Canada before the Canadian actually exits from Canada to become a U.S. tax-paying resident. Several things that advisors should have done for their clients prior to the clients exiting, primarily through qualified cross-border planning specialists, are outlined throughout this chapter. Some of these strategies that need to be followed are deceptively simple, but mistakes are also very easy and potentially very costly to the clients to more than justify, in the best interest of clients, the expense and time to involve the necessary cross-border planning specialists. In addition, those professionals attempting to do cross-border work where they don't have the training, experience or credentials to do such work are opening themselves up to potential malpractice issues.

THE CANADA/U.S. TAX TREATY

One of the key benefits of using a country like the United States for your business or retirement planning is that Canada and the United States have a very good well-established tax treaty. The Canada/U.S. Tax Treaty can be the most important tax planning document for the protection of a Canadian's financial assets in the United States (see some of the actual examples earlier in the previous section). When dealing with traditional tax haven countries that have no treaty with Canada, the taxpayer without treaty protection is vulnerable to the ability of the CRA to tax the taxpayer in whatever way it sees fit or can unilaterally get away with. A simple but very illustrative example is that under the Canada/U.S. Tax Treaty, the treaty withholding rate on dividends can be as low as 5%, whereas with a non-treaty country, the withholding rate is five times that, or 25%, and there is nothing preventing the CRA at any time from increasing the tax beyond 25%.

Most Canadians, however, are completely unaware of the treaty's existence and the benefits that it gives them. Even though tax planning is an important part of cross-border planning, it is my experience that few financial advisors on either side of the Canada-U.S. border have ever cracked the cover of this treaty on behalf of their clients to look for planning opportunities. They tend to focus instead on the domestic tax rules of their own individual countries, which in itself is a tough job. Consequently, it is usually in the clients' best interest for advisors to team up with or refer clients to specialists who deal with cross-border tax and other related issues on a regular basis.

The Canada/U.S. Tax Treaty is one of the most important tools used in cross-border financial planning for two key reasons:

1. The terms of the treaty take precedence over almost all the Canadian *Income Tax Act* (ITA) rules in Canada and the *Internal Revenue Code* (IRC) tax rules in the United States. It is an important trump card to play at appropriate times when doing cross-border planning. The value of this cannot be overemphasized for any cross-border planner.
2. The terms of the treaty seldom change. In addition, when a change to the treaty is requested by one country or the other, there is a protocol that requires substantial communication and negotiation between the tax authorities of both countries. Then once the changes

are agreed to, there is a complex legislative process that requires the treaty changes to be authorized and voted on by the full Parliament in Canada and the U.S. Congress with a presidential signature. The Canada/U.S. Tax Treaty has been amended only six times in its more than 65-year history and can be relied on to a much greater degree for long-term planning than either the Canadian ITA or the American IRC. The ITA and IRC are subject to constant revision without notice and are affected by annual budgets, bipartisan politics and election campaigns. In fact, since the last major treaty negotiations of 1989, the IRS has changed the U.S. domestic tax rules an estimated 15,000 times, and the CRA likely a similar number of times. The 1989 treaty revisions took until 1995 before they were signed into law, and the most recent revisions, the Fifth Protocol, started in the year 2000 and was submitted for final approval to the respective federal legislators in 2008.

One of the foremost roles of the Canada/U.S. Tax Treaty is its tiebreaker rules for determination of residency. These rules prevent a situation where an individual is taxed as a resident of Canada and the United States at the same time on his or her world income. Technically speaking, the treaty states that an individual is only required to pay tax on his or her world income in either Canada or the United States, but not both. By following these four tiebreaker rules and passing just one of the tests clearly in favour of one or the other country, the taxpayer will be protected from having to face two complete sets of tax rules at the same time. The tiebreaker rules in Article IV of the Canada/U.S. Tax Treaty are outlined here, along with comments to explain them:

1. The individual shall be deemed to be a resident of the country in which he or she has a permanent home available. If a permanent home is available in both countries, or neither, an individual is deemed to be resident in the country in which his or her personal and economic relations are closer (centre of vital interests). Generally, a permanent home is any accommodation that is considered permanent. The home may be rented or owned. It is considered permanent where it is available for the individual's use throughout the year. A person's centre of vital interests would be objectively determined and would be based upon his or her familial, social, occupational, political and cultural activities. Economic relations are also considered and are generally linked with the locality of the main source income.
2. If the country in which the individual has his or her centre of vital interests cannot be determined, he or she shall be determined to be a resident of the country in which he or she has an habitual abode.

What constitutes habitual abode requires an evaluation of the individual's lifestyle over a sufficient length of time. In most circumstances the length of time spent in one country over any other may be determinative. Also the transient nature of the stay may be examined, *e.g.*, living at a seasonal vacation cabin at the lake versus at a typical year-round residence in the city.

3. If the individual has an habitual abode in both countries or in neither country, he or she shall be deemed to be resident of the country of which he or she is a citizen. The immigration status is very important; for example, if one was to have a permanent residence status, then that would most definitely be considered. Ultimately though, citizenship is the final determination.
4. If the individual is a citizen of both countries (generally the most recent citizenship obtained will be considered the primary citizenship barring other dominant factors) or of neither of them, then competent authorities of the contracting countries shall settle the question by mutual agreement. The competent authorities are committees of individuals from both Canada and the United States who sit down and examine the facts and make a determination. This process should be avoided at all costs, as it is lengthy and heart-wrenching. It is difficult to determine in advance what the outcome may be.

A retired person or person who has a business which no longer requires that he or she be present on a daily basis in Canada has control over almost all of the factors discussed above in these treaty tiebreaker rules; in effect, he or she can control the company from the country in which he or she is taxed on his or her world income. In an attempt to plug what the CRA considered a loophole in the famous Bronfman rules, where Canadians could use the Canada/U.S. Tax Treaty to reduce their taxes payable without actually exiting Canada for tax purposes, the CRA amended the ITA. The amendment the CRA added to the ITA was subsection 250(5). To paraphrase this subsection, it states clearly that if a taxpayer, under the Canada/U.S. Tax Treaty, is a resident of the United States, he or she is automatically a non-resident taxpayer of Canada. This new rule certainly achieved the results the CRA was looking for, which was to force Canadians through an exit process and pay exit tax before they could enjoy the lower treaty rates. However, a major side benefit was also provided to Canadians living in the United States. They no longer had to worry about Canadian domestic rules being used against them so that the CRA could tax them on their world income because they left some minor financial ties with Canada when they exited or spent a significant amount of time in Canada after their exit. As long as Canadians followed the provisions of the tiebreaker rules in the treaty, noted above, they could have full confidence that the lower treaty tax rates and the lower U.S. tax rates would be applied to them so they could enjoy the tax haven status discussed in this chapter. We recommend that it is never prudent to wave a red flag at the CRA by maintaining significant Canadian ties after a tax exit from Canada even when one is moving to the United States. However, subsection 250(5) means that Canadians taking up U.S. residency could, for example, maintain a Canadian cottage or spend reasonable visiting time in Canada annually without losing treaty benefits, providing they followed the treaty tiebreaker rules for all the major items that really count in determining the country in which they are taxed on their world income. This subsection 250(5) provision of the ITA does not apply to Canadians using the traditional tax haven countries.

The treaty tiebreaker rules in themselves are not enough to give Canadians wanting full tax haven status in the United States full protection; they must also be prevented from being double-taxed on all sources of income. The treaty accomplishes this in three key ways:

1. *Foreign Tax Credits* — The treaty allows for a system of credits so that tax paid to one country on specified income will be allowed as a full credit against any tax due on that same income in the country of residence. For example, a non-resident who earns a taxable rental income in Canada files and pays tax as required by the CRA. The tax paid to the CRA after netting income and expenses on a non-resident T1 under section 216 is converted to U.S. funds and is used on the U.S. return as a full credit against U.S. taxes payable on the same income. This reduces or eliminates U.S. taxes due to IRS on that same rental income, adjusted for U.S. depreciation and rental expense rules. (The CRA limits these credits to the amount of the stated Canada/U.S. Tax Treaty withholding rates on any specific taxable income source, regardless of what foreign tax was actually paid, whereas the IRS allows full foreign credits for actual tax paid, a very important benefit.)
2. *Exemptions* — The Canada/U.S. Tax Treaty provides for certain exemptions from filing or reporting income of a non-resident in Canada that would otherwise be taxable by the CRA. For example, there is a treaty provision that allows Canadians in the United States to earn up to $10,000 annually in Canada through employment without being taxed in Canada on that income. With the latest treaty protocol, there is no withholding on interest earned in Canada by residents of the United States.

3. *Withholding Rates* — Provisions in the treaty establish the amount of maximum withholding tax either country can take on various forms of income in that country from residents of the other country. The provisions for maximum withholding rates prove very useful when one does cross-border planning. These withholding tax rates are: 15% on dividends (5% on dividends between related companies); 15% on periodic withdrawals from Canadian registered plans or the equivalent U.S. plans; 0% on CPP, QPP, OAS and U.S. Social Security, 0% on interest not effectively connected with a trade or business; 0% on capital gains other than gains on real property (withholding taxes on gains on real property are determined by the respective domestic rules of each country); 15% on pension income; and 25% on the gross rental income (most taxpayers can reduce this withholding amount to the net taxable income by filing non-resident tax returns).

The Canada/U.S. Tax Treaty can be used to reduce the level of taxes on residual Canadian income for Canadians living in the United States to levels well below that of traditional tax havens. For example, if you have a Canadian pension or large RRSP/RRIF (or any other Canadian registered plans for that matter), the treaty withholding rate for Canadians living in the United States for the periodic payments is only 15%, whereas a tax haven without the benefit of the treaty withholding rate would be 25%. The treaty rate for Canadian dividends collected in the United States is 15%, whereas the non-treaty rate is 25%, and the treaty rate for Canadian rental income is 25% versus 50% for the non-treaty rate. Consequently, if one has these sources of income, one can cut income taxes substantially without any great deal of planning by moving a few miles to the south across the 49th parallel. However, with planning, someone with a large RRSP cannot only reduce his or her taxes from, say, 46.4% in Ontario to the treaty rate of 15% for periodic withdrawals (25% on lump-sum withdrawals), which is a substantial reduction in taxes by itself, but also have the opportunity to recover the taxes withheld by the CRA through foreign tax credits. The IRS has a very generous foreign tax credit recovery set of rules which, when applied correctly to RRSP withdrawals, can realize an even lower effective net tax rate or in many cases a zero net tax rate on the withdrawal of the RRSP from the U.S. side of the border. Planning required to reduce the tax rate on the RRSPs or other Canadian registered plans to as close to a net of zero as possible requires planning of the skilled cross-border financial planner and is not a do-it-yourself project. The tax savings can be tremendous, particularly if the taxpayer is one of the fortunate Canadians who have a seven-figure RRSP.

SMALL BUSINESS OWNERS CAN REAP HUGE REWARDS

There is nothing in cross-border financial planning that offers owners of small, closely held businesses more income tax-saving potential than moving to the United States. Consequently, a good cross-border financial plan can save a business owner several thousand to several million dollars, depending on the size or the nature of the business. Most of these planning opportunities arise solely because a cross-border move is contemplated and possible. They would not be available to business owners if they were not in the process of moving across the border or at least willing and able to relocate to the United States for about five years or more. Unfortunately, the business owner's Trusted Advisors of many years sometimes become the major deterrent to making these savings happen. As a result, the business owner may be inadvertently misled or discouraged from taking advantage of great opportunities to realize a much higher net value after taxes on the sale of his or her business — a business that he or she worked hard on for many years of his or her career. To help advisors avoid being caught by these misconceptions, particularly the two more common ones such as dealing with Canadian exit tax and avoiding U.S. estate tax, I have discussed both of these misconceptions thoroughly in other sections of this chapter. In addition, because very few Canadian or U.S. advisors are aware of cross-border financial planning techniques, they tend to discourage the business owner from moving. Consequently, the business owner must look elsewhere for cross-border advice and bypass his or her long-time Trusted Advisors, finding a new team that will work in the owner's best interest to make the move successful.

Canadian small business owners are currently limited to a once-in-a-lifetime tax-free capital gains exemption of $750,000 if they meet the CRA requirements to qualify for this exemption on the shares of personal business. If the proper planning has been done, then this exemption may be effectively doubled or better by including a spouse and/or children as co-owners of the business(es). What happens if you have no exemption remaining, you need to sell the assets of your company rather than shares, your business does not qualify for the exemption or your capital gains exceed the $750,000 exemption limitations? A tax rate, which is currently nearly 25% in most provinces, is applied to the amount of capital gains not eligible for the exemption, and when assets are sold, often there is recapture of previous depreciation write-offs that attract an even higher rate of tax, close to 50%, depending on your province of residence.

So how much tax can you save by making the sale using cross-border planning techniques? A properly drafted cross-border financial plan using certain provisions included in the Canada/U.S. Tax Treaty can legally reduce this tax liability to just 15%. The 15% tax paid to the CRA may then be partially or completely recovered in the United States through foreign tax credits on income generated by a properly designed investment portfolio or other foreign tax credit planning methods. Between the Canada/U.S. Tax Treaty and the IRS's generous rules concerning foreign tax credits, this tax paid on the sale of the business can normally be fully recovered over about ten years. The net result is that a successful business owner can sell his or her business and effectively pay very low or even no net tax with a full recovery of all the tax credits. This low/no-net-tax scenario can apply if the proceeds from the business are $500,000, $5 million, $50 million or more!

These potentially enormous tax savings can be obtained based on sound legal precedents, but the rules are much too complex to even attempt to explain in a general guide such as this book. The key point is that business owners should be aware that major tax savings are still possible and available. To use a cross-border plan to their maximum advantage, business owners and/or their advisors need to seek out the services of a qualified cross-border financial planning specialist early in the process of retiring and/or selling their businesses. In fact, if the cross-border planning specialist is brought in early enough, the planning can actually facilitate the retirement process — or transition to family members or third parties — while simultaneously providing major tax advantages to the purchaser as well as the owner. Often, the business owner's current advisors just don't have the answers to assist the business owner and the family members to do what they want to do in the manner they want to do it.

A good example of such a situation is a case we dealt with in which two brothers equally owned a multi-million-dollar business in Calgary. The older of the two brothers wanted to retire to his winter home in Arizona, but a study the brothers had commissioned from one of four big accounting firms in Calgary (and for which they had paid thousands of dollars) told them there wasn't enough cash flow from the business for the younger brother to buy out the older one and pay all the taxes due. The accountants and company bankers also told them that if they borrowed the money to complete the sale, the debt load would likely sink the business. For more than two years these brothers sought someone to help them through this dilemma. They were referred to me by another client, and within a year the older brother was golfing in Arizona, free and easy; the younger brother owned the business, and because the tax burden on the sale between the brothers was reduced dramatically, there was more than enough cash flow to pay out the retired brother and allow the business to carry on unimpeded by debt. This transaction also successfully survived a CRA audit. Now, nearly ten years later, the younger brother has transitioned this very successful business to a third party and his son, using cross-border planning to save several million dollars in income taxes for himself and his family.

Another client from Vancouver who owned a $15 million business had long-time advisors who were unable to help him successfully retire and transfer the business to a son who was actively involved in the running of the business. With our assistance, he was able to utilize several cross-border planning techniques to transition the business to his son free from income tax on a net basis, and save himself and his family nearly $500,000 per year in income taxes.

Many other business owners have been helped in a similar manner. The key is that cross-border planning can provide business owners and their advisors with an additional set of options to help business owners keep their hard-earned business assets and achieve their retirement goals.

A Canadian business owner living in the United States who continues to own an active Canadian business or holding company needs to create new entities or reorganize his or her existing corporation to prevent potential double tax on corporate income. If the Canadian company is largely a passive one earning income from rentals and investments, it will likely be considered a foreign personal holding company or controlled foreign corporation by the IRS and be subject to a myriad of reporting and other requirements. For example, if the company's fiscal year is not December 31, calendar-year reporting of the corporate income must be provided, and tax must be paid as if the shareholder(s) personally owned the corporate assets. This tax must be paid whether or not income is actually distributed to the shareholders during that year. Considering all of the IRS reporting requirements on foreign holding companies, there is little or no advantage, and there are many disadvantages, including higher taxes, to maintaining a Canadian company of this type. We would normally recommend the company be unwound before or shortly after the business owner takes up residence in the United States or that it be converted to a B.C., Nova Scotia or Alberta unlimited liability company (BCULC, NSULC or ABULC). A BCULC/NSULC/ABULC is taxed like a partnership for U.S. purposes, so all income follows the owner, to be taxed only once he or she is in the United States, with full foreign tax credits for taxes paid in Canada by the corporation.

Canadian companies owned by U.S. residents or citizens who are reporting active business income are also subject to special rules on reporting income. The earnings and profits from an active Canadian company that are retained in the company will not flow through to the U.S. shareholder on an accrual basis, and, generally, the tax to this shareholder may be deferred until the earnings and profits are withdrawn. However, deferring tax on the accrued income in the corporation does not eliminate the double-tax problem on this income unless the corporation is converted to an unlimited liability company, as noted above. With an active Canadian company, and to a lesser extent a holding company, one very good method to reduce corporate income from the operation is to collect a reasonable management fee, which could zero out the corporate net income. The Canadian corporation would be able to deduct the management fee in full, and under the Canada/U.S. Tax Treaty, management fees are subject only to a maximum 15% withholding tax, as long as the management services were provided from the U.S. side of the border.

The 15% withholding tax is fully recoverable in the United States, through the foreign tax credits allowed by the IRS.

If the actual management work is done on the U.S. side of the border, the Canadian company can pay a reasonable management fee to the owner, or to a related U.S. company exempt from Canadian withholding. Care must be taken when paying these kinds of fees on a cross-border basis in order not to violate CRA transfer pricing rules. The net result is that income can be removed from the Canadian company without Canadian tax, and taxed at the lower U.S. rates. The final tax rate paid will be determined by the owner's marginal tax rate and his or her state of residence. If U.S. resident shareholders take Canadian salaries for services provided in Canada, the shareholders would have to file non-resident Canadian returns and pay tax on the Canadian salary. The Canada/U.S. Tax Treaty states that if the salary is under $10,000 annually, no Canadian return need be filed or Canadian tax paid.

MEDICAL ACCESS — DOUBLE DIP

There are a great many myths about Canadians finding effective and affordable medical insurance when they take up permanent residence in the United States. I have prepared many plans for Canadians, both winter visitors and permanent residents, for a good number of years, and have successfully discredited most of these myths. There are a variety of alternatives that ensure Canadians receive and have access to the best of both medical systems.

Canadians and Americans like to debate which country's medical system is the best. My nearly 30 years' experience in this area has taught me that you can never answer this question in advance unless you can determine when, where and what medical assistance you will need in advance. Of course, this is the million-dollar question, because if you knew when, where and what illness you were going to have, you could shop the medical purveyors in either country to get the best care, or work to prevent the problem altogether. However, this is equivalent to trying to plan your spending in retirement so that the last cheque you write on the day you die bounces. By combining the best benefits from both countries and planning it so you can double dip and easily access either the Canadian or the U.S. medical systems, you can obtain the best protection with maximum flexibility. Generally speaking, Canadians leaving Canada lose their provincial health care plan coverage within 30 to 60 days, depending on the province. However, to reinstate this coverage, if one deems it necessary, all one needs to do is retake up residency in the province and 90 days later (returning residents to Alberta or Prince Edward Island have no waiting period to become eligible once again), one is back on the provincial health care plan. Consequently, for Canadians using the United States as a tax haven, the medical care options are greatly improved as these Canadians have access to two of the best medical systems in the world when they need it. With the protection afforded by the Canada/U.S. Tax Treaty under the tiebreaker rules noted above, there is little chance of a taxpayer's tax status being jeopardized because of necessary extended medical treatment administered in either Canada or the United States. If the taxpayer goes to a tax haven offshore, spending time in either Canada or the United States for medical treatment could subject him or her to full resident tax rates in the country in which he or she received the treatment. In addition to the tax concerns of getting medical treatment, if one is not a citizen of the country in which one is getting the treatment, one can also have substantial immigration problems if one overstays one's visitor visa status because of the length of treatment. If the treatment is in Canada, without the treaty protection from the Canada/U.S. Tax Treaty, the CRA may attempt to tax the individual as if he or she never left Canada, and collect taxes, interest and penalties for all income earned since he or she exited the country to go to the tax haven.

Canadians over the age of 65 who have resided in the United States legally for at least five years, or who are U.S. citizens, are eligible for complete U.S. Medicare regardless of any pre-existing conditions. The cost is approximately US$600 per month each, or US$100 per month if the individual or his or her spouse has contributed at least the minimum amount to U.S. Social Security programs on U.S. employment earnings. There are also numerous private insurance carriers that provide Medicare supplements to fill any gaps in U.S. Medicare coverage. If the individual does not qualify or is waiting to qualify for U.S. Medicare and is over the age of 65, there is limited but quite adequate choice of coverage available from among some private insurance carriers, most of which originate outside the United States. If the individual taking up residence in the United States has a pre-existing condition that prevents him or her from getting private medical insurance, there are numerous U.S. states that have programs that will cover these people adequately until they can get on U.S. Medicare.

Those under the age of 65 have a wide variety of health insurance options. Health insurance works much like car insurance in the United States. If one wants a zero deductible, with one's auto insurance company paying for the slightest scratch, one will pay a substantially higher premium than someone with a $1,000 deductible. With health insurance in the United States, individuals can choose their coverage and their deductible. For example, a healthy person aged 60 can get a health insurance policy with a $2,500 deductible and a $2-million coverage limit from an A.M. Best A-rated company for less than $350 per month, depending on the state of residence.

FAMILIAR LIFESTYLE

Most of what I discuss in this section is very obvious and simplistic. However, advisors should not underestimate the fact that simple lifestyle issues are important to clients of all income levels when they are choosing where they are going to call home for likely the rest of their lives.

The first advantage the United States has over a number of tax havens is that English is the primary language. For Canadians going to the United States as a tax haven, other than dropping a few "ehs" and adding a few more "uhs", there is no adjustment period or language difficulty understanding and dealing with the local population.

Purchasing or building a dream home in the U.S. Sunbelt is very much like building or purchasing a home in Canada so that there is an effective transfer of experience and knowledge to make this less stressful to the clients' lives. Building materials, construction techniques and construction workers would all be much more familiar in the United States than in an offshore island or country. In fact, most wealthy Canadians either currently or at some point in their lives have purchased or constructed U.S. real estate before considering the United States as their tax haven. Similarly, new furniture, effects and appliances are going to be very similar, if not identical, to what clients have been familiar with all their lives. One pleasant surprise to Canadians using the United States as their tax haven of choice is that the purchase and furnishing of the new residence can be actually much cheaper than an equivalent property in Canada; the same cannot be said for most offshore jurisdictions.

It goes without saying that Americans drive on the same side of the road as Canadians in vehicles that are virtually identical in all respects. Consequently, Canadians can simply import their vehicles to the United States when they take up residency there without any concern other than a bit of government paperwork. This would be a near impossibility if the taxpayer was going to an offshore tax haven, and the vehicle he or she owns would have to be sold, often at a loss, and then new vehicles that may even have steering wheels on the opposite side, with different manufacturers and options, would have to be purchased at outrageous prices in an offshore tax haven. Purchases of vehicles in the United States are, in the majority of cases, less expensive and without GST.

Medical facilities, procedures and professional practitioners are very similar in both Canada and the United States. Many Canadian and American professional doctors and nurses are actually trained in the same facilities. Consequently, there is little adjustment clients have to make to receiving and understanding their medical treatments and options. My experience with clients who have gone offshore have had considerable difficulty in getting the medical treatment and access to familiar facilities and procedures, and in most cases, end up coming back to Canada or the United States, taking the risk of jeopardizing their tax haven status as noted in the previous section of this chapter.

In summary, there are far fewer lifestyle adjustments with far fewer unpleasant surprises for Canadians moving to the U.S. Sunbelt than for Canadians choosing to go to a traditional tax haven island. There are substantial savings in costs for Canadians purchasing homes and vehicles using the United States versus the traditional tax haven; this is one of many hidden costs which I define as the hidden taxes for Canadians not using the United States as their primary tax haven.

NUMEROUS IMMIGRATION OPTIONS

To immigrate to the traditional island tax haven, there is normally a financial requirement such as purchasing a home of a certain dollar value or investing a minimum sum in one of the local banks, along with spending a minimum period of time there to get legal status as a resident.

There are normally two legal ways to immigrate to the United States. The first is through a business or a professional relationship. The second is through the sponsorship of a close family member. Within these two broad family and business categories there are numerous options available to Canadians. The number of combinations and permutations as a result of all these options can get very confusing and seem quite complex. In this section I will outline only a few of the family and business immigration options just to illustrate the ease with which U.S. immigration can be obtained by those who like to use the United States as their tax haven rather than go offshore.

The North American Free Trade Agreement (NAFTA), which came into existence in the early 1990s, provides a variety of visas for a Canadian citizen to work or live in the United States from a few days to a few months, or possibly a few years. However, these visas are non-immigrant visas, which must be renewed periodically, and some can be renewed only a certain number of times, all depending on the type of visa obtained. None of these visas can be used to obtain U.S. citizenship; therefore, anyone attempting to live permanently in the United States for long-term tax benefits should use these visas only as a temporary bridge to obtaining Legal Permanent Status (LPR) or so-called "green card status". Green card status is the Holy Grail for Canadians wishing to live in the United States permanently and become dual citizens of Canada and the United States. Once a green card is obtained, a Canadian is eligible for U.S. citizenship after five years (three years if the green card was obtained through marriage to a U.S. citizen). Those who have recently retired or are about to retire should consider keeping open any business or professional relationships long enough to assist them in getting permanent immigration status. For those who are retired, investing in a small U.S. business with a full-time manager or just a U.S. Citizenship and Immigration Services (USCIS) specially authorized investment can be a suitable means of obtaining a visa or legal permanent resident/green card that allows one to legally live in the United States year-round. For those who have sold their businesses and have no desire to be involved in business directly again, there is one great new green card opportunity that makes it relatively easy for wealthy Canadians to obtain permanent U.S. status.

This is sometimes referred to as the "gold card". This permanent resident status option is technically referred to as the EB-5 Immigrant Investor program. It is similar to the program Canada has used for years to attract foreign business entrepreneurs. In 2002, USCIS introduced an EB-5 Regional Center program, which is ideal for the retiree or inactive investor who wishes to immigrate to the United States. This EB-5 program (discussed in more detail below) provides for a Conditional Lawful Permanent Residence (in other words, a conditional green card) for two years until all the requirements listed below are met; then full green card or LPR status is granted.

The investment amounts for these EB-5 Regional Center programs require a $500,000 amount invested in the targeted areas of high unemployment or areas of desired economic expansion as preapproved by the Regional Center program. The regional program the immigrant investor subscribes to must prove, as a result of the investment, at least a "ten indirect job creation". Consequently, the investor can qualify by presenting evidence that ten jobs will be created throughout the Regional Center economy. This is done for the investor and is a relatively easy hurdle to face for the experienced Regional Center program sponsor. The EB-5 management requirement is minimal in that the investor can be a limited partner and still qualify, making this program much more acceptable for those who are not interested in day-to-day management or actively running a business. The investor is not required to live where the investment is made; he or she can, for example, live in Florida and invest in Washington State.

There are generally several Regional Center programs for the investor to choose from. Thus, the only major concern an investor has is choosing the right investment. The program managers do the rest, and in approximately ten months the investor has his or her conditional two-year green card. At the end of the two years, the green card becomes permanent, with full rights of permanent residency and a path to U.S. citizenship. The investment can be sold at any time after the permanent green card has been obtained; in fact, most of these investments self-liquidate in five to seven years after inception. Choosing the right investment cannot be overemphasized, as the program should give investors a fair return on their investment, and the green card should be considered a secondary benefit or just the icing on the cake. Under mandate by Congress, USCIS gives Regional Center EB-5 petitions priority, which, among other benefits, often results in a quicker path to approval.

The procedure for obtaining an EB-5 investor green card is relatively straightforward. The investor must produce five years of tax returns to substantiate the legal source of investment funds. The source of the funds can also be in the form of a loan or gift from a friend or relative. The investor must also present evidence that traces the capital, through bank transfers and other documentation, from the investor directly to the enterprise being invested in.

If the investor is already in the United States, he or she then applies for a green card through USCIS. Customarily no interview is required, and approval takes approximately ten months. If the investor still lives in Canada, an application for the green card is generally made at a U.S. consulate; however, for consular processing purposes, an interview is necessary, which for Canadians means a trip to Montreal. Approval of the green card in this case takes on average about 10 or 11 months, approximately the same as through USCIS.

The key U.S. family sponsorship programs for green cards involve having U.S. citizen parents, children, siblings or spouses. In some cases, even having U.S. citizen grandparents can be of help. Depending on the relationship to the green card applicant, it can take from a few months to several years to get a green card through a family member sponsorship.

This section of the chapter has offered a general discussion of American immigration rules and policies. Individual factors can greatly influence the course of any immigration undertaking. Immigration can be a complex and lengthy procedure under current law and should not be attempted without the services of a good U.S. immigration attorney in court along with a cross-border financial planning specialist. This co-ordination of the financial planning with immigration planning is critical as many immigration attorneys have been known to ignore tax issues entirely and create incredible tax problems for their clients.

TAX-FREE ROLLOVERS ON INVESTMENT REAL ESTATE

One of the greatest deterrents for Canadians owning or wishing to invest in real estate, either as their living and their sole business or just as a pure investment strategy to supplement their investment portfolio, is the tax when the time comes to sell. If they have a buyer and the time is right, capital gains tax and recapture taxes, depending on the province, can take from just under a quarter to just under half of their gains. Not only does this create cash flow problems for the investor but if they wish to reinvest the net proceeds into a new project or some other investment they have substantially less cash available for new investment.

Another reason why the United States can be an excellent tax haven for Canadians wishing to take advantage of real estate investments is the IRS section 1031 exchange program. The 1031 exchange allows any real estate investor to take all of the gains from one real estate investment (or other business property) and roll the gain without tax into a new or series of real estate projects that need to be identified within a reasonable period of time after the sale of the current property. In short, this means that a real estate investor has a use of his or her money that would otherwise have gone in taxes to purchase more investment real estate. This allows the investor to make even further gains on money that he or she would never have had available for his or her own use. These gains can be deferred for an entire lifetime, and then at death, the IRS allows a free tax holiday by giving a step up on the cost basis on all of the property gains so any beneficiaries can sell all of the property owned by the decedent without capital gains or recapture tax.

Even though real estate investors living in traditional tax havens have no income tax to pay in the country of residence, they virtually always have to pay tax to the country in which the real estate is located. Consequently, Canadians living in the United States who wish to invest in real estate and use the 1031 exchange program to its fullest (although the 1031 exchange is available to non-resident investors, it is very difficult for them to get the same advantage as a U.S. resident) can get substantially better tax results on their U.S. real estate investments than persons living in Canada or outside the United States in one of the island tax havens. Zero % income tax on a lifetime of U.S. real estate gains, which could be in the millions of dollars, is very difficult for any Canadian to achieve when comparing the United States to the traditional tax haven countries.

DEALING WITH THE CANADIAN DEPARTURE TAX

It would be nice to be able to say that the Canadian departure tax (also known as the exit tax) is much ado about nothing, but most Canadians give it a great deal of thought when considering moving to or retiring to any tax haven, including the U.S. Sunbelt. I believe that the departure tax does get more attention than it deserves and that many Canadian advisors incorrectly throw it up as a barrier or reason for their clients not to consider exiting when they otherwise wish to pursue moving from Canada to a tax haven. Dealing with the departure tax is difficult, and the reason why I say advisors may incorrectly throw it up as a barrier for their clients wishing to explore moving as a tax reduction strategy lies in the very essence of this chapter. When a Trusted Advisor understands all of the issues in dealing with a cross-border move with his or her clients, the Trusted Advisor will have the understanding that there are specialists available to provide the expertise to assist him or her in achieving the goals of his or her clients in an accurate and expedited manner.

As almost all Canadian advisors understand, the departure tax is the tax that the CRA levies on a taxpayer's capital assets when he or she becomes a non-resident of Canada. First of all it should be mentioned that this exit tax or deemed disposition tax on leaving the country is not an additional or a punitive tax; it is simply accelerating the time from when the assets would normally be sold to the exit date. The CRA requires that a taxpayer who is exiting Canada has to go through a deemed disposition or a deemed sale of certain assets on the date of departure. For tax purposes, under the CRA rules, a deemed sale is always taxed as an actual sale of assets. Canada taxes residents on their world income only while they are actually living within its borders. Consequently, all one has to do is to depart Canada and no longer be subject to Canadian tax rules. Canada's answer to this simplistic method of avoiding Canadian tax is to collect all the taxes due on any capital gains that have not yet been taxed prior to the taxpayer's departure, hence the departure tax. The best way to understand the departure tax better is to understand what is not subject to the tax, since there are many myths and misunderstandings as to what is included in this tax. The following is a list of assets that are *not* subject to any departure tax when taxpayers move from Canada:

1. Canadian real estate or resource properties;
2. Canadian business capital property (including inventory) if the business is carried on through a permanent establishment in Canada;
3. pensions, all registered plans including RRSPs, registered retirement income funds, locked-in retirement accounts, retirement compensation arrangements and deferred profit-sharing plans;
4. employee stock options subject to tax in Canada;
5. interest in life insurance policies or annuities in Canada;
6. rights to certain benefits under employee profit-sharing plans, employee benefit plans, employee trusts, retirement allowances and salary deferral arrangements; and
7. interests in certain trusts in which the trustee and the trust assets will remain in Canada.

Now that we've looked at what is not subject to tax, it is a little bit easier to understand what is subject to the departure tax. This is the list of what is subject to departure tax:

1. all stocks (including closely held Canadian-controlled private corporations), bonds, mutual funds, exchange traded funds, limited or general partnership interests and other similar securities that are not inside registered plans noted in (3) above;
2. U.S. real estate and other foreign real estate;
3. certain rights or interests in foreign trusts; and
4. personal property that has appreciated in value, such as artwork or antiques.

If you compare the two lists above as to what is and what isn't subject to departure tax, you can easily surmise that a large number of Canadians would not be subject to any departure tax at all. Those Canadians who may be subject to departure tax have several options to mitigate, defer or eliminate this tax altogether.

When Canadian residents move to the United States, the CRA requires that they file exit tax returns for the year of their departure. This exit return is a regular T1 form filed by the usual April 30 deadline following the year of departure, with the exit date clearly indicated on the first page of the T1, and all the appropriate schedules, forms and disclosures completed as required. The important forms to be filed with an exit T1 are Form T1161, List of Properties by an Emigrant of Canada, and Form T1243, Deemed Disposition Property by an Emigrant of Canada, which lists and calculates the net capital gains on those owned items subject to the exit tax. Each property deemed to be disposed of is deemed to have been reacquired by the individual at the time of emigration at a cost equal to the proceeds of the disposition of the property. Any capital gains tax due may be paid with the return, or deferred using the procedures noted in the next paragraph.

To elect to defer this exit tax, the exiting taxpayer must complete and file Form T1244 with his or her exit tax return. He or she is required to post suitable security with the CRA equal to the tax due. The tax due need not be paid until the assets subject to the deemed disposition tax are actually sold. It is important to realize that since the CRA charges no interest on the tax due, by electing to defer, the taxpayer is in exactly the same situation as if he or she stayed in Canada, holding the same securities or properties. Given this, why are so many emigrants overly concerned about leaving Canada and paying an exit tax? Unfortunately, all too often, concern with the exit tax is a result of not knowing the basic rules or of relying on advisors who are not able to or don't want to explain the rules to the taxpayer. Many times during my cross-border planning career, I have heard individuals say to me, "My accountant, who has been my advisor for too many years to mention, told me I can't leave Canada because I would have way too much departure tax to pay." If you are or have been one of these advisors, in the clients' best interests, now might be the time to consider the United States as a potential tax haven for these clients.

Using the election to defer taxes is just a worst-case scenario; there are many cross-border options to legitimately minimize or eliminate any exit tax that may be due. These options include, but are not limited to, the following:

- Most investment portfolios at any given time have some securities in a gain position and some in a loss position. On exit, the taxpayer may offset the losses against gains and therefore be subject to tax only if there is any net gain on the portfolio.
- Use the Canada/U.S. Tax Treaty to eliminate the tax entirely on a net basis by turning the so-called exit tax into foreign tax credits

that can be used to reduce U.S. income taxes on a dollar-for-dollar basis once the taxpayer has taken up residency in the United States. This is a powerful but complex option that is available when Canadians move to the United States with treaty protection, but that is not available if they go offshore to a tax haven island.

- Use the small-business capital gains exemption (for husband and wife, this could mean up to $1.5 million of tax-free capital gains, and with good planning, an additional $750,000 for each child).
- Utilize capital losses carried forward from previous investment losses or failed investments.
- If a taxpayer's spouse is not emigrating from Canada with him or her, then the emigrating spouse should transfer appreciated assets to the Canadian resident spouse on a tax-free basis, and he or she, as the exiting taxpayer, will have no exit tax when he or she departs Canada. The Canada/U.S. Tax Treaty tiebreaker rules, as you can see from the treaty section noted earlier in this chapter, apply separately to each spouse. Although having one spouse resident in one country and the other in the United States is technically achievable under the treaty, it is generally not recommended as a long-term strategy because it is difficult to achieve as there are many "t"s to cross and "i"s to dot on a continuing basis. However, for a short-term strategy, when, for example, one spouse can move to the U.S. tax haven with a large income-producing investment portfolio while the other stays in Canada to clean up other tax issues or sell a business, this can be quite tax-effective. This kind of strategy would never be available to Canadians choosing a traditional tax haven without treaty protection, since having a spouse remaining in Canada is a significant tie under the CRA domestic rules.
- If the exiting taxpayer has any assets that are not deemed to be disposed of when he or she crosses the border, and the assets have a net loss built into them — such as a terrible real estate investment — the taxpayer may elect to go through a deemed disposition of this property on his or her exit and use the loss to offset other capital gains that are subject to the exit tax.

If the taxpayer did not sell or does not wish to sell his or her Canadian principal residence before departing Canada, he or she needs to be aware of some special rules under the Canada/U.S. Tax Treaty that can help him or her reduce future capital gains tax on the sale of his or her Canadian home while he or she is a U.S. resident. The treaty helps the taxpayer around this problem by making it appear, for tax purposes, that he or she purchased the Canadian home at its fair market value the day he or she entered the United States, provided he or she file the appropriate treaty election with his or her U.S. tax return for that tax year. As a result, he or she is responsible to the IRS for gains on this property only from the date that he or she became a resident. Note that this step up in basis for the taxpayer's principal residence applies only to non-U.S. citizens or non-green card holders. Other capital property (thanks to changes to the Canada/U.S. Tax Treaty in September 2000) that is subject to the deemed disposition on exit from Canada may also get a new cost basis for U.S. tax purposes equal to the fair market value of the property on the exit date. To receive the special tax treatment, the individual must file a treaty election Form 8833 with the U.S. tax return for the year of departure from Canada. Upon exit from Canada, taxpayers who have not elected for the deemed disposition of their principal residence on their exit tax return may convert it to rental property or transfer it to a specially designed cross-border trust. This will step up to the Canadian cost basis on the ultimate sale of the property to further reduce possible capital gains taxes in Canada, as they would have received the tax-free principal residence exemption had the residence been sold before their departure from Canada. It is highly recommended that Canadians who keep their principal residences when they move to the United States get a fair market appraisal just before leaving Canada and keep it for future tax reference when making the treaty or other elections.

ELIMINATING THE U.S. ESTATE TAXES

Another important issue for wealthy Canadians looking to go offshore so that they can escape Canadian taxes is the potential estate or inheritance taxes in the jurisdiction which they are considering. The United States actually does have an estate tax, and this fact is often misunderstood by the Canadian advisor or the taxpayer in the decision-making process of whether to move to the United States. Consequently, this is another major reason why the United States is often overlooked as a potential tax haven for high net-worth Canadians. However, with the use of a good cross-border estate planning specialist prior to the exit date from Canada, the U.S. estate tax, for the most part, can be entirely eliminated. Not only can the U.S. estate tax be avoided with good cross-border planning, but so too can the Canadian deemed disposition tax at death also be greatly reduced or eliminated if the taxpayer chooses to still hold Canadian real estate or other assets once he or she has exited Canada.

Necessity is often the mother of invention. Since there is a greater need for comprehensive estate planning in the United States, a number of very good and proven techniques have been developed to help make management of a U.S. taxpayer's estate easier while the taxpayer is alive, and then provide for a smooth transition to his or her heirs. Many of these techniques will work equally well for Canadians who become residents of the United States, and can be used to cover assets remaining in Canada.

When a taxpayer is moving or contemplating a move to the United States, cross-border estate planning needs to be a top priority, as there are many complex issues that could lead to unnecessary estate settlement costs and death taxes if these planning needs are not addressed before the taxpayer takes up residency in the United States.

Normally, the first matter of business in cross-border estate planning is doing a comparison of a client's estate costs and taxes in Canada, and then in the United States, to see if there is any advantage in either country. It is not very often in cross-border estate planning that I can state a general rule that applies in almost every case, but I can say that couples with estates of less than US$7 million, which is 99.5% of the general population, have an unquestionable death tax advantage as residents of the United States under current rules. Since there are spousal trusts in Canada and qualified domestic-marital deduction trusts in the United States to permit the transfer of assets tax-free between spouses, it is generally best to concentrate on estate tax and settlement costs at the death of the second spouse, to measure the full impact of these costs and make a proper Canadian-U.S. comparison. When comparing U.S. and Canadian taxes, many Canadian accountants, financial planners and attorneys are quick to pontificate that Canada does not have an estate tax. I was raised on the Canadian prairies, and we had a simple saying: "If it looks like a duck, walks like a duck, quacks like a duck — it is most likely a duck." Just because the CRA does not call the tax at death an "estate tax", it doesn't mean that most Canadians won't face a much higher estate tax in Canada than U.S. residents who own similar estates. If there are no other tax or other personal objectives a client is attempting to achieve, eliminating the Canadian deemed disposition tax at death could be reason enough to look at moving to the United States or other tax havens. The IRS does not try to disguise its estate tax, and because of the high exemptions allowed, less than 1% of all U.S. residents are subject to an estate tax.

A Canadian couple with an estate of $7 million would likely have a very large RRSP or other registered plan and possibly highly appreciated investments or businesses which in total could produce Canadian deemed disposition taxes or, in other words, estate taxes at the time of death well in excess of $1 million. If this couple took up residence in the United States and had a similar asset mix at the time of death, the couple would have absolutely no U.S. estate taxes due, since the size of the couple's estate would be less than the couple's combined total of US$7 million in U.S. estate tax exemptions. The husband and wife could deal with their RRSPs, as noted earlier in this chapter, to get them out of Canada at no or very low income taxes on a net basis. In addition, the beneficiaries of the estate from the U.S. residents would receive a free step up in basis on any appreciated assets left in the estate so that they could be sold without capital gains taxes.

For estates of more than US$7 million per couple, or US$3.5 million for individuals, other estate-planning techniques can be used to deal economically with almost any size of an estate or estate tax liability. A primary recommended technique for Canadians coming to the United States with an estate exceeding their U.S. estate tax exemptions is to set up a trust or series of trusts prior to becoming subject to the U.S. estate tax rules. Not only can these trusts achieve all of their personal goals but at the same time they can provide income or use of assets from the trust for family members for the balance of the trust settlors' lives and also those of their beneficiaries. A side benefit of these Dynasty Trusts being drafted properly is that they provide creditor protection of the family assets throughout many generations.

Wealthy Canadians who become U.S. residents and who are concerned about leaving a larger estate for their beneficiaries may use some or all income tax savings from their reduced tax burden by moving to the United States to purchase life insurance inside specially designed trusts. This type of planning can provide a nice tax-free highly liquid legacy for the family beneficiaries.

It should be noted that the U.S. estate taxes, under current rules, are set to be eliminated in the year 2010 and then come back again in 2011 with lower personal exemptions than currently available. The main reason for this situation is the fact that U.S. President George W. Bush was never able to get enough votes in the U.S. Senate to make his election promise of eliminating the U.S. estate taxes permanent. Consequently, Congress is undergoing complex negotiations to, rather than eliminate the tax, just freeze personal exemptions at the current $3.5 million per person level. We will have to wait, probably well into 2009, before we know what the U.S. Congress will settle on for estate tax exemptions beyond 2010.

The complexity of these issues underscores the necessity of consulting with a cross-border financial planning specialist to ensure clients maximize the opportunities and minimize the pitfalls of cross-border estate planning.

THE HIDDEN TAX OF TAX HAVENS

When Canadians and their advisors look at and discuss tax havens, the focus is quite logically on the issue of tax reduction. This focus and/or assumption that the cost of doing business is the same in the tax haven as it is in other countries such as the United States often leads to some unpleasant surprises. These unpleasant surprises come in a myriad of hidden costs from your typical island tax haven, such as the cost of building or buying a home or an automobile, which I have already talked about earlier in this chapter. However, these additional costs pale in comparison to what I see as the major cost of wealthy Canadians moving to an offshore tax haven island rather than considering the United States.

The major cost or "a hidden tax" of the traditional island tax haven is by far the cost of managing one's financial affairs. These costs manifest themselves in numerous ways, such as investment management fees, security trading costs, legal costs, accounting fees, wealth management fees, trustee fees and custodial fees, to name a few, but not all of these incredible costs that traditional tax havens depend on are even financially viable.

I will focus on just a couple of these fees that every investor must deal with and that I can give concrete examples of, backed up by public data that is readily available to any prudent investor who chooses to seek these fees out. The fees I will spend some time on are investment management and trading costs of an investment strategy primarily in the public markets. In other words, these are the costs of simply maintaining a large investment portfolio that was likely created by some family-liquidating event like selling a very successful business or possibly an inheritance, which was likely the wealth that triggered the Canadian advisor's recommendations to the clients to consider going offshore.

An actively managed offshore mutual fund or portfolio of investments of virtually any combination and type of stocks and bonds typically averages management fees of 2.5%, called management expense ratios (MER) and will also have trading costs and other administrative costs of at least an additional 1% for a total of about 3.5% per year. These annual costs can easily exceed this 3.5%, depending on the type of actively managed funds and the more conservative funds holding bonds can be significantly less than this amount. What do these costs mean? Most people, clients and non-investment trained advisors alike, underestimate the cost or the drag of such high fees on an investment portfolio. For example, a $10 million portfolio of average cost offshore mutual funds would pay $350,000 a year in management and trading costs. If the portfolio was earning a relatively good rate of return of, say, 7%, then

50% of the total portfolio return would be eaten up in fees, leaving a net return after cost of only $350,000 per year. Does this 50% skimming off the top of one's return not suspiciously look like an income tax, particularly for Canadians who have been used to paying close to 50% of their income to taxes? Why should one consider this portfolio expense a hidden tax when comparing a traditional tax haven island to the United States which does have a tax on investments?

Because the United States has one of the most highly developed and competitive financial markets in the world, the competition keeps the cost of investing down significantly. We at KCA typically recommend mutual funds or exchange traded funds that have expense ratios of 0.1% to 0.5%, with no commissions and no loads to purchase or redeem them. The average American fund has MERs of around 1.5%. Comparing the numbers on the $10 million portfolio noted above earning 7%, we can see that a 0.5% annual management expense leaves $650,000 after cost for a net investment return. However, because the United States has an income tax to get to the net spendable return for the investor, this tax must be taken into consideration. The typical tax rate on an investment portfolio would be less than 20%, or $130,000 in this portfolio example, leaving a net after-cost and after-tax return of $520,000. This is $170,000 or approximately 50% better after-tax and after-cost return than the portfolio in the typical island tax haven. This is the "hidden tax" of the tax havens, and the sad thing is that this major expense is year after year an ongoing hidden tax, and most people using the tax havens do not even realize they would be better off possibly living in the United States and paying a little bit of a tax but keeping more of their investment return. The United States also has a substantial number of investment options like tax-free bonds and tax-deferred annuities, all of which can be used to eliminate or reduce income taxes on investments to bring in the average tax rate well below the 20% used in this example.

A wealthy Canadian family whose name nearly every one in Canada would recognize, and who had gone offshore but for all the reasons I have already noted in this chapter, decided to move to the United States. The family had one of the major Canadian banks in one of the offshore traditional tax haven islands as its investment manager and trustee. When I initially asked the members of the family what it was costing them for this Canadian bank to look after their portfolios, they said it was around 1.5% per year. However, on further examination, with all the other hidden fees, I noted that the annual cost was in excess of 3%. The disclosure requirements in the tax havens with respect to security transactions are very limited at best, particularly when compared with those in the United States. This allows investment managers to take fees and self-deal with impunity without any regulations forcing them to disclose or act in a fiduciary capacity for the client. These offshore tax haven facilitators certainly do take advantage of their situation and the tax motivation of the Canadians fleeing Canada to charge much higher fees and in a manner that they would never get away with in the United States. In the United States, the regulations by the Securities and Exchange Commission force all independent financial advisors not only to charge reasonable fees but also disclose all fees and all conflicts of interest to all of their clients all of the time, a far superior standard of consumer protection than the tax havens have ever come close to. The brokerage firms and banks that were largely responsible for the subprime mortgage financial crisis of 2008, unfortunately, were subject to different regulation which did not force them to disclose conflicts of interest adequately or act in a fiduciary capacity to their clients.

Another hidden cost which manifests in tax havens is the result of a simple fact that there are no stocks, bonds or other investment vehicles directly resident in the tax haven. In other words, when one has an investment portfolio, one needs to invest it somewhere, and, invariably, those investments are not located in the tax haven. Because those investments are from other countries that actually do have an investment and a tax system, the tax haven resident is usually stuck with non-resident withholding taxes on their investments. These withholding taxes are significantly higher for investors living in tax havens than for investors residing in a country that has a treaty with the country in which the investments are located or created. For example, someone living in a tax haven would pay a non-resident withholding tax of 30% on dividends paid by Coca-Cola or any other U.S. company, whereas if he or she were resident in a country that has a treaty with the United States, the withholding rate would be 15% or less. In a large well-diversified portfolio, these withholding taxes on stocks and bonds from the various countries around the world can add up to a very significant ongoing cost.

In summary, although there are many ways that investment portfolios can be managed, the bottom line is that costs for someone in the traditional tax havens are significantly higher than for someone moving to the United States and paying the taxes that the IRS levies that he or she gets no net benefit and, more often than not, a significant reduction in net after-tax income from the tax haven versus the United States.

CONCLUSION

I hope this chapter has enlightened most advisors such that when they talk about tax havens with their clients, they will at least include the United States as one of their potential choices. By using this chapter as a guide, they will be able to discuss intelligently why the United States could actually achieve the tax results the client is seeking without the lifestyle disruption and the hidden taxes of the traditional offshore tax havens. The one thing that this chapter is not designed to do, though, is instruct the advisor how to assist a client with a move to the United States without a knowledgeable and experienced cross-border planning specialist.

CHAPTER 61

OFFSHORE INVESTING MAY BE MORE A PANDORA'S BOX THAN THE PANACEA

Peter J. Merrick

Overview

This chapter describes the follies that might be associated with offshore investing that advisors should keep in mind when they are speaking about the topic of offshore investing with their clients. It asks the question: "Are there other options available to offshore investing that can produce the same or better results by staying in Canada"?

Learning Objectives

By the end of this chapter, you should be able to:

- understand that prior to considering any form of offshore structures, one should always first look at structuring within Canada. Domestic structures may be appropriate in terms of ease of establishment and cost.

We have often heard that the best way for the wealthy in this country to reduce their tax bill and protect their assets from creditors is for them to move their money offshore. This was popularized in Alex Doulis's 1994 best selling Canadian business book called *Take Your Money and Run!* (Toronto: Uphill Pub., 1994). However, the offshore option often has inherent assumptions within it which are left unquestioned by the client and their Trusted Advisors. In this chapter I would like to share a personal story that makes the case for questioning underlying assumptions as it relates to the offshore abyss, and having the wisdom to know when to bring in other experts to help.

Several years ago, early on in my career, my best client called to tell me that he had just been pitched by one of the in-house Chartered Accountants at a large bank-owned brokerage firm on a structure that would move the account he held with me and the professional advice he received from his public accountant all offshore. He was seriously considering this option because he was presented with the possibility of saving on taxes and protecting his assets from creditors. As I got off the phone with my client, I knew that there was a very real possibility that I would lose my influence with him or lose the client altogether or, worse, both! Either way, the prospect did not seem very appealing to me.

The next morning I had a moment of pure synchronicity. As I was working out on the cross-trainer at the Cambridge Club in Toronto, I noticed that Bob was working out on the next machine. Bob was a very successful tax lawyer with over 30 years' experience under his belt. I had talked to Bob several times and had read his book on tax, cross-border and benefit planning for the very successful business owner. At that moment I decided to take the opportunity to ask him about the benefits of offshore investing and the downside of it if there were any. I did this, hoping for the slim chance that Bob would tell me something of true value that I could bring back to my client to save the account and restore my relationship as the client's Trusted Advisor.

I shared with Bob what had transpired the day before and I asked him about offshore investing. In our conversation Bob told me the following follies of offshore investing that most people are unaware of until it is way too late:

- When taking money offshore legally, you, as an individual, most often receive no tax relief; the money must be removed after tax.
- If you take money offshore legally and compliantly, you would have to give up ownership of your money for a moment in time, meaning you would have to trust someone else with all your hard-earned money to be the settlor of your account.
- For the money to grow tax-free offshore, the money would have to stay out of the country. Your money could be brought back to this country, but it would be very difficult and costly, generally speaking.
- To go offshore in most situations you would have to pay large set-up fees and annual fees to maintain whatever structure you settle on.
- There is no compliant offshore structure that allows you to invest pre-tax dollars offshore.

As Bob finished explaining the pros and cons of offshore investing, he then smiled. He began describing an alternative solution that was superior to moving money offshore in a number of ways. He believed that the implementation of this solution should be the alternative option presented to all financially successful individuals considering offshore investing. Bob then shared that the implementation of this solution would result in the following outcomes:

- Your money would stay in Canada, where you can see it, touch it, feel it and smell it.
- Corporate deposits can be structured to be deductable.
- All personal deposits can be structured to be deductable over time.
- Large annual deductions are provided each year against income for the rest of your life or sooner.
- Money would be invested on a deductable basis, the money growing tax free. You, as an individual, retire tax free and die tax free, all the while having your savings protected from your creditors.
- The corporation or personal deduction creates a cash-on-cash return every year, year in and year out, in a plan where tax will never be paid as you use the funds for either retirement or investing.

As I was nearing the end of my workout, I knew that I had just been listening to the solution I could present to my client that would save our relationship and put an end to his account moving into the offshore structure that was pitched to him by the in-house Chartered Accountant at one of the large bank-owned brokerage firms.

I asked Bob if he could tell me more about the solution. Bob said that he had spent over 30 years understanding this solution as it met all the tax and regulatory compliance requirements. He further told me that he had a policy where I would first have to engage his firm before he could go into more detail, especially as to how this solution would specifically relate and apply to my client's situation. Bob said, "All I have to sell is my time, experience, knowledge and my wisdom!"

I knew that Bob's billing rate was over $1,100 per hour, much higher than I thought I could afford at the time. As Bob got off his machine and headed towards the shower, he turned to me and said these words, which I will never forget:

> *"I like you Peter, so I will tell you this: for the solution, start by learning what is in section 148 of the Income Tax Act."*

I did not take Bob up on his offer to engage him on this particular client situation to learn how to implement the solution for this client. What resulted is something I am not proud of admitting: my best client took the advice of the in-house Chartered Accountant at one of the large bank-owned brokerage firms and moved his money offshore. He said goodbye to me, and I said goodbye to my largest account at the time.

It's an experience that I am glad to have learned from, and I promised myself that I would never repeat it. I have learned that if it happens once, it's a fluke; if it happens twice, then we may be able to call it a coincidence; but if it happens a third time, it's me. Years have passed since this happened to me, and the wisdom I would like to impart to you is this: it pays to bring in experts rather than be "penny wise and pound foolish". Section 148 of the *Income Tax Act*, R.S.C. 1985, c. 1 (5th Supp.), holds the solutions to many wealthy clients keeping their money within our nation instead of moving it offshore. Those of us who provide tax advice owe it to ourselves and our clients to know what is in this section of the *Income Tax Act*. For those of you who have guessed right, section 148, speaks directly to the structured use of a life insurance policy. In the next part of this book, we will be exploring the *Income Tax Act* and the different applications of insurance to assist clients achieve their long-term goals.

I ask you to ask yourself the following questions I routinely ask myself. Who are my best clients speaking to other than me? What advice are they giving my best clients? Do I know what my clients' true issues are? Do I have the expertise needed to solve my clients' problems or am I prepared to bring in the experts to solve my clients' needs? Remember, if a client's needs are not being solved by you, he or she will find another professional to bring him or her solutions to solve his or her needs.

PART IX

PERSONAL RISK MANAGEMENT AND MAXIMIZING ESTATE BENEFITS

CHAPTER 62

THE ABCs OF PERSONAL INSURANCE AND ANNUITIES

Peter J. Merrick

Overview

Insurance is an important component of a client's holistic financial plan. It allows a client to preserve his or her wealth, income and estate. This chapter's sole purpose is to act as a primer for the Trusted Advisor to understand the true value of life insurance, disability insurance, critical illness insurance, long-term care insurance and insured annuities. Knowledge equals choice, and with the material contained within this chapter you will be better prepared to assist your clients and yourself achieve your goals of wealth preservation, income tax minimization, creditor protection, wealth accumulation and wealth distribution.

Learning Objectives

By the time you complete this chapter you should be able to:

- understand the importance of key person insurance in protecting your firm and your client's companies from a disruption caused as a result of disability, sickness or premature death of one of the key people;
- understand how risk management can be achieved through the inclusion of life insurance into one's holistic plan and the process applied when buying insurance;
- understand how a life insurance solution for wealthy clients can increase their cash flow and decrease their taxes while they are alive, resulting in accumulating money in a tax-efficient manner, accessing that money for investment purposes and using the policy to retire in the most tax-efficient way;
- understand the value of including disability insurance and protecting a client's income potential, and what clauses should be placed in a disability policy to achieve maximum protection;

- understand how the inclusion of critical illness and coverage it provides can assist in helping clients to have a choice during times of illness to pay for the type of medical care they desire while preserving their wealth and estate;
- understand how long-term care insurance can help your clients live in dignity when they are no longer able to take care of themselves; and
- understanding how an insured annuity solution used properly can increase a client's cash flow while he or she is alive and secure the maximum estate value while eliminating taxes after death.

KEY PERSON INSURANCE

When a senior partner at a mid-sized accounting firm in his early 50s was suddenly killed in a car crash, his firm could have been greatly impacted financially. Instead, his practice transitioned smoothly within the firm, and his spouse was paid handsomely for her husband's interest in the practice.

The best way to protect your firm and your clients' companies from financial hardships and to meet their financial obligations is through proper planning with the right professionals. By having key person insurance in place, this will ensure your firm's and your clients' companies' survival and help each person meet his or her financial and estate planning needs.

How did this accounting firm manage to stay financial healthy after one of its senior partners was gone? A year earlier, all the partners at this firm purchased key person life, disability and critical illness insurance policies to insure two years' profits in the event that any of the partners became critically ill, disabled or died. The result? As I write this chapter, the practice continues to flourish today while having provided for the deceased partner's family.

It should be mandatory for every accounting, law and wealth management firm across Canada to have key person insurance coverage in place, but it is not. This type of insurance protects a firm against various financial setbacks that can result from an accident, a sickness or the death of a key member of the practice. This key person could be you or anyone else critical to your firm's continued operation and success. Key person coverage can provide enough cash to replace lost revenue due to the death of a key member of your firm or a key employee of one of your clients, the repayment of business loans, recruitment and training of a replacement.

Key person insurance can improve your client's or your firm's chances for loan approval. Lenders look favourably on a firm and company with key person insurance, since it shows responsible planning and makes it more likely that creditors will be repaid.

How much key person coverage should be purchased? That depends on the impact that the key person's death would have on the practice or company. Although this may be difficult to determine, aspects to consider include the person's salary, industry knowledge, goodwill generated by the person, the cost of hiring a replacement and the firm's outstanding loan balance. One rule of thumb is to buy five to ten times the key person's salary. Another is to purchase two years' net earnings that the firm produces.

Imagine a two-partner firm that has worked hard to establish a thriving accounting practice. Then, suddenly, one of the partners dies due to a massive heart attack. This event could put the surviving partner into debt and cause him to close up the practice. However, by having a buy-sell agreement in place that is funded through a key person insurance policy, the practice will continue almost uninterrupted.

The buy-sell agreement had established the value of the firm and the funds necessary for the surviving partner to buy out his deceased partner's interest. The CA practice survives, and the heirs of the deceased partner are paid in full for their interest in the firm.

If a firm is a partnership or closely held professional corporation, a properly funded buy-sell agreement is vital. When there is more than one partner, a buy-sell agreement allows the remaining partners to purchase the business interest of the deceased, retired or permanently disabled owner.

A buy-sell agreement funded by a life, disability or critical illness insurance policy can accomplish the following:

- help eliminate potential lawsuits stemming from the business valuation;
- help assure the continuation of the business for the remaining partner(s);
- allow the surviving partner(s) to maintain control of the firm or company by requiring the deceased partner's interest to be sold; and
- help assure that the partner's heirs are quickly paid in full for their share of the firm, even if the surviving partners are not able to run the firm successfully.

Do you or your clients need key person insurance?

You should consider purchasing key person insurance if any one of the following is true:

- Your firm or your clients are likely to falter if you or they are no longer there;
- Your firm or your clients are likely to falter if another key person is no longer there; and
- You or your clients do not have adequate funds to offset any losses until an appropriate replacement for the key person can be found.

Whether your practice or your clients are considering key person coverage, a buy-sell agreement or both, it is important that the documents and insurance policies be reviewed periodically to ensure that the valuation formula is current and that the plan is funded adequately. This should be done at least once every three years or if there is a major change occurring within your firm or your clients' companies.

RISK MANAGEMENT — LIFE INSURANCE

Recently, I finished teaching a course called Risk Management and Life Insurance. This course leads graduates to earn a Bachelor in Financial Services and enables them upon completion to write the Certified Financial Planning qualifying exam. When the topic of life insurances comes up, both in the financial planning community and the general public, there arise several misconceptions. These misconceptions unfortunately can result in inadequate coverage and unnecessary financial hardship for families who suffer the loss of a loved one.

It has often been said that there are only two certainties in life (in Canada): death and taxes! During my career in the financial service industry, I have rarely met anyone who bought life insurance and then found any enjoyment from spending his or her hard-earned money on paying the premiums. However, over the last decade I have never heard of a life insurance beneficiary say after making a claim that his or her dearly departed had bought too much life insurance.

The reasons an individual purchases life insurance arise from his or her basic desire/need to protect someone or something financially in the event of his or her premature death. For most people, not owning life insurance at death would otherwise leave outstanding unfulfilled financial obligations, such as not having enough funds to support dependants, educate their children and pay taxes or mortgages. In essence, one buys life insurance because one either loves someone or owes someone.

In my financial planning classes and professional career, the question that often arises is: "What steps should Canadian consumers embrace when considering buying life insurance?" My stock reply is that Canadian consumers should apply the Six-Step Life Insurance Needs Process. This process first determines if there is a need for insurance, and then, if there is, allows for the consumer to decide how much life insurance to buy so he or she will mitigate his or her financial risk. These steps can be applied to you or your clients.

- *Step 1: Determine whether you need life insurance.*

  For most people, the primary reason for purchasing life insurance is to protect those who are dependent on their income. For example, if you are the owner of your own business and you die prematurely, you might need insurance to contribute to the company's cash flow to replace yourself as a contributing member to the bottom line. Or if you are married with children, by having the proper amount of insurance, your family will receive enough money to replace you as the breadwinner of your family. Some of your needs for life insurance coverage might be temporary in nature, such as paying for your children to go to university or to pay off the mortgage. If you have accumulated a lot of assets in your lifetime, you may need life insurance to pay taxes after your death on your estate.

  It is a major misconception that only the family breadwinner needs life insurance. Although the stay-at-home parent may not contribute cash income to the family, he or she provides important services, such as caring for the children and keeping up the home, which would be costly to replace; therefore insurance is also required on the stay-at-home parent.

  On the other hand, if you are young and single, with no children and no ageing parents, chances are you don't need life insurance. Understandably, some single people want life insurance for covering funeral expenses, paying off accumulated debt or making bequests to charities or special individuals. However, this is the exception rather than the rule.

- *Step 2: Estimate the amount of life insurance you need.*

  Life insurance needs vary from individual to individual and can even vary throughout a person's lifetime. Determining the right amount takes homework. This step of the process involves completing a life insurance needs analysis. You need to take inventory on all of your other financial resources and think long and hard about how much it would take for your family to maintain its lifestyle without you.

  Also included in this step is the creation of a balance sheet, which adds up all of your life insurance policies and other financial and material assets, and then subtracts from that amount all of your financial liabilities. A person's liabilities don't just include his or her mortgage and credit card debt but they also include the loss of his or her human value. Human value is calculated based on the present value of a person's contribution to his or her family's income and lifestyle, today and in the future.

For example, for an individual who earns $100,000 today, his or her family may require 60% of his or her gross income to meet current and future financial obligations. To calculate the life insurance needs of a stay-at-home parent, determine how much it would cost each year to pay someone to provide those same services for as long as the family would need them. The difference between a person's assets, liabilities and his or her human value is the amount of new life insurance that should be purchased/owned.

If you own life insurance and neither you nor your agent has done this step in the Six-Step Life Insurance Need Process, most likely you own the wrong policy and have the wrong amount of insurance coverage.

- *Step 3: Decide the best type of insurance for you.*

  The next step in the process is to decide what type of insurance best suits your individual situation. The best policy is the one that best meets your financial needs. If the amount of money you can spend on life insurance is limited, or if you have a temporary need, consider only term insurance. If you need lifetime protection, consider permanent life.

  Term life insurance is "pure" insurance with no investment component. You buy term insurance for the duration of time you will need coverage. Your premiums typically go up each year unless you opt for a level premium term policy. The premiums for this type of policy are higher but remain constant for the term of the policy. While the primary reason for any life insurance purchase should be income protection for your family, permanent insurance policies, including whole life, universal life or variable life, provide long-term, investment-like features that some people find appealing.

  For example, with these policies, you can build a cash accumulation value from which you can withdraw during your lifetime, though doing so may affect your death benefit and have tax consequences.

  Note: At all cost, avoid purchasing a life insurance policy that you cannot afford. Twenty per cent of life insurance policies lapse for non-payment of premiums during the first year.

- *Step 4: Shop around for a low cost policy.*

  How much you pay for life insurance will depend on a number of risk factors, including your health, your age, your family's medical history and the type and amount of insurance you are looking to purchase. Each insurance company has different cost structures for their term, permanent and universal life insurance products. Although life insurance products are becoming more commodity-like, and insurance companies are continuing to lower premiums to remain competitive, there are still price variables. Shopping around for low-cost life insurance policies can save you thousands of dollars during the lifetime of a policy.

- Calculating Premiums

  Understanding how life insurance premiums are calculated will help you determine which type of policy to buy, at what level and when. Life insurance companies operate on the principle of group risk-sharing. By selling individual policies to a large group of people, the company establishes a fund with the money it collects as premiums. The fund is available for the insurance company to use elsewhere, usually for investment, until benefit claims are made against it. Premiums are based on the number of deaths expected annually among the group of people buying life insurance from the company.

  For example, suppose that 100,000 35-year-olds all buy insurance policies with a $100,000 death benefit. Actuaries have calculated that in the normal course of events, 123 people in the group will die in the next year. The insurance company should, therefore, expect to pay $12.3 million during the next year as the result of death claims (123 × $100,000 = $12,300,000). To cover the $12.3 million payout, the insurance company should charge each policy buyer an annual premium of $123. But this amount would, in fact, be decreased for the following reasons: one can expect that the 123 insured individuals will not die at the same time — benefits will likely be payable throughout the year. Surplus funds not immediately needed to pay death benefits may be invested for additional profits, and the company may adjust the premium rate downward. In addition, the insurance company adds to its cost of doing business plus any reserves for unforeseen circumstances and arrives at a final calculation — the actual premium you pay. Therefore, insurance premiums equal the expected benefit payout, plus a general business charge, including a protection fee, minus some percentage of profits from the investment of surplus funds.

- *Step 5: Consider the financial strength of the insurance company.*

  Do you remember Confederated Life? This was an insurance company that was founded before the Confederation of Canada in 1867 which went bankrupt several years ago. Yes, insurance companies do have the potential to go bankrupt. However, there is the Canadian Life and Health Insurance Compensation Corporation (CompCorp), founded in 1990 to protect Canadian policyholders against loss of benefits or unpaid claims under their life insurance contracts should a CompCorp insurance company member collapse.

  However, it should be noted that CompCorp does not receive any financial support from the federal or provincial governments and it is a voluntary organization. Thus, there is no guarantee that either CompCorp or the insurance company providing the life insurance will be able to pay the death benefit. Therefore, it is important to buy life insurance only from financially sound insurance companies. There are a number of rating organizations that periodically grade the strength of these companies. It is important to know how your life insurance company rates.

- *Step 6: Deal with a competent Certified Financial Planner (CFP) or Chartered Life Underwriter (CLU).*

  To receive the right advice and to be sold the right policy, you should consider your agent's experience and professional qualifications. Certified financial planners (CFPs) and chartered life underwriters (CLUs) are technically competent in the area of life insurance. These individuals who have attained either the CFP or CLU designations must continually meet education, examination, experience and ethical standards. A CFP or CLU familiar with your overall financial situation can provide you with useful advice concerning what type and how much life insurance you should own.

  There is one last thing to remember: as our life changes, so do our needs with the amount of life insurance we should own. Thus, it is important as a rule of thumb to sit down with your CFP or CLU every year to take you through the Six-Step Life Insurance Need Process to make sure you have the proper amount of coverage that best suits your life circumstances now and in the future.

CREATIVE WAYS TO USE LIFE INSURANCE

A close colleague of mine, Richard Segal, author of the 1990 CCH book classic called *Wealth Creation for the Salaried Executive*, is a financial planner who has spent a career spanning over 30 years specializing in tax reduction and cash-flow solutions for business owners. Richard recounted a personal story involving a company's cash-flow situation and the use of insurance. I believe the moral contained within it has true intrinsic value for each successful Canadian business owner, executive and his or her Trusted Advisor.

When Insurance Is More Than Insurance

It begins one perfect summer day about 15 years ago. Mark, a very successful automobile dealer, and Richard were about to tee off on the fourth hole. Almost out of nowhere Mark looked up from his tee and said, "Rich, I have recently bought this life insurance policy. I am paying a lot of premium and I want a second opinion." "Sure, Mark. What kind of policy is it?" Richard asked. "Well, if I remember correctly I think it's a universal life policy," said Mark. "Do you pay premiums for a limited number of years?" asked Richard. "No, I think I pay for as long as I have the policy," Mark said.

Mark shared that the reason he had purchased the policy in the first place was to provide his wife and his two sons, who were now taking over the family business, with cash flow when he died, as all his assets were tied up in real estate, shares in private businesses and stock market investments. Mark did not want his wife or children to be forced to sell assets in a fire sale, as they probably would not receive their true value, nor did he want them to be forced to sell investments, as it could be at a time when there was a market meltdown. Having a solid cash flow had always been Mark's main motivating factor driving all his most important decisions as an entrepreneur. Even though Mark had created cash flow upon his death through the purchase of the life insurance policy, what continued to plague him was the loss of his use of his premium dollars while he was still alive.

Richard asked, "Do you have to leave your deposit in the policy or can you take the money out each year and use it?" Mark responded, "Rich, I have to leave the money in, and this is what I have a problem with. If I had access to my own money, I would reinvest it in my business and make ten times more money than any stock broker could do with it." Richard's next question was the big question: "How much net do you take from your cash flow each year and lock up permanently to pay these premiums, Mark?" "$100,000."

With this information, Richard asked the following: "Mark did you know that there are solutions that are sanctioned within the *Income Tax Act* that allow you to take your premium deposits out each year? Did you know these solutions can be structured so that you are able to take money out of your company and not pay tax? These solutions result in an increase in both your personal and corporate cash flow." Mark took a moment to digest this and then spoke: "I know one thing! We need to meet immediately to discuss this in more detail!"

The Second Meeting

When Mark and Richard resumed their discussion at their next meeting, Richard learnt that Mark was paying his premiums personally, and the policy did not provide for a payout before death if Mark contracted a critical illness or suffered a disability.

After reviewing the policy, Richard made the following recommendations to help Mark achieve his real stated objective of achieving maximum cash flow during his lifetime and after his death for his family. "Mark, there are four changes/outcomes we need to accomplish first for you to achieve your real goal of creating greater cash flow:

> *First*, you need to make changes to have your company own the policy. The beneficiary would also be the company. Premiums are paid by the company, and since the company is the owner and beneficiary of the policy, there is no taxable benefit to you.
>
> Presently, you personally pay $100,000 a year out of your own pocket. To pay $100,000 after tax you have to earn $186,600 before tax. When the company pays the premium, the cost before tax is $156,543, and $122,880 if the Ontario Small Business Tax Rate is applied. By your company paying for the premiums rather than you personally paying, the end result is within ten years you will experience an actual increase to your cash flow derived alone from the tax savings ranging from $305,700 to $637,720.
>
> *Second*, the solution should include a provision for a payout if you suffer a disability or critical illness before death.
>
> *Third*, the solution should allow the company to borrow at a guaranteed rate as well as crediting interest at a guaranteed rate to the amount held as collateral in the policy. This yields the company a guaranteed return on borrowed funds resulting in building up corporate accessible assets. For example, if the company borrows from the policy it can invest the money in an eligible investment or use the money while the interest is deductible. So if you borrow at 10%, your after-tax cost is 5.359%. The money held in the collateral account of the policy is earning 8% tax-free. This is a 49% cash-on-cash return.

Let's take a closer look at how you will achieve a greater actual return on your investment and increase your cash flow:

After-tax collateral account return — 8.000%

After-tax loan interest — 5.359%

Guaranteed return on borrowed money — 2.641%

Before tax return on borrowed money — 4.928%

This is a guaranteed return and you still have the money to invest and earn you additional revenue. More than 90% of the money deposited can be borrowed back within ten business days of deposit and used to increase your cash flow.

Fourth, at a desired point in time such as retirement, the company can repay the loan. You can then obtain a loan annually from a bank for which the company signs as guarantor and the company assigns the policy to the bank as collateral, thus creating an additional annual tax-effective cash flow for you. The insurance company has this arrangement with a number of banks. The interest each year is added to the amount of the loan. On death the cash value retires the loan and the death benefit is paid to the beneficiary tax-free."

Nearing the end of the meeting after Richard had shown only a few of the countless improvements that could be made, the following dialogue commenced: "Rich, will I have to cancel my present policy? Will I lose money?" Rich replied, "Absolutely not! What we will do is restructure your present policy if circumstances permit while implementing the improved solution. Our end goal is to enhance your company's cash flow, earn you higher returns in your company than you would if you invested the money in an insurance company's funds, and, in addition, your company will receive guaranteed returns on the borrowed money."

"Why didn't my trusted accountant, who does all my personal and corporate tax returns, or my insurance agent recommend this solution to me in the first place, since this is what I actually intended?" gasped Mark. "I can only assume that your trusted accountant and your insurance agent were not aware of this solution, or do not have the expertise and resources to properly implement, maintain and wind down this simple yet complicated structure," replied Richard.

Now for the Rest of the Story

Mark was in good health, and he did augment his policy with the solution. After five years, Mark earned substantially more money just from the guaranteed return on the borrowed money, resulting in an increase to his cash flow. Also, by borrowing the money from the policy, the dealership had further increased its cash flow and return on investment by expanding its pool of accessible funds for its leasing department. This generated more sales and higher revenue for the dealership than it would have received by leaving the money invested in an insurance company's funds.

A few years later, Mark did contract a critical illness and received a tax-free payment of $509,000 equivalent to the policy's cash value at the time. He would not have received any payment if he had not implemented the solution. I am happy to say that Mark recovered from his illness. Since the benefit was payable if he contracted a critical illness, there was no obligation for Mark to repay the amount that he received when he became ill.

The moral behind this story is simple: because of the tax savings, an insurance solution of this nature makes sense even if there is no need for insurance but a great need for an improved cash flow statement. If you have a universal life policy, it is definitely in your best interest to have the policy reviewed by an expert to ensure that you have not been paying for a BMW only to find when it is too late that you have actually been driving a Ford Focus.

RISK MANAGEMENT — DISABILITY INSURANCE

Most Canadians don't protect themselves against the loss of their earning power. This year, one in eight working Canadians will become disabled for more than three months, and half of these individuals will be disabled for more than three years.

When people are asked: "what is your most valuable asset?" the usual responses are their homes, cars or investment portfolios. Usually, most people don't think of what allows them to buy and maintain these material things and pay for food, utilities, the mortgage and other living expenses.

The answer is simple: it is our ability to earn an income. Our personal income allows us to repay debts, accumulate wealth and develop a lifestyle for our families and ourselves. Unless we are independently wealthy and we do not need to work, disability insurance is an essential part of risk management when we implement a comprehensive financial plan for our clients and ourselves.

Consider a 35-year-old lawyer earning $120,000 today who plans to work to age 65. Using the historical average rate of inflation of 4% for the 20th century, this lawyer will earn $5.7 million over the next 30 years. A disability insurance policy is a contract between the insured (you or your client) and an insurance company. The monthly income benefits that you buy will only be paid to you based upon the definitions and wording in your contract.

The most important definition in the disability contract is the definition of "disability". This definition is the heart of your plan. If, as a reasonable person, you cannot easily understand the definition of "disability" and how/when disability income will be paid out, then you should not have purchased that plan or dealt with your current insurance agent. If the definition appears unclear, be aware that an insurance company at the time of claim has the power to define what constitutes a disability through its own interpretation.

Own Occupation

Own occupation is the most clearly defined coverage and the most expensive to buy. It is usually sold as a rider to the regular coverage of a disability policy. Owning a policy with the own occupation definition pays you an income when you are disabled and not able to perform the duties of your chosen occupation. You would be eligible to collect full disability benefits, for example, when you are no longer able to work as a lawyer, even if you decided to work in another occupation, such as a cashier at a fast food restaurant, earning less, the same or more money than you did when you were a practising lawyer.

Regular Occupation

Regular occupation is the most common coverage found in privately purchased disability policies today in Canada. You will be paid a benefit when you can no longer work in your chosen profession because of disability or sickness and do not have employment at all. If you choose to work in another profession, the definition of your occupation then changes to that of your new work situation. So if you are a lawyer and can no longer do this type of work but choose to be employed as a cashier at a fast food restaurant, the definition of your regular occupation changes to that of cashier and the insurance policy will no longer pay you a disability income.

Any Occupation

This definition is found in most group and employer-sponsored disability policies after the first two years of disability and is the most misunderstood. This definition gives the insurance company the most leeway to interpret what constitutes a disability and to determine what the insured can or cannot do to earn a living. With the any occupation definition you will only receive a disability income from an insurance company provided you could not work at all in a job that you are "reasonably suited to do by your education, training or experience".

So if you are a lawyer and can no longer perform this type of work, the insurance company will have the power to make the determination if you are qualified to be a cashier at a fast food restaurant.

Even if you choose not to be a cashier, just because it determines that you are qualified to do so, the insurance company can legally deny you your disability income and it would be up to you to fight for your benefits.

Benefit Term

Many people have a difficult time deciding how long a benefit period they should buy. The average length of disability is about three years, and your options for a disability policy benefit period range from two years to five years, or to age 65.

If you are a young professional and do not have considerable financial assets, a benefit period to age 65 is highly recommended.

Consumer Price Indexing

It is very important to consider purchasing a Consumer Price Indexing rider/coverage when buying a disability policy. An inflation rate of 4% cent per year means that $1 today will have the buying power of $0.50 within 18 years. A cost-of-living adjustment rider is designed to help you keep pace with inflation after your disability has lasted for more than a year.

Future Insurability

This optional rider is designed to protect your future income. This rider is a must for young professionals. It offers the ability to increase your disability coverage, regardless of your health, as your income rises. With the earlier example of our 35-year-old lawyer earning $120,000 today, if his or her income only increased with inflation, he or she would have an annual income of $177,000 ten years from now.

By purchasing this option with his or her original disability policy, this lawyer would be able to buy additional coverage without any additional medical underwriting requirements. In essence, if he or she was diagnosed with a heart condition, as long as he or she had future insurability on his or her policy, he or she could buy more coverage and have no fear of being declined by the insurance company.

Individual vs. Group

Individual disability insurance offers several advantages over group disability plans. Some of the advantages are as follows:

(1) Most group plans, until recently, have not covered partial disability, nor have they indexed benefits to reflect increases in the cost of living.

(2) Group plans are generally not portable; individual policies are.

(3) Individual plans are usually not cancellable by the insurance company, whereas coverage under group plans can usually be terminated after one year.

(4) Premiums for group plans may vary from year to year; individual disability insurance plan premiums are fixed for the duration of the policy.

(5) Group policies define disability in stricter terms. For instance, group plans may not consider you disabled if you are able to perform any work after a certain period of time. An individual plan would consider you disabled if you are unable to do the duties of your regular occupation.

(6) Group policies may have exclusions for disabilities suffered as a result of attempted suicide, self-inflicted injuries or a criminal offence. (Speeding, as an example, is a criminal offence so this exclusion could be serious.)

While it is true that individual disability policies may seem more expensive initially, they are far more comprehensive and provide a higher level of benefit than group plans. If the premiums are paid by a management company, they are tax-deductible, but any benefits received would be taxable. If premiums are not taken as a tax deduction any benefits received are tax-free.

RISK MANAGEMENT — CRITICAL ILLNESS INSURANCE

The year was 1998, and it was a beautiful Sunday afternoon in the month of May when I received the call that I will never forget. My father who was only 58 years old at the time had just been admitted to North York General Hospital, in Toronto. What brought him there was that that afternoon he had a major brain seizure, which we later found out was caused by a level-four brain tumour.

My father had always been responsible with his financial planning; he was a Chartered Accountant by profession, and he was very conservative with his financial affairs. What happened in the months that followed were: he had to sell his tax practice, live off of savings until he could start collecting from his disability insurance policy, put his affairs in order and go through numerous cancer treatments in both Canada and the United States, to try to prolong his life.

My father had purchased more than adequate life and disability insurance. If he had lived to age 65, he would have received over $900,000 in after-tax disability benefits, and upon death $2 million from the death benefit of his life insurance policy. His disability insurance provided a hefty monthly income; what his disability and life insurance policies did not provide was a lump sum that was desperately needed for the expensive cancer therapies he received in Virginia. A huge financial burden would have been lifted off my parents' shoulders if someone had introduced the concept of the critical illness insurance to my father and explained its importance as a part of risk management during the financial planning process, when he was well.

The personal story that I just related is not a unique one. It is a sad fact that many of us know or will know someone who has or will suffer from a critical illness. Despite medical advances, critical illness is still all too common. Being diagnosed with a critical illness doesn't only spell emotional and physical turmoil. It can also mean financial disaster for all those involved. If you are unable to work due to a critical illness, or if you have to give up work to look after a parent, spouse or child with a serious medical condition, you could quickly find yourself struggling to meet your financial obligations such as the mortgage and other regular bills, all this at a time when you may have to find additional money to pay for medical treatment.

The first critical illness insurance was introduced by Dr. Marius Barnard. Dr. Barnard was the brother of Christian Barnard, the first doctor in the world to perform a successful heart transplant surgery.

Dr. Marius Barnard realized that many patients who had heart transplant surgery performed by his brother suffered financially from the loss of their income and the increase in their expenses due to the high cost of treatment and their new lifestyles. To alleviate this financial burden, he approached an insurance company in South Africa to create the first critical illness insurance, which would financially support patients before, during and after treatment by providing a non-taxable lump-sum benefit, paid out when a critical illness was diagnosed.

Fortunately for us, because of Dr. Barnard's foresight, critical illness insurance can now be purchased in Canada.

One of the most important things to be aware of when choosing a critical illness policy is the list of illnesses and conditions covered by the policy, as this varies from one insurance provider to another. The illnesses covered vary from policy to policy, but they usually include six core conditions: cancer, heart attack/coronary bypass surgery, kidney failure, major organ transplant, multiple sclerosis and stroke. The total number of conditions now covered exceeds some 30 different conditions.

Is having critical illness insurance coverage worth the cost? Or is it better for you or your clients to self-insure if you or your clients become critically ill?

Responsible Canadian adults have invested the time and money planning for their retirement. But what would happen to those wonderful plans if these individuals had heart attacks or strokes or were diagnosed with cancer today or a few years from now? How would their retirement plans be affected? Let's look at an example.

Imagine a couple named John and Joan Williams, both 40 years of age. John is a dentist and Joan is an accountant. Both have made maximum contributions to their RRSPs for the last 15 years and neither owns critical illness insurance. One day Joan finds out from her doctor that she has inflammatory breast cancer; the news is devastating. The good news is Joan has been accepted into a gene therapy trial program at Scripps Mercy Hospital, in San Diego, that has had promising results for women with the same condition. However, the treatment will cost $100,000 U.S. and it is not covered by the Williams' provincial medical insurance or their private medical and dental plans. The only place where they can come up with this money fast is from their RRSPs.

Between the 20% U.S./Canadian exchange rate and a top marginal tax rate of 46%, the Williams will have to collectively withdraw $223,000 out of their RRSPs to pay for Joan's gene therapy. Joan responds terrifically to the treatment and is in full remission from her cancer, after one year. Now let's fast forward 25 years. Joan and John are now 65 and are about to retire. They never regret withdrawing money out of their RRSPs for Joan's treatment but wish that 25 years earlier they had owned a critical illness policy on both their lives. For a monthly premium of approximately $60, Joan would have received a non-taxable lump-sum benefit of $125,000 from owning a critical illness insurance policy. The opportunity cost that the Williams lost by taking $223,000 out of their RRSPs 25 years earlier at a compound growth rate of 7% per year would have added $1,210,317 to their retirement nest egg. I honestly believe that anyone who benefits from owning a critical illness policy would never complain about its premiums or say that he or she owns too much insurance coverage.

RISK MANAGEMENT — LONG-TERM CARE INSURANCE

Our health rarely improves with age. After the age of 65, 41% of Canadians are likely to use nursing homes or some type of home care. Usually, the last five years of an individual's life will make up 50% of his or her total health care cost spent during his or her entire lifetime, according to the Canadian Institute for Health Information.

Traditional financial planning as it has been sold to the public encourages Canadians to save enough personal capital to generate 65% to 75% of their pre-retirement income during their retirement.

This rule of thumb operates under the premise that when an individual retires, his or her expenses will be less than when he or she was working. The principle behind this type of thinking is that by that point in time, those retiring are likely to have paid down their mortgage on their homes, they are no longer responsible for their children's post-secondary education and they have enough money to spend on vacations and other luxury items.

However, this type of thinking has proven to be based more on myth than reality. People are living longer today than ever before, and this will impact their ability to provide for themselves as they age.

The cost of long-term care can cause post-retirement living costs for many retirees to be greater than when they were working. This cost reality of old age can quickly eat away at one's retirement nest egg.

Many Canadians believe that the government will look after them in their old age. If they become chronically disabled or mentally impaired, their provincial government plan may cover only a portion of their care for the assistance and supervision they may need. Each province subsidizes long-term care to a different degree. In many instances, long-term care is not necessarily medical care as outlined in the *Canada Health Act*, but custodial care.

Canadians will pay more long-term care costs out of their pockets, with an ability to pay usually based solely on monthly income from pensions and investments. Thus, considering the already high costs of living and health care today, most Canadians may not be able to afford the full cost of their care in the future.

If a person is over 40 years old and has assets to protect, but is not wealthy enough to comfortably pay for long-term care out of savings, he or she should consider purchasing long-term care insurance as part of his or her risk management strategy in his or her financial plan. This is especially important if there is a history of serious illness and longevity in the family.

Long-term care insurance is another coverage that is rapidly growing in popularity. Long-term care insurance pays a daily or monthly benefit for medical or custodial care received in a nursing facility, in a hospital or at home.

It is very important to apply for long-term insurance while you are still healthy. These policies are usually guaranteed renewable, meaning that once you qualify, you'll remain eligible as long as the premiums are paid.

The premiums are based on a person's age at the time he or she purchases the insurance, and rates are usually locked in for the life of the policy. Since most premiums for this type of insurance are paid with after-tax dollars, the long-term care insurance benefits are tax-free.

When choosing a long-term care insurance policy, it is important to find a policy that allows customized coverage. Some of the options one may purchase in one's personal policies include:

- location of care — in-home, in a nursing home, in an adult day centre, or in an assisted living facility;
- type of care — skilled nursing care, custodial care, home health aides;
- options for size of daily benefit and length of coverage;
- flexibility in applying benefits (sometimes called "alternate plan of care");
- choice of waiting periods before coverage begins;
- coverage of organic mental illness, such as Alzheimer's; and
- benefit inflation indexing.

In essence, owning long-term care insurance can take away the financial insecurity that may accompany old age. By planning one's future today, it is indeed possible to have nothing to worry about financially during old age.

RISING HEALTH CARE COSTS CALLED A NATIONAL CORPORATE DILEMMA

About six years ago, I experienced the most frightening event of my life. I had just arrived home one evening after seeing the *Lord of the Rings — Two Towers*. My daughter, Leslie, who was one year old at the time, was running a high fever. As we prepared to take her to the hospital, and as I held her tightly in my arms, she started to have convulsions. Then her head cocked back, and suddenly she stopped breathing. It was the longest minute of my life. She then awoke and started to cry. Thank God this life-altering experience only lasted a minute before she was out of danger.

The ambulance arrived a few minutes later, and, within 15 minutes, she was admitted into the world-renowned Sick Kids Hospital in Toronto. Not once during that entire ordeal did the emergency 911 services, the ambulance medics, the doctors or the nurses ask me: "Mr. Merrick, do you have medical insurance to pay for these medical expenses?"

The fact that this question should never be asked of anyone in this country during and after a medical emergency is a purely Canadian reality that we all take for granted. Whether or not a person has private medical insurance, our Canadian society demands that each person be entitled to receive the proper medical attention when it is needed. This innate principle of our culture makes me proud to call myself a Canadian.

What many Canadians believe creates our sense of unity/community as a nation and a people distinct from the United States is our universal health care system. Our Canadian identity is directly tied to the *Canada Health Act*, which makes the promise "to protect, promote and restore the physical and mental well-being of residents of Canada and to facilitate reasonable access to health services without financial or other barriers".

Is Government Cash Infusion Enough?

In the early 1990s there developed a negative attitude towards the Americanization of our health care system. The federal government started cutting transfer payments to the provinces; much of this money had been earmarked to fund provincial health care plans. To reduce costs, the provinces started to delist medical services that were not deemed essential by the *Canada Health Act*, services the provinces had previously provided and paid for.

To address this coming crisis in Canada's health care system, Finance Minister Greg Sorbara took very proactive steps in his first Ontario Liberal Government's 2004 provincial budget by stating: "None of us can afford to believe any longer that the problems in our healthcare system, from ever longer waiting times, to the lack of family doctors, to deteriorating long-term care, can be solved without additional revenue."

So the Ontario Liberal government at the time introduced for low-income earners a $300 tax per year, going up to $900 for high-income earners. The Ontario government then said that the $1.63 billion raised in taxes in the first year from that new tax would be dedicated to covering the $4.8 billion in additional health care spending planned for the next four years. These measures are being taken by governments across Canada today to help meet their commitments to provide all Canadian residents with access to health care when they need it.

The Ontario government, like the federal and other provincial governments, recognized that the money generated from new taxes will not fully cover its health care funding obligations. Both federal and provincial cutbacks in health care services have left both employers and private insurers across this country having to alter and redesign their medical and dental plans to keep up with emerging trends of higher claims and new cost realities.

Managing Medical and Dental Corporate Costs in the 21st Century

The traditional corporate employee medical and dental benefit plan in Canada provided coverage for semi-private hospital rooms, prescription drugs, dental care, chiropractors, physiotherapists, vision care and travel medical insurance. The vast majority of employer medical and dental plans were designed to be supplementary to the government plan and were never meant to be the employee's primary plan.

With traditional plans, insurance companies charged large sums of money in premiums, and, in exchange, insurance companies assumed the risk for poor health within employee groups. On average, Canadian insurance companies aim to generate a margin each year of between 20% and 40% on every medical and dental plan they administer.

The money collected in premiums is then used to pay the employee claims. In the midst of these economic pressures on the current health care system, employees are demanding an enriched company medical and dental benefit plan. Opinions on what to add are divided by age and experience — things like teeth whitening compete with orthotics. Older employees want expanded drug coverage, while younger workers are concerned about their deductibles. The end result is that employees want choice, and employers want/need to contain their costs.

The Emerging Trend in Employer-Sponsored Medical and Dental Coverage

As mentioned in previous chapters, many employers find that to continue to offer even basic medical and dental plans for employees in the future, they will need to understand where their costs are being generated. The most innovative method to date being adopted by employers across Canada to manage their employee medical and dental plan costs is to replace their traditional plans with health spending accounts (HSAs).

In essence, an HSA is a bank account whose deposits are spent exclusively on health care expenses. The HSA converts health care expenses into 100% Canadian Revenue Agency-sanctioned business deductions and a non-taxable benefit for the employee enrolled in the HSA. The employee makes the decision on how to spend his or her medical and dental benefit dollars.

With the creation of a group HSA, the premiums are reduced to a fraction of the cost, and the employer pays for claims from a pool of funds that an independent trustee administers with a management fee ranging from 5% to 10%, on the total pool of funds placed in the HSA. All moneys remaining in the pool at the end of the plan year are returned to the employer. The employer assumes the health risks of its group but is protected by a predetermined maximum payout per employee (deductible).

An additional measure/strategy that employers may put into practice to mitigate potential risk for their health care costs getting out of control are for employers to attach a stop-loss medical and dental insurance policy onto the HSA. This is done by purchasing an insurance policy with a high deductible.

For example, the first $5,000 spent on eligible medical expenses per employee will be reimbursed by the HSA. Once the annual deductible ($5,000) has been met, the eligible claims will be reimbursed by the insurance carrier, with no further expense to the plan sponsor. The combination of a group HSA and a stop-loss insurance policy can reduce corporate medical and dental expenses by 30% to 50% per annum.

DEMYSTIFYING THE INSURANCE UNDERWRITING PROCESS

As I said earlier in this chapter, responsible people buy life insurance for one of two reasons: they either love someone or owe someone. However, purchasing life insurance is not as easy as buying any other type of financial product. Just because someone wants life insurance and is willing to pay for it does not automatically mean that an insurance company will offer to insure him or her. Once someone applies for life insurance coverage, the application must go through a strict underwriting process by the insurance company before an individual is eligible to even purchase the policy.

Today in the 21st century, the underwriting process of a life insurance policy is still a mystery to most financial professionals and especially to their clients. In Chapter 64, "Memories of an Underwriter in the Real World", Bob Kirk goes in depth with the basic questions of how to help your clients through the process by arranging tests, preparing for tests, understanding the art and the science in underwriting, when to ask for help and how to create value with your clients as you, the Trusted Advisor, help them to obtain the best products for their needs. In this section, we will look at just the essence of the underwriting process, which includes three basic steps:

1. Examination of the application
2. Decision as to whether to insure
3. Determination of the premium

So when you sit down at your next annual review meeting with a client and recommend that he or she purchase life insurance for tax or estate planning purposes, you will have a basic understanding of what it will take for your client to follow through on your recommendation and own a life insurance policy. These steps can also be applied to other types of personal insurance, including medical and dental insurance, disability insurance, critical illness insurance and long-term care insurance.

The Life Insurance Applicant's Responsibilities

The Insurance Act in each jurisdiction in Canada details that an applicant for insurance is obligated to report all relevant information about his or her health and financials that will allow an insurance company to properly evaluate a potential insured's suitability for coverage. The applicant is required to provide four types of personal information on his or her application for insurance coverage:

1. Details on income and lifestyle
2. Medical history of applicant
3. Medical history of applicant's family
4. Hazardous occupation/activities

An insurance policy is referred to as a contract of "*uberrima fides*". This term means "in utmost good faith". The insurer depends on the applicant for complete disclosure. The range of negative consequences that can result from making misrepresentations on an insurance application may range from a delay in approval to the voiding of the policy.

The Insurance Agent's Role

Across Canada, for an individual to be authorized to sell life insurance, he or she has to be registered as an agent with the provincial licensing regulator and hold an errors and omissions insurance policy. The agent's primary role in the underwriting process is to record the client's information on an application on the insurance form. This process is called field underwriting. The responsibilities the agent has regarding the application include collecting information accurately and completely, educating the client on consequences of incorrect information and witnessing the client's signature on the application.

The types of information that the agent will collect in the application for insurance include the applicant's name, age, gender, SIN, annual "earned" income, net worth, date of birth, gender, smoking status and medical history. The agent will write down the product details, which include the amount of coverage, type of policy, dividend option if relevant, duration of policy, premium payment period and riders. As well, the agent will collect general information from the applicant such as: Is there existing insurance coverage? Have previous applications been declined? Are there other pending applications? Does the applicant engage in hazardous activities? Has the applicant had his or her driver's licence suspended? Does the applicant have a criminal record? Who will be the named beneficiary and what is his or her relationship to the life insured?

If the applicant qualifies, he or she may receive a Temporary Insurance Agreement (TIA) after the application is completed. The TIA provides coverage while the underwriting process is completed. Applicants can receive the TIA provided that they qualify as a standard risk and include one month's premium with the application. The TIA insures the applicant for 90 days after the application has been signed or when the insurance company has completed the underwriting process. For example, the maximum amount that can be insured for under the TIA is $500,000 for a life insurance application.

The agent must inform and educate the applicant that by signing the application for insurance, the applicant is authorizing his or her medical history to be released to the Medical Insurance Bureau (MIB). The MIB is somewhat like a credit bureau and exists to share medical information among insurers. There is an MIB pre-notice form that is left with the applicant to read after the application is signed.

Lastly, after the applicant signs the application and before the application is delivered to the insurance company, the agent is required to fill out what is referred to as an Agent Report. The Agent provides notes and comments about the applicant on the application that might assist in the underwriting process.

The Insurance Company's Role

Insurance legislation across Canada states that once someone is offered an insurance policy by an insurance company that was based on truthful information provided by the insured, the insurer most honour the contract for the duration of the policy and for as long as the premiums are paid. Therefore, the insurance company must be sure that providing coverage to an insured is a good investment for the company. In essence, both the insurance company and the policyholder make a bet with each other. The insured is betting that one day he or she will die or become sick, and the insurance company is betting that the insured is not going to die or become ill today.

The policy is issued only after the insurance company underwriters have reviewed the inspection and medical report. This report is prepared by a third party interviewing the applicant to confirm the information. The objective of the inspection report is to determine whether or not the face value applied for is justifiable. The size of the face amount being insured will determine whether there is to be a medical exam, either by a paramedical service or by a physician. The "inspection report" verifies information on the application, especially information which relates to financial matters. After all this information has been collected and reviewed, only then can the coverage be approved, and the premium rates are determined based on the insured's age, gender and health.

Delivery of the Contract

The final requirement in creating a legal contractual agreement between the policy owner and the insurance company is met only when the policy is delivered to the applicant. The policyholder is bound to the insurance contract only after his or her receipt, examination and acceptance of the policy. The prompt delivery and proof of delivery are very important for insurance policies because a delayed delivery may create a danger of a change in insurability of the insured from the time the underwriting is completed to the time the policy is delivered. The insured must sign a delivery receipt with a health statement that certifies no change in insurability status before the permanent policy is in force. If there is a change in the health of the insured and the policy is signed without the insurer being notified of this change, at the time of an insurance claim, the insurance company can legally deny the claim and may be required only to return paid premiums. The end result is the full insured benefit will not be paid out to the beneficiary.

The Bottom Line

At your next annual review meeting with a client, you may recommend that he or she purchase a personal insurance policy for personal, tax or estate planning purposes. As the client's fiduciary, it is absolutely imperative that your client receive the right advice and be sold the right policy.

MITIGATING A CLIENT'S RISK DURING THE INSURANCE CLAIM PROCESS

When I think about the insurance claim process, what immediately pops into my head is John Grisham's 1995 bestseller *The Rainmaker*. This is a modern-day "David vs. Goliath" fictitious story, of course. The lead character, Rudy Baylor, a recent graduate from law school, is hired to represent his client Donny Ray Black, a 22-year-old who is dying of leukemia, in a civil litigation lawsuit against Black's insurance company. The insurance company has flatly denied paying Donny Ray's claim for medical treatment. At the end of the novel, Rudy triumphs and wins against that all-powerful insurance company, but only after his client has succumbed to his cancer and died before the final judgment.

The aim of this section is to demystify the insurance claim process, point out some very real hazards that may prevent a client from justifiably receiving his or her insurance benefit and present solutions that will protect your clients from being denied at the time of claim.

The agent's role in the insurance claim process is to provide help to the claimant or to his or her beneficiaries in preparing and filing the claim. The problem that arises with most insurance contracts at the time of a claim lies with the lack of experience of the agent who sold the policy. A British study of the insurance industry found that 93% of agents who entered the insurance business had left the profession within three years. In John Grisham's *The Rainmaker*, the insurance agent who had sold the policy to Donny Ray Black (the client) was nowhere to be found when his client was being denied his life-saving claim.

Beware! The lesson that hopefully will never have to be learnt is this: the agents who sell your clients their insurance policies may not be in the business at the time of claim to help your clients through the claim process. This reality makes it even more imperative for a client's Trusted Advisor to understand the insurance claim process to help their clients avoid the damaging pitfalls of faulty insurance underwriting.

The Claims Process

In a perfect world, the claims process is similar for all types of life, disability, critical illness, long-term care and health insurance — it involves a five-step process.

1. Claim forms must be submitted with supporting documentation.
2. The claims department at the insurer will review claims for accurateness and completeness.
3. The claims department may contact the claimant and/or physician if more information is needed.
4. If the claim is approved, the insurer must pay the claim within 30 days from proof of claim.
5. The insurer pays the claim, and everyone is happy.

When a life insurance death claim is made by a beneficiary or the trustee of the deceased's estate, some of the typical requirements to process a death claim will include the deceased's death certificate, proof of age, beneficiary claim form and the attending physician's statement. There is no time limit for the filing of a life insurance claim. If the claim is not paid for a long period of time, the death benefit is paid with interest.

It is important to be mindful that an official death certificate rather than one issued by a funeral director may be required when the policy is for a large amount or has been recently issued. If the insured dies within two years after the policy has been issued, the insurance company will want information about the cause of death so it can rule out suicide. Life insurance policies prohibit a benefit being paid out for the first two years after a life insurance policy has been issued when the insured has committed suicide during that period. If this is the cause of death, only the premiums will be paid out to the insured's estate or beneficiaries.

In order for an insurance company to process a disability, critical illness or long-term care insurance policy claim, the information it needs includes the nature of disability or illness, the date of disability or illness, the details surrounding disability or illness and the name of the insured's physician. The time limits regarding the notification and filing of these types of insurance claims are 30 days of the insured becoming disabled or ill, and these claims must be filed within 90 days that the insured has become ill or disabled.

Under federal and provincial laws, an insurance company can possibly deny an insurance claim if it can prove that had a material misstatement made by the insured in the application been fully and truthfully disclosed, the insurer would have refused to issue the policy, at least on the terms and conditions it issued the policy. To mitigate this risk and to make sure that an insurance policy has been properly underwritten so your client receives what he or she has paid for, it is recommended that a professional who specializes in reviewing insurance contracts review any existing insurance policies to uncover any issues that may arise during the claim process leading to a denial of a claim.

Imagine that you had recommended to a client that he or she purchase a $10 million life insurance policy to meet his or her estate planning needs. The client follows your recommendation, and over a ten-year period, the client pays over $800,000 in insurance premiums. At the time of the claim, his or her beneficiaries (or estate) are expecting the $10 million death benefit, but through an innocent material misstatement of facts, the beneficiaries (or estate) are only entitled to receive the premiums paid. What type and how much potential liability might you incur as the client's fiduciary/Trusted Advisor as a result of you in anyway advising the client during the implementation of this strategy? As a Trusted Advisor, ask yourself the following: "What am I doing today to protect my clients' and my practice's interests from long-term loss?"

INSURED ANNUITIES — THERE IS SOMETHING BETTER THAN YOUR GICs!

GIC Alternatives

Several years ago, a gentleman 70 years old walked into my office and shared the following with me: "My interest in an independent Certified Financial Planner is based on the poor performance of my existing portfolio. My experience over the past few years is that I have a knack for making poor choices. I'm considering switching to something that will actually give me a positive return. Given my history, I would like something that would produce a greater rate of return on my money than a GIC could ever accomplish, and still give me peace of mind, while at the same time preserving my capital for my heirs."

Like many retirees, this client was exhausted by the fluctuations he had experienced by being exposed to the equity markets. In addition, he did not like the interest rates he could obtain from his local bank by purchasing their proprietary GICs. He sensed that there existed something out in the financial universe that would make better use of his money than what he had been offered by the main stream financial community. He knew that he could achieve his goals of higher secure investment returns, minimize his taxes, preserve his wealth and creditor-protect his estate. His intuition was right on the mark!

The solution to achieve this client's desired financial outcome has been utilized by skilled CFPs and public accountants for over 30 years. It is referred to as the back-to-back annuity or insured annuity. Done properly, the insured annuity will increase guaranteed cash flow and reduce taxable income on non-RRSP and other non-registered moneys, while preserving one's overall estate.

This solution is the most attractive option for older clients who are relatively conservative in today's low interest rate environment. Back-to-back annuities give the best of both worlds because this solution will achieve a higher after-tax cash flow for the lifetime of a client, and at the end of the day, this solution will return all his or her capital to either his or her estate or beneficiary upon his or her death. Depending on a person's age and health, this solution provides a minimum of 25% to upwards of 400% greater income on an after-tax cash flow basis than ownership of a GIC, earning a real rate of return of 8% to 18% annually.

How Does It Work?

"Back-to-back" annuities or insured annuities are a combination of two financial instruments that create extraordinary results on a guaranteed basis. The first financial instrument involves the purchase of a "prescribed annuity", which provides income for life. The prescribed annuity is extremely tax-efficient, since it is taxed at a very low rate. The tax advantages of a "prescribed" annuity are derived from the fact that the bulk of the money coming back to the client is the return of capital and therefore not taxable while the interest is annuitized over the lifetime of the client. The second financial instrument of an insured annuity involves the purchase of a life insurance contract equal to the amount invested into the annuity. This guarantees that the original capital will be paid back upon the death of the annuitant tax-free to the beneficiaries or the estate or charities depending on who is named in the insurance contract or in the insured's will.

The secret behind why the back-to-back annuity solution works so eloquently in producing such spectacular returns is found in the differing actuarial mortality tables used by each of these distinct financial instruments. The mortality tables show the frequency of death within a particular group of individuals related to their age and sex. Insurers use these tables for calculating premiums on their various products.

Annuities use mortality rates found in the general population. Life insurance premiums are based on the mortality rates of people who have been found healthy enough to pass the required physical and financial examinations. This basically means that the life expectancy of an annuity owner is much less than someone who owns a life insurance policy of the same age. Therefore, the annuity can afford to pay out a greater income than any other fixed income product while insuring the original principle.

Another positive result of implementing the back-to-back annuity solution for a client is that the full investment into this solution is segregated from the rest of the client's estate. This results in the death benefit passing to the client's beneficiaries tax-free while avoiding all probate fees. The life insurance is absolutely creditor-protected provided the proper beneficiary designation has been made.

What conservative clients also like about this solution is that it provides them with risk-free investment returns while diminishing the high management fees charged by investment firms on investment portfolios in their care. On average, management fees charged on managed money investment portfolios range between 1.5% and 3.5% per annum. Depending on the size of the investment portfolio, these fees over a 20-year period can add up to be in the range of hundreds of thousands and even the millions of dollars.

The back-to-back annuity solution can be structured in such a way that it provides the option to pay a steady flow of income for the entire lifetime of both the annuitant and his or her spouse. This solution also allows for income-splitting opportunities between spouses, thus further reducing the already low amount of tax associated with implementing the back-to-back annuity solution.

Again, with the proper structuring of the back-to-back annuity, it will minimize the clawbacks of Old Age Security. As mentioned previously, this is due to only a portion of the income from the annuity being included in the annuitant's taxable income in any given year. The payments will also qualify for the client to claim the pension credit when he or she is over the age of 65.

Now for the Rest of the Story

Our 70-year-old client mentioned at the beginning of this column. This client had a $5 million dollar investment portfolio sitting at a bank-owned brokerage firm when we first met with him. His major problem at the time was that he was losing money in his portfolio. As a result, he was worried about his financial livelihood and future.

This client's investment managers at his old brokerage firm had delivered an average rate of return of approximately 3% per year. This produced $80,000 of after-tax income on his $5 million investment portfolio. Today, after implementing the back-to-back annuity solution, this client receives an annual tax-free payment of $250,000-$300,000. Even better, he now has an insurance policy that will, upon his passing, return the $5 million to his family. The back-to-back annuity solution changed this gentleman's world.

It is important to note that not just anyone in the financial advisory industry is familiar with the back-to-back annuity solution. Only a small percentage of advisors truly understand and know how to implement it, and of those only a handful across Canada have the infrastructure in place to support this robust solution for the long haul.

In many situations, clients will place a large portion of their investable net worth into the insured annuity solution. It is absolutely essential that the Trusted Advisor have the expertise that empowers him or her to understand the annuities and life insurance marketplace. This ensures that the client makes use of all the best financial information and instruments available at the time this solution is put into place. Along with having a high level of sophistication that a solution requires, a Trusted Advisor must be licensed as a life insurance agent.

The last element that needs to be taken into consideration before implementing this solution is the credit rating/risk of the insurance company(ies) used to purchase these instruments, because both the annuity and life insurance involved in the back-to-back annuity solution should be a part of a well-formed long-term financial, tax and estate plan. Thus, it is absolutely imperative that the company(ies) issuing these instruments have the economic strength to ensure that they will be around long after the client has met his or her maker.

It is very important not to dismiss the use of the back-to-back annuity solution as an essential part of a holistic financial and estate planning tool for conservative clients. This solution should be considered and investigated by clients and their Trusted Advisors if the client has a desire to increase his or her guaranteed cash flow, reduce taxable income and creditor-proof assets while preserving the maximum estate legally possible.

INSURED ANNUITIES — THE HOLY GRAIL — THE CORPORATE CAPITAL GAINS SOLUTION

Lessening the Capital Gains Issue

It was a winter afternoon in Toronto when Richard Segal and I were meeting with Robert, a successful business owner in his early 70s. Robert had spent over $100,000 in fees to his lawyers and public accountants to create an estate plan that would reduce his taxes upon his death.

Even though his estate plan resulted in alleviating much of his tax issues, Robert still had over $10 million in cash or near cash held in his corporate structure that would be fully taxable as capital gains once he died. His estate plan had not fully provided him and his heirs with a satisfactory solution to reduce or eliminate these taxes. Robert had come into our offices to find out if there were alternative or complementary solutions that would alleviate this pending tax burden.

In the financial planning community, the Holy Grail of all strategies is the little-known structure called the Corporate Capital Gain Solution. It has been used successfully for over 20 years. Some may have heard of the Corporate Capital Gain Solution, fewer know about this strategy and only a very few skilled professionals have the expertise and wisdom to implement it successfully for corporate clients. Richard Segal was one of those rare professionals.

This solution was perfect to resolve Robert's dilemma and that of other business owners who find themselves in the same predicament. In essence, the Corporate Capital Gain Solution is the following: a corporation acquires an annuity and an insurance policy on the life of its key shareholder. The corporation then borrows funds to replace the capital used to purchase the annuity. The annuity payment pays the insurance premium and the loan interest. The capital gain on disposition of the shares of the company is reduced by the amount of the loan. The end result is, upon your client's death, capital gains taxes are eliminated on the disposal of the client's corporate shares. One of the nice results is that the client is cash-neutral during the entire process. Here is an overview of how the Corporate Capital Gain Solution works.

The first stage of the plan involves the purchase by a corporation of an immediate annuity on the life of a key shareholder. This is generally accomplished with the payment of a lump-sum amount to the life insurance company. In order to maximize income, the annuity will generally be paid for the life of the annuitant with no guarantee period.

The second stage involves the purchase of an insurance policy on the key shareholder's life.

The third stage involves the corporation borrowing funds to replace the capital and, where desired, using the funds to reacquire any liquidated assets.

While the shareholder is alive, the corporation will receive payments under the annuity contract. The annuity payments after tax are sufficient to pay the after-tax insurance premium and the after-tax interest on the loan. Interest paid on the borrowed funds is deductible.

In addition, as the insurance policy acquired by the corporation is required as collateral for the loan, the lesser of the policy premium and the policy's net cost of pure insurance will be deductible from the corporation's income.

Now for the really great stuff. Immediately before death, the shareholder is deemed to have disposed of his or her shares of the corporation for their fair market value.

The amount of the loan reduces the value of the shares; however, the value of the annuity and of an insurance policy without cash surrender value is nil. Therefore, there would be a reduction in the value of the corporation for income tax purposes.

This results in significant tax savings to the deceased's estate.

The amount of any insurance proceeds paid to the corporation, net of the adjusted cost basis of the insurance policy, would be credited to the corporation's capital dividend account. This would allow the payment of capital dividends to the estate of the deceased shareholder, *i.e.*, a tax-free distribution that would be unavailable without the life insurance component of the Corporate Capital Gain Solution. Funds received by the estate in this fashion could be used for the payment of bequests, income tax and other estate liabilities.

The Final Result

In Robert's situation, his savings were very substantial as a result of implementing the Corporate Capital Gain Solution. A $10 million annuity was purchased along with a $10 million insurance policy. A loan using the life insurance and annuity as collateral for the $10 million was set up. On Robert's death, the value of the company will be reduced by the $10 million loan. This reduces the capital gain by $10 million. This will be a tax saving to Robert's estate of $2,320,050, assuming a 46.41% tax rate (Ontario tax rate). This results in the $10 million of assets held in Robert's corporate structure that would have been fully taxable as capital gains on his death passing on to his heirs tax-free.

As Richard said to Robert in closing, "This is one occasion where you are able to eliminate a substantial amount of tax at no cost to you. In addition, the way we have structured this has reduced the risk of an increase in interest rates."

When implemented properly and for the right reasoning, the Corporate Capital Gain Solution should be considered as a cornerstone of a well-planned and balanced financial and estate plan. This solution is a powerful and an attractive alternative within the Trusted Advisor's tool bag.

WHAT CAN INSURANCE REALLY ACCOMPLISH IN THE LIFETIME OF A CLIENT BY HELPING HIM OR HER LEAVE A LEGACY?

Over the years, we have all heard that we can do more with much less effort by understanding the power behind knowledge. It has been said that the quality of our decisions is only as good as the information we had access to. In this closing section of the chapter, I would like to shed light on some powerful tools that you may want to consider during the estate planning process with clients that may involve the advanced use of life insurance.

Pose a problem and ask for a solution from four different advisors (insurance professional, investment professional, attorney and an accountant), and you will get four different solutions, each from a different perspective. This is because different advisors have different opinions, and it's difficult to know who's right. When this occurs, more often than not, the end result is ... *nothing*! The client does nothing, because he or she isn't sure who or what is correct. "This is why estate planning doesn't work! That's right, traditional estate planning does not work." This is exactly what Gordon, a successful planner in the wealth preservation and wealth distribution field, said during a recent meeting we had with mutual clients. As the clients sat listening intently in our office, Gordon successfully recreated the thinking behind their dad's decision to create a wealth preservation and distribution plan that modelled his life values.

"Didn't our dad already have an estate plan?" David's son and daughter asked. They just couldn't understand why their dad, as a retired land developer, had engaged in wealth planning at age 78, after he had already done estate planning when he had retired from his business over 13 years ago.

As I listened to their questions and concerns, Gordon answered, "David, your dad wanted to leave his family an inheritance of more than just his money. He wanted to pass on his ethical will and values, and he wanted to leave a lasting legacy to his community."

"When we get older, it's all about dreams and legacies. That's what people want to use their wealth for," Gordon continued. "Have you ever said, 'One day when I have more money I'll do this and that?' Well, those are dreams. Legacies are those things that you want to leave your mark on even after you are gone, the people, causes, and institutions you care deeply about."

"Even at age 78, your dad still had dreams he wanted to accomplish. Unfortunately, nobody had ever asked him about them. Did you wonder why all of a sudden he bought a new boat, looked up his old high school friends and started visiting the grandkids every month from Florida?" Gordon asked. "Well, those were some of his dreams."

As Gordon went on, he related David's passion: "You know that your dad's Great Aunt had brought him over to Canada after WWII as a refugee, and she made it possible for him to be the first in his family to go to university. It was important for your father to make that same opportunity available for each of his grandchildren, as well as other deserving students. And you know how much he loved his community. Those were some of the things he wanted to leave his legacy on. Traditional estate planning never addressed the things that were nearest to his heart."

"This new approach goes way beyond traditional estate planning. It begins where traditional estate planning leaves off. You have heard about some of the living results; let us outline some of the financial results."

"Your dad was able to increase his financial security by reducing his exposure to CIBC stock, which made up one third of his total wealth. He was able to reduce the capital gains taxes normally due on the sale of that stock, increase his after-tax cash flow by $40,000 per year, increase the inheritance to heirs by almost 20%, and create and leave $1 million to charity."

"Oh!" they interrupted. "One million dollars to charity! Wow, that's a lot!"

I jumped in and said, "Besides the benefits to him personally, let's review the impact on you and the family again. Under traditional estate planning, the Canada Revenue Agency would have received $1 million, you would have received $3.3 million and the charity would have received nothing."

"Now, the Canada Revenue Agency will only receive $300,000, you will receive $3.9 million — instead of $3.3 million — and the charity will receive $1 million."

It took them a few times to understand the power of using planning vehicles and financial tools to create more wealth at the end of the process than ever before. Finally, the light bulb went on! The reasons their dad, at age 78, chose to transform his traditional estate plan were becoming clear: for his peace of mind, a richer life, increased financial security, more inheritance for his children and grandchildren, and tax dollars directed to his cherished charities.

Gordon continued, "The problem with traditional estate planning is that it is one-dimensional and narrowly focused on just the financial dimension."

"As we travel around the country," I said, "teaching accountants, lawyers and other financial professionals about advanced wealth preservation and wealth distribution options, I'm surprised how few advisors know the real problems or real solutions! Clients want to simplify their financial lives; they want to stay in control of their money and their decisions; they want to know they have enough for the future; they want to give their heirs more and yet ensure that their wealth doesn't hurt them; and they want to leave a legacy that makes a positive difference."

Gordon and I couldn't help but smile as we thought about David, how during the last few years of his life he saw some of his dreams come true and how happy he was when he talked about the students who would go to school because of his planning and the lives of the people who would be touched through his local charities.

I can't help smiling as I include this in this chapter about how all of that will continue long after David's gone because of his desire to leave a lasting legacy. I am sad that David is gone, but deeply satisfied knowing that his influence is not, and we had some small part in making this happen.

What about you and your clients? Are there any dreams you and your clients would still like to accomplish? Will you leave your legacy to the people, causes and institutions that you really love? There are over one hundred tools, tactics, strategies, options and opportunities to help you and your clients live out your dreams and leave your legacy, and some have been discussed throughout this book.

If, as a client's primary Trusted Advisor, you are not comfortable with starting the conversation leading to what is involved in the essential insurance and estate planning process, perhaps you might want to direct your clients to work with a CFP® who specializes in this area. The CFP® is an internationally recognized professional certification owned by the Financial Planners Standards Council. Through education, training and experience, CFP® professionals are called upon to be "financial psychologists" who understand life and what clients want to create for themselves, their families and charities in the future and the life they live today. Through training in the Six-Step Financial Planning process, CFP® professionals are able to help their clients bridge their estate planning gaps.

Remember, if a client has an insurance or an estate planning need and if that need is not being addressed, the client will eventually find a way to satisfy that need. So think and be a proactive and creative force in your clients' lives by providing solutions for your clients' very real planning needs today by being a legacy-maker.

CHAPTER 63

THE LAST SANTA (SANCTIONED TAX SHELTER)

Richard Segal*

Overview

This chapter will explore in depth the tax shelter aspects of a universal life policy and give you the tools to allow you to recognize situations where it can be beneficially used as well as to critically evaluate different policies so that you are able to select the policy that is the most advantageous.

Learning Objectives

By the end of this chapter, you should have:

- a grasp of the various ways that universal life can be used as a tax shelter;
- an understanding of the key elements and components of a universal life policy;
- the knowledge to evaluate universal life policies even if the make-up of each policy is different; and
- the tools to determine which policy is the most advantageous.

INTRODUCTION

I recently met with a client, Gary, who asked me if there was any tax-effective way of increasing his retirement income. He is an executive with a large financial services company and earns a salary of $360,000 a

---

* Richard Segal, B.Com., CFP is a financial planner in Toronto and has been advising clients for the past 30 years. He has authored numerous articles as well as a book. He appeared weekly on TV and radio and has taught seminars for the University of Toronto and Seneca College.

year. The company has no pension plan, and he already contributes the maximum to his RRSP each year.

"Gary", I said, "I have just the plan for you. It complies with the *Income Tax Act* [R.S.C. 1985, c. 1 (5th Supp.)] and the CRA (Canada Revenue Agency) rules and regulations, there is almost no limit to your contribution, your investment grows tax-exempt and you can use your investment without paying tax." "That's exactly what I'm looking for," Gary said. "Gary, there is one more benefit. It can be used to withdraw funds from your RRSP without paying tax."

"This sounds too good to be true," Gary said.

"Gary," I said, "let me tell you a story:

"There was once a tiny nation in which everyone not in the king's palace contracted food poisoning. They discovered that whenever people with this condition prepared food, they unavoidably contaminated it and spread the epidemic. Being unable to keep down contaminated food, and unable to prepare food without contaminating it, they were in a desperate predicament.

"Alarmed by this, the king prepared from his own supplies a magnificent, endless feast to which everyone was invited. Protocol, however, demanded that no one could attend a royal feast without presenting the king with a highly prized delicacy that he would sample and then add to the banquet. Knowing that none of the invitees could provide uncontaminated food, the king, himself, at great expense, provided everyone with food fit for a king that they could then give back to the king as their own gift.

"Some, having a low opinion of the king, could not believe his generosity. They decided it was too good to be true that the king would accept the gift he, himself, had provided. So they refused to attend the feast and resigned themselves to starving to death.

"But some accepted the king's generosity and, as the king had always intended, they gratefully gave his own gift back to him. Upon receipt of the gift, the king welcomed them into the feast, where they were not only saved from starvation but enjoyed festivities beyond anything they had ever known.

"You can choose to which group you belong."

"That was an illuminating story," Gary said. "It certainly let's me see this from a different perspective. How does the plan work and how do I get started?"

"Well, Gary, you may be shocked to learn that what I have described is a universal life insurance policy."

"Let's look at how it works.

"A deposit is made each year into a universal life policy. Five business days later, a loan for most of the premium is made to you by the insurance company. Assuming premiums are paid for only five years, then over the five-year period, 95% of the premium paid is returned as a loan. You now can invest the loans in an investment of your choice. Provided the investment is an eligible investment, the interest is tax-deductible.

"The loan interest is fixed at 10% for the life of the policy. If you are in the top tax bracket, the interest paid after tax is 5.36% (10% taxed at 46.4%). The insurance policy guarantees an 8% return on the amount equal to the loan. You have now earned a guaranteed rate of 2.64% (8% less 5.36%) on borrowed funds. Interest is paid until you wish to use the funds.

"When you wish to use the funds, a portion of the investments that were generated by the loan proceeds are used to repay the policy loan, and the balance is pooled with the funds in the policy.

"A loan is obtained annually from a bank, and the policy is used as collateral for the loan. The insurance company has an arrangement with most of the banks. Each year the interest charged is not paid but added to the loan. As the amount you receive annually is a loan, there is no tax payable.

"For you and your wife, Janet, who are both 45 years old, assuming the same contributions to an investment, the amount received annually is 66% greater than it would have been if you had not purchased a universal life policy. So, as an example, if you received $60,000 annually after tax from an investment, you would now receive $100,000 a year instead of $60,000.

"In addition, there is a death benefit and a payment if you or Janet contracts a critical illness or suffers a disability."

"That's great," Gary said. "But what about being able to withdraw money from my RRSP without paying tax?"

"Well, if you withdraw an amount from your RRSP equal to the interest payment, there is no tax payable, because although the RRSP withdrawal is taxable, the interest payment is deductible. Effectively, you are transferring funds from your RRSP to the universal life policy without paying tax. The funds grow within the policy at a guaranteed rate of 8% tax-free, and you have the ability to use the funds without paying tax."

"Wow, that's excellent," Gary said, "but I already have a universal life policy. Can I use that policy?" "That would depend on the policy, Gary. Let's examine it."

Gary, a 48-year-old non-smoker, had a $1 million universal life policy and was paying $15,000 a year premium. His policy at age 85 would have a cash value of just over $135,000 but would expire two years later, at age 87. With a different insurance company, Gary would pay the same premium, and if we used the same assumptions, at age 85 his policy would have a cash value of just under $610,000 and would never expire!

Gary replaced the policy on his life with a joint last-to-die policy on his and his wife Janet's life. This reduced his insurance costs even more and increased the cash in his policy.

QUESTIONS THE TRUSTED ADVISOR SHOULD BE ABLE TO ANSWER

Does this work if the person is a business owner?

Yes, and it allows a shareholder to withdraw funds from his or her company without paying tax.

The policy is purchased by the company. The company is the owner and beneficiary. Premiums are paid by the company, loans are received by the company and interest is paid by the company.

At retirement, the shareholder obtains a bank loan annually, and each year the interest is added to the loan. The company guarantees the loan, and the policy is held as collateral by the bank.[1]

On the shareholder's death, the proceeds are paid out almost tax-free through the capital dividend account, the loan is retired and the death benefit is paid out.

Can it be used as a retirement plan by a professional firm?

I recently had a meeting with Jack, the managing partner in a firm with 55 partners. We were discussing a major problem that the firm had: how to provide a pension for partners that retire, in a way that the firm could afford.

"The problem I have, Rich," Jack said, "is that the younger partners do not want to pay for a pension for older partners. The middle-aged partners who bring in most of the business feel that they can earn more on their own, and there is no pension to tie them to the firm. The older partners have spent a long time building the firm and are disillusioned because they have no pension and will only receive their capital account and WIP (work in progress). Their disillusionment is bad for morale and increases the dissatisfaction of the middle-aged partners. At the same time, the firm cannot afford to pay the large sums of money that are required to fund a pension plan for the partners."

---

[1] CRA document no. 2000-0002575, March 29, 2000. The value of a benefit arising from the right to use someone else's property as security for a loan is a question of fact. One method of calculating the fair market value of such a right might be to compare the difference between the interest rates charged with and without the corporation's collateral security. Another method might be to determine what the shareholder would have to pay a third party to provide a similar collateral security.

"I completely understand, Jack, and I am happy to say there is a solution. Assuming a 40-year-old partner retiring at 65, the firm over a 15-year period makes an annual contribution of 14% of the before-tax pension to the partner. This means that the firm pays $25,000 annually for 15 years (a total of $375,000), and the partner, assuming a 46% tax bracket at retirement, receives a before-tax pension of $185,185 a year.

"For a 50-year-old partner retiring at 65, the firm over a 15-year period makes an annual contribution of 15% of the before-tax pension to the partner. This means that the firm pays $27,000 annually for 15 years (a total of $405,000), and the partner, assuming a 46% tax bracket at retirement, receives a before-tax pension of $185,185 a year.

"For a 60-year-old partner retiring at 75, the firm over a 15-year period makes an annual contribution of 38.7% of the before-tax pension to the partner. This means that the firm pays $38,700 annually for 15 years (a total of $530,500), and the partner, assuming a 46% tax bracket at retirement, receives a before-tax pension of $185,185 a year.

"In addition, it is an insured plan. On the death of the partner, the death benefit is paid to the firm. The firm receives substantially more than the contribution that it paid."

Needless to say, the firm instituted the plan, and no partners have left since.

What are the components that make up a universal life policy?

Not only is it important to recognize situations where universal life may be applicable, but it is just as important to understand the components that make up a universal life policy in order to evaluate and determine the most beneficial policy. Let's look at the components.

1. *Maximum Tax Actuarial Reserve (MTAR)*

   Simply put, this is the tax exempt value of the policy at any point in time.

   This is the maximum that an insurance company can deduct from income as a policy reserve (subparagraph 138(3)(a)(i) of the *Income Tax Act*). The *Income Tax Regulations* (the Regulations) prescribe the formula for calculating the policy reserve (the maximum tax actuarial reserve or MTAR) that may be deducted.

   The MTAR calculation has a substantial impact on the maximum amount of cash you can accumulate in your policy. The factors that are used in an MTAR calculation can substantially change the MTAR.

   (a) Maximum premium calculations

   When calculating the yearly maximum premium, you can base the premiums on the accumulation of funds value, which in most companies contains surrender charges, or the actual cash value of the contract after surrender charges are applied. The method you use will make a big difference in the calculation of yearly maximum premiums during the surrender charge period. If the company chooses to interpret that the yearly maximum premium is based on fund values, the maximum deposits will be lower than for a company that chooses to base the maximum on cash value.

(b) Interest rate considerations

Another important consideration is the interest rate used in determining how these yearly maximum premiums are calculated. Companies that use a high rate of interest will have a lower maximum premium than companies that use a low rate of interest. If a high interest rate is used but not achieved, it would have been possible to put in more money. Therefore, you would not have maximized the policy.

If a low interest rate is used, there is less chance of the investment earning less than the rate used in the calculation, but there is more chance of the policy becoming taxable.

This leads to the next consideration — exempt test failure. What action does the insurance company take if the policy does become taxable?

(c) Exempt test failure

The insurance company checks each year that the policy will not become taxable. If the policy would become taxable, the insurance company has three options:

(i) Increase the amount of insurance by a maximum of 8%. The 8% increase is the maximum permitted in the Regulations. As the amount of insurance has increased, the MTAR has increased. If the policy is now tax-exempt, no further action is necessary. If the policy is still taxable, option 2 or 3 has to be exercised.

(ii) Transfer money to a side account. Money is taken out of the policy and transferred into a separate account, often known as a side account. Any returns earned in the side account are fully taxable. Should the MTAR allow, money can be transferred back into the policy at a later time.

(iii) Refund sufficient premium to the policy owner so that the policy is once again tax-exempt.

(d) The 250% rule, also known as the anti-dump-in rule

The purpose of this rule is to prevent a company from making minimum premiums in the early years and then, in a later year, depositing a very large premium.

Beginning at the tenth policy anniversary, the MTAR of the policy cannot exceed 250% of the value that existed at the seventh policy anniversary. From the tenth year on, this test is applied every year based on the previous three years.

From this discussion, you can see that how a policy is formulated has a substantial impact on the amount that can be accumulated on a tax-exempt basis. This is not readily apparent by comparing different companies' illustrations.

2. *Management Fees of Investments*

Not only is the MTAR going to vary from company to company, but so is the management fee for different types of investments. For example, if company A charges a management fee of 2% and company B charges a management fee of 3% for the same investment, even if the MTAR is the same for the two companies, company A will accumulate more cash in its policy than company B. If there is a policy illustration, the rate of return shown should be evaluated. Is the rate of return feasible after management fees have been paid? A 6% return shown on a policy illustration for an investment that has a 3% management fee requires that investment earn 9%.

3. *Guaranteed Minimum Rates of Return*

Companies also have different minimum guaranteed rates of return. If the investment selected does not perform as projected, the minimum guaranteed rate of return is what is credited to the policy. So, a company with a higher guaranteed rate of return will accumulate more cash.

4. *Provincial Premium Tax*

Most, but not all, companies charge the provincial premium tax. This does not have an impact today as even if the provincial premium tax is not charged, it is priced into the premium. It could have an impact in the future if provincial premium taxes increase. The company that is not charging provincial premium tax cannot increase the premium on existing policies. Companies charging provincial premium tax can increase their premiums.

5. *Bonus*

Most companies pay a bonus. The bonus can be guaranteed or based on certain conditions. Obviously, a guaranteed bonus is far better. Conditions that the bonus could be based on are, for example, the amount of cash accumulated or the period of time that the policy has been in force or both.

6. *Factors Affecting Loan Strategies*

It is possible to borrow from a financial institution or an insurance company and use your universal life policy as collateral. Provided you are investing the loan proceeds in an eligible investment, the interest may be deductible. Any return earned in the policy is tax-exempt. Assuming a 10% loan rate and an 8% rate of return within the policy, you would have a positive rate of return of 2.6% on borrowed funds (assuming a 46% tax bracket), the difference between 5.4% (10% taxed at 46%) and 8%.

The key factors are as follows:

- Is the loan from a financial institution or from the insurance company?

  A loan from a financial institution is subject to financial underwriting and affects debt service ratios and borrowing.

- Are the loan and interest rates guaranteed for the life of the contract?

  The rates could drop so that the strategy is no longer viable. For example, a 6% loan rate and a 4% return yield 0.76% rate of return.

- Is it possible to select the interest rate?

  It may be deemed unreasonable by the CRA if you are allowed to select the interest rate.

- Is the formula for calculating the loan specified in the contract?

  With no formula in the contract, the insurance company can arbitrarily change the amount of the loan.

- Does the insurance company adjust the death benefit so that the cash value in the policy is maximized?

  The cash value in the policy of an insurer that does not do this will be substantially lower.

- Are all charges guaranteed for the life of the contract?

  Any change in the charges over a period of time will substantially reduce the amount of cash accumulated.

- Are there any other benefits in the contract?

Some insurance companies provide a disability and critical illness benefit.

- If the policy is a joint last-to-die, can the cash be paid out on the first death? Can the survivor continue the insurance?

  On the first death, the surviving insured can elect to have the cash value in the insurance policy paid out as a death benefit or choose to continue to have the policy in force until his or her death.

- Is it possible to terminate the policy without negative consequences?

  A loan from a financial institution has to be repaid. If all of the cash you have borrowed is from the policy and you have lost the money that you borrowed, you will have to find the money elsewhere to repay the loan. A loan from an insurer has to be repaid as well, but there is sufficient cash in the policy to do this. If this is done correctly, negative tax consequences can be minimized. You also may be able to set off the loan against the cash value of the policy.

- Is there a reasonable expectation of profit from the investment?

  If you borrow at 10% and invest in a guaranteed investment at 4%, there is not a reasonable expectation of profit. If you invest in publicly traded stock or shares in a private corporation, there could be a reasonable expectation of profit. If there is no reasonable expectation of profit, all or some of the loan interest deduction can be disallowed.

IF YOU ARE IN NEED OF A TRUSTED ADVISOR

As you can see, comparing different universal life policies is extremely difficult. It is essential to find a knowledgeable independent insurance advisor. The advisor needs to be aware of all these differences, not just look at and compare company illustrations.

You are unlikely to get objective advice from an advisor who primarily represents one company. In this case, you will probably be presented with a proposal to purchase a policy of the company that the advisor represents. You will also probably be told that the advisor is able to sell any insurance company's policies, yet the best policy happens to be from the company that the advisor represents.

An educated advisor who stays current with recommended continuing education courses will be more knowledgeable. Look for an advisor with a CFP, ChFC, CLU or TEP.

A referral from someone whom you trust and respect is a very good way to find an advisor.

Ask the potential advisor questions. Find out whether the advisor works with clients who are similar to you in age, financial circumstances and occupation. Does the advisor have specialized knowledge in any areas that are applicable to you? What kind of analysis, planning and review is done by the advisor? What services and products does the advisor provide? Is the advisor part of a firm, or a sole practitioner? It is preferable if the advisor is part of a firm. If anything happens to the advisor, there is someone to replace him or her with a similar level of expertise. Tell the advisor what you expect from the relationship and ask whether the advisor can meet these expectations. Establish the level of knowledge that the advisor has with respect to taxes. There are a number of ways you can use universal life that can generate very substantial tax savings and benefits. Only an advisor with an excellent knowledge of tax can provide this kind of information.

CONCLUSION

To fully understand the importance of working with a knowledgeable advisor, I would like to illustrate with the following parable.

Once, the face of the earth was covered with caterpillars of all kinds, shapes, sizes and colours. These caterpillars led fairly mundane lives spent constantly foraging for food, occasionally fighting with each other over a choice leaf and generally trying to avoid being eaten by the ravenous birds that wheeled overhead.

One day several of the caterpillars hit upon an idea. They had this thought that they could protect themselves from the elements and from the always hungry birds by constructing a type of blanket they produced from their own bodies. This wrapping they called a "cocoon" and, once a few of the wiser caterpillars demonstrated how this cocoon was built and how well it protected them, soon nearly all of the other caterpillars began building their own.

Some, however, thought the idea not only silly — after all, there was no proof a cocoon would really protect them from anything — but, worse, it was nothing more than a feeble attempt to escape the brutal realities of the caterpillar life, so they refused to build their own. They would stay on the ground and carry on as before, thank you; they didn't need any of this "cocoon" nonsense.

But the overwhelming majority of the caterpillars thought the cocoon a great idea, and soon the trees and bushes were filled with their handiwork.

One day something strange happened. Some of the cocoon-bound caterpillars began to change. They began to grow wing-like appendages on their backs, which seemed to suggest that a caterpillar could somehow, in some strange way they could not quite understand, be more than a caterpillar. In fact, some of them began to believe that which was clearly impossible for any caterpillar to do, and that was that they might fly.

The problem was that they would never find out if they remained in the tight confines of their cocoon. In order to spread their wings it would be necessary to break the cocoon — even, perchance, destroy it — in order to test their theory.

It was a frightening idea. The cocoon had given them the security and safety they had sought. Some — many, in fact — took their elder's advice and remained locked in their cocoons, safe and secure the rest of their lives, always wondering what it might have been like to fly but never finding the courage to break out and see. Some, however — just a few at first, but then others — decided to take a chance. In doing so, they discovered that the wings they had kept so tightly folded behind them were, when spread, things of breathtaking beauty.

Free! They were free from the confines of their cocoons for the first time in their life, and they wheeled higher and higher into the sky until they could clearly see the forest below them in all its radiant glory. The other caterpillars below — both those in their cocoons and those on the ground — refused to look up or even acknowledge the strange, new creatures flying peacefully overhead. There was nothing to see up there, they shouted in unison. It was one of the few times that the ground dwellers and the cocoon dwellers ever agreed on anything.

Make sure that both your advisor and the policy that you purchase are at the butterfly level.

CHAPTER 64

MEMORIES OF AN UNDERWRITER IN THE REAL WORLD

Bob Kirk

Overview

This chapter discusses underwriting with a goal of understanding the basic premises, how to help your clients through the process by arranging tests, preparing for tests, understanding the art and the science of underwriting, when to ask for help and how to create value with your clients as you, the Trusted Advisor, help them to obtain the best products for their needs.

Learning Objectives

By the time you finish reading this chapter you should be able to:

- understand the importance of working with an insurance underwriter to help place a large insurance case;
- understand how to prepare a client application to undergo both the financial and medical underwriting stages; and
- understand the importance of writing a good letter explaining why an insurance policy should be placed for your client.

INTRODUCTION

Over the years, a lot of people have asked me: why do insurance companies underwrite? Beyond the obvious pricing and risk management objectives that insurance companies have, I can assure most people that they don't underwrite just to make our lives miserable, to slow things down and to test our patience before we can place the case. Believe it or not we want the insurance companies to underwrite because that protects the products that we can sell both now and in the future. Our real goal should be that *we* manage the underwriting process and not the insurance company, that we proactively solve any problems the underwriter from the insurance company might have before they occur and that *we* make sure that the path the business will follow is to ensure that the client gets an equitable policy, the insurance company makes money and we make a living. Sounds easy, doesn't it? So why doesn't it happen? Why do I hear complaints all the time that insurance companies are too conservative, there are too many requirements, it takes too long for the underwriting of an insurance policy and the Underwriter creates too many problems?

More than likely, it is because we don't anticipate what it is that insurance company Underwriters are trying to accomplish on a case-by-case basis, that particular day, at that particular moment of the insurance company's life. Why is it that we research every objection our prospect might have, and every way to overcome objections is understood, catalogued and anticipated so that we not only get the sale, but we provide our client with expertise that adds value, creates future value and builds a stronger relationship, and, yet, when it comes to underwriting, we like to complain rather than create?

Let's spend some time and create with the Underwriter. In his ancient Chinese text, Sun Tzu once said, "know your enemy and know yourself and you will always be victorious!" While I think that the word "enemy" goes much too far, most Trusted Advisors think of Underwriters as adversaries trying to stop their case from making it to the finish line and preventing us from getting it issued and getting paid. Let's see if we can't change that together.

As a former Underwriter with 20 years of working in the head office, I have moved out into the real world and found that I had to spend the first couple of years in the "real world", or "the dark side" as my former colleagues might put it, forgetting much of what I thought and learned when working in the head office environment. The real difference is that people in the real world, contrary to my belief at the time, do not follow the head offices rules and that sometimes the insurance company does not fully understand its customers' goals and expectations, especially as customers become more and more astute, knowledgeable and focused on their objectives.

THE ART AND SCIENCE OF UNDERWRITING

But I digress. Back to underwriting. We have all heard that underwriting is both an art and a science and that the best Underwriters are those who can mesh the two together and have some understanding of what the Trusted Advisor is trying to achieve. I fully endorse this viewpoint by the way, in spite of many pundits who feel that it would be better to remove the human element from underwriting and create an entire science-based industry using genetic markers and other sophisticated tools to determine not only the risk profile of an applicant but also virtually the exact moment and cause of the applicant's death or disability. I know you are chuckling right now, but it is coming. Tests are becoming more sophisticated, and insurance companies would dearly love to be able to use some of them even though they are currently prohibited from doing so.

Back to the art and the science question: what is the breakdown, how much is art and how much is science? Often we talk about the fact that underwriting is both an art and a science. For the artistic types, Underwriters do this to increase the level of mystique in the underwriting field, and for the scientific types it is more a matter of how much is art and how much is science. Through a number of different approaches, I have reasoned that underwriting is about 76% science and about 24% art. Where do the numbers come from? They don't come from anywhere! They are made up! The important thing to note about underwriting is that it is a combination of a myriad of factors, and as any probability statistician knows, the more predictions that have to be made correctly, the less probability (exponentially, I might add) that the answer will be correct. Everyday Underwriters are confronted with the task of making guesses (the art), combining them with the empirical evidence (the science) and coming up with an accurate guess of someone's life expectancy or morbidity. What we want to encourage from a sales perspective is that the Underwriter continues to exercise what we would call "judgement" on every case, because often science and art may digress from each other. Here is a story to illustrate:

I once saw a very large case while I was sitting at my desk, underwriting. I might add that I was very busy that day with a number of meetings and a lot of phone calls from brokers, but I still had to move my 25 cases that day to meet my handling criteria as set out by my boss. Yes, sometimes people do silly things, as we all know, in the name of "efficiency". For example, Underwriters spend an inordinate amount of time doing administration rather than actually risking selecting and other lovely things like not talking to brokers because that would slow them down. Hmmmm, it seems to fly in the face of the "art", doesn't it? Anyway, now that you have my mood down for that day, here is the case as received from the broker:

Application
$300,000 application on 72-year-old female born in the Philippines
$50,000 insurance already in force
CPP income only
Daughter is owner and beneficiary

Life assured resides with daughter
Purpose of insurance — estate taxes

I can assure you that this is how I received the case. Given that the information made no sense at all, I delayed the case and put all medicals, *etc.* on hold. Why? Because in the early 1980s, $300,000 on a 72-year-old was a lot of money and required a fair number of medicals, and judging by a perceived lack of resources and ability to pay, my initial impression was that this would be a decline from a financial perspective, and I didn't want to waste the money completing the medicals on a useless case. I decided instead to interview the broker on the case, and called him directly. Of course, at first I received indignation that I was challenging his case, and how dare I, and he would call his sales representative, Managing General Agent and anybody else he could think of because this was clearly a persecution of him as a broker. I stopped him dead in his tracks when I said, "Listen, stop for a second. I would like to help." I then proceeded to ask him a number of questions about his client, and here is what I found out:

> *"Mrs. F, a 72-year-old widow, immigrated to Canada in 1947 from the Philippines. She met Mr. F, a wealthy Canadian engineer, while he was working in the Philippines on a bridge project. They returned to Canada, were married, and had four children. Mr. F owned a cottage property where the family spent its summer vacations. All of the children have an attachment to the property. Because of its location and the 12,000 feet of undeveloped lake frontage, the property value has increased significantly. The property has a current capital gains tax liability of $300,000. According to the family will, the cottage property will be divided equally amongst the children on Mrs. F's death. The balance of Mrs. F's estate was liquid and has already been passed to the children. The family has contacted me for advice and would like to proceed with an insurance policy to cover the tax liability. The four children will share in the cost, the insurance, but the family has asked that the policy owner and beneficiary be the eldest daughter, since she is executor to the estate, and her mother resides with her."*

Remarkable! The case was proceeded with and subsequently issued and settled. The science said to decline the case (really because of lack of information) on a cost benefit basis, and the art said that maybe the case could make sense, and it did. Now, let me ask you a question: does your Underwriter do this for you? Yes, yes, I hear the resounding *no*! Does your Managing General Agent do this for you? Again, *no*! Who can put the case together for you then? You can, but probably with some help.

The result here was a lost case being placed, and everybody being happy. If only ...

But, before you can do this, it is important that we all take the time to understand underwriting a little better. Underwriting is the art and science of risk selection. It exists, if you really think about it, in all aspects of our business. The Underwriter has input into product development. The actuary designs products with underwriting predictions in mind using mortality and morbidity statistics. The marketing and sales department looks for ways to get the products placed in spite of underwriting. The new business department uses underwriting to determine which policies go on the books. The policy service department underwrites the changes that occur to products, and we all know that the claims area is the other end of the underwriting process, no pun intended to my friends in claims areas.

What is it that we as Trusted Advisors are trying to do? Get our clients what they need? Earn a living? Build our future? Be responsible to our clients? Show strong ethics, morals and values? I hope so. What do we want to do with the Underwriter?

Get the Underwriter working for *us*!

Stop the adversarial relationship!

Make it easy for the underwriter to issue what we want!

Don't frustrate the underwriter along the way!

We really want it to be all about creating a partnership between the Trusted Advisor and Underwriter. We want to understand them, help them and guide them. Why? Because we want to add value to our clients and earn a living. Sounds simple, but again it is not. This is not an easy process because few Trusted Advisors would ever like to take the time to understand underwriting with all that medical and financial stuff. We can, however, understand the basics, try to help make it work better where our contribution matters and get help when we need it.

What we also need to do though is to support the right of the Underwriter to make judgements. This is becoming a lost art, very much like the lost art of "sales speak". We all know good judgement when we see it, but don't you notice that Underwriters are less and less able to exercise that "judgement" and seem to more and more be following an academic approach to thinking. This is happening as actuarial tools such as "predictive modelling", "data mining and segmentation" and "advanced probability tools" become more and more scientific during the product design process, and the Underwriter becomes excluded from that process. This removes the "art" from the Underwriter because the rules are very tightly defined. The "science" should in fact be at the point of sale because this is where the real data is collected, and the real "art" of the sale should be in making complex ideas simple.

You can see that I am making a case for the underwriting judgement. True enough, but there may be an even bigger problem for us. That is, where are all the Underwriters going? There just don't seem to be as many around any more and not very many new ones coming up through the ranks with what I like to think of as practical experience, just as I notice there are getting to be fewer and fewer true salespeople around any more. More brokers, fewer salespeople. Anyway, it seems to me that the Underwriters are quitting, retiring, going part-time, working from home or going to work for the reinsurers. Why? Probably because they can, as the old saying goes. Most of them I talk to say, they just want things a little easier and that they miss the "old days", whenever that was.

Underwriting is becoming more and more complex, frustrating, political and simply "not worth it any more", as many of the veterans feel. I agree with them; it's not what it used to be, but what does that have to do with us? The answer is quite obvious I think. If we can make it easier for the Underwriter to deal with our business, then our business will get the best consideration possible. In real terms, this is why the "my client plays golf three times a week so he must be healthy" or "my client is just a social drinker" reasons just won't cut it any more. Underwriters have been feeling the pinch from the reinsurers over the past several years as well. What are the reinsurers? Reinsurance companies are risk-taking entities where a direct writing company, for a cost, can offload some or all of the risk with an insurance contract. This allows companies to "spread the risk" and prevent a catastrophic claim from destroying a company's results or even putting it out of business. Reinsurance companies have been a great help to our industry because they have allowed us to write larger cases and they have helped to standardize much of the thinking out there by providing credible surveys of mortality and morbidity data to give the industry the opportunity to price more accurately. The problem that occurs is when the reinsurers don't meet their goals or when the results of underwriting audits from the reinsurers (yes, they review the business the insurance companies give them to see the results) are poor and the industry tightens up. This has happened cyclically a number of times over the past 20+ years. An insurance company may become "hungry for business" and relax its underwriting. If an insurance policy is not priced properly, then it may be the reinsurer who pays the price. The result of this is that reinsurers then increase costs and become more conservative on the underwriting side. This leaves Underwriters and all of us feeling very confused when we see sudden, unexplained changes. To dance through this minefield, we need to be very mindful of what is going on in the entire industry as well as the companies that we deal with.

Aggressive insurance companies can create what is called a "business exception" which could be based upon a series of logical inferences — *i.e.*, a good story or what is called a "business decision" which is based upon no logic at all, just that the "company wants the case badly". Differences in the results of these cases should be obvious, and quite often lead to belt tightening in the reinsurance community.

As a result of this, we have seen a lot of different actions on the reinsurers' part, including:

- Underwriting rules
- More stringent claims handling
- Price increases
- Mortality loading
- Leaving the market
- Consolidation
- Adjudication

Again, what is the goal of underwriting? Quite simply put, it is to:

1. provide a policy equitable to the client;
2. provide a policy deliverable by the agent; and
3. provide a policy profitable to the company.

First, we need to talk about the stereotypes. It is important that we understand that not all Underwriters are middle-aged, decrepit, sporting the latest in horn-rimmed glasses and on their last legs who could not find jobs working in the local library and flunked out of everything else.

By the same token, it is important that no Trusted Advisor is an unreformed swashbuckler whose only goal involves the pillage and plunder and the placement of the case to earn the most commission possible.

It is everybody's role to ensure that the Underwriter and the Trusted Advisor can work together as partners so that underwriting can fulfill its goals as defined above.

Now, to move on to the underwriting itself. Why do we do this? To better understand what the Underwriter is doing will allow the Trusted Advisor to achieve quicker issuance of an insurance policy and quicker commission payments, and, most importantly, it will allow the Trusted Advisor the opportunity to grow the sale.

We know that there are two basic types of underwriting — medical and financial. If we try to break it down further we will see that there are a number of distinct factors that affect insurability from an insurance perspective:

- Age
- Genetic Inheritance
- Health and Physical Condition
- Occupation
- Avocation
- Lifestyle
- Habits

THE APPLICATION PROCESS

The application is the single most important tool that the Underwriter has access to. Why? This is simply because the application is the information that forms a part of the contract. It is what the claims person can use later to try to deny a claim. While the blood profile, medical exam and electrocardiogram may initially appear more important, they do not form a part of the insurance contract, and, therefore, once the Underwriter has reviewed them and accepted the case, the company has "waived" its right to contest the results from a medical perspective unless *new* information is disclosed. An Underwriter sees a "snapshot" of your client at that precise moment in time when the contract is formed. There is a very distinct difference between insurance and clinical medicine, but more on that later.

To the Underwriter, the application is:

- the primary source for all personal data on your client;
- a sketch of your client from both a personal and medical perspective;
- the legal document;
- the document for all the facts and the accurate facts; and
- the most detailed picture the Underwriter has the chance to obtain on the client and, therefore, a key ingredient to determining insurability.

Many elite advisors provide cover letters with the application to try to "enhance" the snapshot for the Underwriter. We have all seen many articles which talk about full disclosure, about giving detail on questions and about providing additional information, but so few Trusted Advisors actually do this that it would surprise you. What might also be a surprise is how valuable and self-serving those cover letters can be. This is because a good cover letter may save the case by providing information that could contradict negative information given elsewhere.

As an example, let's say the Underwriter received an application and all the medical information came in. On the paramedical examination, it was noted that the blood pressure was 160/100. That's all the Underwriter often receives. This leads to attending physicians' reports and ratings.

Let's try again. A cover letter contained the following information. The Trusted Advisor had already asked the client about blood pressure, and the client told the advisor that he had something called "white coat syndrome", where he became extremely nervous in strange situations with unknown medical personnel, and this would increase his blood pressure dramatically. Furthermore, he took weekly blood pressure readings at home and went to his doctor once a month for readings, which had all been in the 110-120/80-85 range.

Like the advertisement says, "You can see the difference quality makes." One case received a rating, while the other one was standard.

A good cover letter may save your case:

1. It provides information that is not on the application.
2. It amplifies the case by providing the purpose of insurance and amounts.
3. It expedites approval and avoids unnecessary requirements.

I can only spell out how important cover letters may be. You can see from the example I have already given that it can turn a rated or declined case into a standard one. The application, while a lengthy and detailed document, provides little opportunity to actually "explain" things to the Underwriter. Why? Because insurance companies don't want the Underwriters seeing things that are not black and white — that might introduce "judgement" into the picture, that nebulous thing that slows down cases and could create a decision other than what the specific facts indicate. That is where the Trusted Advisor fits in. People's lives, jobs and insurability are not "cookie cutter" even though insurance companies might want them to be. It is our job to provide the Underwriter with information that clarifies the many grey areas of people's lives. Once an explanation has been given, and in fact volunteered, the Underwriter will be much more open to that elusive thing that all Trusted Advisors seek — understanding. Understanding and empathy for a situation can help create a much clearer picture for the Underwriter because we all must remember that that is all the Underwriter is getting — a snapshot into a specific moment of a person's life.

The cover letter allows the Trusted Advisor to develop the financial picture of the client for the Underwriter; after all, most applications merely have a slot for income and net worth. This doesn't tell anything about how the client got there, what he or she has built and why it is worth protecting — all very important elements of the underwriting picture.

The cover letter can really be the difference between an approval or a slow death due to "requirementitis", a specialized, underwriting term which when loosely translated means ordering more and more requirements until you or your client goes away. If you receive a request for a liver biopsy, you know you have reached the pinnacle!

It requires a special talent to write the underwriting letter, however, and my belief is that it is this fear and indecision that prevents many of us from writing them when we probably should. What would make us feel better is if someone could help us with those letters or proofread our statements to ensure that we are not merely trying to "sell" the Underwriter but are providing real, value-added information. A job opportunity? Sure, but only for the right person. If you, as a Trusted Advisor, don't have the luxury of an Underwriter to help you with the letter, then my suggestion would be to stick as much to the facts as possible, providing sources, specifics and information that the Underwriter can check for himself or herself.

Next, let's talk for a few minutes about missing information. There is nothing that makes the Underwriter roll his or her eyes faster than missing information on the application or the agent's report. I have personally seen applications without the client's name, without the reason for the application and without signatures, and wondered who is applying. These become the drivel of water cooler discussions between the Underwriters at the latest reinsurance conference, and their stories can be pretty graphic. When we call ourselves Trusted Advisors, it is our job and responsibility to get these things right the first time. An application with missing information not only slows down the process and can ultimately lose the business, but it hurts our credibility and can feed into the Underwriter's stereotype that we don't know what we are doing. Let's change that. Here is a checklist that you can use to go over your application *before* you send it to your Managing General Agent or the company.

Missing Information Slows Down the Process

Full name
Beneficiary
Plan and face amount
Identification documentation
Reason for the last visit to the doctor
Smoking status and nicotine products
All medical questions answered
Signatures and extra authorization signatures if applicable
Pre-authorized chequing cards and void cheques
Occupation(s)
All temporary insurance questions answered
Justification and purpose of insurance
Agent's report completed fully

The Non-medical Part II — Avoiding APSs

Give test results if known — *e.g.*, blood pressure readings
Add detail around illness — type, diagnosis, date, frequency, last attack, treatment
Clearly indicate any doctor's consultations

Medications

Disclose them!
Give dosage and frequency
Length of treatment
Response to meds — are they working?
Herbal remedies
Interactions

MEDICAL UNDERWRITING

Next, let's have a little primer on the Dreaded MIB — yes, that's a capital D — what it is and isn't and how the Trusted Advisor can understand what this means to the client and the underwriting process.

The MIB (Medical Information Bureau) is a clearing house for insurance company data and contains a database with client information, medical information and insurance activity over a number of years. It is encoded to protect the confidentiality of the client, and medical information is allocated by a series of codes and contains positive (meaning normal) medical information as well as disease encoding and abnormal test results. It does not provide any underwriting information or the outcome of cases or ratings that may have occurred. Why is this important to the Trusted Advisor? It is simple. If the information is already out there and can be added to, then it could change the outcome of the case. For example, I have often seen an MIB record for an abnormal electrocardiogram (a heart test) but received an MIB result as part of the underwriting process that was interpreted as normal. Working with Medical Directors it may then be possible to ignore previous tests, issue the coverage and amend the client's MIB record with a normal test result, in effect cleaning up the client's record as standard coverage was provided.

Essential facts of the medical history include the following:

- What exactly did the client have?
- When was it diagnosed?
- How often does it happen?
- When, precisely, was the last attack?
- How is it being treated?
- What are the names and addresses of all doctors consulted?

Clinical and Insurance Medicine

It is important here to digress for a minute and look at the difference between clinical and insurance medicine. Quite simply, there are two different types of medicine, and this is very important for us because the Underwriter is only able to use one of them. Clinical medicine is what your doctor practises. It is about keeping someone in good health, preventing future disease and ultimately prolonging life. Insurance medicine is about trying to anticipate where things will go wrong based upon a "snapshot in time" taken today and on the application of large numbers to determine or predict probable outcomes.

Clinical Medicine	Insurance Medicine
Emphasis on maintenance of good health	Present health status
Diagnosis and treatment of ailments	Risk sorted into broad groupings
No time or expense restraints	Groupings based on mortality
Seeing patient many times	Assumptions used for pricing
	Budgets allocated for testing
	Applicant seen only once

Let's now delve into how to get the most for your client from the underwriting process. The goal here is to successfully guide your client through the medicals and lab tests. Remember before when we discussed the Trusted Advisor controlling the underwriting process rather than the insurance company or the Underwriter? Here is where it becomes important.

Preparing the Client

The difference here is preparation, preparation, preparation! The Trusted Advisor will take the time to prepare clients for the following:

- Medical examinations
- Precautions for blood pressure, urine and blood tests
- How to avoid attending physicians' statements (APS) from being ordered
- How and why to record medications
- Special issues related to alcohol, pregnancy, the elderly and smokers

Medical Examinations

Preparing the client for the medical examination (by a doctor) or the paramedical examination (by a nurse) could be the most important thing the Trusted Advisor can do to ensure the best possible outcome for the application. But how many advisors actually know how to do so? Very few. I know this because, as an Underwriter, I saw the outcome far too many times: ill-prepared clients, rushing to the exam and many other errors. So how do *we* fix this? Preparation. Tell your clients the following when they are preparing for the medical:

- Don't eat just before going into the medical examination.

- Get a good night's sleep — it is especially important to the results to make sure the client is well rested and feels good the day of the exam. If the client is sick with the flu or exhausted because he or she has not slept for days, then have the client reschedule the appointment.
- Be early — not late. Getting there late rushes everything, including the client's emotions.
- Answer questions directly and fully.
- Disclose all medications. Prospects who have forgotten to take their medications, who have stopped taking them without the advice of their physician or who are taking medications recommended by a friend should not complete their examination until the issue has been resolved.
- Be careful what is volunteered. This doesn't mean to hide information in any way. What it means is don't speculate about what you as the client do not know. For example, if you have a rash on your face, providing information like "I knew a guy once who had a rash like this that turned out to be lupus" really just tells the Underwriter that you have been watching too many episodes of *House* or spending way too much time on the Internet. It simply tells the Underwriter to be more cautious with this case.

Blood Pressure, Electrocardiograms, Urine and Blood Tests

Blood Profiles

Insurance companies use multicomponent blood tests to evaluate a prospect's current health status. A full blood profile may contain as many as 15 to 20 individual tests, and a number of reflex tests may be required if appropriate. A reflex test occurs when the individual test is abnormal and, therefore, warrants more investigation through a more specific test.

For example, the blood test will test for glucose levels (called a random glucose test). If abnormal, the lab will then, and only then, perform a glycohemoglobin A1C test, which looks at past blood sugar control, and will provide evidence supporting or disclaiming a diagnosis of diabetes. Underwriters are not in the business of diagnosing disease, however. They just know what the results of the test mean in terms of the insurance application. In our example, a positive glucose and glycohemoglobin A1C will probably mean a postponement until the prospect is reviewed by his or her doctor, and the insurance company will likely volunteer to send its results to the client's physician.

Urine Tests

These work on much the same principle as the blood profile, and insurance companies have become very sophisticated with the tests performed to get the most out of a urine test. This reduces their costs significantly because a urine test is much cheaper than a blood profile. They test for several different items in the urine, including sugar, protein, blood, cocaine and cotinine (a derivative of nicotine in smokers) amongst others. While I have seen many methods of trying to "beat" the test, it is very difficult to do so.

But, many will try anyway. Many years ago when urine testing was at the forefront of the underwriting protocol, I had a number of cases where several clients all tested positive for sugar in their urine at the same time. Without much thought, we went back and ordered blood tests as a result of this because we were worried the clients may potentially be diabetic, a condition which may significantly affect life expectancy. For some strange reason, all of the blood profiles came back negative, and we couldn't figure out why until we reviewed things in a little more detail. All of the applications came from the same broker! Upon questioning it turned out that the broker had not wanted to trouble his clients with doing a urine test and had provided the specimens himself. It turned out that he was diabetic and didn't know it! The most amazing thing was that the broker probably saved his own life by his actions — although he is no longer a broker for obvious reasons.

My point here is that the Trusted Advisor will help the prospect improve his or her chances of doing well on the tests — not "beat" the tests. There are no free lunches, as they say! On the other hand, false positives do occur in many tests, and sometimes a repeat or a fasting sample may be the appropriate response before action is taken. However, this is where the knowledge of what is going on is important because some insurers may not want to pay for additional testing, or the product may not warrant further expenditure (especially on term business). If there are abnormal test results found, then someone with an underwriting background should be called in before the prospect receives a decline or rating which may unnecessarily follow him or her around for years to come.

Key Precautions for Blood, Urine and Blood Pressure Tests

- Don't eat!
- Be calm!
- Be rested!

- Don't talk during blood pressure (BP) readings!
- Make sure the BP cuff fits. The BP cuff should not be too small for your arm. This could result in an abnormally incorrect reading. Make sure that there is significant cuff that wraps around your arm at rest when the cuff is being attached.
- Be aware of "white coat" syndrome. This very common condition occurs because many people fear the doctor's office and become extremely nervous when a stranger comes to take their blood pressure. The nervousness results in higher than anticipated readings. If the initial readings are high, a resting period may be in order and additional readings taken.
- Don't exercise within 24 hours!

How and Why to Record Medications

- Date medication began
- Illness being treated or prevented
- Dosage
- Frequency
- Interactions

The why is simple. Providing more information at the application level can reduce the number of Attending Physician Reports ordered and, therefore, speed up the underwriting process on your case. This is not to "beat" the Underwriter at his or her own game but is merely full disclosure, which is what the Underwriter is looking for anyway.

Special Issues Related to Alcohol, Pregnancy and Smokers

- Do not drink alcohol prior to testing — at least 48 hours.
- If you are pregnant, tell the doctor. Outline medications, *etc.*
- If you smoke, drink lots of water for two or three days before the test.
- Don't smoke just before testing.

ECGs (Electrocardiograms and Treadmill Stress Tests)

Electrocardiograms and stress tests are a wonderful tool for the underwriting process. Due to their cost they are only used for increased amounts of insurance and as age advances. Electrocardiograms measure the electrical conductivity through the heart muscle and can reveal many cardiovascular impairments, including coronary artery disease.

- Performing an ECG is easy; interpreting it may not be.
- Treadmill stress tests are becoming routine to screen for large amounts of insurance coverage.
- The "thallium" stress test is a more sensitive type of test where radioactive dye is injected into the blood system and used to determine an area of weakness in the heart.

We have spent a lot of time discussing missing information, how to deal with the Underwriter from a preparation point of view and reviewing the medical underwriting process that the Underwriter will go through. Remember, this is all about making the Trusted Advisor the Underwriter's partner in obtaining the prospect's insurance approval and being prepared for any objection which may come up along the way. You could have the best completed application, a medical standard or even preferred risk and still not obtain the underwriting approval. Why? Because we are still missing one of the most important aspects of the underwriting process.

FINANCIAL UNDERWRITING

Financial underwriting is the process that the Underwriter goes through to determine if the prospect should have the coverage that is applied for, if there is insurable interest (does the beneficiary have a reason why he or she would prefer the client to stay alive) and if the application makes sense. As we start this journey, the real question we always need to answer is the why. Why underwrite financially as well as medically? There are a number of reasons beyond the obvious, such as to keep the client alive, to protect the products we have and to ethically provide the right amount for the client. The specific reasons of underwriting financially include the following:

- Avoid fraudulent claims and early lapses
- Avoid anti-selective claims
- Avoid potential punitive damages
- Potential for fraud and anti-selection increases as the face amount increases
- Anti-money laundering and ability to pay
- Make sure the client is not worth more dead than alive
- You can't price for financial underwriting

Always keep in mind that the Underwriter has not been a part of the sales process, has not met the client and is only aware of the details presented on the application and attachments given to him or her. The Underwriter must establish the purpose for the insurance and justify the amount, based solely on the application and supporting information you have provided and the Underwriter's company rules, so it is important to fit your application and supporting information into the company's rules. If the Underwriter is concerned about the financial justification on a case, or suspects potential fraud, an unscheduled inspection report or other discretionary requirements may be requested, complicating the sale.

So let's spend some time reviewing what it is the Underwriter is looking for.

What most concerns the Underwriter?

- Overinsurance
- Insurable interest
- Ability to pay

Overinsurance is simply having too much insurance. It is amazing how more people with grossly exaggerated amounts of insurance in force seem to die than those people who have a more prudent amount of coverage on their lives. Based on large amount insurance mortality studies by the Society of Actuaries accidental death mortality rises as the amount of coverage rises, both with and without Accidental Death Benefit.

By the same token I have found it fascinating how underinsured most people are. Even those people with Trusted Advisors sometimes find themselves underinsured usually because information has not been disclosed to their Trusted Advisor so that he or she can take action to help ensure that adequate protection is in place. As we have seen earlier, missing information will and does slow down the processing, lead to uninformed and erroneous decisions and ultimately affect a person's ability to provide for those who need it most, at the time when they require it the most.

Insurable interest is an identifiable financial loss to the beneficiary on the death of the insured. Quite simply, if there is a financial gain, there is no need for the insurance. A person is always deemed to have an insurable interest in his or her own life.

Ability to pay premiums is the prospect's ability to afford the coverage he or she requires or is requesting. This is important from a lapse prevention standpoint as policies that can't be afforded will not stay in place for long. The Underwriter will review gross family income and net worth, and the maximum life insurance premium should not be more than 15% to 20% of net income. This, of course, varies from company to company. For business insurance, the evaluation may involve ownership percentage, net income and corporate value.

Now for the $60,000 question: How much insurance will be allowed? There is a lot of "grey area" in the financial underwriting world, but usually it begins with a process of evaluation of the purpose for insurance and will begin with a formula. Of course, the Underwriter does have a lot of discretion in this regard. Usually the determination of amount for personal insurance follows a formula based upon the present value of the future earnings of the prospect. The formula follows something like this:

Amount of insurance needed = income to life expectancy adjusted for inflation and discounted for interest rate.

Example

Male non-smoker age 30 currently earning $30,000 per year and using a 3% inflation rate will earn approximately $3.2 million to age 65 (the normal retirement age). The present value of this number at 7% is approximately $531,000. Divide the present value by the prospect's income to develop the factor. In this case, $531,000/$30,000 = 17. So a 30-year-old male should have 17 times his income in insurance death benefit for adequate protection. (Please note this is a sample only and varies by company to company, and usually the actual table used by the Underwriter is somewhat more generous than shown here.)

An actual table:

Age	Income Factor
Under age 30	20
30-39	17
40-49	12
50-59	8
60-64	5
65+	3

Insurance Coverage Considerations

- Estate Conservation
  - Current liabilities — capital gains taxes
  - Will consider additional insurance for growth in liabilities at 5% per year
- Creditor Insurance
  - 100% of outstanding loan balance(s)
- Buy-Sell

- Percentage ownership in business multiplied by company fair market value
- Will consider company growth of 5% per year for five years
- All shareholders should be insured for appropriate coverage

- Key Person
  - Generally five to ten times income
  - Employee must be key to the operation of the company based on skills and experience
  - Make sure other key people are also insured
  - Most common type of business application
  - Protects employer against financial loss on death of employee
  - Key person defined as:
    - Executive employee of company
    - Employee with specialized technical skills
    - Employee whose productivity and personality skills are so great that his or her death would result in significant loss in sales
- Always Communicate
  - Existing coverage, the purpose of the existing coverage and any replacement
  - Purpose of proposed coverage
  - How the amount of coverage was determined and sales concept(s) used
  - Rationale for owner and beneficiary designations
  - Include Certified Financial Questionnaire and supporting documentation such as financial/net worth statements
- Creditor Insurance: Debt Repayment
  - Percentage of obligation × loan amount
  - Requires loan agreement or letter from creditor
- Charitable Giving
  - Age 65 minus current age × amount of annual contribution
  - Require past three years' contribution record
- Juvenile
  - 25% to 50% × amount on parent with highest income
  - May require covering letter
- Who May Not Be Covered

- Elderly parents dependent on their children
- Welfare recipients (may be exception for single parents)
- Large amounts on children (except for need like trust fund)
- Individuals who do not appear to be likely to be self-supporting

Cases of Insurance Fraud

Does fraud and anti-selection occur?

The simple answer is *yes*.

How often does this happen?

Nobody knows the answer to this.

Below are some examples of insurance fraud:

- Application on Mrs. C
  - $250,000 applications sent to eight companies
  - All policies approved as applied for and kept in force until claim
  - Death claims submitted two years and three weeks following issue
  - Four companies paid death claim and four companies in the process of settling claim when contacted by RCMP fraud squad as Mrs. C did not actually exist
- Application on Mr. M
  - $1 million application owned by brother and paid by single premium
  - Medical indicated proposed insured was mentally handicapped, suffered from dental caries, poor hygiene and severe malnutrition
  - Inspection report representative could not locate client, as he lived on the street and in shelters

Putting the Jumbo Case Together

The "Jumbo" case is one that eludes most Trusted Advisors. Everybody wants to be in this field but very few people are successful time and again. Again, we must ask ourselves why? The answer is really quite simple, and we have already discussed it. Jumbo cases can be completed by those people who are diligent in preparing the case, are good at all aspects of the sale and take the time, care and attention to look after their clients. A couple of easy rules that we always try to live by can help here:

- The client comes first.
- Do what you say you are going to do.
- Do it on time.
- Do it with service excellence.
- Do your personal best.
- Always say please and thank you.

That's enough for the sales part of the case. Now let's *prepare* it to be successful. It is important to build the case from the ground up for the Underwriter, remembering that he or she has not been a part of your brilliant sales process and doesn't yet have your level of excitement with the prospect. Many Trusted Advisors also feel that information is the key to these cases but fail to provide the needed information to the Underwriter because they feel the Underwriter should be looking at them and not the client. "I am trustworthy so the case must be valid." This syndrome causes the delay and potential failure of many a large case.

The Jumbo case will always be subject to review based on a "good story" and will be reviewed by both the insurance company Underwriter and the reinsurers' Underwriters. You have done a needs analysis which reveals a greater amount of insurance needed, so now how do you get it? It is a fact that "exceptions to all limits may be considered if well documented and well explained".

Apply common sense here.

- Does an insurable loss exist between the life assured and the beneficiary?
- Does the owner of the policy make sense?
- Does the purpose of the insurance make sense?
- Does the amount of coverage make sense?
- Does the financial evidence that has been provided make sense?

What is the Underwriter trying to prevent?

- Speculation — buying insurance on someone in the hope that he or she will die soon
- Overinsurance — buying too much insurance
- Selective Lapsation — policies that do not stay in force and affect companies' "bottom line" profitability
- Potential for Violence
- Accident/Suicide/Homicide

- Large Claims

Reinsurance

Reinsurance is the process by which insurance companies "share risk" with third parties. In order to prevent an unwanted claim from adversely affecting the bottom line of a company, insurers will purchase insurance on a given life from third party reinsurance companies, allowing them to spread the risk. The reinsurer will want to underwrite the risk as will the insurance company where the application for insurance was first made, and information will be shared with the reinsurer by the insurance company for its approval. Worldwide capacity on any one individual is limited by the size of the reinsurance market and is currently approximately $100 million in Canada. Capacity is based on the personal risk profile and is affected by many factors, including health, finances and insurance in force.

What Is Different About a Jumbo Case?

- Reserving facilities with the reinsurer
- Requirements — large cases require many additional underwriting requirements
- Medical assessment — review by both the direct company and the reinsurer
- Financial assessment — many additional financial requirements
- Controlling the total line and the amount of insurance in force

All large cases should include at a minimum:

1. Properly completed application
2. A cover letter outlining how the case was built
3. Illustrations and sales materials
4. Financial questionnaires
5. Financial statements
6. Accountant letters
7. Corporate information, brochures, Internet information, *etc.*

Packaging this material for the Underwriter is essential. It communicates how the case was built and why it is being applied for in the way that it is, and provides the justification for the case itself. This is where underwriting knowledge for the Trusted Advisor is key. Use of the resources available here can result in a placed Jumbo case.

Insurance as an Investment

The most difficult case to build is the case that uses insurance as an investment like any other. It is a well-known fact that an insurance policy is one of the last few true tax shelters available in Canada. Money that grows inside a universal life or whole life policy can be tax-sheltered investment growth and will pay out tax-free upon the insured's death to the beneficiaries. While beyond the discussion here, estate bonds, insured retirement policies and leveraged cash values can all provide significant tax benefits to the astute investor. Insurance companies have recognized this and provide many investment options to the discerning applicant. There is one problem. Underwriters still apply the same rules to these cases, and, therefore, justification of the death benefit becomes a limiting factor for many of these cases rather than the amount invested, and it may encumber the applicants' ability to obtain insurance for other needs if their "total insurable amount" has been used up by this methodology. Excellent field underwriting is mandatory in these types of cases, and an expert should be consulted to work this model into the prospects' overall investment, insurance and tax strategy. Premiums must be justified based upon investable assets and should be spread over a number of years to allow for changes in the overall client plan. The valuation of assets in these types of plans may necessitate insurance amounts well in excess of "reasonable" limits to ensure tax exempt status of a policy with large deposits. The key here again is to make sure you tell the entire story to the Underwriter and make him or her your partner in the process.

Possible Scenarios for Large Insurance Coverage

- Buy-Sell/Cross Purchase
    - Arrangement between "partners" to purchase sufficient insurance on all insurable partners
    - Insurance proceeds are used to buy out deceased partner's share
    - Coverage must be related to percentage of ownership
    - Coverages should be reasonable re age and insurability
- Stock Purchase/Redemption
    - Agreement between corporation and major stockholder
    - Provides right (and funds) to purchase stock on death of shareholder
    - Insurable interest of company = value of stock owned
    - Provide a copy of the contract/agreement to justify insurance

- Split Dollar/Deferred Compensation
  - Business insurance with an element of personal insurance
  - Premiums or a portion of premiums are paid by employer
  - On death, cash value paid to employer; insurance value is paid to beneficiary

Financial Statements

Providing the financial statements, especially on the Jumbo case, may be of extreme value to the Underwriter. It is important to have some understanding of the key elements of a financial statement to present the information to the Underwriter in a way that helps the case the most. There are three elements to most financial statements (as listed below), and an audited statement is always better than an unaudited one.

1. Balance Sheet
2. Income Statement
3. Notes

Balance Sheet

What are the various elements of the balance sheet?

- **Asset:** anything of value owned or receivable by the company
- **Current Asset:** cash on hand and in banks, items convertible to cash, accounts receivable
- **Fixed Asset:** real property such as land and buildings, machinery, furniture, fixtures
- **Liability:** any debt incurred or obligation owed by the company
- **Current Liability:** any obligation that has to be met in the next 12 months (*e.g.,* accounts and notes payable, dividends, salaries, taxes)
- **Long-Term Debt:** liability which stretches out beyond one year
- **Net Worth or Book Value:** amount by which the total assets exceed total liabilities; includes capital stock, retained earnings and other surplus accounts
- **Capital Stock, Owner's or Shareholder's Equity:** accumulated amount invested in the organization by its owners
- **Retained Earnings:** accumulated amount of earnings from net income left in the business at the end of a given period

The Income Statement

- a summary of fiscal activity for a period
- shows revenue and its sources
- shows expenses incurred in producing revenue
- bottom line shows net income (loss)

Income Statement Format

Expenses (selling, general and administration) = Income (loss) before taxes – Income taxes = Net income (loss) for the period

Total sales or revenue from services rendered – Cost of goods sold or services rendered = Gross profit (loss)

Industrial Ratios

Industrial ratios are ratios used by financial professionals to assess the ability of a company to sustain itself.

- Current or Working Capital Ratio

  Current Assets ÷ Current Liabilities

  (should be at least 2:1)
- Quick Ratio (Acid Test)

  Current Assets Less Inventories ÷ Current Liabilities

  (should be at least 1:1)
- Working Capital Ratio

  Current Assets – Current Liabilities = Working Capital

  (should be at least equal to total debt)
- Debt to Equity Ratio

  Total Liabilities ÷ Net Worth

  (high ratio is an indicator of problems)

Other Ratios (from Income Statement)

- Profit Margin

  Operating Profit ÷ Net Sales
- Net Income Ratio

  Net Income ÷ Net Sales

  (these ratios are intended to indicate the ability of the business to produce a return on investment; usually the higher the ratio, the better the return)

Notes

The notes section of a financial statement can be very important. It often gives breakdowns of unusual circumstances, equipment and depreciation and is the accounting methodology to tell the reader something about what is going on at the company and how it is structured. Often it will reveal much more about long-term debt, share structure and repurchase plans, shareholder loans and many other elements of a company's business. Understanding this information can help the Trusted Advisor explain things to the Underwriter and develop the case in its best possible light.

APPLYING THE PRINCIPLES

Okay, so now we have gone through the basic gambit of the elements of underwriting life insurance applications and what the Underwriter is looking for and why. Let's now take the opportunity to apply all that we have learned and look at a couple of real life cases. While there is no *right* answer, I will let you know that neither of these cases would have ever been approved without the documentation provided herein.

Case Study #1

Application

- 42-year-old male born in Lebanon
- Occupation — President of A Imports Inc.
- $2 million key-person coverage
- A Imports is owner and beneficiary
- Business and home address are the same
- Salary $200,000
- Business — retained earnings of $1.2 million
- Travel to Middle East to purchase inventory

You Be the Underwriter

- Does an insurable loss exist between the life assured and the beneficiary?
- Does the owner of the policy make sense?
- Does the purpose of the insurance make sense?
- Does the amount of coverage make sense?
- Does the financial evidence that has been provided make sense?

Covering Letter

Upon arriving in Canada from Lebanon 10 years ago, Mr. A started a small sporting goods store. The store grew quickly through advertising and innovative products/pricing. Two additional locations were opened in the city over the past three years. The retained earnings for the companies exceeds $2.2 million. The three stores are currently managed by Mr. A's brothers. This allows Mr. A to concentrate on his newest interest — an importation business that he currently runs from his home, called A Imports. Mr. A expects to travel to the Middle East four times per year to locate interesting products for importation and distribution in Canada.

Mr. A. draws a management salary of $200,000 annually from his sporting goods stores. He has no insurance in force and although his accountant has indicated an insurance need for key-person and estate conservation needs, Mr. A does not really believe in life insurance. His accountant introduced me last week. After meeting with the client, Mr. A has agreed, somewhat reluctantly, to $2 million of key-person insurance. Against my advice, Mr. A has asked to use A Imports Inc. as the owner/beneficiary. The final structure will be determined after discussions with his lawyer and our Estate Practioners group.

Attachments to Application

- Covering letter
- Foreign travel questionnaire
- Financial statements for sporting goods stores documenting retained earnings

Case Study #2

Application

- $4 million key-person corporate-owned
- Beneficiary Z-master Toys Inc.
- Mr. Z's income is $100,000
- Insured is president and 60% owner of company
- The 40% owner is a "silent partner", and he does not require insurance
- Purpose of insurance — to pay off silent partner

You Be the Underwriter

- Does an insurable loss exist between the life assured and the beneficiary?
- Does the owner of the policy make sense?

- Does the purpose of the insurance make sense?
- Does the amount of coverage make sense?
- Does the financial evidence that has been provided make sense?

Covering Letter

Mr. Z left university and worked for a few years in various businesses as an accountant. He always had a fascination with toys and, after his marriage in 1995, decided to pursue this interest, starting his own toy distribution company. Attending trade markets, he discovered a pressurized air piston engine that he envisioned as the power-plant for a new line of air-powered model airplanes and boats.

Two years later, Mr. Z developed the top toy of the year for 1997 and 1998, and his toy distribution company was valued at $10 million. His wife, who is 50% owner, wants to be bought out of the company as part of a divorce settlement. She agreed to a $4 million payout. Mr. Z draws a modest income of $100,000.

Mr. Z has found an investor who will pay $4 million for 40% of the business, but has insisted the shareholder agreement provide for $4 million of key-person coverage on Mr. Z to protect his investment. The investor will not be involved in the company but anticipates excellent growth potential in this venture.

Attachments to submission

- Covering letter
- Copy of financial statements
- Copy of insurance provision from shareholder's agreement

It is quite apparent that a good cover letter cannot only save a case but result in an easy approval rather than delays and Not Proceeded With applications!

CONCLUSION

Now how do we tie all this information together? It can be summed up quite easily. Prepare your case for the Underwriter! Whether you are the accountant, the Trusted Advisor or a financial advisor, it is important to recognize that the sale to the Underwriter is every bit as important as the sale to the client, as it will put the Underwriter in your court and help to get those approvals you are looking for. Some quick checklist items follow:

- Use an underwriting process
- Document your case
- Fill the application out fully
- Provide sales and supporting information
- Build your story
- Anticipate and overcome objections
- Be practical
- Take away any "surprises"
- Consult subject matter "experts"
- Win the Underwriter to your cause

CHAPTER 65

APPLICATIONS OF UNIVERSAL LIFE INSURANCE WITH OTHER FINANCIAL SOLUTIONS TO GET TWICE THE BANG

Gordon Berger
Bob Kirk

Overview

In this chapter you will learn how to complement the Individual Pension Plan (IPP) with the universal life insurance solution.

Learning Objectives

By the end of this chapter, you should be able to:

- understand the value of utilizing universal life insurance to create and maximize wealth; and
- understand the value of leveraging the cash value within a universal life insurance policy to fund IPP contributions.

WHY UTILIZE UNIVERSAL LIFE INSURANCE?

It is quite clear that the most elusive strategies from a financial planning perspective are those that provide integrated solutions to real problems. To create a vehicle that will provide the user with "the missing link", the piece that draws everything together into a package that provides the client with a unique financial solution for now and tomorrow is the real goal or nirvana of wealth creation.

A lot has been said about using leveraged life insurance programs, but there are different ways in which they can be utilized. Select clients can take advantage of the universal life concept through the use of this seamless strategy that provides value with the following benefits:

- allows deposits to be deductible over time;
- has low captive capital;
- grows deposits tax-sheltered;
- transfers the growth to the next generation tax-free; and
- allows for the use of the growth tax-free.

There are only four "real" tax shelters in Canada today:

- principal residence (home);
- Individual Pension Plans (IPPs);
- RRSPs; and
- life insurance.

Sometimes it is not possible to use your home, although recently, lines of credit and concepts such as the reverse mortgage have become all the rage. RRSPs are entirely too constrictive in that they have limited deposits, must be unwound at age 69 and are taxable when used, often at the highest marginal tax rate. That leaves life insurance …

Section 148 of the *Income Tax Act*, R.S.C. 1985, c. 1 (5th Supp.) (ITA), allows for properly structured life insurance plans to "grow deposits sheltered of tax" and "transfer the growth to the next generation tax free". This is why life insurance policies can provide the essential value that makes them a viable chassis for the universal life solution.

However, generally speaking, deposits to life insurance are not deductible. This process allows for the creation of tax deductions using the above section 148 of the ITA.

THE SCENARIO

The scenario below illustrates how a life insurance policy provides the greatest flexibility for a business owner to maximize his or her wealth.

- Business owner is a 55-year-old businessman.
- Business was incorporated in 1985.
- Company can sponsor and fund for our business owner an IPP for past service back to 1991 and current service for $161,851 in 2006.
- Qualifying transfer needed to fund for past service is $242,600.
- The second year (2007) after the IPP has been created, the contribution made into the IPP by the company will be $27,934. These corporate deposits into the IPP for the years that follow will increase at 7.5% per year.

- The business owner did a reorganization in 1999 and opened a holding company (HoldCo).
- He has flowed over $2 million from his operation company (OpCo) to his HoldCo, where it sits in retained earnings.
- The business owner has $1.5 million sitting in his RRSP.

THE PROCESS

The client has already moved money from OpCo to HoldCo and, therefore, has already placed cash into retained earnings of HoldCo.

HoldCo could make a large deposit to the insurance contract — let's say $1 million — and then could subsequently borrow by way of a policy loan back to HoldCo. In actual terms, approximately $700,000 could be borrowed back to HoldCo; the additional $300,000 will pay the cost of insurance and grow tax-sheltered within the insurance policy and provide funds for future policy loans as they become available. HoldCo now needs to invest the $700,000 to provide for the possibility of interest deductibility on the policy loan.

When the funds are withdrawn from the insurance company, the client must invest that money. The investment must be an investment that would allow for the deduction of interest expenses. Why?

Because the withdrawal from the insurance contract is by way of a loan.

Perhaps HoldCo loans a portion of the funds to OpCo at an interest rate slightly higher than that being charged by the insurance carrier — this creates a reasonable expectation of profit scenario. HoldCo could also take out a general security agreement or other security to ensure that it is "first in line" in the event of insolvency of OpCo.

Each year, the insurance carrier will ask for interest on the policy loan, and each year HoldCo will ask OpCo for interest on its loan. The net result is that the deduction in HoldCo offsets the income from OpCo to HoldCo, and there is no tax on this transaction other than a small amount on the income difference between the loan interest paid to the policyholder from OpCo and the loan interest paid by the policyholder to the insurance carrier. In essence, HoldCo has a deduction it did not have before.

Now to the funds, which are now in OpCo. A portion of the funds can be used to deposit into the Individual Pension Plan to satisfy the past service requirement, and funds would be moved from the RRSP into the IPP as well. This is completed in satisfaction of the opportunity to deposit 15 years of past service to the IPP. In order to make these deposits, our client would have to have enough funds in his RRSP to allow for a transfer from the RRSP into the IPP as well. In our example above, this would mean that a deposit of $161,851 would be made into the IPP, and $242,600 would be transferred into the IPP from the RRSP. The main benefit of this is that the deposit from OpCo to the IPP will be deductible, thereby building a retirement plan with deductible funds. It is of special note that funds can be borrowed to contribute into an IPP and are still deductible.

THE OUTCOME

The client would now have a number of benefits as a result of implementing this structure. One benefit would be a deductible interest payment into a life insurance contract every year. These funds would grow tax-sheltered within the insurance contract and could be used to pass funds to heirs or can be leveraged in retirement to create tax-free retirement payments — an IPP with significant, defined benefit, and enhanced retirement benefits. What has been created as a result is a twofold retirement structure. By the use of an integrated plan, the client would have two streams of retirement funds: a defined benefit pension plan and a large cash value life insurance contract both built with deductions. In essence, this planning technique allows for the creation of several retirement structures with high tax efficiency.

THE POSSIBILITIES

Through planning, the client could potentially unwind his RRSP by making withdrawals on an annual basis equal to the interest payable on the policy loan. Therefore, although money withdrawn from an RRSP is taxable, the funds are used to pay deductible interest. The RRSP could potentially be exhausted by the time the client reaches age 69, which means the funds do not have to be transferred to an RRIF or annuity and be withdrawn, since they would now reside as cash within a life insurance contract.

After many years of accumulating funds, the client has several choices as to how to utilize these funds for retirement:

1. The policy loan could be paid with outside funds and then leveraged with a bank for a bank loan or a series of bank loans.
2. After a period of time, the policy loan could be paid with internal cash that has accumulated within the insurance contract and then leveraged as in 1, above.

3. The client could use other retirement sources first, knowing that this cash is available in the future.
4. The client could make withdrawals directly from the insurance contract, albeit with certain tax consequences.
5. The client could potentially even sell HoldCo with the insurance policy asset within it.

As can be seen from the numerous choices, the client has the control, the opportunity and the flexibility to make choices that suit a desired lifestyle and with the capability of making the decisions on the client's own timetable.

If the funds are not needed, the client could pass the funds to the next generation or pay capital gains taxes with the insurance death benefit, having now accumulated excess funds that would not have been present otherwise. This could potentially make it very easy for the estate to be preserved into the hands of the next generation by providing funds to pay the taxes rather than using up a portion of the money the client built over a lifetime of hard work.

The flexibility of the concept lies in its simplicity. There is no financial underwriting for insurance policy loans. They are secured by the contract itself, and interest payments even have flexibility as to timing and amount. In fact, it is even possible to miss an interest payment once there are funds within the plan.

Moreover, the plan can be structured to fit the circumstances of most entrepreneurs and can even use cash flow from the business to be built or can be placed within the all too familiar "bonus out and loan back" structure that is utilized by many principals of individually owned corporations or partnerships. The investments can be structured in numerous ways to fit the most conservative to highly aggressive investment goals. The plan is also available to high-income earning employees although without the IPP component. The OpCo/HoldCo planning is not always necessary but often works best depending on where the funds are located.

The universal life solution provides clients with a means to enhance their retirement, create funds for the future of their family and pass money to their heirs on a tax-free basis. All this is built with funds that are potentially deductible and which provide clients with the control, flexibility and capability of managing their own financial future.

Often, clients find pieces of the puzzle to enhance their future wealth creation goals, but it is rare to find a plan that can create a myriad of possibilities the way that this one can, especially in its flexibility. Isn't that what the nirvana of wealth creation should be all about?

Diagram 1. Universal Life Insurance with an Individual Pension Plan

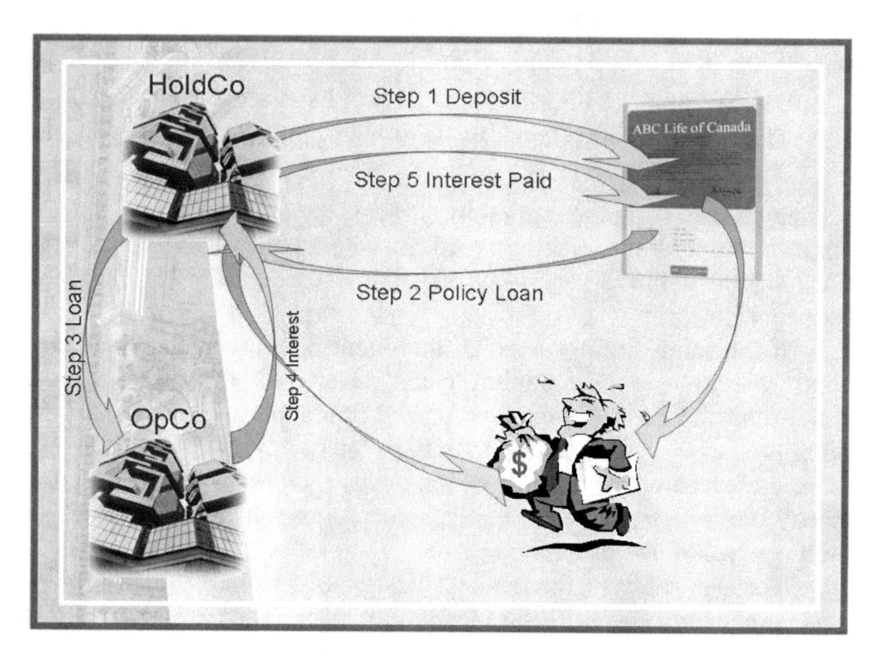

Diagram 2. Universal Life Insurance without an Individual Pension Plan

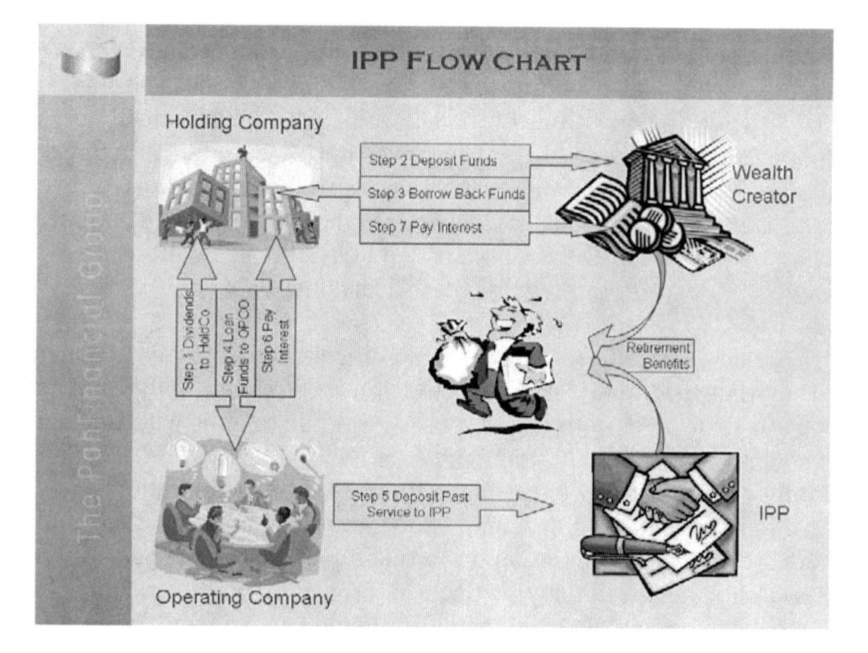

CHAPTER 66

INSURANCE LAW PRIMER

David Bertschi*

Overview

Within this chapter I will discuss insurance law in Canada in detail and provide a method to assist clients whose insurer has denied the insurance benefit at the time of claim. The aim of this chapter is to provide the Trusted Advisor answers to help their clients, their beneficiaries and estates to justly receive the insurance benefit upon time of claim.

Learning Objectives

By the time you complete this chapter you should be able to:

- understand the legal definition of "insurance" in Canada;
- understand Canadian contract and negligence law;
- understand Canadian civil procedure;
- understand the basics of both life and property and causal insurance; and
- understand the steps that should be taken to make sure that clients are paid the insurance benefits that they paid for.

> We cannot always know what new issues might arise before the courts in the future, but we can trust that the law will grow and evolve as necessary and when necessary in response.[1]

---

* David Bertschi is a Senior Partner at the Insurance and Commercial Litigation Boutique Firm of Bertschi Orth Smith LLP in Ottawa, Ontario, Canada. He restricts his practice to insurance and commercial litigation. David is fluently bilingual and has appeared before all levels of the Court in Ontario and at the Federal Court of Appeal. He has been widely quoted on Insurance Law by print, radio and television. A special thanks are owed to David's partners and associates at Bertschi Orth Smith LLP, especially to Kelly Fitzpatrick for assisting in the research and preparation of this chapter.

[1] *R. v. Hape*, [2007] S.C.J. No. 26, 2007 SCC 26, [2007] 2 S.C.R. 292 at para. 95 (S.C.C.).

Successful business people expect their financial advisors not only to increase but to protect their accumulated wealth.

Insurance, and insurance law, is an important component in protecting the wealth and assets of individuals and businesses alike.

INSURANCE

Insurance, including insured services and products, is a means by which individuals and groups of people with an interest or asset in common pay a specific amount of money known as a premium to protect themselves and their property or interests from certain events such as fire, theft, disability or liability when a manufactured product causes harm to others. Critical to the concept of insurance is that the individual(s) that pay for insurance have acted in good faith (full and frank disclosure), they have an interest in the property or item or individual, and the loss or damage is accidental or is not caused intentionally by the individual(s) insured. Should a loss or claim fall within the policy, then, pursuant to the terms, conditions and exclusions of the policy, the insurer may be required to pay or indemnify the insured pursuant to the terms of the insurance contract.

Insurance law is a body of law enacted by the legislatures which is interpreted with the contract or policy of insurance by the judiciary.

While the famous English barrister and novelist John Mortimer stated in reference to counsel,

> The law seems like a sort of maze through which a client must be led to safety, a collection of reefs, rocks, and underwater hazards through which he or she must be piloted.[2]

the financial advisor can assist his or her clients in discerning legal issues and piloting the client to a competent lawyer.

While this chapter will attempt to highlight certain potential legal issues that may befall clients and businesses, it is by no means a comprehensive recitation and analysis of the law. This chapter is meant to give the reader information of a general nature, and it is for discussion purposes. This chapter is not intended to be a substitute for legal advice. Should legal issues arise, one should hire a lawyer immediately to review the specific facts and the law in question, including all the statutes, regulations and jurisprudence on the issue in dispute to provide the client with a comprehensive and accurate legal opinion that would apply to his or her specific circumstances.

---

[2] *Clinging to the Wreckage: A Part of Life* (Penguin Non-classics, 1982).

CONTRACT AND NEGLIGENCE LAW

A critical component to insurance law is an understanding of the doctrines of contract and negligence.

An important component in interpreting the rights of the parties to a contract of insurance involves looking at the terms of the contract and the reasonable expectation of the parties. An unjustified breach of contract will result in the wronged party being placed in the position he or she would have been but for the breach, with a likely award of additional damages, costs and interest by the court.

The doctrine of negligence provides that when an individual is so closely and directly affected by the act of another, it is expected that he or she should take reasonable care to avoid an act or omission which causes harm to that other individual. If the wrongdoer does not take reasonable care to avoid harming the other person, then the wrongdoer's action is deemed negligent for which the perpetrator is responsible in law for his or her actions and the resulting damages. When an individual is negligent and causes harm to his or her "neighbour", the courts will compensate the injured party so as to put the aggrieved party in the position as if the negligent act never occurred. Because the courts cannot make people whole (*i.e.*, by making them physically better), in lieu they provide the injured party with compensation.

To enforce contracts or award damages, the public has recourse to the justice system by a process known collectively as civil procedure.

CIVIL PROCEDURE

Civil litigation in Ontario is governed by the *Rules of Civil Procedure*.[3] There are several steps and considerations that you must look at before commencing an action. Accordingly, you should consult a lawyer to determine your rights and obligations should you decide to proceed with litigation. The lawyer will advise you whether you are required to provide notice of your action, which can vary depending on the nature of your case. You should also be aware of the applicable limitation period, which currently is generally two years under the *Limitations Act, 2002*,[4] as amended.

Another issue to consider is the relief sought and the corresponding monetary jurisdiction. Presently under the *Rules of Civil Procedure*, matters claimed up to $10,000 would proceed in Small Claims Court. For matters up to $50,000, the case would fall under Simplified Procedure

---

[3] R.R.O. 1990, Reg. 194.

[4] S.O. 2002, c. 24, Sched. B.

(Rule 76), where the procedural steps are time limited or curtailed. All matters in excess of $50,000 proceed under the regular regime, incorporating all aspects of the litigation process. The monetary limits will be changing in January 2010 in that the Small Claims Court will have jurisdiction for matters up to $25,000, and the monetary jurisdiction for Simplified Procedure matters will be $100,000.

Generally, an action is commenced by way of a statement of claim. The claim must be served personally upon the named defendant within six months of issuance by the court. The defendant served in Ontario has 20 days to respond to the claim once he or she has been served. If served outside Ontario, a defendant may have 40 or 60 days to respond. The plaintiff or defendant must decide whether to have the matter heard by a jury or by judge alone prior to the "close of pleadings", which occurs once all the pleadings have been exchanged. A jury is not available in matters against a municipality. After the close of pleadings, there is an exchange of Affidavits of Documents (a listing of relevant documents in the control or possession of a party) together with relevant, non-privileged productions and a list of relevant privileged documents that are not being produced.

Examinations for discovery of the parties, where lawyers question the parties about the facts and allegations in dispute, are held shortly thereafter. Provisions do exist under the *Rules of Civil Procedure* to examine non-parties. Examinations for discovery are not available in Small Claims or Simplified Rules and are reserved solely for matters in the regular regime. In Simplified Procedure, the matter moves directly to mediation after the exchange of productions, and Small Claims matters move directly to a Settlement Conference before a judge.

Any undertakings provided at the examination for discovery are answered in the following months leading up to a mediation. Experts may be retained to provide an opinion on matters at issue in the litigation. Offers to settle may be exchanged at any point in the litigation process.

Following examinations, a mediation is held. A mediation is a conference amongst all parties and their legal representatives in an attempt to settle or otherwise resolve the matter with the assistance of a mediator.

If the matter cannot be settled at mediation, the matter moves to a Pre-trial or Settlement Conference. The parties present their positions before a judge or master, who would advise the parties of the strengths and weaknesses of their respective cases. If the matter cannot be resolved, the parties proceed to trial.

At the conclusion of the litigation, the issue of costs is addressed. After trial, costs may be awarded on a partial indemnity basis or substantial indemnity basis to the successful litigant. Any offers to settle will be considered in awarding costs if the nature of the offer attracts the costs consequences under Rule 49. Unlike in the United States, successful litigants in Ontario are often awarded a portion of their costs to hire a lawyer paid by the unsuccessful litigant.

AUTOMOBILE ACCIDENTS IN ONTARIO

In 1990, the Ontario Government significantly changed the way that insured parties in Ontario could be compensated for their injuries and losses arising out of motor vehicle accidents.

The Right to Sue for Personal Injuries Sustained in Motor Vehicle Accidents

Since 1990, Ontario residents have lived through four successive changes in motor vehicle insurance legislation.

As of October 1, 2003, someone who is injured in a motor vehicle accident by the fault of another can sue that individual if his or her injuries and damages meet a statutory "threshold". Subsection 267.5(3) of the *Insurance Act*[5] provides *inter alia* that the prohibition on suing the owner and operator of motor vehicle by the insured person is lifted or removed if the injured party has either (a) died, (b) sustained permanent serious disfigurement or (c) sustained a permanent serious impairment of an important physical, mental or psychological function.

Ontario Regulation 381/03[6] specifically provides for the nature and extent of evidence required and a definition that the injured parties must satisfy in order to be able to sue in tort in Ontario for injuries occasioned by a motor vehicle accident. Jurisprudence (case law) has adopted the definition and requirements to include *inter alia* that the impairment interfere with the activities that are essential tasks to the person's employment or training, or for his or her own care or well-being. For the impairment to be permanent, it must have been continuous since the accident, and it is not expected to improve substantially in the foreseeable future.

Additionally, pursuant to subsection 267.5(8), once the courts have determined that an individual's injuries are sufficiently serious to allow him or her to sue for pain and suffering ("general damages"), the legislature requires an automatic deduction of $30,000 if the general damages claim is worth less than $100,000. Similarly, for claims for loss of care,

---

5 R.S.O. 1990, c. I.8.

6 Amending O. Reg. 461/96 — *Court Proceedings for Automobile Accidents That Occur on or after November 1, 1996.*

guidance and companionship under the *Family Law Act*,[7] the sum of $15,000 is deducted from the assessed *Family Law Act* claim if it is less than $50,000.

General Damages

When it is determined by the Ontario courts that a loss can be monetarily remedied, damages will be awarded in an attempt to place the plaintiff in the position in which he or she would have been had the loss not occurred.[8]

General damages, most often referred to as "generals" or "non-pecuniary damages", cannot be precisely determined and include compensation for such things as pain and suffering, loss of amenities and expectation of life. They are damages which are a direct, natural and probable consequence of the act giving rise to the damage.[9] Loss of future earning capacity and future care costs are also classified as general damages, as there may arise various contingencies which impede an injured party to specifically prove the loss. Although these types of damages may be classified as general, the claim for same are most often made separately (*i.e.*, general damages for pain and suffering, general damages for loss of earning capacity/loss of competitive advantage and general damages for future care costs).

Pain and Suffering

In 1978, the Supreme Court of Canada through a trilogy of cases opined that a cap on general damages awarded for pain and suffering was necessary in Canada.[10] In 2006, the British Columbia Court of Appeal in *Lee v. Dawson*[11] confirmed that an upper limit for an award in general damages for pain and suffering continues to exist.

Taking into account the rates of inflation since 1978, when the Supreme Court imposed a rough upper perimeter on non-pecuniary general damages of $100,000, the highest possible amount of general damages which can be awarded for pain and suffering rests as of January 2009 at

---

7 R.S.O. 1990, c. F.3.

8 *Canadian Encyclopedic Digest*, 4th ed., Damages, I.1 § 1.

9 *Karas v. Rowlett*, [1943] S.C.J. No. 46, [1944] S.C.R. 1 (S.C.C.).

10 See *Thornton (Next Friend of) v. Prince George School District No. 57*, [1978] S.C.J. No. 7, [1978] 2 S.C.R. 267 (S.C.C.); *Andrews v. Grand & Toy Alberta Ltd.*, [1978] S.C.J. No. 6, [1978] 2 S.C.R. 229 (S.C.C.); and *Arnold v. Teno (Next friend of)*, [1978] S.C.J. No. 8, [1978] 2 S.C.R. 287 (S.C.C.).

11 [2006] B.C.J. No. 679 (B.C.C.A.), leave to appeal refused [2006] S.C.C.A. No. 192, 2006 CarswellBC 2594, 2006 CarswellBC 2595 (S.C.C.).

approximately $312,000. If a jury, which is unaware of the existence of the cap, awards general damages for pain and suffering in excess of the above noted amount, a "trial judge should reduce the award to conform with the 'cap' set out in the trilogy and [adjust it] for inflation. While a trial judge does not sit in appeal of a jury award, the trilogy has imposed as a rule of law a legal limit to non-pecuniary damages" and a judgment entered in an amount which exceeds this limit is "as a matter of law" excessive.[12]

Loss of Future Earnings Capacity/Loss of Competitive Advantage

An award for damages for loss of earning capacity recognizes the plaintiff's ability to earn money as a benefit that has been lost to him or her. The calculation is based upon the potential earning level which would reasonably be achieved by the plaintiff subject to contingencies.[13] The process of quantifying a loss of earning capacity is speculative, as the considerations of life such as early retirement, re-injury and surgery must all be taken into account. The courts often make inferences from the plaintiff's personal background, level of education and general life expectancies when trying to ascertain one's loss of future earning capacity; however, statistical evidence is often helpful when making such a determination. Where damages are to be assessed on the basis that a plaintiff was going to follow a particular career path, the plaintiff must show that the career path was a reasonable possibility in his or her life, or he or she risks being awarded nominal damages.

It is important to note that the assessment of future loss of income or earning capacity relies on predictions which might or might not bear any relation to the disabilities that led to past loss of earnings. As a result, loss of future earning capacity need not correspond with past loss of earning, as these damages are based on different considerations and are measured by different kinds of losses.[14]

Family Law Act Claims

In Ontario, damages are awarded to spouses, children and dependants of an injured plaintiff who have sustained a loss of care, guidance and companionship as a result of an accident and injuries to an individual. Claims pursuant to section 61 of the *Family Law Act* are also available to

---

[12] *Ibid.* at para. 42 (B.C.C.A.).

[13] *D'Amato v. Badger*, [1996] S.C.J. No. 84, [1996] 2 S.C.R. 1071 (S.C.C.).

[14] *Cipriano v. Cipriano*, [1996] B.C.J. No. 639, 22 B.C.L.R. (3d) 148 (B.C.C.A.), affg [1994] B.C.J. No. 2779, 1994 CarswellBC 1792 (B.C.S.C.), as cited in the *Canadian Encyclopedic Digest*, 4th ed., Damages IV.1.(c)(ii.)D §324.

unmarried life partners who have sustained such a loss.[15] As noted above, the *Family Law Act* claims are subject to the statutory deductible in place in the province of Ontario.

Special Damages

The calculation of special damages is generally accomplished with reasonable precision. In the context of personal injury claims, special damages consist of pecuniary losses incurred to the date of trial which can be reasonably and accurately proven such as claims for past wage loss, expenses incurred for medical care and/or medical reports, housekeeping and home maintenance costs and the costs of services provided such as yard work and/or renovations to make the plaintiff's home more accessible. These costs are in addition to those incurred for out-of-pocket expenses, which can include the cost of travel. As is the case with general damages, although a certain category of the claim can be classified as special damages in that they are quantifiable pecuniary damages, the claims made for same are usually separately classified in a statement of claim (*i.e.*, claims for past wage loss, claims for housekeeping and home maintenance and claims for out-of-pocket expenses).

Past Wage Loss/Pre-trial Loss of Wages

Income received from all sources (*i.e.*, employment income, unemployment income and assistance) is included in a claim for past loss of income, and the courts have also compensated the plaintiff for lost commissions and/or lost bonuses in certain circumstances.[16] Evidence regarding a person's type of employment, rate of pay and the length of time for which he or she was employed will help him or her prove his or her claim for past income loss. In cases where the plaintiff is self-employed or unemployed, determining his or her pre-trial loss of income can be more difficult, and the self-employed plaintiff must produce evidence to justify his or her estimated pre-trial wages claimed. In Ontario, pre-trial wage losses are reduced by available collateral benefits and subject to a formula approach under the *Insurance Act*.

---

[15] *Miron v. Trudel*, [1995] S.C.J. No. 44, 124 D.L.R. (4th) 693 (S.C.C.).

[16] *Kinsella v. McLean*, [1991] A.J No. 821, 82 Alta. L.R. (2d) 216 (Alta. Q.B.) and *Isert v. Santos*, [1997] B.C.J. No. 912, 1997 CarswellBC 662 (B.C.S.C.), vard on other grounds [1999] B.C.J. No. 113, 65 B.C.L.R. (3d) 104 (B.C.C.A.), leave to appeal refused [1999] S.C.C.A. No. 129, 253 N.R. 196 (note) (S.C.C.).

Future Care Costs

Future care costs are awarded when a person is entitled to compensation as a result of his or her need for assisted daily living. Damages are awarded in circumstances where the plaintiff requires future care over and above that which his or her own insurer is willing or required to compensate pursuant to statute.

Housekeeping and Home Maintenance

In order to enable an injured plaintiff to properly maintain his or her home at pre-accident levels, there may arise a need for the provision of services such as housekeeping or home maintenance. Entitlement to an award for these types of damages depends on concrete functional barriers evidenced by medical and or rehabilitative assessments.

Additional Considerations

A critical, but often overlooked component in advising clients of proper insurance requirements relates to available coverage to protect the client from motorists who are either uninsured, unidentified or underinsured.

Uninsured, Unidentified and Underinsured Motorist Coverage

Uninsured and unidentified motorist coverage is a standard part of every automobile insurance policy in Ontario. Subsection 265(2) of the *Insurance Act* defines an "uninsured automobile" as being "an automobile with respect to which neither the owner nor driver thereof has applicable and collectible bodily injury liability and property damage liability insurance for its ownership, use or operation, but does not include an automobile owned by or registered in the name of the insured or his or her spouse". This section also defines an "unidentified automobile" as being "an automobile with respect to which the identity of either the owner or driver cannot be ascertained".

In the case where a person is injured through the fault of someone who did not have insurance (*i.e.*, an uninsured driver), the injured victim can commence an action as against his or her own insurer for the damages the victim suffered. The insurer for its part then has a right of subrogation as against the at-fault driver and can attempt to recover the payout from him or her.

Where a person is injured by an unidentified driver, he or she can claim as against his or her own insurer for the damages sustained up to the minimum policy limits in place in the jurisdiction in which the accident occurred. It is important to note that although the minimum policy liability limits in the province of Ontario are set at $200,000, these minimum limits are not standard across all provinces and states. According to the *Insurance Act*, the insurer is not liable for any amount in excess of the minimum limits set out in the jurisdiction in which the accident occurs regardless of the number of persons injured or killed. At present, subsection 265(1) of the *Insurance Act*, requires the inclusion of uninsured or unidentified motorist coverage in every contract and the payment of all sums to which the insured is legally entitled to recover from the owner or driver of an uninsured or unidentified automobile or to which any person is legally entitled to recover as a result of the injuries sustained by the insured.

In Ontario, underinsured motorist coverage has been available in its present form since January 2001 when one purchases additional coverage under the OPCF-44R Family Protection Endorsement Coverage. This additional coverage, which can be obtained through payment of an additional premium, entitles the insured to coverage, up to his or her own policy limits, when the defendant in an action does not have enough liability coverage to cover the injured person's claim. In other words, the OPCF-44R affords the plaintiff the opportunity to claim excess coverage as against his or her own insurer up to the policy limits prescribed by his or her insurance policy.

No Fault Benefits

In order to avoid the situation where innocent parties who were injured by an uninsured person were left with little to no compensation, the government of Ontario developed a system whereby the injured party would apply to his or her own insurer for a basic level of compensation for lost income and/or medical and rehabilitation expenses, attendant care and housekeeping expenses thereby ensuring that there was some coverage available. This current "no fault" regime which currently exists is the Statutory Accident Benefit Scheme.[17]

When an insured person is injured in a motor vehicle accident and reports the injury to his or her insurer, an application for accident benefits must be provided to the injured party. The insured is advised either in writing or verbally of the different benefits which are potentially available to him or her, and he or she is requested to have his or her employer fill out an Employee's Confirmation of Income if he or she is unable to return to his or her employment. The injured party is also

---

[17] O. Reg. 403/96 — *Statutory Accident Benefits Schedule — Accidents on or after November 1, 1996,* as amended (SABS).

required to have a Disability Certificate completed by his or her treating medical specialist in order to identify the injury that occurred in the accident and to provide the insured with some background medical information.

Income Replacement Benefits

In order to qualify for an income replacement benefit, the injured party must sustain an impairment as a result of an accident. Subsection 2(1) of the SABS stipulates that an "accident" means "an incident in which the use or operation of an automobile directly causes [the] impairment", which differs from the broader definition in the previous regulations, in that the use or operation of the automobile could indirectly cause the impairment. From there, the injured party must then meet a test of eligibility as set out under subsection 4(1) of the SABS.

As is generally the case for disability benefits, the period of the benefit from a motor vehicle accident in Ontario is defined by applying two different tests, the first being for the first 104-week period and then a more stringent test is for after the 104-week period. To qualify for benefits in the first 104 weeks, the injured party must suffer a substantial inability to perform the essential tasks of the employment in respect of which he or she qualifies for the benefit under section 4 (see subsection 5(1) of the SABS). For any time after the 104-week period, the injured party must suffer a complete inability to engage in any employment for which he or she is reasonably suited by education, training or experience (see clause 5(2)(b) of the SABS).

If the insured is diagnosed with solely a whiplash injury in the category of a WAD I or WAD II level (whiplash associated disorder), the insured is limited to claiming 12 or 16 weeks, respectively, of income replacement benefits. As with any legislation, this is subject to exceptions.

The income replacement benefit is calculated based on 80% of the net weekly income earned prior to the motor vehicle accident up to a statutory maximum of $400 per week, and is subject to deduction for collateral benefits as defined under the SABS. Typically, collateral benefits include but are not limited to disability benefits. If a person continues to qualify for the income replacement benefit, he or she can potentially claim this amount up to age 65, at which time the amount diminishes based on a formula.

Medical/Rehabilitation Expenses

The legislation makes a distinction between catastrophic and non-catastrophic injuries. If an injury comes within the definition of "catastrophic" as set out under subsection 2(1.1) of the SABS, a significantly higher level of benefits is available to the insured. In catastrophic cases, the injured party would have available to him or her the amount of $1 million for medical and rehabilitation expenses incurred over his or her lifetime and a further $1 million for attendant care benefits incurred over his or her lifetime. Conversely, a non-catastrophic claim for medical and rehabilitation expenses would be limited to $100,000 over ten years after the accident, and attendant care benefits would be limited to a maximum of $3,000 per month for a two-year period. In order to qualify for these benefits, again the injured party must suffer an impairment as a result of the accident, and the expenses incurred must be found to be reasonable and necessary. Much case law has developed to determine whether an expense has been "incurred". There is a very detailed procedural system in the regulation for the submitting, approval and denial of any expenses incurred which is subject to very strict timelines. There is a separate regulatory body, the Financial Services Commission of Ontario, which has been tasked with handling the dispute resolution of these matters between the injured party and the insurer.

Of note, however, is that the Accident Benefit insurer, unlike the insurer of the car that may have caused someone else an injury, is not subject to an order from the court to pay out benefits in the future, nor is there any obligation on the insurer to settle out the injured parties' claim into the future. However, often in catastrophic cases, structured settlements are agreed to by the insured and his or her insurer. Insurers, however, are precluded from settling out all past, present and future benefits with an injured party within the first year of the accident. The *Insurance Act* has provisions which allow for the deduction of the moneys received by the injured party from the Accident Benefit insurer from what may be owed by the tortfeasor to the injured party in a damages claim.

HOMEOWNER'S PROPERTY

A homeowners insurance policy is a legal contract between the insured and the insurer to protect the insured, his or her home and belongings if they are damaged. The types of coverage and conditions that apply to policies of insurance vary greatly, and each policy must be carefully reviewed before contracting with an insurer.

Most homeowners policies have a standard format which includes the following types of coverage:

1. coverage for the actual structure;
2. coverage for the contents of the premises;
3. coverage for additional living expenses; and
4. liability coverage.

There are often exceptions to a policy of insurance, typically sewer back-up and earthquakes; however, additional coverage can usually be purchased to cover these types of losses.

To ensure that coverage is maintained, the insured must report any material change in circumstances to the insurer. The time frame in which this notice must be given varies from policy to policy. A failure to report a material change in circumstances can result in a denial in policy coverage, and this can expose the insured to personal liability. Homeowners policies also contain exclusions to coverage, which depend upon the specific contract of insurance. Leaving the premises vacant for a period of time, using the premises for illegal purposes and using the premises for commercial purposes are often uses which can exclude coverage under the policy.

Liability coverage in a homeowners policy of insurance will protect the insured from personal liability should a person visiting your home be injured. The liability coverage in most standard policies of insurance will also cover the actions of household pets. Intentional acts are excluded.

Any claims paid out under an insurance policy may be recovered by the insurer in a subrogated claim. That is, the insurer can bring an action in the name of the insured to recover moneys against another person at fault.

Should your insurer cease to operate its business, the Property and Casualty Insurance Compensation Corporation (PACICC) can pay out moneys owed and not paid by your insurer. However, the maximum that can be claimed is $250,000 for losses from a single incident. The PACICC is an industry-funded corporation.

Slips and Falls on a Homeowner's Property

As a property owner, you are obligated to maintain your property in a reasonably safe manner, failing which you could be sued in negligence. Every province in Canada has Occupiers' Liability legislation to address the issue of slips and falls. In Ontario, the relevant legislation is the

Occupiers' Liability Act.[18] The legislation stipulates that an occupier has a duty to take reasonable care to see that all persons entering a premise are reasonably safe while on the premises.

Under section 1 of the *Occupiers' Liability Act*, an "occupier" is defined as "(a) a person who is in physical possession of premises, or (b) a person who has responsibility for and control over the condition of premises or the activities there carried on, or control over persons allowed to enter the premises".

Under section 3 of the Act, an occupier of the premises has "a duty to take such care as in all the circumstances of the case is reasonable to see that persons entering on the premises, and the property brought on the premises by those persons are reasonably safe while on the premises".

The test as to what is "reasonable care" has been addressed in various case law, and the following guiding principles have been established:

- An occupier has a duty to ensure that the premises are reasonably safe for persons entering; however, this duty is not absolute.
- What constitutes reasonable care will vary according to the relevant factors in each situation.
- If there is a known danger on the premises, the occupier must have a reasonable system in place, and that system must be operating properly in order to meet the required standard of care.
- There is also a standard of care required of persons entering the property. Persons entering the property must meet the standard of "a reasonable person exercising average ordinary prudence" to ensure their own safety.
- Finally, even uninvited persons have been successful in recovering damages for injuries they sustain on poorly maintained premises.

Municipally Owned Properties

There are special considerations if a slip and fall takes place on a municipally owned property. In particular, the notice requirements are stringent, and, without compliance, the ability to recover damages may be compromised. Subsection 44(10) of the *Municipal Act, 2001*[19] stipulates that "[no] action shall be brought for the recovery of damages under subsection (2) unless, within 10 days after the occurrence of the injury, written notice of the claim and of the injury complained of has been served upon or sent by registered mail to … the clerk of the municipality".

---

[18] R.S.O. 1990, c. O.2.

[19] S.O. 2001, c. 25.

On the basis of the legislation, it is best to ensure that written notice is provided within the ten days to ensure that the ability to recover damages is preserved. However, if notice is not provided within ten days, subsection 44(12) of the *Municipal Act, 2001* provides that failure "to give notice or insufficiency of the notice is not a bar to the action if a judge finds that there is reasonable excuse for the want or the insufficiency of the notice and that the municipality is not prejudiced in its defence".

COMMERCIAL GENERAL LIABILITY, BUILDERS RISK AND WRAP-UP POLICIES

Three common policies held by businesses include: commercial general liability, builders risk and wrap-up policies.

Commercial General Liability

This is a broad form of insurance coverage for the legal liability of an insured. Some will know this coverage by its former title, "Comprehensive General Liability Insurance". Coverage under this form of policy will include: bodily injury and property damage liability, personal injury liability, medical payments and tenants legal liability.

Bodily injury and property damage liability will provide coverage for the company and its employees for physical injury to third parties, or damages to a third party's property or belongings. The policy also includes coverage for compensatory damages.

Commercial general liability policies are not meant to act as a performance bond for the actual work or services performed by the business. Further, bodily injury or property damage arising out of the use and operation of an automobile, motorized snow vehicle, trailer or watercraft are excluded. Similarly, damage to the business' own product or work, including deficiencies in the product or work, are also excluded. Further exclusions include intentional acts, injuries to employees and claims for punitive damages.

With respect to personal injury liability coverage, the policy covers damages to a person's character, reputation and position in the community as a result of libel and slander. It can protect the business and employees operating within the scope of their duties when they are accused of libelling or slandering another individual. The coverage is of course subject to specific exclusions.

Coverage is usually afforded for all minor medical expenses that are incurred as a result of an accident that happens at the company's premises or as a result of company operations, even though the company may never be found legally liable. Exclusions for medical payments typically include the same as those listed under "bodily injury and property damage" in addition to the exclusion of casual workers and tenants who injure themselves in their own units.

Tenants liability includes coverage for fire, explosion, smoke damage or other damage caused by fire protection, such as when sprinklers become activated. When legal responsibility is determined, compensatory damages will be paid. However, all personal property is excluded from coverage under the insured's business commercial liability policy, as is intentional damage to property.

Builders Risk Insurance

Builders risk insurance is a special type of *property insurance* which indemnifies a business against property damage during the course of construction. This coverage is comprehensive and includes damage to property owned by the insured or for which it is legally liable, property of others to be used in a part of or incidental to the construction project, property in the course of construction, installation, reconstruction or repair, property while in transit anywhere in the world and debris removal.

Special conditions under this policy may include:

- Business interruption — delayed opening, extra expense, margin of profit extension
- Insureds include contractors, architects, engineers, lender and others involved in construction whether named or not
- Basis of settlement — full replacement value

The main exclusions under this form of the policy include damage to the contractor's equipment and motor vehicles, and penalties for non-completion and non-compliance with contract conditions. Similarly, the cost of making good faulty or defective workmanship is also excluded; however, the exclusion does not extend to resultant damage caused to the property as a result of the faulty or defective workmanship.

Wrap-up Liability Insurance

Wrap-up liability insurance provides protection for the owners, developers, engineers, architects, project managers and contractors and subcontractors against property damage and liability exposures associated with the project for a period of time after construction is substantially complete. Under a wrap-up policy, there is no need to allocate blame for any third party injury or property damage, since all participants are insured by the same policy. This type of policy allows a consolidated claims handling process between the owner and the claimant, leading to a speedy and early resolution.

DISABILITY INSURANCE

The purpose of disability insurance is to provide some form of financial independence in the event of an unfortunate accident and/or sickness. Unlike motor vehicle accident policies, disability insurance policies are contractual and not statutory. It is a contract between the insured and the insurance company. There are, however, pursuant to section 300 of the *Insurance Act*, statutory requirements for the specific content of such policies (*i.e.*, term of the insurance, methods of commencement of the term, *etc.*). In determining an individual's entitlement to disability insurance, one must always refer to the policy wording. Disability insurance policies differ in many respects, and the specific language of the policy may vary from policy to policy and from company to company. Although the underlying concepts are the same, the courts must interpret the terms of the policy in question. It is, therefore, important to carefully review the provisions of the policy, as there may be some differences which can impact on the outcome of the claim.

Most disability policies will likely contain a waiting period. After the waiting period has expired and the individual is able to demonstrate that he or she is unable to perform all of the functions of his or her regular employment, then, subject to other terms, including that the claimant's condition requires both regular and continuous medical care, the individual will likely qualify for the appropriate level of contracted benefits. Generally, after a 104-week period of time, should the claimant remain disabled, the policy will contain a definitional change which will likely require the policyholder to meet a different and more demanding test for long-term disability benefits, namely one of "total disability". A standard definition of "total disability" is a state of complete or continuous incapacity, resulting from illness or accidental injury, which wholly prevents the claimant from performing any work for which he or she is or may be reasonably suited by training, education or experience. Again, it is imperative that the policy be closely reviewed to ascertain the unique terms that may apply.

The Supreme Court of Canada has interpreted the term "total disability" in the case of *Sucharov v. Paul Revere Life Insurance Co.*[20] It

---

[20] [1983] S.C.J. No. 86, [1983] 2 S.C.R. 541 (S.C.C.).

has been widely followed by the lower courts. Total disability was defined as follows:

> The test of total disability is satisfied when the circumstances are such that a reasonable man would recognize that he should not engage in certain activity even though he literally is not physically unable to do so. In other words, total disability does not mean absolute physical inability to transact any kind of business pertaining to one's occupation, but rather that there is a total disability if the insured's injuries are such that common care and prudence require him to desist from his business or occupation in order to effectuate a cure; hence, if the condition of the insured is such that in order to effect a cure or prolongation of life, common care and prudence will require that he cease all work, he is totally disabled within the meaning of health or accident insurance policies.[21]

Most cases are fact-driven, meaning that in determining "total disability", the courts will not only review the medical records and weigh expert evidence but they will also consider the claimant's own credibility in deciding on whether he or she is capable of obtaining other employment.

Failing to report any pre-existing medical condition and/or making any misrepresentations, may jeopardize coverage.

Pre-existing Medical Condition

A pre-existing condition exclusion clause is standard in disability insurance agreements. These exclusions require a policyholder when applying for coverage to disclose any past medical condition. Although each contract of insurance may be different, generally speaking, a "pre-existing condition" is defined as a sickness or injury for which the individual received medical treatment, care or services, or has been prescribed medication in a specified period prior to the policy taking effect. There are some cases where a pre-existing condition is easily identifiable in that the individual would have been receiving treatment and/or he or she may have undertaken some form of diagnostic testing prior to the commencement of disability. The more difficult cases involve the pre-existing medical underlying conditions that were either passive or asymptomatic. The courts generally have taken the approach of applying the concept of "proximate cause", which requires a detailed analysis of the medical documentation as interpreted by the various medical experts.

---

[21] *Ibid.* at 546 (S.C.R.), quoting from *Couch on Insurance*, 2nd ed. (revised ed., 1983) at ss. 53:118.

Misrepresentation

It is settled law that an applicant for disability insurance coverage has a duty to disclose all material facts in an application to an insurer. The purpose is to allow the insurer to make an informed decision as to whether or not it will provide insurance coverage to the individual in question. A misrepresentation does not automatically deny coverage. Rather, the courts have found that the misrepresentation must be examined on a case-by-case basis, and it must be determined whether the misrepresentation was material and relied upon in the circumstances. In other words, a misrepresentation exclusionary clause will be upheld if it is found to have been material to the risk and the misrepresentation would have influenced the insurer in its decision to decline issuing the insurance policy in dispute.

Jurisprudence has established that the wording of disability policies must be interpreted liberally, and the benefit of the doubt will be given to the insured. This means that an exclusion clause should not be interpreted in a way that is inconsistent with the expectations of the parties or with the purpose of the insurance coverage.

Many employers offer disability coverage, commonly known as group insurance. Typically, the terms of the policy are not negotiable, but it is imperative to carefully review the provisions to understand the policy's applicability in the event of an individual's disability. If an individual disability insurance policy is purchased, although it is most likely more expensive than group insurance, it may be tailored somewhat to the individual's own personal circumstances.

Good Faith

The insurance contract between an individual or group and the insurer is one which requires the utmost good faith or *uberrima fides* on behalf of all parties. A breach of the standard by an insured or insurer can result in an award of punitive damages, which is a sum over and above the monetary amount in dispute in the contract.

DIRECTORS AND OFFICERS LIABILITY

What Is a Company?

The first thing to understand about corporate/business law is that companies are legal entities. In a nutshell, when it comes to doing business, they have the same powers and privileges as real people. They can carry on business, they can own property, pay taxes and sue or be sued. So although it may not be possible to commit an assault against a company, it is certainly possible to steal from a company by converting its property.

Companies are generally managed by their officers, controlled by their directors and owned by their shareholders. This is essentially true whether we are dealing with a sophisticated multinational, a mid-sized single provincial company or a company that is operated by one person who is the sole shareholder.

Shareholders take the financial losses when stock prices drop, and profit when stock prices rise. Their exposure is usually limited to the initial amount of their investment.

Officers of a corporation are usually responsible for the day-to-day operations of a company. The number of officers will vary depending upon the jurisdiction in which the company is incorporated and the requirements of the company. Officers' positions are usually those of President, Secretary and Treasurer. The officers are retained by the board of directors and are employees of the company.

Directors and officers liability is grounded in their relationship of trust with the corporation and its shareholders. This duty may be termed a "fiduciary duty". It should be noted that as indicated above, corporations can be incorporated in different jurisdictions.

In Canada, the *Canada Business Corporations Act* is the enabling legislation for federally incorporated companies. Provincially incorporated businesses are governed by their respective Business Corporation Acts. There can also be provincial society legislation or not-for-profit organization statutes. There are very real advantages and disadvantages to incorporating under all of the above potential styles. These advantages and disadvantages are beyond the scope of this section, and should be canvassed with qualified counsel prior to one making a decision.

Legal Duties

In their representation of shareholders or members of any organization, directors and officers have three basic duties:

1. **The Duty of Due Diligence:** This has been defined as the reasonable care expected from a person who is discharging or attempting to satisfy an obligation, or the duty to act prudently in good faith and reasonably with the view to the best interests of an organization and its members.

2. **The Duty of Loyalty:** This is the duty to place the interests of an organization ahead of one's own. It is important to note that one must not use one's position for personal gain or to further one's

own interests. It is also important that one avoid conflicts of interest which would put one's own interests in conflict with those of the organization.

3. **The Duty of Obedience:** This is very simply the duty of obedience to the organization and the duty of one to act within the governing policies and rules as well as the laws and regulations which apply to the organization.

The duty of diligence extends only as far as that of a reasonable person with similar abilities would exercise in similar circumstances. However, if a director or officer has special skills such as that of an accountant or a lawyer, he or she will then have to maintain a standard of care that corresponds with his or her special knowledge or higher professional abilities. The duty of obedience extends to ensuring that the corporation meets its obligations under statutes and regulations with regard to occupational health and safety, human rights, taxation and other related legislation.

A duty of confidentiality flows from the duty of loyalty. Not only must directors avoid putting themselves in situations where they are in a conflict of interest, but they must also keep the business of the corporation private. They must not discuss the matters with spouses, the press or any outside individual or organization.

Liability of Directors

Directors who fail with regard to the above duties may be found liable for their failure. Liability of directors may flow from three main areas:

1. **Tort:** Tort liability is essentially liability flowing from an unintentional or negligent act or failure to act in a way that causes damages or injury to another person. Again, it is important to note that the definition of "person" refers to other companies as well.
2. **Contract:** Where a contract is breached, the remedy might be either the correct performance of the contract or the payment of damages in lieu of performance.
3. **Liability for Breach of a Statute:** This can be a breach of a statute or regulation which will result in the payment of fines, restrictions on the company or potentially penal sanctions.

Indemnification

Typically, corporations have provisions to indemnify their directors and officers, or to protect them from the above liabilities as much as possible.

This is usually done through the purchase of directors and officers liability insurance. It is important to note that different policies cover different areas with different limits. It would be appropriate to consult an insurance broker to canvass what is appropriate coverage for your client.

DUTY TO DEFEND VS. DUTY TO INDEMNIFY

The insurer's duty to defend a claim made against its insured is part of its contractual obligation to the insured. The duty must be specified in the contract of insurance. In addition, it is broader and independent of the duty to indemnify in the sense that the duty to defend arises if the originating pleadings (statement of claim, third party claim, *etc.) allege* acts or omissions that, if proven, might fall within the policy coverage, while the duty to indemnify arises only where such allegations are *proven* at trial.

In other words, the originating pleadings govern the insurer's duty to defend. If the claim alleges a state of facts which, if proven, would fall within the coverage of the policy, the insurer is obliged to defend the insured. If the allegations do not come within the policy coverage, the insurer has no such obligation.[22]

The Ontario Court of Appeal 2002 decision in *Alie v. Bertrand & Frère Construction Co.*[23] confirmed that when it comes to assessing the coverage issue, one must undertake a two-step process in the interpretation of the insuring agreement (*i.e.*, the policy). First, the insured must demonstrate that the claim advanced comes within the insuring agreement. If the insured satisfies this burden, then it is for the insurer to establish that a claim that would otherwise be covered is excluded by some term in the policy.

In *Nichols v. American Home Assurance Co.*,[24] Justice McLachlin comprehensively reviewed the jurisprudence surrounding the duty to defend and noted the following basic principles:

- The duty to defend arises only where the pleadings raise claims which would be payable under the contract of insurance ("the pleadings rule").[25]
- It is not necessary to prove that the obligation to indemnify will in fact arise in order to trigger the duty to defend. The "mere possibil-

[22] See *Bacon v. McBride*, [1984] B.C.J. No. 2813, 1984 CarswellBC 39 (B.C.S.C.).
[23] [2002] O.J. No. 4697, 222 D.L.R. (4th) 687 (Ont. C.A.).
[24] [1990] S.C.J. No. 33, 1990 CarswellOnt 619 (S.C.C.).
[25] See *Bacon v McBride*, [1984] B.C.J. No. 2813, 6 D.L.R. (4th) 96 (B.C.S.C.).

ity" that a pleaded claim may succeed within the terms of the policy is sufficient to trigger the duty to defend.[26]

- The duty to defend is restricted to claims for damages which, if proven, would fall within the scope of coverage provided by the policy.[27]
- Where it is clear from the pleadings that the suit falls outside the coverage of the policy by reason of the exclusion clause, the duty to defend does not arise.[28]

It is noteworthy that in most situations, an insurer who has a duty to defend some, or only one, of the claims made against an insured has a duty to defend the entire claim. This is the case even where there is only a "mere possibility" that a pleaded claim may fall within the terms of the policy.[29]

Non-waiver Agreement and Reservation of Rights

Non-waiver agreements and reservation of rights letters are used by the insurance company to put its insured on notice that it may refuse to defend or indemnify him or her once it has completed its investigation of the claim.

A *reservation of rights letter* is a letter in which the insurance company puts the insured on notice that although it has received the claim, it may decide to deny indemnification under the policy and that it may refuse to defend the claim.

A *non-waiver agreement* is an agreement in which the insurance company is asking the insured to agree that although the insurer investigates the claim and may defend the claim on behalf of the insured, carries out negotiations towards the possible settlement of the claim or settles and pays the claim, it does not constitute a waiver of the insurance company's right to attempt to recover the amount of any settlement paid by the insurer from the insured.

Should an individual be faced with either of the above documents, he or she should consult counsel.

---

26 See *Prudential Assurance Co. v. Manitoba Public Insurance Co.*, [1976] M.J. No. 71, 67 D.L.R. (3d) 521 (Man. C.A.).

27 See *Thames Steel Construction Ltd. v. Northern Assurance Co.*, [1988] O.J. No. 2055, 1988 CarswellOnt 731 (Ont. C.A.).

28 See *Opron Maritimes Construction Ltd. v. Canadian Idemnity Co.*, [1986] N.B.J. No. 111, 19 C.C.L.I. 168 (N.B.C.A.).

29 See *Hanis v. University of Western Ontario*, [2003] O.J. No. 4167 (Ont. S.C.J.) and *E.M. v. Reed*, [2003] O.J. No. 1791 (Ont. C.A.).

LIMITATIONS ACT

The time during which an individual can commence an action is governed by various provincial limitation Acts throughout Canada. The *Limitations Act, 2002*[30] in Ontario came into force on January 1, 2004. The Act provides for a limitation period of two years from the day the cause of action is discovered. The Act contains certain exceptions to the general rule. Section 5 of the Act codifies the discovery principle. The discovery principle essentially provides that the limitation period will begin to run when the party who is affected or injured knew or ought to have known that a claim should or could be advanced. Time will not run against minors or incapable parties who are not represented by a litigation guardian. The Act also provides for an ultimate limitation period as prescribed by subsection 15(2) that no proceedings shall be commenced in respect of any claim more than 15 years after the day on which the act or omission on which the claim is based took place. When an individual first determines that he or she has been aggrieved, he or she should seek immediate legal representation, for, as previously noted at the outset of this chapter, the law is constantly changing.

CONCLUSION

The information included in this chapter is intended to highlight certain areas of interest in insurance law and to assist the financial advisor in piloting his or her valued client to appropriate counsel. We do hope that the information garnered from reading this chapter assists the advisor in protecting and minimizing his or her clients' exposure to insured or insurance losses.

The legal system is critical in the preservation of wealth:

> No civilization ... would ever have been possible without a framework of stability to provide that wherein for the flux of change. Foremost among the stabilizing factors, more enduring than customs, manners and traditions, are the legal systems that regulate our life in the world and our daily affairs with each other.[31]

This primer on insurance law is being provided to the reader for general purposes, and does not constitute nor should it be relied upon as an opinion with respect to insurance law. Statutory, regulatory and jurisprudential thought is constantly evolving. This chapter is meant to give the reader information of a general nature, and is not a substitute for

---

[30] S.O. 2002, c. 24, Sched. B.

[31] Hannah Arendt, *Crises of the Republic*, "Civil Disobedience" (New York: Houghton Mifflin Harcourt, 1972) at 79.

legal advice. Should you require legal advice, you should hire a lawyer who can acquire an understanding of your specific problems and apply the current state of the law to your specific circumstances.

CHAPTER 67

CREDITOR PROTECTION 101

Peter J. Merrick

Overview

This chapter provides a basic primer that could be used as a basis for providing creditor protection for businesses and their owners.

Learning Objectives

By the end of this chapter, you will:

- know about Bill C-45 (2003) and how it impacts business owners across Canada;
- understand the importance of providing creditor protection solutions to your clients;
- understand the ten most effective creditor protection solutions used today; and
- be conscious of how important it is for you and your clients to start conversations about creditor protection today.

INTRODUCTION

It was the summer of 2007 when I received my first call from Tina, a financial advisor in Northern Ontario, otherwise known as Tina of the North. What struck me most was when Tina, with urgency in her voice, said: "We are experiencing an economic boom in Northern Ontario, and many of the business owners enjoying this explosive growth are not receiving the proper advice to help them manage their growth and plan for their eventual exits from their companies gracefully. Peter, you have to visit Northern Ontario immediately to see what I mean and help!"

At the time, mineral prices worldwide had increased dramatically. This had translated to increased corporate earnings, higher executive compensation, higher worker salaries, ambitious capital investment commitments, and generous flows of tax and royalty payments to governments for Northern Ontario businesses.

While I met business owners in Timmins, Sudbury and North Bay, some themes/concerns/needs began to emerge. One particular conversation with an owner of one of the largest private sector mining supply and service companies in Sudbury continues to stand out in my mind when he said: "Even though I have success now, I live in constant fear that I am one event away (a lawsuit, a downturn in the economy, a personal disability or my premature death) from losing everything and I don't know where to start to protect my family."

For many Canadian businesses, their owners now live in constant fear of the potential corporate criminal liability they face under Bill C-45 as of March 31, 2004. This bill was prompted by the federal government's review of the Westray mine disaster in Nova Scotia in 1992. Bill C-45 holds corporate decision-makers responsible for the health and safety of their employees. It establishes a higher standard of care for employees and the public, and extends the responsibility to individuals who directly work for the company. If found guilty, those in charge may possibly face criminal prosecution, high fines and civil liability that may lead to corporate and personal bankruptcy.

Over the last few years, since the passing of Bill C-45, business owners have not received much advice on how to put in place the procedures to protect against criminal prosecution, and even less focus has been placed on creditor protection strategies.

Today in Canada, there are 1.1 million active incorporated businesses; of these, 75% employ fewer than five people. It is these companies that drive our economy. The owners of these businesses have become very successful at building businesses and have learned how to make their own money and success. Many of these businessmen and businesswoman turn to their accounting, financial and legal professionals to help them legally structure their companies and financial affairs to achieve five glorious outcomes: wealth preservation, legal tax minimization and deference, *creditor protection*, wealth accumulation and wealth distribution.

Of these five glorious outcomes, I have always been fascinated by how many times I have met very smart and successful business owners who have neglected to put in place strategies that creditor-proof what they have spent a lifetime to build. Too late in the process, owners of incorporated businesses who have personally guaranteed loans for their companies, or non-incorporated business owners who have left themselves exposed to creditor attacks, personally finally reach out for help. If only they had invested the time and money to structure their financial affairs in such a way that their money would have stayed in their pockets, and not in the pockets of someone else, while the opportunity was there!

Every successful business person can learn a lesson or two from the Reichmann family. In May 1993, Olympia & York, it one of the world's largest privately held real estate companies, filed for bankruptcy; it owed over $20 billion to various banks and investors. The company was finally dismembered in February 1993, and the Reichmann family was left with only Olympia & York Properties Corporation in Toronto. Sixteen years later, the new company has again grown into a multi-billion dollar firm. In September 2006, Paul Reichmann announced that he was bored with retirement and that he would be setting up a new $4 billion equity partner fund. What this story of the Reichmann family teaches is that smart business people can't stay down if they have the right Trusted Advisors at their side who help them plan for the best-case scenario, the *status quo*, and especially for the worst-case scenario.

CREDITOR PROTECTION STRATEGIES

What follows is a basic primer that could be used as a basis for providing creditor protection for businesses and their owners. This is in no way a complete list.

Note: It is highly recommended before applying any of these strategies that you consult with the proper financial, accounting and legal professionals to find out if they work for your client's particular situation.

Strategy One: Incorporated Businesses

The problem in Canada is that proprietorship and partnership businesses in Canadian law are seen and deemed to be the same legal entity as the person and people who own and operate them. This means that creditors can sue the owners of these types of businesses and take aim at their personal assets, such as their homes and non-registered investments.

When a business is incorporated under Canadian law, it is considered a separate legal entity from the individual or individuals who own the incorporated business. What this means is that if an incorporated business is sued successfully, the personal assets of the business owner(s) are protected from creditors in most situations.

Strategy Two: Create a Holding Company

Holding companies may be placed between shareholders and their operating companies for reasons of taxation and legal protection. The income in the operating company remains subject to a lower tax rate using small business deductions. Dividends may be paid from the operating company to the holding company at a preferred tax rate to build up assets in the holding company, keeping the active company mean and lean, free from creditor intrusions.

Strategy Three: Avoid Signing Personal Guarantees

The main reason a person chooses to incorporate his or her business is to segregate his or her personal assets from his or her corporate assets and liabilities. If a person signs a personal guarantee for corporate debt, he or she voids this separation from business and personal assets, and the creditors of the business can successfully attack personal assets.

Strategy Four: Create an *Inter Vivos* Trust (Living Trust)

A living trust is created while a person is alive. This type of trust enables a person to control the distribution of his or her estate while he or she is alive. An individual is able to transfer ownership of his or her property into a trust. A revocable living trust is a vehicle that is very helpful in avoiding probate and completing an estate freeze.

In some cases, non-revocable trust assets that are transferred to the trust may remain available to creditors. However, a living trust will make it much more difficult for creditors to have access to the assets of the trust. Creditors will first have to petition the court for a changing order to be able to attack the assets held in the trust.

Strategy Five: Make Sure the Ownership of Personal Property Is in a Spouse's or in Grown Children's Names

When the ownership of personal assets is in a spouse's or grown child's name, these assets are separated from the business owner's assets and liabilities. Creditors will not be able to attack assets of a spouse or grown child provided that neither the spouse nor the grown child is a director or guarantor for either the business or personal debt of the contributing spouse.

Strategy Six: Make Shareholder Loans to Become a Secured Creditor

An owner of an incorporated business can make shareholder loans back to his or her company and become a secured creditor, having first rights to corporate assets if the company has debt and other financial troubling issues.

Strategy Seven: Spousal RRSP

In all provincial jurisdictions, RRSPs as of 2008 are creditor-protected only upon bankruptcy of the owner. However, it is a wise strategy for a business owner to consider making part or all of his or her RRSP contributions into a spousal RRSP. The business owner takes the tax deduction, and the asset becomes the spouse's property. Creditors will not be able to attack the assets of the spousal RRSP provided that the spouse is not a director or guarantor for either the business or the personal debt of the contributing spouse.

Strategy Eight: Create Individual Pension Plans and Retirement Compensation Arrangements for Business Owners

Incorporated business owners who have a T4 income of over $100,000 per year should consider creating a "supercharged RRSP" in the form of an Individual Pension Plan (IPP) or a Retirement Compensation Arrangement (RCA). Contributions to these two vehicles exceed the maximum allowable RRSP limits, are fully deductible by a company and are a non-taxable benefit for the beneficiaries of these plans. Assets held within the IPP or RCA cannot be seized by creditors of an incorporated business. IPPs and RCAs offer significant amounts of additional tax-deferred income which is to be set aside for a business owner's retirement and which could protect hundreds of thousands and even millions of dollars from corporate creditors.

Strategy Nine: Create a Health and Welfare Trust (HWT)

Incorporated business owners should consider creating a Health and Welfare Trust (HWT) for themselves. A HWT is a bank account whose deposits are spent exclusively on health care expenses. By having a HWT, business owners may convert health care expenses into 100% business deductions and a non-taxable benefit for themselves. All moneys deposited into a HWT are only to be used for health care expenses; therefore, these moneys are segregated from both personal and corporate assets, and are immune from creditors.

Strategy Ten: Create Employee Profit-Sharing Plans (EPSPs) for Business Owners

An Employee Profit-Sharing Plan (EPSP) is a special purpose trust that allows the beneficiaries of the plan to share in the profits of a company. The allocation to an EPSP is taxable in the hands of an employee and a deductible expense for an employer. An EPSP is a non-registered savings plan in which the employer contributions are computed by reference to a company's profit. Advantages of an EPSP are that they attract neither Employer/Employee Canada Pension Plan nor EI contributions. EPSPs allow for more control over retirement assets. They are treated as pension or RRSP eligible earnings. Source deductions and withholdings are not required by the EPSP trustee or employer. More importantly, while the money stays in the EPSP, the money is protected from creditors.

Strategy Eleven: Purchase Investment and Retirement Products Through Insurance Companies

Investment products held in insurance companies such as RRSPs, universal life policies, segregated investment funds and annuities may be protected from an individual's creditors if the named beneficiary of these insurance products is a spouse, parent or grandchild of the annuitant, or if the named beneficiaries on these insurance products are irrevocable.

It is as true today as it was 2,500 years ago when Lao Tzu said: "When the student is ready, the teacher will appear." For the last five years I have been teaching risk management solutions at the university level. During this time I have learned that in order to be a good teacher, one must also be a persistent researcher in the search of better solutions for clients' most common needs.

I would like to share the lesson I learned from a lunch I had in 2007 with Andrew Rogerson, one of my teachers and a lawyer who has developed a specialty niche in Toronto that focuses on estate planning and asset protection both on and offshore. Our conversation was primarily focused on legal solutions a client may employ in order to avoid asset protection strategies being set aside by the courts.

At the beginning of our lunch, Andrew made the point that all credit protection strategies should be made at a time when the client is clearly not insolvent or on the eve of bankruptcy. Andrew clarified this by stating: "Planning must be justifiable in terms of non asset-protection objectives."

He illustrated this concept by recounting the merits of the case of Ramgotra (*Royal Bank of Canada v. North American Life Assurance Co.*,

[1996] S.C.J. No. 17, [1996] 1 S.C.R. 325 (S.C.C.) where the Supreme Court of Canada held that the settlement of funds transferred from non-exempt RRSPs into a RRIF managed by an insurance company should maintain its exemption status from creditors' hands. The Supreme Court's rationale was that the transaction was part of a legitimate retirement planning exercise. This was so, even though the end result was the transfer of funds out of the reach of Dr. Ramgotra's creditors. The exact process by which Dr. Ramgotra managed to keep his RRIF proceeds was as follows: he transferred non-insurance-managed RRSPs into an insurance-administered RRIF in 1990. This was done in good faith at the suggestion of his Certified Financial Planner. The disposition took place within five years of bankruptcy.

The Supreme Court held, however, that although the assets vested in the trustee in bankruptcy, the trustee could not deal with them and had to return them to the bankrupt (Dr. Ramgotra) upon the bankrupt's discharge. This was because the *Bankruptcy and Insolvency Act* precludes the trustee from dealing with assets that are exempt from execution or seizure. The Supreme Court held that there was no evidence of fraudulent intent. The transfer was done in good faith as part of normal prudent retirement planning.

The Insurance Advantage

As it stands, as a general rule of thumb, all assets of an individual or entity are security for unpaid debts owing to a creditor. This applies whether or not the individual or entity is bankrupt. Traditionally, life insurance products have been given special protection against the claims of creditors under provincial legislation. The legislation, which is fairly consistent across Canada, is intended to protect the rights of the beneficiaries under the contracts. Thus, products offered for sale by a life insurance company are generally creditor-protected.

The definition of "insurance products" in all provinces includes annuity contracts. Most RRSPs and non-registered investments issued by insurance companies take the form of an undertaking to provide an annuity and, as such, fall under the definition of life insurance under provincial legislation. Many provinces do not provide creditor protection for non-insurance RRSPs, and no province provides creditor protection for non-registered moneys held in non-insurance investment vehicles.

Creditor protection during the lifetime of the owner can be achieved in two ways: by making an irrevocable beneficiary designation in a life insurance contract or by designating as beneficiaries certain family members specified in provincial insurance legislation.

After the death of the life insured, where an appropriate beneficiary has been designated, the creditors of the deceased are prevented from seizing the policy. The death benefit of the policy is specifically excluded from the estate of the owner. This is because the proceeds flow directly to the beneficiary and are exempt from the claims of creditors.

It should be noted that creditor protection exists only where the policy is owned by an individual. Policies owned by a corporation offer no direct creditor protection; however, a properly implemented corporate structure can achieve creditor protection. Where creditor protection is important, it is advisable to name alternative or contingent beneficiaries within the protected class, since the exemption from seizure can be lost if the designated beneficiary dies.

Insurance products fall into two categories: life insurance policies and deferred annuity contracts. When hearing of "a life insurance contract", most people think of a traditional life insurance policy where one pays a regular stream of premium payments, and a death benefit is paid to a designated beneficiary upon the insured's death. However, accumulation and investment products sold by life insurance companies are "deferred annuity contracts" and, as such, also qualify as life insurance policies.

Cash can be accumulated within a traditional life insurance policy subject to certain maximums imposed by the *Income Tax Act*. Within these maximums, the investment growth is not subject to accrual taxation. This is commonly referred to as an "exempt policy". Furthermore, in most circumstances, the policy fund or cash value is paid out to the designated beneficiary as a tax-free benefit in addition to the face amount of the policy. This feature makes accumulating and investing funds within an exempt policy by an individual an attractive tax deferral and estate planning tool, particularly when combined with the added value of creditor protection.

These structures offer tax minimization solutions that cannot be obtained by run-of-the-mill investments. For example, there are specialized instruments governed under insurance legislation that provide benefits that create the following end results:

- All personal deposits can be structured to be deductible over time.
- Large annual deductions are provided each year against income for the rest of your life or sooner. Money would be invested on a deductible basis; the money grows tax free.
- The individual retires tax-free and dies tax-free, all the while having his or her savings protected from his or her creditors.
- The personal deduction creates a cash-on-cash return every year, year in and year out, in a plan where tax will never be paid as long as the individual uses the funds for either retirement or investing.

Strategy Twelve: Corporate Sponsored Non-registered Senior Executive Retirement Plans (SERPs)

Only corporations are able to sponsor non-registered retirement plans. These plans are governed by insurance and pension Acts. Only insurance segregated funds and non-registered pension funds can protect non-registered investment assets from creditors, not individually held securities held at a bank or investment house.

In the case of Ramgotra, the Supreme Court of Canada held that, provided a transfer of assets to an insurance plan is a legitimate retirement planning exercise, the assets are protected from creditors. It is therefore wise to have the plan set up by someone who is *only* insurance licensed, meaning, the advisor who sells and manages these investment assets is not registered to sell either investment securities or mutual funds. It is important to ask your advisor what licences he or she holds.

All business owners or executives also have the ability to transfer all of their non-registered investments to these types of Senior Executive Retirement Plans (SERPs) and receive the same creditor protection benefits. This is provided the transfer of assets is not done with the contemplation of future bankruptcy; the assets are protected from creditors as it cannot be anything else but a legitimate retirement planning exercise, since the advisor only sells insurance and pension investment products.

The advantage of setting up these types of plans is that it allows a business owner or executive to transfer all of his or her non-registered assets to these plans and to gain the following benefits:

(1) lower management fees (the average management fee for a mutual fund in Canada is 2.5% and for funds held in a non-registered SERP these fees range from 1% to 1.5%);

(2) one has access to top rated money managers;

(3) the sponsoring company has the ability to write off all management fees associated with the investment funds (these fees are a tax-deductable expense for the business and a non-taxable benefit for the individual whom the SERP was set up for);

(4) creditor protection as investments that are governed under both insurance and pension Acts are creditor-protected, and investments held under both the banking and investment Acts can be seized by creditors of an individual; and

(5) funds held in these types of SERPs bypass probate because they have a named beneficiary attached to them.

THE BOTTOM LINE

As Andrew and I finished our lunch, Andrew left our meeting having shared a truism that I found to be the gem of the entire afternoon: "Peter, the sign of a true professional is someone who knows when it's time to seek out other professionals with complementary skills in areas of asset protection and insurance contracts. A dangerous professional is someone who does not know that they don't know, but acts as if they do. The problem with this is clients don't know the difference until it's too late!"

For all Canadians subjected to personal liabilities as a result of their professional activities, creditor protection is absolutely critical. All creditor protection strategies should be made at a time when you are clearly not insolvent or on the eve of bankruptcy. Planning must be justifiable in terms of non-asset protection objectives.

A wise person is someone who does not live in fear of the worst-case scenario, but is aware of it and has prepared to the best of his or her ability to prevent it from happening or lessen its impact. Taking the time to put strategies into place today to ward off creditors of the future just makes good business sense.

EPILOGUE — THE TRUSTED ADVISOR'S WORK MANIFESTO FOR THE 21ST CENTURY

> "Everything that can be counted does not necessarily count; everything that counts cannot necessarily be counted."
>
> Albert Einstein

In the Information Age, the only thing we can count on is change itself. After more than two decades in which millions of people's working lives have been disrupted by corporate outsourcing, downsizing and re-engineering, individuals have come to realize that Canadian companies can no longer offer them job security for life.

In the New Economy, "we have a better chance of getting a gold watch from a street vendor than we do from a corporation", said one former Vice-President of Human Resources with 20 years' experience who had been let go due to corporate restructuring.

Before globalization and the Information Age, the old trappings of success were a secretary, a company car and a corner office. These are now things of the past. Today, we are all responsible for managing our own careers. All jobs, whether contract or permanent, eventually end and should be viewed as temporary. What is not temporary is we who live out our lives.

The true difference between an entrepreneur and an employee is his or her mindset. An employee fears not having a cheque from his or her employer at the end of the week. An entrepreneur fears just the opposite of just receiving his or her cheques from one source. Which mindset do you hold dear to you?

Signs of career trouble have also changed. In the old economy, the rules of success were simple — one would receive incremental promotions every few years. If you did not get a promotion, or were offered partnership in your firm, you would have taken that as a warning that your job might be in jeopardy. Over the last few years, the warning signs have become much more subtle. So in this new era, we must become aware of these signs and be prepared for change.

QUESTIONING UNDERLYING ASSUMPTIONS

It is important for each and every one of us from time to time to question why we do what we do. When I think about questioning our underlying assumptions, I am often reminded of a story about a newlywed couple that drives this point home to me, and I hope it helps you as well.

One evening a husband came home as his new wife prepared dinner. That night they were having roast beef. He noticed that his wife had cut off the ends of the roast beef and thrown them in the garbage. He found this very puzzling so he asked his wife why she had cut off the ends of the roast beef and put them in the garbage. She politely replied that this was the way her mother had "always" prepared roast beef. After receiving her answer, he decided to follow the advice his father had given him on the day of his wedding, which was to pick your battles wisely, so he let it go.

About six months later, the husband was having dinner at his mother-in-law's, and the main dish she was preparing that evening was roast beef. He noticed that she had also cut off the ends of the roast beef and put them into the trash can. He shook his head as he remembered the conversation he had had with his wife several months before and decided that he would ask his mother-in-law why she made roast beef this way. So he asked, and his mother-in-law replied that this was the way her mother, his wife's grandmother, had made roast beef when she was a little girl. He was more confused then ever, so he let it go.

Several months passed, and his wife's grandmother flew in from Florida to visit the family. At dinner one night when the entire family was gathered together, the husband, still puzzled over the roast beef mystery for almost a year, turned to his wife's grandmother and asked her: "I was wondering why, when your daughter, my wife's mother, was young that when you made roast beef you cut off the ends and threw them out?"

The grandmother laughed out loud at the top of her lungs. After she settled down a bit, she turned to him and began to tell him the story that when she first got married, she and her husband were so poor that the pot that she cooked in was too small to fit an entire roast beef in, so she had to cut off the ends so it would fit in the pot. And she said "I never threw away the ends. I used them in the soup the next day."

ARE YOU ASKING THE RIGHT QUESTION?

Asking the right questions is sometimes more valuable than the answers to your questions. Ask yourself the key questions below to provoke insight into what drives and motivates you — embark on the journey of taking ownership of your career and destiny.

Are you learning? If you can't say to yourself that you have learned anything of value in the past year, nor do you think that you will learn anything of value next year at your job, you should be concerned about your position. In the New Economy our greatest assets are the new marketable skills we acquire. When your learning stops at your present job, you have to be prepared to leave and move on. This rule applies even when a promotion might be involved. If your job has become easy for you to do, remember that either your position can be automated or someone else can be hired to replace you for a lot less pay.

Educators have identified four stages of learning that everyone acquiring a new skill set must pass through in order to achieve mastery of those new skills. The financial industry is constantly evolving, requiring you to be a lifelong learner. As you grow as a person and transition from one way of doing something to moving to the next level, it is helpful to identify what stage you are at on your learning curve, so that you can consciously direct your course of study towards mastery. These distinct stages of learning are as follows:

(1) *Unconscious Incompetence* — We are not aware that we can't do something.

(2) *Conscious Incompetence* — We know that we can't do something.

(3) *Conscious Competence* — We can now perform the new task but we have to really think about it while performing it. This is a state of extreme concentration.

(4) *Unconscious Competence* — We no longer have to think about the skill. This is the stage when we can pay attention to other things and new learning while still performing the acquired skill.

If your job were advertised in the career section of the newspaper and you applied for it, would you get it? If you were applying for your current position, would your firm be looking for the skill set that you currently have?

Has your current firm taken advantage of you? Were you asked to sacrifice long-term career growth for very short-term gains that only benefit your firm and not you? For example, a Chartered Accountant wants to learn forensic accounting but is encouraged by senior partners at the firm to stay put and continue doing audit, while others in the firm are paid to learn these skills. If you have answered yes, your firm has stopped investing in you and you are expendable!

Do you know what you contribute to the bottom line of your firm? How about your contribution to your firm's success? If you are not able to describe what you do and how it benefits your firm from the time it takes for a traffic light to turn from red to green, most likely your partners and your clients can't either.

What would you do if your job vanished tomorrow? Can you honestly say that you have invested enough into yourself and your career by developing marketable skills, built contingency into your plans and developed support networks to help you through a transition to new career opportunities?

Do you enjoy what you do for a living? Life is too short to live the delayed life plan — doing the things you don't like, in hopes that one day you will be living your true life plan. There are two major flaws with this type of thinking. One, will you know when it is time to switch to living your true life-plan? If you have not taken the necessary steps towards making your dreams happen today, what makes you think you will embark on your true life path tomorrow? And two, do you really have all the time in the world to make this change? Do you believe that you will be the only one in human history to live forever? Ask yourself: "Have I accomplished anything in my life that has real meaning to me, my family and the greater community as a whole?"

Sure, many of us suffer from the collective illusion that by continuing our delayed life plan we are earning a living and that this is the best we can hope for in this lifetime. But if our hearts are not into our work, are we not just making a "dying" for ourselves? If each day we lose a little more of our dreams, our self-respect and ourselves, what type of legacy do we create?

Do you know what you stand for, and what your core values are? Have you ever sat down and asked yourself what you stand for, and what you believe? Values are the principles and standards we set for ourselves either consciously or unconsciously. These are the qualities that we consider worthwhile to fight for, to uphold and to even die for.

A perfect example of someone who has a very concise value system is a gentleman named Major G. Scott Bowman, founder and headmaster of Robert Land Academy (RLA). Major Bowman had a vision in his mind's eye in the early 1970s to turn a 168-acre pig farm in the heartland of the historic Niagara Peninsula in Ontario, Canada into a school for boys, based on a military theme that would reinforce the importance of organization, teamwork, discipline and personal responsibility. These boys would become true citizens, in the very sense of the word, to their communities, nations and the world. They would value their responsibilities and obligations to their society and know that each right and freedom they enjoy needs to be earned, respected and appreciated every day of their lives. Major Bowman believed that these values were strongly missing in our modern day society. For a baby boomer he was very counter-culture.

Major G. Scott Bowman is a direct descendant of Robert Land, who was a United Empire Loyalist during the American Revolution, an early settler of the Niagara region and a man of significant character and achievement. The Academy was named after Robert Land in honour of his spirit of independent resourcefulness, courage and responsibility.

Students admitted to the Academy are chosen for their potential for success. Students admitted to the Academy have, while trying to succeed in the public school system, experienced difficulties related to attitude, concentration, focus and respect. Today as a testament to Major Bowman's vision, spirit and values, stands "Robert Land Academy, an Island Oasis in a Sea of Mediocrity". Today, from nothing more than one man's vision, determination and hard work stands a school, physically resembling a British colonial fort, that has helped thousands of boys become contributing members to our society. Major Bowman's vision has become a model for hundreds of other schools and institutions around the world.

The driving force behind Major Bowman's creation and success of RLA has been the value system that he first wrote down on a napkin over 35 years ago, when the idea of the school was only a vision in his mind. The Academy emphasizes five core values in everything it strives to teach to its students, within and beyond the bounds of the class: *Loyalty*, *Labour*, *Courage*, *Commitment* and *Honour*. As the excerpt from the Academy's parents' handbook explains below (reprinted with the explicit permission of Robert Land Academy):

The Five Values of Robert Land Academy

> **Loyalty** as a concept is self-explanatory. How one makes it tangible as a value determines the nature of one's conduct. Modeling plays an important role. It is paramount that loyalty is displayed to each other and the Academy. We expect loyalty as a matter of course and it is rewarded when displayed. The necessity and benefits of loyalty to something outside and other than oneself must be demonstrated in a concrete fashion, through verbal explanations and providing opportunities to demonstrate its value in life situations. By graduation, each Cadet should understand and be capable of displaying loyalty to something greater and other than himself.

> **Labour** for Robert Land Academy Cadets entails far more than the routine performance of menial jobs. We are committed to labour as a way of life and to the importance of fulfilling one's life work with an attitude of self-respect as well as respect for the labour of others. We view life itself as labour, in the sense that one must work for what one earns, whether rights or remuneration. This is not to say that we believe life to be drudgery; rather, as Robert Land himself believed, life is a toiling after the best, in the realms of work, rest and play. We instill this value in our Cadets by demanding from them their best in all activities. All Cadets share in the work done at the Academy, and their work must meet our standard of excellence. Our Cadets also labour in academics, life skills and extra curricular activities, and again, they must labour to be the best they can be.
>
> **Courage:** Our Cadets are taught to have the Courage to speak their minds, act on their convictions and be able to finish what they start, despite hardships. With courage our Cadets will learn to master their limitations and exploit their strengths in order to achieve maximum success. It should be noted that courage is not the absence of fear, but its conquest. The person who has never been afraid has never had to display courage.
>
> **Commitment** is perhaps the most fundamental of our values. Robert Land's life was based on a commitment to principles and institutions, which were not accepted universally. For this he suffered considerably. Commitment breeds endurance in adversity, a necessary attribute for anyone seeking success. Cadets must learn that commitment means binding one's self to someone or something else, and that such binding is both necessary for one's development and beneficial to one's personality. Cadets will be taught to show commitment to each other, to the Academy and its values, and to excellence in all their endeavors.
>
> **Honour:** Cadets at Robert Land grow to Honour themselves, their families, their friends, the Academy the greater community. The service theme facilitates the development of all of the values in our Cadets, especially honour. Through the continual insistence of honour for the values of our Academy, our Cadets will learn respect for a code of conduct that will stand them in good stead for the rest of their lives. The honour associated with the life of Robert Land should be a fine example to the entire Robert Land community.

By no means do I imply that you should adopt or accept the five values of Robert Land Academy. However, what is important is to understand the importance of becoming conscious of what your core values are and that you never stray from what you know is right for your community, your family and friends, your clients and you.

After you become conscious of your core values, it is very important that you begin to rank and prioritize them in importance to you. This theory was put to the test at a recent workshop I ran in Toronto for financial planners. The attendees were given an exercise to write down what they valued most and then to list them in order of importance to them. One of the participant's came up with the following "value system", which I would like to share with you now as an example:

Sample "Value System"

(1) I believe in living in truth because when there are no lies, one is not beholden to anything. This results in being congruent in everything one does and empowers one to do what is true and right.

(2) I believe change and success happens explosively and exponentially in one's life. To fully appreciate one's success, one has made the conscious commitment prior to one's success to work towards becoming emotionally and spiritually prepared so one will fully appreciate one's success. This preparation empowers one to enjoy one's success, resulting in it being enjoyable, long and enduring.

(3) I believe in the importance of health; as long as I am healthy, my universe is open to me.

(4) I believe that an individual should strive for personal control over his or her own destiny. I know that this personal power for me only comes after I have taken complete ownership of my own life, attitudes, dreams and hopes. Life is not a dress rehearsal! If it is to be, it is up to me!

(5) I believe my happiness and success in my life will be based on the quality of my relationships with others. Less is more! Quality is better than quantity! Depth not breadth!

(6) I believe in living in appreciation for all that has been brought into my life and will come into my life. Everyday I say "please" and "thank you". I understand that life is a gift and every experience both good and bad is a part of the journey. I expect of myself to get true value from this ride called life. Through the incorporation of "please" and "thank you" and forgiveness, I have come to the personal understanding that these habits release me to travel forward and be a powerful force in my life and the world I create around me.

(7) I believe in life, and that if money can solve a problem, it truly is not a problem!

(8) I believe life is too short and one should find balance with family, friends and work in a synergic way so one can get the most out of one's human experience. As the old saying goes, "Don't sweat the small stuff because in the end it's all small stuff."

(9) I believe through ongoing financial planning and continually putting my plans into action, I will only then be moving in the direction of turning my dreams into my living reality.

(10) Money to me is something I choose to trade my life energy for. I place no limit to my energy. Nor will I let outside influence and forces place a limit on me either.

(11) I choose that the role money is to play in my relationships with others is to foster creative, stimulating and productive mediums of exchange. If we do not all win in a relationship, it is not a relationship I choose to be in. I believe true power is having the ability to choose my relationships and associations.

(12) I believe that we should all strive to play great financial offence in how we earn our living and to play equally, as well, defence in how we store our wealth.

Have you spoken out loud about your vision and do you have a written plan of how you are going to specifically achieve your most important financial and life goals?

"Where there is no vision, the people perish."

Proverbs 29:18

On May 25, 1961, President John F. Kennedy delivered in person before a joint session of Congress his vision of putting a man on the moon and safely returning him back to earth before the end of the decade. What was so powerful about Kennedy's statement at the time he made it was that over a million calculations that had not yet even been thought of needed to be figured out to turn this human vision into an actualized reality. His vision was so compelling that an entire nation mobilized to turn his words and this vision into a fact. On July 20, 1969, Commander Neil Armstrong became the first man on the moon. This historic event was marked by one of the most important declarations ever spoken by a single human being: "One small step for man, one giant leap for mankind."

There is no substitute for a good step-by-step, goal-oriented plan. A Harvard study in 1952 showed that 3% of the graduates had written out their career goals in a plan. Twenty years later, in 1972, those same 3% were worth more than the other 97% of that 1952 class. Remember, these were Harvard graduates; the wealth of that 3% must have been staggering! That's the power of setting a goal, having a plan and working the plan.

Most people spend more time planning a vacation or a car purchase than planning their life and financial future. The average person will work

90,000 hours in his or her life, yet spends less than 24 hours asking himself or herself what he or she wants to accomplish in his or her lifetime, or what his or her legacy will be.

The Ancient Greeks often compared men to ships. However, most do not have rudders, so they go this way and that way and eventually end up crashing on rocks. Any route will do because they don't have a plan. But those who do have a plan make life look so easy for the rest of us. They go from one port to the next, from one success to the next success. If you don't have a plan for your life, there are plenty of other people who will step up to the plate and make decisions for your life. Is this what you want?

All highly successful people I have ever worked with have had very clearly defined, written life, career and financial plans. They believed implicitly and unshakably in their plans and were impervious to external circumstances. So they didn't alter their plans every time the wind changed direction, and continued to work their plans steadfastly, no matter how long it took, until their plans inevitably succeeded. People succeed because they believe and they are believed!

What is your purpose in life? Viktor Frankl, an Austrian psychiatrist, heir to Sigmund Freud (1865-1939), who was the father of psychoanalysis, and a survivor of Auschwitz and the Holocaust, wrote about his experiences in the Nazi death camps in his 1946 book *Man's Search for Meaning: An Introduction to Logotherapy* (Boston: Beacon Press, 1963). In this book he describes what he observed in Auschwitz of humans' free will and character. He tells the story that no one survived in the camps for a prolonged period of time unless he or she had a reason to live, be it for revenge, to find loved ones or to tell his or her story.

Frankl observed that each person needs to be fulfilled as a human being, to have a purpose and to have a meaning for his or her existence. Frankl developed an entire modern movement in therapy based on his experience called Logotherapy. Logo in Greek literally means "meaning". The aim of Logotherapy was to help people find their purpose in life and to help them live out their purpose. To be truly successful in your life it is absolutely imperative that you find a meaning for your life and live your purpose to the fullest. Frankl believed that if a person discovered his or her "why" to life, the "how" of his or her life would fall into place.

In order to do this, one must first make a commitment which actually creates the capacity for one to be an instrument of good. It is a calling to something larger than ourselves. When we find our place, we will find our purpose.

> "The last of the human freedoms — to choose one's attitude in any given set of circumstances, to choose one's own way."
>
> Victor Frankl — *Man's Search for Meaning*

TAKE THE QUANTUM LEAP

In the introduction to James Carse's book *Finite and Infinite Games* (New York: Ballantine Books, 1987), he introduces and then defines that "there are at least two kinds of games. One could be called finite, the other infinite. A finite game is played for the purpose of winning, an infinite game for the purpose of continuing the play".

It absolutely makes a world of difference whether we consider ourselves as pawns in a game whose rules we call reality or as players of the game who know that rules are "real" only to the extent that we have created or accepted them, and that we can change them.

One way or another, most of us believe circumstances are the driving forces of our lives. But if we step back, we will slowly realize it is not our circumstances but how we have structured our lives and thinking. The underlying structure of one's life determines the path one takes. By changing our structure, we change our lives. We need to have discipline that will help cultivate our wisdom, and by writing down our dreams and goals into a plan that represents our purpose, we will not need to use force to create it into our lives because we will be drawn towards it like metal filings being drawn towards a magnet.

The first step is understanding that any relationship or process can be characterized in "finite" or "infinite" terms. The second step is recognizing that characterization is almost always a matter of choice and that, by choosing to see a relationship as "infinite", you can redefine it in a meaningful and healthy way.

I have observed that when people see life as an infinite game and are living out their life purpose, they come up with more ideas, see more associations between ideas and see more similarities and differences among things than people who see life as a finite game. What emerges is more of a partnership ordination towards family, friends, work, communities, environment, ourselves and life.

It has been said that when a person has one way of doing something, he or she is stuck; if that person has two ways, he or she is in a bind; and only when that person has three or more ways of doing something, he or she has true choice. The Chinese symbol for "crisis" has a duel meaning, which also translates into the word "opportunity". Each player in the game of life who is perceptive enough to see himself or herself playing in an infinite game has the uncanny ability to see all crises as opportunities to continue to play. So all that happens to this kind of person in life is a part of the play, and there are no failures in the mind of this kind of player; there is only feedback so play can continue.

Fred Alan Wolf, in his award-winning book titled *Taking The Quantum Leap: The New Physics for Nonscientists* (New York: Harper Perennial, 1989), describes a quantum leap as:

> The explosive jump that a particle of matter undergoes in moving from one place to another … in a figurative sense, taking the quantum leap means taking a risk, going off into uncharted territory with no guide to follow.

In 2001, a few days after 9/11 and after I had had my own epiphany that my business model would need to change if I were going to continue to prosper in the financial industry going forward, I just happened to be watching a television interview with Sir Paul McCartney. Call it synchronicity or not, but when the interviewer turned to McCartney and asked him how he, John Lennon, George Harrison and Ringo Starr started writing their now classic songs for the Beatles that defined a generation, contained within McCartney's answer to the interviewer's question was the insight I had been searching and longing for, of how an individual could live an authentic life.

Paul McCartney answered with a short story. He told the interviewer that when the Beatles were getting started, in 1961, they performed 92 days straight in Hamburg, Germany, where they perfected their talents. At the beginning of their tour, the Beatles were little more than a cover band, playing other bands' top 40 hits.

McCartney recounted how frustrated both he and John Lennon were feeling because many of the bands that the Beatles were performing with were going on stage just before them and playing the same cover songs. So out of this great frustration and some creative flare both McCartney and Lennon found their own voice and made their own quantum leap. One night just before they were to go out on stage to perform, they decided to work on a song that McCartney had written sometime earlier. Together they jotted down some lyrics and improvised a melody.

That cold night in April 1961, the Beatles sang "Love Me Do". It is that little momentous event when the Beatles started writing their own music and performing it themselves that made all the difference. Perhaps if the Beatles had not performed that single authentic act, we might not be experiencing their genius today.

Little, seemingly unconnected events can create huge changes halfway around the globe. The best way to understand this concept is to adopt the metaphor that is used to explain Chaos Theory known as the Butterfly Effect: a butterfly fluttering its wings in China could set off a tornado in Texas.

Now, ask yourself, are you making an authentic change today that will make all the difference in your life today and tomorrow, and will cause you to have your very own butterfly effect?

BE A LIFETIME LEARNER!

If you have read this far, congratulations! You have completed a long unique journey, considering that 80% of U.S. families did not buy or read a book last year (source: Jerold Jenkins, online: <www.jenkinsgroupinc.com>). In January 2007, *The CSI Exchange*, the Canadian Securities Institute's online magazine, reported that "according to a number of studies, business people who read at least 7 business books a year earn over 2.3 times more than people who read only 1 book per year". The report stated that the reason why readers earn more money than non-readers is because they receive "a constant stream of new ideas and strategies they can use to help their careers, their clients and their companies".

Joseph Campbell (1904-1987), who was considered the world's greatest scholar in mythology, was the author of *The Hero with a Thousand Faces*, commemorative ed. (Princeton, N.J.: Princeton University Press, 2004), which inspired George Lucas to write his *Star Wars* script in 1975. Campbell, through his years of studying the world's mythology, came to the understanding that there is very little human knowledge that has not been spoken or written before. Human wisdom that seems new is actually "old wine in new bottles". The things not known is the history not studied.

There is nothing that has not been thought of before. Our minds do not create thought; we amplify it. Our minds can be compared to radio receivers; if we have the right equipment we can tune it into the wisdom of the world. All the wisdom of the world has been written down somewhere in the annals of great literature, and this is mankind's greatest accomplishment and legacy.

Ideas are like viruses of the mind. A profound thought once spoken or written down has the ability to replicate itself and be passed on from one mind onto the next, and from one generation onto future generations. Every idea that enters our mind has the ability to influence our behaviour. History has shown that good ideas always prevail and endure over bad ones in the long run. Aim to tune your mind to great ideas and vaccinate yourself from evil ones.

> "People with extraordinary minds, talk about ideas.
> People with average minds, talk about events.
> People with simple minds, talk about other people."
>
> Anonymous

I have personally found that the books I treasure the most and recommend to others are the ones that say the things that I have been thinking and did not have the right words to properly express myself at the time. These are the books that have provided me with a language empowering me to crystallize my own thoughts and beliefs. These are the books that have a prominent place in my library.

Returning to the discussion of Joseph Campbell, there is a famous story about him when he was a college professor. At the beginning of each course, Campbell would give out a large reading list to his students. Several weeks into one of his classes, a student raised her hand and asked, "Professor Campbell, this is not the only class we are taking. How do you expect us to read all the books on your reading list in one semester?" Campbell turned to his class and replied, "I am not expecting you to read all these books this semester; you have the rest of your life to discover them."

This book will have achieved its primary purposes if you finish it with a brand new kind of lexicon and have many more meaningful and insightful questions than you started out with and your thirst for more knowledge has expanded exponentially. As mentioned throughout this book, a question is ten times more valuable than its answer because when you formulate the right question, what you have accomplished is the focusing of your attention and the presupposing that an answer to your question is out there for your own discovery. Depending on how much importance and how exact your question is will determine how much energy you expend to find out your own unique answers.

An act, a deed and a word have the power to change our world and the worldview of others. When I begin teaching either a financial planning course or a workshop, I always preface my talks by sharing with my students and participants that I am not any smarter than they are. I have, however, been on the path a little longer, and if they have the desire, and the determination to invest their most precious asset, their time, they will be further along the path and know a whole lot more than I. And I look forward to becoming their student.

Each Remembrance Day in Canada, on the 11th hour of the 11th day of the 11th month, we are asked to stop for a minute to reflect on and remember those courageous men and women who served in our armed forces and laid down their lives in war so that today we could all live in peace and enjoy all the rights and freedoms they fought for, and so that we could enjoy a free and democratic society. Every fall across Canada, primary school children are taught and recite "In Flanders Fields", the poem written by Lieutenant-Colonel John McCrae (1872-1918), who had fallen while serving our country during World War I. This legacy belongs to all of us and is a call for both you and me, together, to take up the torch from those who have come before us to have the freedom to be our very best in all our pursuits.

In Flanders Fields the poppies blow
Between the crosses, row on row,

That mark our place; and in the sky
The larks, still bravely singing, fly
Scarce heard amid the guns below.

We are the Dead. Short days ago
We lived, felt dawn, saw sunset glow,
Loved, and were loved, and now we lie
In Flanders fields.

Take up our quarrel with the foe:
To you from failing hands we throw
The torch, be yours to hold it high.
If ye break faith with us who die
We shall not sleep, though poppies grow
In Flanders fields

My father, Marvin S. Merrick (1939-1999), just before he died in March 1999, bequeathed to me his Ethical Will, his spiritual legacy, which he had accumulated throughout his lifetime, and which he believed was important enough to be passed on after he was gone so his values would live on. In one of the last conversations that I had with my father, he imparted the following wisdom:

> "*Tikkun olam,* 'repairing the world'. One's only concern and focus should be on what one has in his pockets and not in the pockets of others. The grass might look greener in someone else's yard, but those lawns need to be manicured as well. Have the wisdom to truly know and appreciate that the grass is always greener on your side of the pond, to always be proud and satisfied with what one has and not to begrudge others for having or not having. Most importantly, it is our responsibility and obligation to take care of that which one loves and to enjoy the best life possible while helping and not harming others. What you do does not define who you are. The world is a looking glass on the self; what one puts before it, is what is reflected back from it. If life serves you up lemons, make lemonade."

THE POWER OF NOW

A successful career in the New Economy results from having a résumé that describes a person with fewer titles, but many more employers and experiences. Whether you are employed permanently or are a sole practitioner, it helps to see yourself as a self-employed person who is always of the mindset of turning work into his or her vocation and purpose — being inwardly directed and outwardly focused. Having a self-employed mindset prepares you mentally for the likelihood of becoming unemployed, looking for new opportunities and turning your dreams into your living reality!

As stated in the Preface of this book, we can all learn from the moral contained within the children's story of the "Tortoise and the Hare". The slow and the steady always win the race. A major influence on Warren Buffett's investment philosophy was the investing legend Philip

Fisher (1907-2004), author of the 1958 investment classic *Common Stocks and Uncommon Profits* (New York: Wiley, 2003). Fisher adamantly believed in never investing money with a man who had never fallen flat on his face, broken some bones, knocked out a few teeth and failed miserably at least once in his lifetime, and then pulled himself up by his own bootstraps through sheer inspiration, determination and perspiration. This individual was a creative force to be reckoned with and could be counted on as a leader in the land of the living.

This type of person, Fisher believed, had an indelible spirit, a moral compass and a strong defining character (an infinite gamer at his or her very best). This was the kind of person whom Fisher wanted on his team and would invest his and his clients' money in for the long haul because this type of person had shown through adversity that he or she would not allow himself or herself to be counted out, and was a serious player in the game of life. Fisher believed that a mistake was an event, the full benefits of which you had not yet turned into your advantage. The people whom Fisher recommended that you would want on your team are people who share this belief.

One of the main tenets behind Kabbalah, the mystical side of Judaism, is the understanding of the "Bread of Shame", which means that you cannot keep what you have not rightfully earned. The only way to be deserving of what you have is to be a proactive force for the purpose of not receiving for the self alone. This belief is in sync with Dr. Laurence J. Peter's (1919-1990) Peter Principle, which became popularized in the late 1960s.

The Peter Principle states that we rise to the highest level of our incompetence and no higher. So by combining both ideas behind the "Bread of Shame" and the "Peter Principle", you and I have as much success, money and fame as we can handle at this moment in time because there is a lesson to be learnt first before we will consciously or unconsciously give ourselves permission to move onto the next level in our maturing process. Winston Churchill (1874-1965) added to this by believing leadership to be "going from failure to failure without losing enthusiasm".

If we aim to achieve more in our life, we will first need to prepare ourselves so we feel deserving of all our successes. So when opportunities present themselves, we will have all the resources needed emotionally, intellectually and physically to identify, act on, incorporate, appreciate and enjoy that which we have learnt. Having acquired new wisdom as a part of who we are at our core will allow us to act appropriately in applying this new wisdom. Only then will we be able to put those experiences and knowledge behind us, allowing us to move on to the next level in our life's quest. The ancient sages teach us that the way out of a rut is to be creative and to give to others. The "ideal" in life is a virtue of good.

At the end of your days, the person whom you will have to answer to for all the things you did or did not do will be you. It is better to regret the things you did than the things you did not do, and live life to its fullest. You are a very powerful person, but first you need to believe this yourself.

"You'll See It When You Believe It"

Dr. Wayne W. Dyer

FIND YOUR OWN ALEXANDER THE GREAT'S GORDIAN KNOT!

When Alexander the Great left Macedonia to conquer Persia, he had heard of the legend of King Gordius who had tied his chariot with a knot to the Temple of the Zeus Basilica. It was prophesied that this knot would only be untied by the one who was destined by the gods to become the king of Persia and the known World.

Alexander the Great went to the chariot and tried to untie the knot, but he could not. Alexander the Great stood there for a moment, staring at the knot, and after a while he then pulled out his sword and with one bold stroke he slashed the knot wide open. Soon after this event Alexander the Great through countless victories became the king of Persia and the known world.

You too have the ability to take any intractable problem you might face in both your life and career and solve it by a bold stroke of genius and determination, cutting your own Gordian knot; it is up to you and only you!

My maternal grandmother, Edith Oretsky, used to like to share with me parables to make her points stick. One of her favorites was this:

When she was young, she wanted to change the world and she found that she could not. So she focused on changing her nation, but she found she could not. She then turned to trying to change her community, and she met with the same obstacles. So she tried to change her family and this resulted in the same outcome. Lastly, she decided to turn towards the most difficult challenges of them all, changing herself through one small act at a time. Thus, through working on herself, she discovered a change in her family, her community, followed by her nation and her world. This was much to her surprise and liking.

What grandmother was teaching me with her parable was that through one small act towards goodness at a time, we all have the power within each of us to change our world and make a positive difference.

A picture might be worth a thousand words, but we all know that an experience is worth a trillion of those. By taking one step forward *today* towards your authentic self and your true purpose in life, the universe will open up to you and make the other 99 steps towards you. It has been said that those who fail to plan, and fail to act, plan to fail. When your life and financial goals are important enough for you, there can be very little that stands between you and your success.

> "Some men see things as they are and say, 'why'; I dream things that never were and say, 'why not'."
>
> Robert Kennedy (1925-1968)

The time is now! It is time to take your own "Quantum Leap" in your life and your career! People are frightened of change because they don't feel they have any control. Remember, you are the producer of your own life; you pick the projects, finance them and choose the directors, writers and actors. You are the one and only unifying and defining principle during your journey. When you take aim at the stars and if you only find yourself walking on the moon, remember you will be in the company of only a few people within human history to have accomplished such a feat. The best place to begin your journey is where you are right now. From the sturdiest foundations the tallest structures are built.

As I finish writing this book, which has been a true labour of love, I am reminded of my children and their favourite bedtime story: Dr. Seuss's (Theodor Seuss Geisel, 1904-1991) last book published just before he died, *"Oh, the Places You'll Go!"* (London: Picture Lions, 2003). This was Geisel's lasting personal message to future generations to go after their dreams.

With any journey as important as your life, this ancient Chinese proverb is very fitting to be mindful of as you finish reading this book and go forward with the rest of your life:

> *"The thousand mile journey begins with the first step!"*

APPENDIX A

CONSULTING, SEMINARS AND WORKSHOPS

Peter Merrick, B.A., FMA, CFP, TEP, FCSI, is one of North America's most sought-after exit and succession planning consultants and speakers. His pioneering insight and work in the areas of tax minimization and deference solutions and employee benefit plan construction have made him the first choice for CAs, CGAs, CMAs, lawyers, financial advisors and organizations seeking a high-profile expert, consultant, keynote speaker or seminar leader whose message and skill set will transform corporations and individual lives, creating tangible results and restoring commitment and productivity in these uncertain times. Peter's extraordinary seminars and consulting services are fully customized through a unique research process, rich in practical content that your people can use immediately.

Learn more about Peter's consulting, seminars and workshops. Visit his website at <www.MerrickWealth.com> or contact him at <peter@merrickwealth.com> or (416) 854-1776.

APPENDIX B

NEHEMIAH

When I sometimes become discouraged and I believe that the world is falling apart around me, and perhaps I will not meet my goals, I remind myself of the story of Nehemiah. Just the name Nehemiah is enough to give me the strength to stay the course to achieve my life goals whatever the obstacles that are placed in front of me. Nehemiah helps me to remember that the important things in life are not easy but are worth achieving.

Nehemiah is a character found in the Old Testament of the Bible. His story to me is the most inspirational in the entire Bible. Nehemiah's story begins in Persia around 446 BC. Here, Nehemiah is a young man who is the King's royal cupbearer at the palace, a very important position.

One day at the palace, Nehemiah met up with some travellers from Jerusalem and heard about the disrepair that had fallen upon Jerusalem, the city of his forefathers. His heart filled with sadness. For many days after this, he couldn't eat or sleep, as he couldn't stop thinking about Jerusalem. The King watched Nehemiah as this was occurring, and one day the King approached Nehemiah and asked:

> "Nehemiah, why are you so sad these last few days?"

Nehemiah explained to the King that he had learned that Jerusalem had fallen on tough times, and he desired to do something to help it rise from its ashes. The King replied:

> "Nehemiah, you have been a loyal servant for these many years, I give you my permission to go to Jerusalem and become the governor of Judea."

On Nehemiah's arrival, he began to survey the city secretly at night, and formed a plan for its restoration. He looked at what could be accomplished, something that would unite the people of Jerusalem. Nehemiah saw that there were great holes in the walls of Jerusalem. He decided that fixing the walls was the project that would unite his people and begin the restoration of the city of his forefathers. The next day, Nehemiah stood up in front of all Jerusalem and proclaimed that he and all who would join him would work to fix the walls, and this would begin the rebirth of Jerusalem and unite its people. Immediately, some of the people saw the value of what Nehemiah planned to do, and joined with him right away. Others who were complacent or threatened by Nehemiah's goal started saying:

"Nehemiah you are crazy, it can't be done, why try?"

Nehemiah replied by restating his goal of fixing the walls of Jerusalem. He focused on his goal and those who supported the goal, and on the restoration and resurrection of an entire people. After the project began, those who had a vested interest in Jerusalem staying the way it was began to try to sabotage the work that was being done. Nehemiah did not become discouraged; no, he focused even more on his goal, and those who supported this goal. He innately knew that this goal was greater than any one person.

Those who tried to stop the work of restoration realized that it was going to happen. Those people made continuous calls to Nehemiah to cease his work and to come meet them to discuss the situation. Nehemiah did not allow those who had tried to co-opt the project of fixing the walls; he stayed focused on the goal and those who supported the goal. Nehemiah and those who had supported him, at great personal risk, and with skill and energy, completed fixing the walls within six months after he had first stood up and stated his goal.

Nehemiah's action is accredited with the return of the Jewish people to Israel after their long exile in the Persian Empire and is seen as the catalyst for the building of the Second Temple.

What I learned personally from the story of Nehemiah, and what we can all learn from Nehemiah, is that it is important to set goals that are greater than ourselves, that are accomplishable either in our lifetime or in future generations.

There will always be people who support us in achieving our goals, and there will always be others who are threatened and fearful of us achieving our goals. Those threatened by us achieving our goals at first may try to discourage us and then may attack us. After they come to terms with the fact that we cannot be put off our chosen path, they may try to pretend that they are beginning to accept our goals in an effort to distract us.

What is very important for us to always remember is never to get distracted from what we know in our hearts to be right for us and to stay committed to our goals, values and ideas, to remain focused and to appreciate those who give us our support while we are journeying towards our goals and destinations. Remember:

"Nehemiah"

APPENDIX C

IT COULDN'T BE DONE

Edgar Albert Guest (1881-1959)

Somebody said that it couldn't be done,
But he with a chuckle replied
That "maybe it couldn't," but he would be one
Who wouldn't say so till he'd tried.
So he buckled right in with the trace of a grin
On his face. If he worried he hid it.
He started to sing as he tackled the thing
That couldn't be done, and he did it.

Somebody scoffed: "Oh, you'll never do that;
At least no one ever has done it";
But he took off his coat and he took off his hat,
And the first thing we knew he'd begun it.
With a lift of his chin and a bit of a grin,
Without any doubting or quiddit,
He started to sing as he tackled the thing
That couldn't be done, and he did it.

There are thousands to tell you it cannot be done,
There are thousands to prophesy failure;
There are thousands to point out to you, one by one,
The dangers that wait to assail you.
But just buckle in with a bit of a grin,
Just take off your coat and go to it;
Just start to sing as you tackle the thing
That "cannot be done," and you'll do it.

APPENDIX D

CHIEF SEATTLE'S LEGACY IS A WARNING TO US ALL!

In December 1854, Chief Seattle of the Suquamish Nation in Washington State's Puget Sound, after whom the city of Seattle is named, delivered what is considered by the Social Responsibility Movement as one of the most insightful environmental declarations of all time. Chief Seattle's speech was given on behalf of his people in response to a proposed treaty offered by the United States that called for the Suquamish Nation to sell two million acres of its ancestral land for $150,000 (U.S.), and to then be relocated to a reserve.

Chief Seattle's Thoughts (1786-1866)

How can you buy or sell the sky, the warmth of the land? The idea is strange to us.

If we do not own the freshness of the air and the sparkle of the water, how can you buy them?

Every part of this earth is sacred to my people. Every shining pine needle, every sandy shore, every mist in the dark woods, every clearing and humming insect is holy in the memory and experience of my people. The sap which courses through the trees carries the memories of the red man.

The white man's dead forget the country of their birth when they go to walk among the stars. Our dead never forget this beautiful earth, for it is the mother of the red man. We are part of the earth and it is part of us. The perfumed flowers are our sisters; the deer, the horse, the great eagle, these are our brothers. The rocky crests, the juices in the meadows, the body heat of the pony, and man — all belong to the same family.

So, when the Great Chief in Washington sends word that he wishes to buy our land, he asks much of us. The Great Chief sends word he will reserve us a place so that we can live comfortably to ourselves. He will be our father and we will be his children.

So, we will consider your offer to buy our land. But it will not be easy. For this land is sacred to us. This shining water that moves in the streams and rivers is not just water but the blood of our ancestors. If we sell you the land, you must remember that it is sacred, and you must teach your children that it is sacred and that each ghostly reflection in the clear water of the lakes tells of events and memories in the life of my people. The water's murmur is the voice of my father's father.

The rivers are our brothers, they quench our thirst. The rivers carry our canoes, and feed our children. If we sell you our land, you must remember, and teach your children, that the rivers are our brothers and yours, and you must henceforth give the rivers the kindness you would give any brother.

We know that the white man does not understand our ways. One portion of land is the same to him as the next, for he is a stranger who comes in the night and takes from the land whatever he needs. The earth is not his brother, but his enemy, and when he has conquered it, he moves on. He leaves his father's grave behind, and he does not care. He kidnaps the earth from his children, and he does not care. His father's grave, and his children's birthright are forgotten. He treats his mother, the earth, and his brother, the sky, as things to be bought, plundered, sold like sheep or bright beads. His appetite will devour the earth and leave behind only a desert.

I do not know. Our ways are different than your ways. The sight of your cities pains the eyes of the red man. There is no quiet place in the white man's cities. No place to hear the unfurling of leaves in spring or the rustle of the insect's wings. The clatter only seems to insult the ears. And what is there to life if a man cannot hear the lonely cry of the whippoorwill or the arguments of the frogs around the pond at night? I am a red man and do not understand. The Indian prefers the soft sound of the wind darting over the face of a pond and the smell of the wind itself, cleaned by a midday rain, or scented with pinon pine.

The air is precious to the red man for all things share the same breath, the beast, the tree, the man, they all share the same breath. The white man does not seem to notice the air he breathes. Like a man dying for many days he is numb to the stench. But if we sell you our land, you must remember that the air is precious to us, that the air shares its spirit with all the life it supports.

The wind that gave our grandfather his first breath also receives his last sigh. And if we sell you our land, you must keep it apart and sacred as a place where even the white man can go to taste the wind that is sweetened by the meadow's flowers.

So we will consider your offer to buy our land. If we decide to accept, I will make one condition — the white man must treat the beasts of this land as his brothers.

I am a savage and do not understand any other way. I have seen a thousand rotting buffaloes on the prairie, left by the white man who shot them from a passing train. I am a savage and do not understand how the smoking iron horse can be made more important than the buffalo that we kill only to stay alive.

What is man without the beasts? If all the beasts were gone, man would die from a great loneliness of the spirit. For whatever happens to the beasts, soon happens to man. *All things are connected.*

You must teach your children that the ground beneath their feet is the ashes of our grandfathers. So that they will respect the land, tell your children that the earth is rich with the lives of our kin. Teach your children that we have taught our children that the earth is our mother. Whatever befalls the earth befalls the sons of earth. If men spit upon the ground, they spit upon themselves.

This we know; the earth does not belong to man; man belongs to the earth. This we know. All things are connected like the blood which unites one family. *All things are connected.*

Even the white man, whose God walks and talks with him as friend to friend, cannot be exempt from the common destiny. We may be brothers after all. We shall see. One thing we know which the white man may one day discover; our God is the same God.

You may think now that you own Him as you wish to own our land; but you cannot. He is the God of man, and His compassion is equal for the red man and the white. The earth is precious to Him, and to harm the earth is to heap contempt on its creator. The whites too shall pass; perhaps sooner than all other tribes. Contaminate your bed and you will one night suffocate in your own waste.

But in your perishing you will shine brightly fired by the strength of the God who brought you to this land and for some special purpose gave you dominion over this land and over the red man.

That destiny is a mystery to us, for we do not understand when the buffalo are all slaughtered, the wild horses are tamed, the secret corners of the forest heavy with the scent of many men and the view of the ripe hills blotted by talking wires.

Where is the thicket? Gone. Where is the eagle? Gone.

The end of living and the beginning of survival.

APPENDIX E

UNIVERSAL DECLARATION OF HUMAN RIGHTS

Universal Declaration of Human Rights

(Adopted and proclaimed by General Assembly resolution 217 A (III) of 10 December 1948)

On December 10, 1948 the General Assembly of the United Nations adopted and proclaimed the Universal Declaration of Human Rights the full text of which appears in the following pages. Following this historic act the Assembly called upon all Member countries to publicize the text of the Declaration and "to cause it to be disseminated, displayed, read and expounded principally in schools and other educational institutions, without distinction based on the political status of countries or territories."

PREAMBLE

Whereas recognition of the inherent dignity and of the equal and inalienable rights of all members of the human family is the foundation of freedom, justice and peace in the world,

Whereas disregard and contempt for human rights have resulted in barbarous acts which have outraged the conscience of mankind, and the advent of a world in which human beings shall enjoy freedom of speech and belief and freedom from fear and want has been proclaimed as the highest aspiration of the common people,

Whereas it is essential, if man is not to be compelled to have recourse, as a last resort, to rebellion against tyranny and oppression, that human rights should be protected by the rule of law,

Whereas it is essential to promote the development of friendly relations between nations,

Whereas the peoples of the United Nations have in the Charter reaffirmed their faith in fundamental human rights, in the dignity and worth of the human person and in the equal rights of men and women and have determined to promote social progress and better standards of life in larger freedom,

Whereas Member States have pledged themselves to achieve, in co-operation with the United Nations, the promotion of universal respect for and observance of human rights and fundamental freedoms,

Whereas a common understanding of these rights and freedoms is of the greatest importance for the full realization of this pledge,

Now, Therefore THE GENERAL ASSEMBLY proclaims THIS UNIVERSAL DECLARATION OF HUMAN RIGHTS as a common standard of achievement for all peoples and all nations, to the end that every individual and every organ of society, keeping this Declaration constantly in mind, shall strive by teaching and education to promote respect for these rights and freedoms and by progressive measures, national and international, to secure their universal and effective recognition and observance, both among the peoples of Member States themselves and among the peoples of territories under their jurisdiction.

ARTICLE 1.

All human beings are born free and equal in dignity and rights. They are endowed with reason and conscience and should act towards one another in a spirit of brotherhood.

ARTICLE 2.

Everyone is entitled to all the rights and freedoms set forth in this Declaration, without distinction of any kind, such as race, colour, sex, language, religion, political or other opinion, national or social origin, property, birth or other status. Furthermore, no distinction shall be made on the basis of the political, jurisdictional or international status of the country or territory to which a person belongs, whether it be independent, trust, non-self-governing or under any other limitation of sovereignty.

ARTICLE 3.

Everyone has the right to life, liberty and security of person.

ARTICLE 4.

No one shall be held in slavery or servitude; slavery and the slave trade shall be prohibited in all their forms.

ARTICLE 5.

No one shall be subjected to torture or to cruel, inhuman or degrading treatment or punishment.

ARTICLE 6.

Everyone has the right to recognition everywhere as a person before the law.

ARTICLE 7.

All are equal before the law and are entitled without any discrimination to equal protection of the law. All are entitled to equal protection against any discrimination in violation of this Declaration and against any incitement to such discrimination.

ARTICLE 8.

Everyone has the right to an effective remedy by the competent national tribunals for acts violating the fundamental rights granted him by the constitution or by law.

ARTICLE 9.

No one shall be subjected to arbitrary arrest, detention or exile.

ARTICLE 10.

Everyone is entitled in full equality to a fair and public hearing by an independent and impartial tribunal, in the determination of his rights and obligations and of any criminal charge against him.

ARTICLE 11.

(1) Everyone charged with a penal offence has the right to be presumed innocent until proved guilty according to law in a public trial at which he has had all the guarantees necessary for his defence.

(2) No one shall be held guilty of any penal offence on account of any act or omission which did not constitute a penal offence, under national or international law, at the time when it was committed. Nor shall a heavier penalty be imposed than the one that was applicable at the time the penal offence was committed.

ARTICLE 12.

No one shall be subjected to arbitrary interference with his privacy, family, home or correspondence, nor to attacks upon his honour and reputation. Everyone has the right to the protection of the law against such interference or attacks.

ARTICLE 13.

(1) Everyone has the right to freedom of movement and residence within the borders of each state.

(2) Everyone has the right to leave any country, including his own, and to return to his country.

ARTICLE 14.

(1) Everyone has the right to seek and to enjoy in other countries asylum from persecution.

(2) This right may not be invoked in the case of prosecutions genuinely arising from non-political crimes or from acts contrary to the purposes and principles of the United Nations.

ARTICLE 15.

(1) Everyone has the right to a nationality.

(2) No one shall be arbitrarily deprived of his nationality nor denied the right to change his nationality.

ARTICLE 16.

(1) Men and women of full age, without any limitation due to race, nationality or religion, have the right to marry and to found a family. They are entitled to equal rights as to marriage, during marriage and at its dissolution.

(2) Marriage shall be entered into only with the free and full consent of the intending spouses.

(3) The family is the natural and fundamental group unit of society and is entitled to protection by society and the State.

ARTICLE 17.

(1) Everyone has the right to own property alone as well as in association with others.

(2) No one shall be arbitrarily deprived of his property.

ARTICLE 18.

Everyone has the right to freedom of thought, conscience and religion; this right includes freedom to change his religion or belief, and freedom, either alone or in community with others and in public or private, to manifest his religion or belief in teaching, practice, worship and observance.

ARTICLE 19.

Everyone has the right to freedom of opinion and expression; this right includes freedom to hold opinions without interference and to seek, receive and impart information and ideas through any media and regardless of frontiers.

ARTICLE 20.

(1) Everyone has the right to freedom of peaceful assembly and association.

(2) No one may be compelled to belong to an association.

ARTICLE 21.

(1) Everyone has the right to take part in the government of his country, directly or through freely chosen representatives.

(2) Everyone has the right of equal access to public service in his country.

(3) The will of the people shall be the basis of the authority of government; this will shall be expressed in periodic and genuine elections which shall be by universal and equal suffrage and shall be held by secret vote or by equivalent free voting procedures.

ARTICLE 22.

Everyone, as a member of society, has the right to social security and is entitled to realization, through national effort and international co-operation and in accordance with the organization and resources of each State, of the economic, social and cultural rights indispensable for his dignity and the free development of his personality.

ARTICLE 23.

(1) Everyone has the right to work, to free choice of employment, to just and favourable conditions of work and to protection against unemployment.

(2) Everyone, without any discrimination, has the right to equal pay for equal work.

(3) Everyone who works has the right to just and favourable remuneration ensuring for himself and his family an existence worthy of human dignity, and supplemented, if necessary, by other means of social protection.

(4) Everyone has the right to form and to join trade unions for the protection of his interests.

ARTICLE 24.

Everyone has the right to rest and leisure, including reasonable limitation of working hours and periodic holidays with pay.

ARTICLE 25.

(1) Everyone has the right to a standard of living adequate for the health and well-being of himself and of his family, including food, clothing, housing and medical care and necessary social services, and the right to security in the event of unemployment, sickness, disability, widowhood, old age or other lack of livelihood in circumstances beyond his control.

(2) Motherhood and childhood are entitled to special care and assistance. All children, whether born in or out of wedlock, shall enjoy the same social protection.

ARTICLE 26.

(1) Everyone has the right to education. Education shall be free, at least in the elementary and fundamental stages. Elementary education shall be compulsory. Technical and professional education shall be made generally available and higher education shall be equally accessible to all on the basis of merit.

(2) Education shall be directed to the full development of the human personality and to the strengthening of respect for human rights and fundamental freedoms. It shall promote understanding, tolerance and friendship among all nations, racial or religious groups, and shall further the activities of the United Nations for the maintenance of peace.

(3) Parents have a prior right to choose the kind of education that shall be given to their children.

ARTICLE 27.

(1) Everyone has the right freely to participate in the cultural life of the community, to enjoy the arts and to share in scientific advancement and its benefits.

(2) Everyone has the right to the protection of the moral and material interests resulting from any scientific, literary or artistic production of which he is the author.

ARTICLE 28.

Everyone is entitled to a social and international order in which the rights and freedoms set forth in this Declaration can be fully realized.

ARTICLE 29.

(1) Everyone has duties to the community in which alone the free and full development of his personality is possible.

(2) In the exercise of his rights and freedoms, everyone shall be subject only to such limitations as are determined by law solely for the purpose of securing due recognition and respect for the rights and freedoms of others and of meeting the just requirements of morality, public order and the general welfare in a democratic society.

(3) These rights and freedoms may in no case be exercised contrary to the purposes and principles of the United Nations.

ARTICLE 30.

Nothing in this Declaration may be interpreted as implying for any State, group or person any right to engage in any activity or to perform any act aimed at the destruction of any of the rights and freedoms set forth herein.

APPENDIX F

PSALM 49

For the director of music. Of the Sons of Korah. A psalm.

Hear this, all you peoples;
listen, all who live in this world,

both low and high,
rich and poor alike:

My mouth will speak words of wisdom;
the utterance from my heart will give understanding.

I will turn my ear to a proverb;
with the harp I will expound my riddle:

Why should I fear when evil days come,
when wicked deceivers surround me —

those who trust in their wealth
and boast of their great riches?

No man can redeem the life of another
or give to God a ransom for him —

the ransom for a life is costly,
no payment is ever enough —

that he should live on forever
and not see decay.

For all can see that wise men die;
the foolish and the senseless alike perish
and leave their wealth to others.

Their tombs will remain their houses forever,
their dwellings for endless generations,
though they had named lands after themselves.

But man, despite his riches, does not endure;
he is like the beasts that perish.

This is the fate of those who trust in themselves,
and of their followers, who approve their sayings.

Selah

Like sheep they are destined for the grave,
and death will feed on them.

The upright will rule over them in the morning;
their forms will decay in the grave,
far from their princely mansions.

But God will redeem my life from the grave;
he will surely take me to himself.

Selah

Do not be overawed when a man grows rich,
when the splendor of his house increases;

for he will take nothing with him when he dies,
his splendor will not descend with him.

Though while he lived he counted himself blessed —
and men praise you when you prosper —

he will join the generation of his fathers,
who will never see the light of life.

A man who has riches without understanding
is like the beasts that perish.

Contributors

Steven Benmor, B.Sc., LL.B, LL.M is a Toronto-based Family Law lawyer who only handles matrimonial cases. Steven is certified as a Specialist in Family Law by the Law Society of Upper Canada. Steven is a recognized lawyer, educator, speaker and writer. He appears before the Court of Appeal, Divisional Court, Superior Courts of Justice and the Ontario Courts of Justice. He was formerly a part-time Professor of Family Law at Seneca College, and served the Bar Admissions Course of the Law Society of Upper Canada as an Instructor of Family Law, a Mentor to law students and as a writer of Bar Examination questions in Family Law. Steven graduated from the University of Toronto with a Bachelor of Science, then from the University of Windsor with a Bachelor of Laws and then from York University with a Master of Laws (Family Law).

Gwen Benjamin, B.Ed., LL.B, TEP is a Partner at Wilson Vukelich LLP in Markham, Ontario. Gwen is a member of both the Ontario and British Columbia bars. Gwen's practice has, since 1989, been concentrated in the taxation area and she continues to practice in that area, focusing on estate planning and business succession planning, in all cases including cross-border matters. Gwen has a particular interest in the area of charity law — including charitable giving and acts for both charities and donors. Gwen has lectured on various income tax topics, including tax-planned charitable giving through the Canadian Institute of Chartered Accountants and other special interest groups. Gwen is a co-author of the Canadian Institute of Chartered Accountants' *Tax Practice Manual*, the *Personal Tax Planner Guide*, *The Family Trust Guide* and *Tax Planning Using Family Trusts*. Gwen is a member of the Canadian Tax Foundation and the Society of Trust and Estate Practitioners (STEP) and the Canadian Bar Association of Ontario, Tax Law, Estates and Trusts and Charity and Non-Profit Subsections.

Gordon Berger, TEP has been in the financial services business since 1972. Gordon was admitted to the "Quarter Century Club", a division of the Million Dollar Round Table (MDRT), and is a life member of "Top of the Table", reserved for the top 400 insurance agents worldwide. Gordon has made numerous appearances on both television and radio on such programs as TV Ontario's *Money Blues*, *Money Talks* on CHFI Radio, and on CFRB. Gordon has participated as co-author of various books, such as *Power of Money* and *Turnaround, The Complete Canadian Guide*. Gordon is a co-author of the *Canadian Guide to Tax Planning, Benefits and Compensation for Executives and Managers* and contributor to *The Essential Individual Pension Plan Handbook*. Gordon has lectured at the University of Toronto, the Schulich School of Business, the Canadian Bar Association and CCH Canadian Limited.

Jeffrey Berger, B.Com. is an analyst at PanFinancial Insurance Agencies Ltd. who has worked in a variety of roles within the financial services industry. Jeff attended Dalhousie University, where he studied finance. He completed the Canadian Securities Course, and has Life Insurance qualifications from the Life Underwriters Association of Canada. He is presently studying for the Certified Financial Planning (CFP) designation, and the Chartered Life Underwriter (CLU) designation.

David Bertschi, B.A., LL.B is a founding partner at Bertschi Orth Smith LLP, a boutique Insurance and Commercial Litigation Law firm in Ottawa Ontario. For over 20 years David has restricted his practice to Insurance and Commercial litigation. His experience includes acting as trial and coverage counsel on complex multi-party, multijurisdictional catastrophic losses. He also provides advice to insurers and self-insured institutions on a multitude of insurance-related issues. In recognition of David's contribution to the International Practice and Substantive Law Section of the FDCC, David was appointed Chair of the Section in 2008. In recognition of his varied and substantial experience in insurance litigation, David has been invited to write and speak on numerous complex issues of interest to insurers and self-insured corporate clients and by the Law Society of Upper Canada, the Advocates Society and the Ontario Bar Association. In addition a special thank you to Partners Debbie Orth and Marc Smith, and Associates Greg Hardy, Kelly Fitzpatrick, Louise Morel, Tamara Hisko and Lori Inglis, who greatly added to his chapter.

Ellen Bessner, B.Com., LL.B is a litigation partner at Gowling Lafleur Henderson LLP in Toronto. She regularly represents financial institutions, brokerage firms, corporations and individuals in all aspects of commercial and securities litigation and regulatory matters, employment law and professional liability, including investment advisors, financial advisors, branch managers, CEOs, CFOs, COOs, CCOs, compliance officers, insurance brokers, insurance agents and MGAs. Ms. Bessner is a regular speaker at Industry (MFDA, IIROC, Provincial Securities

Commissions, IFIC, Advocis, ACCP) and Dealer conferences. She writes regularly for the *National Post* and has written extensively for financial industry publications on matters of risk management and compliance, has co-written a paper on investment advisors' liability for the Canadian Securities Institute's continuing education program, and published several papers. Ellen is the author of the book *Advisor at Risk, A Road-map to Protecting Your Business,* available at Chapters/Indigo stores across Canada and through her publisher at Shore Publishing.

G. Scott Bowman has dedicated his entire adult life and professional career to one registered non-profit company: the Creative Centre for Learning and Development (CCLD). He started it in 1973 while still at university. In 1978, at the age of 27, Scott saw a real need in our society to create Robert Land Academy, which is considered by its peers to be one of the premier military schools in the world. With his vision and determination, Robert Land Academy has served boys from grades 6 through 12 who required challenge, structure, discipline and adventure in order to reach their full intellectual, physical and emotional potential. Over the last thirty years, Robert Land Academy has served over 3,000 boys and their families and developed a thriving campus in rural southern Ontario. Scott is also a sought out expert and speaker. He lectures throughout North America on leadership and ethics. He is a graduate of McMaster University, and served over 20 years in the Canadian Forces Reserve, CIC, retiring at the rank of Major.

Garry M. Cass, B.A., LL.B, TEP has been practising law in Toronto since 1977. Garry was one of the first legal practitioners to advocate a team approach to estate planning and to encourage clients to get an integrated solution that included input from all of their trusted professional advisors. The primary focus of Garry's practice is all aspects of estate and succession planning including developing and implementing estate plans, preparing wills, powers of attorney and living trusts and assisting trustees administer estates. Related areas of practice include real estate and corporate/commercial. For the past several years, Garry has worked closely with financial planners. He has frequently been a guest speaker at client events and has written many timely articles for their clients and advisors. Garry is member of The Society of Trust and Estate Planners. He received his B.A. from the University of Toronto and law degree from Queen's University.

Marie L. Cassis, B.A., LL.B is a Barrister, Solicitor & Notary Public working with Kenneth C. Pope's boutique law practice, which specializes in Estate, Tax and Trust Law, with an emphasis on helping special needs families. Previously, Marie was Manager of Legislated Programs with Nav Canada and prior to that, worked for the International Forum of Federations and for the House of Commons. As a Parliamentary Attaché, Marie gained significant insight into the legislative process while speechwriting, handling media, researching and working on various critic portfolios, including participation on Standing Committees for Members of Parliament, including the Office of Her Majesty's Loyal Leader of the Opposition.

Harish Chauhan is an international corporate and brand strategy practitioner, presenter and the author of *Unconventional Business — 33 insights on how to create a prosperous company*. As founder and CEO of Business by Philosophy® and the Unifying Philosophy (UPh®) strategy, Chauhan helps private and family-owned businesses achieve extraordinary business performance and well-being. His internationally renowned system successfully overcomes complex challenges facing even the most profitable companies, while helping them further maximize and protect their success. Since 1991, Harish has created, built and implemented over 150 brand identities and established over 40 UPh strategies for leading private and family-owned enterprises in Canada, the United States, Bermuda, India and England. Harish provides Trusted Advisors with a unique value add by helping their clients unlock the full potential of their businesses. He is featured at leading-edge conferences, courses and workshops worldwide and delights in mentoring youth and contributing his insights to non-profit organizations.

Stephen Cheng, B.Sc., M.B.A., FCIA, FSA is an actuary and managing director of Westcoast Actuaries Inc. He is a Fellow of the Canadian Institute of Actuaries (F.C.I.A.) and a Fellow of the Society of Actuaries (F.S.A.) with over 20 years of pension and actuarial consulting experience. Mr. Cheng is a graduate of UBC (B.Sc. 1980; M.B.A. 1982). He is an expert with the Supreme Court of British Columbia, providing both oral testimony and written evidence. He is a member of the Communications Committee and the Retirement Benefits Practice Education Course Examination Committee of the Canadian Institute of Actuaries. He has often presented to professional organizations and contributed to books and journals on pension as well as actuarial evidence.

Thomas Deans, Ph.D. is the President of Détente Financial Corp., which specializes in teaching business wealth protection strategies to advisors and business owners. By combining humour and his experience as president of a family-owned multinational corporation for almost a decade, Tom has shown thousands of business owners how to protect the retained earnings in their businesses. Tom's best-selling book *Every Family's Business* provides the framework for his public lectures and seminars. Tom has worked in banking and in government relations, has been the president of a railway, holds patents and chaired a federal government committee on tax credits. Deans earned a B.A. from Mount Allison University, an M.A. from McMaster University and a Ph.D. from the University of Warwick (United Kingdom). Tom has been featured in numerous magazines and journals, including *Profit*, *Money Sense* and *Investment Executive*. A frequent guest on CBC, CTV, MoneyLine and BNN, Tom is a highly sought after international public speaker on succession planning, wealth management and philanthropic giving.

Jordan Dolgin, LL.B. is a principal of Markham, Ontario-based Dolgin Professional Corporation (DPC). DPC is a dynamic business law firm dedicated to helping entrepreneurs start, grow and sell their businesses. For almost 20 years, Jordan has been assisting clients build better businesses through strong business relationship management. His practice focuses primarily on addressing daily corporate-commercial matters, completing M&A transactions and facilitating corporate divorces. Jordan believes in the importance of continuous professional development, is a frequent speaker and writer and was a contributor to *The Essential Individual Pension Plan Handbook*.

Kurt Dreger, B.Sc., ASA, CFP has over 17 years of pension plan experience in Canada, working in many capacities. He has written many articles and was a contributor to *The Essential Individual Pension Plan Handbook*. He has spoken on the subject of executive retirement planning, in particular, Individual Pension Plans (IPPs) and Retirement Compensation Arrangements (RCAs). Kurt graduated in 1991 from the University of Western Ontario with a B.Sc. (Honours) in Actuarial Science. He became an Associate of the Society of Actuaries (ASA) in 1991 and a Certified Financial Planner (CFP) in 2000. From 1991-1998, Kurt worked as a Pension Consultant to Canada's largest pension plans. He continued in the pension field from 1998-2004 as Manager of Business Development at Standard Life. Since 2004, Kurt has been with the Group Pension department at Industrial Alliance Insurance and Financial Services Inc. as Business Development Manager. He is a member of, and plays active roles with, CPBI and ACPM.

Andrew Duckman, B.A., GBA Candidate, RIBO is a seasoned corporate benefits and general insurance consultant. Andrew is the Managing Director of SeveranceOptions.com. This is a fee-for-service employee benefit consulting firm providing employee benefit analysis of severance packages and providing expert witness expertise to the legal community. He has over a decade of experience within the risk management, merchant banking and information technology sectors. His core competencies are employee benefit cost containment and executive and business owner benefit construction and business analysis. Andrew began his career at Unum Provident (now RBC), developing unique financial solutions to serve the specialized needs of Canada's small and medium-sized businesses, and was responsible for integrating special risk solutions into the product lines of some of Canada's largest financial and insurance firms. In 2003, he joined one of Canada's leading Third Party Administrator and Brokerage firms, where he served as the Vice-President of Corporate Development. Andrew recently began his own independent financial consulting firm called Client First Financial. Andrew has authored a number of articles about corporate benefits to Trade Publications, including OTR (*Over the Road Transportation Publication*), Benefit Pension and Monitor, and was a chapter contributor to one of Canada's leading Financial Planning books *The Essential Individual Pension Plan Handbook*.

Eugene Ellmen is Executive Director of the Social Investment Organization (SIO), Canada's association for socially responsible investment (SRI). He is widely regarded as one of Canada's leading authorities on SRI. He is the author of the critically acclaimed *Canadian Ethical Money Guide* (Toronto: Lorimer Press), published in five editions between 1988 and 1998. Eugene was also a contributor to *The Essential Individual Pension Plan Handbook*. Before joining the SIO in 1999, Eugene had a varied career as business writer for Canadian Press, public affairs advisor for Credit Union Central of Ontario, communications advisor to a number of Ministers in the Ontario government, and advisor in private consulting on behalf of companies and non-profit organizations.

Ian M. Hull, B.A., LL.B, TEP co-founded Hull & Hull LLP in 1998, a law firm that specializes in estate, capacity and trust litigation and provides advice in complex estate planning and administration matters. He was called to the Bar in 1990 and is a Certified Specialist in Estates and Trusts Law and in Civil Litigation. He is a Fellow of the American College of Trust and Estate Counsel and a member of the Society of Trust and Estate Practitioners. He is the author of *Advising Families of Succession Planning: The High Price of Not Talking*; *Power of Attorney Litigation; Challenging the Validity of Wills*; as well as the co-author of *Probate Practice*, 4th ed., and was a contributing author of *Key Developments in Estates and Trusts Law in Ontario, 2008* and also a contributing author of *Widdifields on Accounts*. He has been named one of the top estate practitioners in a national survey of his peers, appearing since 2007 in the Canadian Legal Lexpert Directory as one of the top practitioners in the estates litigation area and since 2006 in the *National Post*'s Best Lawyers in Canada list in the Trusts and Estates category.

Robert Keats, B.Sc., CFP, RFP, MSFP is an internationally known expert in cross-border financial planning. His views on how Canadians can better manage their financial affairs have been featured on the Internet and numerous Canadian and U.S. television and radio programs. He has also been featured in numerous publications and magazines, as well as other international media. Keats is author of a Canadian bestseller, *The Border Guide*, now in its 9th edition. He is a founding partner of Keats, Connelly & Associates, Inc. (KCA), which has offices in Arizona, Florida and Michigan. KCA was first established in early 1990 and is the largest U.S. based fee-only firm to specialize in cross-border financial planning. It is regarded as the premier cross-border financial planning firm in North America. Keats is a resident of Phoenix, Arizona. His interests include family, church and volunteer work.

Bob Kirk, B.A., FLMI, ACS is a partner of PanFinancial Insurance Agencies Ltd. and has worked in the financial services industry for over 28 years. He has held executive positions with PanFinancial, Transamerica Life, Unum Provident and ING Life/NN Financial, management positions with MONY Life and North American Life, and has served as the Chief Underwriter at a number of large insurance carriers with Underwriting experience in Life, Group, Special Risk and Disability Insurance. Bob's background is in Sales, Risk Management, Strategic Planning, Underwriting, Claims, Customer Service and Mergers. Bob has lectured at numerous industry and business functions, including the Schulich School of Business. His work has been published in a number of trade journals, including *Underwriter Alert* and *On The Risk*. He has served as a Canadian Editor of *On the Risk*, the pre-eminent Underwriting journal, and has also served as a director of the Canadian Institute of Underwriters. He was also a contributor to *The Essential Individual Pension Plan Handbook*.

Herb Koplowitz, Ph.D. is the President of Terra Firma Management Consulting, based in Toronto. Herb consults to executives and trains managers to enable a more effective and efficient implementation of strategy through aligning structure to strategy, filling roles with the right people, training managers to direct and support employees and to hold them accountable. He has worked extensively in the financial sector and has consulted and taught performance management and organizational design to business leaders in Canada, the United States, Jamaica, South Africa, Russia and India. Herb holds a B.A. in mathematics and philosophy from Cornell University, a Ph.D. in psychology from the University of Massachusetts and registration as an organizational psychologist in Ontario.

David Leonhardt is CEO of The Happy Guy Marketing, a Canadian-based business that specializes in providing freelance writing, editing and Web site search engine ranking services. David was one of Canada's most interviewed spokespeople, often topping 500 media interviews a year, and helped to influence legislation and regulations across Canada. That expertise has since helped position his own business and those of his clients for success on the Internet and in the written word. David publishes *A Daily Dose of Happiness*, an ezine that is read by 40,000 people daily, and has been published in hundreds of books, newspapers, magazines and Web sites. David was a contributor to *The Essential Individual Pension Plan Handbook*. He has also made cameo appearances with such luminaries as Zig Ziglar and Brian Tracy.

Cary List, CA, CFP is President and CEO of Financial Planners Standards Council of Canada. Cary has spent the better part of the last two decades dedicated to the advancement of financial planning as a profession, and over the past six years he has overseen CFP certification in Canada. Under his leadership, CFP certification continues to be the gold standard for professional financial planning. Cary sits on the Council and the Certification Committee of the International Financial Planning Standards Board. Cary was a contributor to *The Essential Individual Pension Plan Handbook*. He holds an honours mathematics degree from the University of Waterloo, is a Chartered Accountant and holds the Certified Financial Planner designation.

J.B. Loewen, B.A., M.B.A. is an experienced corporate consultant, lecturer and writer of business strategy. Loewen assists owner-managed Canadian companies and family businesses in seeking capital and private equity. Currently, as a partner with Loewen & Partners Inc., J.B. Loewen finds capital for companies ranging from $10 million in revenues and up, as well as for family-owned enterprises. Loewen & Partners has raised over $100 million in private equity for owners of companies. J.B. Loewen shares experience and business knowledge of Private Equity in *Money Magnet: How To Attract Investors to Your Business*.

Scott Maclagan entered the employee benefit consulting field in March 1964 with William M. Mercer Limited in Toronto. He has provided consulting services to many of Canada's largest employers, including the CAF, RCMP, federal government and many Crown corporations and private sector employers on both domestic and international benefits. In November 1996, he took early retirement and incorporated E.S. Maclagan & Associates Inc. in order to continue to provide consulting services while also developing the Menu*flex* Benefits Program™. In the fall of 2005 he sold Maclagan & Associates and incorporated Maclagan Inc. In 2008 Maclagan Inc. launched the cost-controlled enVia Benefits Program designed to enable an employer to essentially "freeze" the cost of health and dental benefits, while providing greater flexibility to employees.

Gilles R. Marceau, CFP, CLU, RFP, PRP is President of Gilles R. Marceau and Associates Inc. He is an accomplished Financial Planning, Retirement and Lifestyle Planning Consultant and Educator. Gilles has had a very successful four-decade career in the life insurance, banking, and investment and securities businesses. He was a contributor to *The Essential Individual Pension Plan Handbook*. Gilles has held the positions of Director of Individual Insurance Marketing for one of Canada's leading life insurance companies; Regional Manager for a financial planning practice directed to high net worth individuals; Managing Partner, Marketing Development for what was Canada's largest trust company; and Managing Partner in a fee-based financial planning/employee benefit firm. He is currently the Chair of the Professional Retirement Planners designation accredited through the Canadian Association of Pre-retirement Planners.

Lynn R. Mason, J.D. is a Principle of Global Capital Markets, Inc., a leading West Coast M&A service provider located in California. Lynn has more than 12 years of M&A experience. He formerly served as president of Business Publications, Inc., a national publisher of corporate finance texts, directories and journals and sponsor of leveraged buyout seminars. He spent several years in private law practice where he focused upon M&A, corporate finance and international joint ventures. Lynn has served on the board of directors of numerous middle market companies. His experience includes identifying, qualifying and acquiring target companies in addition to a broad range of other merger and acquisition activities. Lynn received his undergraduate degree in Political Science from United States International University and his J.D. degree from the University of San Diego School of Law.

John Nicola, CLU, CHFC, CFP is CEO and Chairman of Nicola Wealth Management. John has been in the financial services industry since 1974. He provides strategic leadership to Nicola Wealth Management and develops innovative solutions to clients' complex problems. His areas of expertise include wealth accumulation and management through the use of trusts, creative pension and insurance arrangements, and professional investment managers. He is a Founding Member of the Conference for Life Underwriters (CALU) and has served as the CALU Chair for 2003 as well as Chair for TOT in 1999. Nicola Wealth Management is a firm focused on finding holistic solutions to the unique challenges facing business owners and high net worth individuals. From the creative use of corporate savings to the use of insurance as an investment vehicle under John's guidance, NWM continues to be a leader in the financial planning industry.

Fred Nickols has been working on and writing about a broad array of issues of interest and concern to managers, executives and other consultants for more than 35 years. Chief among these are work and work control systems; human behaviour; organizational and process performance and improvement; strategy; change and change management; communities of practice; knowledge management; organization development (OD); and management itself. His almost 100 papers, articles and book chapters are available online at <www.skullworks.com>. A former career Navy man, Fred also has experience at the executive level in for-profit and non-profit organizations. Currently, he is managing partner of The Distance Consulting Company, LLC. He draws on his extensive and varied background to make his ideas accessible, relevant and useful to his readers.

John Parkinson, Ph.D. is Professor of Accounting & Finance and Director of the Atkinson School of Administrative Studies at York University. He graduated with a Ph.D. in finance from Bradford University Management Centre in England, and he holds professional memberships as Fellow of the Institute of Chartered Accountants in England & Wales and Fellow of the Chartered Institute of Management Accountants. His main research interests are the application of process costing in modern manufacturing companies, and the interaction of personality measurement with accounting research and practice and the development and use of case studies.

Trevor R. Parry, M.A., LL.B is Executive Vice-President responsible for Sales and Marketing for Gordon B. Lang & Associates Inc. In addition to leading the consulting group for Lang, Trevor works directly with clients, financial planners and advisors, accountants and lawyers in helping to develop and implement advanced financial planning strategies. Trevor was called to the Ontario Bar in 1996 and is a graduate of Queen's University Faculty of Law. Trevor also holds Masters and Undergraduate degrees in History from the University of Toronto. A dynamic public speaker, Trevor has presented at many conferences, including those presented by Advocis and the Canadian Bar Association. He has also been widely published in professional periodicals. Trevor was a contributor to *The Essential Individual Pension Plan Handbook*.

Greg Pashke, CMC, M.B.A., CPA, CMA, CFM, CBA is President of Pashke Consulting, a strategic, tactical and valuation consulting resource. Greg is a generalist committed to continuous learning and his mantra is "to get a lot done and have a lot of fun". Greg worked for an international accounting firm, served as CFO of a transportation enterprise and was managing partner of a regional CPA firm prior to forming Pashke Consulting. Greg graduated from Gannon University, has an M.B.A. from the University of Pittsburgh, has lectured at Penn State University and holds certifications in consulting, finance, accounting and business valuation. Greg has served on professional and community governing boards including the American Institute of Certified Public Accountants and the Pennsylvania Institute of CPAs. His articles have appeared in *The Futurist*, *Strategic Finance*, the Pennsylvania and New York CPA Journals, and *Renaissance Executive Forum* publications.

Kenneth C. Pope, LL.B, TEP started his law practice in 1980. He travels throughout Ontario to meet with clients and to present seminars on disabilities and estate planning issues. Ken is a Henson Trust specialist, providing financial security for families who have a family member with disabilities or special needs. Ken has written dozens of articles on how guardians and parents of disabled children can financially and legally plan their affairs to protect the interest of their loved ones. He was a contributor to *The Essential Individual Pension Plan Handbook*.

Ian Quigley, M.B.A., CFP, CIM is an independent financial planner specializing in topics related to pension and small business tax planning. Ian holds an M.B.A. from the University of Alberta and is currently a candidate in the Chartered Business Valuator's program (CBV). He has his own consulting firm, Quigley Consulting Inc. He was a contributor to *The Essential Individual Pension Plan Handbook*. Ian is the author of the highly acclaimed book *Compensation and Tax Strategies* (Toronto:

Thomson Carswell, 2004). This book is widely used to teach accountants and financial planning professionals advanced solutions in executive compensation.

Stanley Risen, CA is the Vice-President of Sales and Consulting for Benecaid Health Benefit Solutions Inc., a Toronto-based financial services company. Benecaid is a leading provider of innovative health benefit solutions in Canada. He was a contributor to *The Essential Individual Pension Plan Handbook*. Stanley is a Chartered Accountant with 22 years of financial and managerial experience that has included senior positions at BDO Dunwoody as a senior audit manager, and CFO at Pet-Pak Containers and IMS Machining.

Grant Robinson, FCA is a Fellow of the Institute of Chartered Accountants of Canada and founder of The SuccessCare® Program, a unique process for enabling a successful transition of privately owned and family businesses. For over 25 years, he has coached entrepreneurs and their families through the process of planning for the future. He has facilitated projects for both high profile and medium-sized Canadian businesses, many of which were in transition crises. Grant actively shares his knowledge and experience with other professional advisors through the SuccessCare training programs. In addition, professionals from all disciplines engage him to provide specialized consulting and coaching for their family business clients. Grant uses his experience and facilitation skills to lead families through the development and execution of practical strategies to resolve their concerns.

Andrew Rogerson, LL.B (Hons), TEP practises in Toronto, visiting London and Dubai. He was called to the Bar of England and Wales in 1981 by Middle Temple, where he was a scholarship recipient. Subsequently, Andrew served as a pupil in the insolvency Chambers of Michael Crystal Q.C. in Gray's Inn. His early practice developed from insolvency to trusts, wills, insurance law and estate planning, with an international focus. Since qualification, Andrew has practised in South Africa, Australia, the Turks and Caicos Islands, Jersey (Channel Islands), Ontario, Alberta and as a barrister in London, England. His experience is evenly divided between advisory and drafting work and litigation, with many appearances as counsel in appellate courts. Andrew spent 11 years in offshore financial centres, establishing asset protection structures and litigating trust and insolvency issues.

James Sbrolla is an entrepreneur with extensive experience in the environmental, clean technology and financial sectors. A veteran analyst of the environmental business sector, he is sought out by the media for his sometimes prescient opinion. He has been widely quoted and published in industry and mainstream media, and pens the business column for three magazines. Following a three-year international business development project, he worked as an Investment Advisor before founding Environmental Business Consultants (EBC), a company whose services include business strategy planning and implementation, market research and raising private and public financing. Recently appointed as the Entrepreneur in Residence for the Ontario Center for Environmental Technology Advancement (OCETA), he coaches fledgling businesses to commercial success. James is Chair of EBC and sits on the boards of Actual Media and Clover Insurance.

Shay Schwartzman, B.F.A. founded LifeStyle Media, a full-service production and post-production company that works hand in hand with Trusted Advisors to "*get the message out there*". Shay works hard to set his clients apart from their competition and uses his expertise, gained from working in this business since 1992, to craft the right message, using the right medium to reach the right market … BETTER, FASTER, FURTHER. Times and technology have certainly changed, but the mission to bring top quality, informative and entertaining media, whatever the format, is still the bottom line. Shay has worked in all facets of production since graduating with an Honours B.F.A. from York University in 1990. He spends his working time consulting with clients on how to further their businesses by using video and multimedia, producing, directing and writing.

Richard Segal, B.Com., CFP has over three decades of professional experience and is a pioneer in Canada in combining business succession planning with sophisticated tax and insurance solutions. Richard is among the top 1% of insurance agents in the world. He is past President of the Chartered Life Underwriters Toronto Chapter and is a past Trustee of the CLU Institute. He is a past Director of the Ontario Chapter of the Canadian Association of Financial Planners and a past President of the Scarborough Estate and Financial Planning Council. He appeared regularly on "Money Talks" on CHFI Radio, Cable Pulse 24, as well as on TV Ontario's "Small Business" program, Rogers Cable Financial planning series and a live national financial planning question-and-answer program on Global TV. Richard has spoken and run seminars for numerous organizations, including the University of Toronto, Seneca College and CCH Canadian Limited. He is a co-author of *Wealth*

Creation for the Salaried Executive, which is a Canadian guide to executive and managerial compensation and tax planning.

Morden (Mort) Shapiro, B.Com., FCA, CMC for over 25 years has consulted with accounting practices throughout Canada. Mort, a regular columnist in *The Bottom Line*, coaches accounting firms and frequently performs a diagnostic review of an accounting practice for practices of all sizes. He was a contributor to *The Essential Individual Pension Plan Handbook*. A well-known teacher, author and facilitator of partners' retreats, he is also a frequent presenter of Professional Development courses and is available to address conferences and other professional meetings. Mort consults on a broad range of practice management issues, including: relationship management; partnership arrangements; succession planning; strategic planning; marketing; integration of technology; growth management; mergers; conflict resolution; and profit improvement strategies. He is available as an expert witness, arbitrator and mediator in professional negligence situations and partnership disputes. Mort offers expert guidance with respect to the federal *Personal Information Protection and Electronic Documents Act* (PIPEDA) and the Quality Control requirements for accounting practices.

Charles L. Stanley, CFP, ChFC, AIF is a person with the unique ability to support his clients through strategic life planning that enables them to make progress toward their individual goals in life. He works as a fee-only wealth coach and often acts as the client's team captain with other expert professionals on the client's advisory team in sunny San Diego, California. He offers Investment Consulting, Advanced Planning and Expert Team Management as a member of the advisory team of Trovena, LLC, a leading wealth management firm with offices in La Jolla, CA, Redondo Beach, CA and Roseland, NJ.

Peter Sokoloski, B.A., graduated from Carleton University in Ottawa, Ontario in 2005, with Bachelor of Arts (Honours) Law with a minor in Political Science. Since that time he has been employed in a variety of positions in the offices of Ken Pope and Tax Fisher. Currently, he provides services for special needs clients to assist them in accessing tax credits available to them, and takes great satisfaction in helping to meet the needs of his clients. Tax law is continually changing, and Peter believes that an informed client is a well-served client.

Norm Trainor is the founder and CEO of The Covenant Group. He is an international speaker, the author of the best-selling book *The 8 Best Practices of High-Performing Salespeople*, and a consultant to organizations around the world. He is also the author of *Best Practices: Training and Development*, Carswell Thomson's international bible on Training and Development. His most recent book is *The Entrepreneurial Journey: a Handbook for Building your Business*. In addition, Norm has written over 300 articles for various leading publications in North America and internationally.

Christopher P. Van Slyke, B.A., M.B.A., CFP is a Managing Director of Trovena, LLC, a fee-only wealth management firm in La Jolla, California. His expertise in comprehensive wealth management is reflected in the firm's emphasis on estate planning, asset protection, tax strategies, risk management, investment selection, business succession and retirement planning. A Certified Financial Planner practitioner, Christopher is also a financial planner member of the National Association of Personal Financial Advisors (NAPFA), an exclusive organization of fee-only planners. Christopher is a past member of the Board of Directors of the Financial Planning Association of San Diego and Los Angeles. Christopher was a contributor to *The Essential Individual Pension Plan Handbook*. He has been quoted or published in *The Wall Street Journal*, *The San Diego Union-Tribune*, *Financial Planning*, *Smart Money*, *Financial Advisor*, *Boomer Market Advisor*, *MSN Money*, *Wealth and Retirement Planner*, *thestreet.com*, *Bloomberg Wealth Manager*, the *Del Mar Times*, *Money Magazine* and *MorningstarAdvisor.com*.

Corina Weigl, B.A., LLB, TEP is a partner with the Trusts, Wills, Estates and Charities Group of the Toronto office of Fasken Martineau DuMoulin LLP. Her practice focuses on estate planning, including resolving the complexities associated with family business succession planning. Corina is a frequent lecturer and speaker on related topics, and has co-authored CICA's *Succession Planning Toolkit for Business Owners* and *Planning and Executing an Estate Freeze*. Corina is recognized for her ability to address complex legal issues while efficiently facilitating solutions. She is acknowledged for her "sensitive and insightful approach" to their affairs and her ability to provide timely, pragmatic advice in a cost-effective manner. In addition to wills and trusts, estate administration and corporate reorganizations, Corina also handles marriage contracts and charities law. Corina is the 2008 recipient of the Hoffstein Book Prize, a peer-nominated award for professional excellence and contribution to the Bar. Corina is Past Chair of the Ontario Bar Association's Estates and Trusts subsection. She is a member of the international organization Society of Trust & Estate Practitioners, as well as other professional organizations. Corina is ranked by Lexpert as "up and coming" in the Estate Planning and Personal Tax area.

Galen Weston is the founder of ProfessionalReferrals.ca Inc., North America's premier online referral generation company. Since its inception, ProfessionalReferrals.ca and AdvisorWorld.com have attracted millions of visitors each year and helped tens of thousands of North Americans in both Canada and the United States begin new successful professional relationships with Trusted Advisors. Galen's vision and leadership has resulted in thousands of lawyers, financial advisors and accountants entrusting ProfessionalReferrals.ca Inc. with their marketing resources, which has resulted in millions of dollars in new business. As a pioneer in the advisory industry, Galen is well recognized by his peers as an expert in the field of optimizing the World Wide Web for quality lead generation for the advisory community, by providing the very best information available, through a network of writers and Internet bloggers, and by positioning their works at the top of thousands of Google search topics.

ACKNOWLEDGEMENTS

Sir Isaac Newton in a letter to Robert Hooke wrote: "If I have been able to see further, it was only because I stood on the shoulders of giants." These are powerful words from one of our history's most influential minds. As this book was being put together I was always mindful of those words.

This book has been a labour of love from the beginning. It would not have been possible without the support and contributions of hundreds of individuals who have provided me with both valuable insights on a variety of topics and their time, which helped me turn my idea of writing this book into the reality which you hold in your hands today.

I would like to make a special acknowledgement to Marvin S. Merrick, CA (1939-1999), an accountant's accountant, my greatest mentor and, most importantly, my Dad, who taught me to appreciate the intricacies of the *Income Tax Act* and never to present a tax minimization and tax deference solution to a client unless it has been sanctioned by CRA. And to Brenda Merrick, who encouraged me to do my very best in her loving way as my mother through "living my bliss". "Dad and Mom, this book is because of you, and its words are for your grandchildren."

I would like to give special thanks to Richard Segal and Gordon Berger, contributors to this publication, who helped me to become a better and more mature practitioner. Special thanks to Major (retired) G. Scott Bowman, also a contributor, who has been to me a living, breathing example of an individual who has gone against the grain to do what is right by helping thousands of boys become productive contributors to our national fabric. I owe another special thanks to Larry Lipiec, my lawyer, my career coach and friend, encouraging me to think outside the box while enjoying the journey. To Charles Stanley, a gifted and empathic Certified Financial Planner, who has shared hundreds of hours of his wisdom and helped me understand what it takes to be a true Trusted Advisor. His genius is shared throughout this book in the many chapters he contributed.

To my fellow contributors and my editors I owe a lifetime of gratitude for gifting me their time, patience and intellectual property: Mort Shapiro, Andrew Duckman, Gilles R. Marceau, Shay Schwartzman, Trevor R. Parry, Christopher P. Van Slyke, Jordan Dolgin, Stanley Risen, Kurt Dreger, Eugene Ellmen, Kenneth C. Pope, Tom Deans, David Leonhardt, Cary List, Ian Quigley, J. B. Loewen, Bob Kirk, Greg Pashke, Fred Nickols, Norm Trainor, Herb Koplowitz, Galen Weston,

Marie L. Cassis, David Bertschi, Ellen Bessner, Stephen Cheng, Bob Keats, Jeffrey Berger, Scott Maclagan, John Nicola, John Parkerson, James Sbrolla, Lynn Mason, Harish Chauhan, Corina Weigl, Grant Robinson, Garry Cass, Ian Hull, Gwen Benjamin, Steven Benmor, Andrew Rogerson, Peter Sokoloski, Gian-Luca Di Rocco, Product Acquisitions Editor, LexisNexis Canada Inc., Janet Kim, Director, Product Acquisitions, LexisNexis Canada Inc., Rose Knecht, Editor, Print & CD-ROMs, LexisNexis Canada Inc., Yolanda Majury, Marketing Manager, Print Product, LexisNexis Canada Inc., Pauline Braithwaite and Elaine Wiltshire, former Associate Editors of *The Bottom Line*, and Adam Malik, Associate Editor of *The Bottom Line*.

I would like to give special thanks to the following individuals who were very inspirational and helpful on this journey of discovery: Benny Levi, Aidan Mullen, Sousie Weston, Lloyd Duckman, Greg Kennedy, Ian Wright, Les Kotzer, Barry Fish, Frank Zucchero, Al Emid, Robert Martini, Marc Roche, Shawna Fattal, Lynn Fields, David Williams, Matthew Ramden, David Stewart, George Dryden, Thomas Nicolle, Ian E. Baker, Barry Braun, Sheldon Levy, Sheldon Miller, Yuni Anava, Jordana Paige, Megan Emily, Eryn Niccole, Jason Benjamin, Michael Sheldon, Robert Kliaman, Parool Joshi, Michael Maslin, Munir Noormohamed, Rob Murray, Duff Young, Ray Hinton, Jim Yih, Rudolph Dorner, Margret Anava, John Otto, Julie Weeden, Mark Husken, Alan Rae, Harry Karalis, Normand Frenette, David Bell, Nancy Elgie, Bruce Ness, Bill Bates, Marshall Beyer, Ed Defort, Ken Macrae, Lorilee Lang, David Wolle, David Gentleman, Greg Edwards, Pierre Simard, Bradley Roulston, Caroline Van Hasselt, David Johnson, Peter Wan, Michael Reid, Kenneth J. Weber, Sandy Bowman, Khurram Hussain, Nancy Estey, George Aguiar, Justin Levine, Rick Sprentz, Michel Ghatan, Kevin Kliaman, Paula Sprentz, Daniel Lavi, Geoff Sternberg, Joseph McCabe, Harry Wolle, Dave Chandler, Irv Pitch, Joe MacDonald, Jason Bell, Christopher Hilkene, David Hawkins, Vince Murton, Coleen Clark, Tina Junkala, Helen Vari, George Vari, Bob Hunter, Naomi Carniol, James Daw, Harry W. Arthurs, Agnes Hilkene, David Chong Yen, Peter Traynor, Oli Levi, Terry Stone, Murray Coulter, Dax Sukhraj, Casey Brandreth, Shirley Levi, Ivan Ivanovic, Mark Schwatz, Jury Kopach, Reed Hilton-Eddy, Blake Glendenning, Derek Hill, Laurie Turner, Sam Albanese, Robert Kliaman, Frazer Lang, Gordan Lang, Harvey Willows, Elizabeth Speers, Glorianne Stromberg, Christian Bellavance, Wanda Buote, Sara Levi, Izzy Nelken, Kevin Trainor, Dennis Santarossa, Brian Robinson, Paul Miller, Clark Steffy, Kira Vonrosenstiel, Joan Binetti, Jamie Golombek, Bob Willard, Lisa Nelken, Brian Eker, Paul Morra,

Heather Merrick, Gordon Pape, Michael Guest, David Gobeil, Chris Robinson, Marie Figueiredo, Evelyn Jacks, Ron Foran, Doug Plache, Ian Portsmouth, Gary Sims, Yinka Egberongbe, Richard Eng, Daniel Levi, Raymond Pitch, Robin Ingle, Aurelia Best, Ona Fletcher, Ann Oneil, Ann Bowman, Paulette Anthony, Craig Wolkoff, Adam Verri, Joan Donnelly, Ron Charles, Evelyn Juan, Shawn Dianne Phelps, Scott Hillier, Steve Johnston, Brian N. Feldman, Beverly Kavanagh, Catherine Wilson, Sheldon Miller, Julia Kuipers, Parminder Parmar, Eileen Chadnick, Tino Corsetti, Peter Goral, Chris Edwards, John Hobel, Gail Balfour, Gerry Malloy, Peter D'Cruz, Merlyn Sollano, Andrew Dilorenzo, Mark Galloway, Ron Charles, Gerald Tritt, Rick Spence, Tina Junkala, John Assaraf, Ketan Desai, Patricia Lovett-Reid, Peter Wolchak, Romana King and Henry Kielar.

Lastly, and most importantly, I want to share that none of this work would have been possible without the loving support of my family, my Bashert and wife, Ronit Merrick, and our children, Adam, Steven, Michael, Leslie and Chailee.

INDEX